MOTOR
Auto Body
Repair, 2nd Edition

Edited by Robert Scharff

 Delmar Publishers Inc.®

NOTICE TO THE READER

Text, Design, and Production by
  Scharff Associates, Ltd.

Delmar Staff
  Executive Editor: Michael A. McDermott
  Development:
    Assistant Editor: Lisa A. Reale
    Editorial Assistant: Patricia Konczeski
  Project Editor: Andrea Edwards Myers
  Production Coordinator: Wendy Troeger
  Art Supervisor: John Lent
  Design Supervisor: Susan C. Mathews

For information, address Delmar Publishers Inc.
3 Columbia Circle, PO Box 15015
Albany, New York 12212-5015

Printed in the United States of America
Published simultaneously in Canada
by Nelson Canada,
a division of The Thomson Corporation

10 9 8 7 6 5

Library of Congress Cataloging-in-Publication Data

Motor auto body repair / edited by Robert Scharff. — 2nd ed.
      p. cm.
    Includes index.
    ISBN 0-8273-4667-0 (text), — ISBN 0-8273-4668-9 (IG)
    1. Automobiles—Bodies—Maintenance and repair. I. Scharff,
Robert.
  TL255.M647 1992
  629.26—dc20   91-34668
                                                            CIP

Contents

Contents

Preface

The entire automobile industry is changing faster than ever before. This is especially true of the auto body repair and refinishing trade. The role of the body technician and refinisher has changed greatly in the past few years. The reason for this is the major shift by vehicle owners to unibody construction.

In unibody construction, as discussed in Chapter 2, the metal body panels are welded together making a structural unit, as opposed to the traditional frame construction where the cosmetic steel body rests on top of a structural steel frame. Virtually all cars manufactured today, and in the foreseeable future, will be unibody vehicles. This change in vehicle preference has had a major impact on the duties, knowledge, procedures, and responsibilities of body technicians. Before the introduction of unibody cars, the body technician's primary concern was to straighten the frame and replace or fix damaged panels or sections. Today, the body technician is responsible for a great deal more.

When working on most collision damaged unibody vehicles, it is necessary to have a complete knowledge of the mechanical components, including the operation, diagnosis of problems, and adjustment of the following: strut suspension system, independent rear wheel suspension, rack and pinion steering, and trailing rear axles.

In addition, Chapter 12 details other knowledge that the modern auto body technician must have, such as mechanical component mounting points, engine accessory systems (power steering, fuel systems, and brake systems, for example), removal of mechanical versus partial assembly, emission control systems and certification of repairs, front wheel drive systems, rear wheel drive systems, and heat and air-conditioning systems. Why does the modern auto body technician need to understand the functions of the car's mechanical components? The answer is simple—most, if not all, are fastened to the body structure. This means that with most major collision damage, these parts must be removed by the technician before any body straightening work is undertaken. While the actual repairs to mechanical components might be done in the body by other persons or it might be "farmed out" to outside vendors, it is usually the responsibility of the body mechanic to reinstall the mechanical parts back onto the repaired body.

With the introduction of unibody vehicles, the body technician has had to learn about the use of new materials and techniques. The conventional body-over-frame vehicle was primarily made of low carbon or mild steel. These materials were usually welded or cut with an oxyacetylene gas torch. However, in unibody construction as mentioned in Chapter 7, high-strength steel is used and all vehicle manufacturers mandate in their service manuals that MIG welding must be used on all structural parts repairs. Only the MIG welding procedures described in Chapter 6 will maintain the structural integrity of the high-strength steel used in today's unibody cars. The gas torch should never be used on a unibody constructed car.

The steel used in unibody construction needs constant protection against corrosion. The various corrosion protection systems, methods of handling corrosion repairs, materials and application equipment used, and the techniques are fully covered in Chapters 8 and 15. True, a few years ago corrosion protection work was usually farmed out to specialty shops. Today, it is the task of auto body technicians to restore the corrosion protection to the car.

As pointed out in Chapter 13, the use of plastics—in both unibody and conventional frame construction—has been on the increase. Body technicians must, therefore, add plastic repair techniques to their skills.

Measurements of a vehicle have always been important to collision repair. But, with unibody construction, measurement is vital because of the close tolerance that is necessary. Chapter 9 covers the principles of operation and basic applications and advantages of each system. Covered are the traditional tram gauge, self-centering and strut gauge systems, universal measuring system, mechanical systems (including the laser beam type), and jig and fixture systems.

The next chapter (Chapter 10) examines the use of existing equipment and application of new systems. Key topics include single pull systems, multiple pull systems, anchoring, power requirements, and accurate control and use. As with all the information in this book, pulling and straightening of frame body vehicles is not excluded.

There is still, and there will always be, controversy in the auto collision repair industry. For years, most American car manufacturers recommended that replacement panels be installed at factory seams. Thanks to research, primarily by Inter-Industry Conference on Auto Collision Repair (I-CAR) and TEC-COR, it was discovered that structural parts replacement at factory seams is not always practical. In some cases, it requires extensive dismantling of the car. In others, it simply was not an efficient repair operation. This realization led experts in the field to identify a need for the development of additional technical information, and procedures on how to section structural components when it is not practical to replace them at factory seams. Chapter 11 covers this important update of sectioning and panel replacement.

Chapter 14 details such other body shop repairs as glass replacement, replacing and repairing vinyl roofs and bumpers, correcting wind and water leaks, and installing body accessories such as seats, moldings, and interior trim. In Chapters 3, 4, and 5 is a description of the tools—both hand and power—that are used in the body work, while Chapters 1 and 2 cover shop procedures and collision estimates. Although the important subject of safety is described throughout the book, a detailed look at shop safety is discussed in Chapter 1.

Of couse, no book on the workings of auto collision repair would be complete without a thorough discussion of refinishing. The latest materials, equipment, and procedures used in the auto industry are covered in Chapters 16, 17, 18, and 19.

ACKNOWLEDGMENTS

To organize a book of this size requires the help of many companies and people. As noted on the next page, nearly one hundred companies provided technical data and illustrations for this book. In addition, I would like to thank the following for permission to use information from their training programs and manuals.

- I-CAR for use of materials and illustrations from their nine-part training program that appears in Chapters 6, 9, 10, 12, 13, and 15.
- Toyota Motor Corp. for use of materials and illustrations from their manual, *Fundamental Body Repair Procedures*, that appears in Chapters 2, 6, 9, 10, and 11.
- Nissan Motor Corp. for use of materials and illustrations from their manual, *Body Repair Fundamentals*, that appears in Chapters 9, 10, and 12.
- Blackhawk Automotive, Inc. for the use of materials and illustrations from their training program, *The New Science of Unibody Repair*, that appears in Chapters 9 and 10.
- Chrysler Corp., Ford Motor Co., and General Motors Corp. for the use of materials and illustrations from their service manuals that appears in Chapters 8, 9, 10, 11, 14, and 20.
- Maaco Enterprises, Inc. for the use of text and photographs from the Maaco refinishing training program that appears in Chapters 8, 17, and 18.
- Toyota Motor Corp. for the use of materials and illustrations from their manual, *Fundamental Painting Procedures*, that appears in Chapters 16 to 19.
- Du Pont Co. for the use of materials from their refinishing handbook that appears in Chapters 16 to 19.
- PPG Industries, Inc., for information from *Ditzler® Repaint Manual* that appears in Chapters 16 to 19.
- Binks Mfg. Co. and DeVilbiss Co. for the use of materials from several of their manuals that were used in Chapters 5 and 17.
- Motor Publications for the use of data and charts from their *Crash Estimating Guides* that appears in Chapters 1 and 20.
- J. Gerard Doneski for use of text and materials from his guide, *How to Select a Squeeze-Type Resistance Spot Welder for Unibody Repair Welding* that appears in Chapter 6.

I would like to thank the following people for reviewing the manuscript at various stages, and for their helpful comments:

Mr. Thomas Bellaw
Mid-Florida Technical Institute
Orlando, Florida

Mr. Herb Mayo
Albany, Schoharie, Schenectady
Vo-Tech
Albany, New York

Mr. Kenneth Zoin
El Camino Community College
Torrance, California

Mr. Philip C. Volpe
Vale Technical Campus
Blairsville, Pennsylvania

Keith Draper
Daytona Beach Community
College
Daytona Beach, Florida

Mr. William Millhouse
Gateway Technical Institute
Kenasha, Wisconsin

Mr. Jerry Shopfner
Cerritos Community College
Norwalk, California

Mr. Jack D'Armond
Central Piedmont Community
College
Charlotte, North Carolina

Mr. Frank L. Yeargain
Golden West College
Costa Mesa, California

Mr. Neal D. Grover
Salt Lake City Community
College
Salt Lake City, Utah

Mr. Ronnie Kendrick
Augusta Area Tech
Augusta, Georgia

James M. Walker
Amtech Institute
Wichita, Kansas

John J. Stockdale
Laramie County Community
College
Cheyenne, Wyoming

Paul A. Lind
Duluth AVTI
Duluth, Minnesota

Roger D. Randall
Cleveland Technical College
Shelby, North Carolina

William Boyer
South Florida Community
College
Avon Park, Florida

Jim Johnson
North Dakota State College of
Science
Wahpeton, North Dakota

Arlin R. Buckwalter
Mt. Joy Vo-Tech School
Mt. Joy, Pennsylvania

Peter Gall
Lakeshore Technical Institute
Cleveland, Wisconsin

One final thank-you should be given to Jeff Silver of I-CAR and Lou Forier of Motor Publications for their help in preparing this book.

Through the generosity of the following companies, photographs were supplied to enhance the book.

3M Corp.
Accuspray
America Sikkens, Inc.
American Best Car-Parts, Inc.
American Motors, Inc.
Arn-Wood Co.
Atlantic Pneumatic, Inc.
Auto Lifts & Machinery Corp.
Babcox Publications
Badger Air-Brush Co.
Bee Line Co.
Bend-Pak, Inc.
Biddle Instruments, Inc.
Binks Mfg. Co.
Black & Decker, Inc.
Blackhawk Automotive, Inc.
Bodycraft Corp.
Brian R. White Co., Inc.
Broncrop Mfg. Co.
Campbell Hausfeld Co.
Car-o-Liner Inc.
Carborundum Abrasive Co.
Century Mfg. Co.
Champion Pneumatic Machinery
    Co., Inc.
Chicago Pneumatic Tool Div.
Chief Automotive Systems, Inc.
Chrysler Corp.
Clements National Co.
Dana Corp.
Dedoes Industries, Inc.
Delta International Machinery
    Corp.
DeVilbiss Co.
Du Pont Co.

Dynatron/Bondo Corp.
Easco/K-D Tools, Inc.
Eastern Safety Equipment
Eurovac, Inc.
Everco Industries, Inc.
Fibre Glass Evercoat Co., Inc.
Fitz & Fitz, Inc.
Florida Pneumatic Mfg. Co.
Ford Motor Co.
Forward Mfg. Co., Inc.
Foulk's Sales & Service
General Motors Corp.
Graco, Inc.
Group 10, Inc.
H & S Mfg. Co. Ltd.
Hankison Corp.
Henning Hansen, Inc.
Heritage Ford, Inc.
Herkules Equipment Corp.
HTP America, Inc.
Hunter Engineering Co.
Hutchins Mfg. Co.
Inter-Industry Conference on
    Auto Collision Repair
Kansas Jack, Inc.
Lenco Inc.
Lincoln Electric Co.
Lincoln St. Louis Inc.
Lisle Corp.
Lors Machinery, Inc.
Maaco Enterprises, Inc.
Majestic Tools Mfg. Co.
Marson Corp.
Martin-Senour Paint Co.
Mine Safety Appliance Co.

Modine Mfg. Co.
Mohawk Resources, Ltd.
Motor Publications, Inc.
National Automotive Dealers
    Used Car Guide Co.
Nicator, Inc.
Nissan Motor Corp.
Norco Industries, Inc.
Norton Co.
Oatey Corp.
Omer, Inc.
OTC Corp.
Plumley Co.
PPG Industries, Inc.
Pull-It Corp.
S & G Tool Aid Corp.
Seelye, Inc.
Sherwin-Williams Co.
Snap-on Tools Corp.
Sparten Plastics, Inc.
Stanley Works, Inc.
Steck Mfg. Co., Inc.
Sun Electric Corp.
Thermal Devices, Inc.
Tom's Salvage Yard, Inc.
Toyota Motor Corp.
Unican Corp.
Urethane Supply Co. Inc.
Vaco Products Inc.
Walker Mfg. Co.
Weaver Corp.
Willson Safety Products, Inc.
YACO Industries, Ltd.

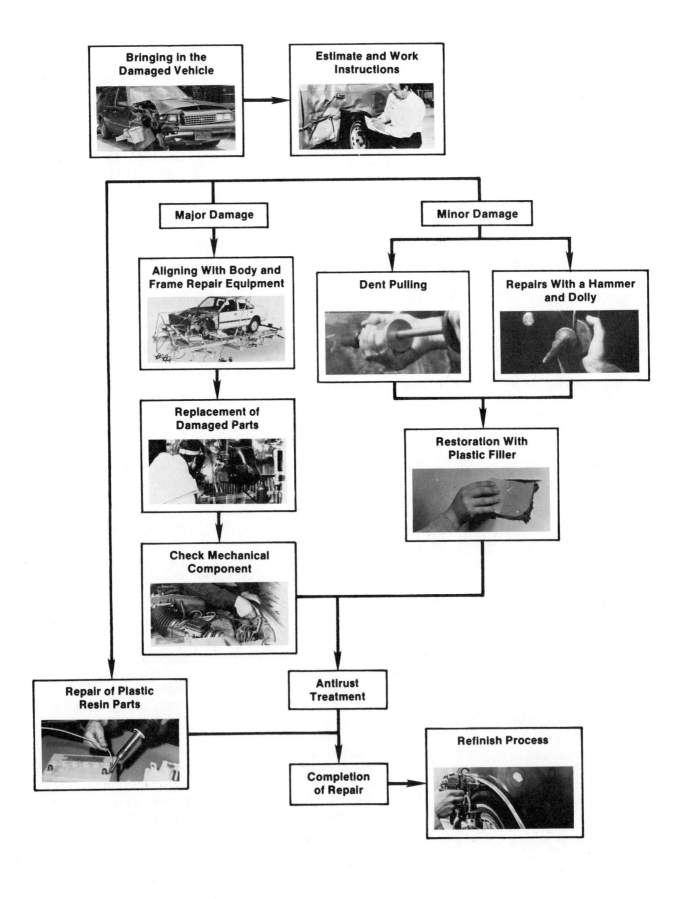

Bringing in the Damaged Vehicle → **Estimate and Work Instructions**

Major Damage
- Aligning With Body and Frame Repair Equipment
- Replacement of Damaged Parts
- Check Mechanical Component

Minor Damage
- Dent Pulling
- Repairs With a Hammer and Dolly
- Restoration With Plastic Filler

Repair of Plastic Resin Parts

Antirust Treatment

Completion of Repair → Refinish Process

CHAPTER 1

Body/Paint Shop Work and Safety Procedures

OBJECTIVES

After reading this chapter, you will be able to:

- list and describe the publications and associations that are available to paint and body shop employees.
- list the rules regarding personal safety, work area safety, tool and welding safety, environmental safety, fire safety, and the methods of handling hazardous wastes safely.
- explain the "right-to-know" law.
- explain the requirements for the ASE Body/Paint Technician Certifications.
- identify the setup and innerworkings of a paint and body shop and its various personnel.
- outline the steps for preparing a car for repair.

Of the nearly 100,000 body and paint shops in the United States, some 25,000 are owned by new car dealers. Whether dealer-owned (Figure 1-1) or independent (Figure 1-2), no two are exactly alike. They vary either in size, in the layout of the work sections, in the location, number of employees, amount or type of equipment, or in the order of procedures that they follow. Yet combined, they do an astounding annual volume of more than $10 billion in the collision repair and refinish business.

1.1 TYPICAL BODY AND PAINT SHOP OPERATIONS

The repair method used for restoring a vehicle damaged in a collision is determined by the area that is damaged, the extent of damage, paint refinishing requirements, the repair costs, and other similar conditions. It must be remembered that nearly any damaged automobile can be restored if the vehicle

FIGURE 1-1   Typical dealership-owned body and paint shop

FIGURE 1-2   Typical independent-operated body and paint shop

FIGURE 1-3   Major front end damage

FIGURE 1-4   Minor front end damage

owner is willing to pay for the repair. It is this cost that is a major consideration for both the vehicle owner and the auto body shop.

For this reason, the vehicle is first brought into the shop where a damage estimate is prepared. Then the decision is made whether the damage is major (a vehicle that requires body or frame repairs, Figure 1-3) or minor (a vehicle that requires only outer panel or cosmetic repairs, Figure 1-4). Repair instructions are written down on the repair order (RO) and the repair operations are carried out according to those instructions. Once the repair order is received in the shop, the repair procedure follows a step-by-step pattern.

Most body and paint shop operations can be classified by size as small, medium, and large. The shop layouts shown in Figure 1-5 are not presented as an ideal arrangement but as examples of some of the things most necessary to include.

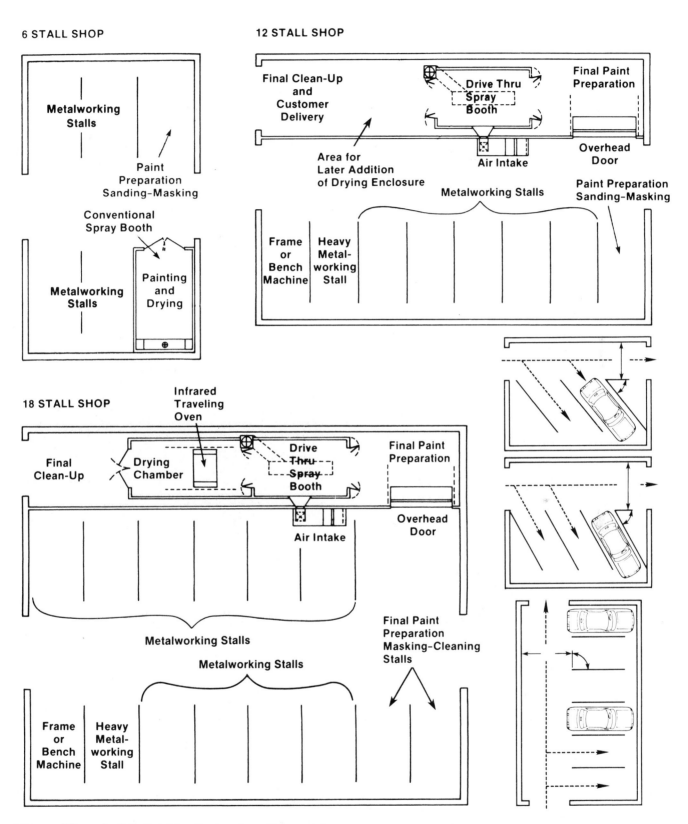

*Concept Downdraft Refinishing System (see Chapter 17) is shown in the 12 and 18 stall illustrations. Standard Conventional Horizontal Flow Booth could also be used.

FIGURE 1-5 Layout of a small (6 stall) shop, a medium (12 stall) shop, and large (18 stall) paint and body shop. Note the driveway widths but note parking should be used where it cannot be avoided.

There are two basic work areas in every collision repair and refinishing shop: (1) metalworking (or body) and (2) paint. Whatever the physical size of the overall shop, the work flow (and the car) should be as continuous as on a factory production line. That is, the vehicle should move from its entrance into the shop to the metalwork area on to the refinishing area. In most shops, however, the vehicle is thoroughly washed to remove mud, dirt, and water-soluble contaminants. The car should be washed and thoroughly dried before moving it to the metalworking area.

Metalworking Shop

The metalworking area (Figure 1-6) is where the vehicle body is repaired. This damage can be either the result of a collision (Figure 1-7) or deterioration (Figure 1-8). The repair tasks in this area of the shop are performed by body technicians or mechanics and their helpers.

In most shops, the estimator makes an appraisal of the damage to the vehicle and how much it will cost to repair. Once the owner and/or the insurance company approves the appraisal, the vehicle is turned over to the body shop supervisor for the start of the repair work. If the shop is large enough, the supervisor and one of the body technicians go over the repair order form (Figure 1-9) that was filled out by the shop manager or estimator.

FIGURE 1-7   Damage can be the result of a collision.

FIGURE 1-8   Damage can be the result of rust deterioration.

FIGURE 1-6   The shop metalworking area is the heart of the body repair operations. *(Courtesy of Du Pont Co.)*

FIGURE 1-9   The shop supervisor and body technician must discuss the repair order. *(Courtesy of Maaco Enterprises, Inc.)*

FIGURE 1-10 Body straightening equipment in use. *(Courtesy of Nicator, Inc.)*

In repairing any type of collision damage, the body technician must first study and diagnose the damage that has occurred. Once the damage has been evaluated, the technician must determine whether it will be cheaper to straighten or repair the damaged section or replace it. Is the cost of repair more or less than the cost of replacement parts plus the cost of installation? In some shops, the estimator, shop manager, or even the owner are involved in these decisions. However, the body technician is usually consulted.

Once the extent of the damage and how it is to be corrected are determined, the repairs must be completed in the body shop. For example, if a panel is creased, torn, or caved in, it can be straightened by hammers, picks, spoons, and hydraulic jacks (Figure 1-10). Accurate adjustment of body assemblies such as hoods, rear deck lids, and doors might have to be made by the technician. If they are not correctly done, the assemblies are difficult to close and will rattle when the car is driven over a rough road. In addition, they are also apt to leak excessive amounts of rain and dust. Such failures on the part of the body technician to perform a job competently are bound to cause customer complaints.

Today, because of changing auto construction design, more and more body shops are offering complete collision services such as wheel alignment (Figure 1-11), cooling system repairs, autoelectric checkouts, and diagnosing strut damage. While

FIGURE 1-11 With the advent of the unibody cars body technicians must consider wheel alignment. *(Courtesy of Bee Line Co.)*

many of these repairs are still done by so-called "auto specialty shops," the interest of body repair shop owners in these jobs has made it necessary for the body technician to have some knowledge of these systems.

The metalworking technician must also be able to correct and repair minor defects such as scratches, chips, dents, surface rust, and rustouts. More and more auto body shops are providing rust-proofing services to their customers either before

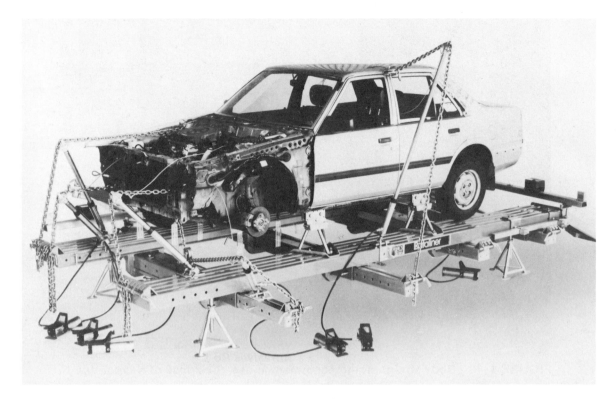

FIGURE 1-12   Hydraulic pulling equipment at work. (Courtesy of Nicator, Inc.)

rustout occurs or after repairing the problem. Except in large shops, methods of applying rustproofing are usually a joint job of both the body and paint technicians.

Today's body technician must have a total knowledge of the tools used in the metalworking area. These include body repair hand tools, air and electric power tools, hydraulic body tools (Figure 1-12), and welding equipment; these are all covered in Chapters 6 through 15.

Paint Shop

Auto refinishing or painting is a very important part of the auto repair business. Not only do major collisions and wrecks and minor damage have to be painted, but also many automobiles are repainted to enhance their beauty. New and used car dealers repaint automobiles to attract buyers. Also, sometimes the owner gets tired of looking at the same old color. Oftentimes, the finish on many automobiles needs attention because it has been neglected or damaged by weather conditions.

The paint shop area (Figure 1-13) is where the car is refinished by refinishing technicians or painters. Here, a series of operations is performed on the vehicle as it passes through the following stages: make-ready, spraying, drying, and final cleaning.

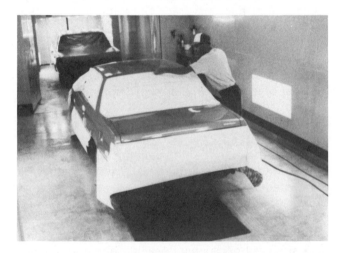

FIGURE 1-13   The heart of the paint shop section is the spray booth and drying area. (Courtesy of DeVilbiss Co.)

Preparation

In the initial make-ready, the car is prepared for the spraying operation. The preparation procedure generally includes:

1. Remove windshield wipers, emblems, nameplate (Figure 1-14), mirrors, and other small pieces of trim.

FIGURE 1-14 To make ready for refinishing, it is often necessary to remove emblems and nameplates.

FIGURE 1-15 Soak a dry cloth with degreasing solvent and apply to remove grease and road tar. While still wet, the surface should be wiped dry with a clean cloth. *(Courtesy of Du Pont Co.)*

2. Degrease the car by wiping down each area with a solvent or degreaser (Figure 1-15) to remove grease and road tar.
3. Machine and hand-sand any chips and scratches (Figure 1-16).
4. Clean both the interior and exterior carefully (Figure 1-17A). All dust is removed with a dusting gun and wiped with a tack rag (Figure 1-17B).
5. Inspect all surfaces to be sure that they are properly cleaned before moving the vehicle to the masking area.

In the masking area, the parts of the car that are not to be painted—windows, chrome, lights, vinyl

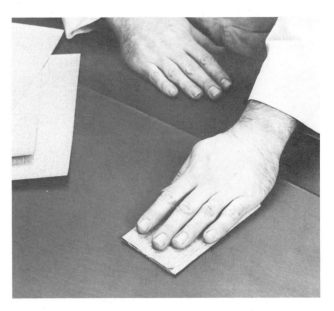

FIGURE 1-16 Sanding removes scratches and minor surface damage. *(Courtesy of Carborundum Abrasives Co.)*

A

B

FIGURE 1-17 (A) Clean the surface thoroughly, then before the finish is applied, (B) wipe the surface with a tack rag to make certain that no moisture or dirt is present.

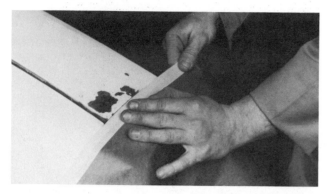

FIGURE 1-18 Masking paper and tape are used to cover the area not to be sprayed.

FIGURE 1-20 Applying a finish topcoat. (Courtesy of Du Pont Co.)

top—are covered with masking paper (Figure 1-18) and held in place with tape. In large shops, the preparation jobs are handled by the **sander,** while the masking operation is performed by a **masker.** In small shops, the make-ready jobs are usually done by the painter or a helper. Complete details of the preparation procedures are given in Chapter 18.

Spraying

When the vehicle moves into the spray booth (Figure 1-19), the **painter** takes over. If a sealer is to be used, it is applied next; followed by the topcoat (Figure 1-20). If the topcoat is fast-drying lacquer, the masking is removed right after the spraying. If the topcoat is enamel, the masking is removed once the paint film is tack free. Complete information on applying paint is given in Chapter 19.

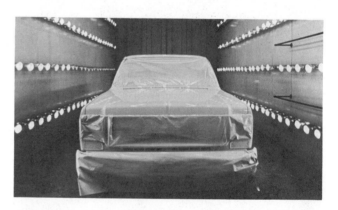

FIGURE 1-21 Typical drive-thru drying area of spray booth

Drying

In the drying room, most shops use drying equipment (Figure 1-21) to speed up the drying. This is especially useful in drying enamel. In some small paint shops the drying operation is often done with portable equipment in the spray area (Figure 1-22).

Final Cleaning

After the finish is dried, the car moves to the final make-ready area. If the car has been refinished with enamel, the masking is now removed. Compounding or polishing is done in the final make-ready area, along with other tasks such as polishing all chrome, cleaning glass and overspray, replacing removed items, vacuuming the interior, and cleaning vinyl top

FIGURE 1-19 Typical spray booth. (Courtesy of DeVilbiss Co.)

FIGURE 1-22 Typical portable drying equipment. (Courtesy of Thermal Devices, Inc.)

and tires. In large shops, these jobs are usually performed by the detailer.

In addition to being able to apply the new finish properly, the painter or refinishing technician must have knowledge about paint products and how to mix and match them. Remember: if the refinishing job looks good and the color matches well, the customer will usually be satisfied with all of the other repair work done while the car was in the shop.

OTHER SHOP PERSONNEL

Foremost in any collision repair business are the body and paint technicians and their helpers. In addition to part time cleanup employees that work one to two hours a day, there are other jobs that must be done as well. The personnel that handle these jobs include the following.

Shop Owner and Manager

The shop owner must be concerned with all phases of work done in the shop. In smaller shops, the owner and shop manager are one in the same person. In larger operations or in new car dealerships, the owner might hire a shop manager to supervise the operation of a collision repair and refinishing shop. In all cases, the person in charge should understand all of the work done in the shop as well as its business operations.

Parts Manager

The parts manager (Figure 1-23) is in charge of ordering all parts (both new and salvaged), receiving all parts, and seeing that they are delivered to the ordering technician. In new car dealerships, these tasks may be taken care of by the parts manager of the franchise.

To locate and order the correct parts, it is important that the repair shop collect all of the necessary information about the vehicle. Not only is accurate

FIGURE 1-23 The parts manager is an important member of the body/paint shop.

ordering of parts vital to the job production, it is equally important to the job cost and profit. For example, the price of a can of paint can vary as much as 200 percent from one color to another. The only way for the parts manager to order the correct color is for the painter to give all information that appears on the body code plate (Figure 1-24). As described and illustrated in Chapters 16 and 20, these tags are located on various parts of the vehicle.

In order to purchase the correct parts, it is sometimes necessary to provide the parts manager with the assembly plant that manufactured the original part. Many body parts require the same reference.

FIGURE 1-24 Typical body code plate. For location of these tags on standard model vehicles, see Chapters 16 and 20.

FIGURE 1-26 Computers are playing a more and more important role in the daily operations of the body and paint shop. The office manager must be able to operate a computer.

To get a wood grain overlay to match a certain vehicle, the parts department must know which assembly plant built the car. The plant code is provided on a body code plate somewhere on the vehicle. The exact location for each vehicle will be explained in the vehicle identification section in front of the collision guide. The VIN (Figure 1-25) will also reveal the build date, trim code, engine size, and all the other data necessary to improve both the estimate writing and parts ordering activities. The VIN plate is described in more detail in Chapter 2.

There are frequent "running changes" made by the vehicle manufacturers. Vehicles built in the same model year can have one of several individual part applications. The only way to keep on track with all of the changes is for the manufacturer to note either the build date when a different part first is installed or to use the VIN or body code plate number as the point of reference.

FIGURE 1-25 Typical VIN plate number. It is located on the front dashboard and is visible through the windshield.

Bookkeeper

The bookkeeper keeps the shop's record books, makes all invoices, writes checks, and pays bills, makes bank deposits, checks bank statements, and takes care of tax payments. Many small shops hire an "outside" accountant to perform these jobs.

Office Manager

The office manager's duties vary from answering the telephone to being a receptionist and handling such secretarial operations as typing and filing letters, estimates, and receipts (Figure 1-26). In many small shops, the office manager also acts as the parts manager and the bookkeeper.

Tow Truck Operator

Larger shop firms generally have trained tow truck operators to operate its wrecker(s). Rather than own this expensive piece of equipment (Figure 1-27), many smaller shops depend on independent towing services or "farm out" such work to other repair garages.

Estimator

Estimating the cost of damage repair and refinishing on various vehicles is important to the success of an auto body shop. Estimates will range from small dents (Figure 1-28A) to major wrecks (Figure 1-28B). Refinishing work must be estimated, too. The person who determines the cost value of the damage plus price required to repair the damaged vehicle is called an **estimator** or **damage appraiser** (Figure 1-29).

FIGURE 1-27 Many body shops offer towing service.

A

B

FIGURE 1-28 Collision damage can range from (A) a small dent to (B) major damage.

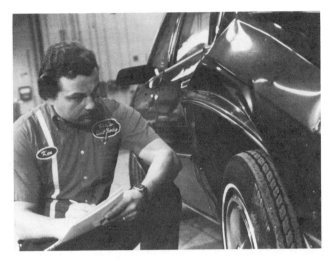

FIGURE 1-29 Estimator making a written estimate

In addition to determining the cost of repairing and refinishing, the estimator must work with insurance companies' adjusters or appraisers. The appraiser is the insurance company's representative who estimates a vehicle's damage and authorizes payment to the shop. All estimates or **damage appraisals,** as they are sometimes called, must be in writing and signed by an insurance company's adjuster or the customer and the shop's estimator. The estimate then becomes a legal commitment among the parties involved as to work to be done, cost, and method of payment. More details on estimating and the importance of the estimator's function in a body/paint shop operation are given in Chapter 20.

SHOP PUBLICATIONS

There are several publications that all body shop personnel should become familiar with. The most important of these to the body technician is the manufacturer's body service manuals (Figures 1-30 and 1-31). On the other hand, the crash estimating guides are vital to the estimator (Figure 1-32); the replacement catalogs are very important to the parts manager; and all shop personnel should be interested in the trade publications (Figure 1-33). These professional publications should be available to all.

1.2 SHOP SAFETY PRACTICES

The most important considerations in any repair and refinishing shop should be accident prevention and safety. Carelessness and the lack of safety habits cause accidents. Accidents have a far-reaching

FIGURE 1-30 The removal and installation instructions are also found in the factory body manuals.

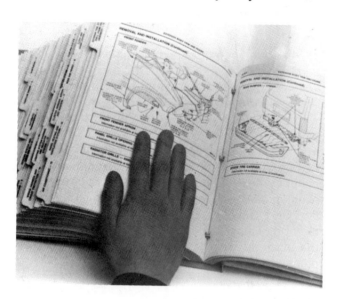

FIGURE 1-31 Typical page from a manufacturer's service manual

FIGURE 1-32 Estimating guides used in the preparation of damage reports.

FIGURE 1-33 Typical trade publications.

effect, not only on the victim, but on the victim's family and society in general. More importantly, accidents can cause serious injury, temporary or permanent, or even death. Therefore, it is the obligation of all shop employees and the employer to foster and develop a safety program to protect the health and welfare of those involved.

In the following chapters of this book, the text contains special notations labeled **SHOP TALK, CAUTION,** and **WARNING.** Each one is there for a specific purpose. **SHOP TALK** gives added information that will help the technician to complete a particular procedure or make a task easier. **CAUTION** is given to prevent the technician from making an error that could

damage the vehicle. **WARNING** reminds the technician to be especially careful of those areas where carelessness can cause personal injury. The following text contains some general **WARNINGs** that should be followed when working in a body and paint shop.

1.3 PERSONAL SAFETY AND HEALTH PROTECTION

The following are very important personal safety rules that must be heeded while working in a body and paint shop.

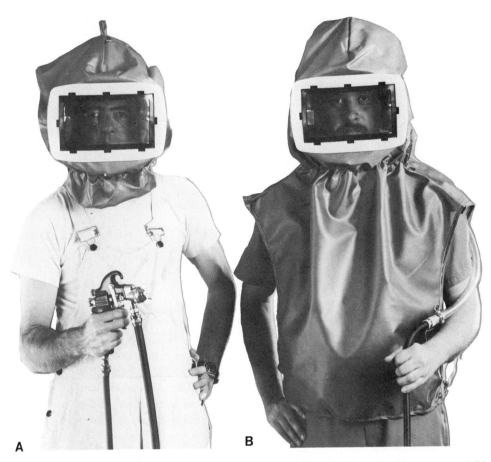

FIGURE 1-34 Air-supplied respirators: (A) neck-length and (B) waist length *(Courtesy of Binks Mfg. Co.)*

Air Passages and Lungs

Abrasive dust, vapors from caustic solutions and solvents, spray mist from undercoats and finishes—all present dangers to the air passages and lungs, especially for workers who are among them day in, day out.

Respirators are usually needed in refinishing shops even though adequate ventilation is provided for the work areas. There are three primary types of respirators available to protect refinishing technicians: the hood or air-supplied respirator, cartridge filter respirator, and dust or particle respirator.

Air-Supplied or Hood Respirators. A National Institute for Occupational Safety and Health (NIOSH) approved air-supplied respirator provides protection from sensitization and other dangers of inhaling isocyanate paint vapors and mists, as well as from hazardous solvent vapors.

Exposure to isocyanates often found in urethanes and other two-pack or two-part materials can lead to a variety of health problems with symptoms that include dizziness, abdominal pain, and vomiting. If a person is allergy-prone or has already suffered from overexposure to isocyanates, a more severe reaction most likely will occur, even at a lower-level concentration.

The air line respirator is comfortable to wear and does not require fit testing (Figure 1-34). It consists of a half mask, full facepiece, hood or helmet, to which clean, breathable air is supplied through a small diameter hose from a separate compressed air source.

The air line respirator should include a self-contained 3/4 horsepower oilless pump (Figure 1-35) to supply air to either one hood or two half mask respirators. The pump's air inlet must be located in a clean air area. Some shops mount the pumps on an outside wall, away from the dust and dirt generated by shop operations. If shop-compressed air must be used, it must be filtered with a trap and carbon filter to remove oil, water, scale, odor, and taste. The air supply must have a valve to match air pressure to respirator equipment and an automatic control to sound an alarm or shut down the com-

FIGURE 1-35 Typical oilless air pump that moves ambient air from a clean environment and supplies it to air line respirators of hood. The 3/4-horsepower unit shown is suitable for two persons. *(Courtesy of Willson Safety Product, Inc.)*

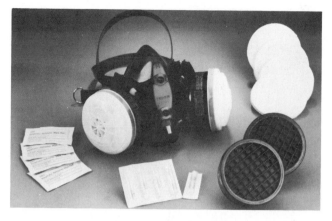

FIGURE 1-36 Half mask, dual cartridge air purifying respiratory kit *(Courtesy of Paint-Safe Products)*

pressor in case of overheating. (Overheating frequently causes carbon monoxide contamination of the air supply.)

Remember that the air source for an air line respirator must be located in a clean, fresh air environment, outside of the spray area.

Cartridge Filter Respirators.

If the refinishing system that is sprayed contains no isocyanates, an air-purifying, cartridge respirator with organic vapor cartridges and prefilters can be used (Figure 1-36). These respirators protect against vapors and spray mists of nonactivated enamels, lacquers, and other nonisocyanate materials.

This type of respirator consists of a rubber facepiece designed to conform to the face and form an airtight seal. It includes replaceable prefilters and cartridges that remove solvent and other vapors from the air. The paint respirator also has intake and exhaust valves, which ensure that all incoming air flows through the filters.

It is very important with air-purifying cartridge respirators that it fits securely around the edge of the face to prevent contaminated air from leaking into the breathing area. To check this, a quantitative fit test should be done prior to using the respirator, performing both negative and positive pressure checks. To check for negative pressure, the wearer should place the palms of the hands over the car-

tridges and inhale. A good fit will be evident if the facepiece collapses onto the wearer's face. To perform a positive pressure check, the wearer covers up the exhalation valve and exhales. A proper fit is evident if the facepiece billows out without air escaping the mask. Another form of quantitative fit testing consists of exposing amyl acetate (banana oil) near the seal around the face. If no odor is detected, a proper fit is evident.

Cartridge respirators are available in several sizes and might or might not contain a face mask (Figure 1-37). The most common size will provide the best protection. But, wearers of this type of respirator should be aware that facial hair might prevent an airtight seal, presenting a hazard to the wearer's health. Therefore, refinishers with facial hair should use a positive pressure-supplied air respirator system, because hair will prevent a seal of mask to face, eliminating the respirator's effectiveness. Remember that cartridge respirators should be used only in well-ventilated areas. They must not be used in environments containing less than 19.5 percent oxygen.

To maintain the cartridge filter respirator, keep it clean and change the prefilters and cartridges as often as directed by the manufacturer. Here are a few other maintenance tips:

- Replace the prefilters when it becomes difficult to breathe through the respirator.
- Replace the cartridge at least weekly, or earlier, at the first sign of solvent odor.
- Regularly check the mask to make sure it does not have any cracks or dents.
- Store the respirator in an airtight container.
- Follow the manufacturer's instructions provided to ensure proper maintenance and fit.

FIGURE 1-37 (Left) Typical cartridge filters with full facepiece *(Courtesy of Mine Safety Appliance Co.)* and (right) cartridge filters with no faceplate *(Courtesy of Herkules Equipment Co.)*

Dust or Particle Respirators. To protect against dust from sanding, use a dust respirator (Figure 1-38). Sanding operations in the body shop create dust that can cause bronchial irritation and possible long-term lung damage if inhaled. Protection from this health hazard is necessary; a NIOSH-approved dust respirator should be worn whenever a technician or someone working close to him/her is involved in a sanding operation. Follow the instructions provided with the dust respirator to ensure proper maintenance fit. Remember that dust masks do not protect against vapors and spray mists.

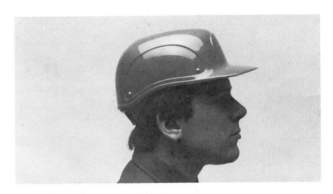

FIGURE 1-39 Bump cap will protect the body shop technician from head bumps or lacerations. *(Courtesy of Willson Safety Products, Inc.)*

FIGURE 1-38 When power sanding, dust and dirt can get into the lungs without proper protection. Always wear safety glasses and a NIOSH-approved dust particle mask before grinding.

HEAD PROTECTION

Be sure to tie long hair securely behind the head before beginning to work on a vehicle. The hair also must be protected against dust and sprays. To keep hair clean (and healthy) wear a cap at all times in the work area and a protective painter's stretch hood in the spray booth.

A body technician should always wear a bump cap (Figure 1-39) or hard hat when working beneath hoods or under the car.

EYE AND FACE PROTECTION

Eye protection is required where there is a possibility of an eye injury from flying particles, chips, and so forth. Clear protective safety goggles, glass-

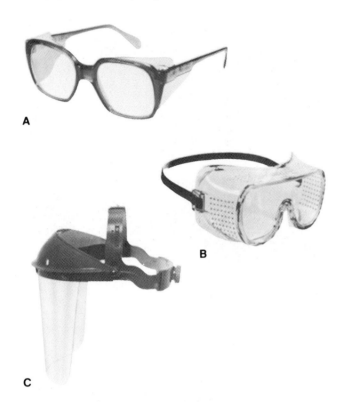

A

B

C

FIGURE 1-40 (A) Safety glasses, (B) goggles, and (C) face shield *(Courtesy of Goodson Shop Supplies)*

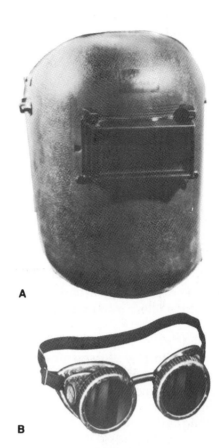

A

B

FIGURE 1-41 (A) Welding helmet and (B) welding goggles

es, or face shields (Figure 1-40) should be worn when using grinders, disc sanders, power drills, pneumatic chisels, removing shattered glass, or when working underneath the auto. Many employers are now requiring **all** employees to wear **safety goggles** or **glasses** when they are in the metalworking or painting areas of the shop even if they are wearing ordinary glasses. This makes sense . . . common sense. Because in any of the shop locations there is always the possibility of flying objects, dust particles, or splashing liquids entering the eyes. Not only can this be painful it can also cause loss of sight. Remember, eyes are irreplaceable. Get in the habit of wearing safety goggles, glasses, or face shields in the working areas.

A welding helmet or welding goggles (Figure 1-41) with the proper shade lens must be worn when welding. These will protect the eyes and face from flying molten pieces of steel and from harmful light rays. Sunglasses are not adequate protection from the latter.

Ear Protection

Panel beating, the piercing noise of sanding, the radio blaring full-blast—it is impossible to hear any-

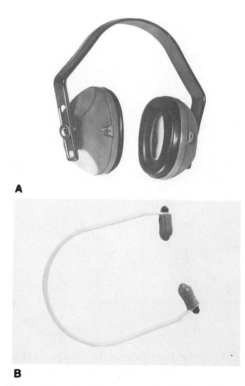

A

B

FIGURE 1-42 Typical (A) ear muffs or (B) ear plugs. *(Courtesy of Willson Safety Products, Inc.)*

thing else. It is enough to deafen a person—and that is exactly what it will do if proper precautions are not taken. When in metalworking areas, wear ear plugs or muffs (Figure 1-42) to protect the eardrums from damaging noise levels.

BODY PROTECTION

Loose clothing, unbuttoned shirt sleeves, dangling ties, jewelry, and shirts hanging out are **very** dangerous in a body shop. Instead, wear approved shop coveralls or jumpsuits.

A clean jumpsuit or lint-free coveralls should be worn when in the spray area. Dirty, solvent-soaked clothing will hold these chemicals against the skin, causing irritation or a rash. Make sure they are long sleeved for complete protection.

Pants should always be long enough to cover the top of the shoes. This will prevent sparks from going down into the shoes especially when using welding equipment. For added welding safety, welder's pants, leggings, or spats are often worn. Upper body protection during this operation should include either a welder's jacket or apron (see Chapter 6).

HAND PROTECTION

The harmful effects of liquids, undercoats, and finishes on the hands can be prevented very effectively by wearing proper gloves. Impervious gloves, such as the nitrile latex type, should be used when working with solvents or two-pack primers and topcoats. These gloves offer special protection from the materials found in two-component systems. See the Material Safety Data Sheets (MSDS) for glove recommendations. Thick, strong work gloves should be worn in the prep area to avoid cuts or abrasions. Always remember to wash hands thoroughly when leaving the shop area. This provides protection from

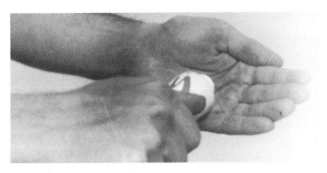

FIGURE 1-43 After working with solvents, use a little silicone-free skin cream.

ingesting any harmful elements that may have been touched.

When washing hands, it is usually recommended that the hands be cleaned with a proper hand cleaner. At the end of a day's work, it is wise to oil the skin a little by applying a good silicone-free skin cream (Figure 1-43). Do not use thinner as a hand cleaner.

WARNING: Before using any solvent as a hand cleaner, be sure there is no manufacturer's warning on the label against this practice. Some of the hardeners and additives used in the newer paints can cause skin rashes and dermatitis.

FOOT PROTECTION

Wear safety work shoes that have metal toe inserts and nonslip soles. The inserts protect the toes from falling objects; the soles help to prevent falls. In addition, good work shoes provide support and comfort for someone who is standing for a long time. While some athletic footwear may be worn, **never** wear gym shoes or dress shoes; they do not provide adequate protection in a body shop.

When spraying, many technicians wear disposable shoe covers. In fact, disposable garments and hoods are becoming more commonly used by sprayers.

DAY-BY-DAY PERSONAL SAFETY GUIDE

The following guidelines are designed to protect the technician while on the job—from the moment he or she determines what steps need to be taken and the products to be used until the time comes to put away the equipment and get ready to head home.

- **Be informed.** Read the warnings on the product labels and in manufacturers' literature. If more information is desired, get copies of the Material Safety Data Sheets for specific products from the shop's office or from the material suppliers. As mentioned later in this chapter, these contain information on hazardous ingredients and protective measures that the technician should use.
- **During power sanding.** When power sanding, dust and dirt fly into the air. These can get into eyes, lungs, and scalp without proper protection. Safety glasses or goggles will protect the eyes. Do not wear contacts when

grinding, sanding, or handling solvents. Head covers provide scalp and hair protection. A NIOSH-approved dust particle mask should also be worn to prevent inhaling dust and particles. All masks should fit tightly to the skin.

- **During cleaning with compressed air.** When using a dust gun to clean doorjambs and other hard-to-reach places, eye protection and particle masks should always be worn.

- **During metal conditioning.** Metal conditioners contain phosphoric acid. Breathing these chemicals or allowing them to come in direct contact with the skin, eyes, or clothing may cause irritation. The use of safety glasses (to prevent splashs into the eyes), coveralls, rubber gloves, and a NIOSH-approved organic vapor respirator is recommended when using these products. If the coveralls become soaked for any reason, make sure they are changed to clean ones to avoid irritation to the skin; or soak with water to dilute the chemicals.

- **During mixing and handling.** Mixing and pouring of refinish materials should be done in a well-ventilated location away from areas used to store or apply the products. When opening cans or mixing, materials might splash. To avoid splashes to the eyes, goggles or other protection should be worn.

- **During spraying of undercoats or topcoats.** Application of undercoats and topcoats requires the use of spraying equipment, which can be hazardous if not used properly. Static electricity is generated when using airless or electrostatic spraying methods. Special attention must be paid to grounding and bonding for this equipment to prevent problems. Technicians should be fully protected when applying undercoat or topcoat products.

- **Storing paint materials.** All refinish products should be stored away from the actual work area. Paint kept in the work area should be limited to a one-day supply. Empty containers should be disposed of daily. All partially used containers should be kept securely closed and should be placed in proper metal (fire-resistant) storage cabinets (Figure 1-44) at the end of the day.

- **Horseplay.** Proper conduct can also help prevent accidents. Horseplay is not fun when it sends someone to the hospital. Such things as air nozzle fights, creeper races, or practical jokes do not have any place in the shop.

- **Lifting techniques.** When lifting and carrying objects, bend with the knees, not the back.

FIGURE 1-44 Large metal safety cabinet (Courtesy of Paint-Safe Products)

Also, do not bend the waist when lifting. Remember, heavy objects should be lifted and moved with the proper equipment for the job.

- **Before leaving the shop.** Solvents, chemicals, and other materials can contaminate clothing and wind up on the hands when removing personal protective equipment or putting away the refinishing tools. They can still enter one's system through the body's digestive tract if the hands are not washed before eating, drinking, smoking, or using the toilet facilities.

1.4 GENERAL SHOP PROCEDURES

In addition to personal safety, the body/painter technicians must be aware of general shop safety procedures. The following are some of the rules and precautions that should be observed to ensure a safe and healthful work environment in the paint shop.

ENVIRONMENTAL CONTROLS

Persons working in body/paint shop facilities are often exposed to dangerous amounts of various gases, dusts, and vapors. Because of this exposure, control measures should be established and practiced for the following frequently observed air contaminants and other hazardous substances.

- **Ventilation.** Proper ventilation is very important in areas where caustics, degreasers, undercoats, and finishes are used. In the shop and the area where vehicles are prepared, ventilation can be provided by means of an air-changing system, extraction floors, or central dust extraction for dust from abrasives combined with spraying area walls with good extraction power. For the spray booth (Figure 1–45), adequate air replacement is necessary not only to promote evaporation and drying of the areas sprayed, but also to remove harmful mist and vapors.

- **Carbon monoxide.** Operate the engine only in a well-ventilated area to avoid the danger of carbon monoxide (CO). If the shop is equipped with a tailpipe exhaust system to remove CO from the garage, use it. If not, use the direct piping to the outside method or a mechanical ventilation system.

Space heaters used in some shops can also be a serious source of CO and therefore should be periodically inspected to make sure they are adequately vented and do not become blocked.

- **Paints, body fillers, and thinners.** Thinners used in most paints have a narcotic effect, and long term exposure can eventually cause irreparable damage. In addition to the ventilation in the spray area or paint booth, respirators should be worn. As previously mentioned, rubber or safety gloves should be worn while handling paints and thinners. If any of these materials get on the skin, promptly wash the affected area with soap and water.

- **Dust.** Dust is a problem in paint shops. It is produced during operations such as sanding paints, primers, body fillers, and so forth. When doing this type of work, wear a dust particle respirator or mask.

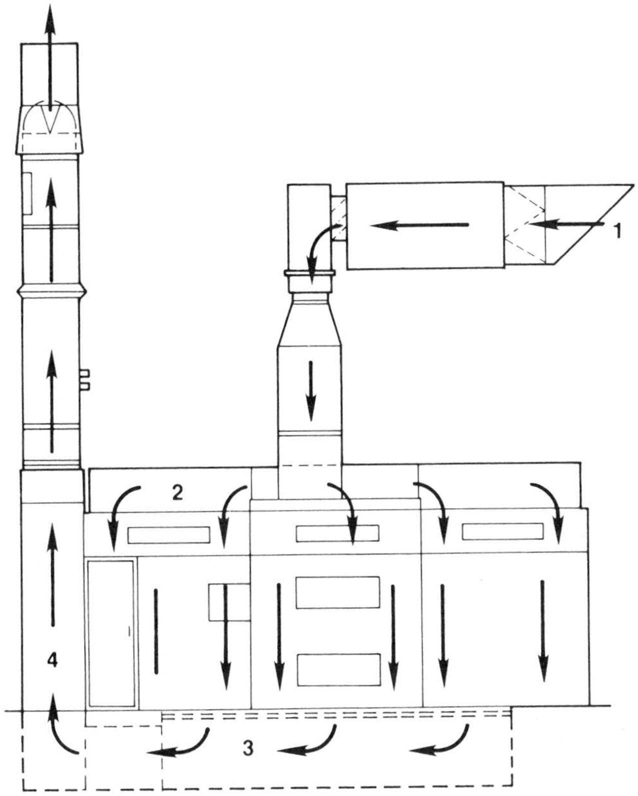

Many shops are installing so-called "dustless" sanding machine systems. Depending on the system, vacuum pumps, vacuum pullers, brush motors, or turbine motors can be used, all in the quest of sufficient air volume and/or velocity to pull airborne sanding dust through either holes in a special sanding pad or a shroud that entirely surrounds the sanding pad. Some systems run constantly, others are started "on-demand" by plugging a vacuum hose into the vacuum outlet or pushing a button at the sanding tool end of the hose. Figure 1–46 shows a portable vacuum system, while Chapter 4 contains an illustration of a central vacuum system.

By using a dustless system, the shop can comply with the Occupational Safety and Health Administration's (OSHA) airborne dust standards and eliminate costly, nonproductive cleanups. Some dustless system manufacturer's claim that their machines can trap over 99 percent of the toxic dust created by sanding lead- or chrome-based automotive paint and primer, which can contaminate the work area.

FIGURE 1–45 Modern air replacement unit for a downdraft spray booth that operates like this: (1) the cycle begins with the outside air being filtered and conditioned to the proper temperature. The processed air then flows through (2) a ceiling plenum and unique filter system and down into the spray booth. As air flows downward it passes around the car and is drawn through (3) a grating in the floor that contains paint arrester filters. The (4) booth fan exhausts the air from the pit, up a duct, and out the stack on the roof.

Vehicle Handling in the Shop

When handling a vehicle in the shop, keep the following safety precautions in mind:

- Set the parking brake when working on the vehicle. If the car has an automatic transmission, set it in PARK unless instructed otherwise for a specific service operation. If the vehicle has a manual transmission, it should

FIGURE 1-46   Portable vacuum system *(Courtesy of Nilfisk of America, Inc.)*

be in REVERSE (engine **off**) or NEUTRAL (engine **on**).

- If for some reason a work procedure requires working under a vehicle, use safety stands.
- To prevent serious burns, avoid contact with hot metal parts such as the radiator, exhaust manifold, tailpipe, catalytic converter, and muffler.
- Keep clothing and oneself clear from moving parts when the engine is running, especially the radiator fan blades and belts.
- Be sure that the ignition switch is always in the **off** position, unless otherwise required by the procedure.
- When moving a vehicle around the shop, be sure to look in all directions and make certain that nothing is in the way.

HANDLING OF SOLVENT AND OTHER FLAMMABLE LIQUIDS

The body/painter technician will be working with various solvents to clean surfaces and equipment and to thin finishes. These solvents are ex-tremely flammable. Fumes in particular can ignite explosively.

The following safety practices will help avoid fire and explosion:

- Do not light matches or smoke in the spraying and painting area, and make sure that the hands and clothing are free from solvent when lighting matches or smoking in other areas of the shop where smoking or an open flame is permitted.
- All ignition sources should be carefully controlled and monitored to avoid any possible fire hazard where a high concentration of vapor from highly flammable liquids might at times be present.
- A UL (Underwriters Laboratories) approved drum transfer pump/drum pump along with a drum vent should be used when working with drums to transfer chemicals.
- Keep all solvent containers closed, except when pouring, and clearly labeled.
- Handle all solvents (or any liquids) with care to avoid spillage. Extra caution should also be used when transferring flammable materials from bulk storage. The most important

thing to remember is to make sure the drum is grounded (Figure 1–47A) and that a bond wire connects the drum to a safety can (Figure 1–47B). Otherwise, static electricity can build up enough to create a spark that could cause an explosion.

- Discard or clean all empty solvent containers as prescribed by local regulations. Solvent fumes in the bottom of these containers are prime ignition sources. Remember: Never use gasoline as a cleaning solvent.
- Paints, thinners, solvents, and other combustible materials used in the body and paint shop must be stored in approved and designated metal (never wood) storage cabinets or rooms. Storage rooms should have adequate ventilation, which takes harmful fumes and pollutants away from the actual working area. Many body shops use a separate facility for the bulk storage of flammable material.

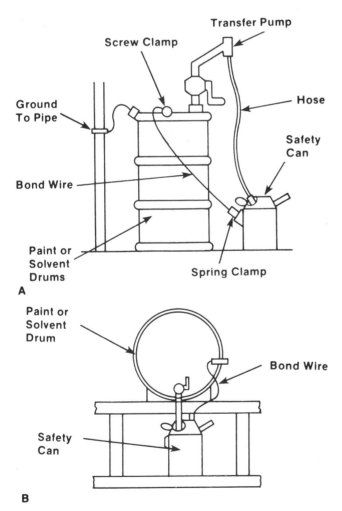

FIGURE 1–47 Two safe methods of moving flammable liquids from a drum to a portable safety can are shown above.

Never have more than one day's supply of paint outside of approved storage areas.

- The connectors on all drums and pipes of flammable and combustible liquids must be vapor- and liquid-tight.
- When spraying paint, follow these procedures:
  —Remove portable lamps before spraying.
  —Ventilation system must be turned on.
  —Spray areas must be free from hot surfaces such as heat lamps.
  —The spray area must be kept clean of combustible residue.
  —Ventilation system must be left on while the paint is drying.
  Complete spraying paint safety precautions are given in Chapter 17.
- When welding and cutting, remember that these procedures produce very high heat and sparks that can travel a long distance. Never weld or cut near paints, thinners, or other flammable liquids or materials. Cover open containers or move them to a safe area. Never cut or weld a container before checking what material was originally in that container.
- Never weld or grind near a battery. The battery charging operation produces hydrogen gas and an explosive atmosphere can exist.
- Fuel tanks should be removed, if necessary, to repair panels next to the filler tube or when the frame and floor is damaged near the tank. If the tank is removed, place it and the gasoline in a safe place. When welding or grinding near fuel filler pipes, close them tightly and cover them with wet rags.
- When welding or cutting near car interiors, remove seats and floor mats. If not, cover them with a water-dampened cloth or a welding blanket. Always have a pail of water handy and a fire extinguisher nearby. Other welding safety tips are given in Chapter 6.

TOOL AND EQUIPMENT SAFETY

The body shop technician must observe the following hand and power tool safety guidelines:

- Hand tools should always be clean and in workable condition. Greasy, oily, or chipped hand tools can easily slip out of one's grasp, causing skinned knuckles or broken fingers.
- Check all hand tools for cracks, chips, burrs, broken teeth, or other dangerous conditions before using them. If any tools are defective, do not use them.

- Be careful when using sharp or pointed tools that can slip and cause injury. If a tool is supposed to be sharp, make sure it is sharp.
- Do not use hand tools for any job other than that for which they were specifically designed.
- Do not carry screwdrivers, punches, or other sharp hand tools in pockets. It is possible to injure oneself or damage the vehicle being worked on.
- When using an electric power tool, make sure that it is properly grounded and check the wiring for cracks in the insulation, as well as for bare wires. Also, when using electrical power tools, never stand on a wet or damp floor.
- Do not operate a power tool without its guard(s).
- Disconnect electrical power before performing any service or maintenance on the tool.
- When doing any power grinding, chipping, sanding, or similar operation, always wear safety glasses. When using power equipment on small parts, never hold the part with the hand. It could slip. Always use vise grips instead.
- Before plugging in any electric tool, make sure the switch is off to prevent serious injury. When not using it, turn it off for the next person.
- Do not attempt to use the tool beyond its stated capacity or for operations requiring more than the rated horsepower of the motor. Never use a tool for operations it was not designed for.
- Keep hands away from moving parts when the tool is under power. Never clear chips or debris when the tool is under power and never use the hands to clear chips; use a brush or chip rake.
- Never overreach. Maintain a balanced stance and avoid slipping.
- Utmost caution should accompany the use of compressed air. Pneumatic tools must be operated at the pressure recommended by their manufacturers. The downstream pressure of compressed air used for cleaning purposes must remain at a pressure level below 30 psi whenever the nozzle is deadended (Figure 1-48). Do not use compressed air to clean clothes. Even at low cleaning pressure, compressed air can cause dirt particles to become embedded in the skin, which can result in infection.

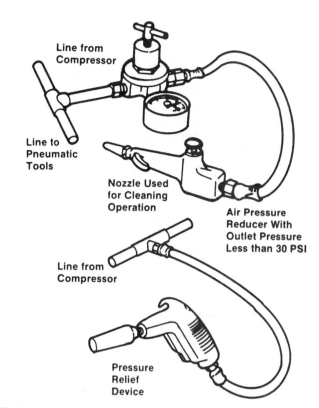

FIGURE 1-48 Air pressure reducing devices

- Store all parts and tools properly by putting them away neatly where other workers will not trip over them. This practice not only cuts down on injuries, it also reduces time wasted looking for a misplaced part or tool.
- When working with a hydraulic press, make sure that hydraulic pressure is applied in a safe manner. It is generally wise to stand to the side when operating the press. Always wear safety glasses.
- If the shop has a hydraulic lift, be sure to read the instruction manual before using it. Check the pads to see that they are making proper contact with the frame. Then raise the vehicle about 6 inches and shake it to make sure it is well balanced on the lift. If there are any rattling or scraping sounds, it means that the vehicle is not locked in place properly. If this happens, lower the lift and realign the pads to the vehicle. Test it again as previously described. Then, after lifting the vehicle to full height, put the safety catch on before working underneath the vehicle. Never permit anyone, either technician or customer, to remain in the car while it is being lifted.
- All bolts, nuts, lock rings, and other fastening components mentioned in the manufactur-

er's service manual are crucial to the safe operation of the car. Failure to use those specific items could cause extensive damage. Manufacturer's torque specifications must be followed.

- Do not risk injury through the lack of knowledge; use shop tools or perform repair operations only after receiving proper instruction. Safety tips as well as operational procedures are given throughout this book.

FIRE PROTECTION

Every body shop requires fire extinguishers (Figure 1-49). Since fires are classified as Class A, B, C, and D type, there are different types of extinguishers specially designed for a particular class of fire. Table 1-1 gives the common classes of fire that are found in body shops and methods of containing them. Some extinguishers are capable of fighting more than one type of fire.

However, the mere provision of a fire extinguisher is useless unless those who might come in contact with it know how to use it properly. If a fire breaks out, there is no time to lose figuring out how to use the fire extinguisher effectively. Operating instructions are imprinted on each listed or approved extinguisher. The approval agencies require information on the front of extinguishers indicating their classification, the relative extinguishing effectiveness (the numeral preceding the classification letter), and the methods of use. However, during an emergency there might be no time to read the label.

FIGURE 1-49 All body and paint work requires plenty of fire extinguishers capable of fighting type A, B, and C fires. (Courtesy of Pittway Corp.)

The basic information should be known ahead of time by anyone who might come in contact with and need to use the fire extinguisher.

A fire can be extinguished by depriving it of its essential ingredients, which are heat, fuel, and oxygen. Most extinguishers work by cooling the fire and removing the oxygen. If the fire extinguisher is going to be used effectively, it must be aimed at the base of the flame where the fuel is located. Fire extinguishers should be checked regularly and placed at strategic shop locations.

GOOD HOUSEKEEPING

Here are some simple good housekeeping precautions that often go unattended:

- All surfaces should be kept clean, dry, and orderly. Any oil, coolant, or grease on the floor can cause slips that could result in serious injuries. To clean up oil, be sure to use a commercial oil absorbent.
- Keep all water off the floor; remember that water is a conductor of electricity. A serious shock hazard will result if a live wire happens to fall into a puddle in which a person is standing.
- Make sure that aisles and walkways are kept clean and wide enough for a safe clearance. Cluttered walking areas contain items waiting to cause accidents.
- Use antiskid floor strips on the floor area where the operator normally stands and mark off each work area.
- There should be a list of emergency telephone numbers clearly posted next to the telephone. These numbers should include a doctor, hospital, and fire and police departments. Also the work area should have a first-aid kit for treating minor injuries. This kit should include some sterile gauze, bandages, scissors, and other related items. Facilities for flushing the eyes should also be in or near the shop area.
- Make sure that so-called hazardous materials are not discharged through floor drains or other outlets leading to public waterways.
- Any dirty rags or other combustible material must be deposited in a metal container with a suitable metal cover and should be removed to a safe place outside the building. Keep used paper towels and other paper products

TABLE 1-1: GUIDE TO EXTINGUISHER SELECTION

	Class of Fire	Typical Fuel Involved	Type of Extinguisher
Class △A Fires (green)	**For Ordinary Combustibles** Put out a class A fire by lowering its temperature or by coating the burning combustibles.	Wood Paper Cloth Rubber Plastics Rubbish Upholstery	Water*[1] Foam* Multipurpose dry chemical[4]
Class ▢B Fires (red)	**For Flammable Liquids** Put out a class B fire by smothering it. Use an extinguisher that gives a blanketing, flame-interrupting effect; cover whole flaming liquid surface.	Gasoline Oil Grease Paint Lighter fluid	Foam* Carbon dixoide[5] Halogenated agent[6] Standard dry chemical[2] Purple K dry chemical[3] Multipurpose dry chemical[4]
Class ◯C Fires (blue)	**For Electrical Equipment** Put out a class C fire by shutting off power as quickly as possible and by always using a nonconducting extinguishing agent to prevent electric shock.	Motors Appliances Wiring Fuse boxes Switchboards	Carbon dioxide[5] Halogenated agent[6] Standard dry chemical[2] Purple K dry chemical[3] Multipurpose dry chemical[4]
Class ★D Fires (yellow)	**For Combustible Metals** Put out a class D fire of metal chips, turnings, or shavings by smothering or coating with a specially designed extinguishing agent.	Aluminum Magnesium Potassium Sodium Titanium Zirconium	Dry powder extinguishers and agents only

*Cartridge-operated water, foam, and soda-acid types of extinguishers are no longer manufactured. These extinguishers should be removed from service when they become due for their next hydrostatic pressure test.

Notes:
(1) Freezes in low temperatures unless treated with antifreeze solution, usually weighs over 20 pounds, and is heavier than any other extinguisher mentioned.
(2) Also called ordinary or regular dry chemical. (sodium bicarbonate)
(3) Has the greatest initial fire-stopping power of the extinguishers mentioned for class B fires. Be sure to clean residue immediately after using the extinguisher so sprayed surfaces will not be damaged. (potassium bicarbonate)
(4) The only extinguishers that fight A, B, and C classes of fires. However, they should not be used on fires in liquefied fat or oil of appreciable depth. Be sure to clean residue immediately after using the extinguisher so sprayed surfaces will not be damaged. (ammonium phosphates)
(5) Use with caution in unventilated, confined spaces.
(6) May cause injury to the operator if the extinguishing agent (a gas) or the gases produced when the agent is applied to a fire are inhaled.

in a separate, covered container, which should be emptied every day.
• Customers and all nonemployees should never be allowed in any of the shop's work areas.

Personal protective equipment, a properly maintained body and paint shop environment, and attention to good safety and health practices all play important roles in the technician's good health. Taking the time to properly prepare **before** working on a vehicle can avoid many accidents or potentially dangerous chemical exposures. Repetition of care-

ful safety procedures will turn them into habits—good habits that will contribute to a long, healthy life.

MANUFACTURER'S WARNINGS AND GOVERNMENT REGULATIONS

In body and paint shops, hazardous wastes are generated. Every employee is protected by Right-to-Know laws. These laws started with the Occupational Safety and Health Administration Hazard Communication Standard published in 1983. This document was originally intended for chemical companies and manufacturers that require employees to handle potentially hazardous materials in the workplace. Since then, the majority of states have enacted their own Right-to-Know laws and the federal courts have decided that these regulations should apply to all including the auto refinishing profession.

The general intent of the law is for employers to provide their employees with a safe working place as it relates to hazardous materials. Specifically, there are three areas of employer responsibility:

1. **Training/educating employees.** All employees must be trained about their rights under the legislation, the nature of the hazardous chemicals in their workplace, the labeling of chemicals, and the information about each chemical posted on Material Safety Data Sheet (MSDS). These sheets (Figure 1-50) detail product composition and precautionary information for all products that can present a health or safety hazard. They are generally prepared by the product manufacturer. Employees must be familiarized about the general

uses, characteristics, protective equipment, and accident or spill procedures associated with major groups of chemicals. This training must be given to employees annually and provided to new employees as part of their job orientation.

2. **Labeling/information about potentially hazardous chemicals.** All hazardous materials must be properly labeled, indicating what health, fire, or reactivity hazard it poses and what protective equipment is necessary when handling each chemical. The manufacturer of the hazardous waste materials must provide all warnings and precautionary information, which must be read and understood by the user before application. Attention to all label precautions is essential to the proper use of the coating and for prevention of hazardous conditions.

3. **Record keeping.** Shops must maintain documentation on the hazardous chemicals in the workplace, proof of training programs, records of accidents and/or spill incidents, satisfaction of employee requests for specific chemical information via the MSDSs, and a general Right-to-Know compliance procedure manual utilized within the shop.

Hazardous waste as determined by the Environmental Protection Agency (EPA) must be in the form of "solid" material, but the EPA includes many liquids in this definition. If the waste is on the EPA list of known harmful materials or has one or more of the following four known dangerous characteristics, it is considered hazardous.

1. **Ignitability.** The waste fails the ignitability test if it is a liquid with a flash point below 140 degrees Fahrenheit or a solid that can spontaneously ignite.

2. **Corrosivity.** A material or waste is considered corrosive if it dissolves metals and other materials or burns the skin. It is an aqueous solution with a pH of 2 and below, or 12.5 and above. Acids have the lower value and alkalis have the higher value.

3. **Reactivity.** Any material that reacts violently with water or other materials or releases cyanide gas, hydrogen sulfide gas, or similar gases when exposed to low pH solutions (acid) is considered hazardous. This also includes material that generates toxic mists, fumes, vapors, and flammable gases.

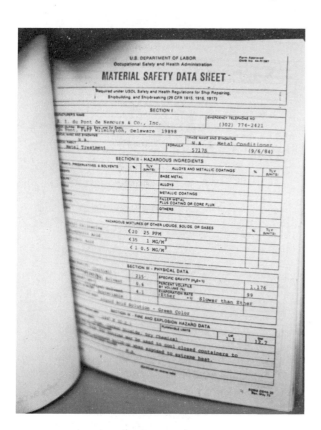

FIGURE 1-50 Typical Material Safety Data Sheet. *(Courtesy of Vulcan Material Company)*

FIGURE 1-51 Many automotive service operations, including body shops, are hiring outside contractors to handle their hazardous waste materials. *(Courtesy of Du Pont Co.)*

Complete EPA lists of hazardous wastes can be found in the Code of Federal Regulations. Materials and wastes of most concern to the body/paint technician are organic solvents: ignitable, corrosive, and/or toxic materials, and wastes that contain heavy metals, especially lead. It should be noted that no material is considered hazardous waste until the shop is finished using it and ready to dispose of it. Now that the shop is ready to dispose of it, it is hazardous waste and must be handled accordingly (Figure 1-51). The EPA says it is the owner's responsibility to determine whether the waste is hazardous, but the owner must have adequate test results to support the shop's claim.

Testing for hazardous wastes can be done by any qualified laboratory that performs tests on drinking water. They should be capable of performing tests for hazardous materials. The shop's owner(s) should contact them to see how they would like the samples taken and shipped to give accurate results.

> **WARNING:** When handling any hazardous waste material be sure to wear the safety equipment (Figure 1-52) covered under the Right-to-Know law and follow all required procedures correctly.

FIGURE 1-52 Handle all hazardous wastes as per EPA regulations. *(Courtesy of Du Pont Co.)*

4. **EP Toxicity.** Materials that leach one or more of eight heavy metals in concentrations greater than 100 times primary drinking water standard concentrations are considered hazardous. These heavy metals include lead, cadmium, chromium, and arsenic.

FIGURE 1-53 ASE body/paint technician's shoulder patch or emblem

TABLE 1-2: ASE CERTIFICATION TESTS

BODY REPAIR (TEST B1)

Content Area	Number of Questions in Test	Percentage of Coverage in Test
A. Preparation	3	7.5%
B. Frame Inspection and Repair	5	12.5%
C. Inspection and Repair of Frame Type Bodies	4	10.0%
D. Unibody Inspection, Measurement, and Repair	10	25.0%
E. Outer Body Panel Repairs, Replacements, and Adjustments	5	12.5%
F. Metal Finishing	3	7.5%
G. Body Filling	2	5.0%
H. Fiberglass Panel Repair	2	5.0%
I. Plastic Repair	4	10.0%
J. Glass, Hardware, and Miscellaneous	2	5.0%
Total	**40**	**100.0%**

PAINTING AND REFINISHING (TEST B2)

Content Area	Number of Questions in Test	Percentage of Coverage in Test
A. Surface Preparation	10	25.0%
B. Spray Gun Operation	5	12.5%
C. Paint Mixing, Matching, and Applying	11	27.5%
D. Solving Paint Application Problems	7	17.5%
E. Finish Defects, Causes, and Cures	5	12.5%
F. Safety Precautions and Miscellaneous	2	5.0%
Total	**40**	**100.0%**

1.5 ASE CERTIFICATION

The certified body shop technician is recognized as a professional by employers, peers, and the public. For this reason, the certified refinisher or body technician usually receives higher pay than the noncertified operator.

Body shop employees can get certified in one or more technical areas by taking and passing refinishing and body repair certification tests. The National Institute for Automotive Service Excellence (ASE) offers voluntary certified programs that are recommended by the major vehicle manufacturers in the United States. The Body Repair Test and Painting and Refinishing Tests each contain 40 questions in the areas noted in Table 1-2.

To qualify to take the appropriate test(s), the technician must have two years of hands-on work experience or a combination of work experience and the appropriate vocational training or education.

Technicians who pass the written exams are awarded a certificate, shoulder emblem, and other credentials attesting to their "know-how" for the subject category passed. If a technician passes both tests, he/she is entitled to be certified as a Body/Paint Technician (Figure 1-53). ASE certification is a badge of proven professionalism.

To help prepare for these programs, the test questions at the end of each chapter are similar in design and content to those used by the ASE. For further information on the ASE certification program, write: National Institute for Auto Service Excellence, 13505 Dulles Technology Drive, Herndon, Virginia 22071. Remember that a certified refinisher or body technician is usually better paid than the general mechanic.

In addition to ASE certification, a professional body/paint technician or the shop should consider membership in the various trade associations. The growth and influence of these trade associations within the industry has lead to increased communication, training, and the sharing of knowledge and ideas from all sides. The Inter-Industry Conference on Auto Collision Repair (I-CAR), Society of Collision Repair Specialists (SCRS), the Automotive Ser-

FIGURE 1–54 Various trade associations work to improve training and communication between all those involved in the collision repair industry.

vice Association (ASA), and the National Autobody Congress and Exposition (NACE) are several examples of organizations that promote professional and consumer education and awareness (Figure 1–54).

1.6 REVIEW QUESTIONS

1. Which of the following presents dangers to the air passages and lungs of the technician?
   a. dust
   b. vapors from caustic solutions and solvents
   c. spray mists from undercoats and finishes
   d. all of the above
   e. both a and b

2. Which of the following respirators covers the entire head and neck area?
   a. cartridge filter respirator
   b. dust respirator
   c. air-supplied respirator
   d. none of the above

3. Technician A and Technician B are both in the practice of spraying continuously for extended periods of time. Technician A changes the cartridges of the respirator every other day. Technician B changes them once a week. Who is correct?
   a. Technician A
   b. Technician B
   c. Both A and B
   d. Neither A nor B

4. Which respirator is used to protect against dust from sanding and grinding?
   a. hood respirator
   b. organic vapor-type respirator
   c. air-supplied respirator
   d. none of the above

5. Eye protection should be worn when using

   _____ .
   a. grinders
   b. disc sanders
   c. pneumatic chisels
   d. all of the above

6. Which of the following should not be worn in a body/paint shop?
   a. jumpsuit
   b. loose clothing
   c. cap
   d. all of the above
   e. both b and c

7. By what means can ventilation be achieved in the body/paint shop?
   a. extraction floors
   b. central dust extraction
   c. air-changing system
   d. all of the above
   e. both b and c

8. Which of the following is not a safety measure to use when applying a lead filler?
   a. Wear a dust mask.
   b. Vacuum the area after the job is complete.
   c. Do not smoke or eat until the hands have been thoroughly washed.
   d. Work in ventilated area.

9. What is the maximum amount of paint that should be left outside of approved storage areas?
   a. 10 quarts
   b. 20 quarts
   c. one day's supply
   d. a half day's supply

10. Technician A discards all empty solvent containers. Technician B cleans them out to be used again. Who is correct?
    a. Technician A
    b. Technician B
    c. Both A and B
    d. Neither A nor B

11. Which of the following is a typical fuel for Class D fires?
    a. plastics
    b. motors
    c. zirconium
    d. wiring

12. Which class of fire can be extinguished with a carbon dioxide extinguisher?
    a. Class A
    b. Class C
    c. Class D
    d. None of the above

13. Which type of extinguisher can be used on all classes of fires?
    a. water
    b. foam
    c. multipurpose dry chemical
    d. none of the above

14. Which type of extinguisher can be used to put out a Class B fire?
    a. carbon dioxide
    b. halogenated agent
    c. standard dry chemical
    d. all of the above

15. What is another name for the cartridge filter respirator?
    a. dust mask
    b. organic vapor-type respirator
    c. air-supplied respirator
    d. hood respirator

16. Technician A will operate a tool beyond its stated capacity only for a limited time. Technician B pays no attention to the limits of the machine. Who is correct?
    a. Technician A
    b. Technician B
    c. Both A and B
    d. Neither A nor B

17. How many years of experience are required to become ASE certified?
    a. one
    b. two
    c. three
    d. five

18. Technician A wears a dust respirator when spray painting, while Technician B wears a cartridge respirator. Who is correct?
    a. Technician A
    b. Technician B
    c. Both A and B
    d. Neither A nor B

19. Technician A often uses gasoline as a cleaning solvent, but Technician B never does. Who is correct?
    a. Technician A
    b. Technician B
    c. Both A and B
    d. Neither A nor B

20. In attempting to find a qualified hauler to remove hazardous waste, Technician A consults local paint suppliers. Technician B checks with the regional EPA office. Who is correct?
    a. Technician A
    b. Technician B
    c. Both A and B
    d. Neither A nor B

CHAPTER 2

Understanding Automobile Construction

OBJECTIVES

After reading this chapter, you will be able to:

- name the different important body shapes.
- describe the general evolution of vehicle body design from early body-over-frame to present-day frame, semiunitized, and unitized construction.
- list the major design characteristics of modern body-over-frame and modern unibody construction and how they affect repair procedures.
- identify the major structural components, sections, and assemblies of body-over-frame vehicles.
- identify the major structural components, sections, and assemblies of unibody vehicles, including front engine/rear drive, front engine/front drive, and mid engine/rear drive vehicles.
- identify the important components or parts of motor vehicles.
- explain how to read a VIN plate number.

The goal of collision and damage repair is to restore the vehicle to its preaccident condition. To accurately estimate the parts, labor, and related materials needed to perform any repair, body shop personnel must fully understand how the vehicle is designed and constructed. They must be capable of accurately identifying all damaged components and the options available for their repair or replacement. And they must know the materials used in constructing the vehicle and how these materials may affect the repair process.

To fully comprehend the challenges faced by the market, consider the radical changes to the industry over the years (Figure 2–1).

With passenger cars, mini vans, and many small pickup trucks, the conventional body-over-frame construction that served the industry for over sixty years has given way to unitized construction, a totally different concept in vehicle design that requires new assembly techniques, new materials, and a completely different approach to collision repairs. In unibody designs, heavy-gauge cold-rolled steels have been replaced with lighter, high-strength steel alloys requiring new handling, straightening, and welding techniques. The ever-increasing use of plastics, modular glass, and advanced paint systems is also changing the face of vehicle repair. And on unibody vehicles, certain mechanical systems, such as suspension and steering, rely on the proper positioning of unibody components for alignment and smooth operation.

But it is not as simple as abandoning an old design concept for a new one. Body-over-frame construction is still being used on one-half and three-quarter ton pickup trucks, some small pickups, and most full-size vans. While literally all passenger car imports built during the 1980s featured unitized construction, some larger domestic models maintained traditional coil spring, body-over-frame setups.

2.1 BODY SHAPES

Various methods of classifying vehicles exist—by engine type, body/frame construction, fuel consumption structure, type of drive, and so forth. The classifications most common to consumers are the use of body shape, seat arrangement, number of doors, and so on. Six basic body shapes are used today:

1. **Sedan.** A vehicle with front and back seats that accommodates four to six persons is classified as either a two or four door sedan (Figure 2–2).
2. **Hardtop.** A vehicle with front and back seats, a hardtop is generally characterized by a lack of door or "B" pillars (Figure 2–3). It can also be classified as either a two or four door hardtop.
3. **Convertible top.** After an absence from the domestic market for several years, the convertible top made a comeback in 1985. Today's convertible top vehicle has a vinyl roof that can be raised or lowered (Figure 2–4). Like a hardtop, a convertible top has no door pillars and, depending on the make, can be purchased with or without a back window. It is available in two and four door models.

A   B

FIGURE 2–1   Great changes have occurred in automotive design since the early years of the automobile: (A) 1897 Oldsmobile and (B) late-model Oldsmobile

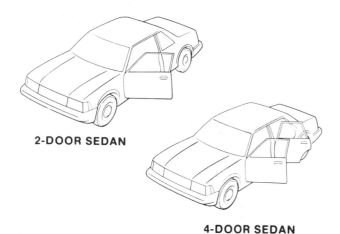

2-DOOR SEDAN

4-DOOR SEDAN

FIGURE 2–2   Typical sedan body shapes

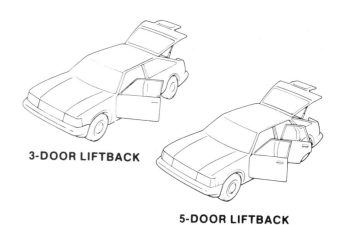

3-DOOR LIFTBACK

5-DOOR LIFTBACK

FIGURE 2–5   Typical liftback body shapes

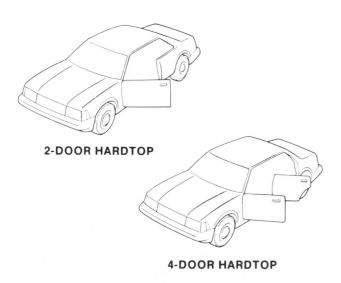

2-DOOR HARDTOP

4-DOOR HARDTOP

FIGURE 2–3   Typical hardtop body shapes

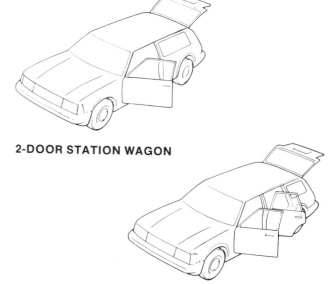

2-DOOR STATION WAGON

4-DOOR STATION WAGON

FIGURE 2–6   Typical station wagon body shapes

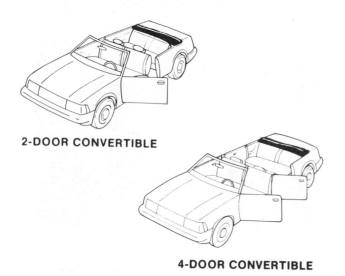

2-DOOR CONVERTIBLE

4-DOOR CONVERTIBLE

FIGURE 2–4   Typical convertible body shapes

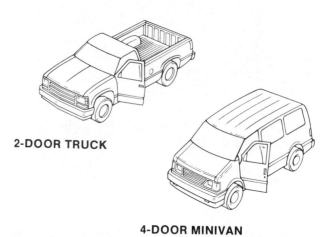

2-DOOR TRUCK

4-DOOR MINIVAN

FIGURE 2–7   Typical sports vehicle body shapes

4. **Liftback or hatchback.** The distinguishing feature of this vehicle is its rear luggage compartment, which is an extension of the passenger compartment. Access to the luggage compartment is gained through an upward opening hatch type door (Figure 2-5). The vehicle comes in three and five door models.

5. **Station wagon.** A station wagon (Figure 2-6) is characterized by its roof, which extends straight back for the length of the vehicle, allowing a spacious interior luggage compartment in the rear. The rear door, which can be opened in various ways depending on the model, provides access to the luggage compartment. Station wagons come in two and four door models and have space for up to nine passengers.

6. **Sports or multipurpose vehicles.** This new classification of vehicles covers a range of body designs (Figure 2-7). They are available in two-wheel-drive, four-wheel-drive (4×4) or all-wheel drive. Pickup truck body designs are available with standard cab designs, with extended (larger) cab areas (some have added seats in back of the front seat) and some with open or closed pickup spaces. While sport utilities appeal to the outdoor enthusiast who wants both road and off-road applications, van designs are considered sport vehicles, but for family use.

Although body types are sometimes classified according to these various descriptions, the body's strength depends on the type of vehicle and its body structure. Factors such as door size, the presence or absence of a center pillar, front body pillar, quarter panels, roof panels, and so forth greatly affect how much or how little the impact from a collision is absorbed. For vehicles with large luggage areas, such as vans or liftbacks, the structural members and reinforcements designed into the body measurably affect overall torsional rigidity.

2.2 CONSTRUCTION TYPES

Passenger cars of today use one of two types of construction:

- Conventional body-over-frame (Figure 2-8)
- Unitized or unibody (Figure 2-9)

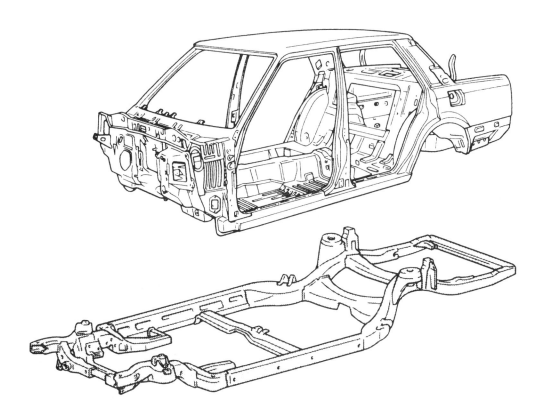

FIGURE 2-8 Typical conventional perimeter frame construction. From the illustration, it is easy to see why this type is called "body-over-frame" construction. *(Courtesy of Toyota Motor Corp.)*

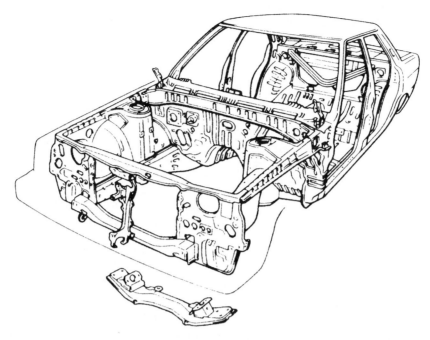

FIGURE 2-9 Typical unibody construction. *(Courtesy of Toyota Motor Corp.)*

Through the 1960s and early 1970s, American automobiles were manufactured in pretty much the same way with similar characteristics. These were:

- Body/frame construction
- Rear drive
- Independent front suspension
- Symmetrical design

In the mid 1970s, 1974 to be exact, a variety of events took place that rocked the foundations of the automobile industry. First of all, the government placed very strict fuel economy and emission control laws and standards on the manufacturers. The economy standard was known as CAFE for Corporate Average Fuel Economy and the emission control standard was set by the Environmental Protection Agency. This meant that American automotive manufacturers had to start designing more efficient methods of combustion and emission control systems for engines.

As a result of a startling revelation by the media of poor safety records and operating conditions of United States automobiles, there came a public demand for safe as well as clean running vehicles. As if clean running and safety were not enough problems for the manufacturers to deal with, the Arab oil embargo occurred at this time also. The price of gasoline escalated; consumers then demanded increased fuel efficiency. Foreign car makers, who had always manufactured smaller, lighter, more

fuel-efficient vehicles, captured an increasing share of the domestic new car market. American automakers were forced to produce smaller, more efficient cars. This resulted in the development of the unitized cars on the roads today.

The five construction areas where domestic automobiles have changed since the mid 1970s are:

1. Body/frame construction
2. Weight (average fleet)
3. Metal composition
4. Suspension/steering
5. Engine location/drive

In 1977, most cars used a perimeter type frame. They averaged around 4500 pounds, used 18 gauge mild steel, and were still conventional in design. In 1978, unitized construction was used for the first time on American-made cars. Body weight began to decrease, thinner gauge metal was used, and the first American-made transverse engine, front wheel drive, strut suspension cars were introduced.

By 1981, unibodies were used in almost half the American-made cars. Fleet average weight decreased 600 pounds, 22 gauge high-strength steel was used in construction, the steering changed to rack and pinion, the suspension to MacPherson strut type, and the drive changed from rear to front wheel drive.

At the present time, most unibodies are constructed of 24 gauge high-strength steel, have a fleet average 900 pounds less than 1980, and feature MacPherson struts, rack and pinion steering, and front wheel drive. Today, 95 to 97 percent of all passenger cars on American roads will be unibodies.

As construction of vehicles has changed over the years, so has the profession of body repairs. In the early days of automobiles, there were no specialized shops for automobile collision repair. When a car was brought in for repair, the damaged part was usually removed and replaced with a new one that was either forged from steel or cut from wood. This method was expensive and time consuming. Many times there was a long wait for parts. Most of the early body/frame technicians were carpenters or blacksmiths.

Because automobile bodies and frames became more complex in design, it became more practical to repair instead of replace. The early repair procedure involved placing the bent member over a massive structure and forcing it back into shape.

With more cars being manufactured, business got to such a point that auto technicians began to specialize as either a body or a frame technician. As repair technicians became more experienced, their techniques improved. Pushing from within the body compartment became accepted as a body alignment method. Frame technicians also used internal pushing as a means of frame alignment.

As procedures were refined, the stationary frame machine evolved. This machine was a more sophisticated version of the railroad iron and mechanical jack the blacksmith used. This stationary frame machine went through some changes to make

it more efficient and easier to use. By raising the machine off the ground, it was easier to gain access to the various components. Ramps were built so cars could be pulled into place. Pits were later dug under the machine to eliminate the ramps.

In conjunction with the racks, hydraulic jacks were used to push heavy upright beams, forcing bent frame members back into place. Frame machine manufacturers had to continuously update their machines to keep their units functional. As the automobile frame design became more complex, so did the repair techniques. The job of the frame technician became a job for a highly skilled technician.

When the Nash Company introduced its unitized body in 1940, a whole new set of collision repair problems occurred. Since there was no frame to apply pushing pressure against, the technique of internal body and frame pushing was of little value. There was not enough material in any one place to push against.

The basic repair technique of pushing out damaged sections changed to that of pulling out damaged sections. Out of necessity, the portable body and frame puller was developed and soon became accepted on a worldwide basis.

The manufacturers of stationary frame equipment again had to modify their equipment. The push technique was changed to a pull technique by adding adjustable pull towers (Figure 2–10). These units remained functional but became more massive, complicated, and expensive.

The portable body and fender puller and the updated stationary frame machine remained in use

FIGURE 2-10   Typical pulling towers at work on a modern aligner

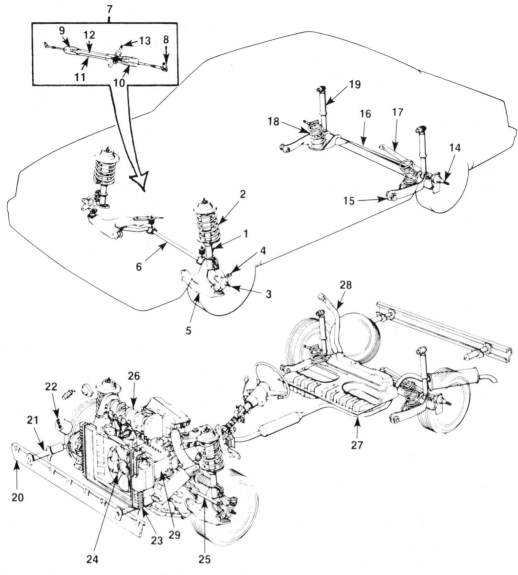

1. MacPherson Strut
2. Front Coil Spring
3. Steering Knuckle/Front Spindle
4. Steering Arm
5. Lower Control Arm
6. Stabilizer Bar
7. Rack and Pinion Assembly
8. Outer Tie Rod End
9. Inner Tie Rod
10. Boot
11. Housing
12. Rack
13. Pinion Gear
14. Rear Spindle
15. Rear Control Arm
16. Rear Axle Support Beam
17. Track Bar
18. Rear Coil Spring
19. Shock Absorber
20. Bumper Reinforcement
21. Energy Absorber
22. Fuel Vapor Canister
23. Radiator
24. Fan and Shroud
25. Drive Axle
26. Engine and Transmission Assembly
27. Fuel Tank
28. Fuel Filler Neck
29. Battery Tray

FIGURE 2-11 Mechanical components of a unibody car

for a number of years. These machines became outdated when automobile engineers again changed their basic frame and body design. When the second generation perimeter frame and unitized bolt-on stub frame became popular, a new repair system was needed. This repair system had to be flexible enough to repair both unitized and frame constructed vehicles. These systems are the ones described in Chapters 9 and 10.

From the body technician's standpoint, it is important to know which type of construction is used. As will be noted in later chapters of this book, repair work is different for each type of construction. For example, the mechanical components of a vehicle—steering and suspension, cooling system, drivetrain, electrical system—are usually done by auto technicians. But with unibodies, because the mechanical components (Figure 2-11) are attached directly to

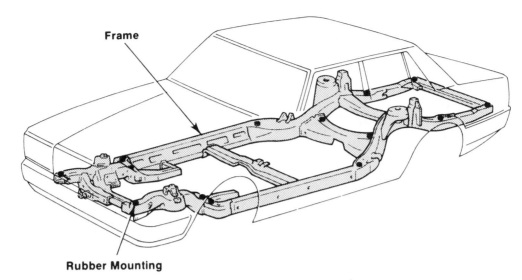

FIGURE 2-12   Location of rubber "biscuits," or mounts. *(Courtesy of Toyota Motor Corp.)*

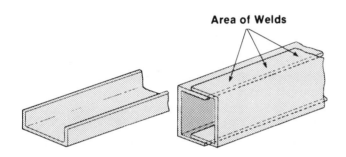

FIGURE 2-13   (Left) U-channel frame section; (right) box channel frame section

the underbody, they require precision and skill. Since the body shop's responsibility is to return the vehicle to the customer totally repaired, the modern body technician requires a great deal more knowledge than the counterpart of this era prior to the advent of the unibody.

2.3 CONVENTIONAL BODY-OVER-FRAME CONSTRUCTION

In the conventional body-over-frame construction, the frame is the vehicle's foundation. The body and all major parts of a vehicle are attached to the frame. It must provide the support and strength needed by the assemblies and parts attached to it. The frame must also be strong enough to keep the other parts of the car in alignment should a collision occur. To the body technician, the frame can be considered the most important part of the vehicle.

The conventional frame is an independent, separate component, because it is not welded to any of the major units of the body shell. The body is generally bolted to the frame and large, specially designed rubber "biscuits," or mounts, are placed between the frame and body structure to reduce noise and vibration from entering the passenger compartment (Figure 2-12). Quite often, two layers of rubber are used in the mounting pads to provide a smoother ride. In higher priced vehicles, a shock absorber is mounted between the body and the rear frame, which serves to minimize vibrations when the car is traveling at high speeds. When repairing a vehicle equipped with such a shock absorber, care should be taken not to damage it.

Today, the strong steel frame side members of the modern conventional design are normally made of U-shaped channel sections or box-shaped sections (Figure 2-13). Cross members of the same material reinforce the frame and provide support for the wheels, engine, and suspension systems. Various brackets, braces, and openings are provided to permit installation of the many parts that make up the automotive chassis. The various cross members, brackets, and braces are welded, riveted, or bolted to the frame side rails.

Most conventional frames are wide at the rear and narrow at the front. The narrow front construction enables the vehicle to make a shorter turn. A wide frame at the rear provides better support of the body. Other characteristics of frame type vehicles are:

- Load-induced vibrations that are transferred to the body via the frame, thus, resulting in a smooth ride.

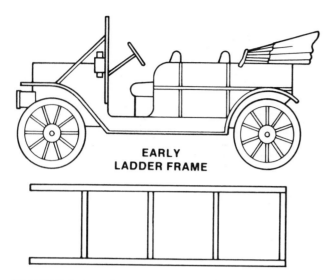

**EARLY
LADDER FRAME**

FIGURE 2-14   Old-fashioned ladder frame

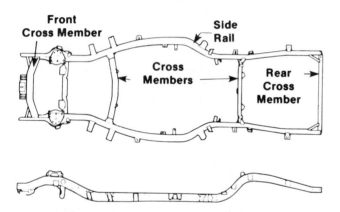

FIGURE 2-15   Modern ladder frame used in some small trucks

- Rubber mountings between the body and frame insulate it from vibrations, providing a quiet interior.
- High amounts of energy are absorbed during a collision.
- Undersurfaces of the body are protected over rough roads.
- Suspension and powertrain parts can be quickly assembled on the basic frame.
- Heavy frame made of thick sheet metal is approximately 3/64 to 1/8 inch.
- The vehicle profile is generally high off the ground.

CONVENTIONAL FRAME DESIGNS

While several conventional frame designs have been used by the auto industry, the three that the body technician may come across are the:

1. Ladder frame
2. X-frame (or hourglass)
3. Perimeter frame

The **ladder frame** consists of two side rails, not necessarily parallel, connected to each other by a series of cross members like a ladder. In fact, as shown in Figure 2-14, some of the early car frames were perfect ladder shapes. While the ladder frame design is no longer used for passenger vehicles because of the "hard" ride, it still can be found on some trucks because of its strength (Figure 2-15).

The **X-frame** (Figure 2-16) narrows in the center giving the vehicle a rigid structure that is designed to

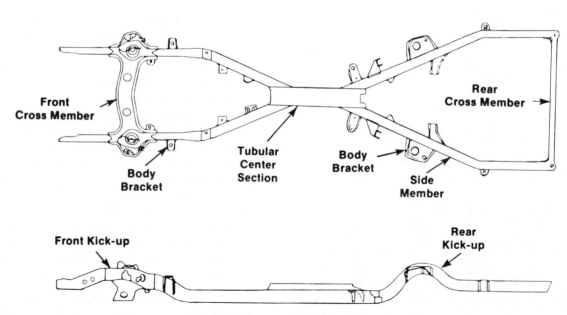

FIGURE 2-16   Typical X-frame

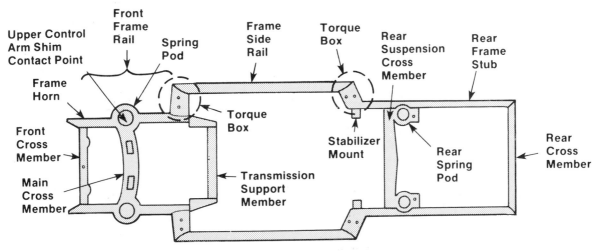

FIGURE 2-17 Perimeter frame terminology

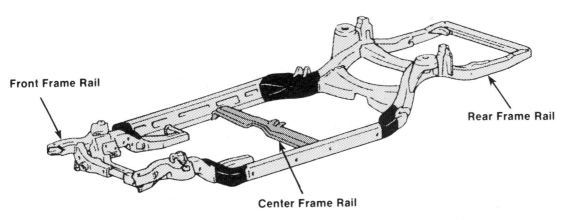

FIGURE 2-18   Perimeter frame featuring a center rail. Shaded portions are torque box structure. *(Courtesy of Toyota Motor Corp.)*

withstand a high degree of twist. A heavy front cross member is used to support the upper and lower suspension control arms and coil springs. The "kick-up" at the rear (that portion of the frame raised above the center section) is to accommodate the rear axle assembly and permit flexing of the rear springs. With the center or main part of the frame dropped down between the front and rear wheels a lower center of gravity results for greater safety. Extended brackets welded to the frame side members provide for the mounting of the body. The X-frame has not been used since the late 1960s and can be considered obsolete.

The **perimeter frame** (Figure 2-17) is similar in construction to the ladder frame. The full length side rails support the body at its greatest width, which provides more protection to the passengers in the case of a side impact to the body. The areas behind the front wheels and in front of the rear wheels are stepped to form a torque box structure. In a head-on collision, the stepped areas absorb much of the

energy, and in a side impact collision, since the center frame rail is near the front floor side member, the passenger compartment is protected from collapse. In rear end collisions, the rear cross members and kick-up absorb the shock. As for twisting and bending, strategic areas are reinforced with cross members.

The perimeter frame shown in Figure 2-18 features a center rail that passes very close to the inside of the front floor side member. Because of this, the passenger compartment floor can be made lower than in cars with other types of frames. As a result, the center of gravity is lower, the vehicle is enlarged, and the vehicle profile is lowered. Most of the conventional frames used today are of the perimeter design and include the following body sections:

Front Body

The front body section is made up of the radiator support, front fender, and front fender apron.

These components (Figure 2-19) are installed with bolts and form an easily disassembled structure. The radiator support is made up of the upper support, lower support, and left and right side supports welded together to form a single structure. The front fender of the separate frame type vehicle differs from the front fender of the unibody. The panels in the upper inside and rear ends of the fender are spot welded. This not only increases the fender's strength and rigidity, it also works along with the front fender apron to reduce vibration and noise transmitted to the passenger compartment and helps to prevent damage to the suspension and engine from side impacts.

Main Body

The main body is made up of the dash panel, underbody, roof, and so on, to form the passenger and luggage compartments, and is similar in structure to that of a unibody. The dash panel is made up of the left and right front body pillars, inner/outer, and cowl side panels. The front of the underbody has a propeller shaft tunnel built into it, forming a channel cross section through the center of the floor pan, and cross members are welded to it where it joins the frame. Thus, the passenger compartment (Figure 2-20), roof side rail, door, and side body are protected from side impact collisions. In addition,

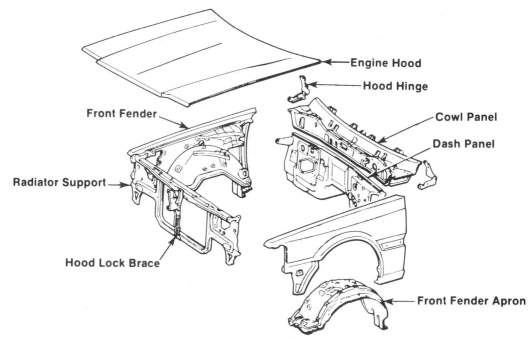

FIGURE 2-19   Front body structural components of conventional constructed vehicle. (Courtesy of Toyota Motor Corp.)

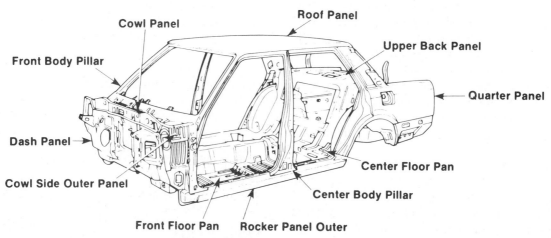

FIGURE 2-20   Main body structural components of conventional constructed vehicle. (Courtesy of Toyota Motor Corp.)

the front, back, and left and right sides of the floor pan are made uneven in the stamping process, increasing the rigidity of the floor pan itself, which reduces vibration.

2.4 UNITIZED FRAME AND BODY CONSTRUCTION

Most, if not all, newer models manufactured in the last few years in small to mid-size classes (and even some full-size) are of the unitized or semi-unitized body construction.

SEMI-UNITIZED OR PLATFORM FRAME BODY

This frame design uses heavy gauge steel "stub" rails that are welded or bolted to the front and rear of the body or platform structure (Figure 2-21). The suspension system, engine, transmission and, of course, rear axle assembly are either attached to the stub rails or sections of the platform type construction. Between the front and rear stub rails is the underbody structure with no frame underneath to act as a support for the unitized body shell or platform. Many of the stub rails and their cross members are welded to both body shell and sheet metal components to form a single integral unit. Today bolt-on stub construction can be considered obsolete.

UNITIZED FRAME AND BODY ASSEMBLY

As previously mentioned, the unitized frame and body assembly has no separate frame (Figure 2-22). The unibody was a design concept used for the bodies of aircraft, and the egg shell is often cited as an example of this type of structure. Even when pressing hard on an egg shell, it is comparatively difficult to destroy since all the strength applied by the fingers is not concentrated in one place but is dispersed effectively through the entire shell. In mechanics, this action is called a **stressed hull structure.**

In a car body, there is no complete stressed hull structure, but generally, a body with a structure that integrates the frame and body to receive and hold outside forces is called a **unibody** and has the following characteristics:

- It is made by combining pieces of thin sheet metal pressed to form panels of various shapes and joined into an integrated struc-

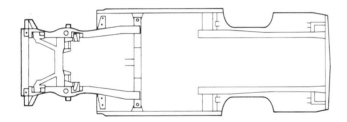

FIGURE 2-21 Typical bolt-on stub frame

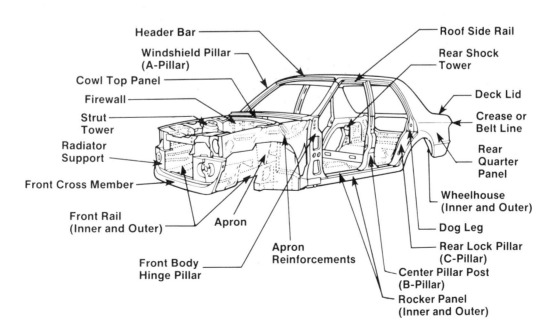

FIGURE 2-22 Unibody terminology. *(Courtesy of Toyota Motor Corp.)*

ture by spot welding. This lightweight structure is highly rigid to bending or twisting.

- The bulk taken by the frame can be used to make the car more compact.
- Vibration and noise from the drivetrain and suspension enter the floor pan and are amplified by the body, which acts as an acoustic chamber making it necessary to add extra components to the body to suppress vibration and noise.
- Once deformed, special procedures which do not cause additional damage are needed to restore it to its original shape.
- With the thin sheet metal body close to the road surface, adequate measures must be taken to prevent the deterioration in strength from corrosion. This is particularly important when dealing with reinforcing materials that make up the underbody.

The major advantage of unibody vehicles is that they tend to be more tightly constructed because the major parts are all welded together. This design characteristic that helps protect the occupants during a collision causes damage patterns that differ from those of frame-type vehicles. Unlike the heavy gauge, mild steel body-over-frame that tends to dampen and localize damage, the stiffer sections used with unibody design tend to transmit and distribute impact energy throughout more of the vehicle, causing misalignment in areas remote from the impact point. Even sections that are buckled or torn loose might have passed along heavy force before deforming. Worse still, much of this remote damage can easily be overlooked in casual inspection but still be sufficient to cause handling or powertrain problems later. Torque boxes are used in the design of some unitized frames/bodies (Figure 2-23).

The extra complexity and stiffness of the structure are especially critical in the front end, which houses not only the front suspension and steering linkage, but also the entire drivetrain—engine, transaxle, drive shafts, and constant velocity U-joints. To keep all these in proper alignment requires support

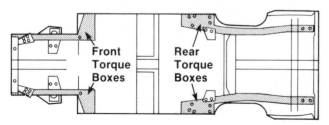

FIGURE 2-23 Torque boxes are used in some unibody designs.

including that supplied by the front end sheet metal. Accordingly, a damaged unibody vehicle requires a more thorough damage analysis than a similar impact would require in a conventional frame/body car. Otherwise, it could mean that after a car is returned to its owner, it might later show unsafe handling qualities, water leaks, or a new family of strange noises in the powertrain.

There are three basic unibody structures: front engine rear drive (FR) vehicle, front engine front drive (FF) vehicle, and mid engine rear drive (MR) vehicle.

FR Vehicle Body Structure

The front engine rear drive vehicle (Figure 2-24) has the engine mounted in the front and the driving wheels in the rear. The body of an FR vehicle is divided into three main sections: front body, passenger compartment (side body), and rear body. The engine, transmission, front suspension, and steering equipment are installed in the front body, and the differential and the rear suspension are installed in the rear body. Also, since all impacts from the road surface are transmitted to the entire body through the front and rear wheels, the body must have enough strength to fulfill its function as an automobile during normal driving. This strength is supplied by the side and cross members welded to the floor.

FR vehicles are characterized as follows:

- Since the engine, transmission, and differential are in separate positions, weight can be distributed uniformly between the front and rear wheels, lightening the steering force.
- In an FR vehicle, the engine is placed longitudinally with respect to the vehicle, and most vehicles have a single suspension cross member placed laterally between the front side members at about the middle of the front body, which supports the engine.
- Since it is possible to remove and install the engine, propeller shaft, differential, and suspension independently, body restoration and repair workability are good.
- Since rear wheel drive equipment is necessary, a tunnel in the floor is necessary, which decreases interior space.
- Since the engine's output is transmitted to the rear wheels by the differential mechanism through the propeller shaft drive, the vehicle, vibration, and noise sources are widely distributed over the front and rear.

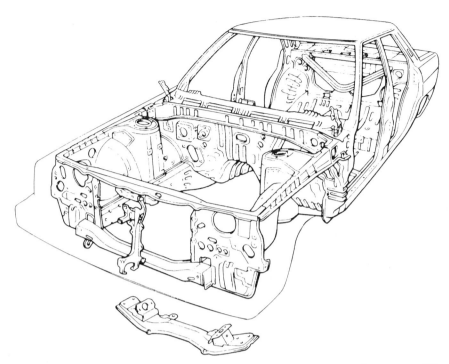

FIGURE 2-24   Main body or shell of front engine rear drive passenger car. (Courtesy of Toyota Motor Corp.)

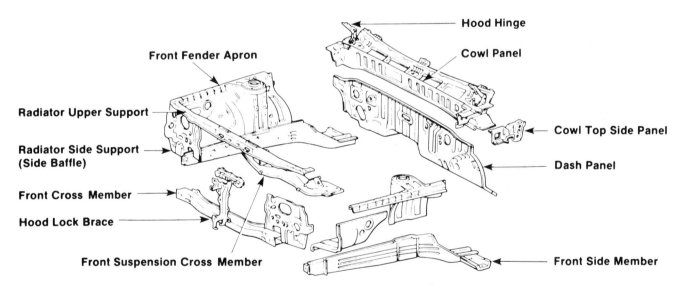

FIGURE 2-25   Front body structure components of typical FR vehicle. (Courtesy of Toyota Motor Corp.)

The engine of an FF vehicle can be mounted either longitudinally or transversely. Engine support methods differ according to orientation. The support method in a four-wheel drive vehicle (4WD) and an FF vehicle with a longitudinally mounted engine is the same.

Front Body

The engine, suspension, and steering equipment are all mounted on the front fender apron and the front side member of the front body. This part is very important because it influences front-wheel alignment and the amount of vibration and noise that are transmitted into the passenger compartment. Therefore, it must be made with great accuracy and strength. With the exception of outer shell parts, such as the engine hood, front fenders, and front valance panel (installed with nuts and bolts) all other exterior parts are welded together, reducing body weight and increasing body strength (Figure 2-25).

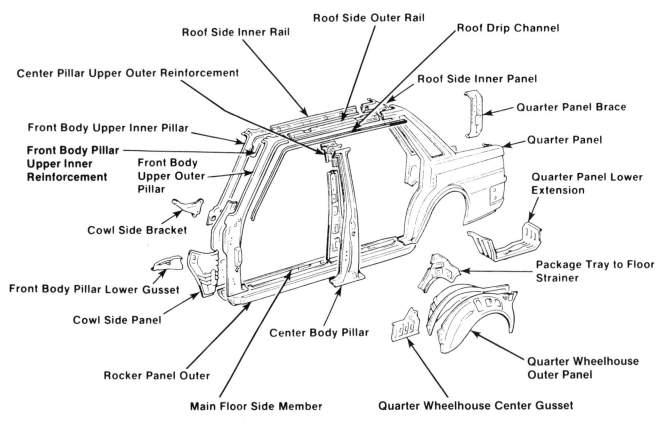

FIGURE 2-26   Side body structure components of typical FR vehicle. *(Courtesy of Toyota Motor Corp.)*

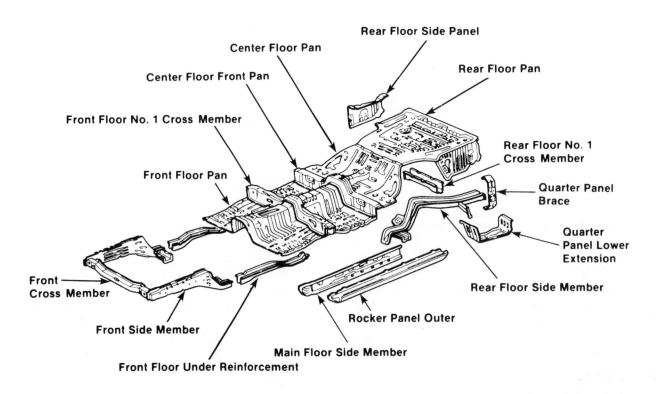

FIGURE 2-27   Underbody structural components of typical FR vehicle. *(Courtesy of Toyota Motor Corp.)*

Side Body

The side body (Figure 2-26) is joined to the front body and roof panel to form the passenger compartment. During travel, these panels distribute the loads from the underbody to the upper part of the vehicle and prevent bending of the left and right sides. The side body members also serve as door supports and maintain the integrity of the passenger compartment if the vehicle should overturn. Since the sides are weakened by large door openings, they are reinforced by joining the inner and outer panels, which forms a very strong boxed type structure.

The front side member, rear floor side member and floor pan, and cross member are the most important structural components. The front and side members resemble the perimeter of a frame structure. The basic arrangement and shapes of these members and floor pan will vary slightly depending on the size and shape of the suspension and the underbody structure (Figure 2-27).

- **Underbody front section (Figure 2-28).** Since the front side members and front cross members of the front underbody section directly affect front-wheel alignment, they are formed into a boxed section made of high-strength steel. To prevent the collapse of the passenger compartment in a head-on collision, the front side members are made with a kick-up so that all the members will bend and absorb shock loads.
- **Underbody center section (Figure 2-29).** The center underbody section is mainly composed of the floor pan, cross member, and

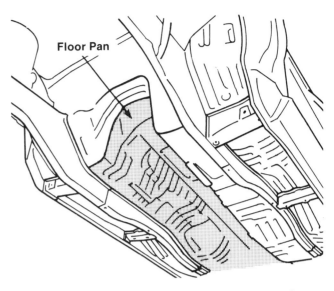

FIGURE 2-29   Underbody center section. *(Courtesy of Toyota Motor Corp.)*

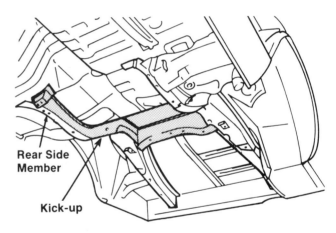

FIGURE 2-30   Underbody rear section. *(Courtesy of Toyota Motor Corp.)*

main floor side member. The center of the floor pan contains the propeller shaft tunnel, which prevents the floor from twisting. In addition, the main floor side member and cross members below the front seats and in front of the rear seats strengthen the left and right sides and prevent the floor from folding in the event of a side collision.

- **Underbody rear section (Figure 2-30).** The rear side member of the underbody extends from under the rear seat to a point near the rear axle, where it forms a large kick-up and extends to the rear floor. This kick-up, like the front side members, is designed to absorb the energy of a rear end collision.

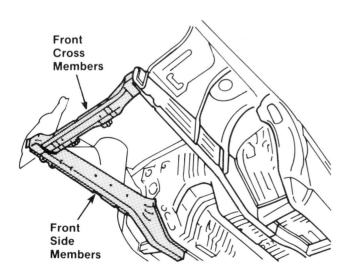

FIGURE 2-28   Underbody front section

Rear Body

The rear body sections are divided into two categories: sedans (Figure 2-31), with the luggage compartment and the passenger compartment separated, and station wagons and liftbacks, with no separation between the luggage compartment and passenger compartment. The upper back panel and rear seat cushion support brace in sedans are joined at the side body and floor pan. The back panel prevents the body from twisting. In station wagons and liftbacks (Figure 2-32) that do not have a rear partition, body rigidity is enhanced by adding enlarged roof side inner rear panels and a back window upper frame and by extending the roof side inner panels to the quarter panels.

FF Vehicle Body Structure

In an FF passenger car (Figure 2-33), the engine is mounted in the front of the vehicle and the engine drives the front wheels. It is also called a **front-wheel drive (FWD)** vehicle. In the space ordinarily taken up by the rear wheels, the passenger compartment can be enlarged and the rear suspension simplified, resulting in substantial weight reduction. Since the engine, transaxle, front suspension, and steering

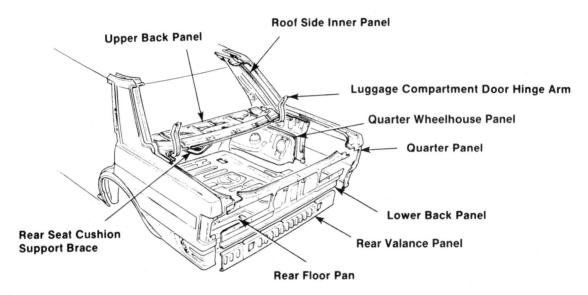

FIGURE 2-31   Rear body structural components of typical FR sedan. *(Courtesy of Toyota Motor Corp.)*

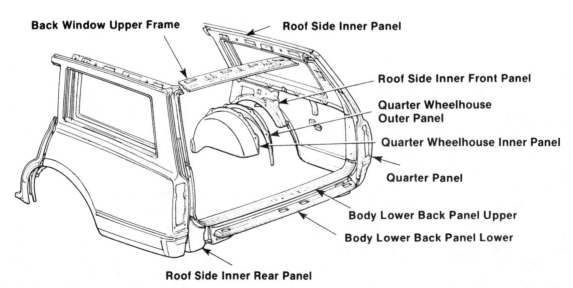

FIGURE 2-32   Rear body structural components for typical FR station wagon. *(Courtesy of Toyota Motor Corp.)*

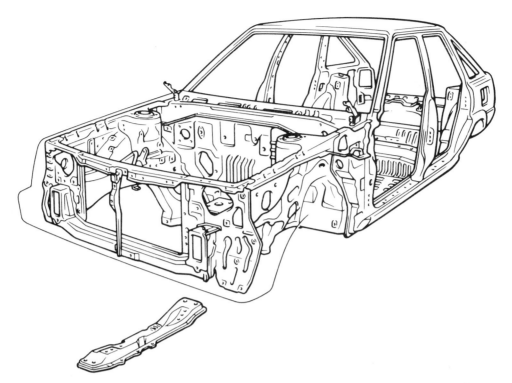

FIGURE 2-33 Typical FF vehicle main body. *(Courtesy of Toyota Motor Corp.)*

equipment are all located in the front body section, the methods of reinforcement are much different than those used in the FR vehicles.

FF vehicles are characterized by the following:

- The transmission and differential are combined, and the propeller shaft is eliminated, providing a substantial weight reduction.
- Overall noise and vibration are reduced because they are confined to the front of the vehicle.
- Since the engine and transmission are located in the front, the load on the front suspension and tires is increased.
- The interior of the vehicle is larger because there is no need for a propeller shaft or rear drive axle.
- Since the fuel tank can be placed under the center of the vehicle, the luggage compartment can be large and flat.
- Because of the location of the engine, there is a greater forward inertial weight in a head-on collision. Therefore, engine mounting components are reinforced accordingly.

The engine of an FR vehicle is mounted longitudinally. The engine of an FF vehicle can be mounted either longitudinally or transversely. Engine support methods differ between longitudinal mount FF vehicles and transverse mount FF vehicles.

1. **Longitudinally mounted FF engine supports.** The engine is supported by the front suspension members connected to the left and right front side members. The FF engine mounting is the same as the FR's engine mounting and is supported in the same manner (Figure 2-34).
2. **Transversely mounted FF engine supports.** The engine is supported at four points, the front and rear of the engine mounting center member, positioned longitudinally through the vehicle's center, and the left and right front side members (Figure 2-35).

Front Body

The front body components consisting of the engine hood, front fenders, radiator upper support, radiator side support, front cross member, front side members, front fender apron, and dash panel are stamped from thin sheet metal. A high-strength structure consisting of reinforced side members and motor mounts capable of supporting the engine transaxle and suspension loads is used in the front section of the vehicle. Lightweight single structure plastic bumpers are also used on FF models.

The front suspension in FF and FR vehicles is almost identical. Both vehicles use an independent

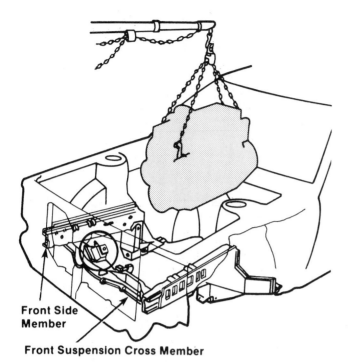

Front Side Member

Front Suspension Cross Member

FIGURE 2-34   Longitudinally mounted FF engine supports

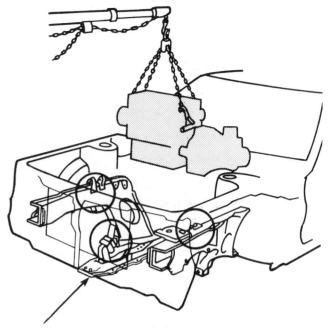

Engine Mounting Center Member

FIGURE 2-35   Transverse-mounted FF engine supports

strut type front suspension. The accuracy of the front body has a direct effect on front wheel alignment, therefore, it is important to check the wheel alignment after performing front body repairs.

- **Longitudinal engine front body.** The front body of a longitudinal FF (including 4WD) is nearly identical to that in an FR. The only differences are in their front fender aprons and front side members (Figure 2-36). The front fender apron is strengthened and rein-

forced by welding together the upper and lower front fender apron to cowl side members. The front side members of the FF are larger and heavier than their FR counterparts, since they must carry a heavier front vehicle load. A torque box is welded onto the rear end of the front side members with the suspension arms connected to it.

- **Transverse engine front body.** The lower dash panel and the front side members of FF

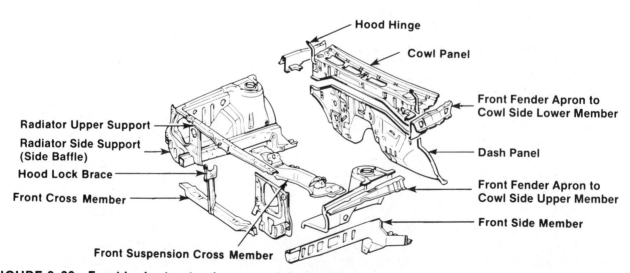

Hood Hinge

Cowl Panel

Radiator Upper Support

Radiator Side Support (Side Baffle)

Hood Lock Brace

Front Cross Member

Front Suspension Cross Member

Front Fender Apron to Cowl Side Lower Member

Dash Panel

Front Fender Apron to Cowl Side Upper Member

Front Side Member

FIGURE 2-36   Front body structural components of a typical longitudinal-mounted engine of a FF vehicle. (Courtesy of Toyota Motor Corp.)

vehicles with transversely mounted engines (Figure 2-37) are quite different from FR or FF vehicles with longitudinally mounted engines. The reason is that the steering gear or rack is mounted in the lower portion of the dash panel. The steering linkage passes through a large opening in the rear portion of the front cross member, and the suspension

arms are mounted to a structure that is directly below the opening.

Rear Body

The rear body section (Figure 2-38) consists of the back door panel, lower back panel, quarter panel, quarter wheelhouse outer panels, quarter wheelhouse inner panel, rear floor pan, and the rear floor

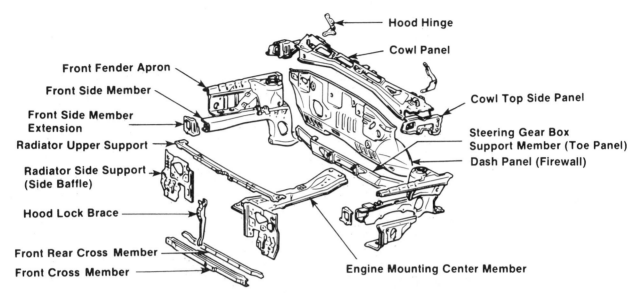

FIGURE 2-37 Front body structural components of a typical transverse-mounted engine of an FF vehicle. *(Courtesy of Toyota Motor Corp.)*

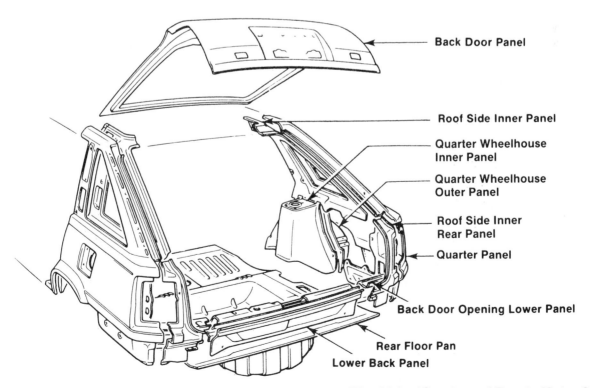

FIGURE 2-38 Rear body structural components of a typical FF vehicle. *(Courtesy of Toyota Motor Corp.)*

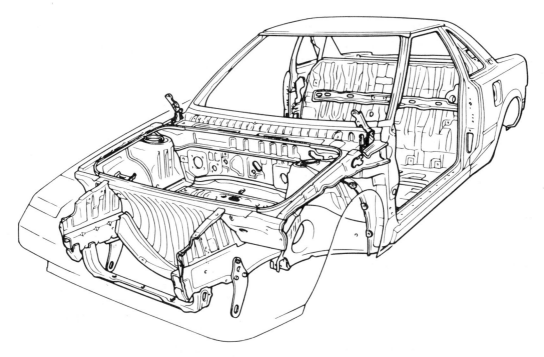

FIGURE 2-39   Main body of a typical MR vehicle. (Courtesy of Toyota Motor Corp.)

side members. Since the entire powertrain is located in the front of FF vehicles, the fuel tank is located below the center floor, which allows the rear floor side member to be lower than in FR vehicles. The lower part of the rear floor side members is then connected to the rear suspension arm. An independent strut suspension is used to improve handling performance and driving stability; therefore, a rear end collision has a greater influence on rear wheel alignment than it would in an FR vehicle. As a consequence, rear wheel alignment should be checked whenever repairs are performed on a rear body section.

In the case of an FR vehicle, the front of the rear floor pan is joined to the end of the center floor pan with spot welds. However, in an FF vehicle, the center and rear floor pan are joined and reinforced with an interlocking structure. The rear body of a 4WD is similar to that of an FR vehicle and no further description is necessary.

MR Vehicle Body Structure

As previously mentioned, MR is the nomenclature derived from a mid engine rear drive vehicle, more commonly known as a mid engine vehicle. The term "mid engine" refers to the central positioning of the engine and powertrain between the passenger compartment and the rear axle. Due to its unique engine placement, a mid engine vehicle (Figure 2-39) has a lower profile and hence a lower center of gravity. Since this type of vehicle has the majority of its heavy components near the center of the vehicle, the strength of the center structure is higher than that of other vehicles to accommodate the increased load. A high-strength box section that runs throughout the vehicle is used in the MR vehicle, resulting in further weight reductions.

MR vehicles are characterized as follows:

- Due to the central location of the heavy components, such as the engine and transmission, the center of gravity is also concentrated toward the center of the vehicle, which gives it improved steering and handling.
- Since the engine is in the rear of the vehicle, the front hood can be sloped downward, improving aerodynamics, lowering the center of gravity, and improving the driver's field of vision.
- Engine access and cooling efficiency are reduced because the engine is located between the passenger compartment and the rear axle assembly.
- A barrier is placed between the engine and passenger compartment to reduce noise, vibration, and heat that might otherwise enter the passenger compartment.

Front Body

The front suspension, steering, radiator, and air condenser are mounted in the front body section (Figure 2-40). Since the engine and transaxle are located toward the rear body, the front body shape is low and sharp. The independent front suspension is supported by the front fender apron and front side members. Because of the engine's unique location, there is room for a front luggage compartment.

Various removable parts, such as the front fenders, hood, and front valance panel, are bolted on. The front fender apron, front cross member, and front side support are spot welded to the front side members. The upper sections of the front luggage end panel and front luggage pan are spot welded to the front cross member, and the front luggage pan is spot welded to the steering gear box support member to form the front luggage compartment. The steering linkage passes through doughnut-like holes in the front side members. The lower control arms are also connected to the side members. The body is reinforced by spot welding the front and rear side members together as well as joining each of the rocker panels together.

Underbody

The underbody receives the various loads from the road surface and distributes them to the side body, the various body pillars, and the roof. Many of the components (Figure 2-41) that make up the underbody are made of high-strength steel. In addition, the underbody is strengthened by raising the tunnel of the front floor pan.

Door Panels

The door is formed by joining a high-strength inner and outer door panel that has inner access holes. The door opens and closes on hinges and is made air- and watertight by weatherstripping. The door reinforcement guard protects the passenger compartment in collisions or if the car should accidentally overturn (Figure 2-42).

Rear Body

The rear body consists of the quarter panels, luggage compartment door, engine hood, body lower back panel, rear floor pan, room partition panel, rear floor partition panel, and rear side member (Figure 2-43). The engine and rear luggage compartment are divided by the rear floor partition panel. The rear floor pan, room partition panel, and rear floor partition panel are reinforced with a deep bead structure and, together with the rear side members, form a rigid body.

The engine is positioned transversely and supported on engine mountings located at four points,

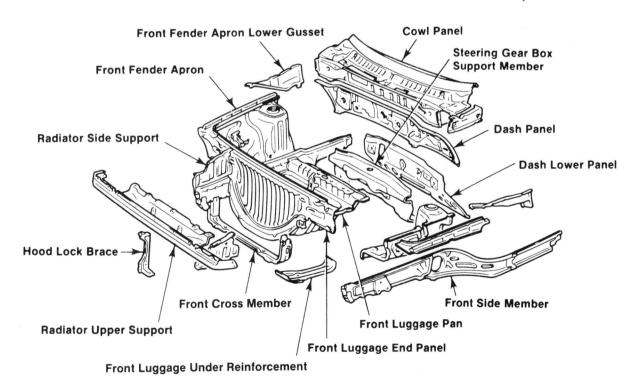

FIGURE 2-40 Front body structural components of a typical MR vehicle. (Courtesy of Toyota Motor Corp.)

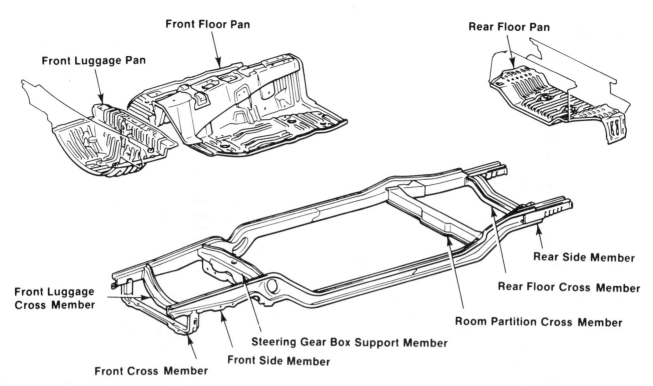

FIGURE 2-41   Underbody structural components of a typical MR vehicle. *(Courtesy of Toyota Motor Corp.)*

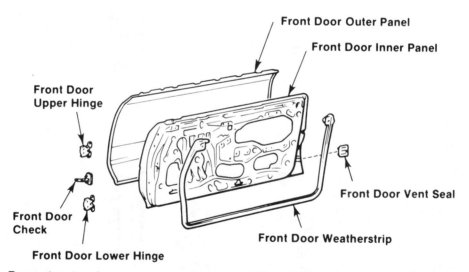

FIGURE 2-42   Door structural components of a typical MR vehicle. *(Courtesy of Toyota Motor Corp.)*

on the left and right rear side members, the room partition cross member, and the rear floor cross member. Since the engine is mounted just behind the passenger compartment, the wall between the passenger compartment and the engine compartment is a three-layered structure to keep out noise, vibration, and heat. Also, since an independent strut suspension is used for the rear suspension, the body structure is made to maintain body accuracy for components that have an influence on rear wheel alignment, such as the rear floor side members and quarter wheelhousings. Therefore, when repairing body damage from a collision, it is necessary to refer to the collision repair manual published for the vehicle being repaired.

2.5 BODY PARTS

As shown in many of the illustrations in this chapter, the body structures or sections are divided

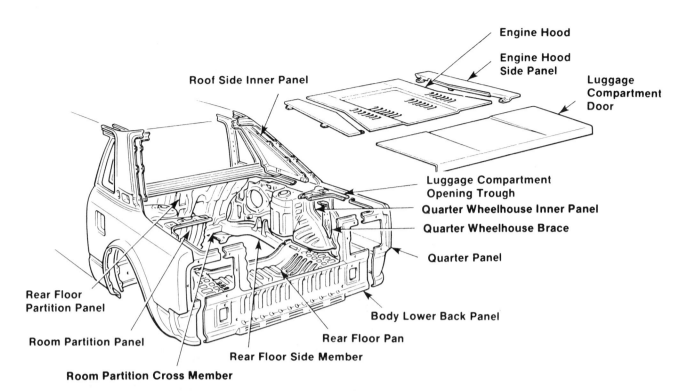

FIGURE 2-43   Rear body structural components of a typical MR vehicle. *(Courtesy of Toyota Motor Corp.)*

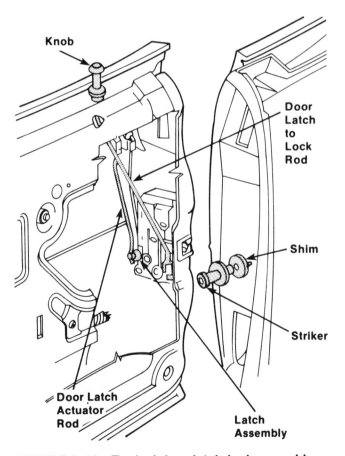

FIGURE 2-44   Typical door latch-lock assembly

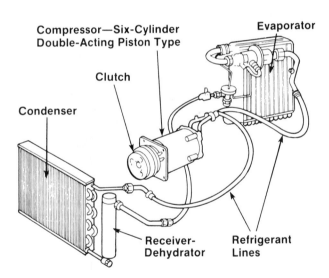

FIGURE 2-45   All air-conditioning systems have these main components or parts. *(Courtesy of Ford Motor Corp.)*

into small units called **assemblies,** (Figure 2-44), which are, in turn, divided into even smaller units, called **components or parts** (Figure 2-45). For example, the front end section, sometimes called **nose section** by veteran body technicians, consists of the following assemblies or parts (Figure 2-46): hood, front right and left fenders and aprons, grille, headlights, radiator and its support, panels, front bump-

TYPICAL FRONT SHEET METAL ON UNITIZED BODY

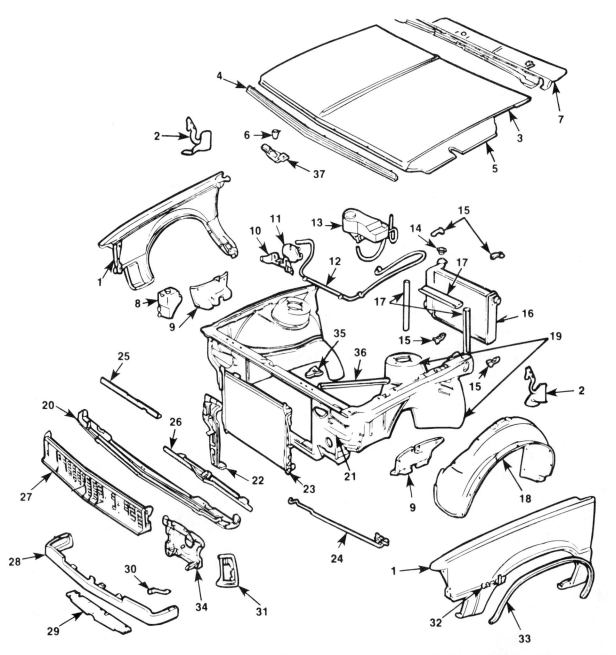

1. Fender	14. Radiator Cap	26. Air-Conditioner Condenser Seal
2. Hood Hinge	15. Radiator Pad	27. Grille
3. Hood	16. Radiator	28. Valance Panel
4. Hood Molding	17. Radiator Air Seals	29. Radiator Air Deflector
5. Hood Insulator	18. Fender Skirt	30. Valance Panel Brace
6. Hood Pop-Up Spring	19. Fender Wheelhouse and	31. Side Market Lamp Bezel
7. Top Vent Panel Cowl	Spring Mounting Panel	32. Name Plate
8. Radiator Overflow Reservoir	20. Tie Bar	33. Wheel Opening Molding
9. Dust Shield	21. Side Baffle	34. Head Lamp Mounting Panel
10. Hood Lock Mounting Bracket	22. Hood Lock Support	35. Head Lamp Mounting
11. Hood Lock	23. Air-Conditioner Condenser	Panel Brace
12. Hood Lock Cable	24. Hood Support Rod	36. Wheelhouse-To-Tie Bar Brace
13. Windshield Washer Bottle	25. Front Hood Seal	37. Hood Lock Striker

FIGURE 2–46   Typical parts and assemblies that make up a front section of a unitized body

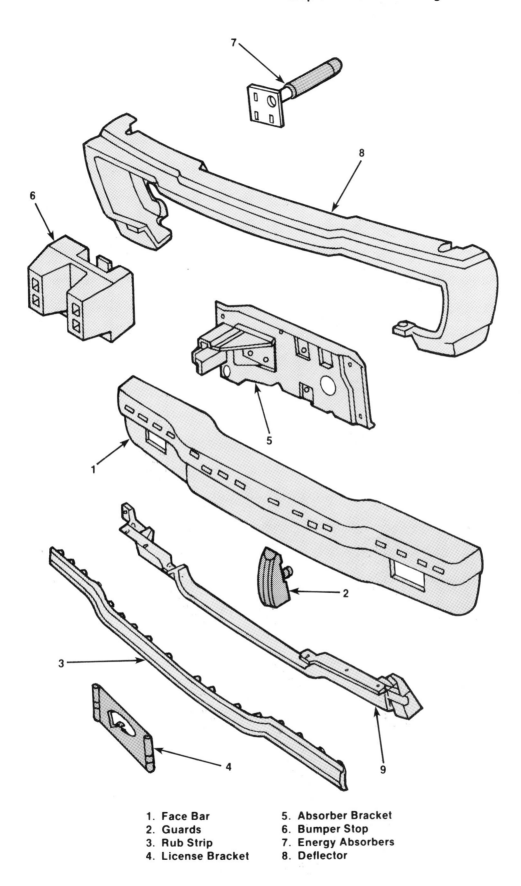

1. Face Bar
2. Guards
3. Rub Strip
4. License Bracket
5. Absorber Bracket
6. Bumper Stop
7. Energy Absorbers
8. Deflector

FIGURE 2-47   Front bumper assembly

TYPICAL BODY PANELS ON UNITIZED BODY

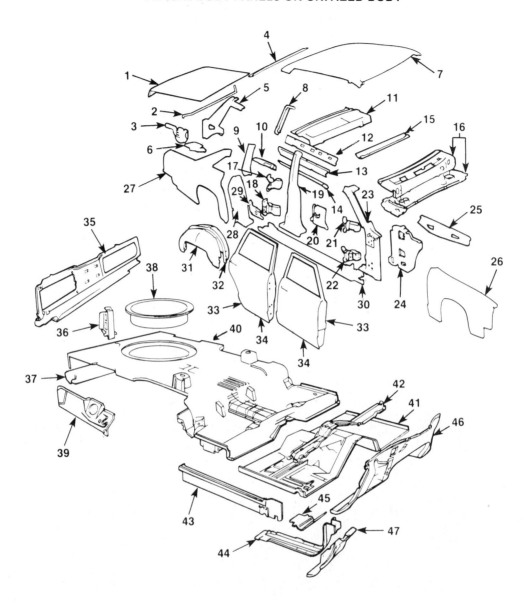

1. Trunk Lid	17. Rear Door Upper Hinge	33. Door Assembly
2. Torque Rod	18. Rear Door Lower Hinge	34. Door Outer Panel
3. Hinge	19. Center Body Pillar	35. Rear Body Panel
4. Rail Above Rear Window	20. Center Body Pillar Extension	36. Rear Body Panel Support
5. Rear Roof Rail	21. Front Door Upper Hinge	37. Rear Floor Cross Member
6. Quarter Window Reinforcement	22. Front Door Lower Hinge	38. Spare Tire Well
7. Roof Panel	23. Hinge and Windshield Pillar	39. Extension From Quarter
8. Roof Rail Extension	24. Cowl Inner Side Panel	Panel to Floor
9. Rear Quarter Upper Lock Pillar	25. Front Fender Reinforcement	40. Rear Floor Panel
10. Quarter Panel Reinforcement	26. Front Fender	41. Front Floor Panel
at Belt Line	27. Quarter Panel	42. Front Floor Panel Support
11. Upper Rear Body Panel	28. Rear Quarter Panel Lower	43. Inner Rocker Panel
12. Inner Roof Side Rail	Lock Pillar	44. Front Side Member
13. Outer Roof Side Rail	29. Lock Pillar Reinforcement	45. Front Side Member
14. Center Roof Side Rail	30. Rocker Panel	Reinforcement
15. Windshield Header Panel	31. Outer Wheelhouse	46. Dash Panel
16. Cowl Top Panel	32. Inner Wheelhouse	47. Gusset-To-Dash Panel

FIGURE 2-48 Typical body panels on unitized body

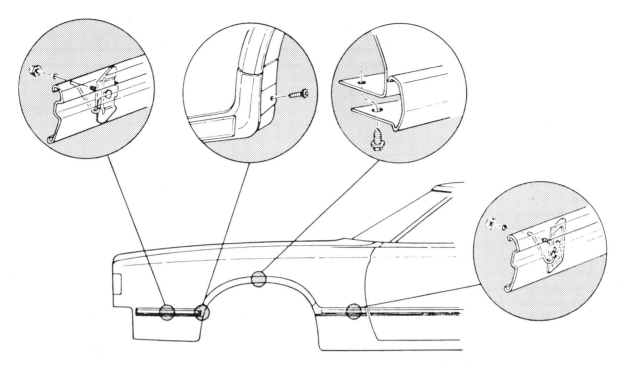

FIGURE 2-49   Side and wheelhousing molding attached with clips and screws

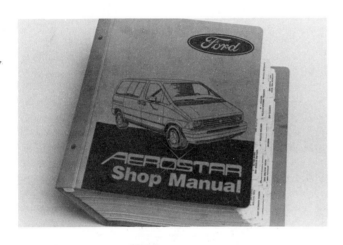

FIGURE 2-50   Typical service manual

er, and its support (Figure 2-47), and trim pieces. Typical unibody body panels are illustrated in Figure 2-48.

The body technician must also be concerned with the decorative trim of the car. Some trim and panel moldings might be attached through the use of foam adhesive tape (also called pressure-sensitive tape) or through the use of several different types of combinations of metal or plastic attachments (Figure 2-49).

A vital element of technical skill that the body technician must have is a complete understanding of commonly used terms that describe and identify

parts, units, components, and assemblies that make up the body structure of a modern passenger car. If the body technician does not know the correct nomenclature (common language) of the parts to be repaired, straightened, replaced, or painted, it becomes extremely difficult to order parts and read a repair order.

All automobile companies supply shop manuals each year that describe the different makes and models of their vehicles. These manuals (Figure 2-50) give important details on body styles and parts.

Before using the manufacturer's shop manual or the crash manuals mentioned in Chapter 1, it is important to accurately identify the body style, model year, engine, and other pertinent details (Figure 2-51). Since 1981, the vehicle identification number (VIN) plate, as mentioned in Chapter 1, is riveted to the upper left corner of the instrument panel, visible through the windshield. Prior to 1981 and in foreign vehicles, check the shop manual for the location of the vehicle identification number, vehicle certification label, or body number plate. In addition the shop manuals, as well as collision repair or estimating guides, contain all of the necessary decoding information. Become familiar with each car maker's method of vehicle identification and the specific information it contains. Remember that it is wise to obtain all of the information possible on the vehicle being worked on.

CHEVROLET

1985-91 CHEVROLET CAR V.I.N. DEFINED

1st POSITION
COUNTRY
1 = United States
2 = Canada
J = Japan

2nd POSITION
MANUFACTURER
G = General Motors
Y = N.U.M.M.I.
8 = General Motors

3rd POSITION
DIVISION
1 = Chevrolet
7 = GM of Canada

4th POSITION
CARLINE CODE
A = Celebrity
B = Impala, Caprice
F = Camaro
G = El Camino, Monte Carlo
J = Cavalier
L = Corsica, Beretta
M = Sprint
R = Spectrum
S = Nova, TVS, Venture
T = Chevette
W = Lumina
X = Citation
Y = Corvette

5th POSITION
CARLINE SERIES
B = Chevette
C = Cavalier Cadet
D = Cavalier CS
E = Cavalier Hatchback, Type 10
F = Cavalier Convertible (1989-91)
F = Cavalier Z24 (1989-91)
F = Spectrum Level I
G = Spectrum Level II
H = Citation
J = Chevette Scooter
K = Nova, TVX
L = Impala, Caprice
L = Lumina
L = Nova Twin Cam
N = Caprice Classic
N = Lumina Eurosport
P = Camaro Convertible
P = Camaro Sport Coupe
P = Lumina Z34
R = Sprint
S = Camaro Berlinetta
S = Sprint E/R
T = Corsica
T = Corsica LT
T = Sprint
U = Caprice Classic Brougham & LS
V = Beretta
W = Celebrity
W = Beretta GT
X = Citation
Y = Corvette
Z = Beretta GTZ
Z = Corsica LTZ
Z = Corvette ZR1
Z = Monte Carlo

6th & 7th POSITION, 1985-86
BODY TYPE
08 = 2 Door Hatchback
19 = 4 Door Sedan
27 = 2 Door Coupe
35 = 4 Door Wagon
37 = 2 Door Coupe
47 = 2 Door Coupe
57 = 2 Door Coupe
67 = 2 Door Convertabla
68 = 4 Door Hatchback
69 = 4 Door Sedan
77 = 2 Door Hatchback
87 = 2 Door Coupe

6th POSITION, 1987-91
BODY TYPE
1 = 2 Door Coupe
2 = 2 Door Coupe
2 = 2 Door Hatchback
3 = 2 Door Convertible
5 = 4 Door Sedan
6 = 4 Door Hatchback
6 = 4 Door Sedan
8 = 4 Door Wagon

7th POSITION, 1987-91
RESTRAINT SYSTEM
1 = Manual Belts
2 = Manual Belts (Built in Safety)
3 = Manual Belts (Driver Inflatable)
4 = Automatic Belts

8th POSITION, 1985-88
ENGINE CODE
A = 3.8-V6, 2 barrel
B = 3.8-V6, 2 barrel
C = 1.6-L4, 2 barrel
D = 1.8-L4, Diesel
E = 5.0-V8, Fuel Injected
F = 5.0-V8, Fuel Injected
G = 5.0-V8, 4 barrel
H = 5.0-V8, 4 barrel
K = 1.5-L4, 2 barrel
K = 2.0-L4, EFI
M = 1.3-L3, 2 barrel
M = 2.0-L4, MFI
N = 5.7-V8, Diesel
P = 2.0-L4, EFI
R = 2.5-L4, TBI
S = 2.8-V6, MFI
T = 4.3-V6, Diesel
V = 4.3-V6, Diesel
W = 2.8-V6, MFI
X = 2.8-V6, 2 barrel
Z = 4.3-V6, TBI
1 = 2.0-L4, EFI
2 = 1.0-L3, EFI
2 = 1.0-L3, Turbo
2 = 2.5-L4, TBI
4 = 1.6-L4, 2 barrel
5 = 1.0-L3, 2 barrel
5 = 1.5-L4, Diesel
5 = 1.6-L4, EFI
6 = 1.0-L3, TBI
6 = 5.7-V8, 4 barrel
7 = 1.5-L4, 2 barrel
8 = 5.7-V8, MFI
9 = 1.5-L4, Fuel Injected
9 = 1.5-L4, Turbocharged

8th POSITION, 1989-91
ENGINE CODE
A = 2.3-L4, MFI
E = 5.0-V8, TBI
F = 5.0-V8, MFI
G = 2.2-L4, TBI
J = 5.7-V8, MFI
R = 2.5-L4, TBI
S = 2.8-V6, Fuel Injected
T = 3.1-V6, MFI
W = 2.8-V6, Fuel Injected
X = 3.4-V6, MFI
Y = 5.0-V8, 4 barrel
Z = 4.3-V6, TBI
1 = 2.0-L4, Fuel Injected
2 = 1.0-L3, MFI
5 = 1.6-L4, MFI
6 = 1.0-L3, TBI
6 = 1.6-L4, MFI
7 = 5.7 V8, TBI
8 = 5.7 V8, MFI

9th POSITION
CHECK DIGIT

10th POSITION
MODEL YEAR
F = 1985
G = 1986
H = 1987
J = 1988
K = 1989
L = 1990
M = 1991

11th POSITION
ASSEMBLY PLANT
A = Lakewood, GA
D = Doraville, Ga
E = Linden, NJ
G = Framingham, Ma
H = Flint, MI
J = Janesville, WI
K = Kosia, Japan
K = Leeds, MO
L = Van Nuys, CA
N = Norwood, OH
R = Arlington, TX
S = Ramos Arizpe, Mexico
T = Tarrytown, NY
W = Willow Run, MI
X = Fairfax, KS
Y = Wilmington, DE
Z = Fremont, Ca
1 = Oshawa # 2, Canada
2 = Ste. Therese, Canada
5 = Bowling Green, KY
6 = Oklahoma City, OK
7 = Fugisawa, Japan (1987)
7 = Lordstown, OH
8 = Fugisawa, Japan (1988)
9 = Oshawa # 1, Canada

12th Thru 17th POSITION
PRODUCTION SEQUENCE
NUMBER

FIGURE 2-51 Typical VIN plate number identification as it appears in service manuals and crash manuals

2.6 REVIEW QUESTIONS

1. Which type of vehicle construction uses a frame only in areas requiring extra support and a strong attachment point?
   a. combination frame construction
   b. semiunitized stub rail construction
   c. first generation unitized perimeter frame construction
   d. fully unitized construction

2. The strength of a unitized vehicle is based on _____ .
   a. mass and weight of components
   b. rigidity and thickness of components
   c. shape and design of components
   d. all of the above
   e. none of the above

3. Which of the following is not an advantage of unitized vehicle design?
   a. increased passenger compartment safety
   b. reduced vehicle weight
   c. higher fuel efficiency
   d. localized collision damage to components

4. Which of the following mechanical components are commonly found on newer unitized constructed vehicles?
   a. MacPherson strut suspensions
   b. rack-and-pinion steering
   c. front wheel drive with CV joints
   d. all of the above

5. In front engine, rear wheel drive unitized vehicles the engine is mounted _____ .
   a. longitudinally
   b. transversely
   c. between the passenger compartment and rear axle
   d. either a or b

6. Which of the following is not a use or characteristic of hot-rolled steels?
   a. used for thicker components such as frame legs and cross members
   b. has a black oxidized surface appearance
   c. highly accurate dimensional thickness
   d. poorer workability than cold-rolled steels

7. Components made of the following type of high-strength steel must always be replaced, never repaired.
   a. high-strength, low-alloy steels
   b. high-tensile strength steels
   c. martensitic steels
   d. all of the above

8. Technician A says that the perimeter frame is similar in construction to the X-frame. Technician B says that the perimeter frame is similar in construction to the ladder frame. Who is correct?
   a. Technician A
   b. Technician B
   c. Both A and B
   d. Neither A nor B

9. Technician A gives a more thorough damage analysis to a unibody vehicle than to a conventional frame vehicle. Technician B says the conventional frame vehicle requires the more thorough inspection. Who is correct?
   a. Technician A
   b. Technician B
   c. Both A and B
   d. Neither A nor B

10. Which of the following are designed to stiffen a unibody structure?
    a. torque boxes
    b. frame horns
    c. crush zones
    d. stone deflectors

11. Which of the following frame designs are no longer used in automobile manufacturing?
    a. perimeter
    b. stub
    c. hourglass
    d. ladder

12. In an FF unibody structure, what panel supports the MacPherson struts?
    a. front cross member
    b. apron
    c. side rails
    d. radiator support

13. Technician A checks the rear wheel alignment whenever he/she is repairing a rear body section. Technician B says this is not necessary. Who is correct?
    a. Technician A
    b. Technician B
    c. Both A and B
    d. Neither A nor B

14. What type of body and frame is welded into one unit?
    a. frame body
    b. unibody
    c. stub frame
    d. nose frame

CHAPTER
3

Body Shop Hand Tools

OBJECTIVES

After reading this chapter, you will be able to:

- list the most common hand tools used in auto repair.
- explain the importance of having a wide range of hand tools.
- choose the correct tool for the job at hand.
- use each tool correctly and in a safe manner.

Having the right tool for the job is a sign of a prepared auto body repair technician. Knowing how to use the tool is the mark of an experienced technician. Knowledge and experience come with study and time, but without the right tools, even the best body technician cannot do quality bodywork.

A full range of bodyworking hand tools includes general purpose tools, metalworking tools, and body surfacing tools. This chapter explains which hand tools an auto body repair technician must have and explains how they are used in the body shop. Subsequent chapters explain the use of power tools, air compressors, welding machines, frame straight-ening equipment, and so on. While most of the power tools used in auto body repair are provided by the shop, every technician is expected to have a full range of personal hand tools. Figure 3–1 shows a typical set of body shop hand tools.

3.1 GENERAL PURPOSE TOOLS

Many of the tools a body technician uses every day are common, general purpose hand tools: wrenches, screwdrivers, pliers, and so forth. An ap-

FIGURE 3–1 A professional set of hand tools. *(Courtesy of Snap-on Tools Corp.)*

prentice auto body repair technician will probably already have many of these in his or her tool collection. The less familiar tools are designed for specific types of industrial fasteners often encountered in bodywork.

Wrenches

A complete collection of wrenches is indispensable for the auto body technician. A variety of auto body parts, accessories, and related parts, not to mention shop equipment, utilize common bolt and nut fasteners as well as special hex screws and fasteners. Depending on the make and model of the vehicle, the fasteners can be standard SAE or metric size fasteners. So, a well-equipped auto body technician will have both metric and SAE wrenches in a variety of sizes and styles (Figure 3-2).

The word wrench means "twist." A wrench is a tool for twisting and/or holding bolt heads and nuts. The width of the jaw opening determines its size (Figure 3-3). For example, a 1/2-inch wrench has a

jaw opening (from face-to-face) 1/2 inch. The actual size is really slightly larger than its nominal size so that the wrench fits around a nut or bolt head of equal size.

The larger the wrench size, the longer the wrench usually is. For example, a 1/4-inch wrench is typically 4-1/2 inches long. A 3/4-inch wrench probably is 10 to 12 inches long. The extra length provides the user with more leverage to turn the larger size nut or bolt.

Most standard wrench sets include sizes from 7/16 to 1 inch. Metric sets usually include 6- to 19-millimeter wrenches. Smaller and larger wrenches can be purchased but are rarely used in auto body repair. Please note that metric and SAE size wrenches are not interchangeable. For example, a 9/16-inch wrench is 3/10 millimeter larger than a 14-millimeter nut (see the conversion chart in Appendix C). If the 9/16-inch wrench is used to turn or hold the 14 millimeter nut, the wrench will probably slip, rounding the points on the nut (Figure 3-4) and possibly skinning knuckles as well. Having the right tool for the job will avoid unnecessary frustration.

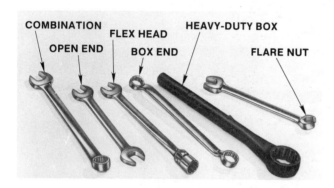

FIGURE 3-2   An assortment of wrenches. *(Courtesy of Snap-on Tools Corp.)*

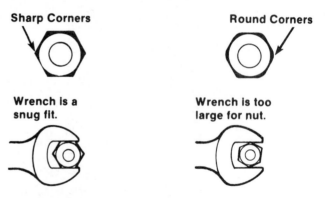

FIGURE 3-4   Use the right size wrench to avoid rounding corners.

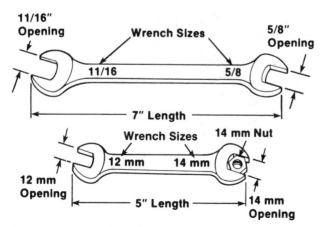

FIGURE 3-3   The wrench size is the size of the nut or bolt it will grasp firmly.

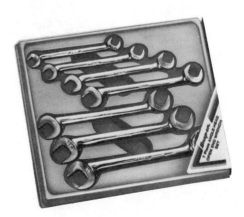

FIGURE 3-5   Typical set of open-end wrenches. *(Courtesy of Snap-on Tools Corp.)*

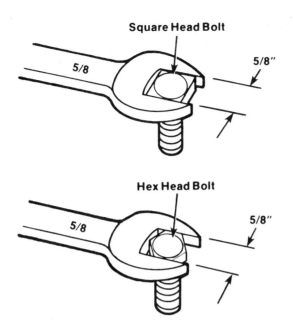

FIGURE 3-6 An open-end wrench grips only two faces of a fastener.

Open-End Wrenches

Every tool chest must have a set of open-end wrenches (Figure 3-5). The jaws of the open-end wrench allow the wrench to slide around bolts or nuts where there might be insufficient clearance above or on one side of the nut to accept a box wrench.

The open-end wrench fits both square head (four-cornered) or hex head (six-cornered) nuts. The disadvantage of using open-end wrenches is that only two faces of the nut are gripped by jaws (Figure 3-6). Thus, there is a greater tendency for the open-end wrench to slip off the bolt or nut. Rounded nuts and injured hands are too often the result. Because of this, the open-end wrench should be used for holding when there is not sufficient room for a box-end wrench to be used.

Open-end wrenches are often angled 15 to 80 degrees at both ends. The offset helps turn a bolt or nut that is recessed or is in a confined area where there is little room to turn the wrench. Flipping the wrench over after each turn maximizes the turning arc (Figure 3-7).

Box-End Wrenches

Figure 3-8 shows box-end wrenches in a variety of sizes, points, and offsets. The end of the box-end wrench is boxed or closed rather than open. The jaws of the wrench fit completely around a bolt or nut, gripping each point on the fastener (Figure 3-9).

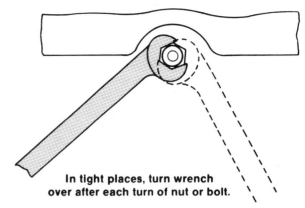

In tight places, turn wrench over after each turn of nut or bolt.

FIGURE 3-7 An offset increases the turning radius.

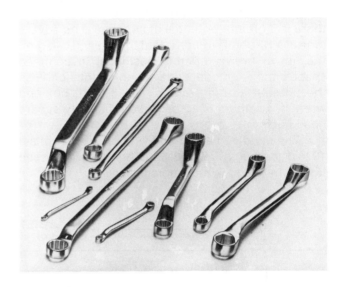

FIGURE 3-8 Box-end wrenches. *(Courtesy of Snap-on Tools Corp.)*

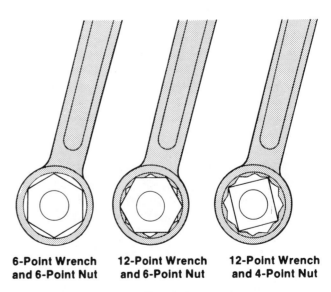

6-Point Wrench and 6-Point Nut   12-Point Wrench and 6-Point Nut   12-Point Wrench and 4-Point Nut

FIGURE 3-9 6- and 12-point wrenches

The box-end wrench is thus the safest to use. More force can be applied without slippage and rounding corners. The handle of many box-end wrenches is offset to provide hand clearance. Each end is usually a different size.

The box-end wrench does have limitations. There must be sufficient clearance for the jaws to fit over and around the head or nut. The box-end wrench must also be lifted off the head or nut and rotated to a new position for each pull.

Box-end wrenches are available in 6, 8, or 12 points (Figure 3-9). The 6-point wrench is the strongest. It completely surrounds the hex nut and brings force to bear on all six sides and points. The 12-point wrench also grips the six points but does not bear on the face surfaces of a hex nut. Thus, there is a greater potential of slippage. The advantage of a 12-point wrench is that the wrench can grab the nut in twelve different positions. In confined spaces, the additional engagement points increase the possible turning radius. The 8-point box-end wrench is seldom used because it fits only square head nuts.

The handle of a box-end wrench is often offset 10 to 60 degrees (Figure 3-10). This allows recessed fasteners to be reached more easily.

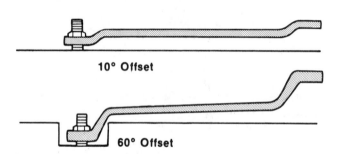

10° Offset

60° Offset

FIGURE 3-10   Offset box wrenches

Combination Wrenches

The combination wrench has an open-end jaw on one end and a box-end on the other (Figure 3-11). Both ends are the same size. Every auto body repair technician should have two sets of wrenches: one for holding and one for turning. The combination is probably the best choice for the second set. It complements either open-end or box-end sets. Combination wrenches are available with 6-, 8-, or 12-point box ends and with or without offset open ends and handles.

Adjustable Wrenches

An adjustable wrench has one fixed jaw and one moveable jaw (Figure 3-12). The wrench opening can be adjusted by rotating a helical adjusting screw that is mated to teeth in the lower jaw. The jaw opening can be adjusted from fully closed (1/2 inch) to its maximum open width (1-3/4 inches). Available in lengths from 4 to 24 inches, the auto body tool chest should have a set of adjustable wrenches. Fig-

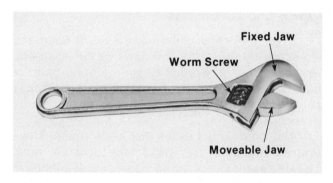

Fixed Jaw

Worm Screw

Moveable Jaw

FIGURE 3-12   An adjustable wrench. (Courtesy of Stanley Works)

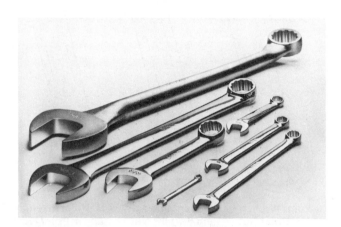

FIGURE 3-11   A set of combination wrenches. (Courtesy of Snap-on Tools Corp.)

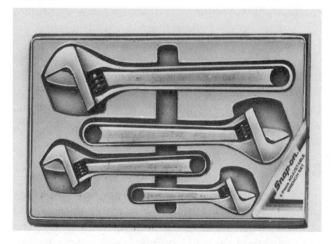

FIGURE 3-13   A set of adjustable wrenches. (Courtesy of Snap-on Tools Corp.)

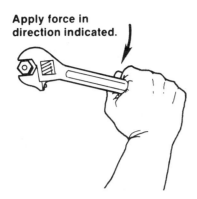

FIGURE 3-14 Pull the adjustable wrench so that the force bears against the fixed jaw.

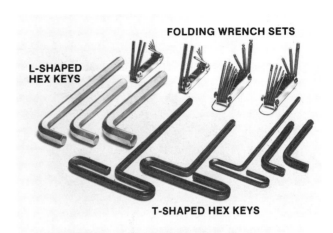

FIGURE 3-16 Typical sets of allen wrenches. *(Courtesy of Snap-on Tools Corp.)*

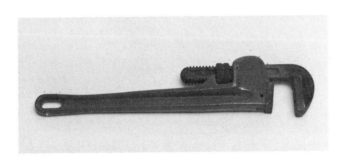

FIGURE 3-15 A pipe wrench

FIGURE 3-17 A hex head socket set. *(Courtesy of Snap-on Tools Corp.)*

ure 3-13 shows a set of 4-, 6-, 8-, and 10-inch adjustable wrenches.

Besides the obvious advantage of fitting various size bolt heads and nuts, the adjustable wrench has the same advantage and disadvantage of an open-end wrench. It can be slipped around bolts or nuts in tight places, but it also bears against only two faces. It, too, slips easier than does the box-end wrench.

As the adjustable wrench wears with use, the adjusting screw will lose some of its holding power. The jaws develop a tendency to loosen as force is applied and then slip off the nut or bolt. Therefore, use only an adjustable wrench when a suitable box-end or open-end wrench is not available. Use it to hold rather than turn when it must be used. If the adjustable wrench is used to turn a bolt or nut, tighten it securely, hold it flush, and **pull** the handle so that the force bears on the fixed jaw (Figure 3-14).

Pipe Wrenches

Another type of wrench that is occasionally used in the auto body shop is the pipe wrench (Figure 3-15). The pipe wrench gets its name from its most common use—turning pipes and pipe fittings. The advantage of the pipe wrench over other wrenches is that it will grab and turn round objects such as pipes and studs.

Like the adjustable wrench, the pipe wrench opening is adjustable. The top or hook jaw is threaded through a stationary adjusting nut. Turn the adjusting nut to increase or decrease the jaw opening. Pipe wrenches are available in maximum openings of 3/8 to 8 inches in various lengths. A 10-inch long pipe wrench is probably adequate for most body shop applications. The best have replaceable teeth on the lower (heel) jaw.

Hex and Torx Wrenches

Setscrews are used to fasten door handles, instrument panel knobs, and even brake calipers. A set of hex head wrenches, or allen wrenches (Figure 3-16) should be in every tool box. Hex head sockets are also available for the task of removing large setscrews (Figure 3-17).

FIGURE 3-18   Torx socket set. *(Courtesy of Lisle Corp.)*

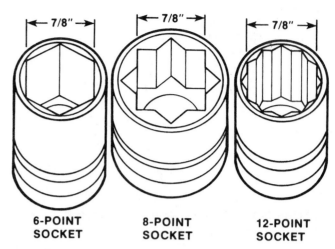

| 6-POINT SOCKET | 8-POINT SOCKET | 12-POINT SOCKET |

FIGURE 3-20   6-, 8-, and 12-point sockets

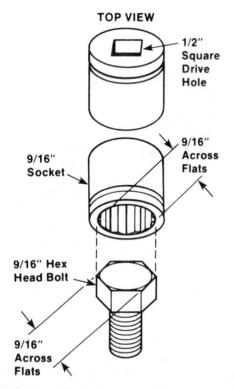

TOP VIEW

1/2" Square Drive Hole

9/16" Across Flats

9/16" Socket

9/16" Hex Head Bolt

9/16" Across Flats

FIGURE 3-19   A size of a socket is the same as the bolt or nut size it fits.

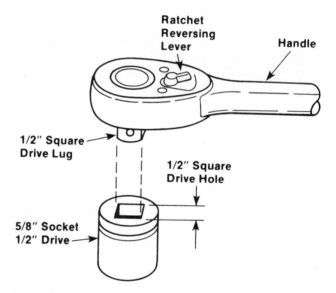

Ratchet Reversing Lever

Handle

1/2" Square Drive Lug

1/2" Square Drive Hole

5/8" Socket 1/2" Drive

FIGURE 3-21   The socket drive size is equal to the diameter of the handle lug.

The Torx fastener is a 6-point fastener that is easier to grip and drive without slippage. Sometimes called a "star" fastener, this relatively new fastener is used on most late model cars. On many American-made vehicles, Torx fasteners are used in luggage racks, headlights, and tail light assemblies, mirror mountings, and exterior trim. Torx wrenches or drivers are sold in sets of five or seven popular metric sizes (Figure 3-18).

Socket Wrenches

In many situations, a socket wrench is much faster and easier to use than an open-end or box-end wrench. Some applications absolutely require one. The auto body repair technician should have several sets of socket wrenches.

The basic socket wrench set consists of a handle and several barrel-shaped sockets. The socket fits over and around a given size nut or wrench (Figure 3-19). Inside it is shaped like a box-end wrench. Sockets are available in 6, 8, or 12 points (Figure 3-20). A 6-point socket gives the tightest hold on a hex nut. The face-to-face fit minimizes slippage and rounding of fastener's points. The 8-point socket, like the 8-point box-end wrench, fits only square head fasteners and is thus limited in its usefulness. The 12-point socket does not have the holding power of the 6-point socket, but its numerous positions maximize the possible turning radius.

The socket is closed on one end. The closed end has a square hole that accepts a square lug on the socket handle (Figure 3-21). One handle fits all the sockets in a set. The size of the lug (3/8 inch, 1/2 inch, and so on) indicates the drive size of the socket wrench. On better quality handles, a spring-loaded

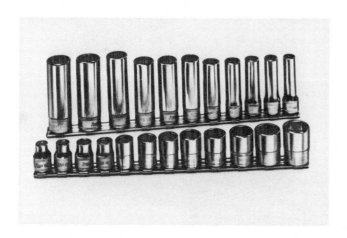

FIGURE 3-22 Regular and deep well sockets. *(Courtesy of Snap-on Tools Corp.)*

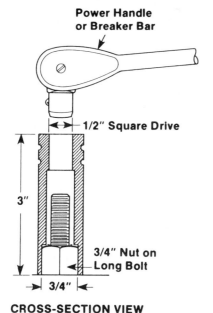

CROSS-SECTION VIEW

FIGURE 3-23 A deep well socket fits over the stud to reach the nut.

ball in the square lug fits into a depression in the socket. The ball holds the socket to the handle.

Socket Sizes

The size of the individual sockets in a socket wrench set depends on the drive size of the set as well as the number of sockets in the set. The socket size is the same as the face-to-face dimension of the fastener it fits. A 1/4-inch set has sockets ranging from 3/16 to 1/2 inch. A good 1/2-inch socket wrench set has sockets ranging in size from 7/16 to 1-1/4 inches. Of course, the actual size is slightly larger than the nominal size so that the socket will fit snugly around a bolt or nut of equal size. Both standard SAE and metric socket wrench sets are necessary for bodywork. A large percentage of the vehicles sold in America are foreign made and metric tools are required to repair them.

Sockets are not only available in standard face-to-face diameters, but they are also available in various lengths or bore depths (Figure 3-22). Normally, the larger the socket size, the deeper the well. Deep-well sockets (Figure 3-23) are made extra long to fit over bolt ends or studs to reach a nut. A spark plug socket is an example of a deep-well socket. Deep-well sockets are useful in a body shop for removing bumper bolts. Deep-well sockets are also good for reaching nuts or bolts in limited access areas. Deep-well sockets should not be used when a regular size socket will do the job. The longer socket develops more twisting torque and tends to slip off the fastener.

Drive Sizes

Socket wrench sets can be purchased in 1/4-, 3/8-, 1/2-, 3/4-, and 1-inch drive sizes. The small drive sizes are used for turning small fasteners on emblems and trim where little torque is required. The larger drive sizes with correspondingly longer handles are used where greater torque is needed. A 3/4- or 1-inch socket wrench is useful for truck and heavy equipment repair.

An auto body repair technician will need a set of 1/4-, 3/8- and 1/2-inch drive sockets (Figure 3-24). The 1/4-inch drive set is a must for disassembly and removal of interior trim components. Socket sizes in 1/4-inch drive sets range from 5/32 to 1/2 inch. The 3/8-inch drive sockets range in size from 3/8 to 3/4 inches and fit almost all sheet metal bolts and nuts found on a vehicle. The sockets in a 1/2-inch drive set range in size from 7/16 to 1-1/4 inches. The 1/2-inch set is useful in removing exhaust systems, sus-

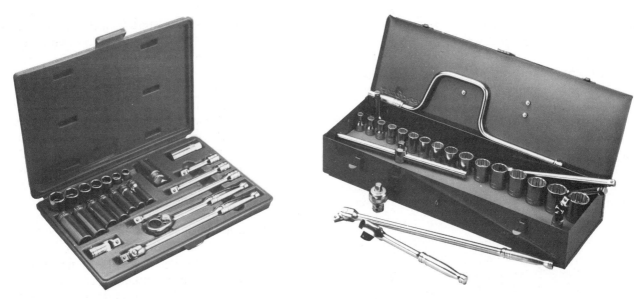

FIGURE 3-24   Typical 3/8″ and 1/2″ socket wrench sets. *(Courtesy of Snap-on Tools Corp.)*

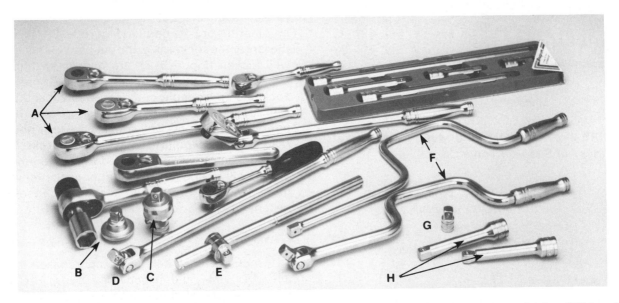

FIGURE 3-25   Socket wrench accessories: (A) ratchet handles, (B) spinner, (C) ratchet adapter, (D) breaker bars, (E) sliding T-handle, (F) speed handles, (G) drive adapter, and (H) extension bars. *(Courtesy of Snap-on Tools Corp.)*

pension parts, bumpers, and other related automotive parts commonly removed in body repair.

Socket Wrench Accessories

Figure 3-25 shows a number of socket wrench set accessories. Accessories multiply the usefulness of a socket wrench. A good socket wrench set has a variety of the following:

- Ratchet handles
- Spinner
- Ratchet adapter
- Breaker bars
- Sliding T-handle
- Speed handles
- Drive adapter
- Extension bars

Handles.   Several different types of handles are available. One is the breaker bar or powerhandle (Figure 3-25D). Held at a 90 degree angle, the extra long handle provides the torque needed to loosen stubborn fasteners. Held in line with the socket, the knurled handle can be spun to turn the nut or bolt. A speed handle (Figure 3-25F) is a bit and brace type handle that can quickly turn off a nut or bolt. Its use requires sufficient clearance for turning the handle.

The ratchet handle (Figure 3-26) is probably the most commonly used handle. The ratchet handle allows removing or tightening without removing the socket from the fastener. A reversing level allows the ratchet mechanism to slip (ratchet) in one direction and turn the socket in the other. The turning direction can be changed by turning the ratchet lever position. Some ratchet handles are equipped with a quick release push button that releases spring pressure on the spring tension ball in the lug. This allows the socket to be easily removed from the handle. Ratchet handles are not only available with flex-heads, but also with offset, or bent, handles to help reach otherwise inaccessible fasteners.

A T-handle or slide bar (Figure 3-27) is another handle that comes in handy when access is limited. The T-handle is similar to a long extension, but a slide bar fits in a hole in the upper end. The slide bar can be centered in the hole and gripped with both hands. The push-pull effort helps to loosen stubborn fasteners with less likelihood of slippage. The slide bar can also be slid to one side or another and used as a breaker bar.

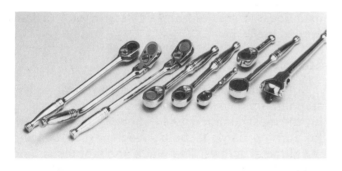

FIGURE 3-26 A variety of ratchet handles. (Courtesy of Snap-on Tools Corp.)

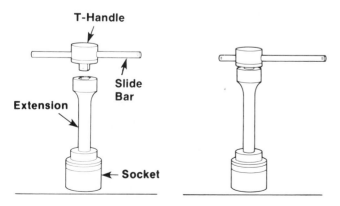

FIGURE 3-27 T-bars can be gripped with both hands or used as a breaker bar.

Many socket wrench sets contain sockets in two drive sizes, such as 1/4- or 3/8-inch and 1/2-inch drives. An adapter, such as the one shown in Figure 3-25G, then is often provided so that the larger drive handle can be used with the smaller drive sockets.

Most socket wrench sets also contain extensions and universal joints. The extensions (3- and 6-inch extensions are common but 1- to 36-inch extensions are available) reach into otherwise inaccessible places. A universal joint (Figure 3-28) allows the work to be done at an angle to the fastener. With a universal joint adapter, one can reach around obstacles and use a socket wrench in places where it would otherwise be impossible.

Flexockets. A flexocket is a combined socket and universal joint (Figure 3-29). The universal joint

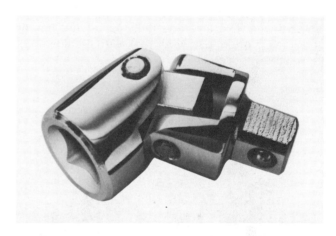

FIGURE 3-28 A universal joint. (Courtesy of Stanley Works)

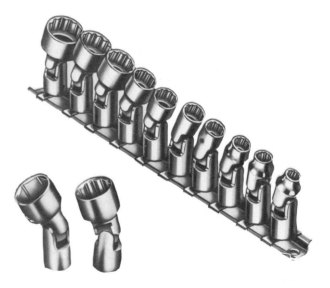

FIGURE 3-29 Flexockets. (Courtesy of Snap-on Tools Corp.)

allows the handle to be held at an angle other than 90 degrees to the fastener. A set of flexockets are generally available in only 3/8-inch drive.

Screwdriver Attachments. Screwdriver attachments are also available for use with a socket wrench. Figure 3-30 shows a typical set of screwdriver attachments and three specialty sockets:

- Hex driver
- Phillips driver
- Flat tip driver
- Clutch head driver
- Torx driver
- Three wing socket
- Double square socket
- Torx socket

These socket wrench attachments are very handy when a fastener cannot be loosened with a regular screwdriver. The leverage that the ratchet handle provides is often just what it takes to break a stubborn screw loose.

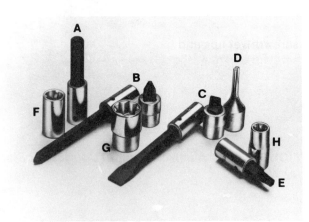

FIGURE 3-30 Typical screwdriver attachment set: (A) hex driver, (B) Phillips driver, (C) flat tip driver, (D) clutch head driver, (E) Torx driver, (F) three wing socket, (G) double square socket, and (H) Torx socket

FIGURE 3-31 Triple square sockets

Two other specialty fastener sockets are shown in Figures 3-31 and 3-32. Triple square and ribe fasteners are common on many European import vehicles.

SCREWDRIVERS

A variety of threaded fasteners used in the automotive industries are driven by screwdriver. Some, like the self-tapping sheet metal screw, are common. Others, like the Torx fastener used to secure exterior side mirrors, are not so common. Each fastener requires a specific kind of screwdriver, and the well-equipped technician will have several sizes of each.

All screwdrivers, regardless of the type of fastener they were designed for, have several things in common. The size of the screwdriver is determined by the length of the shank or the blade. The size of the handle is important, too. The larger the handle diameter, the better grip it has and the more torque it will generate when turned.

No screwdriver should be used as a chisel, punch, or prybar. Screwdrivers were not made to withstand blows or bending pressures. When misused in such a fashion, the tips will wear, become rounded, and tend to slip out of the fastener. Its usefulness is impaired, and a defective tool is a dangerous tool.

Standard Tip Screwdriver

A slotted screw accepts a screwdriver with a standard tip. The standard tip screwdriver is probably the most common type (Figure 3-33). It is useful for turning carriage bolts, machine screws, and sheet metal screws. The blade and lengths should match the job. Small screws will accept a blade 3/16-inch wide. For turning larger, heavier screws, use a 1/4- or 5/16-inch wide blade. A good set of standard tip screws will have five to seven screwdrivers from the 1-1/2-inch snubby to a 10-inch driver with a

FIGURE 3-32 Ribe sockets

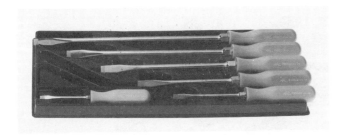

FIGURE 3-33   Standard tip screwdrivers. (Courtesy of Stanley Works)

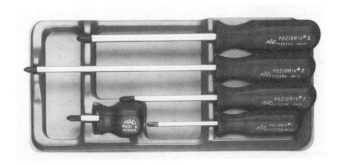

FIGURE 3-34   Phillips screwdrivers. (Courtesy of Stanley Works)

heavy duty 5/16-inch blade. Buy only screwdrivers with insulated handles.

Phillips Screwdrivers

Phillips screws have a four prong funnel-shaped depression in the screw head. The tip of a Phillips screwdriver has four prongs that fit the four slots in the screwhead. This type of fastener is very often used in the automotive field. Not only does it look nicer than the slot head screw, but it also is easier to install. The four surfaces enclose the screwdriver tip so that there is less likelihood that the screwdriver will slip off the fastener. Phillips screws, unlike the standard tip, can also be installed by automated machinery. This is the primary reason they are used on vehicles today.

A set of three Phillips screwdrivers (Figure 3-34) with a number 1, number 2, and number 3 tip will handle most body shop requirements. Purchase a set with large, insulated handles. They are easier and safer to use.

Phillips screwdrivers have one disadvantage. The prongs of the tip tend to wear and round off. Unlike a standard tip screwdriver, a worn Phillips cannot be sharpened. Therefore, it should be discarded and replaced.

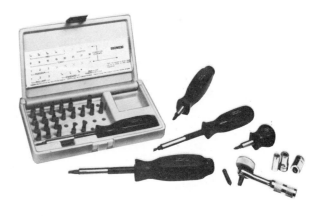

FIGURE 3-35   Magnetic screwdriver and bit set. (Courtesy of Snap-on Tools Corp.)

Specialty Screwdrivers

A number of specialty fasteners have been replacing the slot and Phillips head screws. These new breeds of fasteners are designed to improve transfer of torque from screwdriver to fastener, slip less, result in less work fatigue, and offer some tamper resistance. Figure 3-35 shows a set of specialty screwdriver tips and assorted drivers. Most of these screwdriver bits (Figure 3-36) will prove useful in auto body repair. Three of the most often used screwdrivers are described below:

Clutch Head Screwdriver. There are two kinds of clutch head screws. The older G-style and the newer A-style. The G-style clutch type screwdriver tip (Figure 3-37) has an hourglass profile. It fits into a similarly shaped slot in a clutch head screw. Used most frequently by General Motors, this type of fastener system provides a more positive engagement with less slippage.

Pozidriv Screwdriver. This screwdriver is also like a Phillips but with a tip that is flatter and blunter (Figure 3-38). The square tip grips the screw head and slips less than a Phillips screwdriver. Less slippage results in less aggravation and fatigue and lengthens the life of the screwdriver as well.

Torx Screwdriver. The Torx fastener is becoming more and more common. It is used in a variety of industries, including the automotive industries. Many American-made automobiles use the star-shaped Torx fastener to secure headlight assemblies, mirrors, and luggage racks. Not only does the six-prong tip provide greater turning power and less slippage, but the Torx fastener also provides a measure of tamper resistance. The popularity of Torx fasteners makes having a complete set of Torx

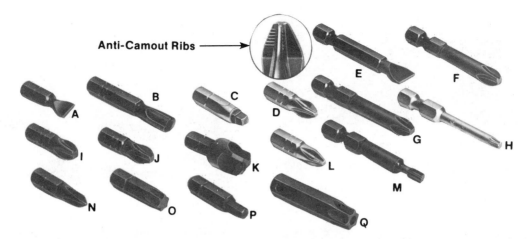

Anti-Camout Ribs →

FIGURE 3-36 (A) Flat tip, (B) Clutch A, (C) Scrulox, (D) Anti-camout ribs Phillips, (E) Flat-tip power bit, (F) Pozidriv power bit, (G) Phillips power bit, (H) Torx power bit, (I) Phillips, (J) Pozidriv, (K) Tri-wing, (L) Anti-camout ribs Phillips, (M) Clutch A power bit, (N) Reed and Prince, (O) Torx, (P) Hex, and (Q) Tamper-proof Torx. *(Courtesy of Snap-on Tools Corp.)*

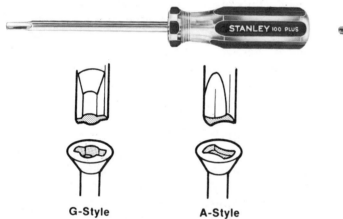

G-Style   A-Style

FIGURE 3-37   Clutch screwdrivers. *(Courtesy of Stanley Works)*

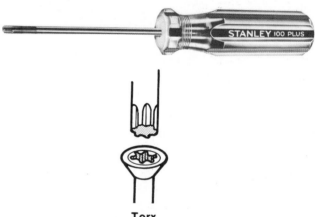

Torx

FIGURE 3-39   Torx screwdriver. *(Courtesy of Stanley Works)*

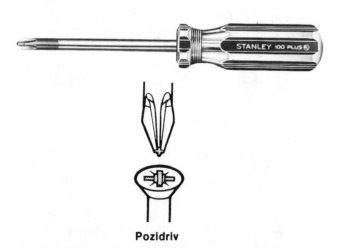

Pozidriv

FIGURE 3-38   Pozidriv screwdriver. *(Courtesy of Stanley Works)*

screwdrivers (Figure 3-39) a necessity for today's auto body repair technician. A set of seven has sizes T8 to T30.

PLIERS

Pliers are an all-around grabbing tool used for working with wires, clips, and pins. The auto body repair technician must own several types: standard pliers for common parts and wires, needle nose for the really small parts, and large adjustable pliers for heavy duty work, including bending sheet metal.

Combination Pliers

The combination pliers (Figure 3-40) is the most common type of pliers and is frequently used in any kind of automotive repair. The jaws have both flat and curved surfaces for holding flat or round objects. Also called slip-joint pliers, the combination pliers has two jaw-opening sides. One jaw can be moved up or down on a pin attached to the other jaw to change the opening.

Adjustable Pliers

Adjustable pliers, commonly called Channel-locks (Figure 3-41), have a multiposition slip joint that allows for many jaw opening sizes. For example a 16-inch adjustable pliers can have a maximum 4-1/2-inch jaw opening. The adjustable pliers then is useful for grasping and turning large objects. The long handle provides plenty of turning leverage. Adjustable pliers are available with flat or curved jaws.

Needle Nose Pliers

Every auto body repair technician should have at least one 6- or 8-inch pair of needle nose pliers. Needle nose pliers have long, tapered jaws (Figure 3-42). They are indispensable for grasping small parts or for reaching into tight spots. Many needle nose pliers also have wire cutting edges and a wire stripper. These are very handy for the minor electrical connections (headlights, for example) often made in the body shop. A needle nose with a 90 degree bend in the jaws is also handy to have for reaching behind or around obstacles.

FIGURE 3-41 Adjustable pliers. *(Courtesy of Snap-on Tools Corp.)*

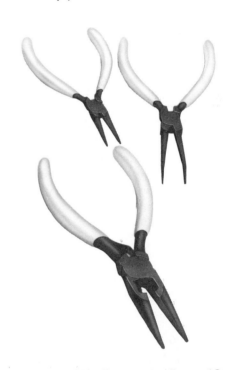

FIGURE 3-42 Needle nose pliers. *(Courtesy of Snap-on Tools Corp.)*

Locking Pliers

Locking pliers (or vise grips as they are commonly called) are similar to the standard kind except that they lock closed with a very tight grip (Figure 3-43). They are extremely useful for holding parts together. For example, several pairs of locking pliers will come in handy when holding a replacement panel in position for spot welding. They are also useful for getting a firm grip on a badly rounded fastener on which wrenches and sockets are no longer effective. Locking pliers come in several sizes and jaw configurations for use in many auto body

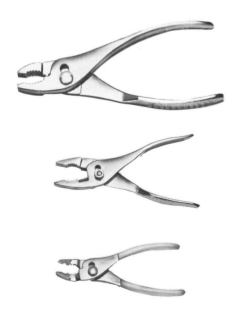

FIGURE 3-40 Slip joint combination pliers. *(Courtesy of Snap-on Tools Corp.)*

FIGURE 3-43 Vise grips

jobs. Of the ones illustrated in Figure 3-44, the C-clamp, welding, and duckbill types are among those frequently used.

The C-clamp type of course is handy for reaching over and clamping pieces with flanges or beads. The welding vise grip has a special shaped jaw for gripping and aligning the weld joints in brazing or welding operations. The duckbill pliers has wide jaws for holding and bending sheet metal.

MISCELLANEOUS HAND TOOLS

A variety of other miscellaneous hand tools will be handy from time to time. Many are inexpensive; most have a variety of uses. A few are very expensive and will probably be provided by the shop.

Tape Measure

A retractable steel rule (Figure 3-45) is a basic ingredient in any tool box. Its uses in the auto body repair shop are many—measuring a repair area for a sheet metal patch, finding centerlines when applying woodgrain transfers, measuring frame dimensions, and so on. A 10- or 12-foot self-winding tape measure is usually sufficient.

Utility Knife

A common utility knife with a retractable razor blade is handy for any general purpose cutting or trimming. Most come with extra blades stored in the handle.

Scrapers

A 1- or 1-1/2-inch scraper is useful for removing old or bad body filler and paint (Figure 3-46). They can also be used for applying body filler and glazing putty when a plastic spreader or squeegee is not available.

Wire Brush

A wire brush should be used sparingly on bare metal because it can leave scratches in the metal. But wire brushes are often used to clean weld joints of welding flux.

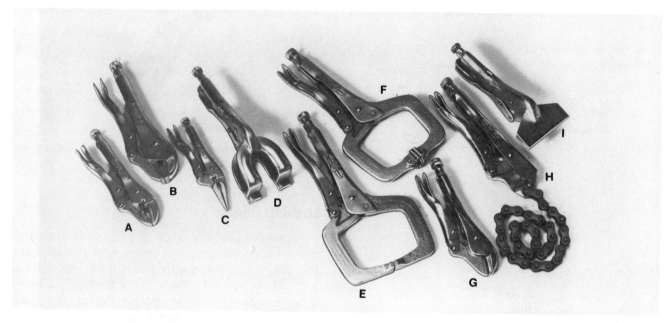

A. Wire Cutter	D. Welding Clamp	G. Hose Pinch Off
B. Standard	E. C-Clamp	H. Chain Wrench
C. Long Nose	F. C-Clamp With Swivel Pads	I. Duckbill

FIGURE 3-44 Assorted vise grip locking pliers. (Courtesy of Snap-on Tools Corp.)

FIGURE 3-45   A retractable tape measure. *(Courtesy of Stanley Works)*

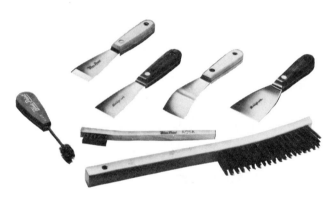

FIGURE 3-46   Various size scrapers and wire brushes. *(Courtesy of Snap-on Tools Corp.)*

C-clamps

When a third hand is needed, a C-clamp is often the answer. C-clamps come in various sizes and a variety will be very useful in a body shop.

Vise

A medium-duty bench vise (Figure 3-47) is normally a shop-provided tool used for holding metal objects when grinding, bending, or welding. Most have a swivel base and serrated jaws. Clamping the workpiece in a vise frees both hands and keeps the workpiece stationary.

Rim Wrench

The rim, or lug, wrench is used to remove wheel lugs (nuts or bolts holding the wheel to the axle flange). A four-way lug wrench (Figure 3-48) has four hex-shaped wrenches, or sockets; each one is sized to fit one of the four popular sizes of wheel lug nuts available.

FIGURE 3-47   A bench-mounted vise

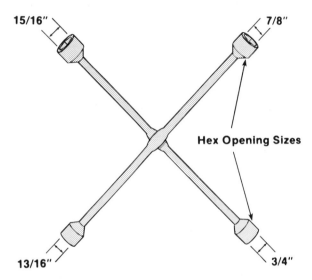

FIGURE 3-48   A four-way lug wrench

Tap and Die Set

A tap is a tool that cleans and rethreads holes. A die straightens damaged threads on bolts or studs. A tap and die set, such as the one shown in Figure 3-49, will perform most rethreading tasks in the body shop. When the correct fastener is not available, a tap and die set can be used to make a bolt or nut.

Tool Chest

A cabinet type tool chest such as the ones shown in Figure 3-50 is standard equipment in the body shop. A portable tool box on top of the chest holds the larger hand and power tools. A chest of drawers organizes wrenches, screwdrivers, hammers, and so forth. The tool chest is on rollers so that

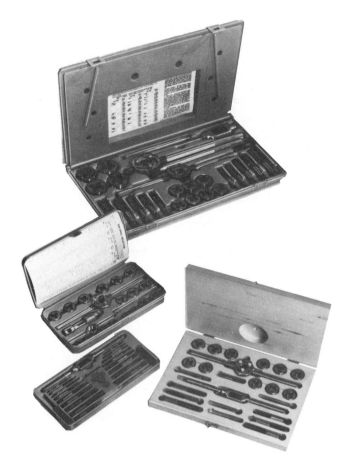

FIGURE 3-49   Tap and die sets

FIGURE 3-50   Heavy-duty tool chests on rollers.
(Courtesy of Snap-on Tools Corp.)

it can be conveniently located in the work area. The box and chest of drawers can be locked to safeguard the tools.

3.2 BODYWORKING TOOLS

Bodyworking tools include some very familiar general purpose metalworking tools as well as specialized tools only used in auto body repair. The following is a description of the most commonly used bodyworking tools. Because of the wide variety of hammers, files, and dollies, some of the less common varieties are not discussed but the tool collection of advanced auto body repair technicians will include all the tools necessary for performing every metal shaping technique, no matter how unusual. A typical set of bodyworking tools is shown in Figure 3-51.

HAMMERS

A number of different hammers are useful in the body shop. Many are specially shaped for a specific metal shaping operation.

Ball Peen Hammers

The ball peen hammer (Figure 3-52) is a useful, multipurpose tool for all kinds of work with sheet metal. Heavier than the bodyhammer, it is used for straightening bent underpinnings, smoothing heavy-gauge parts, and roughly shaping body parts before work with a bodyhammer and dolly begins. A good ball peen hammer, which weighs between 10 and 16 ounces (depending on how much can be swung comfortably), will see a lot of action in a body shop.

Mallets

The rubber mallet (Figure 3-53) gently bumps sheet metal without damaging the painted finish. Its most frequent use is with the suction cup on soft "cave-in" type dents. While pulling upward on the cup, the mallet is used to tap lightly all around the surrounding high spots. A popping sound occurs as the high spots drop and the low spot springs back to its original contour.

A steel hammer with rubber tips is another mallet useful in bodywork. The hammer shown in Figure 3-53B has both hard and soft replaceable rubber heads. The soft-faced hammer, as it is sometimes called, is used to work chrome trim and other delicate parts without marring the finish.

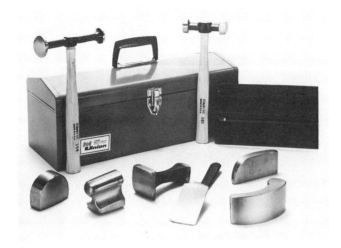

A

B

FIGURE 3-51 (A) Basic bodyworking set; (B) master bodyworker's bumpset. *(Courtesy of Majestic Tools Mfg. Co.)*

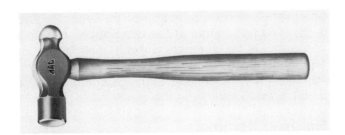

FIGURE 3-52 A ball peen hammer. *(Courtesy of Stanley Works)*

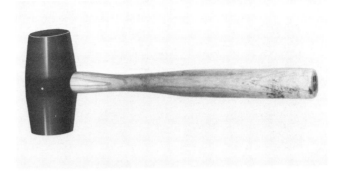

A

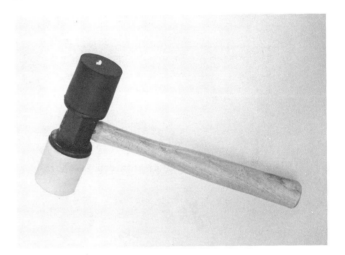

B

FIGURE 3-53 (A) Rubber mallet and (B) soft-faced hammer. *(Photo B courtesy of Majestic Tools Mfg. Co.)*

Sledgehammer

A light sledgehammer (Figure 3-54) is an essential tool for the first stages of re-forming damaged sheet metal. It should weigh 3 to 5 pounds and have a short handle so that it can be used in tight places. The sledgehammer can be used to knock damaged metal roughly back into shape and to clear away damaged metal when replacing a panel.

BODYHAMMERS

Bodyhammers are the basic tools for pounding sheet metal back into shape. They come in many different designs. As shown in Figure 3-55, some have flat, square heads; some have rounded heads; and some, called picking hammers, have pointed heads. Every style is designed for a special use for which it is ideal.

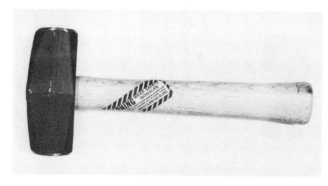

FIGURE 3-54　Light sledgehammers. *(Courtesy of Stanley Works)*

Wide Nose Peen

Picking and Dinging

Long Spot Pick

Spot Pick

Wide Nose Cross Peen

Cross Peen Shrinking

Shrinking

Long Picking

Shrinking Hammer

Wide Face Bumping

Reverse Curve, Light Bumping

Short-Curved Cross Peen

FIGURE 3-55　Bodyhammers. *(Courtesy of Snap-on Tools Corp.)*

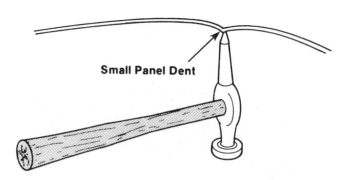

Small Panel Dent

FIGURE 3-56　Raising a dent with a pick hammer

Picking Hammers

The picking hammer will take care of many small dents. The pointed end is used to hammer out small dents from the inside; a gentle tap in the center usually does it (Figure 3-56). The flat end is for hammer-and-dolly work to remove high spots and ripples. Picking hammers come in a variety of shapes and sizes (Figure 3-57). Some have long picks for reaching behind body panels. Some have sharp "pencil" points; others have blunted bullet points.

Be careful when using the pick hammer. If swung forcefully, the pointed end can pierce the lighter sheet metals used in late model cars. Use the pick only on small dents.

Bumping Hammers

Larger dents require the use of a bumping hammer. Bumping hammers can have a round face or a square face. The surfaces of the faces are nearly flat. The faces are large so that the force of the blows is spread over a large area. These hammers are used for initial straightening on dented panels or for working inner panels and reinforced sections that require more force but not a finish appearance.

Sharp concave surfaces, such as the reverse curves on quarter panels, headlights, doors, and so on, require the use of a reverse curve light bumping hammer. The faces of this hammer are crowned—one in the opposite direction of the other (Figure 3-58). The tight curve of the faces allows concave contours to be bumped without the danger of stretching the metal. Remember, the contour of the hammer must be smaller than the contour of the panel to avoid stretching the metal.

Finishing Hammers

After the bumping hammer is used to remove the dent, final contour is achieved with the finishing

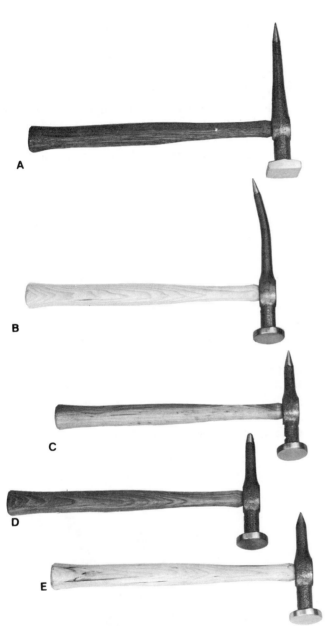

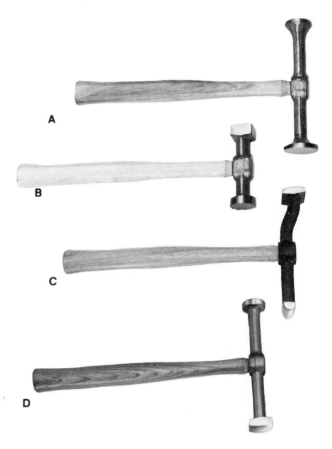

FIGURE 3-59 Finish hammers: (A) double round; (B) shrinking hammer; (C) off-set bumping; and (D) dinging hammer. *(Courtesy of Majestic Tools Mfg. Co.)*

FIGURE 3-57 Pick hammers. (A) long pencil point; (B) long-curved pencil point; (C) short pencil point; (D) short bullet point; and (E) short chisel point. *(Courtesy of Majestic Tools Mfg. Co.)*

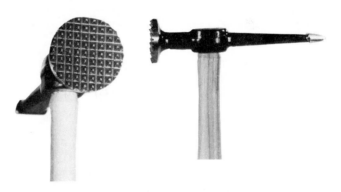

FIGURE 3-60 Serrated face of a shrinking hammer. *(Courtesy of Majestic Tools Mfg. Co.)*

hammer (Figure 3-59). The faces on a finishing hammer are smaller than those of the heavier bumping hammer. The surface of the face is crowned to concentrate the force on top of the ridge or high spot. A shrinking hammer (Figure 3-60) is a finishing hammer with a serrated or cross-grooved face. This

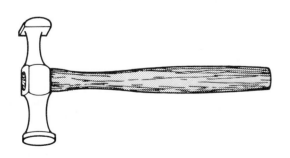

FIGURE 3-58 Bumping hammers

hammer is used to shrink spots that have been stretched by excessive hammering.

Dollies

The dolly or dolly block is used like an anvil. It is generally held on the backside of a panel being struck with a hammer. Together the hammer and dolly work high spots down and low spots up (Figure 3-61).

There are many different shapes of dollies (Figure 3-62). Each shape is intended for specific types of dents and body panel contours—high crowns, low crowns, flanges, and others. It is very important that the dolly fits the contour of the panel. If a flat dolly or one with a low crown is used on a high crown panel, additional dents will be the result.

A general purpose dolly has many contours. It can be used in most situations. A rail type dolly is another commonly used dolly with many contours. Toe and heel dollies are used for bumping in tight places, and the flat right angle edge is used for straightening flanges.

Spoons

Body spoons (Figure 3-63) are another class of bodyworking tools that are used sometimes like a hammer and sometimes like a dolly. Available in a variety of shapes and sizes to match various panel shapes, the flat surfaces of a spoon distribute the striking force over a wide area (Figure 3-64). They are particularly useful on creases and ridges. A spoon dolly can be used as a dolly where the space behind a panel is limited. A dinging spoon is used with a hammer to work down ridges. Inside spoons can be used to pry up low places or can be struck with a hammer to drive up dents. Bumping files have

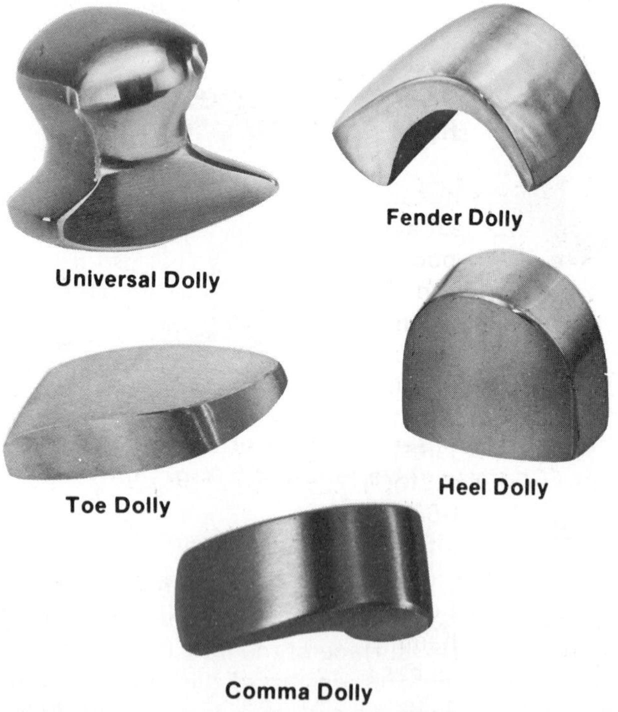

FIGURE 3-61 Bumping a dent with a hammer and dolly

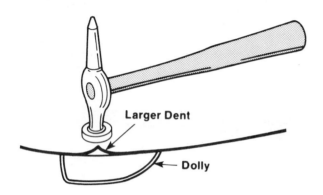

Universal Dolly

Fender Dolly

Toe Dolly

Heel Dolly

Comma Dolly

FIGURE 3-62 Commonly used dolly bars

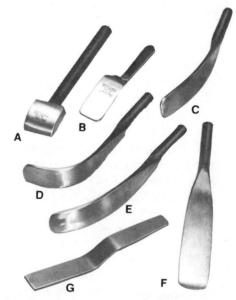

A. Spoon Dolly
B. Light Dinging Spoon
C. Surfacing Spoon
D. Inside High Crown
E. Inside Medium Crown
F. Inside Heavy-Duty Spoon
G. Bumping File

FIGURE 3-63 Various body spoons. (Courtesy of Snap-on Tools Corp.)

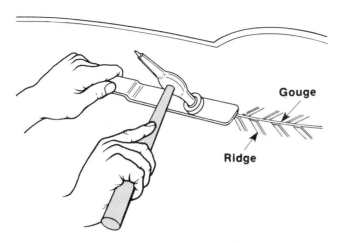

FIGURE 3-64   Lowering a ridge with a hammer and spoon

serrated surfaces and are used to slap ridges or the underside of creases to bump the metal back to its original shape.

PICKS

Picks (Figure 3-65), like spoons, are used to reach into confined spaces. The pick is used only to pry up low spots. They vary in length and shape and most have a U-shaped end that serves as a handle. Picks are commonly used to raise low spots in door, quarter panels, and other sealed body sections (Figure 3-66). Picks are often preferred to slidehammers and pull rods because they do not require drilling holes in the sheet metal.

FIGURE 3-65   Several different body picks. (Courtesy of Snap-on Tools Corp.)

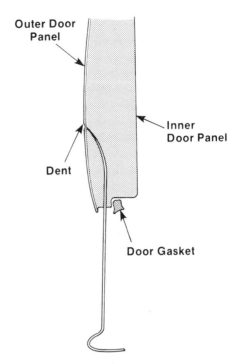

FIGURE 3-66   Prying a dent with a pick

FIGURE 3-67   A dent puller. (Courtesy of Easco/K-D Tools)

DENT PULLERS AND PULL RODS

Creases in sealed body panels or panel sections that cannot be reached from the backside even with the longest spoon can be pulled out with a dent puller or pull rod. Either tool requires one or more holes drilled or punched in the crease.

A dent puller usually comes with a threaded tip and hook tip (Figure 3-67). Either tip is inserted in the drilled hole and a hammer is slid on a steel shaft and struck against the handle. Tapping the slide-hammer against the handle slowly pulls up the low spot (Figure 3-68).

Working with a dent puller is faster when a metal piercing tip is used. When the metal tip is forced through the sheet metal, the angular rings grip the metal as the hammer is tapped against the metal. When the metal has been pulled back to shape, the tip can be backed out of the hole by turning it counterclockwise.

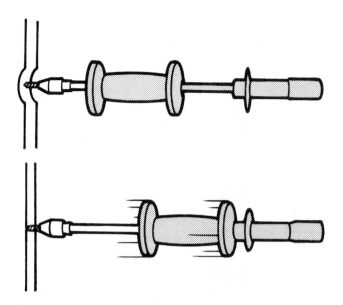

FIGURE 3-68   Pulling a dent with a dent puller

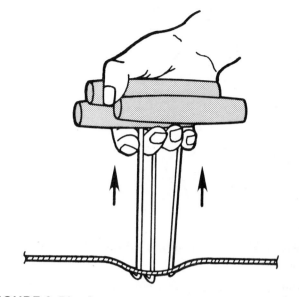

FIGURE 3-70   Several pull rods can be used to pull up larger dents.

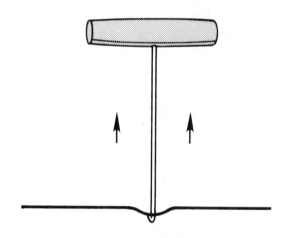

FIGURE 3-69   Pulling a small dent with a pull rod

A pull rod is used in this manner. The curved end of the pull rod is inserted in the drilled hole. A small dent or crease can be pulled up with a single pull rod (Figure 3-69). Three or four pull rods can be used simultaneously to pull up larger dents (Figure 3-70). A bodyhammer can also be used with a pull rod. The high crown of a dent can be bumped down, while the low spot is pulled up (Figure 3-71). Simultaneous bumping and pulling returns the panel to its original shape with less danger of stretching the metal.

It is important to close the holes created by using dent pullers and pull rods by soldering or welding. Simply patching the holes with body filler will not provide sufficient corrosion protection.

SUCTION CUPS

The suction cup (Figure 3-72) is a simple tool that makes short work of shallow dents if they are

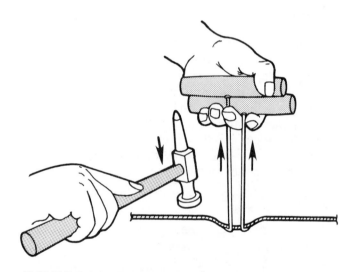

FIGURE 3-71   Bumping and pulling lowers crowns, while raising dings.

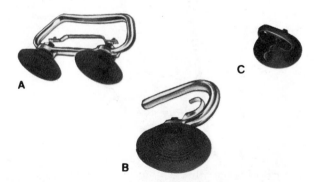

FIGURE 3-72   Suction cups: (A) two-finger cup, (B) heavy-duty suction cup, and (C) heavy-duty dual cup. (Courtesy of Snap-on Tools Corp.)

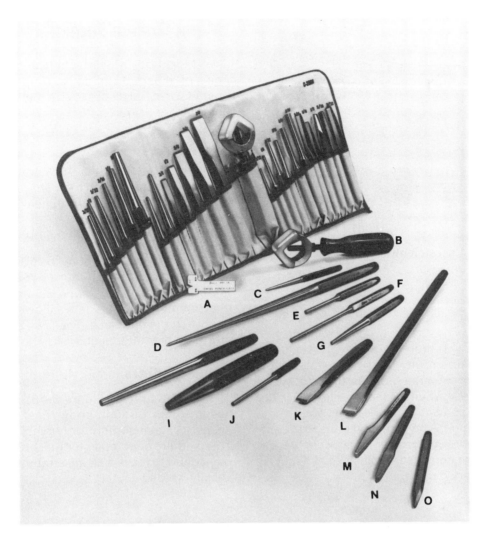

A. Chisel Gauge
B. Punch/Chisel Holder
C. Center Punch
D. Long Center Punch
E. Pin Punch

F. Long Pin Punch
G. Starter Punch
H. Long-Tapered Punch
I. Short-Tapered Punch
J. Roll Pin

K. Flat Chisel
L. Long Flat Chisel
M. Round Nose Cape Chisel
N. Cape Chisel
O. Diamond Point Chisel

FIGURE 3-73 Punches and chisels. *(Courtesy of Snap-on Tools Corp.)*

not locked in by a crease in the metal. Simply attach the suction cup to the center of the dent and pull. The dent might come right out with no damage to the paint and no refinishing required. It is an easy tool to use and can make a simple repair. However, once a dent is locked in, some hammer and dolly work will be necessary to smooth the metal. Even so, the suction cup method is usually worth a try.

PUNCHES AND CHISELS

A good set of punches and chisels (Figure 3-73) is absolutely necessary in every bodyworking tool chest. Center punches are used to mark the location of parts before they are removed and for marking a spot for drilling. (The punch mark keeps the drill bit from wandering.) A drifter or starter punch has a tapered point with a flat end that is used to drive out rivets, pins, and bolts. A pin punch is similar to the drifter except its shaft is not tapered; thus, it can be used to drive out smaller rivets or bolts. An aligning punch is a long tapered punch used to align body panels for welding or other body parts (such as fender bolt holes and a bumper).

A chisel is a steel bar with a hardened cutting edge for shearing steel. These chisels come in various sizes and a set is necessary for both light- and heavy-duty work. The cold chisel is used to split frozen nuts, shear off rusted bolts, cut welds, and separate body and frame parts.

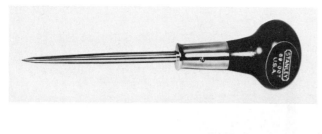

FIGURE 3-74 A scratch awl. *(Courtesy of Stanley Works)*

Scratch Awl

A scratch awl (Figure 3-74) is very similar in appearance to an ice pick, but the pointed steel shank is heavier. A scratch awl is used to pierce holes in their metal when a specific size hole is not required. It is also used to mark metal for cutting, drilling, or fastening. A hammer can be used to lightly drive the awl through heavier metal. Keep the awl ground to a sharp point so it can be used effectively and safely in every job.

Metal Cutting Shears

Most body repair technicians have at least one pair of shears or tin snips. Snips are used to trim panels or metal pieces to size. Several types of metal cutters are useful.

Tin Snips

Tin snips (Figure 3-75A) are perhaps the most common metal cutting tool. They can be used to cut straight or curved shapes in heavy steel.

Metal Cutters

Metal cutters (Figure 3-75B, C, and D), also called aviation snips (Figure 3-75F), are used to cut through hard metals such as stainless steel. The narrow profile of the jaws allows the snips to slip between the cut metal. The jaws are serrated to cut through the tough metal.

Panel Cutters

Panel cutters (Figure 3-76) are special snips used to cut through body sheet metal. These are used to make straight or curved cutouts in panels that require spot repair for rust or damage. They are designed to leave a clean, straight edge that can be easily welded.

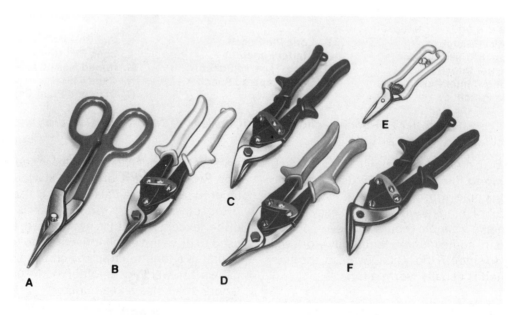

A. Tin Snips
B. Straight Cut Shears
C. Right Cut Shears
D. Left Cut Shears
E. Light-Duty Snips
F. Aviation Snips

FIGURE 3-75 Sheet metal cutting shears. *(Courtesy of Snap-on Tools Corp.)*

FIGURE 3-76 Panel cutter, or two-way nibbler. *(Courtesy of S & G Tool Aid Corp.)*

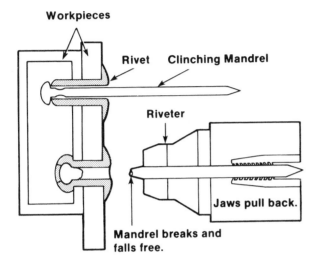

FIGURE 3-77 Riveting two panels together

RIVET GUN

Pop rivets are one of the handiest inventions for auto bodywork. They can be inserted into a blind hole through two pieces of metal and then drawn up with a riveting tool, locking the pieces of metal together (Figure 3-77). There is no need to have access to the back of the rivets, and if enough rivets are used, the joint created is extremely strong. For any kind of sheet metal replacement such as rust hole repair, the pop rivet is by far the easiest and least expensive joining system available. In fact, most body shops use rivets extensively, either as a permanent repair or as temporary fasteners. They are used as temporary fasteners before the replacement sheet metal is welded in places where extreme heat would distort the metal or create a safety hazard (such as around the gas tank). A good rivet gun (Figure 3-78) does not cost much. The most commonly used rivets in bodywork are 1/8- and 3/16-inch. A few others of assorted sizes might be needed for special jobs.

A heavy-duty riveter, such as the one shown in Figure 3-79, is used to rivet hard-to-reach places and heavier mechanical assemblies such as a win-

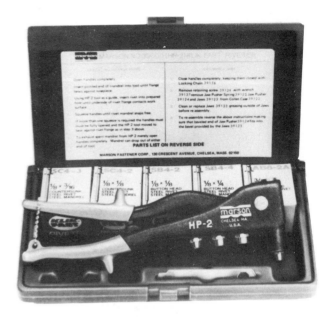

FIGURE 3-78 A pop rivet gun. *(Courtesy of Marson Corp.)*

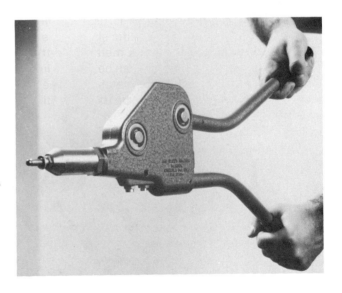

FIGURE 3-79 A heavy-duty pop rivet gun. *(Courtesy of Marson Corp.)*

dow glass regulator. It has long handles, a long nose, and sets 3/16- to 1/4-inch blind rivets.

UPHOLSTERY TOOLS

Any repair work that requires removing interior trim will be facilitated with an upholstery tool (Figure 3-80). This prong-shaped prying tool is used to slip under and pry up upholstery tacks, springs, clips, and other fasteners.

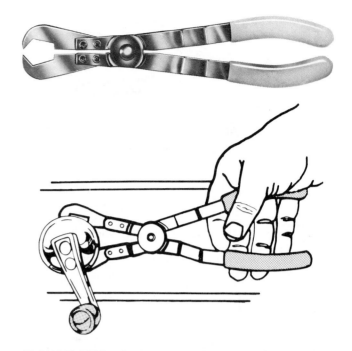

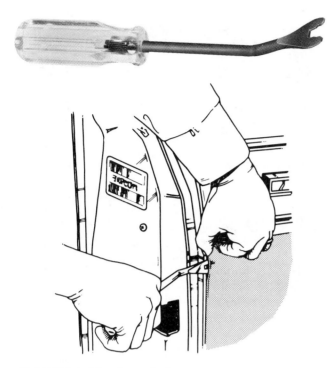

FIGURE 3-80   An upholstery tool

FIGURE 3-81   A door handle tool. *(Courtesy of Lisle Corp.)*

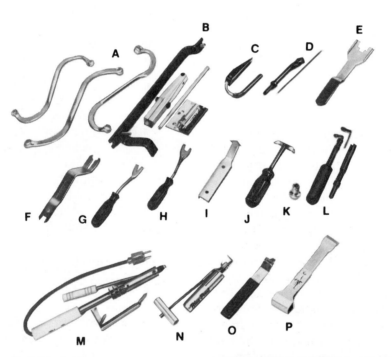

A. Door Hinge Bolt Wrenches
B. Door Removal Kit
C. Door Panel Remover (GM and Ford)
D. Door Panel Remover
E. Door Handle Tool (GM, Some Fords)
F. Door Handle Tool (Chrysler)
G. Trim Pad Remover (GM, Ford, Chrysler)
H. Trim Pad Remover (GM)

I. Window Molding Release Tool
J. Windshield Locking Strip Installation Tool
K. Window Sash Nut Spanner Socket
L. Windshield Remover
M. Hot-Tip Windshield Removing Kit
N. Windshield Wiper Removal Tool
O. Windshield Wiper Tool
P. All-Purpose Window Scraper

FIGURE 3-82   Window and door tools. *(Courtesy of Snap-on Tools Corp.)*

Door Handle Tool

Interior door handles are often secured to the door panel by wire spring clips. These clips, shaped like horseshoes, fit over the handle shaft and hold the handle tightly against the interior panel trim. Clip pullers or door handle tools (Figure 3-81) are needed to reach inside the door and remove the clip. Some door handle tools pull the clip out; others push the clip off the shaft.

Figure 3-82 shows an assortment of window and door tools.

Sheet Metal Brakes

Many body repairs require metal patches to be riveted or welded into place. A tool that comes in handy for bending and breaking sheet metal is shown in Figure 3-83. This sheet metal brake bends sheet metal up to 20 gauge and sheet aluminum up to 16 gauge. Clean, smooth bends up to 90 degrees can be made with a brake. The brake is also used for cutting sheet metal to size. This is done by first bending the metal 90 degrees. Then the metal is worked back and forth by hand until the metal breaks along the crease.

3.3 BODY SURFACING TOOLS

A number of surfacing tools are used to give a repair its final shape and contour. Some are used to shape the repaired metal. Others are used to apply and shape plastic body filler and putty.

FIGURE 3-83   A sheet metal brake is used to bend, shape, and break sheet metal. *(Courtesy of Majestic Tools Mfg. Co.)*

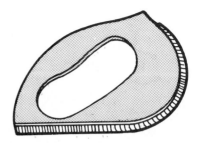

FIGURE 3-84   A reveal file is used to shape tight curves.

Metal Files

After working a damaged panel back to its approximate original contour, a metal file is used to remove any remaining high spots. Two special files are necessary for most bodywork.

Reveal File

The reveal file (Figure 3-84) is a small file that is available in numerous shapes. Generally it is curved to fit tightly crowned areas such as around windshields, wheel openings, and other panel edges. The reveal file is pulled, not pushed, when used. Pushing causes the file to chatter, resulting in nicks and an uneven surface.

Body Files

Body files are used to level large surfaces. After a dent has been bumped or pulled back into shape, the body file will hone down high spots and reveal any low spots that might require additional bumping. Keep in mind that it is possible to file through thin metal used in some vehicles.

The blade of the body file is held in a holder. Figure 3-85A shows a flexible holder with a turnbuckle. The turnbuckle can be adjusted to flex the file. The flexible holder allows the shape of the file to fit the contour of the panel.

Fixed file holders (Figure 3-85B) are also available for filing flat or slightly convex shapes.

Surform File

Body filler can be made level to the adjacent panel with a surform file (Figure 3-86). Commonly referred to as a "cheese grater," the surform file is used to shape body filler while it is semihard. Shaping the filler before it hardens shortens the waiting period while the filler cures and reduces the sanding effort later in the repair process.

FIGURE 3-85 A body file (A) in a flexible holder and (B) rigid file holders. *(Photo B courtesy of Snap-on Tools Corp.)*

SPEED FILE

Once the body filler has hardened, the repair can be shaped and leveled with a speed file (Figure 3-87). The speed file is a rigid wooden holder about 17 inches long and 2-3/4 inches wide. Also called a flatboy, the speed file allows a repair area to be sanded quickly with long, level strokes. This eliminates waves and uneven areas.

The lightweight aluminum sander shown in Figure 3-88A is designed to quickly level body filler. The extra long length helps avoid creating a waxy surface. The sander also flexes to match the panel contour. Adhesive-backed sandpaper is applied from a roll (Figure 3-88B). This particular sander can also be attached to a straight-line air sander.

SPREADERS AND SQUEEGEES

Spreaders and squeegees are two important tools used in auto body resurfacing. Spreaders are used to apply body filler. Spreaders (Figure 3-89) are made of rigid plastic and are available in various sizes. Be sure to use one that is large enough to apply plastic filler over the repair area before the filler begins to set up.

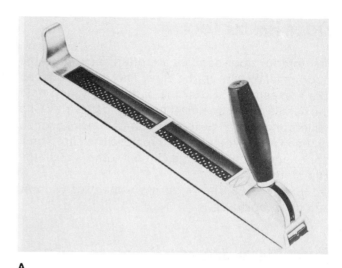

FIGURE 3-86 (A) Surform "cheese grater" and (B) replacement blades. *(Photo A courtesy of Bond-Tite Products; photo B courtesy of Du Pont Co.)*

FIGURE 3-87 Speed files. *(Courtesy of Du Pont Co.)*

FIGURE 3-88   A flexible sander. (Courtesy of Body-craft Corp.)

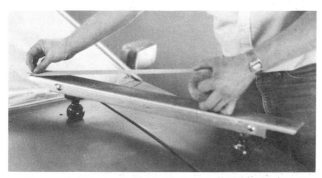

FIGURE 3-89   A body filler spreader. (Courtesy of Du Pont Co.)

FIGURE 3-90   A rubber squeegee

A squeegee (Figure 3-90) is a flexible rubber block approximately 2 inches by 3 inches and 3/16-inch thick. Squeegees are used to apply glazing putty and light coats of body filler. They are also used when wet sanding to skim water and sanding grit from the repair area.

3.4 HAND TOOL SAFETY

Hand tool safety begins with purchasing quality tools. Quality tools might require a greater investment in money, but the dividends—safety and durability—are worth the expense and, in the long run, cost less than cheap tools. Many quality tools are also warranted to ensure their quality and protect the investment.

The second step in safe tool usage is knowledge. Read the manufacturer's instructions and use the tool only for tasks it was designed to do. Misuse of a tool not only frequently results in accidents, but also tends to wear or weaken the tool, increasing the likelihood of slipping, chipping, or shattering.

The final step in tool safety is maintenance. Body shop tools must be kept clean, rust-free, sharp, and safely organized in a tool cabinet or chest. A tool should be maintained as close to the original condition as possible. Damaged and broken tools should never be used.

GENERAL PURPOSE TOOLS AND SAFETY

General purpose tools often have a variety of uses, but never use a tool for any tasks other than the ones for which it was designed. Proper use and proper care of tools will eliminate most accidents in the body shop. Follow these precautions when using general purpose hand tools.

Safety Rules for Pliers

The following basic safety rules should be applied to the use of pliers:

- Pliers should not be used for cutting hardened wire unless specifically manufactured for this purpose.
- Never expose pliers to excessive heat. This might draw the temper and ruin the tool (Figure 3-91).
- Always cut at right angles. Never rock the tool from side to side or bend the wire back and forth against the cutting blades.

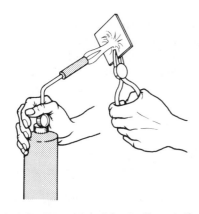

FIGURE 3-91 Do not subject pliers to heat.

- Do not bend heavy metal with light pliers. Needle nose pliers can be damaged if the tips are used to bend body metal, large wires, and so on. Use a sturdier tool.
- Never use pliers as a hammer (Figure 3-92) or use a hammer on the handles. They might crack or break, or the blades might be nicked by such abuse.
- Ordinary plastic-dipped handles are designed for comfort, not electrical insulation. Tools having high-dielectric insulation are available and are so identified. Do not confuse the two.
- Never extend the length of the handles to secure greater leverage. Use a larger pair of pliers or a bolt cutter.
- Pliers should not be used on nuts or bolts. A wrench will do a better job with less risk of damage to the fastener.
- Safety glasses should be worn when cutting wire or other such tasks to protect the eyes from being struck by the end of the object being cut.

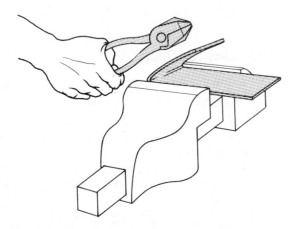

FIGURE 3-92 Do not hammer with pliers.

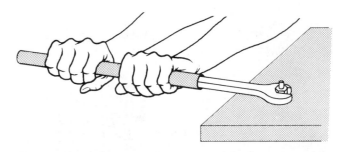

FIGURE 3-93 Do not use pipe extensions on wrench handles.

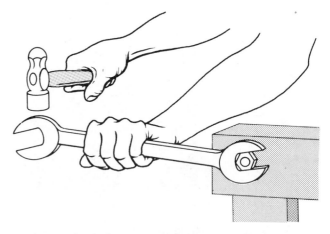

FIGURE 3-94 Do not hammer on wrenches.

Safety Rules for Wrenches

Here are a few basic rules that should be kept in mind when using wrenches:

- Keep wrenches clean and free of oil. Dirt and grit will prevent them from seating firmly around a nut. Oil and grease will make them slippery.
- Do not use a wrench to do the job of another tool. The job will not be done as well, and the wrench might be damaged or even broken. Using a wrench as a hammer or a pry bar or as anything but a wrench can be dangerous. Take the time to get the right tool.
- Never use a wrench opening that is too large for the fastener. This can spread the jaws of an open-end wrench and batter the points of a box or socket wrench. A wrench that has an opening that is too large can also spoil the points of the nut or bolt head. And, when selecting a wrench for proper fit, take special care to use inch wrenches on inch fasteners and metric wrenches on metric fasteners.
- Match the wrench to the job, using box or socket wrenches for heavier jobs, open-end

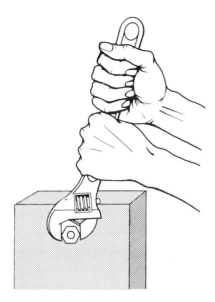

FIGURE 3-95 Do not use adjustable wrenches to tighten nuts or bolts.

wrenches for medium-duty work, and adjustable wrenches for light-duty jobs and odd-sized nuts. A pipe wrench should be used only on pipes, never on a nut, because its teeth will damage the nut. Always use a straight, rather than offset, handle if conditions permit.

- Never push a wrench beyond its capacity. Quality wrenches are designed and sized to keep the leverage and intended load (torque) in safe balance. The use of an artificial extension (such as a pipe "cheater") on the handle of a wrench can break the wrench, spoil the work, and hurt the user (Figure 3-93). Instead, get a larger wrench or a different kind of wrench to do the job. The safest wrench is a box or socket type. Never hammer a wrench not made to be struck (Figure 3-94). (To free a "frozen" nut or bolt, use a striking face box wrench or a heavy-duty box or socket wrench. Never use an open-end wrench. And apply penetrating oil beforehand.)
- Determine which way a nut should be turned before trying to loosen it. Most nuts are turned counterclockwise for removal. This might seem obvious, but even experienced people have been observed straining at the wrench in the tightening direction when they wanted to loosen the nut.
- If possible, always pull on a wrench handle, and adjust your stance to prevent a fall if something lets go. That is, assume a natural stance that will allow correct motion of the

tool without causing danger if something should slip. There might be situations, of course, in which a wrench handle must only be pushed to loosen or tighten a nut or bolt. But always pull on a wrench to exert even pressure and avoid injury if the wrench slips or the nut breaks loose unexpectedly. (If it is necessary to push the wrench, do it with the palm of the hand, and hold the palm open.)

- Never expose a wrench to excessive heat. Direct flame can draw the temper from the metal, weakening and possibly warping it, and making it unsafe to use.
- Place the tool in its correct position. For instance, never cock or tilt an open-end wrench. Always be sure the nut or bolt head is fully seated in the jaw opening, for both safety and efficiency. A box or socket wrench should be used on hard-to-reach fasteners. Adjustable wrenches should be tightly adjusted to the work and pulled so that the force is applied to the fixed jaw (Figure 3-95).
- Do not depend on plastic-dipped handles to insulate from electricity. Ordinary plastic-dipped handles are for comfort and a firmer grip. They are not intended for protection against electric shock. (Special high-dielectric strength handle insulation is available, but it should only be used as a secondary precaution.)

Safety and Striking Tools

The following safety precautions apply generally to striking tools:

- Check to see that the handle is tight before using any striking tool. Never strike a tool or use a striking tool with a loose or damaged handle.
- Always use a striking tool of suitable size and weight for the job. Do not use a tack hammer to drive a spike, nor a sledge to drive a tack.
- Discard or redress any striking or struck tool if the face shows excessive wear, dents, chips, mushrooming, or improper redressing.
- Rest the face of the hammer on the work before striking to get the feel or aim. Then grasp the handle firmly with the hand near the extreme end of the handle.
- Strike squarely, but lightly, until the punch or tool to be driven is set. Make sure that the fingers of the other hand are out of the way before striking with force.

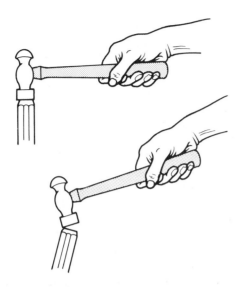

FIGURE 3-96 Strike squarely to prevent damage.

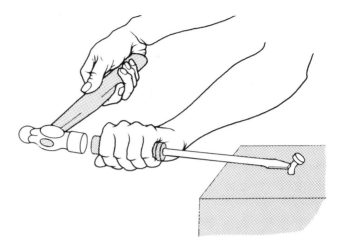

FIGURE 3-98 Do not use screwdrivers as chisels.

- A hammer blow should always be struck squarely with the hammer face parallel to the surface being struck (Figure 3-96). Always avoid glancing blows and over-and-under strikes.
- For striking another tool (cold chisel, punch, wedge, and so on) the face of the hammer should be proportionately larger than the head of the tool. For example a 1/2-inch cold chisel requires at least a 1-inch hammer face.
- Never use one hammer to strike another hammer (Figure 3-97).
- Do not use the end of the handle of any striking tool for tamping or prying; it might split.

Screwdriver Safety

The screwdriver is a very safe tool; it only presents a hazard when misused or when the user lacks the knowledge or skill to use it. Keep the following safety tips in mind:

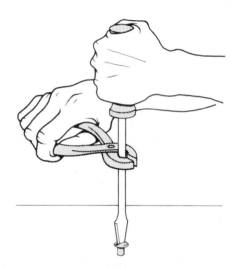

FIGURE 3-99 Do not force screwdrivers with vise grips or pliers.

- Do not hold your work in your hand while using a screwdriver; if the point slips, it can cause a bad cut. Hold the work in a vise, with a clamp, or on a solid surface. If that is impossible, follow this rule: Never get any part of your body in front of the screwdriver blade tip. That is a good safety rule for any sharp or pointed tool.
- All screwdrivers should have smooth, firm handles, and the blades should be kept in good condition. The screwdriver becomes useless and dangerous if the blade is broken.
- Do not use screwdrivers as chisels, hammers, can openers, crowbars, or for any purpose other than to turn screws (Figure 3-98).
- Never try to turn a screwdriver with a pair of pliers (Figure 3-99).

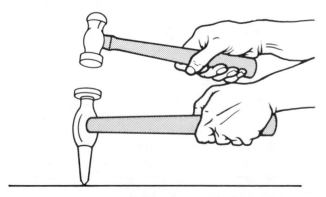

FIGURE 3-97 Do not hit hammers with hammers.

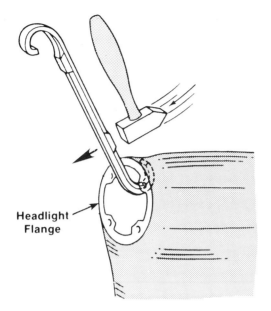

FIGURE 3–100 Driving out dented fender with double-end heavy-duty driver spoon

- Employ the right screwdriver for the job. That is, always use a screwdriver with a blade that fits the screw to be turned. The blade of the screwdriver should be seated squarely against the bottom of the screw slot.
- Screwdrivers with insulated handles and/or blades should be used for electrical repairs or installations. Be sure the battery is disconnected before attempting such work.

Safety and Snips

Although snips are very safe tools, keep the following tips in mind:

- Learn to use snips properly. They should always be oiled and adjusted to permit ease of cutting and to produce a surface that is free from burrs. If the blades bind or are too far apart, the snips should be adjusted.
- Never use snips as screwdrivers, hammers, or pry bars. They break easily.
- Do not attempt to cut heavier materials than those that the snips are designed for. Never use tin snips to cut stainless steel or other hardened sheet metals. Such use will dent or nick the cutting edges of the blades.
- Never toss snips in a tool box where the cutting edges can come into contact with other tools. This dulls the cutting edges and might even break the blades.
- When snips are not in use, the safest thing to do is hang them on hooks or lay them on an uncrowded shelf or bench.

BODYWORKING TOOL SAFETY

Hammers and other striking tools are perhaps the most widely used and probably the most often abused of all bodyworking tools. They are made in various types and sizes with varying degrees of hardness and different configurations for specific purposes. They should be selected for their intended use and used only for those purposes.

For example, do not use a bodyhammer to drive a light spoon that was not designed to be struck. Only driving spoons (Figure 3–100) and spoons designed for spring hammering should be hit with a bodyhammer. Also, do not try to use an adjustable body file to file high-crown or concave surfaces. Overflexing the adjustable file will cause the file to break.

Bodyhammers are highly specialized tools used almost exclusively by automotive technicians for bumping and dinging sheet metal in the repair of automotive bodies and fenders. Drop-forged tools are made from selected steel and heat treated to specific hardness.

Never use these hammers for other than bodywork. Always use a hammer of suitable size and weight for the job. Do not use a lightweight small hammer to pound out a heavy section, or a heavy hammer to lightly finish metal. Use hand tools only for their designed purposes and within their size range.

Never strike cold chisels, punches, or other hard objects with a bodyhammer; the face can chip and possibly cause damage not only to the hammer, but also to the tool user. Eye protection, through the use of safety glasses or hood, is recommended for any job involving the use of tools, particularly when using hammers.

Do not drive nails with a bodyhammer. Do not strike one hammer with another hammer. Never use a hammer by striking with the side or cheek of a hammer. Do not use a body pick hammer as a punch. Cold chisels, punches, and rivets should not be struck with a bodyhammer. Use the proper ball peen or light sledgehammer when applicable. They are made for their specific applications and are designed dressed and heat treated to perform their tasks safely.

Keep tools in proper working condition. Discard any striking or struck tools if the face and its edges show excessive wear, dents, chips, mushrooming, or improper redressing. Mushroomed heads can chip and cause injury. Never use a hammer with a loose or damaged handle. Keep hammer heads tightened on handle. If only the handle is damaged, replace it with a new high-grade hickory handle.

Never redress hammers without proper redressing instructions. The tool must be returned to its original shape. Redressing and reshaping of tools having chipped, battered, or mushroomed heads is **not** recommended.

Tool manufacturers cannot be held responsible for injury or damage caused by tools improperly used or from tools which have been abused or badly worn.

3.5 REVIEW QUESTIONS

1. When should the handle on a hand tool be replaced?
   a. when it is cracked
   b. when it is chipped
   c. when it cannot be refitted securely
   d. all of the above

2. A striking tool should be discarded when it is _____ .
   a. improperly redressed
   b. mushrooming
   c. chipped
   d. all of the above

3. Technician A says that a 1/2-inch drive socket set is required to disassemble and remove interior trim components. Technician B says that a 1/4-inch drive set is a necessity for this task. Who is correct?
   a. Technician A
   b. Technician B
   c. Both A and B
   d. Neither A nor B

4. Technician A says that a wire brush scratches bare metal and thus should be used sparingly on it. Technician B uses a wire brush on bare metal frequently. Who is correct?
   a. Technician A
   b. Technician B
   c. Both A and B
   d. Neither A nor B

5. Which of the following wrenches provides the safest grip on a fastener?
   a. open-end wrench
   b. box-end wrench
   c. adjustable wrench
   d. none of the above

6. Technician A sometimes uses a screwdriver as a chisel. Technician B sometimes uses a screwdriver as a pry bar. Who is correct?
   a. Technician A
   b. Technician B
   c. Both A and B
   d. Neither A nor B

7. Technician A says that a tap cuts external threads. Technician B says that a die cuts internal threads. Who is correct?
   a. Technician A
   b. Technician B
   c. Both A and B
   d. Neither A nor B

8. Which of the following wrenches are used with a ratchet handle?
   a. combination
   b. Allen
   c. socket
   d. box

9. Which of the following screwdriver tips provides the most resistance to slipping out of a fastener?
   a. standard
   b. Torx
   c. Phillips
   d. slotted

10. Which of the following pliers is often used in electrical work?
    a. adjustable pliers
    b. needle nose pliers
    c. retaining ring pliers
    d. snap ring pliers

11. Which of following hammers would be best used for driving gears or shafts?
    a. brass
    b. ball peen
    c. plastic

12. An extractor is used for removing broken _____ .
    a. seals
    b. bushings
    c. pistons
    d. bolts

CHAPTER
4

Body Shop Power Tools

The body shop technician and painter have a wide range of power tools available to make their tasks easier. These tools can be powered by air (pneumatic), electricity, or hydraulic fluid. Most of the tools mentioned in this chapter are general purpose tools; specific use tools are described in their appropriate chapters.

Although electric drills, wrenches, grinders, polishers, drill presses, and heat guns are found in body and refinishing shops, the use of pneumatic (air) tools is a great deal more common. Pneumatic tools have four major advantages over electrically powered equipment in the auto repair shop:

- **Flexibility.** Air tools run cooler and have the advantage of variable speed and torque; damage from overload or stalling is eliminated. They can fit in tight spaces.
- **Lightweight.** The air tool is lighter in weight and lends itself to higher rate of production with less fatigue.
- **Safety.** Air equipment reduces the danger of fire hazard in some environments where the sparking of electric power tools can be a problem.
- **Low cost operation and maintenance.** Due to fewer parts, air tools require fewer repairs and less preventive maintenance. Also, the original cost of air driven tools is usually less than the equivalent electric type.

Actually, the most common causes for any pneumatic or air tool to malfunction are:

- Lack of proper lubrication
- Excessive air pressure or lack of it
- Excessive moisture or dirt in the air lines

Installation of an air transformer and lubricator (Figure 4-1) will greatly reduce the causes for an air tool malfunction. With these units installed, it is possible to assure clean air, proper lubrication of internal wear parts, and control of air pressure to suit different tool applications.

There are pneumatic equivalents for nearly every electrically powered tool, from sanders to drills, grinders, impact wrenches, and screwdrivers. Furthermore, there are some pneumatic tools with no electrical equivalent, in particular: the needle scaler, rotary impact sealer, chisel, ratchet wrench, grease gun, and various auto tools (Figure 4-2).

Hoists, lifts, and frame and panel straighteners can be used in conjunction with a compressed air system. However, in most cases, these pieces of equipment are hydraulically operated. As described later in this chapter, hydraulic tools play a very important role in any body shop operation.

4.1 AIR-POWERED TOOLS

The automotive industry was one of the first industries to see the advantages of air-powered tools. Today they are known as "the tools of the professional auto body/painter technician."

PAINT SPRAY GUNS

The spray gun is probably the most used air-powered tool in the body/paint shop. It is used to do the majority of the refinishing work. Spray guns are also one of the most efficient of all pneumatic tools.

A conventional atomizing air spray gun (Figure 4-3) is a precision tool using compressed air to atomize sprayable material. Replacing the conventional system in many body shops is the high volume, low pressure (HVLP) gun (Figure 4-4). Air and

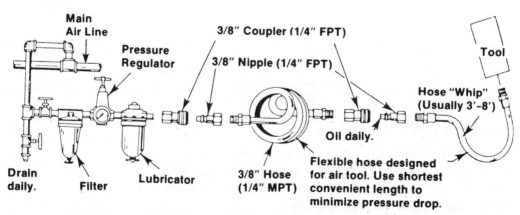

FIGURE 4-1 Typical auto shop air system arrangement for tools

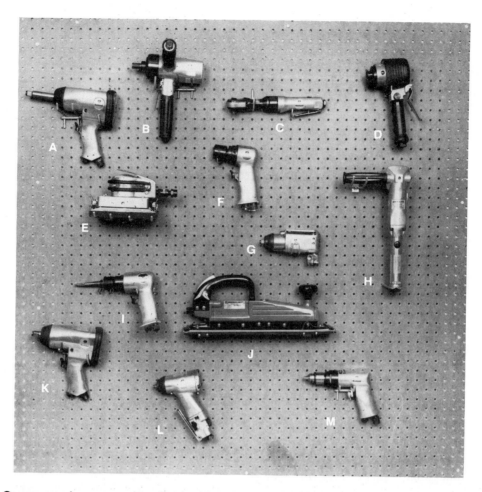

FIGURE 4-2   Common air-powered tools used in a body shop are: (A) 1/2-inch impact wrench with 2-inch extended anvil; (B) vertical air polisher (buffer); (C) 3/8-inch ratchet wrench; (D) orbital sander; (E) finishing sander; (F) disc sander; (G) 3/8-inch palm grip impact wrench; (H) angle polisher; (I) air chisel; (J) straight-line sander; (K) 1/2-inch impact wrench; (L) 3/8-inch angle head impact wrench; (M) 3/8-inch drill

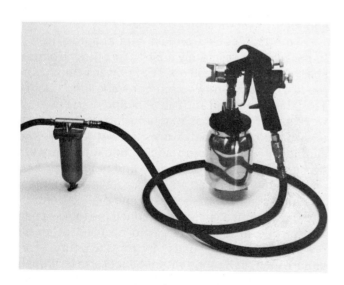

FIGURE 4-3   Conventional atomizing paint spray gun air system arrangement

paint enter both types of guns through separate passages and are mixed and ejected at the air nozzle to provide a controlled spray pattern.

Pulling back slightly on the trigger opens the air valve to allow use of the gun as a blow gun. In this position the trigger does not actuate the fluid needle and no fluid flows. As the trigger is further retracted, it unseats the needle in the fluid nozzle and the gun begins to spray. The amount of paint leaving the gun is controlled by the pressure on the container, the viscosity of the paint, the size of the fluid orifice, and the fluid needle adjustment. In industrial finishing where pressure tanks or pumps are used, the fluid needle adjustment should normally be fully opened. In suction cup operation, the needle valve controls the flow of paint.

Complete details on the operation of the various types of spray guns and their use can be found in Chapter 17.

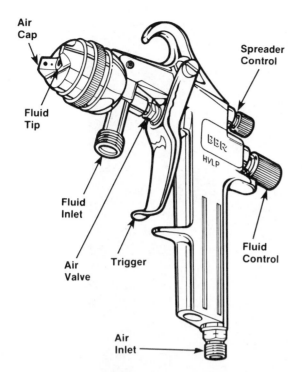

FIGURE 4-4 Components of an HVLP gun. *(Courtesy of Binks Mfg. Co.)*

FIGURE 4-5 The impact socket (left) is tougher than the normal socket (right). The impact type has thicker walls and a stronger six-point design.

Air-Powered Wrenches

Any job that involves threaded fasteners can be done faster and easier with air-powered wrenches. There are two basic types of wrenches: the impact and the ratchet.

WARNING: The use of any air driven power tools described in this chapter requires the wearing of safety glasses or face shield. For hazardous operations, wear both. Never wear loose clothing that might get caught in a tool.

Impact Wrenches

The impact wrench is a portable hand-held reversible wrench. When triggered, the output shaft, onto which the impact socket is fastened, spins freely at anywhere from 2000 to 14,000 rpm, depending on the wrench's make and model. When the impact wrench meets resistance, a small spring-loaded hammer, which is situated near the business end of the tool, strikes an anvil attached to the drive shaft onto which the socket is mounted. Thus each impact moves the socket around a little until torque equilibrium is reached, the fastener breaks, or the trigger is released.

When using an air impact wrench, it is important that only impact sockets and adapters be used with impact wrenches (Figure 4-5). Other types of sockets and adapters, if used, might shatter and fly off, endangering the safety of the operator and others in the immediate vicinity. Therefore, before using any air-powered tool of this type, make certain that sockets and adapters are clearly marked or labeled "For Use With Impact Wrenches," or just with the word "Impact." Impact sockets are sold in both SAE and metric system sizes.

To attach socket chucks and adapters to air-impact wrenches, merely push them onto the output shaft as far as they will go. True power wrench output shafts come in two common variations (Figure 4-6): the detent ball and the retaining ring. For most work, either method of attaching sockets and adapters to the output shaft works fine. Always use the simplest possible tool-to-socket hookup. Every extra connection absorbs energy and reduces power.

An adjustable air regulator is part of most pneumatic impact wrenches (Figure 4-7). Controlling the amount of air lets one adjust the tool's speed and torque. It also allows it to be used at an air pressure above the usual 90 to 125 pounds per square inch (psi) range without excessive tool wear. Usually numbered, air regulators are not so accurate that they can be trusted for final torquing of fasteners. When important, final torque should be done by hand with a torque wrench. Of course, the air tank has a regulator, too.

Air impact wrenches work equally well for tightening and loosening. Direction of the rotation is usually controlled by a switch or two-way trigger (Figure 4-8). Remember, do not change the direction of rotation while the trigger switch is ON.

To remove fasteners, set the switch for left-hand rotation. Place the socket over the nut or fastener head. Exert forward pressure on the wrench while depressing the trigger switch. As soon as the nut or fastener becomes loosened, relax the forward pressure on the wrench to let it spin the nut or fastener free.

To install fasteners, set the switch for right-hand rotation. By hand, start the nut on the stud or the bolt on the threads; this helps to avoid crossthreading,

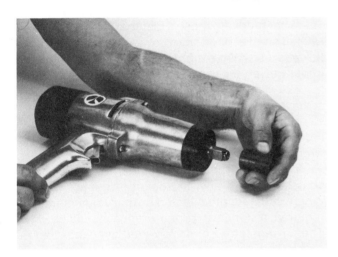

FIGURE 4-6   Two types of output shafts: (top left) detent ball and (top right) retaining or hog ring. (Bottom) Installing a retaining type or an impact wrench.

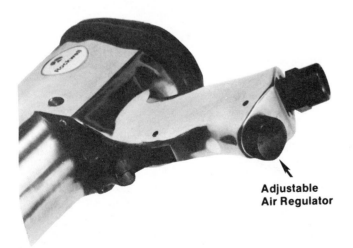

FIGURE 4-7   The adjustable air regulator on a typical impact wrench.

Adjustable
Air Regulator

A

B

FIGURE 4-8   Impact wrenches can be triggered by (A) trigger switch or (B) butterfly throttle switch. The butterfly switch acts as a forward and reverse lever for this palm grip air impact wrench, permitting either a forward right-hand rotation or a reverse left-hand rotation.

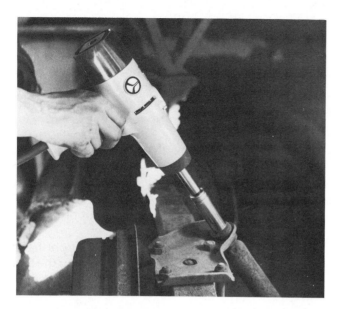

FIGURE 4-9 Loosening a nut using an extension socket on an impact wrench

which would ruin the fastener. Place the socket over the nut or fastener head. Depress the trigger switch to drive the nut or fastener until it rests on the material being fastened, and then exert forward pressure on the wrench to bring the hammer into action to snug the nut or fastener firmly (Figure 4-9). Deep flex sockets permit out-of-line fasteners to be reached without time consuming socket and extension changes. When loose, the bolt drops into the socket.

CAUTION: Remember that when using an impact wrench on wheels, be careful not to warp rotor plates. The final torque is best done by hand.

 SHOP TALK _____

When using an impact wrench, keep the following pointers in mind:
- *Always make sure the impact wrench socket is properly retained. To prevent injury, use an impact type socket. If the impact wrench has a pin retainer, do not substitute a bent nail or piece of wire.*
- *If an air wrench fails to loosen a bolt in 3 to 5 seconds, use the next larger wrench. Soak large rusted nuts with penetrating oil before using the wrench.*
- *Check the clutch lubricant regularly. Typically, a 1/2-inch air wrench should*

have a 1/2 ounce of lubricant in its clutch mechanism. Check parts list for amount and type of lubricant needed, and add only the amount and type specified.

Air Ratchet Wrenches

This air ratchet wrench, like the hand ratchet, has a special ability to work in hard-to-reach places. Its angle drive reaches in and loosens or tightens where other hand or power wrenches just cannot work (Figure 4-10). The air socket wrench looks like an ordinary ratchet, but has a fat handgrip that contains the air vane motor and drive mechanism (Figure 4-11).

After breaking loose a fastener by pulling the air ratchet handle, power can be used easily to move the threads out. When tightening, run in the threads under power, then make it secure by hand-pulling.

For all their torquing power, air impact wrenches have practically no recoil. Holding one is rather easy, but can be misleading. The stream of air blowing through the socket is very strong. Therefore, the wrench should be held tightly.

Remember that there is no consistently reliable adjustment with any air socket or impact wrench. Where accurate preselected torque adjustments are required, a standard torque wrench should be used. The air regulator on air-powered wrenches can be

FIGURE 4-10 Loosening a nut using an air ratchet wrench

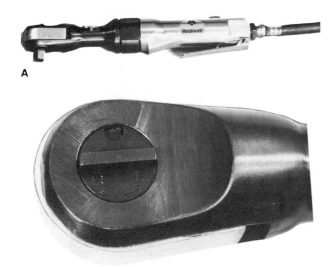

A

B

FIGURE 4-12   (Left) 3/8-inch air drill and (right) 3/8-inch electric drill. The air drill weighs 2-1/2 pounds, while the electric type weighs 4-1/2 pounds.

FIGURE 4-11   (A) Typical air ratchet wrench and (B) the forward and reversing lever is used to change the rotation of the tool. When the lever is set in the forward position, the tool will turn in a right-hand rotation to fasten nuts and bolts. When the lever is moved to the reverse position, the tool will run in reverse or left-hand rotation to nuts and bolts.

employed to adjust torque to the approximate tightness of a known fastener; a 75 foot-pound torque handles most automobile jobs.

 SHOP TALK ─────

Actual torque on a fastener is directly related to joint hardness, tool speed, condition of socket, and the time the tool is allowed to impact.

Air Drills

Air drills are usually available in 1/4-, 3/8-, and 1/2-inch sizes and operate in much the same manner as an electric drill. But, as can be seen in Figure 4-12, they are smaller and lighter. This compactness makes them a great deal easier to use for drilling operations in auto work (Figure 4-13).

To drill with an air tool into any material, the following general procedures should be kept in mind:

 1. Accurately locate the position of the hole to be drilled. Mark the position distinctly with a center punch or an awl to provide a

FIGURE 4-13   Air drill at work

seat for the drill point and to keep it from "walking" away from the mark when applying pressure.
2. Always know what is on the other side. Do not drill a wiring harness or through a trim panel.
3. Unless the workpiece is stationary or large, fasten it in a vise or clamp. Holding a small item in the hand might cause injury if it is suddenly seized by the bit and whirled out of grip. This is most likely to happen just before the bit breaks through the hole at the underside of the work.
4. Carefully center the drill bit in the jaws, while securely tightening the chuck. Avoid

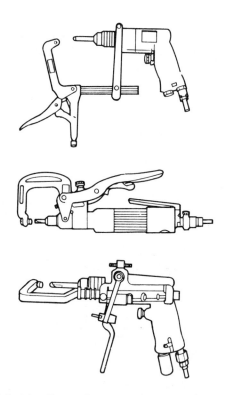

FIGURE 4-14   Several types of spot weld remover air drills

inserting the bit off-center because it will wobble and probably break when it spins. After centering, place the drill bit tip on the exact point to drill the hole, then start the motor by pulling the trigger switch. (Never apply a spinning drill bit to the work.)

5. Except when it is desirable to drill a hole at an angle, hold the drill perpendicular to the face of the work.

6. Align the drill bit and the axis of the drill in the direction the hole is to go and apply pressure only along this line with no sidewise or bending pressure. Changing the direction of this pressure will distort the dimensions of the hole, and it could snap a small drill. To avoid stressing the drill bit, try to extend the index finger along the side of the drill housing with the middle finger on the side.

7. Use just enough steady and even pressure to keep the drill cutting. Guide the drill—do not force it. Too much pressure can cause the bit to break or the tool to overheat. Too little pressure will keep the bit from cutting and dull its edges due to the excessive friction created by sliding over the surface.

8. When drilling deep holes, especially with a twist drill, withdraw the drill several times to clear the cuttings. Keep the tool running when pulling the bit back out of a drilled hole. This will help prevent jamming.

9. Reduce the pressure on the drill just before the bit cuts through the work.

There are special spot remover air drills and/or attachments that are used for cutting out spot welds (Figure 4-14). When cutting out spot welds, the drill can be fastened to the weld area with a clamp attachment that makes the operation easier (Figure 4-15). The cutter will not deviate from the weld center during cutting.

There are two types of spot cutter available that can be mounted in an air drill for cutting out spot welds:

- **Drill type (Figure 4-16A).** This type does not damage the bottom panel, nor does it leave a nib in the bottom panel, so finishing is easy.
- **Hole saw type (Figure 4-16B).** The cutting depth of this type can be adjusted so that the bottom panel is not damaged. It will be necessary to sand off the remaining portion of the weld.

When performing any air drill operation, keep the following maintenance and safety pointers in mind:

- Clean chuck jaws occasionally to prolong concentricity. Use sharp drills; they require far less effort and put less strain on the tool.

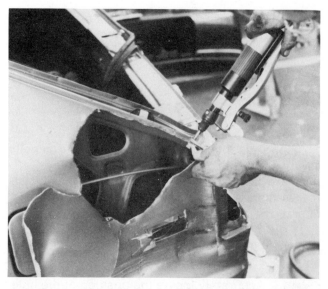

FIGURE 4-15   Spot weld remover air drill at work. (Courtesy of N.C.G. Co.)

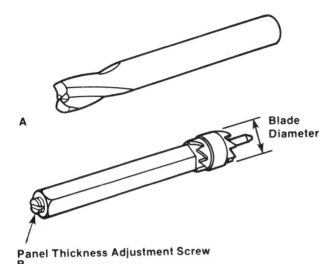

A

Blade Diameter

Panel Thickness Adjustment Screw
B

FIGURE 4-16 Spot cutters: (A) drill type and (B) hole saw type

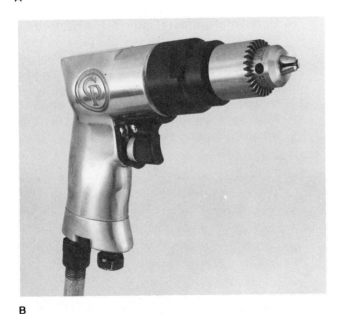

A

B

FIGURE 4-17 Air screwdriver handle types: (A) straight and (B) pistol grip. *(Courtesy of Florida Pneumatic Mfg. Corp.)*

- To avoid the danger of breakage from high break-through torque, use properly sharpened twist drills and reamers, and select proper drill speed.
- Start drilling at low speed and gradually increase it. Avoid kickback by easing up at break through.

AIR SCREWDRIVERS

Unlike electric screwdrivers, the air style runs cool and will not burn out, even under constant use. They are designed to perform well in a wide variety of applications: machine screws in tapped holes, self-tapping screws in plastic, sheet metal screws, self-drilling screws in metal sandwiches, fine-threaded screws in delicate assemblies, thread forming screws in blend die-cast holes, and many more similar shop jobs. Pneumatic screwdrivers are available with straight- or pistol-grip handles (Figure 4-17).

AIR SANDERS

In general, air sanders are used in the paint shop. There are two basic types of air sanders: disc and orbital (finishing). Most rough sanding done in automotive work is done with a disc sander (Figure 4-18) or its counterpart, the dual-action (DA) orbital sander (Figure 4-19). The orbital sander oscillates while it is rotating thus creating a buffing pattern rather than the swirls and scratches often caused by the disc sander.

The finishing orbital sanders, also called "pad" or "jitterbug" sanders (Figure 4-20), are designed for fine finish sanding. It is possible to use a wider variety of abrasives with finish sanders than with any other type of power sanding, but for the most part,

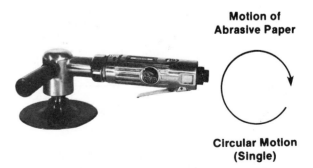

Motion of Abrasive Paper

Circular Motion (Single)

FIGURE 4-18 Disc sander and its motion. *(Courtesy of Florida Pneumatic Mfg. Corp.)*

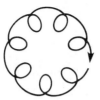

FIGURE 4-19   Dual or double action sander and its motion. *(Courtesy of Chicago Pneumatic Tool Division)*

FIGURE 4-20   Pad or jitterburg sander and its motion. *(Courtesy of Chicago Pneumatic Tool Division)*

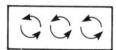

A

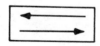

B

FIGURE 4-21   Two types of board sander: (A) orbital and its motion and (B) straight line and its motion. *(Photo A courtesy of Florida Pneumatic Mfg. Corp.; photo B courtesy of Chicago Pneumatic Tool Division)*

the best work is done with comparatively fine grit abrasive paper. Finish sanders are also especially designed for hard-to-reach places and tight corners.

Another sander found in auto body shops is the long board type sander (Figure 4-21). It operates in either an orbital or straight line motion that will cover about 40 square inches of working area per minute.

Details on operating sanders can be found in Chapter 18.

AIR GRINDERS

The most commonly used portable grinder in body and paint shops is the disc type grinder (Figure 4-22). It is operated in the same manner as the disc sander.

> **CAUTION:** Avoid grinding too close to the trim, bumper, or any other projection that might snag or catch the edge of the disc (Figure 4-23). Also do not stop a disc grinder while in contact with the work surface. Start any grinding operation just before the machine makes contact with the work surface.

There are, of course, several other grinders used in the body shop. The more common ones include

- **Horizontal grinder (Figure 4-24A)** is used for heavy-duty grinding.
- **Vertical grinder (Figure 4-24B)** is a larger version of the disc grinder. With a sanding pad, this grinder can be converted into a disc sander. Most vertical grinders can be used with both straight wheels as well as cup wheels (Figure 4-24C).

FIGURE 4-22   **Disc type grinder at work**

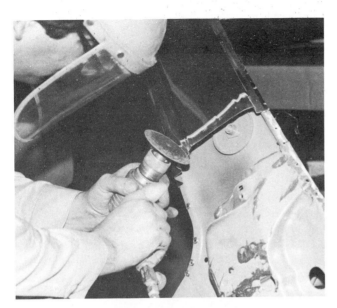

FIGURE 4-23 Take care not to catch projections.
(Courtesy of Marson Corp.)

- **Angle grinder (Figure 4-24D)** is used primarily for smoothing, deburring, and blending welds.
- **Small wheel grinder (Figure 4-24E)** can be used with cone wheels, wire brushes, or collet chucks and burrs in addition to a straight grind.
- **Die grinder (Figure 4-24F)** is used with mounted points and carbide burrs for a vari-

ety of applications such as weld cleaning, deburring, blending, and smoothing. Available in both straight and angle head designs.
- **Cut-off grinder (Figure 4-24G)** cuts through muffler clamps and hangers with ease. It also slices through sheet metal and radiator hose clamps.

POLISHER/BUFFERS

Polisher/buffers (Figure 4-25) are used in compounding, rubbing, and final polishing. Their uses are fully described in Chapter 18.

One of the most important considerations when operating a polisher/buffer is the selection of the proper buffing pad. Here are some points to consider when making a selection:

- Match the pad to the needs of the job. Low pile heights (1 to 1-1/4 inches) work best for the early stages of cutting and compounding. High pile heights (1-1/2 to 2 inches) are better for light compounding and critical jobs, such as touchups and blending (Figure 4-26) where raised body lines demand cushioning. For final finishing and waxing, use a clean lamb's wool bonnet or a final finish disc with long even pile. These will run the coolest and offer the most polishing action. For further protection, consider using pads with rounded-up edges.

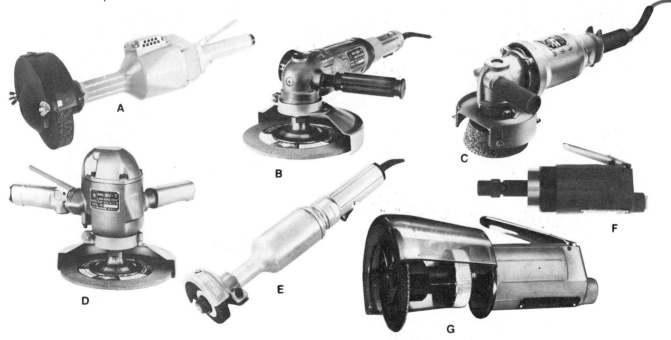

FIGURE 4-24 Various types of grinders found in a body shop: (A) horizontal grinder; (B) vertical grinder; (C) vertical grinder with cup wheel; (D) angle grinder; (E) small wheel grinder; (F) die grinder; and (G) cut-off grinder.

A

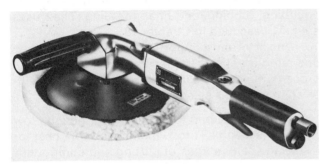

B

FIGURE 4-25 Two types of polisher/buffers: (A) angle and (B) vertical. (Photo A courtesy of Florida Pneumatic Mfg. Corp.; photo B courtesy of Chicago Pneumatic Tool Division)

FIGURE 4-26 Typical polishing/buffing pads

- Let the pad do the work. Using the design of a pad to its best advantage means changing pads at the various stages of the job.
- Be sure that the pad does not load up too fast, does not burn (a rounded-up edge helps prevent edge burns), and is constructed tightly enough to prevent wool flyout.
- Remember that 100 percent wool pads are best for automotive finishes. Wool runs cooler, cushions more, and lasts longer than syn-

A

B

FIGURE 4-27 Two types of sandblasters: (A) standard pressure and (B) captive

thetics, because wool breathes, and its fibers retain their natural spring longer.

- It is poor practice to intermix the use of a buffer with a grinder. Employ a buffer for buffing only or surface scratches can result.

SANDBLASTERS

Another pneumatic tool that is fully described in Chapter 18 is the sandblaster. Sandblasting is the most effective way to remove all finishes from any vehicle. Care must be taken, however not to damage the underlying substrates. The use of plastic media has replaced sand in many body shops. The process is very similar in principle to sandblasting, but, instead of using hard silica sand, much softer reusable plastic particles are used at low blasting pressures of 20 to 40 psi. (Sandblasting operations are usually done at 60 to 100 psi.) At the lower pressures, the plastic media removes paint coatings without damaging the underlying substrates, including thin aluminum, fiberglass, and even plastics.

As shown in Figure 4-27, there are two basic types of sandblasters:

- Standard sandblaster
- "Captive" sandblaster

The standard sandblaster is usually operated outdoors, while the captive units can be used indoors. The indoor sandblasters have a nozzle assembly that confines the blasting action, while a vacuum in the machine sucks the abrasive and debris. Plastic can be used in both types of blasters.

AIR CHISELS OR HAMMERS

Of all auto air tools, the air chisel or hammer (Figure 4-28) is one of the most useful, especially as a spot weld remover. Used with the accessories illustrated in Figure 4-29, this tool will perform the following operations:

- **Universal joint and tie rod tool.** It helps to shake loose stubborn universal joints and tie rod ends.
- **Smoothing hammer.** A good accessory for reworking metal.
- **Ball joint separator.** The wedge action breaks apart frozen ball joints.
- **Panel crimper.** It forms a "step" in a panel where a damaged section has been removed. The "filler" panel will then fit flush, resulting in a strong, professional joint.
- **Shock absorber chisel.** Quick work of the roughest jobs is made without the usual

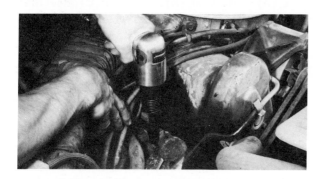

FIGURE 4-28 Typical air chisel at work

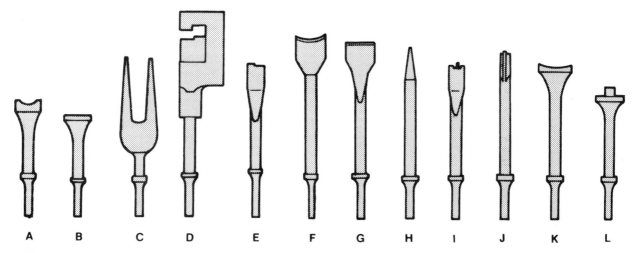

FIGURE 4-29 Typical air chisel accessories: (A) universal joint and tie rod tool; (B) smoothing hammer; (C) ball joint separator; (D) panel crimper; (E) shock absorber chisel; (F) tail pipe cutter; (G) scraper; (H) tapered punch; (I) edging tool; (J) rubber bushing splitter; (K) bushing remover; and (L) bushing installer

bruised knuckles and lost time. It easily cracks frozen shock absorber nuts.

- **Tail pipe cutter.** The cutter slices through mufflers and tail pipes.
- **Scraper.** Removing undercoating in addition to other coverings is this accessory's function.
- **Tapered punch.** Driving frozen bolts, installing pins, and punching or aligning holes are some of many uses for this accessory.
- **Edging tool (claw ripper).** It is utilized to slice through sheet metal leaving a smooth edge.
- **Rubber bushing splitter.** Old bushings can be opened up for easy removal.
- **Bushing remover.** This accessory is designed to remove all types of bushings. The blunt edge pushes but does not cut.
- **Bushing installer.** The installer drives all types of bushings to the correct depth. A pilot prevents the tool from sliding.

In addition to special chisels, there are the so-called "standard" types that can be used for cutting rivets, nuts (Figure 4-30), and bolts, plus removing weld splatter and breaking spot welds.

 **SHOP TALK** _____

When using an air chisel or hammer, keep the following pointers in mind:

- *Always use a chisel retainer when operating an air hammer.*
- *Position tool by starting slowly, then increasing power. Avoid running into hardware, frames, and so forth with sheet metal cutting tools.*
- *Check chisel shanks periodically for peening, and grind a new chamfer when required.*
- *Do not let the chisels ride out of the air hammer.*
- *Keep cutters sharp.*

OTHER PNEUMATIC BODY SHOP TOOLS

There are several other air tools that can be found in some auto body repair shops. They include:

- **Needle scalers (Figure 4-31A).** Used for derusting and cleaning of metals as well as for peening welded joints.
- **Metal shears (Figure 4-31B).** Cuts, trims, outlines, and shears plastic, tin, aluminum, and other metals up to 18-gauge rolled steel.

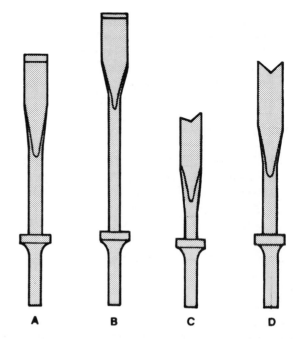

FIGURE 4-30 Standard types of air chisel accessories: (A) rivet cutter; (B) flat chisel; (C) sheet metal cutter; and, (D) spot weld breaker

- **Air nibbler (Figure 4-31C).** Sheet metal—up to 16-gauge—can be cut in any configuration and also cuts holes as small as 1 inch in diameter.
- **Panel saw (Figure 4-31D).** Cuts mild steel (up to 16-gauge), plastic up to 3/8-inch, and aluminum up to 1/4-inch.
- **Power riveter (Figure 4-31E).** Sets rivets up 3/16-inch steel or closed end rivets. It provides an effective, high-strength fastening technique.
- **Air hacksaw (Figure 4-31F).** Has many metal cutting functions in any metal shop.
- **Reciprocating saw/file (Figure 4-31G).** Dual action tool that trims or shapes sheet metal and plastic.
- **Air blow gun (Figure 4-31H).** Possibly the smallest air tool in the shop, it is one of the most worthwhile. It blows away dust and dirt from any small hard-to-reach place.

There are some specialized air-powered auto mechanic tools that are found in commercial garages. These tools—their names usually imply their use—include a radiator tester, cylinder hoist, air filter cleaner, body polisher, brake tester, transmission flusher, engine cleaner, and spark plug cleaner. They are, however, seldom found in a typical auto body and refinishing shop.

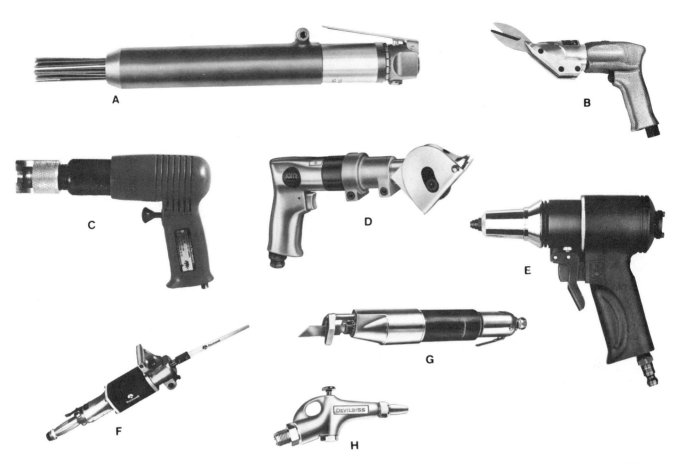

FIGURE 4-31 Other popular air tools found in auto body shops: (A) needle scalers; (B) metal shears; (C) air chisel; (D) panel saw; (E) power riveter; (F) air hacksaw; (G) reciprocating saw/file; and (H) air blow gun

PNEUMATIC TOOL MAINTENANCE

Air tools require little maintenance but could easily cause big problems if that little maintenance is not performed. For instance, moisture gathers in the air lines and is blown into the tools during use. If a tool is left with water in it, rust will form and the tool will experience reduced efficiency and will wear out much more quickly.

To prevent this from happening, remember that most air tool motors need daily (or as often as used) lubrication with a good grade of air motor oil. If the air line has no line oiler or lubricator, run a teaspoon of oil through the tool. The oil can be squirted into the tool air inlet (Figure 4-32) or into the hose at the nearest connection to the air supply; then run the tool. Most air tool manufacturers recommend the use of their special oil for lubricating tools; however, when this is not available standard automatic transmission fluid may be substituted.

All tools have recommended air pressure (Table 4-1). If the tool is overworked, it will wear out sooner. If something goes wrong with the tool, fix it. If not, a

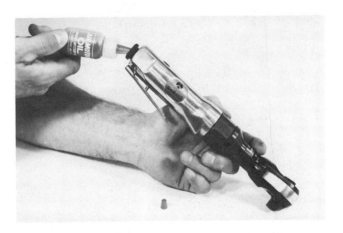

FIGURE 4-32 Hand oiling of an air-powered tool

chain reaction might occur and the other parts will require maintenance also. For example, if the gearing must be replaced and the tool is used anyway, the rotor and end plate might soon wear out as a result. A tool with worn parts will also use more air pressure. The air compressor, in turn, will then be-

TABLE 4-1: AIR CONSUMPTION CHART†

Tool	Scfm*	Psi*	Tool	Scfm*	Psi*
Air brush	1	10–50	Needle scaler	3–4	70–90
Air chisel	4	70–90	Nibbler	8	70–90
Air filter cleaner	3	70–90	Nutsetter	6–7.5	70–90
Air hammer	6–10	70–90	Paint sprayer	0.7–5	10–70
Blow gun	1–2.5	40–90	Panel saw	4–8	70–90
Brake tester	3.5	70–90	Pneumatic garage door	2	90–150
Burring tool	5	70–90	Polisher	2	70–90
Car washer	8.5	40–90	Ratchet wrench	4	70–90
Cut-off grinder	4–8	80–90	Riveter	4.5–5.5	70–90
Drill 3/8 inch	4–6	70–90	Sandblast gun	2.2–4	30–90
Engine cleaner	4–6	70–90	Sandblast gun/hopper	2–6	40–90
Grease gun	3–4	90–150	Sander, disc	4–6	60–80
Grinders, die	4–6	70–90	Sander, double action	6–8	60–80
Grinders, vertical	6–12	70–90	Sander, finish	6–8	60–80
Hacksaw	6–8	70–90	Sander, straight line	6–8	70–90
Hoist (1 ton)	1	70–90	Screwdriver	2–6	70–90
Hydraulic lift	5–7	90–150	Shears	5–8	70–90
Impact wrench 1/4 inch	1.4	70–90	Spark plug cleaner	5	70–90
Impact wrench 3/8 inch	3	70–90	Tire changer	1	90–150
Impact wrench 1/2 inch	4	70–90	Tire chuck	1.5	10–50
Material tank	1.8	10–50			

* SCFM: Standard cubic feet per minute
  PSI: Pounds per square inch
†Always check with the tool manufacturers for the actual air consumption of the tools being used. These figures are based on averages and should not be considered accurate for any particular make of tool.

FIGURE 4-33 Electric-powered impact wrench. (Courtesy of Black & Decker, Inc.)

come overworked and put out air that is not as clean or dry and is shot right back into the tools. Air tool troubleshooting procedures are given in Table 4-2.

Full information on pneumatic air system operation is given in Chapter 5.

4.2 ELECTRIC-POWERED TOOLS

As mentioned earlier in this chapter, shop tools such as sanders, polishers, impact tools (Figure 4-33), and drills can also be powered by electric motors. But, for most auto repair shops, the most important electric only tools are drill presses, bench grinders, vacuum cleaners, heat guns, and plastic welders. The two most popular automotive metal welding systems—MIG and spot—are electrically operated (Figure 4-34). Complete data on metal welders is given in Chapter 6 while plastic welders (Figure 4-35) are described in Chapter 13. For metal cutting operations the electric-powered plasma arc cutting is the one most recommended (Figure 4-36).

Other than these specialized electrically driven power tools, electric drills, polishes, sanders, and so on perform the same shop tasks as their pneumatic counterparts.

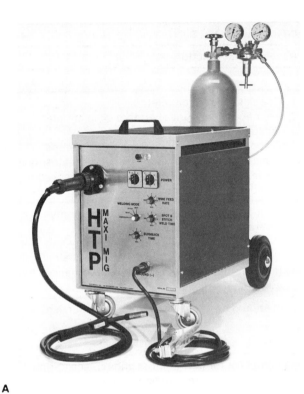

A

FIGURE 4-36   Typical plasma metal cutter. *(Courtesy of Century Mfg. Co.)*

B

FIGURE 4-34   (A) MIG welder and (B) squeeze type resistance spot welder

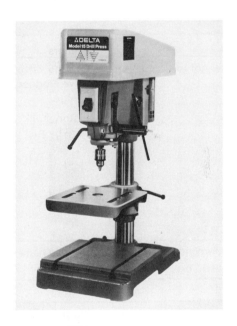

FIGURE 4-37   Typical bench type drill press. *(Courtesy of Delta International Machinery Corp.)*

DRILL PRESS

Some large auto repair shops use a permanently mounted drill press (Figure 4-37). It can be floor mounted or bench mounted. All drill work is performed on a table attached to the stand. The worktable can be adjusted up or down. The drill speed is variable for various materials and thicknesses.

FIGURE 4-35   Typical hot-air plastic welder. *(Courtesy of Brian R. White Co., Inc.)*

TABLE 4-2: TROUBLESHOOTING AIR TOOLS

Problem	Probable Cause	Recommended Action
Air Drills		
Tool will not run or runs slowly, air flows slightly from exhaust, spindle turns freely.	Motor or throttle plugged with dirt	1. Check for dirt in air inlet. 2. Pour liberal amount of air tool oil in air inlet. 3. Operate trigger in short bursts. 4. Disconnect air supply, then turn empty and closed drill chuck by hand. Reconnect air supply. 5. If still not functional, tool should be checked by authorized service center.
Tool will not run, air flows freely from exhaust, spindle turns freely.	Rotor vanes stuck with dirt or varnish	1. Pour liberal amount of air tool oil in air inlet. 2. Operate trigger in short bursts. 3. Disconnect air supply, then turn empty and closed drill chuck by hand. Reconnect air supply. 4. If still not functional, tool should be checked by authorized service center.
Tool locked up, spindle will not turn.	Broken motor vane Gears broken or jammed by foreign object	Tool should be checked by authorized service center.
Tool will not shut off.	Throttle valve O-ring blown off seat	See parts list for part number and replace O-ring or send to authorized service center.
Air Hammers		
Tool will not run.	Cycling valve or throttle valve clogged with dirt or sludge Piston stuck in cylinder bore by rust or dirt	1. Pour liberal amount of air tool oil in air inlet (check for dirt). 2. Operate trigger in short bursts (chisel in place and against solid surface). 3. If not free, first disconnect air supply, then tap nose or barrel lightly with plastic mallet, reconnect air supply, and repeat above steps. 4. If still not free, disconnect air supply, insert a 6-inch piece of 3/8-inch diameter rod in nozzle and lightly tap to loosen piston in rearward direction. Reconnect air supply, and repeat Steps 1 and 2.
Chisel stuck in nozzle.	End of shank peened over	Tool should be sent to authorized service center.
Air Ratchets		
Motor runs, spindle doesn't turn or turns erratically.	Worn teeth on ratchet or pawl Weak or broken pawl pressure spring Weak drag springs fail to hold spindle while pawl advance for "another bite"	Replacement parts should be installed by authorized service center.
Motor will not run, ratchet head indexes crisply by hand.	Dirt or sludge in motor parts	1. Pour a liberal amount of air tool oil into air inlet. 2. Operate throttle in short bursts. 3. With socket engaged on bolt, alternately tighten and loosen bolt by hand. 4. If motor remains jammed, tool should be checked by authorized service center.

TABLE 4-2: TROUBLESHOOTING AIR TOOLS (CONTINUED)

Problem	Probable Cause	Recommended Action
	Air Wrenches	
Tool runs slowly or not at all, air flows only slightly from exhaust.	Airflow blocked by accumulation of dirt Motor parts jammed with dirt particles Power regulator might have simply vibrated to closed position	1. Check air inlet strainer for blockage. 2. Pour liberal amount of air tool oil into air inlet. 3. Operate tool in short bursts—quickly reversing rotation back and forth. 4. Repeat as needed. 5. If this fails to improve performance, tool should be serviced at authorized service center.
Tool will not run, exhaust air flows freely.	One or more motor vanes stuck due to sludge or varnish buildup Motor jammed due to rust	1. Pour a liberal amount of air tool oil into air inlet. 2. Operate tool in short bursts of forward and reverse rotation. 3. Tap motor housing lightly with plastic mallet. 4. Disconnect air supply, then attempt to free motor by rotating drive shank manually. (Some clutches will not engage sufficiently for this operation.) 5. If tool remains jammed, it should be serviced by an authorized service center.
Sockets will not stay on.	Worn socket retainer ring or soft back-up ring	1. Wear safety glasses. 2. Disconnect air supply. 3. Using external retaining ring pliers, expand old retaining ring and remove OR if retaining ring pliers not available, clamp tool "lightly" in soft jaw vise. 4. Holding square drive with appropriate open-end wrench, pry old retainer ring out of groove with small screwdriver. 5. Always pry off ring away from body; it can be propelled outward at high velocity. 6. Replace backup O-ring and retainer ring with correct new parts. (See parts lists that accompanied tool.) 7. Place retaining ring on table, press tool shank into ring in a rocking motion. Snap into groove by hand.
Premature shank wear.	Use of chrome sockets or excessively worn sockets	Discontinue use of chrome sockets. Remember that chrome sockets have a hard surface and relatively soft core. Drive hole will become rounded, but still be very hard. Besides the danger of splitting, they will wear out wrench shanks prematurely.
Tool gradually losing power but still runs at full free speed.	Clutch parts worn, perhaps due to lack of lubricant. Engaging cam of clutch worn or sticking due to lack of lubricant.	*Oil Lubed* 1. Check for presence of clutch oil (where oil is specified for clutch) and, removing oil fill plug, tilt to drain all oil from clutch case. Refill with 30 weight SAE oil or that recommended by manufacturer, but only the amount specified. 2. Check for excess clutch oil. Clutch cases need only be 50 percent full. Overfilling can cause drag on high-speed clutch parts. A typical 1/2-inch oil-lubed wrench only requires 1/2 ounce of clutch oil.

TABLE 4-2: TROUBLESHOOTING AIR TOOLS (CONTINUED)

Problem	Probable Cause	Recommended Action
Tool gradually losing power but still runs at full free speed (continued).	Clutch parts worn, perhaps due to lack of lubricant. Engaging cam of clutch worn or sticking due to lack of lubricant.	*Grease Lubed* Vibration and heat usually indicate insufficient grease in the clutch chamber. The average greasing interval is specified in parts list. Severe operating conditions might require more frequent lubrication. 1. Check for excess grease by rotating drive shank by hand. It should turn freely. Excess is usually expelled automatically. 2. If disassembly is required for greasing, it should be done carefully to maintain orientation of mating parts.
Tool will not shut off.	Throttle valve O-ring broken or out of position Throttle valve stem bent or jammed with dirt particles	1. Remove assembly and install new O-ring. 2. Lubricate with air tool oil and operate trigger briskly. If operation cannot be restored, tool should be checked by authorized service center.

Bench Grinder

This electric power tool (Figure 4-38) is generally bolted to one of the shop's workbenches. A bench grinder is classified by wheel size; 6- to 10-inch wheels are the most common in auto repair shops. Three types of wheels are available with this bench tool:

- **Grinding wheel.** For a wide variety of grinding jobs from sharpening cutting tools to deburring.
- **Wire wheel brush.** Used for general cleaning and buffing, removing rust and scale, paint removal, deburring, and so forth.
- **Buffing wheel.** For general purpose buffing, polishing, light cutting, and finish coloring operations.

When using a bench grinder (these safety rules also apply to portable air grinders), remember to:

- Always use a wheel with a rated speed equal to or greater than the grinder's.
- Always use a wheel guard.
- Inspect wheels for wear or cracks before using them. Use correct wheel for job and mount it properly.
- Always wear safety goggles or face shield and make sure the eye shields of the grinder operator are in position.
- Adjust the rest as needed whenever the gap between it and the grinding wheel exceeds 1/3 inch.

Vacuum Cleaner

A must in every body and refinishing shop is a vacuum cleaner (Figure 4-39). Actually, it should be one of the first tools used when a vehicle comes in for refinishing. That is, an incoming vehicle should be completely washed and vacuumed before it is prepared for refinishing. This will greatly reduce the chance of dirt getting into the complete job.

There are two basic types of shop vacuum cleaners: the dry pick-up type and wet/dry unit. The latter, in the 20- to 30-gallon capacity, is the one found in most shops. For interior vehicle cleaning the portable vacuum cleaner is popular (Figure 4-40).

Power washers can be used in exterior car preparation, engine cleaning, undercarriage cleaning, shop degreasing and cleaning, and snow and salt removal from vehicles. Figure 4-41 shows typical stationary and portable units. Before using a power washer check with OSHA regulations.

To keep dust out of the refinishing shop, some power orbital sanders—both electric and air pow-

FIGURE 4-38   Typical bench grinder. *(Courtesy of Snap-on Tools Corp.)*

FIGURE 4-39 Typical portable body shop vacuum cleaner

FIGURE 4-42 Sander equipped with dust collecting bag. *(Courtesy of Hutchins Mfg. Co.)*

ered—have a sanding dust pick-up arrangement. Figure 4-42 shows a straight line sander equipped with its own vacuum system and a catching bag while Figure 4-43 illustrates an adapter that connects to a central vacuum cleaner system.

HEAT GUN

Heat guns (Figure 4-44) have many uses in the auto body shop. They are used in almost all vinyl roof repairs as well as other plastic repairs. They can be used in some panel shrinking jobs as well as speeding up drying times. The overall use of heat guns can be found in several chapters of this book.

FIGURE 4-40 Vacuum cleaner suitable for the interior of a vehicle.

FIGURE 4-41 Typical electric power washer: (A) stationary and (B) portable. *(Courtesy of Graco, Inc.)*

FIGURE 4–43   Typical central vacuum system. *(Courtesy of Eurovac, Inc.)*

FIGURE 4–44   Typical heat gun. *(Courtesy of Black & Decker, Inc.)*

Electric Power Tool Safety

To protect the operator from electric shock, most power tools are built with an external grounding system. That is, there is a wire that runs from the motor housing, through the power cord, to a third prong on the power plug. When this third prong is connected to a grounded, three hole electrical outlet, the grounding wire will carry any current that leaks past the electrical insulation of the tool away from the operator and into the ground of the shop's wiring. In most modern electrical systems, the three prong plug fits into a three prong, grounded receptacle. If the tool is operated at less than 150 volts, it has a plug like that shown in Figure 4–45A. If it is for use on 150 or 250 volts, it has a plug like that shown in Figure 4–45B. In either type, the green (or green and yellow) conductor in the tool cord is the grounding wire. This grounding wire should be connected to the longer, rounded prong of the plug and never to the shorter flat prongs.

Some of the new electric power tools are self-insulated and do not require grounding. These tools have only two prongs since they have a nonconducting plastic housing. In shop operations, never use a three prong to two prong adapter plug.

Extension Cords

If an extension cord is used, it should be kept as short as possible. Very long or undersized cords will reduce operating voltage and thus reduce operating efficiency, possibly causing motor damage. Actually, an extension cord should be used only as a last resort. But, when an extension cord must be employed, the following wire gauge sizes are recommended for different lengths:

Length	115 Volts	230 Volts
Less than 25 feet	12	14
25 to 50 feet	10	12
50 to 100 feet	8	10

The smaller the gauge number, the heavier duty the cord. These are recommended minimum wire sizes.

Tools with three prong, grounded plugs must only be used with three wire grounded extension cords connected to properly grounded, three wire receptacles (Figure 4-46).

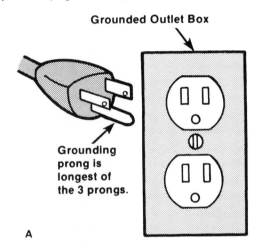

Grounded Outlet Box

Grounding prong is longest of the 3 prongs.

A

Grounded Outlet Box

Grounding prong is longest of the 3 prongs.

B

FIGURE 4-45 (A) Approved type of three prong grounding plug and outlet box for 115 volts AC; (B) approved type of three prong grounding plug and outlet box for 230 volts AC.

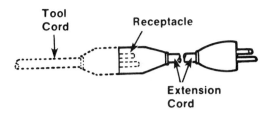

Tool Cord

Receptacle

Extension Cord

FIGURE 4-46 Typical three wire extension cord with an approved connector cap to ensure continuity of the tool's grounding wire

🚗 SHOP TALK ——————

Here are some safety tips to keep in mind when using extension cords:

• Always plug the cord of the tool into the extension cord before the extension cord is inserted into a convenience outlet. Always unplug the extension cord from the receptacle before the cord of the tool is unplugged from the extension cord.

• Extension cords should be long enough to make connections without being pulled taut, creating unnecessary strain and wear.

• Be sure that the extension cord does not come in contact with sharp objects. The cords should not be allowed to kink, nor should they be dipped in or splattered with oil, grease, hot surfaces, or chemicals.

• Before using a cord, inspect it for loose or exposed wires and damaged insulation. If a cord is damaged, it must be replaced. This advice also applies to the tool's power cord.

• Extension cords should be checked frequently while in use to detect unusual heating. Any cable that feels more than comfortably warm to the bare hand, which is placed outside the insulation, should be checked immediately for overloading.

• See that the extension cord is in a position to prevent tripping or stumbling.

• To prevent the accidental separation of a tool cord from an extension cord during operation, make a knot as shown in Figure 4-47A, or use a cord connector as shown in Figure 4-47B.

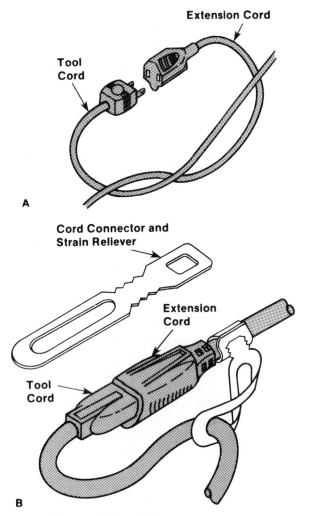

FIGURE 4-47 (A) Knot will prevent the extension cord from accidentally pulling apart from the tool cord during operation; (B) cord connector will serve the same purpose effectively.

Many insurance companies are now requiring automatic shut-off switches on electrical equipment to prevent it from inadvertently being left on. As an alternative, in recent years a few cordless tools—drills and sanders (Figure 4-48)—have made their way into the auto body shop. These tools require no air hose or electric cord, but they require recharging.

4.3 HYDRAULICALLY POWERED SHOP EQUIPMENT

Hydraulic body shop equipment uses an oil-like liquid (called hydraulic fluid) to develop the pressure necessary to operate it. This pressure is achieved manually (pumping on a handle or lever to build up the fluid pressure) or by a small motor—

either air or electrically driven—that provides the necessary pressure needed to force the hydraulic fluid into the equipment's cylinder. The equipment cylinder then causes the tool to operate when a button or a lever is turned.

Hydraulic power equipment is usually classified as "manual," "air over hydraulic," or "electric over hydraulic." Air or electric over hydraulic means that either an air-powered or an electric-powered motor is used to force the hydraulic fluid into the tool's cylinder.

4.4 POWER JACKS AND STRAIGHTENING EQUIPMENT

Hydraulic power equipment in the auto shop is used to operate various jacks. These range from body jacks (Figure 4-49) to large frame/panel pulling and straightener units (Figure 4-50). There are small jack stands used for holding a vehicle after it has been raised in position by a floor jack.

A

B

FIGURE 4-48 Typical cordless tools: (A) drill and (B) sander

The average shop has approximately a dozen jacks, either air, hydraulic, or a combination of both, depending on the preference of the technicians. (Manual jacks are practically obsolete except for use in confined spaces.) The most popular jacks are:

- **Hand and bottle jacks (Figure 4-51).** These tubular-shaped jacks are not specialized. Rather, they perform a variety of functions and range from 1-1/2 tons to 100 tons lifting capacity. Handy for when a service jack is too much.

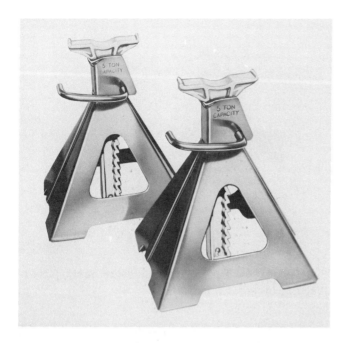

FIGURE 4-49   Typical jack stands. Note capacity is stamped on the jack. (Courtesy of Lincoln, St. Louis)

WARNING: Remember, jacks are for lifting not for supporting. Consequently, jack stands **must** be used at all times to properly support the vehicle.

FIGURE 4-51   Typical hand or bottle jack. (Courtesy of Lincoln, St. Louis)

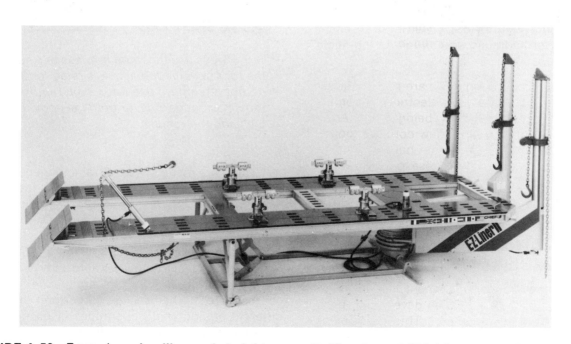

FIGURE 4-50   Frame/panel pulling and straightener unit. (Courtesy of Chief Automotive Systems, Inc.)

FIGURE 4-52 Typical service jacks. *(Courtesy of Blackhawk Automotive Inc.)*

FIGURE 4-54 Typical transmission jack. *(Courtesy of Lincoln, St. Louis)*

- **Service jacks (Figure 4-52).** These four-wheeled jacks with a pump handle are by far the most commonly used jack in the body shop. Ranging in lifting capacity from 1-1/2 tons to 5 tons, these jacks are easily "dollied" around the shop and rolled under the car to lift a section of it, as opposed to the entire structure. Compact and portable, these jacks were developed for a variety of in-shop uses on full-size, intermediate, compact, or subcompact cars. It is also used for road service calls. Service jacks are recommended for all automotive, agricultural, and light truck repair facilities.

- **End lifts (Figure 4-53).** These jacks are either air-over-hydraulic or manual. As the name

implies, they lift only a section of the vehicle by adhering to the bumper. They do not lift the sides of the vehicle. Lifting capabilities range from 1-1/2 to 7 tons.

- **Transmission jacks (Figure 4-54).** Often it is necessary to remove the transmission, engine, or drivetrain from a unibody before servicing a repair. This jack was developed specifically for this purpose. The lifting capacity ranges from 1/4 to 1 ton and jacks are mechanical, air-over-hydraulic or manual.

 **SHOP TALK** _____

Always use the rated tonnage of a jack for the tons specified. If a jack is rated for 2 tons, do not attempt to use it for a job requiring 20 tons. It is dangerous for both the body technician and the vehicle.

There are many styles of frame/panel straighteners on the market. But, there are only two basic types: portable and stationary. Portable units (Figure 4-55) are less expensive to purchase, but they cannot make as many push and pull actions at one time as can the stationary units (Figure 4-56).

Body jacks (also known as auto body repair kits) can be used with frame panel straighteners or they can be used by themselves. To perform the many different straightening operations involving pushing, pulling, or holding a panel to straighten or align metal, a large assortment (Figure 4-57) can be obtained. The hydraulic body jack is usually sold in sets

FIGURE 4-53 Typical end lift jack. *(Courtesy of Lincoln, St. Louis)*

FIGURE 4-55 Portable frame/panel straightener unit. *(Courtesy of Nicator, Inc.)*

FIGURE 4-56 Stationary frame/panel straightener unit

FIGURE 4-57 Typical body jack or body power repair kit. *(Courtesy of Blackhawk Automotive Inc.)*

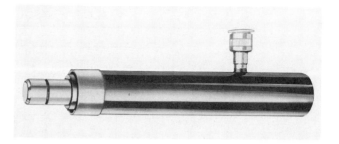

FIGURE 4-58 Typical ram with a 10-ton capacity. *(Courtesy of Lincoln, St. Louis)*

or kits for general work. There is also a bodywork set, a mechanical set, and even a rescue set, which is used during vehicle accidents.

The basic hydraulic jack unit consists of a pump—manual, electrical, or air—a hydraulic hose, and a ram (Figure 4-58). Rams are available in various lengths from approximately 2-5/16 inches for confined areas to 16-1/4 inches with the average being about 12 inches. Included under rams are two wedge type or spreader rams used for getting into tight locations.

Body shop technicians must understand how to make hookups for correcting body or frame damage with power jacks. Complete information on using body jacks and frame/panel straighteners is given in Chapters 9 and 10.

4.5 HYDRAULIC TOOL CARE

Hydraulic tools always seem to be there when they are needed. Otherwise, they are duly ignored. They also require their share of preventive maintenance to avoid failure at a critical moment.

Just because a hydraulic tool is filled with hydraulic fluid does not mean it has been lubricated properly. Moving parts should be lubricated regularly with 30 or 40 weight oil. Included are the moving mechanism, the pump roller, the universal joint, the handle socket, pivot pins, the wheels, and the bearings. Grease at the fittings and sliding points used in pumping.

As with air tools, dirt can be a problem. It will act as an abrasive and scratch the bore of the ram. Where does it come from? Look around the shop at all of the body filler or metal shavings. If the hydraulic tool has an air motor, that dirt might have come from the air hose sitting in dust. After the hose is connected, the dirt shoots right into the tool. The solution is to just clean it before connection.

When filling the hydraulic tool, avoid overfilling it. A certain amount of air is supposed to be left in the

TABLE 4-3: TROUBLESHOOTING CHART

Problem	Reservoir Low on Hydraulic Fluid	Reservoir Over Full	Air in System	Bent Plunger	Release Valve Not Fully Closed	Dirt in Release Valve	Dirt in Check Valve	Loose Dirt or Air Bubble in Valve System	Damaged Quick-Coupler
Spongy effect			X						
Ram will not extend all the way	X	X							
Ram will not retract		X		X					X
Ram leaks down under pressure					X	X			
Handle kickback							X		
Works properly one time but not the next								X	

reservoir. If it is completely filled with fluid, too much vacuum is created and the fluid will not move out of the reservoir.

Following are major problems (Table 4-3) of hydraulic tools and equipment operation:

- **Spongy effect.** Air trapped in the hydraulic system easily compresses under pressure and causes sponginess. To bleed the system, place the pump at a higher elevation than the hose and ram. The objective is to "float" the air bubbles uphill and back to the reservoir where they belong. Close the valve and extend the unit as far as possible. Open the valve fully allowing the oil and air to return to the reservoir. Repeat this procedure until the tool starts to extend on the first stroke of the handle. Usually two or three times will do the trick.

- **Tool will not extend all the way.** This is usually a sign of low hydraulic fluid. Fill to the mark on the dipstick. Do not overfill. The tool should be fully retracted to check oil level. If the tool does not have a dipstick, refer to the manufacturer's filling procedures and fluid level. The hydraulic unit needs the prescribed amount of air chambered in the reservoir, because it works on a partial vacuum to avoid venting to the outside.

- **Tool will not retract.** Usually just too much oil and/or air in the system. Bleed the system and fill to the proper level. If that does not correct the problem, inspect for a bent plunger. If neither is the cause, the quick-coupler is probably damaged. Replace it.

- **Tool leaks down under pressure.** Make sure that the release valve is fully closed. If it still leaks down, there is probably dirt in the return. Check the ball valve. Flush the system with mineral spirits or kerosene. If the problem still exists, the valve is damaged and the unit should go to a repair facility.

- **Handle kickback.** Dirt is in the check valve; flush the system. A damaged check valve should be taken to a repair facility.

- **Works properly one time, but not the next.** Loose dirt or air bubble in the valve system. Flush and refill the system.

A

B

C

D

E

F

FIGURE 4-59 Several ways to get vehicles off the ground: (A) portable lift; (B) side lift; (C) in ground lift—front to rear frame support; (D) in ground lift—side to side support; (E) two post above ground hoist; (F) four post above ground hoist; (G) drive-thru above ground scissor lift; and (H) drive-on above ground ramp plus a scissor lift.

G

H

FIGURE 4-59 Continued

CAUTION: Do not use the brake, transmission, or any fluid other than a good hydraulic oil. Fluids other than hydraulic oil can damage cups and packings, corrode metal parts, and void the warranty. For air-operated hydraulic pumps, refer to the instruction manual for that specific product.

4.6 HYDRAULIC LIFTS

Another hydraulic tool that is found in the body shop is the lift. The traditional stationary in-the-ground unit was usually found only in the service stations, muffler shops, transmission shops, and tire dealers for reasons such as oil and lube jobs, brake service, and other underbody repairs. Today, all body shops, because of unibody construction, are looking for ways to get the vehicle off the ground to estimate and repair. Technicians work better with cars on a lift. Damage reports are easier to write on a vehicle that has been up on a lift.

As shown in Figure 4-59, there are several ways to get the vehicle off the ground. Four-post and two-post hoists are neat and allow total movement under the vehicle, but they take up more than a work stall in length and width. Side post hoists are great to estimate, but some access to the sides of the vehicle is impaired. And lastly, old center post hoists make some areas under the vehicle hard to reach but take up less space.

The using of lifts is a much less physical and mental task on the body technicians since they can work at a level that is comfortable for them. But lifts are a specialized piece of equipment and a technician using it needs to know exactly what is to be done, especially if there are any vehicle weight problems. It is important to note that the quality of today's lifts, as well as the number of safety devices on each model, makes them very safe to operate. Many companies report that almost 100 percent of the lift errors reported to them were the result of operator error or poor maintenance policies on the part of the owner.

WARNING: Before operating any lift, carefully read the owner's manual and understand all the operating and maintenance instructions.

The maintenance on above-ground lifts is minimal, but important. Depending on the lift, pulleys, pivoting lift links, and wheels should be greased. Bearings, pins, and other moving parts should be oiled, and cables and chains should be checked for worn or frayed areas. Again, follow the manufacturer's directions.

On auto side lifts, the rear wheels and center post should be greased, and the front wheel shaft should be oiled.

General maintenance on lifts includes inspecting the lift pads and bumper cushions regularly and replacing them if necessary. Also, it is advisable to appoint a knowledgeable person to inspect the jacks and lifts daily, especially if the units are subjected to abnormal loads or shocks.

Finally, it is important that any jack or lift that appears to be damaged, is found to be badly worn, or operates improperly be immediately removed from service until the necessary repairs are made.

Lift Safety

Raising a vehicle on a lift or a hoist requires specific care. Drive-on lifts are fairly safe. However, it is important to make sure that vehicles equipped with a catalytic converter have enough clearance between the hoist and the exhaust system components before driving the vehicle onto the ramps.

Adapters and hoist plates must be positioned correctly on twin post and rail type lifts to prevent damage to the underbody of the vehicle. The catalytic converter, tie rod, rod bracket, and shock absorbers are some of the components that could be damaged if the adapters and hoist plates are incorrectly placed.

There are specific contact points to use where the weight of the vehicle is evenly supported by the adapters or hoist plates. The correct lifting points can be found in the vehicle's service manual.

🚗 SHOP TALK

Here are some other lift safety tips that should always be kept in mind and followed when getting a vehicle up in the air:

- *Never overload the lift. The manufacturer's rated capacity is shown on the nameplate affixed to the lift.*
- *Employees should stand to one side of a vehicle when directing it into position over a lift. Do not allow customers or bystanders to operate the lift or be in the lift area during its operation.*
- *Positioning of the vehicle and operation of the lift should be done only by trained and authorized personnel.*
- *Always keep the lift area free from obstructions, grease, oil, trash, and other debris.*
- *Operating controls are designed to close when released. Do not block, open, or override them.*
- *Before driving a vehicle over a lift, position the arms and supports to provide*

unobstructed clearance. Do not hit or run over lift arms, adapters, or axle supports. This could damage the lift or vehicle.

- *Load the vehicle on the lift carefully. Check to make sure adapters or axle supports are in secure contact with the vehicle, per the manual instructions, before raising to the desired working height. Remember that unsecured loads can be dangerous.*
- *Make sure the vehicle's doors, hood, and trunk are closed prior to raising the vehicle. Never raise a car with passengers inside.*
- *Position the lift supports to contact at the vehicle manufacturer's recommended lifting points. Raise the lift until the supports contact the vehicle. Check supports for secure contact with the vehicle and raise the lift to the desired working height.*

WARNING: When working under a car, the lift should be raised high enough for the locking device to be engaged.

- *After lifting a vehicle to the desired height, always lower the unit onto mechanical safeties.*
- *Note that with some vehicles, the removal (or installation) of components can cause a critical shift in the center of gravity and result in raised vehicle instability. Refer to the vehicle manufacturer's service manual for recommended procedures when vehicle components are removed.*
- *Make sure tool trays, stands, and so forth are removed from under the vehicle. Release locking devices as per instructions before attempting to lower the lift.*
- *Before removing the vehicle from the lift area, position the arms, adapters, or axle supports to assure that the vehicle or lift will not be damaged.*
- *Inspect the lift daily. Never operate it if it malfunctions or if it has broken or*

damaged parts. It should be removed from service and repaired immediately. A lift requires immediate attention if it:
—*Jerks or jumps when raised*
—*Slowly settles down after being raised*
—*Slowly rises when not in use*
—*Slowly rises when in use*
—*Comes down very slowly*
—*Blows oil out of the exhaust line*
—*Leaks oil at the packing gland*

Repairs should be made with original equipment parts only.

4.7 REVIEW QUESTIONS

1. To locate the position of a hole to be drilled, Technician A uses an awl, while Technician B uses a center punch. Who is correct?
   a. Technician A
   b. Technician B
   c. Both A and B
   d. Neither A nor B

2. Technician A uses a low pile height buffing pad for light compounding, touchups, and blending. Technician B uses a high pile height pad for these tasks. Who is correct?
   a. Technician A
   b. Technician B
   c. Both A and B
   d. Neither A nor B

3. Which of the following operations can the air hammer perform?
   a. bushing installer
   b. bushing remover
   c. shock absorber chisel
   d. all of the above

4. Which type of wheel is used for sharpening cutting tools?
   a. grinding wheel
   b. wire wheel brush
   c. buffing wheel
   d. cutting wheel

5. Which of the following is used to lift the entire automobile?
   a. floor jack
   b. hoist
   c. hydraulic press
   d. all of the above

6. When working with a piece of hydraulic equipment that will not extend all the way, Technician A says the likely problem is low hydraulic fluid. Technician B says the likely problem is dirt in the check valve. Who is correct?
   a. Technician A
   b. Technician B
   c. Both A and B
   d. Neither A nor B

7. What causes a pneumatic tool to fail?
   a. lack of lubrication
   b. excessive air pressure
   c. lack of air pressure
   d. all of the above
   e. both a and c

8. Which air sander creates a buffing pattern?
   a. disc sander
   b. dual-action orbital sander
   c. long board type sander
   d. all of the above

9. Which pad should be used on a polisher/buffer to do the early stages of cutting and compounding?
   a. 1/2 to 1 inch pile height
   b. 1 to 1-1/4 inch pile height
   c. 1-1/4 to 1-1/2 inch pile height
   d. 1-1/2 to 2 inch pile height

10. Which type of sandblaster can be used indoors?
    a. standard
    b. captive
    c. both a and b
    d. none of the above

11. What is the recommended air pressure for a disc sander?
    a. 60 to 80 PSI
    b. 70 to 90 PSI
    c. 40 to 90 PSI
    d. 10 to 50 PSI

12. Which type of vacuum cleaner is most often found in shops?
    a. dry pick-up type, 20 to 30-gallon capacity
    b. dry pick-up type, 30 to 40-gallon capacity
    c. wet/dry unit, 20 to 30-gallon capacity
    d. wet/dry unit, 30 to 40-gallon capacity

CHAPTER
5

Compressed Air Supply Equipment

OBJECTIVES

After reading this chapter, you will be able to:

- identify the various types of air compressors used in a body shop.
- explain the operation of the various air compressors.
- describe the function of air and fluid control equipment.
- use the different accessory equipment of the air compressor.
- properly maintain an air supply system.
- list the air system safety rules.

The compressed air supply system is designed to provide an adequate supply of compressed air at a predetermined pressure to insure efficient operation of all air-operated equipment in the body shop. The system can vary in size from small portable units (Figure 5-1) to large in-shop installations (Figure 5-2). The following basic requirements and considerations for these systems are the same (Figure 5-3):

- An air compressor, sometimes referred to as a **pump,** can be one compressor or a series of compressors.
- The power source is generally an electric motor. (Portable gasoline driven compressors are available for work outside the shop.)
- A control or set of controls to regulate the operation of the compressor and motor.
- Air intake filters/silencers are designed to muffle intake noises as well as filter out dust and dirt.
- The air tank or receiver must be properly sized. It cannot be too small or it will cause the compressor to cycle too often thus causing excessive load on the motor. It should not be too large because of space problems and also unnecessary capacity.
- The distribution system is the key link in the compressed air system. This is the hose or piping, or arrangement of hose and piping, from the air receiver to distribution points requiring compressed air. This distribution system consists of the proper sizes of hose or pipe, fittings, valves, air filters, oil and water extractors, regulators, gauges, lubricators and other air and fluid control equipment

FIGURE 5-2 Multicompressor setup from large body shops. *(Courtesy of Binks Mfg. Co.)*

that will provide for the effective and efficient operation of specific air devices, tools, and spraying equipment.

5.1 THE AIR COMPRESSOR

The compressor—the heart of any air system—is designed to raise the pressure of air from normal atmospheric to some higher pressure, as measured in pounds per square inch (psi). While normal atmospheric pressure is about 14.7 pounds per square inch, a compressor will typically deliver air at pressures up to 200 psi.

TYPES OF AIR COMPRESSORS

There are three basic types of air compressors: the diaphragm type, the piston type, and the rotary screw type.

Diaphragm Type Compressor

In this type of compressor (Figure 5-4), a durable diaphragm is stretched across the bore of a very shallow compression chamber. A connecting plate, operated by an eccentric mounted on the motor shaft, alternately pulls the diaphragm down and thrusts it upward. As the diaphragm is pulled down (Figure 5-5A), air is drawn into the small space above the diaphragm. When the diaphragm is thrust upward (Figure 5-5B), the air trapped in the compression chamber is squeezed and forced out into the delivery chamber and supply lines. Although only a very small amount of air—in the 30 to 35 psi

FIGURE 5-1 Typical portable piston compressor mounted on wheels. *(Courtesy of DeVilbiss Co.)*

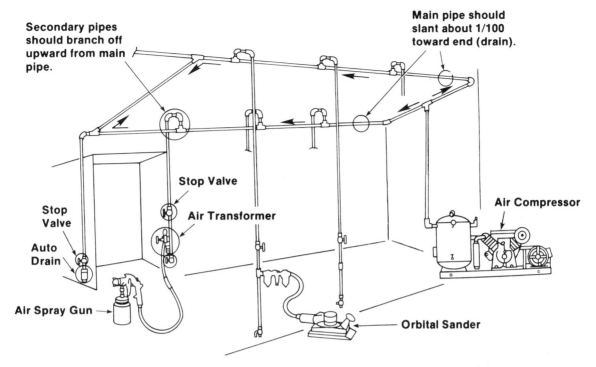

Secondary pipes should branch off upward from main pipe.

Main pipe should slant about 1/100 toward end (drain).

Stop Valve

Air Compressor

Stop Valve

Air Transformer

Auto Drain

Air Spray Gun →

← Orbital Sander

FIGURE 5-3   Typical piping arrangement found in a body/paint shop

FIGURE 5-4   Typical diaphragm type compressor

range—is compressed during each cycle, the action is very rapid—in excess of 1500 strokes per minute.

Because most body and refinishing operations consume large quantities of compressed air at relatively higher pressures, the diaphragm compressor is seldom found in the average shop. The exception to this is a refinishing shop that specializes in custom painting and airbrush work.

Piston Reciprocating Type Compressor

The piston type air compressor pump develops compressed air pressure through the action of a reciprocating piston. As shown in Figure 5–6, a piston, which is actuated by a crankshaft, moves up and

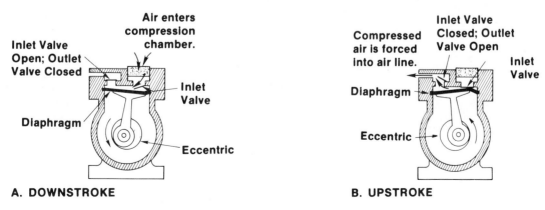

Air enters compression chamber.

Inlet Valve Open; Outlet Valve Closed

Inlet Valve

Diaphragm

Eccentric

Compressed air is forced into air line.

Inlet Valve Closed; Outlet Valve Open

Inlet Valve

Diaphragm

Eccentric

A. DOWNSTROKE

B. UPSTROKE

FIGURE 5-5   The operation of a diaphragm compressor

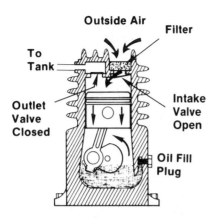 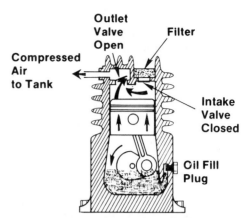

A. DOWNSTROKE—AIR BEING DRAWN INTO COMPRESSION CHAMBER

B. UPSTROKE—AIR BEING COMPRESSED AND FORCED TO TANK

FIGURE 5-6 The operation of a piston type compressor

down inside a cylinder, very much like a piston in an automobile engine. On the downstroke (Figure 5-6A), air is drawn into the compression chamber through a one-way valve. On the upstroke (Figure 5-6B), as the air is compressed by the rising piston, a second one-way valve opens and the air is forced into a pressure tank or receiver. As more and more air is forced into the tank, the pressure inside the tank rises.

Piston compressor pumps are available in single or multiple cylinder and single- or two-stage models, depending on the volume and pressure required. When the air is drawn from the atmosphere and compressed to its final pressure in a single stroke, the compressor is referred to as a **single stage** compressor. Single-stage units normally are used in pressure ranges up to 125 psi for intermittent service. Most single-stage compressors are rated at 50 percent duty cycle (1/2 the time ON, 1/2 the time OFF). They are available in single- or multicylinder

compressors (Figure 5-7). The principal parts of a typical piston type compressor are shown in Figure 5-8.

When the air drawn from the atmosphere is compressed first to an intermediate pressure and then further compressed to a higher pressure, it is done in a **two-stage** compressor (Figure 5-9). Such a compressor has cylinders of unequal bore. The first stage of compression takes place in the large bore cylinder. In the second stage, the air is compressed for a second time to a higher pressure in the smaller bore cylinder (Figure 5-10) after passing through an intercooler. Two-stage compressors are usually more efficient, run cooler, and deliver more air for the power consumed, particularly in the 100 to 200 psi pressure range; this range of pressure is enough for most body or finishing applications.

The advantage of the piston compressor is that it is generally more durable and has a greater capacity than diaphragm types, which makes them more

FIGURE 5-7 Single-stage compressor pumps (left to right): single cylinder, angled V-cylinders, and two cylinders

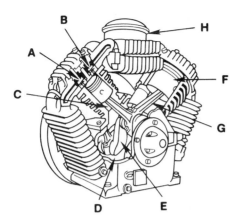

FIGURE 5-8   The principal parts of a four-cylinder, two-stage piston type compressor: (A) intake and (B) exhaust valves; (C) second-stage piston; (D) crankcase; (E) crankshaft; (F) first stage piston; (G) connecting rod assembly; and (H) air intake filter

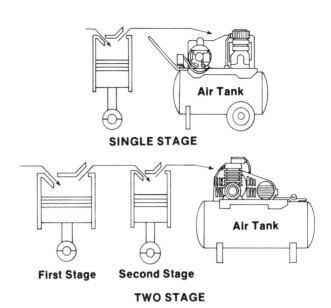

FIGURE 5-10   Comparison of a single- and two-stage compressor

FIGURE 5-9   Typical two-stage compressor. *(Courtesy Binks Mfg. Co.)*

FIGURE 5-11   Three mountings for oilless compressors

suitable for heavier duty work. However, since the piston rides in a cylinder, lubrication is necessary.

In recent years, an oilless or oil-free piston compression system has been introduced that employs self-lubricating materials that do not require an oil lubricant. Until recently, most oilless compressors, like the diaphragm type, were considered compacts and limited in both output and pressure. However, there are oilless compressors (Figure 5-11) now on the market of up to approximately 5 horsepower that will nearly equal, in output and pressure, oil-lubricated compressors of the same

FIGURE 5-12 Typical rotary screw air compressor *(Courtesy of Champion Pneumatic Machinery Co., Inc.)*

horsepower. All oilless compressors produce a clean air output.

Rotary Screw Air Compressor

Rotary screw type air compressors (Figure 5-12) have been a standard in industry, but because of an oil output problem, it was never accepted by the automotive refinishing profession. Recent innovations have greatly or completely eliminated the oil problem but, except in certain areas of the country, the rotary air compressor is not overly used in auto body shops. The rotary screw air compressor is a highly efficient and dependable machine.

How Compressors Are Rated

The following terms are used to measure the performance of a compressor.

Horsepower (hp)

Horsepower is the measure of the work capacity of the motor or engine that drives the compressor. Compressors found in body and paint shops usually range from 3 to 25 hp. As a general rule, the greater the horsepower, the more powerful the compressor. Also, in most cases, as the horsepower increases, so will the other compressor ratings that follow:

- **Cubic feet per minute (cfm).** Cubic feet per minute is the volume of the air being delivered by the compressor to the spray gun or air tool and is used as a measure of the compressor's capabilities. Compressors with higher cfm ratings provide more air through the hose to the tool, thus making higher cfm outfits more practical for larger jobs. Actually, compressors have two cfm ratings:

—**Displacement cfm.** This is the theoretical amount of air in cubic feet that the compressor can pump in 1 minute. It is a relatively simple matter to calculate the air displacement of a compressor if the piston diameter, length of stroke, and rpm are known. For example, the area of the piston multiplied by the length of the stroke and the shaft revolutions per minute equals the displacement volume. The formula for computing it is as follows:

$$\frac{\text{Area of piston} \times \text{stroke} \times \text{rpm} \times \text{number of pistons}}{1,728}$$

$$= \text{Displacement in cfm}$$

—**Free air cfm.** This is the actual amount of free air in cubic feet that the compressor can pump in 1 minute at working pressure. The free air delivery at working pressure, not the displacement or the horsepower, is the true rating of a compressor and should be the only cfm rating considered when selecting an air compressor. Keep in mind that compressor units are frequently rated in standard cubic feet per minute (scfm), which is really cfm corrected for a given barometric pressure and temperature.

It should be remembered that free air delivery is always less than the displacement rating since no compressor is 100 percent efficient. The volumetric efficiency of a compressor is the ratio of free air delivery to the displacement rating, expressed in percent. For example, if a compressor unit for 100 pounds service has a displacement of 8 cfm and its volumetric efficiency is 75 percent, at this pressure the free air delivery will be: 8 cfm × 75 percent, or 6 cfm.

 **SHOP TALK** _____

The displacement of a two-stage compressor is always given for that of the first stage cylinder or cylinders only. This is because the second stage merely rehandles the same air the first stage draws in and cannot increase the amount of air discharged.

- **Pressure (psi).** Pounds per square inch (psi) is the measure of air pressure or force delivered by the compressor to the air tool. This is usually expressed in two figures:
  —Normal or continuous working pressure
  —Maximum pressure
  Average psi and free air delivery requirements for various air tools and accessories

Tank Size

As previously mentioned, with most piston types of compressor pumps, air is forced into a tank or receiver. Working pressure is not available until the tank pressure is above the required psi of the air tool. The compressor puts more into the tank than is required for application. Thus, the larger the tank, the longer a job can be done at the required pressure before a pause is necessary to rebuild pressure in the tank. Since the air tank acts as a reservoir, the unit may for a short time exceed the normal capacity of the compressor. This reservoir action of the tank also reduces the running time of the compressor, thereby decreasing compressor wear and maintenance.

Air tanks or receivers usually have a cylindrical shape (Figure 5–12), and the compressor motor and pump are usually mounted on top of it. Tanks can be purchased with either horizontal (Figure 5–13A) or vertical stationary mountings (Figure 5–13B) or can be mounted horizontally on wheels for portability (see Figure 5–1).

Compressor Outfits

As already illustrated, there are two types of compressor outfits used in body shops: portable and stationary. A portable outfit is designed for easy movement. It is equipped with handles, wheels, or casters and usually a small air receiver or pulsation chamber.

 SHOP TALK

Another source of compressed air found in many body repair/paint shops is the high volume, low pressure system's turbine generator (Figure 5–14). The HVLP system is fully described in Chapter 17.

A stationary outfit is one that is permanently installed. It is usually equipped with a larger air re-

A

B

FIGURE 5–13 (A) Horizontal- and (B) vertical-mounted piston compressors

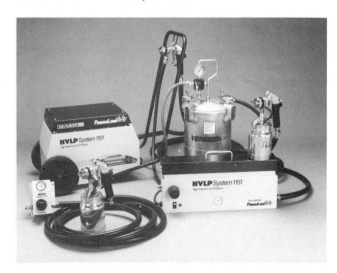

FIGURE 5–14 The basic components of a portable HVLP system, including a portable turbine generator *(Courtesy of DeVilbiss Co.)*

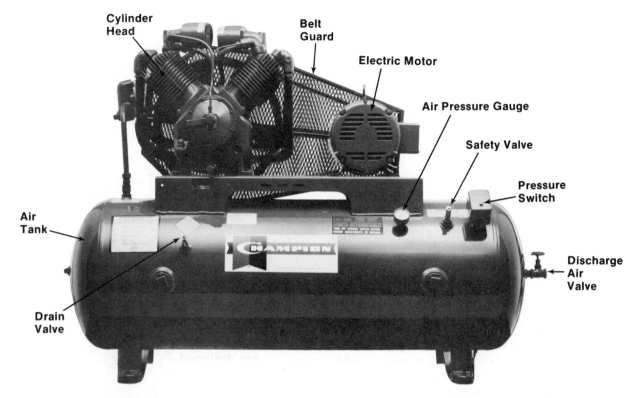

FIGURE 5-15 Parts of stationary compressor. (Courtesy of Champion Pneumatic Machinery Co., Inc.)

ceiver than the portable type and might have a pressure switch as found on service station compressors or an automatic unloader as found on larger industrial units. Larger stationary models are generally equipped with a centrifugal pressure release.

As shown in Figure 5-15, the typical parts of a stationary compressor are:

- Air compressor pump
- Electric or gasoline engine (powers the compressor)
- Air receiver or storage tank (holds the compressed air)
- Check valve (prevents leakage of the stored air)
- Pressure switch (automatically controls the air pressure)

On Large Models

- Centrifugal pressure release (relieves the motor of starting against a load)
- Safety valve (protects air lines and equipment against excessive pressure)
- Drain valve at the bottom of the air receiver (drains condensation)

Because of the importance of the system's safety controls, it is wise to know how they operate to protect excessive pressure and electrical problems. The most common of these are:

- **Automatic unloader** is a device designed to maintain a supply of air within given pressure limits on gasoline and electrically driven compressors when it is not practical to start and stop the motor during operations. When the demand for air is relatively constant at a volume approaching the main capacity of the compressor, an unloader is recommended.

  When maximum pressure in the air receiver is reached, the unloader pilot valve (Figure 5-16A) opens to let air travel through a small tube to the unloader mechanism (Figure 5-16B) and holds open the intake valve on the compressor, allowing it to run idle. When pressure drops to a minimum setting, the spring loaded pilot automatically closes, air to the unloader is shut off causing the intake valve to close, and the compressor resumes normal operation. Maximum and minimum pressures can be varied by resetting the pressure adjusting screw on the pilot.

- **Pressure switch** is a pneumatically controlled electric switch for starting and stopping electric motors at present minimum and maximum pressures. That is, this switch maintains a "cut-in" low pressure point; for example, 80 psi. When the pressure in the air

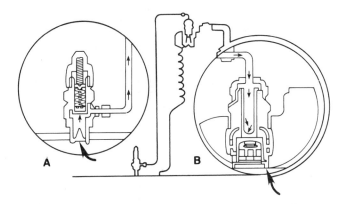

FIGURE 5-16 Automatic unloader. *(Courtesy of DeVilbiss Co.)*

receiver drops to this low point, the motor will start and the compressor will then pump up to its cut-off high pressure point, which might be 100 psi, thus breaking contact and stopping the motor; when the pressure drops to its low point, the cycle is repeated. The time to pump as shown in Table 5-1 varies by compressor size and type and cut-in/cut-out pressure.

- **Motor starter** is an electrical switch designed to provide overload protection or other necessary electrical control for starting motors of various types. The design of the switch varies with different motor sizes and current characteristics.

- **Overload protection** is usually provided on small units by fuses and on larger ones by thermal overload relays on the starting device. Relays are recommended with time delay features so that circuits will not be opened by overloads of short duration not harmful

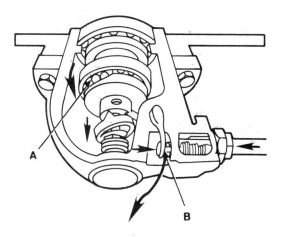

FIGURE 5-17 Centrifugal pressure release. *(Courtesy of DeVilbiss Co.)*

enough to injure the motor. Overload protection should be employed on all compressor installations, except the smaller types that are designed to operate from the standard wall socket.

- **Centrifugal pressure release** is a device that allows the motor to start up and gain momentum before engaging the load of pumping air against pressure. When the compressor slows down to stop, rotating the crankshaft more slowly, steel balls (Figure 5–17A) move toward the center where they wedge against a cam surface forcing the cam outward. This opens a valve (Figure 5–17B) "bleeding" air from the line connecting to the check valve. With air pressure bled from the pump and aftercooler, the compressor can start up free of back pressure until it gets up speed. When normal speed is reached, balls move out by

Outfit	HP	Cut-In pounds pressure	Cut-out pounds pressure	Time to pump from Cut-In to Cut-out (In seconds)	Tank Size
TABLE 5-1: TYPICAL CUT-IN/CUT-OUT COMPRESSION TIMES					
Single Stage	1	80	100	83	30 gal.
Single Stage	2	80	100	69	60 gal.
Single Stage	3	80	100	51	60 gal.
Two Stage	1	140	175	284	60 gal.
Two Stage	3	140	175	115	80 gal.
Two Stage	5	140	175	75	80 gal.
Two Stage	10	140	175	56	120 gal.
Two Stage	15	140	175	42	120 gal.
Two Stage	20	140	175	36	200 gal.
Two Stage	25	140	175	30	200 gal.

centrifugal force, releasing the cam, closing the valve, and allowing air to again be pumped into the air receiver.

- **Fused disconnect switch** is a knife type, OFF/ON switch, containing the proper size fuse. This should be used at or near the compressor unit with the line going from the fused disconnect to the starter. Fuses should be large enough to handle 2-1/2 times the current rating stamped on the motor. A qualified electrician should always make the electrical hookup of an air compressor.

5.2 AIR AND FLUID CONTROL EQUIPMENT

The control of the amount, pressure, and cleanness of the air going to the pneumatic tools, especially spray guns, is of critical importance in the system. The intake air filter located on the compressor is very important as all the air going into the compressor must pass through this filter. The filter element must be made of fine mesh or felt material to insure that small particles of grit and abrasive dust do not pass into the cylinders, thus preventing excessive wear on cylinder walls, piston rings, and valves.

Once the air leaves the compressor, any equipment installed between the air pump and the point of use modifies the nature of the air stream. This modification could be a change in pressure, in volume, in cleanliness, or some combination of them. It must be remembered that raw air piped directly from a compressor is of little use to the refinishing shop. The air contains small but harmful quantities of water, oil, dirt, and other contaminants that will lessen the quality of the sprayed finish. And the air will likely vary in pressure during the job. Furthermore, there will probably be a need for multiple air outlets for compressed air to run various pieces of equipment. Any type of item installed in the air line that performs one or more of these functions is a piece of air control equipment.

DISTRIBUTION SYSTEM

The interconnecting piping, that is, the piping from the compressor to the tool input, can be copper tubing, or galvanized or black iron pipe. Table 5-2 shows the correct pipe size in relation to compressor size and air volume.

TABLE 5-2: MINIMUM PIPE SIZE RECOMMENDATIONS*

Compressing Outfit		Main Air Line	
Size	Capacity	Length	Size
1-1/2 and 2 HP	6 to 9 CFM	Over 50 feet	3/4"
3 and 5 HP	12 to 20 CFM	Up to 200 feet	3/4"
		Over 200 feet	1"
5 to 10 HP	20 to 40 CFM	Up to 100 feet	3/4"
		Over 100 to 200 feet	1"
		Over 200 feet	1-1/4"
10 to 15 HP	40 to 60 CFM	Up to 100 feet	1"
		Over 100 to 200 feet	1-1/4"
		Over 200 feet	1-1/2"

*Piping should be as direct as possible. If a large number of fittings are used, large size pipe should be installed to help overcome excessive pressure drop.

The location of the compressor unit is important. If possible, the compressor should be placed where it can receive an ample supply of clean, cool, dry air. If necessary, connect the air intake to the outside of the building. Distance between the intake and the compressor should be as short as possible for best efficiency and the outside intake should be protected from the elements with a hood or suitable weatherproof shield. The compressor air intake should not be located near steam outlets or other moisture-producing areas.

The pump unit itself should be at least 1 foot from any wall or obstruction so that air can circulate around the compressor to aid in proper cooling. The compressor must be level. Mounting pads or vibration dampeners are generally used under the feet of the compressor. These absorb the vibration, eliminating excessive wear in the area where the feet are welded to the tank. Normally the air compressor is mounted with the fly wheel facing the wall for additional safety.

The compressor should be located as near as possible to operations requiring compressed air. This cuts down lengthy air lines that cause needless pressure drop. It is good practice if the shop is long and narrow to install an extra air receiver at the far end to act as a cushion and help reduce pressure drop when peak loads are placed on the compressed air supply. Pressure drops, to a great extent, can be avoided by encircling the shop or looping the distribution system. This is accomplished by running the piping in a full circle or loop from the air receiver around the shop and back to the air receiver. A double loop or circle is accomplished by installing a

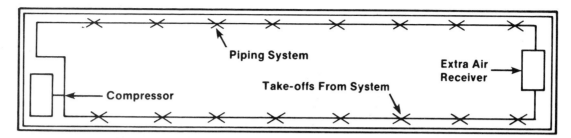

FIGURE 5-18   Some body/paint shop layouts require an extra air receiver.

tee in the line and then running a loop or circle in both directions back to the air tank. For this type of installation, it is recommended that an extra air tank (Figure 5-18) be installed at the far end to balance out peak loads. All piping should be installed so that it slopes toward the compressor air receiver or a drain leg installed at the end of each branch, to provide for drainage of moisture from the main air line. This line should not run adjacent to steam or hot-water piping.

In the air distribution or supply system, there should be a shut-off valve on the main line, close to the storage receiver tank. This valve is used to shut off the air at the air receiver. Keeping the air shut off at the storage tank overnight insures a full tank of air when the shop is opened each day.

Other air control devices come in a very wide variety of types, but they basically all perform one or more of the following functions: air filtering and cleaning; air pressure regulation and indication of pressure; and air distribution through multiple outlets. Some typical devices to perform these functions are called air transformers, air condensers, air regulators, and in some circumstances, air lubricators.

Air Transformer

An air transformer, sometimes called a moisture **separator/regulator,** is a multipurpose device that removes oil, dirt, and moisture from the compressed air; filters and regulates the air; indicates by gauge the regulated air pressure; and provides multiple air outlets for spray guns, dusters, air-operated tools, and so on. Figure 5-19A illustrates a typical air transformer. Some air transfers (Figure 5-19B) are equipped with a second gauge that indicates main line pressure.

Air transformers are used in all spray finishing operations that require a supply of clean, dry, regulated air. They remove entrapped dirt, oil, and mois-

ture by a series of baffles, centrifugal force, expansion chambers, impingement plates and filters, allowing only clean, dry air to emerge from the outlets. The air regulating valve provides positive control insuring uniformly constant air pressure. Gauges indicate regulated air pressure, and in some cases, main line pressure as well. Outlets with valves allow compressed air to be distributed where it is needed. The drain valve provides for elimination of sludge consisting of oil, dirt, and moisture. The air transformer should be installed at least 25 feet from the compressing unit.

A

B

FIGURE 5-19   Two types of air transformers. *(Courtesy of DeVilbiss Co.)*

Air Condenser or Filter

An air condenser is basically a filter that is installed in the air line between the compressor and the point of use. It separates solid particles such as oil, water, and dirt out of the compressed air. No pressure regulation capability is supplied by this device. A typical air condenser is illustrated in Figure 5-20.

Air Pressure Regulator

An air pressure regulator is a device for reducing the main line air pressure as it comes from the compressor. It automatically maintains the required air pressure with minimum fluctuations. Regulators (Figure 5-21) are used in lines already equipped with an air condenser or other type of air filtration device.

Air regulators are available in a wide range of cfm and psi capacities, with and without pressure gauges, and in different degrees of sensitivity and accuracy. They have main line air inlets and regulated air outlets (Figure 5-22).

Lubricator

Certain types of air-operated tools and equipment described in Chapter 4 require a very small amount of oil mixed in the air supply that powers them. An automatic air line lubricator (Figure 5-23) should be installed on leg or branch line furnishing air to pneumatic tools. (Never install a lubricator on a leg or branch air line used for paint spraying since the small oil supplied by it could damage the finish.)

FIGURE 5-22   Typical filter/air regulator

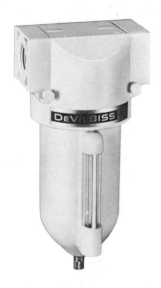

FIGURE 5-20   Typical air filter. *(Courtesy of De-Vilbiss Co.)*

FIGURE 5-21   Simple air regulator

FIGURE 5-23   Typical air line lubricator. *(Courtesy of DeVilbiss Co.)*

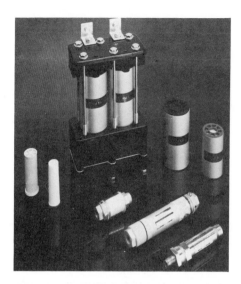

FIGURE 5-24 There are several types of extractor/dryers, filters, and lubricating units that provide clean, dry air to spray guns, tools and other compressed air applications. The lubricating units supply the correct amount of oil to air tools to help keep them running smoother and longer. *(Courtesy of DeVilbiss Co.)*

Lubricators are often combined with air filters and regulators in a single unit. Figure 5-24 shows a lubricator/filter/regulator unit with a built-in sight glass for determining reserve oil level.

THERMAL CONDITIONING AND PURIFICATION EQUIPMENT

While the air control devices already described in this chapter will remove contaminants from the

FIGURE 5-26 Air-cooled aftercooler for system requiring drier air. It is installed between the two compressor stages. *(Courtesy of Hankison Corp.)*

compressed air most satisfactorily, there are some special problems in some shops in the country with heat, dampness, and dirt that require special thermal conditioning and purification equipment. This equipment is usually installed between the compressor and the air storage receiver tank (Figure 5-25). It includes the following:

- **Aftercooler.** The primary purpose of this device is to reduce the temperature of compressed air. Heat, as well as some impurities, can be removed by installing an aftercooler in the system (Figure 5-26). Aftercoolers are very efficient in lowering air temperature and removing most of the oil and water; the residue of oil and water will be removed before

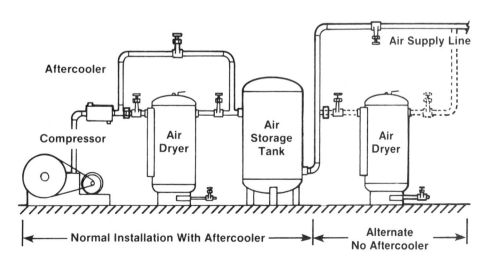

FIGURE 5-25 Arrangement where dry air supply is required.

it enters the air receiver. There are several different designs or types of aftercoolers available. The most common is the water-cooled "air tube" design in which air passes through small tubes and recirculating water is directed back and forth across the tubes by means of baffles and moves in a direction counter to the flow of air. This cross-flow principle is accepted as the most efficient means of heat transfer.

- **Automatic dump trap.** This trap, installed at the lowest point below the air receiver, will collect condensed moisture. It is so designed that the trap opens automatically to discharge a predetermined volume. Due to the air pressure behind the water, the trap opens and closes with a snap action that insures proper seating of the closing valve. A small line strainer should be installed ahead of any automatic device to keep foreign particles from clogging the working parts. If this unit is properly installed, with a line strainer, it will give long and satisfactory service with minimum maintenance.

- **Air dryers.** Good aftercoolers will remove the greatest percentage of water vapor, but the residue can still cause problems. To prevent such problems an air dryer (Figure 5-27) is used. There are many designs of air dryers available; among these the most common are chemical, desiccant (a drying agent), and refrigeration types. All dryers are designed to remove moisture from the compressed air supply so that no condensation will take place in the distribution system under normal working conditions.

5.3 COMPRESSOR ACCESSORIES

The various types of hose used to carry compressed air and fluid to the spray gun are important parts of the system. Improperly selected or maintained hose can create a number of problems.

HOSE TYPES

There are two types of hoses in a compressed air system: air hose and a fluid or material hose (Figure 5-28). The air hose in most compressed systems is usually covered in red rubber, although in smaller, low pressure systems it might be covered

FIGURE 5-27 Typical air dryer used in paint shops. (Courtesy of Hankison Corp.)

with a black and orange braided fabric. The fluid or material hose is normally black or brown rubber.

 SHOP TALK _____

*The air hose is **not** to be used for solvent-based paints.*

The air hose is usually a simple braid-covered hose that consists of rubber tubing (1) reinforced and covered by a woven braid (2), as shown in Figure 5-29A. The single braid, rubber-covered hose (Figure 5-29B) consists of an inner tube (1), a braid (2), and an outside cover (3), all vulcanized into a single unit. The double braid hose, illustrated in Figure 5-29C, consists of an inner tube (1), a braid (2), a separator or friction layer (3), a second layer of braid (4), and an outer rubber cover (5), all vulcanized into one. Double braid hose has a higher working pressure than single braid hose.

 SHOP TALK _____

Since the solvents in some coatings used in refinishing would readily attack and destroy ordinary rubber compounds, fluid hose is lined with special solvent-resistant material that is impervious to all common solvents.

HOSE SIZE

With both the air and fluid (material) hoses, it is important to use the proper size and type to deliver the air from the compressor and the material from its source to the air tools and guns. When compressed, air must travel a long distance; its pressure begins to drop. However, for a distance of up to 100 feet, this air pressure drop can be considered minimal when the proper hose is used. That is, make certain to employ only the hose constructed for compressed air use and with a rating of at least four times that of the maximum psi being used.

Table 5-3 indicates just how much pressure drop can be expected at different pressures with hoses of varying length and internal diameters. At low pressure and with short lengths of hose this drop is not particularly significant, but as the pressure is increased and the hose lengthened, the pressure drop rapidly becomes very large and must be compensated for. Too often a tool is blamed for malfunctioning when the real cause is an inadequate supply of compressed air resulting from using too small an inner diameter (ID) hose.

TABLE 5-3: AIR PRESSURE DROP				
Size of Air Hose (ID)*	Air Pressure Drop			
	5-Foot Length	15-Foot Length	25-Foot Length	50-Foot Length
1/4 Inch	PSIG	PSIG	PSIG	PSIG
@ 40 PSIG†	0.4	7.5	10.5	16.0
@ 60 PSIG	4.5	9.5	13.0	20.5
@ 80 PSIG	5.5	11.5	16.0	25.0
5/16 Inch				
@ 40 PSIG	0.5	1.5	2.5	4.0
@ 60 PSIG	1.0	3.0	4.0	6.0
@ 80 PSIG	1.5	3.0	4.0	8.0
3/8 Inch				
@ 40 PSIG	1.0	1.0	2.0	3.5
@ 60 PSIG	1.5	2.0	3.0	5.0
@ 80 PSIG	2.5	3.0	4.0	6.0

*ID: Inner diameter
†PSIG: Pounds per square inch gauge

FIGURE 5-28   Two types of hoses used in most compressed air systems. (Courtesy of Binks Mfg. Co.)

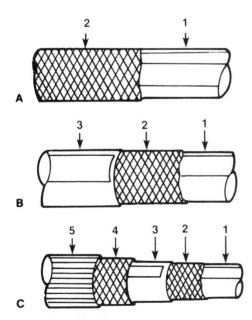

FIGURE 5-29   Construction of hoses used in compressed air system: (A) braid-covered hose; (B) single braid hose; and (C) double braid hose

MAINTENANCE OF HOSES

A hose will last a long time if it is properly cared for and maintained. Caution should be taken when it is dragged across the floor. It should never be pulled around sharp objects, run over by vehicles, kinked, or otherwise abused. Hose that ruptures in the middle of a job can ruin or delay the work.

The fluid hose can be cleaned using a hose cleaner, a device that forces a mixture of solvent and air through the fluid hose and spray guns, ridding them of paint residue. A valve stops the flow of solvent and allows air to dry the equipment. Clean the fluid hose internally with the proper solvent when the gun is cleaned.

The outside of both the air and fluid hose should be wiped down with solvent at the end of every job, then stored by hanging up in coils.

CONNECTORS

Connections are necessary among the compressor, the ends of hoses, and the air tools. Of the many different types used, the most common are the threaded and quick-connect types. The former is a screw type fitting and is usually tightened with a wrench, while the quick-connect is readily attached and detached by hand (Figure 5-30).

Both types of connections use the compression ring system to mount the fittings to the air or fluid

FIGURE 5-30   Quick-connect coupler kit

hose. The system employs a ring that is slipped over the end of the hose. The stem on the fitting is inserted into the hose, and then a sleeve is slipped on and tightened. It forms a perfect seal against the ridges of the stem. The compression ring fitting has a number of advantages. It is economical, in that all of the parts are reusable, it forms a perfect seal free of leaks, and there is no pinching or distortion of the hose cover. The fittings are easily removed and reattached without special tools.

To install a compression ring connection, slip the sleeve (1) and the compression ring (2) over the end of the hose as shown in Figure 5-31. Hold the body (3) of the connection in a vise, and push the hose into the body as far as it will go. Slide the compression ring up to the body and bring the sleeve over the ring and thread it on by hand. Tighten it with a wrench.

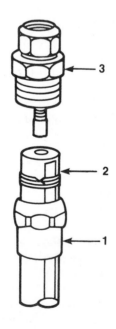

FIGURE 5-31   Compression ring connection installation

Most paint spray guns require either 1/4- or 5/16-inch hoses; air hoses for pneumatic tools usually have 5/16 to 3/8-inch inside diameters. A few of the air tools described in Chapter 4 require hoses of specified inside diameters, which the tool manufacturers usually supply.

Adapters and Couplings

An adapter is a type of connection that is male on one end and female on the other. It is used to convert the connections on the hose and other equipment from one thread size to another. Adapters are available in a very wide variety of sizes and threads.

A coupling is a type of connection that is male on both ends. It is used to couple two pieces of hose or pipe together or to convert a female connection of one size thread to a male connection of another size thread.

5.4 AIR SYSTEM MAINTENANCE

The manufacturer's specific maintenance schedule given in the owner's manual should be followed exactly. In general, however, all air systems require the following periodic maintenance:

Daily

- Drain the air receiver and drain the moisture separator/regulator or air transformer. If the weather is humid, drain them several times a day.
- Check the level of the oil in the crankcase. While it should be kept at full level, do not overfill. Overfilling causes excessive oil usage.
- SAE 10W-30, a multigrade oil, can be used as a substitute when SAE 10 or 20 weight oil is not readily available. Multigrade oils do contain additives that can cause harmful carbon residue and varnish. Detergent type oils are satisfactory if used before hard carbon deposits have developed. Before changing to a detergent type oil, pistons, rings, valves, and cylinder head should be cleaned since the detergent oil can loosen hard carbon deposits that can plug passages and damage cylinders and bearings.

WEEKLY

- Pull the ring on the safety valve and unseat it. If the valve is working properly, it will release air as follows:

  —Valves located on the air receiver or check valve release air when the tank contains compressed air.

  —Valves located on the compressor inner cooler release air only during compressor operation.

  Reseat the safety valve by pushing down the stem with your finger. If the valve malfunctions, repair or replace immediately.

- Clean air filters. Felt and foam air filters should be washed in nonexplosive solvent, allowed to dry, and reinstalled. A dirty air filter decreases compressor efficiency and will increase oil usage.

- Clean or blow off fins on cylinders, heads, intercoolers, aftercoolers, and any other parts of the compressor or outfit that collect dust or dirt. A clean compressor runs cooler and provides longer service.

- Check the oil filter in the air line and change the filter element if necessary.

MONTHLY

- Add or change the compressor crankcase oil. Under **clean** operating conditions, the oil should be changed at the end of 500 running hours or every six months, whichever occurs first. If operating conditions are **not clean,** change oil more frequently.

- Adjust the pressure switch cut-in and cut-out settings.

- Check relief valve or CPR for exhausting head pressure each time the motor stops.

- Tighten belts to prevent slippage. A heated motor pulley is a sign of loose belts. Overtightening of belts can cause motor overload or premature failure of motor and compressor bearings.

- Check and align a loose motor pulley or compressor flywheel. It will be necessary to remove the front section of the enclosed belt guard.

- Tighten all valve plugs and covers on the compressor head to insure that each valve does not become loose and damage the valve or piston.

- Check for air leaks on the compressor outfit and air piping system.

- Check compressor pump up time when the air receiver outlet valve is closed.
- Listen for unusual noises.
- Check and correct oil leaks.

5.5 AIR SYSTEM SAFETY

An air compressor system is a very **safe** arrangement to operate. Accidents seldom happen, but the few that do occur can usually be traced to **human error.** To lessen the chance of human error, keep in mind the following safety precautions that should always be observed:

🚗 SHOP TALK

- **Read the instructions.** *Learn what each part of the compressor does by carefully reading the owner's manual that comes with the unit.*

- **Inspect before each use.** *Carefully check the hoses, fittings, air control equipment, and overall appearance of the compressor before each use. Never operate a damaged unit.*

- **Proper electrical outlets.** *Electrical damage often results from using improperly grounded outlets. Use only a properly grounded outlet that will accept a three-prong plug.*

- **Always run the compressor on a dry surface.** *The compressor should be located where there is a circulation of clean, dry air. Avoid getting dust, dirt, and paint spray on the unit.*

- **Starts and stops.** *Most compressors start and stop automatically. Never attempt to service a unit that is connected to a power supply.*

- **Keep hands away.** *Fast moving parts will cause injury. Keep fingers away from the compressor while it is running. Do not wear loose clothing that will get caught in the moving parts. Unplug the compressor before working on it.*

- **Keep the belt guard on.** *Use all the safety devices available and keep them in operating condition. Also, remember that compressors become hot during operation. Exercise caution before touching the unit.*

- **Release air slowly.** *Fast moving air will stir dust and debris. Be safe! Release air* slowly by using a pressure regulator to reduce pressure to that recommended for the tool.

- **Keep air hose untangled.** *Keep the air, power, and extension cords away from sharp objects, chemical spills, oil spills, and wet floors. All of these can cause injury.*
- **Depressurize the tank.** *Be sure the pressure regulator gauge reads zero before removing the hose or changing the air tools. The quick release of high pressure air can cause injury.*

5.6 REVIEW QUESTIONS

1. Which type of compressor is seldom found in a body shop?
   a. piston reciprocating type compressor
   b. diaphragm compressor
   c. one-stage compressor
   d. two-stage compressor

2. The piston compressor is _____.
   a. less durable than the diaphragm compressor
   b. more durable than the diaphragm compressor
   c. one that requires lubrication
   d. both b and c

3. This is the actual amount of free air in cubic feet that the compressor can pump in 1 minute at working pressure.
   a. cfm
   b. displacement cfm
   c. free air cfm
   d. psi

4. What does the displacement of a two-stage compressor equal?
   a. the sum of the two stages
   b. the difference between the stages
   c. that given for the first stage
   d. none of the above

5. Air tanks have _____.
   a. horizontal mountings
   b. vertical mountings
   c. horizontal mounted wheels
   d. all of the above
   e. both a and c

6. Which safety control is designed to maintain a supply of air within given pressure limits on gasoline and electrically driven compressors when it is not practical to start and stop the motor?
   a. pressure switch
   b. automatic unloader
   c. centrifugal pressure release
   d. overload protection

7. What is the recommended fuse rating for a fused disconnect switch?
   a. equal to the current rating stamped on the meter
   b. twice the current rating stamped on the motor
   c. three times the current rating stamped on the motor
   d. none of the above

8. The intake air filter must be made of _____.
   a. fiberglass
   b. fine mesh
   c. felt material
   d. all of the above
   e. both b and c

9. How far away from the compressor unit should an air transformer be installed?
   a. at least 5 feet
   b. at least 15 feet
   c. at least 25 feet
   d. at least 35 feet

10. Which of the following is often combined with a lubricator in a single unit?
    a. thermal conditioning equipment
    b. air condenser
    c. air pressure regulator
    d. both b and c
    e. none of the above

11. How much pressure is dropped at 60 PSIG when using a 50-foot length 1/4-inch (ID) air hose?
    a. 20.5
    b. 6.0
    c. 4.5
    d. 1.5

CHAPTER

6

Welding Equipment and Its Use

OBJECTIVES

After reading this chapter, you will be able to:

- identify the three classes of welding.
- explain how to use a MIG welding machine.
- name the six basic welding techniques employed with MIG equipment.
- determine where and how to use resistance spot welding.
- identify oxyacetylene welding equipment and techniques.
- explain general brazing and soldering techniques used in a body shop.
- describe plasma arc cutting of body panels.
- explain plasma cutting techniques.
- list safety procedures important in each welding operation.

There are two basic methods of joining metal together in the automobile assembly:

- Mechanical methods (Figure 6-1)
- Metal welding methods (Figure 6-2)

Welding is one method of repair in which heat is applied to the pieces of metal to fuse them together into the shape desired. For all practical purposes, welding can be divided into three main categories:

- **Pressure welding.** This is a method in which the metal is heated to a softened state by electrodes, pressure is applied, and the metal is joined. Of the various types of pressure welding, electric resistance welding (spot welding) is an indispensable welding method used in automobile manufacturing and to a lesser degree in repair operations.
- **Fusion welding.** Pieces of metal are heated to the melting point, joined together (usually with a filler rod), and allowed to cool.
- **Braze welding.** Metal with a melting point that is lower than the pieces of base metal to be joined is melted over the joint of the pieces being welded (without melting the pieces of base metal). Braze welding is classified as either soft or hard brazing, depending on the temperature at which the brazing material melts. Soft brazing is done with brazing material that melts at temperatures below 850 degrees Fahrenheit and hard brazing is done with brazing materials that melt at temperatures above 850 degrees Fahrenheit.

As shown in Table 6-1, there are distinct welding methods within each respective category. Many of these methods can be used in the auto body shop.

Welding Characteristics

Joint welding is indispensable in the restoration of collision damaged vehicles. The characteristics of welding can be summarized as follows:

- Since the shape of welding joints is limitless, it is the perfect method for joining a unibody structure, while still maintaining body integrity.
- Weight can be reduced (no fasteners are necessary).
- Air and water tightness are excellent.
- Production efficiency is very high.
- The strength of a welded joint is greatly influenced by the level of skill of the operator.
- The surrounding panels will warp if too much heat is used.

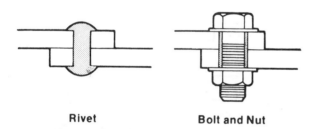

Rivet   Bolt and Nut

FIGURE 6-1   Mechanical joining methods

FIGURE 6-2   One metal welding method used in automobile work

Welding in the Auto Body Shop

New welding techniques and equipment have entered the auto body repair picture, replacing the one time popular arc and oxyacetylene processes (Figure 6-3). The reason for this is that the new steel alloys used in today's cars **cannot** be welded properly with the latter two processes. At the present time, gas metal arc welding (GMAW)—better known as metal inert gas (MIG) welding—offers more advantages than other methods for welding high-strength steels (HSS) and high-strength, low-alloy (HSLA) steel component parts used in unibody cars. As described in Chapter 7, most of the applications of HSS and HSLA steels are confined to body structures, reinforcement gussets, brackets, and supports rather than large panels or outer skin panels.

The advantages of MIG welding (Figure 6-4) over conventional stick electrode arc welding (Fig-

TABLE 6-1: WELDING METHODS

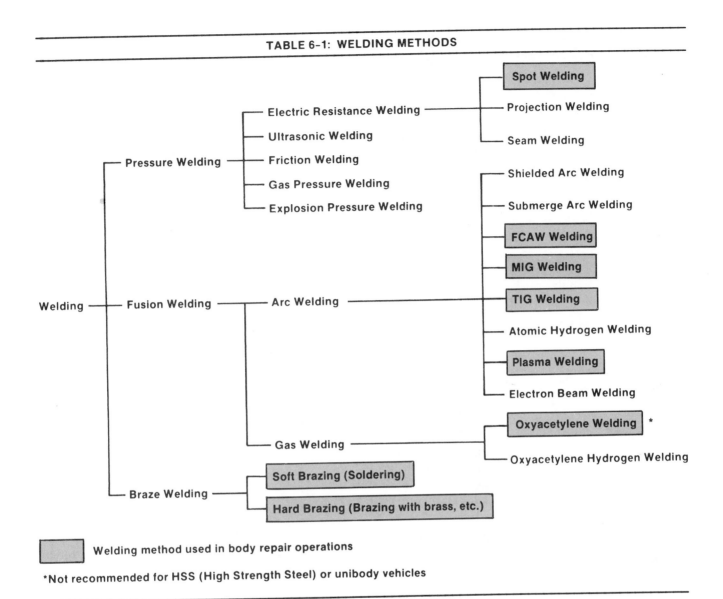

```
                                                                    ┌─ Spot Welding
                                    ┌─ Electric Resistance Welding ─┼─ Projection Welding
                                    │                                └─ Seam Welding
                                    ├─ Ultrasonic Welding
             ┌─ Pressure Welding ───┼─ Friction Welding
             │                      ├─ Gas Pressure Welding        ┌─ Shielded Arc Welding
             │                      └─ Explosion Pressure Welding  ├─ Submerge Arc Welding
             │                                                     ├─ FCAW Welding
             │                                                     ├─ MIG Welding
Welding ─────┼─ Fusion Welding ──┬─ Arc Welding ───────────────────┼─ TIG Welding
             │                   │                                 ├─ Atomic Hydrogen Welding
             │                   │                                 ├─ Plasma Welding
             │                   │                                 └─ Electron Beam Welding
             │                   │                                 ┌─ Oxyacetylene Welding  *
             │                   └─ Gas Welding ────────────────────┤
             │                                                     └─ Oxyacetylene Hydrogen Welding
             │                      ┌─ Soft Brazing (Soldering)
             └─ Braze Welding ──────┤
                                    └─ Hard Brazing (Brazing with brass, etc.)
```

▢ Welding method used in body repair operations

*Not recommended for HSS (High Strength Steel) or unibody vehicles

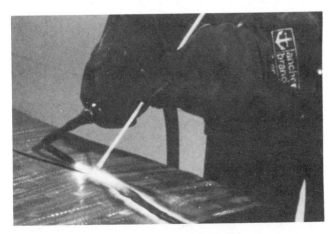

FIGURE 6-3   The once popular oxyacetylene welding process is no longer recommended for automobile work.

FIGURE 6-4   MIG is the number one welding method in auto repair work.

FIGURE 6-5 Conventional stick electrode or shielded arc welding

ure 6-5) are so numerous that car manufacturers now recommend that it be used in all of their dealerships, not only for HSS and unibody repair, but for **all** structural collision repair. This recommendation extends also to independent collision repair shops. Here are some of the advantages of MIG welding.

- MIG is easy to learn to use. The typical welder can learn to use MIG equipment and actually reach a peak level of proficiency in just a few hours of instruction and practice. Moreover, experience shows that even an average MIG welder can produce higher quality welds, faster and more consistently than a highly skilled welder using conventional stick electrode welds.
- MIG produces 100 percent fusion in the parent metals. This means MIG welds can be dressed or ground down flush with the surface (for cosmetic reasons) without loss of strength.
- Low current can be used for thin metals. This prevents heat damage to adjacent areas that can cause strength loss and warping.
- The arc is smooth, the weld puddle small, so it is easily controlled (Figure 6-6). This ensures maximum metal deposit with minimum splatter.
- MIG welding is more tolerant of gaps and misfits. Several gaps can be spot welded by making several spots on top of each other—

immediately. (No slag to remove.) Therefore, the area can be easily refinished.

- Almost all steels can be welded with one common type of weld wire. What is in the machine is generally right for any job.
- Metals of different thicknesses can be welded with the same diameter of wire. Again, what is in the machine is right for any job.
- The MIG welder can control the temperature of the weld and the time the weld takes place.
- With MIG welding, the small area to be welded is heated for a short period of time, therefore reducing metal fatigue, warpage, and distortion of the panel. Vertical and/or overhead welding is possible because the metal is molten for a very short time.

The other type of welding that is being recommended in collision repair work of newer vehicles is portable resistance spot welding (Figure 6-7). This

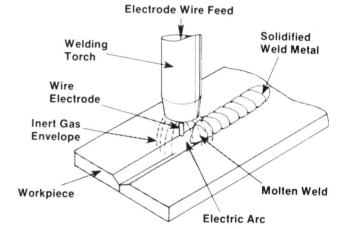

FIGURE 6-6 Basic MIG welding process

FIGURE 6-7 Use a portable squeeze type resistance spot welding gun to weld a left rear quarter panel to the body lower back panel. (Courtesy of Lors Machinery, Inc.)

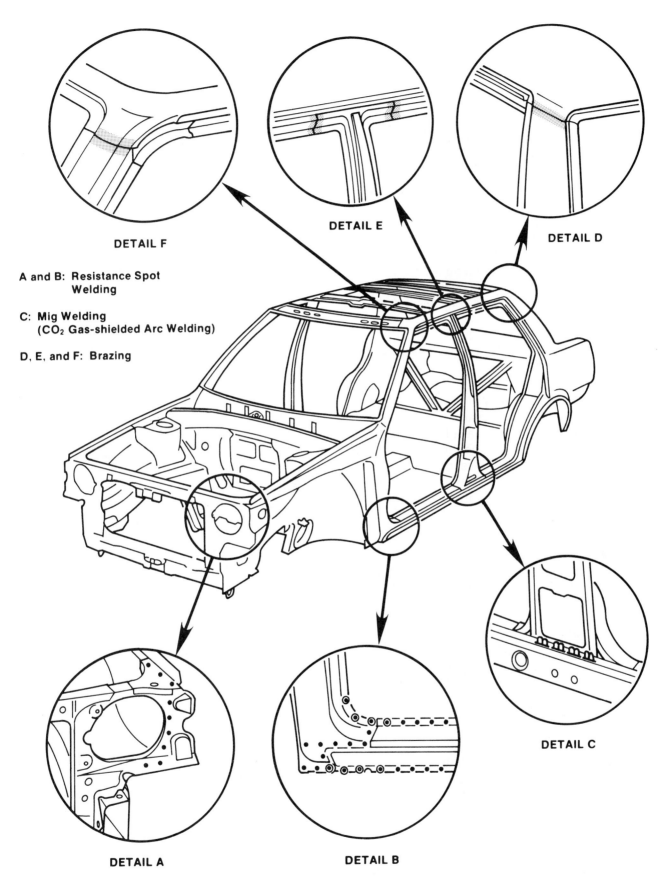

DETAIL F

DETAIL E

DETAIL D

A and B: Resistance Spot
Welding

C: Mig Welding
(CO₂ Gas-shielded Arc Welding)

D, E, and F: Brazing

DETAIL C

DETAIL A

DETAIL B

FIGURE 6-8 Welding methods used in vehicle production. *(Courtesy of Nissan Motor Corp.)*

type of equipment is used to form spot weld attachments like the production welds. To use this kind of spot welding equipment the operator must install the proper extensions and electrodes on the welder to provide access to the area being welded. The clamping force on the so-called squeeze type resistance spot welder for the panels being welded must be properly adjusted. On some equipment, the amperage current flow and timing are all made with one adjustment. After the adjustments are made, the spot welder is positioned for the panels being joined, making sure the electrodes are directly opposite to each other. The trigger is squeezed and the spot weld takes place.

The resistance spot welder provides very fast, high-quality welds while maintaining the best control of temperature buildup in adjacent panels and structure. It also probably requires the least skill to operate.

In the body shop when reference is made to resistance type spot welders, it generally describes the type of welding that requires the actual weld to take place on both sides of all panels at the same time, not the type of spot weld that welds panels together from the same side at the same time. Opposite side spot welding is a structural weld.

Be sure to consult the car manufacturer's recommendations in the vehicle's service manual before welding. When replacing body panels, all the new welds should be similar in size to the original factory welds. Except when spot welding, the number of replacement welds should be the same as the original number of welds in production. Strength and durability requirements differ depending on the location of the part that is to be welded to the body. The factory decides what is the most appropriate welding method (Figure 6–8) by first determining the intended use, the physical characteristics, and the location of the part as it is assembled onto the auto body.

It is essential that appropriate welding methods, which do not reduce the original strength and durability of the body, be used when making repairs. This will be accomplished if the following basic points are observed:

- Try to use either spot welding or MIG/MAG (metal inert gas/metal active gas) welding.
- Do **not** braze any body components other than those brazed at the factory.
- Do **not** use an oxyacetylene torch for welding late model auto bodies.

 SHOP TALK

Regardless of the type of welding that is going to be undertaken, the surface must be properly cleaned before starting the welding procedure. Remove all surface materials back to the bare metal (Figure 6–9). When dirt, rust, sealers, paint, or galvanized or other zinc-rich materials are left in the area of the weld, these materials will burn during the application of heat and the ash or oxidized material can become a part of the weld. The dirt and foreign material cause the weld to be weakened and, in some cases, prevent a proper weld from being made.

6.1 MIG WELDING

As already mentioned, MIG became popular in body shops when auto manufacturers began using thin-gauge, high-strength, low-alloy (HSLA) steels. Car makers insisted that the only correct way to weld HSLA and other thin-gauge steel was with MIG (or similar gas metal arc welding [GMAW] system). And once the MIG welder was in place, it was easy to see that it provided clean, fast welds for all applications. Welding a rear quarter panel with an oxyacetylene welder averages about 4 hours. A MIG welder can do the same job in about 40 minutes.

MIG welding is not limited to body repairs alone. It is also ideal for exhaust work, repairing mechanical supports, installing trailer hitches and truck

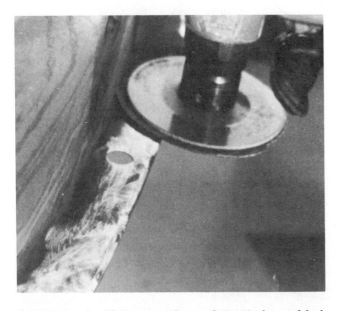

FIGURE 6–9 Make sure the surfaces to be welded are completely free of rust and scale. This is best removed by grinding, sanding, or sandblasting.

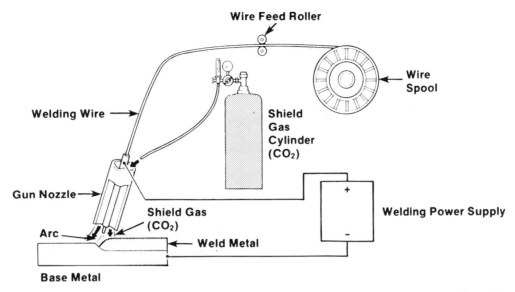

FIGURE 6-10   The principle of MIG welding. *(Courtesy of Toyota Motor Corp.)*

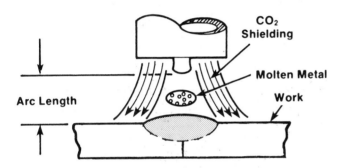

FIGURE 6-11   Carbon dioxide (CO_2) protects the molten metal from contamination by the atmosphere.

bumpers, and any other welds that would be done with either an arc or gas welder. In addition, it is possible to weld aluminum castings like cracked transmission cases, cylinder heads, and intake manifolds.

Principles and Characteristics

The MIG welding method uses a welding wire that is fed automatically at a constant speed as an electrode. A short arc is generated between the base metal and the wire, and the resulting heat from the arc melts the welding wire and joins the base metals together. Since the wire is fed automatically at a constant rate, this method is also called semiautomatic arc welding. During the welding process (Figure 6-10), either inert or active gas shields the weld from the atmosphere and prevents oxidation of the

base metal. The type of inert or active gas used depends on the base material to be welded. For most steel welds, carbon dioxide (CO_2) is used (Figure 6-11). With aluminum, either pure argon gas or a mixture of argon and helium is used, depending on the alloy and the thickness of the material. It is even possible to weld stainless steel by using argon gas with a little oxygen (between 4 and 5 percent) added.

 **SHOP TALK**

MIG welding is sometimes called carbon dixoide arc welding. Actually, MIG welding (metal inert gas) uses a fully inert gas such as argon or helium as a shield gas. Since carbon dioxide gas is not a completely inert gas, it is more accurately called MAG welding (metal active gas). Although most auto body shop welding is done with carbon dioxide gas as the shield gas, the term MIG is used to describe all gas metal arc welding processes. In fact, many welders on the market can use carbon dioxide (a semiactive gas) or argon (inert gas) by simply changing the gas cylinder and the regulator.

MIG welding uses the short circuit arc method that is a unique method of depositing molten drops of metal onto the base metal. Welding of thin sheet metal for automobiles can cause welding strain, blow holes, and warped panels. To prevent these problems, it is necessary to limit the amount of heat

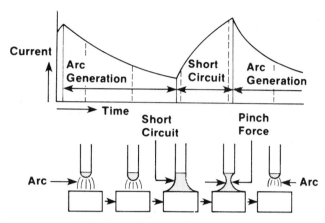

FIGURE 6-12   How the short arc method operates

near the weld. The short circuit arc method uses very thin welding rods, a low current, and low voltage. By using this technique the amount of heat introduced into the panels is kept to a minimum and penetration of the base metal is quite shallow.

As shown in Figure 6-12, the end of the wire is melted by the heat of the arc and forms into a drop, which then comes in contact with the base metal and creates a short circuit. When this happens, a large current flows through the metal and the shorted portion is torn away by the pinch force or burnback, which re-establishes the arc. That is, the bare wire electrode is fed continuously into the weld puddle at a controlled, constant rate, where it short circuits, and the arc goes out. While the arc is out, the puddle flattens and cools; but the wire continues to feed, shorting to the workpiece again. This heating and cooling happens on an average of 100 times a second. The metal is transferred to the workpiece with each of these short circuits. Generally, if current is flowing through a cylindrically shaped fluid (in this case molten metal) or current is flowing through an arc, the current is pulled toward the weld. This works as a constricting force in the direction of the center of the cylinder. This action is known as the pinch effect, and the size of the force is called the **pinch force** (Figure 6-13).

In summary, the MIG process works like this:

- At the weld site the wire undergoes a split-second sequence of short circuiting, burn-back, and arcing (Figure 6-14).
- Each sequence produces a short arc transfer of a minute drop of electrode metal from the tip of the wire to the weld puddle.
- A gas curtain or shield surrounds the wire electrode. This gas shield prevents contamination from the atmosphere and helps to stabilize the arc.

- The continuously fed electrode wire contacts the work and sets up a short circuit, and resistance heats the wire and the weld site.
- As the heating continues, the wire begins to melt and thin out or neck down.
- Increasing resistance in the neck accelerates the heating in this area.
- The molten neck burns through, depositing a puddle on the workpiece and starting the arc.
- The arc tends to flatten the puddle and burn back the electrode.
- With the arc gap at its widest, it cools, allowing the wire feed to move the electrode closer to the work.
- The short end starts to heat up again, enough to further flatten the puddle but not enough to keep the electrode from recontacting the workpiece. This extinguishes the arc, re-establishes the short circuit, and restarts the process.
- This complete cycle occurs automatically at a frequency ranging from 50 to 200 cycles a second.

6.2 MIG WELDING EQUIPMENT

Most MIG welding equipment that is used in and designed for collision repair work, as mentioned ear-

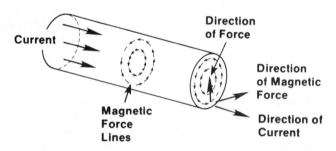

FIGURE 6-13   Typical pinch force and how it is formed

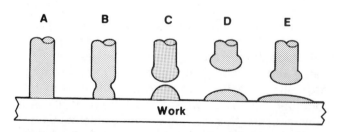

FIGURE 6-14   Here is the typical action of the welding wire as it burns back from the work during the MIG welding process.

• Welding gun and cable assembly that the welder holds to direct the wire to the weld area.

The gas that is most commonly used for collision repair welding is either carbon dioxide (CO_2) or a mixture of argon/carbon dixoide, in a ratio of 75 percent argon, 25 percent carbon dioxide. This latter mixture is usually referred to as C-25 gas.

Generally speaking, fine diameter welding wires are used—1/64 through 1/32 inch (roughly equivalent in diameter to the fine-line and ultra-fine leads of today's mechanical pencils). A wire becoming more commonly used today is 1/64 inch. Once a specialty wire, it is now stocked by most wire manufacturers. These small diameter wires can be used at low currents and voltages, thus greatly reducing heat input to the base material.

Because of the power demands in this process, it is necessary to use a constant potential, constant voltage power source. For auto body applications, these power sources are usually self-contained, meaning the power source, wire feed equipment, and wire are all in one unit (Figure 6–16). The controls found on this type of power source would be a

FIGURE 6–15 Basic components of a MIG setup

lier, is considered semiautomatic. This means that the machine's operation is automatic, but the gun is hand controlled. Before starting to weld, the operator sets:

• Voltage for the arc
• Wire speed
• Shielding gas flow rate and presses the power button

Then the operator has complete freedom to concentrate entirely on the weld site, the molten puddle, and whatever welding technique that is used.

Regardless of the type of MIG equipment used, it will comprise the following basic components (Figure 6–15):

• Supply of shielding gas with a flow regulator to protect the molten weld pool from contamination
• Wire/feed control to feed the wire at the required speed
• Spool of electrode wire of a specified type and diameter
• MIG type of welder machine connected to an electrical power supply
• Work cable and clamp assembly

FIGURE 6–16 A self-contained MIG unit

FIGURE 6-17 Typical control panel of MIG welder unit

voltage adjustment and wire feed speed adjustment. Some optional controls available on this type of equipment (Figure 6-17) are a spot control and pulse control.

MIG spot welding is termed consumable spot because the welding wire is consumed in the weld puddle. Consumable spot welds can be made in a variety of methods and in all positions using various nozzles supplied with this option.

When spot welding different thicknesses of materials, the lighter gauge material should always be spotted to the heavy material.

Spot welding usually requires greater heat to the weld than for continuous or pulse welding. It is best to use sample materials when setting the controls for spot welding. To check a spot weld, pull the the two pieces apart. A good weld will tear a small hole out of the bottom piece. If the weld pulls apart easily, increase the weld time or heat. After each spot is complete, the trigger must be released and then pulled for the next spot. MIG spot has the advantage of an easily grindable crown. The procedure does not leave any depression requiring a fill.

The pulse control allows continuous seam welding on the material with less chance of burn-through

or distortion. This is accomplished by starting and stopping the wire for preset times without releasing the trigger. The weld "on" time and weld "off" time can be set for the operator's preference and metal thickness.

The burnback control on most MIG gives an adjustable burnback of the electrode to prevent it from sticking in the puddle at the end of a weld.

In MIG welding the polarity of the power source is important in determining the penetration to the workpiece. DC power sources used for MIG welding typically use DC reverse polarity. This means the wire (electrode) is positive and the workpiece is negative. Weld penetration is greatest using this connection.

Weld penetration is also greatest using CO_2 gas. However, CO_2 gives a harsher, more unstable arc, which leads with increased spatter. So when welding on thin materials, it is preferable to use argon/CO_2 (Figure 6-18) and if the material is super thin, weld in straight polarity. In straight polarity, the wire (electrode) would be negative and the workpiece would be positive. This would put more heat in the wire, providing less penetration. The disadvantage of using straight polarity would be a high rope-like bead, requiring more grinding.

Voltage adjustment and wire feed speed must be set according to the diameter of the wire being used. It should be noted that when setting these parameters, manufacturers' recommendations should be followed to reach approximate settings. When rough parameters are selected, change only one variable at a time until the machine is fine tuned for an optimum welding condition. MIG welders can be tuned in using both visual and audio signals.

75% Argon 25% CO_2	50% Argon 50% CO_2	CO_2

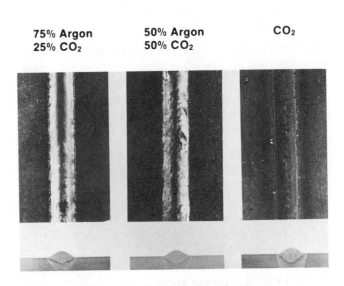

FIGURE 6-18 Typical weld penetration

FIGURE 6-19 Check the manufacturer's manual before hooking up the equipment.

A

B

FIGURE 6-20 (A) Install the shielding gas cylinder with care and (B) chain or strap it in place.

FIGURE 6-21 Installing the regulator on the cylinder

FIGURE 6-22 Attaching the clamp to clean metal

6.3 MIG OPERATION METHODS

Match the welding power unit in the MIG machine to the available input voltage, following the procedure prescribed on the machine or in the manufacturer's manual (Figure 6-19).

Handle the cylinder of shielding gas with care. It might be pressurized to more than two thousand pounds per square inch. Chain or strap the cylinder to a support sturdy enough to hold it securely to the MIG machine's running gear (Figure 6-20), if it is so equipped, or to a wall, post, or the like. Install the regulator, making sure to observe the recommended safety precautions (Figure 6-21).

When the clamp is attached to clean metal on the vehicle (Figure 6-22) near the weld site, it completes the welding circuit from the machine to the work and back to the machine. This clamp is not

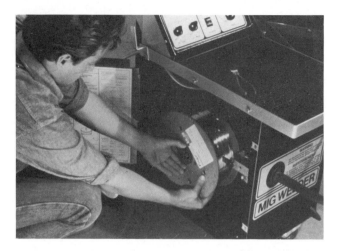

FIGURE 6-23 Adjusting the wire feeder

referred to as a ground cable or ground clamp. The ground connection is for safety purposes and is usually made from the machine's case to the building ground through the third wire in the electric input cable.

Consult the manufacturer's manual as to the specific procedure for assembling, installing, and adjusting the wire feeder components (Figure 6-23). In general, the adjustment of the wire feeder can be done as follows:

- Mount the wire. Feed the wire manually for about 12 inches making sure that it travels freely through the gun assembly.
- A correct setting on the drive rollers will assure just enough pressure on the wire to pull it off the wire spool and through the gun/cable assembly (Figure 6-24). The tension

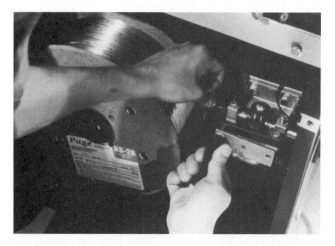

FIGURE 6-24 Making sure the drive roll grooves, wire guides, cable liner, and gun contact tube correspond with the size of wire being used

FIGURE 6-25 The tension should be light enough so the wire slips at the rollers when it is stopped at the nozzle of the gun.

must be set so that the wire will slip at the rollers when the wire is stopped at the nozzle, but tight enough to withstand a 30 to 40 degree deflection. If too much pressure is applied, the wire will be deformed, creating a spiral effect through the liner and erratic feed.

- Stopping the wire at the tip with this much pressure will also cause the wire to bird-nest between the rollers and cable entrance. The tension on the wire spool spindle should also be set so that the wire can be pulled off easily but just tight enough to stop the spool from free wheeling when the trigger is released (Figure 6-25).

The proper handling of any welding equipment is an essential ingredient in successful welding. When tuning the MIG welder for any given welding job, the operator has to deal with a number of parameters, meaning values that are variable: input voltage to the welding equipment, welding current, arc voltage, tip-to-base metal distance, torch angle, welding direction, shield gas flow volume, welding speed, and wire speed. Most manufacturers of MIG welders provide tables that show the variable control parameters that apply to their machines.

Welding Current

The welding current affects the base metal penetration depth (Figure 6-26), the speed at which the wire is melted, arc stability, and the amount of weld spatter. As the electrical current is increased, the penetration depth, excess metal height, and bead width also increase (Table 6-2).

Arc Voltage

Good welding results depend on a proper arc length. The length of the arc is determined by the arc voltage. When the arc voltage is set properly, a continuous light hissing or cracking sound is emitted from the welding area.

When the arc voltage is high, the arc length increases, the penetration is shallow, and the bead is wide and flat.

When the arc voltage is low, the arc length decreases, penetration is deep, and the bead is narrow and dome shaped.

Since the length of the arc depends on the amount of voltage, voltage that is too high will result in an overly long arc and an increase in the amount of weld spatter (Figure 6–27). A sputtering sound and no arc means that the voltage is too low.

Tip-to-Base Metal Distance

The tip-to-base distance (Figure 6-28) is also an important factor in obtaining good welding results. The standard distance is approximately 1/4 to 5/8 inches.

If the tip-to-base metal distance is too long, the length of wire protruding from the end of the gun

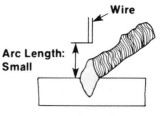

Low-Arc Voltage

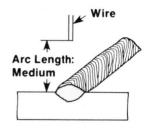

Medium Arc Voltage

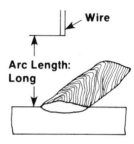

High-Arc Voltage

FIGURE 6-27   Arc voltage and bead shape

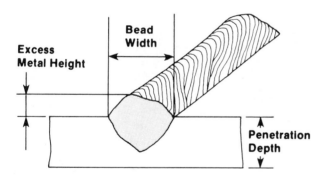

FIGURE 6-26   Penetration depth, excess metal height, and bead width. (Courtesy of Toyota Motor Corp.)

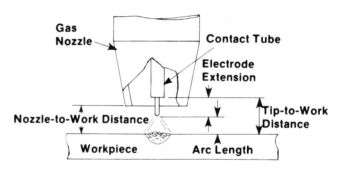

FIGURE 6-28   Tip-to-base metal distance

TABLE 6-2: RELATIONSHIP BETWEEN WIRE DIAMETER, PANEL THICKNESS, AND WELDING CURRENT							
	Panel Thickness						
Wire Diameter	1/64"	1/32"	Less Than 3/64"	3/64"	1/16"	3/32"	1/8"
1/64"	20-30A	30-40A	40-50A	50-60A	—	—	—
1/32"	—	—	40-50A	50-60A	60-90A	100-120A	—
More Than 1/32"	—	—	—	—	60-90A	100-120A	120-150A

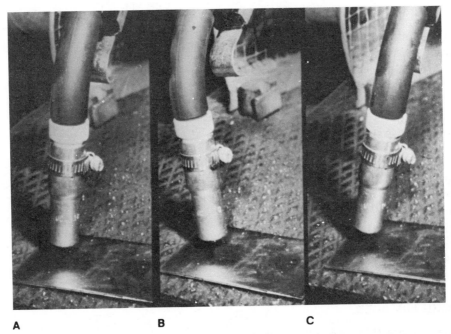

A   B   C

FIGURE 6-29 (A) Hold the torch at a transverse angle of 90 degrees directly over the center of the joint. Find the longitudinal angle by experimentation. (B) The trailing or dragging torch angle—where the torch is pointing opposite or reverse to the direction of travel—should be tried first at about 10 degrees perpendicular. (C) A leading or pushing torch angle—where the torch is pointing forward in the direction of travel—should be used at the same inclination.

increases and becomes preheated, which increases the melting speed of the wire. Also, the shield gas effect will be reduced if the tip-to-base metal distance is too long.

If the tip-to-base metal distance is too short, it becomes difficult to see the progress of the weld because it will be hidden behind the tip of the gun.

Gun Angle and Welding

There are two methods: the forward or forehand method and the reverse or backhand method (Figure 6-29). With the forward method, the penetration depth is shallow and the bead is flat. With the reverse method, the penetration is deep and a large amount of metal is deposited (Figure 6-30). The gun angle for both methods should be between 10 and 30 degrees.

Shield Gas Flow Volume

Precise gas flow is essential to a good weld. If the volume of gas is too high, it will flow in eddies and reduce the shield effect. If there is not enough gas, the shield effect will also be reduced. Adjustment is made in accordance with the distance between the nozzle and the base metal, the welding current, welding speed, and welding environment

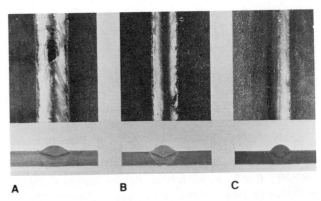

A   B   C

FIGURE 6-30 **The penetration and weld pattern for the three travel methods: (A) forehand; (B) transverse angle of 90 degrees; (C) and backhand (reverse)**

(nearby air currents). The standard flow volume is approximately 1-3/8 to 1-1/2 cubic inches per minute.

Welding Speed

If the operator welds at a rapid pace, the penetration depth and bead width will decrease, and the bead will be dome shaped. If the speed is increased

TABLE 6-3: WELDING SPEED	
Panel Thickness	Welding Speed (in./min.)
1/32"	41-11/32-45-9/32
More Than 1/32"	39-3/8
3/64"	35-7/16-39-3/8
1/16"	31-1/2-33-15/32

even faster, undercutting can occur. Welding at too low of a speed can cause burn-through holes. Ordinarily, welding speed is determined by base metal panel thickness and/or voltage of the welding machine (Table 6-3).

Wire Speed

An even, high-pitched buzzing sound indicates the correct wire-to-heat ratio producing a temperature in the 9000 degrees Fahrenheit range. Visual signs of the correct setting occur when a steady reflected light starts to fade in intensity as the arc is shortened and wire speed is increased.

If the wire speed is too slow (Figure 6-31), a hiss and a plop sound will be heard as the wire melts away from the puddle and deposits the molten gob back. The visual signal will be a much brighter reflected light.

Too much wire speed will choke the arc. More wire is being deposited than the heat and puddle can absorb. The result is spitting and sputtering as the wire melts into tiny balls of molten metal that fly away from the weld. The visual signal is a strobe light arc effect.

Before this critical ratio can be obtained, a thorough understanding of what is happening to produce these signals is essential. Using wire and C-25 gas, a heat setting producing approximately 24 volts and 45 to 50 amperes; approximately 200 to 230

FIGURE 6-31   If the wire speed is too slow, increase the dial setting on the welder.

FIGURE 6-32   Prior to contact, the wire has been charged and the gas flow started.

short circuits and deposits take place per second producing a high-pitched sound.

When the trigger is first activated, a solid steel wire makes its initial contact with a solid steel plate. Prior to contact, the wire has been charged with current and the gas flow has been started (Figure 6-32). The first contact produces tiny sparks of oxide being burned off the wire and base metal.

Immediately after the oxide sparks, tiny molten balls are produced as the wire melts prior to having a molten puddle that will absorb them. Once the heat creates the puddle, the balls stop. A consistent transfer and sound with only oxide sparks are present as they burn off the wire and base metal during the weld process.

In slow motion, after the arc transfer has been started, an on-off action occurs. It is off approximately from 1 to 230 deposits per second. Every time the metal is deposited a plop is heard. When it pulls away, a hiss is heard. Speeded up to 200 plops and hisses per second creates a smooth buzz.

Increasing and decreasing the wire speed causes the ball to burn farther back at 150 transfers than it does at 230. Similarly the sound is a lower buzz at 150 or visually a brighter light compared to a high-pitched buzz at 230 and a much dimmer light. The longer time the ball has to burn back, the more time the arc has to heat the molten puddle. Therefore, a flatter weld is produced with a slow wire speed.

When welding overhead, the danger of having too large a puddle and ball are obvious. The ball is pulled by gravity down onto the contact tip or into the gas nozzle where it can create serious problems.

TABLE 6-4: ADJUSTMENTS IN WELDING PARAMETERS AND TECHNIQUES

Welding Variables to Change	Desired Changes							
	Penetration		Deposition Rate		Bead Size		Bead Width	
	Increase	Decrease	Increase	Decrease	Increase	Decrease	Increase	Decrease
Current and Wire Feed Speed	Increase	Decrease	Increase	Decrease	Increase	Decrease	No effect	No effect
Voltage	Little effect	Little effect	No effect	No effect	No effect	No effect	Increase	Decrease
Travel Speed	Little effect	Little effect	No effect	No effect	Decrease	Increase	Increase	Decrease
Stickout	Decrease	Increase	Increase	Decrease	Increase	Decrease	Decrease	Increase
Wire Diameter	Decrease	Increase	Decrease	Increase	No effect	No effect	No effect	No effect
Shield Gas Percent CO_2	Increase	Decrease	No effect	No effect	No effect	No effect	Increase	Decrease
Torch Angle	Backhand to 25°	Forehand	No effect	No effect	No effect	No effect	Backhand	Forehand

Therefore, overhead welding should always be done with a higher wire speed with the arc and ball kept tiny and close together. Pressing the gas nozzle against the work insures that the wire is not moved out of the puddle. If it is moved out, the balls are produced by melting wire until a new puddle is formed to absorb them.

Normal buildup of oxide sparks in the gas nozzle area must be carefully removed before they fall inside and short out the nozzle. Balls caused by too slow a wire speed must also be removed before a short is formed.

As a summary, Table 6-4 outlines the various effects of several welding parameters and the changes necessary to alter a variety of weld characteristics.

Gun Nozzle Adjustment

The guns used on automotive MIG welders serve two main functions:

- To provide proper gas protection
- To allow pressure to be applied to the work area, thus preventing the wire from moving out of the puddle

If the insulation is bypassed, the power intended for the wire is transferred to the gas nozzle, causing the wire to glow and sputter and the nozzle to be burned up. Welding on dirty or rusty material can cause heavy bombardment into the nozzle and will require immediate cleaning if proper welding performance is to be achieved. To successfully weld on a poor rusty surface, slow the wire speed to approximately 130 transfers per second. Set the burnback control to its maximum and tap the trigger floating the ball on and off the material.

Of the four main components in a MIG welder, the nozzle area is the most crucial. The wire feed delivery is second. A clogged or damaged liner will cause erratic wire speed and produce molten balls that, in turn, will short out the gas nozzle.

To summarize the basic adjustment procedure of the gas nozzle, proceed as follows:

- **Arc generation.** Position the tip of the gun near the base metal. When the gun switch is activated (Figure 6-33), the wire is fed at the same time as the shield gas. Bring the end of the wire in contact with the base metal and create an arc. If the distance between the tip and the base metal is shortened a little, it will be easy to generate an arc (Figure 6-34). If the end of the wire forms a large ball, it will be difficult to generate an arc, so quickly cut off the end of the wire with a pair of wire cutters (Figure 6-35).

CAUTION: Hold the tip of the gun away from the face when cutting off the end of the wire.

FIGURE 6-33 Activating the gun switch starts the wire feed.

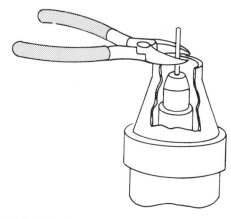

FIGURE 6-35 Cutting off the end of the wire with side cutters

A

B

FIGURE 6-34 (A) Typically, the contact tip should be flush with the nozzle to 1/8 inch inside it. (B) The wire should extend from 3/16 to 5/16 inch beyond the contact tip.

FIGURE 6-36 The use of antispatter compound

- **Spatter treatment.** Remove weld spatter promptly. If it adheres to the end of the nozzle, the shield gas will not flow properly and a poor weld will result. Antispatter compounds are available that reduce the amount of spatter that adheres to the nozzle (Figure 6-36). Weld spatter on the tip will prevent the wire from moving freely. If the wire feed switch is turned on and the wire is not able to move freely through the tip, the wire will become twisted inside the welder. Use a suitable tool, such as a file, to remove spatter from the tip and then check to see that the wire comes out smoothly.
- **Contact tip conditions.** To ensure a stable arc, the tip should be replaced if it has be-

FIGURE 6-37   Checking the tip condition

come worn. For a good current flow and stable arc, keep the tip properly tightened (Figure 6-37).

Clamping Tools for Welding

Locking jaw (vise) pliers, C-clamps, sheet metal screws, tack welds, or special clamps, described in Chapter 3, are necessary tools for good welding practices. Anybody can clamp panels together (Figure 6-38), but clamping panels together correctly to guarantee a sound weld will require close attention to every detail. As shown in Figure 6-39, a hammer and dolly can often be used to fit panels closely together in places that cannot be clamped.

Many times clamping both sides of a panel is not possible. In these cases, a simple technique using sheet metal screws can be employed to gain proper clamping during welding operations. To clamp panels together with sheet metal screws, the panels being welded together should have holes that are punched and drilled through the panel closest to the operator. In the case of plug welding, every other hole is filled with a sheet metal screw. The empty holes are then plug welded using proper plug welding techniques. After the original holes are plug welded, the sheet metal screws are removed and the holes left from the sheet metal screws are then plug welded.

Fixtures can also be used in some cases to hold panels to be welded in proper alignment. Fixtures alone, however, should not be depended upon to maintain tight clamping force at the welded joint. Some additional clamping will be required to make

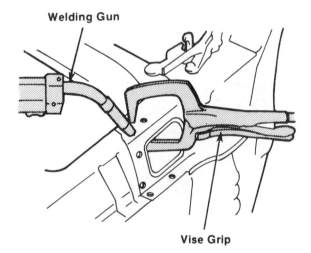

Welding Gun

Vise Grip

FIGURE 6-38   Clamping for front fender apron welding. *(Courtesy of Toyota Motor Corp.)*

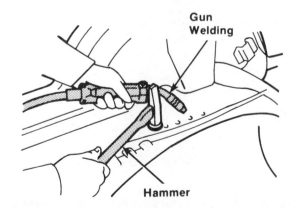

Gun Welding

Hammer

FIGURE 6-39   Clamping for floor pan welding. *(Courtesy of Toyota Motor Corp.)*

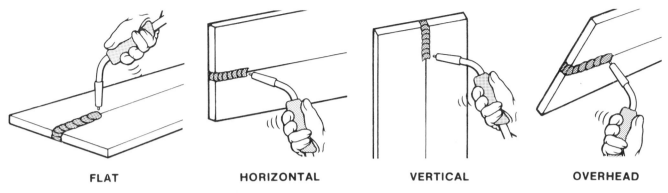

FLAT   HORIZONTAL   VERTICAL   OVERHEAD

FIGURE 6-40   Typical welding positions

FIGURE 6-41   Typical flat welding position

FIGURE 6-44   Typical overhead welding position

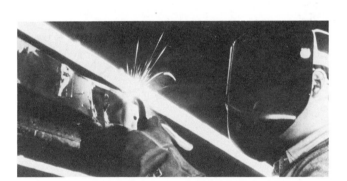

FIGURE 6-42   Typical horizontal welding position

FIGURE 6-43   Typical vertical welding position

sure that panels are tightly clamped together and not just held in proper alignment.

WELDING POSITION

In collision repair, the welding position is usually dictated by the location of the weld in the structure of the car. And both the heat and wire speed parameters can be affected by the welding position (Figure 6-40).

Flat welding is generally easier and faster and allows for the best penetration (Figure 6-41). When welding a member that is off the car, try to place it so that it can be welded in the flat position.

When welding a horizontal joint (Figure 6-42), angle the gun upward to hold the weld puddle in place against the pull of gravity.

When welding a vertical joint (Figure 6-43), the best procedure is usually to start the arc at the top of the joint and pull downward with a steady drag.

Overhead welding, as mentioned previously, is the most difficult. In this position (Figure 6-44), the danger of having too large a puddle is obvious; some of the molten metal can fall down into the nozzle, where it can create problems. So always do over-

163

head welding at a lower voltage, while keeping the arc as short as possible and the weld puddle as small as possible. Press the nozzle against the work to ensure that wire is not moved away from the puddle. It is best to pull the gun along the joint with a steady drag.

6.4 BASIC WELDING TECHNIQUES

As shown in Figure 6-45, there are six basic welding techniques employed with MIG equipment.

- **Tack weld.** The tack weld is exactly that: a tack—a relatively small, temporary MIG spot weld that is used instead of a clamp or sheet metal screw to tack and hold the fit-up in place while proceeding to make a permanent weld. And like the clamp or sheet metal screw, tack weld is always and only a temporary device. The distance between each tack weld is determined by the thickness of the panel. Ordinarily, a length of 15 to 30 times the thickness of the panel is appropriate (Figure 6-46). Temporary welds are very

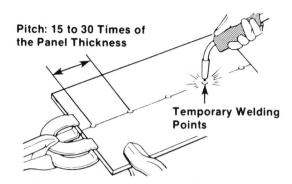

FIGURE 6-46   Temporary or tack welding. (Courtesy of Toyota Motor Corp.)

important in maintaining proper panel alignment and must be done accurately.

- **Continuous weld.** In a continuous weld, an uninterrupted seam or bead is laid down in a slow, steady, ongoing movement. Support the gun securely so it does not wobble. Use the forward method, moving the torch continuously at a constant speed, looking frequently at the welding bead. The gun should be inclined between 10 to 15 degrees to ob-

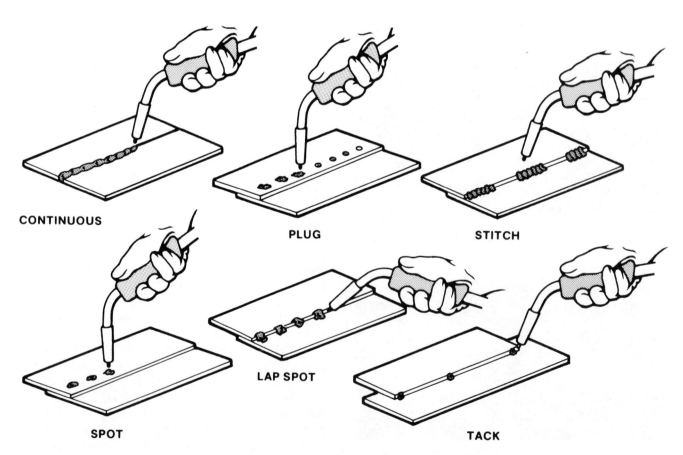

CONTINUOUS

PLUG

STITCH

SPOT

LAP SPOT

TACK

FIGURE 6-45   Basic welding techniques

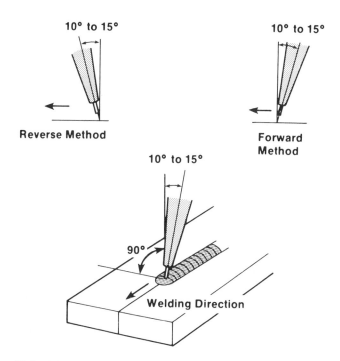

FIGURE 6-47 Continuous welding. (Courtesy of Toyota Motor Corp.)

tain the best bead shape, welding line, and shield effect (Figure 6-47). Maintain proper tip-base metal distance and correct gun angle. If the weld is not progressing well, the problem might be that the wire length is too long. If this is the case, penetration of the metal will not be adequate. For proper penetration and a better weld, bring the gun closer to the base metal. If the gun handling is smooth and even, the bead will be of consistent height and width, with a uniform, closely spaced ripple.

- **Plug weld.** To do a plug weld, a hole is drilled or punched through the outside piece (or pieces), the arc is directed through the hole to penetrate the inside piece, and the hole is filled with molten metal.

- **Spot weld.** In a MIG spot weld, the arc is directed to penetrate both pieces of metal, while triggering a timed impulse of wire feed.

- **Lap spot weld.** In the MIG lap spot technique, the arc is directed to penetrate the bottom piece and the puddle is allowed to flow into the edge of the top piece. The plug weld, MIG spot weld, lap spot weld, and stitch weld are discussed in detail later in this chapter.

- **Stitch weld.** A stitch weld is a series of connecting or overlapping MIG spot welds, creating a continuous seam.

BASIC WELDING METHODS

The types of MIG welds used for the repair or reattachment of damaged or replacement sections are butt welds, lap welds, flange welds, and plug or spot welds. Each type of joint can be welded by several different techniques. This depends mainly on the given welding situation and parameters: the thickness or thinness of the metal; the condition of the metal; the amount of gap, if any, between the pieces to be welded; the welding position; and so on. For instance, the butt joint can be welded with the continuous technique, or the stitch technique. And it can be tack welded at various points along the joint to hold the fit-up in place while completing the joint with a permanent continuous weld or a stitch weld. Lap and flange joints can be made using all six welding techniques.

Butt Welds

Butt welds are formed by fitting two edges of adjacent panels together and welding along the mating or butting edges of the panels.

In butt welding, especially on thin panels, it is wise not to weld more than 3/4 of an inch at one time. Closely watch the melting of the panel, welding wire, and the continuity of the bead. At the same time, be sure the end of the wire does not wander away from the butted portion of the panels. If the weld is to be long, it is a good idea to tack weld the panels in several locations (stitch weld) to prevent panel warpage (Figure 6-48). Figure 6-49 shows how to generate an arc a short distance ahead of the point where the weld ends and then immediately move the gun to the point where the bead should begin. The bead width and height should be uniform at this time.

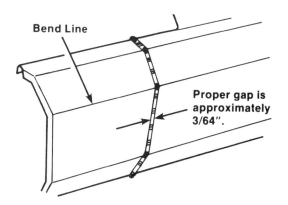

FIGURE 6-48 Tack weld of panels will help prevent warpage. (Courtesy of Nissan Motor Corp.)

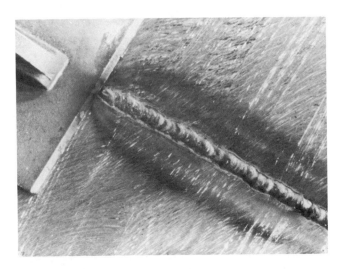

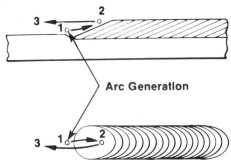

FIGURE 6-49 If the gun handling is smooth and even, the bead will be of consistent height and width, with a uniform, closely spaced ripple.

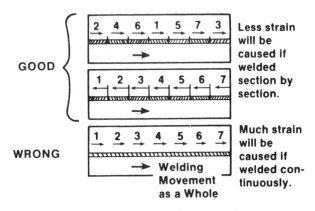

FIGURE 6-50 Right and wrong welding sequence. *(Courtesy of Nissan Motor Corp.)*

A sequence should be established to allow an area that is butt welded to cool naturally before the next area is welded (Figure 6-50). While butt welds of outer panels are far less sensitive, the same sequencing procedure should be allowed to prevent warpage and distortion from temperature buildup. To fill the spaces between intermittently placed

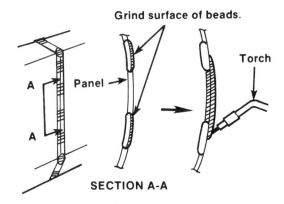

FIGURE 6-51 Filling space between intermittently spaced beads

beads, first grind the beads along the surface of the panel using a sander or grinder, then fill the space with metal (Figure 6-51). If weld metal is placed without grinding the surface of the beads, blowholes can be produced.

When welding thin panels that are 1/32 of an inch or less, an intermittent or stitch welding technique is a **must** to prevent burn-through. The combination of the proper gun angle and correct cycling techniques will enable the operator to achieve a satisfactory weld bead (Figure 6-52). The reverse welding method (Figure 6-29) can be used for moving the gun because it is easier to aim at the bead.

Figure 6-53 shows a typical butt welding procedure for installing a replacement panel. If the desired results are not obtained by using this method, the cause for the problem can be that the distance between the tip of the gun and the base metal might be too great. Weld penetration decreases as the distance between the tip and the base metal increases. Try holding the tip of the gun at several different distances away from the base metal until the proper distance is found that gives the desired results (Figure 6-54).

Moving the gun too fast or too slowly (Figure 6-55) will give poor welding results (even if the speed of the wire feed is constant). A gun speed that is too slow will cause melt through. Conversely, a gun speed that is too fast will cause shallow penetration and poor weld strength.

Even if a proper bead is formed during butt welding, panel warpage can result if the weld is started at or near the edge of the metal (Figure 6-56A). Therefore, to prevent panel warpage, disperse the heat into the base metal by starting the weld in the center of the panel and frequently changing the location of the weld area (Figure 6-56B). The thinner the panel thickness, the shorter the bead length.

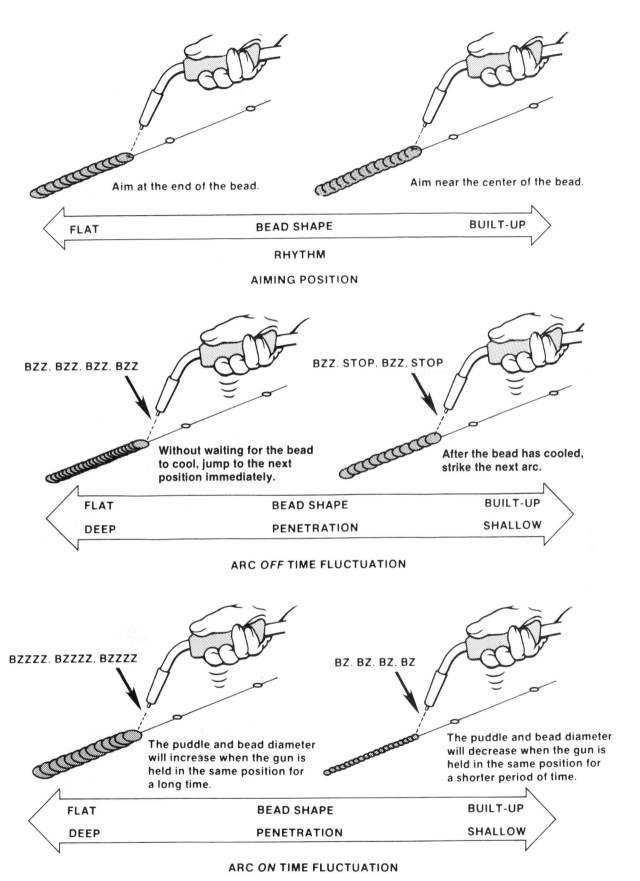

Aim at the end of the bead.

Aim near the center of the bead.

FLAT BEAD SHAPE BUILT-UP

RHYTHM

AIMING POSITION

BZZ. BZZ. BZZ. BZZ

Without waiting for the bead to cool, jump to the next position immediately.

BZZ. STOP. BZZ. STOP

After the bead has cooled, strike the next arc.

FLAT BEAD SHAPE BUILT-UP

DEEP PENETRATION SHALLOW

ARC *OFF* TIME FLUCTUATION

BZZZZ. BZZZZ. BZZZZ

The puddle and bead diameter will increase when the gun is held in the same position for a long time.

BZ. BZ. BZ. BZ

The puddle and bead diameter will decrease when the gun is held in the same position for a shorter period of time.

FLAT BEAD SHAPE BUILT-UP

DEEP PENETRATION SHALLOW

ARC *ON* TIME FLUCTUATION

FIGURE 6-52   Steps in achieving a proper bead. *(Courtesy of Toyota Motor Corp.)*

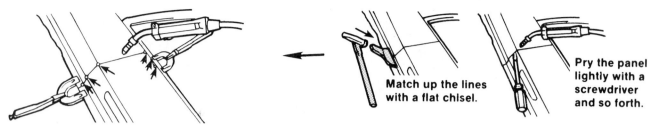

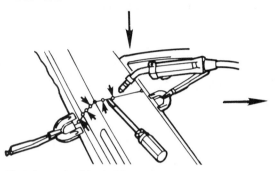

Align the body lines and tack weld the panel in several locations.

Match up the lines with a flat chisel.

Pry the panel lightly with a screwdriver and so forth.

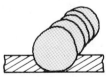

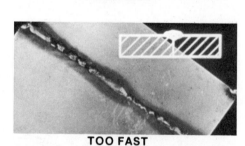

Match up the level differences in the panel surfaces and tack weld the panel in place.

Do **NOT** weld continuously from one point to another. Use an interrupted (stitch type) weld.

FIGURE 6-53 Procedure for butt welding sectional areas. *(Courtesy of Toyota Motor Corp.)*

INCORRECT

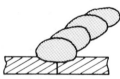

Insufficient penetration. Weld strength is poor and the panel could separate when the panel is finished with a grinder.

INCORRECT

There is good penetration but finish grinding will be both difficult and time consuming.

CORRECT

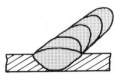

Good Penetration and Easy to Grind

FIGURE 6-54 Bead cutaway shape

CORRECT

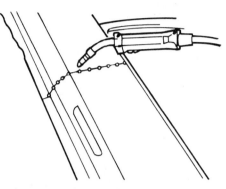

TOO FAST

TOO SLOW

FIGURE 6-55 Gun movement speed and bead shape

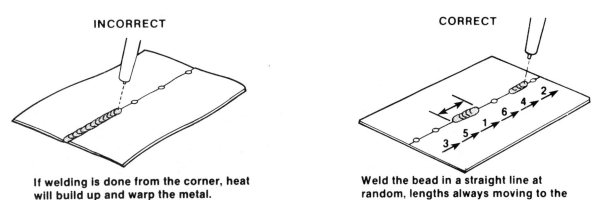

INCORRECT

If welding is done from the corner, heat will build up and warp the metal.

A

CORRECT

Weld the bead in a straight line at random, lengths always moving to the coolest area for the next weld.

B

FIGURE 6-56   Preventing panel warpage. *(Courtesy of Toyota Motor Corp.)*

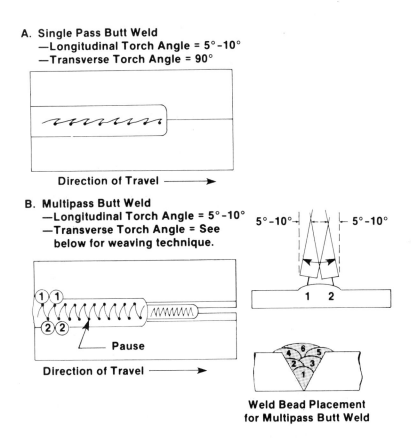

A. Single Pass Butt Weld
—Longitudinal Torch Angle = 5°-10°
—Transverse Torch Angle = 90°

Direction of Travel

B. Multipass Butt Weld
—Longitudinal Torch Angle = 5°-10°
—Transverse Torch Angle = See below for weaving technique.

Pause

Direction of Travel

5°-10°   5°-10°

Weld Bead Placement for Multipass Butt Weld

FIGURE 6-57   Torch manipulations for flat position butt welding

When welding a butt joint, be sure the weld penetrates all the way through to the backside of the joint. Where the metal thickness at a butt joint is 1/16 inch or more, a gap should be left to assure full penetration. If it is not practical to leave a gap, grind a V-groove in the joint (Figure 6-57) so the weld can penetrate to the backside.

Do not reinforce butt welds. Reinforcement can create a weaker condition than nonreinforced welds because of stress or structural buildup at the area of reinforcement.

Lap and Flange Welds

Lap and flange welds (Figure 6-58) are made with identical techniques. They are formed by melting two surfaces to be joined at the edge of the top one of two overlapping surfaces. This is similar to

FIGURE 6-58 Welding a lap or flange joint

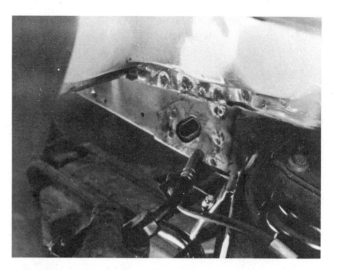

FIGURE 6-59 Plug welding is similar to spot welding

butt welds except only the top surface has an edge. Lap and flange welds should only be made in repairs where they replace original factory lap or flange welds, or where outer panels and not structural panels are involved. These welds should not be used to join more than two thicknesses of material together.

The same technique used for temperature control in butt welding should be followed for lap and flange welding. Welds should never be made continuously but should be sequenced to allow for natural cooling and prevent temperature buildup in the welding area.

Plug Weld

The plug weld is the body shop alternative to the OEM resistance spot welds made at the factory, because it can be used anywhere in the body structure that the factory used a resistance spot weld. Its use is not restricted. It has ample strength for welding load bearing structural members. It can also be used on cosmetic body skins and other thin-gauge sheet metal.

Plug welding (Figure 6-59) is a form of spot welding—spot welding through a hole. That is, a plug weld is formed by drilling or punching (Figure 6-60) a hole in the outer panel being joined (Figure 6-61). The materials should be tightly clamped together. Holding the torch at right angles to the surface (Figure 6-62), put the electrode wire in the hole, trigger the arc **briefly,** then release the trigger. The puddle fills the hole and solidifies.

When plug welding, try to duplicate the number and the nugget size of the original factory spot welds. The hole that is punched or drilled should not

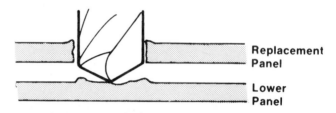

FIGURE 6-60 Plug welds are formed by drilling or punching a hole in the outer panel being joined.

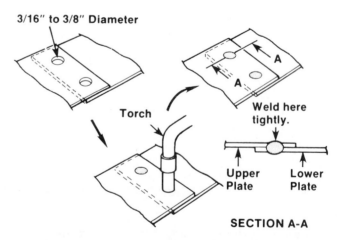

FIGURE 6-61 Steps in making a plug weld. (Courtesy of Nissan Motor Corp.)

be larger in diameter than the factory weld nugget. The 3/16-inch hole customarily used for plug welding cosmetic panels is not sufficient for plug welding structural members. Most of the structural members

FIGURE 6-62 Plugging the weld hole

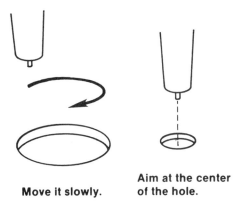

Move it slowly.   Aim at the center of the hole.

FIGURE 6-63 Gun movement to fill plug weld

FIGURE 6-64 Remove oxide film with a wire brush or sealer.

require a 5/16- to 3/8-inch hole to achieve an adequate nugget and acceptable weld strength. When filling a larger hole, move the gun in a circular motion slowly around the edges of the hole (Figure 6-63), filling in the cavity. For smaller holes, it is best to aim the gun at the center of the hole and keep it stationary. A flat, gently sloping bead gives a nice appearance, reducing the grinding or sanding operations.

Proper welding wire length is an important factor in obtaining a good plug weld. If the length of the wire protruding out of the end of the gun is too long, the wire will not melt properly, causing inferior weld penetration. The weld will improve if the gun is held closer to the base metal. Be sure the weld penetrates into the lower panel. Round dome-shaped protrusions on the underside of the metal are good indicators of proper weld penetration.

 **SHOP TALK**

Intermittent welding leads to the generation of oxide film on the surface and this causes blowholes. If this occurs, remove the oxide film with a wire brush (Figure 6-64).

The area welded should be allowed to cool naturally before any adjacent welds are made. Areas around the weld should not be force cooled using water or air. It is important that they be allowed to cool naturally. Slow, natural cooling without using water or air will minimize any panel distortion and keep the strength designed into the panels.

Plug welds can also be used to join more than two panels together. When more than two panels are being welded together, a hole is punched in every panel except the lower panel (Figure 6-65). The diameter of the plug weld hole in each additional panel being joined should be smaller than the diameter of the plug weld hole on top. Likewise, if panels of different thicknesses are being joined, a larger hole is punched in the thinner panel to assure that the thicker panel is melted into the weld first. When

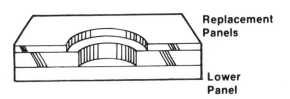

Replacement Panels

Lower Panel

FIGURE 6-65 Welding two or more holes using the plug welding technique

welding panels of different thicknesses using the plug weld method, the thinner panel should be on top.

A plug weld using a MIG welder can be accomplished automatically and in a minimum amount of time, creating less temperature buildup in adjacent panels. While adjacent welds should not be made immediately, the area being welded will cool in a very short period of time.

 **SHOP TALK**

Considerations important to high quality plug welds are: proper time; current flow; temperature; adjustments to the equipment; materials must be tightly clamped together; filler rod must be compatible with the materials being joined; the bottom surface should be melted first; and the clamp of the welder must be positioned near the location of the weld.

Spot Weld

It is possible to spot weld (Figure 6-66) with MIG equipment. In fact, most of the major MIG machines now available and designed for collision repair work have built-in timers that shut off the wire feed and welding arc after the time required to weld one spot (Figure 6-67). As mentioned earlier in this chapter, some MIG equipment also has a burnback time setting that is adjusted to prevent the wire from sticking in the puddle. The setting of these timers depends on the thickness of the workpiece. This information can usually be found in the machine's owner's manual.

FIGURE 6-67 Controls on a typical body shop MIG machine. *(Courtesy of HTP America, Inc.)*

For MIG spot welding, a special welding nozzle (Figure 6-68) must replace the standard nozzle. Once this gun is in place and with the spot timing, welding heat, and backburn time set for the given situation, the spot nozzle is held against the weld site and the gun triggered. For a very brief period of time, the timed pulses of wire feed and welding current are

FIGURE 6-66 Spot welding can be accomplished with most MIG machines.

FIGURE 6-68 Special spot welding nozzle

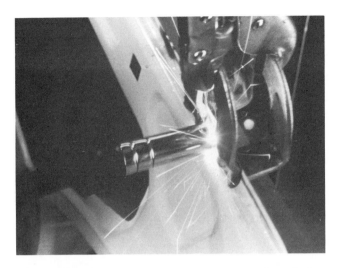

FIGURE 6-69   During one brief, timed pulse of wire feed and welding current, the arc melts through the outer layer and penetrates the inner layer.

FIGURE 6-71   Results of combining the spot welding process with the continuous welding gun technique and gun travel

activated during which the arc melts through the outer layer and penetrates the inner layer (Figure 6-69). Then the automatic shut-off goes into action and no matter how long the trigger is squeezed, nothing will happen. However, when the trigger is released and then squeezed again, the next spot pulse is obtained.

Because of varying conditions, the quality of a MIG spot weld is difficult to ascertain. On load bearing members, therefore, the MIG plug weld or resistance spot welding technique described later in this chapter is the preferred method.

The MIG lap spot technique is a popular one for the quick, effective welding of lap joints and flanges on thin-gauge nonstructural sheets and skins (Figure 6-70). Here again the spot timer is set, but this

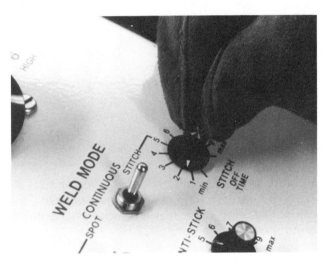

FIGURE 6-72   Setting the spot-off, or interval, timer.

time the spot nozzle is positioned over the edge of the outer sheet—at an angle slightly off 90 degrees. This will allow contact with both pieces of metal at the same time. The arc melts into the edge and penetrates the lower sheet.

Stitch Welding

In MIG stitch welding, the standard nozzle is used, not the spot nozzle. To make a stitch weld, combine the spot welding process with the continuous welding gun technique and gun travel (Figure 6-71). To do this, set the automatic timer—either a shut-off or pulsed interval timer—depending on the MIG machine (Figure 6-72). The spot weld pulses

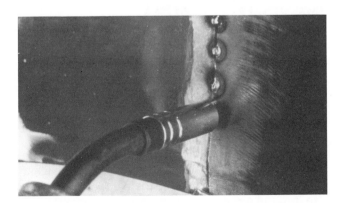

FIGURE 6-70   Lap spot technique is a popular one for the quick, effective welding of lap joints and flanges on thin-gauge nonstructural sheets and skins.

and shut-offs recur with automatic regularity: weld-stop-weld-stop-weld-stop as long as the trigger is held in. It sounds like this: buzz-stop-buzz-stop-buzz-stop-buzz-stop and so on.

Another way to look at this is weld-cool-weld-cool-weld-cool and so on, because the arc-off period allows the last spot to cool slightly and start to solidify before the next spot is deposited. This intermittent technique means less distortion, less melt through or burn through. These characteristics make the stitch weld preferable to the continuous weld for working thinner-gauge cosmetic panels.

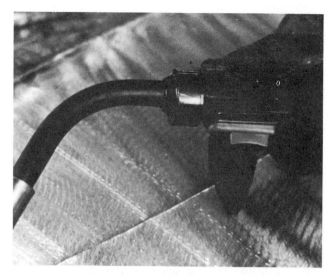

FIGURE 6-75   Hand triggering the welding gun

FIGURE 6-73   The intermittent cooling and solidifying of the stitch weld makes it preferable to continuous welding on vertical joints where distortion is a problem.

The intermittent cooling and solidifying of the stitch weld also makes it preferable to continuous welding on vertical joints where distortion is a problem (Figure 6-73). The welder does not have to contend with a continuous weld puddle that gravity is trying to pull down the joint ahead of the arc. By the same token, stitch welding is also preferable in the overhead position (Figure 6-74). There is virtually no weld puddle for gravity to pull.

If the MIG machine does not have the automatic stitch modes, the spot and stitch welds can be made manually. The operator merely has to be capable of triggering the gun on-off, on-off, on-off—the same way the automatic system does (Figure 6-75).

6.5 MIG WELDING GALVANIZED METALS

When MIG welding galvanized or zinc-metallized steels, also called zinc-coated steels, do **not** remove the zinc. If zinc is ground away, the thickness of the metal is reduced and so is its strength. And when creating a zinc-free area around the weld site, it is an inviting target for corrosion.

With galvanized or zinc-coated steels (Figure 6-76), use a slower gun travel speed than when welding uncoated steels because the zinc vapors tend to rise into the arc zone and interfere with arc stability. A slower travel speed allows the zinc to burn off at the front of the weld pool. How much to reduce the gun travel speed will depend on the thickness of the zinc coating, the joint type, and the welding position.

FIGURE 6-74   Stitch welding is also preferable in the overhead position.

FIGURE 6-76 When welding galvanized or zinc-coated steels, use a slower gun travel speed.

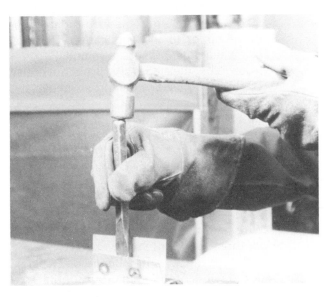

FIGURE 6-77 Checking the quality of the MIG weld

Experience is the best teacher with these variable conditions.

Since there is slightly less weld penetration with galvanized or zinc-coated steels than with uncoated steels, a slightly under gap in square edge butt welds is needed. To prevent burn through or excessive penetration of the wider gap, the welding gun should be handled with a side-to-side weaving motion.

It must be remembered that there is more spatter when welding galvanized or zinc-coated steels than with uncoated steels. Therefore, it is a good idea to apply antispatter compound inside the gun nozzle and to clean the nozzle frequently.

WARNING: Zinc fumes are noxious. Adequate exhaust ventilation must be used and the operator should wear an air-supplied respirator.

6.6 TESTING THE MIG WELD

Repair welds should be tested from time to time on every job. This can be done simply with test panels. Before welding anything on a vehicle, make some welds on pieces of sheet metal like the panels that are going to be welded on the vehicle. If the proper settings on the MIG welder are obtained on the test pieces, the quality of the weld on the car can be assured. To check the quality of the weld, try to break it apart as illustrated in Figure 6-77 or as described later in this chapter under destructive testing of resistance spot welds.

6.7 MIG WELD DEFECTS

Defects in MIG welds and their causes are summarized in Table 6-5. Proper welding techniques assure good welding results. If welding defects should occur, think of ways to change the method of operation in order to correct the defect.

When making any MIG repairs, the materials and panels must be similar enough to allow mixing when they are welded together. The melting and flowing of metals can be accomplished by many methods, depending upon the materials being joined. The combinations of cleanliness of the welded area, the mixing of proper metals, and the right heat application will result in a good MIG weld.

6.8 FLUX-CORED ARC WELDING

Flux-cored arc welding (FCAW) is an electric arc welding process that uses a tubular wire with flux inside. With the development of 0.030 self-shielded flux-cored wire, the flux-cored welding process has proven to be valuable for work on high-strength steel (coated or uncoated). The FCAW process uses the same type of constant potential power source as MIG. It also uses the electrode feed system, contact tube, electrode conduit, welding gun, and many other pieces of equipment that are used in MIG. Nevertheless, the process itself differs somewhat from MIG.

There is no external shielding gas in FCAW. As the flux within the wire melts in the heat of the arc, the created gases shield the weld puddle, stabilize the arc, help to control penetration, and reduce porosity. The melted flux also mixes with the impurities on the metal surface and brings them to the top of the weld where they solidify as slag. The slag can then be chipped or brushed away.

Two very important advantages of the FCAW process over MIG are its ability to tolerate surface impurities (thus, it requires less precleaning) and to stabilize the arc. Other beneficial characteristics of the process include the following:

- High deposition rate
- Efficient electrode metal use
- Requires little edge preparation
- Welds in any position
- Welds a wide range of metal thicknesses with one size of electrode
- Produces high-quality welds
- Weld puddle is easily controlled and its surface appearance is smooth and uniform even with minimal operator skill.
- Produces a weld with less porosity than MIG when welding galvanized steels.

 **SHOP TALK** _____

If the nozzle is removed when using self-shielded wires, visibility is improved.

While the FCAW process has a number of advantges over MIG it has the following drawbacks:

- FCAW wires are more expensive than MIG hard wires. However, the cost is quickly recovered through higher productivity.
- The flux from the wire changes to slag as it cools. Until it does cool, the slag is sharp and hot and should be considered an eye and skin hazard. Once it cools, this slag must be removed prior to the application of fillers, seam sealouts, primers, or paint.
- Spatter is worse when using flux-cored wires. Use nozzle gel and keep the nozzle scraped clean. Spatter buildup in the gun nozzle can jam the wire in the contact tip; it can also fall off during welding and mix with the molten puddle, diminishing the quality of the weld.
- Excessive tension on the drive rollers or using the incorrect style of drive rollers can

collapse the tubular wire. Check the owner's manual for flux-cored wire requirements.
- Only ferrous metals can be welded.

If a machine is used for both MIG and FCAW, the welder must have polarity switching capabilities. FCAW with .030- or .035-inch wire uses straight polarity while .023-, .030-, and .035-inch hard wires for MIG use DC reverse polarity. Many of the gas metal arc welding machines sold over the past few years were originally designed to run DC reverse. Without going inside the machine to change polarities, which is difficult and time consuming, this type of machine will not run DC straight polarity. Check the owner's manual for polarity reversing capabilities.

1. FCAW wires are more expensive per pound than hard wires for GMAW.
2. The .030 self-shielded cored wire contains fluoride compounds. **Use adequate ventilation.**
3. The flux in the core of the wire changes to slag upon cooling. This slag must be removed prior to the application of fillers, seam sealouts, primers, or paint.
4. In addition, the slag is sharp and hot until it cools, so it must be considered an eye and skin hazard.
5. Spatter is worse when using cored wires. Use nozzle gel and keep the nozzle scraped clean. Spatter buildup in the gun nozzle can jam the wire in the contact tip or fall off during welding, mixing with the molten puddle and contributing to a poor quality weld.
6. Wire feed problems for FCAW are similar to those encountered with GMAW, but with one important difference. Because cored wires are not solid but tubular, excessive tension on the drive rolls or the incorrect style of drive rolls may collapse the tubular wire which leads to feeding problems. Again, check with the owner's manual for correct drive rolls and tension requirements for flux-cored wire.

6.9 TIG WELDING

Tungsten inert gas (TIG) welding, another form of GMAW, has somewhat limited use in body shop repair applications. In a general auto repair or engine and radiator rebuilder's shop operation, however, it does things that make it a valuable tool.

TABLE 6-5: WELDING PRECAUTIONS

Defect	Defect Condition	Remarks	Main Causes
Pores/Pits		There is a hole made when gas is trapped in the weld metal.	1. There is rust or dirt on the base metal. 2. There is rust or moisture adhering to the wire. 3. Improper shielding action (the nozzle is blocked or wind or the gas flow volume is low). 4. Weld is cooling off too fast. 5. Arc length is too long. 6. Wrong wire is elected. 7. Gas is sealed improperly. 8. Weld joint surface is not clean.
Undercut		Undercut is a condition where the overmelted base metal has made grooves or an indentation. The base metal's section is made smaller and, therefore, the weld zone's strength is severely lowered.	1. Arc length is too long. 2. Gun angle is improper. 3. Welding speed is too fast. 4. Current is too large. 5. Torch feed is too fast. 6. Torch angle is tilted.
Improper Fusion		This is an unfused condition between weld metal and base metal or between deposited metals.	1. Check torch feed operation. 2. Is voltage lowered? 3. Weld area is not clean.
Overlap		Overlap is apt to occur in fillet weld rather than in butt weld. Overlap causes stress concentration and results in premature corrosion.	1. Welding speed is too slow. 2. Arc length is too short. 3. Torch feed is too slow. 4. Current is too low.
Insufficient Penetration		This is a condition in which there is insufficient deposition made under the panel.	1. Welding current is too low. 2. Arch length is too long. 3. The end of the wire is not aligned with the butted portion of the panels. 4. Groove face is to small.
Excess Weld Spatter		Excess weld spatter occurs as speckles and bumps along either side of the weld bead.	1. Arc length is too long. 2. Rust is on the base metal. 3. Gun angle is too severe.
Spatter (short throat)		Spatter is prone to occur in fillet welds.	1. Current is too great. 2. Wrong wire is selected.

TABLE 6-5: WELDING PRECAUTIONS (CONTINUED)

Defect	Defect Condition	Remarks	Main Causes
Vertical Crack		Cracks usually occur on top surface only.	1. There are stains on welded surface (paint, oil, rust).
The Bead Is Not Uniform.		This is a condition in which the weld bead is misshapen and uneven rather than streamlined and even.	1. The contact tip hole is worn or deformed and the wire is oscillating as it comes out of the tip. 2. The gun is not steady during welding.
Burn Through		Burn through is the condition of holes in the weld bead.	1. The welding current is too high. 2. The gap between the metal is too wide. 3. The speed of the gun is too slow. 4. The gun-to-base metal distance is too short.

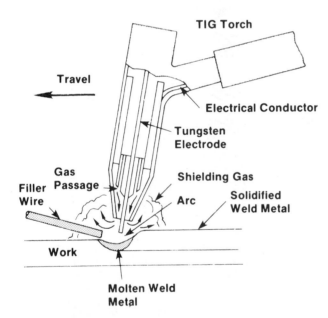

FIGURE 6-78 Principles of the TIG process. If filler metal is required, it is fed into the pool from a separate filler rod.

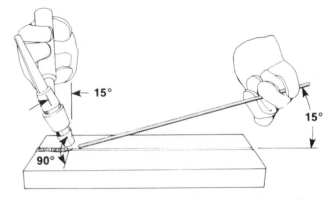

FIGURE 6-79 Proper position of the torch and filler rod for manual TIG welding

MIG welders lay down weld beads at the average of 25 inches per minute. TIG welding is much slower, with weld speeds ranging between 5 to 10 inches per minute. However, this slower speed gives much more control, and the end result is the best looking weld obtainable. A TIG unit can be used to repair cracks in aluminum cylinder heads, reconstruct combustion chambers, and other automotive components that need to be welded.

Like MIG welding (Figure 6-78), TIG welders use an inert gas such as argon or helium to surround the weld area and prevent oxygen and nitrogen in the atmosphere from contaminating the weld. But instead of having a wire feed welding electrode like MIG units, TIG machines use a tungsten electrode with a very high melting point (about 6900 degrees Fahrenheit) to strike an arc between the welding gun and the work.

Since the tungsten electrode has such a high melting point, it is not consumed during the welding process, so a filler rod must be used when welding thicker materials. Because the torch is held in one hand and the filler rod is held in the other (Figure 6-79).

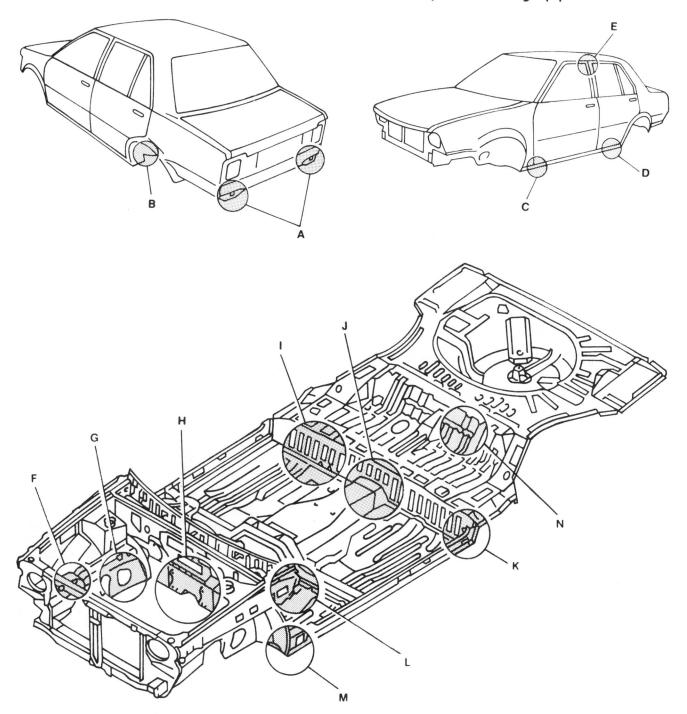

Construction	Location
Suspension mounting	G
Steering gear mounting	H
Fuel tank mounting	N
Engine, transmission mounting	F

Construction	Location
Belt anchor	E
Jack-up point	C, D
Major construction portions	A, I, J, K, L, M

FIGURE 6-80 Typical important locations of the body in spot welding that are done during production of the vehicle. *(Courtesy of Nissan Motor Corp.)*

6.10 RESISTANCE SPOT WELDING

Resistance spot welding is the most important welding process used by automobile manufacturers on their assembly lines to make many of the OEM welds on the unibody cars (Figure 6–80). It is estimated that between 90 to 95 percent of all factory welds in a unibody structure are spot welds. In this country, it is also widely used in the automotive aftermarket for sunroof installations and vehicle conversions, including recreational vehicles (RVs) and stretch limousines.

Although resistance spot welding has been proven in the European and Japanese unibody collision repair industry for more than 30 years, many collision repair specialists in this country first learned of it when they read the new factory body repair manuals published by the auto makers and import car companies. Since resistance spot welding is now specified by a growing number of automobile manufacturers for repair welding their vehicles, the repair specialist must know how to use a resistance spot welding gun.

The squeeze type resistance spot welder (Figure 6–81) is ideal for repair welding many of the unibody's thin gauge sections that require good weld strength and no distortion. Typical applications include roofs, window and door openings, rocker panels, and many exterior panels (Figure 6–82). Due to the strength requirements of unibody repairs, it is often important that a squeeze type resistance spot welder be used and that the repair specialist know how to set it up, make test welds, and use it.

Resistance spot welding has several advantages:

- Reduces welding costs.
- No consumable filler wire, rod, or gas required.
- Clean; no smoke or fumes.
- Allows use of weld through conductive zinc primers to restore corrosion protection to repair joints.

A

B

C

FIGURE 6–82 Typical application of squeeze type resistance spot welder: (A) welding side quarter window pinch weld flange; (B) welding right quarter panel to rear side member, trunk floor pan, and lower back panel; and (C) welding left rear quarter panel to rear valance. *(Courtesy of Lors Machinery, Inc.)*

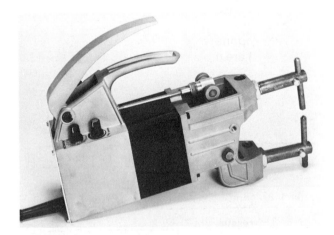

FIGURE 6–81 Typical squeeze type resistance spot welder. *(Courtesy of Lors Machinery, Inc.)*

- Duplicates OEM factory weld appearance.
- Eliminates need for grinding of welds.
- Fast; weld times of 1 second or less make strong welds on HSS and HSLA steels as well as mild steels with a very small heated zone, eliminating distortion of metal.

How Resistance Spot Welding Works

Resistance spot welding relies on the resistance heat generated by low voltage electric current flowing through two pieces of metal held together, under pressure, by the squeeze force of the welding electrodes. Thus, the three important factors in the operation of resistance spot welding are:

- **Pressurization.** The mechanical welding bond between two pieces of sheet metal is directly related to the amount of force exerted on the sheet metal by the welding tips. As the tips squeeze the sheet metal together, an electrical current flows from the tips through the base metal causing the metal to melt and fuse together. Weld spatter (internal or external) is the result of low pressure on the tip or excessive electrical current flow. A high tip pressure causes a small spot weld (Figure 6-83) and a reduced mechanical bond of the weld. In other words, the high tip pressure forces the tip into the softened area, thinning and weakening the weld.
- **Current flow.** When pressure is applied to the metal, a high electric current flows through the electrodes and through the two pieces of metal. The temperature rises rapidly at the joined portion of the metal where the resistance is greatest (Figure 6-84A). If the current continues to flow, the metal melts and fuses together (Figure 6-84B). If the electrical current becomes too great or the pressure too low, internal spatter will result. However, if the current is decreased or the

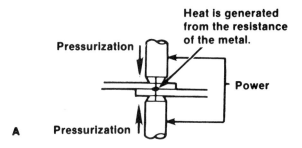

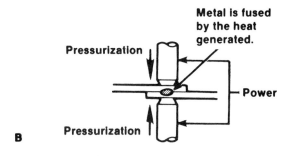

FIGURE 6-84 Electrical current (amperage)

pressure is increased, weld spatter will be held to a minimum. As can be seen, there is a mutual relationship between the electrical current and the pressure applied to the spot weld.

- **Holding.** If the current flow is stopped, the melted portion begins to cool and forms a round flat bead of solidified metal (nugget) (Figure 6-85). This structure becomes very dense due to the pressurization force, and its subsequent mechanical bonding is excellent. Pressurization time is very important. Do not use less time than specified in operator's manual.

Resistance Spot Welding Components

The components of a resistance spot welder (Figure 6-86) are the welding transformer, the weld-

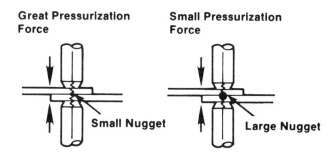

FIGURE 6-83 Electrode (tip) pressure

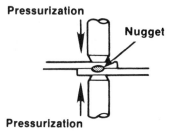

FIGURE 6-85 Electrical current (holding) flow time

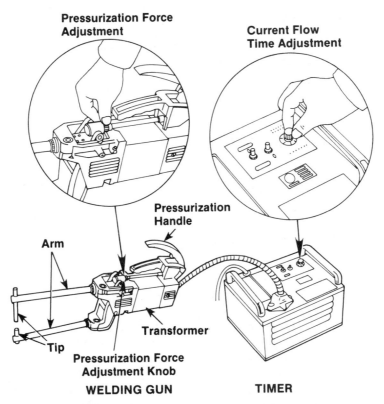

Pressurization Force Adjustment

Current Flow Time Adjustment

Pressurization Handle

Arm

Transformer

Tip

Pressurization Force Adjustment Knob

WELDING GUN

TIMER

FIGURE 6-86 Components of a resistance spot welding system. *(Courtesy of Toyota Motor Corp.)*

er control, and the welding gun with interchangeable arm sets.

The transformer converts low-amperage 200-volt shop line current to high secondary amperage, low voltage (2 to 5 volts) welding current, safe from electrical shock. The welder transformer can be either built into the welding gun or mounted remotely and connected to the gun by means of cables. A built-in transformer is electrically more efficient since there is little or no loss of welding current between the transformer and the gun. A remote transformer must be larger and draw more shop line current to compensate for power losses through the long cables connecting it to the gun. Remember that this high weld current will decrease when long reach or wide gap arm sets are used. A high weld current output can be adjusted to a lower intensity by use of the welder control.

The welder control adjusts the transformer's weld current output and permits precise adjustment of the weld time during which the welding current is switched on and allowed to flow through the metal being welded and then switched off. It is desirable to have a range of timing adjustment from approximately 1/6 of a second to 1 second (10 to 60 cycles) for typical collision repair welding applications. A repeatable accuracy of at least 1/10 of a second is desirable for consistent weld quality.

The welder control should be capable of providing a full range of adjustment of the welding current. Weld current settings vary, depending upon the thickness of the steel to be welded and the length and gap of the arm sets needed to reach into the area being welded. It might be necessary to decrease weld current when welding with short reach arm sets, or increase weld current when using long reach or wide gap arm sets.

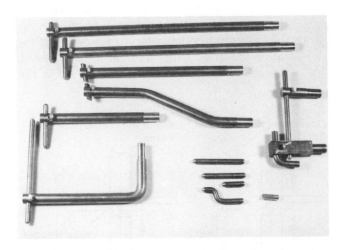

FIGURE 6-87 Type accessory arms. *(Courtesy of Henning Hansen, Inc.)*

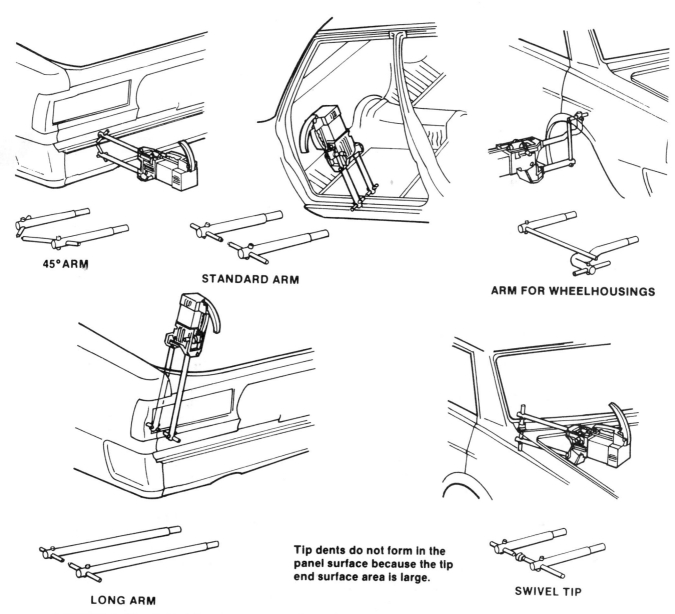

45° ARM

STANDARD ARM

ARM FOR WHEELHOUSINGS

LONG ARM

Tip dents do not form in the
panel surface because the tip
end surface area is large.

SWIVEL TIP

FIGURE 6-88   Select the proper type of arm for the job. *(Courtesy of Toyota Motor Corp.)*

Some manufacturers of resistance spot welders designed for unibody repair work offer additional control features that compensate for small amounts of surface scale or slight rust on the metal. Such features permit the repair specialist to determine when a poor weld condition exists.

The welding gun applies the squeeze force and delivers the welding current through the welder arms to the metal being welded. Most resistance spot welders are designed with a force multiplying mechanism to produce the high electrode force required for consistent weld quality. These force multiplying mechanisms can be spring or pneumatically assisted. Squeeze type resistance welders that do not use a force multiplying mechanism and rely solely on the operator's manual grip for pressure are not recommended for repair welding unibody structures.

The majority of welding guns in auto body shops should have a maximum capacity of up to two times 5/64-inch-thick steel when equipped with short reach arm sets of 5 inches or less. Capacity with long reach or wide gap arm sets should be at least two times 1/32-inch-thick steel. These capacities comply with the specifications listed in most factory body repair manuals.

Resistance spot welders used for unibody repair welding are available with a full range of interchangeable arm sets. Standard arm sets (Figure 6-87) are designed to reach difficult areas on most makes of cars, such as wheel well flanges, drip rails, tail light openings, and other tight pinch weld areas as well as floor pan sections, rocker panels, and window and door openings. Repair shops doing work for new car dealers should check the factory repair manuals and look for availability of special arm sets for the hard-to-reach areas on specific makes of cars.

Spot Welder Adjustments

To obtain sufficient strength at the spot-welded portions, perform the following checks and adjustments on the squeeze type resistance spot welding gun before starting the operation:

- **Arm selection.** It is important to select the arm according to the area to be welded (Figure 6-88).
- **Adjustment of arm.** Keep the gun arm as short as possible to obtain the maximum pressure for welding (Figure 6-89). Securely tighten the gun arm and tip so that they will not become loose during the operation.
- **Alignment of electrode tips.** Align the upper and lower electrode tips on the same axis (Figure 6-90). Poor alignment of the tips causes insufficient pressurizing, and this results in insufficient current density and insufficient strength at the welded portions.
- **Diameter of electrode tip.** The diameter of the spot weld decreases as the diameter of the electrode tip increases. Also, if the electrode tip is too small, the spot weld will not increase in size. The tip diameter (Figure 6-91) must be properly controlled to obtain the desired welding strength. Before starting operation, make sure that the tip diameter (D) is kept the proper size, and file it cleanly to remove burnt or foreign matter from the surface of the tip. As the amount of dirt on the

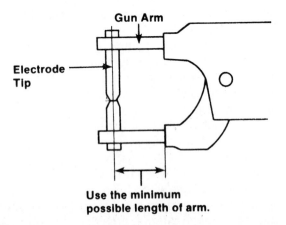

FIGURE 6-89 Adjusting the gun arm. *(Courtesy of Nissan Motor Corp.)*

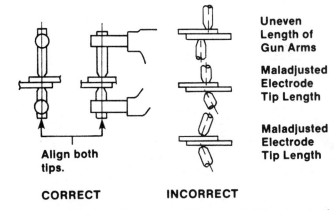

FIGURE 6-90 Correct and incorrect alignment of the electrode tips. *(Courtesy of Nissan Motor Corp.)*

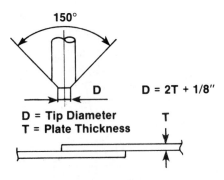

FIGURE 6-91 Method of determining tip diameter. *(Courtesy of Nissan Motor Corp.)*

tip increases, the resistance at the tip also increases, which reduces the current flow through the base metal that in turn reduces weld penetration resulting in an inferior weld. If the tips are used continuously over a long period of time, they will not dissipate heat properly and will become red hot. This will result in premature tip wear that also increases resistance and causes the welding current to drop drastically. If necessary, let the tips cool down after five or six welds. If the tips are worn, use a tip dressing tool to reshape the tips (Figure 6-92).

- **Electrical current flow time.** Current flow time also has a relationship to the formation of a spot weld. When the electrical current flow time increases, the heat that is generated increases the spot weld diameter and penetration. The amount of heat that is dissipated at the weld increases as the current flow time increases. Since the weld temperature will not rise after a certain amount of time, and even if current flows longer than that time, the spot weld size will not increase.

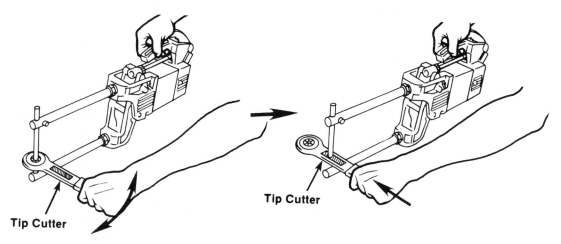

Tip Cutter

Tip Cutter

FIGURE 6-92   Reshaping the ends of the tips. *(Courtesy of Toyota Motor Corp.)*

However, tip pressure marks and heat warping might occur.

The pressurization force and welding current of many spot welders cannot be adjusted and the current value might be low. However, welding strength can be assured by lengthening the current flow time (letting low current flow for a long time).

The best welding results can be obtained by adjusting the arm length or welding time according to the thickness of the panels. While the welder instruction manual has these values listed inside, it is best to test the quality of the weld using the methods described later in this chapter as adjustment is carried out.

SHOP TALK

While spot welding antirust steel panels used in auto bodies, offset the drop in current density by raising the current value 10 to 20 percent above that for ordinary steel panels. Since the current value cannot be adjusted in spot welders ordinarily used for body repairs, lengthen the current flow time a little. It is important to differentiate between antirust sheet metal and ordinary sheet metal since the protective zinc coating on the antirust panels should be removed along with the paint, when sanding in preparation for welding.

OPERATING A SQUEEZE TYPE RESISTANCE SPOT WELDER

In use, the repair technician holds the welding gun and positions it so that the welder arm elec-
trodes contact the body parts to be welded. The technician then uses the squeeze mechanism to apply weld force to both sides of the metal being welded. As force is applied and maintained on the metal, the force mechanism initiates an electrical signal to the welder control that switches on the flow of weld current for a preset time and then switches it off. Since the weld time is usually less than 1 second, the entire process is very fast.

Other important operational procedures that should be considered when using a squeeze type resistance spot welder are:

- **Clearance between welding surfaces.** Any clearance between the surfaces to be welded causes poor current flow (Figure 6-93). Even if welding can be made without removing such gap, the welded area would become smaller, resulting in insufficient strength. Flatten the two surfaces to remove the gaps, and clamp them tightly with a clamp before welding.
- **Metal surface to be welded.** Paint film, rust, dust, or any other contamination on the metal surfaces to be welded cause insufficient current flow and poor results. Remove such

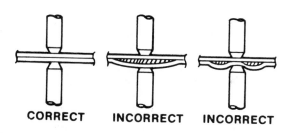

CORRECT   INCORRECT   INCORRECT

FIGURE 6-93   Correct and incorrect clearance between welding surfaces

foreign matter from the surfaces to be welded (Figure 6–94).

- **Corrosion prevents processing on metal surfaces.** Coat the surfaces to be welded with an anticorrosion agent (see Chapter 15) that has higher conductivity. It is important to apply the agent uniformly even to the end face of the panel (Figure 6–95).

- **Performance of spot welding operations.** When performing spot welding operations, be sure to:
  —Use the direct welding method. For the portions to which direct welding cannot be applied, use plug welding by MIG welding.
  —Apply electrodes at a right angle to the panel (Figure 6–96A). If the electrodes are not applied at right angles, the current density will be low, resulting in insufficient welding strength.
  —For the portion where three or more metal sheets are overlapping, spot welding should be done twice (Figure 6–96B).

- **Number of points of spot welding.** Generally, the capacity of spot welding machines available in a repair shop is smaller than that of welding machines at the factory. Accordingly, the number of points of spot welding should be increased by 30 percent in a ser-

vice shop compared to spot welding in the factory (Figure 6–97).

- **Minimum welding pitch.** The strength of individual spot welds is determined by the spot weld pitch (the distance between spot welds) and edge distance (the distance of the spots from the panel edge). The bond between the panels becomes stronger as the weld pitch is shortened. However, over a certain point, the metal becomes saturated and further shortening of the pitch will not increase the strength of the bond because the current will flow to the spots that have previously been welded. This reactive current diversion in-

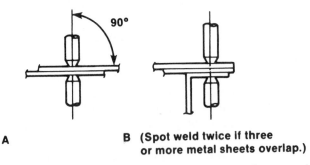

A **B (Spot weld twice if three or more metal sheets overlap.)**

FIGURE 6–96 Precautions in performing spot welds

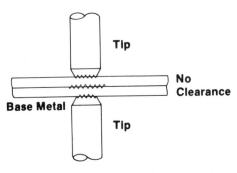

FIGURE 6–94 Condition of base metal surfaces

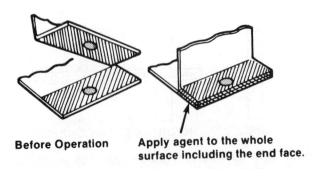

Before Operation   **Apply agent to the whole surface including the end face.**

FIGURE 6–95 Areas to be protected with an anti-corrosion agent

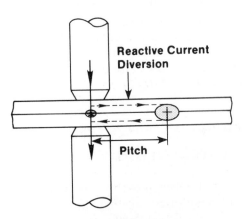

FIGURE 6–97 Number of points to spot weld

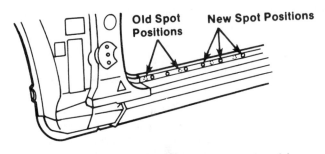

FIGURE 6–98 Minimum welding pitch

TABLE 6-6: SPOT WELDING POSITION

Panel Thickness	Pitch S	Edge Distance P
1/64"	7/16" or more	13/64" or more
1/32"	9/16" or more	13/64" or more
Less Than 3/64"	11/16" or more	1/4" or more
3/64"	7/8" or more	9/32" or more
1/16"	1-9/64" or more	5/16" or more

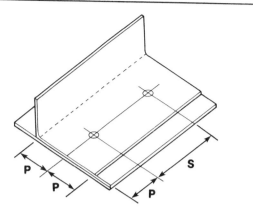

TABLE 6-7: POSITION OF WELDING SPOT FROM THE END OF PANEL

Thickness (t)	Minimum pitch (ℓ)
1/64"	7/16" or over
1/32"	7/16" or over
Less than 3/64"	15/32" or over
3/64"	9/16" or over
1/16"	5/8" or over
5/64"	11/16" or over

creases as the number of spot welds increases, and the diverted current does not raise the temperature at the welds (Figure 6-98). The distance of the weld pitch must be beyond the area influenced by the reactive current diversion. In general, the values given in Table 6-6 should be observed.

- **Position of welding spot from the edge and end of the panel.** The edge distance is also determined by the position of the welding tip. Even if the spot welds are normal, the welds will not have sufficient strength if the edge distance is insufficient. When welding near

the end of a panel, observe the values for the distance from the end of a panel given in Table 6-7. If the distance is too small, it results in insufficient strength and also in a strained panel.

- **Spotting sequence.** Do not spot continuously in one direction only. This method provides weak welding due to the shunt effect of the current (Figure 6-99). If the welding tips become hot and change their color, stop welding and allow the tips to cool.

- **Welding corners.** Do not weld the corner radius portion (Figure 6-100). Welding this portion results in concentration of stress that leads to cracks. For example, the following locations require special consideration:

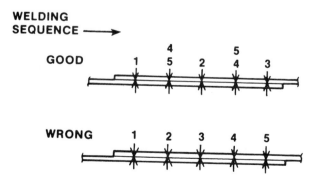

FIGURE 6-99 Proper welding sequence. (Courtesy of Nissan Motor Corp.)

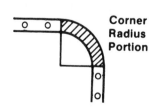

FIGURE 6-100 Proper method of welding corners. (Courtesy of Nissan Motor Corp.)

—Upper corner of front and center pillars
—Front upper portion of the quarter panel
—Corner portion of front and rear windows

Inspection of Spot Welds

Spot welds are inspected either by outward appearance (visual inspection) or destructive testing. Destructive testing is used to measure the strength of a weld and a visual inspection is used to judge the quality of the outward appearance.

Appearance Inspection

Check the finish of the weld visually and by touching. The items to check are:

- **Spot position.** The spot weld position should be in the center of the flange with no tip holes and have no spot welds overriding the edge. As a rule, old spot position should be avoided.
- **Number of spots.** There should be 1.3 or more times the number made by the manufacturers. (For example, 1.3 times 4 original factory spot welds equals roughly 5 new repair spot welds.)
- **Pitch.** It should be a little shorter than that of the manufacturer and spots should be uniformly spaced. The minimum pitch should be at a distance where reactive current diversion will not occur.
- **Dents (tip bruises).** There should be no dents on the surfaces that exceed half the thickness of the panel.
- **Pinholes.** There should be no pinholes that are large enough to see.
- **Spatter.** A glove should not catch on the surface when rubbed across it.

Destructive Testing

Most destructive tests require the use of much sophisticated equipment; a requirement that most body shops are unable to meet. For this reason, simpler methods described here have been developed by general use in body shops.

- **Destructive check.** A test piece of the same metal as the welded piece and with the same panel thickness is made and welded in the positions shown in Figure 6–101. Next, force is applied in the direction of the arrow and the spots are separated. It is then judged by how cleanly the weld has broken whether it is

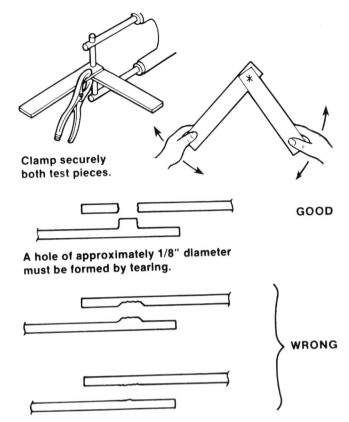

Clamp securely both test pieces.

A hole of approximately 1/8" diameter must be formed by tearing.

GOOD

WRONG

FIGURE 6–101   Performing the destructive check. (Courtesy of Nissan Motor Corp.)

satisfactory or not. If the weld pulls out cleanly as a cork from a bottle, the weld is judged to be good. It should be noted here that since the weld performance cannot be exactly duplicated by this test, the results should only serve as a reference.

- **Nondestructive check.** To confirm a spot weld after it has been made, use a chisel and hammer and proceed as follows:
  —Insert the tip of a chisel between the welded plates (Figure 6–102) and tap the end of the chisel until a clearance of 1/8 to 5/32 inches (when the plate thickness is approximately 1/32 inch) is formed between the plates. If the welded portions remain normal, it indicates that the welding has been done properly. This clearance varies with the location of the welded spots, length of the flange, plate thickness, welding pitch, and other factors. Note that the values given here are only reference values.
  —If the thickness of the plates is not equal, the clearance between the plates must be limited to 1/16 to 5/64 inches. Note that

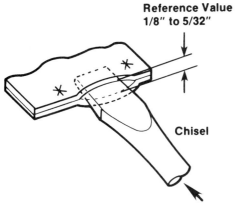

Reference Value 1/8" to 5/32"

Chisel

Tap with a hammer.

FIGURE 6-102   Performing the destructive check. *(Courtesy of Nissan Motor Corp.)*

FIGURE 6-103   Typical panel spotter. *(Courtesy of Lenco Inc.)*

further opening of the plates can become a destructive test.

—Be sure to repair the deformed portion of the panel after inspection.

6.11 OTHER SPOT WELDING FUNCTIONS

While the squeeze type welding gun is the most used in the repair shop, there are other types of guns used with spot welding equipment. With the proper gun attachment the spot welder can be used as a panel spotter, stud welder, spot shrinker, and mold rivet welder.

PANEL SPOTTING

At one time spot welding equipment was called a panel spotter (Figure 6-103). When operating a panel spotter, the two electrode guns are placed on the nonstructural replacement panel. Figure 6-104 shows how both lap and flange joints can be made with a spliced panel or full panel installation. After the adjustments are made following the manufacturer's directions, push both electrodes against the panel and apply moderate pressure to close any gaps. Press the weld button on the switch handle and hold it down until the welding cycle stops automatically. The finger is released from the weld button and the electrodes are moved to the next welding location.

Here are some other panel spotter operational tips:

- As in any spot welding operation, thoroughly clean the surfaces along the weld seam. If a new replacement has been primed, strip off this coat on both sides of the panel and along the weld seam with a coarse abrasive paper. If the panel has a rust preventative film coating instead of a primer, merely wipe off both sides of the weld seam with a clean rag and some solvent.

- Use vise grips on all flange joint and drip rail applications (Figure 6-105) to bring the parts closely together. Weld near the vise grip jaws where the fit-up is tight.

- A few sheet metal screws can be used on lap joints to position the panel for spot welding. Make sure that the paint has been removed from the joints.

- On long splice jobs, start in the middle of the panel and spot weld in one direction; for example, from the middle of the panel to the door post. Start again in the middle and complete the panel welds to the tail light area. This is an additional aid in eliminating distortion.

- Removal of burrs on the newly cut panel insures getting good metal-to-metal contact when body pressure is applied to the electrodes. Burrs and dents cause an air space between mating parts and prevent positive metal contact.

The twin electrodes of the panel spotter often permit spot welding in spaces where the squeeze

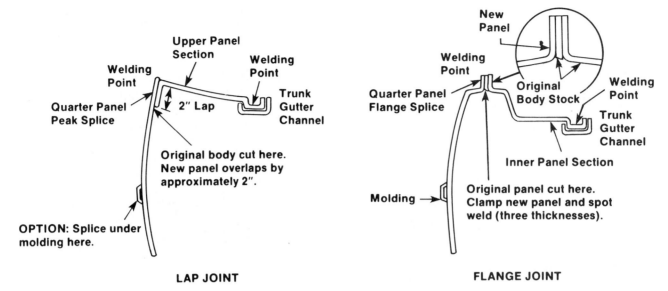

LAP JOINT   FLANGE JOINT

FIGURE 6-104   Panel spotting lap and flange joints

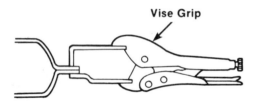

FIGURE 6-105   Using vise grips to hold a flange joint together

type has difficulty operating. In addition the panel spotter can be converted in a squeeze type spot welder with a gun attachment. However, this arrangement should be used only on nonstructural parts; never on structural parts.

6.12 STUD SPOT WELDING FOR DENT REMOVAL

Studs used in dent removal can be resistance welded with a special stud welder (Figure 6-106) or a panel spotter equipped with stud welding attachments (Figure 6-107). With either method, a stud pulling kit (Figure 6-108) containing all the necessary items (including a slidehammer) is a must for dent removal.

To remove a dent properly with either a stud or stud spot welder, a good quality stud is necessary. The stud should offer the necessary combination of pull strength and tensile strength, while remaining extremely flexible. The flexibility allows the stud to be bent out of the way when working on adjacent studs then bent back when required. The impor-

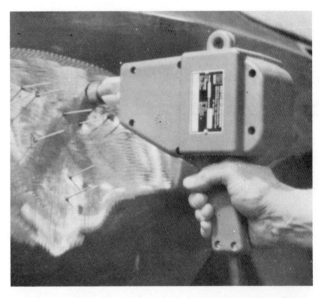

FIGURE 6-106   Typical stud or pin welder for removing dents. *(Courtesy of Henning Hansen, Inc.)*

FIGURE 6-107   Typical panel spotter installing spot studs. *(Courtesy of Lenco Inc.)*

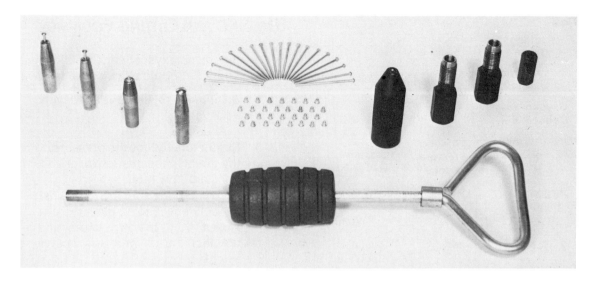

FIGURE 6-108   Typical panel spotter stud kit. *(Courtesy of Lenco Inc.)*

tance of this stud is to minimize the heat required and, therefore, maintain the flexibility of the steel when being applied and removed. Complete details on using stud or panel welding for dent removal can be found in Chapter 7.

6.13 MOLD RIVET WELDING

Although many decorative strips are applied with adhesive, a large number of moldings are still applied with mold rivets and clips; for example, chrome strips on rocker panels and window and vinyl roof moldings.

When patching or refinishing areas that are susceptible to moisture, salt, or high humidity, a technician is usually apprehensive about drilling holes ex-

posing inner panels. Mold rivet welding with a stud or spot welder is a logical solution. (As shown in Figure 6-109, one electrode has the mold rivet welding tip, while the other has the ground tip.) No holes are made; rivets can be relocated or replaced while not exposing vulnerable areas to outside elements. This one-step operation achieves a factory replica and is ideal for placing rivets on new skins. If rivets need to be removed or relocated, they require very little grinding.

6.14 OXYACETYLENE WELDING

Oxyacetylene is a type of fusion welding. Acetylene and oxygen are mixed in a chamber, ignited at the tip, and used as a high-temperature heat source (approximately 5400 degrees Fahrenheit) to melt and join the welding rod and base metal together (Figure 6-110).

FIGURE 6-109   Panel spotter also welds molding rivets. *(Courtesy of Lenco Inc.)*

FIGURE 6-110   Operation of oxyacetylene welder

191

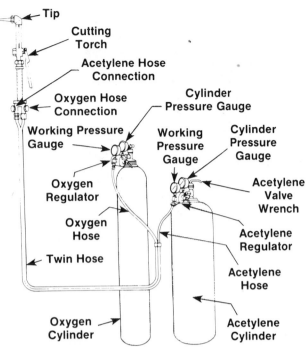

Tip
Cutting Torch
Acetylene Hose Connection
Oxygen Hose Connection
Working Pressure Gauge
Oxygen Regulator
Oxygen Hose
Twin Hose
Oxygen Cylinder

Cylinder Pressure Gauge
Working Pressure Gauge
Cylinder Pressure Gauge
Acetylene Valve Wrench
Acetylene Regulator
Acetylene Hose
Acetylene Cylinder

FIGURE 6-111 Typical oxyacetylene welding and cutting outfit

Since it is difficult to concentrate the heat in one area, the heat affects the surrounding areas and reduces the strength of steel panels. Because of this problem, auto makers do not recommend the use of oxyacetylene in repairs of damaged vehicles. Although oxyacetylene is in disfavor with most automobile manufacturers—with good reason—it has some use in the body shop. The oxyacetylene flame is still used to repair other damaged auto bodies, some heat shrinking operations, brazing and soldering, surface cleaning, and cutting of nonstructural parts. Oxyacetylene should not be used to cut structural parts of any vehicle unless special care is taken.

WELDING AND CUTTING EQUIPMENT

In general an oxyacetylene welding and cutting outfit (Figure 6-111) consists of the following:

- **Steel tanks (cylinders)** filled with:
  —Oxygen
  —Acetylene
- **Regulators** reduce the pressure coming from the tanks to the desired level and maintain a constant flow rate.
  —Oxygen pressure: 15 to 100 psi
  —Acetylene: 3 to 12 psi
- **Hoses** from the regulators and cylinders connect the oxygen and acetylene to the torch.
- **Torch.** The torch body mixes the oxygen and acetylene from the tanks in the proper proportions and produces a heating flame capable of melting steel. There are two main types of torches:
  —Welding torch
  —Cutting torch

The low-pressure torch is generally used for acetylene welding. This torch can be used at an extremely low acetylene pressure and has an injector nozzle. The gases are mixed by the discharge of oxygen from the center nozzle. The important operation control is shown in Figure 6-112.

As shown in Figure 6-113, the cutting torch has an oxygen tube and valve for conducting high-pressure oxygen attached to a welding torch. The flame outlet has a small oxygen hole located in the center of the tip that is surrounded by holes arranged in a spherical pattern. The outer holes are used for preheating.

To round out the equipment, safety gear described in Chapter 1 should be worn. Welding

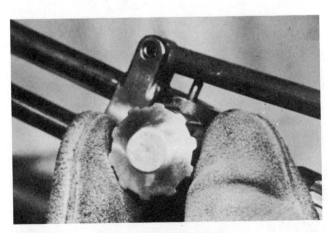

FIGURE 6-112 It is important to be familiar with the cutting torch adjustments.

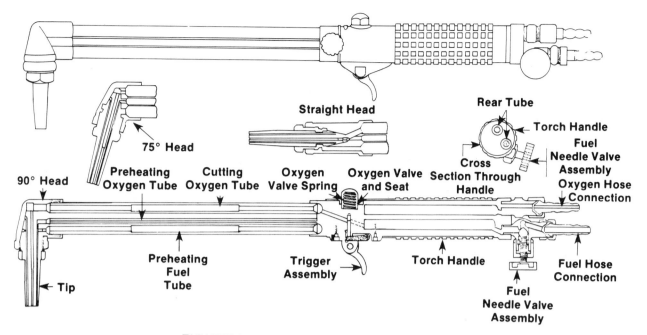

FIGURE 6-113   Parts of a typical cutting torch

should be done with either a number 4, 5, or 6 tinted filter shade. A spark lighter (Figure 6–114) is another necessity.

Types of Flame and Adjustment

When acetylene and oxygen are mixed and burned in the air, the condition of the flame varies depending on the volume of oxygen and acetylene. There are three forms of flame:

- **Neutral flame.** The standard flame is said to be a neutral flame. Acetylene and oxygen mixed in a 1 to 1 ratio by volume produces a neutral flame. As shown in Figure 6–115A,

FIGURE 6-114   Typical spark lighter

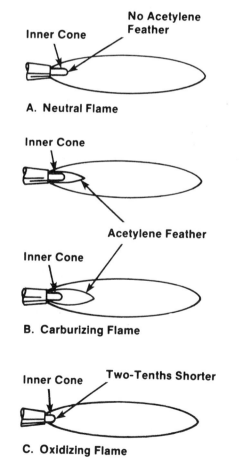

FIGURE 6-115   Types of cutting flames

this flame has a brilliant white cone surrounded by a clear blue outer flame.

- **Carburizing flame.** The carburizing flame, also called a surplus or reduction flame, is obtained by mixing slightly more acetylene than oxygen. Figure 6–115B shows that this flame differs from the neutral flame in that it has three parts. The cone and the outer flames are the same as the neutral flame, but between them there is an intermediate light-colored acetylene cone enveloping the cone. The length of the acetylene cone varies according to the amount of surplus acetylene in the gas mixture. For a double surplus flame, the oxygen-acetylene mixing ratio is about 1 to 1.4 (by volume). A carburizing flame is used for welding aluminum, nickel, and other alloys.
- **Oxidizing flame.** The oxidizing flame is obtained by mixing slightly more oxygen than acetylene. The oxidizing flame (Figure 6–115C) resembles the neutral flame in appearance, but the acetylene cone is shorter and its color is a little more violet compared to the neutral flame. The outer flame is shorter and fuzzy at the end. Ordinarily, this flame oxidizes melted metal, so it is not used in the welding of mild steel, but it is used in the welding of brass and bronze.

Welding Torch Flame Adjustment

As stated in the overview of welding, oxyacetylene welding is **not** used for welding modern auto bodies, but it is used for brazing certain nonstructural panels at factory-brazed seams. When using a welding torch, proceed as follows:

 1. Attach the appropriate tip to the end of the torch. Use the standard tip for sheet metal (each torch manufacturer has a different system for measuring the size of the tip orifice).
2. Set the oxygen and acetylene regulators at the proper pressure:
   - Oxygen—8 to 25 psi
   - Acetylene—3 to 8 psi
3. Open the acetylene valve about half a turn, and ignite the gas. Continue to open the valve until the black smoke disappears and a reddish yellow flame appears. Slowly open the oxygen valve until a blue flame with a yellowish white cone appears. Further open the oxygen valve until the center cone becomes sharp and well defined.

This type of flame is called a neutral flame and is used for welding mild steel (other than automobile bodies).

If acetylene is added to the flame or oxygen is removed from the flame, a carburizing flame will result.

If oxygen is added to the flame or acetylene is removed from the flame, an oxidizing flame will result.

Gas Cutting Torch Flame Adjustment

The cutting torch is sometimes used in collision repair shops to rough cut damaged panels. Gas cutting torch flame adjustment and cutting procedures are as follows:

 1. Adjust the oxygen and acetylene valves for a preheating neutral flame.
2. Open the preheating oxygen valve slowly until an oxidizing flame appears. This makes it difficult for melted metal to remain on the surface of the cut panel allowing for clean edges.
3. **Thick panel cutting method.** Heat a portion of the base metal until it is red hot. Just before it melts, open the high-pressure oxygen valve and cut the panel. Advance the torch forward while making sure the panel is melting and being cut apart. This method is widely used for thick panels (when there are several pieces overlapped together) or for a side member (even when there is an internal reinforcement).
4. **Thin panel cutting method.** Heat a small spot on the base metal until it is red hot. Just before it melts, open the high-pressure oxygen valve, and incline the torch to cut the panel. When cutting thin material, incline the tip of the torch so that the cut will be clean and fast (this prevents unwanted panel warpage).

 **SHOP TALK**

As soon as the cutting operation is completed, quickly turn off the high-pressure oxygen flow used for cutting and pull the torch away from the base metal. This action prevents sparks from entering the tip and igniting the oxygen-acetylene mixture in the torch handle (in extreme cases the ensuing fire could melt the torch handle).

Cutting HSS for Salvage Purposes

Salvage components must be cut with a grinding wheel disc, an air chisel and/or metal cutting saw, or with a plasma cutter. If the use of a gas torch is necessary when cutting HSS sheet metal components for salvage purposes or cutting a body structure for a "front/rear clip," factory engineers advise the following approach:

- Cut the metal structure at least 2 inches away from the desired cut line. Sheet metal within the heat-affected area will lose strength when subjected to the high heat levels of a torch.
- After torch cutting, use a grinding wheel disc, an air chisel, or a metal saw to make the final cut at the originally intended dimension line. HSS damage will then be "cut out" of the salvaged part.

As stated previously, oxyacetylene equipment should not be used on HSS components for welding or cutting. Vehicle manufacturer's engineers stress this point. There is just too much heat buildup that can reduce structural strength. However, in some instances an oxyacetylene torch can be used to heat HSS components or parts ("hot working") provided the critical 1400 degrees Fahrenheit temperature is not exceeded. (Check the manufacturer's shop manual on this point because some say 1000 degrees Fahrenheit is the critical temperature.)

High-strength steels should only be exposed to high temperatures from an oxyacetylene torch for a very short period of time. Three minutes is the recommended maximum time span for exposing HSS to a 1400-degree Fahrenheit temperature in order to reduce the amount of scaling that normally takes place on the metal surface. High-temperature exposure causes discoloration as shown in Figure 6–116.

In order to determine and control temperatures of high-strength steel parts and components being "heat worked" with oxyacetylene equipment, it is necessary to use a temperature indicating crayon (Figure 6–117).

The metal should be marked closely adjacent to the area being worked with a crayon rated no more than 1400 degrees Fahrenheit. Using such a crayon will indicate to the welder whether or not an excessive amount of heat is being applied. Thus metal temperatures can be controlled within safe levels and HSS damage easily prevented.

Cleaning With a Torch

As stated earlier in the chapter, it is important before starting any welding operation that the surfaces to be joined are thoroughly clean. The weld site must be completely free of any foreign material that might contaminate the weld. The finished weld is quite likely to be brittle, porous, and of poor integrity.

To remove heavy undercoating, rustproofing, tars, caulking and sealants, road dirt and primers, and the like, first use a scraper and an oxyacetylene torch. Then do the first cleaning with a wire brush and the torch, using a carburizing flame (Figure 6–118). In any event, keep the torch at a very low, controlled heat—just enough heat to get the job done.

Flame Abnormalities

When changes occur during the welding operation—for example, overheating of the flame outlet, adhesion of spatter, or fluctuations in the gas ad-

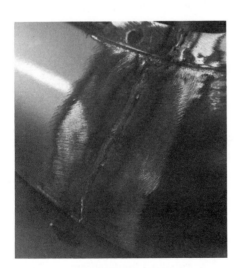

FIGURE 6–116   Discoloration of HSS heat-affected steel

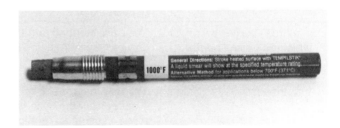

FIGURE 6–117   Typical heat indicating crayon that can be purchased locally from automotive supplier or welding outlet

FIGURE 6-118 Cleaning of metal with a gas torch and wire brush

justment pressure, the result will be variations in the flame. Therefore the operator must always be aware of the condition of the flame. Flame abnormalities and their causes and remedies are described in Table 6-8.

6.15 BRAZING

Brazing is applied only to places for sealing. This is a method of welding whereby a nonferrous metal, whose melting point (temperature) is lower than that of the base metal, is melted without melting the base metal (Figure 6-119). Brass brazing is frequently applied to automotive bodies.

TABLE 6-8: FLAME ABNORMALITIES AND REMEDIES

Symptom	Cause	Remedy
Flame Fluctuations	1. Moisture in the gas, condensation in hose. 2. Insufficient acetylene supply.	1. Remove the moisture from the hose. 2. Adjust the acetylene pressure and have the tank refilled.
Explosive Sound While Lighting the Torch	1. Oxygen or acetylene pressure is incorrect. 2. Removal of mixed-in gases are incomplete. 3. The tip orifice is too enlarged. 4. The tip orifice is dirty.	1. Adjust the pressure. 2. Remove the air from inside the torch. 3. Replace the tip. 4. Clean the orifice in the tip.
Flame Cut Off	1. Oxygen pressure is too high. 2. The flame outlet is clogged.	1. Adjust the oxygen pressure. 2. Clean the tip.
Popping Noises During Operation	1. The tip is overheated. 2. The tip is clogged. 3. The gas pressure adjustment is incorrect. 4. Metal deposited on the tip.	1. Cool the flame outlet (white letting a little oxygen flow). 2. Clean the tip. 3. Adjust the gas pressure. 4. Clean the tip.
Reversed Oxygen Flow (Oxygen is flowing into the path of the acetylene.)	1. The tip is clogged. 2. Oxygen pressure is too high. 3. Torch is defective. (The tip or valve is loose.) 4. There is contact with the tip and the deposit metal.	1. Clean the tip. 2. Adjust the oxygen pressure. 3. Repair or replace the torch. 4. Clean the orifice.
Backfire (There is a whistling noise and the torch handle grip gets hot. Flame is sucked into the torch.)	1. The tip is clogged or dirty. 2. Oxygen pressure is too low. 3. The tip is overheated. 4. The tip orifice is enlarged or deformed. 5. A spark from the base metal enters the torch, causing an ignition of gas inside the torch. 6. Amount of acetylene flowing through the torch is too low.	1. Clean the tip. 2. Adjust the oxygen pressure. 3. Cool the tip with water (letting a little oxygen flow). 4. Replace the tip. 5. Immediately shut off both torch valves. Let torch cool down. Then relight the torch. 6. Readjust the flow rate.

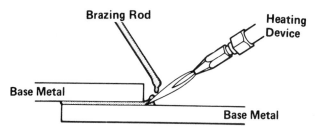

FIGURE 6-119   The brazing principle. *(Courtesy of Toyota Motor Corp.)*

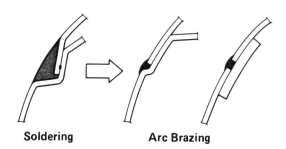

Soldering   Arc Brazing

FIGURE 6-120   **Typical body construction using solder or arc brazing.** *(Courtesy of Toyota Motor Corp.)*

Brazing is similar to joining two objects with adhesives; melted brass sufficiently spreads between the base metals to form a strong bond. The bending intensity against impact is less than that of the base metal, but the same as the melted brass. Therefore, under no circumstances should brazing be applied to any portions other than those to which it is applied at the factory.

There are two types of brazing:

• Soft brazing (soldering)
• Hard brazing (brass or nickel)

Ordinarily, the term **brazing** refers to hard brazing. The basic characteristics of brazing are:

• The pieces of base metal are joined together at a relatively low temperature where the base metal does not melt. Therefore, there is a lower risk of distortion and stress in the base metal.
• Because the base metal does not melt, it is possible to join otherwise incompatible metals.
• Brazing metal has excellent flow characteristics; it penetrates well into narrow gaps and it is convenient for filling gaps in body seams.
• Since there is no penetration and the base metal is joined only at the surface, it has very low strength to resist repeated loads or impacts.
• Brazing is a relatively easy skill to master.

Automobile assembly plants use arc brazing to join the roof and quarter panels together (Figure 6-120). Arc brazing uses the same principles as MIG welding. However, argon is used with brazing metal instead of CO_2 or an argon/CO_2 mixture (Figure 6-121). Special brazing wire is also required. Since the amount of heat applied to the base metal is low, overheating is minimized and there is little distortion or warpage of the base metal. When compared to the previously used methods of depositing brass on the base metal, arc brazing shortens both the time for making the weld and finishing. Also, there is no danger of lead poisoning.

In the body shop, the brazing equipment is usually about the same as oxyacetylene welding. For brazing, an oxyacetylene torch, brass filler rods, flux welding goggles, gloves, and a torch lighter are needed. While the oxyacetylene torch can be used in

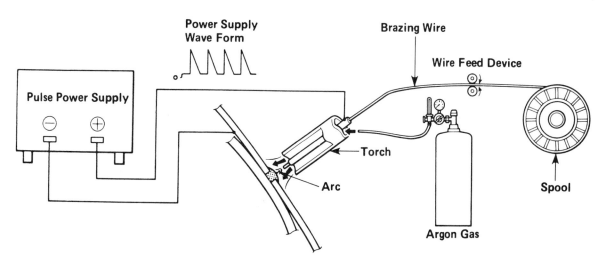

FIGURE 6-121   Arc brazing principles. *(Courtesy of Toyota Motor Corp.)*

TABLE 6-9	
Types of Brazing Materials	**Main Ingredients**
Brass brazing metal	Copper, Zinc
Silver brazing metal	Silver, Copper
Phosphor copper brazing metal	Copper, Phosphorus
Aluminum brazing metal	Aluminum, Silicon
Nickel brazing metal	Nickel, Chrome

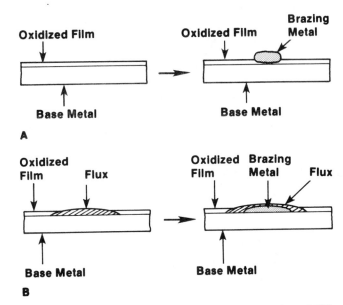

FIGURE 6-122 (A) When flux is not used and **(B)** when flux is used. *(Courtesy of Toyota Motor Corp.)*

soft brazing (soldering), it is best to use one designed for soldering.

In order to have brazing material with good qualities, such as flow characteristics, melting temperature, and compatibility with base metal and strength, it is made of two or more metals that form an alloy (Table 6-9). Copper and zinc are the main ingredients of the brazing rods used on auto bodies.

THE INTERACTION OF FLUX AND BRAZING RODS

Generally the surfaces of metals exposed to the atmosphere are covered with an oxidized film, which, if heat is applied, thickens. Flux not only removes this oxidized film, but prevents the metal surface from reoxidizing. It also increases the bond between the base metal and the brazing material.

If a brazing material is melted over a surface that has an oxidized film and foreign matter adhering to it, the brazing material will not adequately bond to the base metal and surface tension will cause the brazing material to ball up and not stick to the base metal (Figure 6-122A).

The oxidized film can be removed by applying flux to the surface of the base metal and then heating it until it becomes liquid (Figure 6-122B). After the oxidation has been removed, the brazing material will adhere to the base metal and the flux will prevent further oxidation.

BRAZING JOINT STRENGTH

Since the strength of the brazing material is lower than that of the base metal, the shape of the joint and the clearance of the joint are extremely

important. Figure 6-123 shows a basic brazing joint. Joint strength is dependent on the surface area of the pieces to be joined. Therefore, make the joint overlap as wide as possible.

Even when the items being joined are of the same material, the brazed surface area must be larger than that of a welded joint (Figure 6-124). As a general rule, the overlapping portion must be three or more times wider than the panel thickness.

BRAZING OPERATIONS

General brazing procedure is as follows:

 1. **Cleaning the base metal.** As previously stated, if there is oxidation, oil, paint, or dirt on the surface of the base metal, the brazing material will not flow properly over the base metal. These contaminants, if allowed to remain on the surface, can cause eventual joint failures. Even though flux acts to remove oxidized film and most contaminants, it is not strong enough to completely remove everything; therefore, first clean the surface mechanically with a wire brush.

2. **Flux application.** After the base metal is thoroughly cleaned, apply flux uniformly to the brazing surface. (If a brazing rod with flux in it is used [Figure 6-125], this operation is not necessary.)

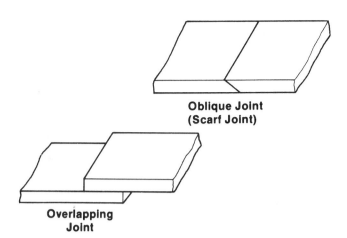

FIGURE 6-123   Two basic brazing joints. *(Courtesy of Toyota Motor Corp.)*

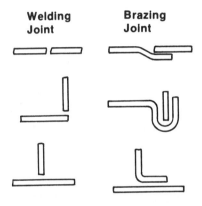

FIGURE 6-124   Comparison of welding and brazing joint. *(Courtesy of Toyota Motor Corp.)*

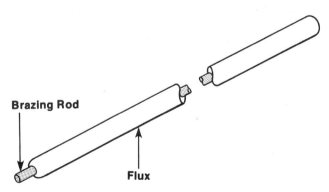

FIGURE 6-125   Brazing rod with flux

3. **Base metal heating.** Heat the joining area of the base metal to a uniform temperature capable of accepting the brazing material (Figure 6-126). Adjust the flame of the gas

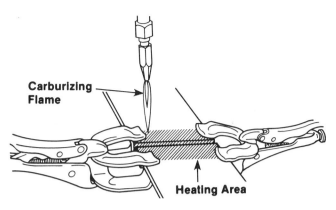

FIGURE 6-126   Base metal heating operation. *(Courtesy of Toyota Motor Corp.)*

welding torch so that it is a slight carburizing flame. By the melting condition of the flux, estimate the proper temperature for the brazing material.

4. **Base metal brazing operation.** When the base metal has reached the proper temperature, melt the brazing material onto the base metal (Figure 6-127), letting it flow naturally. Stop heating the area when the brazing material has flowed into the gaps of the base metal. Other points to consider are:

    *   Since brazing material flows easily over a heated surface, it is important to remember to heat the entire joining area to a uniform temperature.
    *   Do not melt the brazing material prior to heating the base metal (the brazing material will not adhere to the base metal).
    *   If the surface temperature of the base metal becomes too high, the flux will not clean the base metal, resulting in a poor brazing bond and inferior strength at the joint.

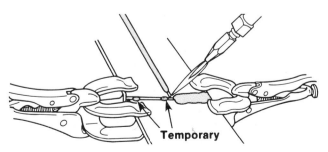

FIGURE 6-127   Base metal brazing operation. *(Courtesy of Toyota Motor Corp.)*

The following additional precautions should be taken when brazing:

- Brazing temperature must be higher than the melting point of brass by 50 to 190 degrees Fahrenheit.
- The size of the torch tip must be slightly larger than the thickness of the panel.
- Preheat the panel to have better deposition efficiency of the brazing filler.
- Secure the panel to prevent the base metal from moving and the brazing zone from breaking.
- Evenly heat the portion to be welded without melting the base metal.
- Control the heat by tilting the torch more horizontally (flatter to the surface) or by removing the flame and allowing the area to cool briefly.
- The brazing time must be as short as possible (to prevent weld strength from lowering).
- Avoid brazing the same place again.

Treatment After Brazing

Once the brazed portion has cooled down sufficiently, rinse off the remaining flux sediment with water and scrub the surface with a stiff wire brush. Baked and blackened flux can be removed with a sander or a sharp-pointed tool. If the remaining flux sediment is not adequately removed, the paint will not adhere properly, and corrosion and cracks might form in the joint.

6.16 SOLDERING (SOFT BRAZING)

Soldering is not used to reinforce the panel joints. It is only used for final finishing, such as in leveling the panel surface and correcting the surface of the welded joints. Because soldering functions by "capillary phenomenon," it has outstanding sealing ability.

Before attempting to solder a joint, remove paint, rust, oil, and other foreign substances from the built-up place and its vicinity.

Soldering Procedure

After the surface has been thoroughly cleaned, proceed as follows:

1. Heat the portion to be soldered. (Wipe it with a cloth after heating.)

2. Stir solder paste well, and apply it with a brush. (Apply it to an area 1 to 1-1/2 inches larger than the built-up area.)
3. Heat it from a distance.
4. Wipe the solder paste from the center to the outside.
5. Make sure the soldered portion is silver gray. (If it is bluish, it is due to overheating; if any spot is not soldered, reapply the paste for soldering.)

When soldering, keep the following points in mind:

- As previously mentioned, it is desirable to use a special torch for soldering. If a gas welding torch is used, the oxygen and acetylene gas pressures must be 4.3 to 5.0 psi.
- The solder must contain at least 13 percent zinc.
- Maintenance of appropriate temperature
  —Move the torch so that the flame evenly heats the entire portion to be soldered (without heating a single spot only).
  —When the solder begins to melt, remove the flame and start finishing with a spatula.
- When additional solder is required, the previously built-up solder must be reheated.

 **SHOP TALK** _____

The use of plastic solder in automotive soldering is not recommended because it is prone to cracking, requires a long time for drying, does not finish smoothly, is prone to rust on the panel, and cannot be recycled as ordinary solder can.

6.17 PLASMA ARC CUTTING

Plasma welding is seldom used in the auto body shop. However, plasma arc cutting is replacing oxyacetylene cutting as the best way to cut modern car metals. It cuts mangled metal effectively and quickly but will not destroy the properties of the base metal. This is important to today's metal shop, which sees more unibody cars with high-strength steel or high-strength alloy steel components. The old method of flame cutting just does not work that well anymore. The high heat, fast travel speed, low-heat input qualities coupled with the fact that plasma air cutting will cut rusted, painted, or coated metal with little difficulty make it an ideal process for the auto body repair field.

Basically, plasma air cutting (or plasma arc cutting) creates an intensely hot air stream over an ultra-small area, which melts and removes metal. Extremely clean cuts are possible with plasma cutting; and, because of the tight focus of the heat, there is no warpage, even if cutting thin sheet metal.

Figure 6–128A shows that there are two areas for gas flow. In air plasma arc cutting, compressed air is used for both shielding and cutting. As a shield gas, air shields the outside area of the torch nozzle, cooling the area so the torch does not overheat. Air also becomes the cutting gas. The air swirls around the electrode as it heads toward the nozzle opening. The swirling action helps to constrict and "narrow" the gas. When the machine is turned on, a "pilot" arc is formed between the nozzle and the inner electrode (Figure 6–128B). When the cutting gas reaches this pilot arc, it is super heated—up to 60,000 degrees Fahrenheit.

The gas is now so hot it ionizes and becomes capable of carrying an electrical current (the ionized gas is actually the plasma). The small, narrow opening of the nozzle accelerates the expanding plasma toward the workpiece. When the workpiece is close enough, the arc crosses the gap, with the electrical current being carried by the plasma (Figure 6–128C). This is the cutting arc.

 **SHOP TALK**

Air ordinarily will not conduct electricity. But during very high voltage, the air molecules ionize and become electrically conductive. The air becomes super heated and forms a path along which voltage can easily flow.

The extreme heat and force of the cutting arc melt a narrow path through the metal, dissipating the metal into gas and tiny particles. The force of the plasma literally blows away the metal particles leaving a clean cut.

Operating a Plasma Arc Cutter

To operate a typical plasma arc cutter such as shown in Figure 6–129, proceed as follows:

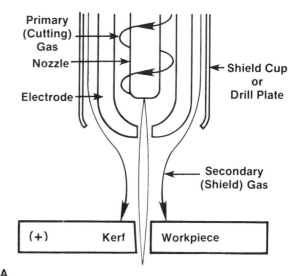

A

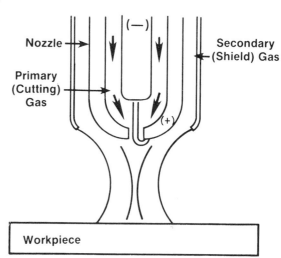

Pilot Arc (Nontransferred)

B

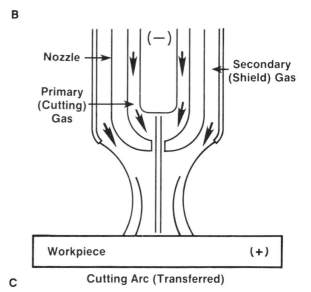

Cutting Arc (Transferred)

C

FIGURE 6–128   Typical plasma arc cutting setup

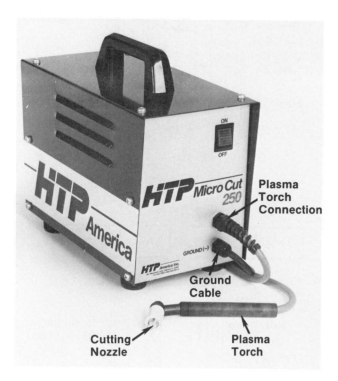

FIGURE 6-129 Typical plasma arc cutter. *(Courtesy of HTP America, Inc.)*

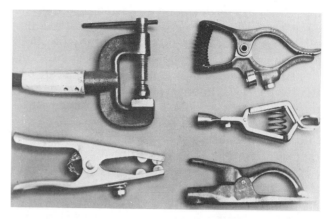

FIGURE 6-130 Various types of clamps

FIGURE 6-131 Position of torch. *(Courtesy of Century Mfg. Co.)*

1. Connect the plasma to a clean, **dry** source of compressed air with a minimum line pressure of 60 psi at the plasma air connection.

2. Connect the torch and clamping wire to the unit. After plugging the cutter into a power source that is recommended by the manufacturer, connect the ground clamp to a clean surface on the vehicle that is as close as possible to the area to be cut. Various types of clamps are shown in Figure 6-130.

3. The cutting nozzle must come in contact with an electrically conductive part of the work before the plasma arc can start. This must be done to satisfy the work safety circuit. However, once the arc has started, the cutter will easily cut through painted surfaces.

4. Hold the plasma torch so that the cutting nozzle is perpendicular to the work surface (Figure 6-131). Push the plasma torch down. This will force the cutting nozzle down until it comes in contact with the electrode, at which time the plasma arc will start. Immediately release the downward force on the plasma torch to let the cutting

nozzle return to its normal position. It is not necessary to keep the cutting nozzle in contact with the work once the plasma arc has started; however, it makes cutting easier. While keeping the cutting nozzle in contact with the work, put very little, if any, downforce on the plasma torch. It is only necessary to drag it lightly on the work surface.

5. Begin to move the plasma torch where the metal is to be cut. The speed of the cut will depend on the thickness of the metal. If the torch is moved too fast, it will not cut all the

way through the workpiece. If moved too slowly, it will put too much heat into the workpiece and might also extinguish the plasma arc.

Other pointers that should be remembered when using a plasma air cutter are:

- When piercing materials that are 1/8-inch thick or more, it is a good idea to angle the plasma torch at 45 degrees until the plasma arc pierces the material. This will allow the stream of sparks to shoot off at a 45 degree angle away from the gas diffuser. If the plasma torch is held perpendicular to the work when piercing heavy gauge material, then the sparks will shoot back up at the gas diffuser. The molten metal will then collect on the gas diffuser, plugging the air holes and greatly shortening the life of the gas diffuser.

- Post cooling of the torch is important to extend the life of the electrode and nozzle. At the end of a cut, the air continues to flow for several seconds after the torch switch has been released to prevent the nozzle and electrode from overheating until the next cut is started. Some equipment suppliers also recommend "idling" the unit for a couple of minutes after the cut is made.

CAUTION: When angling the torch, be aware of the fact that the sparks will shoot off as far as 20 feet away. Be sure that there are no combustibles or bystanders in the area that might be ignited or hurt by the sparks.

- When making long straight cuts, it might be easier to use a metal straightedge as a guide. Simply clamp it to the work to be cut. For elaborate cuts, make a template out of thin wood and guide the tip along that edge.
- When cutting 1/4-inch materials, it is beneficial to start the cut at the edge of the material.
- When making rust repairs, it is possible to piece the new metal over the rusted area and then cut the patch panel at the same time when cutting the rust out. This process also works when splicing in a quarter panel.
- Be aware of the fact that the sparks from the cutting arc can damage painted surfaces. The sparks will also pit glass. Use a welding blanket to protect these surfaces.
- Remember that these variables will have a bearing on cut quality (Figure 6–132).

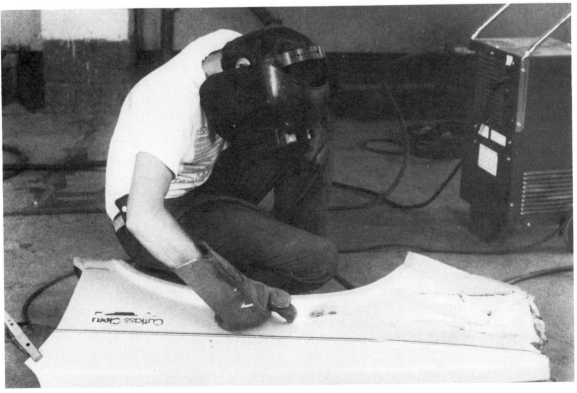

FIGURE 6–132   Making a quality cut. *(Courtesy of Century Mfg. Co.)*

—Travel speed. The thicker the material, the slower the speed. Travel is faster for thin material.

—Parts wear. The tip and electrode will erode with use. The more wear, the poorer the quality of the cut.

—Air quality. Moist or oil-contaminated air will also contribute to a poor quality weld.

Plasma Air Cutter

For plasma cutting with air, power sources can range in output from 10 to 100 amperes. The output of the power source helps determine maximum thicknesses that can be cut. A 10 to 15 ampere plasma cutter is generally adequate for mild steel up to 3/16-inch thick, a 30-ampere unit can cut metal up to 1/4-inch thick, and a 60 ampere unit will slice through metal up to 1/2-inch thick.

Controls are usually quite simple (see Figure 6–129). Plasma cutters made specifically for thinner metals may only have an off/on switch and a ready light to show when conditions are proper for cutting. More elaborate equipment can include a built-in air compressor, variable output control, on-board coolant and other features. Some equipment has a built-in safety protection system to protect the operator. This type of system cuts output power automatically if the safety cup is removed from the torch, if the tip and electrode are accidentally short circuited, because of insufficient air pressure or if the duty cycle is exceeded. The open circuit voltage of plasma cutting equipment can be very high (in the range of 250 to 300 volts) so insulated torches and internally connected terminals are also essential.

On some units, a switch is provided that allows the operator to alter the current mode when cutting bare metal or painted metal. When cutting painted or rusty metal, a continuous high frequency arc is best for punching through the nonconductive surface layer and for keeping the arc going while cutting. When cutting bare metal, on the other hand, a high frequency arc is only needed to start the arc. Once the torch starts to cut, a direct current pilot arc is all that is needed to keep things going. The bare metal position gives the longest electrode and nozzle life.

For automotive work, the cutting torch must be compact and easy to handle, to help you get into tight areas. Two critical parts of the torch are the nozzle and the cutting electrode. These are the only consumables (besides air) in plasma cutting. If either the nozzle or the electrode is worn or damaged, the quality of the cut will be affected. They wear somewhat with each cut, but such things as mois-

ture in the air supply, cutting excessively thick materials or poor operator technique will make them deteriorate prematurely. Keep a supply of electrodes and nozzles on hand and replace the ones on the torch when wear appears.

The electrode is actually quite small and is said to be an "insert," held in place by a metal jacket. Plasma cutting electrodes are often made of hafnium or zirconium because of the hardness and durability of these metals. In heavy-duty industrial cutting, tungsten electrodes are recommended for cutting with gases besides air, such as argon, nitrogen, and hydrogen. These shielding gases are seldom found in the collision shop.

Today's plasma air cutters do an excellent job using clean, dry compressed air. The air can be supplied with an external or built-in air compressor or by using a cylinder of compressed air. Look for equipment designed to run on less air pressure. Cylinders of air can be expensive, and so can shop air. To reduce possible contaminants in the air, use a regulator with a filter. Also, check the air pressure. Using the wrong air pressure can reduce the quality of the cuts, damage consumables, and actually decrease the cutting capacity of the machines.

6.18 Review Questions

1. Technician A uses a forward gun angle to achieve a deep penetration in the metal. Technician B uses the reverse gun angle to achieve a flat bead. Who is correct?
   a. Technician A
   b. Technician B
   c. Both A and B
   d. Neither A nor B

2. Technician A says that the main function of the gun nozzle is to provide gas protection. Technician B says the main function of the gun nozzle is to allow pressure to be applied to the work area. Who is correct?
   a. Technician A
   b. Technician B
   c. Both A and B
   d. Neither A nor B

3. Welding current affects which of the following?
   a. base metal penetration depth
   b. arc stability
   c. amount of weld spatter
   d. all of the above

4. When MIG welding, what happens if the tip-to-base metal distance is too long?
   a. The shield gas effect is reduced.
   b. The wire protruding from the end of the gun increases and becomes preheated.
   c. The melting speed of the wire increases.
   d. All of the above

5. Technician A starts a butt weld in the center of the metal. Technician B starts a butt weld at the edge of the metal. Who is correct?
   a. Technician A
   b. Technician B
   c. Both A and B
   d. Neither A nor B

6. Which of the following welds is the body shop alternative to the OEM resistance spot welds made at the factory?
   a. spot
   b. plug
   c. stitch
   d. all of the above

7. What determines the length of a tack weld?
   a. operator preference
   b. thickness of the panel
   c. type of base metal being welded
   d. type of shielding gas being used

8. In addition to very small surface cracks, what is penetrant inspection used to locate?
   a. porosity
   b. undercut
   c. overlap
   d. burn-through

9. Technician A installs a larger diameter electrode tip to increase the diameter of the spot weld. Technician B installs a smaller diameter electrode tip to increase the diameter of the spot weld. Who is correct?
   a. Technician A
   b. Technician B
   c. Both A and B
   d. Neither A nor B

10. How many spot welds should be made in a panel?
    a. a number equal to the original factory welds
    b. 50 percent more than the number of original factory welds
    c. 30 percent more than the number of original factory welds
    d. none of the above

11. Dross is a direct result of plasma arc torch speed that is _____ .
    a. too fast
    b. too slow
    c. both a and b
    d. neither a nor b

12. Which of the following statements concerning plasma arc cutting is incorrect?
    a. The plasma arc process cuts mangled metal effectively.
    b. Plasma cutting is an extension of the TIG process.
    c. The nozzle must come in contact with an electrically conductive part of the work before the arc can start.
    d. When piercing material that is more than 1/8-inch thick, hold the torch perpendicular to the work.

13. The typical acetylene pressure for oxyacetylene welding is _____ .
    a. 15 to 100 psi
    b. 3 to 12 psi
    c. 3 to 25 psi
    d. 30 to 120 psi

14. Mixing slightly more acetylene than oxygen will obtain what type of flame?
    a. neutral
    b. standard
    c. carburizing
    d. oxidizing

15. Which of the following is not characteristic of brazing?
    a. relatively high strength
    b. can join parts of varying thickness
    c. greater risk of distortion in the base metal
    d. can join otherwise incompatible metals

16. Which rollers are best suited for large-diameter wires?
    a. V-shaped grooves
    b. smooth U-shaped grooves

    c. knurled U-shaped grooves
    d. all of the above

17. Which of the following indicates the correct wire-to-heat ratio?
    a. an even, high-pitched buzzing sound
    b. a steady, reflected light
    c. both a and b
    d. neither a nor b

18. Which of the following statements is true?
    a. FCAW is less tolerant than MIG to surface impurities.
    b. FCAW has greater arc stability than MIG.
    c. FCAW wires are less expensive than MIG.
    d. None of the above

19. Welding current affects which of the following?
    a. base metal penetration depth
    b. arc stability
    c. amount of weld spatter
    d. all of the above

20. Technician A says that all steels can be MIG welded with one common type of weld wire. Technician B says that metals of different thicknesses can be MIG welded with the same diameter wire. Who is correct?
    a. Technician A
    b. Technician B
    c. Both A and B
    d. Neither A nor B

CHAPTER
7

Basic Auto Sheet Metal Work

Metalworking skills are probably the most important craft a body technician can bring to a shop, and probably one of the most neglected skills, too. The development of high-quality plastic body fillers in recent years has made it easy to bump the low spots up, bang the high spots down, and coat the damaged area with filler. In many cases, body repair technicians, spend more time shaping and sculpting plastic filler than they would spend properly reworking the damaged metal. Not only is the inexperienced body mechanic wasting valuable shop time, but in many cases the quality of the repair suffers also. A damaged panel improperly straightened will have tensions that can cause the plastic filler to crack, even lose adhesion, and fall off. That, of course, does nothing to build a reputation of customer satisfaction.

But quality work and customer satisfaction are not the only reasons, nor even the best reasons, for properly reworking damaged sheet metals. In today's unitized frames, the driver's safety and that of his or her family are at stake. All kinks and buckles in the vehicle's boxed rail sections, inner braces, and interlocking panels affect the structural strength of the frame. The damaged unibody frame must be restored to its original condition.

Body repair procedures not only vary according to the type of damage encountered and the contour and construction of the damaged panel, but the type of sheet metal steel in the damage area also affects metalworking techniques. These considerations will be covered in this chapter.

7.1 AUTOMOTIVE SHEET METAL

There are two types of sheet metal used in automobile construction—hot rolled and cold rolled. Hot-rolled sheet metal is made by rolling at temperatures exceeding 1472 degrees Fahrenheit, has a standard manufacturing thickness range of 1/16 to 5/16 inches, and is used for comparatively thick components of auto bodies such as frames and cross members. Cold-rolled sheet metal is acid-rinsed hot-rolled sheet metal that is cold rolled thin, then annealed. Since this sheet metal is worked by cold rolling, it has a dependable thickness accuracy, surface quality, and good press workability. Most unibodies are made from cold-rolled steel. In places around the suspension in which corrosion resistance is particularly required, cold-rolled sheet met-

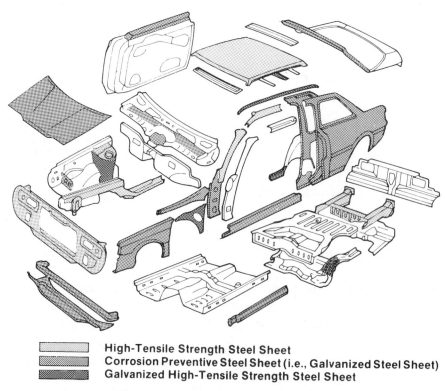

High-Tensile Strength Steel Sheet
Corrosion Preventive Steel Sheet (i.e., Galvanized Steel Sheet)
Galvanized High-Tensile Strength Steel Sheet

FIGURE 7-1 Typical areas where high-strength steels are used on unibody vehicles

al subjected to surface treatment is used to make antirust sheet metals. High-strength steels, instead of the "mild" steel traditionally used in automotive metals, are becoming more and more common on today's unibody frame.

Low-Carbon Steel

Much of the sheet metal used in auto body repair today is low-carbon or mild steel. Steel with a low level of carbon is relatively soft and easy to work. It can be safely welded, heat shrunk, and cold worked without seriously affecting its strength. But because it is easily deformed and relatively heavy, car manufacturers have begun using high-strength steels in load carrying parts of the vehicle.

High-Strength Steels

The term **high-strength steel** has been used arbitrarily to describe types of steel having a higher strength than mild or low-carbon steel that has been used for most automotive structural applications for many years.

In the mid 1970s, automakers were faced with solving the problem of reducing vehicle weight to improve fuel economy. The new unitized body vehicles being designed were usually smaller than those they replaced. Front structures were designed to handle potentially far greater load carrying and energy absorption requirements. Higher strength steel was used to solve both problems.

Today's unitized construction means that a component such as an apron or rail assembly, which is no longer just a splash shield, has to not only be lightweight but also carry a portion of the suspension reaction load and support a transverse-mounted engine, battery, ignition module, and bumper system. It is also designed with buckling sections to limit damage transmitted to the passenger compartment. In order to successfully achieve these objectives, many manufacturers made this new apron/rail assembly of stronger, lighter weight, high-strength steel. Figure 7–1 shows some typical body parts where high-strength steels are used.

However, these same properties that contribute strength and light weight offer some unique challenges to the repair industry. When high-strength steel is deformed on impact, it is more difficult to dimensionally restore than mild steel. Normal repair procedures, which dictate using heat to either aid in relieving the stresses of pulling or welding in a new

part, must be carefully controlled, or not used at all, to avoid structural damage to the part.

Types of High-Strength Steel

Many types of steels are generally classified as high-strength steel. Three types are often used in automotive structures. Before explaining the differences between these types of steel, it is important to understand the definition of strength. Actually, there are two types of strength and they both relate to the ability of steel and other metals to resist permanent deformation. Steel strength can be increased by a variety of manufacturing processes that include heat treatment, cold rolling, and chemical additives. Depending on the type and extent of heat treatment and chemical additions, any further heating beyond specific time and temperature limits can alter the strength of the steel significantly and permanently.

- **Yield strength,** or yield stress, is measured as the minimum force per unit of area, which causes the material to begin to permanently change its shape.
- **Tensile strength,** or tensile stress, is measured as the maximum force, per unit of area, which causes a complete fracture or break in the material.

Both stress and strength are expressed in pounds per square inch (psi) or kilograms per square millimeter (kg/mm^2).

Among other problems, high-yield strength and tensile strength mean that workability is poor and weld strength is inferior. Because of these traits this steel was not used very much in automobile bodies in the past. Recently, high-strength thin sheet metal, which has better formability and weldability, has been developed for automotive use.

High-strength sheet metal is divided in the following three types according to its strengthening process:

- **High-strength, low-alloy (HSLA) steel,** or rephosphorized steel, is produced by adding phosphorus to mild steel to upgrade its strength level. It has working characteristics that are similar to those of mild steel and was developed in recent years to provide better tensile strength to the exterior panels or auto bodies.
- **High-tensile strength steel (HSS),** or Si-Mn solid solution hardened steel, contains increased amounts of silicon, manganese, and carbon to give it a higher tensile strength. It has been used in the past for suspension-

related components, frames, and so on. Precipitation-hardened steel is another HSS steel that is strengthened by the formation of colombium (niobium) carbonitride precipitation. It was developed in the early 1970s as a high-tensile strength steel with excellent working and stamping characteristics. It is used mainly for door side guards, bumper reinforcements, and so on.

- **Ultra-high-strength steel (UHSS),** or dual phase steel, is made by quenching the steel on a continuous annealing line or in a hot-strip mill. This steel has a two phase microstructure (quenched martensitic structure and ferritic structure). Dual phase steel has good formability for HSS with more than 78,000 psi of tensile strength. Martensitic steel is the best known of UHSS.

High-Tensile Strength Steel

High-tensile strength steel (HSS) is stronger than low-carbon or mild steel because of heat treatment. Most Japanese import cars contain HSS in body structural components. Conventional heating and welding methods will not adversely affect the strength level of HSS. This is because HSS has a yield strength of up to 35,000 psi and a tensile strength of more than 45,000 psi. The material will experience an increase in stress, exceeding the yield strength, as it is deformed during a collision. When heat is applied to a HSS component to assist in straightening, the stresses resulting from collision are decreased thereby restoring the strength to a lower or normal level. If the collision stresses exceed the tensile strength, the material will tear or fracture. Normal welding practices, including oxyacetylene, can be used to aid in restoring the component. However, extreme caution must be exercised when using oxyacetylene. Temperature indicating methods should be applied around the area to be heated with an oxyacetylene torch to restrict these temperatures to 1200 degrees Fahrenheit. Door guard beams and some bumper reinforcements cannot be straightened and should be replaced. (Minor damage on door guard beams can be ignored if it does not interfere with door alignment or function. If the corrugations in the beam are dented or deformed, the door beam should be replaced.)

All new or used replacement parts should be MIG welded using AWS-E-70S-6 wire, which has the same strength level of HSS.

High-Strength, Low-Alloy Steel

High-strength, low-alloy steel (HSLA) is used in many United States domestic cars for body structur-

al components such as front and rear rails, rocker panels, bumper face bars, bumper reinforcements, door hinges, and lock pillars. Its strength is mainly due to the addition of special chemical elements.

> **CAUTION:** Use extreme care when using heat to relieve stress on HSLA panels. After exposure to a temperature of 1200 degrees Fahrenheit, or higher, for several minutes, the special hardening elements are absorbed by larger, softer elements in the heated area, resulting in lower strength.

To avoid substantially reducing the ability of the structure to react to normal road loads or collision forces, never exceed the factory-recommended temperatures. A safe rule of thumb is to never heat over 700 to 900 degrees Fahrenheit and do not apply heat longer than 3 minutes. MIG welding is an acceptable practice for HSS and HSLA; most automobile manufacturers do not recommend using oxyacetylene to weld either type.

Ultra-High-Strength Steel

Ultra-high-strength steels are alloy-free with tensile strength almost ten times that of typical mild steel. All door beams and some bumper reinforcements are martensitic, or ultra-high-strength steels. In these steels, the unusually high-strength properties are a result of a special grain or crystalline composition imparted during forming and fabricating. Any reheating for repair destroys this unique composition and reduces strength to that typical of mild steel. In addition, these steels are so hard that they cannot be straightened cold with typical shop equipment. Therefore, a damaged martensitic, or ultra-high-strength, steel member must not be repaired; it must be replaced. New parts should be installed by MIG plug welding.

PROPERTIES OF STEEL SHEET METAL

Regardless of the type of steel used in manufacturing the modern unibody, all sheet metal used by the manufacturer must be soft enough to be pressed into a variety of shapes that satisfy both safety and styling considerations.

The difference in grades of automotive sheet steel is not usually noticeable to the body technician, because he or she never works on flat unworked sheets. The panels he or she works on have already been shaped and formed. When flat sheet

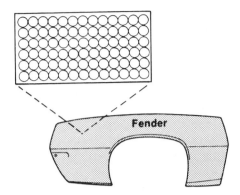

FIGURE 7-2   Granular structure of steel

steel is formed to a shape, it takes on certain properties or characteristics that harden the sheet steel.

For example, the roof panel found on most small economy cars is relatively flat. If hit in the center with the palm of the hand, the panel is likely to bend and then pop back to its original shape. Try the same thing on a roof panel that has a corrugated shape. The panel will hardly move at all. Although both roofs might be made of the same grade of steel, the one that has been changed the most is said to be harder and more resistant to deformation. During this stamping process the properties of the metal in the corrugated roof were changed to more of a degree than the flat roof.

The same is true for panels whose shape has been changed during a collision. The structure of the metal in the affected areas has changed, causing the metal to become harder and more resistant to corrective forces. In order to repair collision damage, a body technician should understand what property changes have taken place in the metal.

Physical Structure of Steel

The best way to define these properties is by first elaborating on the physical structure of sheet metal. Steel, just like all matter, is composed of atoms. These minute particles of matter are combined to form grains (Figure 7-2). Grains are large enough to be seen with the aid of a microscope. Grains are formed into patterns called the grain structure.

The condition of the grain structure in a piece of steel determines how much it can be bent or shaped. In order to change the shape of flat sheet steel, change the shape and position of all the individual grains that are located in the area of the creases, folds, or curves.

In mild steels, the individual grains can withstand a considerable amount of change and movement before splitting or breaking occurs. To demonstrate this, take a welding rod and bend it back and

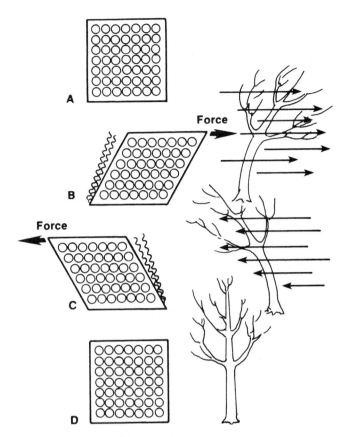

FIGURE 7-3   Elastic deformation: under pressure, the metal bends; when the force is released, the metal returns to its original shape.

forth several times. Notice that in the area of the bend the metal will become very hot. The heat is generated by the internal friction created as the individual grains move against each other in the area of the bend.

Effect of Impact Forces

The atomic structure and grain pattern of a metal will determine how it reacts to force. The sheet metal's resistance to change has three properties:

- Elastic deformation
- Plastic deformation
- Work hardening

All of these properties are closely related in that they are different aspects of the effect of force applied to sheet metal. They all are related to the "yield point." The yield point is the amount of force that a piece of metal can resist without tearing or breaking.

Elastic Deformation

Elastic deformation (Figure 7-3) is the ability of metal to stretch and return to its original shape. For example, take a piece of sheet metal and gently bend it to form a slight arc. When released it will spring back to its original shape. This spring back tendency makes it necessary for the body technician to recognize elastic deformation in damaged panels. This will enable the technician to plan his or her work to take advantage of any tendency of the damaged metal to spring back. Spring-back will be found in any area that is still relatively smooth even though it has been carried out of position by buckles formed in adjoining areas. Many such areas will spring back to shape if they are released by relieving the distortion in the buckled areas that hold them out of place.

Plastic Deformation

Plastic deformation is the ability of metal to be bent or formed into different shapes. When metal is bent beyond its elastic limit, it will have a tendency to spring back, but not all the way to its original shape (Figure 7-4). A piece of sheet metal, if bent into a tight U-shape, will spring back when released but not to its original shape.

This is because the grain structure has taken on a new set. Plasticity is important to the body techni-

cian because both stretching and permanent deformation take place in various areas of most damaged panels that he or she works with.

Elasticity and plasticity are illustrated in Figure 7-5. The graph shows the relationship between the size of the load and the elongation of a sheet metal when a tensile load is applied to the sheet metal.

If the load is increased a little at a time, the elongation increases proportionally. However, if the load exceeds a certain limit, internal slipping of the grain pattern occurs, and even if the rate of load increase is kept constant, elongation will suddenly increase. If even more load is applied, elongation will suddenly increase and the maximum load will be reached. After that, partial elongation will occur in one portion of the material and it will break.

Point A in the figure is called the elastic limit. If the load is lower than point A, deformation of the sheet metal will disappear when the load is removed and it will return to its original shape. This is called elastic stress. If the load exceeds point A, even if the load is removed, the deformation will remain and the panel will not return to its original shape. This is called permanent plastic, or stress. For example, if the load is removed at point P, the elongation of the panel will return to point E but permanent stress OE will remain. When a car is damaged in a collision, the stress sustained from the impact will remain unless it is taken out. This is a condition in which there is an area with permanent stress surrounded by a neighboring area with elastic stress that cannot be removed. When repairing body panels with this type of damage, first remove the permanent stress that is restricting the elastic stress. When that is done, the

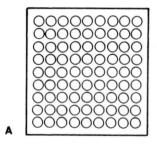

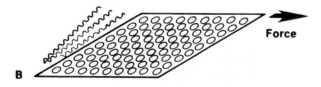

Force

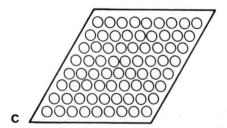

FIGURE 7-4 Plastic deformation occurs when the grain structure is forced beyond the elastic limit and takes on a new set.

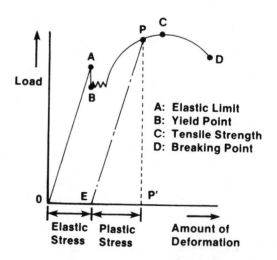

A: Elastic Limit
B: Yield Point
C: Tensile Strength
D: Breaking Point

FIGURE 7-5 Load and deformation characteristics

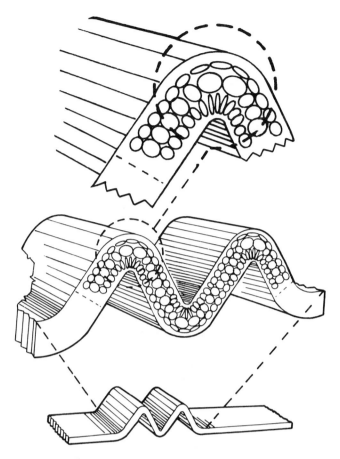

FIGURE 7-6 Grain realignment in bend results in work hardening

elastic stress will disappear naturally and the body panel will return to its original shape by itself.

Work Hardening

Work hardening is the upper limit of plastic deformation causing the metal to become very hard in the area where it has been bent. For example, if a welding rod is bent back and forth several times, a fold or buckle will appear at the point of the bend. The plastic deformation has been so great at this point that the grain structure has been radically forced out of alignment, causing the metal to become very hard and stiff (Figure 7-6). This increased hardness is called work hardening.

The importance of understanding how metal stiffens, making it stronger in areas that are bent or worked, cannot be overemphasized. It is the basis of practically all damage repair.

Some work hardness will be found in any undamaged body panel. It is the result of the original forming process. The bending caused by a collision adds still more work hardening in the areas affected.

Sometimes much more will be added by the cold working used by the body technician as he or she straightens the damaged area. If excessive work hardening is caused by working the metal improperly, the job will be made more difficult.

For this reason, it is important that the body technician be familiar with the properties of sheet metal just discussed. It has been estimated that the average body technician creates as much damage during the repair as was done in the original impact. This is due to a lack of knowledge and skill. It is impossible to correct all the damage without creating some during straightening, but the point is to keep it to the absolute minimum. Do not create damage, repair it.

7.2 CLASSIFYING BODY DAMAGE

The first step in auto body repair is analyzing the damaged area. A number of conditions that the body technician must recognize are present in any damaged panel. Each of the items listed below is a condition that occurs when metal is damaged by impact.

- Direct damage—tear, gouge, or scratch
- Indirect damage—Buckle (simple hinge, collapsed hinge, simple rolled, collapsed rolled) or pressures (tension areas, pressure areas)
- Work hardening—normal and impact created.
- Direction of damaging force.

Damaged metal has two classifications:

- Direct damage
- Indirect damage

DIRECT DAMAGE

Direct damage is very simple. Direct damage is usually visible as a gouge, a tear, or a scratch. It is the damaged portion of the panel that came in direct contact with the object that caused the impact (Figure 7-7). Direct damage is usually only 10 to 15 percent of the total damage; however, it can be as much as 80 percent of the total damage if the impact was limited to a long gouge or crease. Direct damage repair is limited. Metal used in today's cars is often too thin to be reworked. Straightening is time consuming and usually not practical on areas containing direct damage. Direct damage usually requires some plastic filler or, on rare occasions, lead, after all indirect damage has been handled. Direct damage varies from job to job.

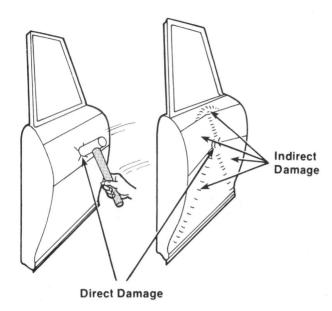

Direct Damage

FIGURE 7-7   Direct and indirect damage

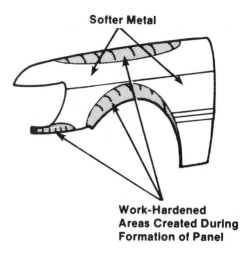

FIGURE 7-8   Factory-formed, work-hardened areas

Indirect Damage

Indirect damage resulting from direct damage, in most cases, represents a large part of the overall damage. What is not direct damage is considered indirect damage. In most collisions there is a combination of both types of damage. Indirect damage does not vary from one job to the next. The buckles created are always the same; the pressure forces are always the same. The repair is always the same, only the tools used vary, because the size, severity, and location will vary.

Indirect damage represents, on the average, 80 to 90 percent of the overall damage. Since indirect damage is basically the same from job to job, 80 to 90 percent of all sheet metal repairs are the same. A few basic techniques will handle most bodywork.

Work Hardening

As has already been stated, work hardening occurs whenever metal bends. It happens when the metal is first formed to shape by the manufacturer and also when it is damaged. To understand this, visualize a flat sheet of metal formed into a body panel such as a fender. The flat sheet is placed in the stamping press; the edges are clamped securely; then the center is stretched into the press until the once flat metal takes the shape of the press. The metal was relatively soft before it went into the press. Now it is quite hard. It has been work hardened by rearranging the grain structure. The areas that are

still relatively flat are softer. In the fender, illustrated in Figure 7-8, there are "soft" areas (unshaded) and "hard" areas (shaded). The shaded areas (crowns and ridges) are harder to damage, but when damaged, are harder to straighten. On the other hand, the flat metal will damage easily during straightening operations, and the correct straightening techniques must be used to avoid damaging the undamaged metal. Work hardening is in all sheet metal panels of a car to varying degrees. It is important to know where the metal was the hardest and softest before it was damaged.

To demonstrate how work hardening affects the repair process, imagine a piece of steel about 12 inches long and 6 inches wide (Figure 7-9). One can bend this metal strip slightly and it will return to its original shape, but if bent past a certain limit (elastic limit), the metal takes a set called a buckle. The metal surrounding the new bend returns to a straight condition. But at the point of the bend work hardening has set in. If an attempt is made to bend the metal back to its original shape, two additional buckles (work hardened) are created adjacent to the original bend because the bend would not open up; it was too hard.

Buckles caused by impact create additional work hardening in an automotive sheet metal panel. Remember: A buckle is created only when the metal is bent to a point where it will not return to its original shape. Bent metal is not necessarily buckled metal. When metal is bent but returns to its original shape later, it is not buckled metal. Work-hardened buckles are represented in Figure 7-10. The other areas are in the damage but are only bent metal not buckled. It is important to recognize these areas as they play an important role in determining a sound repair procedure.

Flat Sheet Before Bending

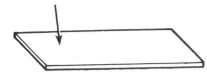

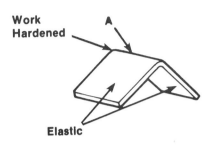

Additional Work Hardening

FIGURE 7–9   Additional work hardening created by trying to bend work hardened metal back to shape

Buckles

As mentioned before, buckles are a result of bending metal past its elastic limit. Bent beyond this

limit, metal will not return to its original shape. New work hardening and a new shape is formed. The buckles in indirect damage are classified as follows:

- Simple hinge
- Collapsed hinge
- Simple rolled
- Collapsed rolled

It is easier to think of them as two types (a hinge and a roll), each of which can be simple or collapsed.

Simple Hinge Buckles

The simple hinge buckle is the easiest to understand. The simple hinge buckle bends like a hinge; that is it bends equally along its entire length (Figure 7–11). The buckle usually causes little stretching or shrinking. If straightened incorrectly, however, it will cause considerable trouble for the technician. When severe, it should be "pulled" out rather than pushed out. Figure 7–11 is a drawing of a simple hinge buckle showing—when it is created—how the top surface pulls, causing stretching on the upper surface, and how the bottom surface pushes together, causing shrinkage on the underside of the metal. If there is stretching on the top and shrinkage on the bottom, it stands to reason that somewhere in the middle there is an area that is unchanged. The correct repair procedures will result in straightening the metal and leaving the overall dimension the same. If corrected properly, the buckle reverses exactly as it was created. If not, additional damage is created to the adjacent metal and to the buckle. A simple hinge buckle always forms a "straight line" buckle. The description of the simple hinge buckle refers to solid sheet metal. The basic rule of metal bending applies to box sections as well as solid metal. There is a difference, however, in the results of bending

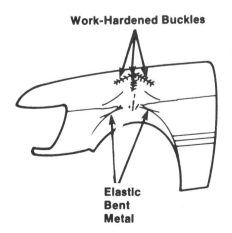

FIGURE 7–10   Work-hardened and elastic areas in a typical dent

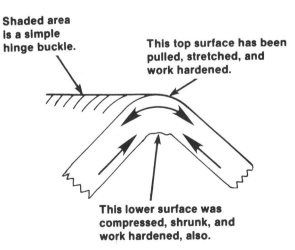

FIGURE 7–11   Analysis of a hinge buckle

215

(Figure 7-12). The box section has no strength in its center, and as a result, the upper (or top) sheet metal is pulled downward instead of stretching. Little or no stretching occurs. The lower (or bottom) sheet metal is under pressure from both sides and buckles easily. If not straightened with care, the top surface will buckle also. Severe overall shrinkage is the result. Unlike the buckle in the solid metal, the box section collapses on both sides, along with the bottom (and the top, when incorrectly straightened).

Collapsed Hinge Buckle

Sheet metal gives very little resistance to pressure forces exerted on its end. It has enormous resistance to a pulling force along its length. To demonstrate this, take a sheet of metal about 1 inch × 8 inches in size and try to push something with it. It takes very little effort to bend the metal. Now secure the metal to a bench or table and pull. The metal strip will pull hundreds of pounds of weight without stretching or creating any damage whatsoever. This simply means that the top metal in the hinge buckle

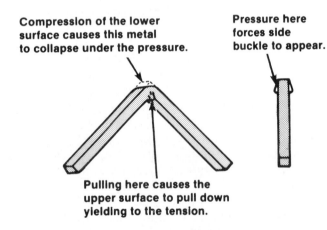

Compression of the lower surface causes this metal to collapse under the pressure.

Pressure here forces side buckle to appear.

Pulling here causes the upper surface to pull down yielding to the tension.

FIGURE 7-12   A collapsed box section

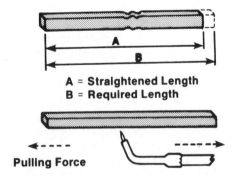

A = Straightened Length
B = Required Length

Pulling Force

FIGURE 7-13   Heat is applied to work-hardened area to soften the metal and allow the rail to be pulled back to its original length.

(Figure 7-12) is relatively undamaged compared with the bottom metal. The pressure side of the buckle is shrunk severely, far more than if the box section were solid metal. This is called collapsing of a hinge buckle or a **collapsed box section.**

When the box section is straightened, further collapsing of the top surface could easily occur. Special effort with heat and pulling equipment is required to prevent it. Figure 7-13 shows the results of improper and proper corrective procedures.

In the new unibody cars of today there are quite a number of complete boxed sections. Boxed structural rails, rocker panels, windshield pillars, center pillars, and roof rails are just a few. Some boxed sections like the door assembly are quite large. Any metal that is bent to form an angle is considered a box section. Late model cars have a great number of ridges and flanges in them. These are all areas where work hardening is built and are considered as **partial boxed sections** (Figure 7-14). Entire fenders can be thought of as partial boxed sections. As did the complete boxed section in Figure 7-12, the partial box also collapses. The results are the same. The name of the buckle is the same: collapsed hinge buckle. Straightening improperly will have the same results as with the complete box—overall shortage in dimensions.

Collapsed Rolled Buckle

When a hinge buckle crosses a panel, it not only shrinks any and all boxed or partially boxed sections, but it will also shrink any crowned surfaces it crosses. When this happens, a new buckle is formed. This buckle tries to turn the panel inside out and rolls along, increasing in length as it does. This "increasing in length" is the characteristic of the buckle. It is called a collapsed rolled buckle. Hinge type buckles (collapsed or simple) increase in depth, but not in length. Any buckles that are on crowned surfaces will shrink the metal. The collapsed rolled buckle is

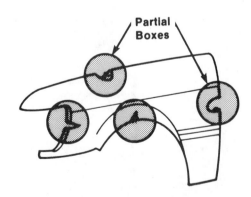

Partial Boxes

FIGURE 7-14   Partial boxed areas

216

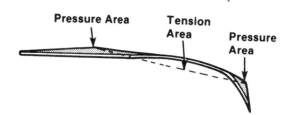

FIGURE 7-16   High and low areas in damaged combination type panel

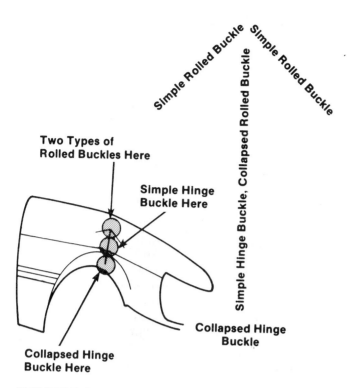

FIGURE 7-15   Combination of buckles in a dented fender

no exception. The shrinkage depends on the severity of the impact.

Simple Rolled Buckle

Two other buckles are also formed whenever a collapsed rolled buckle occurs. These two are adjacent to the collapsed roll. They are called simple rolled buckles. These are also shrinking type buckles because they are on the crown of the panel. The identification of the rolled type buckles is not difficult. The collapsed and simple rolled buckles form an arrow design on the crown of the panel. At first glance, the fender in Figure 7-15 looks like it has only a single buckle crossing it vertically. Actually it has five buckles, four types. Rolled buckles (simple and collapsed) occur only on crowned surfaces. This is because the crown is what causes them. If the metal was flat, it would bend like a hinge and a simple hinge buckle would occur. If the panel is crowned, the buckle crossing it tends to roll as it travels deep into the metal, not just because of the folding action on the surface, but because the metal shrinks within itself. Later if the metal is laid flat (no folds), the shrinkage will still be there, within the metal. Collapsed rolled buckles always occur crosswise to all crowns they are in. The shrinkage they create is also in that direction. Simple rolled buckles

shrink the metal as do collapsed rolled buckles, but in a different direction. The body technician should learn the four different kinds of buckles that are in the indirect damage area. The examples given here have been on only a few specific panels. Recognize the bulges that give clues to possible shrinkage somewhere. Be able to identify the buckles at a glance. Practice by examining many dents. Ask "Where is the direct damage?" and "What is the resulting indirect damage?" Find the work-hardened areas. Find the bent, but undamaged areas. Look for the collapsed rolled buckle. Examine damage found in the repair shop or parking lot. Make note of the buckles found and try to figure out a procedure to correct the damage.

Pressure Forces

The terms **pressure** and **tension** are descriptive words that are commonly used to describe the conditions in metal after damage. These conditions are often described as **high spots** and **low spots.** The main thing is to understand their meanings. There are pressures and tensions (stresses and strains) within the metal before any damage occurs. All crowns, for instance, are under pressure. This "pressure," however, is not the type of force being discussed here—the forces that occur (or start) at the time of the damage. Metal that is forced up has a new pressure applied to it. The pressure is being held there by the work-hardened buckles. If they were to suddenly disappear, the metal would return to its original shape. Consider the metal as being without pressure or tension before it was damaged when evaluating the changes that have taken place and the corrections that must be made.

The metal that is pushed up is called a **pressure area.** Areas that are pushed down are called **tension areas.** The drawing in Figure 7-16 shows a typical cross section of a crowned panel that is damaged. The movement of the metal is obvious.

All panels are crowned to some degree. A highly crowned panel is called a **high crowned.** A nearly flat

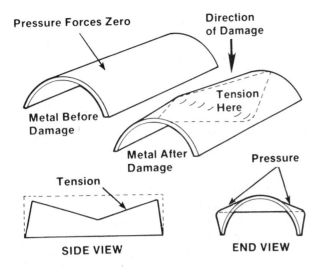

FIGURE 7-17 High and low spots created in crowned panel

panel is called a **low crowned.** When a low-crowned panel is damaged, it is pulled into the center of the damage. This pulling brings the panel below its original level. Damaged areas that are below the normal level are called tension areas. Any area of the panel that moves above the original level is called a pressure area. There are three types of outer panels:

- Single crown
- Combination crown
- Double crown

The important thing about this information is that the repair procedure and the application of tools are determined by whether the area is under tension or pressure. A hammer should never strike in a tension area; the dolly should never strike the underside of a pressure area. Power hook-ups are determined by the direction of pressure forces. No plastic filling can be done when there are pressure areas present.

Single Crown Panels

Figure 7-17 shows a drawing of a **single crowned panel.** This panel is flat in one direction (left to right) and crowned in another (90 degrees or crosswise). The damage shown in the drawing has tension in one direction and pressure in another. Look at the damage from the flat side (the side view of the drawing); it appears similar to that in Figure 7-18. Look at it from the end view; it appears similar to that of Figure 7-19.

This means there is a three dimensional effect on all pressure and tension areas. An area that is low is accompanied by a high (or pressure) area adjacent to it. This is true on all crowned areas.

 **SHOP TALK**

All damage to the crowned areas of a panel must be straightened first rather than just filled with plastic.

"Parking lot" dings are a good example of pressure and tension areas (Figure 7-20). The impact creates a shallow tension area surrounded by a ridge or pressure area. The ridge must be filed level with the panel and the low area must be leveled with the plastic body filler.

Combination Crown Panels

The shifting of the pressure areas on a combination panel is shown in Figure 7-21. The direction of damage shown is from above and almost straight down, yet there are two collapsed rolled buckles

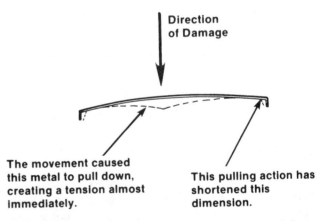

FIGURE 7-18 Tension area in a damaged low-crown area

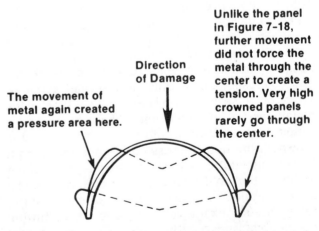

FIGURE 7-19 Pressure areas in a damaged high-crown panel

(P to BF and P to BC) that are of different lengths. This is because the crown is stronger than the flatter area and resisted the pressure forces more. Actually, during the damage, the same force was applied to both sides of the arrow (at P), yet the metal to the left has a greater area of damage. The significance here is that if the novice body technician merely "drives" the

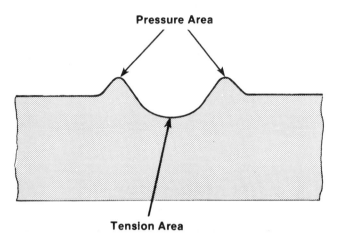

FIGURE 7-20 Pressure and tension areas in a door ding

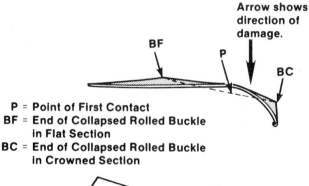

P = Point of First Contact
BF = End of Collapsed Rolled Buckle in Flat Section
BC = End of Collapsed Rolled Buckle in Crowned Section

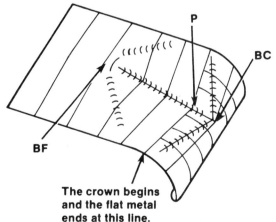

FIGURE 7-21 Work-hardened areas in damaged combination panel

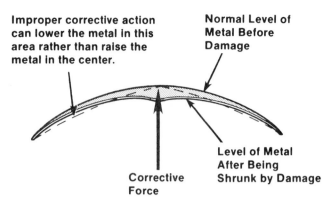

FIGURE 7-22 Shrunken panel must be stretched to return it to its original contour.

metal upward to correct it, he or she would further damage the flatter area of the panel. The flat area would yield to corrective forces (blows), and the greatest resistance area (P to BC) would remain intact. The correction here is to unroll the buckle (P to BC) because it is the "key" to opening up the metal in the flatter area, and it is the area of greatest resistance.

If a crowned panel has a shrunken area on it (caused by either welding, improper hammer and dolly techniques, or the results of a buckle in the crown), the level of that area will be lower than the normal level yet have no pressure areas present. Whenever a low area on a crown is not accompanied by a nearby pressure area, the low area is shrunken and can be corrected only by stretching. To attempt straightening by picking up the low area will only lower the adjacent metal, as shown in Figure 7-22. A damaged crown panel will always have some pressure areas present somewhere, unless it is damaged from underneath. In this case the metal will be pulled inward creating the opposite condition from those described in Figures 7-18 and 7-19.

Understanding these principles will help the body technician determine his or her repair procedures. For instance, when welding on a concave surface (panel sectioning, perhaps), is the metal going to sink inward because of the weld shrinkage or rise? The answer is that the metal will rise. A high area will be created. This problem can be corrected by the metal (hammer-on-dolly technique), and thereby lower the metal. Normally the novice feels stretching will raise metal. On a crowned panel, it will.

Double Crowns

For simplicity the various buckles were discussed as they occurred on panels that are curved or

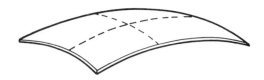

FIGURE 7-23   A double-crowned panel

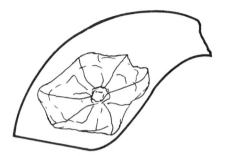

FIGURE 7-24   Collapsed rolled buckles in double crown panel

crowned in one direction and flat in another direction. Most panels are reasonably close to this type of construction. Some, however, are crowned in both directions (Figure 7-23). These are called **double crowns.**

Rolled buckles occur on crowned surfaces and roll (or travel) toward the nearest flat area. In the case of a panel that has a double-crowned surface, the rolled buckles will travel normally in all directions from the point of impact. The collapsed rolled buckles spread out from the impact point, like spokes of a wagon wheel, the hub being the initial point of impact. The damage shown in Figure 7-24 is typical of an impact on that type of panel.

DETERMINING THE DIRECTION OF DAMAGE

All the information given so far is to help the auto body technician analyze the repair job for the methods he or she should use to correct the damage. This information helps determine the direction of damage. Collision damage must be reversed exactly as it occurred. Visual inspection can usually tell what happened, but sometimes it becomes complicated when there are overlapping conditions.

Collapsed rolled buckles always move away from the point of first contact. When two or three of them are present, it becomes easier. Where they all converge (like spokes of a wheel to the hub) is the point of first contact. It is also usually approximately

90 degrees straight out from the collapsed rolled buckle (Figure 7-25).

It helps to visualize the accident happening in slow motion. Then, by reversing the accident visually—in slow motion, studying each buckle, and unfolding each work-hardened section of metal, one can visualize how the repair operations should be formed. Of course, it is not possible to always reverse the damage conditions in the order that they occurred. Buckles cannot be unfolded simultaneously. Shrunken metal that is work hardened cannot be "softened" in reverse. Tears in the metal will not reweld themselves. But before the damaged area can be repaired, the auto body technician must know how the damage occurred, recognize the conditions existing in the metal, and use the correct repair tools and procedures.

7.3 METAL STRAIGHTENING TECHNIQUES

Analysis and theory tell the technician what is wrong. Next he or she must have the basic skills to repair the damage. After this he or she must know how to put these things together to produce the overall results required of a good body technician. The technician must develop a good procedure for repair. A good procedure can save a great deal of "technician-created" damages so that the entire corrective time is spent fixing only the damage that was originally done to the car.

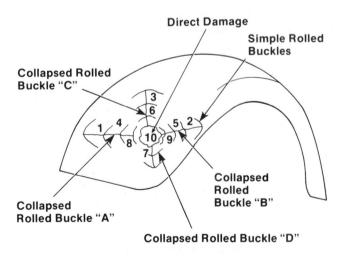

FIGURE 7-25   Procedure for bumping out collapsed rolled buckle

SHOP TALK

The way to achieve success as a body technician is to concentrate on the prevention of damage.

The repair procedure begins with a diagnosis of the damage. The actual work on the metal begins with the **rough-out stage.** Rough-out must be done properly if finishing operations are to succeed. When finishing operations are started too soon, it becomes difficult to do a good job. Rough-out is not usually completed on a damaged panel until 80 to 90 percent of the paint can be removed without turning the grinding disc on its edge (Figure 7–26).

The rough-out operations change with each damage, with each car, and with each different location of the damage on the car. In other words, the rough-out is very important to the particular car being worked on. The analysis must be good for each damage and set of circumstances. Proper analysis in the rough-out stage can mean the difference between making money on the job or taking a loss. Poor rough-out always costs the body technician money in lost time.

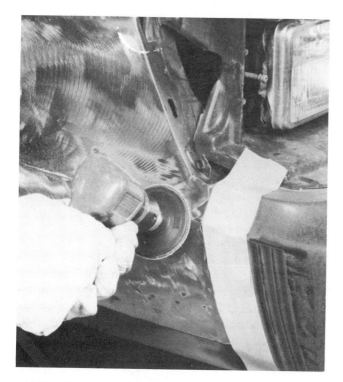

FIGURE 7–26 Grinding paint from roughed-out dented area. (Courtesy of 3M)

Typical of this is the situation in which the technician "hits up" all low areas and "beats in" all high ones thinking that eventually the metal will become straight.

A body technician with a clear understanding of damage analysis knows metal is just not straightened that way. Rolled buckles (simple and collapsed) require special handling, as do hinge-type buckles. Flat low-crowned metal must be protected more than straightened. Hitting up a low-crowned flat area to straighten a work-hardened buckle could create severe damage to the (up to now) undamaged metal in the flat area. Every buckle has a definite method of correction. The basic rules always apply. If an area must be stretched, it might be done with pull clamps, solder plates in combination with a hydraulic jack, hammer and dolly, or several other means.

The rest of the chapter is devoted to explaining some of the common skills utilized by the technician from the rough-out stage of repair up to the plastic filling stage.

Using a Disc Sander

Many sheet metal repairs require removing the paint finish first. Usually this is done with a disc sander or grinder. The disc sander is used throughout the repair for removing paint and removing metal. Most body technicians utilize a 7-inch diameter disc and a sander that operates at least at 4000 rpm or more. Low-speed sanding can be used for paint removal. Grit sizes range from #16 to #60. Size 16 is most commonly used for removing paints. Use #24 or #36 for grinding away metal and the higher grits for removing file marks and polishing metal. Two types of backing pads are used. An inflexible pad is used for removing metal and a softer back-up pad should be used when removing paint or polishing metal. The softer pad allows the disc to "roll" and give with the metal.

There are two different types of disc actions. One, called **buffing,** is used to remove paint and smooth the filler, and the other, called **cross cut,** is used to remove metal (Figure 7–27).

When using the grinder, only the top 1-1/2 to 2 inches should contact the surface. Do not use excessive pressure; the weight of the grinder should just about be enough. On vertical surfaces, use pressure equal to the weight of the grinder. The grinder should be held so the back of the disc is raised 10 to 20 degrees off the metal. It is sometimes

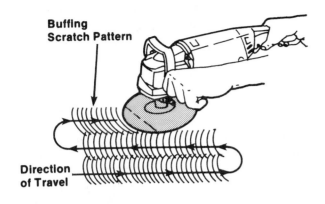

A

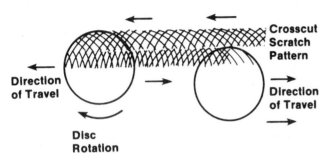

B

FIGURE 7-27   Two grinding actions: (A) buffing method and (B) crosscutting method

difficult to use the round sanding disc in a sharp reverse crown area. The edge of the disc will cause a deep groove to be cut in the metal. This can be avoided by cutting the edge of the disc into points commonly called a star disc (Figure 7-28).

7.4 METALWORKING TECHNIQUES

The buckles and creases in a dented panel can be unlocked in a variety of ways. On panels where the backside of the panel is accessible, hammers and dollies or spoons are used for the initial roughing out. On sealed panels or in areas where the backside of the panel is difficult to reach, slide hammers, picks, and welded studs can be used to reverse the damage.

Damage in an exterior panel can be locked in by indirect damage to structural panels or inner reinforcements. Before the metalworking techniques described in this chapter are used, structural damage must be repaired by pushing or pulling the damaged understructure into alignment. Usually when

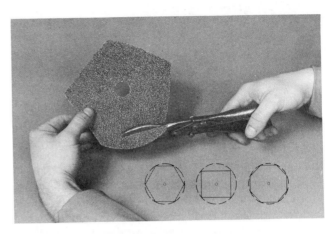

FIGURE 7-28   Profiles of star discs

this is necessary, it is best to maintain the hydraulic push or pull until the exterior panels have been straightened using one of the techniques described here.

BUMPING DENTS

The body repair hammer is designed to strike the sheet metal and rebound off the surface rather than be driven down as in driving a nail. A driving action would create additional damage in the sheet metal.

The secret of metal straightening is knowing to hit the right spot at the right time, with the right amount of force. The hammer should be held as shown in Figure 7-29. The lower two fingers are the "pivot" fingers, in that they allow the hammer to pivot slightly on the rebound off the metal. The other fingers and thumb control the downward thrust of the hammer. Swing in a circular motion, using the wrist rather than the whole arm and shoulder. Hit squarely and let the hammer rebound off the metal. Space each blow 3/8 to 1/2 inch apart until the damaged metal is level.

Carefully select the hammer. The face of the hammer must fit the contour of the panel. Use a flat face hammer on flat or low-crown panels. Use a convex-shaped or high-crown hammer face when bumping inside curves. Heavy bumping hammers should be used for roughing out the damage. Be careful, though, not to create additional damage. Finishing, or dinging, hammers should be used for final shaping.

Finishing hammers are lighter than bumping hammers and usually have heads. The secret to finish hammering is light, rapid taps. It is also important to hit squarely. Hitting on the face edge with the hammer will put additional nicks in the metal.

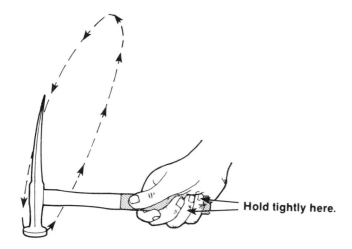

FIGURE 7-29 Hold the hammer with third and fourth fingers and swing with a circular motion.

🚗 **SHOP TALK** _____

Before bumping any sheet metal, make sure that both sides of the panel are clean of road tars, mud, undercoating, and so on, to ensure that the tools come in direct contact with the metal.

Bumping Dents With Spoons

Spoons can be used in a number of ways, depending on their design. Spoons can be used to pry out dents, certain kinds can be struck with a hammer to drive out dents, and others are used as a dolly in hard-to-reach areas. Some are even designed to be used in place of a hammer.

Spring hammering is done with a hammer and a dinging spoon. The dinging spoon is the one most commonly used on sheet metal. It is lightweight and has a low crown. When used, it is held firmly against the high ridge or crease. The spoon is then struck with a ball peen or bumping hammer (Figure 7-30). The force of the blow is distributed by the spoon over a large area of the crease or ridge. This reduces the likelihood of stretching the metal. Always keep firm pressure on the spoon when spring hammering. It must never be allowed to bounce. Part of the corrective force is the pressure of the spoon. Begin at the ends of a ridge (hinge buckle) and work toward the high point on the ridge, alternating from side to side.

Slapping files are sometimes used instead of hammers. They can be driven down harder and more often without damaging the panel. They can be used with a dolly. Remember that hammer blows on top of a panel can be a corrective force only when they are placed on pressure (high) areas of the damage. A bumping file can also be used to "slap" down ridges. It has a serrated surface that shrinks the stretched metal.

🚗 **SHOP TALK** _____

The effect of hammering is increased when pressure is kept on the underside of the panel. This can be done with a dolly, spoon, or hydraulic jack.

Spoons can be used to back up the hammer or in combination with a slapping spoon. With a long body spoon, the body technician can often reach

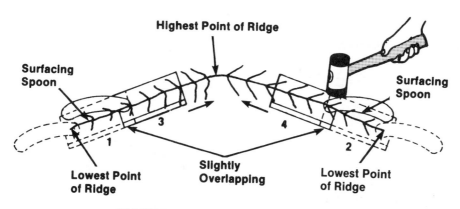

FIGURE 7-30   Spring hammering ridge

into places inaccessible to a hammer or dolly. Pressure can be applied to tension areas with the spoon, while pressure or high areas are bumped down (Figure 7-31).

Spoons can also be used to pry metal up in the rough-out stage or to drive deep dents out. Figure 7-32 shows a double end lower back and quarter-panel spoon being used to pry out a dent in a door panel. The door is supported on blocks of wood to provide clearance for the door panel to move. Care must be taken, of course, not to stretch the metal by prying the metal beyond the original contour of the door shim. Once the dent is roughed out by prying with a spoon or dolly, it can be used with a body hammer to finish the area.

BUMPING DENTS WITH DOLLIES

The dolly block is used throughout the repair process. In the rough-out phase, it is used as an impact tool. The underside of the metal can be hit with the dolly to raise low areas and to unroll buckles. The dolly is also used as a backing block for the hammer. When it is used this way, there are two techniques:

- Hammer-on-dolly
- Hammer-off-dolly

Hammer-on-dolly is used to stretch metal, while hammer-off-dolly is used to straighten metal. The contour of the dolly must fit the contour of the underside of the damaged area or additional damage will result. As each hammer blow is struck, the dolly tends to rebound slightly from its position against the metal, creating somewhat of a secondary lifting action (Figure 7-33). The amount of rebound force is determined by the pressure exerted against the dolly and by the size and shape of the dolly face in relation to the shape of the metal. A greater lifting action is also obtained when the hammer blows are closest to the dolly. The further away the blows are from the dolly, the less the metal is moved.

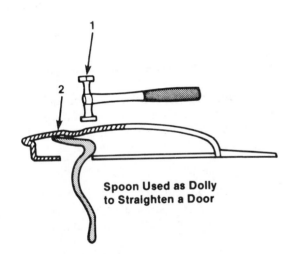

FIGURE 7-31 Using a spoon as a dolly

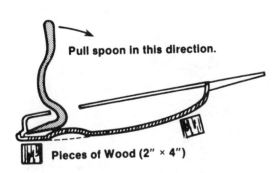

FIGURE 7-32 Using a spoon to pry out a dent in a door panel

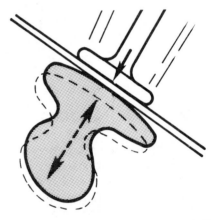

FIGURE 7-33 The rebound of the dolly forces metal up.

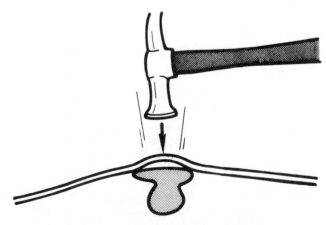

FIGURE 7-34 Hammer-on-dolly repairing

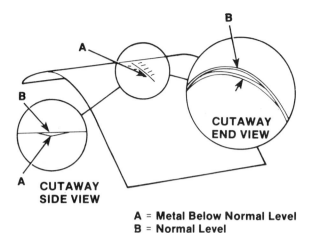

A = Metal Below Normal Level
B = Normal Level

FIGURE 7–35 Shrunken area must be stretched with hammer-on-dolly method.

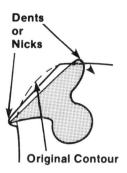

FIGURE 7–36 Using a dolly whose contour does not fit the contour of the panel will result in additional damage to the panel.

Hammer-On-Dolly Method

Hammer-on-dolly repairs are used to smooth small, shallow dents and bulges and to stretch metal so that it can return to its original shape. This occurs usually on crowns and occasionally on flat panels. To flatten a bulge, place a dolly against the backside of the panel directly behind the bulge and use a hammer from the front side (Figure 7–34). There will be a slight rebound as a result of the hammer hitting the dolly. The dolly will hit the backside of the panel and as the force of the dolly pressing against the panel is increased, the flattening action will also increase.

The body technician should calculate the amount the panel to be worked will stretch as it is hammered. If this is not done, the panel will stretch and elongate too much. Since a great deal of body repair experience is needed to accurately judge how much a panel will stretch, an inexperienced technician should not rely entirely on this type of repair method.

Any shrunken metal on a crown can be stretched up to its normal level faster and easier by the hammer-on-dolly than by any other method. The technique of on-dollying is used, provided that there is access to the underside of the panel. If not, sliding hammers and/or filling is done. Figure 7–35 shows a drawing of a typical low area (in this case a collapsed rolled buckle).

This panel was damaged and has been roughed out but is still low in the area of the collapsed rolled buckle (circled). Because this panel shows no evidence of a pressure area adjacent to the buckle, the panel is shrunken at A as shown in the drawing. The only way A can be raised to the original level B is by

stretching. The stretching has to be along the line of the rolled buckle. Picking up the low area will not correct the condition. The hammer-on-dolly method should be used here on line A.

In the hammer-on-dolly action, there are actually two actions:

- When the hammer strikes the metal
- When the dolly rebounds upward and strikes the underside of the metal.

Tension is kept on the dolly at all times. The greater the tension, the greater the rebound action and the faster it returns. When hammering fast, the tension is increased on the dolly to ensure a quick rebound. When low metal is being raised each rebound action should be deliberately driven up by the hand action.

Note that improper hammer blows placed on a crown will shrink rather than stretch. All blows that are designed to stretch should be hard and accurate. An inaccurate hard blow can also cause damage to the panel. Light hammer blows are for straightening, not stretching. In other words, when using the on-dolly technique, hit hard and do not miss!

Be sure to choose the properly shaped dolly. Figure 7–36 shows what will happen when the contour of the dolly is larger than the contour of the panel. Additional dents will inevitably be the result.

Hammer-Off-Dolly Method

The hammer-off-dolly method is used to straighten metal just before the finishing stage. In it the hammer does not actually strike the dolly. The dolly is held under the lowest area, and the hammer hits the high area nearby (Figure 7–37). The dolly, like the hammer, is designed to correct damage in that it must strike in only tension areas to be effective as an impact tool (when used under the panel in the normal way).

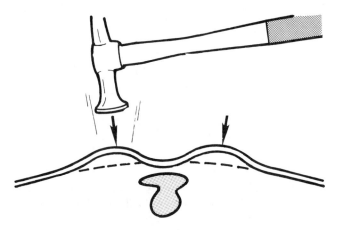

FIGURE 7-37   Hammer-off-dolly position

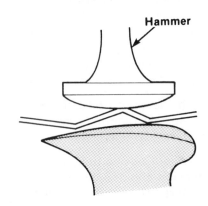

FIGURE 7-38   Variation of the hammer-off-dolly method

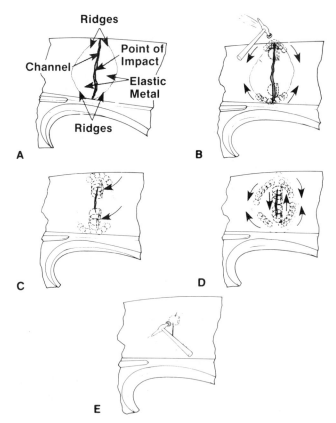

FIGURE 7-39   Steps in repairing a dented panel with hammer and dolly

The hammer-off-dolly method is used mostly on flat or low-crown panels. These panels are soft in comparison with crowned panels. Sometimes the dolly is directly under the hammer but does not actually strike it, as shown in Figure 7-38.

UNLOCKING DENTS WITH A HAMMER AND DOLLY

The damaged metal in a minor dent as shown in Figure 7-39A is straightened by using the hammer and dolly methods to "roll out" the metal in the reverse order to which it went in. For example, the point of impact (POI) was the first area touched by the impact. As the metal is pushed in, a channel is gradually formed on either side of the point of impact. This channel (collapsed rolled buckle) is usually deepest next to the POI, decreasing in size toward the outward end of the channel. At the same time as the channels are being pushed in, ridges (simple rolled buckles) are being formed around the outer area of the dent. They also have the greatest degree

of bend in their center, gradually decreasing in size toward each end. Both the ridges and channels contain work hardening, the amount depending on the degree of bend.

To remove the dent, the damage must be rolled outward from the outside, working toward the center in a reverse order to which it went in. The dolly is held tightly under the channel at the outer end where the least degree of bend is (Figure 7-39B). A flat-faced dinging hammer is used to direct light to medium blows at the outer ends of the ridge closest to the dolly (off-dolly blows). The force from the hammer gradually forces down the ends of the ridges, the arm pressure held against the heavy dolly forces the end of the channel upward. The same procedure is then repeated on the other end of the channel and the adjacent ridges (Figure 7-39B).

The off-dolly method is gradually worked toward center or greatest degree of bend in the ridges and channels. As the pressure is released in the ridges and channels, the surrounding elastic metal tends to move back to its original position. The dolly can also be used as a driving tool to help up the channel (Figure 7-39C). However, if the dolly does not move when the channel is hit upward, there is still too much pressure on either or both the ridges and/or channel. More dollying must be done to relieve the tension (Figure 7-39D).

Once the area has been brought back to its basic shape, the light on-dolly method is used to smooth and level the area (Figure 7-39E). It is then ready for either the metal finishing or filling procedure.

PICKING DENTS

There are several methods of picking up metal with the use of a pointed (not necessarily sharp) tool. Pick hammers, long picking tools, the edge of a dolly, and even a scratch awl can be used. When picking up a small dent with a striking tool, it is better to use several light blows rather than one or two hard blows. After an area has been picked up, a file or grinder can be used to level the damaged area. Figure 7-40 shows a low spot being raised with a pick. A certain amount of stretching has occurred; so, the metal must be filed after the low spot is eliminated. Hard filing will heat the metal causing it to shrink partially back to shape.

Long picking tools can also be used to pry up metal in areas that cannot be reached with a dolly or spoon. A car door is a good example (Figure 7-41). A pick can sometimes be inserted through a drainage hole or a hole drilled behind the door gasket. This eliminates the need to remove the inside door trim or to drill holes in the outer panel for pulling the dent.

When prying with a pick, be careful not to stretch the metal by exerting too much pressure. Start with the original point of contact or the lowest point and slowly pry the crease up. On larger dents, use a flat blade pick rather than a pointed one. Tap down pressure areas, while prying up low tension areas.

PULLING DENTS

Dents can be pulled out with a number of tools: suction cups, pull rods, dent pullers, even a sheet metal screw and vise grips. Figure 7-42 shows a

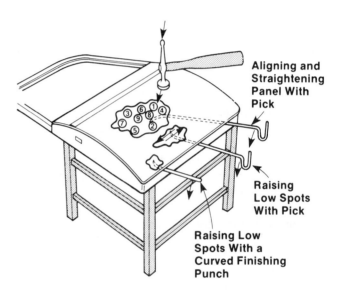

Aligning and Straightening Panel With Pick

Raising Low Spots With Pick

Raising Low Spots With a Curved Finishing Punch

FIGURE 7-41 Raising dents with a pick

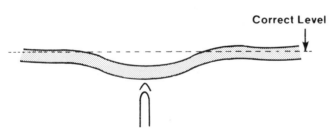

Correct Level

A. The metal is low and irregular.

Correct Level

B. The stretched metal is raised above the normal level.

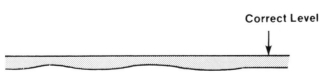

Correct Level

C. The metal is filed hard and is leveled to the desired amount.

FIGURE 7-40 Raising a dent with a pick hammer

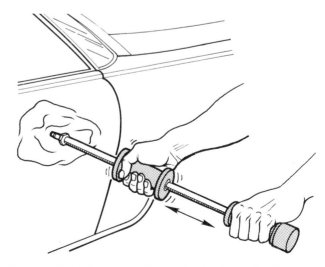

FIGURE 7-42 Removing a dent with a dent puller

227

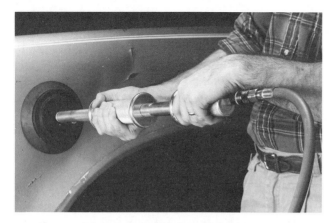

FIGURE 7-43 Pulling a dent with a pneumatic dent puller. *(Courtesy of Atlantic Pneumatic, Inc.)*

FIGURE 7-44 A welded stud dent removal kit. *(Courtesy of H & S Manufacturing Co. Ltd.)*

pneumatic dent puller in use. Vacuum is pneumatically supplied to the suction cup on the end of the puller and a slide hammer provides the force to pull the metal back into shape. By far, though, the most common method of pulling dents is with a dent puller.

The purpose of a dent puller is to lift out simple dents that cannot be reached easily or lifted out by other means.

The dent puller is probably one of the body technician's most used tools. One reason is the growing complexity of automobile body construction. Access to the inside of many panels is blocked by welded-in inner panels and window mechanisms. Using a dent puller, the body technician can often repair a simple dent in less time than would be required to make the disassembly necessary to start the repair by other means.

After scrutinizing the dent to determine the point and angle of the initial impact, drill or punch holes 1 inch apart along the length of the initial crease. Punching is preferred to drilling because punching leaves more metal for the screw tip to grab.

Beginning at the point of initial impact, thread the screw tip on the dent puller into the first hole. Hold the handle of the dent puller in one hand and forcefully slide the weight straight back against the handle (Figure 7-43).

CAUTION: Be careful not to pinch your fingers between the weight and the handle.

Gradually work the crease out. Pull the first hole slightly. Then, go on to the next hole; work from the lowest spot to the crease ends in both directions.

After pulling each hole out slightly, repeat the process. Work the surface as close to the finished contour as possible without pulling the metal beyond the original surface. Tap high spots down with a bodyhammer to relieve pressure in ridge areas. Low spots can be filled with body filler.

Shallow, small dents in enclosed panels can be pulled out with one or more pull rods. Again, a bodyhammer should be used to tap high spots down while pulling.

 **SHOP TALK** _____

The dent puller is an important tool, however, its simplicity of use can lead to its misuse.

It is senseless to pierce a large number of holes in the surface of a panel that could have been straightened by other means. The result is often an unsatisfactory job. Worse, it might be that more time was required to do it wrong than would have been required to do it right.

Pulling With Studs

The most advanced way to pull dents is with a stud welded to the dent. The stud might be a washer, a pull tab, or a pin. Regardless of the system used, pulling with spot-welded studs avoids drilling or punching through the metal and undercoating, potentially a corrosion creating technique.

Figure 7-44 shows a complete set of stud pulling equipment. A specially designed spot welder fuses a metal pin to the dent area (Figure 7–45A). Fusing the pin to the panel takes only a fraction of a second. Then, the pin or pins can be pulled with either a dent puller (Figure 7–45B) or a power jack (Figure 7–45C). When the dent is corrected, the pins can be snipped off with cutters and ground flush with the panel (Figure 7–45D). The whole process is very quick with no damage to the panel. It is especially useful in pulling out small door dings where the backside of the panel is inaccessible.

SHRINKING DENTS

It is safe to assume that the panel has been stretched if the strain on the panel cannot be removed even after the panel has been worked properly. The damaged area can be easily filled with plastic

body filler to give the proper appearance but road vibrations can cause the panel to make a flapping noise as the vehicle is driven on the road. In addition, the owner can see and feel the surface irregularities when he or she waxes the car. Eventually, the body shop will be confronted by the dissatisfied owner and be required to spend extra time correcting the work that should have been done properly the first time.

Stretched Metal

When metal is severely damaged in a collision, it is often stretched in the badly buckled areas. These same areas are also sometimes stretched slightly during the straightening process. Most of the stretched metal will be found along the ridges, channels, and buckles in the direct damage area.

A

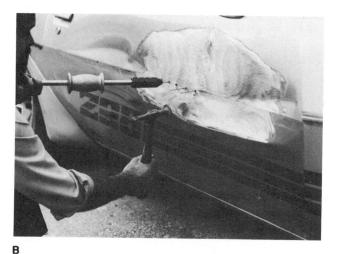

B

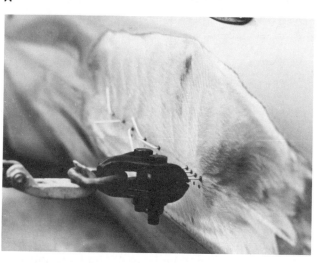

C

D

FIGURE 7–45 **(A) Welding the stud to the dented panel, (B) pulling the dent with puller and hammer, (C) pulling dent with power equipment and (D) grinding off welded studs.** *(Courtesy of H & S Manufacturing Co. Ltd.)*

When there are stretched areas of metal present in the panel, it is impossible to correctly straighten the area back to its original contour. The stretched area can be compared to a bulge on a tire. There is no place for the stretched surfaces to fit within the correct panel contour (Figure 7–46).

When an area of metal is stretched, the grains of metal are moved further away from each other. The metal is thinned and work hardened. Shrinking is the method used to bring the molecules back to their original position and thus to restore the metal to its proper contour and thickness. The object of shrinking is to remove the stretched metal without disturbing the relatively undamaged elastic metal in the surrounding area.

Before any shrinking is attempted, the damaged area must be dollied back as close to its original shape as possible. Then the body technician can accurately determine whether or not there is any stretched metal in the damaged area and, if so, where shrinking should be done.

Principles of Shrinking

Figure 7–47 shows that a steel bar, with both ends free to expand or contract, will expand when heated and contract to its original length when cooled.

If the same steel bar is heated while it is blocked or restricted at both ends, then cooled, its size will decrease. This is accomplished by the following:

- When heated, the steel bar tries to expand (Figure 7–48A), but since it is prevented from

expanding at both ends, a strong compression load is generated inside the bar.
- When the temperature is increased even more, and the steel becomes red hot and soft, the compression load concentrates in the red hot area and is relieved as the diameter of the red hot area increases (Figure 7–48B).
- If the steel bar is suddenly cooled down, the steel contracts and the length of the bar is

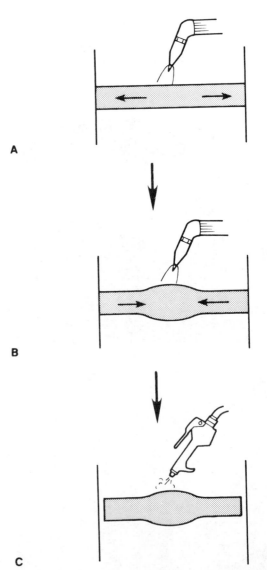

A

B

C

FIGURE 7–48 (A) Shrinkage occurs when expansion forces are restricted by panel rigidity, (B) causing the heat-softened metal to expand and thicken. (C) When the metal cools, the panel contracts and, due to the increased area of the hot spot, shrinks to an area smaller than its original size.

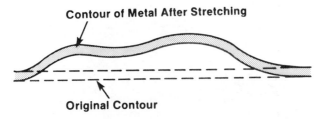

Contour of Metal After Stretching

Original Contour

FIGURE 7–46 Stretched metal that must be shrunk

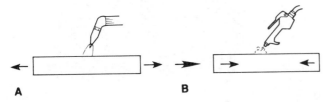

A

B

FIGURE 7–47 (A) Heat causes metal to expand; (B) cooling causes the metal to contract.

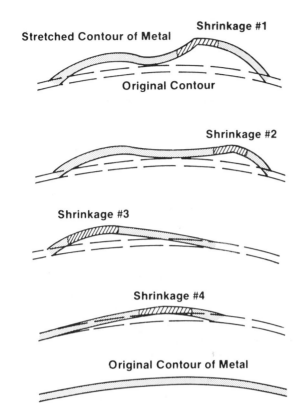

FIGURE 7-49   **Shrinking stretched metal usually requires more than one hot spot. Always heat the highest spot.**

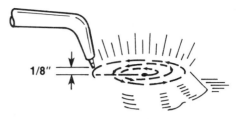

FIGURE 7-50   **Keep the flame cone 1/8 inch from the metal and move the torch in a circular motion from the center out.**

shortened by the amount of the increased diameter of the red hot area (Figure 7-48C).

The above stated principle of shrinking steel also applies to the shrinking of a warped area in a piece of sheet metal. A small spot in the center of the warped area is heated to a dull red. When the temperature rises, the heated area of the steel panel swells and attempts to expand outward toward the edges of the heated circle (circumference). Since the surrounding area is cool and hard, the panel cannot expand, so a strong compression load is generated.

If heating continues, the stretching of the metal is centered in the soft red hot portion, pressing it out, which causes it to thicken, thus relieving the compression load.

If the red hot area is suddenly cooled while in this state, the steel will contract and the surface area will shrink to less than its area before heating. As the panel contracts from the cooling, a tensile load is generated in the panel as opposed to the compression load generated during heating.

A variety of pieces of welding equipment can be used to heat metal for shrinking. Attachments are available for spot and MIG welding equipment to transform them into shrinking equipment. But the most commonly used tool is the oxyacetylene torch with a #1 or #2 tip.

Shrinking Operation With a Gas Torch

To shrink an area with a torch, a small spot of the stretched area or bulge is heated to a cherry red. The "shrink" is placed in the highest spot of the stretched area, then in the next highest spot, and so on, until the attached area has been shrunk back to its proper position (Figure 7-49).

The size of the "shrink" or "hot spot" is determined by the amount of excess metal in the area to be shrunk. The "shrinks" can be anywhere in size from a silver dollar down to the head of a thumbtack. The larger the hot spot, the harder the heat is to control. An average-sized "shrink" is usually about the size of a quarter. Small shrinks should always be used on flat panels, as such panels tend to warp easily.

A very small hot spot would be used to take an oil can out of a flat panel. The term **oil can** is used to describe an area of a panel that is stretched very slightly. It can be pushed in. As soon as the pressure is released, the area will pop back out again, just as the bottom of an oil can does.

A neutral flame and a #1 or #2 tip used for welding sheet metal are used to heat the hot spots. The point of the cone is brought straight down to within 1/8 inch of the metal and held steady until the metal starts to get red. The torch is then slowly moved outward in a circular motion until the complete hot spot is cherry red (Figure 7-50).

 **SHOP TALK**

Do not heat the metal past a cherry red. It will start to melt, and a hole might be burned through the metal.

231

As the heat from the torch enters the small spot in the panel, the heated metal expands. The cooler metal surrounding the hot spot resists the expansion forces. As the temperature increases, the heated metal becomes softer. This soft metal piles up and forms a bulge in the hot spot (Figure 7–51).

The metal usually bulges up instead of down because the top of the metal is heated first. When it starts to bulge, the rest of the metal in the hot spot follows.

When the spot has been heated, tap around the spot with several sharp hammer blows to drive the molecules of metal closer together (Figure 7–52).

During this procedure, it is not necessary to support the metal with the dolly unless the metal collapses. If it is necessary to support the panel, the dolly should only be held lightly under the metal. As soon as the redness disappears, off-dolly blows and light, on-dolly blows are used to smooth and level the area around the hot spot.

 SHOP TALK ────────────

Never use hard, on-dolly blows to level the area. This will restretch the area of metal.

Once the redness has disappeared and the area has been dollied smooth, the "shrink" can be cooled with a wet rag or sponge. When this is done, a greater degree of contraction occurs, and a slight amount of distortion could result. The warpage should be straightened before the next "shrink" is attempted.

It is very hard to determine accurately the amount that each "hot spot" will shrink. One "shrink" can remove far more excess metal in one area than the same size would in another.

It is not uncommon to find that an area has been overshrunk when the "shrink" has completely cooled. When the area has been overshrunk, the metal in the area of the last "shrink" is usually collapsed or pulled flat and sometimes the metal surrounding the "shrink" area can even be pulled out of the proper contour. Overshrinking is corrected by using hard, hammer-on-dolly blows to stretch the last "shrink." The last shrunken area is usually the direct cause of overshrinking.

SHRINKING A GOUGE

A gouge is an example of metal that has been stretched by impact. The gouge must be shrunk to its original size to repair the damage. Simply picking up the low area would distort the panel, and filling the gouge with filler without restoring the panel's original contour will leave tensions in the panel that could cause the filler to fail.

Follow this procedure for shrinking gouges:

1. Heat the lowest point of the gouge with a gas torch or welding rod until the metal is a dull red.
2. Use a dolly to hammer up the hot spot. As explained earlier in this chapter, this will increase the tension on the soft spot, forcing it to swell and return to its original position.
3. While the metal is still hot, hold the dolly directly under the groove and tap down the ridges that will have developed on either side of the groove. This will not only drive

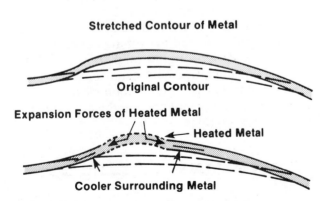

FIGURE 7–51 Heat-softened metal will usually bulge up.

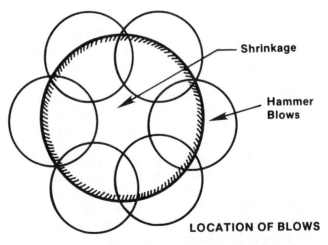

FIGURE 7–52 Hammer around the hot bulge to shrink it.

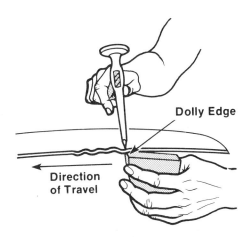

FIGURE 7-53 Shrink metal by kinking the high spot.

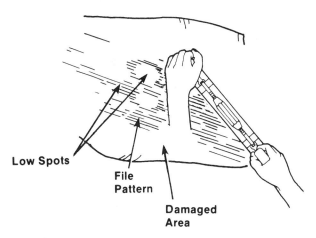

FIGURE 7-54 File the repaired metal to reveal low spots.

down the ridges but will also bump up the gouged metal.

4. If the gouge is a long one, this process will have to be repeated several times to raise the whole length of the gouge. Only heat as much of the gouge that can be worked before the metal cools.

Kinking

Kinking is another way to deal with stretched metal. Instead of using heat to shrink the metal, a hammer and dolly are used to create pleats, or **kinks,** in the stretched area. This is done by striking the stretched area with a pick hammer slightly off-dolly (Figure 7-53). Kinking the metal will lower the area slightly below the rest of the panel. The low spot should be filled with plastic body filler and filed and sanded level with the panel.

Filing the Repair Area

When the damaged area has been bumped and pulled as level and smooth as possible, the body file must be used to locate any remaining high and low spots (Figure 7-54).

Begin filing in the undamaged area on one side and progress across the damaged area to the undamaged metal on the opposite side. This way the correct plane can be maintained from undamaged metal to damaged area. The file should be pushed forward by the handle for the cutting stroke. Downward pressure and direction is controlled by hand holding the front of the file. As long a stroke as possible should be taken. On the return stroke, the

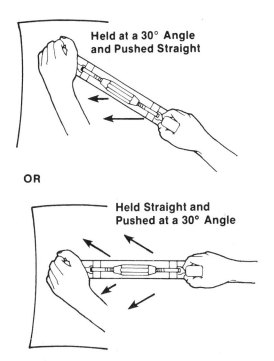

FIGURE 7-55 Push the file at a 30 degree angle on flat or low-crown panels.

file is pulled back over the metal by the handle. When filing relatively flat areas, the file is either held at a 30-degree angle and pushed straight or held straight and pushed at a 30-degree angle (Figure 7-55). On a crowned panel, the file is either held straight and pushed straight along the flattened crown of the panel, or held straight with the length of the flattest crown and pushed to one side at a 30-degree angle or less (Figure 7-56).

The scratch pattern created by the file identifies any low spots. The technician then "picks" up the

233

Held Straight With Length of Crown
and Pushed Straight

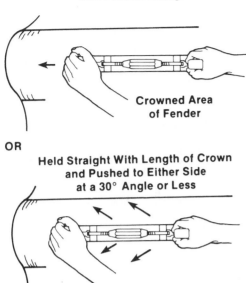

Crowned Area
of Fender

OR

Held Straight With Length of Crown
and Pushed to Either Side
at a 30° Angle or Less

FIGURE 7-56 Filing a crowned panel

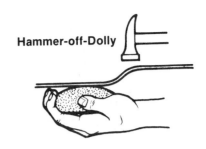

Hammer-off-Dolly

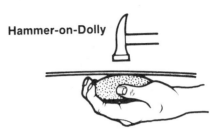

Hammer-on-Dolly

FIGURE 7-57 The hammer-off-dolly method is preferred when straightening aluminum.

low spots, bumps down the high spots, and files the area with the body file. This process is repeated until all the low spots disappear and the area has been filed smooth.

7.5 WORKING ALUMINUM

Aluminum is used for a variety of automotive panels, such as hoods and roof panels. It is used more often on truck vehicles, but the use in car bodies is growing. Pure aluminum is lightweight and useful more for its ability to be formed than for its strength. When used on vehicles, it is alloyed with other elements and heat treated for more strength.

Aluminum's natural resistance to corrosion is a special advantage. When first exposed to air, a thin oxide film forms on the surface. This aluminum oxide serves as self-protection and prevents further corrosion. These properties vary depending on the type of alloy and whether or not it is heat treated.

The repair of aluminum panels requires much more care than working steel panels. Aluminum is much softer than steel, yet it is more difficult to shape once it becomes work hardened. It also melts at a lower temperature and distorts readily when heated. It is important to keep in mind that body and frame parts are usually 1-1/2 to 2 times as thick as

steel parts. When damaged, aluminum feels harder or stiffer to the touch because of work hardening. These characteristics must be taken into consideration when working damaged aluminum panels.

Hammers and Dollies. Straightening by using a hammer and dolly is basically the same with aluminum as for previously described steel, with the following exceptions:

- The hammer-off-dolly method is generally recommended for aluminum panel straightening (Figure 7-57). Because aluminum is less ductile than steel, it does not readily bend back to its original shape after being buckled by an impact. Therefore, aluminum does not respond well to off-dolly hammering. Care must also be exercised not to create additional damage when attempting to lower ridges with hammer and dolly blows.
- Aluminum alloys bend too quickly when the panel is sandwiched between the hammer and dolly, as with the hammer-on-dolly method. When it is necessary to hammer on a dolly, hammering too hard or too much can stretch the panel. Use many light strokes rather than a few heavy blows.
- Shrinking hammers for working steel, should not be used since they can cause cracking. That is, separate sets of tools should be used on steel and aluminum.

 **SHOP TALK**

Do not apply the filler or putty to the bare surface of aluminum. Always apply an epoxy primer first. Also never use lead filler. Lead reduces aluminum's resistance to corrosion.

Picking. Raising small dents with a pick hammer or pry bar is an excellent way to repair aluminum panels. However, be careful not to raise the panel too far, stretching the soft aluminum.

Spring Hammering. Spring hammering with hammer and spoon is an excellent way to unlock stresses in high-pressure areas. The spoon distributes the force of the blow over a wider area, minimizing the possibility of creating additional dents in the unyielding buckle.

Filing. Because aluminum is soft, reduce hand pressure on the body file. Use a file with rounded edges to avoid scratching and gouging the metal.

Grinding. Grinding must be done very carefully on aluminum panels. Not only will a coarse grit grinding disc on a high-speed grinder quickly burn through the soft metal, but the heat from the grinding operation can quickly warp the panel. A #36 grit open coat disc can be used, but grind carefully in order to remove only paint and primer, and not the metal. Make two or three passes; then, quench the area with a wet rag to cool the metal and minimize heat gain in the panel. Grinding small areas and featheredging should be done with a dual-action sander or an electric polish machine that rotates less than 2500 rpm. Use #80 or #100 grit paper and a soft, flexible backing pad.

Heat Shrinking. There is one major difference with straightening aluminum by heat shrinkage. With steel, the use of heat is avoided whenever possible to prevent reducing the strength of the metal. With aluminum, heat must be used to restore flexibility that was reduced by work hardening. This will cause it to crack when straightening force is applied.

Before attempting to straighten aluminum, heat the damaged metal with a torch. It is easy to apply too much heat, because aluminum does not change color with high temperatures. Aluminum melts at a low 1220 degrees Fahrenheit, so careful heat control is very important. Use a temperature sensitive paint

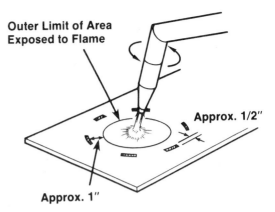

Outer Limit of Area Exposed to Flame

Approx. 1/2"

Approx. 1"

FIGURE 7-58   Using temperature sensitive paint to prevent excessive heat buildup.

or a heat sensitive "crayon" made to change color at 230 degrees Fahrenheit.

- Apply temperature sensitive paint or crayon in a circular pattern around the area that will be exposed to the flame (Figure 7-58).
- Heat the area, keeping the flame moving constantly.
- Stop heating when the color changes. The surface temperature at the center of the heated area will be between 750 and 800 degrees Fahrenheit, a safe margin from aluminum's melting point. A lack of caution will result in a melted panel. Also the shrink spot must be very slowly quenched to avoid distorting the panel by excessive contraction.

Welding. Because aluminum panels conduct heat so well, it is most suitable for MIG welding. With MIG, it is easier to produce good results than with most other shop welding methods (see Chapter 6). MIG also causes a cleaning action during welding. By pushing the welding gun, the arc cleans the area in front of the gun. Pushing, in effect, scrubs away aluminum oxide on the surface at the site of the weld.

Welding steel and welding aluminum panels requires similar conditions:

- Use aluminim wire and 100 percent argon gas.
- Set wire speed faster than with steel.
- Hold the gun closer to vertical when welding aluminum. Tilt it only about 5 to 15 degrees from the vertical in the direction of the weld.
- As in Figure 7-59, use only the forehand welding method. Do not backstep with aluminum. Always push, never pull. When welding on a vertical, start at the bottom and work up.

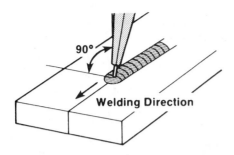

FIGURE 7-59 Forehand or "push" welding method. Keep the angle of the gun more vertical when welding aluminum than when welding steel.

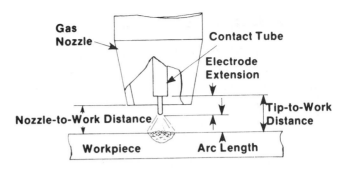

FIGURE 7-60 Recommended stickout is 5/16 to 9/16 inches.

- Set the tension of the wire drive roller lower to prevent twisting. But do not lower the tension too much or the wire speed will not be constant.
- Use about 50 percent more shielding with aluminum.
- Because there tends to be more spatter with aluminum, use an antispatter compound to control buildup at the end of the nozzle and contact tip.

The best way to compare aluminum panel welding to steel is to try some butt welds on 1/8 inch scrap.

1. Clean the weld area completely, both front and back, using a wax and grease remover and a clean rag.
2. Set two square edge pieces on a solid metal table and secure the welding clamp to the table.
3. If the pieces are coated with a paint film, sand a strip about 3/4 inch wide to the bare metal, using a disc sander with a #80 disc. A double action sander can also be used. Do not press too hard or the sander will heat up and peel off aluminum particles, clogging the paper.
4. Clean the metal until shiny with a stainless steel wire brush.
5. Load 0.030 inch aluminum wire into the nozzle and trigger it to extend about an inch beyond the nozzle.
6. Set the voltage and wire speed according to the instructions that came with the welder. This is only an estimate, and you will probably have to adjust these settings. Remember the wire speed is faster than for steel.
7. Nip off the end of the wire to remove the meltdown.
8. Position the two pieces together and lay a bead along the entire joint. Keep a **stickout**

(the distance between the contact tip and the weld) of 5/16 to 9/16 inches (Figure 7-60).

7.6 REVIEW QUESTIONS

1. Which type of sheet metal is most often used in unibody construction?
   a. hot-rolled
   b. cold-rolled
   c. both a and b
   d. neither a nor b

2. Which of the following is not a high-strength steel?
   a. HSLA steel
   b. HSS
   c. martensitic steel
   d. none of the above

3. The ability of metal to stretch and return to its original shape is called _____.
   a. elastic deformation
   b. plastic deformation
   c. both a and b
   d. neither a nor b

4. Whenever a collapsed rolled buckle occurs, there are two other buckles adjacent to the collapsed roll. What type of buckles are these?
   a. simple hinge buckles
   b. collapsed hinge buckles
   c. simple rolled buckles
   d. none of the above

5. The cross cut disc action is used to _____.
   a. remove paint
   b. smooth the filler

c. remove metal
d. both a and b

6. Which kind of spoon can be used instead of a hammer?
   a. dinging spoon
   b. slapping spoon
   c. both a and b
   d. neither a nor b

7. What is the most common tool used to pull dents?
   a. suction cups
   b. pull rods
   c. dent pullers
   d. none of the above

8. When filing a relatively flat area, Technician A holds the file at a 30-degree angle and pushes it straight. Technician B holds the file straight and pushes it at a 30-degree angle. Who is correct?
   a. Technician A
   b. Technician B
   c. Both A and B
   d. Neither A nor B

9. Technician A says that aluminum has a higher melting point than mild steel. Technician B says that martensitic steel loses strength when welded. Who is correct?
   a. Technician A
   b. Technician B
   c. Both A and B
   d. Neither A nor B

10. Technician A says that 80 percent of sheet metal damage is direct damage. Technician B says that bent metal is not necessarily buckled metal. Who is correct?
    a. Technician A
    b. Technician B
    c. Both A and B
    d. Neither A nor B

11. To remove a vehicle's finish prior to sheet metal repairs, Technician A uses a grinder and Technician B uses a disc sander. Who is correct?
    a. Technician A
    b. Technician B
    c. Both A and B
    d. Neither A nor B

12. When picking up a small dent with a striking tool, Technician A uses several light blows. Technician B uses only one or two hard blows. Who is correct?
    a. Technician A
    b. Technician B
    c. Both A and B
    d. Neither A nor B

13. Which condition is the result of the sheet metal grain structure being forced out of alignment and into a new set?
    a. elastic deformation
    b. plastic deformation
    c. work hardening
    d. tensile strength

CHAPTER 8

Minor Auto Body Repairs

The metalworking techniques discussed in Chapter 7 are fundamental to any repair job. Dented metal must be restored to its original contour by unfolding buckles, relieving stresses in work-hardened ridges, shrinking stretched metal, and stretching shrunken areas. The permanence of the repair depends on how successfully the metalworking techniques are applied. After the damaged panel has been bumped, pulled, pried, and dinged to within at least 1/4 inch of the original contour, most shops fill, shape, and smooth the repair with an application of plastic body filler.

Plastic body filler is the finishing touch to most sheet metal repairs. Restoring bent and stretched metal to its exact original shape and dimension would be very time consuming and almost impossi-

ble in many instances. But after the basic shape and soundness of the damaged panel have been restored with proper metalworking techniques, the remaining minor blemishes can be quickly and easily masked with a thin coat of body filler. However, very careful attention must be given to preparation and application of plastic fillers. The permanence of the repair and the quality of the final finish is adversely affected by filler improperly mixed and applied.

Plastic body filler is not only used to finish areas requiring metalworking but is also used to fill scratches, dings, pitted areas, and rustouts. The filler is then filled and sanded level with the panel, and putty and/or primer is applied to fill any remaining surface imperfections. A summary of minor metalworking procedures is given in Table 8-1.

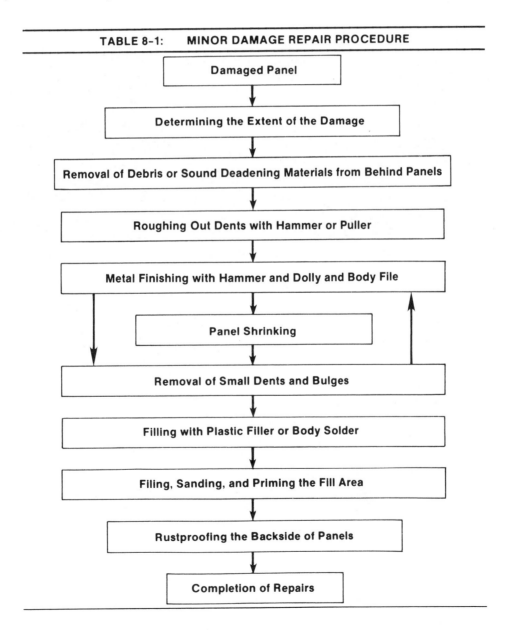

TABLE 8-1: MINOR DAMAGE REPAIR PROCEDURE

Damaged Panel

Determining the Extent of the Damage

Removal of Debris or Sound Deadening Materials from Behind Panels

Roughing Out Dents with Hammer or Puller

Metal Finishing with Hammer and Dolly and Body File

Panel Shrinking

Removal of Small Dents and Bulges

Filling with Plastic Filler or Body Solder

Filing, Sanding, and Priming the Fill Area

Rustproofing the Backside of Panels

Completion of Repairs

8.1 BODY FILLERS

Most auto body repairs require some application of plastic body filler. Plastic body filler is a fast, inexpensive way to restore the final contour of a damaged panel. But many body shops tend to skimp on the sheet metal repairs and simply hide the damage under a thick layer of filler. Body fillers were never meant to replace proper metalworking techniques. Before any fillers are applied, the damaged panel should be returned to its correct shape and dimension by bumping, stretching, and pulling (see Chapter 7) (Figure 8-1). Stretched metal should be shrunk and high spots should be lowered. After the panel has been filed to locate low spots, low areas

should be bumped or picked up so that no area is more than 1/8 inch below the original contour of the panel.

Before any filler is applied, all holes, cracks, and joint gaps must be welded or brazed. Some body fillers are hygroscopic, which means they absorb moisture when exposed to humid conditions. Unless filled with a waterproof pigment, these fillers will absorb moisture through holes or cracks in the metal. The moisture will penetrate to the metal where rust will begin to form. Eventually, the rust will destroy the bond between the filler and the metal.

Body fillers and putties can also be used to repair minor defects, such as dings, stone chips, surface rust, and rustouts. Procedures for making these minor auto body repairs are given in this chapter. Be

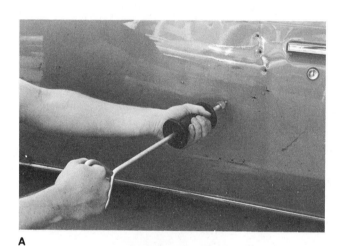

A

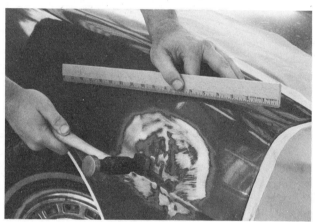

B

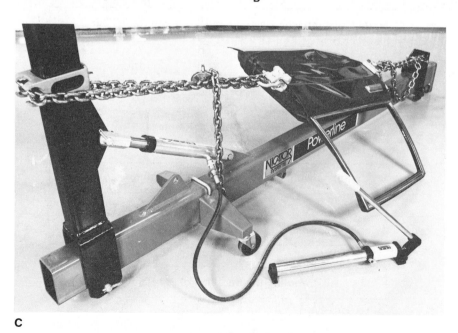

C

FIGURE 8-1 Proper metalworking techniques: (A) pulling, (B) bumping, and (C) stretching. *(Photo C courtesy of Nicator, Inc.)*

aware, though, that plastic body fillers have limitations. Large panels such as hoods, deck lids, and door panels tend to vibrate violently under normal road conditions. Vibrations can crack and dislodge filler that is applied over an area that is too large or applied too thickly.

Care must also be taken when applying filler to semi-structural panels in unibody frames. Panels such as quarter panels and roofs absorb road shocks and torque flexing. Excessive fillers applied in these areas can be popped off by stresses in the panels. Plastic filler should also be used sparingly on rocker panels, lower rear wheel openings, and other areas subject to flying stones and rock chips. Nor should protruding body lines, fender or door edges, or other edges and corners that are subject to scrapes and bumps be shaped with filler.

> **CAUTION:** Plastic body fillers are hazardous materials. Always wear an approved dust mask when sanding filler. Filler dust can damage the eyes, throat, lungs, and liver.

General Description

Plastic body filler is very similar to paint in composition. Both are made of resins, pigments, and solvents. Most plastic body fillers have a polyester resin that acts as a binder. When the filler is applied and the solvents evaporate, the binders hold the pigments together in a tough, durable film. The basic pigment or filler in conventional fillers is talc. Talc, also used in baby powders, absorbs moisture. That is good for the baby but bad for the car if proper steps are not taken to shield the filler from moisture. If holes in the metal or cracks in the paint expose the filler to the atmosphere, the talc in the filler absorbs moisture, which attacks the metal substrate and forms rust. The rust destroys the filler-to-metal bond, causing the filler to fall off. Waterproof fillers are available. Fiberglass strands or metal particles are used instead of talc as pigments.

Like enamel paints, plastic fillers harden by chemical action. Hardening, or curing, produces a molecular structure that will not shrink or soften. The chemical reaction is set off by oxygen. If the container of plastic filler is open and left exposed to the oxygen in the atmosphere, it will slowly harden. To speed up the process, a chemical catalyst is provided by the manufacturer. The catalyst, in liquid or cream form, is called **hardener** (Figure 8–2). Hardener is basically a chemical compound called perox-

TABLE 8-2: EFFECT OF TEMPERATURE ON WORKING TIME

Temperature	Working Times
100°F	3 to 4 minutes
85°F	4 to 5 minutes
77°F	6 to 7 minutes
70°F	8 to 9 minutes

ide. The oxygen in the peroxide drastically speeds up the curing process. As Table 8–2 shows, the filler will soon become too stiff to work in just a few minutes after adding hardener, depending on the ambient air temperature.

As the filler cures and hardens, the chemical reaction produces a tremendous amount of heat. For this reason, unused filler should not be discarded in trash cans containing solvent-wet paper or cloths.

Curing fillers also produce a waxy coating, or paraffins, on the surface. The purpose of the paraffins in the filler is to form a film that prevents oxygen absorption from the atmosphere. The paraffins are suspended in the filler solvent and are carried to the surface when the solvents evaporate. The paraffins must be either removed with a wax and grease remover before being sanded or else filed off with a surform cheese grater.

Types of Body Fillers

During the first 50 years of auto body repair, blemishes in sheet metal panels were corrected by applying lead filler. Lead filler or solder is an alloy of lead and tin. A welding torch is used to soften the solder and bond it to the body sheet metal. Before World War II, automobiles were made with heavy

FIGURE 8-2 Chemical catalyst called hardener. (Courtesy of America Sikkens, Inc.)

gauge steel panels that were unaffected by the heat used in the "tinning" operation. But changes began to take place in automotive construction in the late 1940s and early 1950s. In the economic boom following World War II, Americans began demanding larger and fancier cars. So, manufacturers responded with vehicles made with thinner, larger, and more complex body panels. The thinner metals, however, made the old lead repair methods almost obsolete. The heat required for the lead filler warped the thin panels, and hammer-and-dolly work stretched metals too thin for filing. There was a real need for an inexpensive, time saving substitute.

In the early 1950s, epoxy-based fillers were developed. Usually mixed with aluminum powder, epoxy fillers cured very slowly and did not harden at all if applied too thickly.

In the middle 1950s the first polyester resin-based body fillers were developed. These fillers were made from the same resin used to make fiberglass boats and required mixing with a liquid hardener and accelerator. Since the fiberglass resin is very brittle when cured and depends on cloth or matte for flexibility, the early polyester body fillers were also very brittle and hard.

The first successful filler was named "Bondo" and many body technicians still refer to plastic body fillers as "Bondo." The early fillers were composed of approximately 40 percent (by weight) polyester resin and 60 percent talc. Because the thin resin was difficult to work with and cured hard and brittle, many applications eventually cracked and fell off the vehicle.

Early fillers had other problems, too. Plastic filler technology had still to develop the inhibitors used today to promote stability. Therefore, shelf life of the early fillers was very short. The original products were sold in quart cans only; yet, a very high percentage of the product hardened in the can before it could be used. Early fillers also used a clear liquid hardener that made it difficult to determine when the filler and hardener were thoroughly mixed. Incomplete mixing often resulted in soft spots in the repair area.

When the filler and hardener were properly mixed together, the filler dried very hard. Early fillers were difficult to file and had to be leveled with a grinder, resulting in choking clouds of dust that blanketed the shop. Low dust, straight-line air fillers had not been developed yet.

Finally, a product was developed, called "Black Magic," that utilized more flexible polyester resins and benzoyl peroxide as a cream hardener. Black pigment was added to the resin and talc mixture

(thus its name) and white pigment was added to the cream hardener. The contrasting colors provided a reference to ensure proper mixing of the two ingredients.

As the technology developed, body fillers became softer, easier to apply, and easier to shape. Fillers soon appeared in black, red, gray, white, and yellow. Cream hardeners in contrasting colors—red, white, green, and blue—were also developed to provide a mixing reference for the various colored polyester fillers. The softer fillers could also be grated while still semicured, thus reducing the amount of sanding required. Note that the addition of color does not affect the working characteristics of the filler.

Conventional body fillers have over 30 years of development backing them today. The premium heavyweights use very fine grain talc to provide superior workability, sandability, and featheredging. High-quality resins ensure excellent adhesion and quick curing properties. Most heavyweights can be grated in 10 to 15 minutes.

Fiberglass Fillers

As thinner gauge sheet metal replaced the heavy gauge steel used on vehicles of the 1940s and 1950s, rust became a problem, especially in areas of the country where road salts are used in winter. A product was needed to repair rustouts. Because talc-filled body fillers absorb moisture readily, the available heavyweight fillers did not provide long lasting protection when used to repair rustouts.

To meet this demand for a waterproof filler, fiberglass-reinforced fillers were developed. Fiberglass fillers use fiberglass strands rather than talc as a bulking agent. These fillers are more flexible and stronger than conventional fillers. Because they are also waterproof, they can be used to bridge holes, tears, and rustouts.

Fiberglass fillers are available in two basic forms. One is formulated with short strands of fiberglass. The other is made with long strands. Short strand fiberglass fillers are generally used to repair small holes (approximately 1 to 1-1/2 inches in size). When used to repair larger holes, a fiberglass cloth or screen should be used as a back support. The short strand fillers can be sanded and finished as any conventional filler.

Long strand fiberglass products are designed to fill holes larger than 1-1/2 inches in size. The longer strands interlock and provide a much stronger patch. The long strand filler might also be used with fiberglass cloths or mattes to bridge even larger rust-

Chapter 8 Minor Auto Body Repairs

FIGURE 8-3 Lightweight fillers with microsphere glass beads

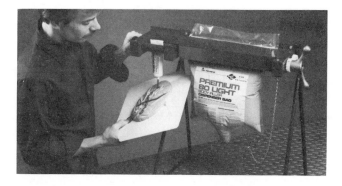

FIGURE 8-4 Roller dispensers for lightweight fillers. (Courtesy of Oatey Corporation)

FIGURE 8-5 5-gallon pneumatic cans or roller dispenser. (Courtesy of Dynatron/Bondo Corp.)

outs. The long strand fillers, however, are used only as a base. Smoother fillers, either short strand fiberglass fillers or conventional fillers, must be used for the final fill. Chopped fiberglass fibers are also available to be added to fillers to increase their strength.

Aluminum Fillers

Some manufacturers attempted to improve water resistance of their products by replacing part of the talc with aluminum powder. This small quantity of aluminum powder did not stop moisture failures because of the talc still remaining in the formula. Another complaint was the short shelf life of the aluminized products since aluminum is, itself, a catalyst for polyester resin.

The first talc-free, 100 percent aluminum auto body filler was developed in England and was introduced into the United States under the name "Alum A Lead." The shelf life problem was solved by packaging the resin and powder separately; mixing was done by the body technician.

The first premixed, 100 percent aluminum auto body fillers were introduced in 1965. This product was waterproof, used a red-tinted liquid hardener, and had a fairly good shelf life. Due to their very high relative costs, the 100 percent aluminum-filled body fillers are used sparingly on special applications, such as restoring antique cars. Today there are several similar 100 percent aluminum products available. Metal fillers are nonshrinking, waterproof, and very smooth. Metal fillers have the look of lead but are easier to work. When cured, they are harder than talc or fiberglass-filled plastic fillers.

Lightweight Fillers

Until the middle 1970s only minor improvements were made to conventional heavyweight fillers. With the invention of microsphere glass bubbles by 3M came the technology to produce the modern, lightweight auto body fillers of the 1980s (Figure 8-3). Lightweight fillers were formulated by replacing about 50 percent of the talc in the filler with tiny glass spheres. The resulting higher resin content dramatically improved the filing and sanding characteristics of the filler as well as improved the filler's adhesion and water resistance. Most lightweight fillers are homogenous. The glass bubbles remain suspended in the resin and do not settle to the bottom of the can. This homogenous composition allows lightweight fillers to be packaged in plastic bags or cans and dispensed with rollers or compressed air or squeezed out with a plastic spreader (Figures 8-4, 8-5, and 8-6). The plastic bags keep

FIGURE 8-6 Lightweight fillers in a plastic pack

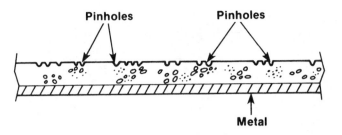

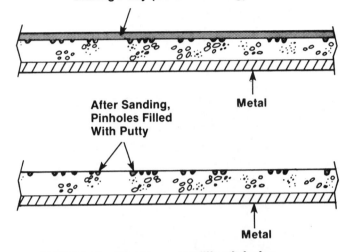

FIGURE 8-7 Glazing putty fills pinholes.

filler fresh and eliminate much of the wasted filler sometimes associated with canned fillers.

By the middle 1980s lightweight body filler technology was shared by most manufacturers, and major brands again became very similar to each other in working characteristics. Lightweight fillers quickly became the most popular filler used. Nationally, lightweight fillers represent more than 80 percent of the total filler used in body shops.

Premium Fillers

Filler manufacturers in the mid 1980s have taken advantage of new technology to produce premium quality fillers. Premium fillers have superior performance qualities that go beyond the capabilities of conventional lightweight fillers. Premium fillers are moist and creamy. They spread easily yet will not sag on vertical surfaces. They dry tack-free without pinholing. Best of all, premium fillers are easy to sand. The smooth finish and ease of sandability reduce the time and labor involved in filling and shaping the repair.

Spot and Glazing Putties

Because mixing, applying, and shaping of body fillers usually creates tiny pinholes and sand scratches, glazing putties have been developed to fill the minor surface imperfections and produce a perfectly smooth surface. Until the mid 1980s a nitrocellulose glazing putty was used for this purpose almost exclusively. Nitrocellulose glazing putties are actually very thick lacquer paints. They have a high concentration of solids and, like lacquer paints, cure by solvent evaporation. Glazing putties should be used only to fill very shallow sand scratches and pinholes (Figure 8-7). Maximum filling depth is only 1/32

inch. Although glazing putties featheredge very nicely, they do not develop the hardness of a body filler. When coated with primer or paint, putties absorb paint solvents and swell. Sufficient time must be allowed for the putty to fully cure again before finish sanding of the finish coats. If sanded too soon, sand scratches will appear in the finish as the putty dries completely and shrinks below the sanded surface.

Polyester Glazing Putty

In the 1980s, the European basecoat/clear coat paint system became popular in the United States. The new basecoat/clear coat paint systems stirred up a problem that had occurred occasionally since the inception of the candy and mother-of-pearl colors in the late 1960s. The rich solvents and multicoats required for these "trick" paint jobs caused the pigment from the cream hardener in the body filler to "bleed" and stain the finish on light colors, usually after several days of exposure to sunlight. The widespread use of basecoat/clear coat products and other multicoat systems has made this staining problem a more frequent occurrence.

Developing a body filler that will not stain results in either extremely high cost or working properties not acceptable to most body technicians. At present, the only absolutely stain-free fillers are liquid hardener-catalyzed aluminum fillers.

To solve the staining problem, body filler manufacturers have developed a fine-grained, catalyzed polyester glazing putty (Figure 8–8). Polyester glazing putty does not shrink, has excellent dimensional stability, and resists solvent penetration (the cause of bleed-through). When applied over traditional body fillers, polyester glazing putties effectively solve the bleed-through problem. Bleed-through problems can also be avoided by using a sprayable polyester filler (Figure 8–9). This type of primer-surfacer has polyester resins and talc fillers and must be catalyzed with a liquid hardener. Sprayed

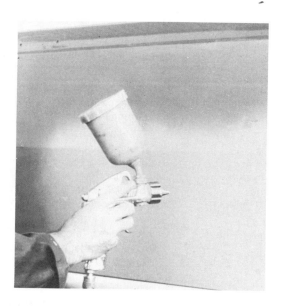

FIGURE 8-10   Applying sprayable filler with a gravity feed gun

from a gravity feed gun (Figure 8–10), polyester primers fill minor imperfections and seal both fillers and old paint finishes.

8.2 APPLYING PLASTIC BODY FILLER

Body fillers are designed to cover up the minor depressions that cannot be removed with proper metalworking techniques. Some, as stated previously, are designed with specific applications in mind. Others are limited to specific applications because of ingredients or cost. Table 8–3 summarizes the ingredients, characteristics, and applications of the currently available body fillers and putties.

Taking shortcuts when mixing and applying fillers might save time, but it affects the quality of the repair. Fillers that are improperly mixed and applied will eventually crack, lose adhesion, permit rust to form on the metal substrate, and fall off the panel. Sooner or later, the repair will have to be redone. The loss in time, money, and reputation is hard to calculate.

PREPARING THE SURFACE FOR FILLING

One of the most important steps in applying plastic body fillers is surface preparation. Begin by washing the repair area to remove dirt and grime. Then clean the area with wax and grease remover to eliminate wax, road tar, and grease. Be sure to use a

FIGURE 8-8   Applying polyester putty

FIGURE 8-9   Sprayable polyester primer-filler. (Courtesy of America Sikkens, Inc.)

TABLE 8-3: COMPARING FILLERS AND PUTTIES

Filler	Composition	Characteristics	Application
Conventional Fillers			
Heavyweight Fillers	Polyester resins and talc particles	Smooth sanding; fine feather-edging; nonsagging; less pinholing than lightweight fillers	Dents, dings, and gouges in metal panels
Lightweight Fillers	Microsphere glass bubbles; fine grain talc; polyester resins	Spreads easily; nonshrinking; homogenous; no settling	Dings, dents, and gouges in metal panels
Premium Fillers	Microspheres; talc; polyester resins; special chemical additives	Sands fast and easy; spreads creamy and moist; spreads smooth without pinholes; dries tack-free; will not sag	Dings, dents, and gouges in metal panels
Fiberglass-Reinforced Fillers			
Short Strand	Small fiberglass strands; polyester resins	Waterproof; stronger than regular fillers	Fills small rustouts and holes. Used with fiberglass cloth to bridge larger rustouts.
Long Strand	Long fiberglass strands; polyester resins	Waterproof; stronger than short strand fiberglass fillers; bridges small holes without matte or cloth	Cracked or shattered fiberglass. Repairing rustouts, holes, and tears.
Specialty Fillers			
Aluminum Filler	Aluminum flakes and powders; polyester resins	Waterproof; spreads smoothly; high level of quality and durability	Restoring classic and exotic vehicles
Finishing Filler/ Polyester Putty	High-resin content; fine talc particles; microsphere glass bubbles	Ultra-smooth and creamy; tack-free; nonshrinking; eliminates need for air dry type glazing putty	Fills pinholes and sand scratches in metal, filler, fiberglass, and old finishes.
Sprayable Filler/ Polyester Primer-Surfacer	High-viscosity polyester resins; talc particles; liquid hardener	Virtually nonshrinking; prevents bleed-through; eliminates primer/glazing/ primer procedure	Fills file marks, sand scratches, mildly cracked or crazed paint films, and pinholes. Seals fillers and old finishes against bleed-through.

remover that will take away the silicones often present in car waxes. Also, wash brazed or soldered joints with soda water to neutralize the acids in the flux. Do not grind these areas before neutralizing the acids. Grinding simply drives the acids deep into the metal.

Grind the area to remove the old paint (Figure 8-11). Remove the paint for 3 or 4 inches around the area to be filled. If filler overlaps any of the existing finish, the paint film will absorb solvents from the new primer and paint, destroying the adhesion of the filler. The filler will lift, cracking the paint and allowing moisture to seep under the filler. Rust will then form on the metal.

Use #24 or #36 grit grinding disc to remove the paint; it removes paint and surface rust quickly and also etches the metal to provide better adhesion.

If applying filler over a metal patch, do not hammer down the excess weld bead. Grind it level with the surface. As shown in Figure 8-12, hammer-

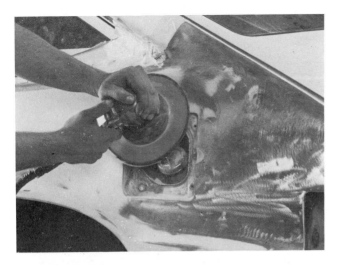

FIGURE 8-11   Removing old paint finish

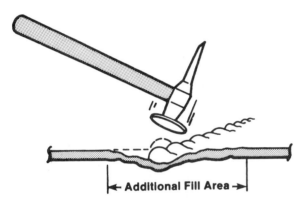

FIGURE 8-12   Beating weld bead down increases fill area.

ing the weld distorts the metal, creates stress in the panel, and increases the area to be filled.

After grinding away the finish from the repair area, blow away the sanding dust with compressed air and wipe the surface with a tack rag to remove any remaining dust particles.

> **CAUTION:** Do not apply a metal conditioner to the repair area **before** applying the filler. The acids in the conditioner will prevent the filler from bonding to the metal substrate.

MIXING THE FILLER

Mix the can of filler to a uniform and smooth consistency free of lumps (Figure 8-13). Preferably,

FIGURE 8-13   Mixing filler in the can

heavyweight fillers should be shaken on a paint shaker for several minutes.

If a heavyweight body filler in the can is not stirred up thoroughly to a smooth and uniform consistency before use, the filler in the upper portion of the can will be too thin. This results in runs and sags in application, slow and poor curing, a gummy condition when sanded, poor featheredge, a very tacky surface, and blistering and lifting when recoated with primers and refinishing materials. If the filler in the lower portion of the can is too thick, the filler will be very coarse and grainy. There will be poor adhesion, rampant pinholing, poor featheredge, and poor color holdout when the repaired area is recoated with primers and refinishing materials.

KNEADING THE HARDENER

Loosen the cap of the cream hardener tube to prevent the hardener from being air bound. Knead the tube thoroughly to assure a smooth paste-like consistency (like toothpaste) when squeezed out (Figure 8-14).

FIGURE 8-14   Kneading hardener

FIGURE 8-15   Mix filler and hardener together on nonporous mixing board.

If the cream hardener is not kneaded thoroughly to produce a smooth, paste-like consistency or ribbon-effect when squeezed out, the hardener can cause slow and ineffective curing, a tacky surface, poor adhesion, poor featheredge, blistering, and peeling after recoating.

If the cream hardener is kneaded thoroughly and remains thin and watery, it is spoiled and should not be used.

MIXING FILLER AND HARDENER

Open the can slowly and remove the desired amount of filler. Using a clean putty knife or squeegee, place the filler on a smooth, clean, nonporous surface such as sheet metal or glass (Figure 8-15). Add the hardener in the proportion indicated on the can instructions.

Too little hardener will result in a soft, gummy filler that will not adhere properly to the metal and will not sand or featheredge cleanly (Figure 8-16). Too much hardener will produce excessive gases, resulting in rampant pinholing (Figure 8-17).

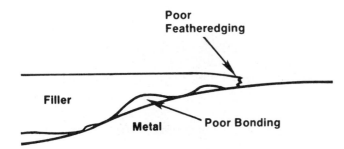

FIGURE 8-16   Too little hardener

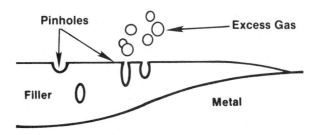

FIGURE 8-17   Too much hardener

 **SHOP TALK** ——————————

Cardboard should not be used as a mixing surface for the filler. Cardboard is porous and contains waxes for waterproofing. These waxes will be dissolved in the mixed filler and cause poor bonding to both the metal repair area and to earlier cured filler. Cardboard also absorbs some of the chemicals in the filler and hardener, reducing its quality. Use glass, plastic, or any nonporous surface. Plastic mixing boards are available for this purpose.

With a clean putty knife or squeegee and using a scraping motion (back and forth), mix the filler and the hardener together thoroughly to achieve a uniform color (Figure 8-18). Do not stir the filler. Stirring whips air into the filler, producing air pockets and pinholes in the application. Do not return the knife or squeegee or mixed filler to the can. Replace the cover on the can and close it tightly.

If the filler and hardener are not thoroughly mixed to a uniform color, soft spots in the cured filler occur. The result is an uneven cure, poor adhesion, lifting, blistering, and so forth.

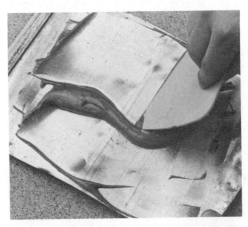

FIGURE 8-18   Mix with a scraping motion.

Always use clean, uncontaminated tools when removing the filler from the can and mixing the filler and hardener together. Otherwise, hard lumps of filler might appear in the can and/or the applied filler, which will give poor adhesion and an uneven cure.

Applying Filler

Apply the mixed filler promptly to a thoroughly clean and well-sanded surface. A first tight, thin application is recommended. Press firmly to force filler into sand scratches to maximize the bond (Figure 8-19). When cured, apply additional thicker applications as needed to build up the repaired area to proper contour (Figure 8-20). Allow each applica-

FIGURE 8-19   Applying filler with a plastic spreader

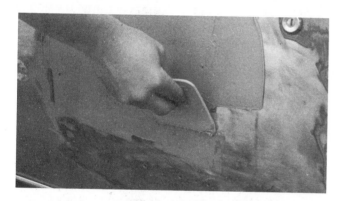

A. Thin skim coat

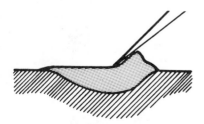

B. Fill slightly above panel.

FIGURE 8-20   Build filler thickness in several coats.

tion to set up before applying the next coat of filler. Conventional body fillers should be built up slightly so that the waxy film that curing produces on the surface of the filler can be removed with a surform grater.

 SHOP TALK _____

Always use a clean plastic spreader or putty knife to apply the filler. Use a different spreader to mix the filler. A small amount of unmixed (uncatalyzed) filler will always remain on the spreader. If any of this is transferred to the metal, soft spots will be present in the cured filler and the paint finish will peel.

Applying the mixed filler thickly without first applying a thin, tight application causes poor bonding and rampant pinholing. Wiping over the repaired area with solvents before applying the mixed filler also causes pinholes and poor adhesion.

Avoid use in cold temperatures. When the filler, shop, and/or body panel temperatures are cold, the body filler will not cure properly. This results in the filler being too soft. It will also have a tacky surface and poor sanding properties. Tremendous pinholes could be created. Filler should be stored at room temperature (65 to 70 degrees Fahrenheit) and a heat lamp should be used to warm cold surfaces.

Avoid moisture on the repair area in conditions of high humidity in the shop. In winter, moisture will form on metal surfaces when a cold car is brought inside. In summer, condensation might form on the metal due to water evaporating from the floor. Use a heat lamp to warm and dry damp surfaces before applying filler. If the repair area is not first warmed to remove moisture accumulation on the surface, poor adhesion, poor featheredge, rampant pinholing, and lifting when recoating with refinishing materials could result.

Shaping the Filler

Allow the filler to cure to a semihard consistency. This usually takes 15 to 20 minutes. If the filler leaves a firm white track when scratched with a fingernail, it is ready to be filed. Filing is perhaps the most important factor in achieving a quality surface and controlling material cost and labor. The surform or cheese grater file is used to cut the excess filler to size quickly. Its long length produces an even, level

A

B

Surform Moving Direction

30° to 40°

Surforming should be done in many directions.

FIGURE 8-21 **(A) Filing the semihard filler. (B) Hold grater to 30° angle and pull across filler.**

surface. The teeth in the file are open enough to prevent the tool from clogging. Grinders, sanders, and air files do not level well; they become loaded quickly, create too much dust, and waste a lot of sandpaper.

To use the grater, hold it at a 30-degree angle and pull it lightly across the filler (Figure 8-21). Work the filler in several directions. Stop filing when the filler is slightly above the desired level. This will leave sufficient filler for sanding out the file marks and for feathering the edges. If the filler is undercut, additional filler must be applied.

After grating, sand out all file marks (Figure 8-22). Use a block or air file. An air file can also be used on large flat areas. Then, follow with #80 grit paper until all grating scratches are removed.

Final smoothing should be done using #180 grit paper until all #80 grit scratches are removed. The DA or air file can again be used or a long speed file can be used. Be careful not to oversand—this results in the filled area being below the desired level, which, again, makes it necessary to apply more filler.

After the final sanding, blow off the area with a high-pressure air gun and wipe with a tack cloth.

This removes any fine sanding dust that might be hiding surface pinholes and exposes holes lying just below the surface (Figure 8-23). These holes and remaining sand scratches must be filled with putty.

Run a hand over the surface often to check for evenness. Do not trust eyeing for accuracy. Remember, paint does not hide imperfections; it highlights them. Do not be satisfied until the repaired surface feels perfectly even.

When satisfied with the smoothness of the filler surface, clean the area with a tack cloth. A tack cloth picks up bits of filler dust—which will mar a smooth surface—that normal cleaning leaves behind. The repair area must then be coated with primer.

APPLYING GLAZING PUTTY

Once the primer is dry, small pinholes and scratches can be filled with glazing putty. If using a polyester putty, mix the putty and hardener according to the manufacturer's instructions. Place a small amount of putty onto a clean rubber squeegee and apply a thin covering over the filler. Use single strokes and a fast scraping motion. Use a minimum number of strokes when applying lacquer-based putties. They skim over or surface dry very fast and repeated passes of the spreader might pull the putty away from the filler.

Allow the putty to dry completely before sanding smooth with #240 grit sandpaper. Sanding the putty before the solvents in it have completely evaporated results in subsequent sand scratches in the finish. The repair is now ready for the priming and painting processes.

FIGURE 8-22 **Sand away file marks.**

FILLER BEFORE SANDING

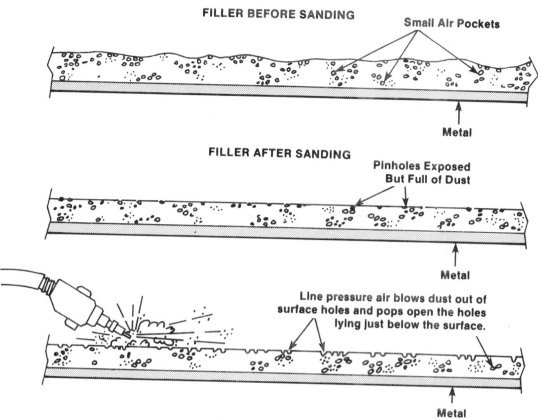

Small Air Pockets

Metal

FILLER AFTER SANDING

Pinholes Exposed
But Full of Dust

Metal

Line pressure air blows dust out of
surface holes and pops open the holes
lying just below the surface.

Metal

FIGURE 8-23   Blow filler dust out of pinholes.

 SHOP TALK

When properly mixed, applied, sanded, and primed, a quality body filler will have very few imperfections. Excessive use of glazing putties is usually an indication of a lack of expertise on the part of the body technician.

Applying Filler to Body Lines

Many cars today have sharp body lines in doors, quarter panels, hoods, and so forth. Figure 8-24

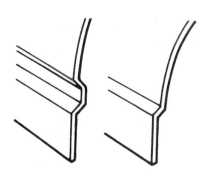

FIGURE 8-24   Typical angular body lines

shows two cross sections of typical angular body lines. Maintaining the sharpness of these lines when doing filler work is difficult, especially in recessed areas. The best way to get straight, clean lines is to fill each plane, angle, or corner separately.

Masking tape is applied along one edge (Figure 8-25). Then filler is applied to the adjacent surface. Before the filler sets up, the tape is pulled off, removing the excess filler from the crease or line. After the first application is dry and sanded, the opposite edge is taped. Masking tape is applied along the body line and over the filler. The adjacent surface is coated with filler. When the tape is removed and the filler sanded, the result is a straight, even line or corner.

Applying Filler to Panel Joints

Many panels on unibody vehicles have joints that are factory finished with a flexible mastic that allows the panel to flex and move. Often both halves of the body joint suffer damage and require filling. Many body technicians make the mistake of covering the damaged joint with body filler. Figure 8-26 shows what happens when the inflexible filler is sub-

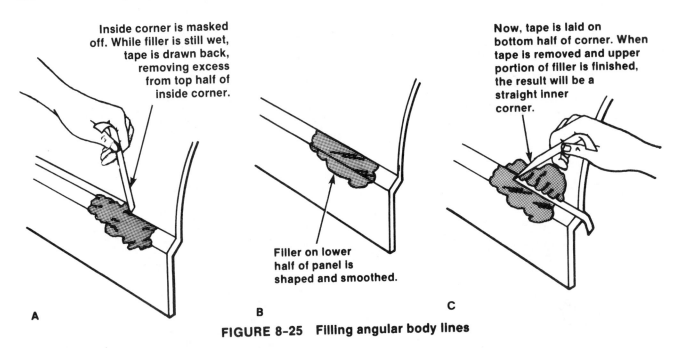

Inside corner is masked off. While filler is still wet, tape is drawn back, removing excess from top half of inside corner.

Filler on lower half of panel is shaped and smoothed.

Now, tape is laid on bottom half of corner. When tape is removed and upper portion of filler is finished, the result will be a straight inner corner.

A   B   C

FIGURE 8-25   Filling angular body lines

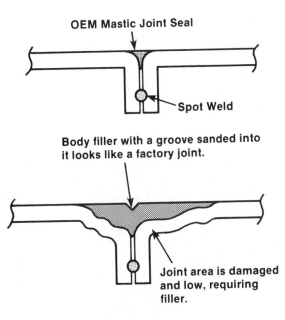

OEM Mastic Joint Seal

Spot Weld

Body filler with a groove sanded into it looks like a factory joint.

Joint area is damaged and low, requiring filler.

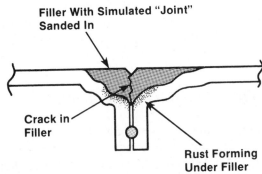

Filler With Simulated "Joint" Sanded In

Crack in Filler

Rust Forming Under Filler

FIGURE 8-26   Body joint covered with filler cracked

jected to the twisting action of the panels under normal road conditions. A crack develops that allows moisture to seep under the filler, which causes rust to form on the metal surface. This eventually results in the failure of the filler-to-metal bond and a weakened sheet metal joint.

The original flexibility of the joint can be preserved by taping its alternate sides. As shown in Figure 8-27, tape is applied to one panel. Filler is then applied to the other panel and the tape is pulled up, removing the excess filler. The other panel is filled in the same way. After the filler in both panels is cured and shaped, a sealer is forced into the joint.

8.3 APPLYING LEAD FILLER

Most body shops use plastic body fillers exclusively in dent repair. Those shops that do use lead filler, or body solder as it is sometimes called, use it only in restoring antique and classic automobiles or in doing custom work. Some shops use lead filler to fill door edges and welded seams, but generally lead work is done only on request by the customer. It is a specialized skill that few body technicians have.

Lead filler is an alloy of lead and tin. Most lead solder used in body repair is 30 percent tin and 70 percent lead; thus, it is often called 30/70 solder. At approximately 360 degrees Fahrenheit, 30/70 body solder becomes soft or plastic. It becomes liquid at approximately 490 degrees Fahrenheit. Within this

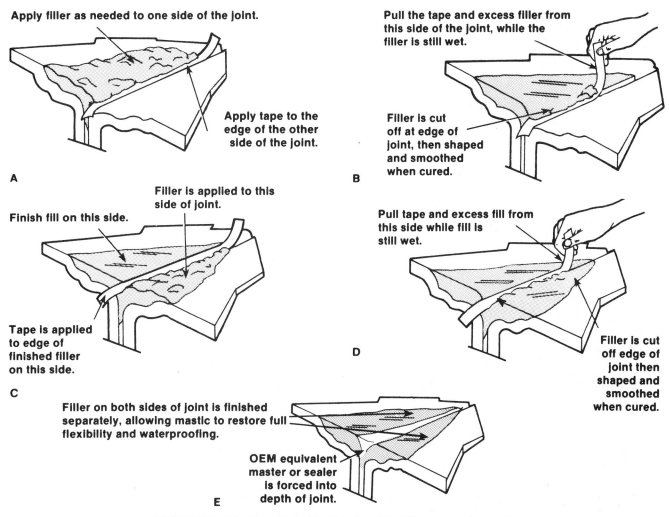

Apply filler as needed to one side of the joint.

Apply tape to the edge of the other side of the joint.

A

Pull the tape and excess filler from this side of the joint, while the filler is still wet.

Filler is cut off at edge of joint, then shaped and smoothed when cured.

B

Filler is applied to this side of joint.

Finish fill on this side.

Tape is applied to edge of finished filler on this side.

C

Pull tape and excess fill from this side while fill is still wet.

Filler is cut off edge of joint then shaped and smoothed when cured.

D

Filler on both sides of joint is finished separately, allowing mastic to restore full flexibility and waterproofing.

OEM equivalent master or sealer is forced into depth of joint.

E

FIGURE 8-27   Creating flexible joint in filler-coated panel

heat range, body solder is plastic enough to be worked and shaped.

An oxyacetylene welding torch, or a specially designed soldering torch, is used to heat and soften the solder. A medium size welding tip is used on the torch. The acetylene pressure is set at 4 to 5 pounds and the tip is adjusted to a carburizing flame. The low heat and wide flame this setting provides is adequate to heat the solder and the repair area without overstressing most mild steel sheet metal panels.

WARNING: High-strength steels used in modern unibody vehicles are heat sensitive. Do not attempt to fill high-tensile strength sheet metal with lead.

After bumping the damaged sheet metal back to the original contour, grind the metal bare and clean

it with a metal conditioner. Then heat the repair area and brush on a tinning flux. Tinning fluxes are used to clean microscopic rust particles from bare metal, prevent rust from forming, and promote adhesion of the solder to the sheet metal. A variety of fluxes is available. Some are acidic; others are nonacidic. Muriatic acid is an example of a flux often used in lead repair. The acid is cut or diluted with a zinc bar and applied to the repair area with an acid brush or swab.

CAUTION: Muriatic acid is very corrosive and poisonous. Do not breathe the fumes produced when cutting with zinc bar and wear heavy rubber gloves when applying it. Always follow the manufacturer's instructions for mixing and applying any kind of tinning flux.

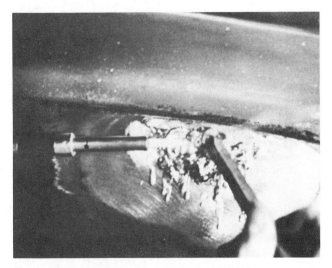

A

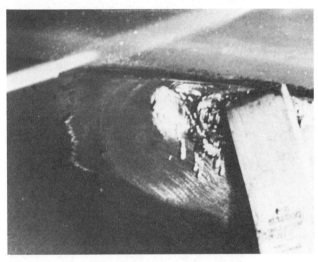

B

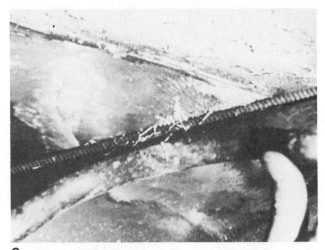

C

FIGURE 8-28 Apply lead filler when (A) melting lead solder, (B) smoothing solder with wooden paddle, and (C) filing the solder.

After applying the flux, heat the metal with the torch and rub the solder bar over the hot metal. This will deposit a thin layer of solder over the repair area. While the solder is still plastic, wipe the area with a clean shop cloth. This will spread the solder over the bare metal and will remove any impurities. The tinned area will be silvery white.

Next, fill the area with solder. Do this by heating 1 inch of the solder rod or bar and the adjacent metal (Figure 8-28A). Press the heat-softened bar against the hot metal. This will deposit the solder on the sheet metal. Do this as much as is necessary to fill the repair area.

Now, shape and smooth the solder. Heat the solder by moving the welding torch with a carburizing flame back and forth over the solder until it begins to sag. Then, with a soldering paddle, spread the solder and smooth it over the repair area (Figure 8-28B). A flat paddle is used on flat and convex surfaces. A curved paddle is used on concave surfaces. The paddle must be clean and properly waxed so that solder will stick to it. The solder level should be slightly above the panel.

While the metal is still hot, quench the area with cool water. Quenching will cool the metal so that it can be filed and will also relieve the heat stress in the panel.

Use a body file as described in Chapter 7 to file the solder level with the panel (Figure 8-28C). Use a dull file if one is available. A sharp file will cut the solder very quickly, and if the solder is undercut, more lead will have to be applied and paddled. File with long strokes, working from the edge across the middle in every direction. Sand the solder to final contour with #80 or #100 grit sandpaper and a speed file. Metal prep before priming.

8.4 REPAIRING SCRATCHES

Most vehicles brought to the auto body shop for damage repair and/or refinishing have a variety of minor imperfections in the paint. Some defects, such as chalking or scuff marks, can be removed with rubbing compound. The abrasive compound removes the damaged surface paint and brings out the luster in the paint beneath. Compounding is discussed at length in Chapter 19. Other defects, such as a scratch, are too deep to buff out with rubbing compound. If the scratch penetrates through the primer and exposes the metal underneath, the scratch must be repaired using the technique for repairing nicks and chips discussed later in this chapter. On the other hand, shallow scratches that

FIGURE 8-29   A shallow scratch

are too deep to be buffed out, but do not reach the metal underneath the paint, can be filled with putty or a polyester primer-surfacer. An example of such a scratch is shown in Figure 8-29.

Preparing the Surface

Wash and clean the repair area with a wax and grease removing solvent; then lightly sand the scratched areas. Use a sanding block when sanding large areas, but a 9 inch by 11 inch sheet of #240 grit paper folded in half and then three ways is fine for small areas. A light sanding will rough up the finish coat so the glazing putty and new primer will adhere to the old finish. Do not press hard on the sandpaper. Excessive pressure can result in low spots or a wavy surface that will require additional filling and sanding. After the rough sanding is complete, clean the sanded area with compressed air or a soft cotton cloth and wipe with a tack cloth.

Applying Glazing Putty

If the scratch is part of a larger panel being refinished, try filling the repair area with the primer-surfacer. Some sprayable polyester primers will provide up to 15 mils of fill. Another solution is to fill the scratch with glazing putty.

Following the instructions on the tube of putty, apply a daub on the edge of a clean rubber contour squeegee. A little bit of putty goes a long way. When filling only scratches, do not squeeze too much putty onto the spreader.

Using moderate pressure, spread putty over the repair area. Apply it with the rubber squeegee (Figure 8-30) and use a fast scraping motion. Apply in

one direction only. Do not pass the squeegee over the same area more than once. Multiple passes can pull the putty away from the body.

Allow the putty to dry completely. Drying time varies with the putty's thickness, but it usually takes between 20 and 60 minutes. For best results, allow the putty to dry overnight before sanding. Sanding the putty before it completely cures will result in sand scratches in the finish.

Sanding the Glazing Putty

After the putty dries, sand the repair area with #240 grit sandpaper. Wet sand to prevent putty from clogging the paper and creating more scratches in the finish. Use a sanding block to avoid making low spots with finger pressure.

When sanding, rub the palm of the hand over the puttied area to feel for high spots on the surface. When finished, rinse the sludge away and wipe the surface dry. Clean the repair area with a tack cloth.

Inspect the scratch for low spots and voids in the putty. If the scratch requires additional putty, repeat the above procedure. When the surface of the previously scratched area is free of imperfections, it is ready for priming and refinishing.

Priming the Glazing Putty

Once the scratched surface is filled with putty and sanded level with the surrounding panel, the repair area must be sanded to a smooth finish and then primed.

FIGURE 8-30   Applying glazing putty to scratch

FIGURE 8-31 Sanding repair area

Use water, a sanding block, and #400 grit or finer sandpaper to finish sanding the puttied scratch (Figure 8-31). Wet sanding prevents the paper from clogging and creating additional scratches. The sanding block helps avoid creating low spots in the finish. Sand with light pressure and long strokes across the face of the repair. Do not concentrate or bear down on any one spot; doing so will almost guarantee a low spot. Low spots created by finish sanding must be filled with additional glazing putty.

When satisfied with the smoothness of the repair, rinse away sanding sludge and wipe the surface dry. Clean the area with a tack cloth. When it is dry and free of dust, spray a medium coat of primer over the entire repair area (Figure 8-32). Allow the primer to flash or surface dry for about 5 minutes; then wet sand the primer with #400 grit or finer sandpaper. Repeat this process until the repair area is glassy smooth. When glassy smoothness is achieved, the surface is ready for painting.

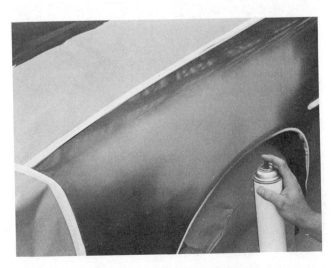

FIGURE 8-32 The primed repair area

8.5 REPAIRING NICKS

Minor bumps and scrapes often leave nicks and scratches in a car's finish. A stone thrown up by a passing vehicle can chip the paint, exposing the sheet metal beneath. Side swipe collisions result in scrapes and gouges. Anytime bare metal is exposed to the air, rust formation must be inhibited with primer before the new finish is applied. A large nick is shown in Figure 8-33.

FEATHEREDGING THE OLD FINISH

After cleaning and dewaxing the repair area, the first step in repairing a nick or deep scratch is sanding the ragged edges of the chipped paint to a smooth surface. This is commonly referred to as featheredging. Featheredging tapers the edges of the paint so that it gradually blends in with the metal surface.

Featheredging chips and nicks is quickly done with a #180 grit disc and a DA. In tight spots, use a sanding block (Figure 8-34). Sand the edges of the

FIGURE 8-33 A sizeable nick in the finish

FIGURE 8-34 Featheredging the nick

old finish to a fine taper. When the sanded area is smooth to the touch, switch to #180 or #240 grit sandpaper and sand any sandpaper scratches away.

APPLYING PRIMER AND PUTTY

After the nicked paint edges are sanded to a smooth surface, clean the metal with a metal conditioner. Metal conditioner is an acid compound that neutralizes microscopic rust particles. The acid also etches the metal to improve the bond between metal and primer. Metal conditioners are discussed fully in Chapter 18. Never leave bare metal surfaces exposed to air. Moisture in the air quickly encourages rust to form on the metal. The slightest film of rust will prevent the paint from properly adhering to the metal. Subsequent lifting and blistering will eventually ruin the paint, and the area will have to be sanded down and refinished again. Priming the bare metal areas with a zinc chromate base primer inhibits rust formation and ensures good bonding of the finish paint.

Blow away any sanding dust and wipe the area with a tack cloth. Then, apply a coat of primer-filler to build up the area and fill any uneven featheredging. After the primer has dried, apply a mist coat of gray primer, block sand the area to identify low spots, and apply glazing putty to fill the low spots (Figure 8–35).

APPLYING FINISHING PRIMER

Final sanding and priming are necessary to achieve a super smooth surface. Wet sand with #400

FIGURE 8-35   Applying glazing putty

grit or finer sandpaper and a sanding block. Sand in long, straight strokes to avoid creating low spots. When sanding curved surfaces, sand very lightly holding the paper with the palm of the hand or use a flexible sander.

Clean, dry, and wipe the sanded surface with a tack cloth. Then, spray the repair area with primer. Completely cover the puttied area and several inches of the old finish around it. Allow the primer to flash (surface dry) for 5 minutes; then sand lightly with water and #240 grit sandpaper.

Clean and prime once or twice more. Between coats, wet sand lightly with #400 or #600 grit sandpaper to achieve an extremely smooth surface. The surface is now ready to be painted.

8.6 REPAIRING DINGS

One kind of surface imperfection that sometimes requires minor metalwork in addition to filling is a ding. Dings are small dents often caused by carelessly opened doors (Figure 8-36). When a pan-

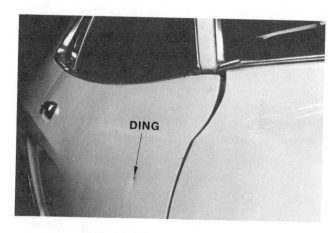

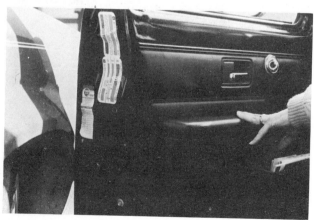

FIGURE 8-36   Minor bumps cause dings.

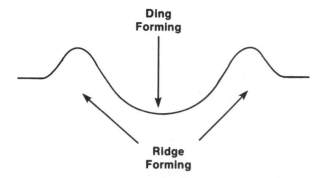

FIGURE 8-37   A high ridge surrounding a ding

el is struck by the edge of another car door, the impact creates a shallow depression in the metal. This small tension area is also usually accompanied by a pressure ridge surrounding the ding (Figure 8-37).

PREPARING THE SURFACE

To repair a ding, first wash and dewax the surface. Then grind the finish from the repair area, using a lightweight air grinder. As shown in Figure 8-38, use up and down buffing strokes to remove the paint. Press the top edge of the disc against the metal and move the grinder up and down.

After removing the paint from the repair area, file down the ridge around the ding. The body file (also called a vixen file) is normally used for this purpose. Sometimes the buffing strokes of the air grinder are enough to remove the high metal areas.

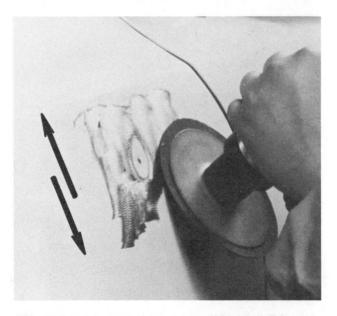

FIGURE 8-38   Buffing strokes with a grinder

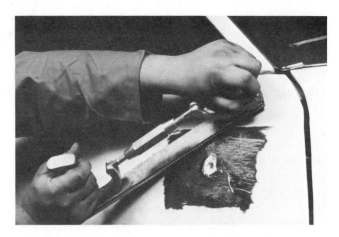

FIGURE 8-39   Filing the bare metal to reveal low spots

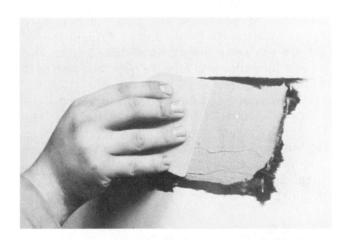

FIGURE 8-40   Applying skim coat of filler

Hold the file at a 30-degree angle and push straight across the ding (Figure 8-39). File until the ridge is completely removed. Using buffing strokes once again, grind deep file scratches away from the metal.

APPLYING THE FILLER

After filing and grinding the ridges even with the panel, apply a skim coat of body filler (Figure 8-40). Allow the plastic to harden; then, block sand the plastic smooth with #80 grit paper (Figure 8-41). Run your hand over the sanded plastic to feel for high and low spots. High metal areas might require additional filing. Low spots will need another application of plastic (Figure 8-42).

Once the ding has been properly filled and leveled, the surrounding paint edges must be featheredged. Featheredging tapers successive coats of paint and primer away from the metal to leave a smooth surface without ridges or ripples. A dual-action sander or a block sander can be used to featheredge the area, depending on the size of the repair.

8.7 REPAIRING RUST DAMAGE

In addition to minor collision damage, the body repair technician will have to be able to recognize and repair corrosion damage created by rusting sheet metal. Rust is produced by a chemical reaction known as oxidation. Oxidation occurs when metal is exposed to moisture and air. The oxygen in the air, water, or other chemicals combines with the steel molecules to form iron oxide. Iron oxide is the reddish brown compound commonly referred to as rust. By turning the metal into flaky or powdery iron oxide, rust will eat completely through a sheet metal panel if not treated. If a crack in the car's finish allows moisture and air to seep under the paint film, the sheet metal beneath will begin to rust (Figure

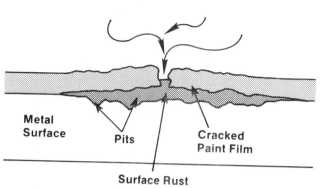

FIGURE 8-43   Example of surface rust

8-43). The same is true if a chip or nick exposes sheet metal to the air and no immediate action is taken to repair it. Left alone to do its work, rust will soon form on the metal surface and begin to eat pits into the sheet metal. These pits harbor rust and prevent sanding the surface rust away. If simply painted over, rust in the pits will eventually bubble up and break through the new paint.

Corrosion damage on a vehicle panel takes two forms: surface rust and rustouts. Surface rust in its early stage can simply leave a reddish coating on the metal surface. Given time, the rust will eat pits into the surface. Eventually the pitting will develop into holes, or rustouts. Both types of damage require different repair procedures. These are outlined in Table 8-4 and are explained in the rest of this chapter.

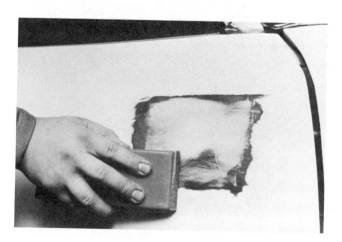

FIGURE 8-41   Block sanding filler

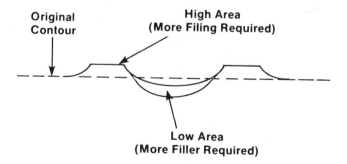

FIGURE 8-42   Feel for high and low spots

PREPARING THE SURFACE

Repairing an area affected by light surface rust can be as simple as grinding the rust film away and chemically neutralizing the area with metal conditioner. However, if the metal is pitted, additional steps are required. The surface rust shown in Figure 8-44 requires minor metalworking and filling.

Prepare the defective area for sanding by first washing with a mild detergent; then clean with a wax and grease remover solvent. Apply masking tape to nearby trim before grinding away paint and rust. The tape will protect the trim from sparks, chips, and accidental contact with the sanding disc.

The lightweight air grinder shown in Figure 8-45 is ideal for doing minor metalwork. Used with a rigid backing plate and a #24 grit sanding disc, this high-speed grinder will quickly cut through paint and rust. Use extreme care when using power tools for

TABLE 8-4: RUST REPAIR PROCEDURES

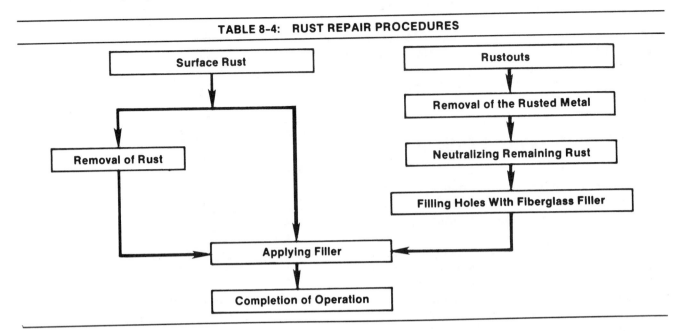

```
┌──────────────────────┐              ┌──────────────────────┐
│     Surface Rust     │              │       Rustouts       │
└──────────────────────┘              └──────────────────────┘
          │                                      │
          │                                      ▼
          │                        ┌──────────────────────────────┐
          │                        │  Removal of the Rusted Metal  │
          │                        └──────────────────────────────┘
          ▼                                      │
┌──────────────────────┐                         ▼
│    Removal of Rust    │          ┌──────────────────────────────┐
└──────────────────────┘          │  Neutralizing Remaining Rust  │
          │                        └──────────────────────────────┘
          │                                      │
          │                                      ▼
          │              ┌──────────────────────────────────────────┐
          │              │  Filling Holes With Fiberglass Filler     │
          │              └──────────────────────────────────────────┘
          │                                      │
          ▼                                      ▼
┌──────────────────────────────────────────────────────────┐
│                      Applying Filler                        │
└──────────────────────────────────────────────────────────┘
                            │
                            ▼
          ┌──────────────────────────────────┐
          │      Completion of Operation      │
          └──────────────────────────────────┘
```

FIGURE 8-44   Surface rust formation

FIGURE 8-45   Lightweight air grinder

grinding. Grind so that the sparks and dust fly down and away from the face and eyes. Always wear safety goggles or a face shield when grinding. Also wear an air filtering mask to avoid breathing paint dust.

With the disc spinning, hold the grinder against the work surface at a 10-degree angle (Figure 8-46). Holding the disc pad flat against the surface causes the grinder to skip uncontrollably. Holding the disc on edge cuts grooves into the metal.

Use a back and forth crosscutting action to remove the rust. When moving the grinder to the right, press the upper left corner of the disc against the metal. When moving to the left, press the upper right corner of the disc against the work surface.

After removing surface rust with the grinder, use a die grinder attachment to remove rust from the

FIGURE 8-46   Hold grinder at a 10° angle to surface.

FIGURE 8-47   Grinding rust from pits

pits, panel edges, and other hard-to-reach places (Figure 8–47).

 **SHOP TALK** _____

Sandblasting, as described in Chapter 18, can be used in place of disc and die grinding.

Applying the Filler

Now, mix plastic filler and hardener together. Remember, do not stir the plastic; stirring results in air bubbles in the hardened filler. Scoop up some filler onto the edge of the spreader and smear a thin skim coat over the pitted area. Apply moderate pressure to force the plastic filler into the pits (Figure 8–48A). Allow the filler to harden; then, block sand with #80 grit sandpaper (Figure 8–48B). Sand until the filler is level with the panel surface. Remember to always wear a dust mask while sanding body fillers. Inhaling filler dust can be harmful.

Use compressed air to blow filler dust from any still visible pits and pinholes. If necessary, apply another tight skim coat of filler. Allow the filler to dry before sanding and priming. Follow the sanding and priming (Figure 8–48C) procedures already described in this chapter.

Then, clean the bare metal with metal conditioner (Figure 8–49). Metal conditioner is an acid compound that neutralizes microscopic rust particles. The acid also etches the metal surface to improve the bond between metal and primer-surfacer. Metal conditioner is bottled in concentrated form and must be diluted with water before use. Always wear rubber gloves and safety glasses when handling conditioners. Follow the manufacturer's instructions carefully when diluting the conditioners.

A

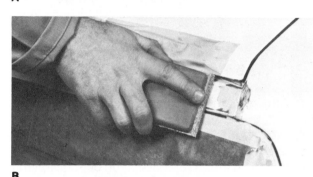

B

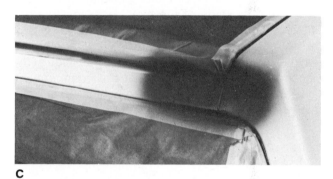

C

FIGURE 8-48   Cover pitted area with filler, sand, and finish.

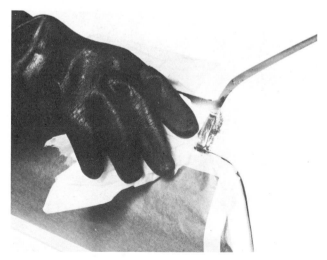

FIGURE 8-49   Clean bare metal with metal conditioner.

8.8 REPAIRING SMALL RUSTOUTS

Rust can form on either side of the metal panel. Rust that is present on the backside of a panel might go unnoticed until the paint begins to bubble and lift. By this time the rust has eaten completely through the panel. Spots of surface rust, as shown on the fender in Figure 8-50, might be a sign that rust has eaten through from the backside of the panel (Figure 8-51). When the surface rust and paint are ground away, small holes called rustouts will be uncovered.

PREPARING THE SURFACE

After grinding the area with the air grinder and a #24 grit rigid disc, use a pick hammer to bevel the rustouts (Figure 8-52). Beveling the edges of the hole dislodges loose scale, brakes away rust-thinned metal, and creates a funnel-shaped depression that prevents the plastic from falling through the hole.

If the backside of the panel is accessible, remove accumulated dirt and undercoating. A wire brush, scrapers, even a wire brush drill attachment can be used to expose the rust on the backside of the repair area. Then, apply one of the commercially available rust deactivators. The chemical reacts with the rust to form a hard, black polymer coating over

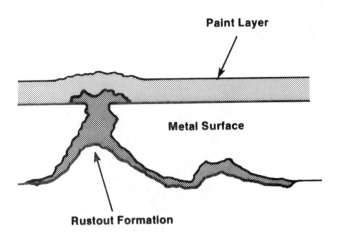

FIGURE 8-51   Rustout formation

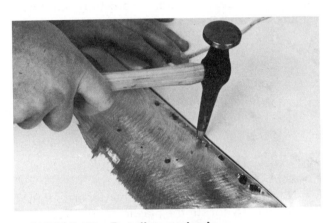

FIGURE 8-52   Beveling rustouts

the rust. This coating seals out air and moisture, preventing any further oxidation.

APPLYING THE FILLER

After cleaning the bare metal with metal conditioner to neutralize the rust particles, plug the rust holes with a waterproof, fiberglass reinforced filler (Figure 8-53). Regular plastic fillers with a talc bulking agent absorb moisture and are not suitable for filling rustouts. Use the plastic spreader to force the filler into the holes.

After the waterproof filler hardens, sand the filler smooth and wipe the dust away with a clean cloth.

Cover the filled holes with a layer of regular plastic. After the plastic turns rubbery but before it hardens, knock off the high spots with a cheese grater (Figure 8-54). Hold the cheese grater at a 10- to 20-degree angle and pull it across the repair

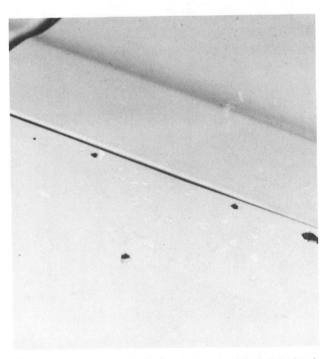

FIGURE 8-50   Spots of surface rust reveal rustout.

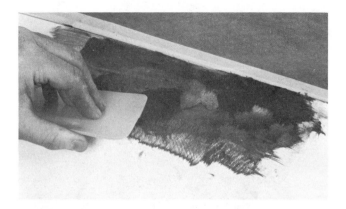

FIGURE 8-53   Filling rustouts with waterproof filler

A

FIGURE 8-54   Filing the filler

B

FIGURE 8-55   Sanding and featheredging the filler

area. If the repaired area is small, it might not be necessary to use a cheese grater.

After the plastic completely hardens, sand it down level with the panel surface (Figure 8-55A and B). The sanded repair is now ready to be primed and puttied.

8.9 REPAIRING LARGE RUSTOUTS

Usually rust on the underside of a panel is not noticed until it has attacked a large area of sheet metal. What might appear as a small spot of surface rust is actually a large area of damaged metal. If left unattended, the rust will continue converting solid steel into flaky ferric oxide and will eat a gaping hole in the metal like the one shown in Figure 8-56.

Not only is the rustout unattractive, but rustouts also affect the structural integrity of the vehicle.

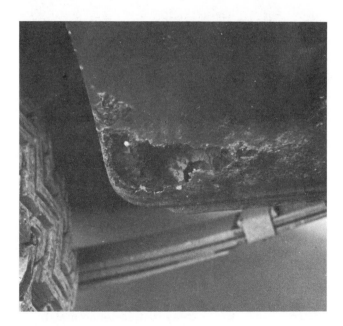

FIGURE 8-56   A large rustout

Structural members with this kind of damage should either be replaced or the rusted area cut away and new metal welded in place.

Preparing the Rustout for Repair

Before sanding away paint and rust from the repair area, cover nearby trim pieces with masking tape. Masking protects the trim from grinding sparks, chips, and accidental bumps of the disc.

Removing Rust

Use #24 or #36 grit sandpaper and a lightweight air grinder to remove paint and rust from the rustout. Exercise extreme care when grinding paint and rust from a rustout area. Rust has often deteriorated a panel until it is very thin and weak. Applying excessive pressure with the grinder against weak sheet metal can burn a hole right through the metal.

Remove as much rust as possible. Use a hammer or tin snips to break away rust-softened metal around the rustout. Hammer down edges of the hole slightly to leave them beveled (Figure 8-57). Use #50 grit sandpaper and a sanding disc to carefully grind away rust on the panel surface. A wire brush or die grinder drill attachment is handy for removing rust from pitted areas.

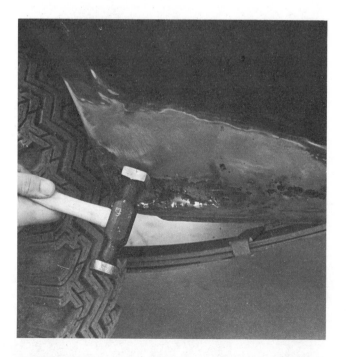

FIGURE 8-57   Break away rust-softened metal.

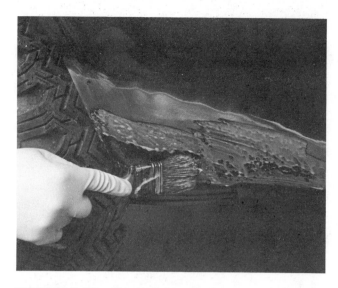

FIGURE 8-58   Neutralize rust with a rust deactivating agent.

Applying Rust Deactivator

After cleaning and sanding the repair area, apply metal conditioner or a rust deactivator (Figure 8-58) to neutralize rust remaining in pitted areas and around the edges of the rustout. Always wear rubber gloves when handling rust deactivator and metal conditioners. Shake the container well before using and follow instructions carefully.

Apply the rust deactivator to the backside of the panel, too. With a wire brush or scraper, first clean dirt and undercoating from the backside of the repair area. Then apply a rust deactivator. Be sure to carefully follow the manufacturer's instructions. A black coating will soon develop over the rust. For maximum protection, this coating should have a solid black color. Wait 1 to 2 hours between coats. If the color is splotchy and uneven, apply additional coats. Two or three thin coats neutralize the rust better than one thick coat. If excess rust deactivator runs over the finish paint, wipe it off immediately. Use a cloth dampened with mineral spirits.

Filling the Rustout

After the repair area is clean, sanded, and conditioned and the hole edges have been beveled, the rustout can be filled with fiberglass-reinforced filler and cloth. Use filler with long fiberglass strands to give maximum strength to the repair. Make sure that the filler is mixed thoroughly before applying.

CREATING A RUSTOUT PATCH

Cut fiberglass cloth 2 inches larger and a patch of plastic film 4 inches larger than the hole. If a stronger patch is desired, make a laminate by cutting additional layers of cloth. Each additional layer should be 1/2 inch smaller than the preceding one.

Mix the filler and hardener as explained earlier in this chapter. Then, spread a thin tinning coat of filler on the repair area and a thin layer of filler on the plastic film (sometimes called release paper). Place the cloth on the filler-coated film (smallest cloth first, the next largest, and so on), and coat each layer with filler. Place the largest cloth on last because this will become the bottom layer.

PATCHING THE RUSTOUT

Pick up the filler-coated patch and place it, cloth side down, over the rustout. With a plastic spreader, smooth wrinkles and high spots from the film (Figure 8-59). When passing the spreader over the center of the rustout, press down to leave a 1/8 to 1/4 inch indentation. Press out all air bubbles. Feather the film edges level with the surrounding surface. Be careful not to press so hard that filler is forced out from beneath the cloth patch. Allow the patch to cure; then remove the plastic film. While the filler is still in a rubbery state, file down high spots with a surform grater.

FIGURE 8-59   Applying fiberglass patch

COMPLETING THE RUSTOUT REPAIR

Following the procedures outlined earlier, mix enough fiberglass filler to fill the depressed area. Using a plastic spreader, apply a coat of filler over the repair area. Press hard on the spreader to force out air bubbles. Spread from the edges to the center. Fill the depression and other low spots. A smoother application can be achieved by placing a second piece of plastic film over the filler and smoothing the filler under the plastic.

SANDING AND PRIMING THE REPAIR

After the filler has dried, it can be sanded and shaped. Remove the plastic film if used, and sand the repair area with #50 grit sandpaper and a sanding block to within 1/16 inch of the finish level. Switch to #80 grit sandpaper and sand to the finish level. Run the palm of the hand over the finish repeatedly to locate high and low spots. Avoid oversanding; this will create low spots that need additional filler. Feather the edges level with the surrounding metal surfaces.

When the filler has been sanded to the desired level and smoothness, clean the area and dry with an unsoiled cloth. Wipe the repair area with a tack cloth and blow with compressed air to remove any remaining dust particles. Spray with primer. After the primer dries, coat the filled area with glazing putty. Apply with a clear rubber squeegee using single, smooth strokes and allow to dry (Figure 8-60).

FIGURE 8-60   Applying glazing putty to rustout repair

Using #240 grit sandpaper and long, even strokes with the sanding block, sand the glazed repair to a smooth surface. If pinholes or voids still remain, fill with additional putty and sand.

Lightly wet sand with #400 grit sandpaper to polish sandpaper scratches from the repaired rustout. Clean with a tack cloth and prime the repair area once more. The repaired rustout is ready to be painted.

More information on rust and corrosion protection can be found in Chapter 15.

8.10 REVIEW QUESTIONS

1. Which of the following is contained in plastic body filler?
   a. resins
   b. pigments
   c. solvents
   d. all of the above

2. Which of the following substances is used in body fillers to prevent oxygen absorption from the atmosphere?
   a. hardner
   b. peroxide
   c. paraffins
   d. both a and b
   e. none of the above

3. Fiberglass fillers are _____ .
   a. waterproof
   b. available in three basic forms
   c. never used to bridge rustouts
   d. all of the above

4. Lightweight fillers have improved _____ .
   a. filing characteristics
   b. sanding characteristics
   c. water resistance
   d. all of the above

5. A body filler that does not bleed through a basecoat/clear coat paint _____ .
   a. is very expensive
   b. is liquid hardener-catalyzed aluminum filler
   c. has excellent working properties
   d. all of the above
   e. both a and b

6. If too little hardener is used, the filler _____ .
   a. will not adhere to the metal
   b. will be subject to rampant pinholing
   c. will be easier to handle
   d. none of the above

7. Wiping over the repaired area with solvents before applying the mixed filler _____ .
   a. improves adhesion
   b. illuminates pinholes
   c. is a mistake
   d. both a and b

8. The first step in repairing nicks is _____ .
   a. sanding the ragged edges of the paint to a smooth surface
   b. featheredging
   c. dewaxing
   d. both a and b
   e. none of the above

9. Once a ding has been properly filled and leveled, Technician A uses a dual-action sander to featheredge the surrounding paint edges. Technician B uses a block sander. Who is correct?
   a. Technician A
   b. Technician B
   c. Both A and B
   d. Neither A nor B

10. Metal conditioner is _____ .
    a. an acid compound
    b. used to etch the metal surface
    c. used to neutralize rust
    d. all of the above
    e. both a and b

11. Technician A grinds a brazed joint before neutralizing the acids in the flux. Technician B neutralizes the acids, then grinds. Who is correct?
    a. Technician A
    b. Technician B
    c. Both A and B
    d. Neither A nor B

12. Technician A uses the same putty knife to mix and apply plastic body filler, while Technician B uses a separate knife for each step. Who is correct?
    a. Technician A
    b. Technician B
    c. Both A and B
    d. Neither A nor B

Diagnosing Major Collision Damage

OBJECTIVES

After reading this chapter, you will be able to:

- distinguish between body-over-frame and unibody vehicles.
- explain how impact forces are transmitted through both frame and unibody construction vehicles.
- describe how to visually determine the extent of impact damage.
- determine damage by measurement of body dimensions.
- analyze impact damage to mechanical components of the vehicle.

Major damage vehicle repairs usually involve correcting a bent body or frame, twisting, deflection, and the replacement of welded panels that are severely damaged. Table 9-1 illustrates the major collision repair processes after the estimate for the major damage vehicle has been made. When the damaged vehicle is brought into the body and paint shop, an estimate is prepared, and it is circulated to the body and paint technician along with the repair procedures or order. The body mechanics should follow the instructions as written, unless they locate damage that was not included or underestimated on the original damage assessment. If the body technicians find hidden damage, it might be necessary to re-evaluate the condition of the vehicle. This is called diagnosis of the damage. After deciding how the repairs should be done, based on the results of the diagnosis, the actual repair can begin. Items that are not marked on the estimate or on the repair instructions, but which are necessary, should be brought to the attention of the person who is responsible for making the estimate of the damage.

TABLE 9-1

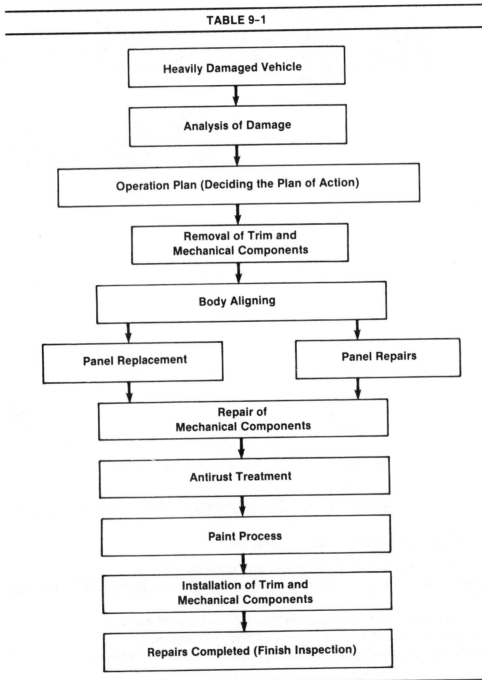

FIGURE 9-1 Measuring is the most important step in major body repair work. *(Courtesy of Pull-It Corp.)*

To repair any vehicle properly, it is necessary to accurately diagnose the collision damage. That is, it is necessary to accurately assess the damage—for example, the severity and extent—and which parts have been affected. Once this has been determined, a plan can be made for repair. A complete, accurate damage diagnosis cannot be overstressed. Damage found from an inaccurately diagnosed vehicle will be uncovered during repair. When this happens, the repair method or procedure must be changed, and the finished product will be less than satisfactory, resulting in the need for further repairs. Therefore, the best person for the body technician to talk to is the person who prepares the estimate.

Generally, physical damage is rarely missed during an inspection by a competent estimator and body mechanic; however, the effects of the damage on unrelated systems and damage occurring next to the impacted part are frequently overlooked. A visual inspection alone is generally inadequate with modern vehicles, therefore, accident damage should be assessed by measurements with the proper tools and equipment.

The following is a basic diagnosis procedure:

1. Know the vehicle construction type.
2. Visually locate the point of impact.
3. Visually determine the direction and force of the impact; once determined, check for possible damage.
4. Determine if the damage is confined to the body, or if it involves functional parts or components (wheels, suspension, engine, and so on).
5. Systematically inspect damage to the components along the path of the impact and find the point where there is no longer any evidence of damage. For example, pillar damage can be determined by checking the door fitting conditions.
6. Measure the major components (Figure 9-1) and check body height by comparing the actual measurements with the values in the repair manual body dimensions chart. Use a centering gauge to compare measurements of the height of the left and right sides of the body.
7. Check for suspension and overall body damage with the proper fixtures.

Generally speaking, vehicle damage conditions are diagnosed from the procedures given in Table 9-2.

Before starting a vehicle damage evaluation, keep the following safety pointers in mind:

- Once the car is in the shop, check for broken glass edges and jagged metal. Edges of broken glass should be masked with tape and labeled "DANGER." Sharp jagged metal edges can be taped, but it is better to grind them down with a portable power grinder or a file.
- If fluids such as lubricants or transmission fluid are leaking from the vehicle, wipe them up to reduce the possibility of someone slipping on the floor.
- Remove the gas tank before welding or cutting is begun on the vehicle. Never just drain the tank because the fumes are explosive.
- Disconnect the battery to open the electrical system circuit. This will avoid the possibility of a charge igniting flammable vapors. It also protects the electrical system.
- Make the damage diagnosis in a well lit shop. If the damage involves functional or mechanical parts, a detailed inspection of the underbody, using a lift (Figure 9-2A) or a bench (Figure 9-2B), is required.
- Other safety measures when diagnosing repair work would include any measures usually followed while in the body shop as detailed in Chapter 1. Being conscious of what one is doing is the most important precaution to adhere to.

TABLE 9-2: FACTORS TO CONSIDER IN THE DIAGNOSIS OF COLLISION DAMAGE

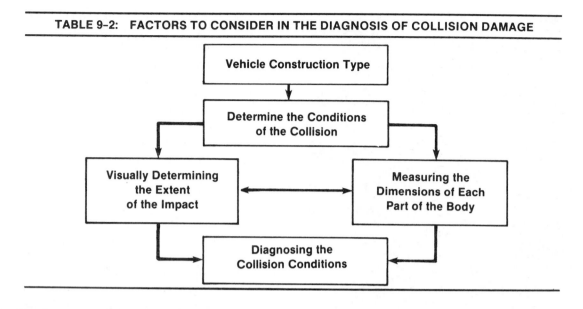

| Vehicle Construction Type |
| Determine the Conditions of the Collision |
| Visually Determining the Extent of the Impact | Measuring the Dimensions of Each Part of the Body |
| Diagnosing the Collision Conditions |

A

B

FIGURE 9-2 Checking a vehicle (A) on a lift and (B) on a bench or rack

9.1 IMPACT AND ITS EFFECTS ON A VEHICLE

The body of a vehicle is designed to withstand the shocks of normal driving and to provide safety for the occupants in the event of a collision. Special consideration is given to designing the body so that it will collapse and absorb the maximum amount of energy in a severe collision, while at the same time minimizing the effects on the occupants. For this purpose, the front body and rear body are to some extent made to deform easily, forming a structure that absorbs impact energy, and at the same time tough in order to preserve the passenger compartment area. During a head-on collision with a barrier at 30 miles per hour (mph) the engine compartment compacts by about 30 to 40 percent of its length, but the passenger compartment is compacted by only 1 to 2 percent of its length.

As described in Chapter 2, there are two basic types of automotive construction:

- Body-over-frame (BOF) cars
- Unibody (or monocoque) vehicles

In the body-over-frame construction, which older body mechanics have been successfully repairing for years, the passenger (pay-load) area is enclosed with cosmetic panels of steel attached to a structural frame that also supports most of the drive-train and mechanical accessories. In the unibody construction, the metal body panels are welded together making a structural unit as opposed to traditional construction where the cosmetic sheet steel body rests on top of a structural steel frame. With

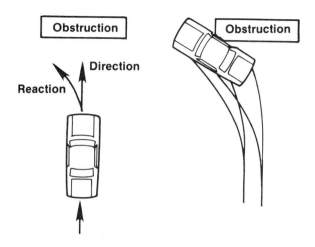

FIGURE 9-3   Driver's first reaction is to turn away from the danger thus forcing the hit to the side, causing sidesway.

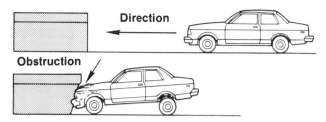

FIGURE 9-4   Driver's second reaction is to slam on the brakes thus forcing the front end to drive down, causing sag.

BOF vehicles, the collision damage can be cosmetic and/or structural. However, when a unibody car is hit, the collision usually results in both cosmetic and structural damage.

Under the force of collision impacts the frame type vehicle and the unibody type vehicle react quite differently. Also, damage assessment and repair techniques are different, even though the basic repair skills are identical.

When the collision damage has been identified using the proper identification and analysis procedures, anyone skilled in the mechanics of collision damage repair is capable of repairing the damage successfully.

DETERMINING THE CONDITIONS OF THE COLLISION

The impact force at the time of the collision and the extent of the damage differ depending on the conditions at the time of the accident. To put it another way, the damage can be partly determined by understanding how the collision occurred. However, in order to understand the circumstances of the collision, it would be necessary to contact persons directly involved or eyewitnesses. Such a task would undoubtedly be a waste of time for a body technician, but it is quite possible for the person responsible for making the estimate to get a direct response from the customer. This method of damage assessment is sometimes necessary in order to estimate the cost of the repair. Therefore, the body technician should speak to the estimator or the person who prepares the estimate.

The body technician should know the following items:

- The size, shape, position, and speed of the vehicles involved in the collision
- Speed of the vehicle at the time of the collision
- Angle and direction of the vehicle at the time of the impact
- The number of passengers and their positions at the time of the impact

A good body/frame technician can usually determine what actually happened in the collision to cause the damage. Because of the predictable nature of a driver's reactions just before a collision occurs, certain types of collision damage almost invariably occur in a rather predictable pattern and sequence. If a driver's first reaction (Figure 9-3) is to turn away from the danger, the vehicle will be forced to take the hit on the side. The results of damage would be similar to those previously discussed.

If the driver's reaction is to slam on the brakes (Figure 9-4), the direction of impact would be frontal. A frontal collision where the point of impact is high on the vehicle could cause the cowl and roof to move rearward and the rear of the vehicle to move downward. Or, if the point of impact is low at the front, the inertia of the body mass could cause the rear of the vehicle to distort upward, forcing the roof forward. This would leave an excessively large opening between the front upper part of the door and the roofline (Figure 9-5).

Given vehicles with similar weights traveling at about the same speed, vehicle damage will vary significantly depending on what is struck, for example, a telephone pole or a wall. If the impact is spread over a larger area, the damage will be minimal (Figure 9-6A).

Conversely, the smaller the area of impact, the greater the severity of the damage (Figure 9-6B). In this example, the bumper, hood, radiator, and so forth have been severely deformed. The engine has

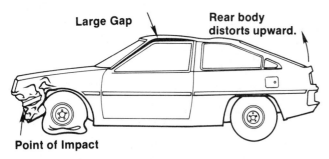

Large Gap

Rear body distorts upward.

Point of Impact

FIGURE 9-5   Results of a front impact

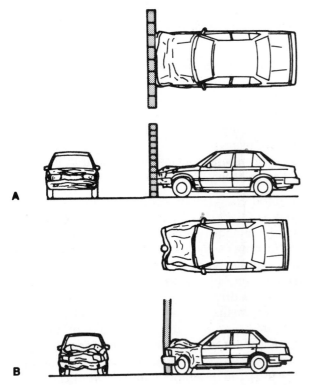

A

B

FIGURE 9-6   (A) Example of a large impact surface area and (B) example of a small impact surface area

been pushed back and the effect of the collision has extended as far as the rear suspension.

Another consideration is when one car hits another while moving. If car Number 1 in Figure 9-7 drives into the side of car Number 2 while Number 2 is moving, the motion of the first car will drive the front end of the car back, but the motion of car Number 2 will also "drag" that same front end to the side.

There is only one collision but the damage is in two directions. On the other hand, there might be two collisions in only one direction. This is a fairly common occurrence in freeway pile-ups.

A car that collides with another car and then leaves the road to hit a pole or guard rail ends up with

two completely separate types of damage. There are many other variables and possible combinations of damage types, and it is important to determine what actually happened before an accurate diagnosis can be made. Get as many facts as possible and combine them with physical measurements and centerline gauge readings to determine exactly the collision repair procedure that should be taken. A little extra time spent here can save many hours in the overall repair procedure. "Think time" saves hard work.

INFLUENCE OF IMPACT ON A BODY-OVER-FRAME VEHICLE

Figure 9-8 illustrates a body with a perimeter frame with its built-in collapsible sections. The circled areas indicate the softer sections of the frame designed to absorb the major impact of a front or rear end collision. The body is attached to the frame by rubber mounts, which reduce the effects of shocks traveling from the frame to the body. It should be noted here that in the event of a large shock, the bolts of the rubber mounts might bend, resulting in a gap between the frame and the body. Also, depending on the magnitude and direction of the shock, the frame might experience damage while the body does not.

Frame deformation can be broken down into five categories:

- **Sidesway (Figure 9-9).** Collision impacts that occur from the side often cause a sidesway or side bending frame damage condition. Sidesway usually occurs in the front or

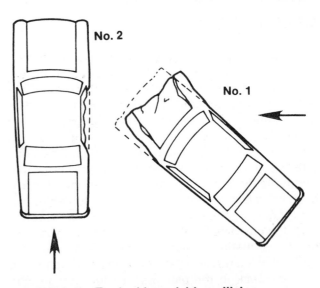

No. 2

No. 1

FIGURE 9-7   Typical broadside collision

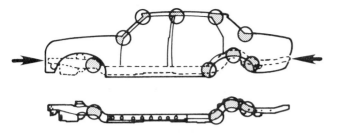

FIGURE 9-8 Typical perimeter frame collapsible sections

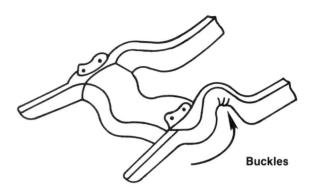

FIGURE 9-10 Good clue to frame misalignment

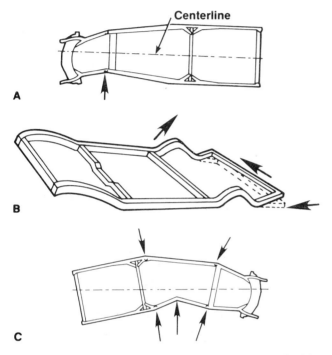

FIGURE 9-9 Various sidesway damage: (A) sidesway at the front of the frame caused by a front end collision; (B) rear sidesway; and (C) double sidesway on the frame's outer section

FIGURE 9-11 Vehicle with front sidesway damage

rear of the vehicle. Generally, it is possible to spot sidesway by noting if there are buckles on the inside of one rail and buckles on the outside of the opposite side rail (Figure 9-10).

Sidesway can be recognized by abnormalities such as a gap at the door on the long side and wrinkles on the short side. Look for impact damage obviously from the side. Hood and deck lid will not fit into proper opening, for example (Figure 9-11).

- **Sag (Figure 9-12).** This type of damage is a condition where the cowl area of the car is lower than normal. The structure has a swayback appearance. Sag damage generally is

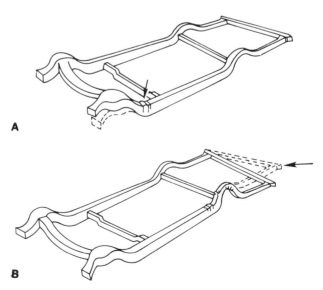

FIGURE 9-12 (A) Typical sag condition on the left front frame section and (B) rear end sag

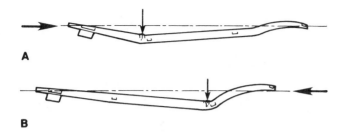

FIGURE 9-13   (A) Side rail sag from front end collision; (B) side rail sag from rear end collision

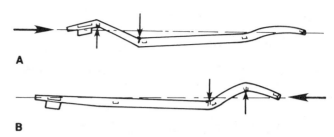

FIGURE 9-15   (A) Frame mashed and buckled from
front end collision. (B) Frame mashed from rear end
collision.

caused by a direct impact from the front or
from the rear. It can occur on one side of the
vehicle or on both sides (Figure 9-13). It can
usually be detected visually by a gap between the fender and the door being narrow
at the top and wide at the bottom. Also look
for the door appearing to hang too low at the
striker. Sag is the most common type of
damage and occurs in most vehicles that are
involved in an accident. Enough sag can be
present in the frame to prevent body panel
alignment even though wrinkles or kinks are
not visible in the frame itself.

- **Mash (Figure 9-14).** Mash is present when
  any section or frame member of the car is
  shorter than factory specifications. Mash is
  usually limited to forward of the cowl or
  rearward of the rear window. Doors might fit
  well and appear to be undisturbed. Wrinkles

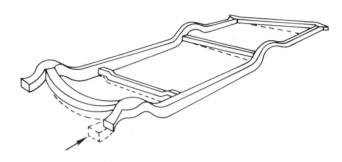

FIGURE 9-16   Typical diamond condition affecting the entire frame alignment

and severe distortion will be found in fenders, hood, and possibly frame horns. The
frame generally will rise upward at the top of
the wheel arch causing the spring housing to
collapse (Figure 9-15). With mash damage,
there is very little vertical displacement of the
bumper. The damage results from direct
front or rear collisions.

- **Diamond (Figure 9-16).** This is a condition
  where one side of the car has been moved to
  the rear or front causing the frame and/or
  body to be out of square. It will attain a figure
  similar to a parallelogram and is caused by a
  hard impact on a corner or off-center from
  the front or rear. Diamond damage affects
  the entire frame, not just the side rails. Visual
  indications are hood and trunk lid misalignment. Buckles might appear in the quarter
  panel near the rear wheelhousing or at the
  roof to quarter panel joint. Wrinkles and
  buckles probably will appear in the passenger compartment and/or trunk floor.
  There usually will be some mash and sag
  combined with the diamond.

- **Twist (Figure 9-17).** Twist is another type of
  total frame damage. It is a condition where
  one corner of the car is higher than normal;
  the opposite corner might be lower than

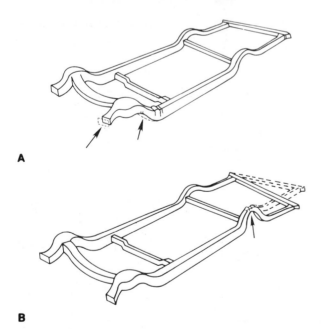

FIGURE 9-14   (A) Mash damage on the left front
side rail; (B) mash damage on the left rear side rail

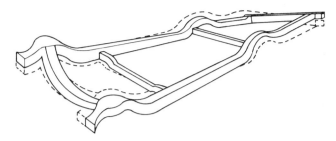

FIGURE 9-17 Typical twist conditions affecting the entire frame alignment

normal. Twist can happen when a car hits a curb or median strip at high speed. It is also common in rear corner impacts. A careful inspection can reveal no apparent damage to the sheet metal, however, the real damage is hidden underneath. One corner of the car has been driven upward by the impact, and more than likely, the adjacent corner is twisted downward. If one corner of the car is sagging close to the ground as though a spring were weak, the car should be checked for twist.

Diamond (Figure 9–18) occurs when the vehicle is struck off center. However, a frame will rarely experience deformation involving the whole frame.

The order of occurrence of the damage is:

- Sidesway
- Sag
- Mash
- Diamond
- Twist

As described in Chapter 10, the most important rule in body/frame alignment is reverse direction and sequence. This means, to correct collision damage on a conventional vehicle, the pulling or pushing of the damaged area must be done in the opposite direction of impact. The repair must be made in the reverse sequence that it happened.

Unfortunately, most collisions or accidents result in a mix of one or more of these damage problems. Sidesway and sag frequency occur almost simultaneously. Also, some of these collision solutions affect the frame's cross members, especially the front member. In a roll-over accident, for example, the front cross member on which the motor mounts are attached will be pulled or pushed out of shape because of the engine's weight. This will result in a sag of this cross member. While cross member damage is rather rare, it must be corrected since cross members affect the handling of the vehicle.

A deformed frame can be inspected by comparing the space between the body rocker panel and the front and back of the frame, and by comparing the space between the front fender and the front and back of the wheel hub (Figure 9–19). To inspect front frame deformation, compare the left and right measurements from the rear hole of the front bumper installation to the front frame rail assembly.

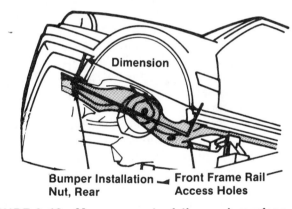

FIGURE 9-19 Measurement of the undersurface dimensions

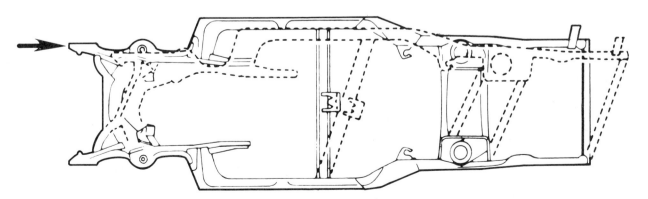

FIGURE 9-18 Typical diamond conditions

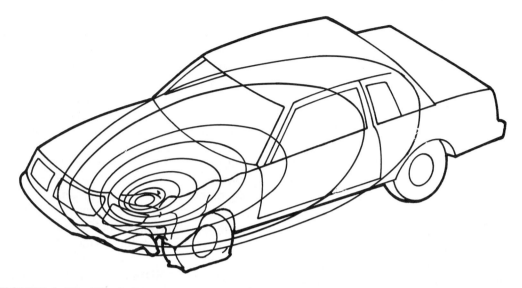

FIGURE 9-20　The best way to describe impact effect on unibodies is the cone concept.

IMPACT EFFECT ON UNIBODY VEHICLES

The damage that occurs to a unibody car as the result of an impact can best be described by using the cone concept (Figure 9-20). The unibody vehicle is designed to absorb a collision impact. When hit, the body folds and collapses as it absorbs the impact. As the force penetrates the structure, it is absorbed by an ever increasing area of the unibody. This characteristic spreads the force until it is completely dissipated. Visualize the point of impact as the tip of the cone.

The centerline of the cone will point in the direction of impact. The depth and spread of the cone indicate the direction and area that the collision force traveled through the unibody. The tip of the cone is the primary damage area.

Since unibodies are structured entirely from the joining of pieces of thin sheet metal, the shock of a collision is absorbed by a large portion of the body shell. But the effects of the impact shock wave as it

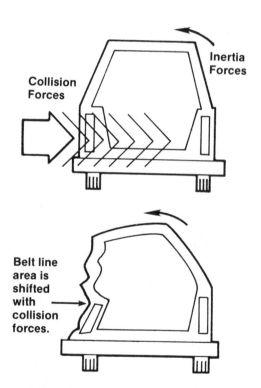

FIGURE 9-22　Roof shifted toward the side of impact, because of weight/mass inertia. *(Courtesy of Babcox Publications)*

travels through the body structure (Figure 9-21) is called "secondary damage." Generally, this damage is toward the inner structure of the unibody or toward the opposite end or side of the vehicle (Figure 9-22).

To provide some control on secondary damage distortion and to give a much safer container or

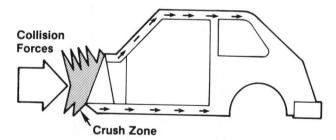

FIGURE 9-21　Collision energy dissipated around passenger compartment through components. *(Courtesy of Babcox Publications)*

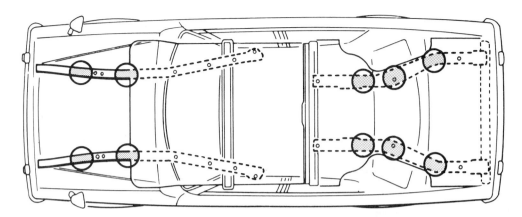

FIGURE 9-23 Typical unibody impact absorbing areas

compartment for the passengers, a unibody vehicle is designed with crush zones or areas at the front and rear (Figure 9-23). These crush zones are engineered to collapse in a predetermined fashion, thus the effects of the impact shock wave to the body structure is reduced as it travels through and is dissipated by the body structure. In other words, front impact shocks are absorbed by the front body and crush zones (Figure 9-24); rear shocks are absorbed by the rear body (Figure 9-25); and side shocks will be absorbed by the rocker panel, roof side frame, center pillar, and door.

Impact damages on unibody vehicles can be described as:

- **Frontal impacts.** The impact of a collision depends upon the vehicle's weight, speed, area of impact, and the source of impact. In the case of a minor impact, the bumper is pushed back, bending the front side members, bumper stay, front fender, radiator support, radiator upper support, and hood lock brace.

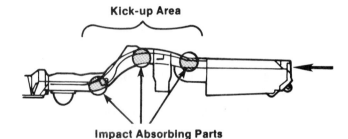

FIGURE 9-25 Rear side member impact absorbing areas

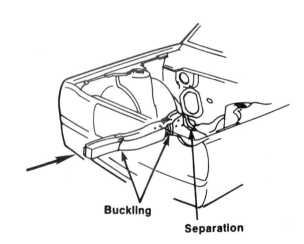

FIGURE 9-26 Buckling and separation action in unibody vehicle. (Courtesy of Toyota Motor Corp.)

If the impact is further increased, the front fender will contact the front door, the hood hinge will bend up to the cowl top, and the front side members will buckle into the front suspension cross member, causing it to bend (Figure 9-26). If the shock is great enough, the front fender apron and front body pillar (particularly the front door hinge

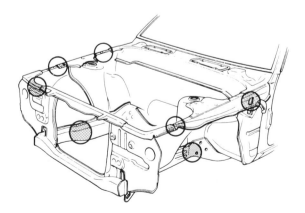

FIGURE 9-24 Typical unibody front crush zones. (Courtesy of Toyota Motor Corp.)

277

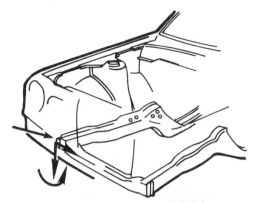

FIGURE 9-27 The lateral and vertical bending movement of a unibody vehicle. *(Courtesy of Toyota Motor Corp.)*

upper installation area) will be bent, which will cause the front door to drop down.

In addition, the front side members will buckle, the front suspension member will bend, and the dash panel and front floor pan will bend to absorb the shock.

If a frontal impact is received at an angle, the attachment point of the front side member becomes a turning axis and lateral as well as vertical bending occurs (Figure 9-27). Since the left and right front side members are connected together through the front cross member, the shock from the impact is propagated from the point of impact to the front side member of the opposite side of the vehicle and causes deformation.

- **Rear end collisions.** The degree of damage will depend on factors such as the impact surface area, the impact speed, the impacting object, and the vehicle's weight. When the impact is comparatively small, the rear bumper, the back panel, the trunk lid, and floor pan will be deformed and the quarter panels will bulge out.

  If the impact is severe enough, the quarter panels will collapse to the base of the roof panel and on four door vehicles, the center body pillar might bend. Impact energy is absorbed by the deformation of the above parts and by the deformation of the kick-up of the rear side member.

- **Side collisions.** In determining the damage from side impacts, vehicle structure is particularly important. Generally, in severe collisions, the door, front section, center body pillar, and even the floor will deform. When the front fender or quarter panel receives a large perpendicular impact, the shock wave

extends to the opposite side of the vehicle. When the central area of the front fender receives an impact, the front wheel is pushed in, and the shock wave extends from the front suspension cross member to the front side member. In this case, the suspension components are damaged and the front wheel alignment and wheel base is changed. Since the steering equipment is usually affected by a side impact, the linkage and steering gear or rack can also be damaged.

- **Top impacts.** When there is damage from falling objects, it not only involves the roof panel but also the roof side rail, quarter panels, and possibly the windows might be damaged as well. When a vehicle has rolled over and the body pillars and roof panels have been bent, the opposite ends of the pillars will be damaged as well. Depending on the manner in which the vehicle rolled over, the front or back sections of the body will be damaged, too. In such cases, the extent of the damage can be determined by the deformation around the windows and doors.

The typical collision damage sequence (Figure 9-28) on a unibody structure goes like this:

- **Bending.** In the first microseconds of impact, a shock wave attempts to shorten the structure, causing a lateral or vertical bending in the central structure. Most of the forces that broadcast impact shock to remote areas occur at this instant. Since the structure is stiff and springy, it tends to snap back to its original shape—at least momentarily. Bending is usually indicated by the height measurement being out of tolerance. This damage—similar to sag in conventional structure—can occur on one side of the car and not the other (Figure 9-29).

- **Crushing or collapsing.** As the collision event continues, visible crushing occurs at the point of impact. Impact energy is absorbed in the deforming structure (helping protect the passenger compartment). Remote areas might buckle, tear, or pull loose. Crush damage, which is similar to mash on BOF vehicles, is indicated by the length measurement being out of tolerance.

- **Widening.** In a well-designed unibody structure, impact forces reaching the passenger compartment cause the side structure to bow out away from the passengers (never in) distorting side rails and door openings. Wid-

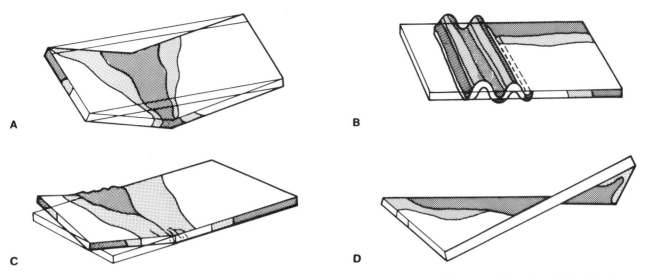

FIGURE 9-28   Typical unibody collision damage: (A) bending; (B) crushing or collapsing; (C) widening; and (D) twisting. *(Courtesy of Blackhawk Automotive Inc.)*

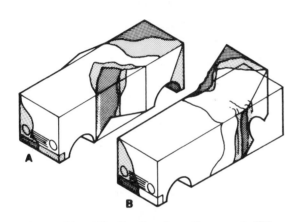

FIGURE 9-29   (A) Center bending and (B) rear bending. *(Courtesy of Blackhawk Automotive Inc.)*

ening is similar to sidesway damage in BOF vehicles and is indicated by the width measurement being out of tolerance.

- **Twisting.** Even if the initial impact is dead center, secondary impact can introduce torsional loads that cause a general twisting of the structure. Unibody structural twisting, like twisting of a conventional vehicle frame, is usually the last collision event. It is indicated by combinations of height and width measurements being out of tolerance.

As can be noted, there is a great similarity between the types of the damage that can occur on body-over-frame and unibody vehicles, although the latter are more complex. (A severe collision will not cause diamond damage on unitized cars.) Also

like conventional aligning, pulling secondary damage (last-in) so that it is corrected first (first-out) is the best way to correct collision damage to a unibody car. Secondary damage is identified by accurate measurement.

9.2 VISUALLY DETERMINING THE EXTENT OF THE IMPACT DAMAGE

In most cases, damaged parts show signs of structure deformations or fractures. When making a visual inspection, stand back away from the vehicle to get an overall view. Estimate the size and direction of the impact (the place where the impact was received). Estimate how the impact was propagated and the damage sustained (Figure 9-30). Also, in-

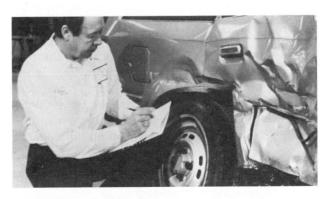

FIGURE 9-30   Visual inspection must be done carefully and repair notes made.

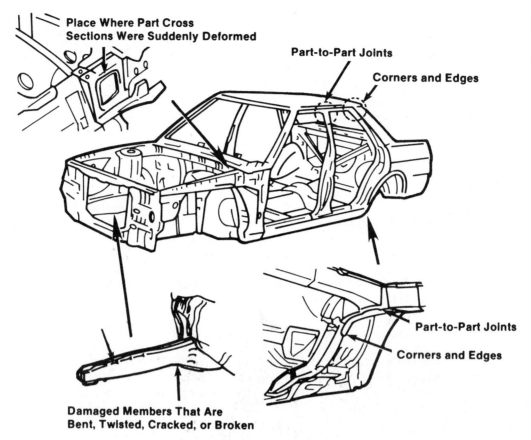

Place Where Part Cross Sections Were Suddenly Deformed

Part-to-Part Joints

Corners and Edges

Part-to-Part Joints

Corners and Edges

Damaged Members That Are Bent, Twisted, Cracked, or Broken

FIGURE 9-31   Parts that show damage easily. *(Courtesy of Toyota Motor Corp.)*

vestigate whether or not there is any overall twisting, bending, or slanting of the vehicle overall. Next, look over the entire vehicle and try to determine where the damage occurred and whether or not all the damage was the result of the same collision.

Impact force propagates and damages many parts of a vehicle. The damage appears in certain portions of the body. (The impact force has the characteristics of passing easily through the strong portions of the body, finally ending up in the weak portions, damaging them, then propagating deep into the body parts.) Therefore, in searching for damage, inspection must be made along the path of propagation of the impact through the weak portions of the body or areas where the stress is the greatest, following in order from place to place, confirming the presence of strain, panel joint misalignment, cracks in and peeling of the paint film, undercoat and sealer, and so on. Damage can be easily seen in the following areas (Figure 9-31).

- Areas where the cross sections of the components were suddenly deformed.
  —Parts that are broken or missing
  —Gaps in strengthening materials such as reinforcements or patches

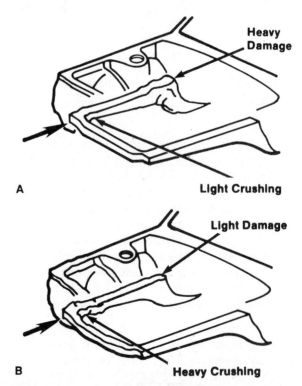

Heavy Damage

Light Crushing

A

Light Damage

Heavy Crushing

B

FIGURE 9-32   Impact and the amount of damage. *(Courtesy of Toyota Motor Corp.)*

—Part-to-part joints
• Corners and edges of components

When surveying the extent of damage to frame components such as side members, it is easier to locate the damage on the concave side of the component because it appears as a sharp dent or kink rather than a minor bulge that would appear on the opposite side of the member.

A body is designed so that the energy received during impact travels along a predetermined path starting at the point of impact and propagating through the structure until all the energy has been dissipated (Figure 9–32). Therefore, the evidence of damage will usually be greater near the point of impact because the extent of damage is reduced as the energy is dissipated into the adjacent structure. However, in some cases, the energy is passed through the impact point (with little evidence of damage showing) and is propagated to a point that is deep into the body.

Inspecting the Clearance and Fit of Each Part

Each door assembly is mounted on the body pillar with hinges making it easy to determine if the body pillar has been damaged by simply opening and closing the door and observing the alignment of the door (Figure 9–33).

In the event of a front end collision, it is important to check the clearances and level differences between the rear doors and quarter panels or rocker panels. Another good method is to compare the clearances on the left and right sides of the vehicle.

Hinges on a vehicle wear over a period of time, and doors tend to drop down. This is especially true of the door on the driver's side, which is opened and closed quite frequently. It is also necessary to exer-

cise caution when the body is lifted up since the fit of the doors can be affected by the flexibility of the body.

Inspecting for Inertia Damage

In the case of heavy objects such as engines mounted on rubber mounts, inertia becomes a powerful force when the vehicle is involved in a collision, and it is easy to follow the damage by tracing it back to its original position. Inspect for damage to the mounts or to surrounding parts and panels. For full frame vehicles, the body is mounted on rubber isolators to make the interior quieter. During a collision, the powerful impact usually causes the body and frame to become misaligned, damaging the body isolator mountings.

Inspecting for Damage From Passengers and Luggage

Passengers and luggage can cause secondary damage to the body as a result of inertia during a collision. The damage will vary depending on the position of the passengers and the severity of the impact. Parts with a high-damage frequency are the instrument panel, steering wheel, steering column, and seat backs. Luggage in the luggage compartment has also been known to cause damage to the body quarter panels.

9.3 MEASUREMENT OF BODY DIMENSIONS

Measuring has always been a requisite for the success of any major repair job regardless of the type of body structure. But with unibody vehicles, measurements are **vital** to successful collision damage repair because the steering and suspension are mounted to the structure. In addition, some of the suspension geometry is built into the mounting design. As a result, the angles of caster and camber have a fixed (nonadjustable) value. Thus, body damage often seriously affects suspension geometry. The rack and pinion control box for the steering assembly is also generally mounted to a panel, resulting in a fixed relationship to the steering arms. The mechanical components, engine, transmission, and differential are mounted directly to body members, or to cradles supported by body members (panels or integral rails).

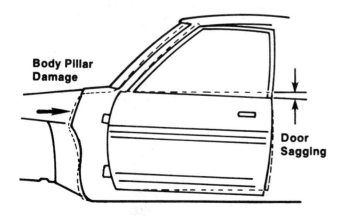

Body Pillar Damage

Door Sagging

FIGURE 9–33 Inspection of door alignment

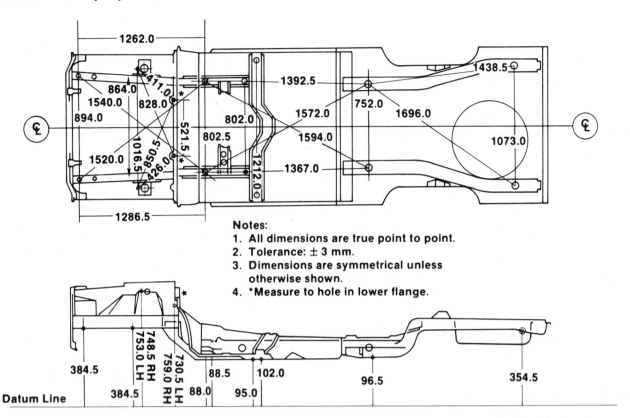

FIGURE 9-34 Underbody unibody dimensions and specifications as taken from a typical manufacturer's manual. Metric conversion chart can be found in Appendix C. *(Courtesy of Ford Motor Co.)*

A distortion of any of these measuring points will change steering or suspension geometry, or misalign mechanical components. This can result in improper steering and handling, vibration and noise in the drivetrain, and excessive wear of tie rod ends, tires, rack and pinion assemblies, universal joints, or other drive or steering components. To maintain proper steering, handling, and driveability, the tolerances of critical manufacturing dimensions must be held to within a maximum value of 3 millimeters, or less than 1/8 inch.

Accurate damage assessment can be made at specific points on the body using a body dimensions chart (this is a widely accepted method). In the body dimensions chart, measurements are based on the diagonal line measuring method. Figure 9-34 shows a typical unibody car dimensions chart, while Figure 9-35 illustrates a conventional frame vehicle. Engine compartment and body dimensional data are recorded in the chart.

Measurement points and tolerances are determined by inspection of the damaged area. Normally, in front end collisions that cause slight amounts of door sag, the damage does not extend beyond the center of the vehicle, so measurement in the rear section is not necessary. In a situation where a large impact has occurred, many measurements must be

taken to assure proper alignment procedures. However, taking and recording too many measurements might cause unnecessary confusion.

In the entire repair process of both conventional and unibody, it is not possible to overemphasize the importance of measuring. A vehicle cannot be satisfactorily repaired unless **all** of the major manufacturing control points in the damaged area are returned to the manufacturer's specifications. To achieve this, the body technician must:

- Measure accurately
- Measure often
- Recheck all measurements

Because of the importance of measuring, many kinds of equipment have been developed and marketed by a large cross section of automotive equipment manufacturers strictly for the purpose of providing the capability to measure quickly and accurately. While there are a number of styles of measuring equipment that can be found in body shops, most of it can be divided into three basic systems:

- Gauge measuring system
- Universal measuring system
- Dedicated fixture system

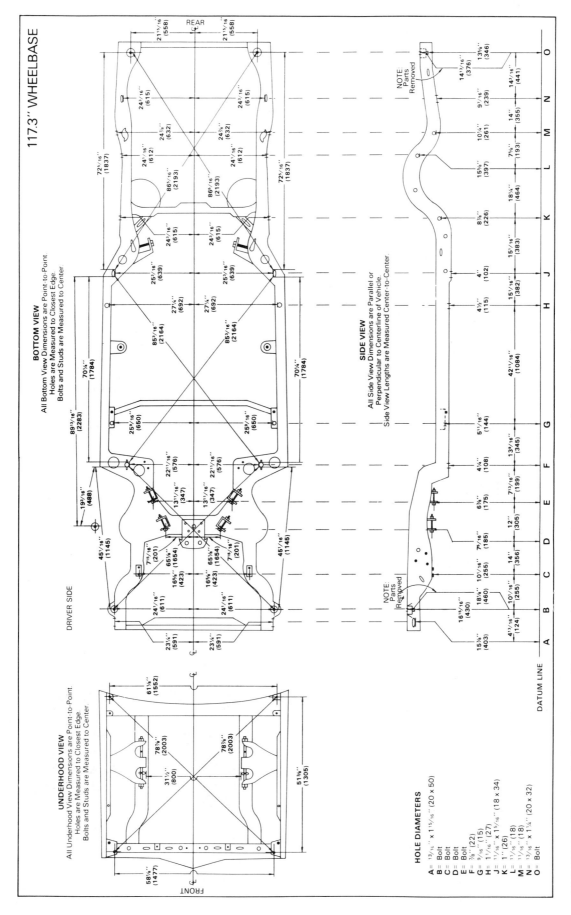

FIGURE 9-35 Underbody/frame dimensions and specifications as taken from a typical manufacturer's manual. *(Courtesy of Kansas Jack, Inc.)*

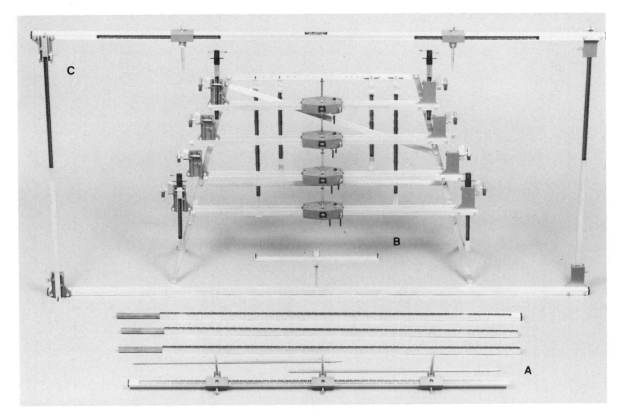

FIGURE 9–36   Typical set gauges: (A) tram gauges; (B) centering gauges; and (C) MacPherson strut center-line gauge. *(Courtesy of Arn-Wood Co., Inc.)*

9.4 GAUGE MEASURING SYSTEMS

The tram gauge, the centering gauge, and the MacPherson strut centerline gauge can be used separately or in conjunction with one another. The tram gauges are used for measurement, while the centering gauges are employed to check for misalignment. Supported by MacPherson strut tower domes, the centerline gauge allows visual alignment of the critical control points of unibody vehicles. The tram centering and strut centerline gauges are available as a unit (Figure 9–36) or as separate diagnostic tools.

Another gauge similar to the tram type is the tracking gauge. This gauge is used to check alignment of the front and rear wheels. If the front and rear wheels are not in alignment, the vehicle will not handle properly.

9.5 TRAM GAUGES

The tram gauge (Figure 9–37) measures one dimension at a time. Each dimension must be recorded and must be cross-checked from two addi-

tional control points—at least one being a diagonal measurement. The best areas to select for tram gauge measurements are the attachment points for suspension and mechanical components, since these are critical to alignment. Throughout the repair operation, critical control points must be measured (and recorded) repeatedly with the tram gauge in order to monitor progress and to prevent over-pulling.

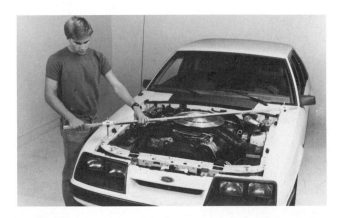

FIGURE 9–37   Using a tram gauge to measure between control points

TRAM GAUGE DATA MEASUREMENT CHART

	Mfg. Spec.	1	2	3	4	5	6	7	8	9	10	11	12
A													
B													
C													
D													
E													
F													
G													
H													
I													
J													
K													
L													
M													
N													
O													
P													
Q													
R													
S													
T													
U													
V													
W													

FIGURE 9–38   Typical tabulation chart

Since these control point tram measurements must be taken and written down several times in a repair operation, a method of tabulation must be devised. One of the ways to accomplish this is to use a data or tabulation chart similar to the one shown in Figure 9–38.

To use this data chart or a similar measurement sheet, the manufacturer's specifications taken from the service manual (Figure 9–39) are written down in the first column. The A-B-C and so on are the actual measuring point dimensions. The 1-2-3 and so on are the readings taken at measurement Step 1, measurement Step 2, and so on. That is, as each step of a restoration repair is made, the measurements should be recorded, including those dimensions that have just been corrected. This measurement data chart tells the body technician at a glance if the job has succeeded in restoring the vehicle to its original state.

The tram gauge might have a scale superimposed on it. However, since almost all manufacturer specifications list measurements in metric, use a steel tape with both fractional inches and metric scales to set the tram gauge up. The tape can also be used to take quick measurements between control points (Figure 9–40). Be sure that the tape has been checked for accuracy.

 **SHOP TALK** ————————

Accurate measurements can be taken if the front end of a tape measure is machined according to Figure 9–41 and is inserted into the control measurement hole.

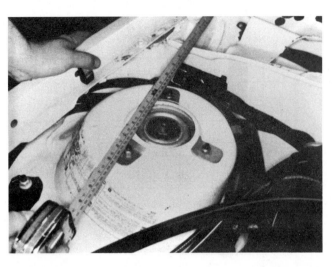

FIGURE 9-40 Quick measurement of control points can be taken with a measuring tape.

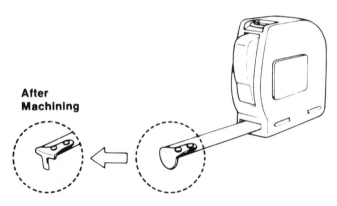

FIGURE 9-41 As shown above, machining the tape measure's tip gives more accurate measurements.

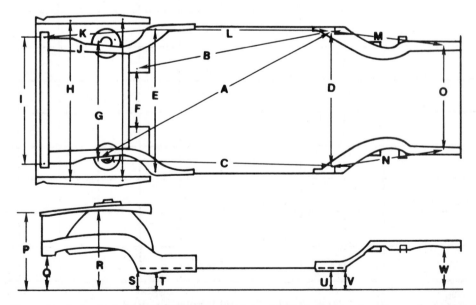

FIGURE 9-39 Many body technicians find it is easier to substitute letters in place of numbers when making up a tabulation chart. *(Courtesy of Chrysler Corp.)*

Measurement With a Tram Gauge

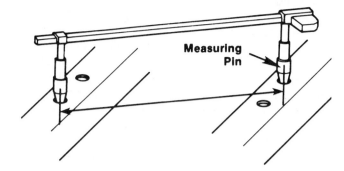

Measurement With a Tape Measure

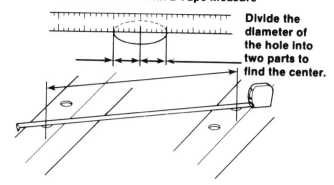

Divide the diameter of the hole into two parts to find the center.

If the measuring pin is inserted securely into the measuring hole, the hole center distance can be measured.

If the reference point is made 4 inches, measurement is easier. Subtract 4 inches from the measured dimension.

FIGURE 9-42   Measuring the distance between hole centers. *(Courtesy of Toyota Motor Corp.)*

Most control points are actually holes in the vehicle structure, and dimensions are center-to-center distances (Figure 9–42). Control point holes are frequently larger in diameter than the tram gauge tip. To measure accurately with the tram gauge (when the holes are the same diameter), measure like-edge to like-edge. A few manufacturer's specific books give the measurement based on the gauge's bar length. Always check the method used for specification measurements.

When the holes are not the same size, they will usually be the same type of hole: round, square, oblong, and so on. In this case, to find the center-to-center measurement, measure inside edge to inside edge, then outside edge to outside edge (Figure 9–43). Add the results of the two measurements and divide by 2. For example, two round holes, one being 1/2 inch in diameter, the other 1-1/2 inches in diameter, have an inside measurement of 30 inches and an outside measurement of 32 inches. The center-to-center dimension is 30″ + 32″ ÷ 2 = 31″ (Figure 9–44). The 31 inches is the dimension for the tram gauge.

In using a tram gauge for measuring, the manufacturer's specifications for the vehicle are needed to accurately assess the damage and to restore the vehicle structure to factory dimensions. If the manufacturer's specifications are not available, use an

In a Situation Where the Hole Diameters Are the Same

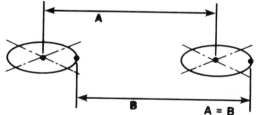

Tracking Gauge

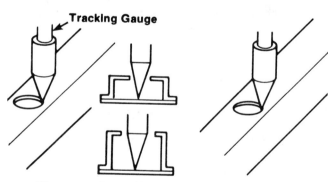

In a Situation Where the Hole Diameters Are Different

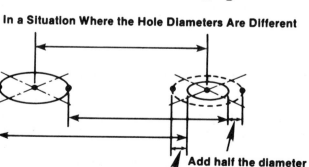

Subtract half the difference in the diameter of the holes.

Add half the diameter of the hole.

The measuring pin hits the bottom of the hole, or the measuring hole is too large.

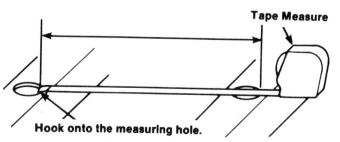

Tape Measure

Hook onto the measuring hole.

FIGURE 9-43   Measuring the distance between the edges of the holes. *(Courtesy of Toyota Motor Corp.)*

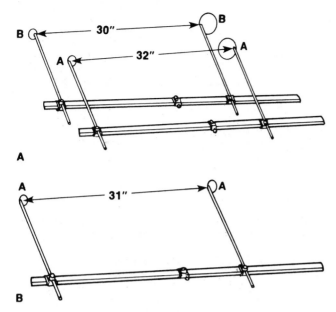

FIGURE 9-44 Example of how to measure holes that are not the same size

undamaged vehicle of the same make, year, model, and body style as a source for correct dimensions. Frequently, if only one side of a vehicle is damaged, it is possible to take measurements on the undamaged side and apply them to the damaged side for a comparison measurement.

UPPER BODY DIMENSIONING

Upper body damage can also be determined by the use of tracking trams and a steel measuring tape. Their use is basically the same as when doing an underbody evaluation. Manufacturers furnish specifications on the most important upper body control points (Figure 9-45).

Measurement of the Front Body

In the case of a damaged vehicle that needs the hood edge and front side member replaced, for example, it is reasonable to take measurements along with the repair. Even if only the front right side of the body received the impact, the left side will usually be damaged also. Therefore, the extent of deformation must be checked before remeasuring. Figure 9-46 shows the typical front body control points, which can be checked against the manufacturer's body dimensions diagram.

When checking front end dimensioning, the best areas to select for the tram gauge measurements are the attachment points for suspension and mechanical components, since these are critical to

proper alignment. Each dimension should be checked from two additional reference points with at least one reference point being a diagonal measurement. The longer the dimension, the more accurate the measurement. For example, a measurement from a lower cowl area to the front mount of the engine cradle is a better gauge than a measurement from a lower cowl area to another lower cowl area because the longer dimension takes in a larger area of the vehicle. The use of two or more measurements from each control point assures greater accuracy and helps identify the extent and direction of any panel damage.

Measurement of the Body Side Panel

Any deformation of the body side structure can be ascertained by the irregularities in the door when it is opened and closed. Depending on where the deformation is located, attention should be given to possible water leakage. Thus, accurate measurements must be taken. The tracking tram gauge is primarily used to measure the body side panel (Figure 9-47).

Warping can generally be detected if the left-to-right symmetry of the body is used for measuring diagonal lines, as shown in Figure 9-48A. Use this measuring method if the data on the engine compartment and underbody is missing, if there is no data available in the body dimensions chart, or if the vehicle has been severely damaged in a rollover.

The diagonal line measurement method is not adequate when inspecting damage to both sides of the vehicle or in the case of twisting, since the left-to-right difference in the diagonal lines cannot be measured (Figure 9-48B). If deformation is the same on the left and the right, a difference will not be apparent (Figure 9-48C).

In Figure 9-49, the measurement and comparison of the left and right lengths between yz, YZ will give an even better indication of damage conditions (this method should be used in conjunction with the diagonal line measurement method). It can be applied where there are parts that are symmetrical on the left and right sides.

Measurement of the Rear Body

Any deformation of the rear body can be roughly estimated by appearance and irregularities (for example, catching) that are evident when the trunk lid is opened and closed. Because of the location of the deformation and the possibility of water leakage, it is essential to take accurate measurements (Figure 9-50). Furthermore, any wrinkle in the rear floor is

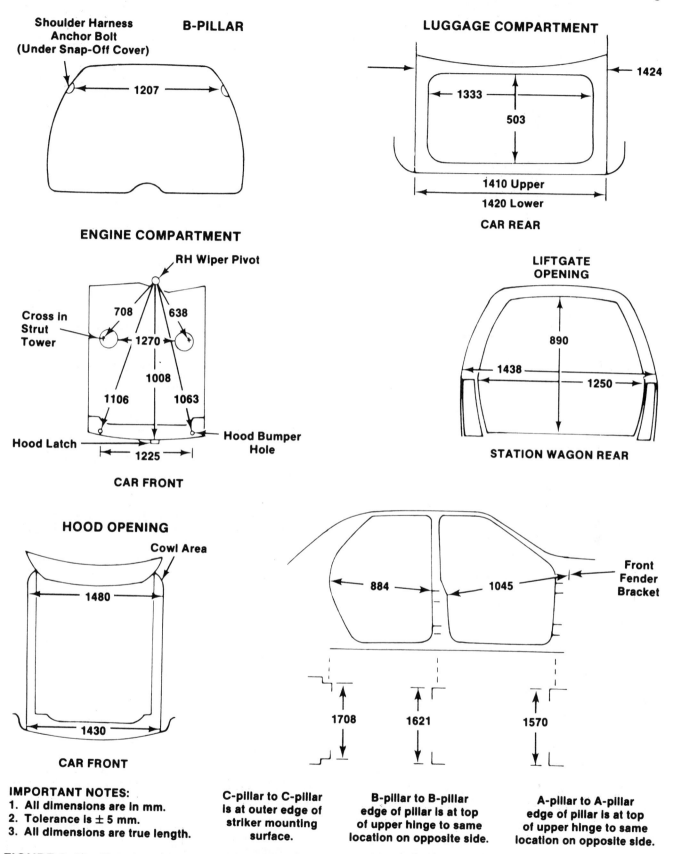

B-PILLAR

Shoulder Harness
Anchor Bolt
(Under Snap-Off Cover)

1207

ENGINE COMPARTMENT

RH Wiper Pivot

Cross in
Strut
Tower

708   638

1270

1008

1106   1063

Hood Latch   Hood Bumper
Hole

1225

CAR FRONT

HOOD OPENING

Cowl Area

1480

1430

CAR FRONT

LUGGAGE COMPARTMENT

1424

1333

503

1410 Upper

1420 Lower

CAR REAR

**LIFTGATE
OPENING**

890

1438   1250

STATION WAGON REAR

884   1045   Front
Fender
Bracket

1708   1621   1570

IMPORTANT NOTES:
1. All dimensions are in mm.
2. Tolerance is ± 5 mm.
3. All dimensions are true length.

C-pillar to C-pillar
is at outer edge of
striker mounting
surface.

B-pillar to B-pillar
edge of pillar is at top
of upper hinge to same
location on opposite side.

A-pillar to A-pillar
edge of pillar is at top
of upper hinge to same
location on opposite side.

FIGURE 9–45   Upper body dimensions and specifications as taken from a typical manufacturer's manual. Most manufacturer body dimension charts are in metric measure. *(Courtesy of Ford Motor Corp.)*

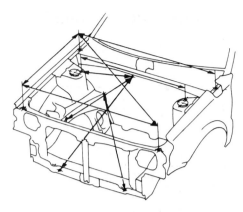

FIGURE 9-46 Typical front body measurement points

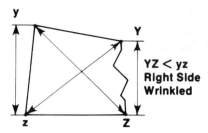

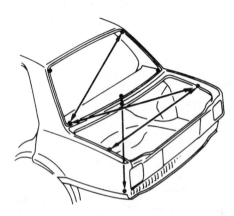

In the diagonal line measurements, YZ < yz, and it is judged that there is deflection on the left.

FIGURE 9-49 Comparison of length dimensions. (Courtesy of Toyota Motor Corp.)

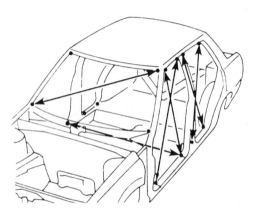

FIGURE 9-47 Typical body side panel measurement points

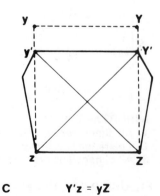

FIGURE 9-50 Typical rear body measurement points

usually due to buckling of the rear side member. Thus, measure the rear body together with the underbody. In this way, the straightening work can be performed effectively.

When using a tram gauge, be sure to keep the following pointers in mind:

- Measurements are made to fixed points on the vehicle such as bolts, plugs, or holes.

- A point-to-point measure is the direct actual measurement between two points (Figure 9-51).
- The tram bar should be parallel to the car body (Figure 9-52). This might require the pointers on the tram bar to be set at different lengths.
- Some body dimension manuals show dimensions in bar length. Other dimension books show dimensions in point-to-point

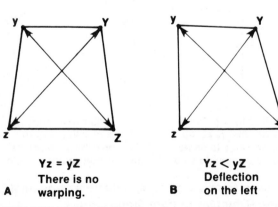

A   Yz = yZ
There is no warping.

B   Yz < yZ
Deflection on the left

C   Yz > yZ
Deflection on the right

C   Y'z = yZ

FIGURE 9-48 Using the diagonal line measurement method

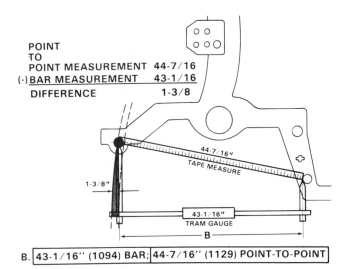

POINT
TO
POINT MEASUREMENT   44-7/16
(-) BAR MEASUREMENT   43-1/16
DIFFERENCE   1-3/8

44-7/16"
TAPE MEASURE

1-3/8"

43-1/16"
TRAM GAUGE

B

B. | 43-1/16" (1094) BAR; | 44-7/16" (1129) POINT-TO-POINT |

FIGURE 9-51   Point-to-point measurement is the direct actual measurement between two points. *(Courtesy of Blackhawk Automotive Inc.)*

FIGURE 9-52   Changing the tram pointer's lengths, it is possible to measure over an obstruction yet still keep the bar parallel to the car's body. *(Courtesy of Blackhawk Automotive Inc.)*

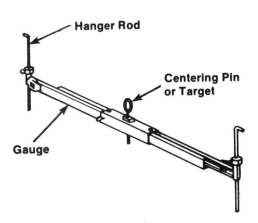

Hanger Rod

Centering Pin
or Target

Gauge

FIGURE 9-53   Typical self-centering gauge

lengths. Some manuals use both. The important point is that the technician must use the same method of measurement as the body manual employs or there is a very good chance of introducing an error.

- Make all measurements on the damaged vehicle at the points specified in the body manual. The amount of damage can usually be determined by subtracting the actual measurement from the specified measurement.

9.6 CENTERING GAUGES

While self-centering gauges (Figure 9–53) are closely related to the tram gauges, as mentioned earlier, they do not measure. They show alignment or misalignment by projecting points on the vehicle's structure into the technician's line of sight and are installed at various control areas on the vehicle. These gauges have two sliding horizontal bars that remain parallel as they move inward and outward. This action permits adjustment to any width for installation on various areas of the vehicle. After the gauges are hung on the car (usually three or four sets), the horizontal bar will be parallel to the portion of the structure to which they are attached.

Place one centering gauge at the extreme front of the vehicle, one at the extreme rear, one rearward of the front wheels, and one forward of the rear wheels (Figure 9–54). When inspecting for warpage, first hang centering gauges from two places where there is no visible damage, then hang two more gauges where there is obvious damage (Figure 9–55). Then, look along gauges hung at both undamaged and damaged locations and check to see if there is a parallel misalignment of the gauges or misalignment of the centering pins.

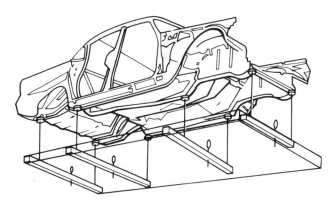

FIGURE 9-54   Typical starting locations for centering gauges. *(Courtesy of Blackhawk Automotive Inc.)*

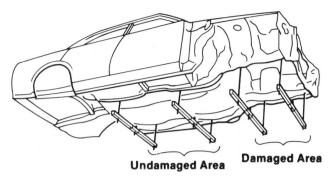

Undamaged Area   **Damaged Area**

FIGURE 9-55   Placement of centering gauges to check a damaged area

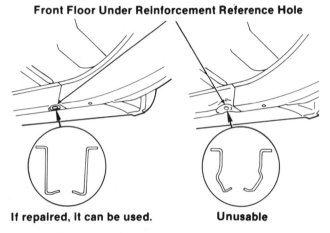

Front Floor Under Reinforcement Reference Hole

If repaired, it can be used.   Unusable

FIGURE 9-56   Centering gauge points that are deformed or damaged and must be corrected before they are used. *(Courtesy of Toyota Motor Corp.)*

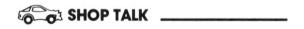 **SHOP TALK** _____

There should not be any deformation at the point the gauge is installed. That is, there are many instances where the alignment of the gauge holes has been deformed by previous collisions or other causes. Do not use deformed holes unless they can be repaired satisfactorily (Figure 9-56).

Centering gauges are also equipped with center pins or sights, which will remain in the center of the gauge regardless of the width of the horizontal bars. This allows the body technician to read the centerline throughout the length of the vehicle.

Each self-centering gauge accommodates two vertical scales—one on the left side, one on the right. These scales can be adjusted vertically to assure that the horizontal bars accurately reflect the true positions of the parts to which they are attached

FIGURE 9-57   Many centering gauges have adjustable, calibrated arms or pointers.

(Figure 9-57). Once hung in specific locations, these gauges generally remain on the car throughout the entire repair operation, unless one or all of them interfere with straightening and clamping or with the tram gauge.

Special centering gauges are available that can be used to check such items as body pillar damage (Figure 9-58). The same system of alignment is employed when using centering gauges to check underbody damage.

The centering gauge reading, as has been pointed out, is the visual alignment of parallel bars and pins, with the final objective being the achievement of square structural alignment in the vehicle. To summarize the use of centering gauges, here are some points to keep in mind when reading and using them.

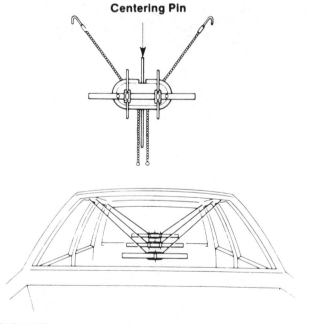

Centering Pin

FIGURE 9-58   Special centering gauges that can be used to check body pillar damage. *(Courtesy of Toyota Motor Corp.)*

- Assuming that the centering gauges have been installed properly, correct alignment will be achieved when all the gauges are parallel to one another. This indicates that the frame is level and all centerline pins are in a straight line.
- When sighting crossbars for parallel, the technician always stands directly in the middle, scanning with both eyes. To ensure accuracy, readings should be made at the outer edge of the centering gauge, not in the middle.
- The farther one stands from the centering gauges while reading, the more accurate the reading will be. Standing close changes the line of sight to the front gauges so drastically that an accurate reading is nearly impossible.
- Centering gauges should always be set at nearly the same height or plane. Different heights will change the angle of sight and give a false reading.
- It is sometimes beneficial to sight over one gauge and under another. Going to the end of the vehicle opposite the damage to make readings will sometimes result in a more accurate reading. This is true because the technician is able to read the base gauges before sighting into the damaged area. With practice and a certain amount of experimentation, the technician can improve the damage analysis.
- The sighting of centerline pins must be done with one eye. Since the center section is al-ways the base for gauging, the line of sight must always project through the pins of the base gauges. Observing pins in other sections of the frame will then reveal how much they are out of alignment.
- Never attach the centering gauges to any moveable parts such as control arms or springs.

Self-centering alignment gauges are used to read three major elements of collision damage: datum, center, and zero planes. As mentioned earlier, critical measurements—the fourth major element of analysis—are handled with tape measure and tram gauge.

THE DATUM PLANE

A datum line, or datum plane, is an imaginary flat surface parallel to the underbody of the vehicle at some fixed distance from the underbody. It is the plane from which all height dimensions are taken by the vehicle manufacturer. It is also the plane that is used to measure the vehicle during repair.

The datum plane is used as a reference for all vertical contour body measurements. A look at a vehicle's dimension data will show the measurements that are made from the datum line (Figure 9-59). Using this line of reference, centering gauges can be strategically suspended under the vehicle from side to side at varying distances along the length of the chassis frame or unibody. First place the base gauges at the main platform: one across the vehicle

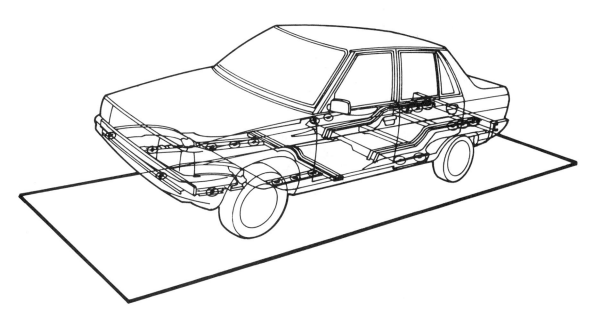

FIGURE 9-59 The datum plane is a reference line for vertical body dimension. *(Courtesy of Blackhawk Automotive Inc.)*

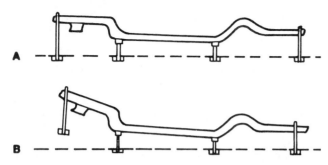

FIGURE 9-60 **(A) Datum is correct and (B) datum is off.**

beneath the rear seat and another under the cowl-toe pan. Add two more gauges before and after the base gauges; one located at the main front cross member and a second at the rear most cross member. Additional gauging of the front cross member area and/or strut tower completes the picture.

To read for datum, all gauges must be on the same plane, as indicated by the spec sheets. After hanging all four gauges, read across the top to determine if datum is correct. If all four gauges are level at the top (Figure 9-60A), the vehicle is on datum. If they are not level, the vehicle is off datum (Figure 9-60B).

Since the datum line is an imaginary plane, datum heights can be raised or lowered to facilitate gauge readings. If the datum height is changed at one gauge location, all the gauges must be adjusted an equal amount to maintain accuracy.

While datum readings are usually obtained from centering gauges, there are individual gauges available for measuring datum heights. These datum gauges are usually held in position by magnetic holders. Remember that the dimensions that allow the vehicle to be level with the road are measured from the datum plane.

THE CENTER PLANE

The datum plane is divided by an imaginary center plane. This center plane or centerline (₵) divides the vehicle into two equal halves: the passenger side and the driver side (Figure 9-61). All width or lateral dimensions of symmetrical vehicles are measured from the center. That is, the measure from the centerline to a specific point on the right side will be exactly the same as the measurement from the centerline to the same point on the left side. One side of the structure would be a perfect mirror image of the other. Since the center pins or sights on the gauges always remain in the center of the vehicle, the body technician can sight along these pins to determine if lateral misalignment is present.

Most vehicles are built symmetrically. But if the vehicle is asymmetrical, the centering gauges will not align and will not indicate a true center reference. Symmetrical means that the dimensions on the right side of the car are equal to the dimensions on the left side of the car. If the car is asymmetrical, these dimensions are not the same. In such a case, a centering gauge that compensates for the asymmetry of the underbody can be used in conjunction with a body dimensions chart that has a built-in compensation factor (Figure 9-62).

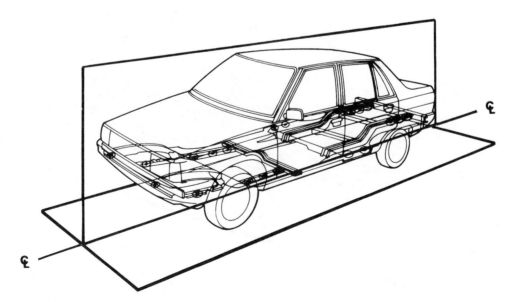

FIGURE 9-61 The center plane or centerline of a vehicle added to the datum plane. *(Courtesy of Blackhawk Automotive Inc.)*

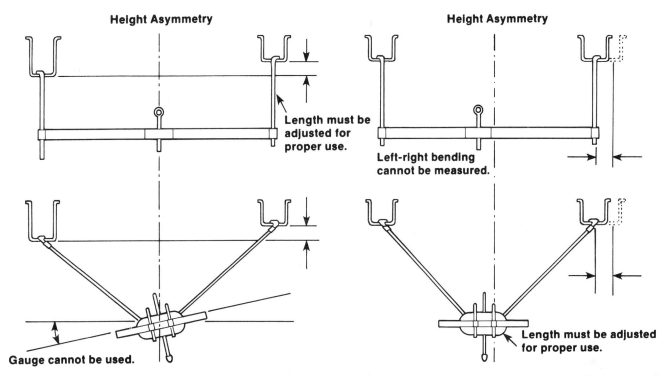

FIGURE 9-62   How gauges are arranged when measuring asymmetric installation points. *(Courtesy of Toyota Motor Corp.)*

To check for centerline misalignment, all four centering gauges must be hung. To establish the true centerline, the center pin on the #2 gauge must be lined up with the center pin on the #3 gauge. Then the center pins of #1 and #4 can be read relative to the centerline of the base. Of course, other damage conditions will affect a centerline reading. If a vehicle has a diamond condition, a shortened rail or subrail, or an out-of-level condition, the centerline reading will be affected. Further inspection by gauging or measuring might be necessary to determine the presence or absence of these conditions.

ZERO PLANES

In order to properly analyze damage to a vehicle, it will be necessary to think of the vehicle as a rectangular structure divided into three zero plane sections (Figure 9-63): front, center, and rear. This three section principle is a result of the vehicle's design and the way it reacts during a collision. In both conventional and unibody construction, the center zone or section is a flat rigid area with considerable strength. It is this rigid center section that will be used as a base for reading structural alignment. All measurements and alignment readings will be taken relative to the center section.

The controlling points of any car underbody are the front cross member, the cross member at the

cowl, the cross member at the rear door, and the rear cross member (Figure 9-64). The center section or the area between the cowl and rear door cross member is the portion used when doing a major straightening operation.

Level in a zero plane means the condition in which all areas of the vehicle are parallel to one another. Level refers to parallel conditions in the vehicle structure only and has nothing to do with any outside reference, such as the floor. Check for an out-of-level condition in the front or rear sections. When the #2 and #3 base gauges are hung, the center section is read for level. When these base gauges are parallel, no twist can exist. However, the front or rear sections could still be out of level. To check for this condition, hang #1 and #4 gauges and read relative to the nearest base gauges. If #1 hangs parallel to #2, the front section is level, relative to the base. If #4 hangs parallel to #3, the rear section is level, relative to the base. If an out-of-level condition exists in the front, #1 would not hang parallel to #2. This same type of reading should be done in the rear section.

9.7 STRUT CENTERLINE GAUGE

Supported by the MacPherson tower domes, the centerline strut tower/upper body gauge (Figure

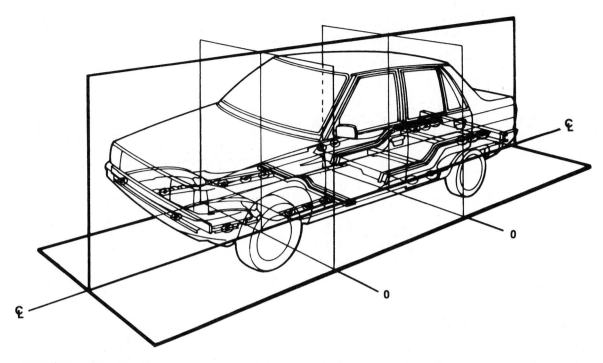

FIGURE 9-63   The three vehicle planes combined. *(Courtesy of Blackhawk Automotive Inc.)*

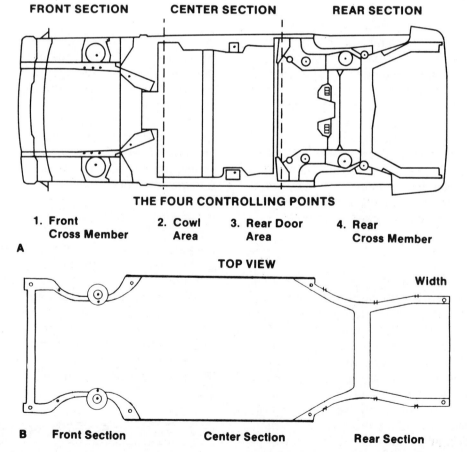

FRONT SECTION   **CENTER SECTION**   **REAR SECTION**

THE FOUR CONTROLLING POINTS

1. **Front**   2. **Cowl**   3. **Rear Door**   4. **Rear**
   Cross Member   **Area**   **Area**   **Cross Member**

A

TOP VIEW

Width

B   **Front Section**   **Center Section**   **Rear Section**

FIGURE 9-64   The three zones (sections) and four controlling points of (A) conventional frame vehicle and (B) unibody car

FIGURE 9-65 Typical MacPherson strut center-line gauge in place. *(Courtesy of Car-O-Liner)*

FIGURE 9-67 Adjusting the upper horizontal bar between two strut towers. *(Courtesy of Chief Automotive Systems, Inc.)*

9-65) allows visual alignment of the upper body area. It shows misalignment of the strut tower/upper body parts in relation to the centerline plane and datum line plane.

The gauge (Figure 9-66) features an upper and lower horizontal, each with a center pin. The upper bar is usually calibrated from the center out. Pointers, which are positioned in an adjustable housing on the upper horizontal bar, are used to mount the gauge to the strut tower/upper body locations (Figure 9-67). Two types of pointers are provided: "cone" and "reverse cone." The reverse cone is notched to provide additional means of mounting on

the vehicle, for example, ridged surfaces. The pointers are usually held in the housing by means of thumbscrews.

In addition to the standard 4-inch length, 7-inch pointers are provided for situations when more length is needed to position the gauge (Figure 9-68). When using the 7-inch pointers to mount the gauge, remember that they change the scale reading by 3 inches.

The vertical scales that link the upper and lower horizontal bars are used to set the lower bar at the datum height of the parts the gauge mounts to (Figure 9-69). The scales fasten in housings at the ends of the horizontal bars. Height adjustments are made at the housings of the upper horizontal bar.

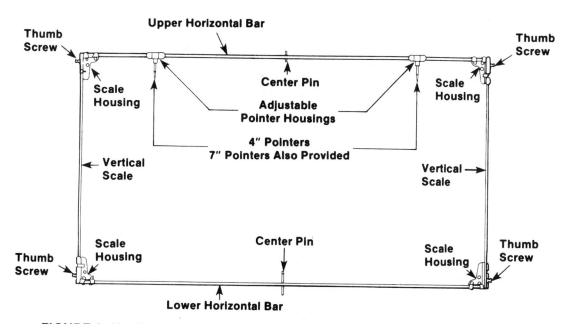

FIGURE 9-66 The parts of a typical centerline strut tower/upper body gauge. *(Courtesy of Chief Automotive Systems, Inc.)*

FIGURE 9-68   Longer pointers can be used to measure roof structures by the extension of its strut tower/upper body bar through the passenger compartment and projection of pointers upward from pointer housings. *(Courtesy of Chief Automotive Systems, Inc.)*

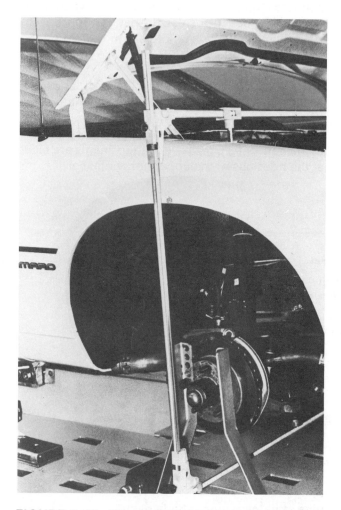

FIGURE 9-69   The vertical side bar of a strut tower/upper body assembly. *(Courtesy of Chief Automotive Systems, Inc.)*

FIGURE 9-70   Check the MacPherson strut for misalignments. *(Courtesy of Chief Automotive Systems, Inc.)*

The strut tower upper body gauge is used most often to detect misalignment of the strut towers (Figure 9-70); however, it can also be used to detect misalignment of a radiator support, center pillar, cowl, quarter panel, and so on.

9.8 DIAGNOSING DAMAGE USING THE GAUGE MEASURING SYSTEM

As previously mentioned, the most common rule in body/frame alignment is: "Reverse direction and sequence." This means that to correct collision damage pull or push the damaged area in the opposite direction of impact. And because the repair must be made in the reverse sequence that it happened, the damage must be measured in the reverse sequence.

When proceeding through the measurement of the damage, keep in mind that a vehicle is similar to a building. If the foundation is not square and level, the rest of the structure will be uneven also. The vehicle foundation, or the center section, is measured for twist and diamond first. These two measurements will tell if the foundation is square and level. The remaining measurements use the foundation as a reference.

TWIST

The first damage condition to look for is twist. Twist is the last damage condition to occur to the vehicle and, therefore, the first to measure. Twist is a condition that exists throughout the entire vehicle. True twist exists when one side of the vehicle is pushed either low or high on one end, either the front or rear, and then moves in the opposite direction (low or high) toward the other end. The opposite side would have exactly the opposite damage.

Twist can only be checked in the center section; otherwise, additional misalignment in the front or rear might give an inaccurate reading of twist. To check for twist, two "base" gauges must be hung. These base gauges are also referred to as the #2 (front center) and #3 (rear center) gauges. The #2 should be hung as far forward of the center section, up to the cowl, as possible. The #3 is hung as far rearward of the center section, to the rear kickup, as possible. The #2 gauge is then read relative to #3. If the gauges are parallel, no twist exists. If the gauges are not parallel, then a twist could exist. Remember that a true twist must exist throughout the entire structure. To check for a true twist versus an out-of-level condition in the center section, hang another gauge. Go to the undamaged section of the car and hang either the #1 (front) or #4 (rear) gauge.

These gauges will be read relative to the nearest base gauge. The #1 will be read relative to #2 and the #4 will be read relative to #3. If the front or rear gauge reads parallel to the nearest base gauge, true twist cannot exist and there is an out-of-level condition in the center section. If a true twist exists, the gauges would read like those shown in Figure 9-71.

DIAMONDING

Diamonding, as mentioned earlier in the chapter, is a condition in which one rail or rocker is pushed either forward or rearward of the opposite rail or rocker. This condition will often be found in conventional frames. The solid nature of unibody construction makes diamonding unusual in these cars, but it is possible. The check for diamonding is simple. Using the tram gauge, measure from the front corner of one rail or rocker to the rear corner of the opposite side.

If a true twist exists, the gauges would read like this.

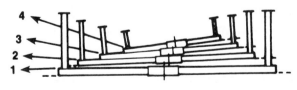

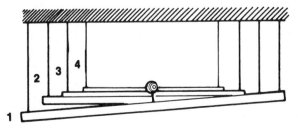

FIGURE 9-71   Example of true twisting. Deviation in the parallel lines of the front gauge is evident.

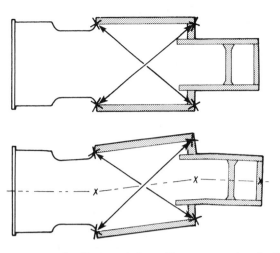

FIGURE 9-72   Determining the amount of diamonding with a tram gauge

An exact dimension is not important here as the desired end result is simply equal measurements for both sides. If one measurement is longer than the other (Figure 9-72), a diamond condition exists. If one measurement is 1-1/2 inches longer than the other, the condition is referred to as 1-1/2 inch diamond.

MASHING (CRUSHING)

Mash is measured with a tram gauge. It is present when any section or frame member of the vehicle is shorter than the factory specifications. When using a tram gauge on a mash damaged vehicle, be sure to make the measurement specified on the manufacturer's specification sheets or in the dimension data book. The amount of mash is determined by subtracting the actual measurement from the specified measurement. The proper methods of measuring various impacts with a tram gauge are shown in Figure 9-73.

SAGGING (BENDING)

Sag is a condition where the cowl area of the vehicle is lower than normal. As mentioned earlier in this chapter, sag can also occur at the front cross member. The ends of the cross member will be closer than normal and the center will be too low.

Three centering gauges are used to check for a sag condition. One gauge is placed at the front cross member, the next one at the cowl area, and the third one at the rear door area. The gauges are on-center and parallel with each other, but the center frame gauge is lower than the others (Figure 9-74). This indicates a sag condition at the cowl area.

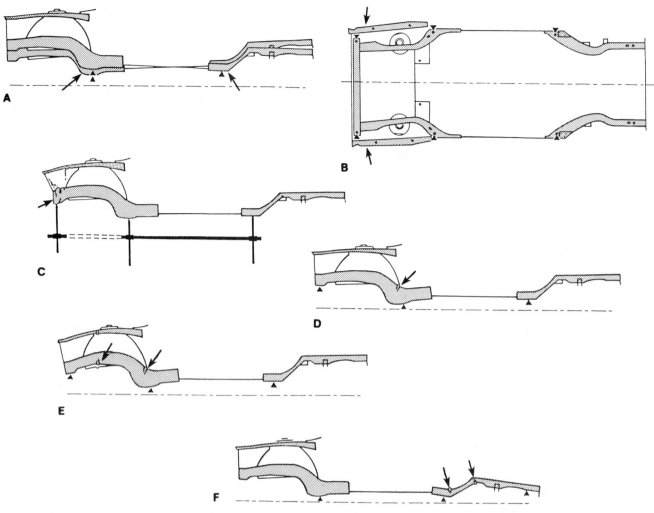

FIGURE 9-73 Typical unibody distortion under impact force. (A) High front impact with secondary damage to rear of assembly; (B) right front corner impact; (C) direct front impact; (D) low front impact; (E) high front impact; and (F) high rear impact.

Up-Down Bending

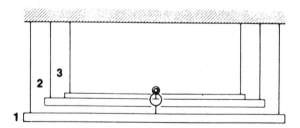

FIGURE 9-74 Cowl area sag

In Figure 9-75 observe the relationship of the centering gauges to each other. Note that the parallel bar in the cowl area is about 2 inches lower than the other bars. This means there is 2 inches of sag.

Sidesway (Widening)

Sidesway is present when the front, center, or rear portion of the vehicle is pushed by a side impact and the frame or body is forced out of alignment. Three centering gauges are used to check for sidesway.

If the vehicle was hit in the front, base gauges #2 (cowl area) and #3 (rear door area) are hung and the sighting gauge #1 is located in the front cross member area. If gauge #1 does not line up with the other two, front sidesway is present (Figure 9-76).

If the vehicle has been struck in the rear, the misalignment would appear on the self-centering gauges in a way similar to front sidesway, except that the rear pin or bull's-eye would be out of alignment. A center hit on a vehicle causes a misalign-

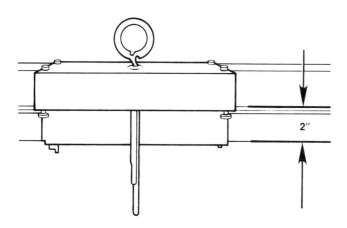

FIGURE 9-75 Position of parallel bar in the cowl area

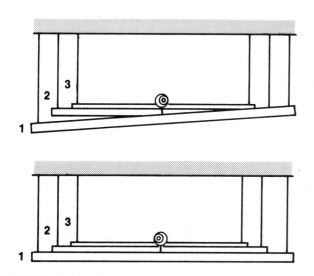

FIGURE 9-76 Example of sidesway

ment known as double sidesway. It results from a severe impact in the center section, but it affects the entire vehicle. The dimensions of both front and rear sections must be checked during the pulling of double sidesway damage.

While the self-centering and datum gauges give a total picture of frame and body damage, their functions can be adapted into a so-called frame gauge. By viewing body damage with a frame gauge arrangement, it is possible to measure the amount of frame or body damage the vehicle has incurred. An undamaged frame would give a frame gauge indication as shown in Figure 9-77. The horizontal bars are parallel to each other, indicating that the frame is level. The targets are centered within each other indicating a perfect centerline. The gauges reveal horizontal and vertical alignment for certain body and frame damages.

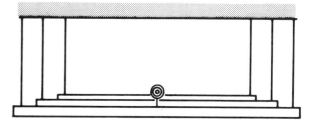

FIGURE 9-77 No deviation should be seen in the parallel or in the centering circles when there is no damage to the vehicle.

Measuring gauges—tram, self-centering, datum, and frame—have been in use for many years and were originally designed for measuring conventional body-over-frame vehicles. However, structurally damaged unibody vehicles can be successfully repaired using the gauge measuring system. In recent years new systems have been introduced for use with both unibody and BOF structures. Today, measuring system gauges are usually limited to light or medium body damage.

9.9 UNIVERSAL MEASURING SYSTEMS

Universal measuring systems are the most efficient application of tram/centering gauge technology. They make parts of the measuring job much easier and more accurate, but still require a degree of skill and attention to detail. These systems have the ability to measure all the control points at the same time. But to get the proper measurement reading, the equipment must be set to the manufacturer's specifications.

Universal measuring systems fall into two groups.

* Mechanical systems
* Laser systems

MECHANICAL MEASURING SYSTEMS

In most mechanical systems, several mechanical pointers are attached to a precision measurement bridge (Figure 9-78). These pointers are positioned on the bridge according to the vehicle's correct factory specifications for horizontal and vertical dimensions, while free-standing type bridges are available (Figure 9-79).

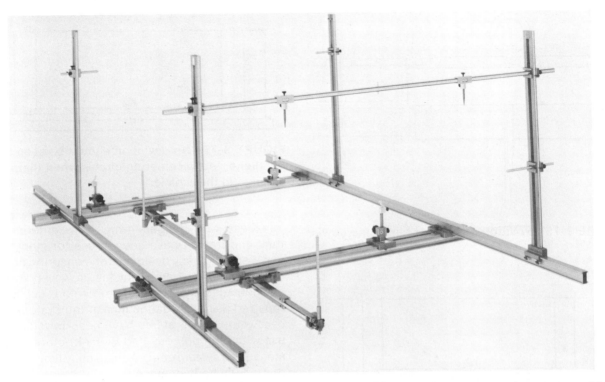

FIGURE 9-78 Universal measuring incorporates the true structural adjustment benefits of gauging with the specific advantages of measuring to form a third dimension of collision damage analysis. This system actually mounts to the vehicle itself, which allows measurements to be taken at any time during the repair. *(Courtesy of Chief Automotive Systems, Inc.)*

FIGURE 9-79 Typical free-standing type universal bridge. *(Courtesy of Nicator, Inc.)*

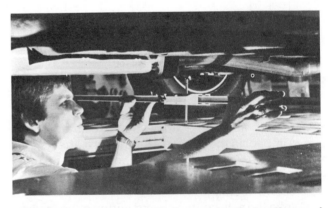

FIGURE 9-80 Adjustments are simple to align and readings are easy to make. *(Courtesy of Chief Automotive Systems, Inc.)*

This system allows simultaneous observation of a number of control points when the pointers are in position. Care must be taken to ensure that the measurement bridge is not stressed or damaged during the repair process. The accuracy of this system is dependent upon the location and precision of the pointers on the measurement.

The advantage of a universal system over a tram gauge is that readings are instantaneous; the pointers either align with the control points or they do not (Figure 9-80).

In practice, a universal measurement system offers the advantage of being able to visually inspect all the control points by just walking around the car and determining where each control point is in comparison to where the control point on the measuring

FIGURE 9-81 An overall view of the vehicle is possible. *(Courtesy of Chief Automotive Systems, Inc.)*

system is (Figure 9-81). If the control point on the car is not in the same horizontal and vertical position as the measurement system says it should be, the control point on the car is wrong.

A

B

FIGURE 9-82 Universal mechanical measuring system can look (A) complex when mounted permanently on a bench or (B) simple when mounted on a vehicle. *(Courtesy of Chief Automotive Systems, Inc.)*

Universal measuring systems vary from the complex units shown in Figure 9-82A to simple ones like the unit shown in Figure 9-82B. The latter is actually a tram/centering gauge system that is fastened to the vehicle. Because of this variation, it would be rather difficult to explain how each measures a vehicle; read the owner's manual for these details. In summary, the fixability of mechanical universal measuring systems enable most of them to work on both the unitized and conventional frame vehicle.

Most mechanical systems measure the lower and upper body reference points of a vehicle as identified in dimension manuals and makes comparison measurements of components from one side of a vehicle to the other. They measure all three dimensions of the vehicle: length, width, and height. Figures 9-83 and 9-84 show how measurements are made in a typical mechanical measuring system.

A universal mechanical measuring system assesses a damaged vehicle by showing how far components are out of alignment. It also remains on the vehicle to guide the technician and verify that components are back in their proper place when the repair is complete.

LASER MEASURING SYSTEMS

The mechanical laser measuring system is extremely accurate when properly installed. The word "LASER" stands for **L**ight **A**mplification by **S**timulated **E**mission of **R**adiation.

All body shop laser measuring systems operate in basically the same way. The laser source is aimed at a target that is either hung or attached to the car. Some systems even use parts of the vehicle as targets.

Measurements are taken by observing the laser beam on the target. Some targets (Figure 9-85) are clear, allowing the laser beam to shine through; thus, several clear targets can be used with one light source. Mirrored targets (Figure 9-86), on the other hand, are capable of reflecting the laser beam to additional targets. (In some laser systems these targets are called "laser guides.") Using combinations of transparent and mirrored targets, it is often possible to simultaneously measure several dimensions on a vehicle using a single laser source.

Some laser systems use up to three laser guns to give length/width/height coordinates anywhere on the vehicle—decks, cowls, door openings, hinges, posts, and rooflines (Figure 9-87). With such a three-dimensional system, a single gun can be used to make measurements in conjunction with measuring devices such as a metal tape (Figure 9-88).

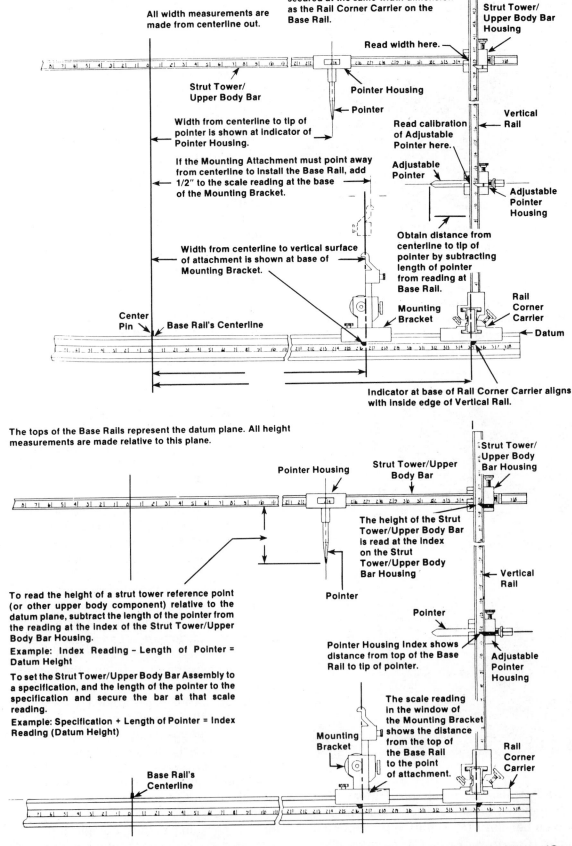

FIGURE 9-83 How widths and heights are measured on a typical mechanical universal system. *(Courtesy of Chief Automotive Systems, Inc.)*

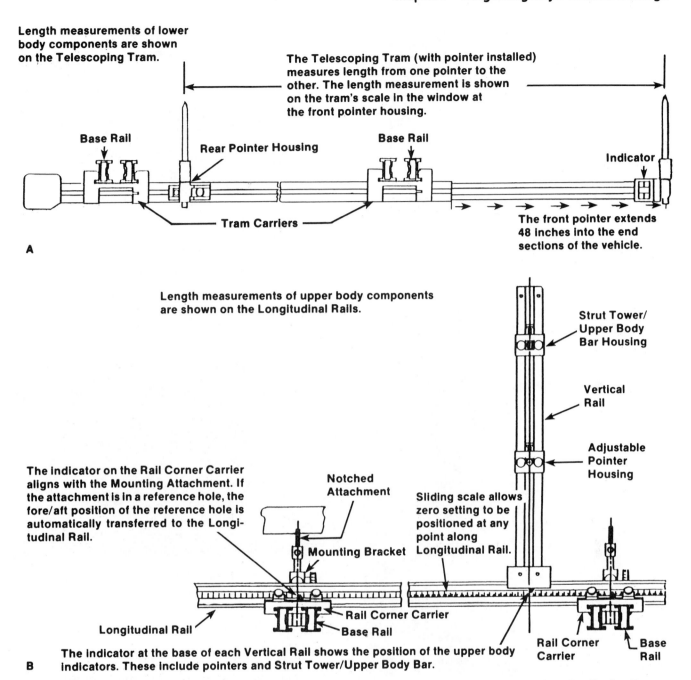

Length measurements of lower body components are shown on the Telescoping Tram.

The Telescoping Tram (with pointer installed) measures length from one pointer to the other. The length measurement is shown on the tram's scale in the window at the front pointer housing.

Base Rail

Rear Pointer Housing

Base Rail

Indicator

Tram Carriers

The front pointer extends 48 inches into the end sections of the vehicle.

A

Length measurements of upper body components are shown on the Longitudinal Rails.

Strut Tower/ Upper Body Bar Housing

Vertical Rail

The indicator on the Rail Corner Carrier aligns with the Mounting Attachment. If the attachment is in a reference hole, the fore/aft position of the reference hole is automatically transferred to the Longitudinal Rail.

Notched Attachment

Adjustable Pointer Housing

Mounting Bracket

Sliding scale allows zero setting to be positioned at any point along Longitudinal Rail.

Rail Corner Carrier

Base Rail

Longitudinal Rail

Rail Corner Carrier

Base Rail

The indicator at the base of each Vertical Rail shows the position of the upper body indicators. These include pointers and Strut Tower/Upper Body Bar.

B

FIGURE 9-84   How lengths are measured (A) using a telescoping tram and (B) using longitudinal rails. (Courtesy of Chief Automotive Systems, Inc.)

Laser measuring systems are made up of both optical and mechanical parts. For example, in the clear target system, the optical parts are:

- Laser power unit or gun (Figure 9–89A), which emits a safe, low-powered laser beam
- Beam splitters (Figure 9–89B) that project beams at a precise right angle so height, width, and length can be measured simultaneously
- Laser guide (Figure 9–89C) to deflect the laser beam at exactly 90 degrees

The mechanical items on laser measuring devices include:

- Calibrated bars that attach to the car or act as support devices for the laser gun itself
- Measurement data specification sheets
- Transparent scales that create a datum plane, which brings the measuring points on the car to a level that can be illuminated with the laser beam. Scales are hung from fixtures or holes on the underside of the car. The laser beam passes through the center of the

FIGURE 9–85   Typical transparent scales or sighting unit used in some laser systems. *(Courtesy of Nicator, Inc.)*

FIGURE 9–87   The "three dimensional" system permits length/width/height measurements. *(Courtesy of Kansas Jack, Inc.)*

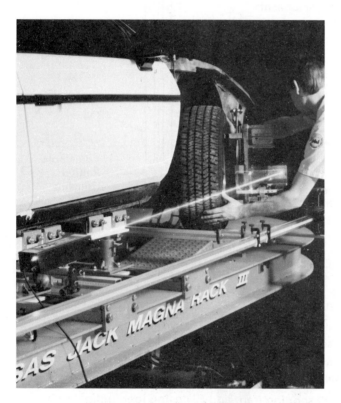

FIGURE 9–86   Typical mirrored laser setup. *(Courtesy of Kansas Jack, Inc.)*

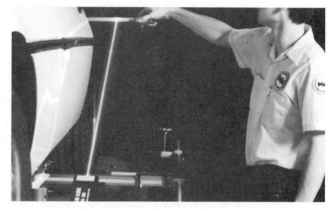

FIGURE 9–88   Using a conjunction with a single laser gun. *(Courtesy of Kansas Jack, Inc.)*

scale target area when the measuring point is in its correct position.

After the laser measuring system is set up and the transparent scales hung under the car (in accordance with data sheets), measuring can be started by using two sets of undamaged measuring points under the car, vertically adjusting the measuring beams, and angling the laser beam using the control on the two laser guides (Figure 9-90). Calibration is completed when the laser beam passes through the two target scales.

Some laser measuring systems will permit the body technician to monitor upper body information, such as pillar locations for windshields. Upper body information allows the technician to have more control when pulling the body back into location for proper alignment (Figure 9-91). It assures that the front door just installed will fit, or that the windshield to be installed is snug. Also, some laser systems offer an integral four-wheel alignment capability (Figure 9-92). This is beneficial because suspension problems can be measured and corrected for unibody repair. Using an accessory as shown in Figure 9-93, MacPherson struts can be measured without removing them.

When properly set up, most laser systems can remain in position during the repair operation unless

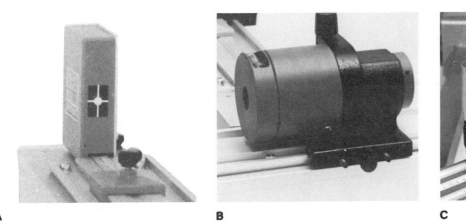

A   B   C

FIGURE 9-89   Optical parts of one type of laser system: (A) laser gun; (B) beam splitter; and (C) laser guide. *(Courtesy of Nicator, Inc.)*

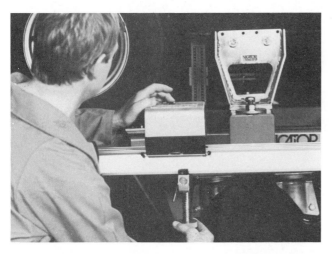

FIGURE 9-90   Adjusting the datum plane of the sighting or gun unit for both the angles of the plane and the height. *(Courtesy of Nicator, Inc.)*

FIGURE 9-92   Using a laser measuring system to perform a four wheel adjustment. *(Courtesy of Kansas Jack, Inc.)*

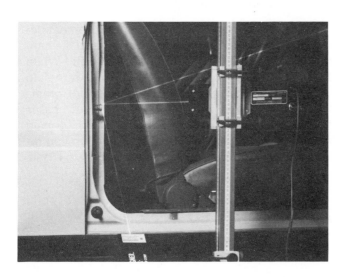

FIGURE 9-91   A three dimensional check of an upper body point. *(Courtesy of Kansas Jack, Inc.)*

FIGURE 9-93   Using a laser measuring system, the MacPherson strut gauge is balanced on two bolts with a counterweight. *(Courtesy of Nicator, Inc.)*

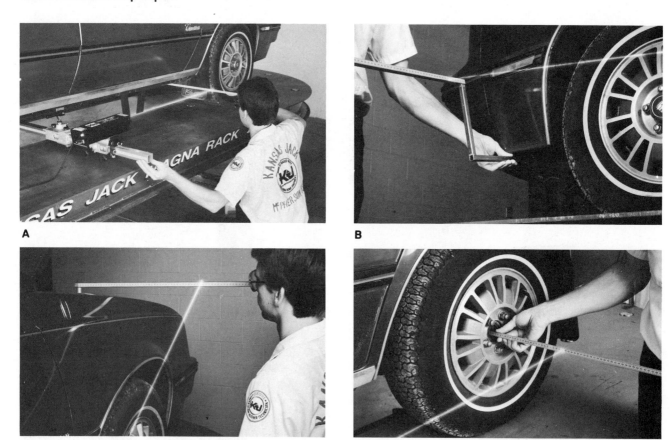

FIGURE 9-94   Checking for structural damage using a laser system is quick and accurate: (A) setting up and aligning the carriage and laser; (B) checking lower front rails; (C) another method of checking strut towers; and (D) checking rear wheel offset *(Courtesy of Kansas Jack, Inc.)*

the mounting hardware or the laser targets interfere with the operation of the pulling and straightening equipment.

Laser equipment, as already pointed out, features few mechanical linkages. Most importantly, laser systems provide direct, instantaneous dimensional readings so that the control points in both the damaged and undamaged areas of the car can be monitored continually during the pulling and straightening operation. In addition, when installed properly (Figure 9-94A), a typical laser system can make approximately forty dimension checks, including the following:

- Lower front rails (Figure 9-94B)
- Upper radiator support
- Strut towers (Figure 9-94C)
- Wheels
- Cross members
- Fender gaps
- Cowl
- Door hinges
- Door strikers
- B-pillars

- Rockers
- Rear wheel offset (Figure 9-94D)
- Front deck lid gap
- Rear deck lid gap
- Rear lower rails

The accuracy of laser system measurement depends upon the accuracy of the targets and the calibration of the laser systems to the targets. When laser beams are projected through one target to another, the targets must be optically perfect, otherwise the laser beam will be deflected as it passes through the targets. The deflection will be magnified by the distance between the targets, which can result in serious error. Laser targets that become scratched or warped should be discarded.

9.10 DEDICATED BENCH AND FIXTURE MEASURING SYSTEMS

Dedicated bench and fixture systems are a completely different type of measuring method. In-

FIGURE 9-95   Typical dedicated bench. *(Courtesy of Blackhawk Automotive Inc.)*

stead of taking actual measurements, the bench acts as a "go-no go" gauge. The bench consists of a flat work surface to which fixtures are attached (Figure 9-95).

Fixtures are designated to duplicate locations of the body control points and other key locations of the underbody. Fixtures bolt to the transverse beams that create a true datum plane and mate with the underbody of the car (Figure 9-96). If the fixtures fit the car properly, the body technician knows that the car is in perfect alignment. All that is necessary is to straighten the car until the factory control points match the fixtures. No other underbody measurements are usually required.

Figure 9-97 shows four of the more common types of fixtures. They are:

- **Bolt-on fixtures.** Used when the attachment is required for suspension or bumper mountings. The studs or bolts normally used to attach these parts to the car are also used to attach the fixtures. Depending on the damage, the fixtures can either be bolted to the car first and lined up with the bench during the repair, or attached to the bench first and lined up with the car during repair.
- **Pin type fixtures.** Used most often to mate with manufacturing control holes in the underbody. They can also be used to mate with suspension mounting holes. These fixtures have the advantage that they can be left in place if overpulling is necessary.
- **MacPherson or strut fixtures.** Used in the same manner as a pin type fixture, a typical MacPherson fixture consists of a bottom plate assembly, a sliding shaft with a cross hole and cross pin, and a bolted-on top plate.
- **Bench extensions.** These are included with certain fixture sets where the length of the car requires that fixtures be positioned beyond the bench surface. The extensions are always used at the rear of the car. Each extension is drilled with seven holes on top

FIGURE 9-96   Fixtures clamped in place. *(Courtesy of Blackhawk Automotive Inc.)*

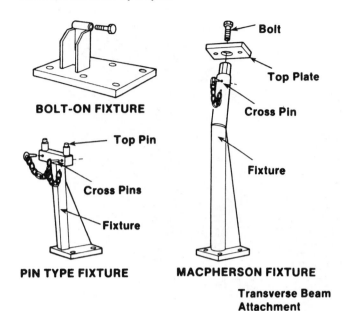

BOLT-ON FIXTURE

PIN TYPE FIXTURE

Top Pin

Cross Pins

Fixture

Bolt

Top Plate

Cross Pin

Fixture

MACPHERSON FIXTURE

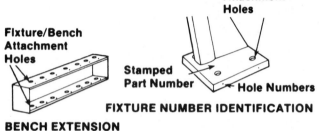

Fixture/Bench
Attachment
Holes

Transverse Beam
Attachment
Holes

Stamped
Part Number

Hole Numbers

FIXTURE NUMBER IDENTIFICATION

BENCH EXTENSION

FIGURE 9-97 Typical fixtures and bench extensions. *(Courtesy of Blackhawk Automotive Inc.)*

and seven holes on the bottom. These holes are directly in line with each other and are numbered beginning with 0 in the center to 3 at either end. The extension is always used between the transverse beam and the bench. The positions are shown on the data fixture diagram.

Most fixtures share a common attachment method to the transverse beams. The base plate for each fixture is drilled with four, eight, or twelve holes and is marked with a part number and also the hole number location on the transverse beam. The part number ends with D for fixtures to be used on the right side of the car and S for fixtures to be used on the left side of the car. Stamped at the rear of each base plate are the numbers that correspond to the numbers on the transverse beam. Always make sure these numbers are on the same side as the numbers on the beam. In cases where there are more than four holes on the base plate, minor length differences in some models require two or three sets of four holes. They are stamped in the base of the fixture and noted on the data sheet.

FIGURE 9-98 Fitting parts using the fixtures. *(Courtesy of Blackhawk Automotive Inc.)*

FIGURE 9-99 Welding parts using fixtures as supports. *(Courtesy of Blackhawk Automotive Inc.)*

A typical fixture consists of 14 to 25 units that can be used individually or together. Many are designed so that they can be used either with mechanical parts in place or removed. One set of fixtures can be used to measure several models or body styles within a given car "family." Each set is shipped in a color-coded container determined by the car manufacturer. In some areas of the country, fixtures are available on a rental basis.

The fixtures perform a number of functions:

- They visually indicate where a control point should be located. If it does not line up with the fixture it must be straightened.
- They provide gauging of all the control points at the same time. No measuring is

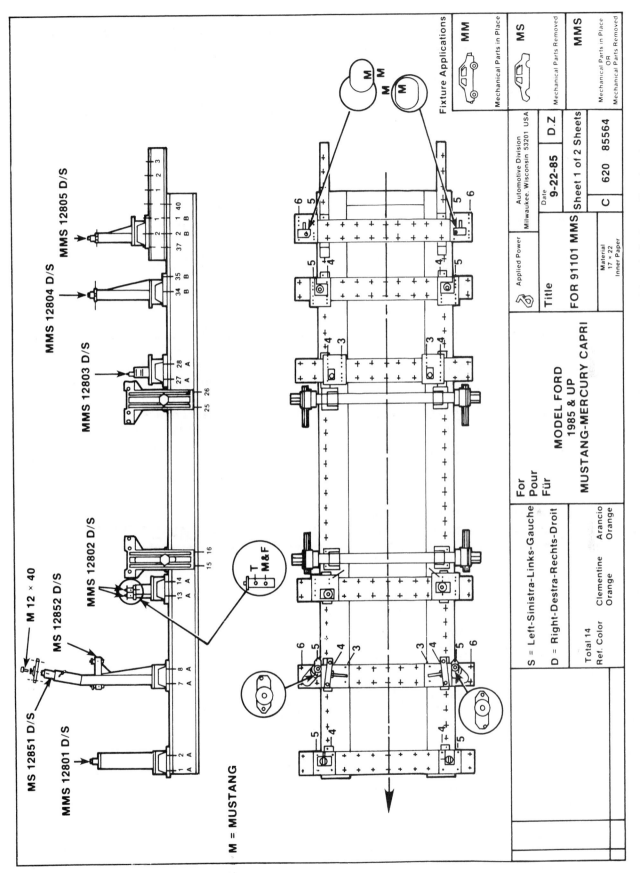

FIGURE 9–100   Typical dedicated bench diagram. *(Courtesy of Blackhawk Automotive Inc.)*

required. If all the points line up, the steering, suspension, engine mounts, and so on are all in the exact position they were in when the car was made.

- As described in Chapter 10, once the damaged parts are properly lined up with the fixtures they can hold these parts in position while further straightening is done (Figure 9–98). This eliminates the "pull-measure" "pull-measure" sequence required with centering/tram gauge or universal systems.

- Dedicated fixtures can allow accurate sub-assembly of parts on a bench before actually welding those pieces together (Figure 9–99). A good example of this would be a lower box rail and tower assembly on some unibody cars. The sequence would go like this:
  —Position and hold the lower rail pieces on the fixtures.
  —Weld them together.
  —Position and hold the strut tower pieces on top of the rail.
  —Weld them in their correct position.

One of the most common errors in bench setup is misreading of the diagram (Figure 9–100). Along the bottom edge of the diagram is a list of each of the fixtures included in the set: an explanation of the letters D for right and S for left; the total number of fixtures in the set and their color; the models on which the fixture set can be used; the part number (title) of the fixture set; and an explanation of the terms MM for mechanical parts, MS for mechanical parts removed, and MMS for fixtures that can be used either with the mechanical parts in place or removed.

The upper illustration in the diagram is a side view and the lower illustration is a top view of the bench with transverse beams and fixtures in place. The front of the bench is to the left of the diagram. Each fixture is numbered with a part number that is also stamped in the base plate of the fixture. In addition, it has numbers corresponding with those on the bench holes and on the A or B holes of the transverse beams. (For example, the first transverse beam in the diagram shown indicates holes 1A and 2A. This means that the A holes in the transverse beam should be lined up with holes #1 and #2 on the bench.)

The top view shows the number on the transverse beam that corresponds with the hole pattern in the base plate of the fixture. These numbers are also stamped in the rear edge of the fixture bottom plate. For example, the front fixtures in the diagram shown are to be lined up with holes 4 and 5 in the transverse

beam. Also shown on the fixture diagram are any special instructions pertaining to specific fixtures, car models, or double-ended pins and base plate with more than four holes.

 **SHOP TALK**

Manufacturers of all measuring systems are constantly furnishing informational updates and bulletins on their products. Be sure to read and study them because they will help to make the repair procedure easier.

More information on the use of a dedicated bench and fixtures in body shop work can be found in Chapter 10.

 **SHOP TALK**

It must be remembered that the proper use of any measuring equipment mentioned in this chapter is the secret of successful vehicle repair. With any measurement system, the key to correct pulling and straightening lies in accurately monitoring all measurements—before starting the pull, while pulling, and immediately after the pull has been made.

9.11 REVIEW QUESTIONS

1. Which type of damage occurs most often in a body-over-frame vehicle?
   a. sidesway
   b. sag
   c. mash
   d. diamond

2. In a unibody structure, which of the following occurs last in the typical collision damage sequence?
   a. bending
   b. widening
   c. twisting
   d. crushing

3. Technician A says that the tolerance of critical manufacturing dimensions must be held to within a maximum value of 5 millimeters. Technician B does no measuring in the rear

section of a vehicle in a front end collision that causes slight amounts of door sag. Who is correct?
a. Technician A
b. Technician B
c. Both A and B
d. Neither A nor B

4. On unibody designs, what has a fixed (nonadjustable) value?
a. camber
b. caster
c. both a and b
d. neither a nor b

5. To accurately measure a vehicle, how many correct dimensions are required as a starting point?
a. at least two
b. at least three
c. at least four
d. one

6. Technician A says that any wrinkle in the rear floor is usually due to buckling of the rear side member. Technician B says that self-centering gauges are used to measure in a manner closely related to the tram gauges. Who is correct?
a. Technician A
b. Technician B
c. Both A and B
d. Neither A nor B

7. Which of the following is a flat surface parallel to the underbody of the vehicle at some fixed distance from the underbody?
a. center plane
b. datum plane
c. zero plane
d. none of the above

8. When proceeding through the measurement of the damage, Technician A measures the center section of the vehicle for twist and diamond first. Technician B measures for mash with a strut tower upper body gauge. Who is correct?
a. Technician A
b. Technician B
c. Both A and B
d. Neither A nor B

9. Technician A says that the larger the area over which the impact is spread, the greater the damage. Technician B says that a visual inspection is sufficient to accurately assess impact damage. Who is correct?
a. Technician A
b. Technician B
c. Both A and B
d. Neither A nor B

10. Technician A says that a laser guide deflects the laser at exactly 90 degrees. Technician B says that beam splitters project beams at a precise right angle so height, width, and length can be measured simultaneously. Who is correct?
a. Technician A
b. Technician B
c. Both A and B
d. Neither A nor B

11. Technician A leaves the laser system in position during the repair operation. Technician B discards a laser target when it is scratched or warped. Who is correct?
a. Technician A
b. Technician B
c. Both A and B
d. Neither A nor B

12. To check for centerline misalignment, how many centering gauges must be hung?
a. four
b. three
c. two
d. one

13. What type of fixture is used when attachment is required to suspension or bumper mountings?
a. bolt-on
b. bench extension
c. pin type
d. strut

14. Technician A frequently uses tram gauges and centering gauges in conjunction with one another. Technician B stands as close as possible to centering gauges in order to read them accurately. Who is correct?
a. Technician A
b. Technician B
c. Both A and B
d. Neither A nor B

15. Which of the following is false?
    a. Pulling secondary damage so that it is corrected first is the best way to correct collision damage to a unibody car.
    b. Pulling secondary damage so that it is corrected first is the best way to correct collision damage on a body-over-frame vehicle.
    c. Bending can occur on one side of the car and not on the other.
    d. None of the above.

16. Technician A uses a strut tower upper body gauge to detect misalignment of a center pillar. Technician B uses the same gauge to detect misalignment of a radiator support. Who is correct?
    a. Technician A
    b. Technician B
    c. Both A and B
    d. Neither A nor B

CHAPTER
10

Body Alignment

Body aligning or pulling is often thought to be a rough and tough physical operation. Actually, it is a relatively easy operation (with the proper equipment) and the most important requirement is accuracy since wheel alignment is directly affected by body alignment. It is, therefore, essential to remove the stress and deformations in the frame and body that were caused by the collision. In order to accomplish this task, it is necessary to use hydraulic equipment such as rams and pulling posts (Figure 10-1). It is essential to use an accurate measuring system such as described in the previous chapter.

Until recently the pulling-out process was actually a matter of applying brute force until the basic damage in the impact area bore a visual resemblance to the proper structure. But today, with unibody construction, precision is the key factor in collision repair. It is not enough to just make the replacement panels fit by shimming and stretching, then turning the handling and mechanical problems over to a mechanic. Mechanics are still necessary, but the body repair technician now has the responsibility for making the basic structure right and leaving only the fine-tuning of suspension and mechanicals to the specialists in those fields.

If, after a vehicle has been repaired following a collision, a customer has a complaint such as abnormal tire wear and pulling to one side, a check might find an enlarged slotted hole for the installation of the front fender, or in an extreme case, an enlarged slotted hole for a door hinge. These procedures produce an excellent finish on the outside at the expense of the problems on the inside of the vehicle. Improper body and frame aligning techniques are the major causes of the frame not being restored to its original dimensions. Body aligning is an extremely important operation. Satisfactory body aligning naturally has an effect on safety, repair time, and finish quality, but its greatest effect is on the confidence of the customer.

FIGURE 10-1 Modern body aligning makes body straightening a great deal easier. *(Courtesy of Car-O-Liner Co.)*

shapes that alter their strength. So to pull only in the opposite direction would not work because of the differences in the strength and the recovery rates of each panel. Therefore, it becomes necessary to apply force according to the recovery rate of each panel and to change the force and the direction in which it is applied to meet the changes that are constantly occurring during the repair operation.

When determining the direction of pull, set the equipment at an angle where the pulling force will be applied perpendicular to the dent (Figure 10-3). One way to alter the direction while pulling is to divide the pulling force into two or more directions (this is the method of changing the direction of the composite force). Use the method that works the best for the given situation (Figure 10-4). Since applying force in only one place will not result in proper repairs, it is, therefore, recommended to exert pulling force on many places at the same time. For convenience, the term **direction opposite to the input** will be used to describe the effective pulling direction.

10.1 BODY ALIGNMENT BASICS

It is a fundamental principle in body aligning that force should be applied to pull the impact area in a direction opposite to the direction of input (Figure 10-2). This method works well when the impact is small and damage is simple but in cases where there is sectional deformation such as folding, or where the impact was severe, the original shape cannot be restored simply by a basic standard pulling operation. Body panels, in these instances, are deformed by the force of the impact into complex

10.2 STRAIGHTENING EQUIPMENT

Every collision repair facility must have equipment that performs many of the basic functions needed for repair. However, unless this equipment has been upgraded to the required level, repairs should not be attempted. More specifically, auto manufacturers feel that their front wheel drive vehicles can be competently repaired and original design safety restored by shops that have equipment that provides:

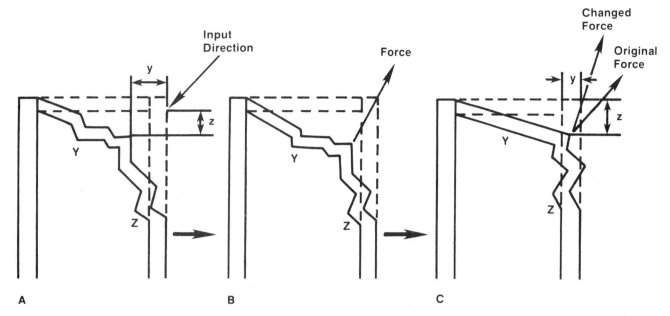

FIGURE 10-2   Pulling direction: (A) input was in the direction of the back arrow causing damage in directions Y and Z; (B) apply force in the direction opposite to the input force; and (C) if a difference in the degree of repair between Y and Z occurs, change the pulling direction accordingly. (Courtesy of Toyota Motor Corp.)

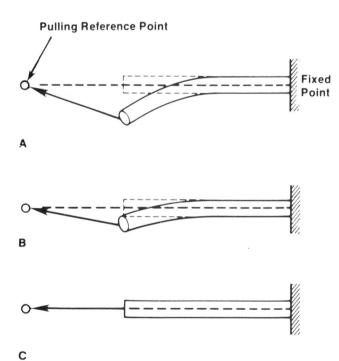

FIGURE 10-3   Basic pulling direction: (A and B) Think of the condition after repairs are completed, set a reference point along an imaginary line extending along the desired axis from which to exert force, and pull from that point. (C) When force is applied and the bend is repaired, the part will be straightened. (Courtesy of Toyota Motor Corp.)

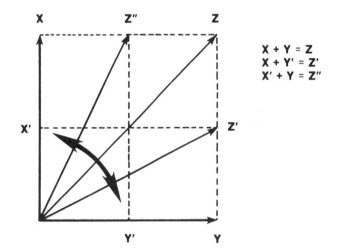

$$X + Y = Z$$
$$X + Y' = Z'$$
$$X' + Y = Z''$$

FIGURE 10-4   If the pulling force is divided between two directions (X, Y), the composite force direction (Z) will change freely with adjustments to the force in the two directions. (Courtesy of Toyota Motor Corp.)

- Precision and full structure alignment
- Multiple structure anchoring and fixturing
- Multiple and full range pulling

On a partial or full frame type vehicle, if the lower structure (the frame) is restored to its proper alignment, generally the suspension and powertrain

A

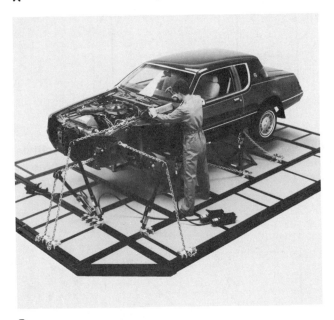

B

FIGURE 10-5 Typical in-floor systems: (A) the anchor-pot system and (B) the modular rail frame. *(Courtesy of Blackhawk Automotive Inc.)*

will be in proper alignment. However, in the unibody vehicle, the "frame" is the entire unibody structure, so some of the alignment reference points are high up in the structure, beyond the range of the usual two dimensional frame alignment equipment. In addition, body-on-frame structures are tolerant of the "trial-and-error" pulling procedure. But, because of the unibody's thin gauge structure, it is very important that the pull setup is right the first time. Therefore, an alignment device that only indicates where there is misalignment is not sufficient. For the unibody repair, the alignment equipment must also show the

- Amount of misalignment at each reference point
- Direction of the misalignment

Only with such equipment can the body technician accurately plan exactly how the total pull sequences

should be set up and how to monitor the progress and effectiveness of each pull while it is being made.

There are several different types of frame corrector equipment on the market that are suitable for both body-on-frame and unibody collision repair work. The most popular systems are:

IN-FLOOR SYSTEMS

Two types of in-floor systems available are the

- Anchor-pot system (Figure 10-5A)
- Modular rail frame system (Figure 10-5B)

Both systems use an in-floor anchoring system (Figure 10-6) that must be balanced both in direction and force of the pull. In addition to the floor rail or anchor pots, this straightening system also has a pump, either hand or air operated, for supplying pressure and a ram for putting that pressure to work. There is a chain for connecting the ram to the car and anchors for anchoring the ram and chain to the grid system. The vehicle is usually supported on a car/truck stand using the cross tube anchor clamps as shown in Figure 10-7. The cross tube anchor clamps are placed over the cross tube and tightened securely. Chains are attached to the cross tube an-

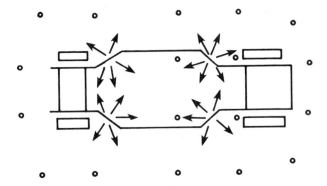

FIGURE 10-6 The anchoring setup must balance in the direction and force of the pull.

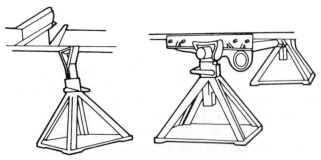

FIGURE 10-7 Arrangement of anchoring clamps. *(Courtesy of Blackhawk Automotive Inc.)*

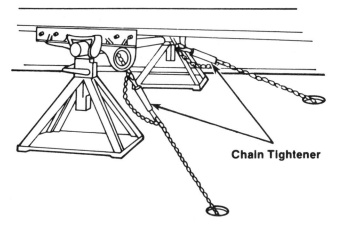

FIGURE 10-8   Method of fastening chains

FIGURE 10-9   Typical power tower. *(Courtesy of Kansas Jack, Inc.)*

chor clamps and the chains are hooked to anchor pots or rails. Pull the chains tight for secure anchoring. Chain shorteners should be used to remove slack from the anchor chain (Figure 10-8).

To make further preparations for the pull, position the ram in the ram foot so it will exert force in the desired direction. Build the ram up to the desired height. Pull the chain tight and lock it in the chain head with the cross pin. Hook the chain onto the anchor. The anchor, ram foot, and attachment point on the car should be in a straight line in the direction of pull. Hook the pump to the ram and connect an air hose to the pump. Engage the pump to take up slack in the chain, and pulling can be started.

An in-floor system is ideal for a small body shop since after the rams or aligners and the other power accessories have been neatly stored away, the aligning area can be used for other purposes. That is, either of the two in-floor systems provide fast hookup, single or multiple pulls, and positive anchoring without sacrificing space.

It is possible with most in-floor systems to use a so-called power tower or post to provide extra pulling power (Figure 10-9). A power tower or post is frequently used to supply pulling power when straightening operations are done on a vehicle lift.

Chainless Anchoring Systems

The low-profile design of this system keeps it close enough to the floor to load a vehicle quickly, yet high enough to allow easy access to the vehicle's underbody. The unit's adjustable length and width allows the body technician to adjust it easily to virtually all vehicle sizes.

The following steps are required to set up a vehicle for pulling with a chainless anchoring system:

1. Raise one end of the vehicle and attach the underbody clamps (Figure 10-10A).
2. Insert the support tube through the underbody clamp and the base (Figure 10-10B). Lower the car onto the base.
3. Secure the system to the in-floor anchors by positioning the lock arm. Hammer the wedges in place to lock the vehicle to the system (Figure 10-10C).
4. Repeat the operation on the opposite end of the vehicle (Figure 10-10D).

Once the car is secured, it is locked to stay. It is possible to pull from any angle, 360 degrees around the vehicle. A power tower or post is often used as a pulling force.

Portable Body and Frame Pullers

This type of pulling of equipment (Figure 10-11) with a hydraulic pressure system installed between the removable main frame and the mast is designed to extract the damaged portion by means of chains and clamps. It is often used for minor damages.

Being easily moveable, this equipment can easily set the traction direction to the damage input (Figure 10-12). Many units of this type, however, are able to pull only in one direction.

Rack Systems

Most rack systems have a pull or power tower or articulating arms that usually give the technician infinite positioning with complete freedom to pull from any angle, any height 360 degrees around the car. It is possible to make up pulls or down pulls (Figure 10-13). In fact, pulls can be made with the

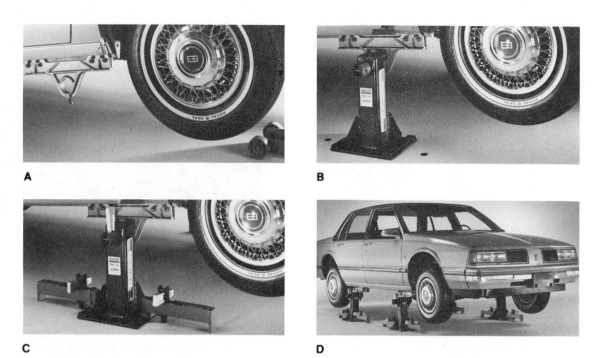

A

B

C

D

FIGURE 10-10   Steps to install a vehicle on the stands of a chainless anchoring system. *(Courtesy of Black-hawk Automotive Inc.)*

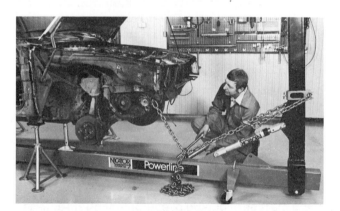

FIGURE 10-11   Typical body and frame puller at work. *(Courtesy of Nicator, Inc.)*

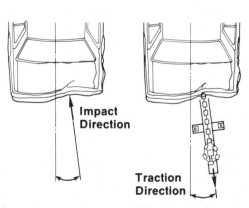

Impact Direction

Traction Direction

FIGURE 10-12   The portable body and frame puller can easily set the traction direction to the damage input. *(Courtesy of Nissan Motor Corp.)*

A

B

FIGURE 10-13   Many racks can make (A) pulls up or (B) pulls down. *(Courtesy of Kansas Jack, Inc.)*

FIGURE 10-14 Some racks can be positioned at full rack height, flush to the floor. *(Courtesy of Kansis Jack, Inc.)*

FIGURE 10-15 Many racks tilt hydraulically so that vehicles can either be driven on or pulled into position with a power winch, shown here. *(Courtesy of Kansas Jack, Inc.)*

FIGURE 10-16 Universal measuring systems can be used on most racks. *(Courtesy of Kansas Jack, Inc.)*

FIGURE 10-17 Typical fixed type alignment bench

rack positioned at full rack height, flush to the floor (Figure 10-14). Most racks tilt hydraulically so that vehicles can either be driven on or pulled into position with the optional power winch, shown in Figure 10-15. Most rack systems also provide an excellent measuring system (Figure 10-16).

Bench Systems

This type of equipment is used to correct the body and the frame on a bench. Alignment benches are available in two types, a fixed type (Figure 10-17) and a moveable type.

To set up a portable alignment bench such as shown in Figure 10-18, proceed as follows:

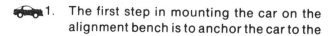 1. The first step in mounting the car on the alignment bench is to anchor the car to the

FIGURE 10-18 Portable or moveable type alignment bench. *(Courtesy of Nicator, Inc.)*

A

B

C

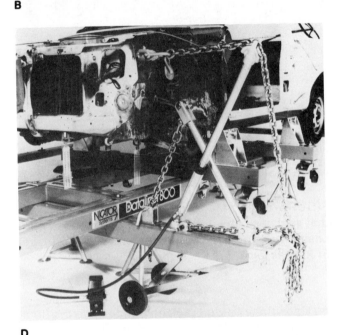

D

FIGURE 10-19 Set-up procedures for alignment on a typical portable bench. *(Courtesy of Nicator, Inc.)*

transport beams. Using a service jack, first lift the front end of the car, roll the transport beams under the car, adjust the chassis brackets, and attach them to the pinch weld of the sill. Tighten the bracket bolts (Figure 10-19A). Lift the end of the car that has the largest overhang in relation to the axles.

2. Perform the corresponding operation for the other end of the car and then ensure that all chassis brackets are fixed tight. As the transport beam and the main frame are both fitted with wheels, the vehicle can now roll to the workplace (Figure 10-19B).

3. Place the jack on the jack attachment under the car. When the frame is raised to meet the transport beams, attach the beam nearest the jack to the frame with a bolt (Figure 10-19C). Continue raising the frame until a suitable working height has been attained and then place the axle stand under the frame. Perform the corresponding operation at the other end, place the remaining bolts in position and tighten.

4. When making a pull, the aligners or rams are mounted on an aligning beam with wheels that are rolled into the desired posi-

tion and bolted in place. The direction of the beam determines the direction of the pull. If, for example, pulling sideways, position the aligning beam at right angles to the main frame (Figure 10–19D).

Another popular bench system shown in Figure 10-20 employs a two part arrangement consisting of the floor anchoring and pulling system (either an anchor pot or modular rail frame type) plus a bench. That is, a floor/bench alignment arrangement offers the best of two aligning systems. Often called a dedicated bench/fixture system, it is discussed in Chapter 9.

Before putting the car on any bench, there are several things that should be done to make the most effective use of the bench. These include preparation of the car and bench itself. One of the most important things to do is to visually determine the degree of damage and begin making a plan for the way to repair it.

As a general rule, a bench system should be used whenever the damage involves the suspension, steering, or powertrain mounting points. This, of course, would include situations such as a side collision where the suspension components and their mountings are not damaged directly, but because of deformation in the center section of the car's structure, the whole body is out of alignment. Determine whether a particular collision meets this rule either by eye, where there is obvious damage, or by making some general measurements with a tape measure or tram gauge. These would include diagonal measurements to check for diamond and length measurements to check for mash. Try to get as good an idea as possible of where the damage begins and ends. Use all the dimension data available, including body/frame dimension books, car manufacturer's manuals, or by checking against an undamaged car. Remember that these are general measurements to help determine whether to use the bench/fixture system and do not have to be made as accurately as when actually straightening the car.

As mentioned in Chapter 9, fixtures (Figure 10-21) are an important component of many bench systems. Using the fixture set-up diagram (Figure 10-22), set the remaining fixtures in place on the

FIGURE 10-21 Fixtures in place on a typical bench. (Courtesy of Blackhawk Automotive Inc.)

FIGURE 10-20 Typical bench of a floor/bench system that is suitable to both types of in-floor anchoring. (Courtesy of Blackhawk Automotive Inc.)

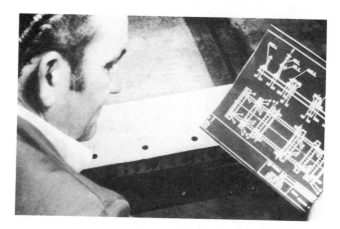

FIGURE 10-22 Referencing the fixture diagram. (Courtesy of Blackhawk Automotive Inc.)

FIGURE 10-23 Positioning the vehicle on the cross tube. *(Courtesy of Blackhawk Automotive Inc.)*

FIGURE 10-24 Attaching locating fixtures in place. *(Courtesy of Blackhawk Automotive Inc.)*

A

B

C

D

FIGURE 10-25 Procedure for fixture setup. *(Courtesy of Blackhawk Automotive Inc.)*

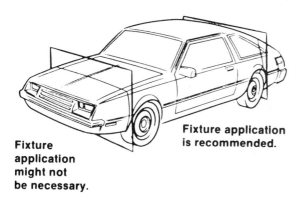

Fixture application might not be necessary.

Fixture application is recommended.

Fixture application might not be necessary.

FIGURE 10-26 Some areas of a car that might not need a fixture. *(Courtesy of Blackhawk Automotive Inc.)*

transverse beams in the damaged area of the car. If bolt-on fixtures are used, they can either be bolted to the car or set on the transverse beams.

It is necessary to have at least three control points on the undamaged part of the car that can be used to set the car up properly on the bench. These three locations will then form the datum plane on which all of the other measurements will be based. If there are more than three locations that are undamaged, they can also be used for setup. The fixtures chosen should require the minimum of disassembly of undamaged components.

For front damage, these set-up fixtures should be located in the center and rear of the car; and for rear damage, these fixtures should be located in the center and front of the car. The fixtures chosen and their location will depend both on the construction of the car and the location and degree of damage. As shown in Figure 10-23, some repair areas might not need fixtures.

In a situation where there are not three undamaged control points, such as a severe side impact, the bench system can still be used. In this case, it might be necessary to do some roughing of the underbody until three points can be secured. The roughing operation can take place on the bench. It might require some shifting of the car on the bench once the roughing operation is completed, however. It can also be done by using conventional measuring methods prior to installing the car on the bench.

Once the car is positioned on the cross tubes (Figure 10-23) and the bench slid under the vehicle, survey the damaged area and the positions of the fixtures to determine exactly the location, direction, and extent of the damage. Loosely attach the outer-

FIGURE 10-27 Pulling power is where it is needed on most bench and rack systems. As shown here the power tower can be used to even pull an engine. *(Courtesy of Kansas Jack, Inc.)*

most set-up fixtures to the proper location on the bench if they are bolt-on fixtures (Figure 10-24). Jack up the bench until the fixtures mate with the proper control point on the car and on the bench (Figure 10-25A). Continue jacking until the weight of the car is off the cross tubes. Remove the cross tubes, stands, and underbody clamps if they are used, and lower the car and bench. The next step is the engagement of the holding clamps with the pinch welds as shown in Figure 10-25B. Repeat the procedure at the opposite end and side of the vehicle and install the remaining set-up fixtures. The car will be set up as shown in Figure 10-25C. Once the body clamp and the chains are fastened in place on the bench (Figure 10-25D), the car is ready for pulling and other repairs. There are some areas of a car that might not need a fixture. These are shown in Figure 10-26.

Power or tilting towers can be installed as part of many bench and rack units. The towers can be positioned (360 degrees) anywhere around the bench or platform giving direct pulling power where needed (Figure 10-27). Like racks, most bench alignment equipment has provisions for body measuring.

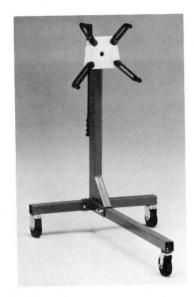

FIGURE 10-28 Engine stand holds the engine in place. *(Courtesy of Blackhawk Automotive Inc.)*

FIGURE 10-29 Typical portable pulling/pushing arm. *(Courtesy of Blackhawk Automotive Inc.)*

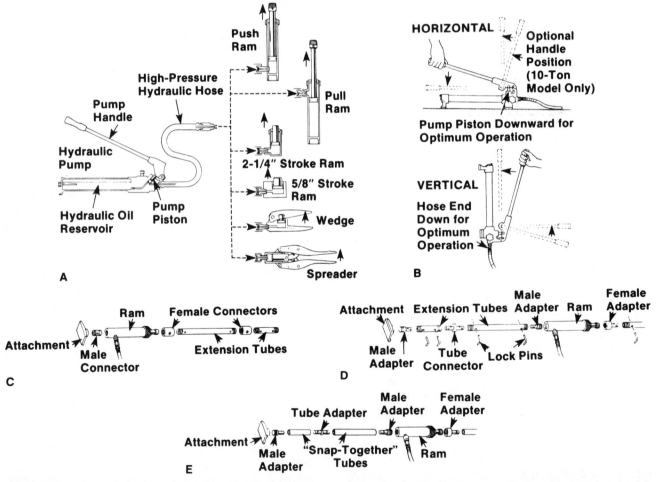

FIGURE 10-30 Major components of a portable hydraulic ram system: (A) the heart of the system—portable pump, high-pressure hydraulic hose and hydraulic ram, wedge, or spreader; (B) positioning and operation of the pump; (C) threaded connection; (D) quick-fitting connection; and (E) snap-together connection. The latter should not be used for pulling. *(Courtesy of Norco Industries, Inc.)*

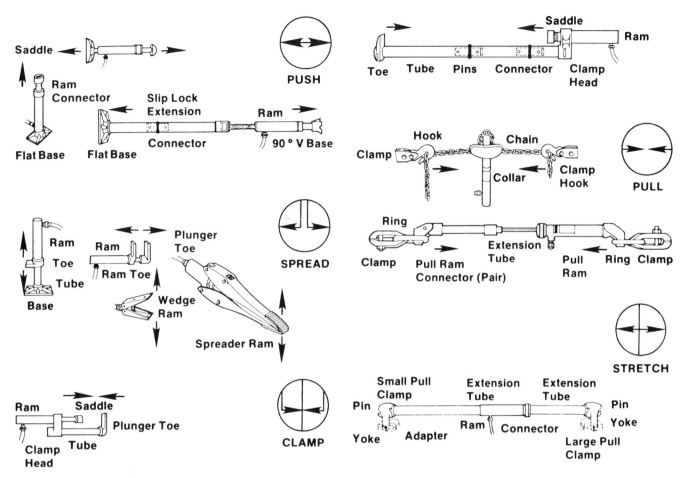

FIGURE 10-31 Basic ram system setup. The standard push, spread, clamp, pull, and stretch symbols tell the technician how each setup will work. *(Courtesy of Blackhawk Automotive Inc.)*

OTHER STRAIGHTENING ACCESSORIES

Two popular accessories that are often used with most alignment systems are the engine stand or holder (Figure 10-28) and a portable pulling or pushing arm (Figure 10-29). Whenever it is necessary to remove the engine or transmission mounts, the engine holder can be used to support the engine during the bench setup. It rests on the inner fenders and is adjustable in width. In the center is an adjustable chain hook that is used to hold the chain attached to the engine.

With a pulling/pushing arm, the unit can pivot completely around the end of the bench from the center position on the special flange. In the other positions, it can reach the end and one side of the bench. The unit can also be used anywhere along the side of the bench by hooking the inner clamp on the outer flange on the opposite side.

Portable hydraulic rams illustrated in Chapter 4 are possibly the most versatile of all aligning tools (Figure 10-30) since they can be used to push,

spread, clamp, pull, and stretch (Figure 10-31). Figure 10-32 summarizes the various applications of portable hydraulic equipment.

10.3 STRAIGHTENING AND REALIGNING TECHNIQUES

The body-on-frame car can usually be straightened and realigned with a series of single-direction pulls. Single, hard pulls in one direction were fairly effective for straightening in older cars. Overpulling or tearing metal was not a very big issue when body metal was 1/8- to 1/4-inch thick in various sections or panels of the vehicle. However, this is seldom the case when repairing modern cars, especially in unibody construction with its 24 gauge steel. Remember that a unibody vehicle is a more complex structure and has a greater tendency to spread collision forces throughout the car. Most unibody repairs demand multiple pulls, which sometimes means

327

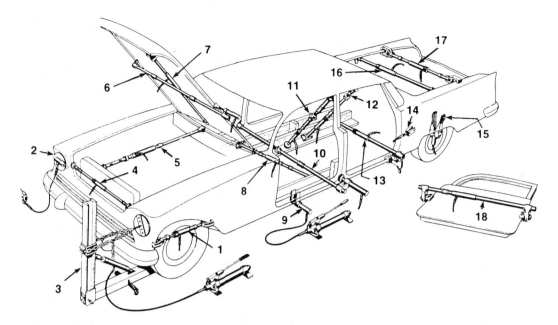

1. Light-duty pulling
2. Light-duty pushing
3. Dozer or tower pulling
4. Light-duty spreading
5. Standard (10 ton) pushing
6. Light-duty clamping

7. Light-duty pushing
8. Standard (10 ton) pushing
9. Standard (10 ton) spreading
10. Standard (10 ton) clamping
11. Standard (10 ton) pushing
12. Standard (10 ton) pushing

13. Standard (10 ton) pulling
14. Wedge spreading
15. Spreader ram spreading
16. Light-duty pushing
17. Light-duty pulling
18. Standard (10 ton) pulling

FIGURE 10-32 Summary of various body straightening operations that can be accomplished with a portable ram. (*Courtesy of Blackhawk Automotive Inc.*)

four or more pulling points and directions during a single straightening and alignment setup. The equipment must be able to do this, and also provide the special clamps that will prevent further damage of the structure during the pull. A single, hard pull in one direction on a unibody car can tear the metal before it is even straight.

The usual sequence for a total structure realignment procedure is:

 1. Understanding the safety considerations of the alignment equipment used
2. Damage analysis (this is fully covered in Chapter 9)
3. Initial clamping with alignment checks
4. Executing the planned pulling sequences with additional clamping and alignment checks

10.4 ALIGNMENT SAFETY CONSIDERATIONS

When using aligning equipment, inadequate attention to any of the prescribed rules given here or other incorrect use can result in material and/or serious physical damage:

- Be sure to use the alignment equipment correctly according to the instruction manual prepared by the manufacturer.
- Never allow unskilled or improperly trained personnel to operate aligning equipment.
- Make sure the rocker panel pinch welds and chassis clamp teeth are tight.
- Always anchor the vehicle securely before making a pull. Check that the chassis clamps and anchor bolts are tightened.
- Always use the size and grade (alloy) chain recommended for pulling and anchoring. Use only the chain supplied with the aligning equipment.
- Drawing chains must be positively attached to the vehicle and/or anchoring locations so that they will not come off during the pulling operation. Avoid placing chains around sharp corners.
- Before powerful side pulls are executed, apply counter supports to prevent pulling the vehicle off the bench.
- Never use a service jack for supporting the vehicle while working on or under it.
- Always use car stands for supporting the vehicle. Use only the stands recommended for the aligning equipment.

- A pull clamp can always slip and cause sheet metal tear. Prevent bodily harm and material damage by always using safety wires.
- Never stand in line with a chain or clamp. Chain breakage, clamp slippage, or sheet metal tearing could cause injury or damage. Remember it can be dangerous to work inside the vehicle at the same time pulls are being made outside.
- Cover pulling chains with a heavy blanket. If a chain breaks, this will keep the chain from being thrown across the shop.

WARNING: Failure to observe any of these precautions or other unsafe use might result in property damage and/or serious personal injury.

Before doing any pulling work, protect the body and externally attached parts as follows:

- Remove or cover interior components (seats, instruments, carpet).
- When welding, cover glasses, seats, instruments, and carpet with a heat-resistant material. (This protection is necessary especially when MIG welding.)
- When removing external parts (moldings and finishers) attached to the body, apply cloth or protection tape to the body to prevent scratching.
- If the painted surface is scratched, be sure to repair that portion: even a small flaw in the painted surface might cause corrosion.

10.5 PLANNING COLLISION REPAIR PROCEDURES

Before attempting any repair work, determine exactly the collision procedure that should be taken. The first step in this procedure is a damage analysis as discussed in Chapter 9. A little extra time spent on such an analysis and operational plan can save many hours in the overall repair procedure.

Unless the damage is really limited to minor cosmetic outer sheet metal, chances are good that parts will have to be removed before pulling can be started. This might be necessary because the unibody's structure tends to spread into remote and often unexpected places, some of which might be hidden behind these parts or systems. In most cases, it is not necessary to remove the sheet metal from the body-over-frame vehicle, except for repair. The technique of removing sheet metal structural panels from a vehicle is fully detailed in Chapter 11.

A general rule to follow when disassembling a car is: Disassemble only those components that must be removed to get to the area of the car being repaired. At one time, it was considered almost automatic to remove the suspension and drive line completely from a unibody car before putting it on the bench. With most of the current fixtures available, and such accessories as the engine holder, this is no longer necessary. Depending on the construction of the car and the location and degree of damage, there will be cases where it will be more convenient to remove these components before proceeding with the repair. Carefully analyze the vehicle and the damage to determine what must be removed. It is sometimes best to remove those components before putting the car on the bench since better access to the fasteners and other attachments is usually available. More components will have to be disassembled when replacing structural members than when using the bench only to straighten those members. Take the time to carefully study the locations of engine and transmission mounts, suspension mounts, and whether or not these components themselves are damaged. Figure 10-33 shows the front suspension cross member removed prior to installing the car on the bench. In most cases these components can be removed as a unit, which reduces the amount of time required for disassembly. Full details on the removal and repair of the vehicle's mechanical components are given in Chapter 12.

When it is determined how far the damage traveled in the unibody structure, and it is fully identified, the damaged area can be pulled and straightened. The corrected control points provide a larger reference for subsequent pulls.

FIGURE 10-33 Front suspension removed

In planning the repair (pulling) sequence, remember the two basic guides to assure that misalignment and damage will be corrected with minimum metalworking and without further damage to the structure.

- Repair the damage in the reverse (first-in, last-out) sequence in which it occurred during the collision.
- Plan the pulling sequence with the pulls in the opposite direction from those that caused the damage.

INITIAL CLAMPING WITH ALIGNMENT CHECKS

There are two pulling systems:

- **Single-pull systems.** A single-pull system (Figure 10-34) is capable of making a single, very directional pull on the damaged area of a vehicle. These systems are effective and will continue to be effective on primary damage on frame-type cars. They do not, however, supply the ability to hold an undamaged or a corrected control dimension while pulling to correct other damaged areas of the car. Other devices must be used to provide the hold capability when making these single, very directional pulls.
- **Multiple-pull systems.** Multiple-pull systems allow hold and pull or bi-directional pull cap-

ability that is often required in correcting secondary damage in unibody cars. Multiple-pull systems, when used, provide the ability to exert a great deal of control over any pulling, improving the precision with which a pull can be made. They also eliminate the need for disconnecting and moving the power posts.

The multiple-pull approach (Figure 10-35) accomplishes these objectives:

- The exact desired direction of pull can easily be achieved from three or four points at one time. This gives the control needed in the repair of modern construction.
- The use of multiple pull points reduces considerably the amount of force required at any single point, thus reducing risk of tearing the new lightweight metals. Due to the design of today's cars, in many cases there simply is not enough material available in any one place to attach to in order to transmit sufficient force to complete a repair. Again, as in the anchoring system, the pull load must be distributed through several attaching points.

A frame type car can be anchored by placing a suitable plug hook in the fixture holes located on the bottom of the frame rail. Blocking should be used to keep the hook in line with the frame rail. If a hard pull

FIGURE 10-34 Single-pull approach. (Courtesy of Nicator, Inc.)

FIGURE 10-35 Multiple-pull approach. (Courtesy of Nicator, Inc.)

FIGURE 10-36 Engagement of clamps with pinch welds. *(Courtesy of Blackhawk Automotive Inc.)*

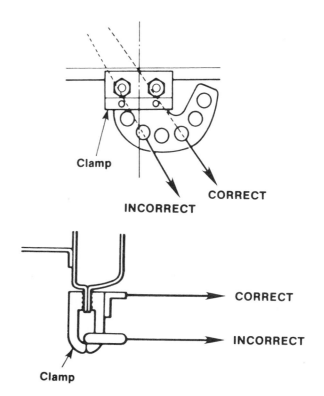

FIGURE 10-38 Right and wrong way to set clamps. *(Courtesy of Toyota Motor Corp.)*

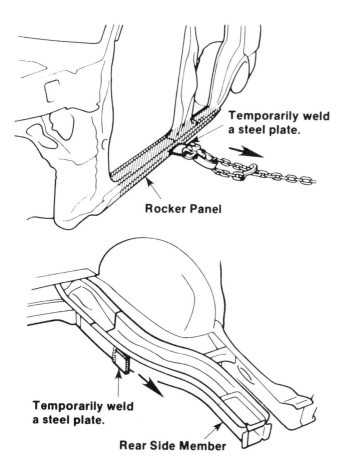

FIGURE 10-37 Examples of welding a temporary metal plate. *(Courtesy of Toyota Motor Corp.)*

is to be made, it is advisable to weld a washer around the hole as a reinforcement. Make an identical hookup on both sides of the vehicle.

A unibody car should be anchored by attaching pinch weld clamps and cross bar as shown (Figure 10-36). To hold the car down and remove slack, pass the chain under the hold down.

When anchoring the car in preparation for pulling, lean toward "over anchoring" or "over clamping." An extra anchor point or two takes very little time and surely cannot hurt anything. But it does little good, of course, to attach a pulling clamp to an area where pulling effect is not needed. However, there are many cases where a clamp cannot be fastened to the exact area of deformation. In such a case, a piece of steel can be temporarily welded to the section (Figure 10-37). After repairs are completed, remove the temporary piece of steel.

It is necessary to set the pulling clamp so that the line extending along the path of the pulling force passes through the middle of the teeth of the clamp. If this is not done, rotational force will act on the clamp to pull it off, further damaging the section (Figure 10-38).

When hooking up to make a pull on a unibody vehicle, consider these pointers:

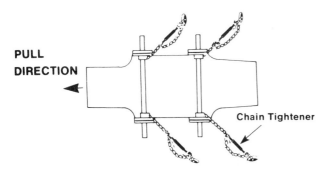

PULL
DIRECTION

Chain Tightener

FIGURE 10-39 Four point anchoring. *(Courtesy of Blackhawk Automotive Inc.)*

- The unitized body has made multiple anchoring a must (Figure 10-39). At least four anchors are required, one on each of the body clamps. Depending on the vehicle construction, additional anchoring might be required.
- Always look for the possibility of more than one hookup for both damage correction and restraints. Twin pulls and/or restraints allow twice the pull potential with less damage being caused at the points of attachment.
- Use multiple hookups on structural members and on sheet metal sections to be worked since today's metals will shift, shrink, and stretch quite readily. This is why an incorrect (too localized) pull can put more damage into a segment than it removes.
- Always install additional security chain or chains to a substantial member on the vehicle chassis.
- Treat each damaged area as individually as possible since the cars of today are manufactured for isolated collapse upon impact.
- Carefully observe the "last-in, first-out" rule in areas of primary as well as secondary damage. This principle can be occasionally violated for initial pulls, but nearly always holds true in the "fine tuning" phases of unibody alignment.
- Use imagination in utilizing available clamps for multiple hookups, including the shaping of straps and other attaching devices.

EXECUTING A PLANNED PULLING SEQUENCE

As mentioned earlier, the overall pulling sequences should be preplanned, but determining the proper attachment points and pulling directions should be fine tuned and evaluated by noting the amount of displacement and its direction of the alignment reference points. The progress toward alignment should be monitored during the pull. Since the body (sheet metal) has elasticity, the structure will partially return to its post damaged condition (to a certain extent) even if the body is pulled back to the prescribed dimensions. Therefore, estimate the amount of return in advance and make allowance for it during the pulling operations.

The pull procedure or sequence simply consists of solving a variety of small problems rolled into one. Find your first problem, and begin working on it. Then move to the next problem and so on.

Because of the power of the rams, the metal will begin moving as soon as the chain slack is taken up. There is no need to worry whether or not the ram has the capability to move the metal—it always will. This frees up the technician to concentrate on the straightening problem.

Simply make the pulls a little at a time, relieve the stress, take a measurement, or, in the case of the bench, check how close the fixtures are to their corresponding control points on the body, and start the sequence again. Work from the center section outward achieving first,

1. Length, then
2. Sidesway removal, and finally
3. Correct height.

The most effective way to perform the pull procedure is to approach the operation as though it was going to be done with bare hands. That is, determine how the metal should be moved to mold it back into shape if the only tools available were hands. How many areas could be moved at one time and in which directions? This is the key to effective pulling.

There are a number of setups for use with this system when pulling or pushing. The pulling arrangement with the vector system is determined by a simple triangle. The setup shown in Figure 10-40 is used for pulling up and out. The ram, the base unit, and the chain form the triangle. As the ram is extended, one side of the triangle becomes longer than it was before. This causes the ram to swing to the right because the chain is locked to the ram. As it swings to its new position, the damaged vehicle is pulled upward and over. This simple procedure is based on the principle of vectors. Tremendous forces can be exerted in a carefully planned direction using this principle.

Figure 10-41 shows a triangular arrangement that will provide more of a straight out pull. Note that the ram is placed at an angle to the right of true vertical. As force is applied, the ram will swing to the right pulling the damaged car sections with it. The

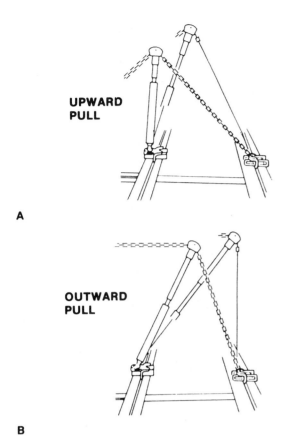

UPWARD PULL

A

OUTWARD PULL

B

FIGURE 10-40 Pulling (A) upward and (B) outward. *(Courtesy of Blackhawk Automotive Inc.)*

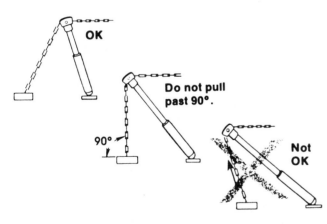

OK

Do not pull past 90°.

90°

Not OK

FIGURE 10-41 Triangular arrangement for more straight out pull. *(Courtesy of Blackhawk Automotive Inc.)*

metal will be pulled outward. It is important that the ram is at the proper height. This can be controlled by adding the proper length of tubing to arrive at the correct height before the hookup is finished. It must be noted that at no time should pulling continue if the chain between the ram and the anchor goes

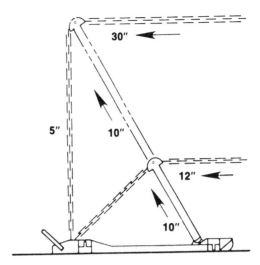

30"

5" 10"

12"

10"

FIGURE 10-42 The vector type pull. *(Courtesy of Blackhawk Automotive Inc.)*

beyond perpendicular. If this condition should occur, the possibility of overloading a chain could occur because of the added stress placed on the anchored end of the chain. To avoid this condition, be sure that the chain lockhead is not placed behind the chain anchor.

By setting up the equipment as designed, the vector system will provide strong pull capabilities at frame horn height and allow 10 inches of chain travel in one continuous pull (Figure 10-42). As higher, longer pulls are needed, the vector system automatically trades power for motion and allows as much as 44 inches of chain travel in one continuous pull. The system can easily pull up, out, or down. These pulls are accomplished by controlling the angle of the ram and by adjusting the length of the tubing used with the ram.

In a typical pull setup at frame rail height, the power ram is set so that the angle between the ram and the pulling chain is equal to the angle between the ram and the anchor (Figure 10-43). With approximately 10 tons of force and 10 inches of pulling chain travel available, there is ample power and chain travel for the lower tough structure pulls.

As the pulls move higher, part of the power available is converted to longer pull chain travel (Figure 10-44). For example, at roof rail height 10 tons of force are not needed to position a top section, but more than 10 inches of continuous pull chain travel might be needed to get it into proper alignment with one setup. In a typical roof rail height pull, approximately 33 inches of continuous pull is usually available automatically. This saves set-up

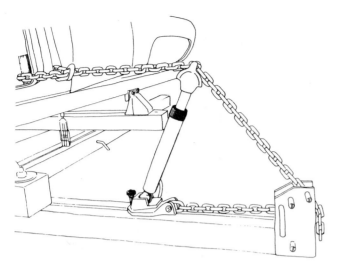

FIGURE 10-43   Lower structure pull. (Courtesy of Nicator, Inc.)

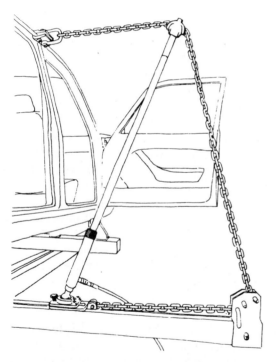

FIGURE 10-44   Typical roof rail height pulls. (Courtesy of Nicator, Inc.)

time and speeds the repair procedure. Again, the mathematical principle involved is the vector principle.

There are other basic single-pull setups when using a ram such as:

- For a high pull, more tubing is required. For an out and down pull (Figure 10-45A) less tubing is needed. Another way to make a

down pull is to attach a chain between the car and floor anchors. By pulling on the chain bridge, the car is forced down (Figure 10-45B).

- A horizontal pull on a rail (Figure 10-45C) can be accomplished by placing the ram at about a 45-degree angle.
- By adding tubing to the ram, a straight out pull on the cowl can be accomplished (Figure 10-45D).
- To pull straight out at the roof line, use the ram with extension tubes as shown in Figure 10-45E.
- Upward pulls are very easy to set up (Figure 10-45F). In most cases, the ram is in a vertical position. This pull setup will produce an upward and slightly outward pull.
- The same type of setup can be used at roof height by adding extensions to the ram (Figure 10-45G).
- Although pushing is not used to the extent it once was in collision damage repair, the capability to push is still important (Figure 10-45H). The vector system provides push capability from any angle around the car by means of a simple triangular setup.
- It is also possible to push from underneath the car at whatever angle that is needed (Figure 10-46A). This push setup can be used to effectively remove sag at the cowl area (Figure 10-46B).
- In most situations, more than one pull will be needed to effectively repair the car for a variety of reasons. Some important multiple pull setups will be discussed later in this chapter.

Due to the high-strength (and, in some cases, heat-sensitive) characteristics of the unibody structure and use, it is usually best not to attempt to make an alignment or straightening pull in one step. Instead, use a sequence that consists of a pull...hold the pull...more pull... hold, and so on. This will allow more time for working the metal, allow the metal more time to relax, and allow more time for checking the progress of alignment (for clamping, repair or reattachment by welding, and so on). That is, start the hydraulics moving, slowly and carefully. Watch the movement closely. Is it doing what it is suppose to do? If it is on the right track, keep on going. If not, determine why and make the angle or direction adjustment and try again. Relieve the stressed or locked-up metal by hammering just as described in Chapter 7. Pull the damaged metal to tension, then loosen it up with hammering. Increase the tension

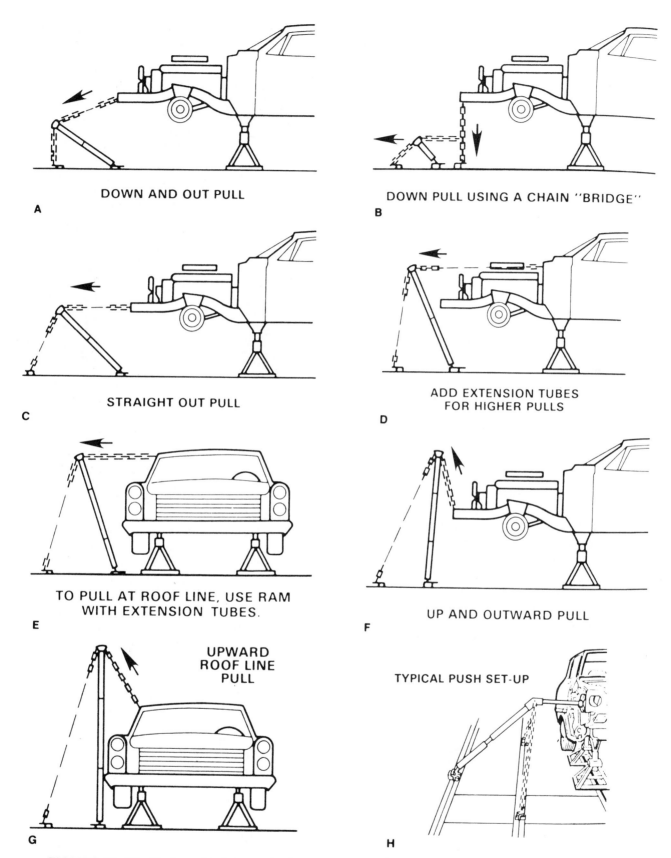

DOWN AND OUT PULL

A

DOWN PULL USING A CHAIN "BRIDGE"

B

STRAIGHT OUT PULL

C

ADD EXTENSION TUBES
FOR HIGHER PULLS

D

TO PULL AT ROOF LINE, USE RAM
WITH EXTENSION TUBES.

E

UP AND OUTWARD PULL

F

UPWARD
ROOF LINE
PULL

G

TYPICAL PUSH SET-UP

H

FIGURE 10-45   Various basic ram single pull setups. *(Courtesy of Blackhawk Automotive Inc.)*

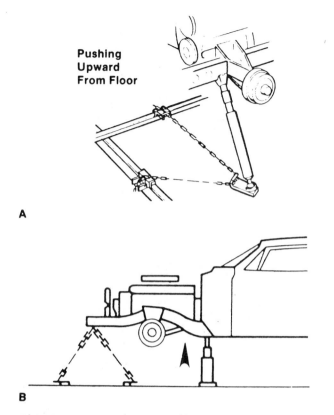

Pushing Upward From Floor

A

B

FIGURE 10-46   Two pushing ram setups. *(Courtesy of Blackhawk Automotive Inc.)*

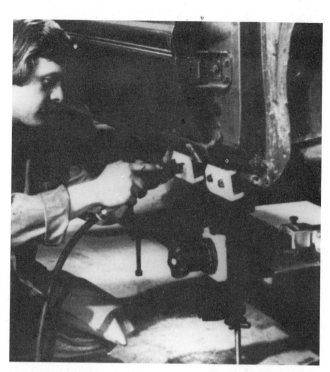

FIGURE 10-47   Attaching additional clamps where needed. *(Courtesy of Blackhawk Automotive Inc.)*

and loosen it again. If the lock-up is not sure, shake it a little with the hammer anyway.

Although these structures are extremely strong in the direction of their design loads, a thin-gauge pulling clamp can still overstress and damage the area where it is attached. It might be a good idea to distribute the load over more of the structure with additional clamps (Figure 10-47).

When using fixtures, begin the pulling operation and straighten the car from the center section outward. As each control point lines up with its fixture without pressure, bolt the fixtures and transverse beams securely in place. Change the angle and location of the pulls as necessary to complete the straightening operation. In the beginning, as already mentioned, apply the pulling force intermittently while checking the movement of the panel and confirming that the force is working effectively on the damaged area. If no effect can be seen, consider changing the pulling direction or the area being pulled.

The repair of a bent closed cross sectional structure such as a side member is done by clamping the surface of the bent-in side and pulling. The pulling direction should be such that force is applied in the direction of an imaginary straight line extend-

ing through the original position of the part. Also, the dented portion of the part can be repaired by welding studs and pulling it with a sliding hammer, or other pulling device, and so on (see Chapter 7).

If some of the buckles are folded so tightly that they threaten to tear, it might be necessary to use a little heat. However, use heat carefully and only on the corners and double panels where the strength is. Heat on a low spot in the side of a frame rail, or box section on unitized, will only drive it deeper. Use heat carefully and as a means of releasing locked-up metal and not as a means to soften up an area. Although a heat torch is not recommended on HSS metals, it can sometimes be used with care as described in Chapter 6.

By bringing the damaged metal back into dimension and shape slowly and carefully, and applying tension in the places and direction desired, while relieving the lock from the bent metal, a first-class solid and safe repair is easy. Although there will be exceptions, a good rule-of-thumb to follow generally is: Concern oneself with achieving length, sidesway, and height, in that order.

Overpulling

Overpulling (Figure 10-48) might not be a correctable error when failing to measure accurately and/or failing to measure often. To prevent overpull damage on unibody cars using any type of pulling equipment, measure the progress when pulling the damaged area. Remember that it is possible to pull a piece of string into a straight line, but there is no way to push it straight. On any damaged metal pulled or stretched beyond the critical control dimension, it is difficult to shrink or compress it. In most instances, the only way the overpulled panel can be repaired is by replacement.

Aligning Front End Damage

The general repair method for front end damage is best covered by going through a typical example of front end collision damage (Figure 10-49) and the replacement of a front cross member, front fender apron on one side, side member, as well as repairs to the front fender on the opposite side, front fender apron, and side member. It is important to begin the repair by restoring the front fender apron and side member to their predamaged condition and to repair the support structure on the replacement side (Figure 10-50).

First, pull the side member on the replacement side in the direction opposite to the impact direction. Then repair the fender apron and side member on the repair side and at the same time repair the front

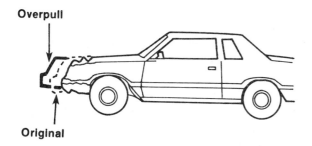

FIGURE 10-48   Example of overpulling

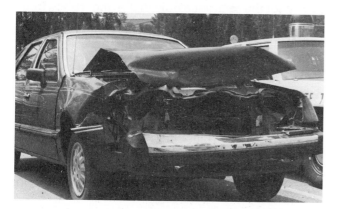

FIGURE 10-49   Example of front end damage

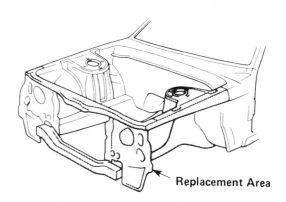

FIGURE 10-50   Restoring the front fender apron. *(Courtesy of Toyota Motor Corp.)*

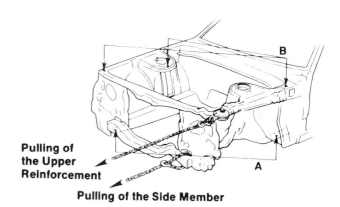

FIGURE 10-51   Checking the front dimensions. *(Courtesy of Toyota Motor Corp.)*

fender apron and side member installation areas on the replacement side. There are many cases where the entire fender apron or side member on the repair side is deflected left or right only. Since there is practically no warping in the lengthwise direction, repairs involve measuring the diagonal dimensions A and B, as shown in Figure 10-51 and correcting that distance while keeping an eye on the repair condition. The operation can be done efficiently if the fender apron upper reinforcement is pulled at the same time as the side member. Nylon pull straps are sometimes used on double pull hook-ups (Figure 10-52).

If there is severe bending damage to the side member on the repair side caused by pulling, separate the front cross member and radiator upper support at the point where the diagonal dimension is correct and repair them separately. Grip the inside broken face of the side member, and while pulling it forward, pull the broken piece from the inside or push it from the outside (Figure 10-53). After repairing the bent portion, match up the dimensions to the standard diagonal dimensions.

FIGURE 10-52   Use of nylon pull straps. *(Courtesy of Bee Line Co.)*

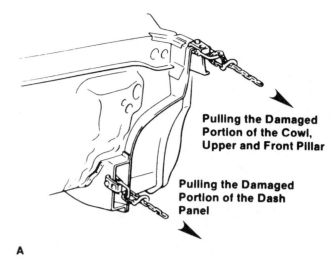

Pulling the Damaged Portion of the Cowl, Upper and Front Pillar

Pulling the Damaged Portion of the Dash Panel

A

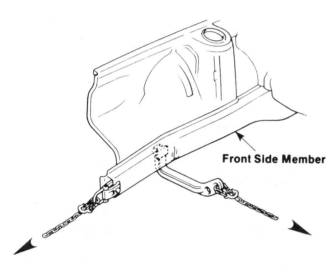

Front Side Member

FIGURE 10-53   Front side member bending repairs. *(Courtesy of Toyota Motor Corp.)*

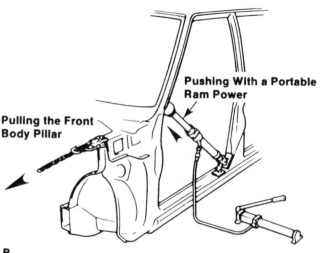

Pulling the Front Body Pillar

Pushing With a Portable Ram Power

B

FIGURE 10-54   Front pillar and dash panel repairs. *(Courtesy of Toyota Motor Corp.)*

To repair the replacement side front fender apron and side member installation area, the main repairs are near the dash panel and the cowl panel, but if the impact was severe, the damage will extend into the front body pillar (the door would fit poorly in this case). Simply gripping the front edge of the side member of the fender apron and pulling will not repair the major damage to the front body pillar or the dash panel (Figure 10-54A). In this case, cut the fender apron and side member near the installation area, clamp near the major panel damage, and pull (keep an eye on the door fit conditions). Good results can be obtained using this method. Also, at the

same time that the pillar is being pulled forward, pushing can be done from the interior side with a power ram (Figure 10-54B).

During body aligning, confirmation of the degree of restoration is made by measuring the dimensions, but the reference hole in the underbody front floor underreinforcement and the rear of the front fender installation hole are the standard reference points. Therefore, it is important if it can be confirmed at the time of the diagnosis that the damage does not extend to these areas (Figure 10-55). If the impact to the front side member structure, which is used particularly for FR vehicles is severe, there is a tendency for it to take the shape shown in Figure 10-56. The height of the standard measuring point might be distorted, so use caution during repair of this nature. Further, the front side member used in

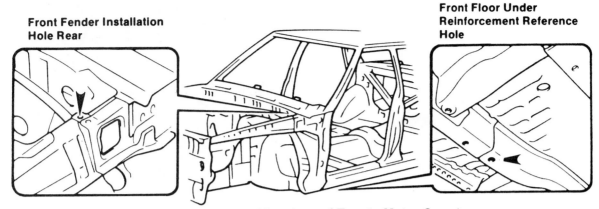

Front Fender Installation Hole Rear

Front Floor Under Reinforcement Reference Hole

FIGURE 10-55   Standard measuring points. (Courtesy of Toyota Motor Corp.)

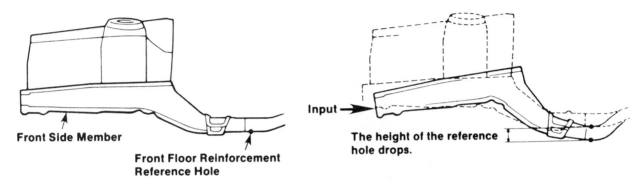

Front Side Member

Front Floor Reinforcement Reference Hole

Input →

The height of the reference hole drops.

FIGURE 10-56   Typical FR vehicle front side member damage. (Courtesy of Toyota Motor Corp.)

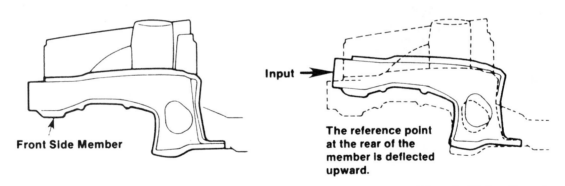

Front Side Member

Input →

The reference point at the rear of the member is deflected upward.

FIGURE 10-57   Typical FF vehicle front side member damage. (Courtesy of Toyota Motor Corp.)

FF vehicles has a reference point in the rear that has a tendency to be deflected upward when damaged (Figure 10–57).

To correct lateral bending damage of the front caused by side impact, frame straightening equipment (best results for this job are obtained with the bench or floor/bench type) is necessary. The clamping point (Figure 10–58) receiving the greatest force is point B, which must be clamped securely. If point C is not secured, point A cannot be pulled. If point C does not have a good clamping location, there is a method for fixing the body sill at four points with underbody clamps.

Rear Damage Vehicle Repairs

Since panel construction of the rear body is more complex when compared to the front body, the path of propagation from an impact is also more complex and the damage can be more extensive. Therefore, the damage diagnosis must be done ac-

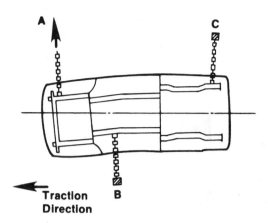

FIGURE 10-58 Correcting lateral bending damage. (Courtesy of Nissan Motor Corp.)

FIGURE 10-59 Typical rear end damage

FIGURE 10-60 Typical rear damage repair pulling setup. (Courtesy of Kansas Jack, Inc.)

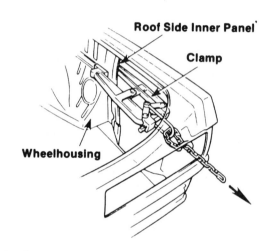

FIGURE 10-61 Rear quarter panel repair. (Courtesy of Toyota Motor Corp.)

curately. In most cases the bumper is impacted during rear end collisions (Figure 10-59) and the impact force will usually propagate through the rear ends of the rear side members or nearby panels and cause damage to the kick-up area. Next, the wheelhousings will deform causing the entire quarter panel to move forward causing clearance problems between other components. If the impact is severe enough, it will have an effect on the roof, door panels, and center body pillar. Attach clamps or hooks to the rear portion of the rear side member, rear floor pan, or quarter panel rear end portion and pull while measuring the dimensions of each part of the underbody and while determining the degree of repairs necessary by the conditions of panel fit and clearances (Figure 10-60).

Do not clamp and pull a quarter panel that has little or no strain on it when the rear side member is

pushed into the wheelhousing or there are clearance problems at the rear door. Relieve the stress in the quarter panel by pulling on the side member only. If the wheelhousing or the roof side inner panel is clamped and pulled along with the rear side member, the clearances with the door panel can be maintained properly (Figure 10-61).

Where there is rear structure twist from a front hit, the rear lower structure should be clamped to the repair bench. The preliminary pulling will restore some of the lower alignment points and clamps can be repositioned to preserve the alignment. Moving forward with subsequent pulls, the alignment and number of anchoring points will, of course, move right along with them.

Install upper structure alignment fixtures as soon as upper damage is reduced enough to permit their positioning. Also, sections too damaged for repairs and requiring replacement can be cut away at this time.

SIDE DAMAGE ALIGNING

If there is a severe impact to the center of the rocker panel, the floor pan will deform and the entire body will take on a curved shape like a banana. To align this type of damage, use a method similar to straightening a piece of bent wire. The two ends of the body are pulled apart and the side that is caved in is to be pulled outward (three-way pulling—Figure 10-62).

Anchoring unitized body vehicles for side pulls can be very difficult due to the limited chain hook-up areas. Figure 10-63 shows an anchoring method. Keep in mind when making a side pull on the end of a vehicle, the center section can be anchored by pass-

A

B

FIGURE 10-64   Tension/anchoring setup. *(Courtesy of Bee Line Co.)*

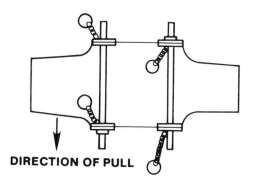

FIGURE 10-62   **For inside damage repairs, it might be necessary to pull in three directions.** *(Courtesy of Nissan Motor Corp.)*

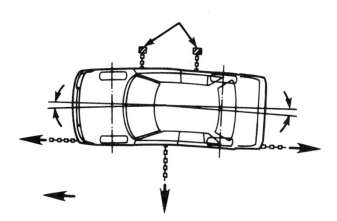

DIRECTION OF PULL

FIGURE 10-63   **Anchoring a side pull.** *(Courtesy of Blackhawk Automotive Inc.)*

ing a chain around the pinch weld clamp and hooking to the edge of the bench (Figure 10-64A). Tension/anchoring can be applied by attaching the pull chain to the pinch weld clamp (Figure 10-64B).

The portable beam and knee can be used as a side anchor with either inside or outside contact (Figure 10-65). By attaching the pull chain to the portable beam and knee, it can be used as a pulling attachment.

It is advisable to make an end-to-end stretch pull whenever pulling outward on the center section of a vehicle. If pulling high on the body, it will be necessary to tie the vehicle down on the opposite side (Figure 10-66). Pulling outward on the center section of the car can also be done with the portable beam and knee attached to the pulling tower or ram (Figure 10-67). The chain roller can be in the lowest position on the power tower.

A

B

FIGURE 10-65   Use of portable beam and knee. *(Courtesy of Bee Line Co.)*

FIGURE 10-66   Making an end-to-end stretch pull. *(Courtesy of Bee Line Co.)*

OTHER ALIGNMENT CORRECTIONS

There are other pull procedures that must be considered when repairing a vehicle. For example:

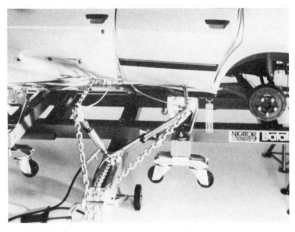

FIGURE 10-67   Pulling outward on the center section. *(Courtesy of Nicator, Inc.)*

FIGURE 10-68   Making upward pull. *(Courtesy of Bee Line Co.)*

- **Upward movement.** Pulling upward can be done by locking two power towers across from each other and connecting pull chains as shown (highest roller position) in Figure 10-68. A suitable sheet metal clamp is attached to the tower pull chains. Direction of the lift can be controlled by opening or closing pull ram valves. The vehicle must also be tied down to the platform or bench.

  Raising the vehicle can be done by positioning towers as shown in Figure 10-69. Wrap nylon straps or chain around the bumper or isolators or pass tower pull chains between the underbody and stabilizers.

- **Sag correction.** Blocking under the low area and pulling down on the high end with pulley and base will correct the datum line (Figure 10-70A). Vehicle must also be tied down to the platform or bench at the opposite end. Anchoring the high portion of the vehicle to

FIGURE 10-69   Raising the vehicle. *(Courtesy of Bee Line Co.)*

A

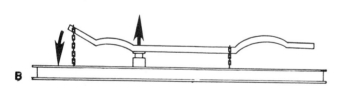

B

FIGURE 10-70   Correcting sag damage. *(Courtesy of Bee Line Co.)*

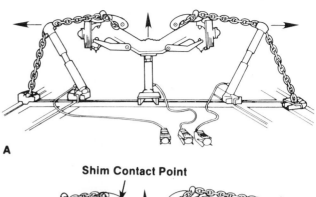

A

Shim Contact Point

B

Tram Gauge Measuring Points

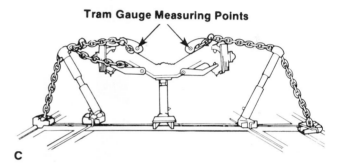

C

FIGURE 10-71   Correcting cross member sag. *(Courtesy of Blackhawk Automotive Inc.)*

the platform or bench with chains and pushing up at the low spot will also correct datum line (Figure 10–70B). When using the pulley and base for the downward pull, the tower pull chain must be in lowest position.

Sag can also occur at the front frame cross member. The ends of the cross member will be closer than normal and the center will be too low. This condition can be corrected by using three hydraulic rams and two chains plus anchoring rail or pots. The correcting hookup for sag on both sides of the cross member is shown in Figure 10–71A, while Figure 10–71B shows the hookup for sag at one side. Check the repair with a tram

gauge and compare the measurements to the specifications in the body manual or chart (Figure 10–71C).

• **Twist correction.** Position and lock a ram or tower on the side of the platform or bench next to the low side of the vehicle. With the tower chain in the highest position, route the chain under the lower horn (on isolator) and over the high horn and attach chain hook to outside edge of the platform bed (Figure 10–72). Make an identical hook-up at the opposite end of the vehicle or tie down and block under the center section of the vehicle. Apply pressure to the pull chain. An alternate method of correcting twist condition can be made by pulling down on the high side as described previously and blocking or lifting under the low side (Figure 10–73). The center section of vehicle should be blocked and tied down.

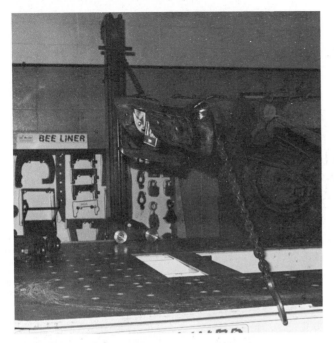

FIGURE 10-72 Correcting twist damage. *(Courtesy of Bee Line Co.)*

FIGURE 10-73 Alternate method of correcting twist damage. *(Courtesy of Bee Line Co.)*

- **Diamond correction.** Place a pulling tower or ram on each end of the bench base on opposite sides. Adjust chain height and attach to vehicle as described for end pull corrections. Block or anchor one side of vehicle to prevent sideward movement of vehicle (Figure 10-74). Activate the pull ram.

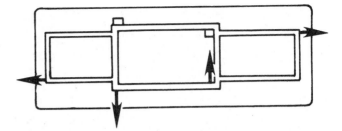

FIGURE 10-74 Correcting diamond damage

- **MacPherson pull.** To pull MacPherson strut tower into position, attach the pull plate to vehicle and connect tower pull chain (Figure 10-75). Most MacPherson adapter plates can also be used on frame horns, hinge mounts, or similar locations. If both towers are tipped left or right, they can be repositioned by mounting adapter plates to both towers and installing a strap to make the pull. After the pull is made, a dimension check should be performed using a MacPherson strut measuring gauge.

Correcting multiple damage conditions can be done by making any of the individual hook-ups in combination with each other (Figure 10-76). Other pull techniques are shown in the color section.

10.6 STRESS RELIEVING

The basic objective of the entire pull procedure is to work the damaged metal back to its original shape and, just as important, to its original state.

It is important to note that shape and state do not necessarily mean the same thing. Something can be manipulated back into its original shape, while its original state is nowhere close. There are two separate problems in the pulling procedure:

- Restoring the vehicle to its original shape.
- Relieving all the stress in the metal accumulated when its shape was distorted in the accident. This is called original state.

State means back to original form. Metal has a "memory" or elastic property, because it "knows" its original state and will be comfortable once it is returned to that condition. The job is to remove all the stress caused by the accident.

Unbent metal (Figure 10-77A) contains layers of grain or molecules all in a relatively relaxed state. As a piece of metal is bent (Figure 10-77B), these grains become slightly distorted, introducing stress.

WELDING AND STRUCTURAL SECTIONING EXAMPLES

1. A typical modern MIG welder

2. Grinding is a good way to clean a surface before welding

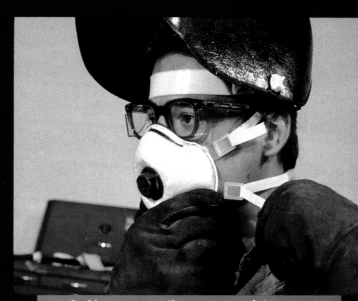

3. Always wear the proper safety gear

4. Welding gloves protect against sparks.

WELDING AND STRUCTURAL
SECTIONING EXAMPLES

5. MIG welding

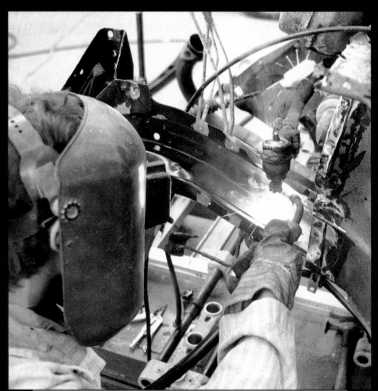

6. Making a spot weld with a MIG welder

7. The continuous weld is ground
away prior to finish grinding
for a smooth joint.

8. Making a horizontal weld

9. Overhead welding can be difficult

10. Some welds are in hard-to-reach places

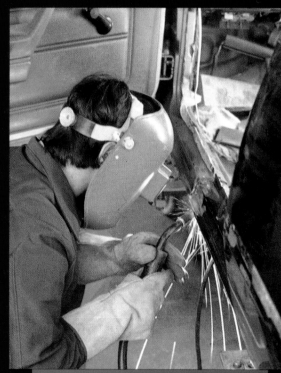

11. Welding a rocker panel

13. Two body sections ready to be...

STRUCTURAL SECTIONING

14. ...pulled together

15. Checking the fit of a quarter section

16. Cutting

STRUCTURAL SECTIONING

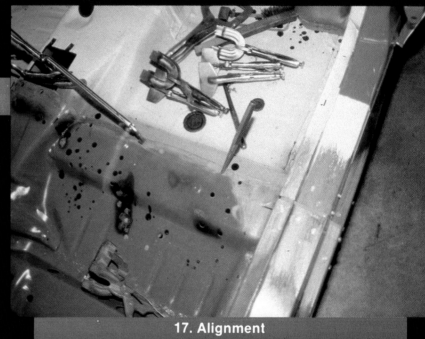

17. Alignment

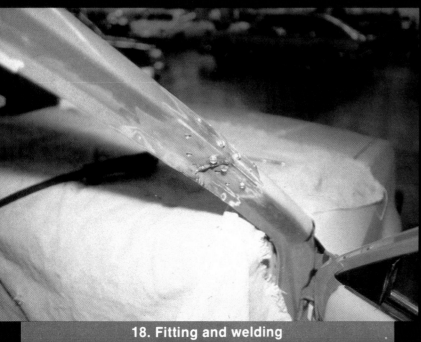

18. Fitting and welding

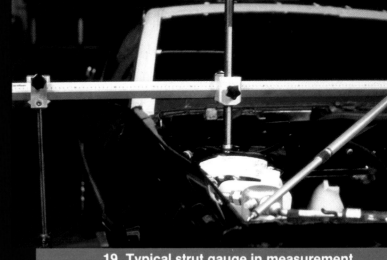

19. Typical strut gauge in measurement

MEASURING AND PULLING

20. Tram can be used for upper and lower body measurements

21. Typical laser measuring set-up

22. Making a single level, single pull

MEASURING AND PULLING

23. Making three forward pulls at two different levels

24. High level or roof pull

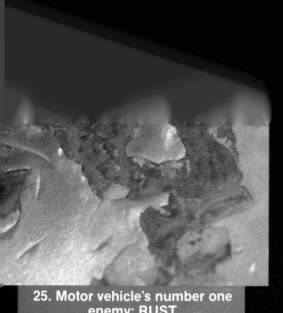

25. Motor vehicle's number one enemy: RUST

$$3Fe + 2O_2 = Fe_2O_3$$

IRON   OXYGEN   IRON OXIDE (RUST)

26. How rust is formed

RUST AND RUST PREVENTION

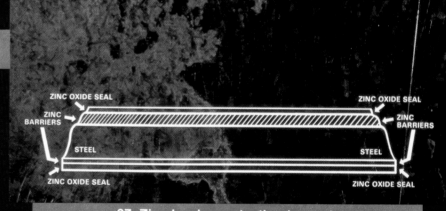

ZINC OXIDE SEAL

ZINC BARRIERS

STEEL

ZINC OXIDE SEAL

ZINC OXIDE SEAL

ZINC BARRIERS

STEEL

ZINC OXIDE SEAL

27. Zinc barrier protection is used by most auto manufacturers

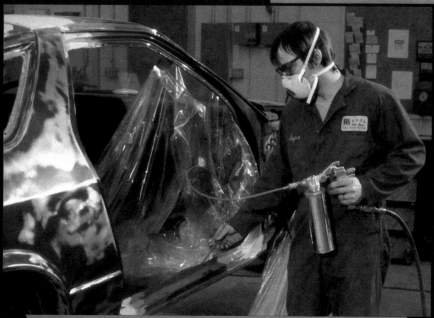

28. Corrosion protection must be restored to any sectioned areas

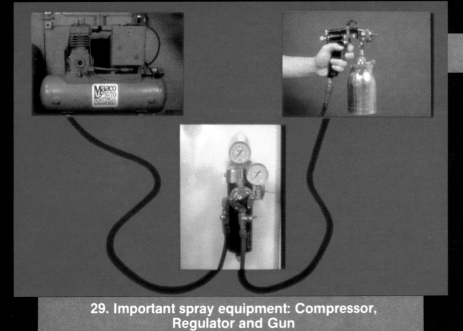

29. Important spray equipment: Compressor, Regulator and Gun

30. Easy way of determining the proper spray gun distance

31. Keep the gun parallel to the surface when spraying horizontally or downward

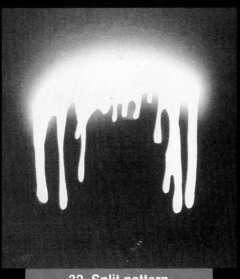

32. Split pattern

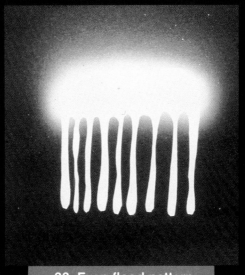

33. Even flood pattern

34. Heavy centered pattern

35. Small scratched and dented area

36. Sand and featheredge the damaged area

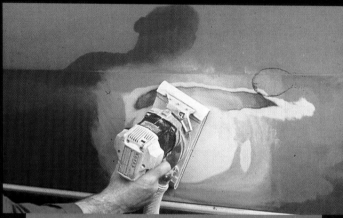

37. Sand the body filler with a flat sander or a sanding block.

38. After two or three coats of primer-surfacer have dried, wet-sand the surface

39. Applying the topcoat finish

40. The completed job

41. Degreasing the area around the damage

DENT AND DEEP SCRATCH PAINT REPAIRS

42. After sanding, fill with body filler. Avoid filling edges and scrape the outside edge away completely.

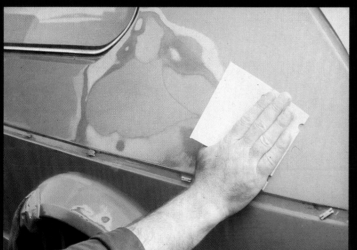

43. Dry sand the surface with a machine or by hand

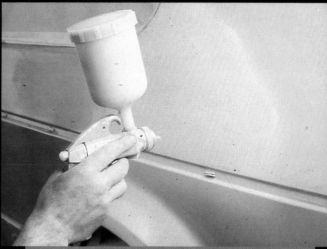

44. Mix with surface-filler and apply with a gravity feed spray gun

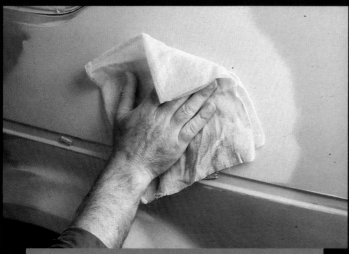

45. Remove the dirt with a tack rag. Keep the pressure light

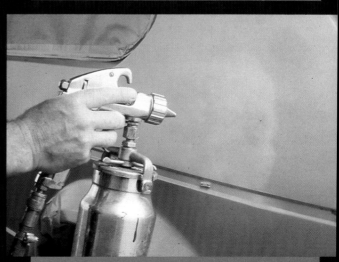

46. Spraying the topcoat

47. The new panel installed

NEW PANEL PAINTING

48. Remove transport primer, if required by panel manufacturer, with paint stripper and clean with scraper and strong solvent

49. Sand surface with #120 or #150 grit, then remove the dust

50. After degreasing, apply 2 or 3 medium coats of primer-surfacer

51. Give the primer-surfacer time to flash off.

52. Applying the final topcoat

53. An undamaged car or a car that has been repaired

54. Apply primer-surfacer or sealer on any spots that need it, then degrease the surface

A COMPLETE RE-SPRAY

55. Abrade the surface with fine or extra fine sandpaper and remove the dust with a tack rag

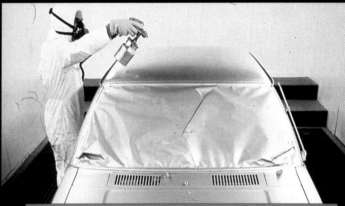
57. Applying the medium coat of sealer.

56. Mix sealer as directed on the container, using a marked measuring stick

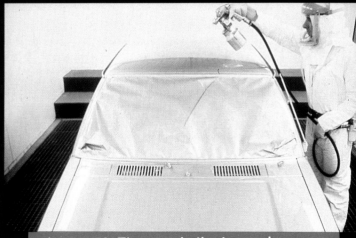
58. Then apply the topcoat.

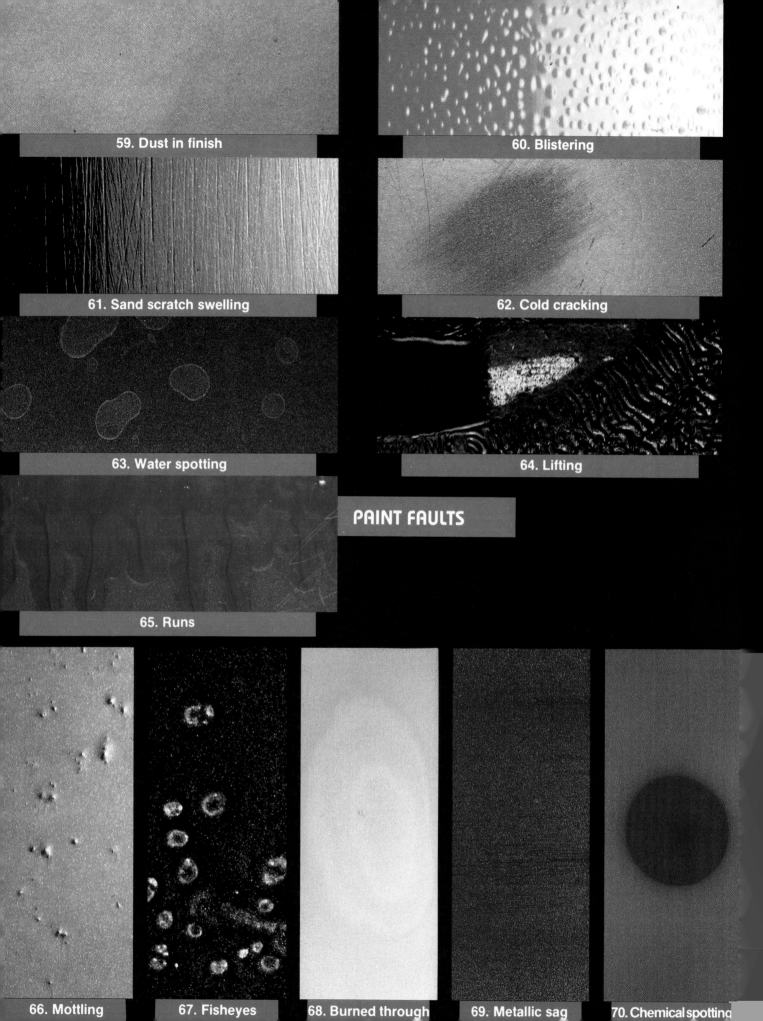

59. Dust in finish

60. Blistering

61. Sand scratch swelling

62. Cold cracking

63. Water spotting

64. Lifting

PAINT FAULTS

65. Runs

66. Mottling

67. Fisheyes

68. Burned through

69. Metallic sag

70. Chemical spotting

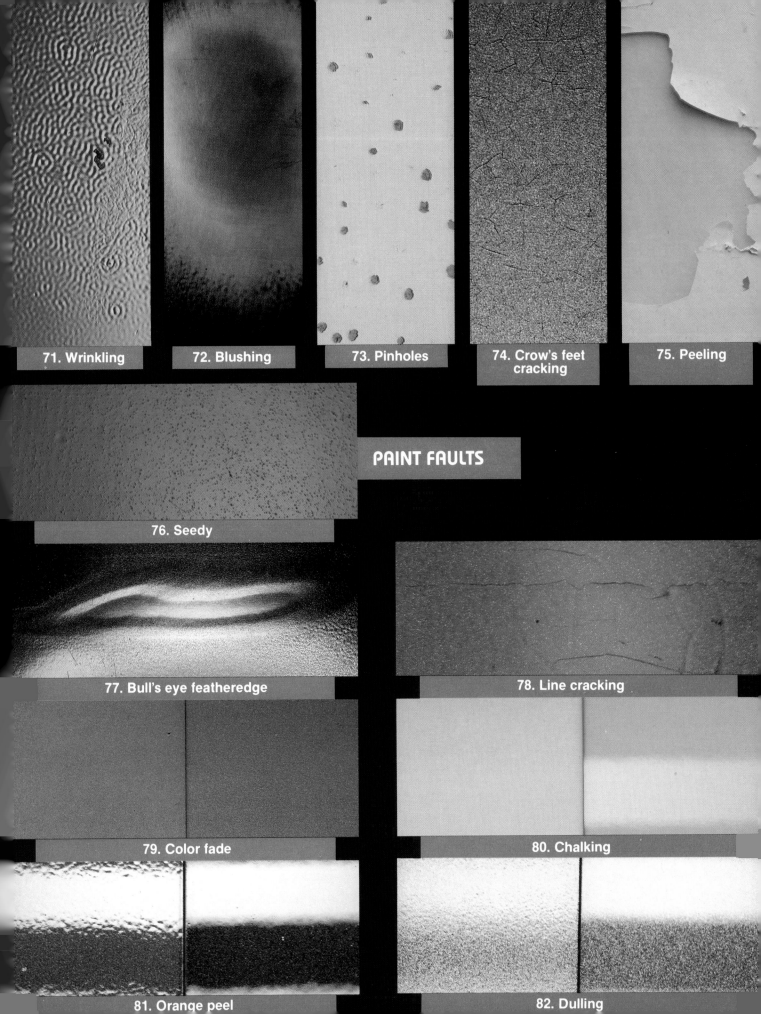

71. Wrinkling

72. Blushing

73. Pinholes

74. Crow's feet cracking

75. Peeling

PAINT FAULTS

76. Seedy

77. Bull's eye featheredge

78. Line cracking

79. Color fade

80. Chalking

81. Orange peel

82. Dulling

TINTING

BASE COLOR	ALUMINUM LETDOWN	MASS TONE	WHITE LETDOWN	BASE COLOR	ALUMINUM LETDOWN	MASS TONE	WHITE LETDOWN
1. Yellow Gold				15. Indo Orange			
2. Lt. Chrome Yellow	*Not to be used with Aluminum Letdown.*			16. Moly Orange (Red Shade)	*Not to be used with Aluminum Letdown.*		
3. Oxide Yellow				17. Red Oxide			
4. Indo Yellow				18. Transparent Red Oxide			
5. Transparent Yellow Oxide				19. Deep Violet			
6. Rich Brown				20. Quindo Violet			
7. Black				21. Magenta Maroon			
8. Strong Black				22. Phthalo Green (Yellow Shade)			
9. Organic Orange (Light)				23. Phthalo Green			
10. Oxide Red				24. Scarlet Red	*Not to be used with Aluminum Letdown.*		
11. Permanent Red				25. Perrindo Maroon			
12. Organic Scarlet				26. Phthalo Blue (Medium)			
13. Phthalo Blue (Green Shade)				27. Phthalo Green			
14. Permanent Blue				28. Phthalo Green (Yellow)			

FIGURE 10-75   MacPherson strut tower pull hook-up. *(Courtesy of Bee Line Co.)*

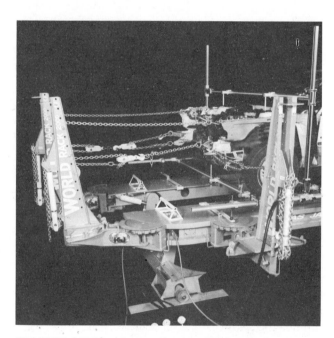

FIGURE 10-76   Correcting multiple damage conditions. *(Courtesy of Kansas Jack, Inc.)*

If a piece of metal is flexible enough once pressure is released, the grain will return to its original state. If the metal is bent too far, as in a collision, the grain on the outside of the bend is severely distorted by tension, while the grain of the inside is distorted by compression (Figure 10-77C). Because a large amount of stress is present, it will remain in this shape. If a pull allows these weak and rather beat up grains back into shape without thinking about state then the piece of metal will look like that shown in Figure 10-77D.

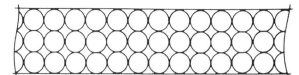

- Metal is unbent.
- Grain (molecules) is in a relaxed, comfortable state.

A

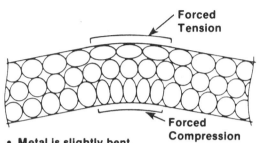

- Metal is slightly bent.
- Grain is forced to expand on outside of bend and compress on inside.
- If metal is flexible, grain will return to comfortable state.

B

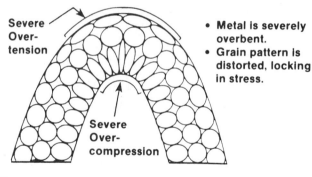

- Metal is severely overbent.
- Grain pattern is distorted, locking in stress.

C

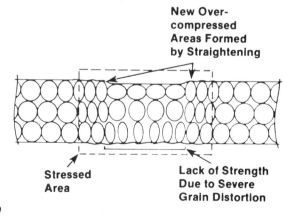

D

FIGURE 10-77   Condition of metal: (A) unbent, (B) slightly bent, (C) overbent, and (D) straightened (without relieving stress)

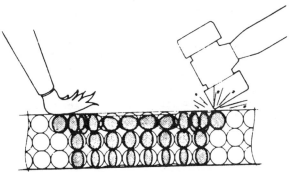

Grain begins to relax and return
to its original state relieving stress.

FIGURE 10-78 Methods of returning metal to a relaxed state

The shape is close to original, but the grains remain distorted and new areas of distortion are formed. The area was straightened but is much weaker than the original, but it can be saved (Figure 10-78). With the use of controlled heat (or no heat) and hammering, the grain can be revived and relaxed back to shape. Begin to add strength back into the metal, relieve the stress, get the metal back to as straight as possible, and, last and most important, have the metal stay where it is supposed to stay. This is original state.

Stress is defined in metallurgical books as the internal resistance a material offers to being deformed when subjected to a specific load (force). In the collision repair industry, stress can be defined as the internal resistance a material offers to corrective techniques. This resistance or stress can be caused by:

- Deformation
- Overheating
- Improper welding techniques
- Undesirable stress concentrations

Signs of stress/deformation (Figure 10-79) on unibody cars:

- Misaligned door, hood, trunk, and roof openings
- Dents and buckles in aprons and rails
- Misaligned suspension and motor mounts
- Damaged floor pans and rack and pinion mounts
- Cracked paint and undercoating
- Pulled or broken spot welds
- Split seams and seam sealer

Since the damaged area will frequently give greater resistance to alignment than adjacent areas, additional holds for clamping are sometimes re-

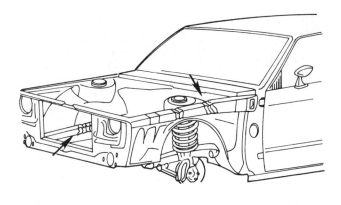

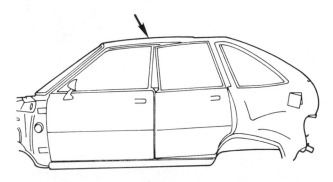

FIGURE 10-79 Signs of stress/deformation on unibody cars

quired; for example, a damaged rail with greater resistance to tension than where it usually attaches to the front cowl/bulkhead. By using a clamp, movement at the front cowl/bulkhead is prevented and corrective forces are applied directly to the rail. During the pulling operation, all critical control points must be measured to monitor direction and prevent overpulling.

Generally, if the strain generated from the propagation of an impact does not lead to buckling, effective pulling force during aligning will alleviate the problem. Use common sense while hammering to remove the strain in a panel or member. Overdoing it will lead to time-consuming surface smoothing operations later on. Use particular caution when pulling large panels such as roof panels that are easily strained when pulled. For example, while applying a backward pulling, use a spoon to press on the backside of the strained area (Figure 10-80).

Once the damage has been analyzed and the angle and direction of the pull decided upon, tension is applied and spring hammering is used to relieve the stress. Spring hammering is usually done with a spoon or a block of wood to distribute the force of the blow over a large area, releasing the tension and allowing the elasticity of the metal to return to its original size and shape. Spring hammering should

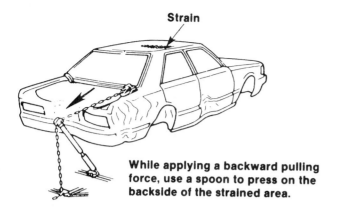

While applying a backward pulling force, use a spoon to press on the backside of the strained area.

FIGURE 10-80   Panel strain repair. *(Courtesy of Toyota Motor Corp.)*

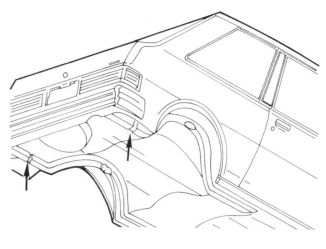

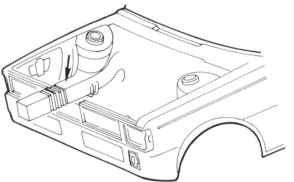

FIGURE 10-81   Stress concentrators

also be applied to areas adjacent to the major damage.

A dolly or 2- by 4-inch wood block and hammer as described in Chapter 7 will work out a lot of stress. Most of the stress relieving will be "cold work." Not much heat will be used. But if heat is needed, use it, but take care and control it.

Heating will usually result in a certain amount of oxidation or scaling and can also result in decarburization. Scaling represents a loss of metal and mars the surface finish. Decarburization results in a soft surface and can seriously affect the fatigue life. The amount of scaling is largely determined by the time and temperature of the heating operation. The scale will always be heavier on the backside of the heated piece than on the side exposed to the flame. The exposed side is protected from oxidation by the burning gas until the torch has been removed. But the backside is subjected to oxidation as soon as the proper temperature is reached. Each reheating of the same area causes more scaling.

If the damage requires the use of heat, follow the car manufacturer's recommendations to the letter. When using heat on a unibody rail, for example, heat only the corners of the rail. If heat is applied to a low spot in the center of the rail, drive it in deeper. Never attempt to cool the heated area by using water or compressed air. Allow it to cool naturally. Rapid cooling can cause the metal to become hard and, in some cases, brittle.

As mentioned in Chapter 6, the best way to monitor heat applications is with a heat crayon. Stroke or mark the cold piece with the crayon. When the stated temperature has been reached, the mark will liquify. Heat crayons are quite precise and far more accurate than the common body shop technique of watching for specific color change. There is a ±1% factor with a heat crayon.

Certain conditions or possible defects of a metal structure can reduce its strength. These conditions are called stress concentrators (Figure 10–81). Stress concentrators, as the name implies, result in a localized concentration of stress as a load is applied. Stress concentrators are designed into unibody vehicles to control and absorb collision forces, minimize structural damage, and increase occupant protection. Do not remove designed stress concentrators. Follow the car manufacturer's recommendations for straightening or replacement of parts that have designated stress concentrators.

A quality repair can be achieved only if function, durability, and appearance have been restored. When stress is not removed, the following possibilities can occur:

- Fatigue caused by loading and unloading of suspension and steering component.
- In the event of a second similar collision, less force is required to cause the same or greater damage and could jeopardize the occupants of the vehicle.
- The vehicle can dimensionally distort causing handling problems.

347

10.7 FINAL CONSIDERATION OF REALIGNMENT

The structural qualities of vehicle construction (especially unibody cars that include heat sensitive, thin gauge, high-strength parts) bring up questions about repairing or replacing severely damaged sections that cannot be restored by the pulling operations. The basic questions are:

- When should the repair or replacement be undertaken in relation to the pull—before, after, or during?
- What procedures and tools should be used to perform the repair or replacement?

The basic rule of thumb here is to make any and all repairs when part alignment permits. In other words, during the pulling, when the torn edges become butted or sheared spot welds move back and line up, that's the time to weld them. When buckled areas start to straighten, use the hammer.

Contrary to what some people think, this when-to-fix rule is not concerned because the damaged section forms a "weak link" in an interdependent unibody strength structure, a weak link that could overstress adjacent structures and possibly damage them further during the pulling operation.

In the beginning, apply the pulling force intermittently while checking the movement of the panel and confirming that the force is working effectively on the damaged area. If no effect can be seen, consider changing the pulling direction or the area being pulled.

Remember that pulling generates forces opposite in direction to those that caused the initial damage. Accordingly, the damaged section can still be practically as strong as it was before it was damaged—in the direction of the restoration forces of pulling. Torn ends butt together to resist compression; buckled sections show considerable strength in tension to resist straightening. Actually the reason for the rule is that alignments of damaged sections that permit repair do not happen at the same time during the pull, but at irregular and unpredictable intervals. For this reason, it is imperative to visually check the progress of alignment during the pull, making all possible repairs at the moment when the alignment is correct and before further pulling pulls them into a new stage of alignment.

The repair of a bent closed cross sectional structure such as a side member is done by clamping the surface of the bent-in side and pulling. The pulling direction should be such that force is applied in the direction of an imaginary straight line ex-

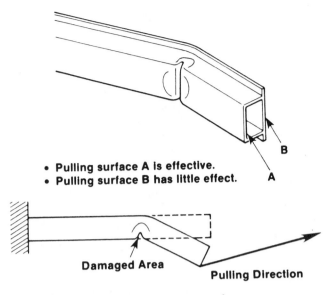

- **Pulling surface A is effective.**
- **Pulling surface B has little effect.**

Damaged Area

Pulling Direction

FIGURE 10-82 Bent portion repair

tending through the original position of the part (Figure 10-82).

In repairing unibody structures, do not try to salvage a member by cutting away a damaged area of a section (tears, fractures, or buckles), and then welding a reinforcing patch over the cut-away area. In a modern, well-designed vehicle structure, some members, such as rails, are designed to provide "controlled damage" in a collision. This prevents or postpones the damage of more critical areas (such as those that surround the passenger compartment).

A reinforcing patch that over-strengthens such a section might prevent "controlled damage" and defeat the design purpose of the section. Consequently, as mentioned earlier, when a fractured, torn, or buckled area cannot be repaired without patching, the only acceptable alternative is to replace the entire section.

Once the parts are welded into place as described in Chapters 6 and 11, restore corrosion protection. Follow the car manufacturer's recommendations for sealing, caulking, and restoring corrosion protection to all the structural parts. As mentioned in Chapters 11 and 15, this is extremely important on a unitized body to assure lasting strength and quality of the repair, particularly where thinner, lighter gauge sheet metal is being used.

Once the repair is completed, including all straightening and welding operations, the alignment procedures are ready for a final check. If the car was repaired without using fixtures, final measurements should be made and compared to the body/frame dimensions book. All measurements must be checked against factory specifications to ensure quality work. This is time consuming, but it must be

FIGURE 10-83 Checking for gaps

FIGURE 10-84 Checking fixture control points

done. Of course, if the car was repaired with fixtures, the technician knows that the underbody of the car is within specifications.

Begin the final checks by slowly walking around the car looking for obvious signs of misalignment. Large gaps between the roof lines and doors (Figure 10-83) are a good sign that small amounts of damage are still present. If fixtures or jigs were used, go back and check all the fixture control points (Figure 10-84). Do they still line up true, without having to force or hammer the fixture? Go back over the repair

order or estimate to be sure everything was done. Remember that it is much easier to set up and make additional pulls now rather than waiting until more steps of the damage repair procedure have been completed and then finding additional damage.

Among other items that should be carefully inspected are:

- Check down low at the alignment between the door and rocker sill. This should be a straight and narrow gap.
- Check the general alignment of all the upper body areas. Make sure everything looks as though nothing was ever out of alignment.
- Then open and close the doors and trunk lid. Do they feel tight and secure when latched? Make sure they close smoothly and open easily just as they are supposed to.

Once the final alignment inspection is made, the car can be left on the bench for replacement of components removed to make straightening easier or the vehicle removed at this point from the bench. The car can be straightened on a bench or other straightening equipment by reversing the sequence of steps used when installing the vehicle originally.

10.8 REVIEW QUESTIONS

1. Which of the following is not an in-floor system?
   a. anchor-pot system
   b. modular rail frame system
   c. chainless anchoring system
   d. none of the above

2. Technician A says that in-floor systems provide fast hookup and positive anchoring without sacrificing space. Technician B says that in-floor systems cannot perform multiple pulls. Who is correct?
   a. Technician A
   b. Technician B
   c. Both A and B
   d. Neither A nor B

3. Technician A says a rack system should be used whenever the damage involves the suspension, steering, or power train mounting points. Technician B says that it is necessary to have at least three control points on the undamaged part of the car that can be used to set the car up properly on the bench. Who is correct?

a. Technician A
b. Technician B
c. Both A and B
d. Neither A nor B

4. When a vehicle has sustained front damage, where should the fixtures be located?
   a. front of the vehicle
   b. front and center of the vehicle
   c. rear and center of the vehicle
   d. front, rear, and center of the vehicle

5. Portable hydraulic rams have the capability to _____ .

   a. pull
   b. push
   c. spread
   d. all of the above

6. Technician A always removes the suspension and driveline completely from a unibody car before putting it on the bench. Technician B says that single-pull systems cannot hold an undamaged or a corrected control dimension while pulling to correct other damaged areas of the car. Who is correct?
   a. Technician A
   b. Technician B
   c. Both A and B
   d. Neither A nor B

7. When anchoring a unibody car in preparation for pulling, Technician A leans toward "over anchoring." Technician B sometimes temporarily welds a piece of steel to a section. Who is correct?
   a. Technician A
   b. Technician B
   c. Both A and B
   d. Neither A nor B

8. Which should the technician work toward achieving first?
   a. sidesway removal
   b. length
   c. height
   d. it depends on the situation

9. Before making a powerful side pull, Technician A applies counter supports. Technician B does not use counter supports for side pulls. Who is correct?
   a. Technician A
   b. Technician B
   c. Both A and B
   d. Neither A nor B

10. When raising a vehicle during an upward pull, Technician A wraps chains around the bumper or isolators. Technician B uses nylon straps in place of the chain. Who is correct?
    a. Technician A
    b. Technician B
    c. Both A and B
    d. Neither A nor B

11. Technician A says that in most instances the only way the overpull panel can be repaired is by replacement. Technician B says that a stress condition is corrected by blocking under a low area and pulling down on a high end. Who is correct?
    a. Technician A
    b. Technician B
    c. Both A and B
    d. Neither A nor B

12. When a vehicle has been hit from the side, _____ .
    a. a "banana" hit results
    b. the ends of the car are pulled in opposite directions to straighten it
    c. the damaged side of the car is pulled in the direction opposite of the hit
    d. all of the above
    e. both a and c

13. Technician A's goal in the entire pull procedure is to work the damaged metal back to its original shape. Technician B defines stress as the internal resistance a material offers to corrective techniques. Who is correct?
    a. Technician A
    b. Technician B
    c. Both A and B
    d. Neither A nor B

14. Which of the following is true?
    a. Cracked paint and undercoating is a sign of stress.
    b. Most of the stress relieving will be "cold work."
    c. The best way to monitor heat applications is with a heat crayon.
    d. All of the above

15. When should the repair or replacement of severely damaged sections that cannot be restored by the pulling operation take place?
    a. before pulling
    b. during pulling
    c. after pulling
    d. repairs during pulling and replacements after pulling

CHAPTER
11

Panel Replacement and Adjustments

OBJECTIVES

After reading this chapter, you will be able to:

- explain the process for removing damaged panels.
- properly align and replace replacement panels.
- name corrosion prevention measurements applied to replacement panels.
- replace outer door skins or panels.
- adjust mechanically fastened panels.

A vehicle that sustains extensive damage in a collision will require a variety of repair operations. Bent structural panels will have to be pulled and realigned using the procedures outlined in Chapter 10. Bulges, dents, and creases must be eliminated using the metalworking skills described in Chapters 7 and 8. Some panels, however, might be so badly damaged that replacing the panels is the only practical and effective procedure. Table 11-1 outlines the general procedure for replacing both bolted and welded panels.

Figure 11-1 shows a collision-damaged door and quarter panel. The collision created a buckle that work hardened in the flange and body line

areas. Because the backside of the panel is inaccessible, the panel was replaced. Section cuts were made in the rear pillars and rocker panel (Figure 11-2) and spot welds were drilled out in the factory seams. The new panel, cut to fit at the pillars, was welded in place (Figure 11-3). The door frame was bent; so, it, too, was replaced.

Panel replacement is often the only permanent remedy for corrosion damage, also. Figure 11-4 shows a rusted out rocker panel and cab corner on a Chevy truck. The repair was made by cutting the rusty metal away and welding new partial panels in place (Figure 11-5). Partial replacement panels for areas commonly subjected to rustout are available

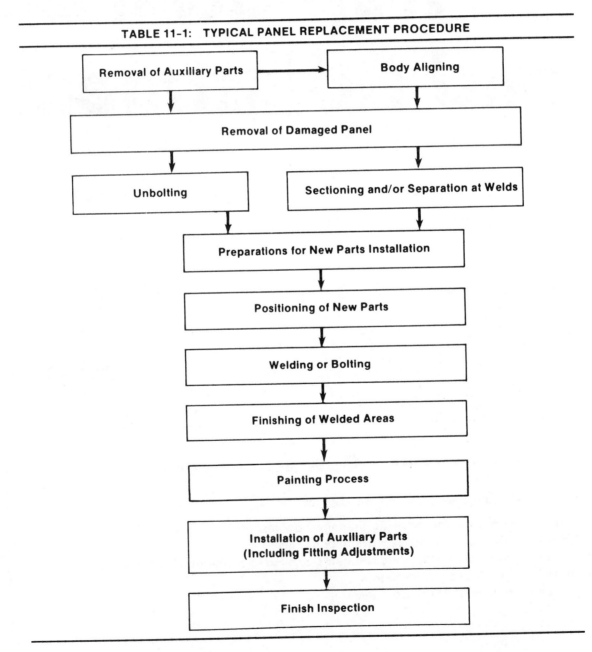

TABLE 11-1: TYPICAL PANEL REPLACEMENT PROCEDURE

Removal of Auxiliary Parts → Body Aligning

Removal of Damaged Panel

Unbolting | Sectioning and/or Separation at Welds

Preparations for New Parts Installation

Positioning of New Parts

Welding or Bolting

Finishing of Welded Areas

Painting Process

Installation of Auxiliary Parts (Including Fitting Adjustments)

Finish Inspection

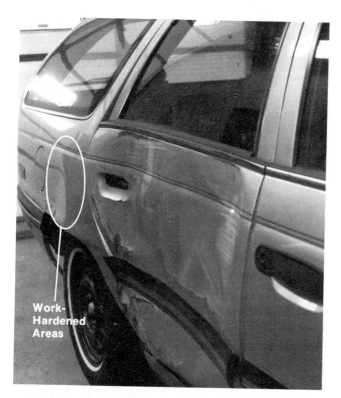

FIGURE 11-1   Collision-damaged door and quarter panel

Work-Hardened Areas

FIGURE 11-2   Vehicle with damaged panel removed

from a number of aftermarket parts manufacturers, local salvage yards, or the original equipment manufacturer.

The numerous panels that make up a vehicle body are joined together in two ways: mechanical fasteners and welds. Nonstructural or cosmetic panels such as fenders, quarter panels, and hoods can be welded to the unibody structure, or they can

FIGURE 11-3   New panel welded in place

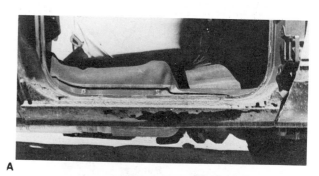

A

B

FIGURE 11-4   Rusted out (A) rocker panel and (B) cab corner

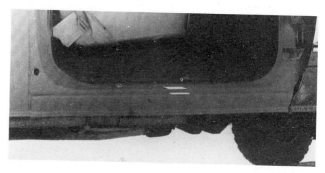

FIGURE 11-5   Replacement rocker panel welded in place and primed

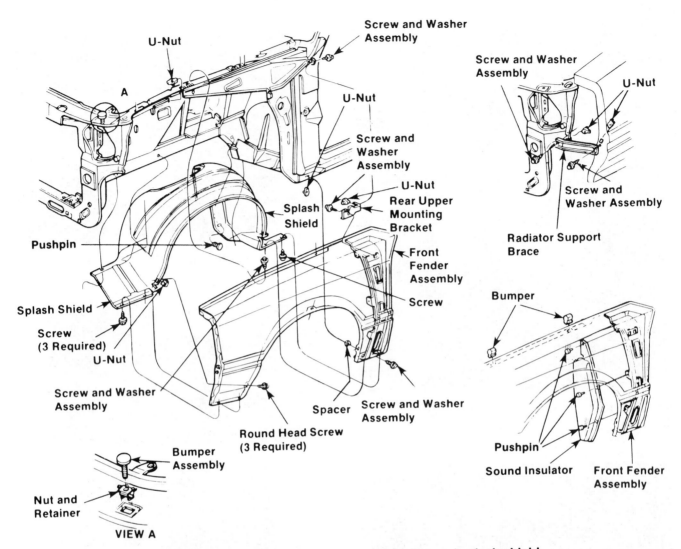

FIGURE 11-6 Typical front fender assembly and splash shield

be attached with bolts, rivets, and screws, among others. Bumpers and related hardware are also usually bolted to the frame. Replacing these panels simply requires removing the fasteners. Figure 11-6 shows the mechanical fasteners used to attach the front fender and splash shield on a Ford Mustang.

In modern unitized construction all the structural panels, from the radiator support to the rear end panel, are welded together to make a one piece frame—a unibody (Figure 11-7). Some examples of structural panels in unibody construction are the radiator supports, the inner fender skirts, the floor pan, the rocker panels, the engine compartment side rails, upper reinforcements, lower body rails in the rear, inner fender wells, luggage compartment floor, and so on.

The integrity of the whole structure is dependent on the interconnection of all the individual panels. The individual panels are joined together at

FIGURE 11-7 Unibody construction

flanges or mating surfaces usually formed at the edges of the panels during factory production.

The structural panels provide the foundation to which all the mechanical components are mounted and all outer panels are attached to them. Therefore, all appearance fits and suspension alignments are

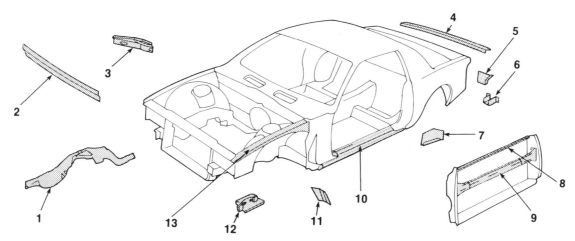

1. Engine Compartment Outer Side Rail
2. Windshield Lower Reinforcement With Extension Support
3. Body Lock Pillar Brace to Wheelhouse
4. Rear End Panel Bumper Retainer
5. Rear End Panel Reinforcement at Bumper Support
6. Compartment Panel Rail Reinforcement at Bumper Mount
7. Inner Compartment Panel Rail Extension

8. Door Inner Panel Reinforcement at Belt
9. Door Outer Panel Bar, Stiffener, and Reinforcement
10. Outer Rocker Panel
11. Engine Compartment Side Rail Reinforcement at Lower Dash
12. Engine Compartment Side Rail Reinforcement at Stabilizer Bar
13. Outer and Lower Engine Compartment Upper Rail Panels

FIGURE 11-8   High-strength steel panels

determined by the accuracy of the positioning of the welded structural panels. Welded panels cannot be shimmed to correct sloppy fit-up procedures. Structural panels must be accurately positioned before final welding.

It is very important to always follow the manufacturer's recommendations when servicing structural panels. This is especially true concerning cutting or sectioning. Some manufacturers do not allow resectioning of structural panels. Others approve of sectioning only if proper procedures established by the manufacturer are followed. All manufacturers stress: Do not section areas that might reduce passenger protection, driveability of the car, or where critical dimensions can be affected.

Another important area is high-strength steel panels, such as bumper reinforcements and side guard door beams (Figure 11-8). These panels must be replaced when damaged. Under no condition can heat be applied to straighten high-strength steel panels.

11.1 REMOVING STRUCTURAL PANELS

Structural body panels are joined together in the factory by spot welding. Therefore, removing

panels mainly involves the separation of spot welds. Spot welds can be drilled out, blown out with a plasma torch, chiseled out, or ground out with a high-speed grinding wheel. The best method for removing a spot-welded panel is determined by the number and arrangement of mating panels and the accessibility of the weld.

Some spot weld areas have a number of layers of sheet metal. The removal tool is determined by the position of the weld and the arrangement of the panels.

DETERMINING SPOT WELD POSITIONS

It is usually necessary to remove the paint film undercoat, sealer, or other coatings covering the joint area to find the locations of spot welds. To do this, scorch the paint film with an oxyacetylene or propane torch and brush it off with a wire brush (Figure 11-9). Propane has a cooler flame than oxyacetylene, subjecting the metal to less heat stress. A coarse wire wheel or brush attached to a drill can also be used to grind off the paint (Figure 11-10).

Scrape off thick portions of undercoating or wax sealer before scorching the paint. Do not burn through the paint film so that the sheet metal panel begins to turn color. Heat the area only enough to soften the paint and then brush or scrape it off. It is

FIGURE 11-9 Removing paint to determine spot weld locations. Use torch with care.

FIGURE 11-10 Removing paint with a wire brush

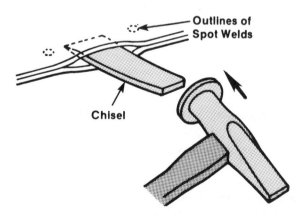

FIGURE 11-11 Determining spot weld location with a chisel. (Courtesy of Toyota Motor Corp.)

not necessary to remove paint from areas where the spot welds are visible through the paint film. Other methods of removing paint can be found in Chapter 18.

In areas where the spot weld positions are not visible after the paint is removed, drive a chisel be-

tween the panels as shown in Figure 11-11. Doing so will cause the outline of the spot welds to appear.

SEPARATING SPOT WELDS

After the spot welds have been located, the welds can be drilled out, using a spot weld cutter (Figure 11-12). Two types of cutting bits can be used: a drill type or a hole saw type (Figure 11-13). Table 11-2 shows when each type should be used to drill out spot welds. Regardless of which is used be careful not to cut into the lower panel and be sure to cut the plugs out precisely to avoid creating an excessively large hole.

Drilling out the numerous spot welds in a panel can be tedious. To make the job easier, use a spot

FIGURE 11-12 Removing spot welds with a spot weld cutter

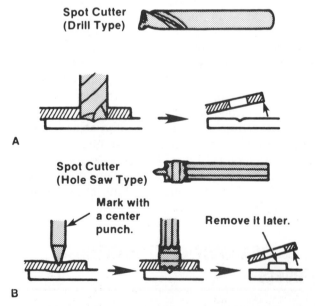

FIGURE 11-13 Spot weld cutters: (A) drill type and (B) hole saw type. (Courtesy of Toyota Motor Corp.)

TABLE 11-2: SEPARATION OF SPOT WELDS

Type			Application Method	Characteristics
Spot Cutter	Drill Type	Small	Places where the replacement panel is between other panels and welding cannot be done from the backside Places where the replacement panel is on top and the weld is small	The separation can be accomplished without damaging the bottom panel. Since the nugget is not left in the bottom panel, finishing is easy.
		Large	When the replacement panel is on top When the panel is thick (places where nuggets are large) Places where the weld shape is destroyed	
	Hole Saw Type		When the replacement panel is on top	Separation can be accomplished without damaging the bottom panel. Since only the circumference of the nugget is cut, it is necessary to remove the nugget remaining in the bottom panel after the panels are separated.
Drill			When the replacement panel is on bottom When the replacement panel is between and welding can be done from the backside (Select a drill diameter that is appropriate for the panel thickness and the weld diameter.)	Lower cost Recently, a labor saving spot weld removing tool has been developed that is easy to use and has a built-in attaching clamp.

FIGURE 11-14   A spot weld removing tool

removing drill with an integral clamping mechanism (Figure 11-14). Hand pressure forces the special rounded bit into the weld.

The removal of spot welds using a plasma torch cutter (Figure 11-15) is much faster. The plasma torch works a little like an acetylene torch. Removing spot welds using a plasma torch blows a hole in all the thicknesses of metal at the same time. Obviously, the use of a plasma torch does not preserve the integrity of the underlying panels.

A high-speed grinding wheel can also be used to separate spot-welded panels (Figure 11-16). Use this technique only when the weld is not accessible with a drill, where the replacement panel is on top, or where a plug weld (from a previous repair) is too large to be drilled out.

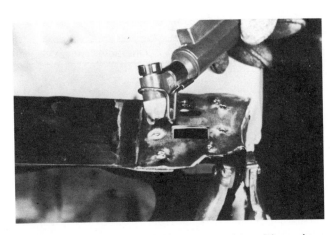

FIGURE 11-15   Removing spot welds with a plasma torch

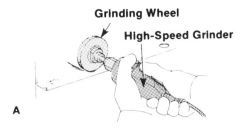

Grinding Wheel

High-Speed Grinder

A

Stop when the round outline is visible.

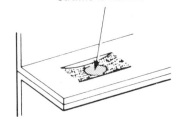

B

FIGURE 11-16   Removing spot welds with a grinder. (Courtesy of Toyota Motor Corp.)

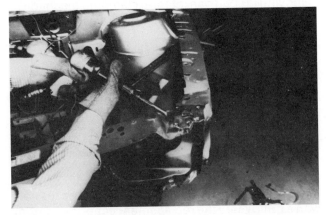

FIGURE 11-17   Separating panels with an air chisel

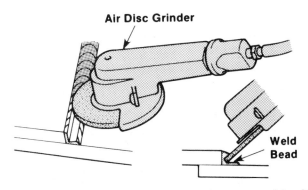

Air Disc Grinder

Weld Bead

FIGURE 11-18   Removing continuous weld with disc grinder. (Courtesy of Toyota Motor Corp.)

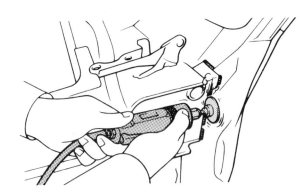

FIGURE 11-19   Using a high-speed grinder to remove continuous weld. (Courtesy of Toyota Motor Corp.)

After the spot welds have been drilled out, blown out, or ground down, drive a chisel between the panels to separate them (Figure 11-17). Be careful not to cut or bend the undamaged panel.

SEPARATING CONTINUOUS WELDS

In some vehicles, panels are joined by continuous MIG welding. Since the welding bead is long, use a grinding wheel or high-speed grinder to separate the panels. As shown in Figures 11-18 and 11-19, cut through the weld without cutting into or through the panels. Hold the grinding wheel at a 45-degree angle to the lap joint. After grinding through the weld, use a hammer and chisel to separate the panels.

SEPARATING BRAZED AREAS

Brazing is used at the ends of outer panels or at the joints of the roof and body pillars to improve the finish quality and to seal the body. Generally, separation of brazed areas is done by melting the brazing metal with an oxyacetylene or propane torch. However, in areas where arc brazing is used, the fusion temperature of the brazing metal is higher than with ordinary brazing, and melting the brazing metal would result in damaging the panels underneath. Therefore, areas that are arc brazed are normally separated by grinding. Ordinary brazing can be distinguished from arc brazing by the color of the brazing metal. Ordinary brazed areas are the color of brass, but arc-brazed areas are a reddish copper color.

First, soften the paint with an oxyacetylene torch and remove it with a wire brush or scraper. Then, heat the brazing metal until it starts to melt and puddle and then quickly brush it off (Figure 11-20). Be careful not to overheat the surrounding sheet metal. Drive a chisel between the panels and separate the panels (Figure 11-21). Keep the panels separated until the brazing metal cools and hardens.

🏎️ **SHOP TALK** ─────────

It is easier to separate the brazed areas after all the other welded parts have been separated.

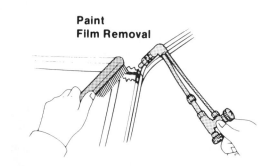

FIGURE 11-20   Removing paint from brazed area. *(Courtesy of Toyota Motor Corp.)*

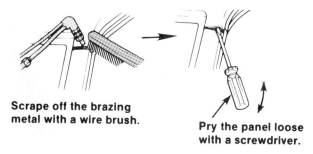

Scrape off the brazing metal with a wire brush.

Pry the panel loose with a screwdriver.

FIGURE 11-21   Separating brazed joints. *(Courtesy of Toyota Motor Corp.)*

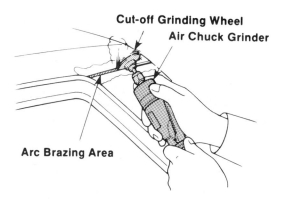

A. Separation of arc brazed areas

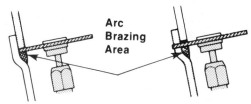

Replacement panel is on top.

Replacement panel is underneath.

B. Cutting depth

FIGURE 11-22   Separating panels connected by arc brazing. *(Courtesy of Toyota Motor Corp.)*

If after removing the paint, the brazed joint is determined to be arc brazing, use a high-speed grinder and grinding wheel to cut through the brazing (Figure 11-22). If replacing the top panel, do not cut through the panel below it. After grinding through the brazing, separate the lapped panels with a chisel and hammer.

11.2 INSTALLING NEW PANELS

As stated earlier, exterior sheet metal panels are attached with either fasteners or welds. The fastener method of installing panels is simple and fast. It is a matter of bolting the new panel in place and adjusting the fit. Inspect and measure the adjacent or adjoining panels for proper alignment before tightening the bolts. If necessary, straighten any adjacent panel that is out of alignment. One indication of misalignment or damaged inner structure is that the bolt holes do not line up with the bolt holes in the new panel. Also, tapered gaps between panels indicate misalignment.

Welding replacement panels require much more preparation and care in alignment. The following procedure is typical of many panel replacement op-

FIGURE 11-23 Removing paint and rust from weld joints

erations. Always refer to the appropriate body repair manual provided by the manufacturer for the type and placement of welds.

VEHICLE PREPARATION

After removal of the damaged panels, prepare the vehicle for installation of the new panels. To do this, follow these steps.

1. Grind off the welding marks from the spot welding areas (Figure 11-23). Use a wire brush to remove dirt, rust, paint, sealers, zinc coatings, and so on from the joint surfaces. Do not grind the flanges of structural panels. Grinding will remove metal, thinning the section and weakening the joint. Also, remove paint and undercoating from the back sides of the panel joining surfaces on parts that will be spot welded during installation.

2. Smooth the dents and bumps in the mating flanges with a hammer and dolly (Figure 11-24).

3. Apply weld-through primer to areas where the base metal is exposed after the paint film and rust have been removed from the joining surfaces. It is very important to apply the antirust primer to joining surfaces or to areas where painting cannot be done in later processes.

REPLACEMENT PANEL PREPARATION

Since all new parts are coated with a primer, the primer and zinc coating must be removed from the mating flanges to allow the welding current to flow properly during spot welding. Also, drill holes for plug welds where spot welding is not possible. Use plug hole diameters that correspond to the thickness of the panels. To prepare the new panel for welding, follow these steps:

 1. Use a disc sander to remove the paint from both sides of the spot welding area. Do not grind into the steel panel and do not heat the panel so that it turns blue or begins to warp.

CAUTION: Wherever possible, grind so that sparks fly down and away. Always wear proper eye protection when grinding.

2. Apply weld-through primer (as an antirust treatment) to the welding surfaces where the paint film was removed. Apply the weld-through carefully so that it does not ooze out from the joining surfaces. If sealer does ooze out, it will have a detrimental effect on painting, necessitating extra work. So remove any excess with a solvent-soaked rag.

3. Make holes for plug welding with a punch or drill. Always refer to the body repair

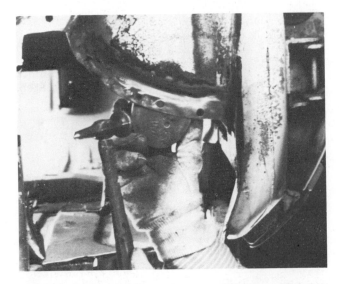

FIGURE 11-24 Smoothing panel flange with hammer and dolly

TABLE 11-3:   PLUG HOLE DIAMETER FOR RESPECTIVE WELDED PORTION

Welded Area Panel Thickness	Plug Hole Diameter
Less than 1/32"	3/16"–1/4"
1/32"–3/32"	1/4"–13/32"
More than 3/32"	13/32" or more

manual for each type of vehicle for the number of plug welding holes. Generally, make more holes than the number of spot welds used on the factory assembly line. Be sure to make plug welding holes of the proper diameter. If the size of the welding holes are too large or too small for the thickness of the panel, either the metal will melt through or the weld will be inadequate (Table 11-3). Space the holes evenly.

4.   If the new panel is sectioned to overlap any of the existing panels, rough cut the new panel to size using an air saw or a cut-off grinding wheel, among others. The edges should overlap the portion of the panel remaining in the sectioning area on the body by 3/4 to 1 inch. If the overlap portion is too large, it will make matching the position of the panel more difficult during temporary installation. More will be said about sectioning and fitting sectioned panels later in this chapter.

Positioning New Panels

Aligning new parts with the existing body is a very important step in repairing vehicles with major damage. Improperly aligned panels will affect both the appearance and the driveability of the repaired vehicle. Basically, there are two methods of positioning body panels. One way is to use dimension measuring instruments to determine the installation position and the other is to determine the position by the relationship between the new part and the surrounding panels. The dimensional accuracy of structural panels making up the engine compartment or underbody parts such as the fender aprons or the front side members and rear side members have a direct effect on wheel alignment and driving characteristics. Therefore, when replacing structural panels in unibody vehicles, use the dimensional measurement positioning method because it is more accurate. There is also a definite relationship be-

tween the fit of the new and old parts and the finish appearance, so whether structural or cosmetic panels are being replaced, the emphasis is on proper fit. Of course, it is desirable to use both methods together and, therefore, assure the accuracy and the finish necessary for a high-quality vehicle repair.

CAUTION: All measurements must be accurate before finish welding structural panels in position, regardless of the measurement system used for replacing structural panels. Because there are no shims on unibodies, no adjustments can be made to the outer panels. Therefore, each panel must be precisely positioned before welding.

Positioning by Dimensional Measurement Methods

When using a dedicated bench system of measurement (Figure 11-25) or a mechanical universal system (Figure 11-26), the vehicle must be properly positioned on the bench before the new panel can be correctly aligned. This will usually have already been done in order to pull and straighten damaged panels that do not require replacing. All straightening must be done before replacing panels. Otherwise, proper alignment of the new panels will be impossible.

So, when using a bench system for panel replacement at a factory joint, place the fixtures or

FIGURE 11-25   Aligning new panel on dedicated bench fixture

FIGURE 11-26   Aligning new panel on universal bench

A

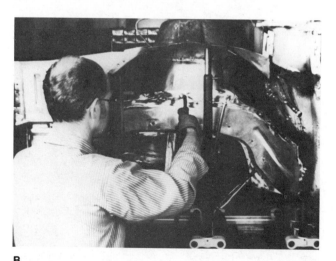

B

FIGURE 11-27   Attaching the new part (A) clamping in place and (B) welding

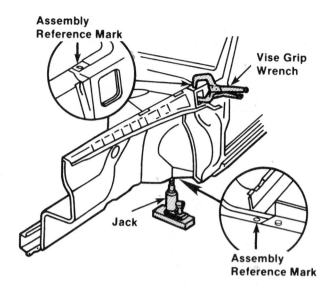

FIGURE 11-28   Clamping new panel in place. (Courtesy of Toyota Motor Corp.)

gauges on the bench in their correct locations and tie them to the bench.

Then, place the new panel in position on the fixtures and see how it lines up with the good panels on the car. Make any necessary adjustments, clamp the panel in place, and weld it to the mating panels (Figure 11-27).

The illustrations in Figures 11-28 through 11-40 demonstrate the use of a tram and center gauge measuring system. In the procedure being illustrated, a vehicle is being fitted with a front fender apron assembly, a front cross member, and a radiator baffle.

1.   Match the assembly reference marks on the installation areas of the front fender apron and the side member, and fasten them in place with vise grips (Figure 11-28). Parts that have no assembly reference marks should be installed in the same location as the old parts.

2.   Match the length dimensions by setting the tracking gauge at the reference values and adjusting the length dimensions so they match those values. Temporarily install the front cross member. Match the panels by tapping a hammer against a block of wood that, in turn, strikes the panel moving it in the desired direction (Figure 11-29).

3.   If the length dimensions match the reference values, temporarily install the front floor reinforcement by tack welding one spot (Figure 11-30). Choose a spot weld location in an area where it will be easy to remove if necessary. Scribe a positioning

line at the end of the part that is not welded and drill a small hole and fasten the parts together with a sheel metal screw. Scribe a line on the apron installation area but do not weld the panels together.

4. Use a centering gauge to match the height of the new components to the components on the opposite side of the vehicle (Figure 11-31). Support the new parts with a hydraulic jack so that the height does not change.

5. Match the diagonal and width dimensions (Figure 11-32). Support the parts with a hydraulic jack so that the height does not change, then move the side member back and forth to match the dimensions.

6. Confirm the height dimensions again.

7. Position the front cross member (Figure 11-33). The strut bar bracket can be installed with a fixture (jig). Install the cross member so that both the left and right ends are uniform.

8. Once the dimensions of the side member match the reference dimensions, secure the member in place. The suspension cross

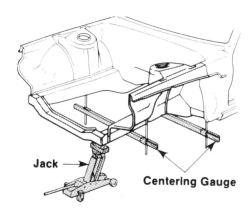

FIGURE 11-31 Checking height adjustments. (Courtesy of Toyota Motor Corp.)

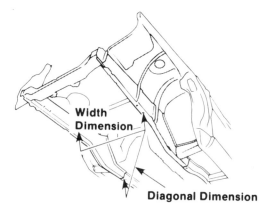

FIGURE 11-32 Checking diagonal and width dimensions. (Courtesy of Toyota Motor Corp.)

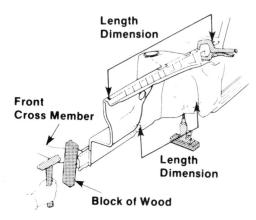

FIGURE 11-29 Making length adjustments. (Courtesy of Toyota Motor Corp.)

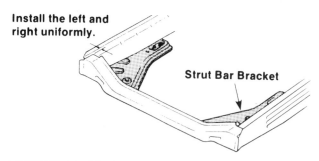

FIGURE 11-33 Locating front cross member. (Courtesy of Toyota Motor Corp.)

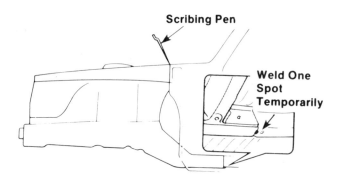

FIGURE 11-30 Temporary installation

member might be installed with fixtures (jigs) (Figure 11-34). Use plug welds at several locations to fasten the joining area of the side member, the under reinforcement and the joining area of the side member to the front cross member.

9. Make sure that the apron upper length has not changed. Confirm by checking for shifting of the scribed line.

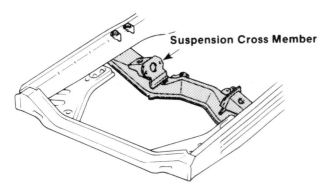

FIGURE 11-34 Attaching the suspension cross member. *(Courtesy of Toyota Motor Corp.)*

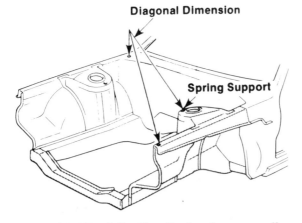

FIGURE 11-35 Adjusting the fender apron dimensions. *(Courtesy of Toyota Motor Corp.)*

10. Match the diagonal dimensions between the fender rear installation hole and the spring support hole or fender front installation hole (Figure 11-35). It is a good idea to match the spring support dimension from side to side at this time also.

11. Verify the width dimension of the spring support and the front of the fender installation hole and fasten them together. If the width dimension does not match the reference value, make a small adjustment, being careful of changes in the diagonal dimensions. Temporarily install and fasten the radiator upper support and the radiator support (Figure 11-36).

12. Match the side support width dimensions (Figure 11-37). Set the tracking gauge to the reference value and adjust the side baffle so that the dimensions match that on the gauge. Lightly fasten it with a vise grip and tap it lightly by hand to move it in place.

13. Match the diagonal dimensions for the side support (Figure 11-38). Be sure the diagonal dimensions of the side supports match. Verify their height and make sure the left and right supports are installed in the same manner.

14. Visually verify the left-right balance (Figure 11-39). Stand back and visually compare the upper support or the spring supports with the cowl panel and so on.

15. Temporarily install the front fender and inspect it for proper fit with the door (Figure 11-40). If the clearance is not correct, it might be because the fender apron or the side member height is off on both the left and right sides.

16. Verify the overall dimensions once more before welding.

When using the tram and centering gauge method of component positioning, it is important to remember that measurement points for the new

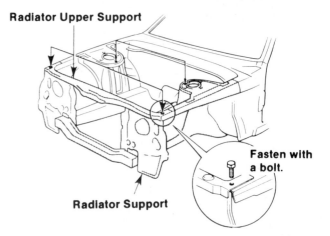

FIGURE 11-36 Checking fender apron width dimensions. *(Courtesy of Toyota Motor Corp.)*

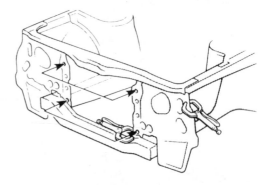

FIGURE 11-37 Matching the width dimensions. *(Courtesy of Toyota Motor Corp.)*

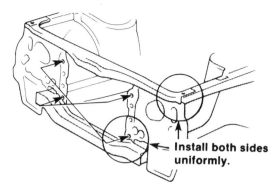

FIGURE 11-38   Match the diagonal dimensions. (Courtesy of Toyota Motor Corp.)

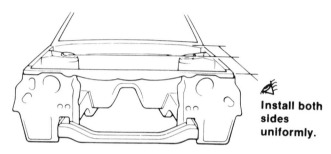

FIGURE 11-39   Visual inspection of parts alignment. (Courtesy of Toyota Motor Corp.)

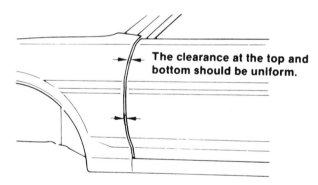

FIGURE 11-40   Inspecting panel clearance for alignment. (Courtesy of Toyota Motor Corp.)

parts should be the same as the opposite side of the vehicle. If the dimensions do not match, or if they are inconsistent, the reference points must be verified and changed if necessary.

Complete information on the use of fixtures and adjusting of panels is given in Chapters 9 and 10.

Positioning by Visual Inspection

Nonstructural outer panels can sometimes be visually aligned with adjacent panels without the precise measurements necessary in replacing structural panels. This is true of both mechanically fas-

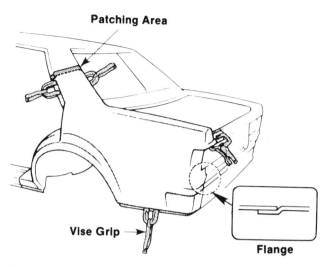

FIGURE 11-41   Temporarily installing the quarter panel. (Courtesy of Toyota Motor Corp.)

tened panels and welded panels. The emphasis here is on appearance. Body lines must be aligned and gaps between panels must be even, not tapered. Figures 11-41 to 11-46 show a new rear quarter panel being installed. The pillar has been sectioned and will be welded to the top portion of the pillar. (Sectioning is explained in detail in another section of this chapter.) The panel is carefully aligned with adjacent body parts and secured with spot welds. The following procedure is typical of a "fitting-by-sight" repair.

Fitting the Panel

Temporarily install the quarter panel and fasten it at several points with vise grips or the equivalent. Make sure that the panel end and flange match (Figure 11-41).

Carefully adjust the fit with the surrounding panels. Adjust the panel so that the clearance with the door and body lines match each other (Figure 11-42). Then, install the trunk lid in its correct position and adjust the clearances and the level difference. Confirm that there is no left-right difference in the diagonal dimensions for the rear window opening (Figure 11-43). Match the rear glass to the opening to verify proper alignment.

After fitting the panel to the door and the trunk lid, drill some small holes and fasten it with self-tapping screws. If it is fastened with vise grips, the fit cannot be verified properly.

Adjust the body line and panel overlap to match the lower back panel and the rear valance panel.

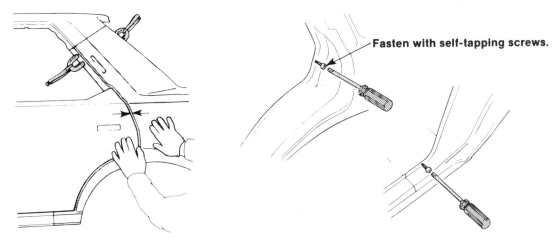

FIGURE 11-42   Adjusting the alignment to the door panel. *(Courtesy of Toyota Motor Corp.)*

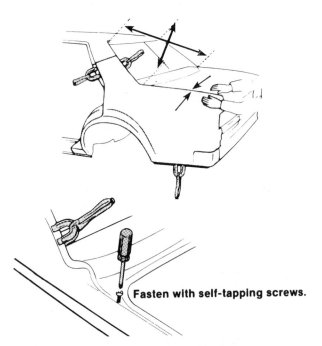

FIGURE 11-43   Adjusting the alignment to the rear window and deck lid. *(Courtesy of Toyota Motor Corp.)*

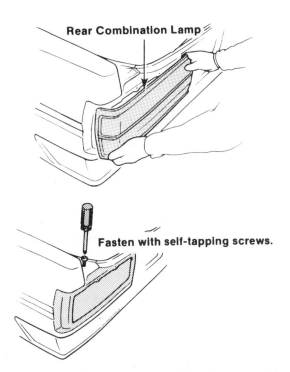

FIGURE 11-44   Attaching lower back panel. *(Courtesy of Toyota Motor Corp.)*

Install the rear combination lamp and fit the panel to the lamp assembly (Figure 11-44).

When the clearance, body line, and level differences of each part have been adjusted, visually check for overall twisting or bending.

CUTTING THE OVERLAPPING PANEL

After the panel is properly positioned, cut the overlapping portion of the joining area with an air saw or cut-off grinding wheel. Be precise when mak-

ing cuts in the sectioning area, because if a gap opens up at the cut or if the panels overlap, welding will be difficult. Therefore, after matching the panel fit at every point, it is important that cutting be done accurately.

Cutting overlapping can be accomplished in these three basic ways: If there is sufficient overlapping, both panels can be cut simultaneously. If the overlapping is small, a line can be scribed at the end of the overlapping panel. When cut along the scribed line, the panels should fit snugly together with little or no gap.

After cutting the overlap to fit, remove the replacement panel and remove any metal chips and other foreign material from the inside of the panel before proceeding.

Apply body sealer around the inside perimeter of the quarter panel and install the panel and other parts with self-tapping screws in the same screw holes as before. Verify the fit once more.

Welding New Panels

Once the dimensions and position of the new part are correct, weld it in place. Welding operations for new panels are fully explained in detail in Chapter 6. The installation of fiberglass (SMC) body panels is given in Chapter 13.

11.3 STRUCTURAL SECTIONING

Structural sectioning has been researched extensively by I-CAR. New repair techniques, based on this research, now make this method widely accepted throughout the industry.

Ordinarily, damaged unibody components are replaced at the factory seams. But this is impractical when many seams have to be separated deep inside the undamaged areas of the vehicle. In such repairs,

sectioning of rails, pillars, and rockers, for example, make the repair less costly. Sectioning structural members makes the repair area as strong as it was before the collision, while preserving the crush zones; thus, allowing absorption of possible future collisions.

The techniques recommended in this book are variations of the basics. These variations take into account unique vehicle designs such as crush zones, internal reinforcements, locations of factory seams, and ideal sectioning areas. Of course, special care must be taken when sectioning HSLA/HSS steels. Repairs of this type should only be performed after determining that sectioning will not jeopardize the structural integrity of the vehicle.

The procedures included here have also been tested by various manufacturers and independent testing agencies, and have been found to provide structurally adequate repairs for the specified areas. However, be sure to follow the car maker's sectioning recommendations. Always given careful attention to detailed damage repair techniques where prescribed for specific vehicle makes and models in technical manuals or bulletins published by the manufacturers.

Major auto manufacturers are continually investigating the sectioning of structural components and are publishing repair procedures as they are developed and verified. Always give careful attention to detailed damage repair techniques where prescribed for specific vehicle makes and models in

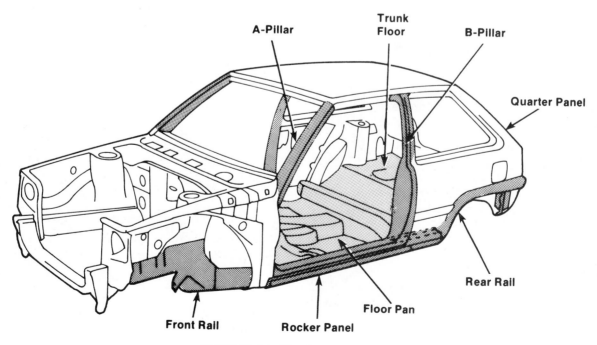

FIGURE 11–45 Section areas

technical manuals or notices published by the manufacturers.

This chapter on panel sectioning and replacement covers the repair of the following components (Figure 11–45): rocker panels, quarter panels, floor pan, front rails, rear rails, trunk floor, B-pillars, and A-pillars.

These unibody structural components involve two basic types of construction design: closed sections—such as rocker panels, pillars, and body rails (Figure 11–46)—and open surface, or single layer overlap joint components, such as floor pans and trunk floors that are discussed later in the chapter.

The closed type sections are the most critical, because they provide the principal strength in the unibody structure. They possess much greater strength per pound of material than other types of sections.

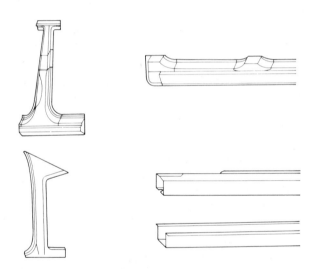

FIGURE 11-46   Closed sections

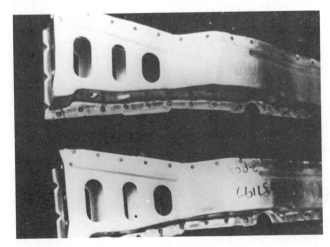

FIGURE 11-47   Crush zones

Crush Zones

Certain structural components have crush zones, or buckling points, designed into them for absorbing the impact energy in a collision. This is particularly true of the front and rear rails because they take the brunt of the impact in most collisions. Crush zones are in all front and rear rails (Figure 11–47). Identify these crush zones by the look of them. Some are in the form of convoluted or crinkled areas, some of them are in the form of dents or dimples, and others are in the form of holes or slots—put in deliberately so the rail will collapse at these points. In virtually all cases, the crush zones are ahead of the front suspension and behind the rear suspension (Figure 11–48).

Avoid crush zones whenever possible. Sectioning procedures can change the designed collapsibility if improperly located. If a rail has suffered major damage, it will normally already be buckled in the crush zone, so the crush zone will usually be easy to locate. Where only moderate damage has occurred, be very careful. The hit might not have used up the entire crush zone. So be aware of other potential areas where designed-in collapse might occur.

Other Caution Areas

There are other areas to stay away from when making cuts. Stay away from **holes** in the component. Do not cut through any inner reinforcements, meaning double layers in the metal. Careless cutting through a closed section with inner reinforcements may make it impossible to restore the area to preaccident strength.

Stay away from anchor points, such as suspension anchor points, seat belt anchor points in the

FIGURE 11-48   Crush zones protect suspension bearing areas.

floor, and shoulder belt D-ring anchor points. For example, when sectioning a B-pillar, make an off-set cut around the D-ring area to avoid disturbing the anchor reinforcement.

Basic Types of Sectioning Joints

Correct structural sectioning procedures and techniques involve three basic types of joints, plus certain variations and combinations of them. One is a butt joint with insert (Figure 11–49) and is used mainly on closed sections, such as rocker panels, A- and B-pillars, and body rails. Inserts help make it easy to fit and align the joints correctly and help make the welding process easier. They also provide a backing that will become part of a solid, continuous joint.

Another basic type is an off-set butt joint without an insert, also known as a staggered butt joint (Figure 11–50). This type of weld joint is used on A- and B-pillars, and front rails. The third type is an overlap joint (Figure 11–51). The overlap joint is used on rear rails, floor pans, trunk floors, and B-pillars.

The configuration and make-up of the component being sectioned might call for a combination of joint types. Sectioning a B-pillar, for instance, might require the use of an off-set cut with a butt joint in the outside piece and a lap joint in the inside piece.

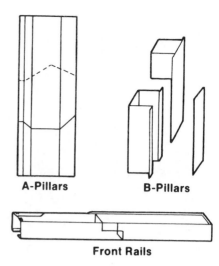

A-Pillars   B-Pillars

Front Rails

FIGURE 11–50   Off-set butt joint without an insert

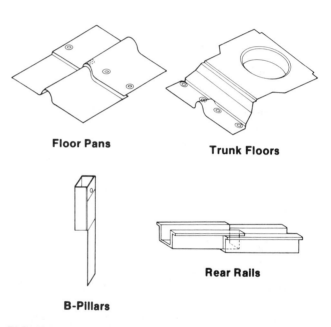

Floor Pans

Trunk Floors

B-Pillars

Rear Rails

FIGURE 11–51   Overlap joints

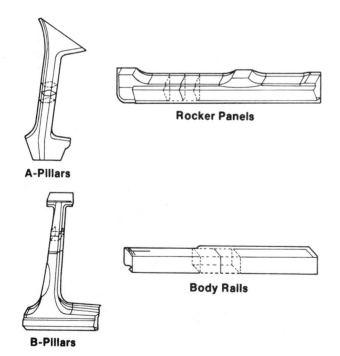

A-Pillars

Rocker Panels

B-Pillars

Body Rails

FIGURE 11–49   Butt joint with insert

Preparing to Section

When preparing to section and replace a panel or any other structural member of a damaged vehicle, certain steps must be taken to ensure the quality of the repair. The first of these is the sectioning of the replacement part by the recycler. Specific instructions must be provided to the recycler as to the placement of the section and the method of sectioning to be used. Other important considerations are the welding techniques used and the cleanliness of the joint metal.

FIGURE 11-52   Sectioning a recycled part

Using Recycled or Salvaged Parts

When using recycled parts, tell the recycler exactly where to make the cuts. Preferably, have the required part removed with a metal saw (Figure 11-52). But if the recycler uses a cutting torch, make sure that at least 2 inches of extra length is left on the part to insure that the heat dispersion from the cut does not invade the joint area. Instruct the recycler to make the cut so that reinforcing pieces that are welded inside the component are not cut through.

When a recycled or salvaged part is received, examine it for corrosion. If it has a lot of rust on it, do not use it. Ask for another one. Before installing a recycled part, check it for possible damage and make sure it is dimensionally accurate (Figure 11-53). Remember: Using quality material is a must to achieve a quality repair.

FIGURE 11-53   Check salvaged parts for dimensional accuracy.

FIGURE 11-54   MIG welding is a must when sectioning.

MIG Welding

To do a proper job of structural sectioning, the body shop must have MIG welding equipment and the body technician must be skilled in its use (Figure 11-54). As stated in Chapter 6, MIG welding is the state-of-the-art in collision repair welding. When it comes to structural sectioning use steel wire—a wire that meets or exceeds the requirements of American Welding Society standard AWS-EX-70S-6 when using 75 percent Argon/25 percent CO_2 gas or other comparable argon-based gas mixtures.

Joint Preparation

Careful preparation of the sectioned joint is another necessity for doing a proper job of structural sectioning. Before starting to weld, be sure to thoroughly clean the surfaces to be joined. The weld site must be completely free of any foreign material that might contaminate the weld. Otherwise a brittle, porous weld of poor integrity will be produced. Use a scraper and an oxyacetylene torch (Figure 11-55) to remove heavy undercoatings, rustproofing, tars,

FIGURE 11-55   Removing coverings with scraper and torch

caulking and sealants, road dirt and oil, primers, and the like.

Do the finish cleaning with a wire brush and torch. Keep the metal at a very low-controlled heat— just enough heat to get the job done. Also, be sure to remove rustproofing, lead, plastic filler, and other contaminants from the inside of structural closed sections when preparing them for welding. The wire brush and torch with a carburizing flame are generally the most effective and efficient cleaning tools. The same goes for removing paint and sealants that have been painted over. The wire brush and torch usually work best.

Make sure the surfaces to be welded are completely free of rust and scale. This is best removed by sanding or sandblasting (Figure 11–56) until there is a clean metal welding surface. In some cases it is possible to do this with a power wire brush. In addition, attach the work cable clamp to a clean surface

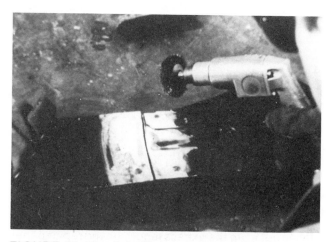

FIGURE 11–56 Grinding rust from flanges

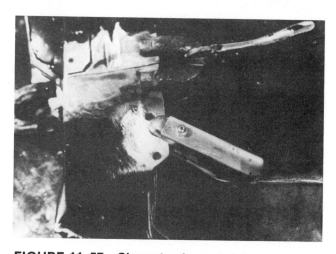

FIGURE 11–57 Clamp to clean metal.

to have a trouble-free welding circuit (Figure 11–57). Application of a weld-through primer is also recommended.

Still another essential for achieving a high-quality job of structural sectioning is that the MIG machine must be properly set up for the specific welding job. The MIG welding machine must be precisely adjusted for the thickness of metal being welded and the type of weld being made.

To make sure that the MIG machine is correctly adjusted for the specific joint being welded, always do a test weld. Especially when welding a closed section where the backside of the weld cannot be checked, a test weld is the only way to ensure that the welding techniques and machine adjustments will restore the original strength, integrity, and alignment of the panel.

To make sure complete penetration and full fusion are achieved, do test welds on sample pieces that duplicate the intended workpiece: the same types of welds on the same type and configuration of joint, and the same gauge metal. The ideal way to do this is to use pieces of excess material from the components being joined on the car: the scrap cut off to make the fit-up. While making the test welds, adjust the MIG machine to suit the given situation.

After completing the test welds, check them for strength as described in Chapter 6.

SECTIONING BODY RAILS

Virtually all front and rear rails are closed sections, but the closures are of two distinct types. One is called a **closed section.** It comes from the factory or the recycler with all four sides intact. Sometimes it is referred to as a box section (Figure 11–58). The

FIGURE 11–58 A closed rail

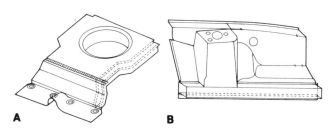

FIGURE 11–59 Typical hat channels: (A) front rail and (B) rear rail

other type comes as an **open "hat" channel** and is closed on the fourth side by being joined to some other component in the body structure (Figure 11–59).

The butt joint with insert is the procedure for repairing a closed section rail (Figure 11–60). Most all rear rails, plus various makes of front rails, are of the hat channel type. Some of the hat channel closures are vertical, such as a front rail joined to a side apron. Some of them are horizontal, a rear rail joined to a trunk floor (Figure 11–59B).

In most cases when sectioning the open, hat channel type of rail, the procedure is a lap joint with plug welds in the overlap areas and a continuous lap weld along the edge of the overlap (Figure 11–61). Whenever sectioning front or rear rails, always remember that all of them contain crush zones that must be avoided when making the cuts. Also remember to stay away from any holes and reinforcements in the rails.

SECTIONING ROCKER PANELS

Rocker panels can come in two piece or three piece designs, depending on the make and model of the unibody (Figure 11–62). In both cases, the rocker panel might contain reinforcements, and the reinforcements might be intermittent or continuous. Depending on the nature of the damage, the rocker panel can be replaced with the B-pillar or without it.

To section and repair the rocker panel, a straight-cut butt joint with an insert can be used (Figure 11–63) or the outside piece of the rocker panel can be cut and the repair piece installed with overlap joints (Figure 11–64). Generally speaking,

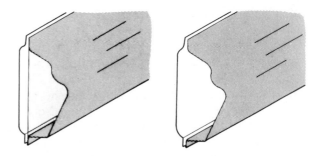

FIGURE 11-62   Rocker panel profiles

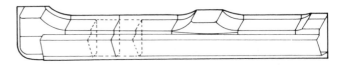

FIGURE 11-63   Joining rocker panel section with butt joint and insert

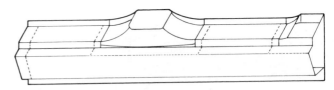

FIGURE 11-64   Replacing the outer rocker panel piece

the butt joint with insert is used when installing a recycled rocker panel with B-pillar attached and when installing a recycled quarter panel.

To do a butt joint with insert, cut straight across the panel. An insert is fashioned out of one or more pieces cut from the excess length on the repair panel or from the end of the damaged panel. The insert should be 6 to 12 inches long and should be cut lengthwise into two to four pieces, depending on rocker panel configuration (Figure 11–65). Then remove the pinch weld flange so that the insert will fit inside the rocker panel. With the insert in place, secure it with plug welds. For structural sectioning, 5/16-inch plug weld holes are required to achieve an adequate nugget and acceptable weld strength. This 5/16-inch hole requires a circular motion of the gun to properly fuse the edge of the hole to the base metal (Figure 11–66).

When installing an insert in a closed section, whether it is a rocker panel, A- or B-pillar, or body rail, make sure the closing weld fully penetrates the insert. When closing the job with a butt weld, leave a gap that is wide enough to allow thorough penetration of the insert. The width of the gap depends on the thickness of the metal, but ideally it should not

FIGURE 11-60   Rear rail with butt joint and insert

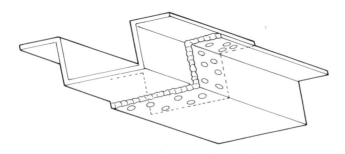

FIGURE 11-61   Joining open rails

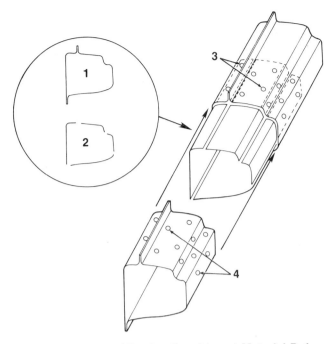

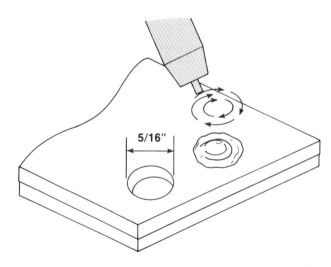

1. Cross Section of Rocker Panel Insert Material Before Cutting Lengthwise
2. Insert Cut Lengthwise into Sections
3. Insert Inside Rocker Panel, Secured With Plug Welds or Sheet Metal Screws
4. 5/16" Holes for Plug Welds

FIGURE 11-65   Cutting an insert to fit a rocker panel

FIGURE 11-66   Circular motion in 5/16-inch hole

be less than 1/16 inch nor more than 1/8 inch (Figure 11-67). Be careful to remove the burrs from the cut edges before welding. Otherwise the weld metal tends to travel around and up under the burr. This can create a flawed weld, resulting in stress concentration that can cause cracks and weaken the joint (Figure 11-68).

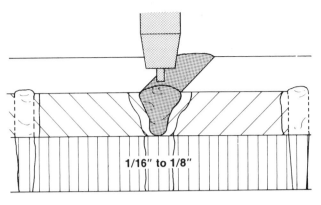

1/16" to 1/8"

FIGURE 11-67   Butt weld gap

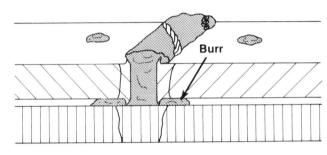

Burr

FIGURE 11-68   Burrs in joint will weaken the weld.

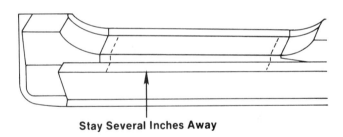

Stay Several Inches Away

FIGURE 11-69   Overlapping the outer rocker panel section

In general, use the overlap procedure on a rocker panel when installing only the outer rocker or a portion of it. Leave the inner piece intact and cut only the outer piece. One way to make an overlap joint is to make the cut in the front door opening and allow for an overlap there when measuring. When making this cut, stay several inches away from the base of the B-pillar in order to avoid cutting any reinforcement underneath it (Figure 11-69).

1. Cut around the bases of the B- and C-pillars, leaving overlap areas around each (Figure 11-70).
2. Cut out the new outer rocker panel so that it overlaps around the bases of the pillars

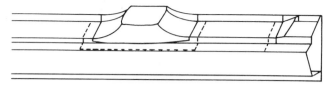

Leave overlap areas.

FIGURE 11-70   Overlap joint around pillar

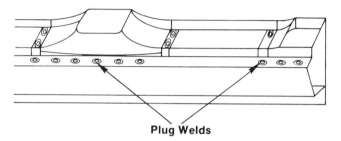

Plug Welds

FIGURE 11-71   Plug weld flanges

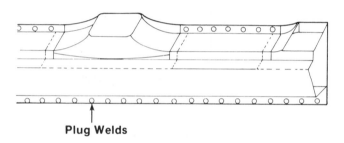

Plug Welds

FIGURE 11-72   Plug weld overlaps

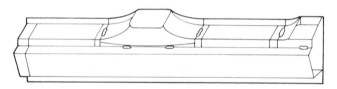

FIGURE 11-73   Intermittent lap weld seams

and also the original piece of the outer rocker still affixed to the car.

3. In the pinch weld flanges, use plug welds to replace the factory spot welds (Figure 11-71).

4. Plug weld the overlaps around the B- and C-pillars, using approximately the same spacing as in the pinch weld flanges (Figure 11-72).

5. Then lap weld the edges with about a 30 percent intermittent seam; about 1/2 inch of weld in every 1-1/2 inches of overlap edge (Figure 11-73).

6. Put plug welds in the overlap area in the door opening, and lap weld around the edges to close the joint (Figure 11-74).

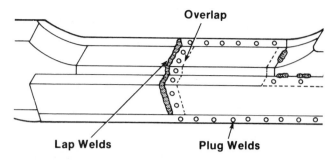

Overlap

Lap Welds   Plug Welds

FIGURE 11-74   Plug weld and lap weld overlapping section

To reverse this procedure, of course, depending on the nature of the hit, make the overlap cut in the rear door opening and cut out and overlap around the bases of the A- and B-pillars. Use this same basic technique to replace the entire outer rocker. In this version, cut around the bases of all three pillars and overlap all three bases in the same way as before.

SECTIONING A-PILLARS

A-pillars can be either two piece or three piece components (Figure 11-75). They can be reinforced at the upper end or the lower end, or both. But they are not likely to be reinforced in the middle. Therefore, A-pillars should be cut near the middle to avoid cutting through any reinforcing pieces. It is also the easiest place to work.

To section an A-pillar, use a straight-cut butt joint with an insert or an off-set butt joint without an insert. The butt joint with insert repair is made in the same manner as already described for the rocker panel. The A-pillar insert should be 4 to 6 inches in length. After cutting the insert lengthwise and remov-

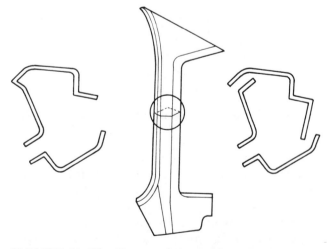

FIGURE 11-75   Two and three piece A-pillar sections

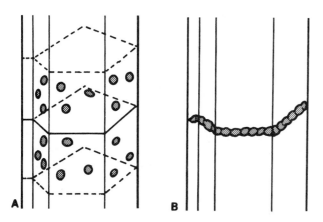

FIGURE 11-76   Welding the butt joint with insert in an A-pillar with (A) plug welds and (B) butt welds

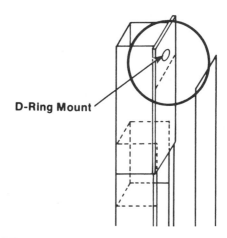

D-Ring Mount

FIGURE 11-78   Two piece B-pillar

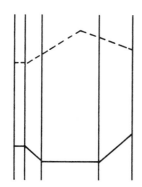

FIGURE 11-77   An off-set butt joint

ing any flanges, tap the pieces into place. Secure the insert in place with plug welds and close all around the pillar with a continuous butt weld (Figure 11-76).

To make the off-set butt joint, cut the inner piece of the pillar at a different point than the other piece was cut, creating the offset (Figure 11-77). Whenever possible, try to make the cuts between the factory spot welds, so that it will not be difficult to drill them out, and make the cuts no closer to each other than 2 to 4 inches. Butt the sections together and continuous-weld them all around.

SECTIONING B-PILLARS

For sectioning B-pillars, two types of joints can be used: the butt joint with insert and a combination of off-set cut and overlap. The butt joint with insert is usually easier to align and fit up when the B-pillar is a relatively simple two piece cross section without a lot of internal reinforcing members. The insert provides additional strength (Figure 11-78).

Be sure to cut below the D-ring mount low enough to avoid cutting through the D-ring anchor reinforcement. The majority of B-pillars have them.

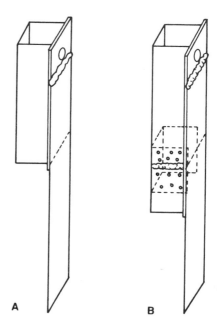

FIGURE 11-79   (A) Lap weld the inner panel; (B) plug and butt weld the outer panel

In the case of the B-pillar, use a channel insert in only the outside piece of the pillar. The D-ring anchor reinforcement welded to the inside piece prevents the installation of an insert there.

Begin by overlapping the new inside piece on the existing one, rather than butting them together, and lap weld the edge (Figure 11-79A). Then, secure the insert in place with plug welds and close the joint with a continuous butt weld around the outer pillar (Figure 11-79B).

On occasion it is expedient to obtain a recycled B-pillar and rocker panel assembly and replace them as a unit, because any time a B-pillar is hit so hard that it needs to be replaced, the rocker panel is almost invariably damaged, too. Install the upper end of the B-pillar with either of the two approved types of joints and make a butt joint with insert in the rocker panel in the manner already shown. If the main damage is in the rear door opening, make the butt joint with insert in the front door opening and install the other end of the rocker in its entirety. If the main damage is in the front door opening, reverse the procedure.

Generally speaking, the combination off-set and overlap joint (Figure 11–80) is used more often when installing new parts and when working with separate inside and outside pieces.

1. Cut a butt joint in the outside piece above the level of the D-ring anchor reinforcement.

2. Make an overlap cut in the inside piece below the D-ring anchor reinforcement.

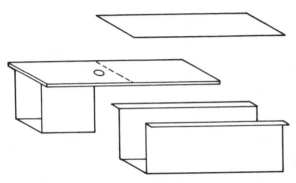

FIGURE 11-80   A combination off-set and overlap joint

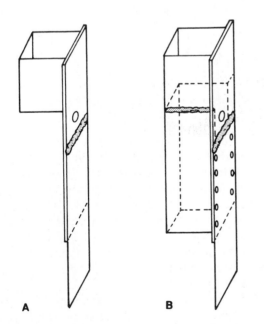

FIGURE 11-81   Creating the combination off-set and overlap joint: (A) lap welding inside and (B) plug and lap weld outside

3. Install the inside piece first with the new segment overlapping the existing segment.

4. Lap weld the edge (Figure 11–81A).

5. Put the outside pieces in place, make plug welds in the flanges, and close the section with a continuous weld at the butt joint (Figure 11–81B).

Usually, it is advantageous to use the off-set and overlap joint on a B-pillar with three or more pieces in its cross section, making it difficult to install an insert. In fact, sometimes the off-set and overlap procedure is mandatory, because it is actually not possible to install an insert.

SECTIONING FLOOR PANS

When sectioning a floor pan, do not cut through any reinforcements, such as seat belt anchorages. Always see to it that the rear section overlaps the front section, so the edge of the bottom piece, under the car, is always pointing rearward. This way road splash, which moves from the front to the rear, streams past the bottom edge and does not strike it head-on (Figure 11–82).

1. Join all floor pan sections with an overlap.

2. Plug weld the overlap, putting the plugs in from the topside, downward (Figure 11–83A).

3. Caulk the topside, forward edge with a flexible body caulk.

4. On the bottom side, lap weld the underlapping edge with a continuous bead.

5. Cover the lap weld with a primer, a seam sealer, and a topcoat (Figure 11–83B). The primer helps the sealer hold better, and the topcoat completes the protection. This as-

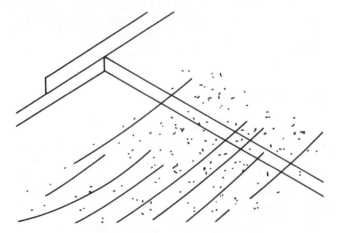

FIGURE 11-82   The rear section overlaps shields joint from windstream.

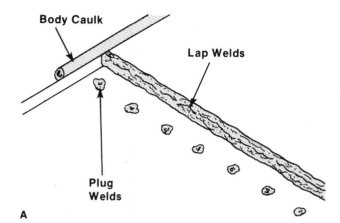

Body Caulk

Lap Welds

Plug Welds

A

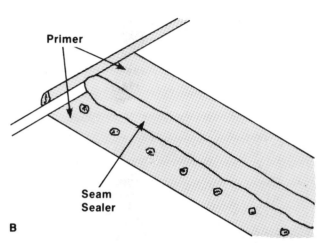

Primer

Seam Sealer

B

FIGURE 11-83 (A) Plug weld from top and lap weld bottom edge; (B) seal and prime bottom edge.

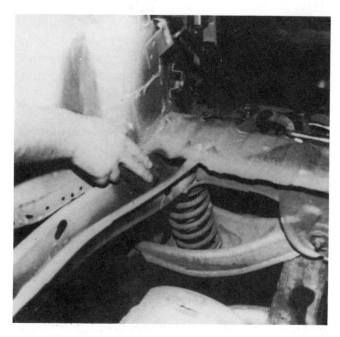

FIGURE 11-84 Section trunk floor above the cross member

sures that there will be no carbon monoxide intrusion through the joint into the passenger compartment.

SECTIONING TRUNK FLOORS

When sectioning a trunk floor, in general, follow the basic procedures just described for the floor pan with some variations.

 **SHOP TALK**

In a collision that necessitates sectioning of the trunk floor, the rear rail usually requires sectioning, too.

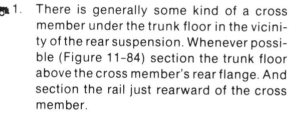

1. There is generally some kind of a cross member under the trunk floor in the vicinity of the rear suspension. Whenever possible (Figure 11-84) section the trunk floor above the cross member's rear flange. And section the rail just rearward of the cross member.

2. Plug weld the trunk floor overlap joint to the cross member, again putting the plugs in from the topside, downward, as in a floor pan (Figure 11-85).

3. Caulk the topside, forward edge just like a floor pan seam (Figure 11-86).

4. On the bottom side a lap weld on the underlapping edge is not necessary because of the strength provided by the cross member. However, on cars where the trunk floor section is not above a cross member, the lower edge must be lap welded.

In both cases cover the bottom-side seam with a primer, a seam sealer, and a topcoat. With the trunk

FIGURE 11-85 Plug weld trunk floor

377

FIGURE 11-86   Caulk the inside seam

floor, the sealing against carbon monoxide intrusion is quite critical because of the proximity of the tail pipe.

SECTIONING WITH LAP WELDS

Recent testing has determined that lap welding of front section frame rails and rocker panels can yield a tighter fitting section and superior corrosion protection when compared to inserts. The following example involves a vehicle that has sustained damage to the left side (Figure 11-87) with the left rail to be sectioned.

1. Locate and drill out the factory spot welds that attach the upper rail to the cowl at the base of the windshield. A propane torch, scraper, and wire brush might be needed to remove sealant or caulk from the spot weld areas. Set the torch on low heat to avoid burning the seam sealer.

2. Remove the two hidden spot welds that secure the upper rail to the rear outer flange of the strut tower. They are visible

FIGURE 11-87   Welding a rocker panel

through a hole at the rear portion of the upper rail (Figure 11-88).

3. Remove the spot welds that attach the strut tower to the rail extension panel at the base of the strut tower (Figure 11-89). Remove any seam sealer covering these welds inside the engine compartment. The under surface is likely coated with sealer and sound-deadening material.

4. The lower rail sectioning is performed forward of the center of the strut tower. The sectioning procedure uses a staggered cut of the inner and outer lower rail, with a lap joint at both cutlines. There is an inner rail reinforcement that is located in the area of

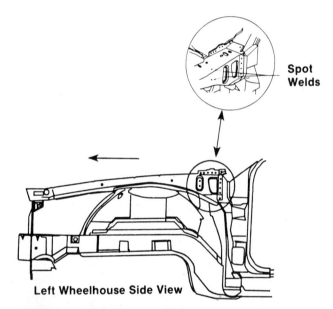

Left Wheelhouse Side View

FIGURE 11-88   The spot welds that secure the upper rail to the strut tower can be seen through the hole at the rear of the upper rail.

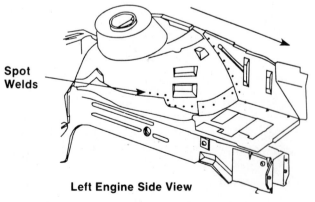

Left Engine Side View

FIGURE 11-89   General location of the spot welds in the strut tower area

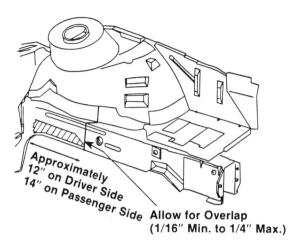

FIGURE 11-90   Sectioning cut on the engine side

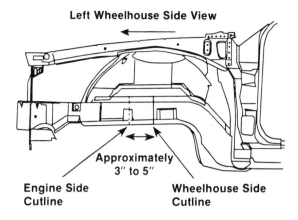

FIGURE 11-91   Sectioning cut on the outer rail

the section. Because of this reinforcement, this part of the rail is ideal for sectioning.

5. There are two spot welds that attach the reinforcement to the inside of the lower rail. These must be removed before any cuts are made, and are visible on the wheelhouse side of the rail.

6. The location of the cut on the engine side is about 12 inches from the cowl (Figure 11-90). This will position the cutline near the end of the inner reinforcement.

CAUTION: If the reinforcement is accidentally damaged with a small cut, it must be welded. If the cut is larger than 1/4 inch in length and completely through the reinforcement, the sectioning process may not be successful even if the reinforcement is repaired. For this reason, it is important that extreme care is used while cutting around an internal reinforcement.

7. The outer rail cutline (wheelhouse side) is made 3 to 5 inches rearward of the engine side cutline (Figure 11-91).

8. To achieve the correct overlap, carefully "split" the corners on the original structure at the exposed end. These splits should not exceed 1/4 inch. Any part of the splits that is exposed after fit-up must be welded closed.

9. It is very important that the replacement structure is positioned **over** the original structure. This will allow the application of the corrosion protection to be more effective, since the open portion of the joint will face the open end of the rail.

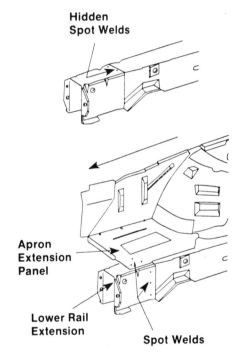

FIGURE 11-92   Fold the apron extension panel up to expose the spot welds.

10. Separate the opposite side lower rail extension from the lower rail by first drilling the spot welds that secure the radiator support and apron extension panel. Next, carefully fold the apron extension panel upward to expose the other spot welds that attach the extension to the rail (Figure 11-92).

11. After all the spot welds have been removed and the offset cuts made, the damaged assembly can be removed from the vehicle.

379

12. Preparation of the used assembly (for example, spot weld removal and the lower rail offset cut) is identical to that of the damaged assembly. It is very important to inspect, measure, and, if necessary, straighten the used assembly to the proper dimensions prior to installing it on the vehicle. Remember to add to the length measurement on the replacement rail to allow for the overlap.

13. All adjoining flanges and weld areas must be cleaned using a propane torch and wire brush. Do not grind or burn off any galvanized coatings. After cleaning and before welding, a weld-through zinc-rich primer must be applied to all bare metal mating surfaces.

14. After the used assembly is installed, measuring equipment can be used to check the correct position. Then the assembly is clamped in place (Figure 11-93).

15. After checking that all dimensions are within tolerance, the assembly can be welded. Continuous welds should be made in alternating segments of 1/2 to 3/4 inch to minimize distortion. Be sure to completely close all seams and do not leave any gaps.

16. Corrosion protection, including refinishing of the replacement pieces, should be completed as detailed in Chapter 15.

FULL BODY SECTIONING

To reconstruct a complete vehicle by full body sectioning, the front portion of one vehicle is joined to the rear portion of another vehicle. This type of repair is generally done on a vehicle that has sustained severe rear end damage. In such a case, sectioning is more practical and cost effective in comparison to conventional methods of repairing severely damaged unitized automobiles. This method reduces the time and labor of dismantling the vehicle and disturbs less of the corrosion protection.

The techniques and procedures just described for sectioning a rocker panel, an A-pillar, and a floor pan are repeated in a full body section. By sectioning both A-pillars, both rocker panels, and the floor pan, a vehicle can be fully sectioned.

When the individual components are properly sectioned, aligned, and welded using the proper techniques and procedures, full body sectioning is a suitable and satisfactory procedure. Vehicles repaired by full body sectioning are completely crashworthy. This has been tested and proved time and again. Keep in mind, however, that full body sectioning is not a frequently required procedure and full disclosure should be given to the car owner before repairs are started.

A discussion between the insurance representative, car owner, and repairer must be conducted and the following points must be covered:

A

FIGURE 11-93   Check dimensional accuracy after the new assembly is clamped into place.

B

FIGURE 11-94   (A) Full body section and (B) replacement rear end

- All repair procedures, including alignment and welding, must be fully explained to the car owner.
- The recycled sections—both body and mechanical—must be of like kind and quality. Always verify that all VIN code identifications and EPA emission control requirements are met and that all suspension, braking, and steering components are in proper working order.
- Carefully inspect front and rear sections for proper alignment before cutting. If either is out of alignment, proper fit and line-up of the section joints will be difficult if not impossible to achieve.

Figure 11-94 shows a popular compact that was fully body sectioned in a commercial repair shop. The undamaged front half of one car was joined to the undamaged rear half of another. Butt joints and inserts were used in the middle of the A-pillars (Figure 11-95) and in the two rocker panels (Figure 11-96) and an overlap joint was used in the floor pan (Figure 11-97). The rocker panel and floor pan cuts were made in the middle of the front door opening to avoid any brackets or reinforcements in the A- and B-pillars.

But remember that the floor pan might have reinforcements and brackets that need to be removed before sectioning. Reinforcements can be left on the replacement rear half to aid in alignment. Proper corrosion protection must be restored when replacing brackets and reinforcements.

JOINING THE FULL BODY SECTIONS

After the front and rear sections have been trimmed to fit, drilled for plug welds, and primed with weld through, follow these steps to join the sections.

1. Install the rocker and pillar inserts. Clamp them in place with sheet metal screws.
2. Place the A-pillar inserts in the upper or lower portion of the windshield pillar, depending on the angle and contour of the windshield.
3. Fit the two halves together by first joining the rocker panels and then the A-pillars. Clamp the rocker and pillar flanges to prevent the sections from pulling apart.
4. Check the windshield and door openings for proper dimension, using a tram gauge or a steel rule. If possible, install the doors and windshield to verify proper alignment.
5. When proper alignment is achieved, secure overlapping areas with sheet metal

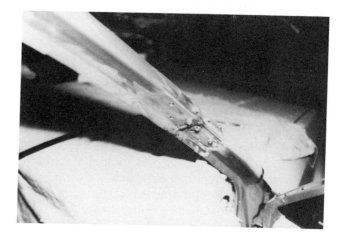

FIGURE 11-95   A-pillar section welded

FIGURE 11-96   Rocker panel butt joint

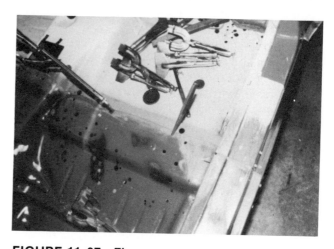

FIGURE 11-97   Floor pan overlap

screws to pull the seam areas together and hold the sections together during welding.
6. Using centerline gauges and a tram gauge, double-check vehicle dimensions and section alignment before welding the sections together.
7. Weld sections together using techniques already described in this chapter for join-

ing rocker panels, A-pillars, and the floor pan.

11.4 ANTIRUST TREATMENTS

The application of antirust agents is necessary not only before welding, but also before and after the painting process. Welded panel joints are treated with weld-through primer before they are joined together. The weld joints must also be sealed with body sealer before finishing undercoating or an antirust treatment must be applied to the joints after finishing to seal out moisture and prevent rust formation. Rustproofing and corrosion protection techniques are discussed fully in Chapter 15.

11.5 DOOR PANEL REPLACEMENT

The repair of vehicle doors can be considered a unique class unto its own. Like other damaged vehicle panels the door can be bumped back to shape, pulled into shape, or replaced. The decision is determined by the amount of work hardening in the buckles, the accessibility of the backside of the door skin, and the amount of door frame damage. Figure 11–98 shows a dented door skin that was repaired with a dent puller. The door in Figure 11–99 requires complete replacement. A third possibility is replacement of the outer door panel.

The outer panel (or door skin) wraps around the door frame and is clinched to the pinch weld flange. The skin is secured to the frame either with plug or spot welds or with adhesives. Typical replacement procedures for welded door skins are given here. Procedures for replacing adhesive-bonded door skins are given in Chapter 19.

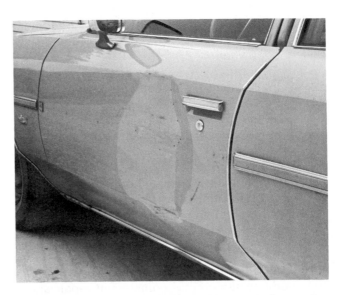

FIGURE 11-98 This dented door panel can be repaired.

FIGURE 11-99 This damaged door must be relaced.

REPLACING WELDED DOOR SKINS

 1. Before removing the door, check to see if the hinges are sprung and observe the alignment of the door with respect to its opening.
2. Observe how the panel is fastened to the door so that it can be determined how much interior hardware must be removed.
3. Remove the trim panel and disconnect the battery to isolate all door power accessories. Remove all hardware from the door.
4. To prevent loss, place parts inside the vehicle. This also applies to the door glass.
5. To remove some of the damage and possibly straighten or align the inner door frame, use a hydraulic or body jack at this time.
6. Remove the door glass to prevent breakage while repairing the door.
7. Now remove the door from the vehicle and move it to a suitable work area.
8. Using an oxyacetylene gas torch and wire brush, remove paint from the spot welds in the panel hem. Using a drill and spot cutter or grinder, remove the spot welds.
9. Apply tape to the door frame and measure the distance between the lower line of the tape and the outer panel edge. Also measure the distance between the front or rear

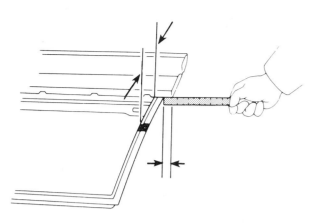

FIGURE 11-100 Measuring panel location and alignment. (Courtesy of Toyota Motor Corp.)

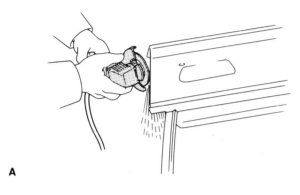

A

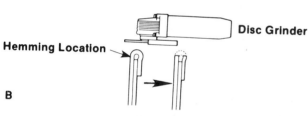

Hemming Location

B

FIGURE 11-101 (A) Grinding off door hemming flange; (B) hemming flange cross section. (Courtesy of Toyota Motor Corp.)

edge of the outer panel and the door frame (Figure 11-100).

10. Use a plasma cutter or cut-off grinder to remove the brazed portion away from the outer panel door frame connections.

11. The quickest way to remove an exterior door panel is to grind off the edge of the hem flange (Figure 11-101). Only grind off enough metal so that the panel can be separated from the inner flange. Do not grind into the inner panel. Do not use a welding torch or power chisel to separate the panels. The inner panel can become distorted or be accidentally cut.

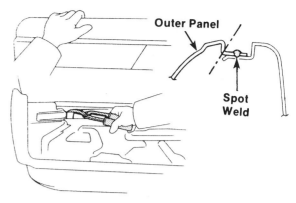

FIGURE 11-102 Cutting around spot welds. (Courtesy of Toyota Motor Corp.)

12. Separate the reinforcing strip on the top of the panel (if installed or used).

13. Using a hammer and chisel, loosen the two panels. Use a pair of tin snips to cut around any spot welds that could not be drilled or ground off (Figure 11-102). When the exterior panel moves freely, remove the panel. Use vise grips or pliers to remove what remains of the inner hem flange. Any remaining spot welds, brazing, and rust should be ground off using a disc grinder.

14. With the exterior panel removed, examine carefully the inner panel and frame construction for damage. If necessary, straighten or repair any remaining inner door damage at this time. Remove dents on the inner flange with a hammer and dolly.

15. Apply weld-through primer to any areas to be spot welded. Cover other bare metal areas with a rust resistant primer or some other rust treatment.

16. Prepare the new panel for installation. Using a drill or hole punch, make holes for any plug welds. Using a sander, remove the paint from the weld and braze locations. Apply weld-through primer to the bare metal seam areas and prime any other bare metal areas.

17. Some outer door panels are accompanied by a silencer pad that must be glued to the outer panel. To do this, clean the outer panel with alcohol or the equivalent. Heat the outer panel and silencer pad with a heat lamp. Then, glue the silencer pad to the outer panel.

18. Before installing the new panel, apply body sealer to the backside of the new panel. Apply the sealer evenly 3/8 inch from the flange in a 1/8-inch thick bead.

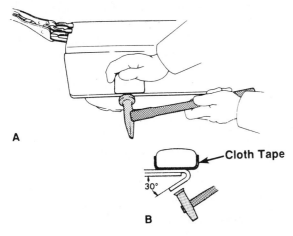

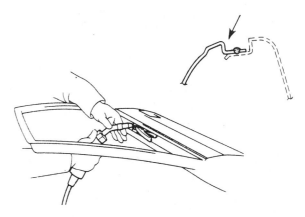

FIGURE 11-105 Spot welding window section. *(Courtesy of Toyota Motor Corp.)*

FIGURE 11-103   (A) Dollying panel flange and (B) cross section. *(Courtesy of Toyota Motor Corp.)*

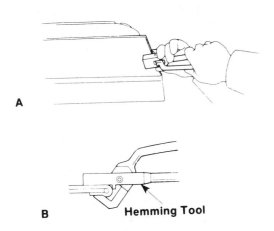

FIGURE 11-104   (A) Forming the panel hem and (B) cross section. *(Courtesy of Toyota Motor Corp.)*

19. Using vise grips, attach the new outer panel to the door and align it properly, using the dimensions determined in Step 2. Braze the outer panel where required.

20. Use a hammer and dolly to bend the outer panel flange (Figure 11-103). Cover the dolly face with cloth tape to avoid scarring the panel. Bend the hem gradually in three steps. Be careful not to tap the panel edge that would throw the panel out of alignment. Do not create bulges or creases in the body lines of the outer panel.

21. After working the flange within 30 degrees of the inner panel, use a hemming tool to finish the hem (Figure 11-104). Again, finish the hem in three steps, being careful not to deform the panel.

22. Weld the plug or spot weld locations of the glass opening and tack weld the hemming edge of the outer panel flange (Figure 11-105).

23. Apply body sealer to the hemming edge of the flange and apply antirust agents on the inside of the spot welds, plug welds, and brazed areas.

24. Drill holes into the new panel for moldings, trim, and so forth.

25. At this point the auto body technician has two possible routes to choose from—continue to prepare the panel for refinishing **OR** place the door on the vehicle to check its alignment, prepare the door for refinishing, and then reinstall the door. The route to take will depend on what the body shop determines to be the most expedient.

26. Before refinishing the door be sure to install the door glass. This will prevent overspray from getting on the interior of the door.

27. Be sure to align the door with all adjacent panels and check for proper closure or latching and panel gaps.

To replace fiberglass plastic door skins, see Chapter 13.

11.6 CUSTOM BODY PANELS

Body customizing is a growing trend. Many car owners, when faced with the need to replace damaged panels, are spending the extra money to give their cars a performance face-lift. A number of com-

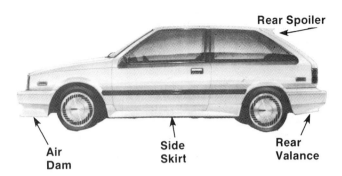

FIGURE 11-106   Car with spoiler and air dam kit

panies are marketing spoiler and air dam kits that can turn any street car into an Indy impression. Figure 11-106 shows what can be done with a Hyundai Excel to give an economy car a sporty look. The accessory panels not only improve the appearance of the car but also improve the aerodynamic performance during high-speed driving (Figure 11-107). Air dams restrict air passing under the car body (minimizing undercar turbulence and reducing resistance to airflow) and prevent the front wheels from lifting. Side skirts channel airflow away from the rear wheels, thus reducing turbulence and resistance to airflow. The rear spoiler alters the airstream at the rear body end to again reduce resistance to airflow and to prevent the rear wheels from lifting.

The spoilers, side skirts, air dams, and so on are made from a molded polyurethane plastic. The product usually comes with a silicone release that must be removed with lacquer thinner or a wax and grease

remover. Then, the panel must be scuff sanded with #240 grit sandpaper followed by #320 grit paper to improve adhesion. The painting of plastic panels is covered in detail in Chapter 19.

Most add-on body panels utilize original fasteners on the vehicle as well as requiring the scribing and drilling of additional mounting holes for the fasteners provided by the kit manufacturer. Double-sided adhesive tape is also sometimes used to keep the plastic panels fitting tightly against the original sheet metal panels. The area to which the tape will be applied should be dewaxed and scuff sanded to ensure a positive bond between the car and new panel. The key to successful add-ons is proper alignment, careful positioning of the new fasteners, and preparation of the mating panel surfaces. A typical procedure for installing a front air dam is given below and illustrated in Figure 11-108.

1. Remove the lower body panel from under the front bumper.
2. Replace the new air dam under the front bumper and align the air dam with the wheel wells. Make sure that the front top lip of the air dam is located inside the front panel.
3. Clamp the corners of the air dam to the wheel well with vice grips.
4. Transfer the front body panel mounting holes with a scribe onto the air dam.
5. Use a scribe to transfer the mounting holes in the ends of the air dam to the wheel well.
6. Using a 1/4-inch drill bit, drill the six holes through the sheet metal and air dam.

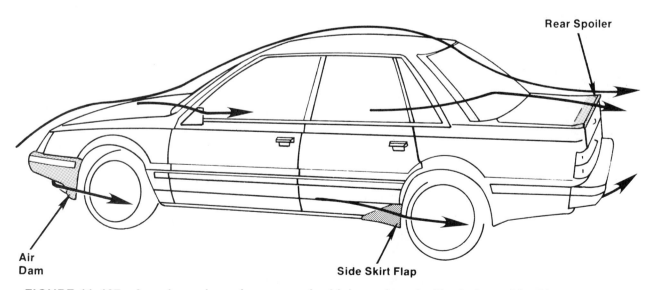

FIGURE 11-107   Aerodynamic performance of vehicle equipped with air dam, side skirt, and spoiler

FIGURE 11-108   Air dam installation

7. Loosely bolt the air dam in position and check it for correct alignment.
8. Tighten all six fasteners securely.

11.7 PANEL ADJUSTMENTS

Manufacturers provide for adjustments of mechanically fastened panels in several ways. One of the most frequent is slotted or oversized holes. Because the openings are larger than the bolts, the panels can be moved up or down, forward or rearward, depending on the size and shape of the hole and its location. Washers are provided under the bolt heads to provide a sufficient bearing surface on which the bolt is to be tightened. The hood hinge

connection shown in Figure 11-109 is an example of an adjustable fastener with slotted holes.

Another common fastener that allows for adjustments to be made is a caged plate (Figure 11-110). The caged plate is like a large nut. It is a heavy steel plate threaded to accept two or more bolts, depending on the number of bolts in the connection. The plate is housed in a "cage" of thin sheet metal spot welded to the supporting panel (Figure 11-111). The cage is larger than the plate, so that the plate can be moved around, but the cage prevents the plate from falling away from the panel. Oversized holes in the panel allow the panel to be adjusted in any direction. Caged plates are often used in doors and door pillars (Figure 11-112) where a cluster of oversized bolt holes would weaken the weight bear-

FIGURE 11-109   Slotted holes permit hood adjustments.

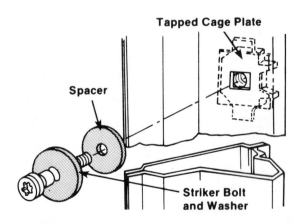

FIGURE 11-110   Caged plate permits striker adjustments.

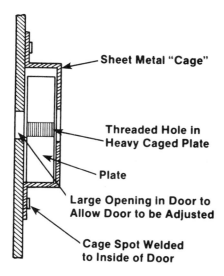

FIGURE 11-111 **Caged plate cross section**

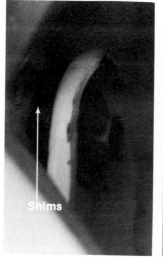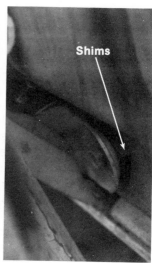

FIGURE 11-113 **Upper and lower fender connections**

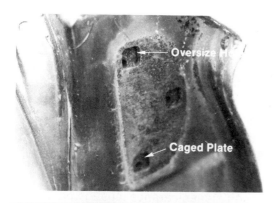

FIGURE 11-112 **Caged plate connections allow door adjustments.**

ing strength of the panel without the reinforcement of the steel backing plate.

A shim is another means of making an adjustment. A shim is a thin U-shaped piece of metal (Figure 11-113). By loosening a bolt, a shim can be slipped under the bolt head and around the bolt. When retightened, the position of the attached panel is thus changed. Shimming body panels was once a very common operation. But with the welded panels of today's unibody construction, there are few body panels that can be shimmed.

Another means of adjusting body parts is the adjustable stop (Figure 11-114). The adjustable stop is a threaded bolt with a rubber cap. It is usually attached to a body panel by a fixed nut in a clip. A locknut secures the stop in position. Adjustable stops are usually found on most cars under the hood. These stops bear against the hood to prevent it from vibrating and rattling on its hinges and to

FIGURE 11-114 **Adjustable stops control hood height**

control the height of the hood. The rubber cap prevents the stop from chipping the paint and denting the hood.

Hood Adjustments

The hood is the largest adjustable panel on most vehicles. It can be adjusted at the hinges, at the adjustable stops, and at the hood latch. The adjustments allow the hood to be moved up and down, forward and rearward to align it with the fenders and cowl. The hood should align with the fender, side to side, with a gap of approximately 5/32 inch between the fenders. The front edge of the hood should be even with the front edge of the fender and there

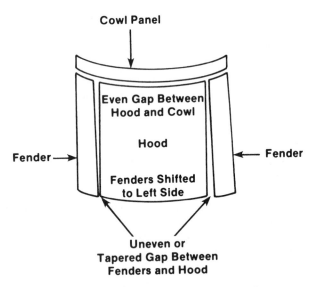

FIGURE 11-115 Uneven hood gaps around hood

FIGURE 11-116 Hood hinge

should be enough of a gap at the back edge to clear the cowl panel (Figure 11-115).

On some models, the rear of the hood is attached to a pair of hinges that are bolted to either the cowl or the inner fender (Figure 11-116). The holes in the hinges are slotted to allow the hinges to be raised or lowered on the cowl or fender and to allow the hood to be moved forward or backward on the hinges.

The front of the hood is held in place by a hood latch (Figure 11-117). This latch is used to secure the front of the hood so that it latches tightly and aligns with the fenders. Slotted holes are usually provided on the latch for alignment purposes. Most vehicles have adjustable bumper stops mounted on the radiator support or along the inner edges of the fenders. These bumper stops provide up and down adjustment points and also prevent hood flutter at the front of the hood. They determine the position of the hood when it is closed. The hood is also equipped with a safety catch to prevent the hood from flying off should it accidentally open when the vehicle is in motion.

Hood-to-Hinge Adjustment

Adjusting the hood forward and rearward can be accomplished by slightly loosening the bolts attaching the hood to the hinges. Then, close the hood and line it up properly, carefully raising the hood far enough for another technician to tighten the bolts. The front of the hood must align with the front of the fenders and sufficient clearance must be permitted between the hood and cowl to allow the hood to be raised without rubbing the cowl.

Hood Height Adjustments

To correct the alignment of the hood up and down, slightly loosen the bolts holding the hinges to the fenders or cowl. Then, slowly close the hood and raise or lower the back side of the hood as necessary. When the back of the hood is level with the adjacent fenders and cowl, slowly raise the hood and tighten the bolts.

Once the rear of the hood is adjusted to the correct height, the adjustable stops must be adjusted (some vehicles have only two stops—one in each front corner, while others have stops in each corner). The rear stops must be adjusted to bear against the hood. This eliminates hood movement and rattle. The front stops control the height of the front of the hood. Turn the stops in or out until the front of the hood is even with the top of the fenders. Be sure to retighten the locknut on the stop after adjusting it.

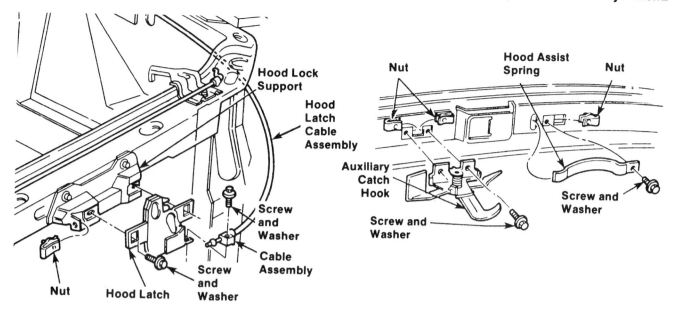

FIGURE 11-117 Hood latches

 SHOP TALK _____

In order to lower the hood, it might be necessary to turn down the adjustable stops under the rear corners of the hood. If the hood is lowered without lowering the stops, it might bend and crease. Additional bodywork will be required to fix the damage.

Hood Latch Adjustments

After making height and lateral adjustments, test the hood for proper latching. If the hood must be slammed excessively hard to engage the latch, the latch should be raised. If the hood does not contact the front stoppers when latched, the latch should be lowered. To adjust the hood latch, do the following:

 1. Remove the hood latch assembly from the radiator support and lower the hood.
2. Check that all the gaps around the hood are properly aligned.
3. Reinstall the hood latch and lower the hood until it engages or contacts the first latch (auxiliary latch or safety catch).
4. Attempt to raise the hood. If it does open, adjust the safety catch so that it engages. Sometimes the hook can be bent until the auxiliary latch "catches."
5. Lower the hood slowly. Check to see if the hood shifts to one side or the other when it is locked. The striker bar bolted to the hood should be centered in the "U" of the

latch. When the hood is latched, it should be even with the surrounding sheet metal and fit tightly.
6. Loosen the hood latch attaching hardware just enough to maintain a tight fit but yet be able to move the latch.
7. Move the latch from side to side to align it with the hood latch hook. Move the latch up or down as required to obtain a flush fit between the top of the hood and the fenders when an upward pressure is applied to the front of the hood.
8. Tighten the hood latch attaching hardware.
9. Open the hood.
10. Close the hood and observe the left and right front corners. If necessary, adjust the bumper stops to eliminate any looseness at the front of the hood and ensure a good, tight fit.
11. Tighten the attaching hardware on the bumper stops.
12. Check to see that the side bumper stops (if any) are in place and in good condition.

Trunk Lid Adjustments

The trunk lid is very similar to the hood in construction. Two hinges (Figure 11-118) connect the lid to the rear body panel and the trailing edge is secured by a locking latch. The trunk lid seals the trunk area from dust and water. Weatherstripping is

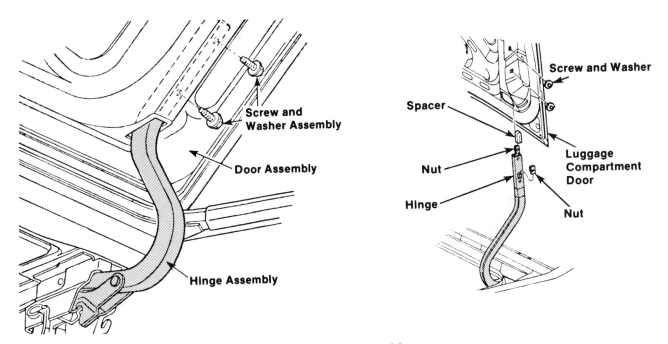

FIGURE 11-118   Trunk hinges

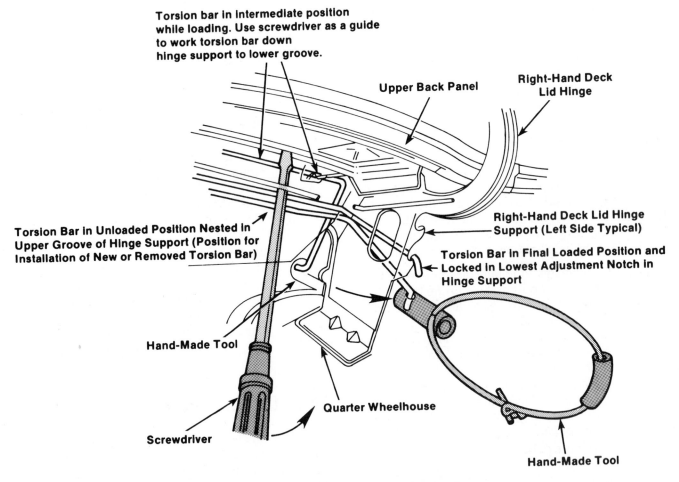

FIGURE 11-119   Adjusting torque rods

used to provide the proper seal. However, for the seal to be effective, the trunk lid must be in continuous contact with the weatherstripping when the lid is closed.

The lid must be evenly spaced between the adjacent panels. Slotted holes in the hinges and/or caged plates in the lid allow the trunk lid to be moved forward, rearward, and side to side. To adjust the lid forward or backward, slightly loosen the attaching hardware on both hinges. Close and adjust the lid as required. Then raise the lid and tighten the attaching hardware.

In some cases, it might be necessary to use shims between the bolts and the trunk lid to raise or lower the front edges. If the front edge must be raised, place the shim(s) between the hinge and the lid in the front bolt area. To lower the front edge of the lid, place the shim(s) at the back of the hinge.

On some vehicles, the trunk lid has hinge assemblies that utilize torque rods to counterbalance the weight of the lid. This arrangement makes the trunk lid easier to raise and hold in the up position. The torque rods can be tightened or loosened by moving the torque rod end to a different hole or slot (Figure 11-119). Using a 1/2-inch pipe inserted over the end of the torque rod is another way to safely move the rod to a new position.

Figure 11-120 shows a typical trunk lid lock assembly. The lock assembly is usually in the trunk lid and the striker plate bolted to the rear body panel. On some cars, this position is reversed. The trunk lid

latch and striker can usually be adjusted up, down, and sideways to properly engage, align, and tightly hold the trunk lid. The necessary adjustments are similar to those given for the hood.

Vehicles with hatchback type trunk lids are usually difficult to align mainly because of their size. For the most part, many lids of this type are nearly horizontal in design, which makes them more prone to water and dust leaks. Some models use adjustable hinges, while others use welded hinges. The hatchback types also use gas-filled door lift assemblies, or springs, one at each upper corner of the lid. Some play might be available in the door lift support brackets to allow adjustment of the hatchback trunk lid (Figure 11-121).

Fender Adjustments

Fenders are bolted (Figure 11-122) to the radiator core support or to the grille, to the inner fender panel in the engine compartment, and to the cowl behind the door and under the car. When these bolts are loosened the fender can be moved forward and backward.

 **SHOP TALK** _____

The screws holding the splash guard to the fender might also have to be loosened.

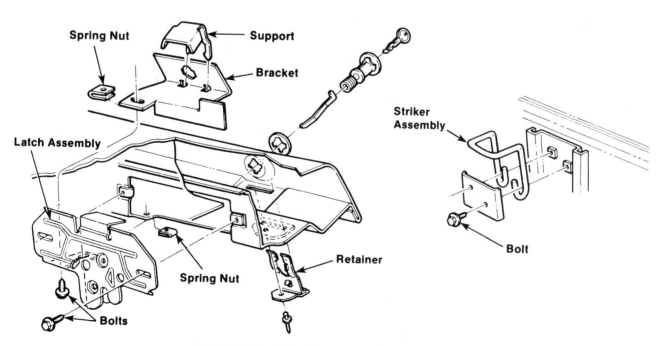

FIGURE 11-120 Typical trunk lock

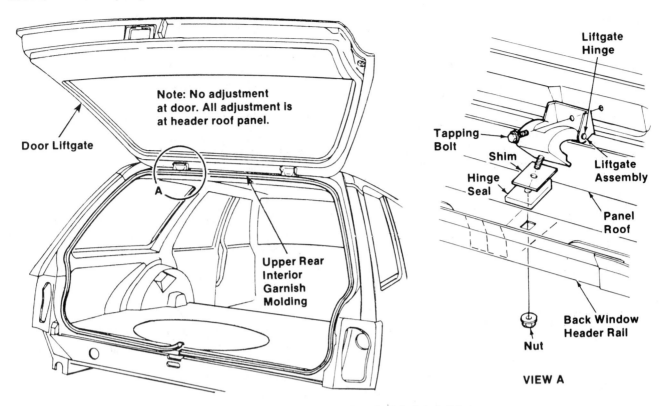

Note: No adjustment at door. All adjustment is at header roof panel.

Door Liftgate

A

Upper Rear Interior Garnish Molding

Liftgate Hinge

Tapping Bolt

Shim

Hinge Seal

Liftgate Assembly

Panel Roof

Back Window Header Rail

Nut

VIEW A

FIGURE 11-121 Adjusting hatch back lid

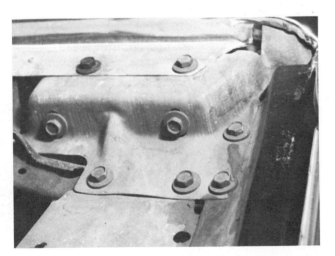

FIGURE 11-122 Fender connections

The fender can also be moved in and out so that it is flush with the door and parallel with the hood. The fender-to-door alignment can be made by shimming the two large bolts attaching the fender to the cowl. The top bolt is usually in the door pillar; the bottom bolt is either in the hinge post or under the car in the rocker panel. By shimming the top bolt, the upper fender can be moved out. Shimming the lower bolt will move the lower portion out. If the fender is in

too far and not flush with the door, the protruding door edge will cause noisy wind turbulence when the vehicle is in motion.

These adjustments allow the fender hood and door to be properly aligned. Often the fender and hood adjustments must be made simultaneously to achieve a pleasing result. The gap between fender and hood should be no more than 3/16 inch. The door-to-fender gap should be no more than 3/16

A

B

FIGURE 11-123 (A) Framed door and (B) hardtop door

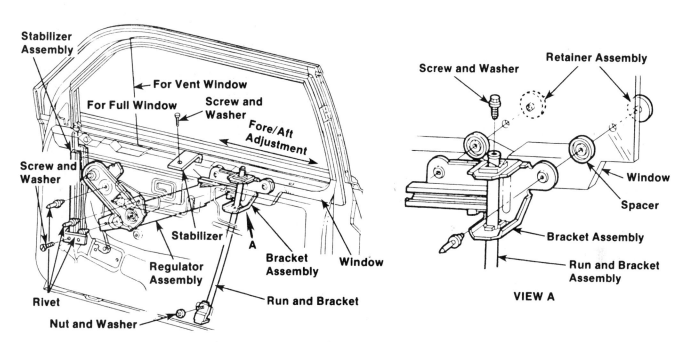

FIGURE 11-124 Window glass secured with rivets and spacers

inch also. And, of course, the front of the fender and the hood should be aligned as well. The result will be even spacing all around the fender.

Complete alignment can be achieved on many fenders without using any shims. Shims should be used only if alignment cannot be achieved without them.

Adjusting Doors

Vehicle doors must be accurately adjusted so that they will close easily; do not rattle when driven

on the road; and do not leak water and dust. This section will describe various door adjustments as well as the servicing of the door glass or moveable glass.

Types of Doors

Two basic types of doors are used on today's vehicle: framed and hardtop (Figure 11-123). The framed door uses an upper door frame structure that surrounds the glass. The hardtop type does not use a frame structure. Both door types use a one-piece glass. Older vehicle types used a vent glass assembly and a one-piece glass section.

The glass mechanism on framed doors is rather simple because the upper frame serves as a guide and support for the door glass. Hardtop doors do not have this advantage, and glass generally rests against the top door opening. A soft rubber gasket is used in the door opening to protect the glass when it is fully raised or closed. The glass must have some means of support and height control when it is lowered or raised. This type of door glass is prone to damage if it is allowed to come in contact with the roof drip rail when the door is closed. The glass must also be properly tilted to make contact with the upper gasket. If it does not, the door will leak water and dust. If it is tilted too far in, the door will be hard to close and the gasket can be damaged. By far the framed door requires the least amount of adjustments for the door glass.

Various methods are used to attach the door glass to the window lifting mechanism:

- Bolt-through method
- Adhesive or bonding method
- Sash channel method

The bolt-through method utilizes bolts or rivets that have plastic or rubber gaskets to prevent direct contact with the glass. The fasteners pass through the window and secure it to the lift channel or bracket. Rubber spacers separate the glass from the bracket and fasteners (Figure 11-124). The bolts are used to attach the lift channel or brackets to the glass. The bolts are inserted through the glass.

The use of adhesives is another method of securing the lower lift bracket to the glass. Usually a U-channel, with insulator stays, is used to prevent the glass from contacting the metal channel (Figure 11-125).

The oldest method of attaching glass to lift channels uses the sash channel. A rubber seal or tape is put on the lower edge of the glass. Then, a channel is positioned and tapped onto the glass by using a rubber mallet. If the channel is too loose, electrical tape can be used as a shim to tighten it. Usually the edges of the channel can be squeezed slightly for an even tighter fit.

Door Adjustments

Doors must fit the openings in which they are hung as well as align with the adjacent body panels. When the doors on a sedan need adjusting, start at the rear door. Since the quarter panel cannot be moved, the rear door must be adjusted to fit these body lines and the opening. Once the rear door is adjusted, the front door can then be adjusted to fit the rear door; next, the front fender can be adjusted to fit the door. On hardtop models, the windows can then be adjusted to fit the weatherstripping. The windows are usually adjusted starting with the front vent assembly and working toward the back. The vent assembly is adjusted to fit the front door pillar, and the front window is then adjusted to it. The rear door window is adjusted to the front window rear edge and the opening for the rear door assembly.

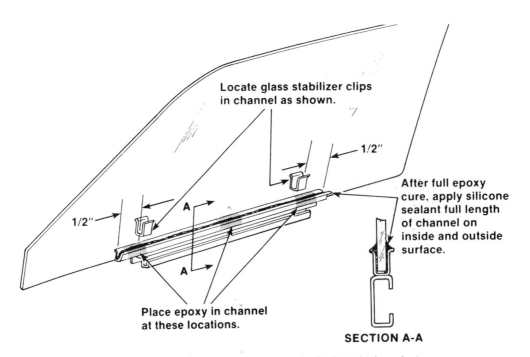

FIGURE 11-125 Adhesive-bonded glass in bracket

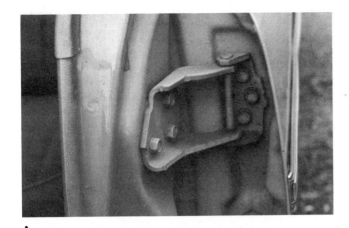

A

B

FIGURE 11-126   (A) Door hinge bolted and (B) welded door hinge

A

B

FIGURE 11-127   (A) Scissor jack and (B) adjusting bar make door adjustments easier.

The doors are attached to the body with hinges. The hinges can be bolted to the door and body or welded to either the body or door. Figure 11-126A shows a hinge bolted to both door and body. Figure 11-126B shows a hinge welded to the door and bolted to the body. Obviously, no adjustments can be made to the welded door side hinge. The body side hinge, however, can be adjusted forward, rearward, up, and down. The use of shims also allows the hinge to be moved in or out as desired.

To adjust a door, follow these steps:

 1. Determine which hinge bolts must be loosened to move the door in the desired direction.
2. Loosen the hinge bolts just enough to permit movement of the door with a padded pry bar or jack and wooden block. Figure 11-127 shows a specially designed pry bar being used to adjust a door. The end of the bar hooks over the striker bar and a U-shaped bracket engages the latch.

3. Move the door the distance estimated to be necessary. Tighten the hinge bolts and check the door fit to be sure there is no bind or interference with the adjacent panel.
4. Repeat the operation until the desired fit is obtained, and check the striker plate alignment for proper door closing.
5. Remove the striker bolt and check the door position in relation to the door opening.
6. On all hardtop models, the door and quarter glass must be checked to assure proper alignment to the roof rail and vertical weatherstrips.

On some vehicles, a special wrench must be used to loosen and tighten the bolts. If the hinges are to be removed, a line should be scribed around the hinge to mark its position, which facilitates the reinstallation and positioning of the hinge. It might be necessary to loosen the fender at the rear bottom edge to enable the body technician to reach the bolts. If the hinge pins are worn out, it might be necessary to change the hinges. Some hinges use bushings in the hinge around the pins. When these bushings are worn out, replace them. This will re-tighten the pin in the hinges and also readjust the door to a certain extent.

In-and-out adjustments are also very important because not only must the door fit the opening but it must also be reasonably aligned in and out to fit the body panels. The door must also provide a good seal between the weatherstripping and the body open-ing. The weatherstrip must be compressed suffi-ciently in the opening to prevent water, dust, drafts, and wind noises from occurring or entering the automobile.

Care must be taken when adjusting the in-and-out movement of the door. If the door is moved out on the top hinge, it will not only affect the top of the door but it will also move the opposite bottom corner in. If the bottom of the door is moved in on the hinge, it will move the top opposite corner out. But if the door is moved in or out equally on both hinges, it will only affect the front of the door because the amount of adjustment decreases toward the back of the door. The center door post, striker bolt, and lock will determine the position of the door at the location. The front leading edge of the door should always be slightly in on the front edge from the rear of the other

panel. This will help to stop wind noises at the lead-ing edge of the door panel. If the front edge is out past the back edge of the other panel, it will likely cause wind noises to occur.

When adjustments of vehicle doors are neces-sary, it is sometimes advantageous to remove the striker plate. Doing so allows the door to be centered in the opening. The striker plate is not adjusted properly if the door rises or it is forced down when the door is closed. The striker should merely provide a slight rise to the door when it is closed. The striker can be moved up and down, in and out, and back and forth.

Another type of hinge used in some compact models is the welded-on type that has no adjustment provisions (Figure 11-128). A pin is provided to re-move the door for servicing of the hinges. The half of the hinge that is to be installed on the door is pre-drilled to permit a bolt-on installation with tapped caged plates and bolts. But the half of the hinge on the hinge pillar must be rewelded on the pillar when it is replaced.

When removing the door hinge pins, take care to cover the spring with a heavy cloth to prevent it from flying and possibly causing damage or personal in-jury. The pin is then removed in each hinge and the door is removed from the vehicle. When the door is reinstalled, it is necessary to use a special spring compressing tool similar to that shown in Figure

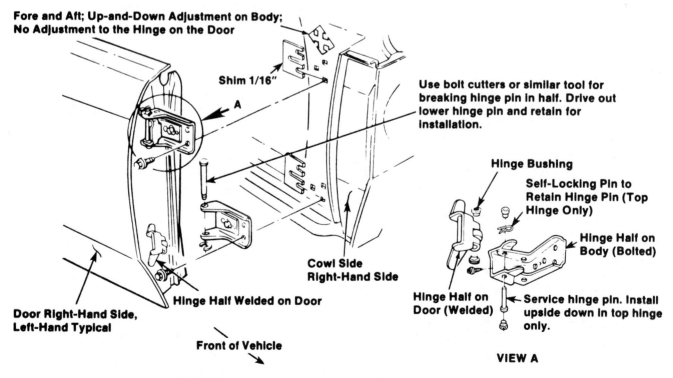

**Fore and Aft; Up-and-Down Adjustment on Body;
No Adjustment to the Hinge on the Door**

Shim 1/16"

A

Hinge Half Welded on Door

**Door Right-Hand Side,
Left-Hand Typical**

Front of Vehicle

**Cowl Side
Right-Hand Side**

Use bolt cutters or similar tool for breaking hinge pin in half. Drive out lower hinge pin and retain for installation.

Hinge Bushing

**Self-Locking Pin to
Retain Hinge Pin (Top
Hinge Only)**

**Hinge Half on
Body (Bolted)**

**Hinge Half on
Door (Welded)**

Service hinge pin. Install upside down in top hinge only.

VIEW A

FIGURE 11-128 Adjustments to welded door hinge

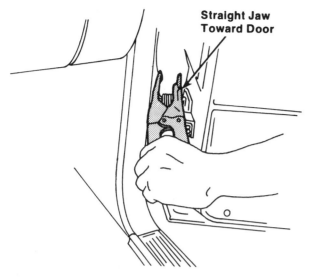

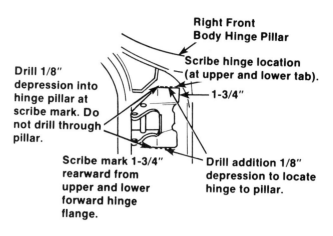

FIGURE 11-129 Spring compressing tool used when reinstalling door hinge

11-129. Again, the spring must be seated properly in the tool before compressing it to prevent it from slipping and causing damage or personal injury.

To replace the door side hinge, first scribe the outline of the hinge on the door. Then, center punch the spot welds and drill a 1/8-inch pilot hole completely through the welds (Figure 11-130). This is then drilled out to 1/2 inch, but only deep enough to penetrate the hinge base to release the hinge from the panel. A chisel is then driven between the hinge and the base to break it free from the panel. The new part is installed on the door by drilling 1/2-inch holes into the attaching holes; this will provide a slight amount of adjustment on the door assembly since the bolts used to attach it are 5/16 inch by 1-1/2 inch.

To remove the body side hinge, scribe the hinge position as shown in Figure 11-131. Measure 1-3/4 inches from the forward edge and scribe a mark above and below the hinge. Drill a slight depression in the 1-3/4 inch scribe mark, using a 1/8-inch drill bit. Do not drill completely through the pillar. Drill another shallow 1/8-inch hole at the corners of the

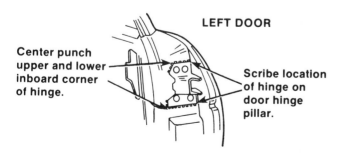

FIGURE 11-130 Scribing hinge location

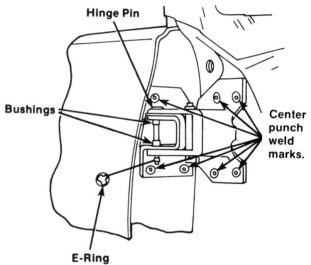

FIGURE 11-131 Scribe hinge position and center punch spot welds.

tabs to mark the hinge position. Then use a cutting torch to cut the tabs holding the hinge together. The door sill plate and carpet should be removed or covered with an asbestos sheet to protect them from the hot slag of the cutting operation.

The welds holding the separated hinge tabs are then twisted or rotated to break them with a suitable tool such as grip type pliers. Once the tabs are removed, the pillar is then ground smooth and prepared to receive the new part.

To install the new hinge strap, the measurements, as shown in Figure 11-132A, must be transferred to the new part. The new part is then lined up to the scribed marks on the hinge pillar as shown in Figure 11-132B. It is tack welded carefully in place and then the door is rehung and pins installed to check the fit of the door to the opening and surrounding panels. If it fits properly, the door is removed and the hinge is then welded completely

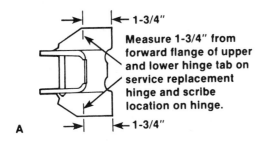

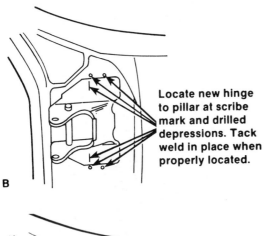

Locate new hinge to pillar at scribe mark and drilled depressions. Tack weld in place when properly located.

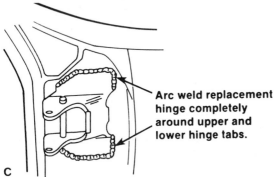

Arc weld replacement hinge completely around upper and lower hinge tabs.

FIGURE 11-132 **(A)** Measurements of hinge, **(B)** transferring these measurements to new hinge, and **(C)** welding hinge tabs

around the upper and lower hinge tabs (Figure 11-132C). The area is cleaned properly and a paintable sealer is applied around the perimeter of the hinge. The area is then refinished to the proper color before the door is reinstalled.

Door Window Alignment and Service

On some vehicle doors, channels are used to control the forward and rearward window adjustments. Some vehicle windows utilize adjustable guide rollers in a moveable channel. Still others have a center lift guide and are adjustable forward and rearward as well as in and out by tilting of the glass. These adjustments are controlled at the bracket that

is attached to the lower sash channel or where the guide attaches to the inner door panel.

If the window binds or is stiff, check the channel or add lubricant to the glass runs or guide channels. A door window that tips forward (or rearward) and that binds can be caused by improper adjustment of the lower sash brackets, a loose channel or cam roller, or a stabilized channel that is out of adjustment.

On some sedan doors, a full or partial length rubber glass run or channel is used (Figure 11-133). If the channels are too tight or lack proper lubricant, the glass or rubber will bind. To free up the glass, a dry silicone spray should be applied to the glass run. Oil is not recommended for use on the rubber channels. It can cause the rubber to swell and deteriorate.

Vehicle doors that use a full trim panel sometimes have a set of brackets at the top of the door. The trim panel is attached to these brackets and if they are set too far inward, the window glass will bind. Another item that can cause the window glass to bind when raised are the antirattle slides or other devices. If not set correctly, they will cause binding.

If the door glass is to be adjusted so that it properly aligns with the edge of the quarter glass, be sure to check and see if the fault is in the quarter glass adjustment. Some of the quarter glasses are moveable and some are stationary. To adjust or remove a quarter glass, some of the interior furnishings such as the rear seat cushion, back rest, inner trim panel, and water shield might have to be removed to gain access to the attaching mechanism. On some types of stationary or swing-out glass, it is not necessary to remove the seats. The stationary glass can be adjusted by loosening the retainer bolts or screws and shift the glass to align it with the door glass. The manufacturer's specifications or procedures should be consulted for specific details.

Operation of the moveable quarter glass is the same as that for door glass. Stops are used to control the up and down movements. The up-stop controls the up and forward movement of the glass. This stop must be set to obtain the proper spacing between the door and quarter glass. Some vehicles use two up-stops—one for the front and one for the rear sections. Just like the door glass, the quarter glass is provided with adjusts for inward and outward tilt of the glass. Consult the manufacturer's service manual or make a careful inspection of what is necessary to remove the quarter glass.

To replace the vent window, it must be aligned as shown in Figure 11-134. An awl or dowel can be used to align the holes in the door frame and vent window. Then, reinstall the mounting screws and torque them to the manufacturer's specifications. Replace the door glass run in the division bar.

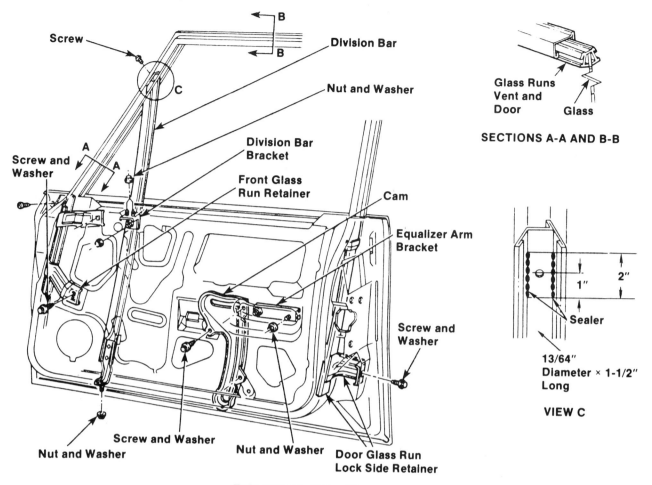

FIGURE 11-133 Glass runs

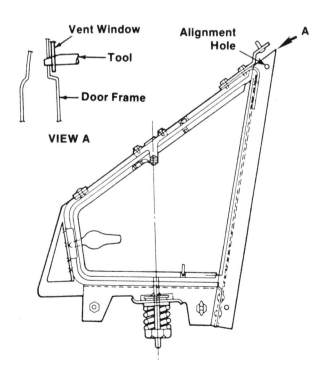

FIGURE 11-134 Vent window alignment

Manual and Power Regulators

Regulators can be manual or powered electrically to raise or lower the door glass and quarter glass. On older vehicles, regulators were also used on vent windows to move them in and out. Both types of regulators are very similar, the only difference being the handle crank mechanism on manual regulators and electromotor-driven gear mechanism on powered regulators. The lift arms are the same for both types.

One or two lift arms can be used depending on the make of the vehicle. If two lift arms are used, it is usually referred to as the X-design (Figure 11-135). The X-design uses an auxiliary arm that is mounted into a cam or stabilizer channel that is adjustable. The cam adjustments allow the glass to be tilted or rocked so that it can be raised in a parallel position.

The regulator and its associated parts are sometimes riveted to the door structure in lieu of being bolted. In this case, drill out the rivets in accordance with good shop practice and reinstall the necessary parts using the appropriate rivet gun and rivets.

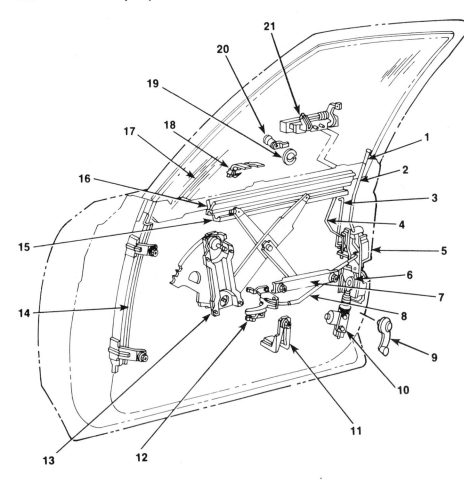

1. Inside Locking Rod Knob
2. Inside Locking Rod
3. Lock Cylinder to Lock Connecting Rod
4. Outside Handle to Lock Connecting Rod
5. Door Lock
6. Inside Locking Rod to Electric Actuator Connecting Rod
7. Inner Panel Cam
8. Inside Remote Handle to Lock Connecting Rod
9. Manual Window Regulator Handle
10. Power Door Lock Actuator
11. Down-Travel Stop
12. Inside Remote Handle
13. Manual Window Regulator
14. Glass Run Channel Retainer
15. Lower Sash Channel Cam
16. Lower Sash Channel
17. Window Glass
18. Lock Cylinder Retainer
19. Lock Cylinder Gasket
20. Lock Cylinder Assembly
21. Outside Handle Assembly

FIGURE 11-135 X-design window regulator

For those window regulators that are spot welded to the inner door panel, use a center punch and hammer to remove visible spot welds. A spot welder cutter can also be used to drill out welds. If necessary, use a chisel between the regulator and inner panel to separate the two structures. Generally, the replacement regulator is reinstalled by the use of U-clips or screws.

If the regulator is to be removed without removing the glass, be sure to secure the glass in an up position to prevent it from dropping inside the door panel. Heavy cloth tape or a wedge can be used for this purpose. Always consult the manufacturer's manual for the proper removal and installation of the regulator.

Power regulators require additional installation care because of the use of counterbalance springs in

their design (Figure 11-136). On some vehicle models, the counterbalance spring must be released before servicing the regulator motor or other associated parts.

• Position the regulator to an access hole in the inner door panel that is large enough to clamp the regulator to the panel. Use a C-clamp. Using a special tool (Figure 11-137), the spring tension is released. After servicing the motor or part, the spring can be reinstalled in its original position. Removing the spring avoids possible hand injury and damage to the door.

• Secure the regulator to the inner door panel by drilling a hole through the regulator gear and back plate and inserting a screw or bolt

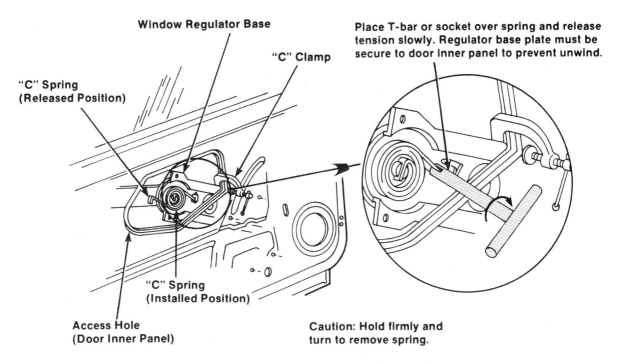

FIGURE 11-136 Counterbalance spring

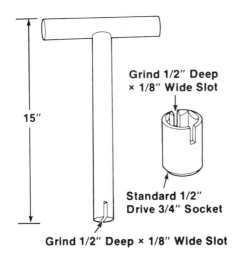

FIGURE 11-137 Shop-fabricated spring removal tools

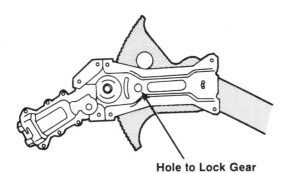

FIGURE 11-138 Secure regulator with bolt.

through the hole (Figure 11-138). Use a nut to lock the assemblies together. Be sure to remove the screw or bolt after servicing the regulator.

Station Wagon Tailgate Adjustments

Most late model station wagons have a three-way tailgate. (Compact cars are the exception; most of these have a hatchback style rear gate.) The three-way tailgate has a unique hinge and locking arrangement that allows the tailgate to be operated as a tailgate with the glass fully down or as a door with the glass up or down. Figure 11-139 shows the hinges and locks in a typical three-way tailgate.

The lock system on the three-way tailgate performs the following blockout functions:

- Allow the tailgate to be opened and closed as a door with glass up or down and at the same time prevent accidental operation of the upper left lock, which allows the gate to be opened as a gate.
- Allow the tailgate to be opened and closed as a tailgate with glass down and at the same time prevent accidental operation of the lower right lock, which allows the gate to be opened as a door.

Before doing any station wagon tailgate alignment, closely examine the area to determine where

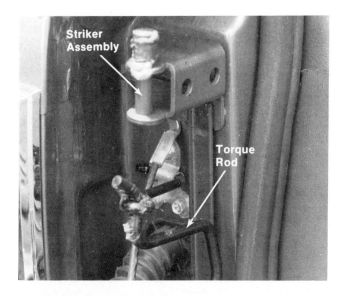

FIGURE 11-139   Tailgate hardware

the misalignment exists. It might be necessary to remove the right upper striker bolt and adjust the tailgate as a regular door. If the right lower striker forces the tailgate up or down and out of alignment, readjust the striker bolt to provide a smooth open/close action.

The left hinges can be adjusted to position the tailgate in the vehicle body opening and for flush alignment with the adjacent body panels. They are also adjustable for smooth lock operation. Closely

examine the hinges to determine what adjustments are available. On some vehicles the lower left hinge provides up and down as well as in and out adjustments for the tailgate. Some vehicles provide for certain types of adjustments on the body side of the hinge; others allow adjustment to the side hinge. After adjusting the left hinges, it is necessary to reinstall and adjust the strikers. If all adjustments have been done correctly, the tailgate should operate smoothly and fit properly.

The following is a typical procedure for adjusting a three way tailgate.

1. The lower left hinge assembly at the body attachment is adjustable up or down and laterally. To gain access to the lower left hinge-to-body attachments, remove the left quarter trim. Loosen the hinge-to-body attachments and adjust the hinge up, down, laterally, or rotate as required.

   Rotating the hinge slightly will raise or lower the right side of the gate. This can be accomplished by loosening the lower hinge-to-body attachments. Then, with the tailgate open as a door, support the right side of the tailgate in the desired position and tighten the hinge attachments. If this adjustment is performed or if the tailgate is moved sideways, it might be necessary to also adjust the left upper hinge striker assembly.

   If the lower left hinge is adjusted upward or downward, clearance between the upper left lock frame on the tailgate and the hinge lock striker on the body pillar should be checked. The specified clearance is 5/16 inch (GM specific) and where required, the upper left lock should be adjusted.

🚗 SHOP TALK _____

Prior to performing any adjustments, the position of the hinge lock, or striker to be adjusted should be scribed or marked to ease realignment.

2. The lower left hinge assembly at the gate attachment is adjustable forward or rearward. This adjustment is primarily for flush alignment of the tailgate outer panel with adjacent panels in the area of the lower left hinge.

   The lower left hinge-to-tailgate attaching nuts are located inside the tailgate. To loosen nuts for the adjustment of the tailgate on the hinge, remove the tailgate trim panel and the left access hole cover to gain access to the hinge-to-tailgate attachments. Adjust the tailgate on the hinge as required, then tighten the nuts and replace the previously removed parts.

3. The upper left hinge lock assembly is adjustable forward and rearward. This adjustment is available to provide a flush alignment of the tailgate outer panel with adjacent body panels in the area of the upper left lock.

   Prior to adjusting the upper left lock, mark the position of the lock on the tailgate. Two of the lock attaching nuts are located inside the tailgate and one on the outside. To loosen inside nuts, remove the tailgate trim panel and access the hole cover. Then loosen the hinge-to-gate attaching nuts. Adjust the lock as required and replace all previously removed parts.

   After any adjustment of the upper left lock, synchronization of the lock system should be checked and where required the lock system should be synchronized. Consult the appropriate manufacturer's service manual for proper synchronization procedures.

4. The upper left striker assembly is adjustable up, down, and laterally. The up or down adjustment is to provide adequate clearance between the bottom of the lock frame (on tailgate) and the top of the hinge pin striker plate.

   To check the clearance, open the gate as a door and measure the distance between the upper surface of the upper left hinge pin and striker plate and the lower surface of the upper left lock frame.

   To make any necessary adjustment, remove the left quarter trim to gain access to the attachments. Loosen the attaching nuts and reposition the striker hinge assembly as required.

   This adjustment is available to provide proper engagement of the hinge pin and lock striker with the lock. It is not intended as a means of raising or lowering the left or right side of the gate.

   To find the correct adjustment, open the tailgate as a gate; then, while closing the gate, carefully observe how the striker pin engages in the slot in the bottom surface of the lock. The striker pin should enter into the slot with side pressure.

5. The right upper and lower lock striker assemblies are adjustable forward or rearward, up or down, and laterally by using spacers. The upper and lower right strikers should be removed prior to performing any other hinge or lock adjustment.

To adjust the upper or lower right strikers, open the tailgate as a door and remove the striker. Check the alignment of the tailgate in the body opening. The tailgate should be aligned with the left upper hinge lock prior to adjustment of the strikers. Install the striker slightly more than fingertight. Then carefully close the gate to allow the striker to self-align. Carefully open the gate and tighten the striker.

Operate the tailgate both as a door and a gate and check for flush alignment of outer panels in the area of the striker. If any further minor adjustment is required, mark the position of the striker on the body pillar, loosen the striker, and make the required adjustments from the marked position and tighten the striker.

Do not use the right upper and lower striker to align the right side of the gate up or down in the body opening.

11.8 REVIEW QUESTIONS

1. Technician A sometimes positions nonstructural outer panels visually, without making precise measurements. Technician B says that measurements must always be made. Who is correct?
   a. Technician A
   b. Technician B
   c. Both A and B
   d. Neither A nor B

2. Rocker panels and pillars are known as what type of sections?
   a. open surface
   b. crush zone
   c. closed
   d. compound

3. Which type of joint is used on floor pans and trunk floors?
   a. offset butt joint without an insert
   b. overlap joint
   c. staggered butt joint
   d. butt joint with insert

4. What is the preferred tool to remove a part for recycling?
   a. metal saw
   b. chisel
   c. cutting torch
   d. none of the above

5. Rocker panels come in which of the following designs?
   a. two-piece
   b. three-piece
   c. four-piece
   d. both a and b

6. Technician A uses a butt joint without an insert to repair a closed section rail, while Technician B uses a butt joint with an insert. Who is correct?
   a. Technician A
   b. Technician B
   c. Both A and B
   d. Neither A nor B

7. Where should A-pillars be cut when sectioning?
   a. at the upper end
   b. near the middle
   c. at the lower end
   d. both a and c

8. When joining full body sections, Technician A uses a steel rule to check the dimension of the windshield and door openings. Technician B uses a tram gauge. Who is correct?
   a. Technician A
   b. Technician B
   c. Both A and B
   d. Neither A nor B

9. Which of the following statements concerning replacement at factory seams is incorrect?
   a. Replacing panels at factory seams is common in unibody repair.
   b. Damaged rails and panels should not be returned to factory specifications until after they have been removed from the vehicle.
   c. It is easy to destroy more of the factory welds than is necessary when doing the job.
   d. All of the above

10. What is the best method for separating spot welds?
    a. blowing them out with a plasma torch
    b. cutting them out with a spot cutter
    c. drilling them out
    d. grinding them down with a high-speed grinding wheel

11. When drilling out spot welds, Technician A uses the same drill speed used for drilling a mild steel. Technician B uses a drill speed

that is faster than that used for mild steel. Who is correct?
a. Technician A
b. Technician B
c. Both A and B
d. Neither A nor B

12. What color is metal that has been arc-brazed?
a. black
b. reddish copper
c. silver
d. brass-colored

13. When preparing a vehicle for installation of replacement body panels, Technician A grinds the flanges of the structural panels, while Technician B does not. Who is correct?
a. Technician A
b. Technician B
c. Both A and B
d. Neither A nor B

14. When a replacement body panel overlaps any existing panels, the overlap portion should be _____ .
a. 3/4 to 1 inch
b. 1 to 1-1/2 inches
c. at least 2 inches
d. no more than 1/2 inch

15. When positioning a nonstructural outer body panel visually, Technician A makes sure that the gaps between panels are tapered. Tech-nician B makes sure that the gaps between panels are even. Who is correct?
a. Technician A
b. Technician B
c. Both A and B
d. Neither A nor B

16. Which of the following should be avoided when making sectioning cuts?
a. structural member mounts
b. compound member mounts
c. dimensional reference holes
d. all of the above

17. To separate an exterior door panel from the inner panel, Technician A uses a power chisel and Technician B uses a welding torch. Who is correct?
a. Technician A
b. Technician B
c. Both A and B
d. Neither A nor B

18. Which of the following welding processes must be used to weld high-strength steel panels?
a. oxyacetylene
b. shield arc
c. metal insert gas
d. all of the above

CHAPTER
12

Analyzing Mechanical, Electrical, and Electronic Components

OBJECTIVES

After reading this chapter, you will be able to:

- explain the procedure for removing a drivetrain from a unibody vehicle.
- identify the principles of how suspension and steering systems work.
- list the elements of proper wheel alignment.
- recognize the typical problems caused by improper suspension system servicing.
- describe the difference involved in aligning vehicles with electronic air suspension.
- perform the diagnosis and servicing of a power steering system.
- list the various drive systems.
- name the service procedures for the major parts of a cooling system, including the radiator, fan and fan clutches, and belts and hoses.
- describe the service procedures for an air-conditioning system.
- perform the diagnosis and servicing of an emission control system.
- describe the test procedures used to repair electrical and electronic systems.

Until a few years ago such repair tasks as wheel alignment, radiator repair, electrical work, air-conditioning reconditioning, transmission problems, and other mechanical component tasks were not jobs generally performed by body shops or body technicians. They were usually "farmed" out to specialty shops or, in the case of a dealership, to auto mechanics. But, with the introduction of unibody cars, it is important for body shops and their technicians to develop some mechanical knowledge and skills.

The repair of collision damage to unibody structures often involves service of the mechanical parts (Figure 12-1). In many cases, major drive line parts such as engines, transmissions, and drive axles are mounted directly to structural unibody panels. In other cases, these parts are mounted to supporting cross members, subframe assemblies, or cradle assemblies that are mounted to the unibody structural panels. The unibody panels provide the structural support for the static load of the mechanical parts mounted to them. Unibody panels must also satisfy dynamic loads developed by the mechanical components. Engine and transmission mounts must satisfy severe torsional loads. Drive axle mountings must also support the loads of acceleration and braking. Proper alignment of mechanical part mountings can be critical to the operation of the part. The dimensional relationship between engine mountings and other drive line component mountings must be maintained.

While mechanical components might not be repaired by the body technician, the components can give the technician leads as to the type and extent of damage that can be passed on to the repair mechanic who is going to make the repairs.

12.1 DRIVETRAIN REPAIRS

The term "powertrain" or drivetrain is used frequently when discussing unibody type cars. A powertrain in a unibody front wheel drive type car includes the engine, transmission, drive shaft, and suspension systems all packaged together, usually located in the front end of the car. It is supported by some cross members that are bolted directly to the body. Drive axle mountings must also support the load of acceleration and braking.

Many mechanical parts such as engine mounts and transmission supports are through-bolted. The position of these through-bolt mountings must be maintained parallel to each other to allow for the correct movement of the mechanical parts. When

FIGURE 12-1 Collision damage in a unibody vehicle often involves mechanical components.

these mechanical mountings are not in proper alignment, free movement of the mechanical parts might be restricted.

Control linkages might not operate properly unless proper alignment is maintained. For instance, engine performance can be affected by the misalignment of the throttle control linkages. Misalignment in transmission linkages can easily cause erratic transmission performance. Proper drive shaft angles must be maintained to prevent vibration and chatter of the drive shaft and universal joints. Drive line components normally vibrate during their operation. These vibrations are isolated from the passenger compartment through the use of specially designed motor mounts.

Motor mounts prevent metal vibrations at the mounting locations from being transferred to the body of the car (Figure 12-2). Misalignment of these

FIGURE 12-2 Typical unibody motor mounts

FIGURE 12-3 Cradle assembly mounting biscuits found on some older unibody cars

motor mounts can cause vibrations to be transferred directly to the passenger compartment. In order to provide the necessary structural support mountings for mechanical parts, special fasteners are frequently used.

An example shown in Figure 12-3 is the use of the cradle assembly mounting biscuits used on some unibody vehicles. These mounting biscuits use a special self-tapping bolt. The special bolt cuts the threads in the mounting biscuit when it is installed at the factory. If possible, the same bolt should be reinstalled in the same mounting biscuit when it is reused. When the new fasteners for these types of applications are required, the correct replacement parts should be used. Generally, common replacement fasteners should not be used because they might not supply the structural support necessary for the mechanical part. These types of special fasteners are more common in unibody construction than they were in frame type construction. Check the individual manufacturer's specifications on the use of all fasteners.

At times it is desirable to completely remove the drivetrain from the unibody to make repairs to the body (Figure 12-4). Removal of the drivetrain allows ready access to structural unibody panels for repair or replacement. In some cases, the time to remove the drivetrain pays off in considerable time savings in the repair or replacement of body panels. Repairs of damaged mechanical parts can sometimes become easier and faster after the piece is removed from the car. The decision whether to remove the drivetrain or to work around it in the car can be made by the repair technician or estimator. When more time is saved in the repair of adjacent panels than is

necessary to remove and reinstall the drivetrain, the drivetrain should be removed. When no time savings will result, the repairs should be made with the mechanical components in the car.

In addition to the usual safety precautions given in previous chapters, which must always be observed when working near a vehicle, car manufacturers' service manuals contain specific cautions that must be followed when disassembling or rebuilding any of these parts. All fasteners must be retightened to their assigned torque values.

At the factory, the drivetrain is installed from the bottom of the car. So the drivetrain assembly in Figure 12-5 will be removed from the bottom of the vehicle by lifting the vehicle away from the engine assembly. The following procedure will describe the use of a floor jack, safety stands, rocker panel clamps, and a cross tube for lifting the vehicle and to efficiently remove and reinstall the drivetrain as an assembly engine, transaxle, and front suspension.

With the car on the ground, start disconnecting the engine and suspension assembly from the top of the engine compartment. But, before starting to disconnect the vacuum lines or electrical lines, make sure to attach a piece of masking tape to both sides of the parts disconnected (Figure 12-6). Mark the same code letter or number on both sides of what has been disconnected. Once all parts have identified all the connections, the technician can feel assured that when putting everything back together it will be possible to fix it right the first time.

The procedure of removing the mechanical components is usually done before the vehicle is straightened. In fact, many of the pointers described in Chapter 10 must be followed when repairing the

FIGURE 12-4 Vehicle with its drivetrain removed

FIGURE 12-5 Removing the drivetrain from the bottom of the vehicle

FIGURE 12-8 Remove air filter to aid visibility.

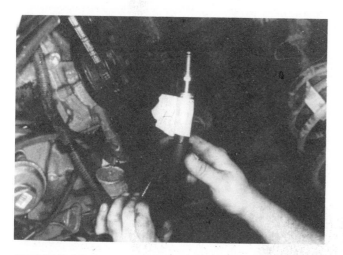

FIGURE 12-6 Label parts as they are disconnected.

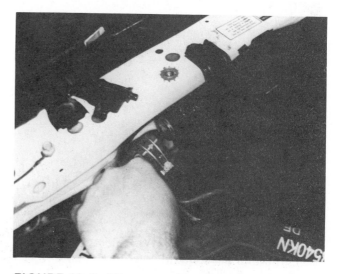

FIGURE 12-9 Disconnecting the radiator hose

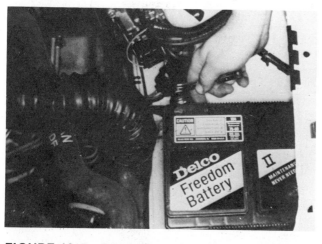

FIGURE 12-7 Disconnect the battery cables before starting any work on the car.

mechanical components. When removing the drivetrain from a unibody vehicle, proceed as follows:

1. Disconnect both battery cables from the battery and the body ground from the battery tray (Figure 12-7). The cables will remain attached to the engine.
2. Remove the air cleaner to aid visibility and to increase the working area (Figure 12-8).
3. Drain the cooling system. The radiator hose can be disconnected at either end (Figure 12-9).
4. Disconnect the vacuum hoses from all components that are not mounted to the drivetrain, for example, the power brake and fuel vapor canister (Figure 12-10).
5. Disconnect carburetor linkage (small horseshoe clip). Disconnect the electrical

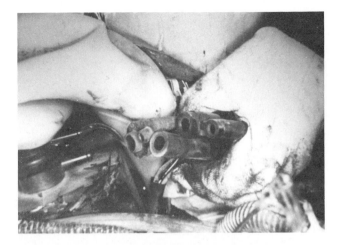

FIGURE 12-10   Disconnect all vacuum hoses.

FIGURE 12-12   Disconnecting shift linkage cable(s) from the transaxle

FIGURE 12-11   Disconnect the electric wire from the carburetor air-conditioning idle solenoid

FIGURE 12-13   Disconnecting the speedometer cable

wire from the carburetor air-conditioning idle solenoid (Figure 12-11).

6. Disconnect shift linkage cable(s) from the transaxle (Figure 12-12). Be careful to separate the cable from the bracket that mounts to the housing of the automatic or standard transaxle. Disconnect manual clutch (if so equipped).

7. Disconnect the speedometer cable at the union located midway on the cable or at the transaxle when not equipped with cable union (Figure 12-13). Disconnect the transaxle cooling lines at the rubber hoses if so equipped.

8. Disconnect the heater hoses (Figure 12-14).

9. Disconnect the power steering pump lines at the inline connection, not at the pump

FIGURE 12-14   Disconnecting the heater hoses

(Figure 12-15). Disconnect the engine electrical harness at the right side of the cowl. Remove the upper front engine stabilizer strap.

10. Remove the air-conditioning (A/C) compressor and set aside or discharge the air-conditioning system and disconnect lines and wiring at the compressor. If the A/C is not damaged and recharge of the system is not required, remove the A/C compressor from its mounting bracket and leave it with the body (Figure 12-16). If there are open lines, they should be plugged. Remove the radiator fan and shroud for additional clearance if necessary. Check for any individual

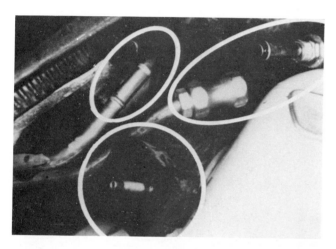

FIGURE 12-15 Disconnecting the power steering system

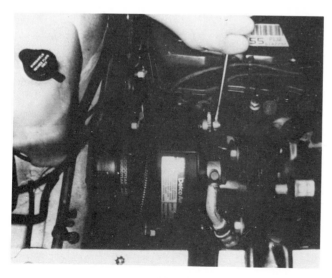

FIGURE 12-16 Removing the air-conditioning compressor

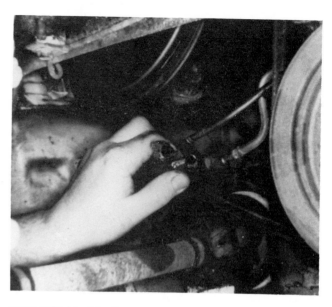

FIGURE 12-17 Disconnecting the fuel flex lines near the fuel pump

wires attached to the engine and traveling to the vehicle body.

11. Disconnect the fuel flex lines near the fuel pump (Figure 12-17). This should be done with the disconnects in the upper engine compartment.

12. To get the vehicle up in the air, install the rocker panel clamps (Figure 12-18A). Install the crosstube as far forward as possible (Figure 12-18B). Place a floor jack under the car and place the stands in position on the crosstubes (Figure 12-18C). A lift or bench can also be used to lift the vehicle off the ground.

13. Once the vehicle is in the air, remove the brake caliper assembly from the disc (Figure 12-19). This prevents the need to bleed the brake system on reassembly, however, the caliper assembly must be fastened to the car and not allowed to hang by the hose.

14. Disconnect the exhaust pipe at the coupling behind the engine. It might be necessary to disconnect the right and left tie rod ends at the steering knuckle (Figure 12-20).

If a bench or platform is not available, place a flatbed cart with 4-inch by 4-inch lumber pieces or whatever else the body technician wishes to use under the drivetrain and lower the vehicle onto the 4 by 4s (Figure 12-21). Be sure to locate the 4 by 4s and the cart in a position that will allow the removal

A

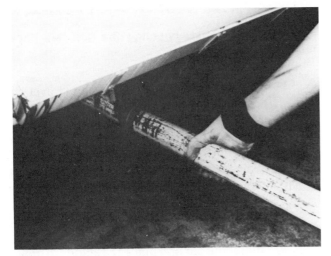

B

C

FIGURE 12-18   Getting the vehicle up into the air:
(A) installing the clamps; (B) installing the crosstube; and (C) placing of the floor jacks

FIGURE 12-19   Removing the brake caliper from
the disc

FIGURE 12-20   Disconnecting the exhaust pipe

FIGURE 12-21   If not using a bench or platform,
carefully support the vehicle with 4 by 4s as shown.

FIGURE 12-22 Removing upper strut tower mounting bolts

FIGURE 12-25 Removing the drivetrain

FIGURE 12-23 Removing the cradle mounting bolts

FIGURE 12-24 Lifting the vehicle from the drivetrain assembly

of the cradle mounting bolts. Remove the three upper strut tower mounting bolts from each side (Figure 12-22). Remove the four cradle mounting bolts (Figure 12-23).

Carefully lift the vehicle away from the drivetrain assembly by raising the floor jack that is under the crosstube (Figure 12-24). As always, support the vehicle with car stands. Care must be taken when lifting the body away from the drivetrain. As the lifting is continued, keep checking all sides for wires or hoses that might not have been disconnected.

Remove the drivetrain (Figure 12-25) and repair the damaged unibody panels as described in Chapters 10 and 11. While the body is being repaired, an auto mechanic can service the drivetrain as required.

Reinstallation of the drivetrain can be accomplished by reversing the removal procedure. After the unibody structure has been accurately repaired, the cradle can be quickly and correctly positioned by using the line up holes located at the right front and right rear cradle mounting points. An incorrectly positioned cradle can give the customer a wheel alignment problem.

It must be remembered that procedures mentioned in this chapter are general. The technician must be aware of the specifics of removal for that particular body style. An example of that would be a body style without a full cradle. On those types of bodies, it is necessary to tie the suspension system to the engine and drivetrain assembly to help prevent the constant velocity, or CV, joints from separating from their assembly.

On a unibody vehicle with a rear wheel drive, the drivetrain removal procedure for the bottom removal would be almost the same. With the car on the ground, disconnect the battery cables, the radiator

FIGURE 12-26 Lifting the vehicle off the ground to disconnect other parts after the drivetrain has been removed

FIGURE 12-27 Removing the drive shaft at the rear of the vehicle

hoses, and the heater hoses. Remove the air cleaner to disconnect the throttle cable, then disconnect the wiring harness, the emission lines that are connected to the smog cannister, and the fuel lines. If the vehicle has air conditioning or power steering, disconnect it the same way as recommended on the front wheel drive car. Raise the vehicle off the ground to disconnect the remaining pieces for the drivetrain removal (Figure 12-26).

 1. Remove the drive shaft at the rear of the car by disconnecting the U-bolts (Figure 12-27). Make sure to mark the U-bolts for identification when reassembling.

2. Remove the bolts from the body that mount the small cross member that helps support the transmission (Figure 12-28). If the car has a manual transmission, remove the clutch linkage and return spring.

FIGURE 12-28 Removing transmission support members

3. Disconnect the transmission cable (Figure 12-29), the wiring for the back-up lights, and the ground strap. All of these are attached to the transmission.

4. Disconnect the drive shaft at the transmission and be sure to protect the spline or gear that sticks out from the end of the transmission (Figure 12-30). Use a plastic plug or a rag. Disconnect the exhaust system at the catalytic converter.

5. Disconnect the steering rack from the steering column at the rack.

6. Disconnect the shocks from the top of the towers or at the bottom of the shock (Figure 12-31). When disconnecting the shock at the bottom, it might be necessary to remove the wheel to have access to the through-bolt that attaches the shock to the rest of the suspension system.

7. Remove the brake lines at the wheel and support the disc brake caliper.

When starting to remove any drivetrain from any unibody, make the actual separation very slowly, while constantly walking around the entire vehicle to make sure everything is clear and disconnected.

 **SHOP TALK** —————

Wire the struts together inboard after removing the engine. This will prevent damage to the CV joints and rubber boots.

FIGURE 12-29 Disconnecting the transmission cable

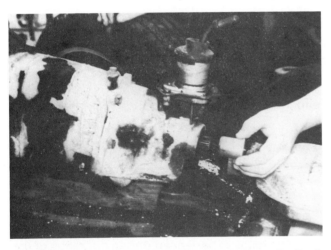

FIGURE 12-30 Disconnecting the drive shaft at the transmission

FIGURE 12-31 Disconnecting the shocks from the towers or at the bottom of the shocks

FIGURE 12-32 The inner fender skirts of a conventional body-over-frame vehicle

12.2 SUSPENSION AND STEERING SYSTEMS

A vehicle's suspension and steering system performs three basic functions:

- It acts as the overall connection between the wheels and the vehicle body.
- It damps and controls the ride; that is, it acts to partially absorb road shock and sway.
- It provides directional control of the vehicle.

Up to a few years ago suspension and steering systems were not the concern of the body technician. Today, however, quality body shop repairs of an automobile must include the return of steering and suspension system parts to their original factory location. In unibody construction, this is especially important because body panels provide the critical mounting positions for the suspension and steering systems. For instance, the inner fender skirts in conventional body frame construction prevent dirt and splash from entering the engine compartment (Figure 12-32). In unibody construction, they are called strut towers and also provide the upper mounting controls for the MacPherson strut suspension system (Figure 12-33).

In some cases, the steering gear of a unibody car is bolted directly to a body panel, like a cowl (Figure 12-34). When this is done, the body panel must hold the steering gear in its correct location. The unibody structure must maintain the proper relationship of the steering and suspension parts to each other.

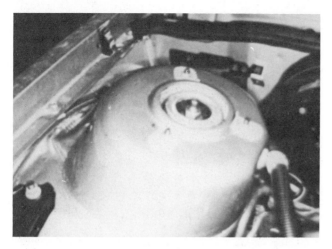

FIGURE 12-33 The strut tower of a MacPherson suspension system

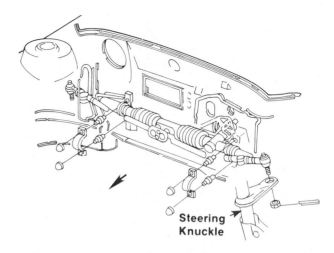

FIGURE 12-34 The steering gear of many unibody cars is bolted directly to the body panel.

Rear suspension components are also mounted directly to the unibody structural panels. The proper relationship of the rear suspension parts to each other and to front suspension parts depends on the position of the unibody structural panels.

> **CAUTION:** The manufacturer has designed certain suspension, steering, and alignment features into the unibody car and when any repairs are made, the manufacturer's specifications must be followed. If the specs are changed or tampered with, they might change the handling and safety features built into the vehicle. As an example, in working with suspension systems, do not straighten or bend any of the pieces that make up the suspension system.

All vehicles—not only those of unibody construction—require an inter-related suspension and body design. The difference in today's vehicles is that safe, efficient collision repairs demand that both body and suspension be corrected together as one system.

Collision repairs on body-over-frame vehicles, where the mechanicals and suspension are connected to the frame only, demand that the frame be restored to within certain tolerances. From there a wheel alignment shop can fine-tune the various suspension angles that affect road handling and safety. Frame vehicles have plenty of suspension adjustments built into their design. The system of repair requires the frame shop to straighten the frame, the body shop to hang sheet metal and straighten pan-

els, and then the wheel alignment shop to adjust the suspension angles.

While the mechanical technician might make the repair to the suspension and steering system, it is a must for the body repair technician to know and understand what is involved and why it is important.

12.3 SUSPENSION SYSTEMS

Proper collision repairs of suspension systems and supporting unibody structural panels must restore the ability of these panels to support the high-dynamic loads experienced during operation of the suspension system. Most body repair technicians focus their attention to suspension system repairs on the ability to restore traditional wheel alignment angles to specification.

FRONT SUSPENSION

There are basic types of suspension systems used in passenger cars and light-duty trucks: coil spring, torsion bar, strut, and twin I-beam (Figure 12-35). Most frame bodies use either the coil spring or torsion bar system. The strut suspension is widely used in unibody cars. Light-duty trucks, vans, and four wheel drive vehicles frequently use the twin I-beam system.

The coil spring suspension (sometimes called the parallel suspension) uses both an upper and lower control arm (Figure 12-35A). These arms are attached with pivots to a structural component, such as the frame. The outer ends of the control arms are

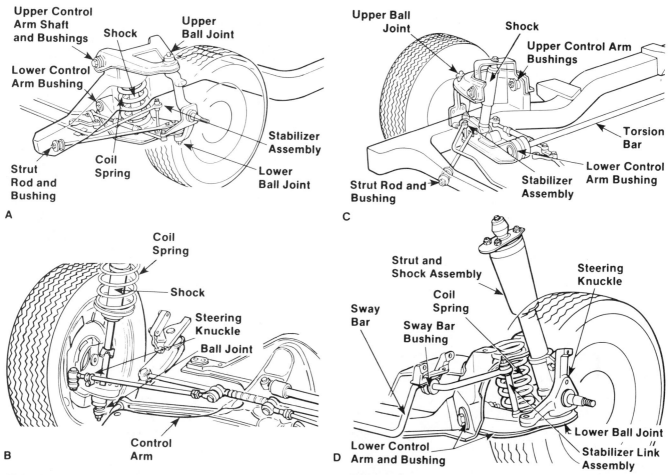

Upper Control Arm Shaft and Bushings

Shock

Upper Ball Joint

Lower Control Arm Bushing

Strut Rod and Bushing

Coil Spring

Stabilizer Assembly

Lower Ball Joint

A

Upper Ball Joint

Shock

Upper Control Arm Bushings

Torsion Bar

Strut Rod and Bushing

Stabilizer Assembly

Lower Control Arm Bushing

C

Coil Spring

Shock

Steering Knuckle

Ball Joint

Control Arm

B

Strut and Shock Assembly

Coil Spring

Sway Bar

Sway Bar Bushing

Steering Knuckle

Lower Ball Joint

Stabilizer Link Assembly

Lower Control Arm and Bushing

D

FIGURE 12-35   Front suspension system: (A) conventional coil spring system; (B) conventional torsion bar system; (C) conventional strut system; and (D) twin I-beam system

attached to the spindle and steering knuckle assembly with ball joints. The spring is usually placed between the lower control arm and the frame. Some types place the spring above the upper control arm and others use torsion bars. A separate shock absorber is connected to one of the control arms and a structural member.

The torsion bar suspension system (Figure 12-35B) uses torsion bars instead of coil springs. Vehicle weight is supported by the torsion bar with the front of the bar attached to the lower control arm and the rear attached to the frame. Torsion bars installed in this manner are commonly called "longitudinal" because they run lengthwise in the vehicle.

The most commonly used front suspension system for unibody vehicles is the MacPherson (conventional) strut suspension (Figure 12-35C) and the modified version (Figure 12-35D). The design and operation of a strut suspension system are simple

compared with the more familiar parallel coil arm suspension system.

Like the parallel coil arm suspension, the MacPherson strut suspension has a lower control arm and spring. The strut replaces the shock absorber and the upper control arm (Figure 12-36). The strut suspension system uses a coil spring that is part of the strut assembly. In some cases, the coil spring is placed between the lower control arm and the unibody structure. In either case, the loads generated by the strut suspension are transferred directly to the unibody structure through the spring mounting.

The twin I-beam front suspension was developed to combine independent front wheel action with the strength and dependability of the mono beam axle. Twin I-beam axles allow each front wheel to absorb bumps and road irregularities independently, while providing sturdy, simple construction. The outer ends of the I-beams are attached to the

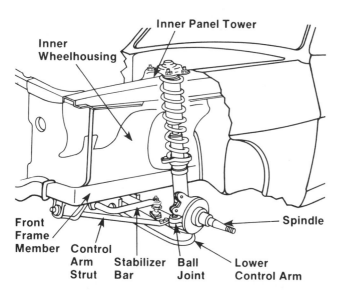

FIGURE 12-36   Major components of a MacPherson suspension system

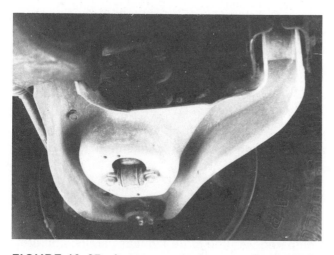

FIGURE 12-37   Lower control arms attached directly to the front body side

spindle and to the radius arms. The inner ends are attached to a pivot bracket fastened to the frame near the opposite side of the vehicle. This type of construction provides good antiroll characteristics. The use of a progressive coil spring (a spring that becomes increasingly stiff as it is compressed) provides good riding qualities on normal roads and sturdiness off the road. The radius arms permit the I-beam to move up and down, stabilize any front to rear movement of the I-beam, and help maintain the proper caster setting. The spindle is mounted to the I-beam by a spindle bolt (kingpin). There are no ball joints.

Many unibody vehicles have lower control arms attached directly to the front body side rails (Figure

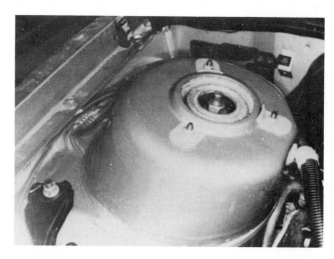

FIGURE 12-38   Suspension system mounted to body side rails

12-37). Other unibody vehicles attach lower control arms to suspension subframes or cross members that are bolted directly to the front body side rails.

The suspension system mounting locations in the unibody structural panels (Figure 12-38) must be able to withstand the load transferred by this vertical movement. In the case of strut suspensions, the vertical load is transferred directly from the upper strut mount to the top unibody panel.

Suspension systems also experience lateral or side-to-side loads during operation; very heavy side loads are transferred through the suspension system during high-speed cornering, the lateral load from the cornering effect is transferred from the wheel of the car through the lower control arm to the supporting structural panels of the unibody.

Front suspension ball joints (Figure 12-39) are used to connect the spindle to the upper and lower control arms. They provide a pivot for the wheel to turn and also allow for vertical movement of the control arms as the vehicle moves over irregularities in the road. While holding the front wheel in position, each ball joint performs a specific function. One joint supports vehicle weight, while the other functions as a steering dampener or resistance joint. But remember, both are subject to the stresses of road shock (up and down movement), braking, and cornering forces.

Rear Suspension

The rear suspension system is an important, often ignored area. Generally, rear suspensions require no special service. Broken or worn parts

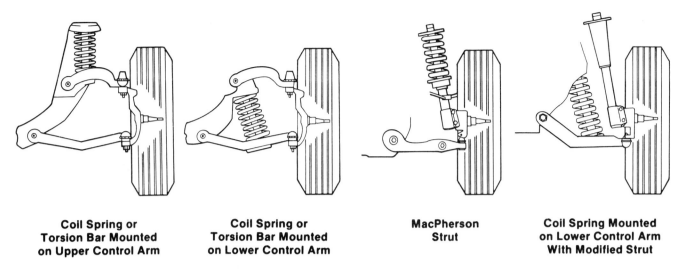

**Coil Spring or
Torsion Bar Mounted
on Upper Control Arm**

**Coil Spring or
Torsion Bar Mounted
on Lower Control Arm**

**MacPherson
Strut**

**Coil Spring Mounted
on Lower Control Arm
With Modified Strut**

FIGURE 12–39 Types of ball joints

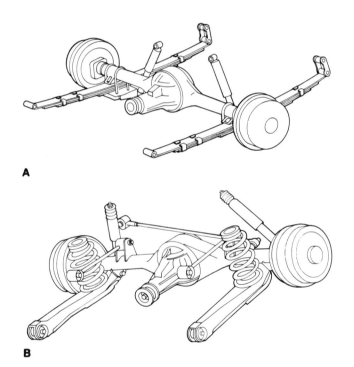

A

B

FIGURE 12–40 Two of the more popular rear suspension systems: (A) leaf spring nonindependent and (B) coil spring nonindependent systems

should be replaced. Remember that rear wheels, just like front wheels, are affected by road shock, acceleration, and braking forces. Control arm or leaf spring bushings are constantly flexing. In addition, bushings keep the rear wheels in line with the front wheels and when worn can upset the settings of the entire suspension and driveshaft systems. Loose, worn, or broken attaching parts will allow the rear wheels to shift, causing premature tire wear as well

as short U-joint service life. A metallic jingling sound when driving over small bumps or unusual tracking (sometimes called dog tracking) also indicate the need for inspection. Usually a visual inspection is enough to determine repair requirements.

The coil spring and leaf spring nonindependent rear suspensions (Figure 12–40) are the most common today on rear drive vehicles. The solid axle design will exhibit some of the same teeter-totter characteristics as noted with solid axle front systems. However, the effect is not nearly as dramatic since the rear wheels do not pivot.

Rear suspension systems on front wheel drive vehicles are usually designed with one of the systems shown in Figure 12–41.

Table 12-1 gives a diagnosis of suspension problems.

COMPUTERIZED SUSPENSION

As already described, conventional systems consist of coil, struts, and absorbers. The new computer suspension systems use sensors to adjust height, leveling of the car, and ride firmness in some models.

Five systems are in current use:

1. Electronic air suspension (EAS)
2. Electronic level control (ELC)
3. Variable damping shock (VDS)
4. Springless electronic suspension (SES)
5. Computer-controlled suspension (CCS)

Some of these systems are relatively new or in the final experimental stages. Repairing these sys-

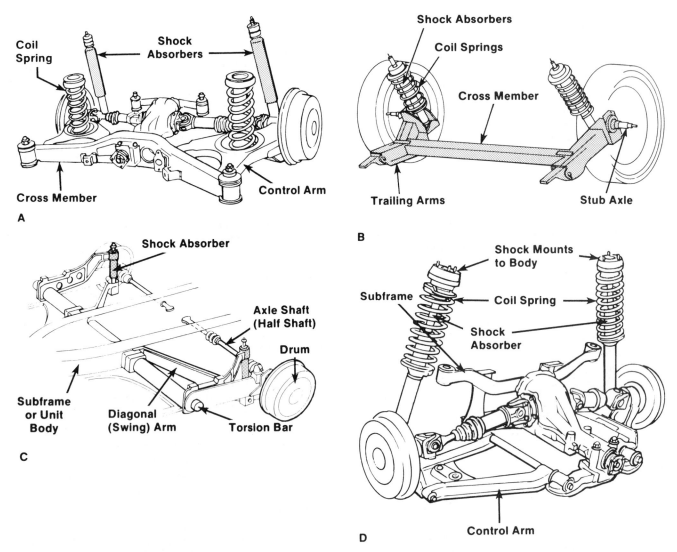

FIGURE 12-41 Rear suspension systems on front wheel drive vehicles: (A) independent rear suspension; (B) independent rear axle suspension; (C) swing arm rear suspension; and (D) strut rear suspension

tems will become more common as more vehicles come equipped with them. Anyone involved in the collision repair process needs a good basic knowledge of how these systems work. The best source of information about these systems is the service manual. Keep in mind that the computer suspension systems are vulnerable to certain problems, any one of which can upset the ability to maintain the desired distance between chassis and road. A plugged or leaky air hose, a bad solenoid, a dead compressor, or a misadjusted or faulty height sensor, for example, can interfere with the suspension's ability to level itself. Because of this, check the operation of the system after a collision to make sure it is functioning correctly.

To understand the basic operation of the EAS and ELC computer systems, look at Figure 12-42. An air bag replaces the coil spring used in a conventional independent suspension system. The computer controls the car's height by either telling a battery driven air compressor to pump air into an air spring or telling a valve to let air out. Three height sensors, two in the front and one in the rear, tell the computer if the car is too high or too low. When the car reaches the right height, the sensors send a trim signal. The pump is shut off, the air spring valve is closed, and the air is trapped in the spring.

The SES and CCS are known as *active* suspension systems. They have the ability to adapt themselves to changing road and driving conditions (Figure 12-43). Instead of conventional springs or air springs to support the vehicle, double-acting hydraulic cylinders (called *actuators*) are mounted at each wheel. Each actuator maintains a sort of hy-

TABLE 12-1: SUSPENSION PROBLEM DIAGNOSIS

Check	Noise	Instability	Pulls to One Side	Excessive Steering Play	Hard Steering	Shimmy
Tires/Wheels	Road or tire noise	Low or uneven air pressure; radials mixed with belted bias ply tires	Low or uneven air pressure; mismatched tire sizes	Low or uneven air pressure	Low or uneven air pressure	Wheel out of balance or uneven tire wear or overworn tires; radials mixed with belted bias ply tires
Shock Dampers (Struts/ Absorbers)	Loose or worn mounts or bushings	Loose or worn mounts or bushings; worn or damaged struts or shock absorbers	Loose or worn mounts or bushings	—	Loose or worn mounts or bushings on strut assemblies	Worn or damaged struts or shock absorbers
Strut Rods	Loose or worn mounts or bushings	Loose or worn mounts or bushings	Loose or worn mounts or bushings	—	—	Loose or worn mounts or bushings
Springs	Worn or damaged	Worn or damaged	Worn or damaged, especially rear	—	Worn or damaged	—
Control Arms	Steering knuckle control arm stop; worn or damaged mounts or bushings	Worn or damaged mounts or bushings	Worn or damaged mounts or bushings	—	Worn or damaged mounts or bushings	Worn or damaged mounts or bushings
Steering System	Component wear or damage	Component wear or damage	Component wear or damage	Component wear or damage	Component wear or damage	Component wear or damage
Alignment	—	Front and rear, especially caster	Front, camber and caster	Front	Front, especially caster	Front, especially caster
Wheel Bearings	On turns or speed changes: front-wheel bearings	Loose or worn (front and rear)	Loose or worn (front and rear)	Loose or worn (front)	—	Loose or worn (front and rear)
Brake System	—	—	On braking	—	On braking	—
Other	Clunk on speed changes: transaxle; click on turns: CV joints; ball joint lubrication	—	—	—	Ball joint lubrication	Loose or worn friction ball joints

draulic equilibrium with the others to carry the vehicle's weight, while maintaining the desired body altitude. At the same time, each actuator serves as its own shock absorber, eliminating the need for yet another traditional suspension component.

In other words, each hydraulic actuator acts as both a spring (with variable-rate damping characteristics) and a variable-rate shock absorber. This is accomplished in an active suspension system by varying the hydraulic pressure within each cylinder

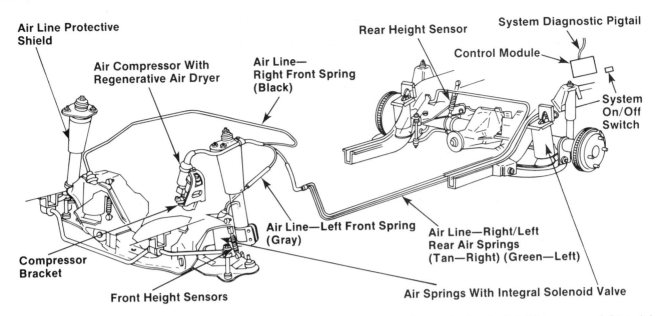

Air Line Protective Shield

Air Compressor With Regenerative Air Dryer

Air Line— Right Front Spring (Black)

Rear Height Sensor

System Diagnostic Pigtail

Control Module

System On/Off Switch

Compressor Bracket

Front Height Sensors

Air Line—Left Front Spring (Gray)

Air Line—Right/Left Rear Air Springs (Tan—Right) (Green—Left)

Air Springs With Integral Solenoid Valve

The system consists of an electric air compressor with regenerative air dryer, electronic height sensors, eight quick connect air fittings, four air springs with integral solenoids, four one-piece air lines connecting each spring to the compressor, and a control module with a single chip microcomputer.

FIGURE 12-42 Typical electronic air suspension system

and the rate at which it increases or decreases. By bleeding or adding hydraulic pressure from the individual actuators, each wheel can react independently to changing road conditions.

A steering angle sensor is used to signal the computer when the vehicle is turning. To monitor body motions, a roll sensor and lateral acceleration and G-sensors are used. The computer also monitors hydraulic pressure within the system and the speed of the pump motor.

Once it has all the necessary inputs, the computer can then regulate the ebb and flow of hydraulic pressure within each individual actuator according to any number of variables and its own built-in program. Bonus features are, for example, leaning into turns or even raising a flat tire on command to change the tire without using a separate jack.

12.4 STEERING SYSTEMS

The steering linkage consists of the pivoting parts necessary to connect the output of the steering box to the front wheel steering arms. Three main types of steering linkage are in common use.

- The **standard or parallelogram steering system** (Figure 12-44) is the most common type

on conventional frame cars. A pitman arm attaches to the steering box either with a ball socket assembly or bushing. Steering action is relayed via the center link, again attached by either ball sockets or bushings. The idler arm supports the center link at the opposite end holding the system parallel, transmitting horizontal steering action. If up and down movement is excessive, toe change might exceed manufacturer's limits thereby creating premature and rapid tire wear. Tie rod ends are the final wearable pivots of the system. Looseness in the ball sockets indicates loss of tension in the internal spring. Even if slight tire motion is evident during the inspection (car off the ground, hand pressure only) when the vehicle is on the ground, moving and subjected to road forces, this motion might be dramatically more substantial.

- The **twin I-beam steering linkage** (Figure 12-45) system is often used with the twin I-beam suspension and is frequently used in light trucks, vans, and four wheel drive vehicles. Its operation is similar to the parallelogram system.

- The **rack and pinion steering system** (Figure 12-46) is fast becoming a standard system for unibody vehicles. It gets its name from

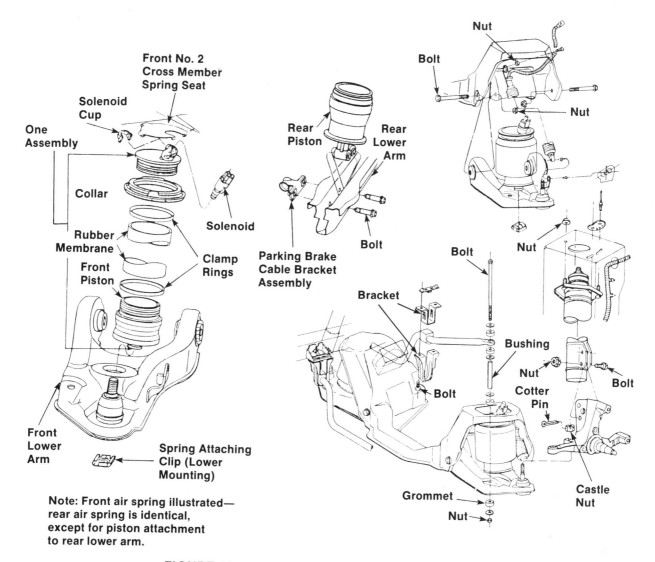

FIGURE 12-43 Typical components of an air spring

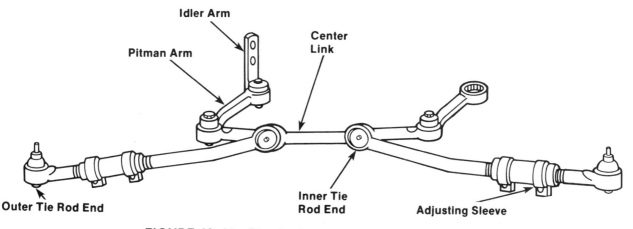

FIGURE 12-44 Standard or parallelogram steering system

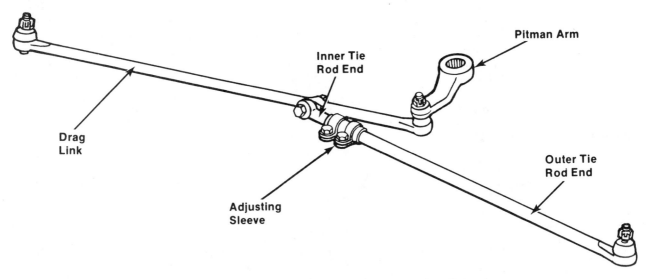

FIGURE 12-45   Typical twin I-beam steering linkage

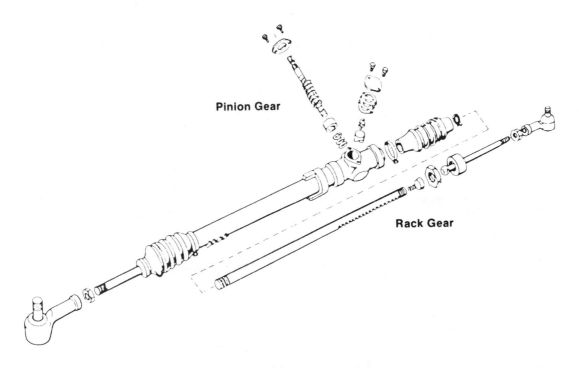

FIGURE 12-46   Rack and pinion steering system

the pinion gear attached to the steering col-umn and the rack gear in the steering gear housing. This rack gear is moved right to left within the housing by the rotation of the pin-ion gear. The ends of the steering rack are attached to the front wheel spindles by tie rods. The rack and pinion gear provides the same combined function as the intermediate rod, idler arm, the pitman arm, and steering gear in a conventional steering system. In unibody construction, the rack and pinion

steering gear assembly on some cars is mounted to the cowl panel. In other cases, the rack and pinion steering gear is mounted to the front suspension cross member or the engine cradle assembly. The rack and pinion steering gear must be mounted securely be-cause any movement will cause the car to wander as it travels down the road.

Rack and pinion has fewer friction points than a traditional steering system, so more energy and movement from road forces get through to the steer-

FIGURE 12-47 Without removing the protective boots, check the condition of the inner tie-rod ends on rack and pinion steering.

ing wheel. This gives the driver a more positive feel of the road. A power-assisted rack and pinion system responds faster to input changes, and the boost can be adjusted to suit driving conditions or individual drivers. It also steers more easily without a boost than hydraulic systems.

To check a rack and pinion system, begin by raising the car and taking the weight off the front suspension. Visually inspect the steering system for any physical damage. Check the boots for leaks, inspect the tie-rods, and examine the mounting points for any distortion. Inspect the tie-rod ends. Grab the tie-rod near the tire and try pushing it up

and down. Any vertical looseness indicates damage or wear.

Check the inner tie-rod socket by squeezing the bellows until the socket can be felt. With the other hand, push and pull on the tire (Figure 12-47). Looseness in the socket indicates damage or wear. Take a front tire in each hand, and see if they can be moved back and forth in opposite directions. If excessive movement is noted, wear or damage is likely. Observe the rack and pinion at the same time. Any movement might indicate a problem.

 **SHOP TALK** _____

Remember that rack and pinion units must be mounted on a level plane. A change as small as 3 millimeters can affect handling. The closer the mounting brackets are to the middle of the rack, the more critical this measurement becomes (Figure 12-48). Misalignment of the rack and pinion will cause changes in the steering geometry during jounce/rebound. This condition cannot be corrected by changing the length of the tie-rods.

POWER STEERING

The power steering unit is designed to reduce the amount of effort required to turn the steering

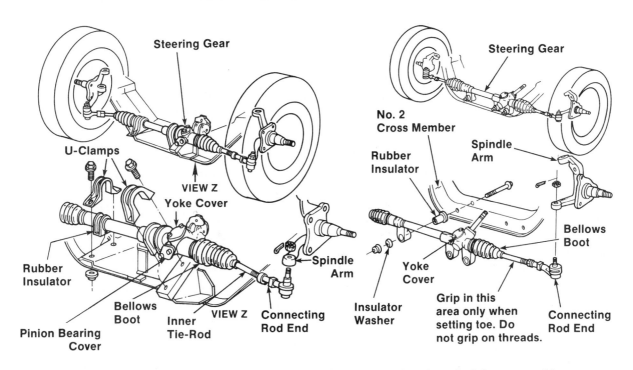

FIGURE 12-48 Typical attaching methods for manual rack and pinion assembly

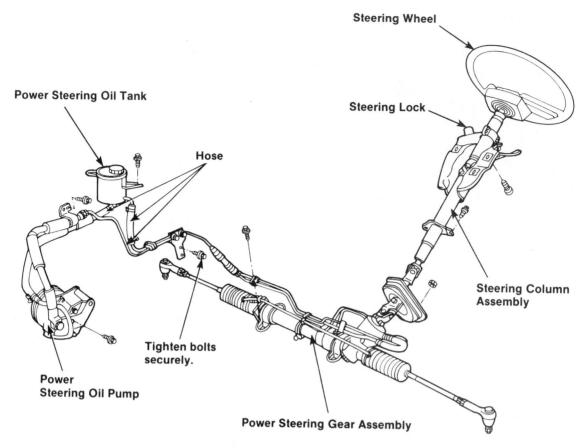

FIGURE 12-49 Typical power steering system

wheel (Figure 12-49). It also reduces driver fatigue on long drives and makes it easier to steer the vehicle at slow road speeds, particularly during parking.

Power steering can be broken down into two design arrangements: conventional and nonconventional or electrically controlled. In the conventional arrangement, hydraulic power is used to assist the driver, while in the nonconventional arrangement an electric motor and electronic controls provide power assistance in steering.

In an electronically controlled power steering arrangement, an electric/electronic rack and pinion unit replaces the hydraulic pump, hoses, and fluid associated with conventional power steering systems with electronic controls and an electric motor located concentrically to the rack itself. The design features a DC motor armature with a hollow shaft to allow passage of the rack through it. The outboard housing and rack are designed so that the rotary motion of the armature can be transferred to linear movement of the rack through a ball nut with thrust bearings. The armature is mechanically connected to the ball nut through an internal/external spline arrangement.

Here are some power steering service tips that should be kept in mind:

- **Protect the system.** Protect the system from invasion by dirt and moisture. If the system must be open, be sure to plug or tie off all openings with a plastic sheet.
- **Use recommended fluid.** Always replace the fluid lost with the manufacturer's recommended type to protect the warranty. Most vehicles require either Dexron or Type F fluid. Some fluids claim to meet the specifications for both of the above types.
- **Bleed the system.** Many systems are self-bleeding. Some have specific bleeding procedures in the service manual to eliminate air. Air in the system can cause noise, vibration, and erratic performance.
- **Check the hose routing.** Check the hose routing when reassembling power steering systems. Always route and hang the same as in the factory installation. Avoid contact with other parts. Especially watch rubbing against moving parts.

TABLE 12-2: STEERING PROBLEM DIAGNOSIS

Check	Problem					
	Noise	Instability	Pulls to One Side	Excessive Steering Play	Hard Steering	Shimmy
Tires/Wheels	Road/tire noise	Low/uneven tire pressure; radial tire lead	Low/uneven tire pressure; radial tire lead	Low/uneven tire pressure	Low/uneven tire pressure	Unbalanced wheel; uneven tire wear; over-worn tires
Tie-rods	Squeal in turns: worn ends	—	Incorrect toe: tie rod length	Worn ends	Worn ends	Worn ends
Mounts/ Bushings	Parallelogram steering: steering gear mounting bolts, linkage connections; rack & pinion steering: rack mounts	Idler arm bushing	—	Parallelogram steering: steering gear mounting bolts, linkage connections; rack & pinion steering: rack mounts	Parallelogram steering: steering gear mounting bolts, linkage connections; rack & pinion steering: rack mounts	Parallelogram steering: steering gear mounting bolts linkage connections; rack & pinion steering: rack mounts
Steering Linkage Components	Bent/damaged steering rack	Incorrect center link/ rack height	Incorrect center link/ rack height	Worn idler arm, center link, or pitman arm studs; worn/damaged rack	Idler Arm binding	Worn idler arm, center link, or pitman arm studs
Steering Gear	Improper yoke adjustment on rack & pinion steering	—	—	Improper yoke adjustment on rack & pinion steering; worn steering gear/ incorrect gear adjustment on parallelogram steering; loose or worn steering shaft coupling	Parallelogram steering: low steering gear lubricant, incorrect adjustment; rack & pinion: bent rack, improper yoke adjustment	—
Power Steering	—	—	—	—	Fluid leaks, loose/worn/ glazed steering belt, weak pump, low fluid level	—
Alignment	—	—	Unequal caster/camber	—	Excessive positive caster, excessive scrub radius (incorrect camber and/or SAI)	Incorrect caster

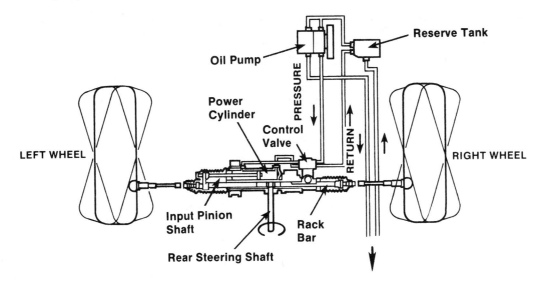

FRONT STEERING SYSTEM

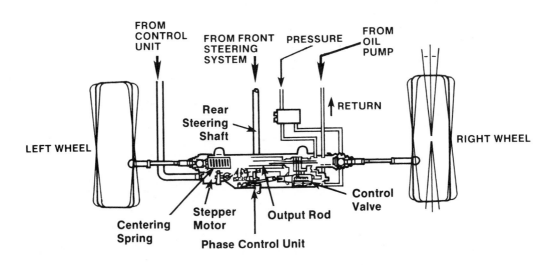

FIGURE 12-50   Mazda 4WS system will operate in relation to speed and steering wheel movement

To perform a diagnostic check of possible steering problems, see Table 12-2.

FOUR-WHEEL STEERING

Four-wheel independent suspensions have been around for years and will continue to be an important part of the automotive industry. Now the industry is offering four-wheel independent steering systems, where the rear wheels also help to turn the car, by either electrical or mechanical means. Because these systems are going to be more common in the future, the repair industry will have to adapt to them.

To understand the advantages of four-wheel steering, it is wise to review the dynamics of typical steering maneuvers with a conventional front-steering vehicle. When turning, the driver sets in motion a complex series of forces that must be balanced against each other. The tires are subjected to road grip, momentum, and steering input. **Grip** holds the car's wheels to the road; **momentum** moves the car straight ahead; and **steering input** causes the front wheels to turn. The tires will momentarily resist the turning motion, causing a slip angle. Once the vehicle begins to respond to the steering input, cornering forces are generated. The vehicle yaws as the rear wheels attempt to keep up with the cornering forces already generated by the front tires (Figure 12-50). This is referred to as rear-end lag, because there is a time delay between steering input and vehicle reaction. When the front wheels are turned back to a straight-ahead position, the vehicle must again try to adjust by reversing the same forces developed by the turn. As the steering wheel is turned, the vehicle body yaws as the rear wheels again try to keep up with the cornering forces generated by the front wheels.

The idea behind four-wheel steering is that a vehicle requires less driver input for any steering maneuver if all four wheels are steering the vehicle. As with two-wheel steering vehicles, grip holds the four wheels on the road. However, when the driver turns the wheel slightly, all four wheels react to the steering input, causing slip angles to form at all four wheels. The entire vehicle moves in one direction rather than the rear half attempting to catch up to the front half (Figure 12-51). There will also be less yaw when the wheels are turned back to a straight-ahead position. The vehicle responds more quickly to steering input because rear-end lag is eliminated.

Currently there are three types of four-wheel steering systems: mechanical, hydraulic, and electrohydraulic designs. Since each system is unique in its construction and repair needs, the service manual for the vehicle must be followed for proper diagnosis, repair, and alignment of a four-wheel system.

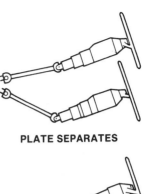

PLATE SEPARATES

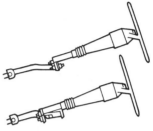

U-JOINTS PIVOT TO ABSORB CRASH IMPACT

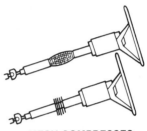

MESH COMPRESSES

FIGURE 12-52   The common types of collapsible steering columns

COLLAPSIBLE STEERING COLUMNS

To reduce the chance of injury to the driver, automotive engineers have designed steering columns that collapse in the event of a collision. Lower steering sections are linked by two or more universal joints; these joints allow the sections to fold (Figure 12-52). The upper column normally incorporates a solid shaft and a tube. The shaft is locked to the tube by one of several methods, each designed to "give" in the event of a collision.

Methods used to lock the shaft to the tube include plastic inserts or steel balls held in a plastic retainer that allow the shaft to "roll" forward inside the tube. There are also collapsing steel mesh or accordion-pleated devices that give way under pressure. During damage analysis, check the steering column for evidence of collapse. Although the car can be steered with a collapsed column that has been pulled back, the collapsed portion must be

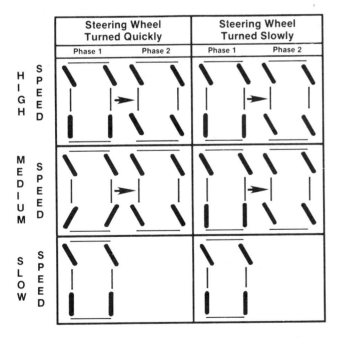

	Steering Wheel Turned Quickly		Steering Wheel Turned Slowly	
	Phase 1	Phase 2	Phase 1	Phase 2
HIGH SPEED				
MEDIUM SPEED				
SLOW SPEED				

FIGURE 12-51   Rear-wheel positions. Wheel angles and scale are exaggerated.

replaced. All service manuals provide explicit instructions for doing this.

> **CAUTION:** When working on a collapsible steering column, do not hammer on or bump column components. With the column removed from the mounts, it is extremely susceptible to impact damage. A slight impact on the column end can collapse the steering shaft or loosen the plastic injections that maintain column rigidity. When removing the steering wheel, use a puller. Do not hammer on any components to aid in removal.

12.5 WHEEL ALIGNMENT

After a thorough inspection of the suspension/steering system and repair or replacement of any

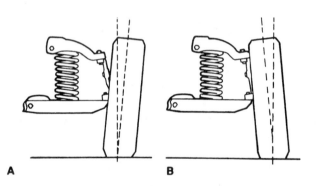

A   **B**

FIGURE 12-53 Two types of camber: (A) positive and (B) negative

damaged parts are completed, wheel alignment is the next important step. The main purpose of wheel alignment is to allow the wheels to roll without scuffing, dragging, or slipping on the road.

 **SHOP TALK** _____

Radial tires cause problems when they have defective belts, unusual wear patterns, uneven air pressure, or are mismatched. These tire problems can cause the technician to misdiagnose steering and alignment problems.

The proper alignment of a suspension/steering system centers around the accuracy of seven control angles:

1. Camber
2. Caster
3. Steering axis inclination (SAI)
4. Scrub radius
5. Toe (in and out)
6. Thrust line
7. Turning radius

CAMBER

This is the inward or outward tilt of the tire as measured at the top. When the tire is tilted out from true vertical, it is positive (Figure 12-53A). When it is tilted toward the center of the vehicle from true vertical, it is negative (Figure 12-53B).

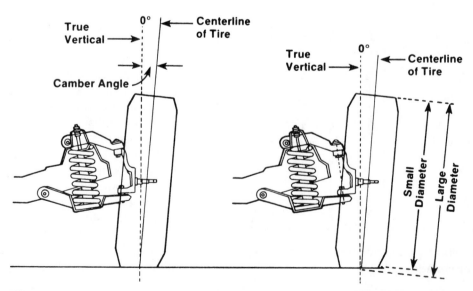

FIGURE 12-54 When camber is out of specifications, it can create changes in the diameter of the tire from inside to outside.

Camber compensates for load and maintains good tire-to-road contact, brings the road contact area of the tire more nearly under the point of load, and works with steering axis inclination in putting the vehicle load on the inner wheel bearing. Camber is usually slightly positive when the car is unloaded and at rest, so that when it is loaded and moving over irregular road surfaces, it will have close to zero camber.

Camber is referred to as a tire wearing angle. When camber is out of specifications, it can create changes in the diameter of the tire from inside to outside. The smaller diameter will be forced to slip in order to catch up with the larger diameter, creating a wear pattern (Figure 12-54). Besides wearing tires, incorrect camber can increase wear on ball joints and wheel bearings. Camber is a directional control angle; incorrect camber can cause the vehicle to pull to one side.

Camber is controlled by the control arms and their pivots. It is affected by worn or loose ball joints, control arm bushings, wheel bearings, and chassis height. Because chassis height affects camber, anything that changes chassis height will affect camber.

However, camber is adjustable on most vehicles. In fact, some manufacturers prefer to include a camber adjustment at the spindle assembly. The adjustment at the spindle assembly attachment provides more correction range for camber. Camber adjustments are also provided on some strut suspension systems at the top mounting position in the body. Very little adjustment of camber or caster will be required by strut suspensions if the tower and lower control arm mounting positions are in their proper place. If serious caster or camber error has occurred and the suspension mounting positions have not been damaged, it is an indication of bent suspension parts. Therefore, diagnostic angle checks and dimensional checks should be made to the suspension parts. Following these checks, the damaged parts should be identified and replaced.

Caster

Caster is the forward or backward tilt of the steering axis. If the steering axis tilts backward at the top, it has positive caster (Figure 12-55A). If the steering axis tilts forward at the top, it has negative caster of the car to force the wheels into a straight ahead (Figure 12-55B). Caster also uses the weight position by pitting the downward force on one side of the car against the downward force on the other side.

While positive caster does aid in directional stability, it also increases steering effort. This can be

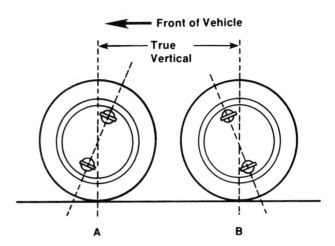

FIGURE 12-55 Two types of caster: (A) positive and (B) negative

compensated for with power steering. Cars with manual steering require a caster setting of almost zero or, in some cases, a negative caster setting. Negative caster settings are required on some newer vehicles.

Caster is not generally a tire wearing angle, but incorrect caster can cause a vehicle to pull to one side and for that reason it is considered a directional control angle and is adjustable. Caster is affected by worn or loose strut rod bushings and control arm bushings. Caster adjustments are usually not provided on strut suspension systems. Where caster adjustments are provided, they can be made at the top or bottom mount of the strut suspension (Figure 12-56).

Steering Axis Inclination

This is the inward tilt of the steering axis at the top (Figure 12-57). It also contributes to directional stability. Because the steering axis is inclined, the spindle is forced to move in an arc downward as the wheel is turned. This action causes the vehicle to rise as the wheel is turned in either direction, so the weight of the car forces the wheels back to the straight ahead position.

Steering axis inclination is not generally considered a tire wear factor unless there is an extreme change. The amount of inclination is preset and should not change unless there is damage to the spindle support arm.

Camber and steering axis inclination are sometimes measured together as the "included angle." The amount of tilt is measured in degrees from vertical.

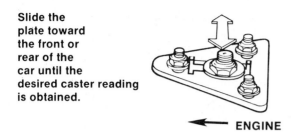

Slide the plate toward the front or rear of the car until the desired caster reading is obtained.

← ENGINE

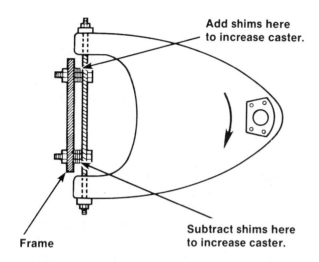

Add shims here to increase caster.

Frame

Subtract shims here to increase caster.

FIGURE 12-56 On some struts, the caster can be adjusted by sliding a plate or by adding or subtracting shims.

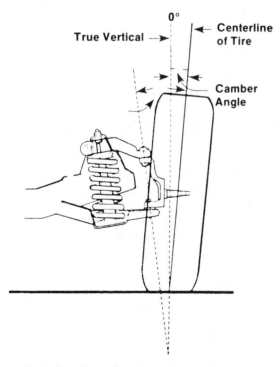

True Vertical →

0°

Centerline of Tire

Camber Angle

FIGURE 12-57 Steering axis inclination

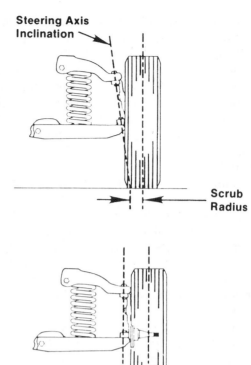

Steering Axis Inclination

Scrub Radius

A

Scrub Radius

B

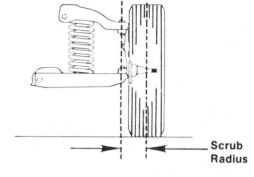

Steering Axis Inclination

Positive Camber

Scrub Radius

C

FIGURE 12-58 Steering scrub radius

Scrub Radius

The importance of steering axis inclination to steering ease and stability centers around the reduction of scrub radius. Scrub radius is the distance between the centerline of the ball joints and the centerline of the tire at the point where the tire contacts the road surface (Figure 12-58A). When the ball joint centerline (pivot point) is inboard of the point of tire contact, the tire does not pivot where it touches the road. Instead, it has to move forward and backward to compensate as the driver turns the steering wheel. Steering effort is greatly increased as the tires scrub against the road during turns.

If the control arm assembly were designed with no steering axis inclination, scrub radius would be quite large, as can be seen in Figure 12–58B.

Both positive camber and steering axis inclination combine to reduce scrub radius to a minimum (Figure 12–58C).

Toe

Toe, in or out, is the difference in the distance between the front and rear of the tires at one end of the car (Figure 12–59). If the tires at one end of the car are closer at the front than at the rear, they have toe-in. If the tires at one end of the car are closer at the rear than at the front, they have toe-out.

Toe is set so that when the car is moving down the road, the wheels are pointed straight ahead. The amount of toe at rest is determined by the amount of play in the steering linkage and suspension. Toe adjustments are made by shortening or lengthening the tie rods on both the conventional parallel arm suspension and the rack and pinion steering system commonly used with the strut suspension system.

Toe adjustments to the rack and pinion gear are made at the tie rod, similar to a parallel steering system. Toe adjustments must be made evenly on both sides of the rack and pinion gear. If toe adjustments are not made evenly, the rack assembly will be off-center in the gear. This off-center rack condition can cause a pulling feeling to the driver as the car runs down the road. This pull condition is especially common with power-assisted rack and pinion gears. When the rack is adjusted off-center, the power assist powers the gear into a corner, causing the driver to feel a pulling effect. The pulling effect can be corrected by making the adjustments equal on both sides of the gear. The steering assembly must be centered before these adjustments are made.

Rear toe condition (Figure 12–60) refers to the angle of the rear wheel in or out at the front of the wheel as viewed from the top. It might or might not be adjustable depending on the design of the car. However, it has an important effect on the handling of the car. Some cars with independent rear suspensions also have at-rest toe settings to compensate for play in the rear suspension.

Rear camber (Figure 12–61) refers to the position of a rear wheel in or out at the top as viewed from

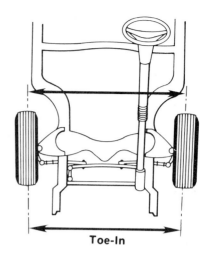

A

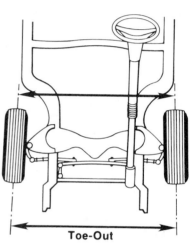

B

FIGURE 12–59   Toe conditions: (A) Toe-in is the amount that wheels are closer together at the extreme front of the tires than they are at the extreme rear. (B) Toe-out is just the opposite of toe-in, with a greater measurement in front than in the rear.

the rear of the rear wheel. It might or might not be adjustable depending on the design of the car. However, it has an important effect on the handling of the car.

Thrust Line Alignment

A main consideration in any alignment is to make sure the vehicle runs straight down the road, with the rear tires tracking directly behind the front tires when the steering wheel is in the straight-ahead position. The geometric centerline of the vehicle should parallel the road direction. This will be the

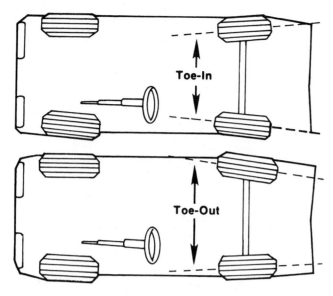

FIGURE 12-60 Typical rear toe condition

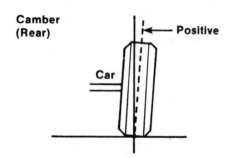

FIGURE 12-61 Rear camber and the position of the rear wheel

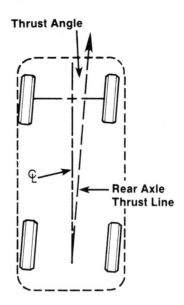

FIGURE 12-62 Thrust line alignment

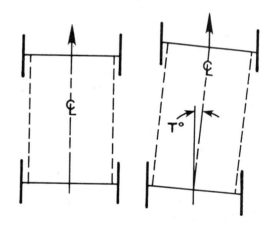

FIGURE 12-63 Tracking is the parallel alignment of the rear wheels to the vehicle centerline and to the front wheels. When the rear wheels are not set parallel to the centerline and to the front wheels, the car will dog track.

case when rear toe is parallel to the vehicle's geometric centerline in the straight-ahead position. If rear toe does not parallel the vehicle centerline a "thrust" direction to the left or right will be created (Figure 12-62). This difference of rear toe from the geometric centerline is called the **thrust angle**. The vehicle will tend to travel in the direction of the thrust line, rather than straight ahead.

To correct this problem, begin by setting individual rear toe equal in reference to the geometric centerline. Four-wheel alignment machines check individual toe on each wheel. Once the rear wheels are in alignment with the geometric centerline, set the individual front toe in reference to the thrust angle. Following this procedure assures that the steering wheel will be straight ahead for straight-ahead travel. If you set the front toe to the vehicle geometric centerline, ignoring the rear toe angle, a cocked steering wheel will result. The direction of the front wheels would be trying to compensate for differences between the vehicle geometric centerline and thrust angle (Figure 12-63).

Turning Radius

Turning radius or cornering angle is the amount of toe-out on turns (Figure 12-64). As a car goes around a corner, the inside tire must travel in a smaller radius circle than the outside tire. This is accomplished by designing the steering geometry to turn the inside wheel more sharply than the outside wheel during a turn. The result can be seen as toe-out on turns. The purpose is to eliminate tire scrubbing on the road surface by keeping the tires pointed in the direction they have to move.

The analysis of ride and handling complaints involves more than just attention to the accuracy of

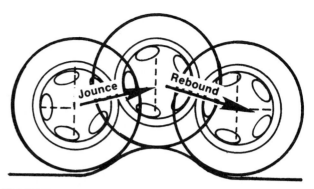

FIGURE 12-65   Reaction of jounce and rebound

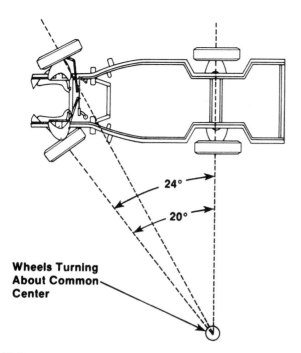

24°

20°

Wheels Turning About Common Center

FIGURE 12-64   Typical turning radius

control angles. The analysis of ride and handling problems involves the consideration of diagnostic angles. Suspension system parts must be considered as moving parts in the operation of the car. Diagnostic angles evaluate suspension parts as they move. When a car comes in with a collision caused steering problem, before the technician starts disassembling the car, the first diagnostic check should be a visual inspection of the entire vehicle for anything obvious: bent wheels, obvious misalignment of the cradle, and the wheels to the wheel opening. If there is not a thing obviously wrong with the car, make the following diagnostic checks without disassembling the vehicle. One of the very useful diagnostic checks that can be made with a minimum of equipment is a jounce-rebound toe-in change check, which can help determine the condition of the suspension system.

- **Jounce** is the motion caused by a wheel going over a bump and compressing the spring. During jounce, the wheel moves up toward the chassis. Jounce can be simulated for in-shop testing by pushing down on the car by sitting on the fender. The car must be jounced equally on both sides.
- **Rebound** is the motion caused by a wheel going into a dip, or returning from a jounce and extending the spring. During rebound, the wheel moves down away from the chassis. Rebound can be simulated for in-shop testing by lifting up on the fender. The car must be lifted equally on both sides.

This jounce-rebound check (Figure 12-65) will determine if there is some misalignment to the rack and pinion gear. For a quick check, unlock the steering wheel and see if it moves during the jounce and/or rebound. For a more careful check, employ a pointer and a piece of chalk. Use the chalk to make a reference mark on the tire tread and place the pointer on the same line as the chalk mark. Jounce and rebound the suspension system a few times, while someone watches the chalk mark and the pointer. If the chalk mark on the wheel moved unequally in and out on both sides of the car, the chances are that there is a steering arm or gear out of alignment. If the chalk mark did not move, or moved equally in and out on both sides of the car, the steering arm and gear are probably all right. Each wheel or side should be checked.

The next diagnostic check is for cornering angle. The cornering angle check evaluates the proper relationship of the two front wheels as they are turned through a steering arc. To measure cornering angle, one wheel is turned on a turn plate or **protractor** a given amount; the amount of rotation of the opposite wheel is measured in a similar manner. The results are compared right to left to determine if the two front wheels are rotating through the same arc.

During a cornering angle check, the left front wheel should be turned out 20 degrees. Then the right wheel rotation is measured. The readings will usually not match those of the right wheel. The right wheel should turn in the same amount or about 2 degrees less. The difference accounts for the turning radius difference between the inside and outside wheels during cornering.

The process is repeated with the right wheel; the right wheel is turned out 20 degrees. The movement of the left wheel is measured on the protractor or turn plate. The left wheel should turn in the same amount or about 2 degrees less.

By design, a vehicle might use a different turning radius from one side to the other. If in doubt, refer to the manufacturer's specifications. If these measurements do not repeat within 2 degrees, damage to the steering arms or gear is indicated. Cornering angle measurements are especially useful in determining whether improper toe conditions are caused by poor wheel alignment or damaged suspension components.

CAMBER CHECKS

Some camber checks can be made to diagnose the condition of a strut and can be measured easily with a camber gauge (Figure 12-66). One is called a jounce-rebound camber measurement (Figure 12-67A) and can be made by loading the suspension in a similar fashion to jounce-rebound toe change and measuring the camber angle from an individual wheel.

The suspension is then unloaded as in the jounce-rebound toe check and a second camber reading of the same wheel is made (Figure 12-67B). The two readings are compared; these readings should not differ more than 2 degrees on a MacPherson strut type suspension. In most cases, the readings will be the same.

The jounce-rebound camber change will tell the technician if the strut is bent either inboard or out-

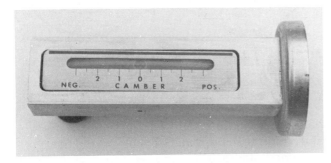

FIGURE 12-66   Gauge used in camber checks

A

B

C

D

FIGURE 12-67   Jounce and rebound camber checks

board. Check each wheel individually before deciding if that one wheel strut is bad based on the readings. If the readings differ between wheels more than 2 degrees, a bent strut is indicated.

A swing camber measurement is made by turning the front wheel "in" a given amount and performing a jounce-rebound camber check (Figure 12-67C).

The front wheel is then turned out the same amount and the camber angle is measured again (Figure 12-67D). If the camber angle change differs more than 3 degrees from left wheel to right wheel, it is likely that either the strut is bent forward or rearward of its normal position or the caster angle is incorrect. As a further test for a bent strut, perform a jounce-rebound check while the wheels are turned in and while they are turned out. Check each wheel and compare the readings. These diagnostic angles are especially helpful in determining the cause of vehicle handling and tracking problems.

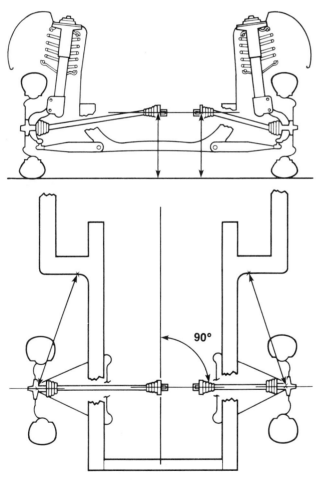

FIGURE 12-68 Drive shafts are a part of the steering and suspension systems. Their positioning can affect those systems. If the drive shaft system parts are bent or damaged, they can cause handling problems.

ENGINE CRADLE POSITION

Proper positioning of the engine cradle will affect the steering angles. Since the cradle provides the lower pivot point, movement of the cradle will cause a camber change. Both wheels will show an equal camber change, one side negative and one side positive. It will also cause an SAI but not an included angle change. Make sure the cradle's position is within the specifications given in the service manual.

The positioning of the drive shaft can also affect the steering and suspension systems. If any of these parts are bent, it can cause a shimmy or handling problems. If there is any doubt about the positioning of the drive shafts measure them as shown in Figure 12-68.

ROAD HEIGHT

For proper alignment, each of the front and rear wheels must carry the same amount of weight. The car is designed to ride at a specific height, sometimes referred to as **curb height** (Figure 12-69). Curb height specs are published in the service manuals and some of the alignment spec books.

If the vehicle leans to one side or seems to be lower on one side than on the other, something is wrong. Either the front or rear suspension on that side of the vehicle can cause the condition. To isolate the problem, place a jack in the center of the main cross member in the front of the vehicle (Figure 12-70). Raise the vehicle several inches, and look at the rear of the car. If the rear of the car looks level, the problem is in the front suspension on the side that shows the lean. If the rear suspension is not level, the problem is the rear suspension on the low side.

ALIGNMENT PROCEDURE

Before making any adjustment affecting caster, camber, or toe-in, the following checks should be made to ensure correct alignment readings and adjustments.

- Make sure the vehicle is sitting on a level surface (side to side and front to rear).
- Rotate the tires if needed. (Check the tires for similar tread design, depth, and construction).
- Make sure all tires are inflated to recommended pressure.

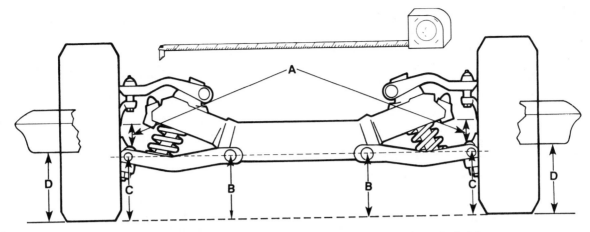

FIGURE 12-69 Methods of measuring curb or ride height

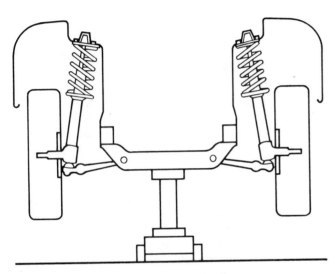

FIGURE 12-70 Raising the vehicle by jacking in the center of the main cross member

- Inspect for worn or bent parts and replace. Much of this should be checked during body/frame correction.
- Check and adjust wheel bearings if necessary. (Spin tires; check for looseness or unusual noises.)
- Check for unbalanced loading (proper chassis height). This should be checked after body/frame correction.

 **SHOP TALK** _____

Caster and camber angles are measured with gauges (Figures 12-71 and 12-72) available from specialty tool manufacturers. They must be used as directed to get proper measurements.

- Check for loose ball joints, tie rod ends, steering relay rods, control arms, and stabilizer bar attachments.
- Check for run-out of wheels and tires.
- Check for defective shock absorbers.
- Consider excess loads, such as tool boxes.
- Consider the condition and type of equipment being used to check alignment and follow the manufacturer's instructions.

The adjustment order—caster, camber, toe—is recommended regardless of the make of car or its type of suspension. Methods of adjustment vary from vehicle to vehicle and, in some cases, from year to year of the same make car. Refer to the manufacturer's service manual for details. A typical alignment procedure could be considered as follows:

 1. Obtain manufacturer's specifications.
2. Camber. Tilt of wheel inward and outward.
3. Caster. Forward or rearward tilt of steering axis.
4. Steering and axis inclination. Inward tilt of steering axis at the top.
5. Turning radius. Wheel angles while turning.
6. Toe. Difference in distance between the front and rear of the tire.

Today most vehicles use a four wheel alignment.

Table 12-2 summarizes a typical steering problem diagnosis. But, it is important to remember that the typical customer judges the quality of a wheel alignment by the position of the "fifth wheel"—the one in his/her hands. It must be straight (Figure 12-73). Make sure all alignments end with a properly centered steering wheel.

A

B

C

D

FIGURE 12-71   Alignment gauge that makes it easy to check wheel alignment while the vehicle is still on the repair bench: (A) measure passenger side to drive side at the front and rear of the gauge for toe; (B) read the bubble level for camber; (C) check the rear suspension; and (D) read the camber with the car on a level surface. *(Courtesy of Steck Mfg. Co. Inc.)*

A

B

FIGURE 12-72 Sophisticated wheel alignment, once found in only alignment specialty shops, has now found its way into body shops because of unibody construction. (A) Typical four wheel alignment system; (B) computerized system. Four wheel and computerized alignments are becoming a "must" today. *(Photo A courtesy of Bee Line Co.; photo B courtesy of Hunter Engineering Co.)*

FIGURE 12-73 The final test—the steering wheel

12.6 DRIVE FUNDAMENTALS

Constant velocity (CV) joints have overcome the design limitations of conventional universal (U) joints and have become common to unibody drivetrains. They can be found on some unibody rear wheel drive (RWD) and four wheel drive (4WD) or all wheel drive (AWD) vehicles, as well as on all front wheel drive (FWD) vehicles.

FRONT WHEEL DRIVE

In a typical FWD application (Figure 12-74) two CV joints are used on each half shaft, or a total of

Plunging
(Inner)   Fixed
(Outer)

FIGURE 12-74 Inner and outer CV joints on a front-wheel-drive half shaft

four CV joints: two outboard joints near the wheels and two inboard joints near the transaxle. The outboard joints are usually fixed and the inner ones are generally plunging types (Figure 12-75).

Front wheel drive half shafts can be solid or tubular, of equal or unequal length, or with or without damper weights (Figure 12-75A). Equal length shafts (Figure 12-75B) help reduce torque steer (the tendency to steer to one side as engine power is applied). In these applications, an intermediate shaft links the transaxle to one of the half shafts. This intermediate shaft uses an ordinary universal joint to couple to the transaxle. At the outer end is a support bracket and bearing assembly. Be sure to inspect these drivetrain components because loose bearings and/or brackets vibrate.

Because the half shafts on a front wheel drive vehicle turn at roughly one-third the speed of the drive shaft in a rear wheel drive vehicle, half shaft balance and runout are not very important. The small damper weight that is sometimes attached to one half shaft serves to dampen harmonic vibrations in the drivetrain and to stabilize the shaft as it spins, not to balance the shaft.

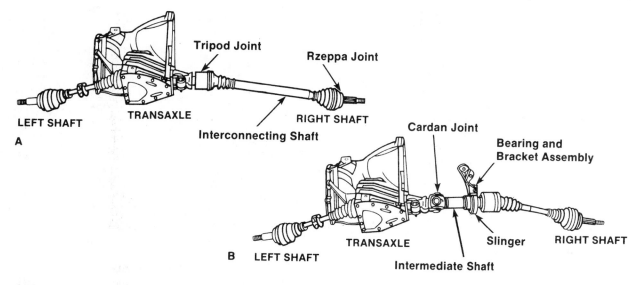

FIGURE 12-75   (A) Unequal and (B) equal length FWD half shafts

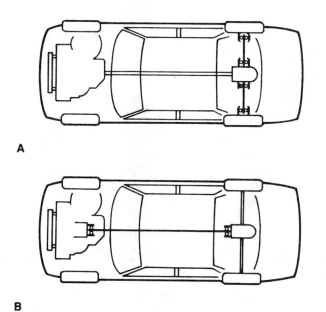

FIGURE 12-76   (A) Rear-wheel drive with independent rear suspension CV joint positions; (B) CV joint applications on the propeller shaft of a RWD vehicle

Rear Wheel Drive

There are two basic types of CV joint applications found on RWD unibody vehicles: independent rear suspension (Figure 12-76A) and main drive propeller shaft (Figure 12-76B). In RWD with independent rear suspension (IRS), CV joints can be found at both ends of the axle shafts (for a total of four). One or both joints on either shaft might be the plunging type.

In RWD with the propeller shaft setup, plunging joints are sometimes used at one or both ends of the

shaft to eliminate high-speed vibrations. That is, a plunging joint will compensate for changes in shaft length that occur with rear suspension travel.

In propeller shaft applications, the CV joint still needs a protective boot, but it is a different design than the boots used on front wheel drive or rear wheel drive axle half shafts. Instead of wrapping around the outside of the joint, it is mounted within the outer housing. This protects the boot but also makes inspection more difficult.

CV-jointed propeller shafts revolve at high speeds and require balancing if removed for service. Remember that many RWD vehicles still use the conventional U-joint drive. Check the service manual whether a CV or U-joint system is used.

Four Wheel Drive

There are several four wheel drive drivetrain configurations; so, the number of CV joints will vary accordingly (Figure 12-77). CV joints and/or universal joints are used on front and/or rear axle shafts, as well as on the front and rear propeller shafts. On the typical 4WD vehicle, a transfer case is mounted to the side, underneath, or the back of the transmission. A chain or gear drive within the case receives the power flow from the transmission and transfers it to two separate drive shafts leading to the front and rear axles.

A selector switch or shifter located in the driving compartment controls the transfer case so that power is directed to the axles as the driver desires. Power can be directed to all four wheels (4WD), to only two wheels—normally the rear wheels (2WD), or to no wheels (neutral). On many vehicles, the

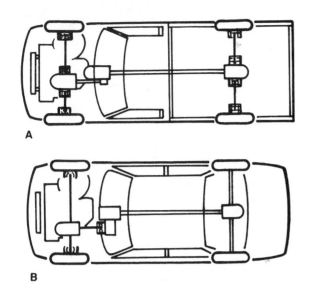

FIGURE 12-79   Squeeze testing a boot *(Courtesy of Dana Corp.)*

FIGURE 12-77   **(A) Four-wheel drive system with independent front and rear suspension; (B) four-wheel drive system with beam axle**

driver is also given the option of a "low" 4WD range for extra traction in especially rough conditions, such as deep snow or mud.

The selector can also permit the driver to choose either a full-time or part-time 4WD setting. In full-time 4WD, all four wheels are constantly open to receiving power from the power train, but they are not necessarily all receiving an equal power flow. Part-time units only deliver power to all the wheels when the driver consciously asks for it, but they deliver equal power to the wheels at all times. But on a full-time 4WD system, the driver is given the option of selecting the equivalent mode of a part-time system. This is done by locking up the differential in the drivetrain transfer case. Part-time units or modes should be used only when poor road conditions require extra traction; otherwise, accelerated and ex-

cessive gear and component wear will result. Part-time systems are frequently called all-wheel-drive (AWD) in many unibody models.

DAMAGE INSPECTION

Begin damage inspection (Figure 12-78) by checking the condition of the CV joint boots. Splits, cracks, tears, punctures, or thin spots caused by rubbing call for immediate boot replacement. If the boot appears rotted, this indicates improper greasing or excessive heat, and the boot should be replaced. Squeeze-test all boots (Figure 12-79); if any air escapes, replace the boot. Also replace any boots that are missing. Keep in mind that any discoloring of the housing at the bearing grooves is normal because all CV joints are especially heat treated. If the inner boot appears to be collapsed or deformed,

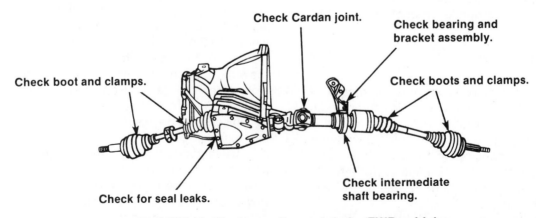

Check Cardan joint.

Check bearing and bracket assembly.

Check boot and clamps.

Check boots and clamps.

Check for seal leaks.

Check intermediate shaft bearing.

FIGURE 12-78   **Inspection points for FWD vehicles**

venting it (allowing air to enter) might solve the problem. Place a round-tipped rod between the boot and drive shaft. This equalizes the outside and inside air and allows the boot to return to its normal shape.

Make sure that all boot clamps are tight. Missing or loose clamps should be replaced. If the boot appears loose, slide it back and inspect the grease inside for possible contamination. A milky or foamy appearance indicates water contamination. A gritty feeling when rubbed between the fingers indicates dirt. In either case, as a minimal service before the joint can be dried, the old grease will have to be cleaned out, the joint repacked with fresh grease, and a new boot installed. However, in many cases a water- or dirt-contaminated joint will have to be replaced rather than regreased.

The drive shafts should be checked for signs of contact against the chassis or rubbing. Rubbing can be a symptom of a weak or broken spring, engine mount, or chassis misalignment.

On front wheel drive transaxles with equal length half shafts, inspect the intermediate shaft U-joint, bearing, and support bracket for looseness by rocking the wheel back and forth and watching for any movement.

Various drivetrain and suspension problems can be confused with symptoms produced by a bad CV joint. The following list of symptoms should help guide the technician to a proper diagnosis:

- **A popping or clicking noise when turning.** This signals a worn or damaged outer joint. The condition can be aggravated by putting the car in reverse and backing in a circle. If the noise gets louder, the outer joint(s) should be replaced.
- **A "clunk" when accelerating, decelerating, or when putting the transaxle into drive.** This kind of noise can come from excessive play in the inner joint of FWD applications, either inner or outer joints in a RWD independent suspension, or from the drive shaft CV joints or U-joint in a RWD or 4WD power train. Be warned, though, that the same kind of noise can also be produced by excessive backlash in the differential gears and transmission.
- **A humming or growling noise.** Sometimes due to inadequate lubrication in either the inner or outer CV joint. It is more often due to worn or damaged wheel bearings, a bad intermediate shaft bearing on equal-length half shaft transaxles, or worn shaft bearings within the transmission.
- **A shudder or vibration when accelerating.** Excessive play in either the inboard or out-

board joints but more likely the inboard plunge joint. These kinds of vibrations can also be caused by a bad intermediate shaft bearing on transaxles with equal length half shafts. On FWD vehicles with transverse-mounted engines, this kind of vibration can also be caused by loose or deteriorated engine/transaxle mounts. Be sure to inspect the rubber bushings in the upper torque strap on these engines to rule out this possibility. Note, however, that shudder could also be inherent to the vehicle itself.
- **A vibration that increases with speed** is rarely due to CV joint problems or FWD half shaft imbalance. An out-of-balance tire or wheel, an out-of-round tire or wheel, or a bent rim are the more likely causes. It is possible that a bent half shaft as the result of collison or

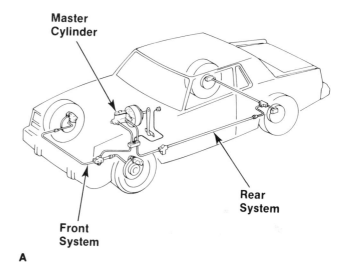

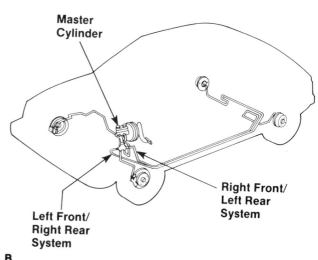

FIGURE 12-80 (A) Front/rear split hydraulic system; (B) dual diagonal split hydraulic system

towing damage could cause a vibration, as could a missing damper weight.

12.7 BRAKE SYSTEMS

In the body shop of yesteryear, brake systems were rarely repaired or serviced by the average service technician; they were farmed out to a specialty shop or, if available, in-house brake specialists. However, in the age of unibodies, it is important that the body technician know how the various brake systems operate, how to check for collision-damaged parts, and how to remove, if necessary, the components from a unibody structure. Most of the repair itself is still done by brake specialists.

In today's front wheel drive automobiles, the front brakes are now doing as much as 80 percent of the work in stopping the car. Thus, the conventional front/rear split hydraulic system (Figure 12–80A) has given way to a dual diagonal split system. This combines a front brake with its opposite rear brake (Figure 12–80B). This system allows straight stopping and provides 50 percent of the braking capacity in case of failure in either of the two hydraulic systems.

The actuating system of today's cars employs hydraulic pressure or power-assisted hydraulic pressure. When the driver steps on the brake pedal, the force from the foot creates a hydraulic pressure in the master cylinder. This pressure is transmitted through lines and hoses to the wheel cylinders where it turns into force again to act upon the drums or discs that stop the car (Figure 12–81).

 **SHOP TALK** _____

Keep the brake system closed to the atmosphere as much as possible. This will keep moisture from entering the system. Moisture is readily absorbed by the fluid and causes sludge and corrosion to form. In time, this will cause partial or complete loss of brake effect. Moisture also lowers the boiling point of the fluid. Boiling results in vapor, which has the same effect as air in the system. Moisture can enter the system in several ways: leaving the system open, improper storage of fluid, and incorrect bleeding equipment or techniques.

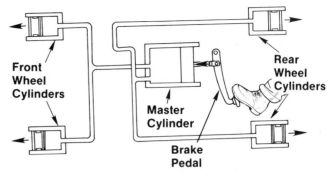

FIGURE 12-81 Simple automotive hydraulic system

Two basic types of hydraulic brakes are used in unibody vehicles. They are drum brakes and disc brakes.

DRUM BRAKES

A drum brake assembly consists of a cast-iron drum, which is bolted to and rotates with the vehicle wheel, and a fixed backing plate to which are attached the shoes and other components—wheel cylinders, automatic adjusters, linkages, and so on (Figure 12-82). Additionally, there might be some extra hardware for parking brakes. The shoes are surfaced with frictional linings, which contact the inside of the drum when the brakes are applied. The shoes are forced outward, against the action of the return springs, by pistons which are actuated by hydraulic pressure. As the drum rubs against the shoes, the energy of the moving drum is transformed into heat, and this heat energy is passed into the atmosphere.

When the brake shoe is engaged, the frictional drag acting around its circumference tends to rotate it about its hinge point, the brake anchor. If the rotation of the drum corresponds to an outward rotation of the shoe, the drag will pull the shoe tighter against the inside of the drum, and the shoe will be self-energizing.

DISC BRAKES

Disc brakes resemble the brakes on a bicycle: the friction elements are in the form of pads, which are squeezed or clamped about the edge of a rotating wheel. With automotive disc brakes, this wheel is a separate unit, called a **rotor**, inboard of the vehicle wheel (Figure 12–83). The rotor is made of cast iron

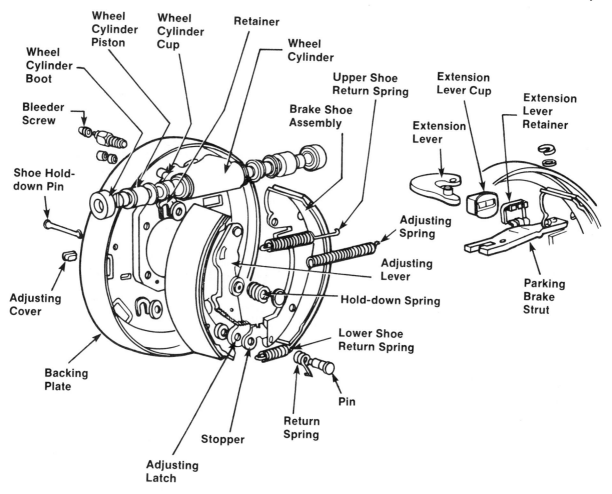

Wheel Cylinder Boot

Wheel Cylinder Piston

Wheel Cylinder Cup

Retainer

Wheel Cylinder

Bleeder Screw

Upper Shoe Return Spring

Brake Shoe Assembly

Extension Lever Cup

Extension Lever Retainer

Extension Lever

Shoe Hold-down Pin

Adjusting Spring

Adjusting Lever

Adjusting Cover

Hold-down Spring

Parking Brake Strut

Backing Plate

Lower Shoe Return Spring

Pin

Return Spring

Stopper

Adjusting Latch

FIGURE 12-82   Rear drum brake components

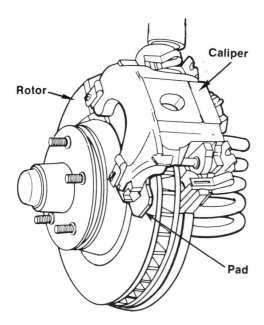

Caliper

Rotor

Pad

FIGURE 12-83   A typical disc brake

and, since the pads clamp against both sides of it, both sides are machined smooth. Usually the two surfaces are separated by a finned center section for better cooling. The pads are attached to metal shoes, which are actuated by pistons, like drum brakes. The pistons are contained within a **caliper assembly**, a housing that wraps around the edge of the rotor. The caliper is kept from rotating by way of bolts holding it to the car's suspension framework.

The **caliper** is a housing containing the pistons and related seals, springs, and boots, as well as the cylinder(s) and fluid passages necessary to force the friction linings or pads against the rotor. The caliper resembles a hand in the way it wraps around the edge of the rotor. It is attached to the steering knuckle. Some models employ light spring pressure to keep the pads close against the rotor; in other caliper designs this is achieved by a unique seal that pushes out the piston for the necessary amount, then retracts it just enough to pull the pad off the rotor.

445

Unlike shoes in a drum brake, the pads act perpendicular to the rotation of the disc when the brakes are applied. This effect is different from that produced in a brake drum, where frictional drag actually pulls the shoe into the drum. Disc brakes are nonenergized and require more force for the same braking effort. For this reason, they are ordinarily used with a power brake unit.

Actual work on hydraulic brake system parts—master cylinder, combination valve, wheel cylinders, brake shoe, and caliper assemblies—is best left to brake specialists. However, disassembly and reassembly, and replacement of some damaged components are skills of the service technician.

Master Cylinder

The master cylinder is the heart of the hydraulic system (Figure 12-84). It is located in the engine compartment, usually on the driver's side, and is connected to the brake pedal by a special rod. The master cylinder initiates braking when the brake pedal is depressed by pushing out a piston inside the cylinder, exerting pressure that is transferred through the system. To protect against total failure of the system, all cars are now required to have two hydraulic systems.

The master cylinder must be checked before the car is put back in service. To check the fluid level, clean all dirt and grease off the unit, then simply pop the wire bracket (or whatever locking device is on the top) and remove the lid. The level should not be more than 1/4 inch below the top of the reservoir. If the level is below this, check the brake line connections and refill the reservoir with fluid. If the system is leaking anywhere but at the brake line connec-

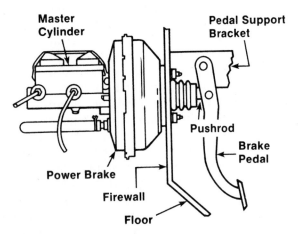

FIGURE 12-84 Typical master cylinder and system components

tions, the master cylinder should be replaced or rebuilt by a brake specialist.

 **SHOP TALK** _____

Never use the master cylinder and other brake mounts as a pulling attachment. If a pull must be made to correct cowl damage, use a plate and different bolts to anchor the pull.

Brake Fluid

WARNING: The chemicals in brake fluid damage most paint finishes. If spilled on paint, a quick flush with water can lessen the damage.

When brake fluid absorbs moisture, it drastically reduces the boiling point of the fluid. This effect is even more pronounced in high-temperature fluids that are used in heavy-duty and disc brake service. Typical vehicles in the field for 18 months accumulate 2 to 3 percent water in the brake fluid. Absorption of a mere 3 percent of moisture reduces the boiling point of these fluids by 25 percent.

This effect bears a bit of investigation. Given a system contaminated with water dispersed throughout the brake fluid, the system acts properly when cold. But after some heavy braking, the fluid in the wheel cylinder or caliper heats up and the contaminated fluid vaporizes. This vapor is now a gas in the system and behaves just like air or any other gas, creating a spongy pedal, or in the extreme case, no pedal at all. The danger of entrapped moisture is that the symptoms do not show up until moments of heavy braking, when the brakes are needed the most.

To prevent contamination, the following precautions must be strictly observed when handling brake fluid:

- Keep the master cylinder tightly covered.
- Always recap it immediately after filling.
- Use the smallest possible can of fluid, and use it all if possible. If, for instance, there is a choice of using two small cans or a portion of a large can, use the two small ones.
- Tightly cap the fluid container after use.
- If using a pressure brake bleeder, keep its fluid reservoir tightly closed, just like the master cylinder.

- If any fluid has become contaminated, throw it out.
- Do not reuse old brake fluid.
- Do not reuse an old brake fluid container since it is not possible to know what else might have been in the can.
- Do not transfer brake fluid from its original container to anything other than a container specifically designed to hold brake fluid, such as a pressure bleeder.

Brake Lines

The brake lines are generally the major brake component that a service technician must repair. When making a collision inspection, check the brake lines for chafing, crimps, loose or missing tube clips, kinks, dents, and leakage. Leaks are evidenced by fluid seepage at the connections or stains around hose ends (Figure 12-85). Blockages are not so readily apparent, but are just as detrimental to the function of the braking system, often acting as a check valve to prevent proper release of the brakes. During a brake application the pressure forces the fluid past the obstruction, but when the pressure is relaxed, the fluid will not readily flow back past the blockage and the brakes drag. Brake lines are usually steel, except where they have to flex—between the chassis and the front wheels, and the chassis and the rear axle. At these places flexible hoses are used.

When replacing damaged brake lines, use the same type of material as OEM. This includes stainless steel, armor plate tubing, or ribbed hose. Local availability might be limited on special types, but it is important to try to match the factory materials.

When cutting tubing to length, it is important to duplicate the factory flare (Figure 12-86). Some cars use a double flare connection, so check for details carefully. Do not use compression fittings in brake line repairs. Replace all supporting clamps removed

Torn inner lining restricts flow, acts as valve.

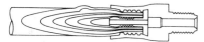

Fitting leakage seeps out or forms bubble.

FIGURE 12-85   Examples of internal defects

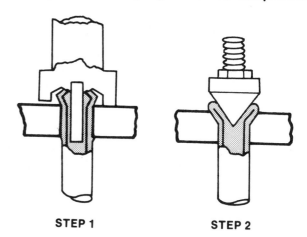

STEP 1   STEP 2

FIGURE 12-86   Steps in making a flare connection

during the repair. Support springs prevent kinking and serve a very important role. Be sure to replace them just as they were, and install new ones if damaged. Always replace brake lines in the original routing to avoid damage to the lines later. Remember, you are repairing the car, not reengineering it. A change in routing may result in rubbing or chafing of brake lines as the suspension moves. Most brake hoses have a male fitting on one end and a female fitting on the other. Disconnect the female end first, remove the clip or jam nut holding it down, then unscrew the male end. Install the new hose by connecting the male end. If a copper gasket was used, replace it with a new one. When the male end is tight, connect the female end. Tighten it in such a way as to keep the hose from touching any part of the chassis or suspension. Check for interference during suspension deflection and rebound and turning of the front wheels.

Bleeding

To remove or replace a brake component, follow the instructions in the service manual. Remember that anytime the brake system is open, it must be bled. Keep the system open for as short a time as possible to prevent moisture from entering and causing sludge and corrosion.

Bleeding removes air from the brake system. Air is lighter than liquid and it seeks high points in the hydraulic system. Bleeder screws are provided at each of these collecting points: calipers, wheel cylinders, and on some master cylinders. Bleeding involves opening up these screws in a specific order to let the trapped air escape. Fluid is added to the master cylinder to replace whatever is lost in bleeding.

Bench Bleeding the Master Cylinder

When the master cylinder is removed for re-building or replacement, bench bleeding is necessary to ensure that air does not remain in the cylinder when it is reinstalled. Mount the cylinder in a vise with the bore angled slightly downward (Figure 12-87). Attach two short brake lines or purge tubes to the outlet ports so they curl back into the reservoirs with the ends below the fluid level. Stroke the piston back and forth. This pumps air out of the cylinder and into the reservoir. Do this until only clear brake fluid comes out of the tubes. The same method will work using threaded plugs instead of purge tubes.

Bleeding the System

Whether the pressure or manual bleeding technique is used, both methods of bleeding follow a common sequence for opening the bleeder screws. Begin at the master cylinder if it has bleeder screws (Figure 12-88). Move to the combination valve if it has bleeder screws. Next, bleed the wheel cylinders or calipers. Start with the wheel located farthest from the master cylinder. Work back from there. The bleeding sequence at the wheels is different for dual front/rear systems than for dual diagonal systems. In addition, each manufacturer might have a preferred sequence for any given model design. Check the service manual for each car.

Some four piston calipers have two bleeder screws. In this case, bleed the lower one first. On diagonal systems, bleed one system at a time. Do one front disc brake first, then the diagonally connected rear drum.

Always check the master cylinder first. If the brake fluid falls below the level of the intake ports, air will get into the system. Refill the reservoir and pump the brake pedal slowly a number of times. Oftentimes this will purge it of all unwanted air. If this does not work, bleed the system.

Manual Bleeding

Manual bleeding should be done only if a pressure bleeder is not available. Begin at the master cylinder. Clean the cover before removing it and the diaphragm gasket. Fill the reservoir to 1/4 inch from the top. Apply pressure to the brake pedal slowly and with a smooth action. Open the bleeder screw on the first wheel in the sequence. Drain the aerated fluid through the bleeder hose into a jar partially filled with clean brake fluid (Figure 12-89).

Keep up a pedal pressure while the bleeder screw is open. When the pedal bottoms out, close

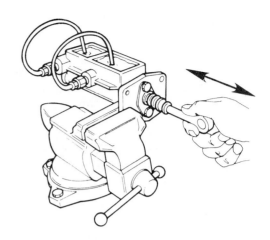

FIGURE 12-87 Stroking the piston back and forth

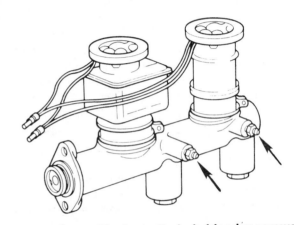

FIGURE 12-88 Master cylinder's bleeder screws

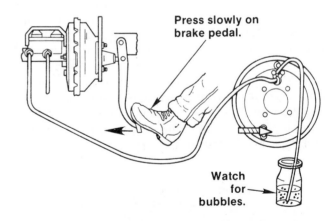

Press slowly on brake pedal.

Watch for bubbles.

FIGURE 12-89 Manual bleeding operation

the screw and release the pedal. If all the air is not yet purged and air bubbles can be seen in the fluid, repeat the process. When only clear fluid with no bubbles appears, go on to the next wheel in the sequence.

While bleeding the brakes, watch the fluid level in the reservoir. About every six pedal applications

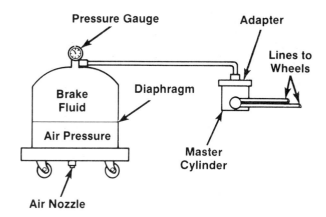

FIGURE 12-90   Pressure bleeding operation

more fluid will have to be added so it does not fall below the level of the intake port. If it does, more air will enter into the system.

Pressure Bleeding

This procedure is the recommended method of ridding the hydraulic system of air. It is the most efficient, requiring only one person to perform it.

The pressure unit used in this process is a tank divided into two sections by a flexible diaphragm (Figure 12-90). Pressurized air comes into the bottom chamber, compresses the fluid in the top, and brings it up to the desired pressure. The fluid then goes into the hydraulic system through a hose attached to a master cylinder adapter cap. In using a pressure bleeder unit, make sure to use the correct adapter for the particular master cylinder.

Bring the pressure unit up to a level of 15 to 20 psi. Make sure the master cylinder cover is clean so that no loose particles of dirt fall into the reservoir. Remove the gasket, and clean the gasket seat. Fill the reservoir and attach the adapter cap and hose. Check the coupling sleeve and make sure it is fully engaged before opening the fluid supply valve.

Follow the sequence for bleeding as recommended by the service manual. Allow the aerated fluid to flow out of the bleeder screws through a short bleeder hose into a jar. Once completed, close the supply valve of the pressure unit. Wrap the coupling sleeve in a rag to prevent brake fluid from dripping onto the car finish. (Flush off brake fluid immediately with water or it will ruin the paint.) Undo the coupler. Disconnect the unit and check to determine that the brake fluid level in the reservoir is not more than 1/4 inch from the top. Replace the gasket and cover and check the vehicle's brakes.

The recommended method of bleeding a brake system is with a vacuum type bleeder. This technique withdraws the fluid from the system rather than pumping it, which has certain advantages:

- Will not create foaming
- Does not activate pressure differential valve
- Less chance of fluid contamination

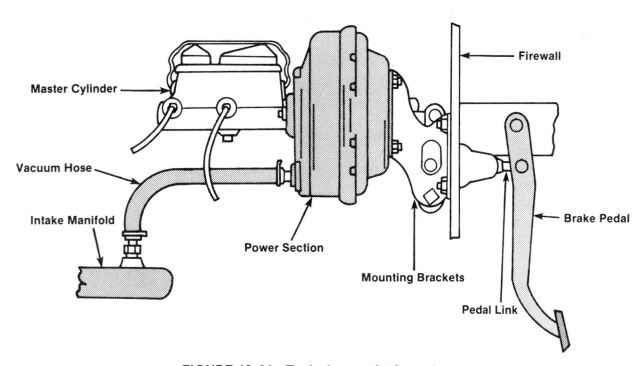

FIGURE 12-91   Typical power brake system

Check the connection pattern of the system's wheels. Some cars have the two front and two back wheels connected; some are crossed diagonally. Others combine the front two with one rear, and the rear two with one front wheel. Always check the service manual.

Final Check

Late-model cars sometimes have air left in the master cylinder bore above the outlet ports. As a final check, raise the rear of the car so the bore angles downward. Take off the reservoir cover and tap the pedal lightly a number of times. Very small bubbles should come up through the fluid to the top of the reservoir. When a spurt of fluid appears and the stream of bubbles ceases, the vehicle is ready to be road tested.

Power Brakes

Power brakes are nothing more than a standard hydraulic brake system with a vacuum assist or booster unit between the pedal and the master cylinder to help activate the brakes (Figure 12-91). Most power brake units consist of a piston, control valves, and a vacuum connection from the engine intake manifold. When the foot is off, the brake and the vacuum unit is in the released position, and the vacuum system intake port is closed. However, a special atmospheric port remains open to allow air to pass from one side of the vacuum piston to the other. This maintains equal pressure on the piston and keeps it in the OFF position. When the brake is hit, the atmospheric port closes and the vacuum port opens. Vacuum from the engine then withdraws the unit's piston forward against the master cylinder operating rod and actuates the brakes.

When a unibody car is involved in a collision, the power brake booster should be carefully inspected. Pay particular attention to vacuum hoses, check valves, fasteners, and the master cylinder itself. Replace all damaged pieces. This system builds up to 2500 psi to make the car stop—do not take any chances with it.

 **SHOP TALK**

Check if the booster is working by pushing the pedal down, hold it down, and start the engine. Note that when the car first starts, the brake pedal will tend to go down. This is normal and is related to the vacuum buildup.

Antilock Brakes

Modern antilock or antiskid brake systems can be thought of as electronic/hydraulic "pumping" of the brakes for straight line stopping under panic conditions. That is, this system is another control arrangement that is used in conjunction with a basic hydraulic braking operation. During hard braking conditions with a conventional hydraulic system, it is possible for the wheels of a vehicle to lock, resulting in reduced steering, as well as braking. On vehicles equipped with the antilock brake system (ABS), however, an electronic sensor constantly monitors wheel rotation (Figure 12-92). If one or more of the wheels begins to lock, the system opens and closes solenoid valves, cycling up to 10 times per second.

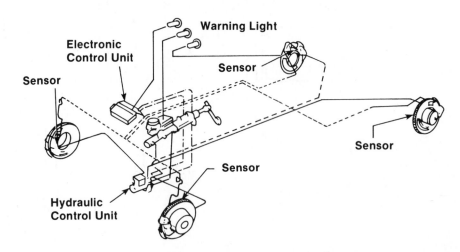

FIGURE 12-92   Basic elements of ABS four-channel or four-sensor system

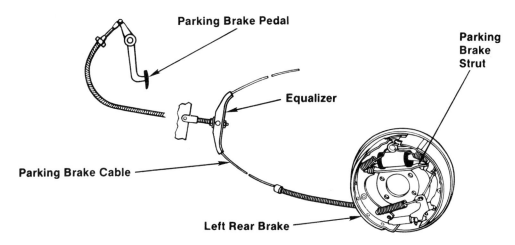

FIGURE 12-93   Typical integral parking brake

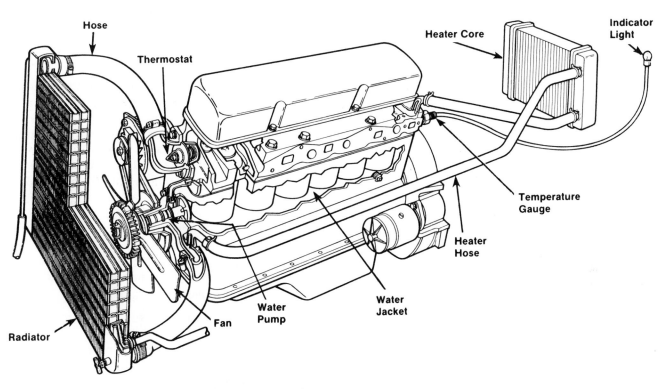

FIGURE 12-94   Cooling system components

This applies and releases the brakes rapidly and repeatedly, so that the front wheels alternately steer and brake. This makes it possible for vehicles equipped with the antilock brake system to avoid skidding under conditions that might cause vehicles not so equipped to handle differently.

The antilock or antiskid brake system has a controller that senses rotation at each of the wheels through wheel sensors. It can apply the antilock brake system to each of the front wheels independently, to the rear wheels as a pair, or to any combi-

nation of these three, as the need arises. Since there are several antilock or antiskid systems, check the service manuals for diagnosis and service procedures.

Parking Brakes

The rear wheel brakes act to hold the car stationary for parking. Although shown in Figure 12-93 as such, parking brakes are not actually a part of the hydraulic brake service system. They are actuated mechanically rather than by hydraulic pressure.

12.8 COOLING SYSTEMS

Whenever a vehicle is in a collision, especially involving the front end, some part of the cooling system probably has been damaged. To be sure, check out some basics in the cooling system (Figure 12-94).

COOLANTS

One of the most frequently missed areas of the cooling system is the strength of the antifreeze. A common idea is that the stronger the concentration, the better. This is not so. Pure water transfers heat better than pure antifreeze, but it does not protect the system from freezing corrosion. In addition, water has a boiling point of only 212 degrees Fahrenheit. Pure antifreeze has a higher boiling point (330 degrees Fahrenheit) than pure water. But, due to its lack of heat transfer ability, it can cause an engine to overheat. In addition, pure antifreeze offers no corrosion protection, since the anticorrosion chemical must be mixed with water to activate it.

WARNING: When working on the cooling system, remember that at operating temperature the coolant is extremely hot. Touching the coolant or spilling the coolant can cause serious body burns.

The ideal antifreeze-to-water ratio is 50/50. This ratio provides freezing protection to –34 degrees Fahrenheit, while increasing the coolant's boiling point to 224 degrees Fahrenheit. Always use an accurate antifreeze checking tool to ensure a proper antifreeze-to-water mixture. Some systems, such as mid-engine cars and vans, and those having dual heaters, can require up to three to four gallons of antifreeze. Check the specifications. Measure the level of installed protection with an antifreeze tester, following the manufacturer's directions.

CAUTION: Never run the engine with the cooling engine dry. Lack of coolant and lubricant in the water pump can cause destruction of the pump or the engine.

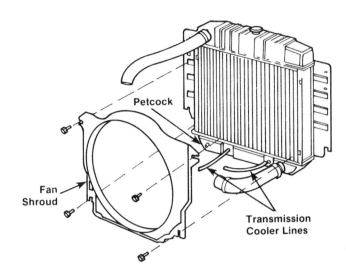

FIGURE 12-95 **The location of transmission cooler lines into radiator**

Coolant Leaks

A low coolant reduces cooling capacity. In addition to obvious leaks resulting in squirting steam and water, coolant leaks may also be internal. Internal leaks can result from a blown head or intake manifold gasket or warped cylinder heads. Another type of internal leak occurs when the automatic transmission fluid (ATF) cooler tank leaks from the inside into the radiator (Figure 12-95). A sure sign of this is a thick, pink solution in the radiator caused by the mixing of coolant and transmission fluid. Due to the impact forces in a collision, this area should be a high priority in any post-repair inspection. The loss of ATF due to a fractured radiator or ATF-to-radiator line connection causes two problems:

- Eventual loss of hydraulic pressure needed to operate the transmission
- Loss of lubricant needed to protect the internal mechanical and friction surfaces

With low pressure and missing lube, it does not take long for the clutch plate to literally "burn up" and the pressure pump and other parts of the transmission to become scored and galled due to metal-to-metal contact. If there is a real transmission problem, most body shops turn the work over to a transmission specialist.

Coolant Recovery Bottle. This bottle is normally plastic and can be easily damaged. Check for cracks or abrasions in the bottle and make sure the hose leading to the radiator is connected and in good shape. These plastic tanks are normally not repaired. If cracked or distorted, replace with new components.

Refilling a System. Before making any replacements in the cooling system, drain the coolant from the system and dispose of it properly (check local regulations). Never reuse the old fluid. When refilling, make sure that the proper coolant is used in vehicles with aluminum engines or radiators. Some warranties will not be honored if the coolant recommended by the manufacturer is not used.

After installation of the engine coolant, bleed the cooling system to ensure proper coating. Always follow the manufacturer's recommendations. On some vehicles there are bleed valves; on others, the thermostat must be taken out to bleed the system; and on others, the upper radiator hose must be removed. Check the directions in the service manual.

RADIATOR

The coolant flows from the engine to tubes located inside the fins of the radiator where the airflow cools it. If these tubes become plugged, either by being bent or through maintenance neglect, the flow of coolant through the radiator is reduced and overheating can result. This condition is more noticeable at highway speeds and/or heavier loads. If the vehicle is not air conditioned, plugged areas of the radiator can be identified by cold spots felt on the front of the radiator after the vehicle is warmed up. Chances are that a collision-damaged vehicle will have damaged or bent areas in the radiator (Figure 12-96), even though leaks might not be present. So always check that area carefully. Use a radiator pressure tester to test the radiator for leaks (Figure 12-97). Pressure testing should always be done if the radiator or any hoses were removed or replaced during collision repair.

Crushed fins can be straightened with a special tool designed for that purpose and tubes that are not too badly mangled can be soldered. But if large hunks of cooling fins have been pulled loose or if multiple tubes have been crushed or ruptured, a new core is recommended. Time is money and if the cost to repair core damage begins to approach the cost of a new core, most shops will opt for the new core. Besides, a new core offers greater reliability, especially if the radiator is showing its age.

Due to the aerodynamic designs of some vehicles, the radiator ends up being the low point in the cooling system. Because the radiator is lower than other areas, the cooling system might not be able to be completely filled after it is drained. This will cause overheating problems due to the cooling system being only partially full. To eliminate this problem,

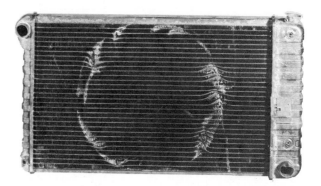

FIGURE 12-96 Typical collision core damage

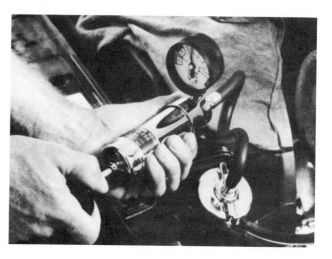

FIGURE 12-97 Testing radiator for leaks

some vehicles will have a separate filler neck that is higher than the radiator. If the vehicle is not so equipped, jacking up the front of the vehicle will place the fill point higher than the rest of the system. This will allow the system to be completely filled.

Radiator Cap

Most cooling systems operate under a pressure of 15 psi. This is because increased pressure on a liquid raises its boiling point. With a 50/50 mixture of antifreeze and water, a boiling point of 263 degrees is achieved. To maintain the correct pressure in the system, the radiator cap must be able to hold the required pressure. A defective radiator cap lowers the boiling point to 224 degrees Fahrenheit. The coolant could boil, even though the engine is not actually overheated.

Dried calcium deposits in a radiator cap can make the radiator inoperative. Use a pressure tester designed to test the radiator cap (Figure 12-98). Replace, if necessary.

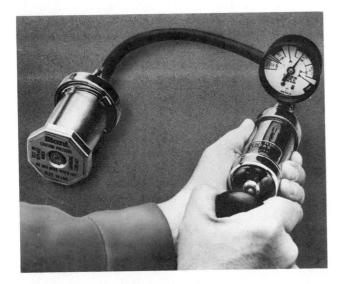

FIGURE 12-98 Testing radiator cap

WARNING: A hot radiator can release hot steam very quickly. When removing a radiator cap from a vehicle, always use extreme caution. Slowly loosen the cap, allowing pressure to escape before removing fully.

Thermostat

The thermostat is the engine's temperature control. It keeps the coolant in the engine until the engine reaches its peak operating temperature (Figure 12-99). Once the proper operating temperature (usually 180 to 195 degrees Fahrenheit) has been reached, the thermostat opens up, allowing the coolant to flow to the radiator for cooling. A thermostat that is stuck closed will cause the engine to overheat. A quick way to tell if this is happening is to feel the upper radiator hose. If it is cold but the engine is hot, the thermostat is probably stuck closed. On the other hand, if the thermostat is stuck open, the engine will take a long time or possibly fail to reach proper operating temperature.

Water Pump

The water pump circulates the coolant throughout the cooling system with internal blades called **impellers** (Figure 12-100). They push the fluid through the system. If they are loose or corroded, the coolant will not circulate properly and will cause overheating. This is more noticeable at highway speeds. Check for coolant movement with the cap

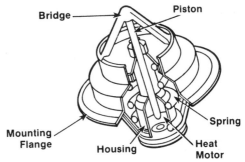
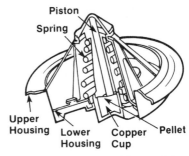

FIGURE 12-99 Types of thermostats: (A) reverse popped (B) balanced sleeve

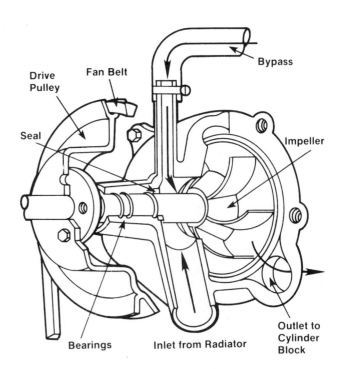

FIGURE 12-100 Impeller-type water pump

removed and the engine warm enough for the thermostat to be open. If the coolant does not flow, replace the pump.

Radiator System Belts and Hoses

While working on the cooling system during collision repair, check that the hoses are in good condition and are securely clamped (Figure 12-101). The lower radiator hose routes coolant from the radiator to the water pump. The turning water pump draws coolant, creating a low-pressure area in the lower hose. A coiled spring inside the lower hose keeps it from collapsing. The lower hose should not show signs of collapse.

Cooling Problems

Although similar, front and rear drive vehicles have some important cooling system differences.

RWD Cooling Problems. Certain cooling system problems are limited to RWD vehicles. This is due to the layout of the engine and cooling fans.

- **Belt tension.** On vehicles where the cooling fan is driven by belts from the engine, proper tension must be maintained or belt slippage

will occur. When this happens, the cooling fan does not turn at full speed, resulting in reduced airflow through the radiator at idle. This is a problem only at idle. At highway speeds, the airflow is sufficient to maintain cooling.

- **Fans and fan clutches.** On vehicles with electric fans, check for loose electrical connections and bare, burnt, or cut wires. Check to make sure the fan blades turn with no interference and that the fan mounts are not rubbing against the radiator or body (Figure 12-102). On some cooling systems there might be two or more fans.

  Some vehicles are equipped with a special type of cooling fan with a clutch built in. Fan clutches can either be filled with a fluid or use a thermostat spring that allows the fan to slip at highway speeds when the fan is not needed for airflow. This reduces drag on the engine, resulting in increased fuel economy. If a fan clutch does not work due to its fluid leaking or its spring becoming defective, fan speed is reduced at idle, causing overheating.

FWD Cooling Problems. Here are some of the more common problems that can occur in a unibody FWD cooling system.

- **Electric cooling fan.** The cooling fan on FWD vehicles is often electric, rather than belt driven. An electric fan is less of a draw on an engine than a belt-driven fan, resulting in better fuel economy.

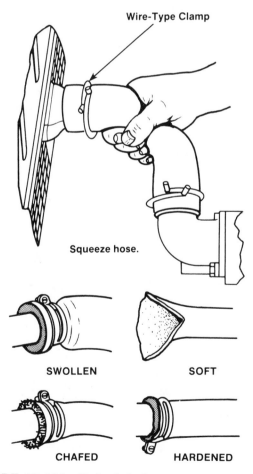

Wire-Type Clamp

Squeeze hose.

SWOLLEN   SOFT

CHAFED   HARDENED

FIGURE 12-101 Defects in hoses

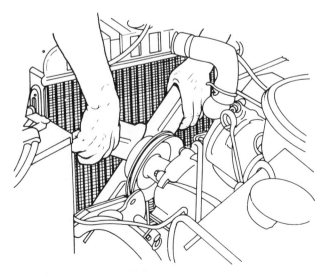

FIGURE 12-102 Checking fan movement (fan shroud not shown for better clarity)

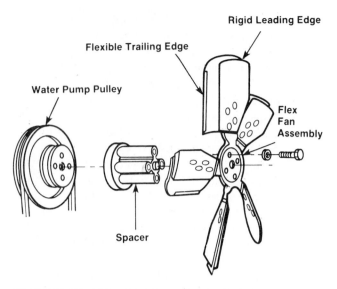

FIGURE 12-103 Single speed flexible fan

Most unibody vehicles have one single-speed cooling fan (Figure 12-103). Some vehicles are equipped with two fans or one two-speed fan. These are designed to increase airflow through the radiator. If engine overheating is present at idle, check to make sure that the fan or fans are operating correctly.

- **Cooling fan and air conditioners.** When the air conditioner is turned on, the cooling fan should also come on, regardless of coolant temperature. This prevents the engine from overheating due to the increased load placed on it from the air conditioning.

Replacing a Radiator

There are two basic types of radiator designs. They are distinguished from one another by the di-

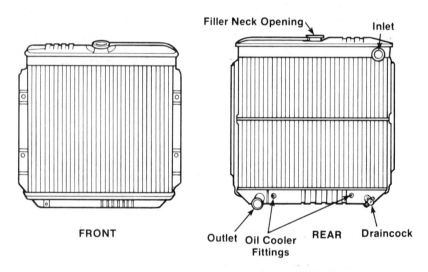

FIGURE 12-104 Downflow style radiator is identified by its upper and lower tanks.

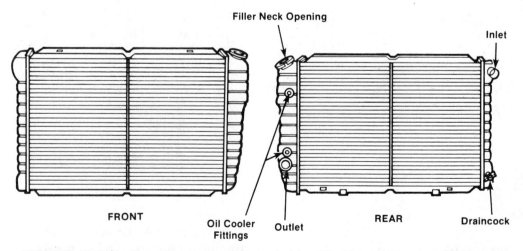

FIGURE 12-105 Crossflow style radiator is identified by its side-mounted tanks.

rection of the coolant flow and location of the two tanks. In the downflow radiator (Figure 12–104), the coolant flows from the top tank downward to the bottom tank. In the crossflow type (Figure 12–105), the tanks are located at either side and the coolant flows across the radiator core from tank to tank.

When replacing a radiator, first measure it upright with the filler neck opening facing up. Determine whether it is a downflow or crossflow type. When measuring either a crossflow or downflow radiator, measure only the core to determine the size (Figure 12–106). The core is the central part of the radiator (between the tanks and mounting brackets) and consists of parallel rows of tubes and fins.

Measure the height from the top edge of the core to the bottom edge, and from side to side to determine the width. To measure the thickness of the core, simply take a piece of straight wire, for example, and insert it through the core until the end becomes flush with the other side. Mark the other end of the wire with the thumb and forefinger (at the point where it is flush with the core), withdraw the wire, measure it, and obtain the core thickness.

When replacing radiators (Figure 12–107) on vehicles involved in collisions, it requires a special check of tolerances, making certain the mounting does not bring the surface of the radiator too close to the fan. This could create a situation in which hitting a bump could result in the radiator hitting the fan. Again, use care in reconnecting the transmission lines, avoiding a connection at an angle where the threads could be stripped. Follow the manufacturer's torque specifications, making certain that connections are tight enough to prevent leaks, but not

FIGURE 12–107 Be very careful when replacing a new radiator

overly tight where damage results to the internal configuration.

12.9 HEATER OPERATION

The heater is a comfort control item especially in colder climates. It may be part of the air-conditioning system or a separate item. Actually, the heater core could be considered a miniature version of the radiator. That is, as hot coolant flows through the heater, a fan blows air over the tubes, warming it and delivering it to the passenger compartment. The blower fan, located in the heater housing, forces air

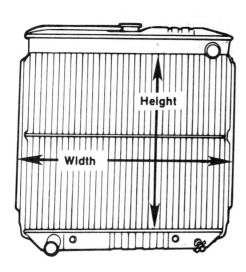

DOWNFLOW RADIATOR

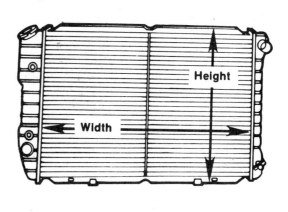

CROSSFLOW RADIATOR

FIGURE 12–106 Measuring a radiator

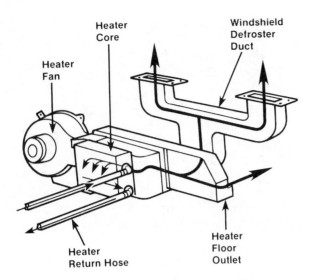

FIGURE 12-108 Typical heat distribution system

through the heater core and into the passenger compartment.

The air heating distributor system is a duct system. Outside air enters the system through a grille, usually located directly in front of the windshield, and goes into a plenum chamber where rain, snow, and some dirt is separated from it. The air from the plenum is directed through the car's heater core, through the air conditioner evaporator, or into a duct that runs across the fire wall of the car. Outlets in the duct direct the airflow into the passenger compart-

ment (Figure 12-108). Doors inside the system either recirculate the air inside the compartment or circulate outside air, according to the control settings. They also route the air inside the system through or around the heater or air conditioner, or to the windshield defroster.

Some cars have an additional distributor system that brings air into the vehicle through intakes located in the engine compartment and carries it through ducts to side vents located in the sidewall of the passenger compartment near the front seat passenger's feet. The airflow through these vents can be controlled mechanically, electronically, or by a vacuum system.

The heating system is controlled by a number of cables, valves, and switches. Be sure the cables are correctly reconnected if you disconnected any of them during repair. Follow the manual for troubleshooting. Also keep in mind that the heating system may have collected some dust during repair. Be sure to run it during cleanup so that the customer is not caught in a cloud of sanding dust after picking up the car.

12.10 AIR-CONDITIONING AND HEATER SYSTEMS

Proper handling of the air-conditioning (A/C) system during collision repair is both one of the

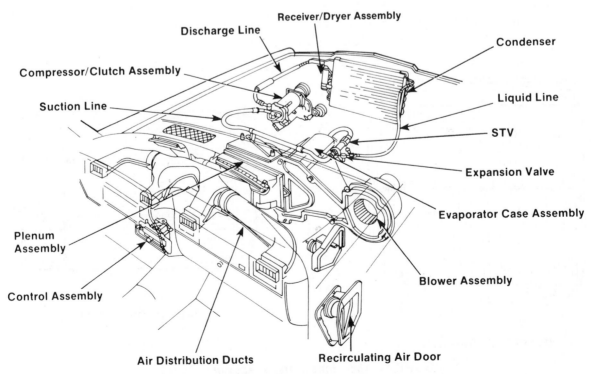

FIGURE 12-109 Typical air-conditioning system

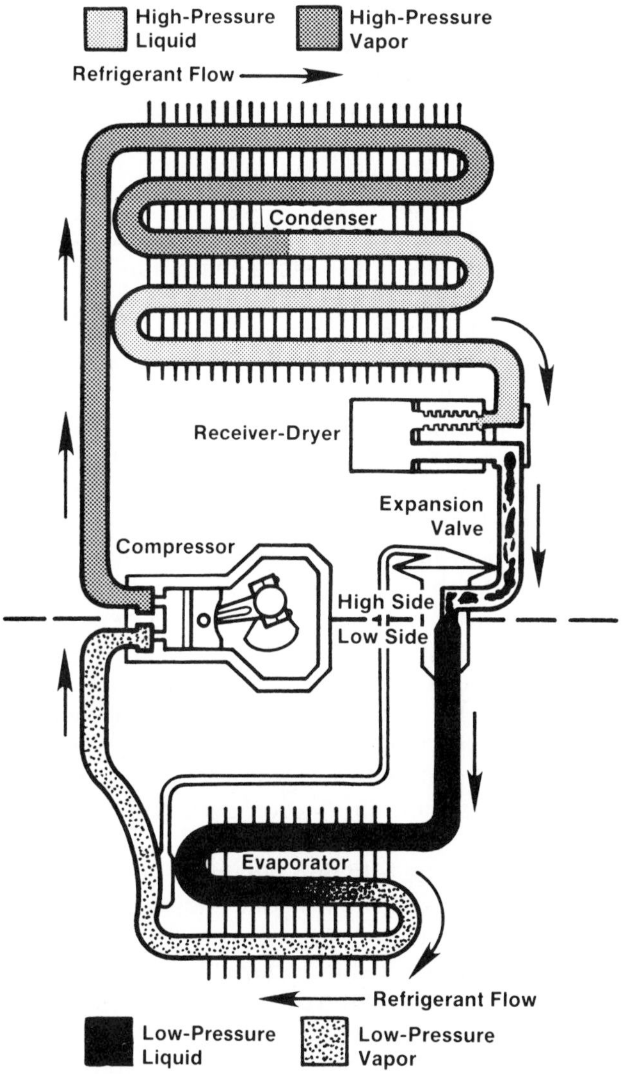

High-Pressure Liquid ☐ High-Pressure Vapor ▨

Refrigerant Flow ⟶

Condenser

Receiver-Dryer

Expansion Valve

Compressor

High Side
Low Side

Evaporator

⟵ Refrigerant Flow

Low-Pressure Liquid ■   Low-Pressure Vapor ▦

FIGURE 12-110   Refrigerant flow cycle

- Compressor
- Condenser
- Receiver/dryer
- Refrigerant control
- Evaporator

In the basic five-part air-conditioner system, the heat is absorbed and transferred in the following six steps (Figure 12–110).

1. Refrigerant leaves the compressor as a high-pressure, high-temperature vapor.
2. By removing heat via the condenser (Figure 12–111), the vapor becomes a high-pressure, lower-temperature liquid.
3. Moisture and contaminants are removed by the receiver/dryer, where the cleaned refrigerant is stored until it is needed.
4. The expansion valve converts the high-pressure liquid into a low-pressure liquid by controlling its flow into the evaporator.
5. Heat is absorbed from the air inside the passenger compartment by the low-pressure, low-temperature refrigerant, causing the liquid to vaporize.
6. The refrigerant returns to the compressor as a low-pressure, higher-temperature vapor.

Refrigerants are the chemicals that transfer heat by absorbing it during evaporation and releasing it during condensation. Refrigerant 12 (R-12) is currently used in most cooling applications because of its unique properties.

most important and least understood aspects of working with mechanical components. Many needless repairs are caused unknowingly by service technicians who do not understand the importance of following some very strict rules for working with air-conditioning systems. What compounds the problem is that malfunctions often occur several months after the collision repair work is completed, so the customer is unaware of who caused the problem.

A/C OPERATION

An air-conditioning unit works on the simple principle that when a liquid is converted to a gas, it absorbs heat from its surroundings. When it is reconverted from a gas back to a liquid, it gives up this heat. The air-conditioning system (Figure 12–109) consists of the following components:

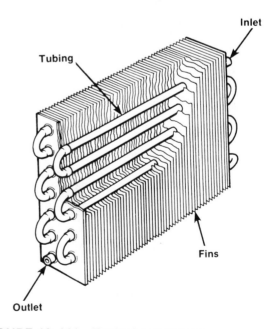

Inlet

Tubing

Fins

Outlet

FIGURE 12-111   Typical condenser

A/C Handling Tips

Although most actual A/C repair and service work is done in specialty air-conditioning shops, here are pointers that the service technician must keep in mind:

- **Moisture, the worst enemy.** Most failures are caused by moisture entering the A/C system. Moisture interacting with refrigerant and air-conditioning oil causes sludge and hydrochloric acid to form. This will attack the delicate parts of the compressor and eat away at the aluminum components of the evaporator and condenser.
- **Precaution before opening.** Sudden release of air-conditioning refrigerant to the atmosphere is dangerous and not recommended. With the establishment of the Montreal Protocol Agreement, there is a worldwide demand to protect the earth's ozone layer. This means the drastic cutting of worldwide production of R-12 over the next few years. For this reason, most A/C shops use R-12 recovery devices (Figure 12–112).
- **Seal the opening.** When removing or opening up the A/C unit, seal all openings with appropriate protective barriers. These can be hydraulic caps and plugs, tight-fitting rubber corks, or plastic wraps. Use sturdy rubber bands or wire ties to hold plastic wraps in place securely.
- **Precautions for reassembly.** If a system has been open to the atmosphere more than a few hours, do the following:
  1. Change the oil.
  2. Flush each component separately with nitrogen gas before charging.
  3. Replace the receiver/dryer.
  4. During evacuating, hold the system at high vacuum for a minimum of 30 minutes.
- **Evacuating guidelines.** Before recharging, the system must be evacuated as directed in the service manual (Figure 12–113). Evacuating removes all atmospheric gases. It also causes all water to vaporize so all moisture is removed. Incidentally, evacuating does not save the receiver/dryer if it has been open more than a short time.
- **Pressure test for leaks.** Test the system for leaks by closing the system under vacuum and checking to see if it holds the same vacuum reading. If it does not hold vacuum, it will not contain the refrigerant under pressure.
- **Role of the bridging dioxide.** The A/C compressor is driven from the engine through an electric clutch. When this clutch cuts in and out, a spike voltage is developed by the building and collapsing of the magnetic field. This spike voltage could damage the delicate computer equipment in the car. To prevent this, a bridging diode is wired into the air-conditioning circuit. The diode does not allow the current to flow in the direction where it could cause damage. When there is air conditioner system damage, the bridging diode might be destroyed. If it is not replaced, the air-conditioning clutch might not energize. In some cases damage to the computer could result. The diode is normally found on the air-conditioning pump wiring and can be checked with a test light or ohmmeter as discussed later in this chapter.
- **A/C oil guidelines.** Use only oil designed specifically for air-conditioning systems. Do not reuse oil that has been drained from the system. Also do not use oil that has been stored in a partially filled container because it will have absorbed moisture. As stated before, even a small amount of moisture can be very damaging.

FIGURE 12-112 Equipment for recovering used refrigerant (Courtesy of Moog Automotive)

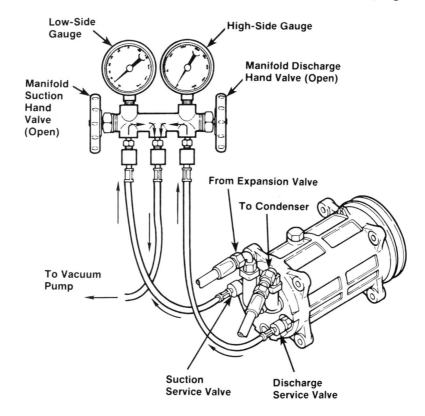

Low-Side Gauge

High-Side Gauge

Manifold Suction Hand Valve (Open)

Manifold Discharge Hand Valve (Open)

From Expansion Valve

To Condenser

To Vacuum Pump

Suction Service Valve

Discharge Service Valve

A

Low-Side Gauge

High-Side Gauge

Manifold Discharge Hand Valve (Open)

Manifold Discharge Hand Valve (Closed)

A

C

B

Scale

From Expansion Valve

To Condenser

R-12

R-12

Suction Service Valve

Discharge Service Valve

B

FIGURE 12–113 (A) Evacuation and (B) recharging

12.11 EXHAUST SYSTEMS

The exhaust system is used to collect and discharge the exhaust gases caused by the combustion of the air/fuel mixture within the engine. The exhaust system found on today's automobile must also aid in the control of exhaust emissions.

WARNING: When inspecting or working on the exhaust system, remember that its components get very hot when the engine is running; contact with them could cause a severe burn.

The engine exhaust consists mainly of nitrogen (N_2). In addition it also contains carbon monoxide (CO), carbon dioxide (CO_2), water vapor (H_2O), oxygen (O_2), nitrous oxides (NO_x), and hydrogen (H_2). Also found are unburned hydrocarbons (HC). Three of these exhaust components, CO, NO_x, and HC are major air pollutants. The emission of these components to the atmosphere must be controlled.

The catalytic converter (CC), mounted in the exhaust system, plays a major role in the emission control system. The converter works as a gas reactor, and its catalytic function is to speed up the heat-producing chemical reaction between the exhaust gas components in order to reduce the air pollutants in the exhaust. Figure 12–114 illustrates the three basic types of CC design.

 SHOP TALK ———————

Because of constant change in EPA catalytic converter servicing and installation requirements, check with the CC manufacturer or the EPA for the latest data regarding replacement, if damaged in a collision.

In addition to the catalytic converter, the exhaust system includes an exhaust manifold, exhaust pipe, muffler, resonator (optional), and tail pipe (Figure 12–115). All the components are designed to conform to the available space of the car's undercarriage and yet be high enough from the road to avoid striking obstructions. Most parts of the exhaust system, especially the exhaust, muffler, and tail pipe, are subject to collision damage.

To check the system's condition, grab the tail pipe (when it is cool) and try to move it up and down and side to side. There should be only slight move-

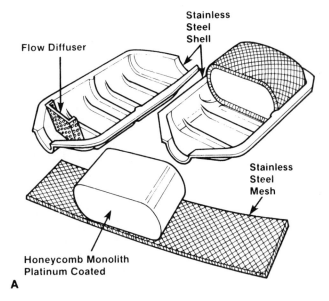

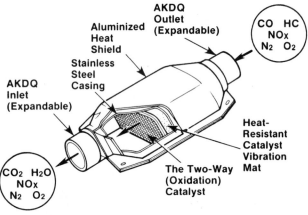

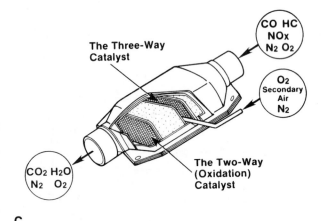

FIGURE 12–114 Types of catalytic converters: (A) single-bed, (B) dual-bed, and (C) three-way

ment in any direction. If the system feels wobbly or loose, raise the rear of the car and check the clamps and hangers that fasten the exhaust system to the

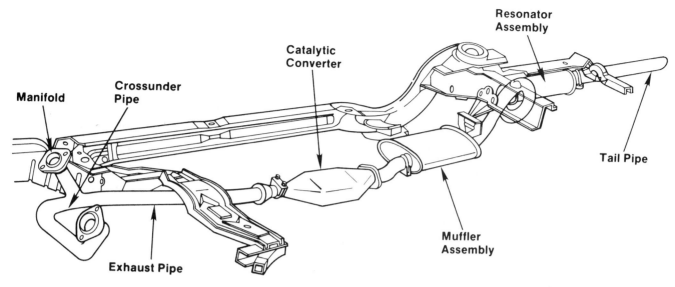

Manifold

Crossunder Pipe

Catalytic Converter

Resonator Assembly

Tail Pipe

Muffler Assembly

Exhaust Pipe

FIGURE 12-115   Typical exhaust system

underbody. Also, jab at all rusted areas in the system with an old screwdriver. If the blade sinks through the metal at any point, that part needs replacing. Tap on parts of the system with a hammer or mallet (Figure 12–116). A ringing sound indicates that the metal is good. A badly corroded part gives out a dull thud.

To check further, start the engine (never in a closed shop). Stuff a rag in the tail pipe and feel around every joint for leaks. If one is found, try tightening the clamp. If this does not stop the leak, it must be repaired.

If a loud rumble is heard during normal operation, either there is a large leak in one of the components or the muffler is not operating properly. There is only one way to repair faulty exhaust system parts, and that is to replace them. To replace a single component such as the muffler, it might not be necessary to take off any of the parts behind it to do the job.

12.12 EMISSION CONTROL SYSTEMS

Many times emission control systems are damaged in a collision and must be serviced as part of the collision repair. The Clean Air Act, which is a federal law, makes the repair technician responsible for the emission control systems. The law requires service technicians to restore emission control systems to their original design. The law prescribes penalties for repair shops and technicians who alter emission control systems or fail to restore them to their original design.

FIGURE 12-116   Tapping the old muffler free from the exhaust pipe

- Damaged parts must be replaced with good parts. Eliminating damaged parts to avoid replacement parts is against the law.
- Using damaged parts that prevent proper operation of the emission control system is also against the law.
- Proper repairs to the emission control system must be made to manufacturer's specifications.
- All replacement parts for emission control systems must satisfy the original design requirements of the manufacturer (Figure 12-117).

The emission control system consists of three subsystems. They are as follows:

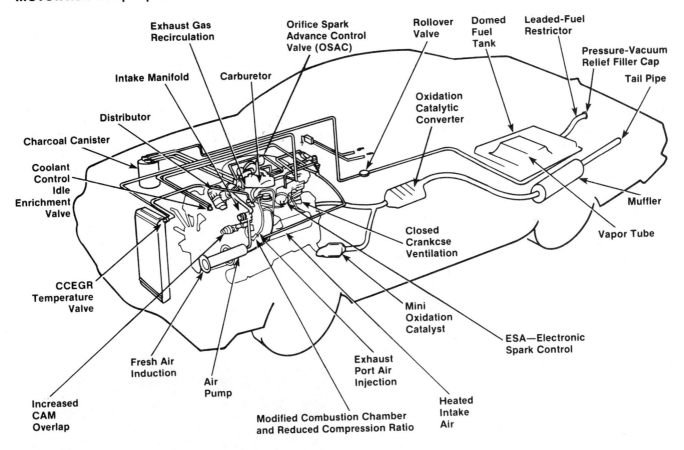

FIGURE 12-117   Emissions systems parts

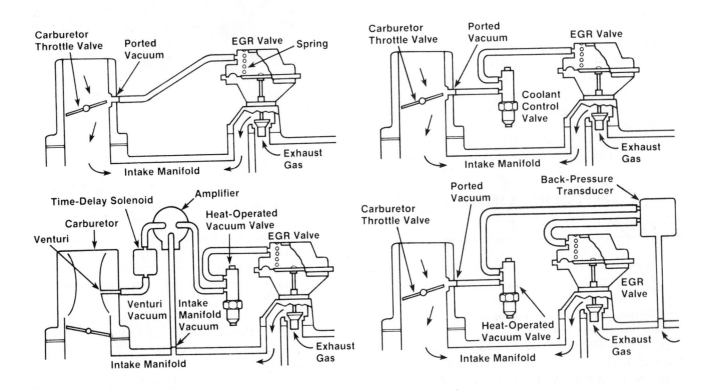

FIGURE 12-118   EGR variations

1. **Exhaust and engine control system.** In addition to the catalytic converter in the exhaust system, the other important control is the exhaust gas recirculation (EGR) valve. This valve opens to allow engine vacuum to siphon exhaust into the intake manifold (Figure 12–118). The EGR valve consists of a poppet valve and a vacuum-actuated diaphragm. When ported vacuum is applied to the diaphragm, it lifts the valve off its seat. Intake vacuum then siphons exhaust into the engine. On many late-model vehicles, a positive back pressure or negative back pressure EGR valve is often used. This type of valve requires a certain level of back pressure in the exhaust before it will open when vacuum is applied.

2. **Crankcase ventilation system.** Crankcase emissions are easily controlled by the positive crankcase ventilation (PCV) system. This system channels blowby gases into the fuel intake area to be drawn into the engine and burned (Figure 12–119).

3. **Evaporative system.** This emission control system filters fumes from the gas tank and the carburetor through a charcoal canister, which absorbs and stores vaporized

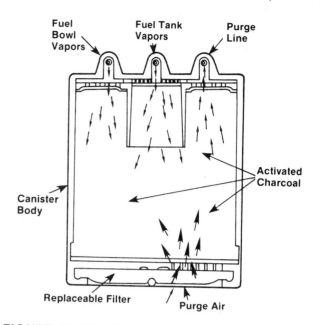

FIGURE 12-120 Typical charcoal canister

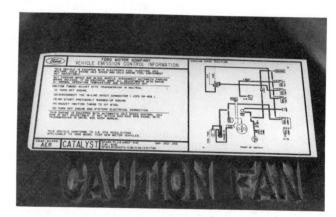

FIGURE 12-121 Typical identification label

fuel (Figure 12-120). When the car is running, these vapors travel into the engine, where they are burned, at the same time restoring the capacity of the canister to store fumes.

Some emission control systems have more controls than mentioned here. The service, repair, and replacement procedures for emission control components are given in the service manual. To make it easier for the technician, manufacturers are required by law to install identification labels (Figure 12-121) and labels supplying vacuum routing and connection information and adjustment specifications when the cars are built. These labels are considered part of the emission control systems under the law. The labels must be replaced when collision

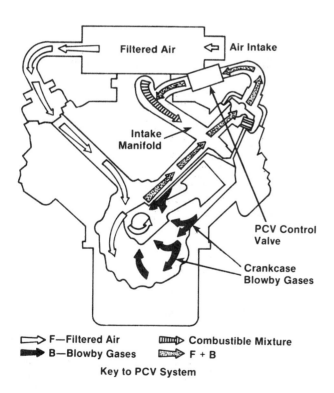

Key to PCV System

➪ F—Filtered Air   ▥▷ Combustible Mixture
➡ B—Blowby Gases   ▨▷ F + B

FIGURE 12-119 PCV system

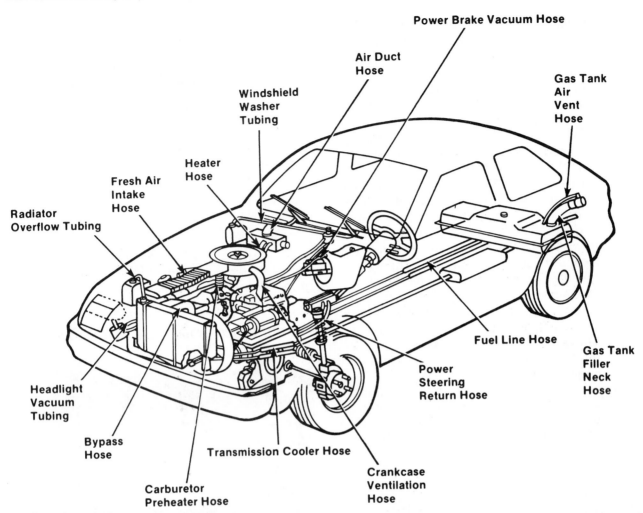

FIGURE 12-122 Typical hoses that should be checked as a result of a collision. *(Courtesy of Plumley Co.)*

repair services require their removal or cause damage to the labels. Part numbers appear on the labels as required by law.

12.13 HOSE AND TUBING INSPECTION

As illustrated in Figure 12-122, there are a number of hoses of various types and sizes in a car. Before the vehicle is returned to the customer they all should be checked. If any hoses, tubing, or clamps appear damaged, they should be replaced. This is especially true of the fuel line system (Figure 12-123).

Hose clamps might not seem like an important item either, but OEM type ring clamps are best discarded rather than reused. The ring type clamps can lose tension and might not hold the hose securely if

reused. Worm screw clamps are the preferred replacement.

12.14 CHECKING ELECTRICAL PROBLEMS

An often overlooked area of collision repair is the electrical system. The modern automobile is threaded with literally miles of wires. Most of these are bundled together in harnesses. These harnesses route the wires from the battery to all electrical body parts—dome lights, headlights, electric door locks, remote control side mirrors, and so on. A typical example of a vehicle's wiring harnesses is shown in Figure 12-124. These harnesses snake along body parts such as windshield pillars, rocker panels, doors, quarter panels, and roof panels, among others. Damage in these areas often cuts or abrades

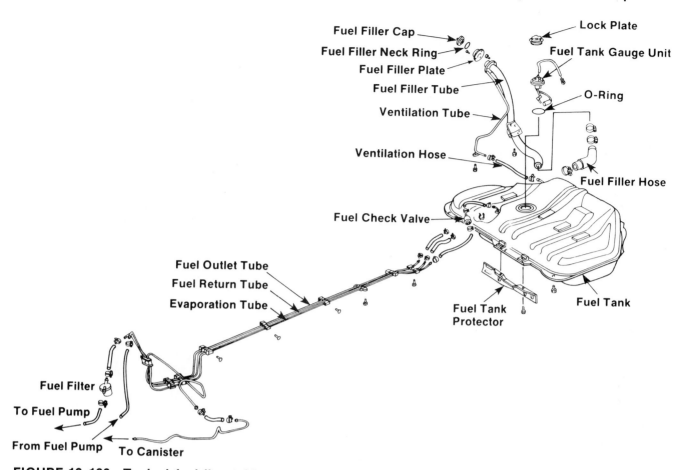

FIGURE 12-123 Typical fuel line tubing that should be visually checked for any leak or damage and looseness of clamps. *(Courtesy of Nissan Motor Corp.)*

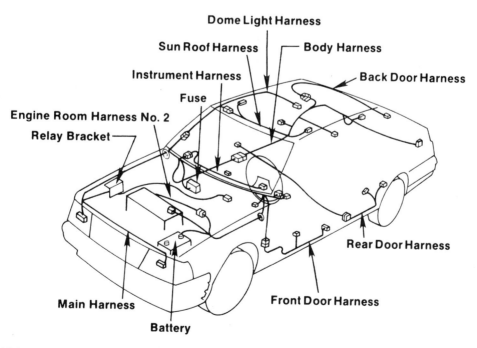

FIGURE 12-124 Typical electrical harness that must be checked for any kinking, missing clamps, and loosening terminals.

467

the insulation protecting the wires, and a short or open circuit is the result. Collision forces can also pull wires from their connections, and corrosion damage can loosen ground wire connections, again breaking electrical circuits.

Before any collision-damaged vehicle is returned to the owner, every electrical component should be operated to verify that it works and that it stops working when turned off. If either condition does exist, the problem must be traced to its source, and the faulty wires or loose connections repaired. Oftentimes, the problem is simply a blown fuse or a loose connection. For example, when replacing the outer door skin, the door, of course, is removed from the vehicle and any electrical components are disconnected from the related wiring harness. If the connectors are not properly connected when the door is replaced, the windows, lock, or exterior mirror will not be operable. Always double-check connections. Make sure harnesses are secured in their clips and that ground wires are tightly secure. Typical ground connections are shown in Figure 12–125.

Most body shops send major electrical problems to a garage for repair—particularly damage to starter and ignition systems. Testing the major components in these systems oftentimes requires expensive diagnostic equipment (Figure 12–126). But there are many minor problems in the lighting and accessory circuits that could be quickly diagnosed and repaired in the body shop. Minor electrical trou-

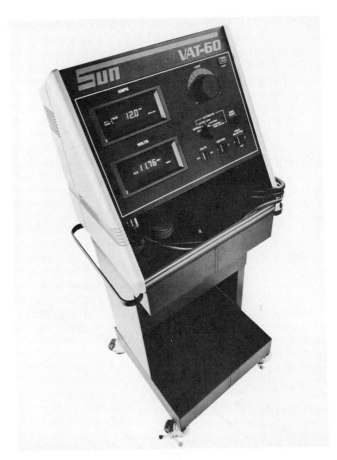

FIGURE 12–126 Typical diagnostic tester used to check electrical components

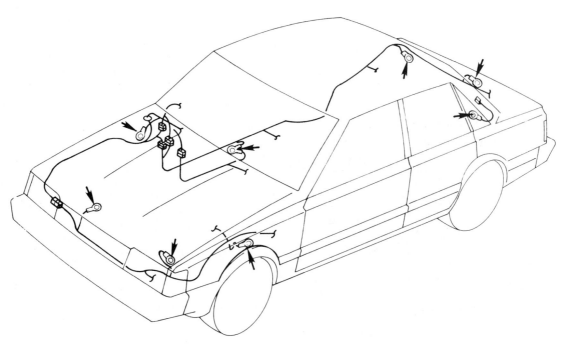

FIGURE 12–125 Typical grounding points in a vehicle

bleshooting requires only basic knowledge of electrical theory and a few simple diagnostic tools.

OPEN CIRCUITS

Most electrical problems are a result of a break in the wiring circuit. A wiring circuit has three major parts:

- Power source. The battery.
- Load. The electrical component that needs the power to function.
- Wires or conductors. Connect the power source to the load.

Figure 12-127 shows a typical automotive electrical circuit. The battery is connected to a starter relay, which houses the terminals for many different circuits. When the starter switch is turned on, power is provided to a lamp. The lamp is controlled by a switch. When the starter switch is on and the lamp switch is on, power (electrical current) flows to the lamp, illuminating it. The current flows through the lamp, through the ground wire, and into the chassis or frame, which serves as the return route to the battery. As long as this circuit or route is unbroken, the circuit is said to have continuity (be continuous). Most electrical problems encountered in the auto body repair shop are the result of a break in the circuit. When the continuity is broken, the circuit is said to be open. Power does not flow to the compo-

nent. Too often this problem is not discovered until the owner has picked up his or her vehicle and (days or weeks later) attempts to turn on the wipers, lock the doors, use the map light, or operate some other electrical device. These problems should be discovered and repaired in the body shop.

SHORT CIRCUITS

Oftentimes a collision will not only create an open, or broken, circuit but will also create a short circuit. Unlike the open circuit that will not conduct electricity, a short circuit provides a very easy route for the current to return to the battery. There are several kinds of short circuits. A dead short to ground is usually a bare conductor touching directly against the vehicle frame. This type of short always opens a circuit breaker, blows a fuse, or pops a fusible link. Sometimes a short is intermittent. It only touches the frame and shorts momentarily when the vehicle bounces heavily or jars. A flickering dash lamp is such as example. A cross circuit short occurs when two hot wires come in contact. This is usually caused by abrasion of the protective plastic coverings or by an overload that causes the coverings to melt. Such a short can cause more than one component to operate on a single switch. For example, when the lights are turned on, the windshield wipers operate. This is because the shorted wires are sharing current. Supplying current to one (by actuating

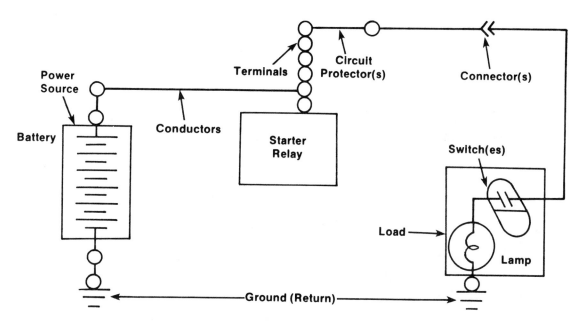

FIGURE 12-127 Typical automotive electrical circuit

a switch) supplies current to both. The last type of short circuit is called a high resistance short to ground. The circuit is not broken but contact is present between the hot wire and the ground. A high resistance ground might not blow a fuse until the circuit is loaded to full capacity. Or it might not blow a fuse at all, but it will slowly drain the battery.

Battery Safeguards

The battery is a power plant. Therefore, it must be treated with respect as well as protected. Because of the potential electrical problems incurred in a collision, always disconnect the battery ground cable as soon as a vehicle is received at the shop. A low amperage shortage will gradually drain the vehicle's battery. Too often this happens and the body shop remedy is to recharge the battery (Figure 12-128). Charging the battery can get the vehicle back to the owner without another battery failure, but this solution is only temporary and does not fully restore the vehicle to full operation.

Another reason to disconnect the battery is to avoid possibly damaging electrical components through which current might be flowing. For example, a high resistance short in the wiring harness can create a constant current flow to the coil and distributor. If the points are closed, they could melt together. A similar problem could also destroy the ignition solenoid and many other electrical sensors or

switches. To prevent this type of electrical damage, always disconnect the battery ground cable when the vehicle is delivered to the shop.

There are several precautions that must be taken when recharging a battery. The following precautions protect the battery, vehicle, and technician:

- Always disconnect the battery ground wire before charging a battery on the vehicle. Charging the battery with it connected might damage electrical components on the vehicle. The transistors and microcircuits on many cars are very sensitive to current levels. The high-amperage chargers can burn out many expensive parts: regulator, alternator, power transistors, computerized control modules, and so on.
- Never disconnect the battery with the ignition switch in the ON position. The resulting voltage "spike" will destroy many microcircuits in today's electronic systems.
- Check the battery carefully before charging. Look for low water level, cracked case, and so forth. Add distilled water or electrolyte if needed. Use a hygrometer to check the state

FIGURE 12-128 Typical battery charger. (Courtesy of Sun Electric Corp.)

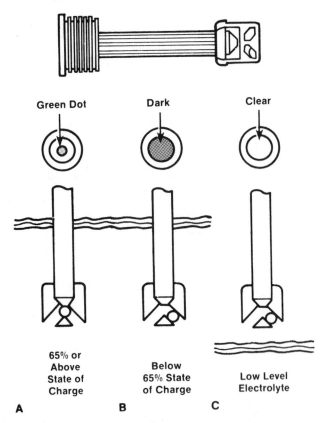

FIGURE 12-129 Typical design and operation of built-in hydrometers on maintenance-free batteries

of charge (specific gravity). Table 12-3 shows the state of charge that corresponds to specific gravity reading.

- Follow the manufacturer's instructions carefully. Do not overheat the battery by charging too long. A standard battery charging guide is usually given in the owner's manual. Test the specific gravity once an hour. Once no change is noticed in readings, disconnect the charger. Overcharging the battery will destroy the active material on the plates.
- Never charge the battery near any welding operations, open flames, or other heat source. Do not smoke near the charging battery. The battery gives off very flammable hydrogen gas while charging. If the gas ignites, the battery will explode.
- Ensure protection from the battery acid. Wear eye protection when handling the battery and immediately wash off acid that splashes on clothing or skin. If battery acid does get in an eye, hold the eye open and flush with water at room temperature. See a physician immediately. Battery acid can cause blindness.

WARNING: Battery charging can be dangerous if done improperly. Follow the manufacturer's instructions carefully to charge the battery. Do not overheat the battery by charging too long. Test the specific gravity once an hour. When no change is noticed in the readings, disconnect the charger. Overcharging the battery will destroy the active material on the plates. Never charge the battery near any welding operations, open flames, or other heat sources. Do not smoke near the charging battery. It gives off very flammable hydrogen gas while charging; if the gas ignites, the battery will explode. Charge only in well-ventilated areas. Also wear eye protection when handling the battery and immediately wash off acid that splashes on clothing or skin. If battery acid gets in an eye, hold the eye open and flush with water at room temperature. See a physician immediately because battery acid can cause blindness.

Although it is a common practice in some repair shops, avoid jump starting whenever possible. The discharged battery can explode or create voltage spikes, which can damage electronic components. This is true of both the car you are trying to start and

TABLE 12-3: SPECIFIC GRAVITY VS STATE OF CHARGE AT 80°F

Specific Gravity	State of Charge	Open Circuit Cell Voltage
1.260	100%	2.10
1.230	75%	2.07
1.200	50%	2.04
1.170	25%	2.01
1.110	0	1.95

the car providing the jump. However, if the car must be jump started, connect the positive terminal to the positive terminal on the batteries, connect the negative terminal of the "good" battery to a ground other than the ground terminal of the "bad" battery. If using another car for the jump, make sure the two vehicles are not touching each other.

In addition, it is important that the following be considered to avoid damage from voltage spikes in the electronic or electrical circuit of a vehicle with a dead battery:

- Make sure every electrical device in that car, including the dome light, is turned off before connecting the batteries.
- Only after the hookups are properly made, turn the key in the "dead" car to get it started.
- Once the "dead" car is running, remove all jumper connections before turning on any electrical devices.

CAUTION: Never jump start a vehicle with a "so-called" maintenance-free battery that is fully discharged. Not all such batteries have the same color "eyes" when discharged (Figure 12-129). Check the top of the battery case to find out the color codes for the battery. Do not attempt to recharge a fully discharged maintenance-free battery. In either of these cases, replace the battery instead. Jumping or recharging a fully discharged maintenance-free battery can create an explosion hazard. These batteries have no way to vent gas buildup.

ELECTRICAL SYSTEM DIAGNOSTICS

After the body damage to the vehicle has been repaired, check the operation of each and every electrical component. Before reconnecting the battery, pull all the fuses. Then, turn all the electrical switches to the ON position, and reconnect the battery. If any lights turn on or motors begin running, a "hot" wire somewhere is bypassing the fuse box. A short exists in the system. Also activate systems that cannot be simply turned on—for example, brake lights or electric windows. If current is flowing to these components, disconnect the battery ground cable and repair the problem.

If the hot side of the system checks out all right, replace the fuses. Make sure that the proper amperage fuses are used. Putting a 30 ampere fuse where a 15 ampere fuse should be could cause an overload that will melt the plastic coating from a wire and create a short. Worse yet, the overload could supply more amperage than the associated component can handle, resulting in a burned out motor or solenoid. If the correct size fuse blows when it is placed in its holder, a short exists. Somewhere two hot wires are in contact, overloading that particular system. The short must be located and repaired.

After checking component operation with the fuses out and after replacing the proper amperage fuses in the fuse holders, turn on each electrical component one by one and check the operation. If trouble is found in any system, the fault should be located and corrected.

The fault will basically be in one of four areas:

- Short in the hot wire from the battery
- Blown fuse, fusible link, or circuit breaker
- Faulty component
- Faulty ground wire connection

The tricky part is finding which area contains the trouble.

The mystery is solvable without major difficulty if the technician uses the tools available. These are a variety of testers, the manufacturer's wiring diagrams, and the troubleshooting trees also provided by the manufacturer.

Test Lights

The most basic testing or troubleshooting tool is a test light (Figure 12-130). The basic test light has a pointed probe attached to one end and a long wire lead with an alligator clip attached to the other. By inserting the probe into an electrical connector and attaching the lead wire to a ground, current flow can be determined. If the tester lights up, current is available. If the tester light does not illuminate, a break in the circuit exists somewhere between the connector and the battery. Figure 12-131 shows a typical area in which a test light can be used.

In this illustration, a solenoid is controlled by two switches—one normally closed and one normally open. To determine if current is available to the

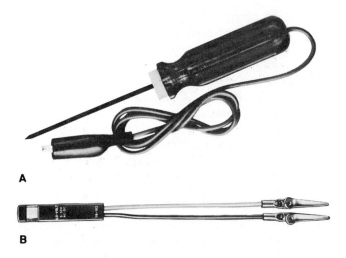

FIGURE 12-130 Test lights: (A) handle of probe light and (B) twin lead tester. *(Courtesy of Vaco Products Division)*

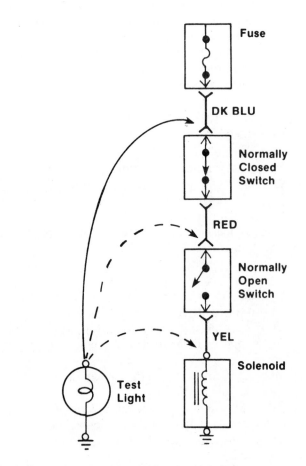

FIGURE 12-131 Test light checkpoints

solenoid, the test light is clipped to a good ground surface (clean metal) and the probe is placed in the solenoid battery side connection. If the tester lights up, the solenoid is probably bad or the solenoid-to-

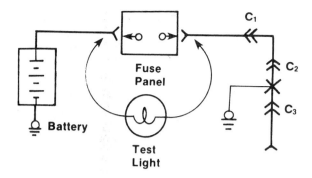

FIGURE 12-132   Short circuit check with test light

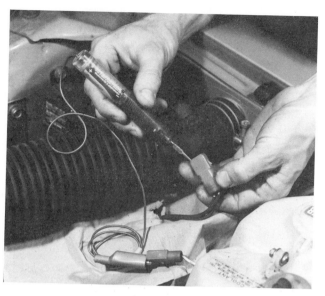

FIGURE 12-133   Continuity tester is used to test the continuity of an electrical harness. *(Courtesy of Easco/K-D Tools)*

ground connection might be bad. If the light does not illuminate, a short circuit exists. The switches can be tested with the probe as shown in the illustration. If power is not available to either switch, the problem might be in the fuse. Connect the test light to the fuse panel (Figure 12-132). If the test light illuminates, the short is probably in the fuse or fuse box. (Make sure all other accessories receiving power through the fuse are turned off.)

Care must be taken when using a test light on a circuit that is computer activated. Holes made in the electrical wires by the probe can allow moisture to enter the circuit. This, in turn, can cause resistance in the circuit that will affect the computer operation.

Continuity Tester

Another handy tool for diagnosing electrical troubles is a self-powered test light or continuity tester. The continuity tester (Figure 12-133) has a battery that will illuminate the light in the handle when continuity (an unbroken circuit) exists. The self-powered test light can also be used to determine ground contact.

> **CAUTION:** To use the battery-powered test light, all power to the circuit being tested must be turned off.

Figure 12-134 shows a typical application of a self-powered test light in a continuity check of a blower switch. With power to the switch turned off or disconnected, connect the wire lead to the load side of the switch. Then using the probe, check for continuity at each switch position. If the tester fails to light up, a short exists in the switch.

A self-powered test light can also be used to check ground connections. After turning off power to the circuit, connect the test light to the ground

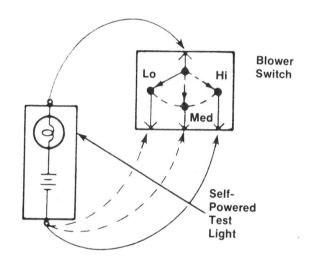

FIGURE 12-134   Using a self-powered test light to make continuity checks

wire in question and to a good body ground. If the tester lights up, the ground connection is good. Look for the fault elsewhere.

Jumper Wire

Another simple tool is a jumper wire. A jumper wire is a wire lead with alligator clips on both ends (Figure 12-135). The wire is used to bypass a suspected open in the circuit. For example, a jumper wire is used to bypass the circuit breaker shown in Figure 12-136. If attaching the test jumper restores current to the nonoperating component, the circuit breaker is faulty and should be replaced.

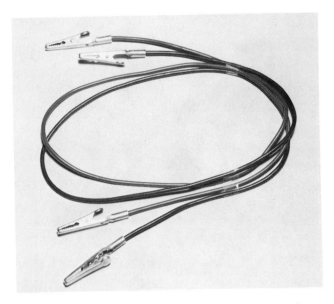

FIGURE 12-135 Typical jumper wires. *(Courtesy of Vaco Products Division)*

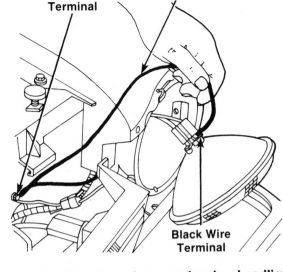

FIGURE 12-137 Using jumper wires in a headlight problem

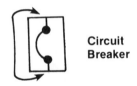

Circuit Breaker

FIGURE 12-136 Using jumper wires around a circuit breaker

To use a jumper wire and test lamp to find an open in a headlamp circuit, connect one end of the jumper wire to a good ground. Then, connect the other end of the wire to the ground side of the lamp (Figure 12-137). Turn the light switch on. If the lamp comes on, the reason for lack of continuity is a poor ground. Check the ground connections.

If the light does not come on, connect the jumper wire between the battery and the hot wire terminal on the lamp. If the light comes on, the open lies between the battery and the lamp.

AVR Multimeter

Another tool indispensable in troubleshooting electrical system faults is a multimeter, or AVR (Figure 12-138). The AVR meter can be set to monitor amperage, voltage, or resistance. The ammeter setting indicates how much current is flowing in a circuit. The voltmeter setting measures the voltage available to the circuit. The ohmmeter setting measures resistance to current flow. All the tests described above with test lights and jumper wires can be done with an AVR multimeter.

FIGURE 12-138 Typical ampere/volt/resistance (ohm) multimeter. *(Courtesy of OTC Division)*

For example, consider the tail light circuit in Figure 12-139A. If the lights do not work, check the voltage available to the fuse. If 12 volts are not displayed on the meter, a short exists between the battery and the fuse box. If 12 volts are available, check the voltage between the switch and the first lamp (Figure 12-139B). If voltage is not available, bridge the switch with a lead wire. If the light comes on or the voltmeter reads 12 volts, the switch is defective. If no voltage shows on the gauge, bridge the fuse box with the jumper wire. The short might be either in the box or in the wiring between the fuse box and the switch.

Assume that after repairing the shortage in the same circuit, only the first two lights come on. Then

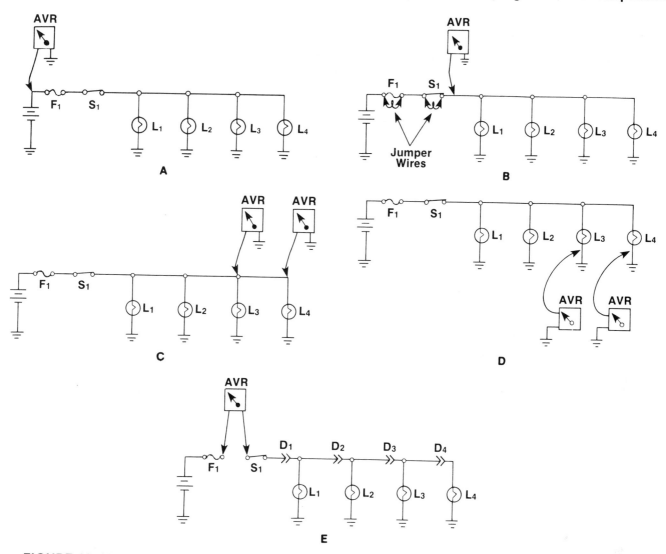

FIGURE 12-139 Checks that can be made with an AVR meter to determine tail light circuit problems

check the voltage available to the third and fourth light (Figure 12-139C). If the meter reads 0 volts, the wire between the two lights is probably broken or disconnected. If 12 volts register on the meter, the problem must be narrowed down to one of the following:

- Defective ground connection
- Defective light socket
- Burned out bulbs

Try new bulbs in each of the sockets. If that does not solve the problem, test the ground wires of the third and fourth lights with the AVR multimeter set to read voltage (Figure 12-139D). Connect the leads to the ground side terminal of the socket and to a suitable ground. If the meter reads 12 volts, this indicates a defective ground. If 0 volts are read, the sockets are probably bad. Verify that no continuity exists in the bulbs by setting the multimeter to read ohms. Con-

nect the leads to either side of a socket. If the ohmmeter reads "infinity," no continuity exists and the sockets are defective.

If the problem with the tail lights is narrowed down to a fuse that "blows" whenever the lights are turned on, the lights are drawing too much current. This indicates a high-resistance short somewhere in the circuit. To determine where the short is, connect the multimeter in series with the circuit (Figure 12-139E). Then, disconnect the hot wire from the first light. If current registers on the ammeter, a shortage somewhere between the switch and the first tail light is grounding the circuit.

If no current flow registers, remove the light bulbs and replace them one at a time. If the circuit is designed to draw 5 amperes, each bulb should draw 1.25 amperes (5 ÷ 4 = 1.25). Replace the first bulb. The ammeter should read 1.25 amperes. When the second lamp is added, the reading should be 2.5

(1.25 + 1.25). Add the third lamp to the circuit, and the reading should be 3.75 amperes; add the fourth lamp, and the reading should be 5 amperes. If a higher than normal reading is achieved at any light, the short drawing the additional current lies between that light and the preceding one.

LIGHTING AND OTHER ELECTRIC CIRCUITS

Automotive lighting systems have become increasingly more sophisticated. Headlights and tail lights have grown into multiple-light systems, turn signal indicators have changed from optional accessories into standard equipment and evolved further into emergency and hazard warning systems. Indicator lights on the dashboard, as mentioned later in this chapter, commonly warn of failure or improper operation of the changing system, seat belts, brake system, parking brakes, door latches, directional lights (Figure 12–140), and other items on the vehicle (Figure 12–141).

Headlights (see Chapter 14) have both a high and a low beam. The two-light systems have one headlight on each side, each of which has a high-beam and a low-beam filament. The four-light systems have two lights on each side. Two of these should be lit for low beam and all four for high beam. The four-light system uses two distinctly different headlights. The headlights used in the two-light system and the four-light system are different in size. Until recently, all headlights were round, but recent styling developments created a need for a rectangular light, which is also supposed to be more efficient.

There are other electrical circuits in modern vehicles that operate such accessories as

- Power seat positioners and heated seats
- Power window and locks
- Power positioned outside mirrors
- Automatic headlight dimmers
- Cruise control

Other electrical devices include radios, cassette players, speaker systems, chimes, buzzers, graphic displays, analog instruments, and computer commands. Speedometers, odometers, and various vacuum/pressure gauges are usually operated mechanically rather than electrically. There are two electric circuits in every automobile: windshield wipers and washers, and horn.

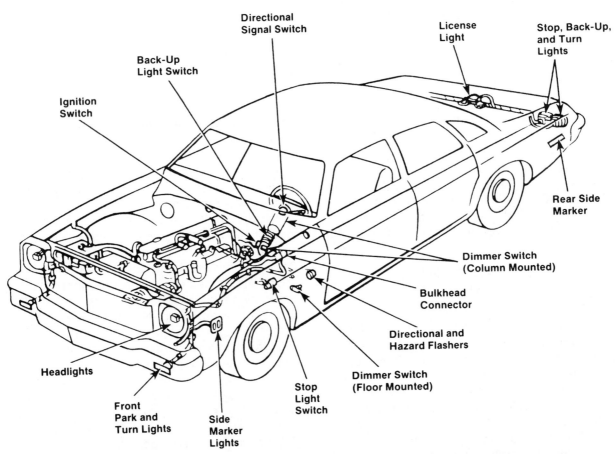

FIGURE 12-140 Typical service manual automotive lighting systems

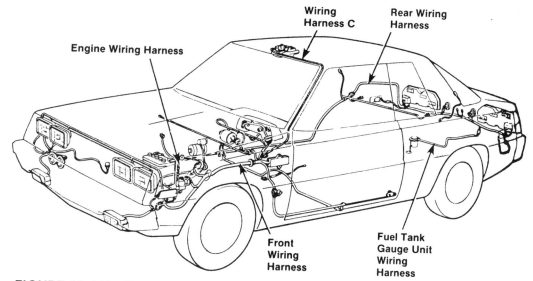

FIGURE 12-141 Be sure the wiring harness groupings are secure in their clips or holds.

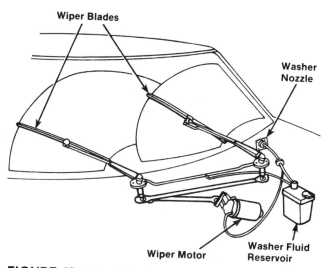

FIGURE 12-142 Windshield wipers and washers

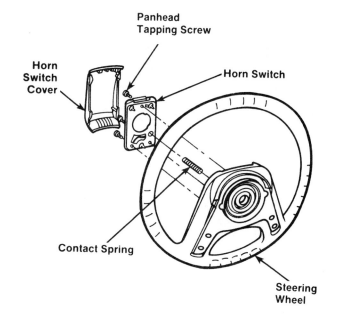

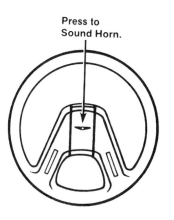

FIGURE 12-143 How a typical horn operates

Windshield Wipers and Washers

A typical windshield wiper operates on a small single- or multi-speed electric motor. A switch on the steering wheel assembly or dashboard activates the motor. The spray washer generally has it own motor, plastic container, or reservoir and pump, which forces liquid through tubing to a nozzle (Figure 12-142). The nozzles spray the liquid washer on the windshield.

Horn

Most horn systems are controlled by relays. When the horn button, ring, or padded unit is depressed, electricity flows from the battery through a horn lead, into an electromagnetic coil in the horn relay to the ground (Figure 12-143). A small flow of

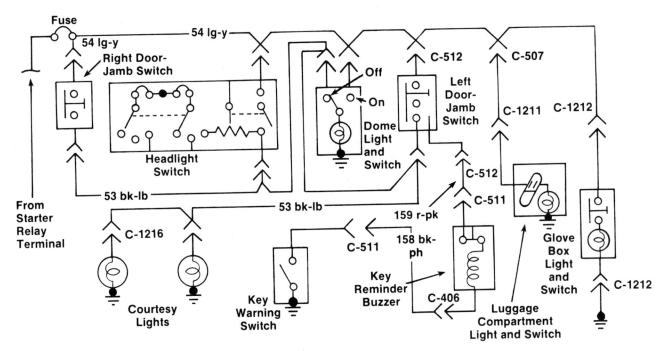

FIGURE 12-144 Typical service manual interior light wiring diagram

TABLE 12-4: COMMON ELECTRICAL ABBREVIATIONS			
A	Ampere	POS	positive
ac	alternating current	PRES	pressure
ACC	accessory	SOL	solenoid
BAT	battery	SPDT	single-pole double-throw
C/B	circuit breaker	SPST	single-pole single-throw
dc	direct current	TEMP	temperature
DPDT	double-pole double-throw	TOG	toggle (switch)
MOM	momentary	V	Volt
MOT	motor	W	Watt
(n)	none	–	negative
NC	(nc) normally closed	Ω	Ohm
NEG	negative	+	positive
NO	(no) normally open	±	plus or minus
PB	push button	%	percent

electric current through the coil energizes the electromagnet, pulling a movable arm. Electrical contacts on the arm touch, closing the primary circuit and causing the horn to sound.

WIRING SCHEMATICS AND TROUBLESHOOTING TREES

In order to determine and isolate the electrical problems, it is often necessary to trace the electrical circuit. The only way to do this properly is with a wiring diagram. Wiring diagrams look extremely confusing to people who do not know how to read them. But wiring diagrams are nothing more than road maps. They trace the route the electrical current takes from the battery to an electrical component and back to the battery. A simple service manual wiring diagram of an interior lights circuit is shown in Figure 12-144. Reading a wiring diagram is not difficult if one understands the symbols used. Some of the most common symbols and abbreviations are given in Figure 12-145 and Table 12-4.

Wires are color coded. Typical color codes are given in Table 12-5. The first letter in a combination of letters usually indicates the base color. The second letter usually refers to the stripe color (if any). Tracing a circuit through a vehicle is basically a matter of following the colored wires.

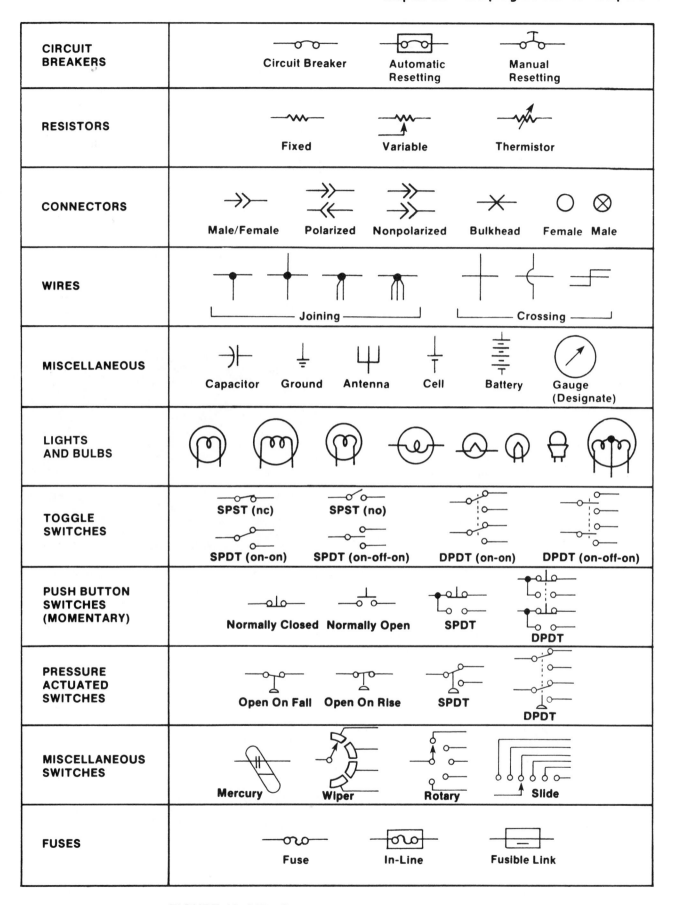

CIRCUIT BREAKERS	Circuit Breaker	Automatic Resetting	Manual Resetting
RESISTORS	Fixed	Variable	Thermistor
CONNECTORS	Male/Female Polarized Nonpolarized Bulkhead Female Male
WIRES	Joining Crossing
MISCELLANEOUS	Capacitor Ground Antenna Cell Battery Gauge (Designate)
LIGHTS AND BULBS	
TOGGLE SWITCHES	SPST (nc) SPST (no) SPDT (on-on) SPDT (on-off-on) DPDT (on-on) DPDT (on-off-on)
PUSH BUTTON SWITCHES (MOMENTARY)	Normally Closed Normally Open SPDT DPDT
PRESSURE ACTUATED SWITCHES	Open On Fall Open On Rise SPDT DPDT
MISCELLANEOUS SWITCHES	Mercury Wiper Rotary Slide
FUSES	Fuse In-Line Fusible Link

FIGURE 12–145 Common automobile electrical symbols

TABLE 12-5: COMMON WIRE COLOR CODES

Color	Abbreviations		
Aluminum	AL		
Black	BLK	BK	B
Blue (Dark)	BLU DK	DB	DK BLU
Blue (Light)	BLU LT	LB	LT BLU
Brown	BRN	BR	BN
Glazed	GLZ	GL	
Gray	GRA	GR	G
Green (Dark)	GRN DK	DG	DK GRN
Green (Light)	GRN LT	LG	LT GRN
Maroon	MAR	M	
Natural	NAT	N	
Orange	ORN	O	ORG
Pink	PNK	PK	P
Purple	PPL	PR	
Red	RED	R	RD
Tan	TAN	T	TN
Violet	VLT	V	
White	WHT	W	WH
Yellow	YEL	Y	YL

 **SHOP TALK**

Wires in a circuit can change color from one terminal to the next. So follow the manufacturer's wiring diagram closely.

Most manufacturers also provide troubleshooting trees (Figure 12–146). The most efficient way to locate an electrical fault is to follow the manufacturer's diagnostic steps. These step-by-step procedures are used hand in hand with the wiring diagrams. If, however, troubleshooting trees are not available, begin at the battery and systematically trace the circuit from there. Do not jump back and forth in the circuit or between circuits. Be patient and narrow down possible trouble spots by a process of elimination.

12.15 ELECTRONIC SYSTEM SERVICE

Many electronic diagnostic and repair procedures are not that difficult. If the technician goes back to the basics of electrical circuits and can follow a few simple rules, he/she can find and fix a lot of electronic problems. Knowledge of electronics is necessary for the technician to perform his/her job (Figure 12–147).

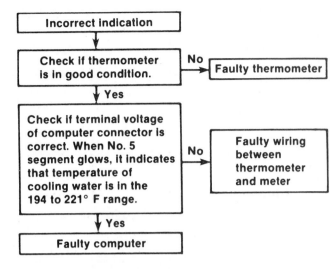

FIGURE 12-146 Manufacturer's troubleshooting tree for diagnosing faulty temperature gauge

FIGURE 12-147 Electronics is now within the technician's field of knowledge.

 **SHOP TALK**

The use of the word electronics in this book refers to on-board computers and other "blackbox" type items, while electrical systems just described means wiring and electrical components such as alternators, lights, heater motors, and so on.

ELECTRONIC DISPLAYS AND ON-BOARD COMPUTERS

Electronic instrument displays are becoming more and more popular. There are two reasons for this. The technology has become less expensive and more reliable. And many customers like the high-tech, state-of-the-art image of electronic displays. But, in collision repair, electronic displays call for some special cautions. These complex and expensive parts must be handled carefully to avoid damage.

Most dashboard gauges are driven by some type of electrical signal. These gauges can either be analog or digital. A digital display uses numbers instead of a needle or graphic symbol. In an analog display, an indicator moves in front of a fixed scale to give variable readout. The indicator is often a needle, but it can also be a liquid crystal or graphic display. An example is a speedometer in which the speed is shown by a set of vertical bars that light up or dim as the speed changes.

The advantage of analog displays is that they show relative change better than digital displays (Figure 12-148). They are useful when the driver must see something quickly, and the exact amount of change is not important. For example, an analog tachometer shows the rise and fall of the engine speed better for shifting than a digital display. Here the driver does not have to know exactly how many rpm's the engine is running. The most important thing is how fast the engine is reaching the red line on the gauge.

A digital display is better for showing exact data such as miles or operating hours (Figure 12-149). Many speedometer/odometer combinations are examples of both analog (speed) and digital (distance). The choice of display types is a matter of designer and buyer preferences. An analog electrical signal is continuously variable. An analog current is like the water flowing from a faucet, which is gradually turned up and down. Sometimes it flows a lot, sometimes only a little, and sometimes not at all. As an example, a temperature sensor causes the current to change as the temperature changes. As the temperature rises, the resistance decreases. This causes an increase in the circuit current. As the sensor cools, the current decreases.

The changing current is used to drive a gauge. The higher the temperature and pressure, the more current flows in the gauge circuit. The current creates a magnetic field that moves the pointer. In a temperature gauge, the higher the current (temperature), the greater the magnetic field and the more the pointer moves. These are called magnetic gauges and are used widely. A digital signal has only two states. It is either on or off. If a switch is turned on and off many times, the number of pulses can be counted. For example, a sensor can be made to turn

on and off each time a wheel moves a certain distance. The number of pulses that are counted in a given period of time allows the computer to display the speed. The pulses can also be used by the computer to change the odometer reading.

ELECTRONIC DISPLAYS

Following are the types of electronic displays used today:

- **Light-emitting diode (LED).** These are used as either single indicator lights, or they can be grouped to show a set of letters or numbers. LED displays are commonly red, yellow, or green. But, LED displays use more power than other displays. They can also be hard to see in bright light.
- **Liquid crystal diode (LCD).** They have become very popular for many uses, including watches, calculators and dash gauges. They are made of sandwiches of special glass and liquid. That is where the term "liquid" comes from. A separate light source is required to make the display work. The display has wires on the glass. When there is no voltage, light cannot pass through the fluid. When voltage is applied, the light passes through the segment. LCDs do not like cold temperatures, and the action of the display slows down in cold weather. These displays are also very delicate, and must be handled with care. Any rough handling or force on the display can damage it.
- **Vacuum fluorescent diode (VFD).** These displays use glass tubes filled with argon or neon gas. The segments of the display are little fluorescent lights, like the ones in a fluorescent fixture. When current is passed through the tubes they glow very brightly. These displays are both durable and bright.

SENSORS

All gauges require input from a sensor. However, with modern computer-controlled displays, the sensor's output is used in two ways. The engine control computer needs the same information as the electronic display, so the information passes through the computer first. It then travels to the gauge. As an example, compare the temperature sensor on the vehicle of ten years ago with a modern

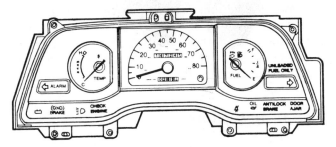

FIGURE 12–148 Typical dashboard display. The temperature gauge, speedometer, and fuel gauge are all analog displays.

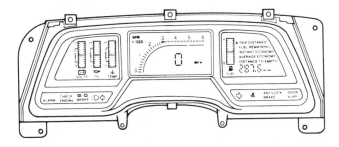

FIGURE 12–149 Typical LCD display. The gauges themselves are electronic digital displays, even though some of the information may be analog.

vehicle. On the car of ten years ago, the temperature gauge was connected directly to a sensor that checked the engine temperature. A rise in temperature resulted in increased current in the gauge circuit. This caused the pointer and magnetic gauge to move, showing the temperature to the driver on an analog scale.

On the modern vehicle the system works identically, with one very important exception. The information from the sensor is first fed through the vehicle's engine control computer. The computer uses the information to manage a variety of systems, including air/fuel ratio, spark timing, and switching of emission control system components. In addition, the computer uses the information to operate the temperature gauge—digital, analog, or just a temperature warning lamp (a form of digital display).

Self-Diagnostic Displays

Most of the electronic displays today have some sort of built in diagnostics. These differ with the vehicle make and year. However, in recent years there has been a trend toward more on-board checks. Each time the key is turned to the ON position, the system does a self-check. The self-check makes sure that all of the bulbs, fuses, and electronic modules are working. If the self-check finds a problem, it might store a code for later servicing. It may also instruct the computer to turn on a trouble light to show that service is needed. For instance, some systems run an instrument cluster self-test on start-up. It goes through a series of nine tests, called **prove out**, checking for function of the display, connectors to the sensors, and the condition of the LCD displays themselves. During prove out, all illuminated parts of the display are briefly lighted. Passing all parts of this test tells that the display is working properly. If portions of the display do not light, there is a problem. The technician should check whether he/she has properly reinstalled all of the connectors to the back of a replacement display.

On-Board Computers

The computer is the brain or decision-making center for the entire engine control system or module (ECM). The unit maintains a constant check on engine performance, making thousands of split-second decisions in response to the demands of the driver and the outside conditions. Sensors act as the eyes and ears of the system. The computer processes the incoming information and compares the data with the specs. If the sensor input does not match the specs, the computer sends signals to controlling devices such as solenoids, switches, and relays. These adjust spark timing, emission controls, and fuel flow to keep the engine running smoothly and efficiently.

Repair and Replacement

Other than replacing bulbs and fuses, and repairing damaged wires, the only "fix" is to replace the unit. Repairs to the instrument cluster cannot be done in the collision shop. However, the assembly is often divided into units that can be replaced individually. For example, the odometer/speedometer unit in some systems can be replaced without replacing the rest of the display.

Replacing a module is a straightforward operation. Before ordering the replacement module, find out if any data needs to be transferred from the old unit. For instance, when replacing the odometer, check the manufacturer's information for dealing with the mileage. On some systems this information is kept in the body computer, and will automatically appear on the display when the key is turned to the

ON position. On other models, the mileage has to be supplied when ordering the replacement. The mileage is then entered before the replacement module is shipped. The service manual will provide the needed information or check with the dealership parts or service department.

Although parts in any computerized system are amazingly reliable, they do occasionally fail due to collision. Diagnostic charts in service manuals and trouble codes will help the technician troubleshoot the system (Figure 12–150).

Before reading the trouble codes, do a visual check to make sure the problem is not a result of wear, loose connections, or vacuum hoses. Inspect the air cleaner, throttle body, or injection system. Do not forget the PCV system and vacuum hoses and make sure the vapor canister is not flooded. Look at the wiring harnesses and connectors and the charging and alternator system. The connectors are especially important. Disassembly and reassembly or damage can cause many intermittent driveability problems. Also check the connectors for signs of corrosion. The low level electrical signals in today's electronic circuits cannot tolerate the increased resistance caused by corrosion in contacts.

Without starting the engine, turn the ignition key on and off three times within 5 seconds, ending with it on. The CHECK ENGINE or POWER LOSS light will glow a short time to test the bulb, then start flashing. Count the first set of flashes as tens. There will be a 1/2-second pause before the light starts

flashing again. This time count by ones. Add the two sets of flashes together to obtain the trouble code. For example, 3 flashes, a 1/2-second pause, followed by 5 flashes is read as code 35. Watch carefully, because each trouble code will be displayed only once. Look it up in the service manual. This will tell which circuit to check. Once the trouble codes are flashed, the computer will signal a code 55. If the light does not flash at all, there are no trouble codes stored. The problem could be a mechanical one, or the computer could be defective. Keep in mind that replacing the computer should be one of the last options. Check everything else first.

PROTECTING ELECTRONICS SYSTEMS

The one thing a technician does not want to do when a vehicle comes into the shop for collision repair is to create problems. This is especially critical when it comes to automotive electrical systems and electronic components. Following are the proper and correct ways to protect automotive electrical systems and electronic components during storage and repair:

- Disconnect the battery (both cables) before doing any kind of welding. To avoid the possibility of explosion, completely remove the battery when welding under the hood or on the front end. Also make sure the ground connection is clean and tight. Position the ground clamp as close as possible to the work area to avoid current seeking its own ground.

 **SHOP TALK**

Whenever disconnecting or removing the battery on a computer-controlled car, remember that the memory for radio station selection, seat position, climate control setting, and any other "driver programmable" options is erased. When delivering the car, advise the customer that he or she must reprogram these settings. Or better yet, record them and reprogram them before delivery.

- Static electricity can cause problems. Avoid it by grounding yourself before handling new displays. One way is to touch a good ground with one hand before handling the display

DIAGNOSTIC CODE DISPLAY

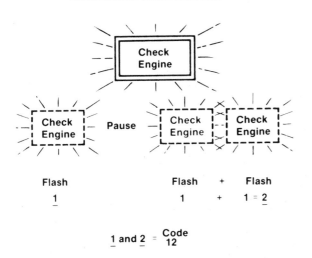

FIGURE 12–150 The CHECK ENGINE light will signal the codes. Code 12 is a signal that the computer's diagnostic program is working properly.

with the other hand. Another way is to use a grounding strap that attaches your wrist to the vehicle. This type of grounding strap should be a 1 megohm resistor in line.

- Avoid touching bare metal contacts. Skin oils can cause corrosion and poor contacts.
- Be careful about the placement of welding cables when welding. Keep a short electrical path in the body by placing the ground clamp near the point of welding. Also do not let welding cables run close to the display or the computer.
- Take care when handling displays and gauges. Never press on the gauge faces because this could damage them.
- Computer diagnostic tests can be performed using a scan tool (Figure 12-151). Connect the tool to the diagnostic connectors on the left fender apron. Follow the same sequence with the ignition key. The trouble codes will be displayed on the scan tool readout. Circuits, switches, and relays can also be used with scan tools.
- If the code indicates a problem with the oxygen sensor, extra caution is required. The oxygen sensor wire carries a very low voltage and must be isolated from other wires. If not, nearby wires could add more induced voltage. This gives false data to the computer and can result in a driveability problem. Make sure that the oxygen sensor wire is kept separate and insulated from the other wires. Some carmakers use a foam sleeve around the oxygen sensor wire.

- The sensor wires that connect to the computer should never be rerouted. The resulting problem might be impossible to find. When replacing this wiring, always check the service manual routing instructions.
- Remove any computer module that is near welding operations or that could be affected by hammering, grinding, sanding, or metal straightening. Protect it with a plastic bag to shield it from moisture and dust.
- Be careful not to damage wiring when welding, hammering, or grinding.
- Be careful not to damage connectors and terminals when removing electronic components. Some may, in fact, require special tools to take them out.
- Identify the blackboxes or sensor wires while disconnecting them. This will make reinstallation and reconnection easier.
- Always route wiring where it was originally. If this is not done, electronic crossover from the current carrying wires can affect the sensing and control circuits. Reuse or replace all electrical shielding for the same reason.

12.16 REVIEW QUESTIONS

1. To begin a cornering angle check, Technician A turns the left front wheel out 20 degrees. Technician B turns the left front wheel out 70 degrees. Who is correct?
   a. Technician A
   b. Technician B
   c. Both A and B
   d. Neither A nor B

2. In unibody construction, what provides the critical mounting positions for the suspension and steering systems?
   a. body panels
   b. drivetrain
   c. upper and lower control arms
   d. cradle assembly mounting biscuits

3. The strut replaces the shock absorber and the _____.
   a. lower control arm
   b. leaf spring bushings
   c. upper control arm
   d. all of the above

FIGURE 12-151   Scan tools can be used to access EEC trouble codes. (Courtesy of All-Test, Inc.)

4. Upon examining a collapsed steering column, Technician A decides to attempt a repair of the collapsed portion. Technician B replaces the collapsed portion. Who is correct?
   a. Technician A
   b. Technician B
   c. Both A and B
   d. Neither A nor B

5. What is the definition of camber?
   a. the forward or backward tilt of the steering axis
   b. the distance between the centerline of the ball joints and the centerline of the tire at the point where the tire contacts the road surface
   c. The amount of toe-out present on turns
   d. The inward or outward tilt of the tire as measured at the top

6. To determine whether an improper toe condition is caused by poor wheel alignment or damaged suspension components, Technician A makes a cornering angle check; Technician B makes a jounce/rebound check. Who is correct?
   a. Technician A
   b. Technician B
   c. Both A and B
   d. Neither A nor B

7. What is the notable feature involved in aligning a vehicle with an electronic air suspension that is not a factor when aligning any other vehicle?
   a. the "fifth wheel"
   b. ride height
   c. turning radius
   d. toe-out

8. Which of the following statements concerning brake systems is incorrect?
   a. All cars are now required to have two hydraulic systems.
   b. The major brake component that a technician must repair is the brake line.
   c. A hose that is blistered does not necessarily have to be replaced.
   d. The wheel cylinder converts hydraulic pressure to mechanical force.

9. When bleeding a four-piston caliper with two bleeder screws, Technician A bleeds the lower one first, while Technician B starts with the upper. Who is correct?

   a. Technician A
   b. Technician B
   c. Both A and B
   d. Neither A nor B

10. Which emission control subsystem is responsible for channeling blowby gases into the fuel intake area?
    a. engine control
    b. positive crankcase ventilation
    c. evaporative
    d. exhaust gas recirculation

11. Never attempt to _____ .
    a. straighten a damaged cooling fan
    b. visually inspect a cooling fan clutch for signs of fluid loss
    c. check the cooling fan power circuit by turning the ignition on and jumping the coolant sensor on the engine
    d. all of the above

12. When discharging an A/C system, Technician A uses hydraulic caps to keep out moisture. Technician B uses plastic wrap held in place with wire ties. Who is correct?
    a. Technician A
    b. Technician B
    c. Both A and B
    d. Neither A nor B

13. An open circuit breaker is an example of what type of short?
    a. intermittent
    b. dead short to ground
    c. cross circuit
    d. high resistance short to ground

14. When soldering an electrical connection, Technician A uses rosin core solder; Technician B uses an acid type flux. Who is correct?
    a. Technician A
    b. Technician B
    c. Both A and B
    d. Neither A nor B

15. What type of safety restraint system operates automatically, with no action required by the vehicle's occupant?
    a. passive
    b. retractor
    c. active
    d. both a and c

CHAPTER
13

Repairing Auto Plastics

OBJECTIVES

After reading this chapter, you will be able to:

- identify and explain the difference between the two types of plastics used in automotive production.
- identify unknown plastics by means of the burn test and a trial-and-error weld.
- repair minor cuts and cracks in plastic using adhesives.
- repair gouges, tears, and punctures in plastic by means of a chemical bonding process.
- set up and operate a typical welding torch.
- explain the keys to good welding technique.
- describe the proper welding repair sequence.
- explain the safety precautions used when working with fiberglass.
- explain how fiberglass is used in adhesives to reinforce the damaged surface.
- make SMC and RRIM repairs.

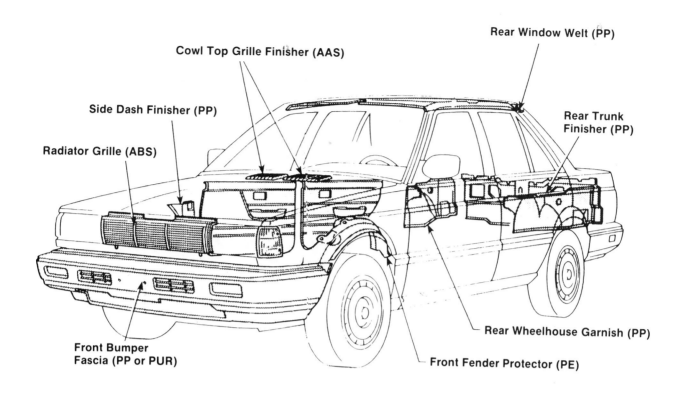

Rear Window Welt (PP)

Cowl Top Grille Finisher (AAS)

Side Dash Finisher (PP)

Rear Trunk Finisher (PP)

Radiator Grille (ABS)

Rear Wheelhouse Garnish (PP)

Front Bumper Fascia (PP or PUR)

Front Fender Protector (PE)

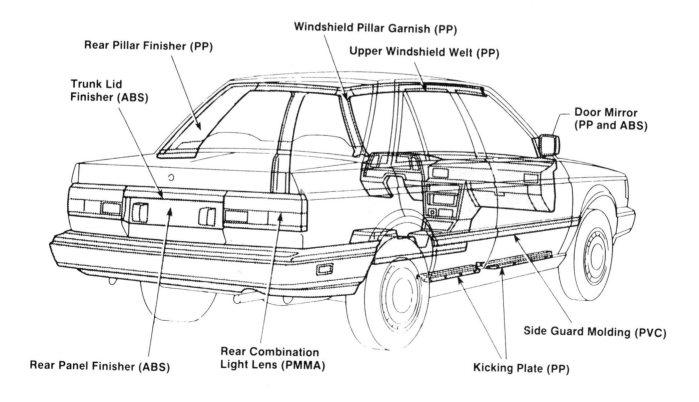

Windshield Pillar Garnish (PP)

Rear Pillar Finisher (PP)

Upper Windshield Welt (PP)

Trunk Lid Finisher (ABS)

Door Mirror (PP and ABS)

Side Guard Molding (PVC)

Rear Panel Finisher (ABS)

Rear Combination Light Lens (PMMA)

Kicking Plate (PP)

FIGURE 13–1   Exterior plastic locations in modern cars

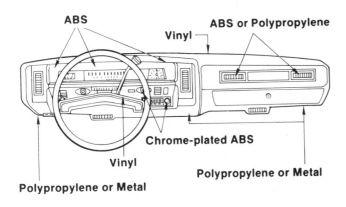

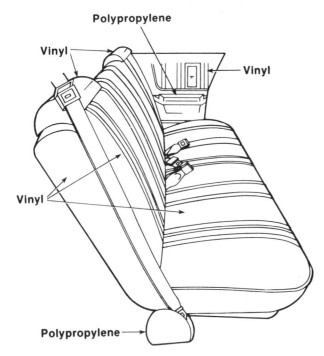

FIGURE 13-2 Common interior uses of plastic in today's automobile

In recent years, more and more plastic has been used in various parts of car bodies, particularly in the front end: in bumper and fender extensions, in soft front fascia, fender aprons, grille opening panels, stone shields, instrument panels, trim panels, and elsewhere. Figure 13-1 illustrates exterior uses of plastics, while Figure 13-2 shows interior uses of plastic in today's cars. Because these parts are much lighter in weight than sheet metal, they have become an important part of every American manufacturer's fuel saving, weight reduction program. And because of the high strength-to-weight ratio of plastic, the weight decrease does not mean a decrease in strength. Every indication is that plastic body parts are here to stay, and new applications for plastic will probably be found in the future. Therefore, plastic repairs can be expected to be a growing part of life in every body shop.

This increasing use of plastic in the automobile industry has resulted in new approaches to collision damage repair. Many damaged body parts can be repaired more economically than they can be replaced, especially if the part does not have to be removed from the vehicle. Cuts and cracks, gouges, tears, and punctures are all repairable; and, when necessary, some plastics can also be re-formed after distortion from their original shapes. Repair is quicker as well since replacement parts are not always available.

13.1 TYPES OF PLASTICS

There are two types of plastics used today in automotive production:

- **Thermoplastics.** These plastics are capable of being repeatedly softened by heating, with no change in their appearance or chemical makeup. They soften or melt when heat is applied to them and harden when cooled. Thermoplastics are weldable with a plastic welder.
- **Thermosetting plastics.** These plastics are materials that undergo a chemical change by the action of heating, a catalyst, or ultraviolet light. They are hardened into a permanent shape that cannot be altered either by reapplying heat or catalysts. Thermosets are not weldable, although they can be "glued" using an airless welder.

Figure 13-3 explains the relationship of heat to the two types of plastics more fully. In general the repair techniques are chemical adhesive bonding for thermosetting plastics and welding for thermoplastics.

PLASTIC IDENTIFICATION

Before deciding on a repair technique, it is necessary to identify the type of plastic in question. This is crucial, because a repair based on incorrect identification of the plastic will likely fail. The use of plastic types can change from vehicle to vehicle, even within the same model year. This can happen if the manufacturer switches suppliers or as a result of design or production changes. Naturally, this can make the job of identification even more difficult.

TABLE 13-1: IDENTIFICATION SYMBOL, CHEMICAL NAME, TRADE NAME, AND DESIGN APPLICATIONS OF MOST COMMONLY USED PLASTICS

Symbol	Chemical Name	Common Name	Design Applications	Thermosetting or Thermoplastic
AAS	Acrylonitrile-styrene	Acrylic Rubber	—	Thermosplastic
ABS	Acrylonitrile-butadiene-styrene	ABS, Cycolac, Abson, Kralastic, Lustran, Absafil, Dylel	Body panels, dash panels, grilles, headlamp doors	Thermoplastic
ABS/MAT	Hard ABS reinforced with fiberglass	—	Body panels	Thermosetting
ABS/PVC	ABS/Polyvinyl chloride	ABS Vinyl	—	Thermoplastic
EP	Epoxy	Epon, EPO, Epotuf, Araldite	Fiberglass body panels	Thermosetting
EPDM	Ethylene-propylene-diene-monomer	EPDM, Nordel	Bumper impact strips, body panels	Thermosetting
PA	Polyamide	Nylon, Capron, Zytel, Rilsan, Minlon, Vydyne	Exterior finish trim panels	Thermosetting
PC	Polycarbonate	Lexan, Merlon	Grilles, instrument panels, lenses	Thermoplastic
PPO	Polyphenylene oxide	Noryl, Olefo	Chromed plastic parts, grilles, headlamp doors, bezels, ornaments	Thermosetting
PE	Polyethylene	Dylan, Fortiflex, Marlex, Alathon, Hi-fax, Hosalen, Paxon	Inner fender panels, interior trim panels, valances, spoilers	Thermoplastic
PP	Polypropylene	Profax, Olefo, Marlex, Olemer, Aydel, Dypro	Interior moldings, interior trim panels, inner fenders, radiator shrouds, dash panels, bumper covers	Thermoplastic
PS	Polystyrene	Lustrex, Dylene, Styron, Fostacryl, Duraton	—	Thermoplastic
PUR	Polyurethane	Castethane, Bayflex	Bumper covers, front and rear body panels, filler panels	Thermosetting
PVC	Polyvinyl chloride	Geon, Vinylete, Pliovic	Interior trim, soft filler panels	Thermoplastic
RIM	"Reaction injection molded" polyurethane	—	Bumper covers	Thermosetting
R RIM	Reinforced RIM-polyurethane	—	Exterior body panels	Thermosetting
SAN	Styrene-acrylonitrite	Lustran, Tyril, Fostacryl	Interior trim panels	Thermosetting

**TABLE 13-1: IDENTIFICATION SYMBOL, CHEMICAL NAME, TRADE NAME,
AND APPLICATIONS OF MOST COMMONLY USED PLASTICS (CONTINUED)**

Symbol	Chemical Name	Common Name	Applications	Thermosetting or Thermoplastic
TPR	Thermoplastic rubber	—	Valance panels	Thermosetting
TPUR	Polyurethane	Pellethane, Estane, Roylar, Texin	Bumper covers, gravel deflectors, filler panels, soft bezels	Thermoplastic
UP	Polyester	SMC, Premi-glas, Selection Vibrin-mat	Fiberglass body panels	Thermosetting

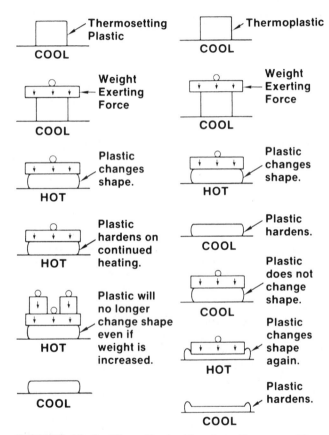

FIGURE 13-3 The effect of heat on thermosetting plastic and thermoplastic

Table 13-1 shows some of the more common plastics with their full chemical name, common name, and where on the vehicle they might be found. Their designation as to thermosetting or thermoplastic is also included. There is another group of plastics that the body technician should be aware of. These are called composite plastics and are blends of different plastics and other ingredients designed to achieve specific performance characteristics.

There are several ways to identify an unknown plastic. One possibility is the use of international identification symbols, or ISO codes, which can often be found molded into plastic parts. Manufacturers are using identification symbols more and more; unfortunately, there are still some who do not. Keep in mind that one problem with this method is that it is usually necessary to remove the part to read the symbol.

In the event that the part in question is not identified by an ISO code, the body repair manual may be of help. While these manuals often name the types of plastic used in a particular application, keep in mind that they are updated frequently, often as much as twice a year. For this reason, it is crucial that the very latest edition be consulted when working on a late-model vehicle.

The so-called burn test has fallen out of favor as a technique for identifying plastics for several reasons. For one, having an open flame in a body shop environment creates a potential fire hazard and is environmentally unsound. Another reason the burn test is not as popular as it once was is because it is not always reliable; many parts are now being manufactured from "hybrids," which are blended plastics that use more than one ingredient. A burn test is of no help in such cases.

A reliable means of identifying an unknown plastic (assuming it is probably a thermoplastic that is potentially weldable) is to make a trial-and-error weld on a hidden or damaged area of the part (Figure 13-4). Try several different filler rods until one sticks. Most suppliers of plastic welding equipment offer only half a dozen or so different types of plastic filler rods, so the range of possibilities is not that great. The rods are color coded, so once the rod that works is found, the base material is identified. Table 13-2 contains additional information on types of automotive plastics.

TABLE 13-2:   HANDLING PRECAUTIONS FOR PLASTICS

Code	Material Name	Heat Resisting Temperature* °F	Resistance To Alcohol or Gasoline	Notes
AAS	Acrylonitrile Acrylic Rubber Styrene Resin	176	Alcohol is harmless if applied only for short time in small amounts (example, quick wiping to remove grease).	Avoid gasoline and organic or aromatic solvents.
ABS	Acrylonitrile Butadiene Styrene Resin	176	Alcohol is harmless if applied only for short time in small amounts (example, quick wiping to remove grease).	Avoid gasoline and organic or aromatic solvents.
AES	Acrylonitrile Ethylene Rubber Styrene Resin	176	Alcohol is harmless if applied only for short time in small amounts (example, quick wiping to remove grease).	Avoid gasoline and organic or aromatic solvents.
EPDM	Ethylene Propylene Rubber	212	Alcohol is harmless. Gasoline is harmless if applied only for short time in small amounts.	Most solvents are harmless, but avoid dipping in gasoline, solvents, etc.
PA	Polyamide (Nylon)	176	Alcohol and gasoline are harmless.	Avoid battery acid.
PC	Polycarbonate	248	Alcohol is harmless.	Avoid gasoline, brake fluid, wax, wax removers, and organic solvents.
PE	Polyethylene	176	Alcohol and gasoline are harmless.	Most solvents are harmless.
POM	Polyoxymethylene (Polyacetal)	212	Alcohol and gasoline are harmless.	Most solvents are harmless.
PP	Polypropylene	176	Alcohol and gasoline are harmless.	Most solvents are harmless.
PPO	Modified Polyphenylene Oxide	212	Alcohol is harmless.	Gasoline is harmless if applied only for quick wiping to remove grease.
PS	Polystyrene	140	Alcohol and gasoline are harmless if applied only for short time in small amounts.	Avoid dipping or immersing in alcohol, gasoline, solvents, etc.
PUR	Thermosetting Polyurethane	176	Alcohol is harmless if applied only for very short time in small amounts (example, quick wiping to remove grease).	Avoid dipping or immersing in alcohol, gasoline, solvents. etc.
PVC	Polyvinylchloride (Vinyl)	176	Alcohol and gasoline are harmless if applied only for short time in small amounts (example, quick wiping to remove grease).	Avoid dipping or immersing in alcohol, gasoline, solvents. etc.
SAN	Styrene Acrylonitrile Resin	176	Alcohol is harmless if applied only for short time in small amounts (example, quick wiping to remove grease).	Avoid dipping or immersing in alcohol, gasoline, solvents, etc.

TABLE 13-3: HANDLING PRECAUTIONS FOR PLASTICS (CONTINUED)

TPO	Thermoplastic Polyolefin	176	Alcohol is harmless. Gasoline is harmless is applied only for short time in small amounts.	Most solvents are harmless, but avoid dipping in gasoline, solvents, etc.
TPUR	Thermoplastic Polyurethane	140	Alcohol is harmless if applied only for very short time in small amounts (example, quick wiping to remove grease).	Avoid dipping or immersing in alcohol, gasoline, solvents, etc.

*Temperature higher than listed here could result in material deformation during repair.
NOTE: When repairing metal body parts that adjoin plastic body parts (by brazing, flame cutting, welding, painting, etc.), consideration **must** be given to the properties of the plastic.
Chart courtesy of Toyota Motor Corporation

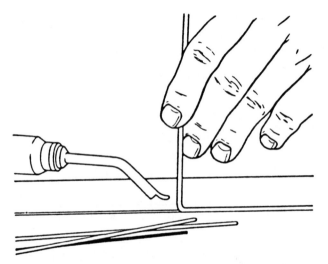

FIGURE 13-4   Making a trial-and-error weld

13.2 PLASTIC REPAIR

Plastic repair, like any other kind of body repair work, begins with an estimation. It must be determined if the part should be repaired or replaced. A minor crack, tear, gouge, or hole in a nose fascia or large panel that is difficult to replace, costly to replace, or is not readily available probably indicates a repair is in order. Extensive damage to the same component or damage to a fender extension or plastic trim item that is cheap and easy to replace would dictate replacement. In short, it is up to the repair person or estimator to decide if it makes more sense to repair a plastic part than to replace it.

If repair is the answer, it must be determined if the part must be removed from the vehicle. The entire damaged area must be accessible in order to do a quality repair; if it is not, the part must be removed. Keep in mind that the part will also have to be refinished, so take this into consideration. In short, parts do not always have to be removed, but in many cases it is the only way to do the job right.

As mentioned earlier, there are two methods of repairing plastics:

- Use of chemical adhesives
- By plastic welding

> **CAUTION:** Keep in mind that while the techniques discussed in this chapter are proven repair methods, no technique is 100 percent reliable when used to repair a fuel tank or in similar critical structural applications.

Table 13-3 indicates the best repair systems for the plastics most often used by the automotive industry.

13.3 CHEMICAL ADHESIVE BONDING TECHNIQUES

The main advantage adhesives have over welding is that not all plastics can be welded. Only thermoplastics soften when heated. Adhesive repair systems are of two types: two-component or cyanoacrylate.

Two-component systems consist of a base resin of polyester, epoxy or urethane, and a hardener or

TABLE 13-3: PLASTIC PARTS REPAIR SYSTEMS

KEY

AR	Adhesive repair	S	Anerobic (instant) adhesive
FGR	Fiberglass repair	PC	Patching compound
HAW	Hot-air welding	AW	Airless welding

ISO Code	Name	Repair System
ABS	Acrylonitrile-butadiene-styrene(hard)	HAW, S FGR, AW
ABS/PVC	ABS/Vinyl (soft)	PC, AW
EPI II or TPO	Ethylene propylene	AR, AW
PA	Nylon	S, FGR, AW
PC	Lexan	S, FGR, AW
PE	Polyethylene	HAW, AW
PP	Polypropylene	HAW, AW
PPO	Noryl	FGR, AW
PS	Polystyrene	S
PUR, RIM, or RRIM	Thermoset polyurethane	AR, AW
PVC	Polyvinyl chloride	PC, AW
SAN	Styrene acrylonitrile	HAW, AW
TPR	Thermoplastic rubber	AR, AW
TPUR	Thermoplastic polyurethane	AR, AW
UP	Polyester (Fiberglass)	FGR

catalyst. A number of different manufacturers supply two-component adhesives to the automotive aftermarket.

Cyanoacrylates, or CAs, have changed significantly in the last few years, with many new formulations becoming available. CAs, sometimes known as super glues, are not a recommended solution for most types of plastic repair. There are some questions about the ability of CA adhesives to withstand weather exposure to ensure longevity of the repair. It should be mentioned that CAs do not work equally well on all plastics. There is no hard and fast rule. If you decide to use CAs, be sure to use products from reliable suppliers and follow the manufacturer's guidelines for using them. Before attempting a repair with either type of adhesive, make sure to read

and understand the product literature and follow all recommendations.

The main advantages of adhesives is their versatility. Not all plastics can be welded, but adhesives can be used in all but a few instances. If adhesive bonding is chosen, the best way to identify the plastic type is by using a flexibility test. In this test, the base material's flexibility is compared to a sample disk of the repair material. Use the repair material that most closely matches the base material. When working with an adhesive system, use the manufacturer's categories to decide on a product. There might be only two categories or as many as five.

There are differences between manufacturers' product lines, so it is very important to choose a product line and use it for the entire repair.

- Most product lines have two or more adhesives designed for different types of plastic.
- The product line usually includes an adhesion promoter, a filler product, and a flexible coating agent.
- Some product lines are formulated for a specific base material. For instance, one manufacturer offers individual products for use on such plastics as TPO, urethanes, or Xenoy regardless of plastic flexibility.
- A product line might also use a single flexible filler for all plastics, or there might be two or more designed for different types of plastic.

REPAIRS OF MINOR CUTS AND CRACKS

Adhesives are usually used for repairing minor cuts and cracks in plastic parts (Table 13-4). First wipe or wash the repair area clean with water and a plastic cleaner. It is most important for the mating surfaces to be clean and free of wax, dust, or grease. It is not necessary to use solvents other than a plastic cleaner for cleaning plastic parts that are to be repaired. Allow the part(s) to warm to 70 degrees Fahrenheit before applying adhesives.

After cleaning, the next step is to prepare the crack with an adhesive kit. The kit should have two elements: an accelerator and an adhesive. The first step is to spray one side of the crack with the accelerator, as shown in Figure 13-5. Then apply the adhesive to the same side of the crack.

Carefully position the two sides of the cut or crack in their original position, and quickly press them together with firm pressure. Hold for a full

TABLE 13-4: ADHESIVE REPAIR SYSTEMS

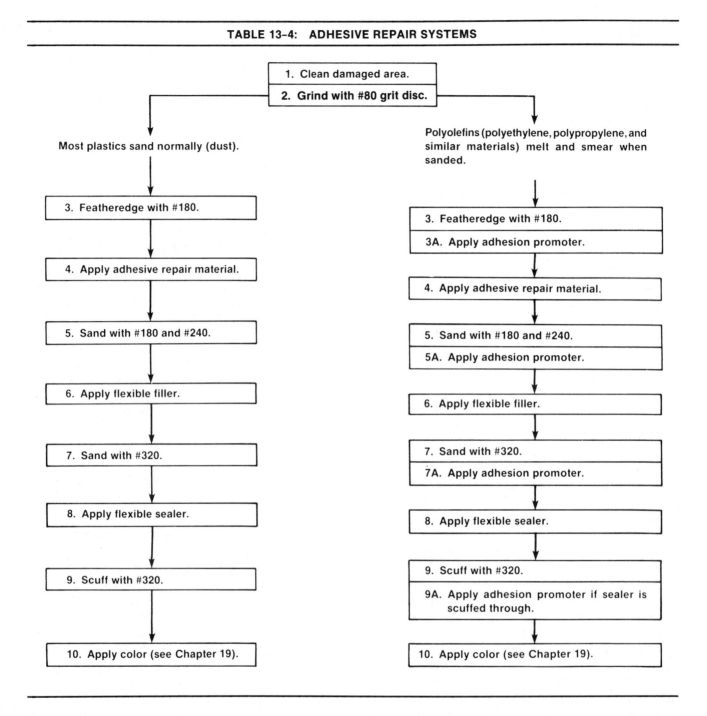

1. Clean damaged area.
2. Grind with #80 grit disc.

Most plastics sand normally (dust).

3. Featheredge with #180.

4. Apply adhesive repair material.

5. Sand with #180 and #240.

6. Apply flexible filler.

7. Sand with #320.

8. Apply flexible sealer.

9. Scuff with #320.

10. Apply color (see Chapter 19).

Polyolefins (polyethylene, polypropylene, and similar materials) melt and smear when sanded.

3. Featheredge with #180.
3A. Apply adhesion promoter.

4. Apply adhesive repair material.

5. Sand with #180 and #240.
5A. Apply adhesion promoter.

6. Apply flexible filler.

7. Sand with #320.
7A. Apply adhesion promoter.

8. Apply flexible sealer.

9. Scuff with #320.
9A. Apply adhesion promoter if sealer is scuffed through.

10. Apply color (see Chapter 19).

minute to achieve good bond strength, and then cure for 3 to 12 hours for maximum strength, according to instructions on the label. Note the precautions and instructions on the container for the adhesive used.

If the original paint was not damaged and the repair was properly positioned, painting may not be required. Where painting is required, special procedures are needed as described in Chapter 19.

Repairs of Gouges, Tears, and Punctures

The procedure for repairs of gouges, tears, and punctures is somewhat more involved than the previous one but requires no special skills or tools. This procedure is a chemical bonding process.

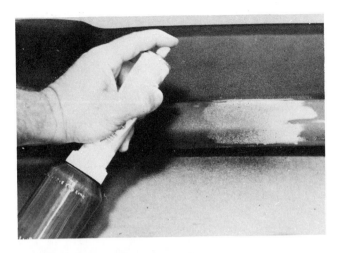

FIGURE 13-5 **Spraying a crack with accelerator.** *(Courtesy of Urethane Supply Company, Inc.)*

FIGURE 13-7 **Using a finer grit disc to featheredge the paint**

FIGURE 13-6 **Beveling damaged area with a 3-inch grinding disc**

The first step in the repair procedure is to clean around the damaged area thoroughly with a wax, grease, and silicone-removing solvent applied with a water-dampened cloth, and then to wipe it dry.

To prepare for the structural adhesive, bevel the edges of the hole back about 1/4 to 3/8 inch. The technician in Figure 13-6 is using a 3-inch grinding disc, medium grit. In this repair, the beveling has left a coarse surface for good adhesion. In any repair, the mating surfaces should be scuffed to improve adhesion. Use a slow speed when grinding (2000 rpm or less). If the sanded area has a "greasy" appearance, it would be wise to apply a coat of adhesion promoter to the surface. Do apply more adhesion promoter after each sanding step.

The next step is to featheredge the paint around the repair area (Figure 13-7). For this purpose, use a finer grit disc. In this step, remove the paint, but very little of the urethane plastic. Blend the paint edges into the plastic.

Continue removing paint until there is a paint-free band around the hole—about 1 to 1-1/2 inches wide. The repair material must **not** overlap the painted surface.

Carefully wipe off all paint and urethane dust in preparation for the next step. The repair area must be absolutely clean.

Then flame treat the beveled area of the hole. This flame treatment improves the adhesion of the structural adhesive. Use any torch with a controlled flame, and develop a 1-inch cone tip. Very carefully direct the flame onto the beveled area. Keep moving the flame all the time until the beveled area is slightly brown. Be extremely careful to accomplish this without warping the urethane and without burning the paint.

The next step is to apply auto backing tape to the repair area. An aluminum foil with a strong adhesive on one side and a moisture-proof backing is recommended. Clean the inner surface of the repair area with silicone and wax remover. Then install the tape. Cover the hole completely, with about a 1-inch adhesion surface around the edges.

Then, before applying the structural repair adhesive material, the back of the opening should be thoroughly cleaned and taped with aluminum auto body repair tape to provide support for the repair. For best results slightly dish the aluminum tape so that the repair materials overlap the repaired area on the backside.

For this repair, it was possible to install the tape without loosening or removing any parts from the

495

car. For repairs in other areas or on other makes, partial disassembly might sometimes be necessary.

Next, prepare the repair adhesive material as directed by the manufacturer. Most adhesive compounds come in two tubes. On a clean, flat, nonporous surface such as metal or glass, squeeze out equal amounts of the repair mix. Then, with an even paddling motion to reduce air bubbles, completely mix the two components until a uniform color and consistency is achieved.

Paddle the structural adhesive into the hole, using a squeegee or plastic spreader (Figure 13-8). This must be done carefully and swiftly, as the structural adhesive material will begin to set in about 2 to 3 minutes. Two applications of the adhesive are usually required. This first application is used to fill the bottom of the hole, and it is not necessary to worry about contour at this time.

In the first application of patch material, try to fill the greater part of the hole's volume. Then cure for about an hour at room temperature, or 20 minutes with a heat lamp or gun at 190 or 200 degrees Fahrenheit.

Before the final application of the adhesive, use a fine grit disc to grind down the high spots of the first application (Figure 13-9). Wipe the dust from the repair area.

After the first application is ground and wiped clean, mix the second application of the adhesive, squeezing the components together as before for about 2 minutes. Then apply the second adhesive mixture, paddling it into an overfill contour of the area (Figure 13-10). A flexible squeegee or spatula is useful in approximating the panel contours.

FIGURE 13-9　Grinding down high spots

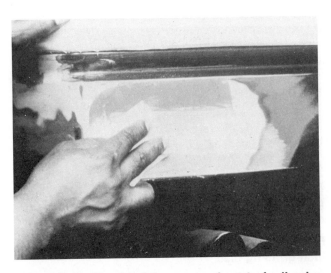

FIGURE 13-10　Applying second coat of adhesive

When the adhesive repair material has dried, establish a rough contour to the surrounding area with a #80 grit abrasive on a sanding block. Feather-sand the area using a disc sander with a #180 sandpaper followed by a #240 sandpaper to achieve an accurate level with the surface of the part. Check the repaired surface to see if there are any low areas, pits, or pinholes in it. If there are, additional material can be spread over them to fill the holes and raise the area as needed.

Final feathering and finish sanding can be done with a disc sander and a #320 grit disc. When the final sanding is completed, the area is cleaned to remove all dust and loose material. The plastic surface is then ready to be painted as described in Chapter 19.

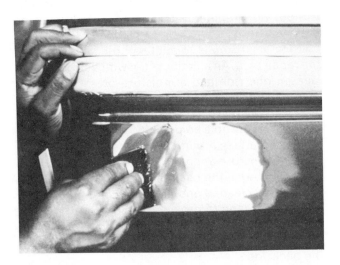

FIGURE 13-8　Applying structural adhesive with a squeegee

Epoxy and Urethane Repair Materials

Adhesive repair materials are made of both epoxy and urethane. Both are two-component materials that must be mixed in equal parts just prior to application. Some types of urethane are available in various degrees of flexibility that can be matched to the particular part being repaired.

Whether to use epoxy or urethane is the choice of the repairer. Both applications are essentially the same. Whenever adhesives are used, the following points should be considered:

- As with welding, surface preparation and cleanliness are extremely important. The part must be washed and a plastic cleaner used before starting any repair.
- Both the part to be repaired and the repair material must be at room temperature (at least 60 degrees Fahrenheit) to achieve the proper cure and adhesion.
- The 2 parts of the repair material must be equally and completely mixed before application.
- Whenever possible, particularly when repairing cuts or tears that go all the way through the paint, a fiberglass mat reinforcement should be used.

Two-Part Epoxy Repair

Until recently, adhesive repairs were limited to urethane plastics only. With the introduction of adhesion promoters, polyolefins can now be repaired using virtually the same adhesive bonding techniques as urethane. The only difference is the addition of the adhesion promoter before each application of repair material. The rest of the procedure is the same. If in doubt as to whether the base material is a polyolefin, grind the damaged area. If it grinds cleanly, do the repair without an adhesion promoter. If the material melts or smears, it is a polyolefin and must have an adhesion promoter.

Use the following procedure to make a two-part epoxy repair of a polyolefin bumper cover.

 1. Clean the entire cover with soap and water, wipe or blow dry, then clean with a good plastic cleaner.
2. With a slow speed grinder and 3-inch #36 grit disc, V-groove and taper the damaged area. Grind about a 1-1/2-inch taper around the damage for good adhesion (Figure 13-11).
3. Use a sander with #180 grit paper to feather-edge the paint around the damaged area;

FIGURE 13-11 Grinding around damage for good adhesion

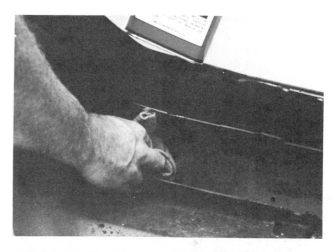

FIGURE 13-12 Cleaning back side with plastic cleaner

FIGURE 13-13 Applying adhesive promoter to back side

then blow dust-free. Depending on the severity of the damage, the back side of the cover might need reinforcement. To do this, follow Steps 4 through 6:

4. Clean the back side with a good plastic cleaner (Figure 13-12). Then apply a coat of adhesion promoter according to the manufacturer's recommendations (Figure 13-13).

5. Dispense equal amounts of both parts of the flexible epoxy adhesive, and mix to a uniform color. Apply the material to a piece of fiberglass cloth (Figure 13-14).

6. Attach the saturated cloth to the back side of the bumper cover. Fill in the weave with additional adhesive material.

7. With the back side reinforcement in place as shown in Figure 13-15, apply a coat of adhesion promoter to the sanded repair area on the front side (Figure 13-16). Let dry completely.

8. Fill the groove with the adhesive material (Figure 13-17). Allow it to cure according to manufacturer's recommendations.

9. Rough grind the repair area with #80 grit paper, then sand with #180 grit, followed by #240 grit. If additional adhesive material is needed to fill in a low spot or pinhole, be sure to apply a coat of adhesion promoter first. Follow up with **a skim coat of adhesive material** to fill in the imperfections.

 **SHOP TALK** _____

Do not use flexible putty on polyolefins—it will not work.

FIGURE 13-14   Applying flexible epoxy adhesive to fiberglass cloth

FIGURE 13-15   Finished back side reinforcement

FIGURE 13-16   Applying adhesive promoter to front side

13.4 PRINCIPLES OF PLASTIC WELDING

The welding of plastics is not unlike the welding of metals. Both methods use a heat source, welding rod, and similar techniques (butt joints, fillet welds, lap joints, and the like). Joints are prepared in much the same manner, and similarly evaluated for strength. Due to differences in the physical characteristics of each material, however, there are notable differences between welding metal and welding plastics.

When welding metal, the rod and base material are made molten and puddled into a joint. And while metals have a sharply defined melting point, plastics have a wide melting range between the temperature at which they soften and the temperature at which

FIGURE 13-17   Filling in groove with adhesive material

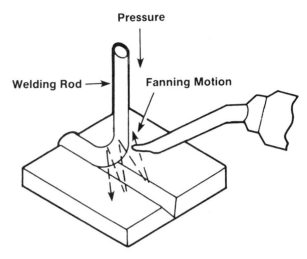

FIGURE 13-18   Successful plastic welding requires the proper combination of heat and pressure.

they char or burn. Also unlike metals, plastics are poor conductors of heat and thus are difficult to heat uniformly. Because of this, the plastic filler rod and the surface of the plastic will char or burn before the material below the surface becomes fully softened. The decomposition time at welding temperature is shorter than the time required to completely soften many plastics for fusion welding. The result is that a plastic welder must work within a much smaller temperature range than a metal welder.

Because a plastic welding rod does not become completely molten and appears much the same before and after welding, a plastic weld might appear incomplete to the technician who is used to welding only metal. The explanation is simple; since only the outer surface of the rod has become molten while the inner core has remained hard, the welder is able to exert pressure on the rod to force it into the joint and create a permanent bond. When heat is taken away, the rod reverts to its original form. Thus, even though a strong and permanent bond has been obtained between the rod and base material, the appearance of the rod is much the same as before the weld was made, except for molten flow patterns on either side of the bead.

When welding plastics, the materials are fused together by the proper combination of heat and pressure. With the conventional hand welding method, this combination is achieved by applying pressure on the welding rod with one hand, while at the same time applying heat and a constant fanning motion to the rod and base material with hot gas from the welding torch (Figure 13-18). Successful welds require that both pressure and heat be kept constant and in proper balance. Too much pressure

on the rod tends to stretch the bead; too much heat will char, melt, or distort the plastic. With practice, plastic welding can be mastered as completely as metal welding.

HIGH-SPEED WELDING

High-speed welding incorporates the basic methods utilized in hand welding. Its primary difference lies in the use of a specially designed and patented high-speed tip (Figure 13-19), which enables the welder to produce more uniform welds and work at a much higher rate of speed. As with hand welding, constant heat and pressure must be maintained.

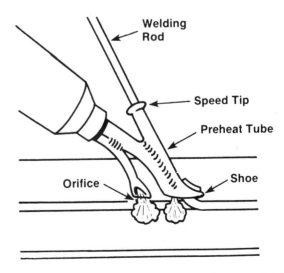

FIGURE 13-19   Plastic welder utilizing a high-speed tip

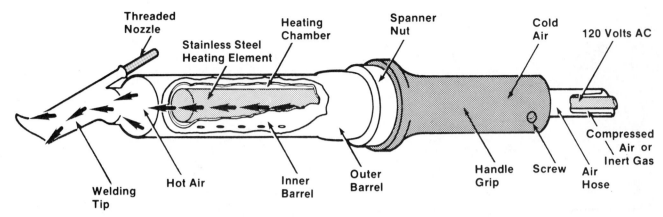

FIGURE 13-20   Typical hot-air welder

FIGURE 13-21   Tacking welding tip *(Courtesy of Seelye Inc.)*

The increased efficiency of high-speed welding is made possible through preheating of both the rod and base material before the point of fusion. The rod is preheated as it passes through a tube in the speed tip; the base material is preheated by a stream of hot air passing through a vent in the tip ahead of the fusion point. A pointed shoe on the end of the tip applies pressure on the rod, thus eliminating the need for the operator to apply pressure. At the same time the shoe smooths out the rod, creating a more uniform appearance in the finished weld.

In high-speed welding, the conventional two-hand method is replaced by a faster and more uniform one-hand operation. Once started, the rod is fed automatically into the preheating tube as the welding torch is pulled along the joint. High-speed tips are designed to provide the constant balance of heat and pressure necessary for a satisfactory weld. The average welding speed is about 40 inches per minute.

High-speed welding does have its advantages. Because increased speeds must be maintained to achieve the best possible weld, the high-speed welding torch is not suited for small, intricate work. Also, when the operator is new to this technique, the position in which the welder is held might seem clumsy and difficult. However, experience will enable the operator to successfully make all welds that can be made with a hand welder, including butt welds, V-welds, corner welds, and lap joint welds. Speed welds can be made on circular as well as flat work. In addition, inside welds on tanks can be speed welded, provided the working space is large enough to manipulate the torch.

13.5 HOT-AIR PLASTIC WELDING

There are a number of manufacturers who make plastic hot-air welding equipment for the body repair industry, and all use the same basic technology. A ceramic or stainless steel electric heating element is used to produce hot air (450 to 650 degrees Fahrenheit), which in turn blows through a nozzle and onto the plastic. The air supply comes from either the shop's air compressor or a self-contained portable compressor that comes with the unit. Never use oxygen or other flammable gases with any type of plastic welder. Most hot-air welders use a working pressure at the tip of around 3 psi. A pair of pressure regulators is required to reduce the air pressure first to around 50 psi, and then finally to the working pressure of 2-1/2 to 3-1/2 psi. A typical hot-air welder is illustrated in Figure 13-20.

The barrel of the torch gets sufficiently hot so that skin contact could cause a burn if the hot air is directed against the skin long enough. The torch is used in conjunction with the welding rod, which is normally 3/16 inch in diameter and made from the same material as the plastic being repaired. This will ensure that the strength, hardness, and flexibility of the repair is the same as the damaged part. Use of the proper welding rod is very important; even a merely adequate weld is impossible if the wrong rod is used.

One of the problems with hot-air welding is that the 3/16-inch-diameter rod is often thicker than the panel to be welded. This can cause the panel to overheat before the rod has melted. Using a 1/8-inch rod with the hot-air welder can often correct such warpage problems. (This works on the same principle as using a 1/64-inch wire instead of a 1/32 inch for MIG welding.)

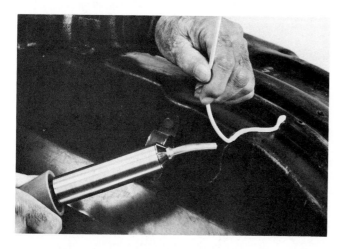

FIGURE 13-22 Round welding tip (Courtesy of Seelye Inc.)

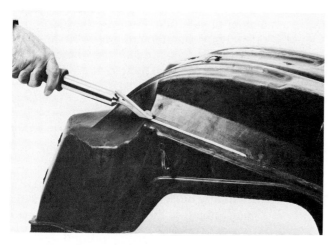

FIGURE 13-23 Speed welding tip (Courtesy of Seelye Inc.)

Three shapes of welding tips are available for use with most plastic welding torches. They are:

- **Tacking tips.** These are used to tack broken sections together before welding (Figure 13-21). If necessary, tack welds can be easily broken apart for realigning.
- **Round tips.** These tips are used to fill small holes and make short welds, welds in hard-to-reach places, and on tight or particularly sharp corners (Figure 13-22).
- **Speed tips.** These are used for long, fairly straight welds. They hold the filler rod, automatically preheat it, and feed the rod into the weld, thus allowing for faster welding rates (Figure 13-23).

SETUP, SHUTDOWN, AND SERVICING

Naturally, no two hot-air welders are exactly alike; their design varies from one manufacturer to another. The setup, shutdown, and service procedures that follow, although typical of all hot-air welders, should nonetheless be regarded as general guidelines only. For specific instructions, always refer to the owner's manual and other material provided by the welder manufacturer. Keep in mind that some manufacturers advise against using their welder on plastic that is any thinner than 1/8 inch because of the likelihood of distortion. In other cases, it is acceptable to weld plastics as thin as 1/16 inch, provided they are supported from underneath during the operation. Again, it is very important to read and follow the specific directions for the welder being used.

Setup and Shutdown

To set up a typical hot-air welder, proceed as follows:

 1. Close the air pressure regulator valve by turning the control handle counterclockwise until it is loose. This will prevent possible damage to the gauge from a sudden surge of excess air pressure.
2. Connect the regulator to a supply of either compressed air or inert gas. The standard rating for an air pressure regulator is 200 pounds of line pressure. If inert gas is used, a pressure-reducing valve is needed.
3. Turn on the air supply. The starting pressure depends on the wattage of the heating element and the air pressure. The operating air pressure requires slightly less air.

4. Connect the welder to a common 120-volt AC outlet. A three-prong grounded plug or temporary adapter must be used with the welder at all times.

5. Allow the welder to warm up at the recommended pressure. It is essential that either air or inert gas flows through the welder at all times, from warm-up to cool down, to prevent burnout of the heating element and further damage to the gun.

6. Select the proper tip and insert it with pliers to avoid touching the barrel while hot.

7. After the tip has been installed, the temperature will increase slightly due to back pressure. Allow 2 to 3 minutes for the tip to reach the required operating temperature.

8. Check the air temperature by holding a thermometer 1/4 inch from the hot air end of the torch. For most thermoplastics, the temperature should be in the 450- to 650-degree-Fahrenheit range. Information supplied with the welder usually includes a chart of welding temperatures.

9. If the temperature is too high to weld the material, increase the air pressure slightly until the temperature goes down. If the temperature is too low for the particular application, decrease the air pressure slightly until the temperature rises. When increasing and decreasing the air pressure, allow at least 1 to 3 minutes for the temperature to stabilize at the new setting.

10. Damage to the welder or heating element will not occur from too much air pressure; however, the element can become overheated by too little air pressure. When decreasing the air pressure, never allow the round nut that holds the barrel to the handle of the welder to become too hot to the touch. This is an indication of overheating.

11. A partially clogged dirt screen in the regulator or a fluctuation in the line voltage can also cause over- or underheating. Watch for these symptoms.

12. If the threads at the barrel's end become too tight, clean them with a good, high-temperature grease to prevent seizing.

13. When the welding is finished, disconnect the electric supply and let the air flow through the welder for a few minutes or until the barrel is cool to the touch. Then disconnect the air supply.

CAUTION: When welding plastics designed to hold liquids (such as gas tanks), keep in mind that the plastic may have absorbed some of the liquid over time. For this reason, the weld may not bond sufficiently.

Maintenance

If it becomes necessary to change the heating element, proceed as follows:

 1. While pushing the end of the barrel against a solid object, hold the handle tightly and push in. The pressure on the barrel will compress the element spring.

2. Use a spanner wrench to loosen the spanner nut. Keep the pressure on the handle and back off the nut all the way by hand.

3. Hold the barrel and place the complete welder on a bench. Remove the barrel.

4. Gently pull the element out of the handle. At the same time, unwind the cable, which is spiraled into the handle, until it is completely out of the handle.

5. Grasp the socket at the end of the wire tightly. Rock the element while pulling until the element is disconnected.

6. To install the new element, reverse the above procedure. Turn the element clockwise (about 1-1/2 turns) while pushing the wire gently back into the handle. This prevents kinking of the wire.

Other, more involved service procedures are best left to qualified repair technicians. Many manufacturers make it clear that disassembling the welder automatically invalidates the warranty.

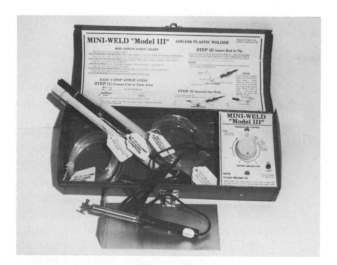

FIGURE 13-24   Typical airless welder

13.6 AIRLESS PLASTIC WELDING

Although only in existence for a relatively short period of time, airless welding has become very popular with the auto body repair industry (Figure 13-24). Compared to the hot-air method, it is less expensive, easier to learn, simpler to use, and more versatile. The hot-air method utilizes 3/16-inch-diameter welding rods, and 1/8-inch-diameter rods are used with the airless method. This not only provides a quicker rod melt, it also helps eliminate two troublesome problems: panel warpage and excess rod buildup.

When setting up an airless welder, the first and most important step is to put the temperature dial at the appropriate setting, depending on the specific thermosetting plastic being worked on. It is crucial that the temperature setting is correct; otherwise, the entire welding operation will be jeopardized. It will normally take about 3 minutes for the welder to fully warm up. As for the selection of the welding rod, there is another factor to consider besides size; namely, compatibility. Make sure the rod is the same as the damaged plastic or the weld will more than likely be unsuccessful. To this end, many airless welder manufacturers provide rod application charts. When the correct rod has been chosen, it is good practice to run a small piece of it through the welder to clean out the tip before beginning.

13.7 ULTRASONIC PLASTIC WELDING

The technology of ultrasonic plastic welding was originally developed solely as a means of assembly, but it is also suitable for making repairs. It relies on high-frequency vibratory energy to produce bonding without melting the base metal. Hand-held systems (Figure 13-25) are available in 20 and 40 kHz; they are equally adept at welding large parts and tight, hard-to-reach areas. Welding time is controlled by the power supply. And although the use of ultrasonics in the auto body shop is still in its infancy, the strong, clean, precise welds that the process produces can only increase its popularity in the years to come.

Most commonly used injection-molded plastics can be ultrasonically welded without the use of solvents, heat, or adhesives. Ultrasonic weldability depends on such factors as the plastic's melting temperature, elasticity, impact resistance, coefficient of friction, and thermal conductivity. Generally, the more rigid the plastic, the easier it is to weld ultrasonically. Thermoplastics such as polyethylene and polypropylene are ideal for ultrasonic welding, provided the welder can be positioned close to the joint area.

In the typical ultrasonic system, the vibration is generated in the transducer and then transmitted through the sonotrode, which is the equivalent of an electrode. The sonotrode tip directly contacts the workpiece, and an anvil supports the assembly. The best results are achieved when the sonotrode tip and anvil are contoured to accommodate the specific geometry of the parts being joined. An automatic ultrasonic welding cycle consists of lowering the sonotrode or raising the anvil, applying a clamping force, introducing the ultrasonic pulse or vibration, and retracting the sonotrode or anvil.

For spot welding of flat sheets, the tip is contoured to a radius of about 50 to 100 times the thickness of the sheet adjacent to the tip. The anvil face is usually flat. This provides a friction-type drive in which slippage can occur between the tip and the top sheet or between the anvil and the bottom sheet.

As in resistance spot welding, wear of the sonotrode tip and anvil depends upon the properties and geometry of the parts being welded. Tips made of high-speed tool steel are generally satisfactory for welding relatively soft materials, such as aluminum, copper, iron, and low carbon steel. Tips of hardenable nickel-base alloys usually provide good service life with hard, high-strength metals and alloys. The material used for the sonotrode tip is also satisfactory for the anvil face.

Frequently, longer tip life and more effective welding are possible using tips and anvils with rough faces because they tend to prevent slippage between them and the workpieces. The roughening can be done by sandblasting.

When sonotrode tips begin to show wear, they may be reconditioned by cleaning and burnishing.

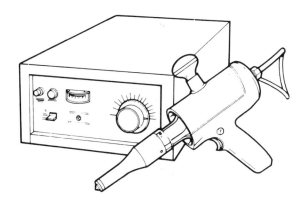

FIGURE 13-25 Typical hand-held ultrasonic welder and power supply

Light sanding with 400 grit paper is usually sufficient. If the wear is excessive, the tips should be replaced. Most ultrasonic welding machines have mechanically attached tips to simplify replacement.

Occasionally, the tip might tend to stick to the weld surface, particularly if improper machine settings are used. The sticking can be alleviated by increasing the clamping force or decreasing the welding time. With some materials, it is effective to apply a lubricant, such as a diluted soap solution, to the surfaces being joined. If these measures are not adequate, tip sticking can usually be eliminated by welding with a tip containing an insert of special grade tungsten carbide.

13.8 PLASTIC WELDING PROCEDURES

The basic procedures for hot-air and airless welding are very similar. To make a good plastic weld with either procedure, keep the following factors in mind:

- **Welding rod material.** Rods are frequently color coded to indicate the material they are made of. Unfortunately, the coding is not uniform among manufacturers, so it is important to use the reference information provided. If the rod is not compatible with the base material, the weld will not hold.
- **Temperature.** Too much heat will char, melt, or distort the plastic.
- **Pressure.** Too much pressure stretches and distorts the weld.
- **Angle between rod and part.** If too shallow, a proper weld will not be achieved.
- **Speed.** If the torch movement is too fast, it will not permit a good weld; too slow a speed can char the plastic.

The basic repair sequence is generally the same for both processes. That is:

 1. Prepare the damaged area.
2. Align the damaged area.
3. Make the weld.
4. Allow it to cool.
5. Sand. If pinholes, voids, and the like exist, bevel the edges of the defective area and add another bead of weld. Resand.
6. Paint or finish.

13.9 GENERAL WELDING TECHNIQUES

Welding plastic is not difficult when done in a careful and thorough manner. The following guidelines cannot be stressed enough:

- The welding rod must be compatible with the base material in order for the strength, hardness, and flexibility of the repair to be the same as the part. To this end, the rods are color coded for easy identification.
- Always test a welding rod for compatibility with the base material. To do this, melt the rod onto a hidden side of the damaged part, let the rod cool, then try to pull it from the part. If the rod is compatible, it will adhere.
- Pay close attention to the temperature setting of the welder; it must be correct for the type of plastic being welded.
- Never use oxygen or other flammable gases with a plastic welder.
- Never use a plastic welder, heat gun, or similar tool in wet or damp areas. Remember: electric shock can kill.
- Become proficient at horizontal welds before attempting the more difficult vertical and overhead types.
- Make welds as large as they have to be. The greater the surface area of a weld, the stronger the bond.
- Before beginning an airless weld, run a small piece of the welding rod through the welder to clean out the torch tip.
- Consult a supplier for the brands of tools and materials that best fit the shop's needs. Always read and follow the manufacturer's instructions carefully.

BASICS OF HOT-AIR WELDING

The typical hot-air plastic welding procedure is as follows:

 1. Set the welder to the proper temperature (if a temperature adjustment is provided).
2. Wash and clean the part with plastic cleaner; do not use conventional prep solvents or dewaxers. To remove silicone-type materials, use a conventional cleaner first, making sure to remove all residue.

3. V-groove the damaged area.
4. Bevel the part 1/4 inch beyond the damaged area.
5. Tack weld or tape the break line with aluminum body tape.
6. Select the proper welding rod and the welding tip best suited to the type of damage.
7. Make the weld. Allow it to cool and cure for about 30 minutes.
8. Grind, sand, or scrape the weld to the proper contour and shape.

Basics of Airless Welding

The typical airless plastic welding procedure is as follows:

 1. Wash the damaged part with soap and water and wipe or blow-dry.
2. Clean the damaged part with plastic cleaner.
3. Align and tape the broken or split sections with aluminum body tape.
4. V-groove at least 50 percent of the way through the panel for a two-sided weld and 75 percent of the way through for a one-sided weld (Figure 13-26).
5. Use a slow speed grinder and a No. 60 or No. 80 grit disc to remove the paint from around the damaged area. Blow dust free.
6. After setting the welder to the proper temperature, slowly feed the rod into the melt tube.
7. Apply light pressure to the rod to slowly force it out into the grooved area.
8. As the rod melts, start to move the torch tip very slowly in the direction of the intended weld. Overlap the edges of the groove with melted plastic while progressing forward.
9. After completing the weld, use the flat "shoe" part of the torch tip to smooth it out.

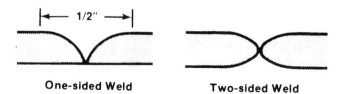

FIGURE 13-26   Proper V-grooves

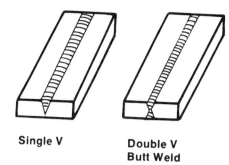

Single V   **Double V Butt Weld**

FIGURE 13-27   Single- and double-V butt welds produce strong joints.

When welding plastic, single- or double-V butt welds (Figure 13-27) produce the strongest joints; lap fillet welds are also good. When using a round- or V-shaped filler rod, the damaged area is prepared by slowly grinding, sanding, or shaving the adjoining surfaces with a sharp knife to produce a single- or double-V. For flat ribbon filler rods, V-grooving is not necessary. Wipe any dust or shavings from the joint with a clean, dry rag. The use of cleaning solvents is not generally recommended because they can soften the edges and cause poor welds.

Tack Welding

For this process, the edges to be joined must be aligned. On long tears where backup is difficult,

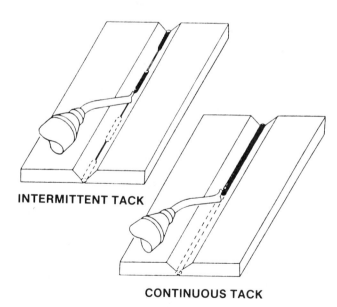

INTERMITTENT TACK

CONTINUOUS TACK

FIGURE 13-28   Two methods of making a tack weld

small tack welds can be made along the length of the tear to hold the two sides in place while doing the permanent weld. For larger areas, a patch can be made from a piece of plastic and tacked in place (Figure 13-28). To tack weld, proceed as follows:

1. Hold the damaged area in alignment with clamps or fixtures.
2. Using a tacking welding tip, fuse the two sides to form a thin hinge weld along the root of the crack. This is especially useful for long cracks because it allows easy adjustment and alignment of the edges.
3. Start the tacking by drawing the point of the welding tip along the joint. Press the tip in firmly, making sure to contact both sides of the crack; draw the tip smoothly and evenly along the line of the crack. No filler material is used when tacking.
4. The point of the tip will fuse both sides in a thin line at the root of the crack. The fused parts will hold the sides in alignment, though they can be separated and re-tacked if adjustment is necessary. Fuse the entire length of the crack. Tack welds can be broken away and re-welded if realignment of the pieces is required.

HAND WELDING

Hand welding involves several different stages, each of which must be mastered for a quality job to be performed.

Starting the Weld

Prepare the rod for welding by cutting the end at approximately a 60-degree angle. When starting a weld, the tip of the welder should be held about 1/4 to 1/2 inch above and parallel to the base material. The filler rod is held at a right angle to the work as shown in Figure 13-29, with the cut end of the rod positioned at the beginning of the weld.

Direct the hot air from the tip alternately at the rod and the base, but concentrating more on the rod. Always keep the filler rod in line with the V while pressing it into the seam. Light pressure (about 3 psi) is sufficient for achieving a good bond. Once the rod begins to stick to the plastic, start to move the torch and use the heat to control the flow. Be careful not to melt or char the base plastic or to overheat the rod. As the welding continues, a small bead should form ahead of the rod along the entire weld joint. A good start is essential because this is where most weld failures begin. For this reason, starting points on multiple-bead welds should be staggered whenever possible.

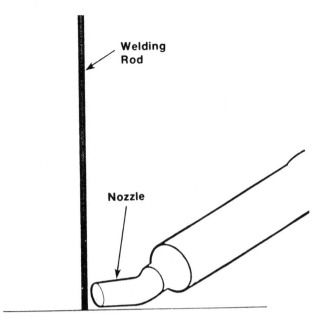

FIGURE 13-29 Keep the nozzle parallel to the base material and the rod at a right angle to the surface.

Continuing the Weld

Once the weld has been started, the torch should continue to fan from rod to base material. But because the rod now has less bulk, a greater amount of heat must be directed at the base material. Experience will help develop the proper technique.

Feeding the Rod

Throughout the welding process the rod is gradually being used up, making it necessary for the welder to renew his or her grip on the rod. Unless this is done carefully, the release of pressure might cause the rod to lift away from the weld and allow air to become trapped under the weld and weaken it. To prevent this, the welder must develop the skill of continuously applying pressure on the rod while repositioning the fingers. This can be done by applying pressure with the third and fourth fingers while moving the thumb and first finger up the rod. Another way is to hold down the rod in the weld with the third and fourth finger while repositioning the thumb and first finger. The rod is cool enough to do this because only the bottom of it is heated. However, care should be observed in touching new welds or aiming the torch near the fingers. Both methods of grip repositioning are shown in Figure 13-30.

Finishing the Weld

As the end of a weld is approached, maintain pressure on the rod as the heat is removed. Hold the

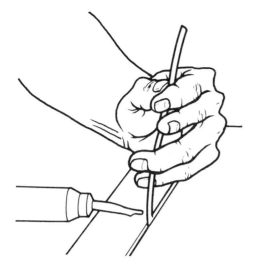

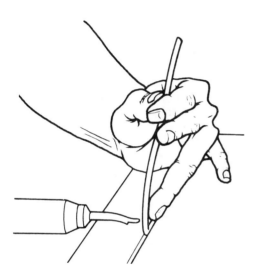

FIGURE 13-30 Methods of repositioning a grip on the rod

rod still for a few seconds to make sure it has cooled enough so it will not pull loose, then carefully cut the rod with a sharp knife or clippers. Do not attempt to pull the rod from the joint. About 15 minutes cooling time is needed for rigid plastic and 30 minutes for thermoplastic polyurethane.

Rough Grinding the Weld

The welded area can be smoothed by grinding with #36 grit emory or sandpaper. A 9- or 10-inch disc on a low-speed electric grinder will smooth large weld beads. Excess plastic can be removed with a sharp knife before grinding. Care must be taken not to overheat the weld area because it will soften. To speed up the work without damaging the weld, periodic cooling with water is necessary.

Checking the Weld

After rough grinding, the weld should be checked visually for defects. Any voids or cracks will make it unacceptable. Bending should not produce any cracks because a good weld is as strong as the part itself. Table 13-5 shows some typical welding defects, their causes, and corrections.

Finishing

The weld area can be finish sanded by using 220 grit sandpaper followed by a 320 grit. Either a belt or orbital sander may be used, plus hand sanding as required. If refinishing is to be done, follow the procedure designed specifically for plastics.

SPEED WELDING

On panel work, speed welding is very popular. Following are some techniques that are essential for quality speed welding.

Starting the Weld

With the high-speed torch held like a dagger and the hose on the outside of the wrist, bring the tip over the starting point a full 3 inches from the material so the hot air will not affect it (Figure 13-31). Cut the welding rod at a 60-degree angle, insert it into the preheating tube, and immediately place the pointed shoe of the tip on the material at the starting point. Hold the welder perpendicular to the material and push the rod through until it stops against the material at the starting point. If necessary, lift the torch slightly to allow the rod to pass under the shoe. Keeping a slight pressure on the rod with the left hand and only the weight of the torch on the shoe, pull the torch slowly toward you. The weld is now started.

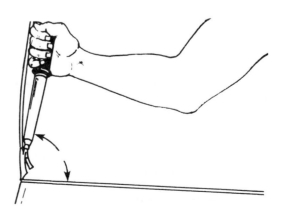

FIGURE 13-31 Starting a speed weld

507

TABLE 13-5: PLASTIC WELDING TROUBLESHOOTING GUIDE

Problem	Cause	Remedy
Porous weld	1. Porous weld rod 2. Balance of heat on rod 3. Welding too fast 4. Rod too large 5. Improper starts or stops 6. Improper crossing of beads 7. Stretching rod	1. Inspect rod. 2. Use proper fanning motion. 3. Check welding temperature. 4. Weld beads in proper sequence. 5. Cut rod at angle, but cool before releasing. 6. Stagger starts and overlap splices 1/2 inch.
Poor penetration	1. Faulty preparation 2. Rod too large 3. Welding too fast 4. Not enough root gap	1. Use 60° bevel. 2. Use small rod at root. 3. Check for flow liners while welding. 4. Use tacking tip or leave 1/32-inch root gap and clamp pieces.
Scorching	1. Temperature too high 2. Welding too slowly 3. Uneven heating 4. Material too cold	1. Increase airflow. 2. Hold constant speed. 3. Use correct fanning motion. 4. Preheat material in cold weather.
Distortion	1. Overheating at joint 2. Welding too slowly 3. Rod too small 4. Improper sequence	1. Allow each bead to cool. 2. Weld at constant speed; use speed tip. 3. Use larger sized or triangular-shaped rod. 4. Offset pieces before welding. 5. Use double V or backup weld. 6. Backup weld with metal.
Warping	1. Shrinkage of material 2. Overheating 3. Faulty preparation 4. Faulty clamping of parts	1. Preheat material to relieve stress. 2. Weld rapidly—use backup weld. 3. Too much root gap 4. Clamp parts properly; back up to cool. 5. For multilayer welds, allow time for each bead to cool.
Poor Appearance	1. Uneven pressure 2. Excessive stretching 3. Uneven heating	1. Practice starting, stopping, and finger manipulation on rod. 2. Hold rod at proper angle. 3. Use slow, uniform fanning motion, heating both rod and material (for speed welding: use only moderate pressure, constant speed, keep shoe free of residue).
Stress cracking	1. Improper welding temperature 2. Undue stress or weld 3. Chemical attack 4. Rod and base material not same composition 5. Oxidation or degradation of weld	1. Use recommended welding temperature. 2. Allow for expansion and contraction. 3. Stay within known chemical resistance and working temperatures of material. 4. Use similar materials and inert gas for welding. 5. Refer to recommended application.
Poor fusion	1. Faulty preparation 2. Improper welding techniques 3. Wrong speed 4. Improper choice of rod 5. Wrong temperature	1. Clean materials before welding. 2. Keep pressure and fanning motion constant. 3. Take more time by welding at lower temperatures. 4. Use small rod at root and large rods at top—practice proper sequence. 5. Preheat materials when necessary. 6. Clamp parts securely.

CAUTION: Once the weld is started, do not stop. If the forward movement must pause for any reason, pull the tip off the rod immediately; if this is not done, the rod will melt into the tip's feed tube. Clean the feeder foot with a soft wire brush as soon as the welding is completed.

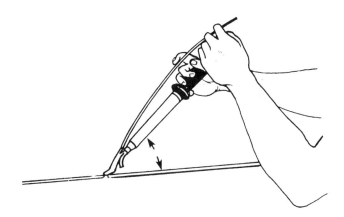

FIGURE 13-32 Continuing a speed weld

Continuing the Weld

In the first inch or two of travel, the rod should be helped along by pushing it into the tube with slight pressure. Once the weld has been properly started, the torch is brought to a 45-degree angle; the rod will now feed automatically without further help. As the torch moves along, visual inspection is needed to monitor the quality of the weld being produced.

The angle between the welder and base material determines the welding rate. Since the preheater hole in the speed tip precedes the shoe, the angle of the welder to the material being welded determines how close the hole is to the material and how much preheating is being done. It is for this reason the torch is held at a 90-degree angle when starting the weld and at 45 degrees thereafter (Figure 13-32). When a visual inspection of the weld indicates a welding rate that is too fast, the torch should be brought back to the 90-degree angle temporarily to slow it down, then gradually moved to the desired angle for proper welding speed. It is important that the welder is held in such a way that the preheater hole and the shoe are always in line with the direction of the weld, so that only the material in front of the shoe is preheated. A heat pattern on the base material indicates the area being preheated. The rod should always be welded in the center of that pattern.

Finishing the Weld

It is important to remember that, once started, speed welding must be maintained at a fairly constant rate. The torch cannot be held still. To stop welding before the rod is used up, bring the torch back past the 90-degree angle and cut off the rod with the end of the shoe (Figure 13-33). This can also be accomplished by pulling the speed tip off the remaining rod. When cutting the rod with the shoe, the remaining rod must be removed promptly from the preheater tube or it will char or melt, clog the tube, and make it necessary for the tube to be cleaned out by inserting a new rod in it.

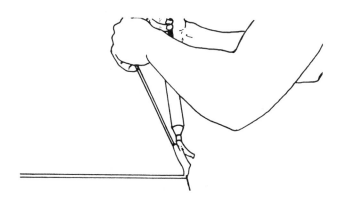

FIGURE 13-33 Finishing a speed weld

A good speed weld in a V-joint will have a slightly higher crown and more uniformity than the normal hand weld. It should appear smooth and shiny, with a slight bead on each side. For best results and faster welding speed, the shoe on the speed tip should be cleaned occasionally with a wire brush to remove any residue that might cling to it and create drag on the rod.

REPAIRING INTERIOR AND UNREINFORCED HARD PLASTICS

Dash pads or padded instrument panels are expensive to replace and are therefore perfect candidates for repair (Figure 13-34). Most dash pads are made of vinyl-clad urethane foam. Surface dents in foam dash covers, armrests, and other padded interior parts are common in collision repair. These dents can often be repaired by applying heat as follows:

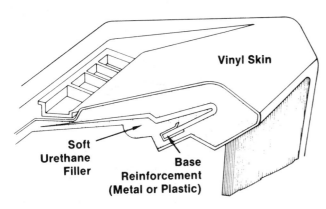

Vinyl Skin

Soft Urethane Filler

Base Reinforcement (Metal or Plastic)

FIGURE 13-34   Working with dash pads

1. Soak the dent with a damp sponge or cloth for about half a minute. Do not wipe dry. Keep the dented area moist.

2. Using a heat gun, heat the area around the dent, holding the heat source 10 to 12 inches from the surface. Keep it moving in a circular motion at all times, working from the outside in.

3. Heat the area to around 120 and 140 degrees Fahrenheit. Do not overheat the vinyl because it might blister.

4. Keep heating the area until it is too uncomfortable to touch.

5. Using gloves, massage the pad, forcing the material toward the center of the dent or deformation. The area might have to be reheated and massaged more than once. In some cases, the heat alone might repair the damage.

6. When the deformation has been removed, cool the area quickly with a damp sponge or cloth.

Repairing Dash Pads

To repair the dash panel, proceed in the following manner:

1. Set up the airless welder for the proper temperature, if adjustable. Use the urethane setting, if so equipped.

2. Wash the pad with soap and water, dry, and clean with plastic cleaner.

3. If the damaged area is brittle, warm with a heat gun. If there are curled or jagged edges, cut them away.

4. V-groove at least 1/4 inch into the foam padding. Bevel the edges as much as possible. Rough up the area for about 1/4 inch around the V-groove.

5. Turn the welder so the shoe is facing up. Feed the filler rod slowly through the welder. Start the weld at the bottom of the groove and completely fill with melted rod until it is flush with the surface.

6. Smooth out the excess rod buildup. Feather it out over the beveled edges for at least 1/4 inch on each side of the groove.

7. Cool the weld and grind away any remaining excess rod buildup. Rough up the vinyl for about 2 inches beyond the weld on each side for good filler adhesion.

8. Use a flexible filler material designed for use on vinyl to get the desired contour. Allow the filler to cure.

9. Contour sand to remove the tacky glaze. If any filler is accidentally sanded through, apply a skin coat and re-sand.

Using Heat to Reshape Plastics

Thermoplastic parts such as urethane bumper covers that are bent, stretched, or deformed in a collision can often be straightened with heat. This is because plastic has a "memory," which means that the piece wants to keep the shape in which it was molded. If it is bent or scratched, it will return to its original shape if heat is applied. Use a concentrated heat source, such as a heat lamp or high-temperature heat gun. To reshape a distorted bumper cover, use the following procedure:

1. Thoroughly wash the piece with soap and water.

2. Clean with plastic cleaner. Make sure to remove all road tar, oil, grease, and undercoating.

3. Blow or wipe dry.

4. Apply heat directly to the distorted area. When the opposite side of the piece becomes uncomfortable to the touch, the piece has been heated enough.

5. Use a paint paddle, squeegee, or wood block to help reshape the piece if necessary.

6. Lastly, quick-cool the area by applying cold water with a sponge or rag.

Tab Replacement for Exterior Plastic Surfaces

The following is the procedure for rebuilding a mounting tab that has been torn off:

1. Begin by cleaning the piece as described before.
2. Bevel back the torn edges of the mounting tabs at least 1/4 inch on both sides.
3. Rough up the plastic and wipe dust free.
4. Use aluminum body tape to build a form in the shape of the missing tab. The edges are turned up to form the thickness of the new tab.
5. Set the temperature dial on the welder for the urethane rod. Allow the unit to warm up.
6. Begin the weld, pushing the rod slowly through the melt tube. Slightly overfill the form, working the filler material into the base material.
7. Smooth and shape the weld. Quick-cool the weld area.
8. Remove the tape and V-groove along the tear line on the other side about halfway through the material.
9. Fill in the groove and quick-cool. Finish the weld to the desired contour using a slow-speed grinder with a 60 or 80 grit disc.

13.10 ULTRASONIC STUD WELDING

Ultrasonic stud welding, a variation of the shear joint, is a reliable technique that can be used to join plastic parts at a single point or at numerous locations. In many applications requiring permanent assembly, a continuous weld is not required. With similar materials, this type of assembly can be effectively and economically accomplished using ultrasonic stud welding. The power requirement is low because of the small weld area, and the welding cycle is short, almost always less than half a second.

Figure 13-35 shows the basic stud weld joint before, during, and after welding. The weld is made along the circumference of the stud; its strength is a function of the stud diameter and the depth of the weld. Maximum tensile strength is achieved when the depth of the weld equals half the diameter of the stud. The radial interference (dimension A) must be uniform and should generally be 0.008 to 0.012 inch for studs having a diameter of 0.5 inch or less. The hole should be a sufficient distance from the edge to prevent breakout; a minimum of 0.125 inch is recommended.

In the joint, the recess can be on the end of the stud or in the mouth of the hole, as shown in the

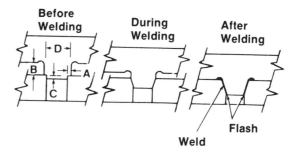

FIGURE 13-35   Basic ultrasonic stud welding joint

examples. With the latter, a small chamfer can be used for rapid alignment. To reduce stress concentration, a good-sized fillet radius should be incorporated at the base of the stud. Recessing the fillet below the surface allows flush contact of the parts.

Other ways in which the ultrasonic stud weld can be used are illustrated in Figure 13-36. A third dissimilar material can be locked in place, as in view A. View B shows separate molded rivets in lieu of metal self-tapping screws. Unlike metal fasteners, this produces a relatively stress-free assembly.

Figure 13-37 shows a variation that can be used where appearance is important or an uninterrupted surface is required. The stud is welded into a boss, whose outside diameter can be no less than twice the stud diameter. When welding into a blind hole, it might be necessary to provide an outlet for air. Two possibilities are shown: a center hole through the stud (view A), or a small, narrow slot in the interior wall of the boss (view B).

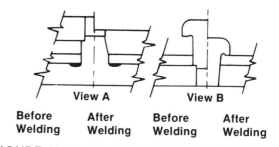

FIGURE 13-36   Variations of the basic stud joint

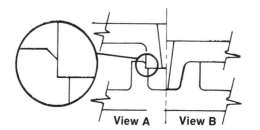

FIGURE 13-37   Welding a stud in a blind hole

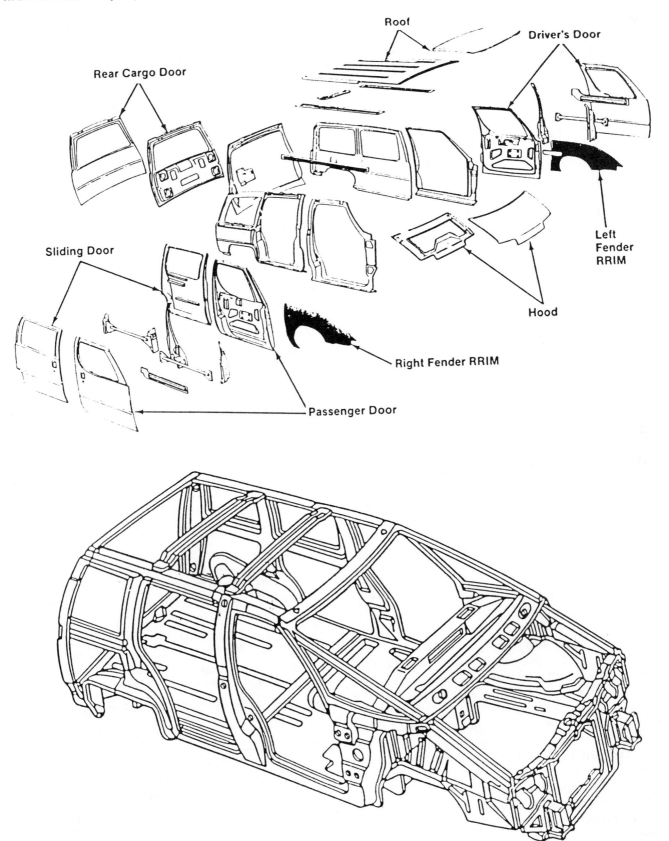

FIGURE 13-38   SMC panels bonded to a steel space frame, introducing a new type of construction for production vehicles

13.11 REPAIR OF REINFORCED PLASTIC

Figure 13-38 illustrates the first vehicle that was to be built of external unibody panels made of plastic that were bonded to the space frame. That is, the space frame is galvanized metal, with the remainder of vehicle exterior panels being urethane composites and sheet molded compounds (SMC), which help with vehicle rigidity. Parts made of SMC are the doors, quarter panels, and roof. Urethane parts consist of the fascias and fenders. Even the fuel tank is made of plastic—a polyethylene composite. Table 13-6 provides an overview of reinforced plastic repair materials.

SMC is very much like fiberglass in its composition. The big difference between the two materials is how they are manufactured and the materials used to make them. Fiberglass is laid up by hand or is sprayed into a mold. SMC, on the other hand, uses a sheet of preformed, partially cured material compressed between the heated halves of both a male and female mold. Pressure and temperature work together to cure the resin. The result is a strong, dense panel of controlled thickness, which has a smooth finish on both sides. The repair procedures are basically the same. Generally speaking, however, do not use traditional fiberglass resin for SMC repairs. The reason is very simple. Traditional fiberglass was made up of about 70 percent polyester resin and 30 percent glass fibers. The repair resin used on fiberglass was a polyester product, so it generally worked well. Fiberglass resin does not have the same type of performance on SMC, because each individual manufacturer might have a different formula. (A common one is 40 percent polyester resin, 20 percent glass fibers, 33 percent calcium carbonate filler material, and 7 percent other materials.) So, fiberglass resin will not provide a uniform performance on all of the SMC panels being produced today. Therefore, it is not recommended for use.

> **CAUTION:** Do not intermix fiberglass and SMC repair products. Though fiberglass and SMC are very similar, their repair materials are not.

WORKING WITH SMC AND FIBERGLASS

Working with SMC and fiberglass requires thinking about safety at all times. The resin and related ingredients can irritate the skin and stomach lining. The curing agent or hardener is generally a methyl ethyl ketone peroxide, which produces harmful vapors. Read and understand the following safety points before using any fiberglass products:

- Read all label instructions and warnings carefully.
- Wear rubber gloves when working with fiberglass and resin or hardener. Long sleeve shirts with buttoned collar and cuffs are helpful in preventing sanding dust from getting on the skin.
- A protective skin cream should be used on any exposed areas of the body.
- If the resin or hardener comes in contact with the skin, wash with borax soap and water or denatured alcohol.

Type of Repair	Applicable Repair Product				
	Panel Adhesive	Patching Adhesive	Structural Filler	Cosmetic Filler	Glass Fiber Reinforcement
Panel Replacement	X				
Panel Sectioning	X		X_1	X_1	X
One-Sided Repairs				X_1	
Two-Sided Repairs	X_2	X_2	X	X	X

TABLE 13-6: REINFORCED PLASTIC REPAIR MATERIAL SELECTION CHART

Notes: 1. Some panel adhesives can also be used as structural and cosmetic fillers, depending on sanding characteristics.
2. Panel adhesives can also be used as patching adhesives, but not vice versa.

- Always work in a well-ventilated area of the shop.
- Wear a respirator to avoid inhaling sanding dust and resin vapors.
- When making fiberglass repairs, mask the surrounding areas to avoid spilling resin on them.
- Clean all tools and equipment with lacquer thinner immediately after use. Dispose of the leftover mixed material in a safe container.

Types of Damage

The damage that generally occurs in SMC and fiberglass panels includes:

- One-sided damage to a plastic panel, such as a scratch or gouge.
- Punctures to and fractures of the plastic panels.
- Panel separation, where the panel pulls away from the metal frame.
- Severe damage to the plastic panel, which requires full or partial panel replacement.
- Bends and distortions of the sheet metal space frame, which can be repaired by pulling and straightening.
- Severe kinks and bends to the space frame, which call for replacement of that piece along factory seams or by structural sectioning.

Remember, it is likely that combinations of these types of damage will occur on a single vehicle. As with conventional unibody designs, damage to the metal space frame will include sidesway, sag, collapse, and twist.

Depending on the location and amount of damage, there are four different types of repairs. These are:

- Single-sided repair
- Two-sided repair
- Panel sectioning
- Full panel replacement

These repairs share some common aspects, such as tools and materials.

Tools and Materials Needed to Make Repairs

Most of the tools used for repairs of reinforced plastics should already be available in a well-equipped body shop. The only special tools will be the adhesive applicators, which allow two-part adhesives to be dispensed at a constant rate. There are two types of applicators:

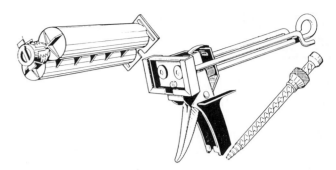

FIGURE 13-39   Typical dual cartridge, shown with a manual applicator

- Pneumatic
- Hand-operated (Figure 13-39)

The pneumatic applicator uses compressed air to force the materials out. The hand-operated applicator works like a caulking gun. Hand-applied pressure is used to force material out of the tubes.

To use either type of applicators, follow these simple rules:

- Follow manufacturer's instructions.
- Check for proper product flow.
- Check for consistent mix of two-component product.
- When changing cartridges, run a new test bead.
- If saving part of a cartridge, leave static mixing nozzle in place.

Types of Adhesives

Many of the materials that are used for SMC repair are two-component adhesive products. That means they have a base material and a hardener, which must be mixed together in the proper ratio. It is very important that they are mixed in the ratio called for by the product manufacturer and that both components are thoroughly and adequately mixed together before use.

After mixing, remember that each product of the system has a work life or open time. This is the time in which it is possible to realign or change the position of the panels being replaced and still have the adhesive set up for a good bond. This work life will be provided by the manufacturer.

Two-component adhesives have a set cure time during which the piece should not be moved. This allows the adhesive to set up properly. The cure time of some of the products used in SMC repair can be shortened with the application of heat.

Temperature and humidity can affect work and cure times. The product manufacturer will provide a temperature range for the product to be used, as well as guidelines for heat curing of the product. Excessive humidity can slow the curing process.

Fillers and Types of Glass Cloth

Two products are specifically formulated for use on SMC. They are:

- **Cosmetic filler.** Typically a two-part epoxy or polyester filler used to cover up minor imperfections. Do not use body fillers designed for sheet metal on SMC.
- **Structural fillers.** Those used to fill the larger gaps in the panel structure. Structural fillers add to the panel's structural rigidity.

There are several different types of glass cloth and matting available. Choose unidirectional cloth, woven glass cloths, or nylon screening. The main thing to remember is that the cloth weave must be loose enough to allow the adhesive to fully saturate the cloth, leaving no air space around the weave.

SINGLE-SIDED REPAIRS

Single-sided damage is surface damage or damage that does not penetrate or fracture the rear of the panel. In some cases damage might pass all the way through a panel, but no pieces of panel have been broken away. If the break is clean and all of the reinforcing fibers have stayed in place, then a single-sided repair would be adequate. In this case, the technician must make the bevel very deep to penetrate the fibers in the panel (Figure 13-40A). The broken fibers must come into contact with the adhesive.

The following is a typical single-sided repair procedure:

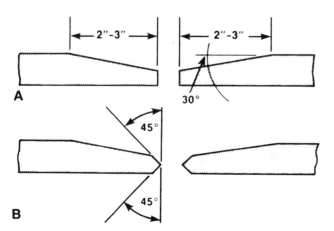

A **B** 30° 45° 45°

FIGURE 13-40 Beveling the inside and outside of the repair area permits better adhesion.

 1. Clean the area with soap and water.
2. Clean the repair area using mild wax and grease remover.
3. Remove paint from the surrounding area by sanding with #80 grit sandpaper.
4. Scuff sand the area surrounding the damage.
5. Bevel the damaged area to provide an adequate area for bonding.
6. Mix two-part SMC-compatible filler according to the manufacturer's instructions. Apply the filler.
7. Apply the filler to cure according to the manufacturer's recommendations.

Once the filler has been sanded, apply additional coats as required and resand. The product manufacturer will provide grit recommendations.

TWO-SIDED REPAIRS

Damage that passes all of the way through the panel involving the reinforcing fibers, such as cracks and holes, usually requires a two-sided repair (Figure 13-40B). A backing strip or patch is used to restore the required strength. The patch also forms a foundation on which to build and form the exterior surface to match the original contour of the panel.

To make either a one-sided or two-sided repair in either an SMC or fiberglass panel, proceed as follows:

 1. Clean the surface surrounding the damage with a good commercial grease and wax remover. Use a #36 grinding disc to remove all paint and primer at least 3 inches beyond the repair area.
2. Grind, file, or use a hacksaw to remove all cracked or splintered material away from the hole on both the inside and outside of the repair area.
3. Remove any dirt, sound deadener, and the like from the inner surface of the repair area. Clean with reducer, lacquer thinner, or a similar solvent.
4. Scuff around the hole with #80 grit paper to provide a good bonding surface.
5. Bevel the inside and outside edge of the repair area about 30 degrees to permit better patch adhesion.
6. Clean the repair surface thoroughly with reducer or thinner.
7. Cut several pieces of fiberglass cloth or mat large enough to cover the hole and the

FIGURE 13-41   Applying resin to the mat strips

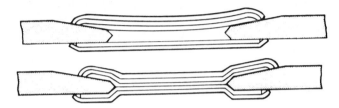

FIGURE 13-42   The layers of saturated glass cloth should contact the outside repair area.

scuffed area. The exact number will vary depending on the thickness of the original panel, but five is usually a good number to start with.

8. Prepare a mixture of resin and hardener following the label recommendations. Using a small paintbrush, saturate at least two layers of the fiberglass cloth with the activated resin mix and apply it to the inside or back surface of the repair area (Figure 13-41). Make sure the cloth fully contacts the scuffed area surrounding the hole.

CAUTION: If working with an SMC panel, be sure to use special resin designed for use with SMC. Standard fiberglass resins will not bond to SMC.

9. Saturate three more layers of cloth with the mix. Apply it to the outside surface, making certain that these layers fully contact the inner layers and the scuffed outside repair area (Figure 13-42).

10. With all of the layers of cloth in place, form a saucer-like depression in them. This is

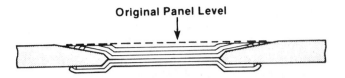

FIGURE 13-43   Sand the patch slightly below the contour of the panel.

FIGURE 13-44   Hardened patching material

necessary to increase the depth of the repair material. Use a rubber squeegee to work out any air bubbles.

11. Clean all tools with lacquer thinner immediately after use.

12. Let the saturated cloth become tacky. An infrared heat lamp can be used to speed up the process; if one is used, keep it 12 to 15 inches away from the surface. Do not heat the repair area above 200 degrees Fahrenheit, because too much heat will distort the material.

13. With #50 grit paper, disc sand the patch slightly below the contour of the panel (Figure 13-43).

14. Prepare more fiberglass resin mix. Use a plastic spreader to fill the depression in the repair area, leaving a sufficient mound of material to grind down smooth and flush.

15. Allow the patch to harden (Figure 13-44). Again, a heat lamp can be used to speed the curing process.

16. When the patch is fully hardened, sand the excess material down to the basic contour, using #80 grit paper and a sanding block or pad. Finish sand with #120 or finer grit paper.

This same repair can be made by attaching sheet metal to the back side of the panel with sheet metal screws (Figure 13-45). Sand the metal and both the inner and outer sides of the hole to provide good adherence for the repair material. Before fastening the sheet metal, apply resin mix to both sides of the rim of the hole. Follow the above procedure for the remainder of the repair.

When the inner side of the hole is not accessible, apply a fiberglass patch to the outer side only. After the usual cleaning and sanding operations, apply

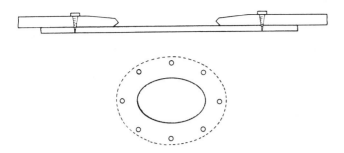

FIGURE 13-45   Sheet metal attached to the back side of a damaged panel

several layers of fiberglass cloth to the outer side of the hole. Before it dries, make a saucer-like depression in the cloth to provide greater depth for the repair material.

Panel Replacement and Sectioning

When replacing a full panel, keep in mind that there are some panels that cannot be replaced in their entirety, but some others should probably be replaced and not repaired.

Proper sectioning requires that the technician understands the areas of the vehicle that are most appropriate for sectioning and how to avoid problems with horizontal bracing, rivets, and concealed parts (Figure 13-46). The replacement panel ordered will depend on the amount and location of the damage. Using the left rear quarter panel as an example, there are three possibilities (Figure 13-47).

The mill and drill pads (Figure 13-48) are used to help the factory hold panels in place while the adhesive cures. These mill and drill pads will also help the technician to hold, align, and level replacement panels. If a panel is to be sectioned, it should be done between mill and drill pad locations.

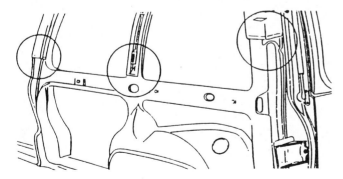

FIGURE 13-46   Sectioning locations and procedures

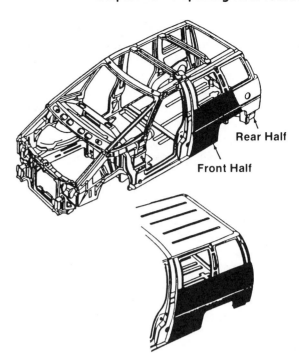

FIGURE 13-47   Replacement panels

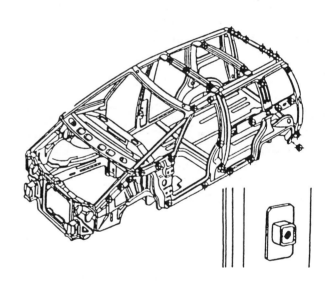

FIGURE 13-48   Mill and drill pads

Preparing for Sectioning

After removing the scrap panel pieces, prepare the space frame to receive the new panel.

- Remove the old adhesive from the space frame.
- Reprime the space frame, if necessary.
- Bevel the edges of the old panel.
- Clean the back side of the old panel.

517

Bevel the outside edges of the remaining panel edges to a 20-degree taper. Sand and clean the back sides of the original panels where the backing strips will be attached. Backing patches are made using scrap material, which duplicates the original panel contour as closely as possible. They should extend to about 2 inches on either side of the sectioning location. Clean the backing pieces and remove the paint from those places where adhesive will be applied.

When fitting the new panel, measure the service panel for fit. Trim the panel to size and check the fit again. Leave a 1/2-inch gap between the old and the replacement panel. When proper fit has been established, the panel can be prepared for the adhesive. Sand or grind the bevels into the panel where they mate to the existing panels on the vehicle (Figure 13-49). Clean and scuff the back sides of the service panel that will receive a backing patch, including any area that mates to a horizontal support on the space frame.

When making a filler patch, build it on a piece of waxed paper (Figure 13-50). Put down a layer of adhesive roughly the width of the gap between the two panels. Cut a strip of fiberglass cloth as wide as the top of the gap between the panels. Lay it on the adhesive. Apply more adhesive and cut a piece of cloth as wide as the panel gap at the bottom of the gap. Lay this down and apply more adhesive. Use the saturation roller.

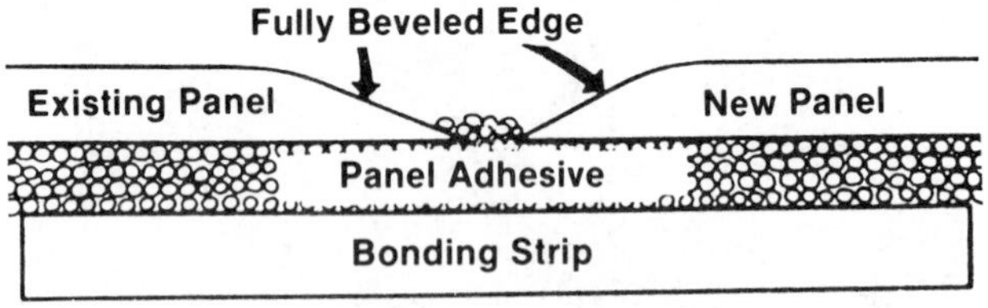

SMC Door Skin Replacement

A door skin replacement is a straightforward repair because most are made of an inner and an outer piece of SMC bonded together. The exterior of the door might be repaired, using a single-sided or two-sided repair, or the door skin might be replaced. Outer door skins are available as service parts.

The outer panel of the door usually overlaps the inner panel slightly. This forms a little lip around the door. Grind away this lip to expose the joint between the outer and inner panels. Use caution to avoid damaging the inner panel that must be saved.

There are two methods of separating the door pieces. They are:

1. Use heat and a putty knife.
   - Remove the lip of the panel with an air grinder.
   - Apply heat to the edge of the panels.
   - Force the putty knife between the panels, separating the adhesive bond.
2. Use an air chisel (Figure 13-51).
   - Force the chisel between the panels.
   - Do not damage the inner panel.
   - If the chisel begins to cut through the panel, remove it and try cutting from the outer direction.

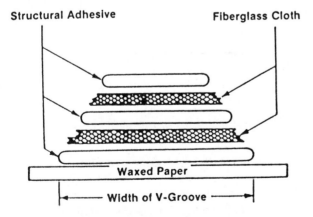

FIGURE 13-49 Fitting the new panel

FIGURE 13-50 Making a filler patch

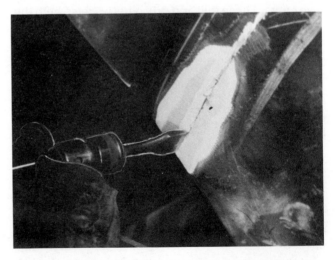

FIGURE 13-51 Using an air chisel to separate the panel from the body

The mating edges of the inner panel are now cleaned of loose adhesive or SMC or fiberglass parts.

Usually there is an inner UHSS reinforcement that runs the length of both front doors and the sliding cargo door. There will also be some inner SMC reinforcements attached directly to the SMC outer door skin itself. Look for any inner reinforcements by removing the inner door skin. The leading and trailing edges inside the doors are bonded with a metal reinforcement to which the intrusion beams are bolted. Look at these areas carefully for damage if there has been an impact to the intrusion beam.

USING MOLDED CORES

Naturally, holes are much more difficult to repair in a curved portion of a fiberglass panel than those on a flat surface. Basically, the only solution in such a case (short of purchasing a new panel section) is to use the mold core method of replacement. This is often the quickest and cheapest way to repair a curved fiberglass surface; the entire process takes almost an hour. While the procedure illustrated in Figure 13-52 and described here relates to a rear fender section, the principle can be applied to any type of curved fiberglass panel damage. The mold core is made as follows:

1. First off, locate an undamaged panel on another vehicle that matches the damaged one; this will be used as a model. A new or used car can be employed, since the model vehicle will not be harmed if care is taken.
2. On the model vehicle, mask off an area slightly larger than the damaged area. Apply additional masking paper and tape to the surrounding area, especially on the low side of the panel. This will prevent any resin from getting on the finish.
3. Coat the area being used as a mold with paste floor wax. Leave a wet coat of wax all over the surface. A piece of waxed paper can be substituted for the coat of wax; be sure that it is taped firmly in place (Figure 13-53A).
4. Cut several pieces of special fiberglass mold veil (thin fiberglass mat material) in sizes ranging from 2 by 4 inches to 4 by 6 inches. Standard fiberglass mats can be used if the panel does not have reverse curves.
5. Mix the fiberglass resin and hardener following the instructions on the label of both products.
6. Starting from one corner of the mold area, place pieces of veil on the waxed area so each edge overlaps the next one; use just one layer of veil (Figure 13-53B).
7. Apply the resin/hardener to the veil material with a paintbrush (Figure 13-53C). Force the mixture into the curved surfaces and around corners with the tips of the bristles.
8. Use the smaller pieces of veil along the edges and on difficult curves. Additional resin can be applied if needed, brushing in one direction only to force the material into the indentations. In all cases, use only one layer of veil.

CAUTION: Be sure that the resin does not get on any part of the model vehicle that is not coated with wax.

9. After the veil pieces have been applied to the entire waxed area, allow the mold core to cure a minimum of 1 hour.
10. Once the mold core has hardened, gently work the piece loose from the model vehicle (Figure 13-53D). The core should be an exact reproduction of this section of the panel.
11. Remove the floor wax protecting the model vehicle's paint finish using a wax and grease remover. Then polish this section of the panel.
12. Since the mold core is generally a little larger than the original panel, place it under the damaged panel and align. If necessary, trim down the edges, the core, and the damaged panel slightly where needed for better alignment. The edges of the damaged panel and core must also be cleaned.

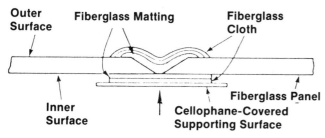

FIGURE 13-52 The repair area covered with fiberglass cloth

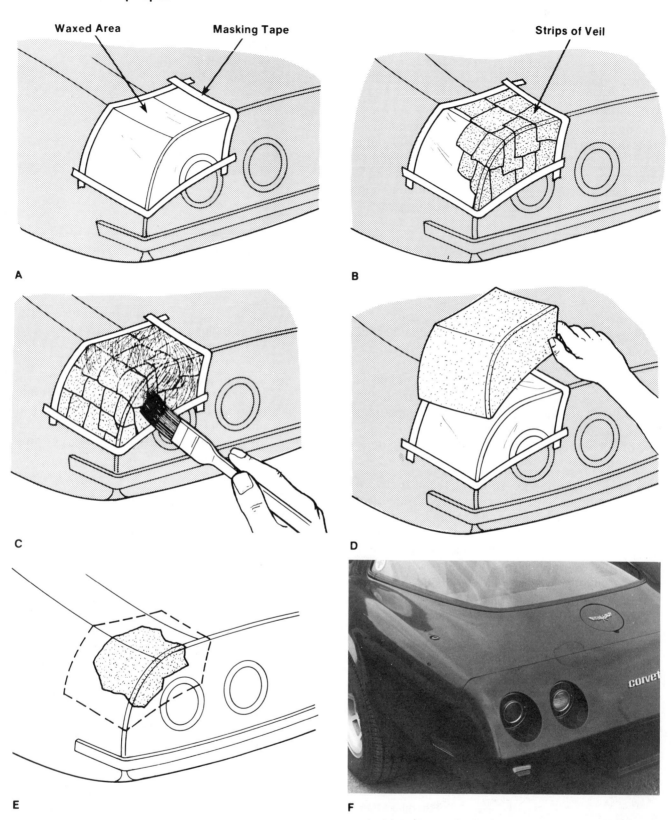

FIGURE 13-53   Steps in making a fiberglass core: (A) coat the area being used as a mold model with paste floor wax or a piece of waxed paper; (B) place pieces of fiberglass veil over the waxed or waxed paper surface; (C) apply resin/hardener to the veil material; (D) remove the mold core from the model; (E) cement the core piece in place; (F) the completed job. *(Courtesy of Unican Corp.)*

13. Using fiberglass adhesive, cement the mold core in place (Figure 13-53E). Allow the core and panel to cure.

14. Grind back the original damaged edges to a taper or bevel, maintaining the desired contour.

15. Lay the fiberglass mat, which has been soaked in resin/hardener, on the taper or bevel and over the entire inner core. Once the mat has hardened, level it with a coat of fiberglass filler. Then prepare it for painting (Figure 13-53F).

In some instances, it might not be possible to place the core on the inside of the damaged panel. In this case, the damaged portion must be cut out to the exact size of the core. After the panel has been trimmed and its edges beveled, tabs must be installed to support the core from the inside. These tabs can be made from pieces of the salvaged fiberglass panel or from fiberglass cloth strips saturated in resin/hardener.

After cleaning and sanding the inside sections, attach the tabs to the inside edge of the panel and bond with fiberglass adhesive. Vise grips can be used to hold the tabs in place while bonding. Taper the edge of the opening and place the core on the tabs. Fasten the core to the tabs with fiberglass adhesive. Grind down any high spots so that layers of fiberglass mat can be added.

Place the saturated mats over the core, extending about 1-1/2 to 2 inches beyond the hole in all directions. Work each layer with a spatula or squeegee to remove all air pockets. Additional resin can be added with a paintbrush to secure the layers. Allow the resin/hardener time to cure sufficiently, then sand the surface level. For a smooth surface, use fiberglass filler to finish the job.

Repairing RRIM

Reinforced reaction injection molded (RRIM) parts are becoming more common. RRIM actually describes a combination of a manufacturing process and the material most commonly used. It is usually found in fenders and bumper covers.

RRIM is a two-part polyurea composite. Part A is the isocyanate. Part B contains the reinforced fibers, resins, and a catalyst. The two parts are first mixed in a special mixing chamber, then injected into a mold. Since it is a thermosetting plastic, heat (100 to 140 degrees Fahrenheit) is applied to the mold to cure the material. The molded product is made to be stiff yet flexible. This allows RRIM material to absorb minor impacts without damage. This makes it an ideal material to use for exposed areas such as front fenders, bumpers, and front and rear fascias. Although minor impacts/bumps might not dent RRIM material, damage will likely occur in a heavier collision.

 **SHOP TALK**

Plastic welding is not the repair choice for RRIM. Damage is repaired using an adhesive.

Gouges and punctures can be repaired using a structural adhesive. If the damage is a puncture that extends through the panel, a backing patch is required. It is very important to follow the adhesive manufacturer's mixing ratio exactly. Mix by beading the proper amount of each part on a flat, nonporous material, then work the two parts together. Make note of the manufacturer's listed work life for the adhesive once it has been mixed. This lets the technician know how long he/she has to apply the product, and provides a gauge of how much to mix at one time. Also, note the cure time. This tells the technician how long he/she must wait before doing more work on the repair. The cure time varies depending on the product used as well as temperature and humidity.

To make a typical backing patch repair, proceed as follows:

 1. Clean the damaged area thoroughly using the plastic cleaner recommended by the manufacturer and a clean cloth. Wipe dry.

2. Remove any paint film in and around the damage with an orbital sander and #180 grit disc.

3. Using a #50 grit disc, enlarge the damaged area, tapering out the damage for about 1 inch. Wipe or blow away any loose particles.

4. Clean the back side of the damaged area with the plastic cleaner.

5. Use a #50 grit disk to scuff sand the area. Extend the area to about 1-1/2 inches beyond the damaged area. Align the face side with body tape, if necessary.

6. Cut a piece of fiberglass cloth to cover the damaged area and the part of the panel that has been scuff sanded.

7. Mix the adhesive according to the manufacturer's recommendations. Apply a layer

of adhesive to the back side of the panel to about 1/8 inch thick.

8. Place the fiberglass patch into position on the adhesive. Cover it with a sheet of waxed paper. Use a saturation roller to force the adhesive into the fibers of the cloth.

9. Remove the wax paper and add another layer of adhesive. Work out the adhesive to just beyond the edges of the cloth. Allow the adhesive to cure following the manufacturer's recommendation.

10. Now move to the face side of the panel. Apply a layer of adhesive, completely covering the damaged area. Build it up to slightly higher than the surrounding contour. Allow it to cure.

11. Apply heat to help speed the cure of the patch.

12. Contour to the adjoining surface by block sanding using #220 grit paper.

13. Finish by feathering with an orbital sander and a #320 disc.

14. Follow the recommendations given in Chapter 16 to prime and paint the RRIM.

13.12 REVIEW QUESTIONS

1. When tack welding, Technician A does not use filler material. Technician B says filler material must always be used. Who is correct?
   a. Technician A
   b. Technician B
   c. Both A and B
   d. Neither A nor B

2. During a burn test, the plastic in question burns with a thick, black, sooty smoke and produces a sweet odor. Technician A says the plastic is polyethylene; Technician B says it is thermosetting polyurethane. Who is correct?
   a. Technician A
   b. Technician B
   c. Both A and B
   d. Neither A nor B

3. In high-speed welding, what applies pressure on the welding rod?
   a. operator
   b. pointed shoe
   c. preheat tube
   d. none of the above

4. Which type of welding tips are ideal for working in hard-to-reach places?
   a. round
   b. speed
   c. both a and b
   d. neither a nor b

5. The recommended welding rod size for airless welding is _____ .
   a. 3/16-inch diameter
   b. 1/32-inch diameter
   c. 1/16-inch diameter
   d. 1/8-inch diameter

6. Ultrasonic weldability depends on the plastic's _____ .
   a. melting temperature
   b. elasticity
   c. impact resistance
   d. all of the above

7. A good speed weld in a V-joint will have _____ .
   a. a smooth and shiny appearance
   b. more uniformity than a normal hand weld
   c. a slightly higher crown than a normal hand weld
   d. all of the above

8. Which of the following statements is incorrect?
   a. CAs work equally well on all automotive plastics.
   b. PP and TPO are examples of plastics that require an adhesion promoter as part of the repair process.
   c. The best way to identify a plastic for adhesion bonding is by using the flexibility test.
   d. Both a and b

9. Which is more versatile?
   a. adhesive bonding
   b. hot-air welding
   c. airless welding
   d. none of the above

10. When Technician A grinds the base material, it melts and smears, so he or she uses an adhesion promoter to make the repair. Under the same circumstances, Technician B says that an adhesion promoter is not needed. Who is correct?
    a. Technician A
    b. Technician B
    c. Both A and B
    d. Neither A nor B

11. At what angle should the welding rod be cut before speed welding begins?
    a. 45 degrees
    b. 50 degrees
    c. 60 degrees
    d. 90 degrees

12. Technician A uses a pneumatic adhesive applicator when repairing a reinforced plastic, while Technician B uses the hand-operated type. Who is correct?
    a. Technician A
    b. Technician B
    c. Both A and B
    d. Neither A nor B

13. Which of the following statements concerning minor cut and crack adhesive repairs is incorrect?
    a. Allow the parts to warm to 70 degrees Fahrenheit before applying the adhesive.
    b. The adhesive is applied after the accelerator.
    c. Both sides of the cut or crack must be sprayed with accelerator.
    d. For maximum strength, allow 3 to 12 hours of curing time.

14. After completing an airless plastic weld, what is used to smooth it out?
    a. disc sander and #320 grit (or finer) disc
    b. cheese grater file
    c. slow-speed grinder and #36 grit disc
    d. flat "shoe" part of the torch tip

15. Which of the following is the correct repair method for RRIM?
    a. adhesive
    b. welding
    c. both a and b
    d. neither a nor b

CHAPTER
14

Other Body Shop Repairs

-- OBJECTIVES --

After reading this chapter, you will be able to:

- describe glass replacement procedures.
- describe how to replace a bumper.
- locate and correct wind and water leaks.
- install body accessories such as seats, moldings, interior trim, and spoiler kits.
- name the types of restraint systems.
- explain how to replace and repair vinyl roofs.

After all sheet metal damage has been pulled into alignment, bumped and filled into shape, or replaced with new panels, there is still much work to be done in order to restore the damaged vehicle to its original condition. A very common replacement item on a damaged vehicle is the front or rear bumper. Windshields, back lights, and door windows cracked by a collision also require replacement. Damage to the roof panel might necessitate replacing the vinyl roof cover. Moldings and weather-stripping often need to be replaced as well as interior trim, seats, dashboards, among others. There is such a wide diversity among manufacturers in these areas that only typical examples of each type of repair can be noted in this chapter. Always refer to a manufacturer's service manual when in doubt as to the best procedure for replacing the following body accessories.

14.1 REPLACING GLASS

Today's vehicles are built with a good amount of glass that affords greater visibility for driving and sight-seeing. Most of the glass built into the vehicle is centered in the front windshield, the doors, and rear window. Frequently this glass is broken out or cracked as a result of a collision, flying gravel, or vandalism. It is, therefore, important for the body shop technician to be familiar with the various techniques to remove and install vehicle glass. Glass must also be removed from areas of major damage before the damage is straightened.

14.2 TYPES OF GLASS

There are two types of glass used in today's vehicles: laminated and tempered (Figure 14-1). Both are considered safety glass, and may or may not be tinted.

Laminated plate glass is used to make all windshields. This type of glass consists of two thin sheets of glass with a thin layer of clear plastic between them. Some glass manufacturers have increased the thickness of the plastic material for greater strength. When this type of glass is broken, the plastic material will tend to hold the shattered glass in place and prevent it from causing injury (Figure 14-2). The plastic or vinyl material is usually clear to provide an unimpeded view from all angles.

Tempered glass is used for side and rear window glass but rarely for windshields. This type of glass is a single piece of heat-treated glass and has more resistance to impact than regular glass of the same thickness. The strength of tempered glass re-

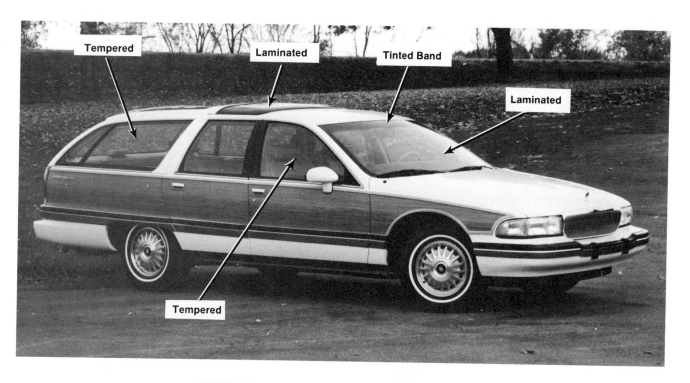

FIGURE 14-1   Types of automotive glass

FIGURE 14-2 Lamination kept windshield glass intact upon impact.

sults from the high compression of its surfaces. This high compression is induced by rapidly heating the glass to approximately 1100 degrees Fahrenheit. The high temperature softens the glass. The glass is then cooled rapidly by blowing air on both flat surfaces. The resulting rapid contraction adds compressive stress to the surface of the glass, which strengthens the glass. Because of this compression, tempered glass cannot be cut, drilled, or ground after the tempering process.

When tempered glass is broken, the pieces of glass are small and have a granular texture. The shattered glass has an interlocked structure to it that obstructs visibility. This is one reason tempered glass is not used in windshields. Another reason it is not used is that this type of glass does not readily give and would, therefore, cause more severe head injuries in a collision. Tempered glass will also shatter if previously damaged or stressed. For example, a chipped edge or a stone striking it can weaken the glass so that it suddenly shatters some time after the initial defect is incurred.

Uniformly tempered glass usually develops thin fractures or cracks when it breaks, which makes it difficult to see through the glass. Zone-tempered glass is a better choice for windshields. Zone-tempered glass, which has a lesser degree of tempering in the area directly in front of the driver, prevents these small cracks from developing in the event of glass breakage.

Tinted glass can be laminated or tempered glass. Tinted laminated glass contains a light green shade of vinyl material to filter out most of the sun's glare. This type of windshield glass is helpful in reducing eye strain, driver tension and fatigue, and prevents fading of the interior furnishings. Some windshields are shaded to reduce the sun's glare.

This type uses only a dark band or section across the top part of the windshield. Tinted or shaded glass is usually recommended if the vehicle is to be equipped with air-conditioning.

Glass can also be tinted by adding minute quantities of metal powder to the other normal ingredients of glass to give it a particular color. The addition of cobalt gives the glass a blue tint. Iron gives the glass a reddish tint.

The above safety glasses can also be fitted with a defrost circuit or antenna or additional plastic laminates. Defrost glass is common in rear windows. Before heat treatment, metal powder, which conducts electricity, is printed on the glass surface in the form of heating wires. The metal powder is baked on the surface during the tempering process.

An antenna wire for radio reception is placed either between the layers of laminated glass (windshield) or printed on the surface of the glass (rear window). Some windows have antenna wires and heating wires side by side. This glass is used in the rear window and front windshield.

Antilacerative glass is similar to conventional multilayered glass, but it has one or more additional layers of plastic affixed to the passenger compartment side of the glass. This glass is used in the front windshield only and is added protection against shattering and cuts during impact.

14.3 REMOVING WINDSHIELD AND REAR WINDOW GLASS

Windshields and rear windows are usually secured in place by rubber weatherstripping or by an adhesive. Generally, moldings are used on the interior and exterior of the body around the glass opening. Interior moldings are called **garnish moldings** and exterior moldings are called **reveal moldings.** The replacement of the windshield and the rear window follow almost identical procedures, varying slightly for different makes of vehicles. One of the first steps is to protect the interior furnishings and equipment by adequately covering them with protective covers. The moldings can be removed and finally the glass itself.

REMOVAL AND REPLACEMENT OF WINDSHIELD GLASS

Replacement of windshield glass involves two different methods based on the materials used: **gasket installations** or **adhesive type installations.** The adhesive type installation is further refined into

FIGURE 14-3   Windshield glass secured with rubber gasket

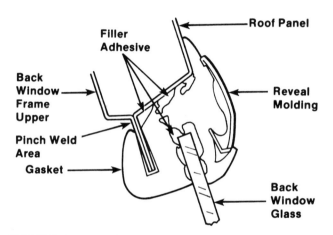

FIGURE 14-4   Cross section of typical back light gasket

two additional methods: the full cutout and the partial cutout method.

The gasket installation was more predominate in older vehicles but still finds use in present day vehicles (Figure 14-3). The gasket is grooved to accept the glass, the sheet metal pinch weld flange, and sometimes the exterior reveal molding (Figure 14-4).

Locking Strip Gaskets

The windshields and rear glass on many older model vehicles are held in place by a locking strip of rubber (Figure 14-5). The locking strip fits into a groove between the glass and the pinch weld flange. The strip forces the gasket tightly against the glass and the flange. This locking strip must be removed before the glass can be removed from the opening. Once removed, the glass can be replaced without removing the gasket from the pinch weld flange.

The adhesive type installation, as the name implies, uses an adhesive material to secure the glass in place in lieu of a gasket (Figure 14-6). The adhesive bond has virtually replaced the gasket method of attachment for the windshield. The use of adhesives permits the windshield to be mounted flush with the roof panel, decreasing wind drag and noise (Figure 14-7). Adhesive-bonded windshields also increase the overall rigidity of the vehicle, minimizing body twist and helping to keep the glass in place during a collision. Rubber stops and spacers separate the glass from the metal. Reveal moldings are held in place by adhesive grooves in the body or by clips. This type is more advantageous than the gasket installation because the pinch welds do not have to be as exact since no pressure is exerted on

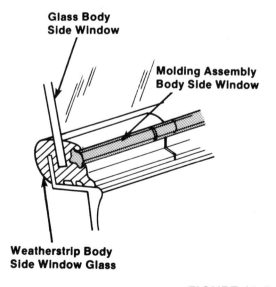

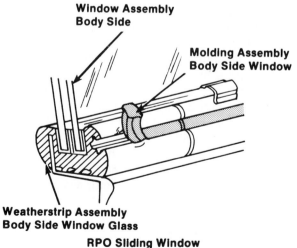

FIGURE 14-5   Locking strip gasket

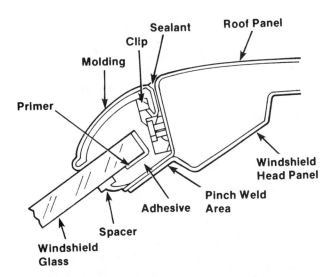

FIGURE 14-6   Cross section of bonded windshield

FIGURE 14-7   Typical adhesive-bonded windshield

the glass outside of the reveal moldings. The adhesive can be extruded from a cartridge or it can be applied in strip or tape form. Typical adhesives in use include polysulfide, urethane, and butyl rubber.

As previously mentioned, adhesive type installations are further subdivided into two methods. The partial cutout method takes advantage of the fact that most of the adhesive in good condition and of sufficient thickness is allowed to remain and be utilized as a base for the application of new adhesive. When the original adhesive is defective or requires complete removal, the full cutout method is utilized.

Removal of Molding

Before removal of the windshield glass or rear window, the interior and exterior moldings must be

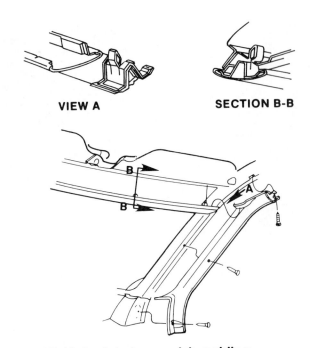

VIEW A   SECTION B-B

FIGURE 14-8   Interior garnish molding

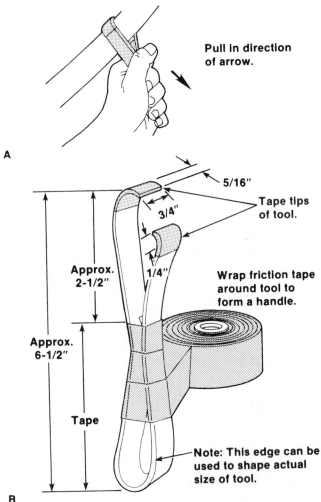

Pull in direction of arrow.

Tape tips of tool.

Wrap friction tape around tool to form a handle.

Note: This edge can be used to shape actual size of tool.

FIGURE 14-9   Spring clip removal tool

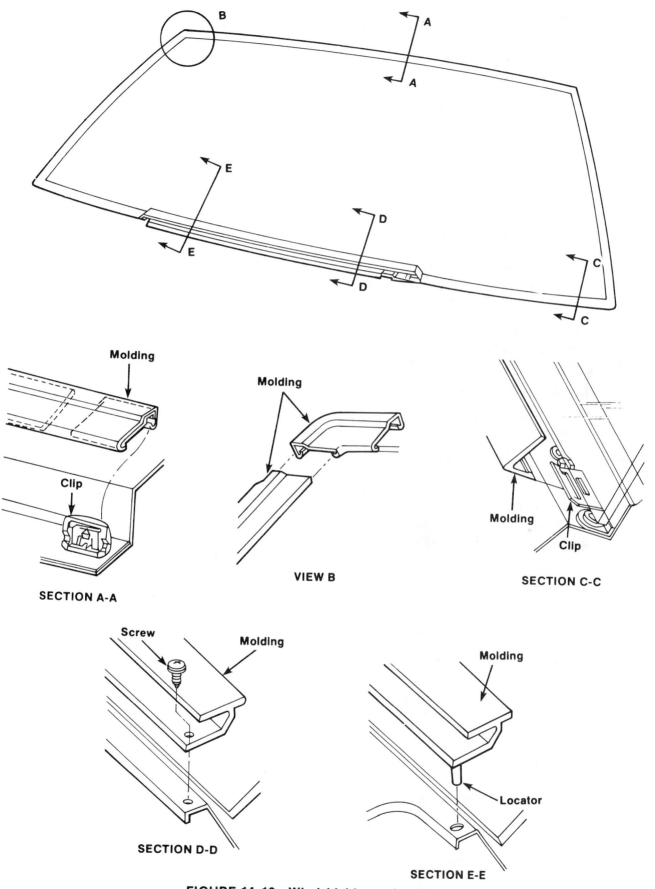

FIGURE 14-10   Windshield reveal molding

removed. In most cases, the garnish moldings used on the interior face of the windshield or rear window consist of several pieces or strips that are secured in place by screws or retaining clips of some sort (Figure 14-8). All of the garnish moldings, as well as the rear view mirror (if possible), should be removed first by using a special tool. If unavailable, a suitable remover can be made from banding strap steel as shown in Figure 14-9.

On the exterior of the vehicle, remove the reveal moldings and other trim or hardware (such as windshield wiper arms) in the adjacent area to the glass being removed. Reveal molding is usually secured in place by clips that are attached to the body opening by welded-on studs, bolts, or screws (Figure 14-10). A projection on the clip engages the flange on the reveal molding, thereby retaining the molding between the clip and body metal. To disengage or remove the molding from the retaining clips, a special tool such as that shown in Figure 14-11 must be used. Reveal moldings can also be anchored in the adhesive material. Exercise care when removing the reveal moldings so that they are not damaged.

Gasket Method

To replace windshield glass using gasket material, perform the following procedures:

 1. Place protective covers on the areas where the glass is to be removed.
2. Be sure all moldings, trim, and hardware are removed.
3. If the glass has a built-in radio antenna, disconnect the antenna lead at the lower

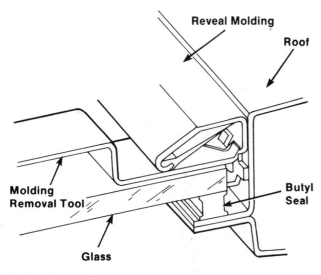

FIGURE 14-11   Clip removal tool

center of the windshield and tape the leads to the glass.
4. Locate the locking strip on the outside of the gasket. Pry up the tab and pull the tab to open the gasket all the way around the windshield glass.
5. Use a putty knife to pry the rubber channel away from the pinch weld inside and outside of the vehicle.
6. With an assistant, push out the windshield glass and gasket.
7. Clean the windshield body opening with an acceptable solvent to clear the area of dirt or residual sealant.
8. If the glass was not cracked and is to be reused, do not exert uneven pressure to the glass or strike it with tools. The technician should always wear safety goggles and gloves when replacing windshield glass or rear window glass—broken or not.
9. Place the removed glass on a suitable bench or table that is covered to protect the glass. If the glass was removed to accommodate body repairs, leave the gasket and moldings intact. If the glass was replaced because it was broken, remove the associated moldings and gaskets from the glass.
10. Cracks that develop in the outer edge of the glass are sometimes caused by low or high spots or poor spot welds in the pinch weld flange. Examine the pinch weld and correct the problem if applicable.
11. Apply a double layer of masking tape around the outside edge of the glass with 1/4 inch overlap onto the inside of the glass. This will prevent chipping or breaking the glass.
12. Install stop blocks and spacers. If the original blocks are not available, cut pieces of used gasket for blocks.
13. Carefully install the glass on the blocks. Center the glass and then check the gap between the glass and the pinch weld. The gap should be even around the entire pinch weld. Remove the masking tape around the edges of the glass.
14. Apply a bead of sealer in the glass channel and install the gasket on the glass.
15. Insert a cord (Venetian type) in the pinch weld groove of the gasket. Start at the top of the glass. The cord ends should meet in the lower center of the glass. Tape the ends of the cord to the inside surface of the

glass (Figure 14-12). Squirt a soapy solution in the pinch weld groove to ease installation.

16. Apply sealer to the base of the gasket.
17. With the aid of an assistant, install the glass and gasket assembly in the body opening and center it. Slip the bottom groove over the pinch weld.
18. Very slowly pull the cord ends so that the gasket slips over the pinch weld flange (Figure 14-13). Work the bottom section of the glass in first, then do the sides, and finally the top section. Be sure to work the sections evenly, otherwise the glass might crack if the cord end is pulled from one side only.
19. Extrude a small bead of sealer around the body side of the gasket.
20. Remove excess sealer with a suitable solvent.
21. Install the reveal and garnish moldings.

22. Check the windshield for water leaks using a low pressure stream of water.
23. Place a soapy solution in the locking strip groove and with a tool designed for the job, replace the locking strip. The wedge-shaped tool shown in Figure 14-14 spreads the groove and feeds the strip into the opening. The soapy solution lubricates the groove and makes it easier to slide the tool through the rubber groove.

Full Cut-out Method of Installing Glass

This method involves the complete removal of all the old adhesive caulking. To remove the glass, the adhesive must be first cut. Several devices are available to do this: a steel wire (piano wire), a hot knife, or a cold, sharp knife. Each device has its own advantages and disadvantages.

A 3-foot length of single strand steel music wire (smallest diameter available) is the safest to use if the glass is being removed primarily for body repairs. The hot or cold knife can crack the glass in the areas where the reveal molding clips are very close to the glass.

Prior to removing the glass, be sure to remove all the reveal and garnish moldings and other accessories such as wiper arms, rear view mirrors, and so on. Also place protective covers inside as well as outside the vehicle in the general area of the glass to be replaced. If a window defogger or windshield

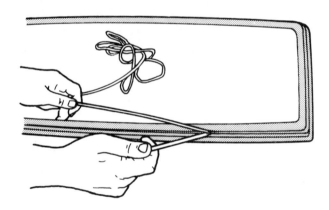

FIGURE 14-12   Cord in pinch weld opening of gasket

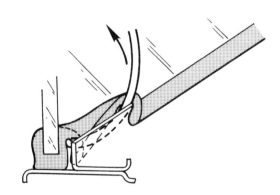

FIGURE 14-13   Pulling cord to slip gasket lip over pinch weld flange

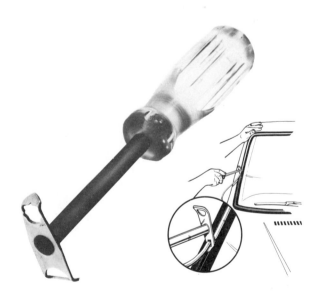

FIGURE 14-14   (A) Windshield locking strip tool and (B) installing a locking strip. (Courtesy of Lisle Corp.)

antenna is installed, be sure to disconnect the appropriate electrical leads. Tape the defogger leads to the inside of the glass; tape the windshield antenna leads to the outside of the glass.

The following procedure for replacing an adhesive-bonded windshield uses both butyl rubber tape and a urethane sealant.

 1. If a steel wire is used to remove the glass, soften up the adhesive by using an appropriate chemical. Cut excessive adhesive from the glass edge to the pinch weld with a sharp knife. Attach one end of the wire to a wooden handle. Force the other end of the wire through the adhesive and under the bottom of the glass. Attach this end to a wooden handle also. With one technician inside the vehicle, work the wire back and forth to cut through the sealant (Figure 14-15). Cut out the bottom, the sides, and lastly the top.

🚗 SHOP TALK _____

A 3/16-inch maximum OD aluminum rod with a notch cut in one end can be used to thread the wire through the seal.

2. If a hot knife, such as the one shown in Figure 14-16, is used to remove the glass, cut excessive adhesive from the edge of the glass to the pinch weld. Insert a hot knife in the adhesive and keep it as close to the glass as possible. Cut around the entire perimeter of the glass. To cut the adhesive

at the corners of the glass, move the handle of the tool as close to the corner as possible. Then rotate the tool to cut the adhesive seal (Figure 14-17). Be careful not to twist the blade of the knife because it will break. Use wedges (wooden, plastic, and so on) if the adhesive tends to reseal itself after being cut.

3. If a cold knife, such as the one shown in Figure 14-18, is used to remove the glass, cut excessive adhesive from the edge of the glass to the pinch weld (Figure 14-19). Soften up the adhesive by using an appro-

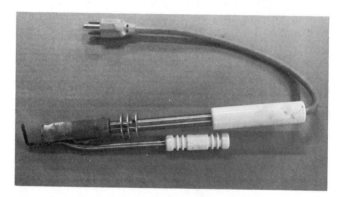

FIGURE 14-16   An electric "hot" knife

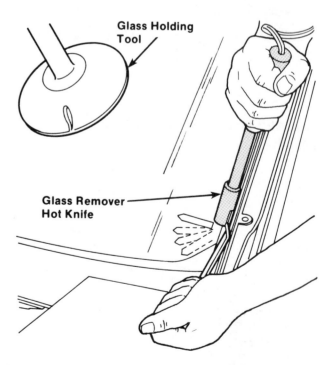

FIGURE 14-17   Cutting windshield adhesive with a hot knife

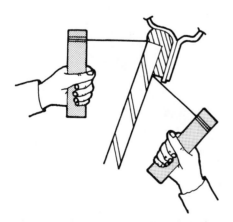

FIGURE 14-15   Cutting through windshield adhesive with a piano wire

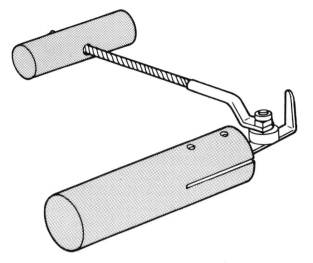

FIGURE 14-18   A cold knife

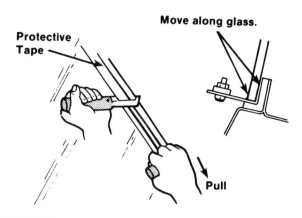

FIGURE 14-20   Pull the cold knife carefully through the adhesive.

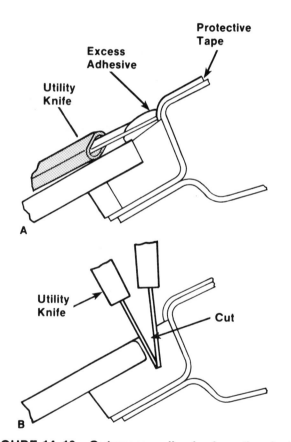

A

B

FIGURE 14-19   Cut excess adhesive from the pinch weld flange.

FIGURE 14-21   Driving a cold knife with an air hammer. *(Courtesy of Lisle Corp.)*

priate chemical. Insert the knife and pull it carefully through the sealant (Figure 14-20). Tip the knife slightly so that the forward edge of the blade scrapes along the glass surface. Cut around the entire perimeter of the glass. Use an additional softening chemical to keep the adhesive soft. Sharpen the knife blade as required.

Figure 14-21 shows a cold knife designed to be driven with an air hammer. This knife cuts through even tough urethane sealants with ease.

4. When the adhesive has been cut, remove the glass and place it in a safe area if it is to be reused. If the glass had been damaged, remove as required and discard. Be sure to wear safety goggles and gloves when handling glass.

5. Position replacement windshield into opening. Align for uniform fit and adjust setting blocks (spacers) as needed. To allow for sufficient bonding of urethane, make sure there is a minimum of 1/4 inch of glass, in addition to the space that will be taken up by the butyl tape around the entire perimeter of the glass. Mark position with a crayon or by applying masking tape to windshield and car body (Figure 14-22). Slit the tape at the edge of the glass. Remove windshield.

6. Remove the remaining adhesive from the body opening using a putty knife or scraper.

7. Inspect all reveal molding clips. Replace all broken or rusted clips; if bent, straighten them.

8. Check the pinch weld flange for rust. Remove any with a wire wheel or #50 grit sanding disc. Treat the bare metal with a metal conditioner, and prime the areas with a urethane primer.

9. Clean the inside surface of the glass thoroughly with a glass cleaner and wipe dry with clean, lint-free cloth or towel. Apply a uniform 1/2-inch-wide coat of urethane primer to the inside edge of the glass. Allow primer to dry 1 to 10 minutes (see manufacturer's instructions for suggested drying time).

10. Ensure the glass supports or spacers are in place (Figure 14-23). Install new ones if necessary. Cement the flat rubber spacers in place using just enough cement to attach the spacers. The spacers should provide equal support around the perimeter of the glass and the spacers on the sides will keep the glass from shifting left or right.

11. If replacing butyl ribbon adhesive, apply appropriate size of rectangular adhesive ribbon sealer to inside edge of the pinch weld (Figure 14-24). Shallow pinch welds will require 5/16 inch × 5/16 inch size, while deeper ones will require 3/8 inch × 3/8 inch size. Start in the center of one A-pillar. Do not stretch the strip of sealer. Cut the ends at a 45-degree angle and butt together.

12. Apply a bead of urethane sealant around the glass or the perimeter of the pinch weld flange as shown in Figure 14-25. Cut the cartridge nozzle at a 45-degree angle with an opening to acheive a bead size slightly larger than the ribbon sealer. Apply the sealant directly behind the ribbon sealer dam on the pinch weld. (Do not apply sealant on antenna lead wires.)

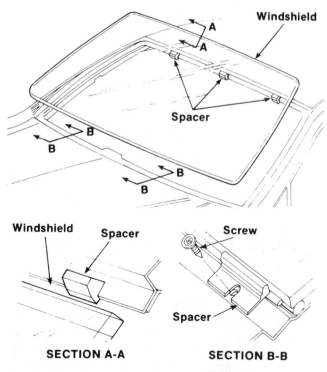

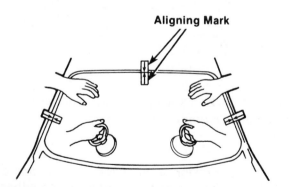

FIGURE 14-22   Marking glass position with masking tape

FIGURE 14-23   Typical spacer positions

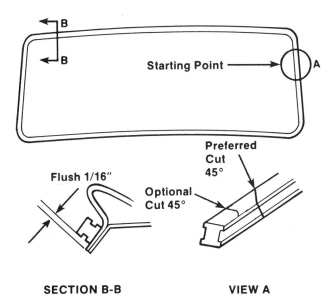

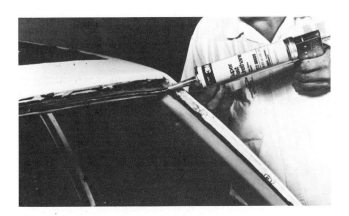

SECTION B-B   **VIEW A**

FIGURE 14-24   Applying ribbon sealer

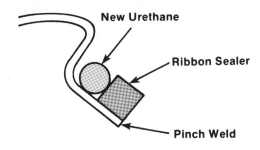

FIGURE 14-25   Applying urethane adhesive

 SHOP TALK _____

*If too much sealant is applied, excessive squeeze-out will occur. Taking time to do the job right **now** will minimize clean up time later.*

13. With the help of an assistant and suction cups, carefully position the glass in the body opening using the masking tape as a guide. Be careful not to smear the adhesive when positioning the glass. Lay the glass in the body opening and press firmly to properly seal the installation.

14. Paddle squeeze-out around the edge of the glass and remove any excess urethane. If necessary, paddle additional sealant between the glass and the car body to fill voids. Remove masking tape and protective coverings.

15. If the glass has an imbedded antenna that uses a butyl strip, put additional adhesive at the ends of the strip to get a watertight seal.

16. Water check the installation with a soft water spray. Do not use a direct water spray on the fresh adhesive. Let water flow over the edges of the glass. If a leak is found, apply additional sealant at the leak point.

17. Install all necessary trim parts and attach the antenna lead and/or defogger lead.

18. Allow the adhesive to cure for 6 to 8 hours at room temperature before the vehicle is returned to its owner. However, since the ribbon sealer will hold the windshield in place while the urethane is curing the car can be moved immediately.

Partial Cut-out Method of Installing Glass

If the partial cut-out method is to be used to install the glass, thoroughly inspect the remaining adhesive first before attempting the procedure. There must be sufficient adhesive remaining in the pinch weld to give adequate clearance between the body and the glass. This remaining adhesive must be tightly bonded to the pinch weld so that a good base exists for the new adhesive to be added. Also check for rust under the adhesive. If it exists, the adhesive must be removed and the pinch weld ground down and refinished. Extensive rusting will require the technician to resort to the full cut-out method of installing glass.

If the original glass is to be reinstalled, remove all traces of adhesive from the glass and clean the areas with either denatured alcohol or a lacquer thinner to clean any residual adhesive from the edge of the glass.

To replace a windshield using the short method, do the following:

535

1. Place protective coverings on the vehicle to prevent damage to the paint or interior.
2. Remove windshield wiper arms, trim, antenna, and so on to expose entire perimeter of glass.
3. Using a utility knife, make a cut into existing urethane sealant around entire perimeter of glass (Figure 14-21). Cut as close to edge of glass as possible.
4. Using a cut-out knife or piano wire, cut out glass keeping tool as close to edge of glass as possible. Remove windshield. Trim any high spots on urethane bed to assure a flat surface. The remaining adhesive should be approximately 3/32 inch thick (Figure 14-26).
5. Inspect the reveal molding clips for damage. Replace any clips if necessary.
6. Select the proper type adhesive that will be compatible with the adhesive used on the body pinch welds. If necessary use the burn test to determine whether it is urethane or polysulfide. Place some small pieces of the adhesive on a painted metal tool and hold it over a flame. Polysulfide burns with a clear flame with little white smoke and a strong odor of sulphur dioxide. Urethane burns with a dirty flame, black smoke, and little or no odor.
7. Replace lower glass supports or spacers where applicable.
8. With the help of an assistant, position the glass in the body opening. Ensure that the gap is equal on both sides and that there is ample clearance on the top. Lower or raise the lower supports or spacers as required to get the correct placement of the glass.
9. Apply two pieces of masking tape from the bottom portion of the glass to the body about 6 to 8 inches in from the corner.

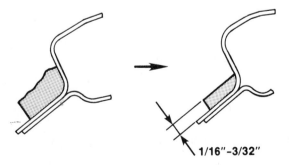

FIGURE 14-26 Trim remaining adhesive to 3/32 inch.

Repeat this procedure at the top of the glass.

Use a razor blade or knife to cut the masking tape strips and remove the glass. The tape strips will help to align the glass when reinstalling it.

10. Using a clean, dry, lint-free cloth, clean the surface of the urethane sealer remaining on the pinch weld. Replace butyl tape strip in antenna area with a new piece of butyl tape.
11. Clean the inside surface of the windshield thoroughly with glass cleaner and wipe dry with a clean, lint-free cloth or towel. Apply a uniform 1/2-inch-wide coat of urethane primer to the inside edge of glass. Allow primer to dry 3 to 5 minutes. Also, apply adhesive primer to the existing or remaining adhesive.
12. If the windshield contains an antenna, place a piece of butyl tape about 8 inches from the antenna pigtail. Do not use urethane or primer near the pigtail because it will interfere with radio reception.
13. Apply the adhesive to be used to the glass or directly over the existing adhesive. Either choice can be made. Also, a ribbon type adhesive or a cartridge type, heavy-bodied adhesive can be used.
14. If the cartridge type adhesive is to be used, apply masking tape about 1/4 inch from the outer edge of the inside of the glass on the top and both sides. This will aid the cleanup process when the glass is installed. Apply a smooth bead of the adhesive, about 1/8 to 3/16 inch in diameter around the outer end of the glass or to the pinch weld.
15. If the ribbon type adhesive is used, masking tape is not required. Apply the ribbon evenly and continuously along the outer edge of the glass for appearances. Do not stretch the ribbon because this will reduce its thickness.
16. With the help of an assistant, install the glass into the body opening. Place the glass on the lower supports or spacers with the masking tape strips properly aligned. (See Steps 5 and 6 above.)
17. Open the vehicle front doors. Place one hand inside the opening and gently lay the glass in position. Use suction cups to control glass movement. An alternate method is to rest the glass on the lower supports or spacers. Then one technician can go in-

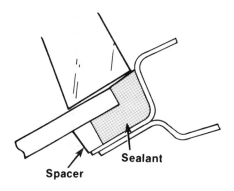

FIGURE 14-27 Smooth adhesive with a putty knife.

side the vehicle and help lay the glass in position.

18. Firmly press the glass in place to set the adhesive material.

19. If adhesive was placed in the pinch weld, a dark line in the glass will indicate a sealed area. The dark line should be completely around the glass. Any light spots that appear will indicate improper sealing.

20. If cartridge type adhesive was used, the adhesive can be smoothed out along the edge of the glass. Additional cartridge adhesive can be applied around the entire perimeter of the glass to ensure proper sealing. Use a putty knife to smooth out the adhesive (Figure 14-27).

21. Water test the installation using a fine water spray. Do not use a direct flow of water on the fresh adhesive. Correct leaks by adding additional adhesive in the applicable areas.

22. Install necessary trim and moldings and connect the antenna and/or defogger pigtails as applicable.

23. Clean excess adhesive from the glass area or body.

24. Allow the adhesive to cure for 6 to 8 hours before moving the vehicle. If butyl was used, the vehicle can be moved as soon as the glass is cleaned up because butyl adhesive does not require a cure period.

REMOVING AND REPLACING REAR WINDOWS

The removal and replacement procedures for back lights and many stationary side windows follow the same methods rather closely. Methods can vary slightly for different vehicle makes. However, many

of the operations that are applied to one make of vehicle can readily be applied to others.

On some vehicles, the rear windows are removed toward the inside of the vehicle rather than to the outside. This procedure will require the removal of certain interior trim parts and accessories and the use of a special knife.

For this type of glass removal, consult the manufacturer's service manual for specific procedures.

14.4 DOOR WINDOW GLASS SERVICE

Removing or servicing door glass will vary between different makes and models of vehicles. As explained in Chapter 11, door window glass is secured in a channel with either bolts, rivets, or adhesive. Doors on sedans are basically the same as are different makes of hardtop doors. Some hardtop doors require the removal of the upper window stops; lower lift brackets or bolts, front or rear glass run channel (if required) upper glass stabilizers, and many other parts. If the glass is to be reinstalled, be sure to store it in a safe place.

Door glass requires servicing when it is broken or must be removed for other body or door repairs. Also, the glass might have to be removed to replace a broken channel assembly. On some vehicle makes, to remove the door glass, it might be necessary to remove the door trim panel, water shield, lower window stop, and the hardware securing the glass channel bracket to the glass channel. The forward edge of the glass assembly must be tilted up to remove it from the door. At this point the channel assembly can be removed from the glass.

Mark the position of the channel on the glass. The sash channel can then be unbolted or rivets drilled out. If the glass is glued into the channel, follow this procedure:

 1. Remove the channel from the glass by applying heat from the welding torch with a #2 or #3 tip along the full bottom length of the channel. Slowly pass the tip back and forth for 60 to 90 seconds, then grip the channel with pliers and pull loose. If the channel does not separate easily, repeat the heating operation.

2. Clean the replacement glass. If the original glass is to be used, scrape all traces of adhesive off with a sharp-bladed tool. If the

original channel is to be reused, clamp it in a vise and burn out the remaining adhesive with a welding torch. While still hot, wire brush adhesive traces from the channel and remove the remaining adhesive from the glass and channel with lacquer thinner. Complete the cleaning operation with water.

When the sash channel is clean and dry, the replacement glass can be glued in place. If using new glass, transfer the position markings from the original glass to the replacement glass. The vehicle manufacturer's service manual can also be consulted for correct channel position. Then, apply an epoxy adhesive to the channel. Position the spacers about 1/2 inch from the ends of the channel and replace the glass in the sash. Tape the channel to the glass using cloth-backed body tape, and allow the adhesive to cure for 1 hour minimim prior to reinstallation into the car. After the adhesive cures, apply a thin bead of silicon adhesive along the length of the channel on both sides of the window.

To reinstall glass in a bolted or riveted channel, a strip of tape of the proper thickness should be applied to the bottom of the glass. Rest the top part of the glass on a piece of soft wood or carpeting. Then position the channel on the glass and use light blows to force the channel on the glass. If possible, use a rubber hammer. If the channel is loose on the glass, use a thicker piece of tape to close the gap in the channel a little to provide the proper width. Then reattach the channel bolts or rivets and spacers.

After the channel has been installed on the glass, the glass and channel assembly can then be positioned into the door and secured with the necessary attaching hardware. Install the lower glass stop and adjust it if necessary. Finally, all the hardware and trim panels can be reinstalled.

To remove quarter glass (on rear doors on some vehicle makes), it might be necessary to remove

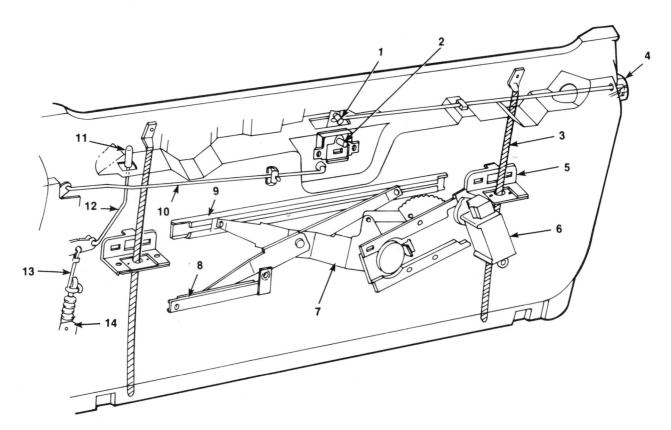

1. **Left Upper Remote Synchronization Lock Rod**
2. **Remote Control**
3. **Guide Tube**
4. **Left Upper Hinge Lock**
5. **Guide Plate Assembly**
6. **Window Regulator Motor**
7. **Tailgate Window Regulator**
8. **Tailgate Inner Panel Cam**
9. **Tailgate Glass Regulator Cam**
10. **Right Upper Remote Locking Rod**
11. **Knob Door Inside Locking**
12. **Tailgate Inside Locking to Lock Rod**
13. **Rod Tailgate Lock to Power Actuator**
14. **Electric Lock Power Actuator**

FIGURE 14-28 Typical tailgate glass regulator

some interior items such as the rear seat, window regulator handle, trim panel(s), and water shield. While supporting the glass, remove the lower frame-to-glass attaching screws and then lift out the glass from the panel. Then remove the spacers from the openings in the glass. To install quarter glass, reverse the procedure.

TAILGATE GLASS SERVICE

Tailgate glass is generally secured to a regulator can with screws or bolts. Figure 14–28 is a typical example of a tailgate window and regulator assembly. Removal or replacement of tailgate glass is similar to that presented for door glass. To remove tailgate glass, run the glass to the down position (manually or automatically) and remove the inner trim panel cover. Run the glass to the up position

and out of the tailgate until the glass channel screws are visible and accessible. Remove the glass channel screws to disconnect the glass from the channel assembly. Slide the glass out of the belt opening. Then, remove the attaching hardware from inside the tailgate. Finally, remove the slides from the glass in four places. The installation procedure is a reverse of the removal procedure.

14.5 DOOR AND TRUNK LOCKS

Door lock assemblies usually consist of the outside door handle and linkage, the inside door lock mechanism, and the inside locking rod (Figure 14-29). Various types of exterior door handles are in use and usually depend on the vehicle model. Among those in use are the pushbutton and the lift

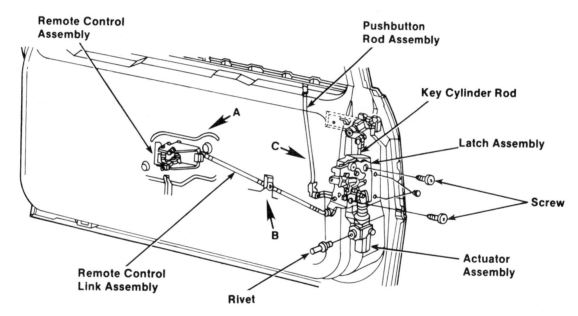

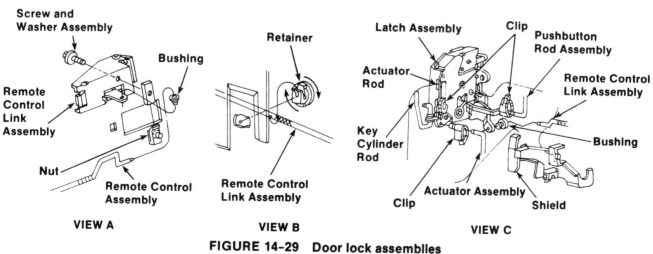

FIGURE 14-29 Door lock assemblies

FIGURE 14-30   Installing trunk lock with rivets

handle type. On the pushbutton type, the button directly contacts the lock lever that releases the mechanism to open the door. Most exterior door handles operate a lock mechanism by using one or more rods. The handles can be replaced by raising the window and removing the interior trim and panel and water shield to gain access to the attaching hardware and linkage.

Some exterior door handles are attached by screws, bolts, or rivets to the door panel. Some causes of malfunctioning exterior door handles are worn bushings; bent or incorrectly adjusted rods; lack of lubrication on the handle, linkage, or latch; and worn or damaged latches.

Inside door lock mechanisms are generally the pull handle type. The mechanisms are connected to the lock by one or more rods and are accessible by removing the interior trim panel and water shield. The mechanism is attached to the door handle with screws, bolts, or rivets, depending on the vehicle make. The rods are usually long and must be supported to prevent them from engaging or getting caught in other components within the door panel. Clips or bushings are used to secure the rods in place.

Trunk or hatch doors usually do not have exterior or interior door handle mechanisms. They operate with a key (or dash switch on powered units) and lock mechanism. Some are adjustable, while others are riveted in place (Figure 14-30).

The lock cylinder on door and trunk lids is usually held in the panel with a retainer. A sealing gasket is also used on the cylinder to protect the paint. The retainer must be disengaged to remove the lock cylinder. A pointed tool or screwdriver can be used to accomplish this. On some vehicles the cylinder can be removed once the linkage is disconnected. The cylinder is either directly connected to the latch or connected by a rod. The lock is usually lubricated with dry graphite for ease of operation.

Optional equipment on some vehicles includes a feature whereby all the latches on the vehicle can be locked at one time from the driver's door control panel. The control panel electrically operates a power cylinder to control the latches. The power unit is bolted or riveted to the inner door frame.

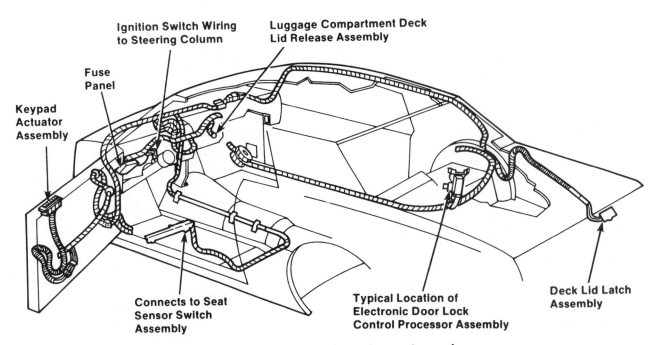

FIGURE 14-31   Typical keyless entry system

Failure of a power unit to operate could be caused by faulty wiring or connections or a defective power unit.

Some vehicles have an interior push rod or button to lock the doors. On this type, the doors cannot be opened from the inside once they are locked. This is a safety feature that is especially useful when small children are placed in the rear seat area.

Keyless door entry systems are becoming a more common feature on late model vehicles. The system consists of two main components:

- Five button keypad on the outside panel of the driver's door
- Electronic microprocessor/relay module

A typical system (Figure 14–31) performs the following functions:

- It unlocks the driver's door. A keypad code is programmed into the system at the factory. The factory-programmed code is permanently recorded on the owner's warranty card (usually located inside the luggage compartment deck lid) and on a separate code card.

    Some systems also allow the owners to select and program their own personal code (a birthdate or part of a social security

number, for example) by pressing a specified sequence of keypad buttons (refer to procedure in the owner's guide). When either the factory-programmed code or the owner's code is entered, the driver's door unlocks.

- It unlocks the other doors of the vehicle if the keypad button is pressed within a certain time limit of the driver's door unlocking.
- It turns on the interior lamps and the illuminated keyhole on the driver's door. The lamps are turned on by pressing any keypad button or lifting the door handle.
- It unlocks the luggage compartment deck lid when the keypad button is pressed within a certain time limit after the driver's door is unlocked.
- It locks all the doors automatically when:
    —The driver's seat is occupied (except Thunderbird with Recaro seats).
    —All the doors are fully closed.
    —The ignition switch is turned to RUN.
    —The transmission selector passes through R position.
- It locks all the doors from outside the vehicle when the keypad buttons are pressed at the same time.

Collision repair or a malfunction in the keyless entry system might require the removal of related

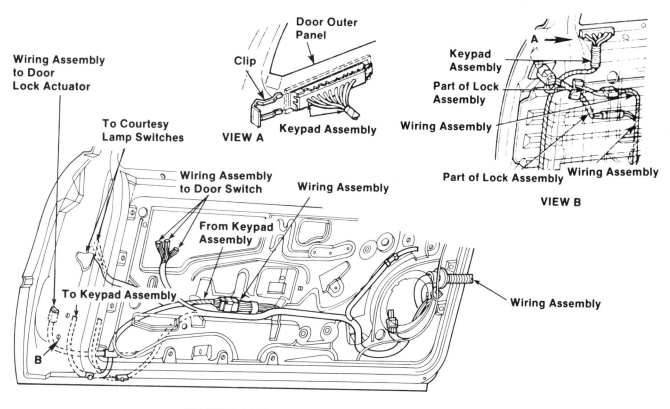

FIGURE 14–32   Door keypad and wiring harness

components from a vehicle. Figure 14-32 shows a keypad and wiring harness. The keypad can be secured by clips or screws. The microprocessor/relay module is located either under the dash or on the package tray in the luggage compartment. It is secured with screws or bolts. After reassembly of the keyless entry system components, test the system to insure that the system is fully operational.

14.6 LOCATING LEAKS

Water leaks and wind noises are frequent customer complaints brought to a body shop. Such problems are often difficult to locate. Water leaks frequently occur at panel joints and glass-to-metal joints due to cracked or insufficient sealer (Figure 14-33A). Dust and water leaks also occur at doors, windows, trunk lids, and windshields whenever the weatherstripping becomes damaged or loose or when the doors or window glass are improperly adjusted (Figure 14-33B).

Wind noises are high-frequency sounds heard while driving. They are heard mainly around the door when the window is closed. This is generally due to loose, worn, or improperly applied weatherstripping, which allows air to leak into the passenger compartment (Figure 14-34A). Wind noise is also produced when the wind hits a projection (Figure 14-34B). This disturbance produces an eddy or swirl behind the object, thus creating a noise (the principle of flute and bugle sounds).

A loose body molding, a poorly aligned front fender, or an improperly adjusted hood are just some examples of causes of wind noises. A troubleshooting chart on how to identify and solve wind noises is given in Table 14-1.

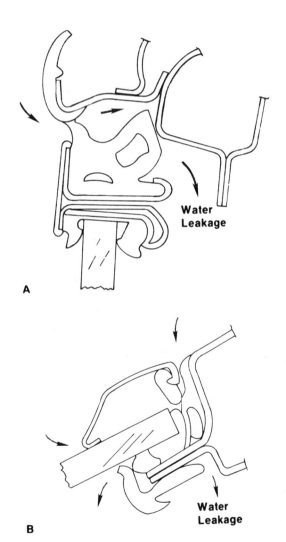

FIGURE 14-33 Water leakage around (A) windshield glass and (B) door weatherstripping

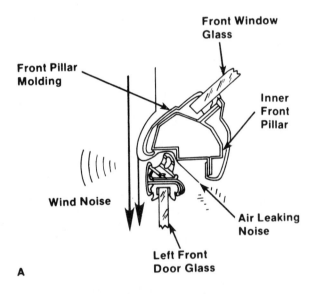

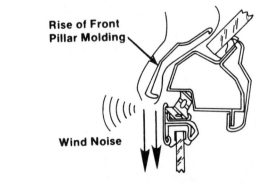

FIGURE 14-34 Wind noise caused by (A) loose fitting weatherstripping and (B) loose molding

TABLE 14-1:   ELIMINATING NOISE LEAKS

Sources	Causes	Corrections
Weatherstrip	Imperfect adhesion to contact surface and improper contact of lip due to separation, breakage, crush, and hardening	Repair or replace weatherstrip.
Door Sash and Related Parts	1. Improper weatherstrip contact due to a bent door sash 2. Gap caused by corner piece improperly installed. 3. Gap caused by corner sash badly finished. 4. Separation and breakage of the rubber on the door glass run	1. Repair. 2. Install properly. 3. Repair with body sealer and masking tape. 4. Repair.
Door Assembly	Improper weatherstrip contact due to improper fitting door.	Correct door fit.
Door Glass	Gap caused due to ill-fitting door glass	Align door glass.
Body	Improper body finishing on contact surface for door weatherstrip (uneven panel joint, sealer installed improperly, and spot welding splash)	Repair contact surface.
Drip Molding	Rise and separation of molding	Repair or replace.
Front Pillar	Rise and separation of molding	Repair or replace.
Waist Molding	Door glass gap due to rise of molding and deformation of rubber seal	Repair.

Three principal methods are often used to locate air and water leaks:

- Spraying water on the vehicle
- Driving the vehicle over very dusty terrain
- Directing a strong beam of light on the vehicle and checking for light leakage between the panels

Before making an actual leak test, remove all applicable interior trim from the general area of the reported leak. The spot where dust or water enters the vehicle might be some distance from the actual leak. Therefore, remove all trim, seats, or floor mats from areas that are suspected as possible sources of the leak. Entrance dust is usually noticed as a pointed shaft of dust or silt at the point of entrance. These points should be sealed with an appropriate sealing compound and then rechecked to verify that the leak is sealed.

Leak Checks Using Water

After all the applicable trim has been removed, place one person inside the vehicle with all the doors and windows closed. Then, spray the vehicle with a low pressure stream of water in the suspected area of the leak. The person inside the vehicle should act as an observer to locate just where the water enters.

The water pressure must be at such a level that when sprayed from the waist, water falls to a place 14 to 16 inches away (Figure 14–35). (The hose should be an ordinary garden hose of about 1/2 inch in diameter.) The hose should be used as it is, or press the end of it lightly with the thumb, according to the condition of the panel joint; water should be sprayed for more than 10 minutes from a distance of approximately 8 inches.

Another way to discover water leaks around a windshield or back light is to apply a soapy solution around the outside edge of the window. Then, from inside the vehicle, apply compressed air to the window to panel joint. Any gap in the sealant will result in bubbling of the soap solution (Figure 14–36).

Leak Checks Using Light

Simple leaks can often be located by moving a strong light source around the vehicle, while an ob-

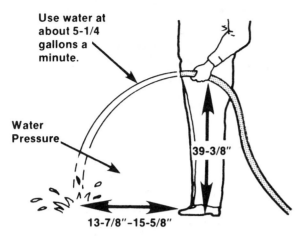

FIGURE 14-35 Proper water pressure for testing for leaks

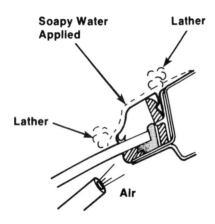

FIGURE 14-36 Testing for leaks using soapy water and compressed air

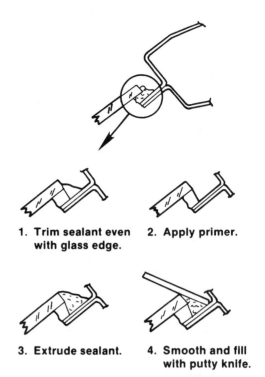

1. Trim sealant even with glass edge.
2. Apply primer.
3. Extrude sealant.
4. Smooth and fill with putty knife.

FIGURE 14-37 Sealing a leaky windshield

server remains inside the vehicle. This method is useful only if the leakage course is in a straight path. If the path is devious, the light beam will not pass through the turns and curves.

Repairing Leaks

Plugs and grommets are used in floor pans, dash panels, and trunk floors of a vehicle to keep out dust and water from the interior. These items should be carefully checked to ensure they are in good condition.

Vehicle windshields and rear windows usually develop water leaks that can be repaired without removing the glass. A majority of leaks occur at the top of the windshield or top and bottom of the rear window. On a station wagon, the leaks usually occur on the rear side windows. If several leaks are de-

tected, it is better to seal all around the area rather than at each leak point. To repair an adhesive glass water leak, first clean the leak area and blow the area dry. Then, trim off the surplus adhesive that extends beyond the edge of the glass (Figure 14-37). After removing the surplus adhesive, dry the area using compressed air again. It is advisable to use a solvent to clean the area of oil or grease that might be present. Prime the repair area with a urethane primer-sealer. Allow the primer to dry according to the manufacturer's instructions (approximately 5 minutes). Then, apply the windshield sealer along the cleaned area and use a putty knife to smooth it out. The sealant should be applied and spread so that it is even with the top edge of the glass and tapered back to the molding clip area. Be sure the sealant is worked into any existing crevices. While the sealant is still soft, water check the area again. Use a very soft stream or spray of water so as not to disturb the sealant. If no leaks are detected, reinstall trim and remove any surplus sealant on the glass or vehicle.

Gasket type glass more commonly develops leaks between the gasket and the glass or between the gasket and the vehicle body. Use the water spray method to locate the exact leaking area. Mark the area and dry using compressed air. Apply bedding compound or joint sealer to the marked area. This type of caulking material never hardens; it remains

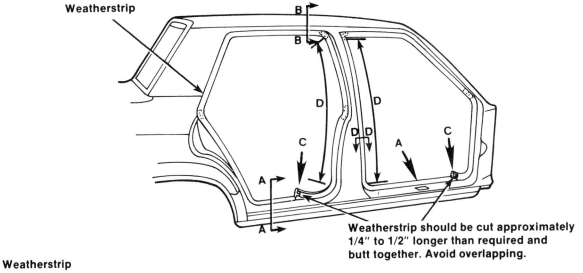

Weatherstrip

Weatherstrip should be cut approximately 1/4" to 1/2" longer than required and butt together. Avoid overlapping.

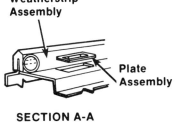

Weatherstrip Assembly

Plate Assembly

SECTION A-A

Apply silicone lubricant jelly to areas marked D. Wipe off excess lubricant.

SECTION B-B

Weatherstrip Assembly

VIEW C

FIGURE 14–38   Typical door gasket installation

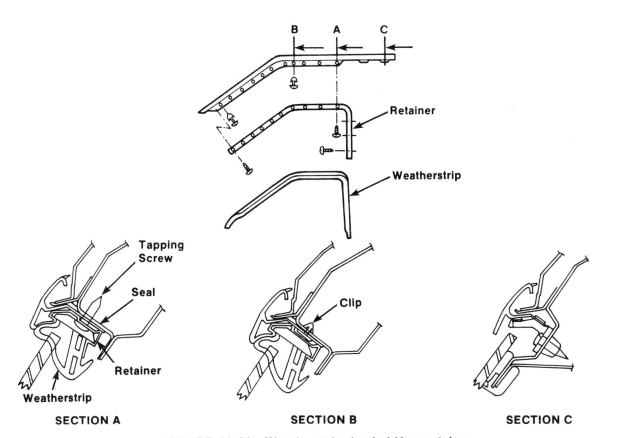

Retainer

Weatherstrip

Tapping Screw

Seal

Retainer

Weatherstrip

SECTION A

Clip

SECTION B

SECTION C

FIGURE 14–39   Weatherstripping held by a retainer

soft and flexible. The sealer is usually packaged in a cartridge with a nozzle. It might be necessary to use a flat, pointed piece of wood to make an opening between the gasket and glass (or body) so that the nozzle can be inserted to apply the sealant. Place the cartridge nozzle adjacent to the wood piece and move forward, filling the opening. Remove surplus sealant with a solvent or enamel thinner. Recheck the area using the water spray method.

Doors and windows are sealed against wind and water with rubber gaskets called weatherstripping. Weatherstripping usually fits over a pinch weld flange or inside a channel. The rubber gaskets can be glued on, held with screws or clips, or simply held securely by the design of the gasket (Figure 14-38). The weatherstripping in Figure 14-39 is held by a retainer that is screwed to the vehicle frame before the gasket is placed in the retainer. When applying weatherstripping around a door or trunk, cut the strip 1/2 inch longer than required and butt the cut ends together. A sponge rubber plug is often used to hold the cut ends together. Some manufacturers require an application of silicone lubricant jelly to the base of the weatherstrip bulb. Be careful not to stretch the weatherstripping during installation. Pulling the strip too tight will result in an improper seal.

When the weatherstripping on doors and trunk lids becomes loose, damaged, or deteriorated, dust and water leakage results. On most vehicles the weatherstripping used on doors or trunks is cemented in place. Check the weatherstrip for correct positioning by placing a feeler gauge (about 1/64 inch thick) or a plastic credit card between the weatherstrip and frame. If there is little or no resistance when withdrawing the gauge or card, the weatherstrip should be moved closer to the edges of the door or trunk or replaced completely.

14.7 HEADLIGHTS

The headlights on today's vehicles are either of the two sealed beam system or the four sealed beam system. If the vehicle was involved in a front end collision, the headlights should be adjusted after they have been replaced.

The two sealed beam system has the low and high beams built into the same sealed beam. In the four sealed beam system, two sealed beams have both low and high beam; the other two sealed beams are used only on the high beam. High or low beam is selected by a switch on the floorboard or on the steering column. Quick-disconnects are used for

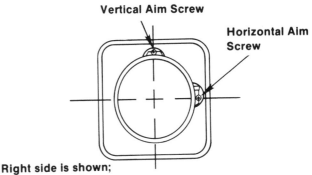

Right side is shown; left side is similar.

A

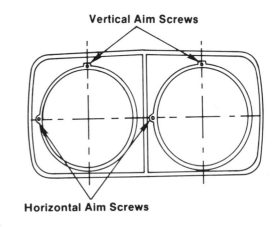

B

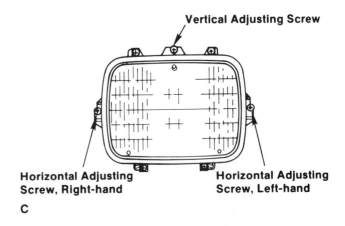

C

FIGURE 14-40   Headlight bulb adjusting screws

the left and right sealed beams. A typical headlight system consists of adjusting screws for horizontal and vertical movement. The headlight bulb is retained to the assembly by screws (Figure 14-40).

Before making adjustments to a vehicle's headlights, make the following inspections to ensure that the vehicle is level. Any one of the adverse conditions listed here can result in an incorrect setting.

- If the vehicle is heavily coated with snow, ice, or mud, clean the underside with a high-pressure stream of water. The additional weight can alter the riding height.
- Ensure that the gas tank is half full. Half a tank of gas is the only load that should be present on the vehicle.
- Check the condition of the springs or shock absorbers. Worn or broken suspension components will affect the setting.
- Inflate all tires to the recommended air pressure levels. (Take into consideration cold or hot tire conditions.)
- If collision damage requires straightening of the frame, make sure that the wheel alignment and rear axle tracking path are correct before adjusting the headlights.
- After placing the vehicle in position for the headlight test, bounce the vehicle by standing on the bumper or pushing down on the front fenders to settle the suspension.

Normally, the body shop will have and use a headlight alignment unit to make the necessary and correct adjustments. Once the vehicle is properly interfaced with the alignment unit, the horizontal and/or vertical adjustment screws on the headlight are adjusted for the proper reading or indication on the unit. If no headlight alignment equipment is available, an alternate method is available whereby an alignment setup can be laid out on the floor and wall of the auto body shop. Figure 14-41 illustrates such a layout that can be used. The high and low beams should be adjusted until they appear as shown in Figure 14-42. The preferred method to

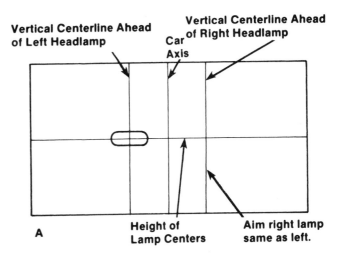

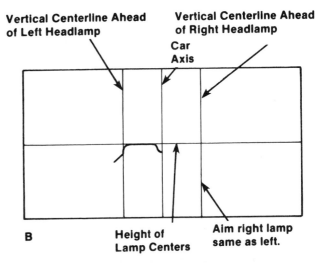

FIGURE 14-42   (A) Correct upper headlight beam alignment; (B) correct lower headlight beam alignment

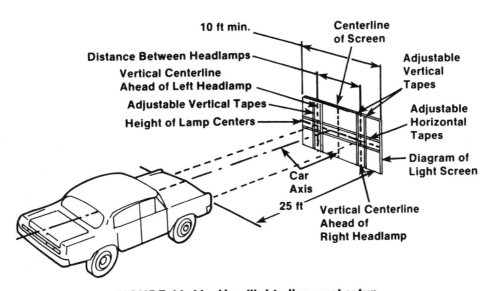

FIGURE 14-41   Headlight alignment setup

align the headlights, however, is to use the headlight alignment unit.

14.8 TAIL, BACKUP, AND STOP LIGHTS

Failure of a tail, backup, stop, or directional light on the vehicle can usually be attributed to a faulty bulb. Oftentimes moisture gets into the bulb socket and causes corrosion of the electrical contacts and the bulbs. Corrosive conditions can be repaired by using sandpaper on the affected areas. For severe cases, replace the socket and/or bulb. After any repair, always attempt to waterproof the assembly to prevent future problems.

These types of lights are also contained within a lens or bezel type assembly, usually amber or red in color. Cracked or broken assemblies are easily replaced; they are secured by attaching hardware readily accessible to the body technician.

14.9 RATTLE ELIMINATION

Rattles and squeaks are normally caused by sheet metal that is loose or rubbing adjacent parts, loose bolts and screws, and loose or improperly adjusted doors, hood, or body panels. Other rather simple things such as a broken or loose exhaust mount or an improperly secured jack, tire, or articles in the trunk can also be causes of rattle.

Oftentimes a noise will be pinpointed by the customer to be in a certain area of the vehicle when in fact it might be caused by something in another area of the vehicle. This effect is caused by the sound traveling through the body. Usually a thorough investigation and a test drive of the vehicle is recommended so that the rattle or noise can be located.

Most rattle or noise repairs involve the readjustment of parts, the replacement of parts, tightening loose attaching hardware, and welding broken parts. Check the hood for proper alignment at the front and the back. If the paint is knocked off or scratched on one end, it is probably hitting another edge or rubbing against it. Check the hood latch pin for looseness and proper fit as well as the rubber hood bumpers. If the back of the hood flutters, readjust the hood so that it properly fits at the back seal. Also check the grill, wheelhousing, trim moldings, and bumper brackets for tightness.

Many areas on the body of the vehicle can also cause rattles, noises, and squeaks. Most susceptible areas are the dash, doors, steering column, and seat tracks. It is also possible for weatherstripping to squeak, especially when it becomes very dry. Lubrication should be applied to applicable moving parts such as door hinges. All attaching hardware should be checked for tightness, especially in the area of the suspected noise source.

14.10 ADJUSTING OR REPLACING BUMPERS

Bumpers are designed to protect the front and rear of a vehicle from damage during a low-speed collision. The traditional bumper is made of heavy gauge spring steel and is plated with bright chromium metal. The chrome-plated steel bumper is still very popular (Figure 14–43). Many larger passenger vehicles and trucks are equipped with chrome bump-

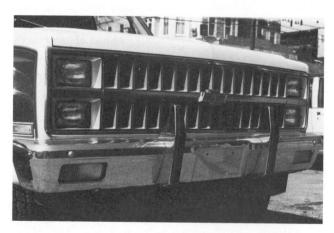

FIGURE 14–43 Chrome-plated steel bumpers

Chapter 14   Other Body Shop Repairs

FIGURE 14-44   An aluminum bumper

FIGURE 14-45   Painted steel bumper

FIGURE 14-46   Plastic-covered bumpers

ers. Many smaller vehicles, however, have aluminum bumpers (Figure 14-44). These are much lighter than the steel bumpers and maintain a bright finish without chrome plating. Painted steel bumpers are popular on many trucks. Figure 14-45 shows a typical painted steel bumper.

Bumpers on many late model cars are covered with urethane or other plastics (Figure 14-46). The use of urethane polypropylene or other plastic allows the bumper to be shaped to blend with the body contour. Plastic bumper covers can also be painted to match the body finish color. Underneath the plastic covers might be a steel or aluminum face bar or reinforcement bar or a thick energy absorbing pad made of high-density foam rubber or plastic. The repair of flexible bumper covers, as well as other plastic bumper parts, such as bumper strips, soft nose parts, gravel deflectors, and filler panels, is explained in detail in Chapter 13.

Chrome bumpers that are severely damaged or that have chipped chrome plating are usually sent to a specialty shop that specializes in repairing and rechroming bumpers. The damaged bumper is exchanged for a refurbished bumper. Painted bumpers that are not too severely bent can be pulled and bumped back to shape, using common shop procedures. The damaged area can then be ground down to bare metal, filler can be applied to surface irregularities, and the bumper primed and painted.

Prior to 1972, bumpers were rigidly bolted to the vehicle's frame. At best, the old bumpers only resisted the bending forces of an impact; they transferred the energy shock directly to the frame and, thus, to the occupants of the vehicle. Modern bumpers are designed to absorb the energy of a low-speed impact minimizing the shock to both vehicle frame and the occupants of the vehicle. Between 1973 and 1983, car manufacturers were required by federal regulations to equip cars with bumpers that could withstand 5 mph collisions without incurring damage to the vehicle. In 1983, the federal standards were relaxed to 2.5 mph. In order to comply with the federal regulations, manufacturers fitted their bump-

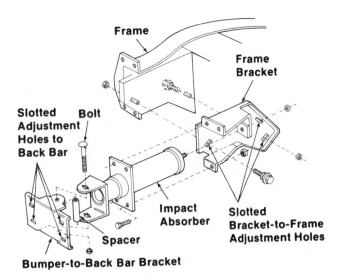

FIGURE 14-47   Bumper shock absorber

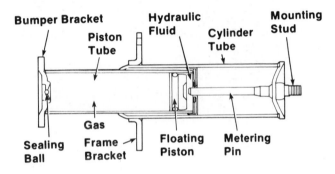

FIGURE 14-48   Cross section of a typical energy absorber

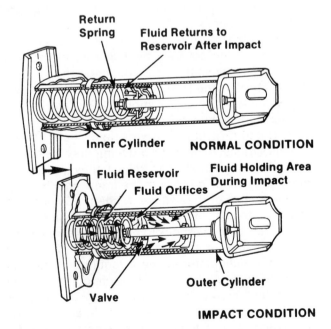

FIGURE 14-49   Spring-loaded bumper shocks

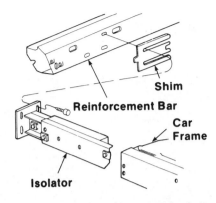

FIGURE 14-50   Typical bonded isolator

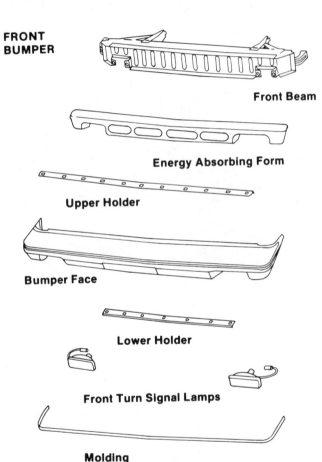

FIGURE 14-51   Plastic-covered bumper with energy absorbing form

ers with energy absorbers. Most energy absorbers are mounted between the bumper face bar or bumper reinforcement and the frame (Figure 14-47).

There are three types of energy absorbers. The most common is similar to a shock absorber. As shown in Figure 14-48, the typical bumper shock is a cylinder filled with hydraulic fluid. Upon impact, a piston filled with inert gas is forced into the cylinder. Under pressure, the hydraulic fluid flows into the piston through a small opening. The controlled flow of fluid absorbs the energy of the impact. Fluid also displaces a floating piston within the piston tube, which compresses the inert gas. When the force of the impact is relieved, the pressure of the compressed gas forces the hydraulic fluid out of the piston tube and back into the cylinder. This action forces the bumper back to its original position.

Another energy absorber design is shown in Figure 14-49. Upon impact, fluid flows from a reservoir through a metering valve into an outer cylinder. When impact forces are relieved, a spring in the absorber returns the bumper to its original position.

Another type of bumper energy absorber is called an isolator (Figure 14-50) and is generally found on Ford vehicles. It works in principle like a motor mount. A rubber pad is sandwiched between the isolator and the frame. Upon impact, the isolator moves with the force, stretching the rubber pad. The "give" in the rubber absorbs the energy of the impact. When the force is relieved, the rubber will retract to its original shape (unless it is torn from its base by the impact), and return the bumper to its normal position.

A third type of energy absorber is found on many light imports and sports model vehicles. Instead of shock absorbers mounted between the frame and the face bar or reinforcement bar, a thick urethane foam pad is sandwiched between an impact bar and a plastic face bar or cover (Figure 14-51). The pad is designed to give and rebound to its original shape in a 2.5 miles per hour collision. On some vehicles the impact bar is attached to the frame with energy absorbing bolts (Figure 14-52). The bolts and brackets are designed to deform during a collision in order to absorb some of the impact force. The brackets must be replaced in most collision repairs.

Replacing a bumper is basically a matter of removing the correct bolts. This job is made easier if the bumper is supported by a scissors jack lift (Figure 14-53). On some vehicles, stone deflectors, parking lights, windshield washer hoses, and other items must be disconnected before the bumper can be removed from the car. Figures 14-54 and 14-55 show typical urethane-covered front and rear bumpers and the related assembly hardware. Bumpers with energy absorbers should be unbolted from the absorber brackets. Fixed bumpers should be removed by unbolting the brackets from the frame. Be sure to torque all bolts to the manufacturer's specifications.

Several cautions must be observed when removing bumpers with energy absorbers.

- The shock type absorber is actually a small pressure vessel. It should never be subjected

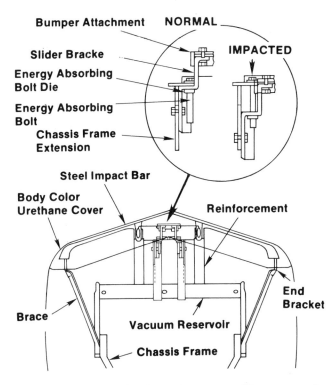

FIGURE 14-52   Urethane bumper with energy absorbing bolts

FIGURE 14-53   Supporting bumper with scissors jack. (Courtesy of Fitz & Fitz, Inc.)

551

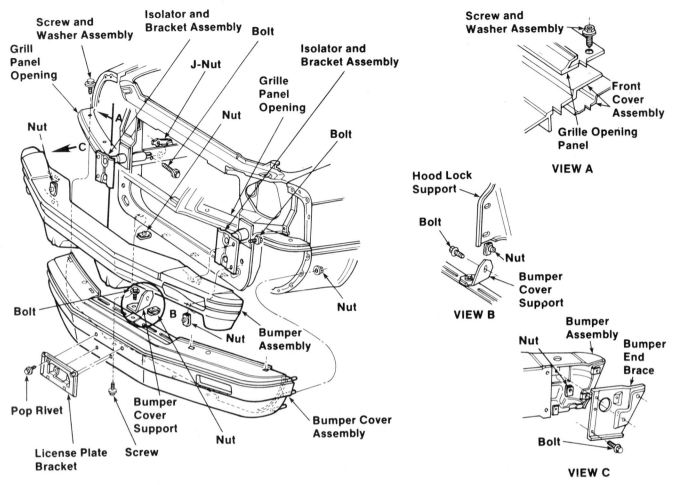

FIGURE 14-54 Typical front bumper attachment methods

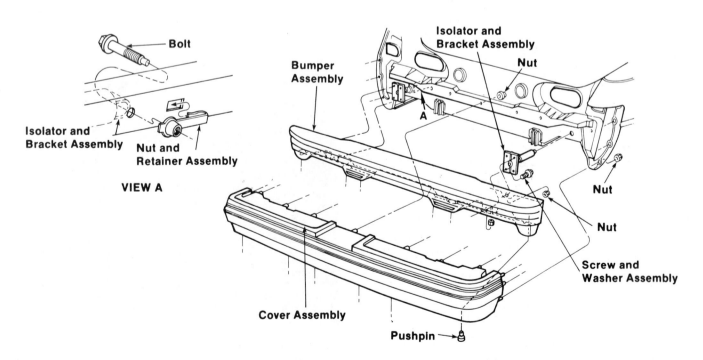

FIGURE 14-55 Typical rear bumper attachment methods

to heat or bending. If cutting or welding near an absorber, remove it.

- If the absorber is bound due to the impact, relieve the gas pressure before attempting to remove the bumper from the vehicle. Secure the bumper with a chain to prevent its sudden release and drill a hole into the front end

of the piston tube to vent the pressure. Then, remove the bumper and absorber.

- Play it safe and wear approved safety glasses when handling, drilling into, or removing a bound energy absorber.

When replacing a bumper, always test the energy absorbers. To do this:

1. Position the vehicle facing a solid barrier (Figure 14–56).
2. Shift the transmission into PARK and fully engage the parking brake.
3. Place a hydraulic jack between the barrier and the bumper. Position the jack squarely over the energy absorber.
4. Compress the absorber 3/8 inch.
5. Release the jack. If the bumper does not return to its normal position, replace the absorber.

After bolting the bumper in place, it must be adjusted so that it is an equal distance from the fenders and front grille. The clearance across the

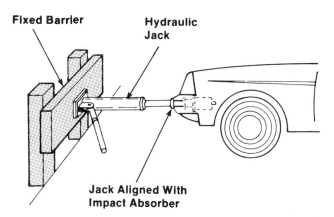

FIGURE 14–56 Testing energy absorber operation

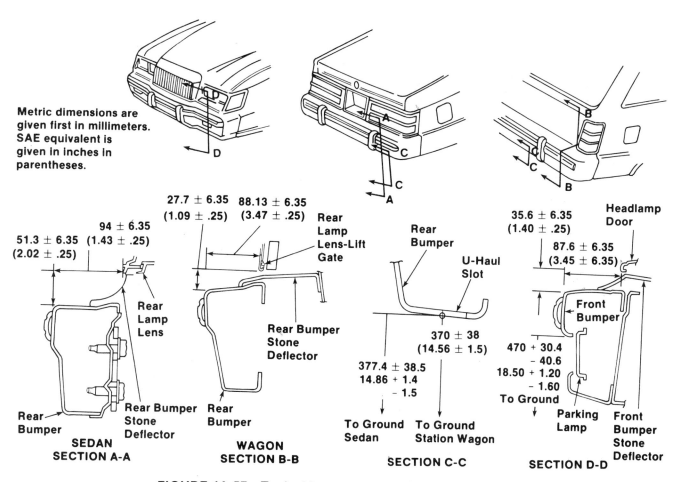

FIGURE 14–57 Typical bumper adjustment specifications

top must be even. Adjustments are made at the mounting bolts. The mounting brackets allow the bumper to be moved up or down, side to side, and in and out. If necessary, shims can be added between the bumper and the mounting bracket to adjust the bumper alignment. Figure 14-57 shows one manufacturer's specified clearances with allowable tolerances.

14.11 RESTRAINT SYSTEMS

The National Highway Traffic Safety Administration (NHTSA) supports a ruling that requires all new cars sold in the United States to be equipped with either automatic seat belts and/or a driver-side air bag. The implications of a recent amendment by NHTSA also will see to it that by 1996, all light trucks, vans, and many vehicles formerly classified as recreational vehicles will also be equipped with some form of passive restraints. In many cases both driver and occupant air bags will be required.

The assertion that lives are saved by the use of a passive restraint mechanism, whether it is an air bag or motorized seat belt, depends on the active participation by drivers and occupants who will still be required to buckle up. Automatic seat belts must also be checked to assure that they work.

There are two types of restraint systems:

- **Active restraint.** This system is one that the occupants must make an effort to use. For example, in most vehicles the seat belts must be fastened for crash protection.
- **Passive restraint.** This system is one that operates automatically. No action is required to make it functional. Two types are automatic seat belts and air bags.

LAP AND SHOULDER BELTS

Most modern coupes have a passive restraint system, while most late-model sedans were built with both passive and active systems. On active systems the front seat belt incorporates a 4- to 8-second fasten seat belt reminder light and sound signal designed to remind the driver if the lap and shoulder belts are not fastened when the ignition is turned to the ON position. If the driver's seat belt is buckled, the audible signal will not sound; however, the fasten seat belt reminder light will stay on for a 4- to 8-second period. If the driver's seat belt is not buckled, the reminder light and sound signal will automatically shut off after a 4- to 8-second interval.

On the passive system, the belt warning light will glow for 60 to 90 seconds and an audible signal will sound for 4 to 8 seconds if the driver's lap and shoulder belt is not buckled. The system will also signal if the ignition is on and the driver's door is

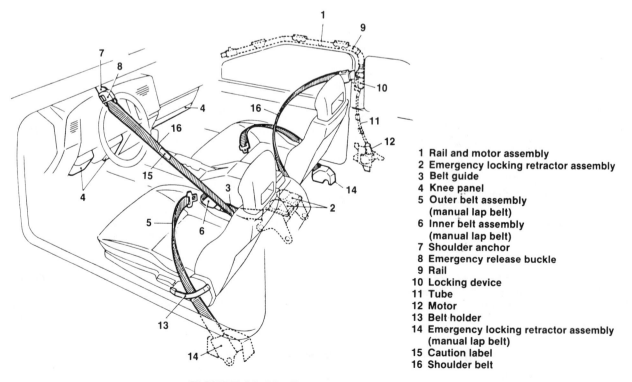

1 Rail and motor assembly
2 Emergency locking retractor assembly
3 Belt guide
4 Knee panel
5 Outer belt assembly
  (manual lap belt)
6 Inner belt assembly
  (manual lap belt)
7 Shoulder anchor
8 Emergency release buckle
9 Rail
10 Locking device
11 Tube
12 Motor
13 Belt holder
14 Emergency locking retractor assembly
  (manual lap belt)
15 Caution label
16 Shoulder belt

FIGURE 14-58 Passive seat belt system

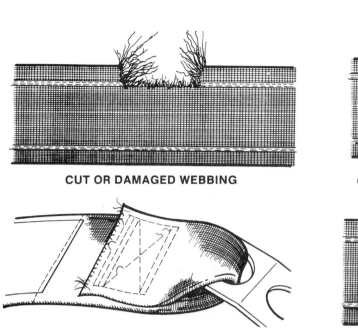

CUT OR DAMAGED WEBBING

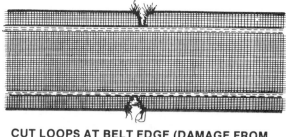

CUT LOOPS AT BELT EDGE (DAMAGE FROM
BEING CAUGHT IN DOOR)

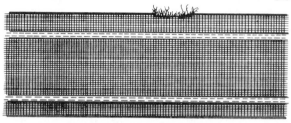

BROKEN OR PULLED THREADS

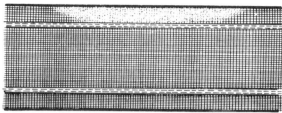

COLOR FADING

CUT LOOPS AT BELT EDGE

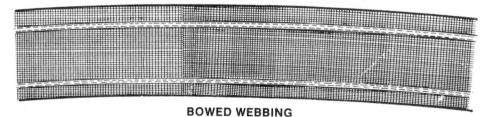

BOWED WEBBING

FIGURE 14-59 Examples of webbing defects

opened or if a system failure occurs wherein the system fails to deactivate the solenoids after the door is closed.

The active belt system consists of a single continuous length of webbing. The webbing is routed from the anchor (at the rocker panel), through a self-locking latch plate (at the buckle), around the guide assembly (at the top of the center pillar), and into a single retractor in the lower area of the center pillar.

The passive system for all coupes and late-model sedans differs from the active in that two retractors are used—one for the seat belt and a second for the shoulder belt (Figure 14-58). Both retractors are located behind the front door trim panels.

When servicing or replacing lap and shoulder belts, refer to the following:

1. Do not intermix standard and deluxe belts on front or rear seats.
2. Keep sharp edges and damaging objects away from belts.
3. Avoid bending or damaging any portion of the belt buckle or latch plate.
4. Do not attempt repairs on lap or shoulder belt retractor mechanisms or lap belt retractor covers. Replace with new replacement parts.
5. Tighten all seat and shoulder belt anchor bolts as specified in the service manual.

A visual and functional inspection of the belts themselves is very important to assure maximum protection for vehicle occupants. The following inspection checklist provides a typical, detailed seat belt inspection.

Front Seat Webbing Inspection

1. Check for twisted webbing due to improper alignment when connecting the buckle.
2. Fully extend the webbing from the retractor. Inspect the webbing and replace with a new assembly if the following conditions are noted (Figure 14-59):
   - Cut or damaged webbing
   - Broken or pulled threads
   - Cut loops at belt edge
   - Color fading as a result of exposure to sun or chemical agents
   - Bowed webbing
3. If the webbing cannot be pulled out of the retractor or will not retract to the stowed position, check for the following conditions and clean or correct as necessary:
   - Dirty webbing coated with gum, syrup, grease, or other foreign material
   - Twisted webbing
   - Retractor or loop on B-pillar out of position

Buckle Inspection

1. Insert the tongue of the seat belt into the buckle until a click is heard. Pull back on the webbing quickly to assure that the buckle is latched properly.
2. Replace the seat belt assembly if the buckle will not latch.
3. Depress the button on the buckle to release the belt. The belt should release with a pressure of approximately 2 pounds.
4. Replace the seat belt assembly if the buckle cover is cracked, the push button is loose, or the pressure required to release the buckle is too great.

Retractor Inspection

1. Grasp the seat belt webbing and, while pulling from the retractor, give the belt a fast jerk. The belt should lock up.
2. Drive the vehicle in an open area away from other vehicles at a speed of approximately 5 to 15 mph and quickly apply the foot brake. The belt should lock up.
3. If the retractor does not lock up under these conditions, remove and replace the seat belt assembly.

Anchorage Inspection

1. Check the seat belt anchorage for signs of movement or deformation. Replace if necessary. Position the replacement anchor-

age exactly the same as in the original installation.

 SHOP TALK _____

Do not bleach or dye the belt webbing (clean with a mild soap solution and water).

Rear Seat Restraint System

Removal and installation of a rear seat restraint system will be obvious upon inspection (Figure 14-60). Check the position of the factory installed lap belt and single loop belt anchors and reinstall the anchor plates in the same position as shown. Torque the bolts as specified in the service manual.

Some models have a rear center seat belt. These belts do not have a retractor. In addition to checking the webbing and anchorages, the adjustable slide locking of the belt must be checked.

- Fasten the tongue to the buckle and adjust by pulling the webbing end at a right angle to the connector and buckle.
- Release the webbing and pull upward on the connector and buckle.
- If the slide lock does not hold, remove and replace the seat belt assembly.

Child Seat

There are three types of child car seats: rear facing, forward facing, or a combination. The car seat is secured with a lap and shoulder seat belt

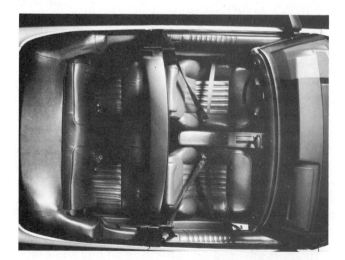

FIGURE 14-60 Rear seat restraint belts are clearly visible.

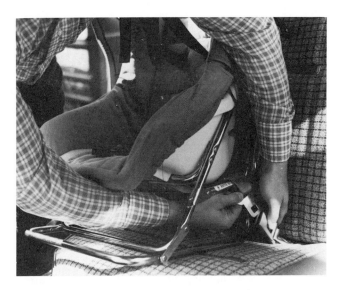

FIGURE 14-61   Typical child car seat

(using a locking clip provided by the car seat manufacturer) or just a lap belt (Figure 14-61). No one can be sure a child car seat will prevent injury in a specific accident but the proper use of the car seat should reduce the risk.

Air Bag Systems

A typical air bag system includes three important elements (Figure 14-62).

1. The electrical system, which includes the impact sensors and the electronic monitor assembly. Its main functions are to
   - Conduct a system self-check to let the driver know that the system is functioning
   - Detect an impact
   - Send a signal that inflates the air bag
2. The air bag module, which is located in the steering wheel and contains the air bag and the ports that cause it to inflate.
3. The knee diverter, which cushions the driver's knee from impact and helps prevent the driver from sliding under the air bag during a collision. It is located underneath the steering column and behind the steering column trim.

The air bag module itself is composed of nylon and is sometimes coated internally with neoprene. All the air bag module components are packaged in

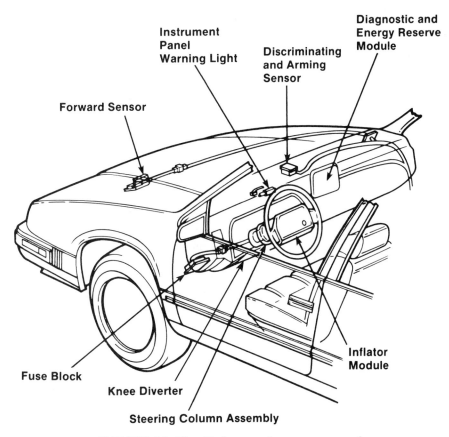

FIGURE 14-62   Air bag system components

a single container, which is mounted in the center of the steering wheel (Figure 14-62). This entire assembly must be serviced as one unit when repair of the air bag system is required.

Inflation of the air bag is caused by an explosive release of gas. In order for the "explosion" to occur, a chemical reaction must be started. The igniter does this when it receives a signal from the air bag monitor. Actually, the igniter is a two-pin bridge device. When the electrical current is applied, it arcs across the two pins, creating a spark that ignites a canister of gas generating zerconic potassium perchlorate (ZPP). This material in turn ignites the propellent. Once it triggers the igniter, the propellent charge is progressive burning sodium oxide, which converts to nitrogen gas as it burns. It is the nitrogen gas that fills the air bag (Figure 14-63).

Almost as soon as the bag is filled, the gas is cooled and vented, thus deflating the assembly as the collision energy is absorbed. The driver is cradled in the envelope of the supplemental restraint bag instead of being propelled forward to strike the steering wheel or be otherwise injured by follow-up inertia energy from seat belts. In addition, there is some facial protection against flying objects.

It is important to remember that the tandem action of at least one main sensor and a safing sensor will activate the system. The microcontroller also provides failure data and trouble codes for use in servicing various aspects of most systems.

 **SHOP TALK** _____

A recent development in the area of air bag research for passenger/occupant protection is the use of a solid propellent and argon. This gas has a stable structure, cools more quickly, and is inert as well as nontoxic.

Passenger-side air bags are very similar in design to the driver's unit. The actual capacity of gas required to inflate the bag is much greater because the bag must span the extra distance between the occupant and the dashboard at the passenger seating location. The steering wheel and column make up this difference on the driver's side.

Air Bag System Servicing

Begin with a thorough visual inspection of the sensors. Damage from a collision, or mishandling during a nonrelated repair, can disarm the air bag system. If possible, use a service code-related procedure to troubleshoot the fault area.

When testing for continuity problems or short circuits, remove the air bag module and substitute a jumper wire or special load simulator. This step will ensure a safe test sequence by preventing accidental bag deployment. Also remove the battery ground cable and any backup power packs, if so equipped.

An air bag module is serviced as a complete assembly in all of the available systems to date. While repairing this system, service the crash sensors, mercury switches, and any other related components. A crash sensor that has been damaged should be replaced. Replace the entire set if a failure of any single sensor is found.

Extreme care must be taken when reinstalling an air bag module (Figure 14-64). The modules should be stored with the horn pad facing up and the aluminum or metallic housing facing down.

FIGURE 14-63 **Crash sequence of a typical air bag system**

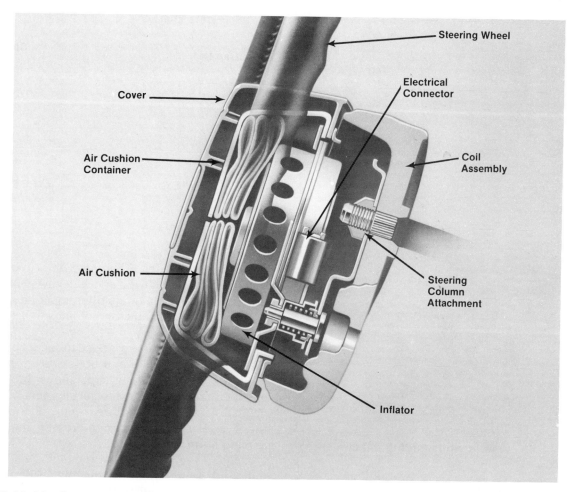

FIGURE 14-64   Cutaway of air bag system components in steering wheel

The steering column clock spring or spiral wrap, used to electrically link the controller to the bag and the crash sensors, should be kept in its correct position at all times. Failure to keep the centering spring relative to the steering wheel's straight-ahead neutral position can cause damage to the enclosure, wiring, or module. Any of these situations can cause the system to default into a nonoperative mode.

Do not pull the steering wheel to compensate for alignment variations or to service the couplings or gearbox seals. This can cause many installation errors—the most serious being damage to the spiral coupler or clock spring device, or altering the deflection attitude of the bag for deployment. Even though the removal of the steering wheel is similar to non-equipped air bag vehicles, caution should be used when servicing these systems.

Follow these safety precautions when working with air bag systems:

- Before beginning diagnostic procedures, as well as the repair, removal, or installation of

any components of an air bag system, disconnect the battery to prevent accidental inflation of the bag. On some vehicles, wait 10 minutes for the auxiliary power supply to discharge (check the service manual).

- When carrying a live (undeployed) air bag module, be sure the bag and trim cover are pointed away from your body as you walk. This will help reduce the chances of serious injury if the bag suddenly inflates.

- When laying a module down on a surface, make sure the bag and trim cover are face up to minimize a "launch effect" of the module if the bag suddenly inflates.

- Defective, or used, air bag modules must be replaced as a whole unit. Do not attempt to service individual parts of these modules.

- Wear safety glasses and protective gloves when handling inflated air bags, and wash hands with soap and water when finished. Inflators often contain irritating and toxic chemicals.

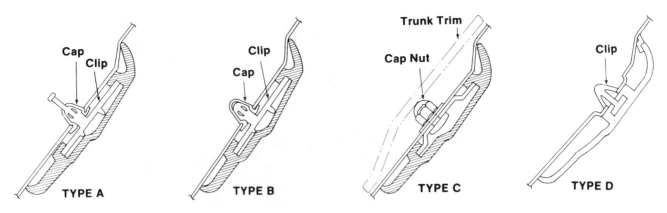

FIGURE 14-65   Typical molding attachments

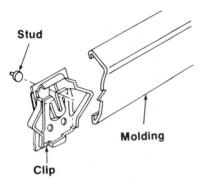

FIGURE 14-66   A weld stud molding attachment

- Never probe electrical connectors on an air bag module. This could set off the air bag.
- Never just toss out a faulty air bag module or uninflated air bag. Some manufacturers stipulate that a deployed air bag must be returned to the manufacturer. Follow specific U.S. Department of Transportation regulations when returning it.

A final inspection of the job should include checking to make sure the sensors are firmly fastened to their mounting fixtures, with the arrows on them facing forward. Be certain all the fuses are correctly rated and replaced. Make sure a final sweep is made for codes or accident information using the approved scan tool. Carefully recheck the wire and harness routing before releasing the car.

14.12 INSTALLING BODY MOLDING

Every vehicle has a variety of moldings. Moldings enhance the appearance of a vehicle by hiding panel joints, framing windshield or back lights, and accenting body lines. They also help to weatherproof by channeling wind and water away from windows and doors. Moldings often must be replaced due to collision damage, or moldings can be added as a custom accessory.

A variety of fasteners is used to secure moldings to a vehicle. The clips and bolts shown in Figure 14-65 are examples. The clips shown in A and B must be removed with a special clip puller. Removing fasteners C and D requires removing the interior trim. Type D is removed by compressing the clip and pushing it through the hole.

One of the most common molding attachment methods is a stud welded to the body. A clip fits over the stud and the molding slides over the clip (Figure 14-66). If a weld stud is bent or broken off, replace it with an oval head blind rivet, or weld a new stud in place with a stud welder equipped with a special rivet electrode.

Other methods of attachment include adhesives and rivets. Body side moldings installed as add-ons by dealers, trim shops, and body shops are installed by one of these two methods. Adhesive moldings, when properly applied, are permanent. Rivet-on moldings, while also permanent, might create buckles in large, low-crown panels and require drilling through the corrosion protection on the body. Instructions for both types are given here.

INSTALLING ADHESIVE BODY SIDE MOLDINGS

 1. Park the car on a level surface. The surface to which the molding will be applied should be cleaned and at least 70 degrees Fahrenheit to ensure proper adhesion.

2. Select the area to which the molding will be applied. For greatest protection, the mold-

ing should be applied to the outermost surface of the vehicle. If the car has an outermost ridge, install the molding 1/8 inch above or 1/8 inch below the ridge (Figure 14-67A), but not on the ridge itself. If the panel does not have a prominent ridge, select the outermost surface of the body contour (Figure 14-67B).

3. After determining the best location for the molding, thoroughly clean the area with water and detergent. Then, use a clean rag wetted with enamel thinner or a wax and grease remover to remove waxes and silicones (Figure 14-68). Use a clean cloth for each side of the vehicle.

WARNING: Before installing body side moldings on newly repainted cars, allow 24 hours for a baked finish to dry and five full days for air dry finish to dry. Also, car body moldings must be applied before polishing the newly finished car with waxes that contain teflon, silicones, or polymers. All traces of these waxes and polishes must be thoroughly removed before applying the adhesive back molding. The molding will not permanently bond to the vehicle if any trace of these substances remains on the panel.

4. If the body molding will not be aligned above or below a body ridge that can be used as a guide, mark the correct height of the molding with a steel rule and a soft lead pencil or a china marker. Mark the height at the rear and front of the car and at each door gap. Then, stretch a piece of masking tape from front to rear connecting the marks (Figure 14-69). Keep the tape taut and sight along its length to ensure a straight line. Magnetic plastic tape can also be used as a straight edge.

5. The next step is cutting the molding to length. Start 3 inches from the front edge of the fender of the car and measure to the edge of the car door. Allow for 1/8 inch clearance between the molding and the edge of the fender. Cut the molding to size (Figure 14-70). Repeat this procedure for the rear quarter panel piece of molding. When measuring for door pieces, leave 1/8 inch clearance at both ends of the molding. To enhance the molding's appearance and to prevent binding when the door is

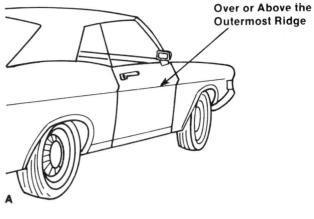

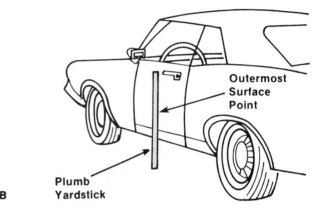

FIGURE 14-67 Apply exterior molding (A) along the outermost ridge or (B) the outermost surface point

FIGURE 14-68 Cleaning with wax and grease remover

FIGURE 14-69 **Applying masking tape as a straight-edge**

opened, cut the ends of the molding at a 45-degree angle, using single edge razor blade (Figure 14-71).

6. Peel 6 inches of the protective backing paper from the cut end of the fender molding. Do not touch or dirty the exposed adhesive after removing the backing. Begin installing the fender molding 1/8 inch from the fender rear edge. Align the molding with the top edge of the tape and lightly press against the panel (Figure 14-72). Progressively remove the backing and press the molding against the surface and along the edge of the tape. Do not attempt to reposition a piece after it is applied. After the whole length of molding is applied,

FIGURE 14-70 **Cutting molding to length**

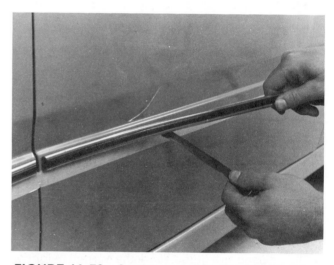

FIGURE 14-72 **Applying molding to front fender**

FIGURE 14-71 **Cutting 45-degree angle on molding ends**

FIGURE 14-73 **The finished application**

press along the entire length with the heel of the hand or with a roller.

Repeat this process with the door moldings and the rear quarter panel molding. Figure 14–73 shows the completed application.

> **WARNING:** The adhesive develops its full strength slowly. Caution the owner to avoid washing the car by hand for several days and to avoid washing by a high-pressure automatic system for three weeks after installation.

INSTALLING RIVET-ON BODY SIDE MOLDINGS

Before applying rivet-on moldings, park the vehicle on a level surface and clean the sides of the

FIGURE 14–74   Vinyl-covered roofs

vehicle where the molding will be applied. Then, determine the best location for the molding, following the procedure described in installing adhesive moldings. After applying masking tape as a guide, hold the molding in position and mark the desired length. Be sure to leave 1/2-inch clearance on both ends for caps and spears.

Cut the molding to length. Use a sharp pair of metal cutters or razor blade to cut the ends square. Duplicate each piece for installation on the opposite side of the vehicle.

Slide the molding out of the track, and hold the track in place. Some moldings have an adhesive backing to assist in positioning the track. With the track in place, use a 9/64-inch drill bit (1/64 inch larger than the rivet diameter) to drill through holes in the track. Also, drill holes 3/4 inch from each end of the molding. Install 1/8 inch × 1/4 inch rivets with a rivet gun.

Replace the molding in the track and install the end caps and spears. If necessary, tape the caps with a rubber mallet to seat them. Be careful not to scratch the finish.

14.13 VINYL ROOF SERVICING

Roof panels are commonly covered with a vinyl-coated fabric (Figure 14–74). Full vinyl roofs and landau roofs (Figure 14–75) can be repaired or completely replaced. Replacement procedures vary depending on the roof design, attachment method, and trim molding design. Most vinyl covers are glued directly to the roof panel. Others are padded with foam rubber. Some typical vinyl roof designs are given in Figure 14–74. Note the methods of attachment at A-pillars, windshields, back windows, door openings, and so on.

Vinyl covers are adhered to the roof panels with adhesive. A number of mechanical fasteners are also used to secure the vinyl cover to the edges of the roof: clips over weld-on studs, reveal moldings, finishing lace, drive nails, screws, drip scalp moldings, weatherstrip retainers, or finishing plugs. While some replacement covers come with a preapplied adhesive backing, this chapter deals only with the adhesive application of an unpadded vinyl top. Foam rubber pads are applied following the basic procedure described for vinyl top installation.

Vinyl top repairs fall into three categories. One is **complete replacement** of the vinyl material. This can be necessary due to direct damage to the roof or due to weathering of the material. If not properly maintained, the vinyl material will discolor, blister,

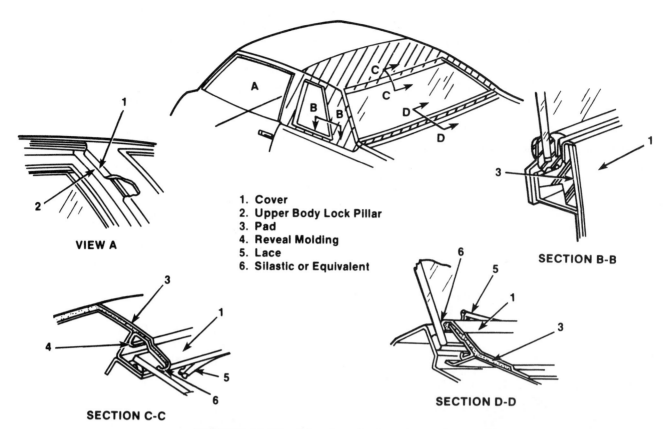

1. Cover
2. Upper Body Lock Pillar
3. Pad
4. Reveal Molding
5. Lace
6. Silastic or Equivalent

VIEW A

SECTION B-B

SECTION C-C

SECTION D-D

FIGURE 14-75   A landau vinyl roof installation

and peel. **Partial removal** of a vinyl roof is sometimes necessary to repair damage to the rear quarter panel or windshield A-pillar. **Minor repairs**—such as cuts and abrasions—can also be made with a patching compound or rebonded with a soldering iron.

COMPLETE REPLACEMENT

When a vinyl top has been damaged beyond repair, replace the vinyl following this procedure.

1. Unpack the new cover and spread it out to remove the wrinkles.
2. Remove the trim moldings that cover the edges of the cloth—windshield and back light moldings, drip rail moldings, upper quarter panel moldings, and any emblems, ornaments, or nameplates attached through the vinyl material. If necessary, remove the blind quarter inner trim to gain access to the ornament retaining nuts. Some vehicles also require removal of interior garnish molding to gain access to weatherstrip retaining screws. Be very careful when removing drive nails. Avoid stretching the holes so that the nails can be reinstalled in the same holes.

3. Clean excess cement and sealer from the roof edges and the windshield and back light. If necessary, use a heat gun to soften the cement and ease removal.
4. Using the hot-air gun, soften the edges of the material so that it can be pulled from the roof. Use a pair of pliers to grasp the vinyl edge and peel the cover from the roof (Figure 14-76). If necessary, use the heat

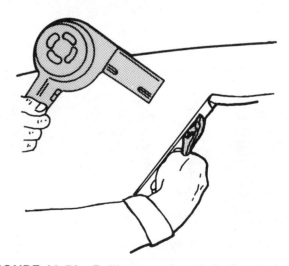

FIGURE 14-76   Pulling up edge of vinyl material

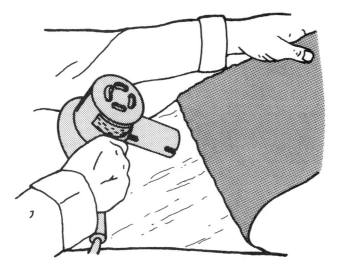

FIGURE 14-77   Use heat to soften glue if necessary.

gun as shown in Figure 14-77 to soften the cement. Carefully observe how the vinyl is fitted to the roof panel. The new cover must be installed identically.

5. After the vinyl has been removed, remove the old cement from the roof, using an xylol-based adhesive remover. It is not necessary to completely remove all of the old adhesive, but the roof must be smooth and level before applying the new vinyl fabric or the finish installation will be lumpy.

6. Mask around the roof to avoid getting cement on the glass and the paint area. Masking is especially important if using a spray adhesive.

7. Lay the new roofing material over the roof and verify that it fits properly.

8. Remove the fabric and use chalk to mark the centerline of the roof. Measure carefully so that the line is accurate. Then, fold the fabric in half and mark the centerline on the cloth side of the vinyl.

9. Place the vinyl on the roof and align the centerlines. Fold one half of the vinyl back to the centerline.

10. Apply a vinyl roof cement to one half of the fabric. Do not apply adhesive to areas that cover the upper quarter panel, roof sides, or the area around the door, windshield, and rear windows.

11. Starting at the centerline, also apply vinyl roofing cement to the exposed half of the roof top. Do not apply adhesive yet to sides or around windows. Be sure to carefully follow the adhesive manufacturer's instruc-

tions. Some adhesives must be brushed or rolled on. Others are designed to be sprayed on. However the cement is applied, it must be applied evenly. There should be no skips, voids, globs, or pools of adhesive.

12. After allowing for the manufacturer's suggested tack time, carefully roll the vinyl over the cement, smoothing out any wrinkles or air bubbles. Be careful to keep the vinyl aligned with the roof. A stiff plastic squeegee can be used to work out air bubbles (Figure 14-78). To work out wrinkles, use a heat gun to soften the vinyl and adhesive. Hold the gun 1 to 2 inches from the vinyl and rotate the gun in a circular motion. Apply pressure with the squeegee to smooth the wrinkles out.

WARNING: Do not blister or scorch the vinyl.

13. Apply adhesive to the remaining half of the roof and cover as described in Steps 10 through 12. Smooth the cover over the roof and stretch out all wrinkles.

14. Apply adhesive to the body and underside of the cover in the area below the rear window (if applicable). Position the cover and remove any wrinkles.

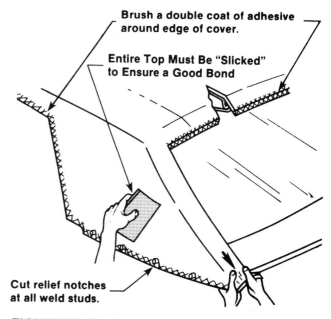

Brush a double coat of adhesive around edge of cover.

Entire Top Must Be "Slicked" to Ensure a Good Bond

Cut relief notches at all weld studs.

FIGURE 14-78   Applying new vinyl to the roof panel

15. Apply adhesive to the roof sides and door openings and to the underside of the cover. Make angle cuts at the corners as necessary. Then, stretch the cover and cement in place. Pull the material taut, using fabric roof cover pliers.

16. On vehicles with frenched backlights carefully apply adhesive around the back light on padding and the plastic panel. Be sure to use a spatula type tool to fold the roof cover back under the rear window opening panel.

17. Trim the roof cover at the windshield and rear window openings. Leave 1/2 inch of material at the openings for cover attachment in the window opening recess.

18. Apply adhesive to the rear window opening and the underside of the roof cover. Make angle cuts as necessary at the corners and cement the material in the rear window opening recess. Trim the cover around the molding retainer weld studs.

19. Apply adhesive to the windshield opening and the underside of the roof cover. Make angle cuts as necessary at the corners and cement the material in the windshield opening recess. Trim the cover around the molding retainer weld studs.

20. At each roof rear quarter, locate and punch two holes for the roof side ornament on models so equipped. Install each side ornament with the studs entering the punched holes. Then, from inside the vehicle, install the retaining nuts on the studs and apply a silicone sealant around the nuts.

21. Reinstall interior trim panels, garnish moldings, weatherstrips, and exterior moldings.

 SHOP TALK _____

Any exterior moldings using positive bolt-on fasteners must be installed prior to installation of interior trim parts.

22. Clean the glass, moldings, top, and surrounding area.

Partial Removal

If partial removal of the vinyl roof is necessary because of damaged roof metal, follow this proce-

dure. Remove trim from the affected area and pull the vinyl material up. Peel it away from the area, following techniques discussed earlier. Place shop rags in the fold of the material to prevent it from creasing. If the repair area requires welding or heat shrinking, make sure that the material is pulled far enough away so that it will be unaffected by the heat. If necessary, place an asbestos dam between the area and the vinyl to absorb the heat. After the area has been repaired and refinished, apply cement to the area and smooth the vinyl back into place. Pull it tight and work out any wrinkles. Clean up excess cement, and reapply the trim.

After the repair has cured for several days, wrinkles can appear in the vinyl. Use an electric household iron pressed over a damp cloth to soften the material and smooth the wrinkles out (Figure 14-79). A heat gun and a stiff squeegee can also be used. If the wrinkles cannot be removed with one of these methods, pull the fabric up and reglue the area.

Patching a Vinyl Roof

A torn vinyl roof can sometimes be repaired with a vinyl patching compound and a grain mold die. The grain mold die is made from a special die material or from body filler. The die is used to impress the vinyl texture in the patching compound. To make the die, clean a 6 to 8 inch square portion of the undamaged vinyl roof with a vinyl cleaner. Then, spray the area with a silicone mold release. Apply a properly catalyzed amount of die material or body filler to the area. Cover the material with a scrap piece of vinyl, place a block of wood on top of the vinyl, and weight it down to force the material into the grain pattern. Allow the die to harden; then, peel the die up, trim the edges, and spray with a silicone mold release.

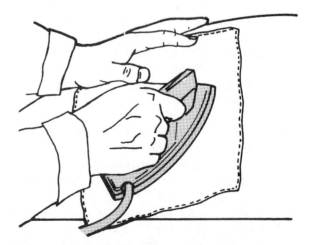

FIGURE 14-79 Smoothing out wrinkles with an iron

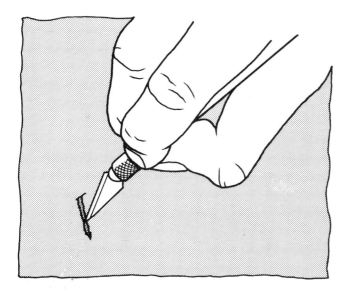

FIGURE 14-80   Trim off frayed edges.

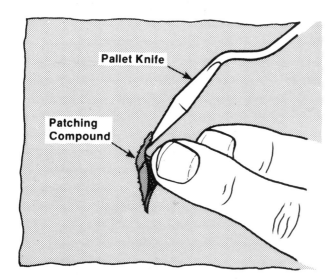

Pallet Knife

Patching Compound

FIGURE 14-81   Glue loose material.

After the grain mold die has been made, patch the torn vinyl following this procedure.

1. If the area is torn, trim off any loose fabric and frayed edges (Figure 14-80). If the damaged area is larger, cement the loose material back into place with trim cement and allow to dry (Figure 14-81). Cut out at least 1/16 inch of material on both sides of the tear line to allow for the vinyl patching compound.

2. Clean the area with a vinyl cleaner by spraying the cleaner onto a clean cloth and wiping the area. Do not spray the cleaner directly onto the repair area.

3. Apply the vinyl patching compound to the repair area with a suitable applicator trow-

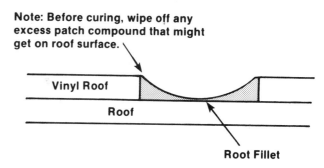

Note: Before curing, wipe off any excess patch compound that might get on roof surface.

Vinyl Roof

Roof

Root Fillet

FIGURE 14-82   Filling the panel to vinyl edges

el. Use a trowel or putty knife to work the compound under any loose edges of the vinyl. Apply the first layer to the metal-vinyl edge to make a root fillet (Figure 14-82). Wipe off any excess compound from the vinyl. Because most vinyl compounds have a thin viscosity, several coats will be necessary to completely fill the void. Be sure to follow the manufacturer's instructions for curing time between coats. Normally, a heat gun is used to speed the curing time. Hold the gun 1 inch above the compound and move the gun in a circular motion to distribute heat evenly. Curing takes about 20 seconds and is complete when the compound turns from white to translucent (almost clear). Press down on the roof material around the repair during the heat curing process to keep the fabric flat.

4. Build up the repair area until the compound is slightly above the level of the vinyl (Figure 14-83). Usually three layers are adequate to complete the job, but larger holes might require up to four or five layers. Before the last application hardens, draw the side edge of the trowel tool over the face of the patch area to strike off the

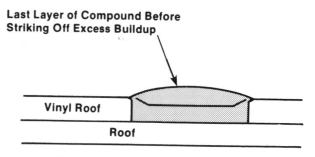

Last Layer of Compound Before Striking Off Excess Buildup

Vinyl Roof

Roof

Do not cure with heat gun at this stage.

FIGURE 14-83   Build last layer above vinyl material.

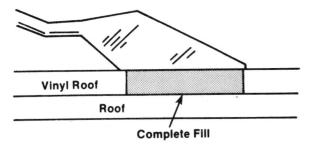

Vinyl Roof

Roof

Complete Fill

FIGURE 14-84 Level the compound with the vinyl material.

excess buildup to get a level surface (Figure 14-84). Also, remove any excess compound that might smear on the vinyl roof material adjacent to the patch area, otherwise, it will cure to the roof material and cause unwanted buildup on the surrounding area. Joint is now ready for the final heat cure and regraining procedure.

5. Cure this last leveled layer by heating the patched area for about 30 seconds at 1-inch nozzle distance (always moving the gun nozzle in a circular motion) until the patched area develops a shiny glazed appearance. Have the grain pattern die ready in the other hand.

6. Remove heat and immediately press grain pattern die with force. Hold die on service area for at least 10 seconds to obtain a good impression.

7. Cool the serviced area with a moist sponge or cold air blast from the gun.

8. Spray vinyl prep conditioner on a clean cloth and lightly dab the area. Do not rub.

9. Spray the repaired area with a matching color vinyl paint. Complete instructions for refinishing vinyl materials are given in Chapter 19.

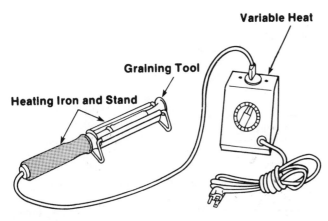

Variable Heat

Graining Tool

Heating Iron and Stand

FIGURE 14-85 Vinyl repair tools

MINOR VINYL ROOF REPAIRS

A variety of minor vinyl roof repairs can be made. Most require special tools not usually found in a body shop. Many minor repairs require the use of a soldering iron connected to a variable transformer (Figure 14-85). The transformer allows the heat of the soldering iron to be set at 225 degrees Fahrenheit. Other "tools" needed for minor repairs are a hypodermic syringe available from any medical supply company, an abrasive sponge, and a rubber cement pick-up block available at most craft or art supply stores. With these tools, the following repairs can be made.

Scuffs or Abrasions

 **SHOP TALK** _____

Before making any vinyl repair, thoroughly clean the vinyl roof with a vinyl cleaner. Use a scrub brush to remove all dirt imbedded in the graining. Repeat the cleaning operation as often as required, particularly on white vinyl tops.

Connect the soldering iron and set the transformer heat range to approximately 225 degrees Fahrenheit.

Clean the soldering iron tip thoroughly with the abrasive pad. This must be done frequently while performing the service to avoid vinyl buildup on the tip.

Lightly slide the soldering tip over the scuff mark several times using short overlapping strokes until the frayed vinyl is fused to the surface.

The vinyl surface might have been removed by the scuff, exposing the cloth backing. Repair the vinyl surface by filling in with vinyl. This is accomplished by stripping a small quantity of vinyl from a piece of scrap material with the hot tip of the solder gun. Carefully fill in as required using short overlapping strokes. Several stripping operations might be required to adequately fill the scuffed area.

The graining effect in the vinyl can be restored by carefully etching the grain pattern into the vinyl with the sharp edge of the soldering tip. The gloss or shiny surface created by the service area can be removed with the dulling agent or by spraying the area with liquid vinyl. Several color coats can be required. The last coat should be a fog coat to minimize gloss.

This service can be applied to scuffs or abrasions in most areas of the vinyl tip.

Minor Surface Cuts

The edges of a surface cut that has not penetrated the cloth backing can be welded together with a soldering iron.

Connect the soldering gun and set the transformer heat range to approximately 225 degrees Fahrenheit.

Clean the soldering iron tip thoroughly with the abrasive pad. Lightly slide the soldering tip across the cut surface using very short strokes—1/4 inch or less—until the cut is covered with vinyl. Go over the cut lengthwise again with the soldering tip to smooth out the surface. The graining effect can be restored by carefully etching the grain pattern into the vinyl with the sharp edge of the soldering tip.

If required, the gloss or shine on the vinyl surface created by the service can be removed with the dulling agent and then spraying the area with liquid vinyl. Several color coats of liquid vinyl can be required. The last coat should be a fog coat to minimize gloss.

Major Cuts

A major cut—one that has penetrated through both the vinyl and the cloth backing—can also be repaired with the soldering iron.

Connect the soldering iron and set the transformer heat range to approximately 225 degrees Fahrenheit. If damage is more than 1 inch long, apply a light coat of adhesive (Figure 14-86). (It is not necessary to use cement if the cut is over a padded area.)

Start at the center of the cut and lightly slide the soldering tip across the cut surface (Figure 14-87), using strokes 1/4 inch or less until the cut is covered with vinyl.

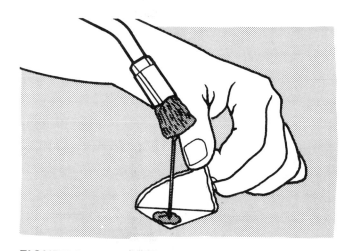

FIGURE 14-86   Gluing loose material

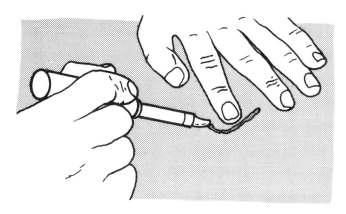

FIGURE 14-87   Soldering cut edges together

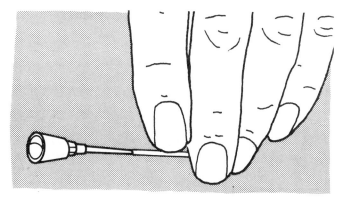

FIGURE 14-88   Removing air bubble with a hypodermic needle

Go over the cut lengthwise again with the soldering tip to smooth out the surface and restore the grain as described.

Bubbles

Generally, an air bubble can be eliminated by removing the air with a hypodermic needle. Insert the needle under the vinyl material as shown in Figure 14-88 and press the air out. It is necessary to activate the adhesive under the vinyl after the air has been expelled by applying heat with the gun until the vinyl surface is hot to the touch. Then, work the material down with the fingers.

To avoid overheating and possible damage to the vinyl, hold the heat gun about 10 to 12 inches from the surface and constantly move the gun in a circular motion. In some cases where a good bond cannot be obtained, insert a small amount of roof adhesive under the vinyl material with a syringe.

Wrinkles

Do not confuse a wrinkle with a bubble. Usually a wrinkle has small radial folds with slack material that cannot be displaced without rearranging the material. The following service procedure describes the correction of a wrinkle at the front corner.

 1. Partially or completely remove any moldings or ornamentation in the immediate area of the wrinkle.

2. Pull the vinyl material free from the roof panel up to the bonded seam and along the side drip rail for approximately 10 inches.

3. Clean the surface thoroughly to remove the old adhesive. Apply a thin film of adhesive both to the vinyl material and along the drip rail. Allow the adhesive to air dry for several seconds.

4. Grasp the material firmly and draw it tight until all wrinkles are removed. Fold the material under the drip rail flange.

5. Secure the front edge of the material with as many drive nails as needed to prevent the material from creeping. Apply sealer under the drive nail to prevent water leakage. Some manufacturers suggest securing the vinyl edge with 1/8 inch × 3/8 inch pop rivets. Caution must be used when riveting the top. If the rivet head is exposed after installing the moldings, the vinyl roof must be replaced.

6. Install the moldings and weatherstrips.

Looseness

Loose vinyl roof material usually occurs at padded areas of the vinyl roof on body styles so equipped. The following is a typical repair of loose material at the blind quarter area and generally applies to other areas such as around the back light opening.

 1. Partially or completely remove moldings or ornamentation in the immediate area to be repaired.

2. Carefully peel the edge of the material free from the sheet metal.

3. Clean the metal surface thoroughly to remove the old adhesive. Apply a thin film of adhesive to both the vinyl and metal surface. Allow the adhesive to air dry for several seconds.

4. Grasp the material firmly and draw it tight. Secure the edge of the material with drive nails or sheet metal screws as needed to prevent the material from creeping.

5. Apply sealer over the drive nails or sheet metal screws to prevent water leaks. Install the moldings.

Gap Between Vinyl Top and Molding

In some instances, vinyl top material that is too short to be concealed under the roof molding can be corrected by adjusting the molding or stretching the material. If it is necessary to stretch the material, pop rivets must be used to prevent the vinyl from returning to its original position. Should there be an insufficient amount of material to allow the use of pop rivets, the complete vinyl top cover must be replaced. To determine whether there is a sufficient amount of material, perform the following procedure:

 1. Loosen the molding retainers and reposition the molding sufficiently to cover the edge of the vinyl roof material. Retighten the molding retainers. If the edge of the vinyl material cannot be covered by repositioning the molding, proceed to Step 2.

2. Partially or completely remove the molding(s) or ornamentation in the area in which the vinyl roof is too short or gaps to the molding(s).

3. Carefully peel the vinyl material free from the roof panel 4 to 6 inches.

4. Using vinyl adhesive remover, clean the sheet metal surface thoroughly, removing all of the old adhesive.

5. Apply a thin film of vinyl roof adhesive to both the vinyl material and the sheet metal surface. Allow the adhesive to air dry for several seconds.

6. With a heat gun, apply heat to the vinyl, then grasp the material firmly and stretch the material so it can be installed beneath the molding(s). If, after stretching the material, it is evident that the edge to be held by pop rivets cannot be hidden by the moldings, the vinyl roof cover will have to be replaced.

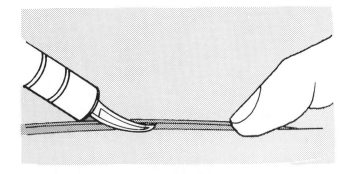

FIGURE 14-89   Soldering underside of seam

CAUTION: To avoid overheating the vinyl, hold the heat gun about 12 inches from the surface and constantly move the gun in a circular motion.

7. Drill a sufficient number of 9/64-inch diameter holes in the edge of the vinyl to be covered by the moldings to assure that it can be adequately secured to the roof panel with 1/8 inch × 3/8 inch pop rivets.
8. Install the necessary pop rivets and reinstall the molding(s) or ornamentation removed in Step 1.

Separated Bonded Seam

Connect the soldering iron and set the transformer heat range to approximately 225 degrees Fahrenheit.

Frequently clean the soldering iron tip thoroughly with the abrasive pad to avoid vinyl buildup on the tip. Start at one end of the separated seam and insert the tip of the soldering iron between the bonded seam (Figure 14-89). Note the position of the curved tip. Slowly move the tip along the underside of the seam. Immediately follow with the fingers to press the seam together.

Reverse the soldering iron tip (Figure 14-90) and again slowly move the tip along the edge of the seam.

This completes the service and, if performed correctly, should not require paint touch-up. Use a dulling agent or liquid vinyl to restore finish if necessary. Several coats might be required. The last coat should be a fog coat to minimize gloss.

Adhesive Smears

Adhesive smears can be removed in most cases, provided this is done immediately and the adhesive

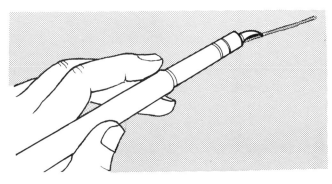

FIGURE 14-90   Soldering outer edge of seam

is not allowed to age on the vinyl roof. It is imperative that the cleanup is performed as soon as possible. Remove fresh sealer smears by rubbing with a rubber cement pick-up block.

14.14 REVIEW QUESTIONS

1. Technician A attempts to repair lap and shoulder belt retractor mechanisms before replacing them. Technician B automatically replaces defective lap and shoulder belt retractor mechanisms. Who is correct?
   a. Technician A
   b. Technician B
   c. Both A and B
   d. Neither A nor B

2. When measuring for door molding pieces, Technician A leaves 1/8 inch of clearance at both ends of the molding. Technician B makes no allowance for clearance. Who is correct?
   a. Technician A
   b. Technician B
   c. Both A and B
   d. Neither A nor B

3. What is used to remove wrinkles from a newly repaired vinyl roof?
   a. heat gun and squeegee
   b. iron and damp cloth
   c. both a and b
   d. neither a nor b

4. Prior to patching a vinyl roof, Technician A cleans the repair area by spraying vinyl cleaner directly on the vinyl. Technician B sprays the cleaner on a cloth and uses it to clean the vinyl. Who is correct?
   a. Technician A
   b. Technician B
   c. Both A and B
   d. Neither A nor B

5. When repairing a major cut in a vinyl roof, when should adhesive be used to secure the loose material?
   a. never
   b. if the cut is more than 1 inch deep
   c. if the cut is more than 1 inch long
   d. always

6. Tempered glass is never used for
   _____ .
   a. windshields
   b. rear windows
   c. side windows
   d. both a and b

7. What is another name for modular glass?
   a. reveal
   b. encapsulated
   c. garnish
   d. venetian

8. Technician A uses a sharp pair of metal cutters to cut molding to length. Technician B uses a razor blade. Who is correct?
   a. Technician A
   b. Technician B
   c. Both A and B
   d. Neither A nor B

9. What type of glass consists of two thin sheets of glass with a layer of clear plastic between them?
   a. tinted
   b. tempered
   c. laminated
   d. antilacerative

10. What type of glass fits the contours of a vehicle very closely?
    a. modula
    b. tempered
    c. laminated
    d. channel

11. When servicing an air bag system, Technician A probes the electrical connectors on the air bag module; Technician B does not. Who is correct?
    a. Technician A
    b. Technician B
    c. Both A and B
    d. Neither A nor B

12. Gasket glass installation is more common in
    _____ .
    a. older vehicles
    b. newer vehicles

c. vehicles with modular glass
d. none of the above

13. Which of the following items is used in the full cutout windshield replacement method?
    a. butyl ribbon sealer
    b. setting blocks
    c. utility knife
    d. all of the above

14. In the partial cutout windshield replacement method, what serves as the base for the new adhesive?
    a. butyl ribbon sealer
    b. butyl tape
    c. masking tape
    d. the old adhesive

15. Where do the majority of windshield leaks occur?
    a. sides
    b. top
    c. bottom
    d. corners

16. Which of the following should not be done before adjusting vehicle headlights?
    a. Inflate the tires to the recommended pressures.
    b. Clean off any snow, ice, or mud from the underside.
    c. Fill the gas tank.
    d. Check the condition of the suspension components.

17. What is required to test an energy absorber?
    a. hydraulic jack
    b. chain
    c. drill
    d. all of the above

18. Which fastening method is used to install add-on body side moldings?
    a. studs welded to the body
    b. bolts
    c. both a and b
    d. neither a nor b

CHAPTER
15

Restoring Corrosion Protection

Corrosion is a problem that has always concerned body shop technicians and refinishers. It requires either repair work (see Chapter 8) or special treatment when refinishing (see Chapter 18). But, with the following recent developments in the automotive industry, the words **corrosion prevention** have taken on new meaning to body shop personnel:

- Corrosion prevention is the phrase that is replacing rustproofing, undercoating, and sound deadening. Corrosion prevention implies a vehicle lifetime maintenance responsibility for the consumer. Rustproofing, undercoating, and sound deadening had suggested a one-time application to the new vehicle by car dealerships and rustproofing franchises.
- Car manufacturers are including in their owner's manual instructions recommendations for sheet metal repair or replacement. They suggest that the body shop should apply an anticorrosive material to the part repaired or replaced so that corrosion protection is restored.
- In affiliation with the Inter-Industry Conference on Auto Collision Repair (I-CAR), the insurance companies are promoting corrosion prevention repair to the body shops.
- The increased usage of replacement panels in the body shops requires widespread corrosion prevention treatment.
- Possibly the major reason, however, is the advent of the unibody car.

In unibody construction, the car's body panels are no longer cosmetic sheet metal. They now constitute the structural integrity of the vehicle. This means that rust is not just an eyesore. The unibody car has more welded joints in critical structural areas where corrosion can do serious damage. It is an ever present danger to the unibody vehicle since rusting of structural panels and rails can affect the driveability of the car and the safety of its passengers.

15.1 WHAT IS CORROSION?

Corrosion—or rust, when it occurs on steel—is the product of a complex chemical reaction with serious and costly consequences (Figure 15–1). Chemical corrosion requires three elements (Figure 15–2):

- Exposed metal
- Oxygen
- Moisture (electrolyte)

In other words, the formula for rust in a car body is:

Iron + Oxygen + Electrolyte = Rust (Iron Oxide)

There are three basic types of corrosion protection used on today's automobiles:

- Galvanizing or zinc coating
- Paint
- Anticorrosion compounds

Galvanizing is a process of coating steel with zinc (Figure 15–3). It is one of the principal methods of corrosion protection applied during the manufacturing process. On galvanized steel, the zinc forms a natural barrier between the steel and the atmosphere. As the zinc corrodes, a layer of zinc oxide will form on the surface exposed to the atmosphere. Unlike iron oxide, or rust, the zinc oxide adheres to the zinc coating tightly, forming a natural barrier between the zinc and the atmosphere. When the surface of the car's finish is damaged by a scratch or nick, the zinc coating undergoes corrosion, sacrificing itself to protect the iron under it. The resulting zinc oxide actually forms a protective coating and repairs the exposed area of the steel. Thus, zinc performs a twofold protective process; first, it pro-

FIGURE 15-1   Closeup of car's number one enemy—rust

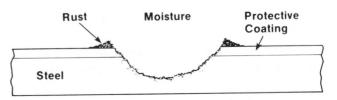

FIGURE 15-2   Breakdown in protective coating causes rapid rust formation.

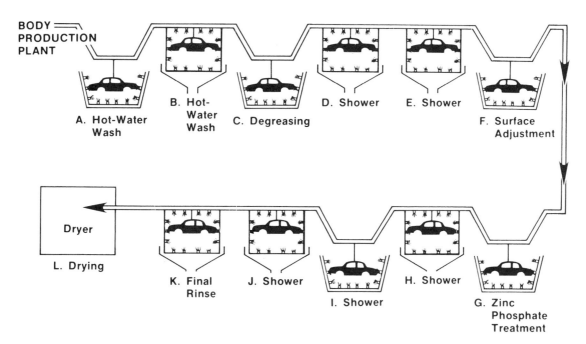

FIGURE 15-3 Zinc corrosion treatment utilizing the full dip method as done by a vehicle manufacturer's body production operator: (A) and (B) metal chips, dirt, and other foreign particles are washed off with 100 to 125 degrees Fahrenheit hot water; (C) press oil and anticorrosion oil are removed with a weak alkali degreasing agent; (D) and (E) the degreasing agent is washed off with water in two stages; (F) nucleus of zinc phosphate film is adhered to panel surfaces; (G) body dipped into tank of zinc phosphate for crystallization; (H), (I), and (J) zinc phosphate liquid washed off by water in three stages; (K) final rinse to prevent blistering; and (L) dried at 212 to 300 degrees Fahrenheit. *(Courtesy of Toyota Motor Corp.)*

vides chemical, galvanic protection, and second, it forms a repair over the exposed steel with a layer of zinc oxide.

A paint system such as those described in later chapters of this book will provide a barrier between the atmosphere and the steel surface. When this barrier is in place (Figure 15-4), the moisture and impurities in the air cannot interact with the steel surface and the steel is protected from corrosion. If the paint surface or barrier is broken by a stone chip or scratch, the steel in this area is no longer isolated from the moisture and impurities in the air. Corrosion will then take place in this region. Corrosion will spread between the paint and steel surface. If the adhesion of the paint to the steel is poor, large sections of the paint can be separated from the steel. This will result in a large area of the steel being left unprotected, and severe rust in this region will quickly follow. If impurities are present between the paint and the steel, then oxygen in the air can pass through the paint, reacting with the impurities and the steel to form rust. In this case, corrosion will take place on the steel surface and the protective paint barrier will be destroyed. Paint, by itself, is only effective as long as the paint film remains intact.

FIGURE 15-4 The paint system used on the vehicle is a barrier against corrosion. *(Courtesy of Sherwin-Williams Co.)*

Anticorrosion compounds are additional coatings applied over the paint film. Protective coatings can be applied either by the manufacturer or as an aftermarket process. The two most popular types of anticorrosion coatings are:

- Petroleum-based compounds
- Wax-based compounds

FIGURE 15-5 Anticorrosion material being applied to an enclosed body section.

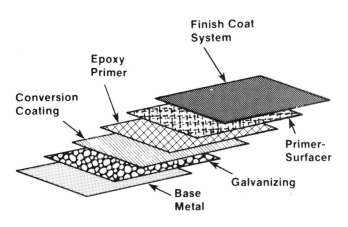

FIGURE 15-6 Typical buildup of corrosion prevention material used by car manufacturers.

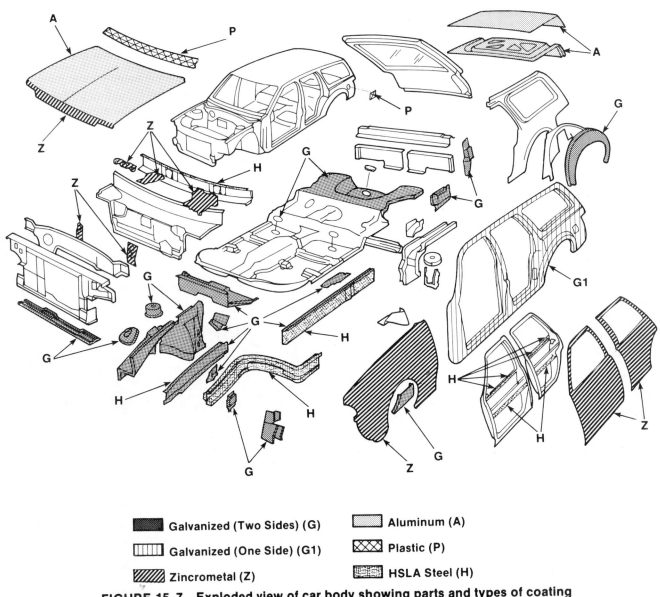

■ Galvanized (Two Sides) (G)		▨ Aluminum (A)	
▥ Galvanized (One Side) (G1)		▨ Plastic (P)	
▨ Zincrometal (Z)		▨ HSLA Steel (H)	

FIGURE 15-7 Exploded view of car body showing parts and types of coating

Anticorrosion compounds are primarily used in enclosed body sections (Figure 15-5) and other rust prone areas.

The auto manufacturers are increasing their corrosion protection measures all the time. New processes and methods, including the use of coated steels, zinc rich primers, and more durable base coatings, have made it possible for modern cars to survive corrosive forces for longer periods than before. The following is a typical new car finishing sequence (Figure 15-6) used by major auto manufacturers:

1. Use coated or galvanized steel (Figure 15-7).
2. Chemically clean and rinse.
3. Apply conversion coating.
4. Apply epoxy primer.
5. Bake primer.
6. Apply primer-surfacer.
7. Apply color coats.
8. Bake color coats.
9. Apply anticorrosion materials.

Because of these better finishing procedures, corrosion protection warranties (Figure 15-8) of up to ten years are likely within the next few years. With these dramatic improvements in the performance of OEM products, the repair industry must rise to the challenge of producing corrosion resistance in repaired areas that matches or exceeds the durability of the original product. Repair work that does not stand up will draw attention to itself next to the outstanding durability of many original finishes. It can also draw liability challenges where issues of vehicle safety are involved. Remember, the body shop technician is responsible for the quality and durability of the repairs completed. Remember that the customer is entitled to a car restored to the way it was before the damage occurred.

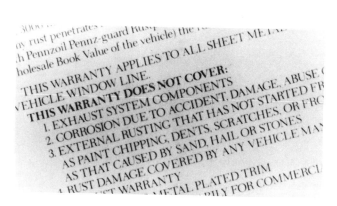

FIGURE 15-8 Typical corrosion protection warranty policy in use today

FIGURE 15-9 Stone chips can lead to rust spots.

15.2 CAUSES FOR LOSS OF FACTORY PROTECTION

Even with all of the care taken to protect vehicles, breakdown still occurs. The breakdown of corrosion protection falls into three general categories:

- Paint film failure
- Collision damage
- Repair process

The paint film is the result of the entire process of coatings, primers, and color coats that the manufacturer applies. When the paint film fails, corrosion begins. Stone chips (Figure 15-9), moisture, and improper surface preparation can all lead to film failure.

During a collision, the protective coatings present on a car are damaged (Figure 15-10). This, as

FIGURE 15-10 During a collision, corrosion protection is usually damaged.

FIGURE 15-11   Heat from welding and cutting operations destroys factory corrosion protection.

mentioned earlier in Chapter 9, occurs not just in the areas of direct impact, but also in the indirect damage zones. Seams pull apart, caulking breaks loose, and paint chips and flakes. Locating and restoring the protection to all affected areas remains a key challenge for the auto body technician.

Vehicle repair is possibly one of the major causes of protective coating damage. For example, repair procedures often require cutting body panels and seams either mechanically or with a plasma torch. Even minor straightening and stress relieving procedures can damage these protective coatings so corrosion can start. Normal welding temperatures cause zinc to vaporize and be lost from the weld area (Figure 15-11). Abrasive operations during repair and refinishing can also leave areas unprotected. After all welding and repair work has been completed, these damage points need careful attention to eliminate contaminants. Then steps must be taken to exclude the atmosphere from the metal by sealing all surfaces thoroughly.

Other precautions that should be taken to protect the factory corrosion protection are:

- Remove only the minimum amount of paint film from affected areas such as welded points.
- Be extremely careful not to scratch any part except that to be repaired. If there is an accidental scratch, take necessary remedial measures.
- When clamping or holding the affected panels during body repair work (Figure 15-12), clamping tools can cause scratches on the panel. They must be treated to avoid rusting.
- While grinding (Figure 15-13), cutting, or welding panels, place protective covers over adjacent painted surfaces and surrounding areas to protect them from the flame or metal chips.
- Cover any opening of the body sills and similar area with masking tape to prevent metal chips from entering during the grinding, cutting, or welding operation.
- Completely remove any metal chips from inside the body. Use a vacuum cleaner, not dry compressed air, to remove metal chips. If dry compressed air is used, metal chips can be blown out and accumulate in corner areas.

There are also some environmental and atmospheric conditions that help to influence the rate of corrosion. They are:

- **Moisture.** As the water on the underside of the body increases, so will the chances of corrosion accelerate. Floor sections that have snow and ice trapped under the floor matting will not dry. Likewise, if holes at the bottom of the doors and side sills (Figure 15-14) are not kept open, water will accumulate. Remember, water is one of the requirements for rust.
- **Relative humidity.** Corrosion will be accelerated in areas of high relative humidity, especially those areas where the temperatures stay above freezing and where atmospheric pollution exists and road salt is used.
- **Temperature.** A temperature increase will accelerate the rate of corrosion to those parts that are not well ventilated.
- **Air pollution.** Industrial pollution (acid rain), the salty air of coastal areas, or the use of heavy road salt accelerate the corrosion pro-

FIGURE 15-12   When clamping for body pulling, be sure that all hold areas are corrosion treated after repairs are made.

FIGURE 15-13 Be sure all metal chips caused by grinding are cleaned up.

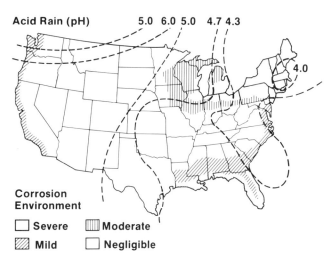

FIGURE 15-15 While corrosive environments are most severe in the northeast and along the southern seaboard, acid rain has become a factor in much of the country.

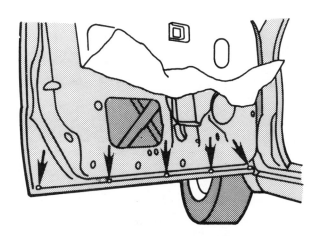

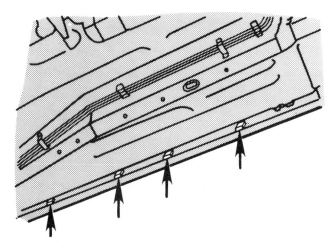

FIGURE 15-14 Keep drain holes open at the bottom of the doors, side sills, and so forth to avoid water accumulation. *(Courtesy of Nissan Motor Corp.)*

cess. Road salt will also accelerate the disintegration of paint surfaces. (Methods for combatting acid rain damage are given later in this chapter.)

 **SHOP TALK**

Acid rain is the term given to rain containing effluents from manufacturing and chemical industries. It causes discoloration and even destruction of the paint surface that could lead to corrosion damage. In Figure 15-15, the higher the pH number the less chance of acid rain problems. Any condition below 6.0 pH is considered acid.

Another type of corrosion that must be considered when working on automobiles is known as galvanic corrosion. This occurs when two dissimilar metals are placed in contact with each other. The more chemically active of two metals will corrode, protecting the other metal in the process. As shown in Table 15-1, this is why zinc will sacrifice itself to protect steel. In the case of other metals, as mentioned later in the chapter, galvanic corrosion can cause problems.

Regardless of the cause, if corrosion prevention is not practiced, the cost to the body shop and insurer is comebacks or lost customers. Inadequate preparation that leaves dirt, grease, or acids on the

TABLE 15-1: RELATIVE ACTIVITY OF METAL	
Magnesium	Most Active
Aluminum	↑
Zinc	
Chromium	
Iron	
Cadmium	
Cobalt	
Nickel	
Tin	
Lead	↓
Copper	Least Active

metal will cause the loss of adhesion. Rust will start, a little at first, creating corrosive "hot spots" at the points of failure. Surface failure will progress quickly in unseen or enclosed areas, spreading under the surface coatings, eating deeper and deeper into the metal. Figure 15-16 illustrates some of the more common hot spots found on an automobile.

The body shop's interest in rust is twofold:

- First, the body technician must be able to repair rust damage
- Second, the body technician must be able to provide treatment that will prevent rusting from recurring

Chapter 8 describes how to repair rust damage, while this chapter is devoted to restoring corrosion prevention to damaged vehicles.

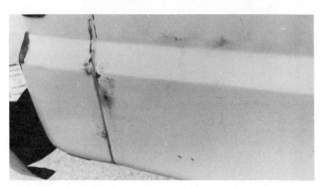

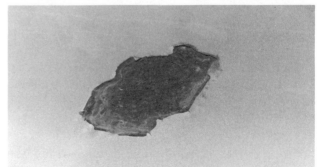

FIGURE 15-16   Common rust hot spots found on vehicles

15.3 ANTICORROSION MATERIALS

The body and paint shop's efforts in protecting car bodies from rusting should focus on creating a clean, chemically neutral surface on the sheet metal, then sealing the material under layers of paint. Under certain conditions, as mentioned earlier in the chapter, a wax- or petroleum-based anticorrosion compound is used to exclude air and moisture from the metal surface.

More and more new vehicles come off the assembly line today with anticorrosive materials that are available to the body shop. Being able to replace or install these wax- or petroleum-based materials is very important to the knowledgeable auto body technician.

Corrosion prevention has not always been a popular body shop operation. The original rust-proofing was called undercoating, and it was an asphalt-based product that was sheer agony to apply, because it got not only on the underside of the car, but also on everything else within 20 feet of the application bay. But, worst of all, it did not work very well. In time, the solvents used would evaporate, the asphalt would harden and crack, and the moisture that causes oxidation would actually become trapped under the undercoating.

The asphaltic undercoats did have benefits in terms of sound deadening and preventing stone marks under fenders. And it is useful today on fiberglass panels for the same reasons. As a rustproofer, however, it probably was not the best.

When selecting a modern anticorrosion material, there are several things that should be considered:

- The material should be thin enough to flow or penetrate pinch weld cracks and to creep adequately to protect the exposed metal of such areas as the steel immediately adjacent to spot welds—a particularly tough rustproofing proposition.
- The material should have good adherence to both bare metal and painted surfaces. In addition to adhering to the surface, it should be highly resistant to water, cutting from stones thrown up from the road, ordinary solvent type materials used in the engine and elsewhere, and so forth. In other words, it should not only protect initially, it should also continue to protect. Material that does not retain some pliability and toughness will not do the job.
- It is important to choose a material without solvents that have a lingering bad odor, which can be present in a car when it is delivered and make the best body work and paint look bad.
- The product should be easy to clean up with ordinary and safe solvents.

Anticorrosion materials or agents can be divided into three broad categories:

- **Anticorrosion compound (Figure 15-17).** As already mentioned, either wax- or petroleum-based compounds are resistant to chipping and abrasion; they can undercoat, sound deaden, and completely seal the surface of a car from the destructive causes of rust and corrosion. They should be applied to the undercarriage and inside body panels so that they can penetrate into joints and body crevices to form a pliable, protective film.
- **Body sealer or sealant (Figure 15-18).** These prevent the penetration of water or mud into

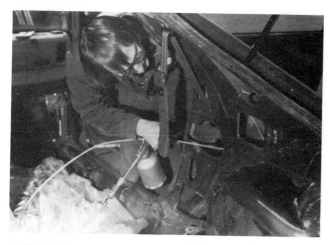

FIGURE 15-17   Applying a typical anticorrosion compound

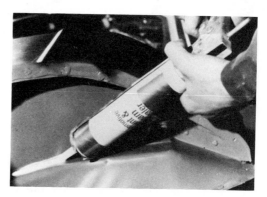

FIGURE 15-18   Applying a typical body sealer or sealant

FIGURE 15-19   Applying a typical antirust agent

panel joints and serve the important role of preventing rust from forming between adjoining surfaces.

- **Antirust agents (Figure 15-19).** Antirust agents are used where it is difficult to get anticorrosion material coverage. This includes such areas as the back sides of welded parts with boxed cross-sectional structures such as side members and body pillars that cannot be painted.

 **SHOP TALK** _____

Be sure to carefully read the manufacturer's instructions on the container (Figure 15-20) and follow them. Several of these anticorrosion materials can be used on the same part or section.

New and better anticorrosion materials are constantly appearing on the automotive market. For example, a new line of anticorrosives is available that is effective for coating over existing rusted areas and retarding any further corrosion. This is especially important on repairs of older vehicles or repairs involving salvage parts. Be sure to check trade publications, I-CAR bulletins, manufacturer's representatives, and automotive suppliers for updated information on anticorrosion materials.

15.4   BASIC SURFACE PREPARATION

Surface preparation is one of the most important steps in assuring long-term corrosion resistance of body panels and other metal parts. Without the proper surface (especially bare metal), the rest of the repair procedure and refinishing efforts might be wasted. The conventional system generally consists of the following three step process called **metal treating.**

- **Cleaning to remove contaminants.** Use a wax and grease remover to dissolve and float off oily, greasy film as well as other contaminants from the surface. Apply the remover with a clean, white cloth (Figure 15-21). Work small areas, 2 to 3 square feet, wetting the surface liberally and keeping it wet. While the surface is still wet, fold a second cloth and wipe the surface to remove the contaminants. Turn the cloth frequently while drying the surface (Figure 15-22).
- **Cleaning with metal conditioner.** The purpose of the metal conditioner is to deep clean

FIGURE 15-20   Always read carefully the manufacturer's instructions and literature before using the product.

FIGURE 15-21   Saturating clean, white cloth with wax and grease remover

FIGURE 15-22 Removing the wax and grease

FIGURE 15-23 Diluting a metal conditioner with clean water

FIGURE 15-24 Applying a metal conditioner with a spray bottle

and etch the metal. Dilute the conditioner with water in a plastic bucket according to label instructions (Figure 15-23). Apply to metal—a spray bottle is recommended (Figure 15-24). Then rinse with clear water and wipe dry with a clean cloth.

- **Applying conversion coatings.** The conversion coating forms a zinc phosphate coating that is chemically bonded to the metal. This layer makes an ideal surface for the primer and prevents rust from creeping under the paint. Use conversion coatings on galvanized and uncoated steels and aluminum. Be sure to use the correct product for each type of surface. Pour the appropriate conversion coating into a plastic bucket and mix with water according to the instructions on the container (Figure 15-25). Using a spray bottle, apply the coating to the metal surface. Then leave the conditioner on the surface 2 to 5 minutes. Work only as much area as can be coated and rinsed before the solution dries. Reapply if the surface dries before the rinsing. Flush the coating from the surface with clean water (Figure 15-26), or mop with

FIGURE 15-25 Read application instructions very carefully.

FIGURE 15-26 Flush off excess conversion coating with clean water.

a damp sponge or cloth that is rinsed occasionally in clean water. Wipe dry with a clean cloth and allow to air dry.

As described in Chapter 18, there are other types of metal treatment protection systems that can be employed, but the conventional system just described is the most popular for general corrosion protection restoration work.

15.5 CORROSION TREATMENT AREAS

The corrosion treatment areas that must be considered when body repair work is done can be grouped in four categories. They are:

- **Enclosed interior surfaces.** Includes body rails and rocker assemblies.
- **Exposed interior surfaces.** Including floor pan, apron, and hood sections.
- **Exposed joints.** Such as quarter-to-wheel-housing and quarter-to-trunk floor joints.
- **Exposed exterior surfaces.** Such as fenders, quarter panels, and door skins.

The term "exposed" as used in this chapter refers to a panel surface that is accessible without having to remove a welded component.

15.6 ENCLOSED INTERIOR SURFACES

Of all the areas to be protected during a repair job, the enclosed interior surfaces (Figure 15-27)

FIGURE 15-27 Enclosed surfaces such as this require anticorrosion attention.

are the most important. These include underbody structures such as front rails, rear rails, and rocker panels. The reason for the importance of these enclosed body sections is that they represent the principal load carrying members of the unibody car (Figure 15-28). Corrosion of these components can have a severe effect on the crashworthiness and durability of the vehicle.

Metal conditioners and conversion coatings described earlier in this chapter under "15.4 Basic Surface Preparation" are not recommended for use inside closed sections. The reason is that the chemicals and moisture might be difficult, if not impossible, to fully remove from the inside seams. Since stone chipping is not a hazard here, the primer should develop adequate adhesion in these areas without conversion coating.

With this in mind, begin the process on closed sections with a thorough cleaning and degreasing. Because of the closed construction of these components, the cleaning must be done before the part is welded into the repair area.

After cleaning and degreasing, the enclosed metal surfaces must be protected with a primer. As described in Chapter 18 there are many different primers used by the auto trade. However, for corrosion protection, especially for enclosed interior surface, the two most used are:

- **Self-etching two-part epoxy primers.** These relatively new materials are recommended by most automobile makers in place of the standard epoxy primer. When using a self-etching two-part epoxy primer, be sure to follow the manufacturer's instructions to the letter.
- **Weld-through primers.** These primers are rich in zinc to protect joints better. Remember the heat from welding can destroy factory corrosion protection.

 **SHOP TALK**

Do not use lacquer-based primers since they do not provide enough adhesion under enclosed interior conditions.

The application of both the primer and anticorrosion materials to the inside of closed sections must be done only with the coating manufacturer's recommended equipment. This is normally of the airless or pressure-feed type of spray guns (see Chapter 17), although some suction equipment is

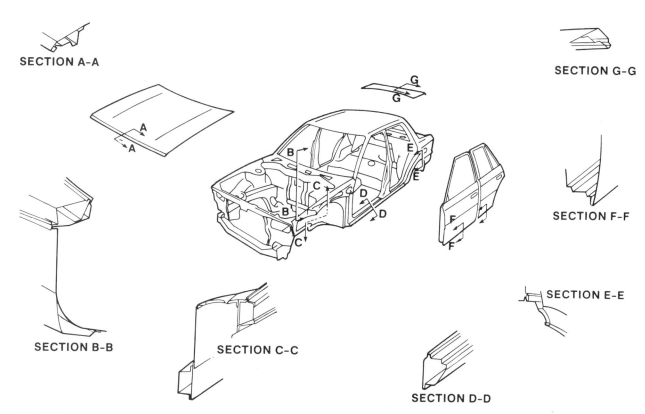

SECTION A-A

SECTION G-G

SECTION B-B

SECTION C-C

SECTION D-D

SECTION F-F

SECTION E-E

FIGURE 15-28   Enclosed interior surfaces that must be protected. *(Courtesy of Nissan Motor Corp.)*

FIGURE 15-29   **Typical spray gun used to spray enclosed interior surfaces**

FIGURE 15-30   **Apply primers with a spray gun. Note "fog" coming out of top hole.**

also recommended (Figure 15-29). Aerosol or conventional spray gun equipment will not do the job in enclosed interior sections because it is not possible to spray the material directly on the surface. This work requires special wands to reach all the inside cavities and joints where the material must go.

This equipment uses compressed air behind the fluid to force the liquid through the wand and nozzle. The fluid is broken up into a very fine atomized state,

sometimes called a **fog.** When the substance is introduced inside the closed section in this atomized state, it spreads rapidly and evenly into all areas including tiny crevices (Figure 15-30).

WARNING: Before using air pressure equipment, be sure to use a respirator and wear proper protective clothing and rubber gloves.

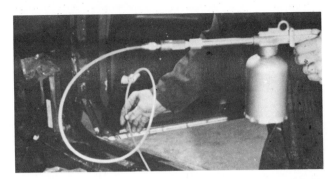

FIGURE 15-31 Be sure that the wand is inserted all the way into the cavity.

To use a spray wand, insert it into the cavity (Figure 15-31) to the farthest point that the coat is needed. Begin the spray, and pull the wand out at an even rate, coating the section of the cavity evenly as it moves along.

There are several wand styles available (Figure 15-32). Before spraying with a wand, be sure that:

- Spray pattern is checked and that it is corrected.
- Pistol or barrel is filled with the desired primer or anticorrosion material.

 **SHOP TALK**

Once a week or as needed:

- *Fill the gun or tank with cleaning solvent or mineral spirits.*
- *Spray cleaning solvent through all wands.*
- *Hang wands to drain overnight.*

Failure to clean the gun and wands on a regular basis can result in clogging or total blockage of the wand, which will prevent proper function.

The general corrosion restoration process for an enclosed interior surface is as follows:

1. Clean the enclosed interior surface with wax and grease remover.
2. Apply weld-through primer to bare steel areas only. Do not apply over paint, primer, or galvanized surfaces.*
3. Apply only in the immediate weld area since this product has poor adhesion characteristics. After welding, thoroughly remove all welding residue and surplus primer from the joint area.*

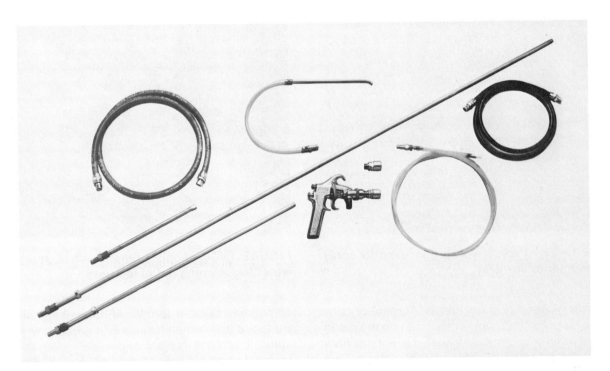

FIGURE 15-32 Typical wands, connecting air hoses, and spray gun used with an airless corrosion protection system. *(Courtesy of Binks Mfg. Co.)*

---

*If heat is not used in the vehicle repair, Steps 2, 3, and 4 can be omitted.

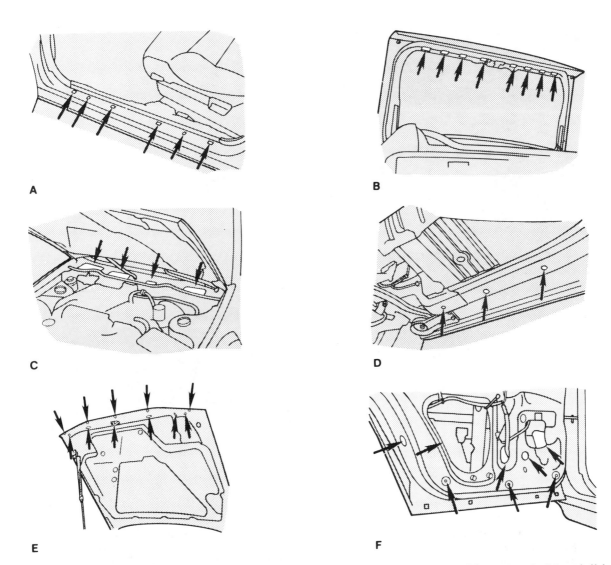

FIGURE 15-33 **Typical service or access clip holes: (A) interior of body sill; (B) rear end of trunk lid; (C) inside cowl top; (D) inside member; (E) front end of hood; and (F) lower part of door. Keep the mechanical parts of the door free of compounds; windows should be in a closed position.** *(Courtesy of Nissan Motor Corp.)*

4. Research has shown that wire brushing is not the best way to clean a weld area. Wire brushing can leave scratches in the original primer, which are not always filled by the new primer. The primer tends to "float" over the scratches, creating minute voids in which corrosion can start. A better way to clean the weld area is to use a plastic abrasive. Another way is to sandblast with a captive sandblaster, if available, or with regular sandblasting equipment. Thorough cleaning after welding should again be stressed here.*

5. After the area is thoroughly cleaned, apply a primer—two-part or self-etching epoxy

type is usually recommended—to the inside area. Be sure to allow sufficient drying time according to the primer manufacturer's recommendations.

6. Apply anticorrosion compound according to manufacturer's direction. The material is applied using service or access clip holes (Figure 15-33) and drain holes. When rustproofing material is dry, approximately 1 hour, the water drain holes must be cleared.

*If heat is not used in the vehicle repair, Steps 2, 3, and 4 can be omitted.

FIGURE 15-34 **Applying anticorrosion to the trunk's enclosed surfaces**

FIGURE 15-35 **Drilling an access hole in the door**

To spray specific enclosed interior surfaces, special techniques might be required. These area considerations include:

- **Trunk.** Remove the spare tire, tools, floor mat, board, and padding on each side of the trunk to spray quarter panels. The rear quarter panel behind the wheels is coated from inside the trunk using the flexible spray wand (Figure 15-34), spraying downward in the recess between the trunk and the quarter panel. Spray the back edge of the trunk getting under the beads.

    Spray the trunk lid by inserting the flexible wand into the existing holes, making sure the material reaches the edges.

    When the spraying is completed, replace the padding, floor extensions, floor mats, tools, and tire. Wipe off overspray with cloth dampened lightly with enamel reducer, stoddard solvent, or kerosene.

- **Doors.** Doors can be treated through their drains after the interior panel has been removed, or a 1/2-inch hole can be drilled in each door, approximately 6 to 9 inches above the bottom. Center punch and drill the hole (Figure 15-35).

    With the windows up, insert the wand into the drilled hole as far as possible. Slowly retract the wand, while spraying the length of the bottom third of the door (Figure 15-36). Just before the wand is withdrawn from the hole, point it down to assure direct coverage into the inside corner of the open door. Plug the hole with a 1/2-inch plastic body plug (Figure 15-37).

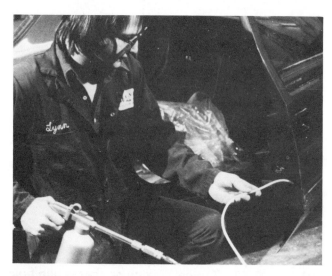

FIGURE 15-36 **Removing a wand from a door access hole**

FIGURE 15-37 **Plugging a hole with a plastic body plug**

- **Rear post and quarter panel.** The reverse side of the rear post and quarter panel can sometimes be sprayed from the trunk area. To ensure coverage, the front edge of the wheel well and the quarter panel area should be coated via one or more 1/2-inch holes drilled in the rear post or by removing the ventilator cover. Insert the flexible spray in the drilled hole in the rear post, and spray while gradually withdrawing the wand. Plug the drilled hole with a plastic plug.
- **Front post (and four door center post).** Drill a hole in the front step plate at the center of the curve where it meets the front supports. Insert the flexible cone spray wand and spray thoroughly. Also spray the lower edge of the front fender and any boxed-in areas in the vicinity. Drill a hole in the center of the curve formed by the step plate and rear support. Spray with the flexible spray wand. If the car is a four door, the wand must reach the rear of this center post. If it does not, drill a hole from the rear of the center post.
- **Behind front fender.** Some cars might have a boxed cavity behind the front fender into which the flexible cone spray can be inserted either from under the hood or alongside the front door post.
- **Rocker panel.** Check to see if the rocker panels are boxed. If not, work from both ends. Before drilling any holes, check both ends of the rockers underneath for existing plugs. If satisfactorily located, these can be used to spray the entire length of the rocker with the flexible cone spray wand. If it is inconvenient or undesirable to do the rocker panel from above, drill a hole from below into the rocker panel at about the center and spray in both directions using the flexible cone spray wand. Be sure to spray on both sides of internal baffles, if present.

15.7 EXPOSED JOINTS

Body panel joints and seams require special attention since they are areas highly vulnerable to corrosion and must be protected correctly. This is true because of the effect of welding on the metal as well as the tendency of water, snow, dirt, mud, and other contaminants to become trapped in the joint area. As a general rule, a body sealant must be applied over all the joints. That is, the sealant must be

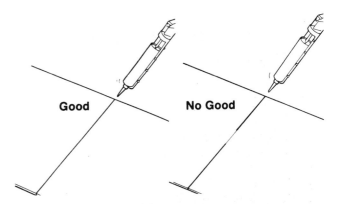

FIGURE 15-38 Proper application (left) of a sealant does not permit gaps as shown at the right.

applied so there are no gaps between the material and the panel surface (Figure 15-38).

The following are some factors that should be known when selecting and applying seam sealers:

- **Paintability.** All sealants must be paintable and have good adhesion to bare and primed metal. A seam sealer should be allowed to adequately dry before painting. The necessary dry time depends on the sealer itself, the thickness applied, and the temperature and humidity during the drying period. Normally, the lower the temperature is below 70 degrees Fahrenheit, the longer the necessary dry time. The higher the humidity is above 50 percent relative humidity, the longer the necessary dry time is.
- **Flexibility.** This is a critical issue with today's unibody automobiles. The sealer must be able to withstand the motion associated with the automobile (cured bead samples of sealers will be provided to demonstrate this).
- **Tooling sealants.** A finger wetted with solvent or water makes tooling easier and helps to keep the sealer from sticking to the finger. This is a good application tip to help improve the finished seam's appearance. Brushable seam sealer should be tooled with a stiff bristle brush and should be stroked in one direction only to help it match an original equipment appearance.
- **Silicone sealants.** These should not be used as a body seam sealer. They typically are not paintable, attract dust and dirt with time, and do not offer the adhesion of other types of sealants.

There are four types of seam sealers that are commonly used in auto corrosion protection work:

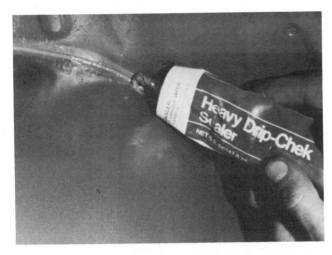

FIGURE 15-39 Application of a thin-bodied sealer

FIGURE 15-40 Application of a heavy-bodied sealer

- **Thin-bodied sealers** are designed to fill seams under 1/8 inch wide. This sealer will shrink slightly to provide definition to the joint, while remaining flexible to resist vibration. Adhesion is good to both primed metal and bare metal surfaces. Since many of the seams are on a vertical surface, sag control is important so the sealer does not run out of the seam. Typically thin-bodied sealants carry the generic names of drip-chek (Figure 15-39) or flow grade.
- **Heavy-bodied sealers** are used to fill seams from 1/8 to 1/4 inch wide (Figure 15-40). These sealers can be tooled to hide the seam or can be left in bead form. Shrinkage should be minimal, with good resistance to sagging, and high flexibility to resist cracking in service. Heavy-bodied sealants are used on both coach joints and overlap seams. They are typically dispensed from cartridges.

Some products are available in squeeze tubes.

- **Brushable seam sealers** are used on interior body seams where appearance is not important. These seams are normally hidden and not seen by the customer, unless under close examination. Brushable sealers are designed to hold brush marks and to resist salt and automotive fluids such as gasoline, transmission fluid, and brake fluid. Any seams such as those under the hood and under the carriage that might be exposed to automotive fluids should have a brushable seam sealer. Applied with a brush, it normally has overlap seams (Figure 15-41).
- **Solid seam sealers** containing 100 percent solids are used to fill larger voids at panel joints or holes. This product comes in strip caulking form, designed to be pressed into place with the thumb (Figure 15-42).

FIGURE 15-41 Application of a brushable seam sealer

FIGURE 15-42 Application of solid seam sealer

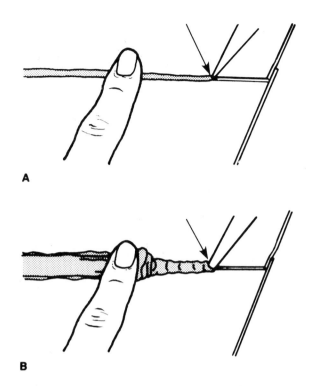

A

B

FIGURE 15-43   Use proper nozzle size. *(Courtesy of Toyota Motor Corp.)*

Be sure to follow the manufacturer's instructions carefully for the use of these versatile products.

The application sequence is basically the same as it is for interior exposed panels with the addition of two more steps. After the welded areas are thoroughly cleaned, seal all body panel joints with a seam sealer. Finish the joints by applying another coat of primer over the seam sealers, then topcoat with the same material used over the rest of the repaired area.

It is important to use a nozzle with a small hole in the end to apply the sealer and then spread out the bead of sealer with a fingertip. If the nozzle hole is small, the finish can be kept neat (Figure 15-43A). If the nozzle hole is too large, the sealer will spread too wide and might cause a poor looking finish (Figure 15-43B).

A neat sealer application can also be obtained if automotive masking tape is used to make a parting line for the sealer application area.

When applying sealant, refer to the shop manual for the vehicle being rustproofed. Determine the sealer application area (Figure 15-44) or look at the other side of the vehicle to see where the sealer is applied.

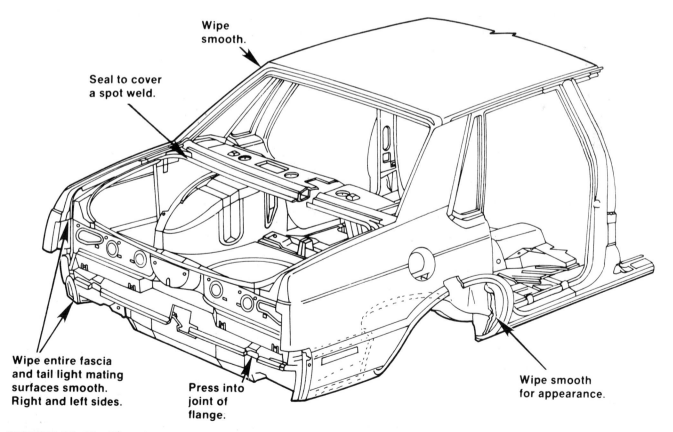

Wipe smooth.

Seal to cover a spot weld.

Wipe entire fascia and tail light mating surfaces smooth. Right and left sides.

Press into joint of flange.

Wipe smooth for appearance.

FIGURE 15-44   Manufacturer's recommendations as given in shop manual should be followed during the applications of seam sealers.

 **SHOP TALK** _____

More than one type of seam sealer can be used on any given joint. For example, a brush-able seam sealer could be used over a thin-bodied sealer.

To summarize the corrosion process for exposed joints and seams, proceed as follows:

 1. Thoroughly clean the joint or seam.
2. Apply primer or primer-sealer (see Chapter 18).
3. Seal the joints with seam sealer.
4. Apply a second coat of primer or primer-sealer.
5. Finish with a color coat in a spray booth.

15.8 EXPOSED INTERIOR SURFACES

The bottom surfaces of the underbody and inside of the wheelhousing can be damaged by flying stones causing rust to develop. These areas are given an undercoat treatment with a material such as shock absorbing wax. As a general rule do not spray anticorrosion material into the passenger compartment; apply treatment from below the underbody.

Metal conditioners and conversion coatings also are not recommended on interior surface protection. There are two reasons for this:

• These surfaces are not exposed to physical damage the way exterior surfaces are.
• These areas contain joints and seams that should not be contaminated with etching and conversion coating chemicals and are generally difficult to rinse clean.

The corrosion protection process begins with a thorough cleaning with a wax and grease remover. Once the surface is completely air dried, spray the first coating of wax- or petroleum-based undercoat compound on all welded areas and panel joints (Figure 15–45A). Then apply a second coat over the entire area (Figure 15–45B). Cover places surrounding the application area with masking paper and/or tape to prevent the undercoating from sticking to areas where it is not wanted.

In areas where there is a moderate or negligible corrosion environment (see Figure 15–15), a proper primer might be all that is needed for exposed interior surface protection. While there are several different types available, the two-part epoxy primers

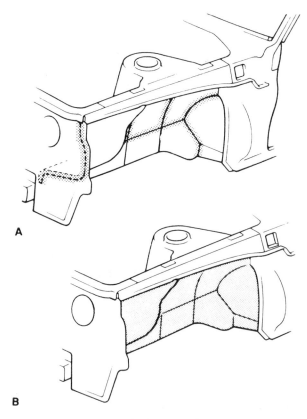

FIGURE 15–45 **(A) Apply undercoat to all welded areas and panel joints; (B) then apply to the entire area. *(Courtesy of Toyota Motor Corp.)***

most closely duplicate the baked-on electrodeposition coating, or E-coat, used by car manufacturers. Nearly any material can be applied over the epoxy primer.

Self-etching primers can also be used for exposed interior surfaces. However, common lacquer-based primers will not provide proper adhesion when used on bare metal, even if it has been properly cleaned and conversion coating was used. This point cannot be overemphasized. Lacquer-based primer should never be used directly on the bare metal of modern unibody cars.

To restore corrosion protection to specific areas such as under the hood, proceed as follows:

 1. Lift the hood and spray the front quarter panel, between it and the wheel well. Be sure to apply the material right down to the fender beads. Use the flexible cone spray wand to reach all recessed areas.
2. Cover the large open spaces with a 45 degree flat spray wand.
3. Spray the leading edge and the side channels of the hood with the flexible cone spray wand.

4. Loosen or remove the battery and coat the battery tray and surrounding areas.

> **CAUTION:** Do not spray radiator core, battery, air conditioner core, fans, belts, hoses, or pulleys.

The headlight areas on some cars might be reached from under the hood. On other makes the headlight areas can be reached from existing holes under the hood by means of the flexible spray wand. If not accessible from under the hood, the headlight areas can be sprayed from under the car, working forward in the front wheel well when the car is put on a lift. This can be a baffled area with a rubber edge that can be depressed to insert a flexible cone spray or flat spray wand. Choose the best method to assure complete coverage.

15.9 EXPOSED EXTERIOR SURFACES

Exterior surfaces are subjected to much greater exposure to chips and nicks than interior surfaces. This is why the use of etching and conversion coating agents is of critical importance on exterior surfaces. Conversion coating provides the kind of superior paint film adhesion that retards creeping rust from working its way under the paint when chips and nicks do occur.

Exposed exterior surfaces are of two types:

- Cosmetic
- Underbody

FIGURE 15-46 Exterior body panels require the most protection. Etch conversion coating to ensure maximum protection.

Anticorrosion procedures for exterior cosmetic surfaces are generally as follows:

 1. Clean with a wax and grease remover.
2. Apply a metal conditioner.
3. Rinse with water.
4. Apply a conversion coating (Figure 15-46) and allow to thoroughly air dry. Drying can be speeded with compressed air or a clean, white rag.
5. Rinse with water.
6. Apply a primer—two-part epoxy primer recommended.
7. Apply a primer-surfacer.
8. Apply color coat system (Figure 15-47).

If a lift is available, it makes underbody corrosion protection work easier. When corrosion-proofing the underbody, start by spraying the fenders and wheel wells, paying particular attention to the fender beads. On some cars it will be necessary to remove the wheels to do an adequate spraying job. Fender skirts should be removed and done separately.

Spray the remaining underbody and splash pans adjacent to the front and rear bumpers. Spray the underside of the floor pan, welded joints, frame, tank straps, and seams. Remove any loose debris or sound deadener, particularly around joints, before spraying. Loose sound deadening materials or dirty surfaces at critical locations will only create pockets for rust to form and will prevent the rustproofing material from reaching the metal.

> **CAUTION:** Never apply undercoating compounds to parts that reach high temperatures such as the exhaust pipe or muffler, and do not apply it to the suspension and drivetrain parts, brake drums, and other related moveable parts.

Anticorrosion procedures for exterior underbody surfaces are generally as follows:

 1. Clean with a wax and grease remover.
2. Apply a metal conditioner.
3. Rinse with water.
4. Apply a conversion coating.
5. Rinse with water.
6. Apply a primer—self-etching primer recommended.
7. Apply anticorrosion compound and sound deadening materials to restore to factory specifications.
8. Most undercoat overspray can be removed with enamel reducer, stoddard solvent, or kerosene and washing.

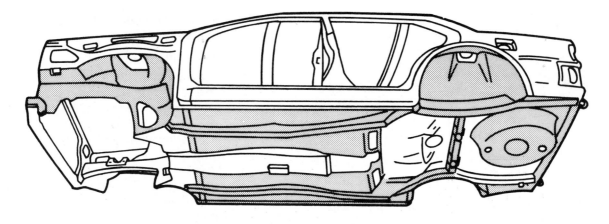

☒ **Indicates Undercoated Portions**

FIGURE 15-47 **These are important to any underbody corrosion protection.** *(Courtesy of Nissan Motor Corp.)*

15.10 EXTERIOR ACCESSORIES

To prevent corrosion, it is very important to install a barrier between dissimilar metal components such as aluminum bumpers and stainless and aluminum body trim. The plastic or rubber isolating pads accomplish this effectively. Mounting stainless and aluminum body trim must be done correctly to avoid galvanic corrosion. For example, when mounting trim requires drilling holes in a new or repaired panel, drill all holes before applying the primer, coating the inside edges of all holes completely. When using a kit for replacement trim, be sure to use all parts supplied with the kit. If parts are not purchased as a kit, duplicate the original assembly exactly. Clearly, there is a great variety of body trim and accessories requiring many different application techniques. In all cases, be sure to follow the manufacturer's recommendations to avoid problems in making these repairs.

15.11 ACID RAIN DAMAGE

As mentioned earlier, air pollutants can damage an automotive finish. Since most of their damage is done to exterior, finished surfaces, they are a major concern of the refinisher.

Acid rain and other pollutants have generated a lot of controversy in recent years, and there has been some confusion as to their causes and effects. Sulfur dioxide or nitrogen oxides create acid rain when released into the atmosphere, and combine with water and the ozone to create either sulfuric or nitric acid. It is estimated that the United States alone pumps out 30 million tons of sulfur dioxide and 25 million tons of nitrogen oxides yearly. More than two-thirds of the sulfur is emitted from power plants burning coal, oil, or gas. Iron and copper smelters, automobile exhaust and natural sources like volcanoes, wetlands, and forest fires account for most of the remaining pollutants.

The standard for measuring acid rain is the pH scale. It runs from zero to 14, with 7 being neutral or equal to distilled water. A pH reading of 4 is ten times more acidic than a solution of acid and water with a pH of 5, and 100 times more acidic than a pH of 6. Once released into the ozone, these acids are readily dissolved into cloud droplets which, if low enough in pH, can cause significant damage.

The level of acid rain varies greatly around the country (see Figure 15-15). For example, South Carolina is reported to be one of the most acidic states in the nation. In Los Angeles, fog has been measured to have the acidic strength of lemon juice.

Rainfall in the northeastern states is extremely corrosive to car paints and finishes. For example, the average pH of rainfall in New Jersey is an acidic 4.3. Several manufacturers now have clauses in some of its new car warranties that exempt them from liabilities involving paint damage in high pH areas.

Acid rain damage generally occurs to the paint pigments, with lead-based pigments the most susceptible. Typically, the damage looks like water droplets that have dried on the paint and caused discoloration. Sometimes the damage appears as a white ring with a clear, dull center. Severe cases show pitting. Discoloration varies depending on the color.

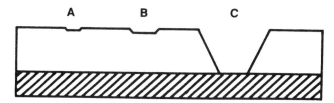

FIGURE 15-48 Levels of acid rain damage

For example, acid rain damage to a yellow finish might appear as a white or dark brown spot. Medium blue might have a whitening look. White might be discolored pink, and medium red, purple.

Metallic finishes can be damaged because the acidic solution reacts with the aluminim particles and etches away the finish. A fresh finish is more easily damaged than an aged finish. Lacquers and uncatalyzed enamel finishes are most susceptible to damage, followed closely by catalyzed enamels.

Clear-coated finishes add a layer of protection against acid rain, so late-model vehicles with two- and three-coat finishes are less susceptible to damage. A clearcoat protects the paint pigments from discoloration, but it is still possible for acid rain to create a peripheral etch, or ring on the clearcoat.

Restoring

The procedure for restoring acid rain damage varies depending on the level and depth of the damage. The following steps outline repair procedures according to the level of damage as illustrated in Figure 15-48. When the problem has been corrected, stop at that stage. Remember that polishing or compounding removes part of the original finish, and thereby reduces its overall life.

If the surface damage is like that shown in Figure 15-48A, proceed as follows:

1. Wash with soap and water.
 2. Clean with wax and grease remover.
 3. Neutralize the area by washing with baking soda solution (1 tablespoon baking soda to 1 quart of water) and rinse thoroughly.

If the damage is embedded in the surface coat (Figure 15-48B), proceed as follows:

1. Follow cleaning and neutralizing steps already listed.
 2. Hand polish problem area (inspect and continue if necessary).
 3. Buff with polishing pad (inspect frequently and remove as little of the original finish as possible to cure the problem).

 4. Use rubbing compound (inspect and continue if necessary).
 5. Wet sand with 1500 or 2000 grit sandpaper and compound. If damage is still visible, repeat with 1200 grit. Do not use grits coarser than 1000.

If the damage is through to the undercoat (Figure 15-48C), proceed as follows:

1. Follow cleaning and neutralizing steps listed in Figure 15-48A.
 2. Sand with 400 to 600 grit sandpaper.
 3. Reclean and reneutralize prior to priming and repainting.

Surface Damage Industrial Fallout

Generally speaking, damage from industrial fallout is caused when small, airborne particles of iron fall and stick to the vehicle's surface. The iron can eventually eat through the paint, causing the base metal to rust. Sometimes the damage is easier to feel than see. Sweeping a hand across the apparent damage will likely reveal a gritty or bumpy surface. Rust-colored spots might be visible, however, on light-colored vehicles.

The steps for repairing damage caused by industrial fallout are similar to those used when repairing acid rain damage, but with the following exception. After washing the car, treat the repair area with a "fallout remover," a chemical treatment product made especially for industrial fallout damage. Do not buff the damaged area before removing the fallout because buffing will drive the particles into the paint surface. If the particles break loose and become lodged in the buffing pad, deep gouges can occur.

15.12 Review Questions

1. Corrosion prevention is the phase that is replacing _____ .
   a. rustproofing
   b. undercoating
   c. sound deadening
   d. all of the above
   e. both a and b

2. Corrosion will be accelerated in areas _____ .
   a. of high relative humidity
   b. where temperatures drop below freezing

c. both a and b
d. none of the above

3. The higher the pH number rises above 6.0, the _____ .
   a. greater chance of acid rain
   b. less likely chance of acid rain
   c. both a and b
   d. none of the above

4. When two dissimilar metals are placed in contact with each other, the more chemically active will corrode, protecting the other metal in the process. This is called _____ .
   a. zinc coating
   b. galvanic corrosion
   c. all of the above
   d. none of the above

5. Which of the following prevents rust from forming between adjoining surfaces?
   a. anticorrosion compounds
   b. body sealant
   c. antirust agents
   d. none of the above

6. Technician A uses a conversion coating and then a metal conditioner. Technician B uses a metal conditioner and then a conversion coating. Who is correct?
   a. Technician A
   b. Technician B
   c. Both A and B
   d. Neither A nor B

7. Technician A uses a conversion coating on inside closed sections. Technician B uses a primer. Who is correct?
   a. Technician A
   b. Technician B
   c. Both A and B
   d. Neither A nor B

8. How often should cleaning solvent be sprayed through the spray wand?
   a. every half day
   b. once a day or as needed
   c. once a week or as needed
   d. once a month or as needed

9. The worst way to clean an enclosed interior weld area is to use a _____ .
   a. plastic abrasive
   b. captive sandblaster
   c. regular sandblaster
   d. wire brush

10. This sealant is not paintable and attracts dust and dirt with time _____ .
    a. silicone sealant
    b. tooling sealant
    c. thin-bodied sealant
    d. heavy-bodied sealant

11. Heavy-bodied sealers are used to fill seams from _____ .
    a. 1/16 to 1/8 inch wide
    b. 1/8 to 1/4 inch wide
    c. 1/4 to 1/2 inch wide
    d. all of the above

12. Technician A uses conversion coating on aluminum. Technician B uses conversion coating on galvanized steel. Who is correct?
    a. Technician A
    b. Technician B
    c. Both A and B
    d. Neither A nor B

13. When restoring corrosion protection to an enclosed interior surface, Technician A applies the weld-through primer over existing paint. Technician B applies the weld-through primer over galvanized surfaces. Who is correct?
    a. Technician A
    b. Technician B
    c. Both A and B
    d. Neither A nor B

14. Any seams that might be exposed to automotive fluid should have a _____ .
    a. thin-bodied sealer
    b. heavy-bodied sealer
    c. brushable seam sealer
    d. solid seam sealer

15. Which of the following can be used for exposed interior surfaces?
    a. epoxy primers
    b. self-etching primers
    c. lacquer-based primers
    d. all of the above
    e. both a and b

16. Undercoating compounds should never be applied to _____ .
    a. the exhaust pipe or muffler
    b. suspension parts
    c. drivetrain parts
    d. brake drums
    e. any of the above

CHAPTER 16

Automotive Refinishing Materials

OBJECTIVES

After reading this chapter, you will be able to:

- explain the uses and properties of paints used in the trade for undercoats and topcoats.
- define the four components of automotive paints.
- define the characteristics of a good primer-surfacer.
- name five types of primer-surfacers.
- identify the types of body finishes and refinishing.
- explain the functions of the four types of undercoats.
- name the types of topcoats.
- discuss the advances made in refinishing by basecoat/clear coat finishes.
- explain the advantages of basecoat/clear coat finishes.
- describe the role of solvents and the variables that affect their spraying.
- determine the proper solvent to be used for a particular paint job.

Automobile finishes perform four very important functions:

- **Protection.** The automobile is constructed primarily of steel sheet metal. If this steel were left uncovered, the reaction of oxygen and moisture in the air would cause it to rust. Painting serves to prevent the occurrence of rust, therefore protecting the body.

- **Appearance improvement.** The shape of the body is made up of several types of surfaces and lines, such as elevated surfaces, flat planes, curved surfaces, straight and curved lines, and so forth. Therefore, another objective of painting is to improve the body appearance by giving it a three-dimensional color effect.

- **Quality upgrading.** When comparing two vehicles of identical shape and performance capabilities, the one with the most beautiful paint finish will have a higher market value. Hence another object of painting is to upgrade the value of the product.

- **Color designation.** Still another objective of painting automobiles is to make them easily distinguishable by application of certain colors or markings. Examples are police and fire department vehicles.

To achieve this, the typical automotive finishing system consists of several coats of two or more different materials:

- Undercoat or primer coat(s)
- Topcoat (color coat or basecoat/clear coat)

The undercoat provides a sound foundation for the topcoat and makes it adhere better. If applying topcoats to bare substrates (metal, fiberglass, or plastic), they might peel or look rough; that is why the undercoat is "sandwiched" between the substrate and the topcoat. The undercoat also protects against rusting and will fill scratches and other flaws in the metal or plastic.

The topcoat is the finish that is seen on the car. From an appearance standpoint, it is smooth, glossy, and eye catching. Functionally, it is tough and durable. The topcoat thickness on a new car when it comes from the factory is only about 2.5 mils.

A refinisher should know the uses and properties of all paints used in the trade—both undercoats and topcoats. That knowledge will help in choosing the best refinishing system for each job.

Refinishing paints are complex. Through the years, those applied to automobiles at the factory have been changing. Many domestic manufacturers have begun to use high-solids finishes, clear coat-

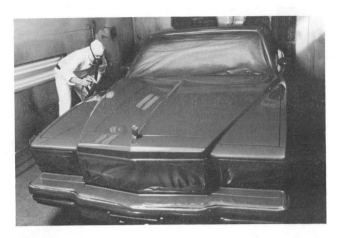

FIGURE 16-1 The painter or refinishing technician is responsible for the final appearance of a vehicle. (Courtesy of DeVilbiss Co.)

FIGURE 16-2 Paint is composed of four ingredients: (A) pigment/metallic flake; (B) binder; (C) solvent; and—on occasion—(D) additives. (Courtesy of Du Pont Co.)

ing, and most recently mica in certain topcoats to provide a pearlescent finish. In response to demands for more fuel efficient cars, body parts that were once steel are now manufactured from one or more of the many choices of plastics available to car manufacturers. Each, though labeled plastic, exhibits its own characteristics and differences that determine its repairability and refinishing requirements.

The body shop painter (Figure 16-1) must respond to these changes in order to provide the perfect matches demanded by the customer on a refinishing job. Keeping up-to-date on the changes is crucial. The paint manufacturers providing finishes for use by the automotive refinisher have quickly responded to the car manufacturer's changes and are getting products to the body shop painter that will enable the painter to effectively repair that new car. In addition to keeping informed and using the right products, the bottom line of a good paint job is the skill and care of the painter in the refinishing process. The techniques employed can vary color, cause loss of adhesion, cause sand scratch swelling, and create a multitude of other problems.

16.1 CONTENTS OF PAINT

Basically, automotive paints are composed of three or—with some topcoats—four components (Figure 16-2).

- Pigment
- Binder
- Solvent
- Additives (with some finishes)

PIGMENT

Pigment is one of two nonvolatile film-forming ingredients (that part which remains in the dried film) found in paint. It provides the color and durability of the finish. It also gives the paint the ability to hide what is underneath. In addition to providing durability and hiding, pigment can also improve the strength and adhesion, change gloss, and modify flow and application properties.

The size and shape of pigment particles are important, too. Pigment particle size affects hiding ability, while pigment shape affects strength. Pigment particles can be nearly spherical or rod- or plate-like. Rod-shaped particles, for example, reinforce paint film like iron bars in concrete.

BINDER

The other nonvolatile film-forming paint ingredient, the binder, holds the pigment in liquid form, makes it durable, and gives it the ability to stick to the surface. The binder is the backbone of paint.

The binder is generally made of a natural resin (such as rosin), drying oils like linseed or cottonseed, or a synthetic resin (such as methyl methacrylate, polyurethane, polystyrene, polyvinyl chloride, and so forth). The binder dictates the type of paint to be produced because it contains the drying mechanism.

Binder is usually modified with plasticizers and catalysts. They improve such properties as durability, adhesion, corrosion resistance, mar-resistance, and flexibility.

SOLVENT

The solvent (or **vehicle** as it is sometimes called) is the "volatile" ingredient of the paint. Most solvents are derived from crude oil. The main function of a volatile in paint is to make it possible to properly apply the material, and it must be of sufficient solvent power to dissolve the binder portion of the film. High-quality solvents improve the application and film properties of topcoats. They also enhance gloss and minimize paint texture, so less buffing is needed. They also help with more accurate color matches.

In addition to the solvent already in paint, so-called **diluent** solvents are used to give the paint a viscosity that makes it easier to apply. When used with lacquer, the diluent solvent is called a **thinner.** When used with enamel, it is called a **reducer.** This is an important distinction in the automobile refinishing business, and the respective products are so labeled. Remember that a lacquer is **thinned,** while an enamel is **reduced.** The ratio of pigment/binder/solvent that makes up paint is given in Figure 16-3.

ADDITIVES

With the extensive changes made in paint technology during the last decade, additives have become a way of life for most refinishers. While comprising no more than 5 percent of the paint at most (and usually much less), additives perform a variety of vital functions. Some speed up drying and improve gloss; others slow drying; and still others lower gloss. And some perform a combination of functions—such as eliminate wrinkling, provide faster through cure (the final drying), prevent blushing (a milky, misty look), and improve chemical resistance.

Those additives that speed up cure and improve gloss are often referred to as **hardeners.** Those that slow drying are called **retarders.** And those that lower gloss are called **flatteners.**

Flexible paint additives are used in various color coat systems to afford the necessary elasticity of an otherwise rigid paint coating. When a flexible part is compressed or crinkled, the part will return to its normal shape. These additives allow the paint system to flex with the part.

16.2 TYPES OF BODY FINISHES

The exterior of an automobile is painted with one of two basic finishes—**lacquer** or **enamel.** Other terms such as nitrocellulose, acrylic, alkyd, or poly-

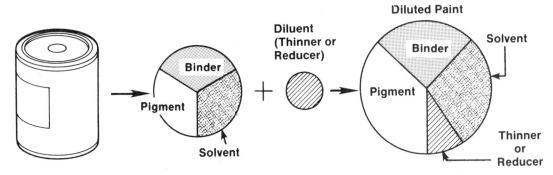

FIGURE 16-3   Ratio of pigment/binder/solvent that makes up paint.

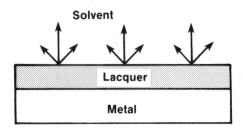

FIGURE 16-4   Lacquers and acrylic lacquers dry by evaporation.

urethane sometimes can be used to describe an automobile paint. However, these products are still either lacquer or enamel. Each of two basic body finishing systems—lacquer and enamel—has its advantages and disadvantages.

Lacquers are physically hardened and dry by evaporation (Figure 16-4). As the solvents evaporate, the binder and pigments left behind combine into a solid state. If the solvents are reintroduced into physically hardened paint products, they will soften and, if enough solvents are added, will eventually return to a liquid state.

Lacquers can be made hard and then soft again and, therefore, are reversible. As solvents evaporate, the painted film shrinks; as solvents are added, it expands. Lacquers are quick to surface dry but take a very long time to dry all the way through. Herein lie some of the problems refinishers encounter with lacquer-primers and putties when not properly used.

Lacquer topcoats usually must be compounded or rubbed with a compound or polish to bring out the gloss (Figure 16-5). Most acrylic lacquer basecoat/clear coat finishes can allow a lacquer basecoat to be clear coated with an enamel topcoat. This helps eliminate the need for compounding or polishing to bring out the gloss.

Enamels dry by evaporation of the solvents as the first stage and by oxidation of the binder as the second stage (Figure 16-6). The oxidation is a

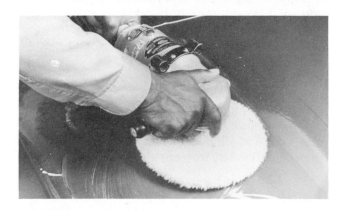

FIGURE 16-5   Lacquer topcoat being compounded by hand or machine to bring out the gloss. (Courtesy of 3M)

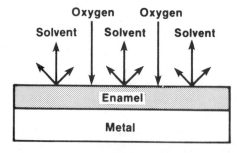

FIGURE 16-6   Enamels dry by evaporation and oxidation.

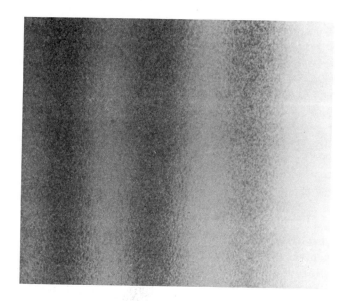

FIGURE 16-7 Orange peel is a fairly common problem. *(Courtesy of PPG Industries, Inc.)*

change in the binder as a result of combining with the oxygen in the air. Heat makes these actions more rapid. Thoroughly dry synthetic films are quite insoluble in ordinary solvents. The longer the drying period, the more insoluble and tougher they become. A thorough sanding when repainting is therefore necessary. Enamel finishes dry with a gloss and do not require rubbing or polishing because of a chemical change rather than simply solvent evaporation. Since enamels generally dry slower, there is more of a chance for dirt and dust to stick in the finish. Also, enamel finishes often dry with a texture called **orange peel** (Figure 16-7). While there is generally a slight amount of orange peel in an enamel film, too much will cause surface roughness or lower gloss.

The bulk of today's passenger cars are finished either in acrylic lacquer, Thermosetting Acrylic Enamel (TAE), or the new high-solids basecoat/clear coat enamel finishes. These finishes are baked

Functional Nomenclature	Resin/Pigment Ratio	Primary Objective	Use and Features
Primer		Adhesion and anticorrosion	Applied directly to panel surface
Primer-Surfacer		Adhesion, anticorrosion, and smoothness	Intermediate between primer and surfacer. Applied to metal surface or over primer.
Putty		Filler	To smooth out rough spots
Sealer		Prevent absorption of topcoat	Intermediate between surfacer and topcoat. Prevents absorption of topcoat and helps avoid troubles arising from old (previous) paint.
Topcoat		Upgrades external appearance	Gives color, gloss, and body to help upgrade merchandising value

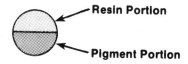

— Resin Portion

— Pigment Portion

(The more resin, the better gloss and less absorption)

(The more pigment, the better covering of rough spots and smoothness, but less gloss and more absorption.)

FIGURE 16-8 Functions of automobile paint materials. *(Courtesy of Toyota Motor Corp.)*

in huge ovens to shorten the drying times and cure the paint. It is important to know what type of finishes the car manufacturers use because there are slightly different methods required for refinishing them.

There is a difference between the lacquer used by the car manufacturers and that used in the paint and body shops. Both are fast drying, but Original Equipment Manufacturers (OEMs) bake lacquers to produce reflow that assures leveling and a mirror-like gloss without need for compounding. Refinish lacquers—on the other hand—are made to air dry and often require compounding to achieve the proper gloss. Since high-temperature ovens are generally not used in the shop, refinishers need faster drying thinners than the OEMs.

The thermosetting acrylic enamel finishes used by the car manufacturers must also be baked in ovens in order to dry and cure properly. Very few, if any, refinish shops have these large bake ovens, but even if they did, the high temperatures might damage a car's upholstery, glass, or wiring. Therefore, finish shops require an easy-to-apply, yet durable enamel that will:

- Air dry without baking.
- Dry when baked at low temperatures. Again, air dry refinish shop conditions require faster drying (and a wider range of) solvents than OEMs.

More information on the various lacquers and enamels used as topcoats in the automobile industry is given later in this chapter. As shown in Figure 16-8, in addition to the topcoat, there are other materials that play an important role in the refinishing operation.

16.3 TYPES OF REFINISHING

With a wide number of refinishing paint materials available, the refinisher uses them to do only one of three types of jobs:

- Spot refinishing repairs (Figure 16-9)
- Panel refinishing repairs (Figure 16-10)
- Overall repainting of the entire vehicle (Figure 16-11)

SPOT REPAIR

This type of repair is often called "ding and dent" work. That is because the damaged area is usually small—either a ding or a dent. Other possi-

FIGURE 16-9 Spot refinishing repair generally involves minor body repair, featheredging, an application of primer-surfacer, and sanding. *(Courtesy of America Sikkens, Inc.)*

FIGURE 16-10 Panel or block refinishing repair, basically the same as spot repair, covers an entire panel or panels of the car (door, hood, and so forth).

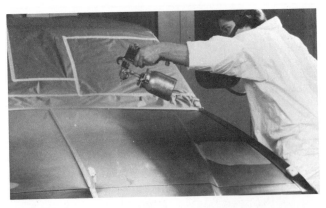

FIGURE 16-11 Overall repainting can be dictated by the extent of the repair, the condition of the finish, or by the owner's preference. *(Courtesy of Maaco Enterprises, Inc.)*

bilities might be scratches or a breakdown of the substrate due to rust or corrosion.

Spot repair generally involves:

- Minor body repair
- Metal conditioning
- Undercoat applications
- Topcoat application that is blended into the old finish surrounding the repair

PANEL REPAIR

Basically, panel repair work uses the same technique as spot repair except that the area covers an entire panel or panels of the car (door, hood, and so on) and the match is made at the panel joints. As in spot repair, any imperfections within the panel must be featheredged and the undercoats applied before the topcoats go on. Sometimes when the color match is especially difficult, it is recommended that the new color be blended into the adjoining panels.

Both spot and panel repair could be considered small area finishing. Oftentimes the refinisher must decide whether to do a spot or a panel repair. If the area to be repainted is large, panel repair can be easier.

OVERALL REPAINTING

Overall repainting is just what it says, the whole vehicle is painted. Some reasons for refinishing the entire car include:

- Size and/or number of spots to be repaired
- Dull, cracked, or worn finish
- Car owner wishes to change color

There are also specialty paint shops that do mostly overall painting as well as custom shops that develop glamour finishes for custom, antique, and classic cars.

16.4 UNDERCOAT PRODUCTS

Proper undercoating is part of the foundation for an attractive, durable topcoat. If the undercoat—or combination of undercoats—is not correct, the topcoat appearance will suffer and might even crack or peel.

Undercoats can be compared to a sandwich filler that holds two slices of bread together. The bottom slice of bread is called the substrate (or sur-

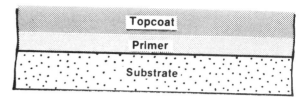

FIGURE 16-12 Primers are generally applied in a thin coat and do not require sanding. Primers are applied over bare substrates. *(Courtesy of Du Pont Co.)*

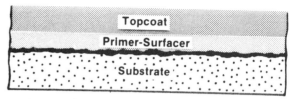

FIGURE 16-13 Primer-surfacers—unlike primers—must be sanded. They can be applied over bare metal or sanded old finishes. *(Courtesy of Du Pont Co.)*

face of the vehicle). That surface can be bare metal or plastic, or a painted or preprimed surface. The undercoat is the sandwich filler applied to the substrate. It makes the substrate smooth and provides a bond for the topcoat. The upper slice is the topcoat, the final color coat that the customer sees.

Undercoats contain pigment, binder, and solvent. There are four general or basic types of undercoats:

- Primer (Figure 16-12)
- Primer-surfacer (Figure 16-13)
- Primer-sealer
- Sealer (Figure 16-14)

Most surfaces must be undercoated (Table 16-1) before refinishing for several reasons: to fill scratches to provide a good base for applications, to promote adhesion of the topcoat to the substrate, and to assure corrosion resistance. A primer alone, however, will not fill sand scratches or other surface flaws. Primer-surfacers are used to provide both priming and filling in one step. Primer-sealers are applied to prevent solvents in the topcoat from being absorbed into the porous primer-surfacer. These three undercoats—primer, primer-surfacer, and primer-sealer—can be used together, singularly, or in various combinations, depending on the surface condition and size of the job (Table 16-2). Sealers are employed to improve adhesion between the old and new finishes. To provide good adhesion, a sealer should always be used over an old lacquer finish when the new finish is to be enamel. Under

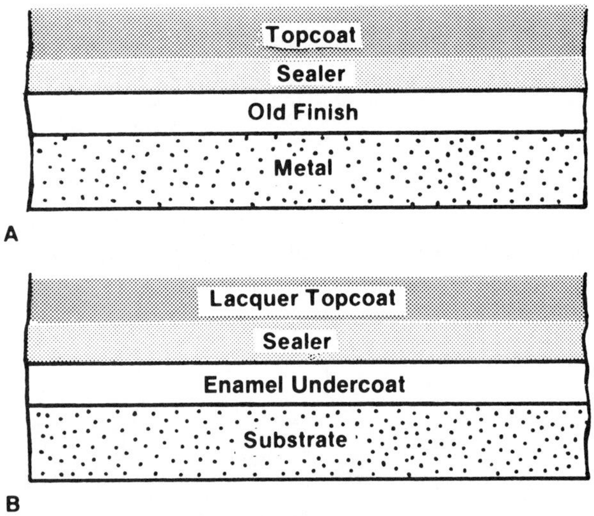

A

B

FIGURE 16-14 **(A) Sealers improve topcoat adhesion. They can be applied over primers, primer-surfacers, or (in this case) old finish. (B) When a topcoat different from the old finish (in quality as well as color) is applied, a sealer should be used.** *(Courtesy of Du Pont Co.)*

TABLE 16-1: FUNCTIONS OF UNDERCOATS

Undercoat Function	Primer	Primer-Surfacer	Primer-Sealer	Sealer
Resists rust and corrosion	Yes	Yes	Yes	No
Makes topcoat adhere better	Yes	Yes	Yes	Yes
Fills scratches and nicks	No	Yes	No	No
Provides uniform hold out of the topcoat	No	No	Yes	Yes
Prevents show through of sand scratches	No	No	Yes	Yes

other conditions, a sealer can be desirable but not absolutely necessary.

With a great number of different kinds of undercoat products on the market, the refinisher is often faced with the problem of what one to use. No matter which type of undercoat product is used, the golden rule for selecting surface preparation and all other refinish products is the same: Never mix manufacturers' products.

Refinish products are formulated to work as systems. Manufacturers spend millions of dollars in research and development to design "systems" of products that work together to provide a specific result. Mixing one manufacturer's reducer with another manufacturer's primer-surfacer or topcoat is almost sure to create a lot of headaches. Putting one manufacturer's primer-sealer over another's primer-surfacer is just as risky. It is important to remember that manufacturers only test and guarantee their own systems.

When selecting an undercoat system, it is best to choose products that match the quality of the topcoat. Especially when refinishing a luxury car or applying a top quality basecoat/clear coat system, it can be worth the extra investment in a premium undercoat system to get the additional assurance against finish failure that these products provide.

Quite often, a premium undercoat system actually might be less costly than an economy grade product when labor and materials costs are considered. Premium primer-surfacers typically provide greater fill, so the surface can be prepared with fewer coats using less product.

TABLE 16-2: SURFACES FOR UNDERCOATS

Undercoat Surface	Primer	Primer-Surfacer	Primer-Sealer	Sealer
Bare substrate (metal, fiberglass, or plastic)	Yes	Yes	Yes	No
Sanded old finish	No	Yes	Yes	Yes

PRIMERS

By definition, a primer (or prep coater as it is sometimes called) is generally the first coat in any finishing system (Figure 16-15). It is designed to prepare the bare substrate and to accept and hold the color topcoat. Primers should provide maximum adhesion to the surface and produce a corrosion-resistant foundation. Primers generally do not fill surface imperfections and therefore often do not require sanding.

Straight primers are predominantly used by original equipment manufacturers rather than paint and body repair shops. Primers are usually enamel type products because they provide better adhesion and corrosion resistance than lacquers. (Where the original surfaces are plastic or fiberglass, some lacquer-primers are used.)

There are several special primers available to the shop refinisher. For example, the two-part, self-etching **epoxy primers** are probably the most versatile and valuable primer products on the market today. An epoxy primer system consists of the primer itself and an activator (or catalyst). When mixed together (known as **catalyzing**), it often requires an induction time; that is, the period of time that the components must be allowed to thoroughly mix with each other before spraying. It must be remembered that these two-part or two-component mixtures have a "pot" life, or a limited time before they become unusable.

Epoxy primers are a good choice where a great deal of fill is required. On sandblasted, coarse surfaces, for example, a high-build epoxy primer adheres to the bare substrate and provides the fill necessary for a smooth finish. As mentioned in detail in Chapter 15, it was stated that two-part epoxy primer was the best way to restore corrosion prevention to a damaged vehicle. The epoxy primers are easy to apply (Figure 16-16) and offer the extra protection that vehicles require because of the high degree of wear and tear to which they are exposed. Virtually any automotive or commercial vehicle topcoat can be used over an epoxy primer. Most epoxy primers are available in lead-free gray and lead- and chromate-free red iron oxide. They enable topcoat color to be sprayed only 1 hour after primer application, with no sanding or sealing.

Zinc chromate primer is a product that has been around for many years. It is a primer designed mainly for adhesion to aluminum. Today, however, epoxy primer will actually do a better job in this application.

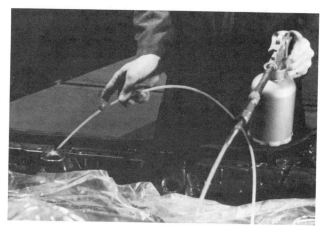

FIGURE 16-16 Application of a two-part epoxy primer to interior enclosed parts of a vehicle

Zinc chromate primer should always be used in applications where dissimilar metals will come in contact with each other, such as in a truck body where steel ribs might be used to support aluminum sides and top. One thin coat of zinc chromate will prevent an electrolysis reaction, which causes rapid corrosion. Most zinc chromate primers are reduced with enamel reducer and can be topcoated only with enamels.

Zinc weld-through primer is a zinc-rich material that protects welded joints against corrosion (see Chapter 15). The zinc in the primer will provide galvanic protection in the weld zone, but provide poor adhesion to other finish material.

When corrosion resistance is very important, **wash-primers** (also called **vinyl wash-primers**) are used under primer-surfacers or sealers. The reducer in a wash-primer contains phosphoric acid that "bites" into the surface to provide superior adhesion to steel, aluminum, rigid and flexible plastics, and certain kinds of zinc-coated metal. The bond is so strong, in fact, that when a primer has been applied to bare metal it is extremely difficult to remove without grinding it off.

To use the wash-primer it must be reduced with a special reducer-catalyst and must be used within a specific period of time. It offers high corrosion resistance to alkalies, oils, grease, and even salt water. Another benefit of this type of resin primer is that it is more forgiving of metal cleaning problems.

Chip resistant primers are specially formulated for use on lower body sections that are prone to gravel and stone impact damage (Figure 16-17). They give improved resistance against corrosion and help to reduce drumming noise.

Adhesion to plastic panels that have come from the factory unprimed can be improved by the use of

FIGURE 16-15 Application of a primer is generally the first step in refinishing. (Courtesy of America Sikkens, Inc.)

FIGURE 16-17   Application of a chip resistant primer provides resistance to chipping, salt spray, and the abrasive action of stones, sand, and other road particles. It dries fast and can be painted 30 minutes after applying. *(Courtesy of 3M)*

FIGURE 16-18   Application of a plastic primer over a flexible plastic part. Apply a wet coat on the part and then after 10 minutes, apply a second coat. *(Courtesy of 3M)*

a special plastic primer. Flexible plastics in particular require **plastic primer** (Figure 16-18). Many rigid plastics also benefit from priming with a plastic primer. Plastic primers promote bonding, eliminating peeling and other adhesion problems.

Another ready-to-spray primer product designed specifically for use with basecoat/clear coat OEM finishes is the so-called **adhesion promoter** or **mid coat primer.** This product is a water-clear primer with good durability and excellent adhesion to the very hard clear coats. It is recommended that it be applied beyond the repaired area on a spot repair before any other primer is used. Its purpose is to provide a surface to which a blend edge can adhere.

 SHOP TALK

Some metal replacement parts are supplied by the car manufacturers with a primed surface. The car manufacturer might recommend that this primer not be removed as it is an anticorrosive as well as for paint adhesion. It is necessary to apply a primer over the factory primers.

Primer-Surfacers

Primer-surfacers are the most popular of all the undercoats in refinish applications. They are used to build up featheredged areas for rough surfaces and to provide a smooth base for lacquer and enamel topcoats (Figure 16-19). A good primer-surfacer should have all of the following six characteristics (Figure 16-20):

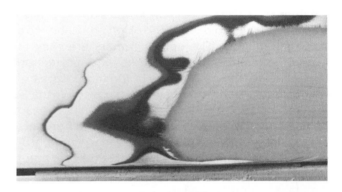

FIGURE 16-19   Primer-surfacers are very important where featheredging has been done. *(Courtesy of Carborundum Abrasives Co.)*

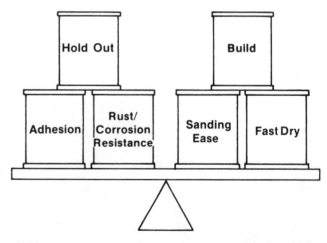

FIGURE 16-20   A "balance of properties" is vital in a primer-surfacer. The three properties on the right build the proper foundation for the topcoat; the three on the left make the job fast and easy. *(Courtesy of Du Pont Co.)*

FIGURE 16-21 Most primer-surfacers are easy to sand. (Courtesy of Carborundum Abrasives Co.)

- **Adhesion.** A strong bond between the metal or the old finish and the topcoat to be applied.
- **Rust/corrosion resistance.** A durability characteristic that prevents loss of adhesion and, ultimately, disintegration of the metal.
- **Build.** A quality that provides the necessary fill for grinder marks and sand scratches in repair work.
- **Sanding ease.** A characteristic that allows the primer-surfacer to be sanded smooth and leveled quickly and easily (Figure 16-21).
- **Hold out.** A sealing quality that prevents the topcoat from sinking into the primer-surfacer, resulting in a dull look.
- **Drying speed.** A time saving quality that permits the refinisher to go on to the next operation. (A good primer-surfacer should be ready to sand in 20 to 30 minutes.)

There are five types of primer-surfacers:

- Nitrocellulose lacquer
- Acrylic lacquer
- Alkyd or synthetic enamel
- Self-etching
- Acrylic urethane

Nitrocellulose primer-surfacer was, until the last few years, the most popular with the majority of painters—primarily because it dries fast and is easy to sand. While it has adequate adhesion in most cases, it does not have these two qualities that the

other four primer-surfacers do: rust and corrosion resistance and a tough, flexible film. And it cannot be used on aluminum. The use of nitrocellulose lacquer primer-surfacers currently is recommended only for small area repairs.

Acrylic primer-surfacers have replaced nitrocellulose-based primer-surfacers as the painter's number one choice because of their good fill and fast dry times. They can be directly recoated with a wider variety of topcoats than nitrocellulose primer-surfacers, making them suitable for more jobs. They offer greater durability, shrink less, and provide the same fill in fewer coats. Other desirable characteristics of an acrylic resin sealer are:

- **Sanding.** Easy sanding.
- **Drying.** It dries in 30 minutes or less when applied correctly.
- **Hold out.** The hold out is good and not porous.
- **Settling.** It does not settle too hard in the cup. It can be stirred back into solution quickly if it stands for a while.

Alkyd or synthetic enamel primer-surfacer is excellent in all respects except one: It requires a much longer drying time—2 to 3 hours. If it is to be wet sanded, dry overnight. Because of its tough, flexible film and high degree of corrosion resistance, it is recommended for surfacing large areas—either panel repair or complete repainting. It also can present an overspray problem.

Though fairly new on the market, **self-etching primer-surfacers** are rapidly gaining in popularity because in one step they etch the bare metal and provide the fill needed for a smooth finish. Etching filler ensures outstanding paint adhesion and corrosion resistance and can reduce surface preparation time and materials costs by more than 25 percent.

The two-component **acrylic urethane primer-surfacers** were created for use with today's more sophisticated and expensive topcoats. Acrylic urethane primer-surfacers provide even higher film build than conventional acrylics, better color hold out, and virtually no film shrinkage, substantially reducing the risk of overnight dull-back. The trade-offs are longer dry times, cost, overspray damage, and the need to apply these products at controlled shop temperatures and in a very clean shop environment. An acrylic urethane primer-surfacer is a good choice for overall refinishing when a long-lasting, superior paint job is the goal.

Another excellent product is the new polyester primer-surfacer that primes, fills, and seals in one easy operation. It develops a tough, flexible polyes-

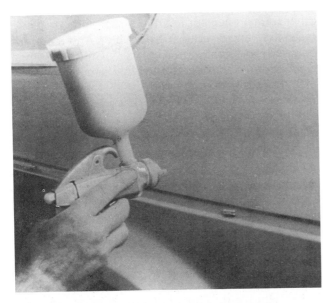

FIGURE 16-22 Spraying a polyester primer-surfacer with a gravity feed spray gun

ter resin that offers its user high build-up capabilities. It quickly levels, fills, and reconditions sand scratches, pinholes, stone chips, grinder marks, crazed and lacquer-checked surfaces, and most minor surface imperfections. Polyester primer-surfacers can be sprayed—preferably with a gravity feed spray gun (Figure 16-22).

All primer-surfacers should be thinned as per label directions and applied in medium coats, allowing 15 to 20 minutes flash time between coats. Applying heavy coats or not allowing enough flash time will result in a thick coat of surfacer that can gum up the sandpaper, featheredge poorly, and cause loss of gloss or peeling of the topcoat. Excessive thickness of a primer-surfacer coat under a topcoat could lead to premature crazing and/or cracking conditions.

Recommended topcoats for both lacquer and acrylic primer-surfacers include lacquer and enamel. In some cases, urethanes can be applied over an acrylic primer-surfacer. Check manufacturers' recommendations regarding proper primer products for urethanes before making any suggestions because they can vary greatly from brand to brand.

Primer-Sealers

A primer-sealer—like a primer—is used to prime bare metal to resist rust and corrosion and to provide topcoat adhesion. In addition, primer-sealers can be used to seal aged painted surfaces that have been sanded. In contrast to primer-surfacers, primer-sealers do not fill and do not have to be sanded.

A primer-sealer is generally an enamel-based product that must be reduced with an enamel reducer. The main reason for using this type of primer is to ensure that the ready-to-paint surface is consistent in color (to prevent primer spots from showing through the finish) and porosity (to prevent topcoat solvents from soaking into the primer spots, causing dull spots or featheredge ring).

Sealers

Sealers differ from primer-sealers in that they cannot be used as a primer. Sealers are sprayed over a primer or primer-surfacer or a sanded old finish. They are used in automotive refinishing for four specific purposes:

- To provide better adhesion between the paint material to be applied and the repair surface (Figure 16-23). Sanding of the surface is usually required before application.
- To act as a barrier type material that prevents or retards the mass penetration of refinish solvents into the color and/or undercoat being repaired.
- To provide uniform hold out. If the old finish is good and hard and if a primer-surfacer with good hold out is used for spot repairing, a sealer is not mandatory. Obviously, if only one or neither of these conditions is present,

FIGURE 16-23 Spraying a sealer will provide better adhesion for the topcoat. (Courtesy of Du Pont Co.)

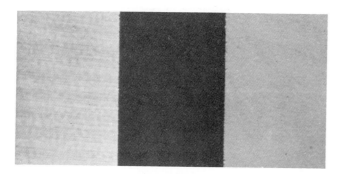

FIGURE 16-24 This stepped up panel—from scratches in the old finish to sealer to new topcoat color—shows how scratches can be minimized or eliminated through the use of the proper sealers. (Courtesy of PPG Industries, Inc.)

a sealer is recommended (Figure 16-24). However, a sealer is always recommended to provide uniform color hold out and to prevent die-back.

- To prevent show through or sand through. If sand scratches (Figure 16-25) are present in the undercoat, particularly if noticeable to the eye, they will show through the topcoat. The safest procedure is to apply a coat of sealer, especially on large areas of sand

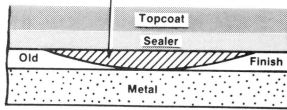

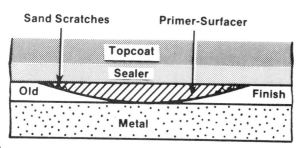

FIGURE 16-25 (A) If a primer-surfacer has been used, there might be a difference in the hold out between the two types of finishes. (B) If so, a sealer will solve the problem, use of a sealer might prevent show through of sand scratches. (Courtesy of Du Pont Co.)

scratches. Small areas, such as sand scratches around a featheredge, can be removed by compounding.

Sealers also provide the following desirable characteristics:

- Improve adhesion of the repair color to very hard undercoats and enamel surfaces
- Improve gloss
- Prevent bleeding (when designed for this purpose)
- Can be used on small, clean bare metal surfaces

There are situations in which some kind of sealer must be used, and there are conditions in which a sealer should be used to improve adhesions, the following application rules must be kept in mind:

- **Alkyd enamel over lacquer.** To ensure adequate adhesion, a sealer must be used.
- **Enamel over enamel.** Adequate adhesion might be present between two enamels, but there is no guarantee, so a sealer should be used.
- **Lacquer over enamel.** Spot repairs generally are not a problem, but a sealer is recommended in panel repair or complete repainting (Figure 16-26).
- **Lacquer over lacquer.** Sealer not required to ensure adequate adhesion but can be desired for hold out and hiding sand scratches.

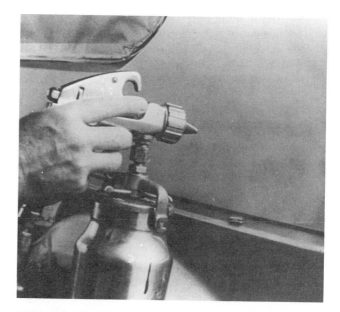

FIGURE 16-26 Sealer should be used when making panel refinishing repairs or when doing a complete refinishing job.

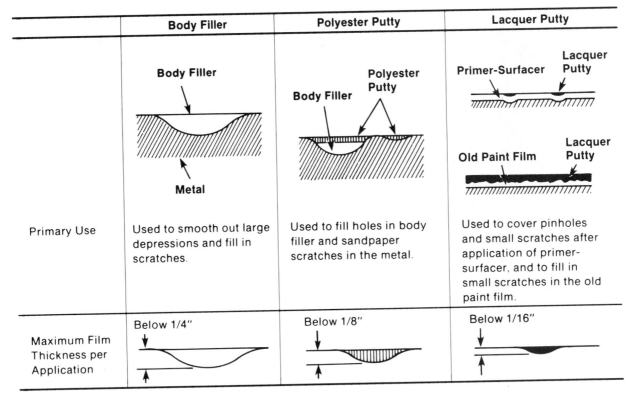

	Body Filler	Polyester Putty	Lacquer Putty
Primary Use	Used to smooth out large depressions and fill in scratches.	Used to fill holes in body filler and sandpaper scratches in the metal.	Used to cover pinholes and small scratches after application of primer-surfacer, and to fill in small scratches in the old paint film.
Maximum Film Thickness per Application	Below 1/4"	Below 1/8"	Below 1/16"

FIGURE 16-27　Use of three major types of putties and body fillers

Two basic types of sealer are available:

- Those designed for an acrylic lacquer paint system. This sealer, when so stated on the label, is not to be topcoated with enamel finishes.
- Those designed for air dry enamel paint systems. This sealer, when so stated on the label, is not to be topcoated with lacquer or acrylic lacquer finishes.

Universal sealers have been developed that can be used under the majority of topcoat systems. For instance, **barrier coat sealers** are designed for extremely sensitive substrates. Old finishes that are on the verge of cracking or that have been exposed to too much sun can require the use of a barrier coat sealer. These sealers eliminate lift when an enamel topcoat is going to be sprayed over a previous enamel paint job that has been buffed through to an OEM lacquer.

Recoat sealer is a special purpose primer that is made only by a few paint companies to be used only with their acrylic enamel system when there is a need to repaint a panel that is in a sensitive stage. Recoat sealer is packaged ready to spray, requires no reduction, and has poor adhesion if it is used on a paint film that is not sensitive. The only way to find out whether or not recoat sealer is required is to test

a small painted area by applying some enamel reducer. If the reducer has no effect or if it dissolves the finish, recoat sealer is not needed. If the finish is wrinkled or lifted by the reducer, recoat sealer must be applied before any repainting. If an isocyanate additive is used in the acrylic enamel, there is no sensitive time and recoat sealer is not necessary.

Bleeder sealer seals colors that contain a bleeding dye pigment. Some reds and maroons contain such a pigment; however, there are others that result in a yellowing rather than the familiar reddish tone. A spot check using a white color will generally tell whether or not a bleeding color is present.

More recently, **tie coat sealers** have been developed that provide extra adhesion when a lacquer topcoat is being sprayed over an OEM enamel. The transparent resin in the tie coat sealer provides the extra "bite" into the OEM enamel that refinish lacquer topcoats require.

Putties and Body Fillers

Putties and body fillers, while not precisely defined as undercoats, might be termed solid undercoats since they are frequently used in conjunction with one or more of the four liquid undercoats and perform many of the same functions. There are several types of putty that are called by different names depending on the manufacturer, but normally putty is classified as body filler, polyester putty, or lacquer putty (Figure 16-27).

Body filler is primarily used during body repair work to smooth out rough spots in the metal (see Chapter 8). Also called plastic filler, it features pliability and can be applied rather thickly (Figure 16-28). There is also a type that contains wax. When applied, the wax rises to the surface and cuts off air contact so as to prevent the adverse effects that oxygen has on the chemical reaction that occurs during hardening. Because it is easy for sandpaper scratches to occur during polishing, it is necessary to later remove the wax with a surform tool after the putty has partially dried (Figure 16-29). However, there is also

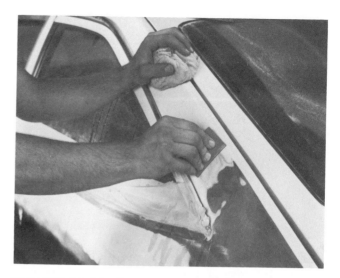

FIGURE 16-30   Polyester putties spread easily. (Courtesy of America Sikkens, Inc.)

a nonwax type that does not require scraping with a surform tool, but it is inferior to the wax type in respect to the maximum application thickness. In the past, wax type body filler was used a great deal, but recently there is wider use of the nonwax type, similar to polyester putty. Because it is also possible to apply polyester putty rather thickly, little distinction is made between body filler and polyester putty.

Polyester putty is used to fill in small holes or slight scratches in the body filler. Its formal name is unsaturated polyester putty, but most body personnel call it "poly putty." It is not as pliable as body filler and cannot be applied as thickly, but it has a fine texture, spreads easily (Figure 16-30), and does not require surform treatment. Like body filler, polyester putty is a two-component type requiring mixing of a main agent and a hardening agent. As there is no volatile component during application, the paint film maintains its body after hardening.

Lacquer type putty is a companion product to lacquer primer-surfacer and is used to fill scratches and flaws that the primer-surfacer cannot. Like primer-surfacers, a quality putty must offer a balance of properties, including fast drying, ease of sanding, good adhesion, and hold out. Lacquer putty is designed for spot applications rather than over a large area (Figure 16-31). It is not designed to straighten or finish straightening metalwork.

In composition, putty is made up of a very high solid material of the same nature as surfacer, but with a low thinner or solvent content. Therefore it is used to fill any small imperfections or flaws remaining in the substrate after primer-surfacer has been applied. Putty must be sanded (Figure 16-32).

FIGURE 16-28   Body fillers are applied rather thick. (Courtesy of America Sikkens, Inc.)

FIGURE 16-29   Body fillers are frequently shaped with a surform tool. (Courtesy of Carborundum Abrasives Co.)

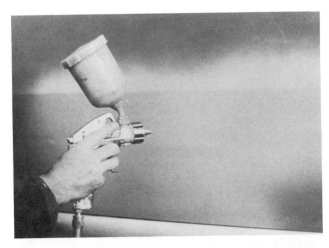

FIGURE 16-31 **Lacquer type putty is best for small areas.** *(Courtesy of America Sikkens, Inc.)*

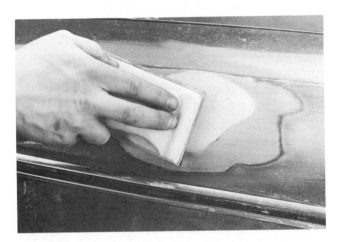

FIGURE 16-32 **All putties usually require sanding.**

CAUTION: After sanding the putty, it is important to recoat the putty with a **thin** coat of primer-surfacer before applying topcoats.

Nitrocellulose-based spray putties are a special type of putty that gives the build of spray fillers coupled with fast drying. They can be applied by a siphon feed spray gun or pressure feed spray gun. The latter is preferable for speed and ease of application. These putties can be applied over large areas with less danger of imperfections than with putties applied with a squeegee or glazing knife. More details on the use and application of putties and body fillers can be found in Chapter 8.

In summary, the selection of one or more undercoats will be determined by the following characteristics of a job:

- **Type of surface.** Bare metal or previously finished.
- **Condition of that surface.** Repaired area or sanded aged finish.
- Whether **hold out** and **show through** are problems.

Depending upon the situation, the painter might use a:

- Primer by itself
- Primer-surfacer by itself
- Primer-sealer
- Primer-surfacer with a sealer
- Sealer over a sanded old finish

While a primer-surfacer will cover small imperfections, it will not handle deep scratches, gouges, or other similar defects. When these conditions exist, the painter has two other options:

- Where the scratches are a bit deeper, it is possible to apply putty over the primer-surfacer (Figure 16-33A).
- When the scratches are too severe for putty, the painter has to use body filler on the metal and then prime it (just as it is used in the metalworking area to repair larger dents) (Figure 16-33B).

No matter what type of refinish job confronts the painter, the purpose of the undercoat is always the

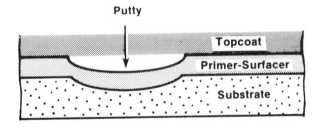

A

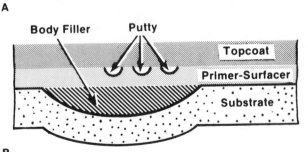

B

FIGURE 16-33 **(A) Where scratches are too deep for primer-surfacers, use a putty after application of the primer-surfacer. (B) When scratches are too severe for putty, use a body filler on the surface and then the primer-surfacer.** *(Courtesy of Du Pont Co.)*

same: to provide the best possible foundation for a beautiful, long-lasting finish. Making the right product choices is an important step in paving the way for a successful paint finish.

16.5 TOPCOATS

From the customer's standpoint, the topcoat (or color coat) is the most important in body repair because that is all he/she sees. The expert refinisher takes special pride in producing a beautiful finish on spot and panel repairs, or in an overall repaint job that matches both the color (or color effect) and the texture of the original finish. Therefore, it is of great importance to fully understand the topcoat materials and how they are applied. The latter is covered in detail in Chapter 19.

AUTOMOBILE COLORS

Like all colors, automotive refinishing colors are a result of the way they react to light. The color seen

FIGURE 16-34 In metallic finishes the light enters the finish and is reflected by metal flakes to produce metallic color effect. (Courtesy of Du Pont Co.)

FIGURE 16-35 Dry spray traps the metallic particles at various angles near the surface and causes a high-metallic color effect. (Courtesy of Du Pont Co.)

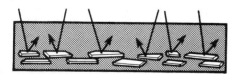

FIGURE 16-36 Wet spray allows time for metallic particles to settle in the paint film and causes a strong pigment color effect. (Courtesy of Du Pont Co.)

is the result of the kind and amount of light waves the surface reflects. When these light waves strike the retina, they are converted into electrical impulses that the brain sees as color. The same color will look very different under natural daylight, incandescent lamps, or fluorescent bulbs. That is why it is so important to check color match in daylight or a balanced artificial light. There are two basic automobile general finish types: solids and metallic colors.

Solid Colors

For many years all cars were solid colors, such as black, white, tan, blue, green, maroon, and so on. These colors are composed of a high volume of opaque type pigments. Opaque pigments block the rays of sun and absorb light in accordance with the type of color they are. That is, the darker the solid color is, the more light it absorbs and the less it reflects. Black will absorb more light and will reflect less; white absorbs less light but reflects a great deal more. When polished, solid colors reflect light in only one direction. Solid colors are still used by the refinisher, but to a lesser degree when compared with a few years ago.

Metallic Colors

Metallic (or polychrome) paint contains small flakes of metal suspended in liquid. The metal particles combine with the pigment to impart varying color effects. The effect depends on the position the flakes assume within the paint film (Figure 16-34). The position of the metal flakes and the thickness of the paint affect the overall color of the painted surface. The flakes reflect light, but some light is absorbed by the paint. The thicker the layer of paint, the greater the light absorption.

When metallic paint is sprayed on dry, the metallic flakes are trapped at various angles near the surface. Light reflection is not uniform, and because the light has less film to travel through, little of it is absorbed (Figure 16-35). The result of nonuniform light reflection and a minimum of light absorption is a painted surface with a metallic appearance and a light color.

When metallic paint is sprayed on wet, the metallic flakes have sufficient time to settle so they lie parallel to and deeper within the paint film. Light reflection is uniform and, because the light has to go farther into the paint film, light absorption is greater (Figure 16-36). The result is a painted surface that appears deeper and darker in color.

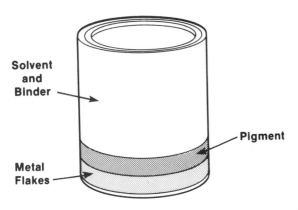

FIGURE 16-37 Metallic paint is composed of solvent, binder, pigment, and metal flakes. The pigment settles below the solvent and binder, while the flakes sink below the pigment.

CAUTION: Metallic color paints must be stirred and mixed thoroughly before using. As shown in Figure 16-37, the pigment settles below the binder; the metal flakes settle below the pigment. If flakes stay at the bottom of the can, the paint will not match the same color on a vehicle being repaired or refinished.

Basic Types of Topcoats

Automotive topcoat finishes range from paints that have been available for 50 years to new multicomponent systems that provide the ultimate in durability. No single finish is the best for all applications; it all depends on a careful matching of finish capabilities and characteristics with the requirements of the application.

Here is a brief review of the history and highlights of various materials used as topcoats. The application of those still being employed by the automotive trade is detailed in Chapter 19.

Starting with 1900 and into the early 1920s, the wooden bodies and spokes of cars built during this period were painted by hand. Using a mixture of lampblack pigment and varnishes, this material was brushed on by hand, coat after coat, until coverage and hiding were achieved (Figure 16-38). This pigment, having very few solids and being weak, could not give enough coverage with 1, 2, 3, 4, or 5 coats. This buildup of material, lacking any modern driers, would take from 40 to 50 days to dry.

When the bodies were finally dry enough to work on again, a pumice stone, water folded into the

damp rag, along with plenty of elbow grease were applied and any flaws—such as remaining brush marks, dirt, or runs—were removed in this manner. No color selection had been developed at this time, nor did this material have any durability. It dulled and cracked within a year after all that hard work.

Nitrocellulose Lacquers

The introduction of nitrocellulose lacquer in 1924 revolutionized automobile finishing. The use of this lacquer, applied with a spray gun, allowed the steel vehicle bodies to be completed in one day, in turn eliminating a major bottleneck in automobile production.

Nitrocellulose lacquer required several coats of color that did air dry very quickly but faded and chalked because of weak pigment. The color range was just beginning to show improvement, with something other than black, as the greens came into focus. Reds, blues, and yellows (Figure 16-39) were also developing, along with solvents and other technology. Nitrocellulose lacquers were used by the American automobile refinishing trade well into the 1950s.

Alkyd Enamels

Introduced in 1929, alkyd resin enamel has been satisfying refinisher needs in the overall repainting of passenger cars and commercial vehicles for more than half a century. This finish is basically the same today as it was when it was first introduced with a slight modification. The name "synthetic" was given to this enamel finish because the resin used in its formulation was modified by synthesizing the enamels with simple petroleum chemical compounds.

FIGURE 16-38 The use of lampblack pigment and varnish was the standard car finish before 1924.

FIGURE 16-39 The introduction of nitrocellulose lacquers brought color to the automotive industry.

FIGURE 16-40 With the introduction of alkyd resin enamels in 1929, cars took on a lustrous high gloss.

Of course, all paint resins are synthesized, but the name synthetic enamel is still used to identify these alkyds.

Synthetic or alkyd enamels dry to a lustrous high gloss (Figure 16-40), requiring no compounding or buffing. It is the least expensive and the least durable of the commercial finishing systems and tends to dry slowly, generally overnight. It is prone to wrinkling in hot weather during the first 24 to 48 hours and cannot be two-toned or repaired for about 8 to 24 hours. Synthetic enamel also has poorer resistance to water, chemicals, and gasoline during the first few days after application.

Over the past few years, alkyd synthetic enamels have given away some of their popularity to newer finishes, namely acrylic and polyurethane enamels. However, many refinishers still select this enamel because it provides an economical two-coat system with high initial gloss that hides surface imperfections better than newer enamels. This is especially true when a synthetic enamel is reduced with hardener. The synthetic is applied the same as without hardeners, but the drying time is shortened when the hardener has been added. The finish can be two-toned when it is dry enough to tape and generally can be recoated at any time without fear of lifting. The hardener also makes the synthetic enamel highly wrinkle-resistant, though it does not improve durability.

Acrylic Lacquers

Introduced in 1956, acrylic lacquer quickly replaced nitrocellulose lacquer because it dried to a higher gloss and retained its appearance longer. It found immediate acceptance as a favored OEM and repair finish. It is used for spot and panel repair of both lacquer and enamel original finishes and in overall repainting. When used over enamel, a sealer is recommended.

Properly applied, an acrylic lacquer system can give excellent results. It combines the features of durability, color and gloss retention, high gloss, and fast drying time. But, to achieve these features, both the undercoats and thinners must be those recommended for acrylic lacquer paints. The manufacturer's instructions should always be followed. If products from different manufacturers are mixed, failure of the paint film might occur by cracking or crazing.

Acrylic lacquers respond readily to hand or machine polishing, using rubbing or polishing compounds. Some degree of polishing is usually necessary, depending on the gloss level required.

Acrylic Enamels

Developed in the 1960s, acrylic enamels are more durable and faster drying than alkyd enamels and eliminate the compounding step associated with acrylic lacquer. Generally recommended for panel repairs and overall repainting, some acrylic enamels are used for spot repair of both lacquer and enamel original finishes. Acrylic enamel costs slightly more than synthetic enamels but is less expensive than other finishing systems available today.

Acrylic enamel combines the properties and advantages of the very durable color and gloss retentive acrylic lacquer with the excellent flow characteristics and gloss of the enamel systems. It is fast drying and is about 50 percent more durable than synthetic enamel. It is also easy to apply, produces a deep luster and high gloss, and has excellent color and gloss retention. Two-toning or recoating is possible within the first 6 hours of drying. During this period, the solvent evaporates from the film, leaving the finish nontacky and dry to the touch.

For the next 6 to 48 hours, however, most acrylic enamels enter the hard-curing period. Recoating must be done before this period since strong solvents of another coat could cause lifting because the original coat has become too cured to be dissolved and melt in with the new coat. If recoating is necessary during this time, most paint manufacturers recommend the use of a recoat sealer that serves as a barrier coat and permits recoating of acrylic enamel during the critical cure period when lifting might otherwise occur.

Some of the problems created when using acrylic enamels can be reduced or eliminated by the use of a hardener or urethane catalyst. The addition of a hardener or catalyst (often referred to as a second stage or second component) provides a greater initial gloss than alkyd or synthetic enamels and acrylic enamel alone. It also improves the DOI (Distinctiveness Of Image, or measurement of the sharpness of images reflected from the surface), chemical resistance, flexibility, and chip resistance of the finish while eliminating the self-lifting that might occur during the recoating within the 6- to 48-hour hard-curing period of the acrylic enamel without hardener. When adding a hardener or catalyst to acrylic enamel, a recoat or barrier coat sealer is not necessary to prevent lifting.

After reducing the acrylic enamel color and just prior to spraying, add the catalyst or hardener to the reduced material as per label directions (Figure 16-41). Once the catalyst is added and mixed, the topcoat should be sprayed immediately. The pot life, or working time, of these paints will generally be in the range of 4 to 8 hours. After this time all mixed paints should be discarded.

The advent of ultraviolet absorbers has greatly increased the durability and exterior weathering of the acrylic enamel. Acrylic enamel with hardeners

FIGURE 16-41 Before applying any paint material, carefully read the manufacturer's instructions on the container.

and ultraviolet absorbers or stabilizers is sprayed in the same manner as acrylic enamel but provides 50 percent greater durability than acrylic enamels and 100 percent greater durability than the alkyd or synthetic enamels.

Polyurethane Enamels

Ordinary polyurethane enamel provides significantly greater durability than alkyd or synthetic enamels, acrylic enamels, and acrylic enamels with hardeners.

The polyurethane enamel—made with a polyester resin—dries by evaporation of the solvents and by chemical cross-linking between the two principal base components to cure the paint film. A high-gloss, extremely durable, chemical and solvent resistant finish results. Without an accelerator, dry time to tape is about 16 hours. With an accelerator, dry time to tape can be reduced to approximately 3 to 5 hours.

Acrylic Urethane Enamels

A recent development in the urethane family is the acrylic urethane enamel. It is formulated with an acrylic resin that is much more durable than any other finish. Because of the characteristics of this resin, an acrylic urethane enamel offers higher gloss retention and, ultimately, a much longer life. Recent manufacturer tests have shown that this finish retains its gloss from 50 percent to 100 percent longer than ordinary polyurethane enamels.

The acrylic urethane enamel also dries tack-free and out of dust faster than polyurethane enamels and is more resistant to film degradation caused by the sun's ultraviolet (UV) rays. While degradation of the finish cannot be totally stopped, chemical composition of this material substantially retards damaging UV effects. When compared to metallic polyurethane colors, acrylic urethane enamel metallic colors have twice the durability. The urethane's durability also offers exceptional resistance to stone chipping and does not break down when exposed to weather, gasoline (Figure 16-42), chemicals, dirt, and road grime. It virtually eliminates sand scratch swelling.

To achieve proper results from this two-component high-quality material, it is necessary to closely follow the manufacturer's instructions to the letter. The pot life of the activated material is 6 to 8 hours. To achieve the best results the material should be sprayed as soon as possible after components are mixed together. Such additives as fish eye eliminators; accelerator (for temperatures below 70 degrees

Fahrenheit) or retarder (for temperatures above 85 degrees Fahrenheit); and acrylic enamel reducers. If these additives and reducers are employed, they must be used in amounts specified by the manufacturer.

Typical application times are as follows:

- **Nonmetallic (nonpolychromatic).** Apply two to three medium wet coats and allow 20 to 30 minutes drying time between coats.
- **Metallic (polychromatic).** Apply three medium wet coats and allow 20 to 30 minutes drying time between coats. If necessary, apply a final mist coat to even out the metallic color (polychromatic).

Urethane clear coats can be applied over polyurethane enamel and properly prepared acrylic enamels 30 minutes after the color coat application. The result is an ultimate wet look that gives the basecoat additional depth, maximum color and gloss retention, plus extended durability.

> **WARNING:** Polyurethane and acrylic urethane enamels as well as the two-component or catalyzed type finishes (acrylic and alkyd) use isocyanates as a hardener. Isocyanates, however, are highly reactive and can become health hazards if not handled carefully. Because isocyanates react with many common substances, they must be used, stored, and disposed of with care. All urethane paints and products contain isocyanates and, therefore, share the same potential health hazards regardless of brand.

FIGURE 16-42 Polyurethane finishes are not affected by gasoline spills.

FIGURE 16-43 When spraying isocyanate-based paints, wear a hood respirator. (Courtesy of Sherwin Williams Co.)

Appropriate measures must be taken to prevent overexposure or sensitization whenever urethane or any other paints containing isocyanates are being sprayed. These paints should only be used in areas with adequate ventilation. For maximum protection when isocyanates are being sprayed, an air line respirator (Figure 16-43) should be worn until the work area has been exhausted of all vapors and spray mist.

Table 16-3 shows the relative durability of the various types of topcoat systems previously discussed and a comparison to Original Equipment (OE) high-baked thermosetting acrylic enamels.

Costs can be deceiving, particularly with the polyurethane and acrylic urethane colors, both of which are substantially more expensive in their un-

TABLE 16-3: COMPARATIVE DURABILITY OF TOPCOATS

```
0   10   20   30   40   50   60   70   80   90  100
```

Acrylic Urethane Enamel

Two Component Acrylic Enamel

Polyurethane Enamel

Acrylic Enamel With Hardener

Acrylic Enamel

Synthetic (Alkyd) Enamel

TABLE 16-4: SUMMARY OF TOPCOAT PAINT FEATURES

Nomenclature		One-Component Type			Two-Component Type	
		Alkyd Enamels	Acrylic Lacquer	Acrylic Enamel	Polyurethane	Acrylic Urethane Enamel
Spray characteristics		Excellent	Excellent	Good	Good	Good
Possible thickness per application		Fair	Fair	Good	Excellent	Excellent
Gloss	without polishing	Fair	Good	Good	Excellent	Excellent
	after polishing	Good	Good	Good	—	Good
Hardness		Good	Good	Good	Excellent	Excellent
Weather resistance (frosting, yellowing)		Fair	Fair	Good	Excellent	Excellent
Gasoline resistance		Fair	Fair	Fair	Excellent	Good
Adhesion		Good	Good	Fair	Excellent	Excellent
Pollutant resistance		Fair	Fair	Fair	Excellent	Excellent
Drying time	to touch	68°F 5-10 minutes	68°F 10 minutes	68°F 10 minutes	68°F 20-30 minutes	68°F 10-20 minutes
	for surface repair	68°F 6 hours 140°F 40 minutes	68°F 8 hours 158°F 30 minutes	68°F 8 hours 158°F 30 minutes	—	68°F 4 hours 158°F 15 minutes
	to let stand outside	68°F 24 hours 140°F 40 minutes	68°F 24 hours 158°F 40 minutes	68°F 24 hours 158°F 40 minutes	68°F 48 hours 158°F 1 hour	68°F 16 hours 158°F 30 minutes

reduced prices per gallon. When costs are viewed in terms of life cycle—for example, the length of time the finish will continue to present an acceptable appearance before requiring refinishing—acrylic urethane enamels prove to be the most economical.

The type of paint used for the topcoat ultimately determines the attractiveness of the color, gloss, and finish. Table 16-4 is a general summary of the properties of paint used for repainting.

Polyoxithane Enamels

Recently introduced, these enamels are part of the first isocyanate-free basecoat/clear coat and single stage system. Developed with health considerations in mind, they provide the highest quality in OEM color and matching. Tests show that these enamels provide excellent hiding, durability against industrial pollution and extreme weather conditions, and protection from fading caused by ultraviolet

light. More information about polyoxithane enamels will be available in the near future, but for now they promise to be the answer to one of the refinishing industries' major health problems.

Basecoat/Clear Coat Finishes

In the past few years, OEMs around the world have increasingly adopted basecoat/clear coat systems as the finish of choice for new cars rolling off assembly lines. The technology for basecoat/clear coat finishes was developed in Europe. The durability and popularity of these finishes prompted Japanese and American automobile manufacturers to begin offering them, too. In fact, most automotive finishing experts agree that the basecoat/clear coat system will be used on the vast majority of refinished vehicles before the turn of the century. When the system was first used, it utilized either an acrylic lacquer clear or a polyurethane enamel clear over an acrylic lacquer basecoat. Early in 1985, the first acrylic enamel basecoat/clear coat refinish system to actually simulate the OEM basecoat/clear coat finish was introduced. Like OEM finishes, the new system loads more transparent pigments into the basecoat and locks the metallic flakes into a flat arrangement, enabling it to match the brightness, the color intensity, and the travel of an OEM basecoat/clear coat finish. This makes it easy to get the best color match available.

An added benefit of this new basecoat technology is a 30-minute recoat time with the clear coat. Conventional basecoats use a "chemical drying" to build solvent resistance. Chemical drying generally requires 4 to 6 hours to prevent the clear coat solvents from redissolving the basecoat and allowing the aluminum or mica flakes to streak and mottle. Another new basecoat technology builds the necessary solvent resistance without chemical drying in just 30 minutes at 75 degrees Fahrenheit and 1.5 mils dry film thickness. These qualities enable this new basecoat/clear coat system to be applied quickly and easily with superior results.

More recently, painters have been switching to the new acrylic urethane basecoat/clear coat system. Many refinish paint manufacturers now offer this excellent two-stage system, which has quickly achieved a strong following. The reason for its popularity stems from not only meeting the practical needs of the painter, but also because of its advanced technology. Acrylic urethanes are fast, offer the best color matches, and provide better coverage and hiding. Thus, they increase productivity and improve customer satisfaction.

In a few years, most cars probably will be finished in basecoat/clear coat colors. This trend is certain to have several effects on the body shop. Surface preparation and a clean shop environment will be more important than ever, as the higher gloss and DOI of the clear coat make imperfections easier to see. A greater emphasis on cleanliness will result in more use of downdraft booths in progressive body shops.

With good surface preparation and a clean shop, however, body shop painters will find that the new acrylic enamel basecoat/clear coats are very easy to apply and result in better looking, more durable finishes. For example, painters no longer have to balance flow for metal control in a metallic color, and streaking and mottling are eliminated. Spot repair is made easy because basecoat/clear coat finishes make it simple to blend in an edge. And the need for buffing is just about eliminated. But most important to body shop painters is the outstanding

color match that state-of-the-art basecoat/clear coat systems provide.

One challenge the body shop painter faces is becoming well-educated about the many different systems available in order to select the best one. No customer likes a streaked finish or color drift. No body shop can afford to lose potential income because shop time is tied up due to the difficult application procedures and long dry times. When choosing a refinishing system, the key factors involved are probably appearance and ease of application.

It is a good idea to look for a system that provides fast dry time and locks in the metallic flakes for consistent color match. Also, the amount of pigment in the basecoat should be considered. A good basecoat will contain enough pigment to achieve hiding in 1 to 1-1/2 mils (two coats basecoat). Some basecoats will require four to six coats of basecoat, which means more application time, more materials, and longer dry times due to higher film thickness. To assure long-term durability and customer satisfaction, the system should contain light stabilizers and ultraviolet light absorbers.

Identifying cars that are clear coated is easy. Looking at the vehicle identification code and the color chip book is a quick way to find out if the car has the basecoat/clear coat system. If the code has

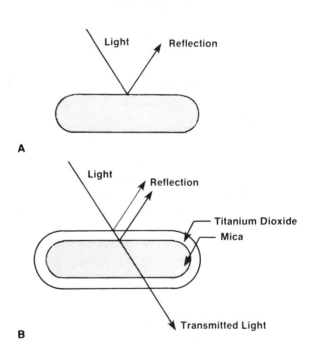

FIGURE 16-44 As opposed to (A) an aluminum flake, which only reflects light off its surface, (B) colored mica particles can be designed to reflect, absorb, and refract differing amounts of light striking them, thereby changing the color.

been removed or destroyed, sanding a small spot in a concealed area of the vehicle to be finished, using a fine sandpaper, can help determine the type of finish. If the dust is white, the car has a basecoat/clear coat finish. If the dust is the color of the car, it does not.

Pearl Luster Finishes

Most recently, in their effort to attract buyers in a market where cars are starting to look alike, car manufacturers are offering highly iridescent colors applied in three layers. The first stage is a mica or "pearl" coat, and the final stage is the clear topcoat.

In 1960, a synthetic pearl luster pigment using a mica particle covered with thin layers of titanium dioxide was developed. The mica particles made very good carriers for the titanium dioxide because of their highly transparent qualities. The titanium dioxide layers provide the rainbow or pearl effect as light reflects and passes through them.

This transparent quality of the pearl luster pigments is what allows a much higher reflective brilliance that cannot be obtained with aluminum flakes. Aluminum flakes act as miniature mirrors that reflect light (Figure 16-44A). However, they will not let light pass through to the color. If too many aluminum flakes are added to a brilliant color, the color will be washed out.

Pearl luster pigments of titanium dioxide-covered mica flakes reflect light while also allowing some to pass through to other mica flakes and colored pigments below (Figure 16-44B). The brilliance and high iridescent effect of the finish are created this way. Because the pearl coat stage of this system is translucent and reflective, the amount of mica is critical for matching.

The repaint formulas available for the pearl colors on new cars usually have colored pigments and mica pigments combined. These formulas are applied like any other two-stage paint, except when they are to be sprayed over an area that has been primed. Several additional coats with the proper flash times between them will be necessary because of the transparent quality of the paint. Allow more spraying time when scheduling jobs with mica finishes.

Several things should be kept in mind when working with pearl luster paints:

- Mica flakes are heavy. Keep the paint agitated to ensure even distribution.
- Spray test panels. Do not test on the car.
- Continually blend.
- Do not rush. Allow enough flash time between coats.

- Spray in a well-lighted booth.
- Ultraviolet light can help in checking the pearlescent effect.
- Direct sunlight is the best source of light for evaluating touch-ups.
- Check work from three angles in direct sunlight: straight in, from a 45-degree angle to the surface with the light behind the observer, and from the opposite 45-degree angle with the light ahead of the observer.

Some experimenting with tinting of the base colors, tinting of the pearl coat with colored pigments or pearl pigments, or a combination of both, might be necessary to accomplish a good match.

Tricoat Finishes

Tricoating, a three-stage basecoat/clear coat technique, has been used for 20 years in glamor coating custom cars and for other special applications. It has now found its way into the production line of several manufacturers' deluxe models.

As the name implies, tricoat finishes consist of three distinct layers that produce a pearlescent appearance: a basecoat, a midcoat or interference coat, and a clear coat. Unlike other coating systems such as metallics and some micas, which change the value of a color (lightness/darkness) when viewed from different angles, tricoats actually change the hue (color) as the angle of view changes (Figure

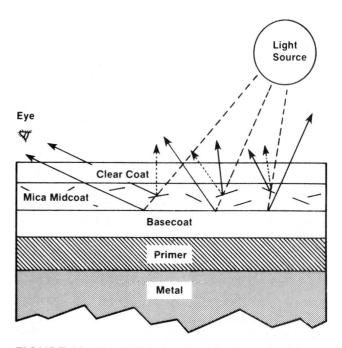

FIGURE 16-45 As this example shows, tri-coat finishes will alter the hue (color) of the finish as the angle of view changes.

16–45). Thus a three-coat finish might look red viewed from straight on and blue when seen from the side. The effect is similar to that of a thin layer of oil floating on water.

In a three-coat finish, the midcoat is the layer contributing the most to the final appearance of the color. Particles making up the midcoat can be designed to reflect, absorb, and refract differing amounts of the light striking them, as in pearl luster finishes. Changing the amount, or color, of the mica flakes' coating drastically alters the color of the finish when viewed from straight on or from an angle. While most of the three-coat finishes currently used by automakers are pastels, darker shades are also feasible. Three-coat finishes have given automotive stylists an exciting new palette of available colors. Anywhere from one to five coats of pearl luster midcoat need to be applied to achieve the desired effect.

Force Drying Enamel Topcoats

Force drying enamels by means of heat convection ovens or infrared lights will greatly reduce the drying period but care must be exercised to avoid wrinkling, blistering, pinholing, or discoloration. It is generally better to force dry at lower temperatures for longer periods rather than to run high tempera-

tures for shorter periods. The following will serve as a guide for force drying times and temperatures for alkyd enamels: 125 degrees Fahrenheit for 90 minutes; 150 degrees Fahrenheit for 45 minutes; 180 degrees Fahrenheit for 30 minutes; and 200 degrees Fahrenheit for 15 to 20 minutes. Usually, acrylic enamel will dry in 15 to 20 minutes at 175 degrees Fahrenheit. While enamel can be force dried up to 200 degrees Fahrenheit, maximum care should be taken to allow sufficient flash-off time for solvents to escape before force drying or blistering is likely. Generally speaking, pastel colors are heat sensitive and extreme caution must be used in force drying them to avoid discoloration.

It is especially necessary to avoid heavy coats of enamel in hot weather or when force drying. The temperature at which the enamel is sprayed, rather than the temperature at which it is dried, determines the reducer selected. Further information on the operation of force drying equipment is given in Chapter 17.

Color Selection

There are two important steps that must be taken before proceeding with any refinishing job:

- Decide what type of repair is called for—spot, panel, or overall repainting.
- Order all materials that are needed to complete the repair—particularly the topcoat color to be used.

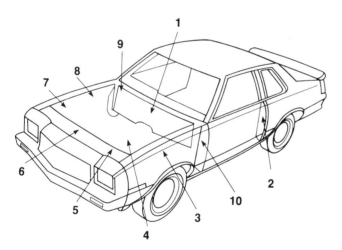

1. Engine Compartment (center)
2. Lock Pillar (left side)
3. Fender Apron (left side)
4. Hood (left underside)
5. Radiator Support (left side)
6. Radiator Support (center)
7. Fender Apron (right side)
8. Fender Apron (right side)
9. Engine Compartment (right side)
10. Front Door Body Hinge Pillar

FIGURE 16–46 Locating the paint code number on various car makes. (Courtesy of Du Pont Co.)

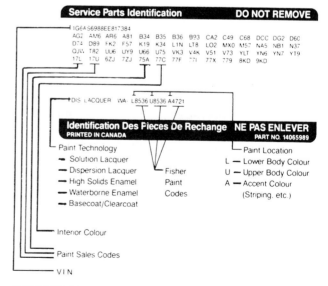

FIGURE 16–47 Typical General Motors' service parts identification label. (Courtesy of Du Pont Co.)

TABLE 16-5:   PAINT CODE LOCATION
(See Figure 16-46)

Manufacturer	Position
AMC	10
	2
ARROW	5
CHALLENGER 1978-82	5
1983	4
CHAMP	3
CHRYSLER	3
	4
	5
CONQUEST	1
COLT 1974-82	3
1983-84	5
COLT VISTA	4
COURIER	2
	5
	8
DATSUN/NISSAN	6
	8
	9
DODGE D50	5
FORD	2
HONDA	2
ISUZU	6
LUV 1972-80	1
1981-82	6
MAZDA	5
	8
	9
MITSUBISHI	
Starion	1
Montero/Pickup	5
Cordia/Tredia	7
OPEL	
SAPPORO 1978-82	5
1983	4
SUBARU	6
TOYOTA	
Passenger	1
Truck	7

If spot or panel repair is planned, it is important to purchase the topcoat color that will accurately match the old color. When planning an overall re-painting, the customer might wish to match an old finish or might want a completely new one.

To order a matching topcoat color, first locate the vehicle identification plate (VIP). Write down the car manufacturer's paint code shown on the plate. Use Figure 16-46 and Table 16-5 to find the position of the paint code number on almost all vehicles, except General Motors. Location of paint code numbers for General Motors is shown in Figures 16-47 and 16-48.

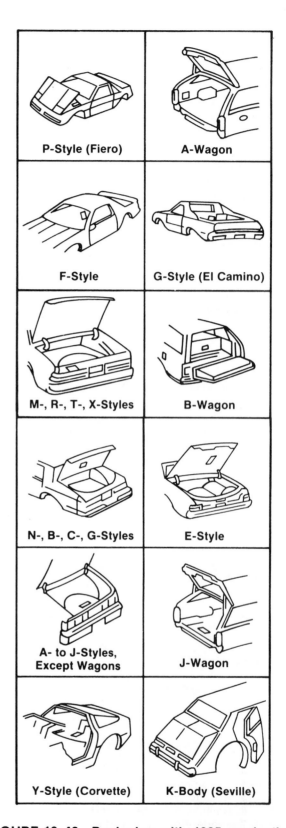

P-Style (Fiero)

A-Wagon

F-Style

G-Style (El Camino)

M-, R-, T-, X-Styles

B-Wagon

N-, B-, C-, G-Styles

E-Style

A- to J-Styles, Except Wagons

J-Wagon

Y-Style (Corvette)

K-Body (Seville)

FIGURE 16-48 Beginning with 1985 production, General Motors has added identification colors used on various parts of the car. These labels or tags define the type of paint used. *(Courtesy of Du Pont Co.)*

FIGURE 16-49 Refer to the shop's color book containing color chips that identify make and model year. *(Courtesy of Du Pont Co.)*

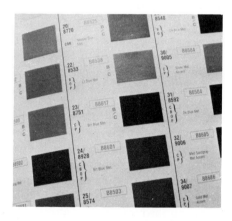

FIGURE 16-50 Locate the manufacturer's paint code number in the book. Identifying color chip is located next to it. *(Courtesy of Du Pont Co.)*

Most auto refinishing shops have a color book (Figure 16-49). This book contains color chips and color information for almost all makes and models worldwide (Figure 16-50). First locate the car manufacturer's code number. This permits the refinisher to identify the color chip next to it. As a double check, it is wise to compare the color chip with the car color, for there is always the chance that the car has been repainted with a different color.

If the color match is correct, order the topcoat from a local supplier by color stock number. Refinish suppliers supply topcoat colors in two ways:

- If it is a recent model or a popular color, chances are they will have it ready-mixed in pint, quart, and occasionally gallon cans. These ready-mixed colors are called **factory packaged** (Figure 16-51).
- If it is an older color, they might have to mix it in pint, quart, or gallon quantities. Paint man-

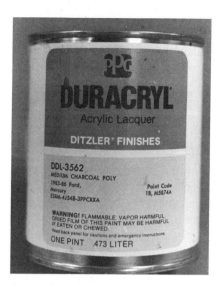

FIGURE 16-51 Factory-packaged paint is mixed and packaged at the paint factory. *(Courtesy of Du Pont Co.)*

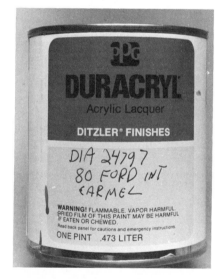

FIGURE 16-52 Custom-mixed paint is mixed and packaged at a local paint dealer or distributor for use on a specific job. *(Courtesy of Du Pont Co.)*

ufacturers work extensively to develop OEM matches with mixing color formulas for all top qualities. Custom-mixed colors are those colors that are mixed to order at the paint supply distributor. Custom-mixed color can always be identified easily because the contents of the container must be written on the label by the paint distributor that mixed the paint (Figure 16-52).

In recent years, most of the major automobile paint manufacturers have made available to refinisher shops a color mixing system. Under such an "intermix" system (see Chapter 17), it is possible to mix thousands of colors at a savings of up to 35 percent of the cost of factory-packaged colors.

With this service, inventory can be reduced, keeping only the fast-moving current colors on hand. Yet, the service takes up little space. It is fast and easy to mix a color that matches car maker's standards.

- Formulas are scientifically developed by the laboratory from base tints, rigidly controlled by plant chemists to assure batch-to-batch uniformity.
- Formulas come completely indexed on microfiche ready to use with directions for mixing exact quantities.
- Measuring by weight, not volume, ensures completely accurate measurements.
- Pour-spout allows precise control of material flow.

If the car, the color, or both are old—and if there is no record of the color type (lacquer or enamel)—there is a simple test that can be made. Rub a small spot of the finish where the repair is to be made with a cloth saturated with lacquer thinner. If the finish softens, it is lacquer (Figure 16-53). If it does not, the finish probably is enamel.

It must be remembered that the color code might not be exactly the right color because all automotive finishes gradually change color when exposed to light. Some colors fade lighter, others go darker. Yellow, for instance, fades fairly rapidly. If the yellow fades from a cream, the color will usually go lighter and whiter. If the yellow fades from a

green composed of blue and yellow, the color will go bluer and usually darker.

Every color weathers a little differently than any other color, depending on its pigment composition. Other factors that affect weathering are the care and the part of the country in which it is driven. In general, cars that are in a garage a good share of the time change less. Those that are rubbed and polished a lot, change more. Those parked under trees change depending on the type of tree spray or drippings. Those in the South change more rapidly due to increased ultraviolet radiation from the sun. Those in industrial areas or in areas of the country where there are natural chemicals in the air, such as alkali flats, change depending on the chemical to which they are exposed. If a refinish material made with the same pigmentation of the original equipment material is used, the weathering will be the same (unless the type of care or exposure has changed) and in a few months, the refinished area will change to the same weathered color as the original finish. Weathering is fastest in the first few months, and then it slows down. For that reason, a fresh touch-up spot will catch up in time.

In order to give the customer the best match at the time the vehicle is delivered, most shops tint colors to match the weathered color on the car. This matching process is made much simpler through the use of test cards. First the original finish must be compounded to bring it up to its original shine. Then, thin cardboard (not corrugated) can be taped to a piece of paper or another protective backing and propped up so that it hangs vertically (Figure 16-54). The cardboard is spray painted and held against the car to see if it matches. A number of adjustments can be made to make slight changes in the paint's color. Several test cards might be needed in order to achieve a good match. The ability to match is mostly a matter of experience and can be honed with practice.

FIGURE 16-53   Simple test to determine if a finish is lacquer.

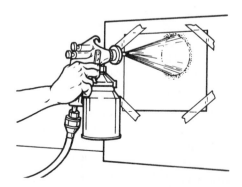

FIGURE 16-54   To match the color exactly, make a test card by spray painting a piece of cardboard.

16.6 SOLVENTS (REDUCERS AND THINNERS)

As mentioned earlier in the chapter, when used with lacquer undercoats or topcoats, the blend of diluent solvents is called a **thinner.** When used with enamel undercoats or topcoats, the blend of diluent solvents is called a **reducer.** While the principles for making automotive paint solvents are similar, the ingredients that go into reducers are entirely different from the ones used in thinners. Therefore, the two materials never should be used interchangeably.

The basic function of diluent solvent such as a reducer and a thinner is to lower the viscosity of undercoats and topcoats that are too thick to spray as they come from the container. To accomplish this, a reducer or thinner must be properly balanced. That is, it must be made of the right ingredients to:

- Provide proper dilution of the material so that it will not only pass through the gun smoothly but also atomize easily as it leaves the gun.
- Keep the material in solution long enough for it to flow out and level a smooth, even surface and not allow the film to sag or run.
- Provide complete evaporation of the solvent so as to leave a tough, smooth, and durable film.
- Aid in blending lacquers and enamel spot repairs.

WARNING: Solvents are also used to clean painting equipment, and frequently the painter. However, before using the solvent to remove paint or undercoats from the skin, check to see if the manufacturer has any warnings against using it for this purpose. Some solvents used with newer finishes contain materials that can cause skin rashes and dermatitis. Always wash the area immediately after solvent, paint, or undercoat is removed.

SELECTING THE PROPER SOLVENT

There are two vital variables that affect the spraying of materials: **temperature** and **humidity.** Unless a shop has year-round temperature control, these variables must be carefully observed and compensated for with use of the proper solvent. Of the two variables, temperature is the most critical.

Here is how temperature and humidity affect sprayed material:

- Hot, dry weather produces a **faster dry time.**
- Hot, humid, or warm, dry weather produces a **fast dry time,** but slower than hot, dry weather. (High humidity can cause problems.)
- Normal weather—70 degrees Fahrenheit with 45–55 relative humidity—produces a **normal dry time.**
- Cold, dry weather produces a **slower dry time** than normal.
- Cold, wet, or humid weather produces the **slowest dry time.**

Thus, to do quality refinishing, many auto paint shops use up to four different types of solvents for each paint system employed during the course of a year:

- **Slow drying solvent.** The flash time evaporation rate for slow lacquer thinners ranges from 3-1/2 to 5 minutes at about 75 degrees Fahrenheit when applied wet. For a slow drying enamel reducer, the flash time is slightly longer.
- **Medium drying solvent.** The average flash time evaporation rate for medium thinner is about 2 minutes when applied wet. Flash time for a medium reducer is slightly longer.
- **Fast drying solvent.** The flash time evaporation rate for fast thinners ranges from 15 to 20 seconds when applied wet at about 72 degrees Fahrenheit. The flash time for a fast reducer is slightly longer.
- **Retarder.** This is a very slow drying solvent. The flash time evaporation rate of retarder is about 30 minutes when applied wet at about 75 degrees Fahrenheit.

A good general rule to follow when selecting the proper solvent is: The **faster** the shop drying conditions, the slower drying the solvent should be.

In hot, dry weather, use a slow drying solvent. In cold, wet weather, use a fast drying solvent. If a solvent evaporates too rapidly, the following problems can be caused:

- **Orange peel.** As illustrated earlier in the chapter (Figure 16–7), the droplets formed in the spray pattern hit the surface and dry before they have time to flow out. This causes a roughness in the surface. In enamel topcoats this condition is referred to as orange peel. In lacquers this texture is often called dry spray. When this occurs with primer-surfacers, excessive sanding is required to make the surface smooth enough to apply the topcoats. With lacquer topcoats, excessive compounding and polishing are required to produce a smooth, high-luster film. While there can be a slight amount of orange peel in an enamel film, too much will cause roughness, low gloss, or both.

- **Blushing.** In hot, humid weather, some of the thinner evaporates as it leaves the gun and some as it hits the surface. This evaporation of the thinner creates a cooling condition that causes the moisture in the air to condense into droplets and mix with the spray stream. As the spray hits the surface and the film forms, the condensed moisture droplets are trapped. This gives the film a dull, hazy, or cloudy look (Figure 16-55A).
- **Overspray.** Similar to dry spray, overspray (Figure 16-55B) occurs where the spray pattern overlaps an area already sprayed. (If a slow-dry thinner is used, the overspray will generally melt into the previously sprayed area.)

If on the other hand, a reducer or thinner evaporates too slowly, look for these problems (Figure 16-56):

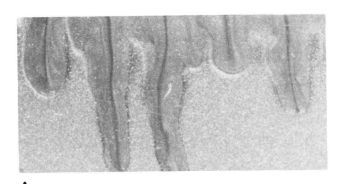

A

B

C

FIGURE 16-56 Too slow an evaporation rate can cause such problems as (A) sags and runs, (B) sand scratch swelling, and (C) mottling. *(Courtesy of PPG Industries, Inc.)*

A

B

FIGURE 16-55 Improper selection of a solvent that drys too fast can cause problems like (A) blushing and (B) overspray.

- **Sags and runs.** A topcoat must lose part of its solvent before and part after it hits the surface. If the evaporation is too slow, the droplets will be too wet when they contact the surface and they will tend to flow. The weight of the film will cause it to slide or roll down the surface. Sags and runs are by far the most common problem where evaporation is too slow.
- **Sand scratch swelling.** A very slow drying thinner will tend to penetrate an old finish. This condition, which makes the sand

scratches more pronounced, is called sand scratch swelling.

- **Mottling.** When metallic colors are sprayed too wet, the metallic flakes float and group together, thus distorting the appearance of the finish.

While the use of an improper thinner or solvent might cause other problems, the six previously outlined cover the most common situations. Perhaps the best rule to follow in selecting reducers or thinners is to choose the slowest drying reducer or thinner that can be handled safely without sags, runs, or mottling (in metallic finishes). This will assure a smooth, glossy surface and generally the best color match. Lacquer topcoats minimize buffing time. Such a selection will also improve the performance of most undercoats (for example, by reducing the sanding time for primer-surfacers and allowing sealers to flow better).

Basecoat Additive

Instead of using a regular paint reducer for a basecoat/clear coat system, many paint manufacturers are recommending the use of a basecoat additive or stabilizer. This material not only acts as a reducer for base colors, but works as a "fixer" to lock the flake in place. This makes it easier to achieve a more accurate color match to today's OEM colors. It also minimizes sand scratch swelling to give a smoother looking basecoat and ultimately a better looking topcoat.

When using most basecoat additives, add the material in a 200 to 250 percent reduction. Use the correct additive for the shop's temperature. The additive label lists this information and other directions.

Thinning Primer-Surfacer

When thinning lacquer-based primer-surfacers, the object of the thinner selection is to be slow enough to provide a relatively smooth surface, which will require a minimum amount of sanding. Faster drying thinners will cause the film to be rough, thus increasing sanding time.

The use of a slower drying topcoat thinner should also be avoided. The reason is that there is a tendency to spray heavy coats of primer-surfacer because of the high-solids content. When slow dry thinners are used, longer flash times and dry times are required. If the refinisher fails to allow sufficient

DIRECTIONS FOR USING MIRACRYL 2 STANDARD COLORS

DESCRIPTION: MIRACRYL 2 is a fast drying, easy to use and durable acrylic enamel for refinishing STANDARD (NON BASECOAT/CLEARCOAT) colors on cars and trucks.

SURFACE PREPARATION: Clean the area to be painted with 900 Pre-Kleano and sand thoroughly with fine or medium sandpaper. Build up all bare metal and damaged areas with R-M Primer-Surfacer. To minimize sand scratches and improve hold-out, appropriate R-M Sealers may be used.

COLOR REDUCTION: To one quart MIRACRYL 2 STANDARD color add one half quart MIRACRYL 2 REDUCER. A complete range of MIRACRYL 2 REDUCERS is available for various climatic and shop conditions. Stir thoroughly and strain through medium strainer.

APPLICATION: MIRACRYL 2 STANDARD colors may be used with or without MIRACRYL 2 HARDENER. Spray single coats until hiding and color match have been achieved. Allow each coat to become tack free before applying the next. Use 45-55 pounds air pressure at the gun. Lower air pressure will darken iridescent colors, higher air pressure will lighten them.

RECOATING: MIRACRYL 2 STANDARD colors may be recoated after air drying 16 hours under normal conditions.

DETROIT, MI 48210 · GRA

FIGURE 16–57   Before thinning or reducing a paint material, check the label for proper percentage.

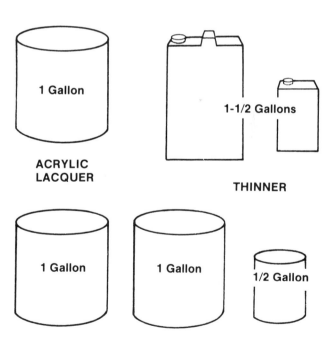

2-1/2 GALLONS READY TO SPRAY

FIGURE 16–58   Various materials work best at given percentages. For example, lacquer primer-surfacers and acrylic lacquer colors work best when thinned 150 percent. (Courtesy of PPG Industries, Inc.)

TABLE 16-6: REDUCTION RATIO GUIDE			
Reduction Percentage	Mixing Ratio	Paint Material	Solvent Material
12-1/2	8:1 =	8 parts	1 part
25	4:1 =	4 parts	1 part
33	3:1 =	3 parts	1 part
50	2:1 =	2 parts	1 part
75	4:3 =	4 parts	3 parts
100	1:1 =	1 part	1 part
125	4:5 =	4 parts	5 parts
150	2:3 =	2 parts	3 parts
175	4:7 =	4 parts	7 parts
200	1:2 =	1 part	2 parts
225	4:9 =	4 parts	9 parts
250	4:10 =	4 parts	10 parts
275	4:11 =	4 parts	11 parts
300	1:3 =	1 part	3 parts

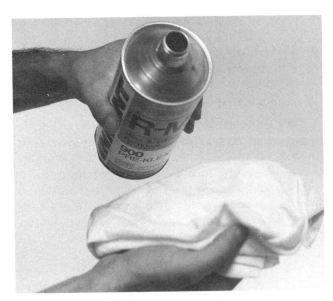

FIGURE 16-59   A dewaxing and degreasing is a very important operation in most refinishing operations. When applying be sure to follow manufacturer's recommendations.

flash and dry time, the primer-surfacer might shrink and crack at the featheredge.

When thinning or reducing, refer to the paint label for the proper solvent percentage (Figure 16-57) so there will be no danger of over or under reducing. Table 16-6 shows how to convert these percentages to the proper proportions of paint and solvent (Figure 16-58).

16.7 OTHER REFINISHING MATERIALS

There are several other products available to the refinisher that will help produce a better finishing job. The application of these products is covered in Chapters 18 and 19.

WAX AND GREASE REMOVERS

The adhesion of any paint film to any surface depends first on whether or not the surface is absolutely clean, not just physically clean, but chemically clean. The slightest film of oil, grease, wax, or moisture will prevent the paint from sticking to the surface.

Wax and grease removers (also called dewaxers) are solvent type materials that will dissolve partly oxidized waxes and greases that are embedded in the old finish (Figure 16-59). They should be strong enough to dissolve the several types of waxes used in automobile polishes but not so strong as to attack the old finish. A final wipe off with a clean rag saturated in wax and grease remover before applying the

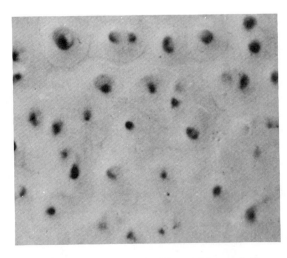

FIGURE 16-60   Fish eyes caused by painting over silicone. (Courtesy of PPG Industries, Inc.)

paint is the best insurance against peeling and silicones. If the silicones are not removed before refinishing, fish eyes might form in the final finish (Figure 16-60). An additive or eliminator can also be put in to prevent fish eyes. However, the surface must be thoroughly cleaned before applying fish eye eliminator.

METAL CONDITIONERS AND RUST INHIBITORS

Some auto paint jobs fail to hold up because the metal over which the finish was sprayed contains microscopic rust particles or pits of rust. Unless this rusting action is eliminated and further rusting prevented, the action will continue and the swelling effect of the rust will eventually pop off the paint.

As described in Chapter 15, metal conditioner and rust inhibitor is an acid that, when it comes into contact with rust, changes the iron oxide (rust) into another compound. This compound is fairly stable and if the surface containing it can be sealed over with paint shortly after its use, there will be no further development of the oxidizing action.

The application of metal conditioner also creates negatively charged ions on the metal surface. The positively charged paint products are thus attracted to the metal, enhancing the paint-to-metal bond. This is the principle of "bonderizing" that is used in the car factories and duplicated in a refinish shop with a metal conditioner. This material also etches the metal to give the primer-surfacer a better tooth and therefore better adhesion.

Rubbing Compounds

Rubbing compounds are composed of an emulsion of water and oils combined with abrasive compounds. Selection and grading of the abrasives determine the difference between good and bad compounds. Uniformity of size and hardness of the grits must be carefully controlled. Sharp, hard abrasives or irregular size results in scratching the surface in place of doing a smooth cutting job.

FIGURE 16–61 Use of a mechanical polishing compound. (Courtesy of PPG Industries, Inc.)

Mechanical polishing compounds (Figure 16–61) are designed for use with a power polisher/buffer. Those classified as rubbing compounds are intended to be used by hand. The very fine grit hand compound is called a polishing compound.

Glaze compounds are used in fine finishing work. Similar to polishing compounds, they can be hand or machine finished. Small areas are best done by hand, while machine compounded is recommended for larger areas.

Luggage Compartment or Trunk Finishes

Abrasion and moisture-resistant spatter finishes are designed especially to duplicate the original car and truck finishes. Most spatter finishes are reduced with water and are easy to apply. White undercoats are recommended, but these spatter finishes will adhere to virtually any clean surface. These finishes are applicable to many other areas where an attractive finish is desired and where high scuff and wear resistance are needed.

Vinyl Spray Colors

Vinyls dry by evaporation of the volatiles. They dry rapidly to a permanent flexible film. The use of vinyl liquid over vinyl that is cleaned and pretreated with vinyl conditioner results in chemical bonding of the two films. Clear coats are essential to provide abrasion resistance and proper gloss level. More refinishing vinyl surfaces are found in Chapter 19.

Some auto finishing shops apply vinyl spray paint on lower body panels. This abrasion-resistant coating protects these panels from being chipped by stones and other flying objects.

Flex (Elastomeric) Additives

Flex additives import flexibility to most topcoat qualities. They can be blended with acrylic lacquers, acrylic enamels, polyurethane acrylic enamels, and acrylic urethanes to produce flexibility for bumpers and fascia. The basic characteristics of the topcoat remain the same except for the flexibility.

There are several other additives available that help to improve the finish. For example, there are fish eye eliminators on the market. This material can be added to acrylic enamels, acrylic enamel basecoat/clear coat, synthetic enamels, and urethane enamels to keep fish eyes under control. However, they cannot be used with acrylic lacquer. All additives must be used as per manufacturer's instructions on the label.

ANTICHIPPING PAINT

Most modern automobiles come with an antichipping paint applied to the rocker panels. Compared with other paints, antichipping paint has better coherence and pliability and helps prevent rust occurrence due to stone damage. When repainting, care is needed to apply antichipping paint at the designated areas so as not to lower the anticorrosion effectiveness.

ROCKER BLACK PAINT

This is either a semigloss or flat enamel coat that is applied to the rocker panel. After first masking off the surrounding area to protect it from paint overspray, the rocker panel is hand sprayed with a two-component urethane paint that has good adhesion qualities. If there are any other panels, such as the back panel, that require blacking, they should also be sprayed.

PAINT REMOVERS

There are many types of paint removers on the market. Two types of chemical paint removers are popular in refinishing shops:

- Paint removers designed primarily to remove lacquer-type products
- Paint removers designed to remove all types of finishes (including enamel and urethane colors) down to the bare metal

Apply chemical strippers freely with a brush. When the old finish bubbles, flush off with a stream of water. Steel wool might be required to remove the finish in the case of acrylic lacquers. Other stubborn old finishes might have to be lifted from the surface with the aid of a putty knife. Further details on the use of paint removers in removing an old finish can be found in Chapter 19.

CAUTION: Never use a paint remover on plastic or fiberglass substrates.

Another chemical remover that is found in most paint shops is the decal remover. This material makes easy work of taking off decals.

ADHESIVES, COMPOUNDS, AND SEALANTS

Perhaps more so than any other refinishing materials, adhesives are used where the action is—on those body parts subject to constantly changing conditions of temperature, moisture, friction, and pressure. Some of the more common adhesives in a refinishing shop include trim cement, glass sealer, weatherstrip adhesive, and caulking compounds and body seam sealer. Instructions for use of most of these materials are given in earlier chapters.

When using any of the paint products mentioned here—as well as when applying undercoats and solvents—be sure to carefully read the instructions detailing how to mix, how to apply, and how long to dry. These instructions on the container are important because they help to do the job right.

16.8 REVIEW QUESTIONS

1. Technician A uses a sealer when applying alkyd enamel over lacquer, but Technician B does not. Who is correct?
   a. Technician A
   b. Technician B
   c. Both A and B
   d. Neither A nor B

2. Which is the volatile ingredient of the paint?
   a. pigment
   b. binder
   c. solvent
   d. none of the above

3. Which additives improve gloss?
   a. hardeners
   b. retarders
   c. flatteners
   d. none of the above

4. Which dries by evaporation of the solvents as the first stage and by oxidation of the binder as the second stage?
   a. lacquers
   b. enamels
   c. both a and b
   d. neither a nor b

5. When is a sealer absolutely necessary?
   a. when an old lacquer finish is to be covered with lacquer
   b. when an old lacquer finish is to be covered with enamel
   c. when an old enamel finish is to be covered with enamel
   d. when an old enamel finish is to be covered with lacquer

6. Which of the following is a characteristic of primers?
   a. They fill surface imperfections.
   b. They require sanding.
   c. They are usually enamel type products.
   d. All of the above
   e. None of the above

7. When working with pearl luster paints, Technician A allows flash time between coats, but Technician B does not. Who is correct?
   a. Technician A
   b. Technician B
   c. Both A and B
   d. Neither A nor B

8. Which is the most popular primer-surfacer used today?
   a. nitrocellulose primer-surfacer
   b. acrylic primer-surfacer
   c. alkyd primer-surfacer
   d. self-etching primer-surfacer

9. The main reason for using a primer-sealer is to _____ .
   a. resist rust and corrosion
   b. provide topcoat adhesion
   c. ensure a surface consistent in color and porosity
   d. none of the above

10. When using a wash-primer, Technician A uses it full-strength. Technician B reduces it with a spec reducer-catalyst. Who is correct?
    a. Technician A
    b. Technician B
    c. Both A and B
    d. Neither A nor B

11. Which provides extra adhesion when a lacquer topcoat is being sprayed over an OEM enamel?
    a. barrier coat sealer
    b. recoat sealer
    c. bleeder sealer
    d. tie coat sealer

12. Technician A says that sand scratch swelling results when a thinner evaporates too quickly. Technician B says that this condition results when a thinner evaporates too slowly. Who is correct?
    a. Technician A
    b. Technician B
    c. Both A and B
    d. Neither A nor B

13. How many coats does it take for a good basecoat to achieve hiding?
    a. one
    b. two
    c. three
    d. four to six

14. Which of the following conditions results when the solvent evaporates too quickly?
    a. sand scratch swelling
    b. mottling
    c. sags and runs
    d. orange peel

15. Which solvent has an average flash time evaporation rate of 2 minutes when applied wet?
    a. slow drying thinner
    b. slow drying reducer
    c. medium drying thinner
    d. medium drying reducer

CHAPTER
17

Refinishing Equipment and Its Use

To do a good refinishing job, the proper equipment must be used in the proper manner. But to achieve high-quality finishes on automobiles, good materials, proper equipment, and correct techniques are necessities.

Spray painting equipment for the auto refinishing shop consists of:

- Spray guns and cups (either suction or pressure feed)
- Air compressor of adequate size
- Oil and water extractor and air regulator combination to filter air and regulate pressure
- Air hose of sufficient size (inside diameter) to convey air from the extractor to the spray gun without causing an excessive drop in pressure
- Spray booth or enclosure to ensure a healthy, safe, dust-free working area.

A separate drying area and force-drying equipment are also important parts of refinishing work.

The selection and use of air compressors, air control equipment, and air hose connectors are thoroughly described in Chapter 5.

17.1 SPRAY GUNS

The spray gun (Figure 17-1) is the key component in a refinishing system. It is a precision engineered and manufactured tool, and each type and size available is specifically designed to perform a

FIGURE 17-1 The proper use of a spray gun is a must in any refinishing paint shop. (Courtesy of Maaco Enterprises, Inc.)

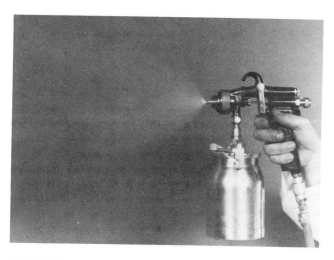

FIGURE 17-2 An atomized spray

certain number of tasks. Even though all spray guns have many parts and components in common, each gun type or size is suited for only a certain, defined range of jobs. As in most other areas of refinishing work, having the right tool for the job goes a long way toward getting a professional job done right in minimum time.

ATOMIZATION AND THE SPRAY GUN

An air spray gun can be defined as a tool that turns a liquid into tiny droplets by means of air pressure. This process is called atomization (Figure 17-2). A thorough understanding of atomization is the key to using a spray gun correctly. Atomization breaks paint into a spray of tiny, uniform droplets. When properly applied to the auto's surface, these tiny droplets will flow together to create an even film thickness with a mirror-like gloss.

Atomization takes place in three basic stages (Figure 17-3):

- In the first stage, the paint siphoned from the fluid tip is immediately surrounded by air streaming from the annular ring. This turbulence begins the breakup of the paint.
- The second stage of atomization occurs when the paint stream is hit with jets of air from the containment holes. These air jets keep the paint stream from getting out of control and aid the breakup of the paint.
- In the third phase of atomization, the paint is struck by jets of air from the air cap horns. These air streams hit the paint from opposite sides, causing the paint to form into a fan-shaped spray.

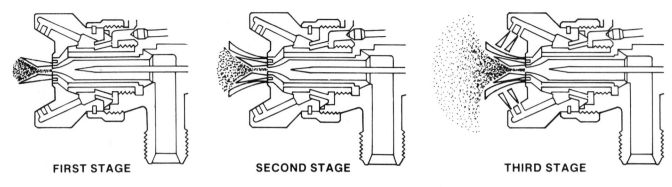

FIRST STAGE   SECOND STAGE   THIRD STAGE

FIGURE 17-3   The three stages of atomization

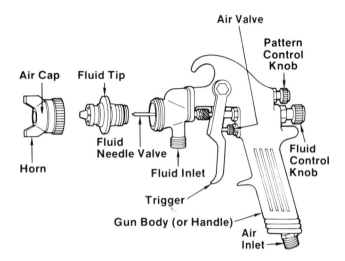

FIGURE 17-4   Parts of a typical air spray gun

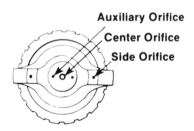

FIGURE 17-5   Nomenclature of air orifices

Little ⟵ Air Discharge Volume ⟶ Much
Poor ⟵ Paint Atomization ⟶ Good

FIGURE 17-6   Number of auxiliary holes and gun performance

PRINCIPAL PARTS OF A SPRAY GUN

The principal parts or components of a typical air spray gun are illustrated in Figure 17-4. Some guns are equipped with a removable spray head unit containing the air cap, fluid tip, and fluid needle.

- Air cap or nozzle
- Fluid tip or nozzle
- Fluid needle valve
- Trigger
- Fluid control (or spreader) knob
- Air valve
- Pattern (or fan adjustment) control knob
- Gun body (or handle)

The air cap directs the compressed air into the material stream to atomize it and form the spray pattern. There are three types of orifices (holes) (Figure 17-5): the center orifice, the side orifices or ports, and the auxiliary orifices. Each of the orifices has a different function. The center orifice located at the nozzle tip creates a vacuum for the discharge of the paint. The side orifices determine the spray pattern by means of air pressure, and the auxiliary orifices promote atomization of the paint. Figure 17-6 illustrates the relationship between the auxiliary orifices and the gun's performance. Large orifices increase the ability to atomize more material for painting large objects with great speed. Fewer or smaller orifices usually require less air, produce smaller spray patterns, and deliver less material to conveniently paint smaller objects or apply coatings at lower speeds.

Air also flows through the two side orifices in horns of the air cap. This flow forms the shape of the spray pattern. When the **pattern control valve** is closed, the spray pattern is round. As the valve is opened, the spray becomes more oblong in shape.

The **fluid needle valve** and the **fluid tip** meter direct the flow of material from the gun into the air stream. The fluid tip forms an internal seat for the fluid needle that shuts off the flow of material. The amount of material that actually leaves the front of the gun depends on the size of the fluid tip opening provided when the needle is unseated from the tip. Fluid tips are available in a variety of sizes to properly handle materials of various types and viscosities and pass the required volume of material to the cap for different speeds of application. The **fluid control knob (valve)** changes the distance the fluid needle valve moves away from its seat in the nozzle when the **trigger** is pulled.

The **air valve,** like the fluid valve, is opened by moving the trigger. When the trigger is pulled partway, the air valve opens. When it is pulled a little farther, the fluid valve opens.

TYPES OF AIR SPRAY GUNS

As pointed out in Table 17–1, there are three basic methods of paint supply or feed to the air spray gun (Figure 17–7):

• Suction (or siphon) feed type (Figure 17–8A)
• Compression feed type (Figure 17–8B)
• Gravity feed type (Figure 17–8C)

The suction feed type air spray gun is by far the most used type in auto paint shops. The paint mate-

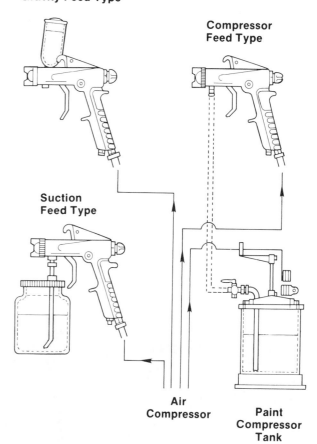

FIGURE 17-7 Paint feed methods to air spray guns

TABLE 17-1: TYPES OF AIR SPRAY GUNS			
Type	**Paint Feed Method**	**Advantages**	**Disadvantages**
Suction Feed Type	Paint container is installed below the spray nozzle and paint is supplied by suction force alone.	Stable gun operation. Easy to refill container or make color changes.	Difficult to spray on horizontal surfaces and some variations occur in discharge volume due to variations in viscosity. Has a larger paint container than gravity feed type, but this causes quicker painter fatigue.
Pressure Type	Paint is pressurized by a compressed air tank or pump.	Large surfaces can be painted without stopping to refill container. A paint with a high viscosity can also be used.	Not suitable for small area painting. Color changes and gun cleaning take time.
Gravity Feed Type	As the paint cup is installed above the spray nozzle, paint is supplied by gravity and a suction force at the nozzle tip.	Because there is no change in paint viscosity, there is no variation in the injection volume. The position of the cut can be changed according to the configuration of the the painted item.	Because the cup is installed above the injection nozzle, it adversely affects gun stability. Cup capacity is small so not useful for painting larger surfaces.

A

B

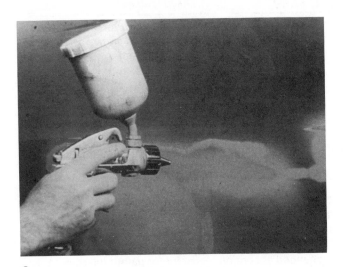

C

FIGURE 17-8   Use of three types of air spray guns: (A) suction, (B) pressure, and (C) gravity

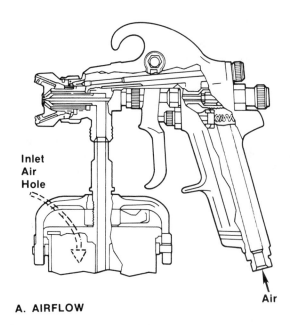

A. AIRFLOW

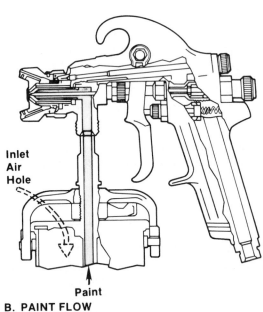

B. PAINT FLOW

FIGURE 17-9   The airflow and paint flow of pressure feed gun

rial is held in a 1 quart cup attached to the gun. When the spray gun trigger is partially depressed, the air valve opens and air rushes through the gun. As the air passes through the openings in the air cap, a partial vacuum is created at the fluid tip (Figure 17-9A). Further squeezing of the trigger withdraws the fluid needle from the fluid tip. The vacuum sucks paint from the cup, up the fluid inlet, and out through the open fluid tip. Air enters through the air hole and replaces the siphoned paint (Figure 17-9B). The inlet air vent holes in the cup lid **must** be open.

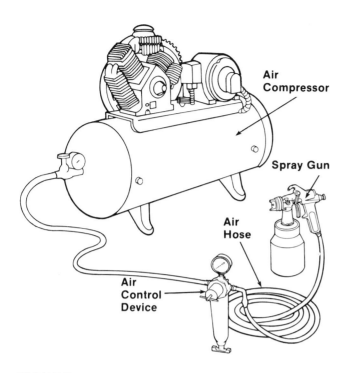

FIGURE 17-10   The suction feed equipment hook-up

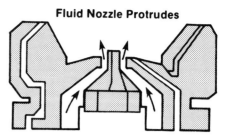

A. SUCTION AIR NOZZLE

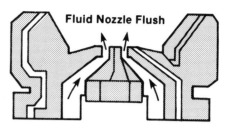

B. PRESSURE·AIR NOZZLE

FIGURE 17-11   The difference between suction and pressure feed gun air nozzles

The suction feed equipment (Figure 17-10) is hooked up for operation as follows:

- Connect air line from the compressor outlet to the air control device inlet.
- Connect air hose leading from the air outlet on the air control device to the air inlet on the spray gun.
- After the material has been reduced to proper consistency, thoroughly mixed, and strained into the cup, attach the gun to the cup.

In the gravity feed system, the paint is supplied by gravity and the material is suction forced at the nozzle tip. This system is ideal for heavier material such as lightweight body filler. The handling of the gun is the same as a suction feed type gun.

It is easy to identify a suction feed gun by its fluid tip that extends slightly beyond the face of the air cap, as shown in Figure 17-11A.

In the design of an air pressure feed gun, the fluid tip is flush with the face of the air cap (Figure 17-11B) and no vacuum is created. The fluid is forced to the air cap by pressure kept on the material in the system: a separate cup, tank, or pump.

Figure 17-12 illustrates how the regulated pressure cup is hooked up for spraying:

- Connect air hose from air control device to air regulator on cup.

FIGURE 17-12   Hook-up for air pressure cup. *(Courtesy of Binks Mfg. Co.)*

- Connect air hose or tank air regulator to air inlet on gun.
- Connect fluid hose from fluid outlet on cup to fluid inlet on gun.

Figure 17-13 illustrates how the equipment of the pressure tank spraying system is hooked up:

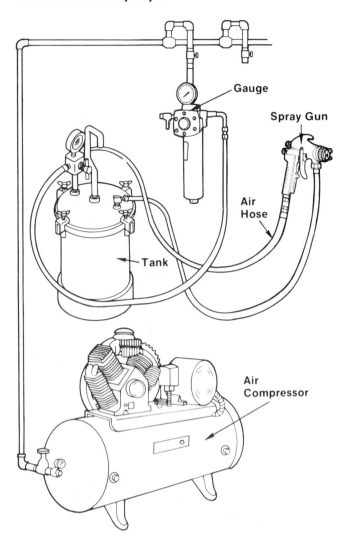

FIGURE 17-13   Hook-up for pressure tank

- Connect regulated air hose from air control device on tank to air inlet on gun.
- Connect mainline air hose from main regulating device to air regulator inlet on tank.
- Connect fluid hose from fluid outlet on tank to fluid inlet on gun.

Paint pressure tanks are available in sizes from 2 to 10 gallons. They are available in dual, single, or nonregulated models (Figure 17-14). Dual air regulators control both material and atomization air pressure; single models regulate material pressure only. Some tanks have an agitation paddle system to keep the pigments and solids thoroughly mixed at all times, assuring color uniformity. Some siphon gun cups also have an agitator system (Figure 17-15). These cups provide constant mixing of all automotive finishes and primers; they even keep metal flakes and metallics in total suspension and complete dispersion.

A

B

C

FIGURE 17-14   Pressure tanks (A) dual regulated, (B) single regulated, and (C) nonregulated. (Courtesy of Binks Mfg. Co.)

FIGURE 17-15   Agitator type paint cup. *(Courtesy of Binks Mfg. Co.)*

The gravity feed gun preceded the present—and now more widely used—pressure feed method of material delivery to the spray gun. The main requirement of gravity feed is that the container be vented so that atmospheric air can replace the material as it is being sprayed.

The gravity feed equipment is relatively inexpensive in initial cost and in operation. The container can be refilled without interrupting the spraying operation because it is at atmospheric pressure. However, this method does have some limitations. Viscosity and flow characteristics of the material directly affect rate of flow to the gun, as do hose size and hose length. Flow is also affected by changes in pressure head, which will vary with vertical position of the gun and with material in the container.

The container can be of any convenient size with 1/2 and 1 pint the most common in auto shops. Its location should suit the material supply requirements of the gun, taking into account that resistance to material flow increases with length of hose and with additional valves and fittings. Its location should also make filling convenient. The container material should be compatible with the contents to avoid corrosion and chemical reaction. It should be covered with a lid that has a vent hole.

The suction feed gun is by far the most popular type of gun in auto refinishing shops for all types of work (spot, panel, and overall). The pressure feed gun is mainly used for overall painting of vehicles (including trucks and vans), for spraying some heavier refinishing materials that are too heavy to be siphoned from a container, or where volume paint-

ing is required. Although gravity feed guns can be used for basecoat/clear coat work, they are employed to spray undercoat refinishing materials such as primers and sealers, as well as some lighter body putties and fillers. Gravity feed guns are especially good for those European and Japanese finishes that are formulated for these types of guns.

17.2 SPRAYING TECHNIQUES

Spraying a vehicle is a skilled job and calls for considerably more experience and knowledge than just holding down the trigger and hoping that the gun will put the paint where it is supposed to be and in the right amount. There are several variables contributing to the quality of the spray finish including spraying material viscosity, spray booth temperature, film thickness, and spray practice.

SPRAYING MATERIAL VISCOSITY

Using an incorrect viscosity paint will result in various paint finish defects. The paint must be thoroughly mixed and be properly thinned or reduced (Figure 17-16) or a good-quality paint finish cannot be attained. Therefore, the paint viscosity is measured by means of a viscometer. The two types of viscometers used for automobile painting are the Ford cup and the Zahn cup. Although the Ford cup is

FIGURE 17-16   To achieve correct atomization, the paint must be reduced with the proper solvent. *(Courtesy of Maaco Enterprises, Inc.)*

very accurate, because of its high cost it is not used as much as the Zahn cup, which is less accurate but less expensive.

The viscosity of a spray material is an indication of its ability to **resist** flow. The flow characteristics of liquids relate directly to the degree of **internal friction;** therefore anything that will influence the internal friction (such as solvents, thinners, or temperature change) will influence flow. Similarly, it is the flow characteristics that determine how well a material will atomize, how well it will "flow out" on the work, and the type of equipment needed to move it.

When preparing material for spraying, thin to the proper viscosity according to the directions on the can, using the thinner or reducer best suited for the shop temperature and conditions. It can be demonstrated that at a given temperature, a 3-second difference in spraying viscosity will have a distinct influence on the flow of the material being

FIGURE 17-17 Robots are used by most car manufacturers for the application of the finishing system. (Courtesy of Sherwin-Williams Co.)

sprayed. It can therefore be seen that exact reduction is essential if the painter is going to spray at the viscosity at which the paint will spray the easiest and the best results can be obtained. In auto factory operations (Figure 17-17), where new cars are sprayed, spraying viscosity is held within a tolerance of 1 second at a given temperature.

No method other than measurement of the thinner or reducer does the job adequately. Because appearance is affected by the temperature, the way the paint runs off the stirring paddle is not a reliable method of determining viscosity.

The amount of reduction should be the same regardless of temperature. At a higher temperature the viscosity of the reduced material is actually slightly lower, but this is offset by the faster evaporation of the thinner as it travels between the gun and the surface being painted. The result is that the paint reaches the surface at the correct viscosity. The reverse is true in a cold shop. The reduced paint is a little thicker, but evaporation in the air is less so that the paint reaches the surface being sprayed at the proper viscosity.

Various automotive finishes are manufactured to spray at ideal viscosities. For instance, lacquer primer-surfacer sprays best at 15 seconds viscosity, acrylic lacquer at 12 seconds, and alkyd enamel colors, lacquer colors, and synthetic primer-surfacers all at 19 seconds.

Ford Cup

The Ford cup (Figure 17-18) used for automobile painting comes in two sizes: #3 and #4. It has a

FIGURE 17-18 Ford viscosity cup with thermometer and stopwatch for testing paint viscosity. In practice, the thermometer is immersed in the paint. (Courtesy of PPG Industries, Inc.)

cylindrical container, made of either aluminum or stainless steel, with a capacity of 6.1 cubic inches. The bottom of the cup is conical shaped with an orifice in the center. The #3 and #4 cups are distinguished by the diameter of this orifice. Ford cups are precision-made and care should be taken to prevent any damage or deformation of the inner surface of the cup or to the orifice. To measure the viscosity of a paint material with a Ford cup, proceed as follows:

 1. Keep the temperature of the paint and Ford cup at about 68 degrees Fahrenheit.
2. Secure the cup with the set bolt and place the glass plate on top.
3. Place the level on top of the glass plate, and adjust the level of the frame with the level adjusting bolts. Then, place a container below the cup.
4. While supporting the bottom of the cup with one hand, place a piece of thick rubber in between to prevent transmission of body heat to the orifice and pour in the paint, being careful that no air bubbles enter.
5. Slide the glass plate horizontally over the top of the cup to remove any excess paint and set it aside.
6. Release the rubber plate supporting the orifice and at the same time begin measuring the time of the continuous downward drain of the paint with a stopwatch. Measure until the continuous paint flow stops. This time is used as an indicator of the paint viscosity. For example, if it takes 15.4 seconds, the viscosity of the paint is said to be 15.4 seconds at 68 degrees Fahrenheit.

Zahn Cup

The #2 Zahn cup is very popular in auto refinishing shops. It is cylindrical in shape and has an orifice (hole) at the bottom. To determine viscosity with a #2 Zahn cup (Figure 17–19), proceed as follows:

 1. Prepare the material to be tested. Mix, strain, and reduce as directed by the manufacturer.
2. Fill the cup by submerging it in the material.
3. Release the flow of the material and trigger the stopwatch. Keep eyes on the floor, not on the watch.
4. When the solid stream of material "breaks" (indicating air passing through the orifice), stop the watch.

5. The result is expressed in seconds. Table 17–2 gives typical desired results of the #2 Zahn cup.

🏎 **SHOP TALK** _____

A stopwatch is necessary for measuring paint viscosity with either viscometer system. Most painters prefer a digital stopwatch to the standard type because it is easily read.

TABLE 17–2: SPRAYING VISCOSITIES USING THE #2 ZAHN CUP

Material	Reduction	Viscosity
Acrylic enamel	33-1/3%	19 seconds
Acrylic enamel	50%	18 seconds
Acrylic enamel with hardener	75%	16 seconds
Acrylic lacquer	150%	15 seconds
Polyurethane enamel	per manufacturer's instructions	20 to 22 seconds

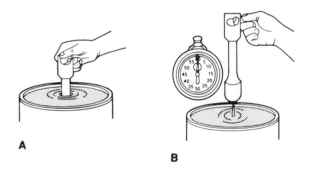

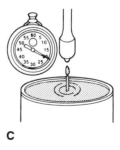

FIGURE 17–19   (A) Dip cup into paint until it is full. (B) Remove cup, and as it clears the surface of the paint, begin timing the flow of paint from the small hole in the bottom of the cup. (A stopwatch is preferred for this step.) (C) Stop the timer when the stream of paint breaks. *(Courtesy of Du Pont Co.)*

TEMPERATURE

The temperature at which material is sprayed and dried has a great influence on the smoothness of the finish. This involves not only the air temperatures of the shop, but the temperature of the work as well. A job should be brought into the shop long enough ahead of spraying time to arrive at approximately the same temperature as the shop. Spraying warm paint on a cold surface or spraying cool material on a hot surface will completely upset flow characteristics. The rate of evaporation on a hot summer day is approximately 50 percent faster than it is on an average day with a shop temperature of 72 degrees F. Appropriate thinners or reducers should be used for warm and cold weather applications.

FILM THICKNESS

As noted in Chapter 16, acrylic lacquers dry by evaporation only. Alkyd and acrylic enamels dry by both evaporation and oxidation. Urethanes dry by evaporation and chemical cross-linking reaction.

The thicker the film applied, the longer the drying time. The difference in film thickness shows up plainly in primer-surfacer and enamels. A lacquer primer-surfacer that can be sanded in 30 minutes at 70 degrees will take over an hour if sprayed twice as heavily. Alkyd enamel of normal film thickness should dry tack free in 4 to 6 hours at 70 degrees and be hard enough for unmasking and handling in 16 hours. If sprayed twice the normal thickness, this will take 2 to 3 times longer. The thicker the film, the greater the depth of paint from which the thinner or reducer must work its way out, or, in enamels, the greater the distance the oxygen from the air must penetrate in order to dry or oxidize the finish. This process is complicated in thick coats by surface skins or crusts as the paint dries.

The technician should develop a technique so that the coat sprayed on a surface will remain wet long enough for proper flow-out, and no longer. Heavier coats are not necessary. They can produce sags, curtains, or wrinkles, as well as strongly influence metallic color when matching.

The amount of material sprayed on a surface with one stroke of the gun will depend on width of fan, distance from gun, air pressure at the gun, amount of reduction, speed of stroke, and selection of thinner or reducer. Many paint shops have a paint thickness measuring meter such as the one shown in Figure 17–20. This instrument is able to determine

FIGURE 17–20   A meter for measuring paint thickness. *(Courtesy of PPG Industries, Inc.)*

the thickness of the paint on a vehicle. Working on a magnetic principle, it measures the thickness of paint and any body filler by sensing the magnetic pull of the metal under the paint and filler. If the paint and filler are too thick, the magnetic pull will be less than if they are thin. The meter then converts this "pull" to read the approximate thickness of the filler/paint base.

Another popular and less expensive paint thickness gauge is the Tinsley gauge (Figure 17–21). This

FIGURE 17–21   The Tinsley gauge is a paint thickness gauge. *(Courtesy of Biddle Instruments)*

gauge consists of a special lightweight magnet attached to a spring and contained within a pencil-like tube. To take a measurement, the exploring head or magnet is placed on the surface and the body of the gauge is drawn away, thus extending the spring. The spring extension, the amount of which is observed on the scale, is proportional to the force required to detach the magnet from the surface. The reading is taken at the point when the magnet breaks away from the surface, and the thickness is read directly from the scale.

Adjusting the Spray

A good spray pattern depends on the proper mixture of air and paint droplets much like a fine-tuned engine depends on the proper mixture of air and gasoline. The sprayed material should go on smoothly in a medium to wet coat without sagging or running. There are three basic adjustments, which under normal conditions will give the proper spray pattern, degree of wetness, and air pressure for suction feed guns.

1. Adjust the pressure (Figure 17–22). Air pressure, as described in Chapter 5, generally is set at the separator-regulator (or transformer). But due to friction as air passes from the regulator through the hose to the gun, pressure will be lost. The difference between the reading at the regulator and the reading at the gun will vary depending upon the length and diameter of the hose. (For example, a 50-foot, 1/4-inch diameter hose will yield a lower reading than a 15-foot, 5/16-inch diameter hose.) For this reason, pressure should be measured at the gun and all recommended pressures in this test are for readings at the gun.

FIGURE 17–23 A gauge installed at the spray gun will give accurate readings of pressure at the gun. (Courtesy of DeVilbiss Company)

A

B

FIGURE 17–24 (A) Turning in fan valve and (B) backing out fan valve. (Courtesy of Maaco Enterprises, Inc.)

FIGURE 17–22 Setting air pressure

The surest method to measure this pressure drop is with an air gauge, which is inserted between the hose coupler and the gun. (Some guns are equipped with regulators that allow for checking and setting pressure at the gun [Figure 17-23], while others have optional accessories to do the same thing.) Another method is to consult Table 17-3.

2. Set the size of the spray pattern using the fan adjustment or pattern control knob. To adjust the fan pattern, turn the pattern control knob all the way in to create a small, round pattern (Figure 17-24A). Backing the pattern control all the way out will produce a wide spray pattern (Figure 17-24B). Use narrower patterns for spot repairs and wider patterns for panel repairs or overall painting. Figure 17-25 represents the evolution of spray pattern from all the way in to all the way out.

3. Set the fluid control knob (Figure 17-26) to regulate the amount of paint according to the selected pattern size; backing the knob out increases the paint flow and turning the knob in decreases paint flow (Figure 17-27).

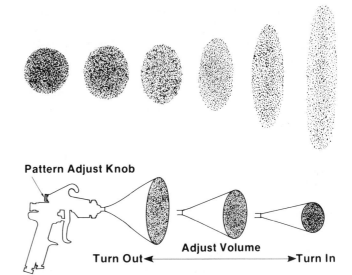

FIGURE 17-25   Pattern width adjustment

🚗 **SHOP TALK** _____

*In most cases the fluid control knob is left set in the full **open** position. The full **open** position is attained when two or three threads are showing on the adjusting valve.*

	Pressure Reading (lbs.) at Gauge	Pressure at the Gun for Various Hose Lengths					
		5 feet	10 feet	15 feet	20 feet	25 feet	50 feet
1/4-Inch Hose	30	26	24	23	22	21	9
	40	34	32	31	29	27	17
	50	43	40	38	36	34	22
	60	51	48	46	43	41	29
	70	59	56	53	51	48	36
	80	68	64	61	58	55	43
	90	76	71	68	65	61	51
5/16-Inch Hose	30	29	28-1/2	28	27-1/2	27	23
	40	38	37	37	37	36	32
	50	48	47	46	46	45	40
	60	57	56	55	55	54	49
	70	66	65	64	63	63	57
	80	75	74	73	72	71	66
	90	84	83	82	81	80	74

TABLE 17-3: ESTIMATED AIR PRESSURES AT THE GUN

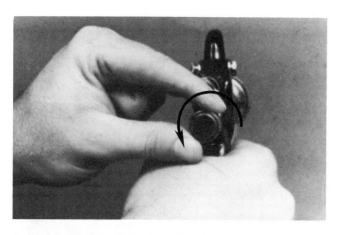

FIGURE 17-26 Adjusting fluid control valve

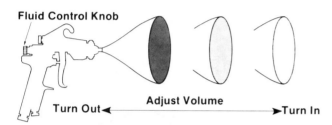

FIGURE 17-27 Paint fluid volume adjustment

The optimum spraying pressure is the lowest needed to obtain proper atomization, emission rate, and fan width. A pressure that is **too high** results in excessive paint loss through overspray (and therefore high usage), and poor flow, due to high solvent evaporation before the paint reaches the surface being sprayed.

A pressure that is **too low** gives a paint film poor drying characteristics, due to high solvent retention, and makes it prone to bubbling and sagging. The recommended pounds of air pressure vary with the kind of material to be sprayed. The typical ranges are given in Table 17-4.

BALANCING PRESSURE FEED GUN SYSTEM

To balance the pressure tank (Figure 17-28) or cup for spraying the procedure is as follows:

1. After paint is poured in the container (Figure 17-29), open the pattern control knob for maximum pattern size and open the fluid control knob until the first thread is visible.

2. Shut off the atomization air to the gun. Set the fluid flow rate by adjusting the air pres-

TABLE 17-4: RECOMMENDED AIR PRESSURE RANGES			
Topcoats	**Pressure at the Gun (psi)**	**Undercoats**	**Pressure at the Gun (psi)**
Polyurethane enamel	50–55 (solids) 60–65 (metallic)	Lacquer primer–surfacers	25–30 (spot) 35–45 (panel)
Acrylic lacquer	20–45	Multipurpose primer–surfacers	30–40 as primer–surfacer
Acrylic enamel	50–60	Multipurpose primer–surfacers as nonsanding	35–40
Alkyd enamel	50–60	Nonsanding primer–sanders	45
Flexible finishes	35–40	Enamel primer–surfacers	45
		Epoxy primer	45
		Zinc chromate primer	45
Sealers	**Pressure at the Gun (psi)**	**Miscellaneous**	**Pressure at the Gun (psi)**
Acrylic lacquer	25–30	Uniforming finishes	15–20
Universal sealer	35–45		
Bleederseal	35–40		

NOTE: Spot repairs should be made at the low end of the air pressure range.

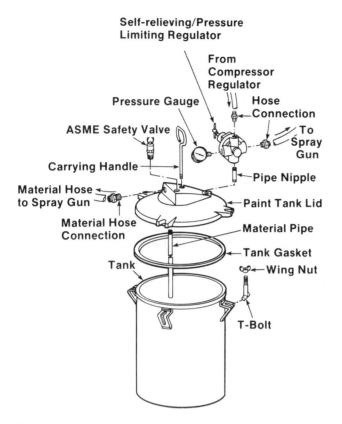

FIGURE 17-28   Major parts of pressure tank

FIGURE 17-29   Pouring paint into tank

FIGURE 17-30   The best way to learn the effects of gun movement and gun adjustments is to experiment on a test surface.

sure in the paint container. Use about 6 psi for a remote cup and about 15 psi for a 2-gallon or larger container. Adjust the fluid flow in **either** of the following ways:

Remove the air cap, aim the gun into a clean container, and pull the trigger for 10 seconds. Measure the amount of material that flowed in that time and multiply by 6 (or 30 seconds and multiply by 2). This is the fluid flow rate in ounces per minute. For standard refinishing it should be about 14 to 16 ounces per minute. If the flow rate is less than this, increase the air pressure in the container and repeat. If it is faster than this, decrease the pressure slightly. When the flow rate is correct, reinstall the air cap.

OR

Pull the trigger and adjust the pressure on the paint container until the stream of paint discharging from the gun squirts about 3 to 4 feet before it starts to drop. This indicates a fluid flow of about 14 to 16 ounces per minute.

3. Turn on the atomization air to about 50 **at the gun.** Then spray a fast test pattern.

TESTING THE SPRAY PATTERN

After setting the air pressure, the fan size, and the fluid flow, test the spray pattern on a piece of masking paper or newspaper (Figure 17-30). Hold the gun 6 to 8 inches away from the paper if spraying lacquer and 8 to 10 inches for enamel. Pull the trigger all the way back and release it immediately. This burst of paint should leave a long, slender pattern on the test paper (Figure 17-31A). Spraying primer-surfacer usually requires a small spray pat-

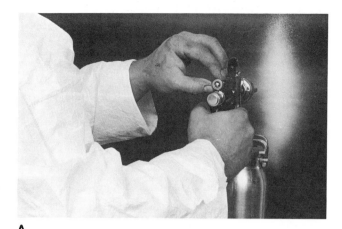

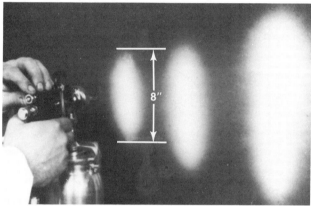

A

B

FIGURE 17-31   Test patterns

FIGURE 17-32   Inspect the texture of the spray pattern.

tern. Turn the pattern control knob in until the spray pattern is 6 to 8 inches high (Figure 17-31B).

For spot repair, the pattern should be about 5 to 6 inches from top to bottom. For panel or overall repair, the length of the pattern should be about 9 inches from top to bottom. A larger pattern can be obtained by opening the pattern control knob.

Carefully inspect the texture of the spray pattern (Figure 17-32). If the paint droplets are coarse and large, turn the fluid control knob in about 1/2 turn or increase the air pressure 5 pounds. If the spray is too fine or too dry, either open the fluid control knob about 1/2 turn or decrease the air pressure 5 pounds.

 SHOP TALK _____

Remember, the objective of spraying on a test surface is twofold. First, make sure all atomized paint particles are of uniform size. Second, make sure this size is fine enough to achieve proper flow out (Figure 17-33).

Next, test the spray pattern for uniformity of paint distribution. Loosen the air cap retaining ring and rotate the air cap (Figure 17-34) so that the horns are straight up and down. The air cap in this position will produce a horizontal spray pattern rather than a vertical one. Spray again, but this time hold the trigger down until the paint begins to run. This is called **flooding** the pattern. Inspect the lengths of the runs. If all adjustments are correct, the runs will be approximately equal in length (Figure 17-35).

The uneven runs in the split pattern shown in Figure 17-36 are a result of setting the spray pattern too wide or the air pressure too low. Turn the pattern control knob in 1/2 turn or raise the air pressure 5

647

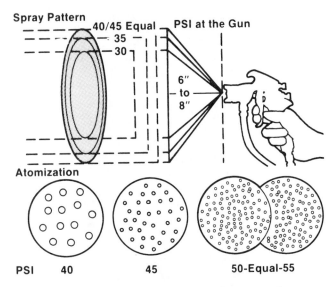

FIGURE 17-35   Balanced spray pattern

FIGURE 17-36   Split pattern

FIGURE 17-33   As shown here, the correct spraying pressure is, therefore, 50 psi.

FIGURE 17-37   Heavy center pattern

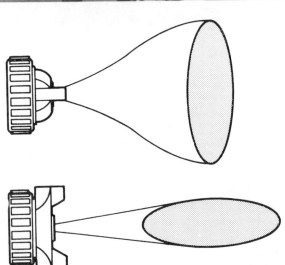

FIGURE 17-38   Be sure to wear an air respirator when spraying. (Courtesy of Maaco Enterprises, Inc.)

pounds. Alternate between these two adjustments until the runs are even in length.

If paint runs are longer in the middle than on the edges (Figure 17-37), too much paint is being discharged. Turn the fluid control knob in until the runs are even in length.

FIGURE 17-34   How rotating the air caps affects the pattern.

WARNING: Always wear a suitable air respirator (Figure 17-38) when spraying test patterns.

The Application Stroke

The proper stroke is most important in obtaining a good refinishing job. To obtain a good stroke technique, proceed as follows:

1. Hold the spray gun at the proper distance from the surface—6 to 8 inches for lacquer, 8 to 10 inches for enamel (Figure 17–39). If the humidity is high, a shorter distance might be necessary. If the spraying is done from a shorter distance, the high velocity of the spraying air tends to ripple the wet film. If the distance is increased beyond that, there will be a greater percent of thinner evaporated, resulting in orange peel or dry film, and adversely affecting color where matching is required. A slower evaporating thinner will permit more variation in the distance of the spray gun from the job but will produce runs if the gun gets too close (Figure 17–40). Excessive spraying distance also causes a loss in materials due to overspray.

2. Hold the gun level and perpendicular to the surface (Figure 17–41). If the spray gun is not kept at a right angle even at curves, an uneven paint film will result (Figure 17–42). On flat surfaces, such as the hood or roof, the gun should be pointed straight down (Figure 17–43).

3. The gun should be in motion before the trigger is pulled, and the trigger should be released before the gun motion stops. This technique gives a fade in and fade out effect, which prevents overloading where one series of strokes is joined to the next by overlapping the stroke ends.

4. Do not fan the gun and do not use wrist motions if a uniform film is desired. The only time it is permissible to fan the gun is on a small spot spray where the paint film at the edges of the spot should be thinner than the center portion.

5. Move the gun with a steady deliberate pass, about 1 foot per second. Moving the gun too fast will produce a thin film, while moving it too slowly will result in the paint running. The speed must be consistent or it will result in an uneven paint film. Never stop in one place or the sprayed coat will drip and run!

6. Release the trigger at the end of each pass. Then pull back the trigger when beginning

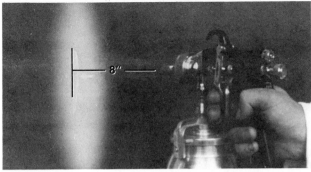

A

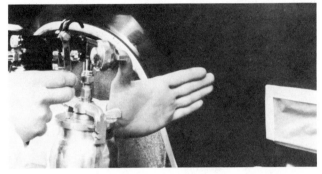

B

FIGURE 17–39   (A) Proper spray distance; (B) easy method of checking spray distance. (Courtesy of Maaco Enterprises, Inc.)

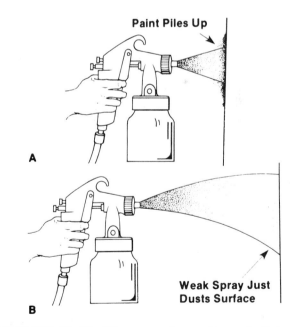

FIGURE 17–40   The correct gun-to-work distance is important. If the gun is too close, (A) the finish material piles up and causes runs and sags. When the gun is too far away, (B) material tends to dry into dust before it reaches the surface. Adjust distance accordingly.

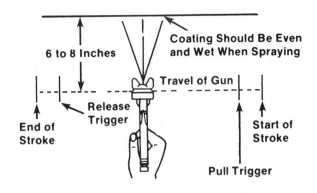

6 to 8 Inches

Coating Should Be Even and Wet When Spraying

Travel of Gun

Release Trigger

End of Stroke

Start of Stroke

Pull Trigger

FIGURE 17-41   Proper parallel motion

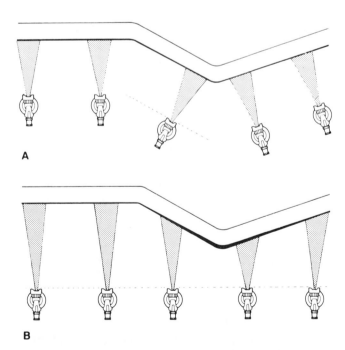

A

B

FIGURE 17-42   (A) Proper spray gun movement. (B) If the spray gun is not kept at a right angle even at curves in the body, an uneven paint film will result.

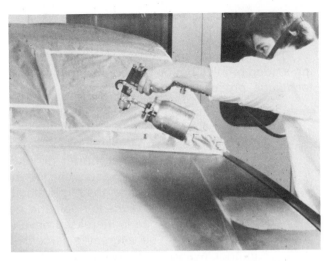

FIGURE 17-43   Proper spraying technique for flat surfaces. (Courtesy of Maaco Enterprises, Inc.)

the pass in the opposite direction. In other words: "trigger" the gun and turn off the gun at the end of each sweep. This avoids runs, minimizes overspray, and saves paint. Proper triggering involves four steps (Figure 17-44): (A) Begin the stroke over the masking paper, triggering the gun halfway to release only air; (B) when the starting edge of the panel is reached, squeeze the trigger all the way to release the paint; (C) release the trigger halfway to stop the paint flow when directly over the finishing edge; and (D) continue the stroke several more inches before reversing the direction and repeating the sequence.

7. Difficult areas such as corners and edges should be sprayed first. Aim directly at the area so that half of the spray covers each side of the edge or corner. Hold the gun an inch or two closer than usual, or screw the pattern control knob in a few turns. Either technique will reduce the pattern size. If the gun is just held closer, the stroke will have to be faster to compensate for a normal amount of material being applied to the smaller areas. After all of the edges and corners have been sprayed, the flat or nearly flat surfaces should be sprayed.

8. For painting very narrow surfaces, switch guns or caps with a smaller spray pattern to avoid having to readjust the full size pattern gun. The smaller pattern guns are easier to handle in critical areas. As an alternate, a full size gun can be used by

A

B

C

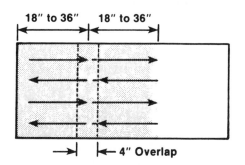

D

FIGURE 17-44   **Proper triggering involves four steps: (A) begin the stroke over the masking paper and as the gun is moved, trigger halfway to release only air; (B) when reaching the starting edge of the panel, squeeze the trigger all the way to release the paint; (C) release the trigger halfway to stop the paint flow when directly over the finishing edge; and (D) continue the stroke several more inches before reversing the direction and repeating the sequence.** *(Courtesy of Maaco Enterprises, Inc.)*

reducing the air pressure and fluid delivery and triggering properly.

9. Generally, start at the top of an upright surface such as a door panel. The spray gun nozzle should be level with the top of the surface. This means that the upper half of the spray pattern will hit the masking.

10. The second pass is made in the opposite direction with the nozzle level at the lower edge of the previous pass. Thus one half (50 percent) of the pattern overlaps the previous pass and the other half is sprayed on the unpainted area (Figure 17–45).

11. Always blend into "the wet edge" of the previous section sprayed (Figure 17–46). Proper triggering technique at the area where the sections are joined will avoid the danger of a double coat at this point and the possibility of getting a sag (Figure 17–47).

12. Continue back and forth passes, triggering the gun at the end of each pass, and lowering each successive pass one half the top-to-bottom width of the spray gun pattern.

13. The last pass should be made with the lower half of the spray pattern below the surface being painted. If it is a door, the pattern would shoot off into space below it.

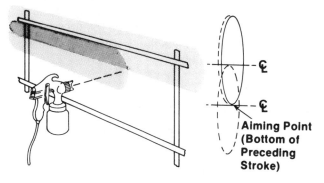

FIGURE 17-45   **How to overlap strokes**

FIGURE 17-46   **Always blend into the wet edge.**

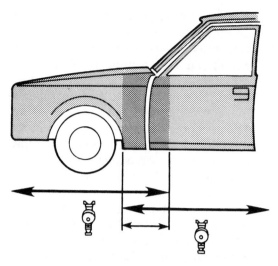

FIGURE 17-47   Gun overlap area where runs occur easily in overall painting jobs

FIGURE 17-48   Heeling is a common gun handling error.

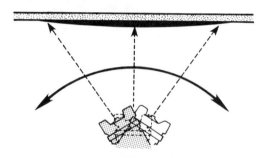

FIGURE 17-49   Another common gun handling error is arcing.

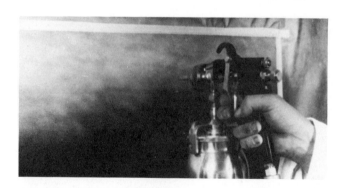

FIGURE 17-50   Gun movement too fast

14. The procedure just followed is called a **single coat.** For a **double coat,** repeat the single coat procedure immediately. Generally, two or more double coats are required to properly apply a lacquer topcoat. Allow for flash time (the time required for the solvents to evaporate and the finish to dull slightly) or several minutes between coats. This can be observed as a slight dulling of the coat's appearance. Two or three single coats are normally required for enamel topcoats. Allow the first coat to set up (become tacky) before applying additional coats.

GUN HANDLING PROBLEMS

The inexperienced painter is prone to several spraying errors including:

- **Heeling.** This occurs when the painter allows the gun to tilt (Figure 17-48). Because the gun is no longer perpendicular to the surface, the spray produces an uneven layer of paint, excessive overspray, dry spray, and orange peel.
- **Arcing.** This occurs when the gun is not moved parallel with the surface (Figure 17-49). At the outer edges of the arced stroke, the gun is farther away from the surface than at the middle of the stroke. The result is uneven film buildup, dry spray, excessive overspray, and orange peel.
- **Speed of stroke.** If the stroke is made too quickly, the paint will not cover the surface evenly (Figure 17-50). If the stroke is made too slowly, sags and runs will develop (Figure 17-51). The proper stroking speed is something that comes with experience.
- **Improper overlap.** Improper overlapping results in uneven film thickness, contrasting color hues, and sags and runs as shown in Figure 17-52.

FIGURE 17-51 Gun movement too slow

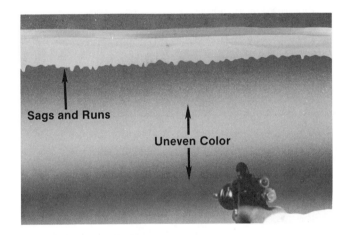

Sags and Runs

Uneven Color

FIGURE 17-52 Improper overlapping can cause problems.

- **Wasteful overspray.** Failure to trigger the gun before and after each stroke results in wasteful overspray and excessive buildup of paint at the beginning and end of each stroke (Figure 17-53).
- **Improper coverage.** Triggering at the wrong time is another common error. Failure to trigger exactly over the edge of the panel results in uneven coverage and film thickness (Figure 17-54).

Types of Spray Coats

There are varying degrees of thickness for a sprayed coat. Generally, they are referred to as light, medium, or heavy. The easiest way to control this degree of thickness is by the speed with which the gun is moved. That is, the slower the speed, the heavier the coat.

There are also six other terms to describe spray coats:

- Tack
- Full wet coat
- Mist
- Dust
- Shading or blending
- Banding

The **tack coat** allows the application of heavier wet coats without sagging or runs. This is a light covering coat applied to the surface and then allowed to **flash** until it is just tacky, which usually takes only a few minutes. The finish wet coats are then sprayed over the tack coat.

A **full wet coat** is a heavy, glossy coat that is applied in a thickness almost heavy enough to run. It requires skill and practice to spray such a coat.

The **mist coat** is an application of slower drying thinners over a color coat. It helps to level the final

FIGURE 17-53 An example of wasteful overspray

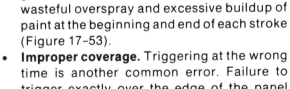

FIGURE 17-54 An example of improper coverage

coat, melt in the overspray, and control mottling of metallics. Uniforming finishes or blenders are applied as mist coats in spot and panel repairing of acrylic lacquers and acrylic enamels.

A **dust coat** is a light, dry coat of finish. It is accomplished by holding the gun a little from the surface being sprayed.

Shading or blending coats are applications of paint on the boundary of spot repair areas so that a color difference between the new paint and surrounding original paint is not noticeable. It is applied in two coats and the second coat is thinner and sprayed over a wider area than the first. Finally a mist coat is applied. Shading can also be done when repainting a panel so that a color difference is not noticeable between adjacent panels.

Banding is a single coat applied in a small spray pattern to the frame in an area to be sprayed. This technique assures the painter of coverage at the edges without spraying beyond the spray area and reduces overspray. Banding is often used in spraying panel repairs with a primer-surfacer.

Sometimes a banding coat is thinned more than the normal application that follows. This is especially true when the paint to be sprayed is of high viscosity. The additional thinning of the paint used for banding allows it to fully enter cracks and seams. A good example is the application of textured vinyl finish. Table 17-5 summarizes the variables that control quality when spray painting.

17.3 CLEANING THE SPRAY GUN

Neglect and carelessness are responsible for the majority of spray gun difficulties. Proper care of a gun requires little time and effort. Thorough cleaning of gun and accessory equipment **immediately after use,** lubrication of bearing surfaces and packings at recommended intervals, and proper care in handling (do not drop or throw gun) are important factors in the care of a spray gun.

To clean a suction feed gun, first loosen the cup from the gun (Figure 17-55A). Keep the fluid tube in the cup. Next, unscrew the air cap two or three turns. Hold a folded cloth over the air cap and pull the trigger (Figure 17-55B). This will force the paint in the gun back into the cup.

 **SHOP TALK**

Use very low pressure (5 pounds). Do not attempt when paint cup is loaded, because paint could be splashed from the container.

TABLE 17-5: SUMMARY OF VARIABLES CONTROLLING QUALITY IN SPRAY FINISHING	
Atomization	1. Fluid viscosity 2. Air pressure 3. Fan pattern width 4. Fluid velocity or fluid pressure 5. Fluid flow rate 6. Distance of spray gun from work
Evaporation Stages	1. Between spray gun and part 2. From sprayed part
Evaporation Variables Between Spray Gun and Sprayed Part	1. Type of reducing thinner 2. Atomization pressure 3. Amount of thinner 4. Temperature in spray area 5. Degree of atomization

Evaporation Variables Affecting	1. Physical properties of solvents (i.e., fast or slow evaporation)
	2. Temperature
	  a. Fluid
	  b. Work
	  c. Air
	3. Exposed area of the surface sprayed

Evaporation Variables from the Sprayed Part	1. Surface temperature 2. Room air temperature 3. Air pressure velocity 4. Flash time between coats 5. Flash time after final coats 6. Physical properties of the solvents (i.e., fast or slow evaporation)

Operator Variables	1. Distance of spray gun from the work surface
	2. Stroking speed over the work surface
	3. Pattern overlap
	4. Spray gun attitude
	  a. Heeling
	  b. Arcing
	  c. Fanning
	5. Triggering

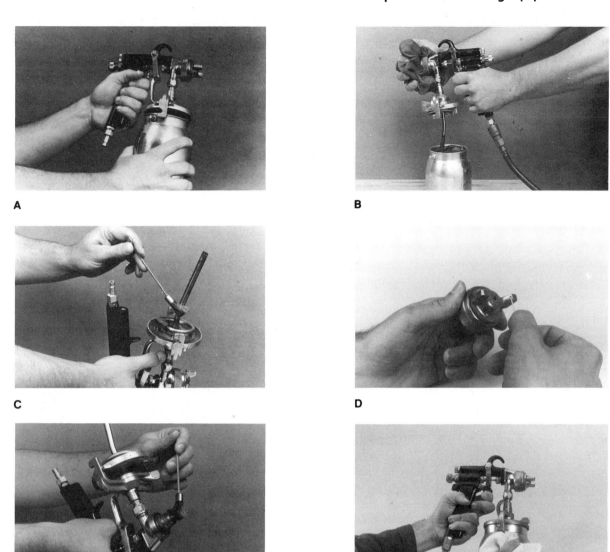

FIGURE 17-55   To clean a spray gun: (A) loosen cup; (B) discharge paint; (C) clean paint pipe; (D) clean clogged holes in air cap; (E) clean paint nozzle; and (F) clean cup cover. *(Courtesy of Maaco Enterprises, Inc.)*

Retighten the air nozzle and pour the paint in the cup back into the original container. Clean the cup and the cup cover with solvent and a thin bristle brush (Figure 17-55C). Wipe up residue with a clean rag soaked with solvent. Then, pour 1 inch of clean solvent in the cup. Spray the solvent through the gun to clean out the fluid passages.

On pressure feed air guns, release the pressure in the cup, loosen the air nozzle and force the material in to the cup by triggering the gun. Take the air nozzle off. Empty the contents into a suitable container and refill the cup with a clean compatible solvent. The air nozzle can be left off. Spray solvent from the gun and repeat this process until clean

solvent is flowing from the gun. If a tank is used, clean as directed by the manufacturer and reassemble for future use.

With either type of gun, remove the air cap and soak it in thinner or solvent. Clean out clogged holes with a soft item such as a round type toothpick or a broom straw (Figure 17-55D). Remember, **never** use wires or nails to clean the precision-drilled openings. Clean the fluid tip with a gun brush and solvent (Figure 17-55E). With a clean rag soaked in thinner, wipe the outside of the gun to remove all traces of paint (Figure 17-55F).

Areas in the United States with air pollution problems, such as southern California, require the use of enclosed spray gun cleaning equipment. The paint spraying equipment—guns, cups, stirrers, and strainers—is placed in the larger tub of the gun washer/recycler (Figure 17–56), the lid is closed, then the air-operated pump recirculates the thinner into the upper portion of the tub. In less than 60 seconds, the equipment is clean and ready for use.

The automatic gun washer/recycler saves the body technician time. Compared with traditional manual cleaning methods, the gun washer/recycler machine saves 10 minutes on each color change. The cleaning system offers increased safety, because the skin no longer is exposed to the drying effects of solvent. The system is designed so that sludge from the cleaning action settles to the bottom for easy drainage and disposal with other shop wastes. Check the owner's manual for complete operational details and the proper solvents to use.

 **SHOP TALK** _____

If the gun is not cleaned soon after use, the nozzle might clog, causing the gun to spit (eject pieces of dried paint) or form the wrong spray pattern. For enamel paints with additives, the enamel paint might harden right in the gun lining.

Most spray gun manufacturers recommend lubricating, at the end of each day, the parts shown in Figure 17–57 with light machine oil. Packings and springs plus needles and nozzles must periodically be replaced due to normal wear and tear. This should be done only in accordance with the manufacturer's instructions. Extreme care should be taken not to overlubricate since the excess oil could overflow into the paint and oil passages, mixing with the paint and resulting in a defective paint film. Oil and paint do not mix to produce a good finish.

 **SHOP TALK** _____

Never soak the entire gun in cleaning solvent. Doing this will dry out the packings and remove lubrication.

For best results in refinishing, use separate guns for topcoats and undercoats. Ideally, there should be at least three guns: one gun for spraying undercoats like primer-surfacers, another for spraying lacquers and acrylic lacquers, and a third gun for

FIGURE 17–56 Typical automatic gun washer/recycler

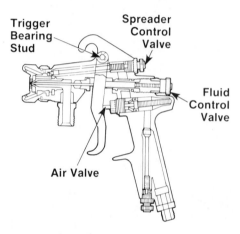

FIGURE 17–57 Parts to lubricate in an air spray gun

spraying enamels. If these guns are kept clean and in good working order, much time will be saved over trying to use one gun and having to adjust it each time that the operation is changed.

17.4 SPRAY GUN TROUBLESHOOTING

If the air spray gun is not adjusted, manipulated, and cleaned properly, it will apply a defective coating to the surface. Fortunately, defects from incorrect handling and improper cleaning can be tracked down quite readily, and then corrected without much difficulty. The most common spray gun application problems, with their possible causes and suggested remedies, are given in Chapter 19.

TABLE 17-6: TROUBLESHOOTING AN AIR SPRAY GUN

Trouble	Possible Cause	Suggested Correction
Spray pattern top heavy or bottom heavy	1. Horn holes partially plugged (external mix). 2. Fluid tip clogged, damaged, or not installed properly. 3. Dirt on air cap seat or fluid tip seat.	1. Remove air cap and clean. 2. Clean, replace, or reinstall fluid tip. 3. Remove and clean seat.
Spray pattern heavy to right or to left	1. Air cap dirty or orifice partially clogged. 2. Air cap damaged. 3. Paint nozzle clogged or damaged. 4. Too low a setting of the pattern control knob.	1. To determine where buildup occurs, rotate cap 180 degrees and test spray. If pattern shape stays in same position, the condition is caused by fluid buildup on fluid tip. If pattern changes with cap movement, the condition is in the air cap. Clean air cap, orifice, and fluid tip accordingly. 2. Replace air cap. 3. Clean or replace paint nozzle. 4. Adjust setting.
Spray pattern heavy at center	1. Atomizing pressure too low. 2. Fluid of too great viscosity. 3. Fluid pressure too high for air cap's normal capacity (pressure feed). 4. Caliber of paint nozzle enlarged due to wear. 5. Center hole enlarged.	1. Increase pressure. 2. Thin fluid with suitable thinner. 3. Reduce fluid pressure. 4. Replace paint nozzle. 5. Replace air cap and paint nozzle.
Spray pattern split	1. Not enough fluid. 2. Air cap or fluid tip dirty. 3. Air pressure too high. 4. Fluid viscosity too thin.	1. Reduce air pressure or increase fluid flow. 2. Remove and clean. 3. Lower air pressure. 4. Thicken fluid viscosity.
Pinholes	1. Gun too close to surface. 2. Fluid pressure too high. 3. Fluid too heavy.	1. Stroke 6 to 8 inches from surface. 2. Reduce pressure. 3. Thin fluid with thinner.
Blushing or a whitish coat of lacquer.	1. Absorption of moisture. 2. Too quick drying of lacquer.	1. Avoid spraying in damp, humid, or too cool weather. 2. Correct by adding retarder to lacquer.
Orange peel (surface looks like orange peel)	1. Too high or too low an atomization pressure. 2. Gun too far or too close to work. 3. Fluid not thinned. 4. Improperly prepared surface. 5. Gun stroke too rapid. 6. Using wrong air cap. 7. Overspray striking a previously sprayed surface. 8. Fluid not thoroughly dissolved. 9. Drafts (synthetics and lacquers). 10. Humidity too low (synthetics).	1. Correct as needed. 2. Stroke 6 to 8 inches from surface. 3. Use proper thinning process. 4. Surface must be prepared. 5. Take deliberate, slow stroke. 6. Select correct air cap for the fluid and feed. 7. Select proper spraying procedure. 8. Mix fluid thoroughly. 9. Eliminate excessive drafts. 10. Raise humidity of room.

TABLE 17-6: TROUBLESHOOTING AN AIR SPRAY GUN (CONTINUED)

Trouble	Possible Cause	Suggested Correction
Excessive spray fog or overspray	1. Atomizing air pressure too high or fluid pressure too low. 2. Spraying past surface of the product. 3. Wrong air cap or fluid tip. 4. Gun stroked too far from surface. 5. Fluid thinned out too much.	1. Correct as needed. 2. Release trigger when gun passes target. 3. Ascertain and use correct combination. 4. Stroke 6 to 8 inches from surface. 5. Add correct amount of thinner.
No control over size of pattern	1. Air cap seal is damaged. 2. Foreign particles are lodged under the seal.	1. Check for damage, replace if necessary. 2. Make sure surface that this sets on is clean.
Sags or runs	1. Dirty air cap and fluid tip. 2. Gun manipulated too close to surface. 3. Not releasing trigger at end of stroke (when stroke does not go beyond object). 4. Gun manipulated at wrong angle to surface. 5. Fluid piled on too heavy. 6. Fluid thinned out too much. 7. Fluid pressure too high. 8. Operation too slow. 9. Improper atomization.	1. Clean cap and fluid tip. 2. Hold the gun 6 to 8 inches from surface. 3. Release trigger after every stroke. 4. Work gun at right angles to surface. 5. Learn to calculate depth of wet film of fluid. 6. Add correct amount of fluid by measure. 7. Reduce fluid pressure with fluid control knob. 8. Speed up movement of gun across surface. 9. Check air and fluid flow; clean cap and fluid tip.
Streaks	1. Dirty or damaged air cap and/or fluid tip. 2. Not overlapping strokes correctly or sufficiently. 3. Gun moved too fast across surface. 4. Gun held at wrong angle to surface. 5. Gun held too far from surface. 6. Air pressure too high. 7. Split spray. 8. Pattern and fluid control not adjusted properly.	1. Same as for sags. 2. Follow previous stroke accurately. 3. Take deliberate, slow strokes. 4. Same as for sags. 5. Stroke 6 to 8 inches from surface. 6. Use least air pressure necessary. 7. Reduce air adjustment or change air cap and/or fluid tip. 8. Readjust.
Gun sputters constantly **Sputtering Spray**	1. Connections, fittings, and seals loose or missing. 2. Leaky connection on fluid tube or fluid needle packing (suction gun). 3. Lack of sufficient fluid in container. 4. Tipping container at an acute angle. 5. Obstructed fluid passageway.	1. Tighten and/or replace as per owner's manual. 2. Tighten connections; lubricate packing. 3. Refill container with fluid. 4. If container must be tipped, change position of fluid tube and keep container full of fluid. 5. Remove fluid tip, needle, and fluid tube and clean.

TABLE 17-6: TROUBLESHOOTING AN AIR SPRAY GUN (CONTINUED)

Trouble	Possible Cause	Suggested Correction
Gun sputters constantly (continued)	6. Fluid too heavy (suction feed).	6. Thin fluid.
	7. Clogged air vent in canister top (suction feed).	7. Clean.
	8. Dirty or damaged coupling nut on canister top (suction feed).	8. Clean or replace.
	9. Fluid pipe not tightened to pressure tank lid or pressure cup cover.	9. Tighten; check for defective threads.
	10. Strainer is clogged up.	10. Clean strainer.
	11. Packing nut is loose.	11. Make sure packing nut is tight.
	12. Fluid tip is loose.	12. Tighten fluid tip. Torque to manufacturer's specifications.
	13. O-ring on tip is worn or dirty.	13. Replace O-ring if necessary.
	14. Fluid hose from paint tank loose.	14. Tighten.
	15. Jam nut gasket installed improperly or jam nut loose.	15. Inspect and correctly install or tighten nut.
Uneven spray pattern	1. Damaged or clogged air cap.	1. Inspect air cap and clean or replace.
	2. Damaged or clogged fluid tip.	2. Inspect fluid tip and clean or replace.
Fluid leaks from spray gun **Nozzle Drip**	1. Fluid needle packing not too tight.	1. Loosen nut; lubricate packing.
	2. Fluid needle packing dry.	2. Lubricate needle and packing frequently.
	3. Foreign particle blocking fluid tip.	3. Remove tip and clean.
	4. Damaged fluid tip or fluid needle.	4. Replace both tip and needle.
	5. Wrong fluid needle size.	5. Replace fluid needle with correct size for fluid tip being used.
	6. Broken fluid needle spring.	6. Remove and replace.
Fluid leaks from packing nut **Packing Nut Leak**	1. Loose packing nut.	1. Tighten packing nut.
	2. Packing is worn out.	2. Replace packing.
	3. Dry packing.	3. Remove and soften packing with a few drops of light oil.
Fluid leaks through fluid tip when trigger is released	1. Foreign particles lodged in the fluid tip.	1. Clean out tip and strain paint.
	2. Fluid needle has paint stuck on it.	2. Remove all dried paint.
	3. Fluid needle is damaged.	3. Check for damage; replace if necessary.
	4. Fluid tip has been damaged.	4. Check for nicks; replace if necessary.
	5. Spring left off fluid needle.	5. Make sure spring is replaced on needle.
Excessive fluid	1. Not triggering the gun at each stroke.	1. It should be a habit to release trigger after every stroke.
	2. Gun at wrong angle to surface.	2. Hold gun at right angles to surface.
	3. Gun held too far from surface.	3. Stroke 6 to 8 inches from surface.
	4. Wrong air cap or fluid tip.	4. Use correct combination.
	5. Depositing fluid film of irregular thickness.	5. Learn to calculate depth of wet film of finish.
	6. Air pressure too high.	6. Use least amount of air necessary.
	7. Fluid pressure too high.	7. Reduce pressure.
	8. Fluid control knob not adjusted properly.	8. Readjust.

TABLE 17-6: TROUBLESHOOTING AN AIR SPRAY GUN (CONTINUED)

Trouble	Possible Cause	Suggested Correction
Fluid will not come from spray gun	1. Out of fluid. 2. Grit, dirt, paint skin, etc., blocking air gap, fluid tip, fluid needle, or strainer. 3. No air supply. 4. Internal mix cap using suction feed.	1. Add more spray fluid. 2. Clean spray gun thoroughly and strain spray fluid; always strain fluid before using it. 3. Check regulator. 4. Change cap or feed.
Fluid will not come from fluid tank or canister	1. Lack of proper air pressure in fluid tank or canister. 2. Air intake opening inside fluid tank or canister clogged by dried-up finish fluid. 3. Leaking gasket on fluid tank cover or canister top. 4. Gun not converted correctly between canister and fluid tank. 5. Blocked fluid hose. 6. Connections with regulator not correct.	1. Check for air leaks or leak of air entry; adjust air pressure for sufficient flow. 2. This is a common trouble; clean opening periodically. 3. Replace with new gasket. 4. Correct per owner's manual. 5. Clear. 6. Correct as per owner's manual.
Sprayed coat short of liquid material	1. Air pressure too high. 2. Fluid not reduced or thinned correctly. (Suction feed only) 3. Gun too far from work or out of adjustment.	1. Decrease air pressure. 2. Reduce or thin according to directions; use proper thinner or reducer. 3. Adjust distance to work; clean and adjust gun fluid and spray pattern controls.
Spotty, uneven pattern, slow to build	1. Inadequate fluid flow. 2. Low atomization air pressure. (Suction feed only) 3. Too fast gun motion.	1. Back fluid control knob to first thread. 2. Increase air pressure, rebalance gun. 3. Move at moderate pace.
Unable to get round spray	1. Pattern control knob not seating properly.	1. Clean or replace.
Dripping from fluid tip	1. Dry packing. 2. Sluggish needle. 3. Tight packing nut. 4. Spray head misaligned on type MBC guns causing needle to bind.	1. Lubricate packing. 2. Lubricate. 3. Adjust. 4. Tap all around spray head with wood and rawhide mallet and retighten locking bolt.
Excessive overspray	1. Too much atomization air pressure. 2. Gun too far from surface. 3. Improper stroking, i.e. arcing, moving too fast.	1. Reduce. 2. Check distance. 3. Move at moderate pace, parallel to work surface.
Excessive fog	1. Too much or quick drying thinner. 2. Too much atomization air pressure.	1. Remix. 2. Reduce.
Will not spray on pressure feed	1. Control knob on canister cover not open. 2. Canister is not sealing. 3. Spray fluid has not been strained. 4. Spray fluid in canister top threads.	1. Set this knob for pressure spraying. 2. Make sure canister is on tightly. 3. Always strain before using. 4. Clean threads and wipe with grease.

TABLE 17-6: TROUBLESHOOTING AN AIR SPRAY GUN (CONTINUED)

Trouble	Possible Cause	Suggested Correction
Will not spray on pressure feed (continued)	5. Gasket in canister top worn or left out.	5. Inspect and replace if necessary.
	6. No air supply.	6. Check regulator.
	7. Fluid too thick.	7. Thin fluid with proper thinner.
	8. Clogged strainer.	8. Clean or replace strainer.
Will not spray on suction feed	1. Spray fluid is too thick.	1. Thin fluid with thinner.
	2. Internal mix nozzle used.	2. Install external mix nozzle.
	3. Spray fluid has not been strained.	3. Always strain before use.
	4. Hole in canister cover clogged.	4. Make sure this hole is open.
	5. Gasket in canister top worn or left out.	5. Inspect and replace if necessary.
	6. Plug or clogged strainer.	6. Clean or replace strainer.
	7. Fluid control knob adjusted incorrectly.	7. Correct adjustment.
	8. No air supply.	8. Check regulator.
Air continues to flow through gun when trigger has been released (on nonbleeder guns only)	1. Air valve leaks.	1. Remove valve, inspect for damage, clean valve, and replace if necessary.
	2. Needle is binding.	2. Clean or straighten needle.
	3. Piston is sticking.	3. Clean piston, check O-ring, and replace if necessary.
	4. Packing nut too tight.	4. Adjust packing nuts.
	5. Control valve spring left out.	5. Make sure to replace this spring.
Air leak at canister gasket	1. Canister not sealing on canister cover.	1. Check gasket, clean threads, and tighten canister.
Leak at setscrew in canister top	1. Screw not tight.	1. Clean threads and tighten screw.
	2. Damaged threads on setscrew.	2. Inspect and replace if necessary.
Leak between top of canister cover and gun body	1. Retainer nut is not tight enough.	1. Check nut to make sure it is tight.
	2. Gasket or gasket seat damaged.	2. Inspect, clean, and replace if necessary.
Pressure Fluid Tank Problems		
Leaks air at the top of the tank lid	1. Gasket not seating properly or damaged.	1. Drain off all of the air from fluid tank thus allowing the gasket to seat. Retighten wing nuts, and fill with air again. Lid will seat tightly.
	2. Wing screws not tight enough.	2. Make sure all wing screws are tight. By following remedy #1 (above), wing screws can be pulled down even tighter.
	3. Fittings leak.	3. Check all fittings and apply pipe dope if necessary.
	4. Air pressure too high.	4. Maximum 60 psi. Normal w.p. 25–30 psi.
No fluid comes through the spray gun	1. Not enough pressure in tank.	1. Increase regulator setting until fluid flows; do not exceed 60 psi.
	2. Out of fluid.	2. Check fluid supply.
	3. Fluid passages clogged.	3. Check tube, fittings, hose, and spray gun. Clean out fittings, hose, tube, and spray gun making sure all residual fluid is removed.

TABLE 17-7: TROUBLESHOOTING A COMPRESSED AIR SUPPLY

Fault	Result	Blistering	Nondrying	Poor Adhesion	Contamination	Poor Atomization	Poor Flow	Overloading	Sags	Popping	Slow Application	Off-shade Metallic	Uneven Application	Dry Spray	Dirt	Remedy
Oil/water not adequately condensed out.	Oil/water at spray gun	A	C	A	C											Ensure regular drainage of air receiver, separator, and transformer. Site transformers of adequate capacity in cool places. Lubricate compressors with recommended grade of mineral oil of good emulsifying properties.
Long air line; inadequate internal bore of air line; connectors, fittings, compressor, air transformers, and regulators of inadequate capacity.	Pressure drop					B	C	C	A	A	C	A				Ensure adequate air supply with 30 feet 5/16 inch (8mm) internal bore air line with appropriate fittings. NOTE: Reduction of viscosity to give improvement may produce other defects.
Inadequate compressor capacity. No pressure regulator. Regulator diaphragm broken.	Pressure fluctuation							A	A	A		A	A	A		Increase capacity. Use pressure regulator. Replace regulator diaphragm.
Compressed air intake filter breached. Transformer filter not properly maintained. Compressor sited in dusty area.	Dirt in compressed air														A	Repair air intake filter. Replace transformer filter. Clean dust and dirt from compressor site.

A Most likely failure to be associated with the fault
B Likely failure
C Failure less likely to be associated with the fault

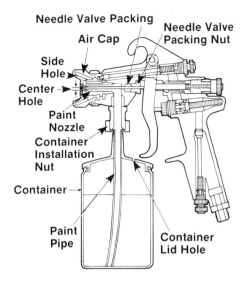

FIGURE 17-58   Possible trouble spots of an air spray gun

If not properly maintained, the air spray gun itself (Figure 17-58) can also create some problems. Table 17-6 contains the causes of and possible solutions to some of the more common spray gun difficulties.

Failure of the compressed air supply system to perform properly can cause the paint problems as shown in Table 17-7.

17.5 OTHER SPRAY SYSTEMS

There are four other types of spray systems that can be found in some shops: airless spray gun, electrostatic system, HVLP system, and the airbrush. Operation is basically the same as the air spray system just described.

Airless Spray Gun System

Airless spraying equipment (Figure 17-59) uses hydraulic pressure to atomize paint rather than air pressure. With the airless spray method, pressure is applied directly to the paint, which is injected at high speed through small holes in the nozzle and formed into a mist. Unlike the air spray method, there is less mixing of air in the paint and, consequently, less mist dispersion. Also, since the paint is pressurized directly, less energy is used for atomization so that with the same amount of power, a degree of atomization is accomplished that is several times that for air spraying. In fact, the pressure developed in airless

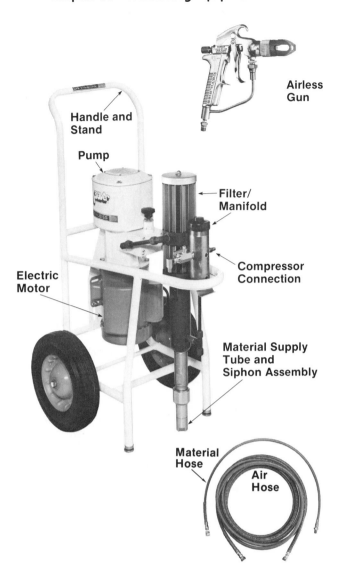

FIGURE 17-59   Typical airless spray equipment. (Courtesy of DeVilbiss Company)

equipment ranges from 1,500 to 3,000 psi. Actual pressure depends on the pump ratio of the equipment.

The airless system reduces overspray and rebound to a minimum, and application of the finish is much faster than with conventional atomized air. Because of higher pressures involved, the airless system can be used with paints and other materials that have a higher viscosity. However, this system of application can only be used where a fine finish is **not** required. It is often employed to apply the finishing coating in the truck fleet commercial vehicle refinishing business. It also has found a place for auto underbody and corrosion work (see Chapter 15). The so-called air-assisted airless system that uses some air to assist in the spraying operation tends to give a better finish.

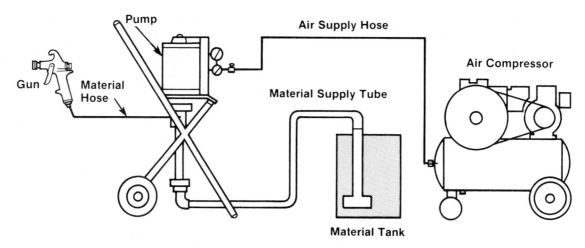

FIGURE 17-60 Typical airless spray equipment setup

Figure 17-60 shows a typical assembly of an airless system. The gun is connected to the pump with a single hose. When the gun is spraying, the pump delivers fluid under pressure adjusted by the air pressure to the pump. When the gun is not spraying, the fluid pressure and air pressure are balanced and the pump stops. The quality and economy of the finish is dependent upon operator skill, fluid preparation, and nozzle size. There are six ways that a painter can control the operation of this system. They are as follows:

- **Orifice size.** This determines the amount of paint sprayed through the gun. The range for automotive coatings is 7/64 inch to 1/64 inch. More paint will be applied through the gun with a larger orifice.
- **Paint viscosity.** This is controlled by the amount of reduction. Viscosity ranges can be from 24 to 36 seconds on a #2 Zahn cup (18 to 28 seconds on a #4 Ford cup).
- **Speed of the reducer.** Generally, use the fastest reducer consistent with flow and sagging. Airless equipment sprays much wetter than conventional air-atomized equipment.
- **Speed of gun movement.** Because of the wetter spray with airless, the painter will generally have to move faster than with conventional spray equipment.
- **Gun distance.** Because of wetter spray patterns, the gun distance to the work should be around 14 inches.
- **Coating material.** Prepare the coating material and use the air pressure as recommended in the manufacturer's instruction manual.

The basic operating techniques of an airless spray gun are the same as those for conventional guns. That is, the gun should be held **perpendicular** and moved **parallel** to the surface in order to obtain a uniform coating of fluid. The wrist, elbow, and shoulder must all be used. Once the best working distance (10 to 15 inches) is determined, the spray gun should be moved across the work at this optimum distance throughout the stroke.

Some object shapes do not allow this practice, but it should be used whenever possible. The proper speed allows a full wet coat application with each stroke. If the desired film thickness cannot be obtained with a single stroke or pass because of sagging, then two or more coats can be applied with a flash-off period between each coat. The spray movement should be at a comfortable rate. If the spray gun movement is excessive in order to avoid flooding the work, then the fluid nozzle orifice is too large or the fluid pressure is too high. If the stroke speed is very slow in order to apply full wet coats, then the fluid pressure should be increased slightly or a larger tip is required.

WARNING: An airless system maintains pressure after the system is shut down. High pressure can cause a serious injury. Before attempting any disassembly of the gun, system pressure must be relieved.

Electrostatic Spraying System

Electrostatic spraying utilizes the principle that positive(+) and negative(–) electricity mutually attract each other but oppose a like charge. Therefore, when paint particles are given a negative charge by a high-voltage generator (Figure 17-61), the particles oppose each other, causing them to become atom-

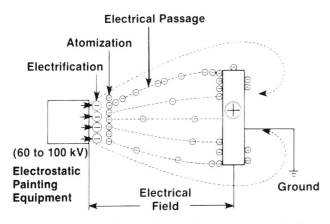

FIGURE 17-61   Principle of electrostatic painting

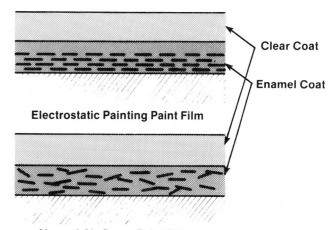

FIGURE 17-62   Electrostatic painting film and spray paint film

ized. On the other hand, because the adherend is grounded, it is under a positive electrical charge. In this manner, when high voltage is applied between the adherend and the electrostatic painting equipment, an electrical field is formed and the air in the field allows the electricity to pass through easily. In other words, electrical passages are formed and the atomized paint passing through these passages is sent to and adheres to the object that is being painted.

Advantages and disadvantages of electrostatic painting are as follows:

• Because the paint particles are drawn to the adherend by electrical attraction, there is less paint loss compared to normal spray painting.

• Because atomization is promoted by opposing electrical forces, a very good quality paint finish can be attained. This is particularly true for metallic painting because the metallic paint particles are formed into rows by the opposing electrical forces, providing an appearance that cannot be attained with the usual air spray gun (Figure 17-62).

• Paint adhesion efficiency is very good and, as a result, painting operations are fast. The reverse side of cylindrical objects, lattice work, and linear objects can be painted simultaneously with the front surface.

• Because the electrical potential in depressed areas is low, the adhesion is not as good, necessitating touchup.

• Unless nonconductors such as plastic, glass, and rubber are made conductive, painting is not possible.

As for portable electrostatic painting equipment, there are both the air spray type (Figure 17-63) and the airless spray type (Figure 17-64).

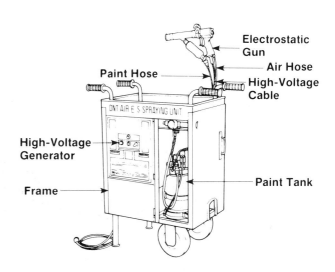

FIGURE 17-63   Air type electrostatic painting equipment

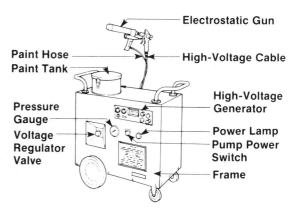

FIGURE 17-64   Airless type electrostatic painting equipment

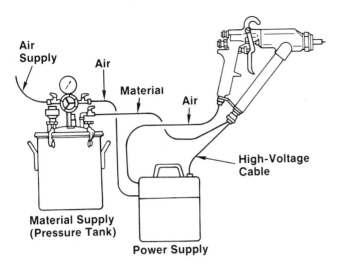

FIGURE 17-65   Atomization electrostatic equipment layout

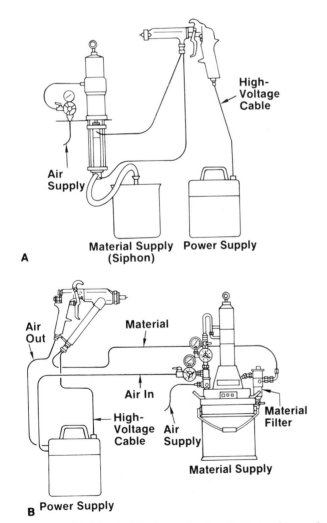

FIGURE 17-66   (A) Airless electrostatic equipment layout; (B) air-assisted airless electrostatic equipment

As with normal air spray painting, an air spray gun is also used for air spray type electrostatic painting and the paint is atomized by the force of compressed air (Figure 17-65). However, atomization is further promoted by the application of a negative electrical charge. Therefore, the paint is sprayed onto the adherend by both the force of the compressed air and electrical attraction. Adhesion efficiency is not as good as with airless electrostatic spraying (Figure 17-66A), but because the air spray gun is easy to use, this method is suitable when delicate spray gun manipulation is required. The air-assisted airless electrostatic equipment overcomes this problem to some degree (Figure 17-66B).

Like the normal airless spray method, airless electrostatic spraying utilizes high pressure to atomize the paint by injecting it through small holes in the nozzle, but it also gives the paint a negative electrical charge to further promote atomization. Paint is adhered by means of both injection pressure and electrical attraction. This method provides a very good adhesion efficiency and work is faster due to the large discharge volume. However, because compressed air is not used, injection energy is not as strong and air spray prepainting of depressed areas like the underside of the hood and inner side of the doors is necessary.

WARNING: Because of the high voltage involved in electrostatic spraying it is very important to follow the manufacturer's instructions on the use of the equipment and all safety procedures. It is important that the vehicle be grounded. It is a good idea to always ground the car's body (or frame) to a good ground source (such as a water pipe) as soon as it enters any spray booth (Figure 17-67). Grounding the car will help prevent dust and dirt from being attracted to the new paint by static electricity.

HVLP Systems

The HVLP, or **h**igh **v**olume, **l**ow **p**ressure, spray system (also known as the "high solids" system) uses a high volume of air, delivered at low pressure, to atomize paint into a pattern of low-speed particles. The most important way it differs from conventional spray systems is its high transfer efficiency.

The high pressure of conventional sprays tends to "blast" the paint into small particles. In the process, it creates a fair amount of overspray. The trans-

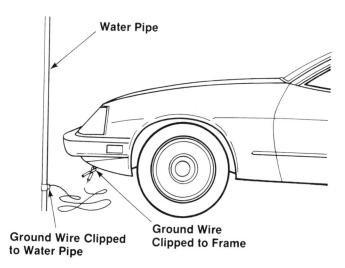

FIGURE 17-67 Grounding a vehicle in spray booth before spraying. *(Courtesy of Binks Mfg. Co.)*

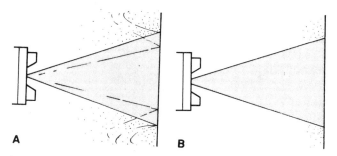

FIGURE 17-68 Operation of HVLP system

fer efficiency of high-pressure systems suffers as a result of overspray, particle "bounce," and blow back. In contrast, HVLP relies on air delivered at 10 psi or less to break the paint into small particles (Figure 17-68). As the material flows into the air stream, far less is lost in overspray, bounce, and blow back, hence the dramatic improvement in transfer efficiency. HVLP will work with any medium solids material that can be atomized by a spray gun. These include two-component paints, urethanes, acrylics, epoxies, enamels, lacquers, stains, primers, and so on.

High transfer efficiency is attractive for several reasons. But, perhaps the most compelling is the trend toward legislated transfer efficiency requirements. In California, for example, several new laws require the use of spray methods, which are at least 65 percent transfer efficient. Low pressure spray (up to 10 psi) has been approved, along with electrostatic spray methods based on the principle of the attraction between positive and negative electricity. Similar legislation is pending or under consideration in many industrial states. The forecast is that soon

high transfer efficiency will be a nationwide requirement.

The purpose of this legislation is to protect the environment, but there are other good reasons for HVLP. Higher transfer efficiency improves the quality of both the workplace and the finished product. Overspray not only makes painting work less desirable, it also reduces visibility, which contributes to mistakes and low productivity. Overspray is one of the main causes of paint operation maintenance, so cutting overspray cuts downtime. All paint spraying equipment can be affected by overspray, but the booth and its filters are affected the most.

To illustrate how much of a difference transfer efficiency makes in booth maintenance, consider that HVLP can be two to three times as efficient as conventional air spray. Depending on how it is used, conventional air spray is as little as 20 to 30 percent efficient. That means for every 3 gallons of paint sprayed, more than 2 gallons are wasted. With HVLP typically between 65 and 90 percent efficient, only 1 pint of paint would be wasted for every gallon applied. That is how a 3:1 difference in transfer efficiency becomes a 16:1 advantage in terms of overspray.

One of the most troublesome problems high transfer efficiency can solve is waste disposal. In air spray systems where overspray volume normally means using a water wash booth, the easy-to-handle dry filter media may now be sufficient, completely eliminating the hazardous waste that is often the byproduct of these systems. High transfer efficiency can also make existing water wash filtration systems virtually maintenance-free, particularly when using the new sludge removal techniques. Conventional air spray productivity usually does not suffer, either. Since more paint is applied per pass, fewer passes are needed to build up the same film thickness.

HVLP systems (Figure 17-69) are simple, consisting of the following:

- High volume air source
- Material supply system
- Special spray guns designed to operate with a high volume of low pressure air

Air sources for HVLP can be centralized, serving multiple guns, or can be dedicated to single-gun use. These sources will provide a range of delivery volumes and pressures. As a general rule, maximum pressure should be limited to 10 psi. It is pressure, not volume, that atomizes the paint.

Material can be supplied through pressure pots, quart cups, or other conventional supply systems. Flow requirements are usually lower than air spray systems for similar applications because of the

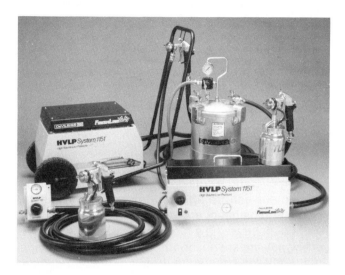

FIGURE 17-69   Typical HVLP system *(Courtesy of DeVilbiss Company)*

FIGURE 17-70   Typical HVLP spray gun *(Courtesy of Binks Mfg. Co.)*

higher transfer efficiency. Special guns (Figure 17-70) are used; they have no obstructions that could restrict the flow and increase the pressure drop. In many designs, the airflow through the gun is continuous; the trigger opens the material flow valve. Special caps and tips are also used to assure proper atomization. Because use of heated air is common, some HVLP guns feature insulated grips.

FIGURE 17-71   HVLP conversion kit used to upgrade a compressed air system *(Courtesy of Accuspray)*

There are two basic air supply designs. One generates airflow from a turbine generator, the other converts 80 to 100 psi shop air to the required 2 to 10 psi (Figure 17-71). Each of these approaches has advantages and disadvantages:

- **Turbine generators.** The turbine approach offers portability (Figure 17-72) that generally is not available when connecting to shop air lines. Existing shop air sources also may not provide sufficient volume. For example, in a body shop with its existing air compressor already working at full capacity, a turbine unit would work well, as it would not draw from the existing shop air. Due to friction, the

FIGURE 17-72   Typical small turbine generator *(Courtesy of DeVilbiss Company)*

turbine generates enough heat to provide moderate air temperatures. However, the temperature of the air is not always controllable, depending on such factors as turbine design, distance from the gun, and the insulating values of the air conduit. Assuming that the air intake system and its filter are well designed and maintained, turbine generators provide relatively clean, oil-free, and dry air. For turbine systems to be used inside the spray booth, they must be of explosion-proof design, which is relatively costly.

- **Air conversion units.** A standard shop air compressor such as described in Chapter 4 and an air conversion unit provide more control over the variables that can affect HVLP application. Heat and pressure are the two most important variables.

When fitted with air heaters (Figure 17-73), air conversion units offer controlled air temperature. The heat can be varied or turned off completely. Furthermore, they can deliver a consistent 10 psi or be regulated to provide somewhat less pressure. Air conversion units eliminate turbine maintenance and reliability problems.

The shortcomings of air conversion units primarily revolve around their relationship with the air supply. The shop air lines must be capable of delivering a sufficient volume of clean, dry, oil-free air. If the system is adequate for conventional air spray systems, however, the same volume of air will suffice with HVLP. Additional equipment and maintenance procedures could be required to assure that the air is clean, dry, and oil-free; otherwise, contaminated air could spoil the paint job. Again, if the air supply

system is maintained for conventional air spray finishing, existing equipment and procedures will do the job for HVLP.

Except for a few subtle differences, the HVLP and conventional air spray gun operate in basically the same manner. For instance, the HVLP gun should be held closer to the surface of the workpiece because of the lower speed of the particles. A rule of thumb would be to hold the gun 6 to 8 inches away when spraying with HVLP, compared to 8 to 10 inches for enamel. Greater distances result in excessive dry spray and lack of film buildup.

Many first time HVLP users get the impression that HVLP is slower than conventional air spray, but this is not always the case. Film thickness is often greater than conventional spray systems. This results in fewer total passes for the desired build. Sometimes the application **is** slower, but this is generally because the air source is not delivering sufficient air pressure. Remember that not all systems deliver their rated pressure under actual conditions. To many people, HVLP also sounds ineffective. Unlike conventional air spray systems, which sound like a leaking tire when airflow is present, HVLP is very quiet.

Table 17-8 details some of the features of the six types of spray painting. Although at the present, airless, air type electrostatic, and airless type electrostatic are used primarily in commercial vehicles, the environmental consideration in some states is toward a 65 percent adhesion efficiency. The only way this seems possible is by using electrostatic and air-assisted airless, and airless techniques. Spray equipment manufacturers are hard at work attempting to improve the quality of finishes obtained from these methods. In the foreseeable future, it is possible that electrostatic and airless spray equipment might be used on topcoat finishes.

AIRBRUSHES

Airbrushes range from simple types used for touch-up work (Figure 17-74) to complex and exacting tools used in custom finishing (Figure 17-75). The latter, of course, is generally found only in paint shops that do custom auto finishes.

It is important to select the correct airbrush for the type of work to be performed. Consider the size and type of the work to be done, the fineness of the line desired, and the fluids to be sprayed. Airbrushes used for custom auto finishing are generally in two categories: double-action and single-action types (Figure 17-76). The double-action brushes are more versatile than are the ones found in most custom

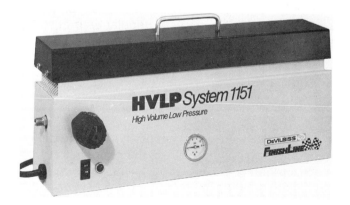

FIGURE 17-73 Typical air conversion unit (Courtesy of DeVilbiss Company)

TABLE 17-8: COMPARISON OF VARIOUS SPRAYING SYSTEMS

	Conventional Air Spraying	Conventional Airless Spraying	Air-Assisted Airless Spraying	Air-Assisted Electrostatic Spraying	Airless Type Electrostatic Spraying	HVLP Spraying
Adhesion of Spray Efficiency	20 to 40%	50 to 60%	40 to 60%	60 to 70%	70 to 80%	65 to 90%
Quality of Finished Surface	Excellent	Poor	Fair to Good	Good	Fair	Good to Excellent
Work Environment (paint mist dispersion)	Poor	Good	Good	Excellent	Excellent	Excellent
Paint Speed	Slow	Fast	Fast	Very Fast	Very Fast	Slow
Paint of Depressed Areas	Excellent	Poor	Fair	Good	Fair	Excellent
Gun Handling (partial repainting and touch up)	Excellent	Fair	Fair	Fair	Good	Excellent

FIGURE 17-74 The airbrush can be used for simple touch-up jobs. (Courtesy of Binks Mfg. Co.)

FIGURE 17-75 The airbrush can also be used in custom finishes. (Courtesy of PPG Industries, Inc.)

paint shops. They are available with a choice of tips to further increase their versatility. The double-action airbrush is usually recommended for projects that require very fine detailing. They produce a variable spray that works by depressing the finger-controlled front lever for air and pulling back on the same lever for the proper amount of color to be sprayed.

With single-action airbrushes, air is released by depressing the finger lever, while the amount of color desired is controlled by rotating the rear needle adjusting screw. While working, it is not possible to change the amount of color being sprayed because the operator must stop spraying to rotate the needle adjusting screw in the rear.

Airbrushes operate on a range of 5 to 50 psi pressure, with the normal operating pressure being approximately 30 psi. A scfm rating of about 0.7 is sufficient for most airbrushes. Compact compressors (Figure 17-77) are very popular with custom auto painters.

17.6 SPRAY BOOTHS

The body shop, by necessity, is continually generating dust and dirt from the pounding out of metal, grinding of welds and fillers, sanding, and similar dirt creating operations—the very worst kind of environment in which to paint cars. Much of this dust is so fine it can scarcely be controlled.

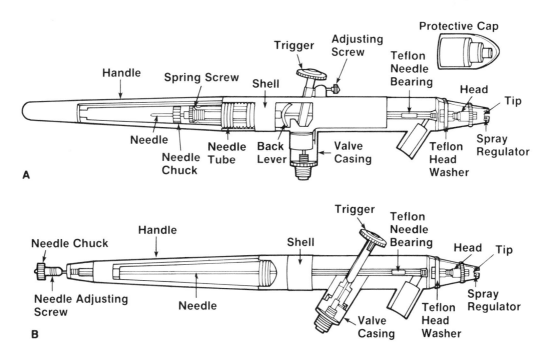

FIGURE 17-76   (A) Double-action and (B) single-action airbrush. *(Courtesy of Badger Air-Brush Co.)*

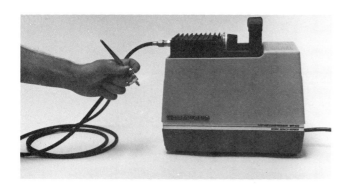

FIGURE 17-77   A typical airbrush operated with a diaphragm type compressor

Providing a clean, safe, well-illuminated enclosure for painting is the primary purpose of a spray booth (Figure 17-78). It isolates the painting operation from the dirt and dust producing activities and confines and exhausts the volatile fumes created by spraying automotive finishes. Modern spray booths are scientifically designed to create the proper air movement, provide necessary lighting, and enclose the painting operation safely. In addition, their construction and performance must conform to federal, state, and even local safety codes, not to mention those of insurance underwriters. In some areas, automatically operated fire extinguishers are required because of the highly explosive nature of the refinishing materials.

The spray booth should be located as far removed as possible from the area where dust and dirt are prevalent. Therefore, it should be isolated from the mechanical and metalworking portions of the shop wherever possible. This can be accomplished with partitions, walls, or a separate building arrangement. A workbench should be handy in the spray booth for thinning the paint and filling the gun cup. Paint storage should, however, be outside the booth, but nearby.

FIGURE 17-78   Inside a well-designed spray booth. *(Courtesy of Sherwin-Williams Co.)*

When a spray booth must be located in the same room with metalworking stalls or other locations where there is excessive dust, the intake air can be drawn from the outdoors, utilizing an air replacement system. This arrangement greatly reduces the number of filter changes required in the booth doors and reduces the chances of ruined paint jobs.

If the volume of paint work is sufficient, a straight line work flow is recommended (Figure 17-79). Utilizing a drive-thru type spray booth, the layout is designed for maximum efficiency of manpower and equipment. Jobs are started in the metalworking stalls in the normal manner. From this point the work flows in a production line manner through each of the various stages all the way to final clean-up. Cleaning preparation should be done outside the booth area. Steam clean the underbody of the vehicle thoroughly and air dust the entire vehicle before moving it into the spray booth. After the vehicle is in the booth, close the booth doors tightly and tack-rag the entire vehicle again before proceeding with the painting operation. All spray booth doors must be kept tightly closed during painting. If it becomes necessary to open the door, be sure the fan and air supply are turned off. In fact, many spray booths are equipped with door switches that shut off the air supply and fan when the doors are opened. The air compressor should be outside the booth with the air delivery pipes slanting back toward the compressor. The drive-thru principle can be used in a one or two booth arrangement (Figure 17-80).

An air make-up or replacement system is important because of the large volume of air exhausted from spray booths. This exhaust is sufficient to produce two or more complete changes every hour. Under such conditions in winter, the spray area can become cold and uncomfortable. Finish problems can arise because of spraying with cold materials on cold products in cold air. An air make-up system will provide even temperatures and clean filtered air as well as to assure proper booth performance. Sometimes paint shops employ an independent air replacement system specifically designed for the spray booth (Figure 17-81). This provides clean, dry, filtered air from the outside to the booth, heating the air in colder weather. Replacement air can be delivered to the general shop area or directly into the booth for a completely closed system.

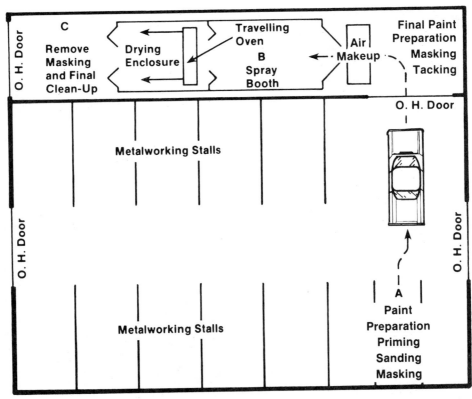

FIGURE 17-79 Typical body shop layout showing straight line work flow finishing operation. The important stops in such an arrangement are: (A) paint preparation, (B) spray booth, and (C) final clean-up.

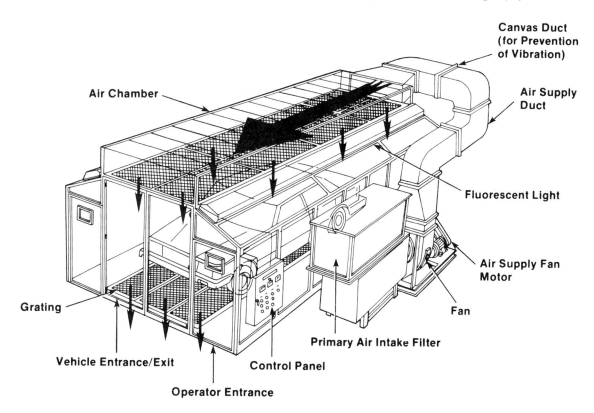

Canvas Duct
(for Prevention
of Vibration)

Air Supply
Duct

Air Chamber

Fluorescent Light

Air Supply Fan
Motor

Fan

Grating

Primary Air Intake Filter

Vehicle Entrance/Exit

Control Panel

Operator Entrance

ONE ROOM BOOTH

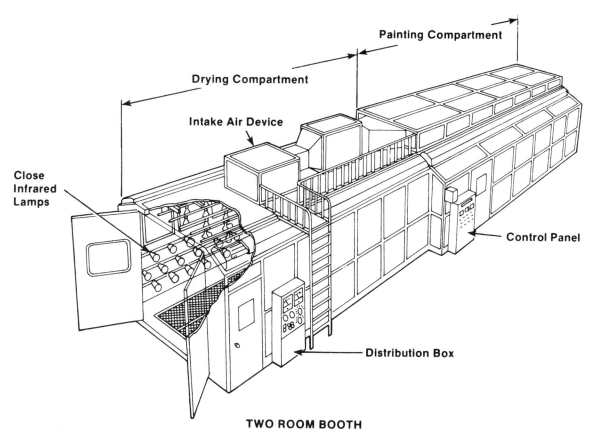

Painting Compartment

Drying Compartment

Intake Air Device

Close
Infrared
Lamps

Control Panel

Distribution Box

TWO ROOM BOOTH

FIGURE 17-80   Typical one and two room booths. *(Courtesy of Toyota Motor Corp.)*

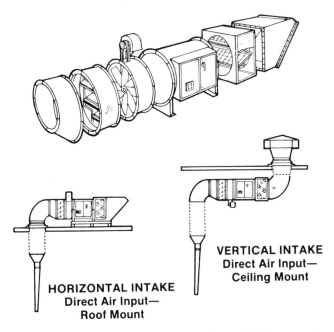

HORIZONTAL INTAKE
Direct Air Input—
Roof Mount

VERTICAL INTAKE
Direct Air Input—
Ceiling Mount

FIGURE 17-81 Air replacement is available in various configurations to fit building needs.

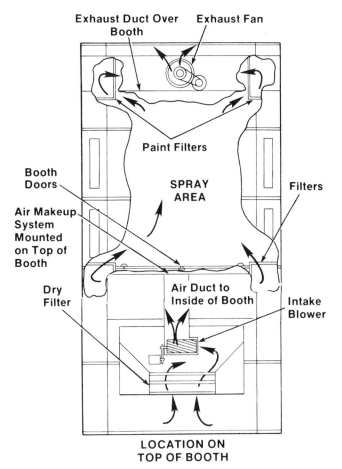

FIGURE 17-82 A typical make-up air system

There are four air make-up systems in use today:

- Regular flow booth
- Reverse flow booth
- Crossdraft booth
- Downdraft booth

Both the regular and reverse flow types of booths were once considered standards in spray booth construction. However, since the late 1970s, they have been replaced to a great degree by crossdraft and downdraft airflow types.

As shown in Figure 17-82, in the regular system, the vehicle enters at the air inlet and follows the airflow to the exhaust area at the other end of the booth; that is, the airflow is from back to front. In the reverse flow process, the airflow is from front to back. The reverse flow type of booth generally has a solid back (Figure 17-83), while a regular flow usually is of the drive-thru style. It is interesting to note a good number of vehicles that were sprayed in a reverse type of booth were backed in.

The most popular air movement system employed in a spray booth today is the downdraft type. This system utilizes the downdraft principle of air movement, the same as huge auto production line spray booths. The downward directional flow of air from the ceiling of the booth to the exhaust pit creates an envelope of air passing by the surface of the vehicle. This process of taking clean, tempered air and directing it downward past the surface of the

vehicle serves to eliminate contamination and overspray from settling on the freshly painted surface of the vehicle (Figure 17-84). This process ensures a cleaner paint job. But just as important, this air movement helps to remove toxic vapors and harmful overspray from the breathing zone of the painter, providing a safer working environment. The downdraft booths as illustrated in Figure 17-85 are available in raised platform models and floor models and are usually of the drive-thru type. Some more important features of this system are shown in Figure 17-86.

Crossdraft systems are less expensive to install since they do not require a raised platform or a pit under the booth. The crossdraft type booth provides a horizontal airflow and many of the advantages of the downdraft system. It is available in solid back and drive-thru models.

Because of the many OSHA, state, and local regulations regarding spray booths, the use of solid concrete or cinder block types has been on a decline. While many are still in use, building a "do-it-yourself" spray booth is seldom done today.

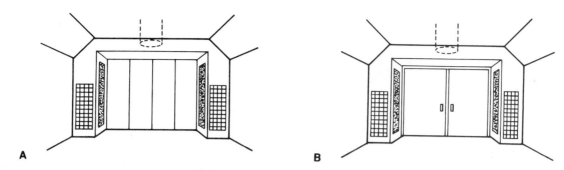

FIGURE 17-83   Two designs of spray booths: (A) solid back and (B) drive-thru. The solid design is generally found in smaller shops.

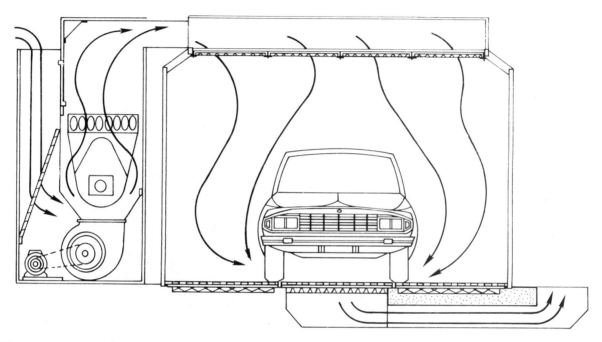

FIGURE 17-84   The airflow pattern of a downdraft spray booth. The location of the intake and exhaust system will depend on the system manufacturer. One downdraft airflow system is illustrated in Figure 1-45.

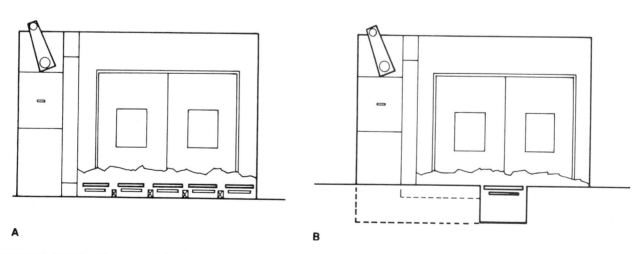

FIGURE 17-85   Two models of downdraft booths: (A) raised platform model and (B) floor model with underfloor pit.

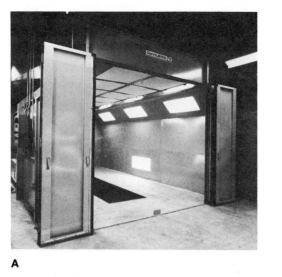

A

B

C

D

FIGURE 17–86   Important parts of a downdraft refinish system include: (A) spray booth itself; (B) air replacement unit; (C) ceiling plenum and filter system; and (D) floor gratings and filter. *(Courtesy of DeVilbiss Co.)*

Air Filtration Systems

The most important safety feature of spray booths is the filtration system. Currently there are two commonly in use (Figure 17–87): wet filtration system and dry filtration system.

Wet Filtration Systems

Although wet or wash filtration has a higher initial cost than a dry filter system, it has grown in popularity with downdraft spray booths because it does an excellent job of removing paint particles from exhaust air regardless of the paint viscosity or drying speed. It can handle a variety of spray materials, is capable of high volume production, eliminates the expense and inconvenience of changing

exhaust filters, and is accepted by most local fire codes.

The typical downdraft booth with a water filtration system has ducts or an open grate floor under which a layer of water circulates to carry away overspray. The contaminated water is routed through the system. Exhaust air from the booth is purified by routing it through a water curtain wash system. A continuous spray mist of water scrubs the paint particles from the air, while baffles reverse the direction of the airflow to help separate out the particles by centrifugal action. The air that emerges is as clean or cleaner than that achieved by a quality dry filtration system (Figure 17-88).

There are wide varieties of wet filtration configurations available, with some offering various advantages over others. There are also "pumpless"

Wet or Wash Type

Filter Type

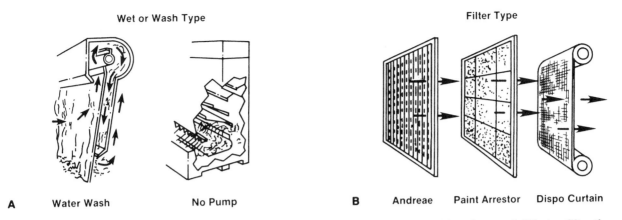

A   Water Wash   No Pump

B   Andreae   Paint Arrestor   Dispo Curtain

FIGURE 17-87   **Different methods of spray booth filtration: (A) wet filtration and (B) dry filtration**

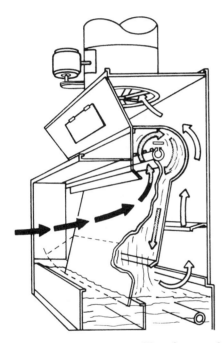

FIGURE 17-88   **Dry air filtration system**

FIGURE 17-89   **Commercial paint waste pickup service**

wash systems. Instead of using a curtain spray wash to clean the air, the air is pulled through a pan of water and series of baffles by a high-pressure fan. This creates a swirling mixture that washes out the paint particles. The water is treated with an anti-coagulant additive so the paint particles settle to the bottom (in pump wash systems, the paint rises to the top). Pumpless wash systems are very sensitive to the water level and air pressure, so proper maintenance is very important.

The paint residue that collects in the water must be removed periodically, and the water kept at the specified level. The rate at which water evaporates from the system will depend on temperature, humid-

ity, the volume of usage, and the design of the system. It is necessary to add makeup water at least once a week unless the booth has an automatic water makeup feature. Water additives must be placed in the water to prevent the growth of bacterial/germ growth and an unpleasant smell.

The paint residue that is separated from the water hardens and can be disposed of by bagging it and, in most areas, sending it to a landfill (Figure 17-89). One innovative approach is to "recycle" it by mixing it with undercoating and spraying it under cars. As for water disposal, there is no reason to worry about it because the water is continuously recycled. If the system has to be drained for some reason, the waste water would have to be disposed of in accordance with whatever local sewer restrictions might apply.

Dry Filtration Systems

Dry filtration systems come in various configurations and filter media (paper, cotton, fiberglass, polyester, and so on). What is notable is the efficiency of this system and how quickly the filters clog up. Dry filters work like a sieve. They mechanically filter out particles of paint and dirt by trapping the particles as air flows through the filter. Some are also coated with a tacky substance so particles will adhere to the surface of the fibers.

Most dry filtration systems can remove virtually 100 percent of the particulates that are large enough to cause a noticeable blemish in a paint job. Anything larger than about 14 microns (0.0005 inch, the smallest particle that can be seen by the naked eye) can leave a noticeable speck in the paint. Anything smaller than 14 microns is usually encapsulated in the paint and will not cause problems. Most of the filters that are used in the ceilings of downdraft booths or the doors of crossdraft booths today will stop anything larger than about 10 microns from getting through.

As a filter traps more particles, it becomes more dense and thus more efficient. But at the same time, it also offers increasingly greater resistance to the flow of air. Eventually the point is reached where the filter restricts airflow through the spray booth. Ideally, the filter should be changed before it reaches that point. It is something that has to be watched very closely.

The best way to judge a filter's condition is to measure its air resistance with a water column pressure differential gauge (manometer or magnehelic gauge). Some booths have built-in gauges, others do not (Figure 17-90). Comparing air pressure upstream of the filter to that which is downstream is a good indication of whether or not it is time to replace filters. The amount of restriction that is considered "acceptable" will vary according to filter construction and media, spray booth construction, and air volume. Some filters should be changed when there is as little as 0.25 inch difference in the water column side to side, while others can handle up to 2-1/2 inches of difference before they have to be replaced.

Because the amount of restriction that is considered acceptable can vary so much from one type of filter to another, it is important to check with the filter supplier before using any replacement filters that are different from those originally supplied. The type of filter media used will also have a significant bearing on maintenance costs, filtration efficiency, and filter longevity. Filters are not a generic product; one type might be much better suited to a particular application than another. That is why spray booth manufacturers typically put such a high emphasis on filter selection.

There are still other considerations to keep in mind when selecting a filtration system. In southern California, for example, shops over a certain size are now facing an additional air filtration expense. Neither dry nor wet filtration can remove harmful chemicals and solvents such as isocyanates from the exhaust air, so additional exhaust filtration is now being required. To date, unfortunately, the only "approved" methods of treating exhaust air are with an afterburner system (which is very expensive) or with activated carbon filtration. Some booth manufacturers claim that water filtration can "neutralize" isocyanates, but this has not yet been approved in California.

17.7 SPRAY BOOTH MAINTENANCE

Regardless of the type of filtration that a paint shop employs, spray booth maintenance is a prime consideration, not only from the standpoint of cost and convenience, but also because it is essential to achieving quality paint jobs. The best air filtration system in the world will not be able to do its job if it is poorly maintained. The first task in learning how to avoid dirt is to understand where it comes from. Anything that is brought into the booth can bring dirt with it. Potential sources of dirt include the air, the vehicle, the painter, the equipment and supplies, and even the paint.

Incoming air is a prime source of dirt. Dirt is generated by dirty filters, imbalanced air pressures, and open doors. Check the intake filters daily and change them as soon as the manometer indicates. When dust and dirt start to clog filters and restrict airflow, the velocity of air passing through the filters

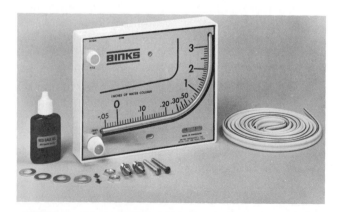

FIGURE 17-90 Manometer and its accessories. (Courtesy of Binks Mfg. Co.)

begins to climb. Increased velocity increases the likelihood of pulling dirt through the filters. Balance the input air pressure against the exhaust air to provide slightly positive pressure in the booth. This balance can change as filters load up and also differs from car to car. Therefore, check and adjust it with each new job.

Enter the downdraft booth only with the fans running. The positive pressure helps keep the dirt out. Once a vehicle is inside, keep traffic flow in and out of the booth to an absolute minimum. Also, make sure that the body shop doors are closed at all times during the painting operation. Opening and closing these doors can cause the booth balance to fluctuate, creating turbulence and dirt inside the booth.

The booth itself can be a main contributor to dirt problems through air leaks, poor housekeeping habits, exhaust air, and floor coverings. There are recommended seals for door frames, light openings, and panel seams that must be installed properly and replaced periodically. Heavy usage and temperature extremes quickly destroy these seals. Use caulking as an inexpensive gap sealant to keep dirt out of the air stream.

When operating the spray booth, keep the following points in mind:

1. Follow the manufacturer's recommendations for the minimum velocity needed to exhaust spray vapors properly. If that recommendation is exceeded, turbulence cancels out the screening performed by the filters. If the velocity is too low, the air will not move fast enough to remove overspray and airborne dirt before it causes defects.
2. Paint arresters are a high-consumption item requiring frequent changing. Check filter resistance daily on the manometer. When paint accumulation builds up, velocity goes down, and air movement is too slow.
3. In a dry filtration system, the filters must be periodically inspected and replaced (Figure 17-91). And when they are replaced, the multistage filters designed for the booth should be used.

WARNING: Clogged filters are a fire hazard; they could catch fire, under certain conditions.

4. Be sure the water level in the wet filtration system is kept at its proper working level and that the correct water additive is used.

FIGURE 17-91 Good spray booth housekeeping includes filter changes. *(Courtesy of DeVilbiss Co.)*

In order to get the best results from any type of spray booth, it is important to follow a good housekeeping program such as this:

- Periodically wash down the booth walls, floor, and any wall-mounted air controls to remove dust and paint particles. Many shops require that floor and walls be wiped down after every job. Always pick up any scrap, rags, and so forth.
- The booth is no place to store parts, paint, trash cans, or work benches because dirt will accumulate on these things and will eventually land on the vehicle. Keep these items in a sealed, ventilated storage area.
- Be sure that all bodywork and most paint preparation procedures are done outside of the spray booth. Make certain no sanding or grinding operations are performed in or near the spray booth. The dust created will spread all over and ruin not only a present job but many future jobs.
- Water is most often used to contain dirt. It is cheap and effective at trapping the dirt. But it can splash on the car midway through the job or, in a heated booth, dry out before the paint job is finished. If water is sprayed on the floor to keep any stray dust down, eliminate all puddles to prevent splashes. Water can also rust the walls of the spray booth, resulting in premature deterioration.
- Roofing felt held to the floor with duct tape provides an inexpensive method of containing dirt. It attracts and holds lint, lasts longer

than water, is not a hazardous waste, and does not deteriorate in the booth.

- Clay tiles look nice and provide an easy-to-clean surface, but are expensive and make it difficult to load a car in the booth on dollies.
- Concrete sealant provides a smooth, easily cleaned surface that is somewhat inexpensive. It should be noted that any slick surface treatment adds to the turbulence, while a textured surface tends to impede the turbulence or at least scrub the air. There are also strippable spray-on coverings. When the overspray becomes too thick, strip and recoat.

The vehicle itself is often the greatest source of dirt in the spray booth. Dirt hides in cracks and crevices, behind bumpers, and in the engine compartment. Even a thoroughly cleaned vehicle collects dirt when left in the general sanding area before being brought into the booth. When the spray gun hits this dirt at 50 psi, it kicks it out of its hiding places and deposits it into the finish. That is why a good prep job is so important.

 **SHOP TALK**

A cotton T-shirt is perhaps the greatest source of contamination and should never be worn in the booth. Lint-free paint suits, rubber form-fitting gloves, a dirt-free head cover, and the appropriate respirator should be worn inside the booth. Remain in the booth between the application of coats rather than risk dragging dirt back inside. If this is not possible, remove the protective suit inside the booth and leave it there. Upon returning, put the suit back on to contain the dirt collected outside the booth. (Anyone not wearing the proper attire should view the work through an observation window rather than risk contaminating the paint.)

Spray guns and cups should always be kept spotless inside and out. Do not use those dirt-collecting cloth wheel covers. Spray guns, masking paper, paint cans, tape, wheel covers, air transformers, hoses, respirators, coveralls, tack rags, and various other supplies can all collect dirt if stored in a dirty environment. All of these items should be kept in a filtered, ventilated storage/mix room. If subject to sanding dust, they will quickly ruin a paint finish.

Unbelievable as it might seem, dirt from compressed air lines often causes blemishes in paint jobs. Air transformers, with properly cleaned and

regularly drained filters, keep the air clean and dry. Oil and water separators are absolutely necessary to eliminate dirt and contamination.

A buildup of overspray can collect on the air cap and turn into a kind of fuzz. Clean the gun frequently to prevent the fuzz from blowing off and ruining a paint job. Paint will set up in and on the gun. If the dried paint flakes, it will land on the job and cause a defect. Clean the gun inside and out after each job.

Improper viscosity can cause excessive overspray, increased booth maintenance, runs or sags, pebble-dry finishes, and color mismatches. Always mix the paint according to the manufacturer's recommendations and check the viscosity with a Zahn cup and stopwatch as described earlier in this chapter.

Paints are complex formulations. A combination of two or more brands of ingredients can result in unbalanced viscosity, poor adhesion, dry spray, mottling, low gloss, off-standard soft finish, and solvent pop. Until wrinkle finishes become popular, avoid this condition at all times by using the manufacturer's recommended products.

Oil the fan pulley and motor bearings of the spray booth regularly, if required. Always switch off the main fan power supply before oiling the fan. If the spray booth is not properly maintained, it can cause finish problems (Table 17-9).

17.8 DRYING ROOM

A dust-free drying room following the spray booth will speed up drying, turn out a cleaner job, and increase the volume of refinishing work that can be handled. The drying rooms of more sophisticated paint shops have permanent infrared or sodium quartz units for the forced drying of paint, particularly enamels. These oven-like units (Figure 17-92) can

FIGURE 17-92 An infrared drying unit in place in a drying room

TABLE 17-9: TROUBLESHOOTING SPRAY BOOTH PROBLEMS

Fault	Result	Dirty Job	Thin Coats	Poor Opacity	Sags	Overloading	Popping	Softness	Overspray	Uneven Application	Recoat Failure	Fire Hazard	Water Splashes
Dirty filters	Vacuum in booth (hot air drawn from oven)	C				B	A	A	C	C,D	A		
	OR												
	Not pressurized (low air movement and dirty air drawn in from preparation area)	A	A*	C	B					C,D			
Breached or damaged filter	Turbulence	A							B	B,D			
	Over-pressurized				A†	A	A	A**	B	C,D	A		
Water level Low	Increased extraction					A	A	A		C,D	A		A‡
High	Restricted extraction		A*	C	B				C	C,D			A‡
Empty	Increased extraction with buildup of dry paint in reservoir	A										A	
Use of incorrect water additive, or incorrect use of water additive	Blocked water jets and filters. Formation of dry powder on anti-splash panels.	A										C	A
	E ⎡ Bacterial/germ cultivation (unpleasant smell)												
	Corrosion of paint. Paint deposits difficult to remove											A	
Flatting paper, rags, masking paper, old cans, and so on in booth.	Dirt accumulation	A										A	
Spraying on walls of booth.	Poor light reflection									C,D			
Loose deposits of dirt, dry spray, rust, and so forth on booth walls.	Dirt in atmosphere	A											

A Most likely failure to be associated with the fault
B Likely failure
C Failure less likely to be associated with the fault
D Will affect color of metallics
E Health hazard

* Poor build
† In oven
** Cold air forced into oven
‡ Alkaline contamination

Note: 1. Use only lint-free overalls and head gear in the spray booth. (Use them only for this purpose.)
2. Clean and blow off prepared vehicles outside the spray booth, paying particular attention to the engine compartment. Do not exceed 40 psi (3 bars).
3. Repair damaged or ill-fitting spray booth doors promptly.
4. Affix clean sheet of paper daily to spray booth wall for testing gun.

speed up the dry time of enamels as much as 75 percent. The use of forced drying on putty, prime, and sealer coats will reduce waiting time between operations and can also be used for fast drying spot and panel finish coats.

Infrared or sodium quartz drying equipment is available in portable panels for partial or sectional drying, or in large travelling ovens capable of moving automatically on track over the vehicle to dry a complete overall job. There are two types of infrared drying equipment:

- **Near drying equipment.** Because drying equipment uses lamps as the heat source, this type of equipment is easy to handle; the radiation angle can be varied easily; and construction, relocation, and assembly are simple, so it is the most common type used for automobiles. There are several shapes and sizes of this equipment, depending on

what it is used for, but the most common types are illustrated in Figure 17-93.

- **Far drying equipment.** Far drying or sodium quartz equipment affects paint drying by means of heat radiated from a tubular or plate type heater. The heat source is either gas or electricity. Far drying equipment also comes in various types and sizes, depending on its use (Figure 17-94).

Drying can best be accomplished in a separate drying chamber attached to the back of a downdraft system or conventional drive-thru booth (Figure 17-95A) where the travelling oven is housed and operated. In this configuration, the highest production is achieved since both the painting and drying operations can be performed simultaneously.

Drying can also be performed directly in the spray booth after painting. A storage vestibule is used to store the traveling oven until it is needed

TABLE 17-10: TROUBLESHOOTING DRYING ROOM PROBLEMS

Fault	Result	Popping	Softness	Dirty Job	Overspray	Impaired Durability	Polishing Impaired	Fire and Explosion Hazard	Loss of Gloss	Recoat Failure	Discolorate
Dirty filters	Diminished air velocity	A[1]	A[3]			C	B			A	
	Diminished oven pressure		A[4]	C	B[5]	C	B				
	Spray booth/oven pressure imbalance			B							
Filters damaged or breached	High velocity jet streams and turbulence	A[2]	B[2]	A		C	C				
Thermostat probe not correctly sited in moving airstream and/or insufficiently sensitive.	Excessive high/low temperature modulation	A	A			C	C				
10% Bleed duct closed 10% Make-up filter clogged	Foul oven Excessive fumes							B	A	A[6]	A[7]
Failure to remove deposits of rust, dust, and flaking paint from oven surfaces	Excessive dirt circulation			A							
Failure to clean unpainted areas on vehicles. Failure to clean masking or remask. Operators entering oven with dirty overalls	Unnecessary dirt introduced into oven			A							

A Most likely failure to be associated with the fault
B Likely failure
C Failure less likely to be associated with the fault
D Will affect color of metallics
E Health hazard
Note: Repair ill-fitting or damaged oven doors immediately.

[1]Upper parts
[2]Local
[3]Lower parts
[4]Cold air drawn from booth

[5]Drawn from spray booth
[6]Microshrivel
[7]Chemical reaction

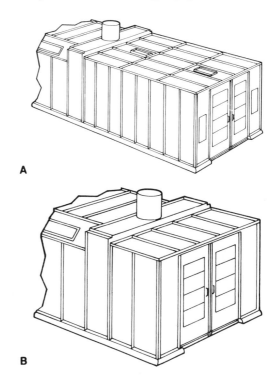

A

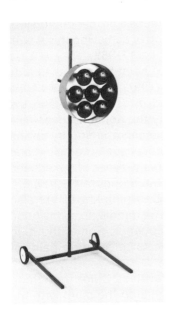

B

FIGURE 17-95   (A) Spray booth with drying chamber; (B) spray booth with storage vestibule

FIGURE 17-93   Typical near infrared drying equipment. The unit on the top has a moveable top and is portable, while the one on the bottom moves over the vehicle on a track. *(Courtesy of Binks Mfg. Co.)*

(Figure 17-95B). After the vehicle is painted, the oven is rolled out of the vestibule and into the spray booth for the drying operation.

When using a drying room, certain precautions must be taken not to destroy the finish. Table 17-10 gives the common difficulties that can be caused in the drying room.

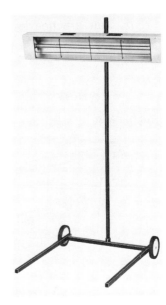

FIGURE 17-94   Examples of portable far drying equipment

17.9 OTHER PAINT SHOP EQUIPMENT AND TOOLS

There are several pieces of paint shop equipment that can help the refinishing technician perform paint jobs better. These items include:

- **Wet sanding stand.** A wet sanding stand (Figure 17-96) is used for wet sanding individual components or small parts. These cabinets are made by individual paint shops with the size and installation location depending on shop requirements and conditions.
- **Paint hanger.** Paint hangers are used to suspend or secure individual components or small parts for spray painting. As with the wet sanding stands, these are made by the individual shop in accordance with the shape of the item to be painted, the quantity required, and so on. Paint hangers keep the panel from dropping during painting. They must be made of a material that will withstand heat during paint drying. An example is shown in Figure 17-97.
- **Panel drying ovens.** These are small ovens used to dry test pieces. There are various types—from a very simple kind using infrared lamps to more complicated kinds with an electric heater, vent fan, and a timer for controlling the temperature and drying time.
- **Paint shakers and paddle agitators.** For a good refinishing job, it is very important that the paint be thoroughly mixed or agitated. In fact, with metallic paint topcoats it is essential. These paints contain metallic particles that are heavier than the paint itself and quickly settle to the bottom of the container. For this reason, metallic paint, as well as

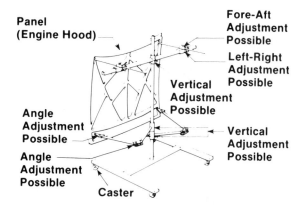

FIGURE 17-97 Typical paint shop hanger stand (Courtesy of Herkules Equipment Corp.)

FIGURE 17-98 The paint shaker shown here is compressed air operated. Paint shakers are also available that are electrically driven. (Courtesy of Broncrop Mfg. Co.)

most other types, needs a proper mixing job. The quickest method of achieving this is with a paint shaker (Figure 17-98).

Another type of paint mixer is the blade agitator (Figure 17-99). The blades of the agitator are dipped into the paint and the paint can sealed by the agitator cover. The cover locks over the can opening by spring action. These agitators usually come in 1 and 4 quart sizes and are the types of mixer used by color mixing centers (Figure 17-100).

- **Churning knives.** Churning knives are also used to stir paint. The handle tip is designed as a paint can lid opener. Some churning knives have a scale for measuring paint or hardening agents.
- **Color matching scales.** Color matching scales are used to match the paint with the original color or tone. There are volume type and weight type scales. The paint is matched

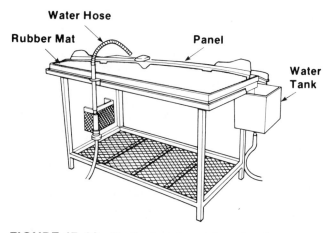

FIGURE 17-96 Typical wet sanding stand

FIGURE 17-99 The blade agitator type mixer unit fits right on the top of paint can. *(Courtesy of Dedoes Industries, Inc.)*

FIGURE 17-101 Weight type scales such as those shown here are used with most color mixing systems. Exact weight scales are available with standard or digital scales. *(Courtesy of Du Pont Co.)*

FIGURE 17-100 Most custom color mixing service centers (see Chapter 16) use blade agitator mixers. As shown here, the blades are built right into the shelf units. *(Courtesy of Du Pont Co.)*

against a color formula card. Use of these scales will enable even a relatively inexperienced person to match paint. However, a final visual check is recommended before using the paint since the scales are not always 100 percent accurate. There are three types of color matching scales:

—**Volume type scale.** This type matches the paint according to volume. The container for the paint to be mixed should have smooth walls. To match the paint, first set the color card into the scale, insert the ingredients as specified, and mix them.

—**Weight type scale.** This type (Figure 17-101) matches paint according to the weight of the ingredients. Weighing must

be accurate, according to specifications on the formula card, in order to obtain a correct color match. First, combine the ingredients and then mix thoroughly to obtain the desired color.

—**Computer type scale.** This type of scale allows very small quantities of paint to be mixed and its accuracy makes ingredients mix easily.

• **Masking paper dispenser.** A masking paper dispenser (Figure 17-102) allows dispensing

FIGURE 17-102 A typical masking paper and tape dispenser. The tape is automatically applied to the edge of paper as it is rolled off. *(Courtesy of Marson Corp.)*

FIGURE 17-103 Portable vehicle lift in refinishing preparation work. (Courtesy of Herkules Equipment Corp.)

of both masking paper and masking tape at the same time; as the paper is pulled, masking tape automatically adheres to the paper edge. Two or three sizes of roll paper can be set in the dispenser to help upgrade work efficiency.

- **Metal paint cabinet.** Paint cabinets are used for storage and stock control of paint, thinner, and putties. These cabinets should be selected in accordance with the amount of paint and thinner normally handled and the conditions of the shop layout.
- **Vehicle lift.** A portable vehicle lift, described in Chapter 4, is handy when preparing a car for refinishing (Figure 17-103).
- **Respirators.** Spray finishing creates a certain amount of overspray, hazardous vapors, and toxic fumes. This is true even under ideal conditions and there is no way to avoid it entirely. Anyone who is around a spray finishing operation must consider wearing some type of respirator or breathing apparatus (Figure 17-104).

🚗 **SHOP TALK** _____

The right-to-know laws and personal protection equipment for the body shop painter were described in Chapter 1. Most of the materials handled in paint areas can generally be considered hazardous. Therefore, the paint technician must know:
- *What the material is*
- *Hazardous properties of the material*
- *Operation of personal protection equipment needed for working with that material (Figure 17-105)*
- *Proper use of the protection equipment*
- *Protective equipment fits properly and is in working order*

FIGURE 17-104 Many painters wear a respirator when mixing paints.

There are two good reasons for wearing a respirator. First, some sort of respiratory protection is dictated by OSHA/NIOSH regulations. And second, even if this were not true, common sense would tell one that inhaling overspray is not healthy. Overspray contains particles of toxic paint pigments, harmful dust, and in some cases vapor fumes, which can be harmful to your health. Depending on design, a respirator can remove some or all of the dangerous elements from the air around a spray finishing operator.

There are three primary types of respirators available to protect the operator: the hood respirator, the cartridge filter respirator, and the dust respirator. These are fully discussed in Chapter 1. But, when there is any doubt about the respirator to be worn, always use the air line hood respirator.

WARNING: The precautionary measures mentioned here should prevent overexposure by inhalation, but if any symptoms of overexposure develop such as breathing difficulty, tightness of chest, severe coughing, irritation of the nose or throat, or nausea, leave the area quickly and get fresh air. If breathing continues to be labored, see a physician immediately.

It is important to note that symptoms of inhalation overexposure might not appear until 4 to 8 hours after the exposure. Depend-

JOB DESCRIPTION	RECOMMENDED PAINTER PROTECTION						
WET SANDING CAR WASHING		Goggles	Gloves	Protective Clothing		Boots	Knee Pads
SOLVENT WAX REMOVAL STRIPPING/PAINT REMOVAL	Air Purifying Respirator	Goggles	Gloves	Protective Clothing		Boots	
MACHINE SANDING BLOWING	Air Purifying Respirator	Safety Spectacles	Gloves	Protective Clothing	Hearing Protection	Boots	Knee Pads
BUFFING POLISHING		Safety Spectacles	Gloves	Protective Clothing	Hearing Protection	Boots	Knee Pads
PRIMERS (NON-CATALYZED) LACQUER AND ENAMEL TYPE	Air Purifying Respirator	Goggles	Gloves	Protective Clothing		Boots	
SPRAYING (NON-CATALYZED) LACQUERS AND ENAMELS	Air Purifying Respirator	Goggles	Gloves	Protective Clothing		Boots	
ALL CATALYZED PRIMERS AND PAINTS	Supplied Air Respirator	Goggles	Gloves	Protective Clothing		Boots	
PAINT AND PRIMER MIXING WET PAINT JOB INSPECTION	Air Purifying Respirator	Goggles	Gloves	Protective Clothing		Boots	

Air Purifying Respirator	Supplied Air Respirator	Safety Goggles	Face Shield	Safety Spectacles	Gloves	Protective Clothing	Hearing Protection	Boots	Knee Pads

FIGURE 17–105   Recommended personal protection equipment

ing upon the severity of overexposure, symptoms might persist for 3 to 7 days.

Because high concentrations of vapor will irritate the eyes, goggles or sufficient eye protection should be worn at all times during application. If spray residue finds its way to the eyes, they should be flushed immediately with water for at least 15 minutes. If irritation persists, see a physician.

17.10 BASIC PAINT SHOP MATERIALS

Paint shop materials differ from refinishing equipment in one key way: Paint shop refinishing materials are expendable. They are used up in the day-to-day operation; whereas, equipment is used over and over. Paint shop materials include:

- **Abrasive paper or sandpaper.** The rough side of paper is called the "grit side." Grit sizes vary from coarse to micro fine and are ordered by number (see Chapter 18). The lower the number, the coarser the grit.
- **Clean cloths or paper towels.** It is important that the areas to be painted are clean. Most

paint shops provide clean cloths or special disposable paper wipes. Whichever is used, these simple tips will help:
—Use clean, dry cloths folded into a pad.
—When using a cleaning solvent, be sure to pour enough onto the pad being used to thoroughly wet the surface to be cleaned.
—Do not wait for the solvent to dry. Wipe it dry with a second clean cloth.
—Refold the cloth often to provide a clean section.
—Change cloths often.
—Once an area is clean, do not touch it with the hands, as it might affect adhesion.

🚗 SHOP TALK ─────────

Cheesecloth strainers can add as much as a tablespoon of lint to the paint. The wrong mesh size can allow dirt to pass through the strainer that will later show up in the finish. Metallics require the coarsest mesh; clearcoats the finest. Clearcoats can develop small globs in the can that show up like dirt in the finish. Therefore, use only approved paper, or better yet, properly maintained metal strainers. Always strain the paint.

- **Tack rags or cloths.** These are specially treated sticky cloths (varnish-coated cheese cloth) that are used in the make-ready operation to wipe the surface clean just before the paint is applied. They should be used on the area to be painted to remove all sanded particles, dirt, old paint chips, and so on. Often the painter will simply blow off the area with an air nozzle or will use an old rag to wipe off the area. These procedures will leave minute impurities on the surface that will detrimentally affect adhesion and performance of the product. A tack cloth will pick up fine particles that are invisible to the naked eye. Tack rags should be stored in an airtight container to conserve their tackiness.

- **Paint paddles.** Made of either wood, metal, or plastic, paint paddles are used to stir the paint material. If the paddle is wood, it is recommended that the end be tapered to a sharp edge like a chisel. This will make it easier to dislodge the pigment and metallic flakes from the bottom of the can.

- **Strainers.** Consisting of a cardboard funnel with cotton mesh, a strainer is used when pouring thinned topcoat and other materials into a spray cup (Figure 17-106). This is done to make sure it is free of any dirt or foreign material.

- **Containers.** Paint shop containers come in six common sizes and/or shapes and contain various materials:

—Tubes that contain putty.
—Round cans such as gallon, quart, and pint containers for topcoats and some undercoats, including putty and body filler.
—Square cans for thinners, reducers, primer-surfacers, sealers, and clear topcoats.
—Pails that contain thinners, reducers, undercoats, and topcoats.
—Drums that contain thinners, reducers, and undercoats.
—Plastic containers that contain metal conditioner, body filler, polish, and buffing compounds.

Lids on round containers of a gallon or less—called "friction lids"—should be carefully opened with a proper opener. After pouring off whatever amount of material is needed from a round can, the lip should be wiped and the lid replaced tightly to form a good seal (Figure 17-107). A pouring spout made of masking tape will keep liquid from collecting in the rim, while a rubber mallet is recommended for tapping the lid around the edge. Proper resealing of the can will keep air out and minimize the formation of the film on the top—called "skinning." It will also prevent the loss of solvents. Screw top cans should be carefully wiped and closed tightly for the same reasons.

FIGURE 17-106 Straining thinned topcoat into a spray cup through a strainer. (Courtesy of Du Pont Co.)

FIGURE 17-107 Device for applying lids. (Courtesy of Dedoes Industries, Inc.)

 **SHOP TALK** _____

Keep the pouring spouts of the stirring heads clean to avoid a buildup of paint residues around the spout that can ultimately affect the accuracy of pouring. Wiping the spout after every pour is the simplest method. Alternatively, application of masking tape around the spout that can be replaced at regular intervals, removing solidified residues, is fairly effective.

Where there is heavy usage of undercoats, thinners, and reducers, the material can be purchased in drums at a considerable savings. When lacquer undercoats are stocked in large containers, the solvents keep the solids properly mixed, so there is less waste of materials. Drums of undercoats should be fitted with a gate valve for pouring, while drums of thinners and reducers should be fitted with either a faucet or a pump.

 **SHOP TALK** _____

Store clean empty containers upside down to prevent entry of dirt or other forms of contamination. Many shops now use can crushers to make container disposal easier (Figure 17-108).

FIGURE 17-108 Typical container crusher (Courtesy of Herkules Equipment Corp.)

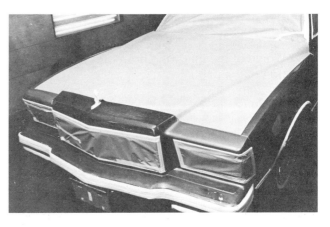

FIGURE 17-109 Masking paper and tape are used to protect areas where paint is unwanted.

Plastic measuring cups are used for matching or thinning paint. Generally, their sizes range from 1 quart to 5 quarts and they are made of easy-to-use and easy-to-clean plastic.

- **Masking paper and tape.** Masking paper is used to cover surrounding areas not to be painted so that paint mist does not settle there (Figure 17-109). It is necessary that the masking paper be capable of preventing solvent in the paint mist from seeping through to the surface of the object. Some paint shops use newspapers for this purpose, but this cannot be recommended because thin fibers from the paper come off and adhere to the painted surface, resulting in dirt. Also, solvent will seep through newspaper or even transfer newsprint onto the area covered.

Masking tape is used to stick the masking paper to the areas to be covered or it can be used by itself. Masking tape is made of different types of materials, such as paper, cloth, and vinyl, so that adhesion performance is assured regardless of the season or weather. The adhesive performance of masking tape does not change when heat is applied and will not leave traces of adhesive when removed. Also, it is easy to cut or tear off.

There are several types of paper masking tape depending on what it is used for, but they can be roughly classified into general masking tape used for air drying and heat-resistant tape used for baking enamel. The proper tape for the job must always be used. Full information on masking paper and tape and how it is used is given in Chapter 18.

17.11 REVIEW QUESTIONS

1. Which of the following promotes atomization of the paint?
   a. center orifices
   b. side orifices
   c. ports
   d. none of the above

2. Which type of spray gun has the disadvantage of having a small cup capacity?
   a. suction feed type
   b. pressure type
   c. gravity feed type
   d. both a and b

3. Which type of spray gun can be used with a high-viscosity paint?
   a. suction
   b. pressure type
   c. gravity feed type
   d. none of the above

4. Which sprays best at 19 seconds viscosity?
   a. lacquer colors
   b. alkyd enamel colors
   c. synthetic primer-surfacers
   d. all of the above

5. A spraying pressure that is too high results in which of the following?
   a. poor flow
   b. poor drying characteristics
   c. bubbling
   d. sagging

6. What happens when testing the spray pattern for uniformity of paint distribution?
   a. A vertical spray pattern is used.
   b. The trigger is pulled all the way back and released immediately.
   c. The pattern is flooded.
   d. None of the above
   e. Both a and b

7. Which coat helps to level the final cost, melt in the overspray, and control mottling of metallics?
   a. banding coat
   b. dust coat
   c. mist coat
   d. blending coat

8. Which spray booth provides the safest environment for the technician?
   a. regular flow booth
   b. reverse flow booth
   c. downdraft booth
   d. crossdraft booth

9. Which spray booth is the most popular today?
   a. regular flow booth
   b. reverse flow booth
   c. downdraft booth
   d. crossdraft booth

10. Technician A monitors the manometer readings hourly. Technician B monitors the manometer readings daily. Who is correct?
    a. Technician A
    b. Technician B
    c. Both A and B
    d. Neither A nor B

11. Which drying room problem will result in a loss of gloss?
    a. dirty filter
    b. damaged filter
    c. 10 percent bleed duct closed
    d. insufficiently sensitive thermostat probe

12. Which type of sandblaster can be used indoors?
    a. standard
    b. captive
    c. both a and b
    d. one of the above

13. What type of spraying system has the best paint spray adhesion?
    a. conventional air spraying
    b. air-assisted airless spraying
    c. conventional airless spraying
    d. HVLP spraying
    e. none of the above

14. Technician A uses the same spray gun for the topcoat that was used for the undercoat. Technician B uses a different spray gun. Who is correct?
    a. Technician A
    b. Technician B
    c. Both A and B
    d. Neither A nor B

CHAPTER 18

Surface Refinishing Preparation

The life of a finish and the appearance of that finish will depend considerably upon the condition of the surface over which the paint is applied. In other words, proper surface preparation is the foundation of a good paint job. Without it, there will be a weak base for the topcoat that eventually can result in the failure of the finish.

The word "surface" as used in the automobile refinishing trade is the stage in the painting process just before the application of the final color coats. To get a smooth, level surface is therefore going to involve the steps necessary to get good adhesion and also the subsequent filling and sanding operations. Any painter knows that the color coat does little filling of rough areas and that the finished job is no smoother than the surface over which these materials are applied.

18.1 DETERMINATION OF SURFACE CONDITIONS

The very first job for the refinisher is to correctly identify the surface and overall condition of the existing paint system. Failure to identify defects at this stage can be very expensive to correct. It could even involve the complete removal of the repair and the original finish.

- Clean the areas to be inspected.
- Look carefully for any signs of surface or other forms of film breakdown—such as checking, cracking, and blistering (Figure 18-1). Horizontal surfaces usually show the greatest film deterioration; careful inspection of the hood and trunk areas will give a

FIGURE 18-2 To check to see if rust has developed under a paint film, sand through a small spot and featheredge it.

good indication of the overall condition of the paint system.

- Note particularly the gloss level. Low gloss will often indicate surface irregularities caused by such defects as checking or microblistering, which will need more thorough investigation with a magnifying glass.
- Any signs of disfigurement or discoloration of the paint film due to attack by industrial fallout/acid rain must be completely removed.
- It must be determined that the old finish has good adhesion and that rust is not developing under the paint film. To test adhesion, sand through the finish (Figure 18-2), and featheredge a small spot. If the thin edge does not break or crumble, it is reasonable to assume that the old paint will stay on when the refinish color is applied over it. Developing rust can be detected by a roughness or pitting of the surface. The paint on those areas where either poor adhesion or rust is found must be removed to bare metal.

18.2 SANDING

Sanding is one of the most important steps of surface preparation. In fact, this operation is a standard part of most surface preparation procedures. Sanding prepares the surface for painting in several ways:

- Chipped paint (Figure 18-3) is sanded to taper the sharp edges that would show up as ridges under the new finish.

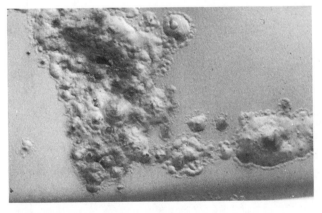

FIGURE 18-1 Carefully check the surface for signs of film breakdown such as blistering.

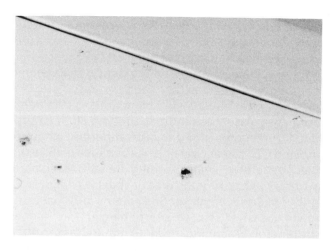

FIGURE 18-3 A chip or chips is a problem that can easily be solved by proper sanding.

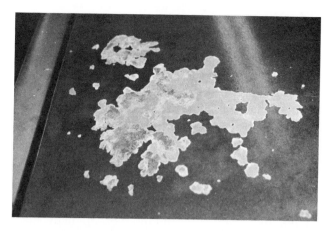

FIGURE 18-5 Rust must be removed by sanding before a new finish can be applied. *(Courtesy of Maaco Enterprises, Inc.)*

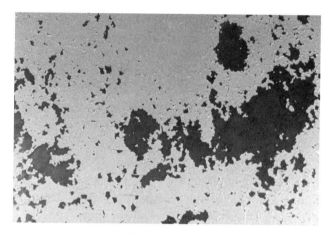

FIGURE 18-4 Cracking or peeling paint can be repaired by sanding. *(Courtesy of Maaco Enterprises, Inc.)*

FIGURE 18-6 Primed and puttied areas must be smoothed and leveled by sanding.

- Cracking or peeling paint (Figure 18-4) and minor surface rust (Figure 18-5) must be removed before applying a fresh topcoat. If not, these conditions will continue to deteriorate and will eventually ruin the new finish.
- Primed and puttied areas must be smoothed and leveled (Figure 18-6).
- The entire surface to be refinished must be scuff sanded to improve adhesion of the new paint (Figure 18-7). Scuff sanding removes any trace of contaminants on the existing finish. A clean, scuffed surface is very important for proper bonding of the new topcoat.

Because coated abrasives (sandpaper) perform the actual cutting and leveling in the sanding operation, selecting the correct abrasive is critical to the quality of the finished work.

FIGURE 18-7 Scuff sanding is used to improve the adhesion of the new paint. *(Courtesy of Maaco Enterprises, Inc.)*

18.3 COATED ABRASIVES (SANDPAPER)

When modern coated abrasives (sandpaper) are constructed, a flexible or semirigid backing attaches to the abrasive grains, which are bonded by an adhesive. Hence, the most efficient results on a particular application depend on the selection and manufacturing of suitable combinations of grains, adhesives, and backings available. The automotive refinisher must then select and correctly use the proper sandpaper product for optimum productivity, material cost efficiency, and the best finish.

ABRASIVE TYPES

The abrasive grains used to manufacture sandpaper products used in automotive refinishing are selected on the basis of their hardness, toughness, resistance to grinding heat, fracture characteristics, and particle shape. The kind of grain a refinisher chooses depends on the purpose for which the coated abrasive is to be used.

As for abrasive types, most body shops stock two: silicon carbide and aluminum oxide. Silicon carbide is a very sharp and fast-penetrating grain, customarily used (in paper sheet and disc form) for featheredging and dry sanding soft materials, such as old paint, fiberglass, and body putty. The major limitation of silicon carbide grain is that it tends to break down and dull rather readily when sanding hard surfaces.

Aluminum oxide is an extremely tough, wedge-shaped grain that better resists fracturing and dulling. Traditionally popular in coarse grits for grinding damaged metal, stripping old paint, and shaping plastic filler, numerous tests have demonstrated the superior performance of aluminum oxide sanding sheets and discs over silicon carbide on today's modern paint systems. Aluminum oxide is also preferred for use with today's paint finishes, which are predominantly basecoat/clear coat, have harder surfaces, and are applied in thinner layers than traditional lacquers and enamels. The blocky shape of the aluminum oxide abrasive when compared to silicon carbide makes it not as likely to create deep scratches right through to the base material and so reduces the risk of overcutting. The greater durability of aluminum oxide versus silicon carbide enables the abrasive sheet or disc to better resist edge wear and dulling for longer effective life on these harder finishes.

A third type of abrasive, zirconia alumina, has been developed through advanced technology and continues to gain widespread preference in auto body repair shops. Zirconia alumina grain has a unique, self-sharpening characteristic that provides continuous new cutting points during the sanding operation for reduced labor and increased efficiency and longer effective life compared to traditional abrasives. Also, the fact that zirconia alumina products run cooler is particularly important when removing OEM clear coat finishes because of the extra heat generated when sanding these harder paint surfaces. A hot-running disc or sheet will load faster as the material being sanded softens and "balls up" in the abrasive. The self-sharpening action reduces the amount of sanding pressure required—and often auto body professionals find that they can save money by using one grit finer and get a better finish. The net result is that zirconia alumina abrasive products are being recognized as the more cost-effective alternative to traditional aluminum oxide and silicon carbide for a growing number of auto body repair and refinish operations.

GRIT NUMBERING SYSTEM

The rough side of the sandpaper is called the grit side. Grit sizes vary from coarse to micro fine grades and are ordered by number (Table 18-1). The lower the number, the coarser the grit (Figure 18-8). For example, a #24 grit is used to remove old paint film; while a #320, #360, or #400 grit is used to sand the gloss of an old finish to be repainted. Very fine and ultra fine abrasive papers are used primarily for color coat sanding. The so-called compounding papers, the #1250, #1500, and #2000 grits, are used to solve problems on basecoat/clear coat paint surfaces such as those shown in Figure 18-9.

All domestic manufacturers conform to the same grading system for uniform consistency of standards. Differences in performance when using the same mineral, grit, bond, and backing from different manufacturers can be attributed to differences in manufacturing processes or quality, and/or operator methods.

As shown in Figure 18-10, the abrasive papers are available in various sizes and shapes. The most common forms found in paint/body shops are sheet stock and discs. The sheet stock—usually 9 by 11 inches—can then be cut into smaller pieces. Sheets are also available in jitterbug and board or body file sizes.

The most common abrasive sanding disc sizes for disc and dual action sanders are 5, 6, and 8 inches. Sandpaper disc grit sizes generally range from #50 to #400 grit. To apply the sandpaper to the backing pad of a disc, orbital, or dual action sander,

TABLE 18-1: TYPES OF GRIT AND NUMBERING SYSTEM

Grit	Aluminum Oxide	Silicon Carbide	Zirconia Alumina	Primary Use for Auto Body Repair
Micro fine	—	2000 1500 1250	—	Used for basecoat/clear coat paint system.
Ultra fine	—	800	—	Used for color-coat sanding.
Very fine	—	600	600	Used for color-coat sanding. Also for sanding the paint before polishing.
	400 320 280 240	400 320 280 240	400 — 280 240	Used for sanding primer-surfacer and old paint prior to painting.
	220	220	—	Used for sanding of topcoat.
Fine	180 150	180 150	180 150	Used for final sanding of bare metal and smoothing old paint.
Medium	120 100 80	120 100 80	— 100 80	Used for smoothing old paint and plastic filler.
Coarse	60 50 40 36	60 50 40 36	60 — 40 —	Used for rough sanding plastics filler.
Very coarse	24 16	24 16	24 —	Used on sander or grinder to remove paint.

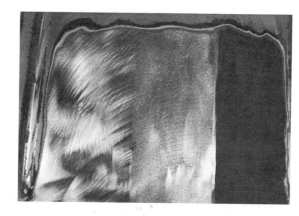

FIGURE 18-8 As the grit number increases, so does the smoothness. *(Courtesy of Maaco Enterprises, Inc.)*

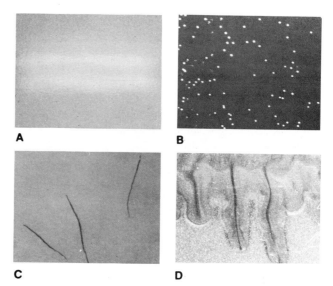

A

B

C

D

FIGURE 18-9 The micro fine grids are frequently used to remove such problems as: (A) orange peel; (B) dust nibs; (C) small surface scratches; and (D) paint sags.

squeeze a few drops of adhesive on the backing pad. Spread the adhesive evenly on the pad (Figure 18-11A). Then center the disc on the pad and press it into place (Figure 18-11B). When using a self-adhesive sandpaper disc (Figure 18-12), be sure to center the paper on the pad before pressing it into place. Immediately after finishing the sanding operation, remove the used sandpaper from the backing pad. If it is not removed right away, the adhesive will harden and cause the disc to stick fast to the backing

FIGURE 18-10 Various sizes and shapes of abrasive papers and discs

A

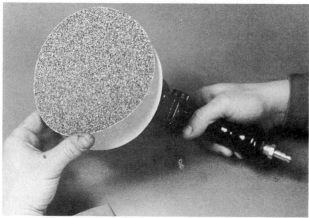

B

FIGURE 18-11 (A) Spread the adhesive on the pad, then (B) press the sandpaper disc in place. *(Courtesy of Carborundum Abrasives Co.)*

FIGURE 18-12 Applying a self-adhesive disc. *(Courtesy of Maaco Enterprises, Inc.)*

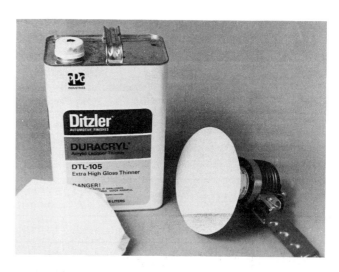

FIGURE 18-13 A solvent can be used to remove the sandpaper from the pad.

pad. Should this occur, use solvent on a rag to dissolve the adhesive and then remove the paper (Figure 18-13).

Grinding abrasive discs are used for rough jobs, such as grinding off rust and paint. They are available in numbers of #16 to #50 grits and in diameters of 3 to 9 inches. A dual action sander can be used to remove light rust, but heavy surface rust must be removed with an air grinder (Figure 18-14). The grinder disc is first assembled to the backing plate (Figure 18-15) and then the disc/plate assembly is attached to the air grinder (Figure 18-16). Some sandpaper discs are available with a center hole and are fastened to the sander in the same manner as the grinding abrasive disc. This manner of fastening is necessary in some wet sanding operations.

Although grinding discs are thicker and stronger than sandpaper discs, they are rather thin and easily bent. For this reason, the backing plate is necessary to provide stiffness for the revolving disc. Two types of back-up pads or plates are shown in Figure 18-17.

Coated Abrasive Surfaces

Coated abrasives are generally manufactured in two types of surface distributions (Figure 18-18):

- Closed coat abrasive paper
- Open coat abrasive paper

A closed coat product is one in which the surface grains completely cover the sanding side of the backing. An open coat product is one in which the

A

B

FIGURE 18-15 (A) Grinder disc and backing plate; (B) assembling the disc and plate using adhesive. *(Courtesy of Maaco Enterprises, Inc.)*

B

FIGURE 18-14 (A) Dual action sander and (B) air grinder can be used to grind rust and paint.

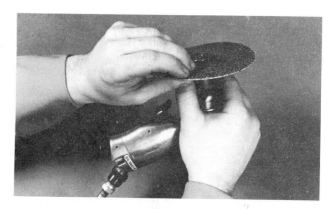

FIGURE 18-16 Attaching abrasive disc/plate assembly to air grinder. *(Courtesy of Maaco Enterprises, Inc.)*

abrasive grains are spaced to cover between 50 and 70 percent of the backing surface.

As for uses, open coat products are the popular choice on softer materials such as old paint, body filler, and putty, plastic, and aluminum—where premature loading of the abrasive would otherwise be a problem. Closed coat products generally provide a finer finish and are most commonly used in wet sanding applications.

In addition to open coat construction, many abrasive sheets and discs are surface coated in manufacturing with a zinc stearate solution to further prevent the premature loading of the sandpaper and to extend its useful life. This is particularly true of fine grit papers commonly used for scuff sanding old

paint and primer-surfacer and finishing body filler. During those applications, the materials tend to soften because heat is generated while sanding and loading the abrasive. Remember also that with zinc stearate-coated products, the coating breaks away from the abrasive grain during use, taking with it sanding residue, and thereby freeing the abrasive to cut longer.

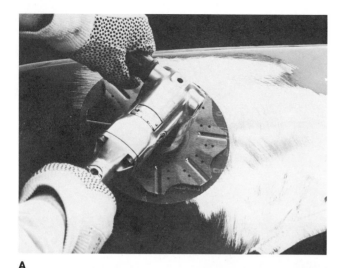

A

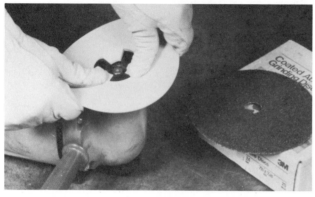

B

FIGURE 18–17   (A) Hard rubber backing plate and (B) a 3-inch fiber back-up plate

FIGURE 18–18   (Top) Closed coat abrasive paper; (bottom) open coat abrasive paper surfaces. (Courtesy of Norton Co.)

Zinc stearate remains an excellent load-resistant feature. However, with the evolution of paints, in particular today's popular basecoat/clear coat paint systems, certain elements of surface preparation become more critical, necessitating a possible alternative to the standard zinc stearate-coated sanding product.

One critical element is a contamination-free surface. Although zinc stearate can extend abrasive life, it also contributes another contaminant to the auto body surface. A clean surface under the basecoat is extremely critical for the success of the basecoat/clear coat paint job—more so than with standard enamels and lacquer. In the past, dust "nibs" or contamination under the first color coat could be sanded down, spot recoated, and blended in without detracting from the appearance of the final finish. With basecoat/clear coat, however, spot sanding of the basecoat is to be avoided without necessitating a complete redo, as any defects or mismatches are

magnified by the clear coat. With metalite flake and pearl color coats, subsurface dirt is a disaster. A key, then, is to minimize the contaminants on the auto body surface whenever possible. To this end, new sanding products have been introduced for auto body and paint professionals that employ high-tech, antistatic bonding agents to retard loading without zinc stearate.

In addition, new advanced abrasives such as zirconia alumina, anchored by resin type adhesives, are becoming more and more popular in the automotive refinishing trade because they cut faster and cooler. In other words, they will cut through paints, primers, and plastic fillers before they can soften and load the abrasive. And from a safety standpoint, sanding with products that do not have a zinc stearate coating creates less nuisance dust in the air as well as on the auto body surface.

WEIGHT OF PAPER

The proper selection of backings likewise depends on the application involved. Paper-backed abrasive products used in automotive refinishing are designated under uniform standards by all manufacturers as A-, C-, D-, or E-weight. A-weight paper is the lightest, most conformable paper backing available. It is popular for wet color sanding and dry finish sanding. The C- and D-weight paper products are progressively heavier, tougher, and less flexible. They are suitable for coarser sanding applications. E-weight paper is being more widely used by refinishing personnel for paint stripping and shaping of filled areas, as it is more durable than the traditional D-weight paper backings once popular for these applications. D- and E-weight papers are sometimes referred to as "production" papers because their construction produces a fast cutting, long lasting abrasive surface.

Cloth backings employed in products used by the auto body trade are likewise designated by a letter code. J-weight is a light, flexible cloth, popular for general clean-up, and deburring in sheet or handy roll form. X- and Y-weight cloths are heavier, more rigid backings often used in small disc form for tight-quarter coarse sanding.

Fiber backings are most common in grinding discs. This very tough, semirigid backing is best suited for heavy operator pressure applications, such as weld grinding and rust removal. The most suitable fiber backing for automotive application is 30 mil vulcanized fiber because of its extra durability and greater resistance to breakdown and edge chipping.

Safety Pointers With Abrasives

The following points must be kept in mind when working with abrasives:

- Grinding discs should never be run if the edges are nicked, torn, or show excessive wear. Whenever in doubt do not use the product. Recommended fiber disc grinding speeds are 5 inch, 7650 rpm; 7 inch, 5500 rpm; 9-1/8 inch, 4200 rpm.
- Fiber grinding discs should be seated flat against a back-up pad and never overhang a pad by more than 1/4 inch.
- When paper discs are used on a slow speed polisher, the recommended speed is 3000 rpm or less.
- Curled discs generally indicate improper storage and should not be used until the shape is corrected. Storage of discs at 65 to 75 degrees Fahrenheit will prevent excessive curling of abrasive products prior to usage.
- Ensure proper ventilation at all times when grinding or sanding and particularly avoid breathing dusts/fumes that are generated by "grinding aid" disc products. Refer to precautions on box labels, discs, or charts for detailed instructions.

18.4 METHODS OF SANDING

Refinishing sanding can be done:

- By hand or
- By power equipment

Most heavy sanding—such as the old finish—is done by power sanders. But some conditions—particularly the delicate operations—dictate hand sanding.

HAND SANDING

Hand sanding is a simple back and forth scrubbing action with the sandpaper flat against the surface. It can be achieved by following a general procedure such as this:

 1.   Cut the sheet of sandpaper in half crosswise and then fold in thirds (Figure 18-19).
2.   Place the paper in the palm of the hand and hold it flat against the surface. Apply even,

FIGURE 18-19   Fold sandpaper in thirds. (Courtesy of Maaco Enterprises, Inc.)

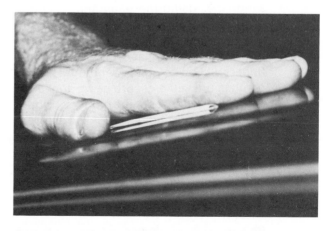

FIGURE 18-20   Method of holding the paper

FIGURE 18-21 Result of finger sanding. *(Courtesy of Maaco Enterprises, Inc.)*

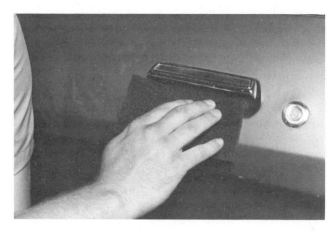

FIGURE 18-23 Sand around trim, handles, molding, and other similar items.

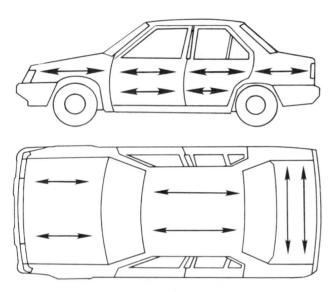

FIGURE 18-22 Sand with body lines.

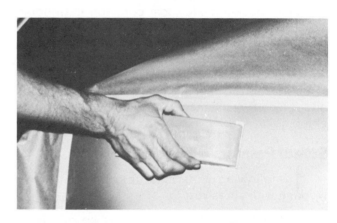

FIGURE 18-24 Use a flexible sponge rubber pad on convex and concave panels. *(Courtesy of Maaco Enterprises, Inc.)*

moderate pressure along the length of the sandpaper using the palm and extended fingers (Figure 18-20). Sand back and forth with long, straight strokes. If the palm of the hand is not flat on the surface, the fingers will be doing the sanding. This will result in uneven pressure being applied in the spaces between the fingers (Figure 18-21). Finger sanding should be avoided.

3. Do not sand in a circular motion. This will create sand scratches that might be visible under the paint finish. To achieve the best results, always sand in the same direction as the body lines on the vehicle (Figure 18-22).

4. Be sure to thoroughly sand areas where a heavy wax buildup can be a problem, such as around trim, moldings, door handles (Figure 18-23), radio antennae, and behind the bumpers. Paint will not adhere properly to a waxy surface.

5. Use a sanding block or pad for best results. To sand convex or concave panels (Figure 18-24), employ a flexible sponge rubber backing pad. Use a sanding block (Figure 18-25) to sand level surfaces.

6. Carefully sand areas where coarser grit paper has been used. Hard-to-reach areas are easier to sand with a small abrasive pad similar to the one shown in Figure 18-26.

7. When hand sanding primer or putty, make certain to sand the area until it feels smooth and level. Rub a hand or a clean cloth (Figure 18-27) over the surface to check for rough spots.

FIGURE 18-25 Use a sanding block on flat sur-faces. *(Courtesy of Maaco Enterprises, Inc.)*

FIGURE 18-26 Use an abrasive pad in tight spots.

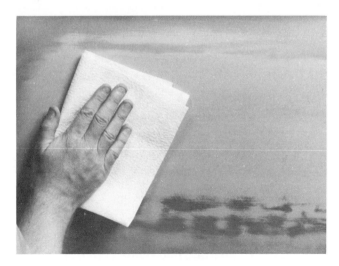

FIGURE 18-27 Feel for rough spots.

FIGURE 18-28 When wet sanding, water can be applied by a sponge. *(Courtesy of Carborundum Abrasives Co.)*

TABLE 18-2: COMPARISON OF WET AND DRY SANDING

Item	Wet Sanding	Dry Sanding
Work speed	Slower	Faster
Amount of sand-paper required	Less	More
Condition of finish	Very good	Final finish difficult
Workability	Normal	Good
Dust	Little	Much
Facilities required	Water drain necessary	Dust collector and exhaust necessary
Drying time	Necessary	Not necessary

—**Dry.** This is basically the back-and-forth procedure just described. But one of the problems with it is that the paper tends to clog with paint or metal dust. Tapping the paper from time to time will remove some of the dust. Another suggestion is to use zinc stearate-coated or dry-lubri-cated sandpaper, which tends to prevent clogging. Special-treated open coat paper resists loading for long life.

—**Wet.** Wet sanding also solves the prob-lem of paper clogging. It is basically the same action as dry sanding except that water, a sponge, and a squeegee are used in addition to the sanding block. Sandpapers are available in dry, wet, or wet-or-dry abrasive types.

When wet sanding, dip the paper in the water or wet the surface with the sponge (Figure 18–28). Use plenty of water, employing short strokes and light pressure. Never allow the surface to dry during the wet sanding operation. Also do not allow paint residue to build up on the abrasive paper. It is possible to tell how well the paper is cutting by the amount of drag felt as it moves across the surface. When the paper begins to slide over the surface too quickly, it is no longer cutting. The grit has become filled with paint particles or sludge. Rinse the paper in water to remove the paint and sponge the surface to remove the remaining particles. Then the sandpaper will cut the surface again. Check the work periodically by sponging the surface off and wiping it dry with a squeegee. This will remove all excess water, so that it is easier to evaluate the surface condition. It is usually wise to complete one panel or body section at a time, then remove the sanding residues with the sponge and dry off with the squeegee before sanding the next panel.

Once the wet sanding operation is completed, be sure that all surfaces are dry. Blow out the seams and molding with compressed air at a lower pressure and tack-rag the entire surface.

A comparison of the advantages and disadvantages of wet and dry sanding is given in Table 18–2.

POWER SANDING

As described in Chapter 4, there are four types of power sanders used by the refinisher (Figure 18–29):

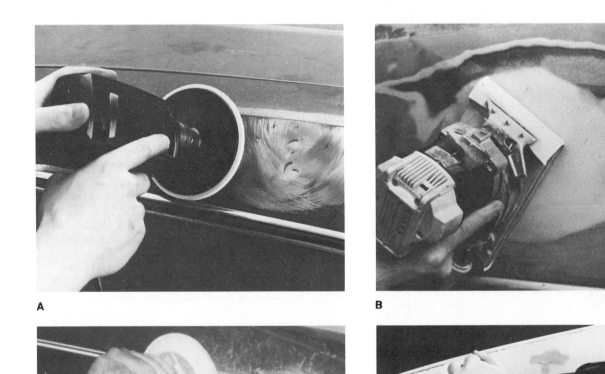

A

B

C

D

FIGURE 18–29   The types of sanders in operation: (A) disc sander; (B) jitterbug pad sander; (C) dual action sander; and (D) straight line sander

- Disc sander or grinder
- Orbital or jitterbug pad sander
- Dual action (DA) sander
- Straight line or board sander

All four types of sanders are powered by air or electricity.

In general, the type of power sander dictates sanding procedures (Table 18-3). Disc sanders or grinders, for example, have high-speed discs that turn from 2000 to 6000 rpm. They use circular discs from 5 to 9 inches in diameter and are used for such operations as grinding off an old finish. Heavier grinders (Figure 18-30) generally take a 9-inch diameter disc and—because of the obvious safety hazard involved—many have both a rear and side handle for better control.

When using a disc grinder, care must be taken to tilt it slightly so that only about 1 inch of the leading edge of the sanding disc contacts the surface (Figure 18-31). Never use the disc flat on the surface because it will twist the grinder and can even cause it to fly out of one's grip. Also when held flat, it makes circular sand scratches, which are difficult to get rid of. Never use a disc grinder at a sharp angle with just the edge of the disc in contact, because this will cause it to gouge or dig deeply into the surface. When a disc grinder is properly held, the sanding marks are nearly straight.

Orbital sanders have an eccentric (off center) action that produces either a partly circular scrubbing action (orbital pad or dual action types) or a straight back-and-forth reciprocating action (flat orbital or straight line type). Unlike the disc sander just discussed, orbital sanders should be pressed flat so they will not leave surface scratches. Orbital and board sanding can be done either dry or wet.

To operate an air sander, set the air pressure at 65 to 70 pounds. Then if right-handed, hold the handle of the sander in the right hand, while using the left hand to apply light pressure and guide the tool (Figure 18-32).

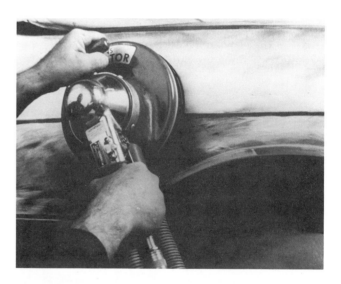

FIGURE 18-30 Heavy-duty sander/grinder in operation

		Normal Use						
Sander Type	Normal Area of Operation	Paint stripping	Feather-edging	Rough sanding of solder	Rough sanding of metal putty	Rough sanding of poly putty	Sanding of metal putty	Sanding of poly putty
Disc Sander		A	C	B	C	C	C	C
Dual Action Sander	Suitable for narrow areas	B	A	C	A	A	A	A
Orbital Sander		B	B	C	A	A	A	A
Straight Line Sander	Suitable for wide open spaces	B	C	C	A	B	A	B
Long Orbital Sander		B	C	C	A	B	A	B

TABLE 18-3: USE OF SANDERS

NOTE: It is important that the correct type of sander and abrasive paper be used for each type of job. Also, always wear a mask or use some sort of dust arrester when using the sander.
A Preferred
B Acceptable
C Least preferred

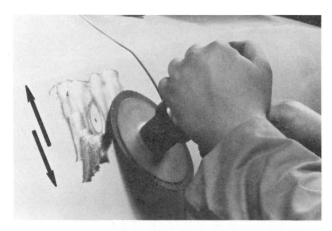

FIGURE 18-31   When using a disc, be sure only the leading edge does the cutting.

FIGURE 18-34   Masking can cut down the chance of surface scratch damage.

A

B

FIGURE 18-32   (A) Setting the correct air pressure; (B) handling a sander correctly. *(Courtesy of Maaco Enterprises, Inc.)*

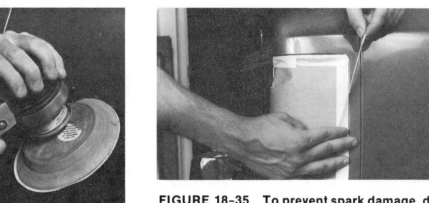

FIGURE 18-35   To prevent spark damage, double-tape all trim in the area. *(Courtesy of Maaco Enterprises, Inc.)*

To protect the chrome from damage, do not machine sand closer than 1/2 inch from the trim and moldings (Figure 18-33). Mask nearby trim, decals, glass, handles, and emblems (Figure 18-34) to prevent metal spraks from pitting these surfaces. In fact, it is a good idea to double-tape (Figure 18-35) all moldings and trim on the panel before sanding.

When using any mechanical sander—and particularly a disc grinder—keep it moving so that no deep scratches, gouges, or burn-throughs develop. And do not, except when sanding bare metal, power sand styling lines as this will quickly distort the styling edge.

FIGURE 18-33   Avoid ornamental and chrome items.

WARNING: Always wear a dust mask (Figure 18-36A) when sanding, and wear both a dust mask and face shield (Figure 18-36B) when grinding.

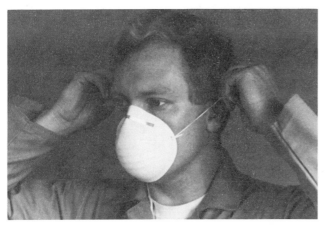

A

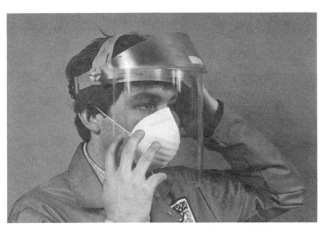

B

FIGURE 18-36   (A) When just sanding, wear a dust respirator, but when sanding and grinding, wear both a dust respirator and face mask. *(Courtesy of Maaco Enterprises, Inc.)*

When power sanding, replace the sandpaper when paint begins to cake or "ball" up (Figure 18-37). This paint buildup can scratch the surface and reduce the sanding action of the disc. Slowing down the speed of the sander will also help prevent paint buildup on the sanding disc and prolong sandpaper life. Generally, 6 to 8 sanding discs or pads will be required to featheredge the chips and scratches on the average automobile.

18.5 TYPES OF SANDING

There are several types of sanding that a refinisher must master. Some can be completed with power sanders alone, others with a combination of power and hand, and still others by hand alone.

FIGURE 18-37   Paint caked on sandpaper. *(Courtesy of Maaco Enterprises, Inc.)*

Most occur during the surface preparation stage, but one—scuffing—is done after undercoating.

BARE METAL SANDING

If the metal work has been done properly, little sanding of bare metal should be required. But once in a while the metal arrives very rough from coarse sanding in the metal shop. In such cases, it might be necessary to sand it with #50 grit to level out the burrs, nibs, and deep scratches. Remember, the smoother the bare metal, the easier the repair work. For more details on bare metal sanding, check **grinding** later in this chapter.

THOROUGH SANDING

Use this procedure for two specific conditions:

- Where the old finish is rough or in poor shape
- To level and smooth primed areas

Since the primer-surfacer is primarily intended to fill low spots and scratches, sanding must be done in a manner that will leave material in the low spots and cut away the high. Block sanding is highly recommended for this purpose. A guide coat is very helpful and assists in pointing out the depressions. Spray a very light coat of a different color material over the primer-surfacer. Quickly sand through the high spots, and the low spots immediately become evident. The sanding itself can be done mechanically or by hand with a sanding block. For the average hand wet sanding job, use #360 or #400 grit when applying an acrylic lacquer or enamel topcoat and #320 when the topcoat is an alkyd enamel.

Light Sanding

This procedure should be done on all areas where the old finish is in good condition. The purpose is to partially reduce the gloss and to improve adhesion. Use an orbital or dual-action sander, or do it by hand (Figure 18-38), but **never** use a disc grinder or sander.

If the new topcoat will be lacquer or enamel, use a #360 or #400 sandpaper. If it will be alkyd enamel, use a #320 sandpaper. For basecoat/clear coat finishes, proper surface preparation is critical. It is important to sand all surfaces to be refinished with #400 grit or finer paper. Sanding can be wet or dry.

FIGURE 18-38   Light sand when the old finish is in good condition.

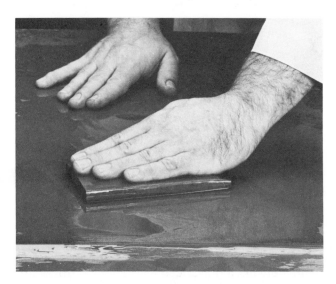

FIGURE 18-39   Use plenty of water when color sanding.

Color Sanding

To achieve the smoothest finish and best results in acrylic work, wet sand (Figure 18-39) the next-to-the-last coat of color with #600 or #800 grit paper.

Featheredging

If a new coat of paint were applied right over the broken areas of the old finish, the broken film would be very noticeable through the topcoat (Figure 18-40). So the broken areas must be featheredged. That is, the sharp edge of the broken film must be tapered down by sanding (Figure 18-41). Then the bare metal areas are filled with a primer-surfacer and the entire area is sanded smooth and level.

FIGURE 18-40   Squeegee helps show the feather-edge areas.

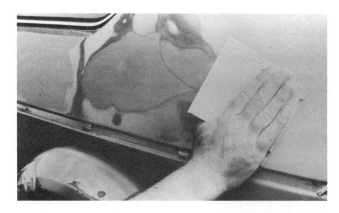

FIGURE 18-41   Featheredging tapers successive coats of paint and primer away from the metal to create a smooth surface.

FIGURE 18-42   Correct angle for featheredging.
(Courtesy of Maaco Enterprises, Inc.)

FIGURE 18-43   Crosscutting with a sander

Featheredging by hand is usually a two-step procedure:

 1. First, cut down the edges of the broken areas with a coarse #220 sandpaper.
2. Then, complete the taper of the featheredge by hand with a sanding block and either a #360 or #400 grit sandpaper and water to produce a finely tapered edge and eliminate coarse sandpaper scratches.

If the old finish is lacquer, an alternate Step 1 can be used. Cut down the edges chemically by using lacquer removing solvent. Roll a cloth into a ball or thick pad and soak with lacquer removing solvent. Then rub back and forth in a circular motion until a tapered edge is obtained. Finish the edge by light sanding with #360 or #400 sandpaper and water.

When featheredging with a power sander, an orbital or dual action type equipped with a flexible backing pad is recommended. Use a #80 grit for the rough cut followed by a #280 or #360 sandpaper for the fine work. When featheredging a chip, start by positioning the sanding disc at a 5 to 10 degree angle from the work surface (Figure 18-42). Using the outer edge, approximately 1 inch of the sanding disc, cut away the rough paint edges. Do not hold the sander at an angle greater than 10 degrees from the surface. Doing so will cut a deep gouge in the paint.

After initially leveling the rough paint edges in this manner, flatten the sander on the panel and finish tapering the paint layers by moving the sander back and forth in a crosscutting pattern (Figure 18-43). Start over the chipped area and work in an outward direction. Stop frequently and run a hand over the sanded area to feel for rough edges (Figure 18-44). When the surface feels smooth, and rings of

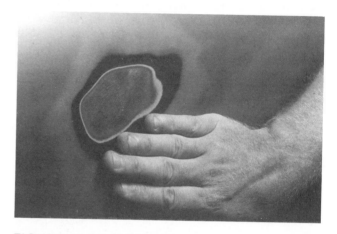

FIGURE 18-44   Feel for rough spots.

old paint and primer color are visible, the featheredging is complete.

Certain localized peeling paint problems can be corrected using the featheredging technique (Figure 18-45). Slowing down the sander's speed helps produce a smooth edge on brittle paint. However, if the paint is extremely brittle, it will continue to chip away as sanding progresses. When this happens, move the sander several inches beyond the edge of the peeling paint and feather an edge in the undamaged finish (Figure 18-46). Once the layers of paint film have been successfully tapered, remove the damaged paint between the feathered edge and the original bare metal area using a buffing action (Figure 18-47).

If the successive layers of paint are not properly tapered, a depression called a "bull's eye" will show up under the new paint finish (Figure 18-48A). This condition can usually be corrected by extending each paint and primer ring farther from the bare metal. Do this until the depression can no longer be

FIGURE 18-45   Featheredging brittle paint. (Courtesy of Maaco Enterprises, Inc.)

FIGURE 18-46   Feathering an edge

FIGURE 18-47   Removing brittle paint

felt when a hand is run over the featheredged area. Occasionally, when featheredging areas with several layers of paint, primer and putty might be necessary to fill the bull's eye to the level of the existing film buildup (Figure 18-48B).

GRINDING

Start grinding with a #24 grit disc (Figure 18-49) followed by a #50 grit disc to remove the #24 sand scratches. If possible, do not operate a grinder at full. The high speed could cause the metal to heat up and warp or cause the disc to break.

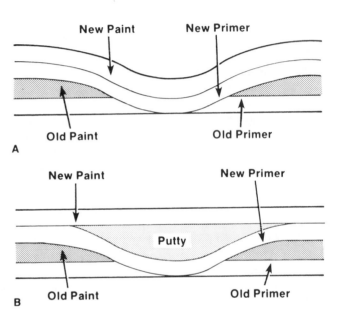

FIGURE 18-48   Causes of "bull's eye" and how to correct it

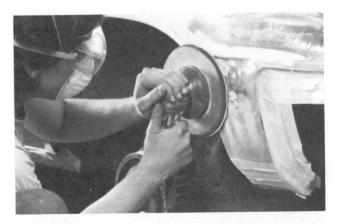

FIGURE 18-49   When grinding, first use a #24 grit disc on a disc sander/grinder. (Courtesy of Du Pont Co.)

Safety Pointers When Grinding

In addition to the safety procedures given in Chapter 4, the following pointers must be remembered:

- When disc grinding, hold the grinder firmly at a low 5 to 10 degree angle to the work surface.
- Grinding should direct dust away from the face and toward the floor.
- Be conscious of the grinder or polisher cord at all times to prevent entanglement.
- Do not grind or sand too close to trim, bumpers, or any projection that might snag or catch the grinding disc's edge.
- Never start or stop a disc grinder in contact with the work surface.
- Never "free run" a grinding disc or set a grinder down until it stops completely.
- Make certain the back-up pads are designed for the work, free of cuts or nicks at the edge or at the center hole. Make certain pads are seated on the shaft properly. Check for proper balance. Retainer nuts should not show excessive thread wear, must have at least three-thread contact, and should not cause damage to the grinding discs.
- Back-up pads for use with the "self-adhesive" type discs must be dry, clean, and dust free. Avoid using pads with frayed, torn, dirty, or paper contaminated surface. If necessary wipe pad face with clean dry cloth. Do not immerse pad or clean pad face with solvent.

Scuffing

Once all surface reconditioning is completed, the final sanding operation is to scuff the surface to remove nibs and dust specks on nonsanding primers, sealers, or where dirt shows up. It should be done with a very fine grit sandpaper such as #400.

Place the paper in the palm of the hand and hold it flat against the surface. Apply even, moderate pressure along the length of the sandpaper using the palm and extended fingers. Sand back and forth with long, straight strokes. Remember that scuffing the surface is only to improve adhesion of the new paint. Care should be taken not to cut into the film. When sanding large panels, one stroke back and forth in an overlapping pattern will be sufficient. More sanding than this is not only a waste of energy, but could possibly risk creating scratches that could show up under the new finish. Do not oversand.

Sand Scratch Swelling

The first requirement for a good paint job is a smooth surface. The body technician can make it doubly hard for the painter if the metal is not properly finished. The best practice is to use a #24 disc for restoring the contours and finishing off the metal with #50 and then #80 paper. Even this method will not eliminate some sources of sand scratches (Figure 18-50) because there are often little burrs or fins on the crests of the scratches, and these cause uneven shrinkage in the surfacer coat (Figure 18-51A). To eliminate them, sand with #220 paper to round off the tops of these crests (Figure 18-51B). Do not

FIGURE 18-50   Any sanding operation, unless extreme care is taken and #800 grit or finer grit is used, is going to produce some scratches.

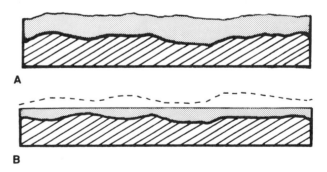

FIGURE 18-51   Enlarged cross-section of rough metal. (A) Some metal coated with primer-surfacer. Surface of undercoat follows approximate contours of original metal when thoroughly dry. (B) Sanding levels off high spots, producing a flat, smooth surface. If not dry when sanded, further shrinking over deep fills produces uneven surface and shows abrasive marks.

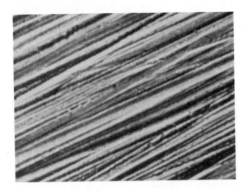

FIGURE 18-52 Sand scratches in primer-surfacers enlarged 40 times. *(Courtesy of PPG Industries, Inc.)*

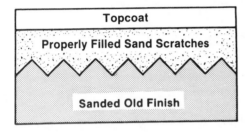

FIGURE 18-53 The best way to prevent sand scratches from showing is to use the proper grit sandpaper and proper sanding technique. In hand sanding always sand in a straight line, never circular. *(Courtesy of Du Pont Co.)*

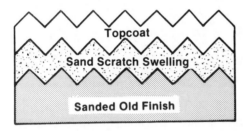

worry about getting the metal too smooth. Sanded metal that looks and feels smooth will still have plenty of "tooth" for the surfacer (Figure 18-52).

Modern primer-surfacers will do a lot of filling in one coat. It is not hard to understand, however, that the thicker the coat, the slower the drying, so spray two or three coats with 5 to 15 minutes between them, and thus save time over spraying a real heavy coat and having to wait a long time for it to dry through. It is difficult to tell when a thick coat is really dry because the surface will appear to be dry while there is still a lot of thinner trapped below the surface and shrinkage is still going on. Where the

imperfections or scratches in the metal are unusually deep, the use of a lacquer glazing putty will save time in getting a smooth surface.

After the primer-surfacer has dried thoroughly, the next thing to consider is the sanding operation. The use of coarse sandpaper such as #220 or #240 will produce scratches in the primer-surfacer that will be hard to fill by the final finish coats. With the present day surfacers, sanding is so easy it is not necessary to use paper coarser than #320 or #360. In order to get the smoothest finish, the use of #400 paper as a final sanding is recommended.

When a lacquer or acrylic lacquer finish coat is used, the thinner penetrates and swells the undercoat and where the undercoat is the heaviest, as in the deep scratches, the swelling will be the greatest. If the color is compounded and polished before all of the thinner has evaporated from the primer-surfacer, there will be further shrinkage at the point of deepest fill. Therefore, it is important to give finish coats plenty of dry time before sanding and polishing.

The danger of sand scratch swelling is greatest on the featheredge. The spraying of a light fog coat for the first color coat keeps the solvent content on the low side when it first comes in contact with the old featheredge finish.

It can be seen from Figure 18-53 that the shrinkage and swelling of lacquer undercoats is an important point to consider in the elimination of sand scratches. If the undercoat is not allowed to dry down to its final position before sanding or applying finish coats, scratches are likely to result.

18.6 REFINISHING SURFACES

It is unwise to apply any kind of finish to a surface that has not been prepared properly. Quality suffers, customer dissatisfaction is inevitable, and finally, costs increase because the job usually has to be done over. A good beginning pays off in a savings of materials and time and in a higher quality refinishing job.

There are two types of automotive refinishing surfaces:

- Previously painted
- Bare metal or substrate

Even if the original paint finish is in good condition, it should be lightly sanded or scuff sanded after washing to remove dead film and to smooth out imperfections. If the surface is in poor condition, all the paint should be removed down to the bare metal. In this way, a good foundation is achieved.

18.7 PAINTED SURFACE IN GOOD CONDITION

It is simple to repaint over an existing paint film in good condition, whatever the type of finish, providing it is stable and does not react to the solvent of the refinish paint. The procedure for surface preparation in good condition is as follows:

CLEANING THE VEHICLE

The vehicle should be washed to remove any mud, dirt, or other water-soluble contaminants before being brought into the shop (Figure 18-54). Hose down the car, sponge with detergent and water, then rinse thoroughly. Wash the top, front and deck, then the sides—and allow to dry.

CLEAN WITH WAX AND GREASE REMOVER

Be sure there is no wax, grease, or other contaminants imbedded in the old finish. Gasoline is a dangerous, poor wax solvent and can itself deposit contaminating substances on the surface. It is ill advised to use synthetic reducers for cleaning up a surface, particularly acrylic lacquer, because they absorb reducer into the paint film and blistering or lifting can result.

Before the job is sanded, use a specially blended wax and grease remover or solvent to thoroughly clean the surface and repeat the operation after sanding. Be sure to thoroughly clean areas where a heavy wax buildup can be a problem, such as around trim, moldings, door handles, radio antennae, and behind the bumpers. Paint will not adhere properly to a waxy surface.

To apply the wax and grease remover (or silicone and wax remover as it is sometimes called) fold a clean, dry cloth, soak it with solvent (Figure 18-55), and apply it to the old painted surface. While the surface is still wet, fold a second clean cloth and wipe dry. Work small areas that are 2 or 3 feet square, wetting the surface liberally. Never attempt to clean too large an area; the solvent will dry before the surface can be wiped. Maximum effectiveness will be achieved by wiping up the wax and grease remover while it is still wet. Always use new wiping cloths because laundering might not remove all oil or silicone residue.

To remove any last trace of moisture and dirt from seals and moldings, blow out with compressed air at low pressure. Wax and silicone can penetrate beneath the surface. This contamination is not easily detectable. It is wise to assume that it is present, so always include some wax and grease cleaner or detergent in the sanding water.

Special attention should be paid to tar, gasoline, battery acid, antifreeze, and brake fluid stains. These can also penetrate well beneath the surface of old

FIGURE 18-54   Wash the car very carefully. (Courtesy of Maaco Enterprises, Inc.)

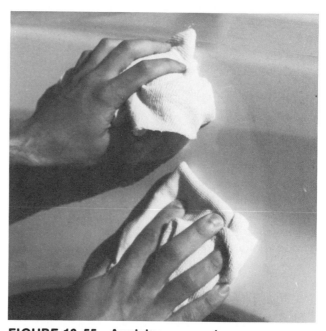
FIGURE 18-55   Applying wax and grease remover

FIGURE 18-56 Grinding a rustout. *(Courtesy of Maaco Enterprises, Inc.)*

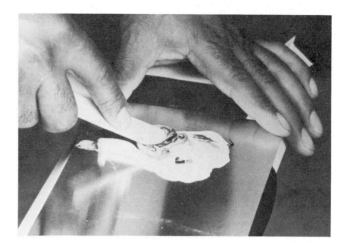

FIGURE 18-57 Mixing a body filler

paint films and their residues must be removed during the sanding operation.

Repair Flaws in Painted Surfaces

First, sand or grind off the rust and old paint in the damaged areas (Figure 18-56). If the grinding operation goes down to bare metal, it will be necessary to perform the appropriate metal conditioning later. These steps are described later in this chapter.

Be sure that all the dings, dents, and built-up areas have been made as described in Chapter 8. Many dings and dents are too deep to be filled by a primer-surfacer and/or putty. In such cases use a lightweight body filler. But when using a body filler, there are some precautions that should be kept in mind:

- **Do not** use body filler directly over a metal conditioner.
- **Do not** use too much hardener because it will cause pinholes.
- **Do not** return any unused mixture to the can.

The following is a review of the procedure for using body filler as given in Chapter 8 concerning minor surface repairs. For small dents, squeeze a 1-1/2-inch ribbon of hardener on a mass of body filler about the size of a golfball. Mix well with a putty knife or paint paddle (Figure 18-57). Mix only as much as can be handled properly because the mixture will harden. Apply immediately with a spreader or squeegee (Figure 18-58). Work to the contour of the surface. Then let it harden for 8 to 10 minutes. Use a grater to shape the repair, bridging the dent to prevent gouging. Sand as needed.

FIGURE 18-58 Applying a body filler

If using a power sander—such as an orbital or dual action sander—use a #80 sandpaper for the rough cut followed by a #180 or #220 grit for the fine work. Next, feather the broken paint edges. This must be done so that a continuous smooth surface can be developed when filled with a primer-surfacer. Featheredging can be done by hand with a sanding block or with an orbital sander.

Taper the broken edges first. If hand sanding, use a #220 grit sandpaper for the rough work. Then complete the job with a #240 or #320 paper and water to produce a fine tapered edge and eliminate sandpaper scratches.

To remove decals from a painted surface, a razor blade slipped under the edge of a decal will start a small area that can be pulled up and the whole decal peeled off. If the decal will not peel off, disc grinding is usually employed or, if a heat gun is available, heat the decal and surrounding surface to soften the adhesive and peel off. There are also decal removers on the market, however, they must be used with care since they may damage the surface on which the decal is applied.

18.8 PAINT WORK IN POOR CONDITION

Most forms of paint failure are progressive. These conditions cannot be stopped by any form of repairing; in fact, repairing will usually accelerate the deterioration of the original finish. If the old finish is badly weathered or scarred, it is **not** suitable for recoating. When this situation occurs, the old finish should be completely removed. There are three common ways of stripping paint from metal surfaces:

- Sanding or grinding
- Sandblasting
- Chemical stripping

With any of these methods, remove all chrome trim strips, lamp surrounds, badges, and so forth that are adjacent to the area to be painted, or in direct contact with it. A chemical paint remover can be trapped and retained by these parts, or they can be accidentally damaged by the sander/grinder or sandblaster. In any case, corrosion is often found beneath exterior trim parts, and this can only be dealt with if they are removed.

SANDING OR GRINDING

Machine sanding/grinding is suitable for removing old finish from small flat areas and gently curved areas. Start with a #24 grit open-coated disc, and by

FIGURE 18-59   Typical bottle type blaster. *(Courtesy of A.L.C. Co.)*

holding the face of the disc at a slight angle to the surface, work forward and backward evenly over the area to get off the bulk of the old finish down to the metal. Follow this with a #50 or #80 close-coated disc, go over the entire area and slightly out on the surrounding surface to clean up the work, and eliminate the troughs or steps caused by the coarse disc. When using the grinder, care must be taken to prevent gouging or scarring the metal.

After all of the paint is removed with the grinder and the coarse grit disc, resand the area with the orbital or dual action sander and #100 grit paper to remove the metal scratches. Then finish sand the panel using #180 grit sandpaper. In this way most of the scratches created by the stripping operation will be eliminated. Remember that any metal that has been scratched with very coarse abrasive paper will require filling to the depth of the scratch plus the height of the burr.

SANDBLASTING

Sandblasting can be done on nearly all types of body construction—even aluminum sheet, with caution—and it leaves a clean, dry surface in an ideal condition for refinishing. It is a very fast method and has the further advantage of revealing rusted areas and places where hidden rusting can result in scaling after the job has been refinished. In addition, sandblasting makes hard-to-reach areas accessible to the technician. Also this method saves time when compared with sanding/grinding and chemical stripping.

A sandblaster concentrates the pressure and flow of air and sand. Usually found in shops in a smaller version (40 to 300 pound models), the technician using it can vary the blast volume, focusing the pattern on the spot at hand, rather than blasting in a wide pattern.

Blasters in the shop are one of two kinds: pressure or siphon. Pressure blasters are pressurized containers filled with abrasive material (such as silica sand). The sand travels down one hose, the high-velocity air comes down another hose. Both meet at another hose and travel out toward the surface together at tremendous speed and force.

In a siphon blaster, compressed air draws the abrasive from the reservoir as suction is applied. The abrasive accelerates and is shot out of the nozzle at the intended surface. Small bottle blasters are available for spot type jobs (Figure 18-59).

The basic procedure in operating sandblasters is as follows:

FIGURE 18-60   Typical safety gear worn by a sand blaster.

3. Before blasting, check the manufacturer's instructions for proper blasting pressures, sand load procedures, and setup arrangements (Figure 18-61). When ready to blast, apply the abrasive material directly on the area to be blasted. Eventually, the area will turn a gray or white color. Blasting has textured the surface by opening the pores of the metal in these colored areas. This etched texture makes an excellent surface for primer adhesion. When the area shows no signs of brown rust, remove the pressure.

    Pressure should be applied by holding the hose 8 to 12 inches back from the area being repaired. It should hit the surface at a 20 to 30 degree angle. That way, the cutting edges of the blasting are away from the operator.

1. Mark off the areas that will not be affected by the spot repair. For instance, when spot repairing a rocker panel, mask the wheel caps and the top of the car (as described later in this chapter).
2. Put on the necessary safety gear. It is a good idea to wear gloves, eye protection, a helmet, and a respirator (Figure 18-60). A respirator should be worn because sand can build up in the lungs over an extended period of time causing silicosis.

CAUTION: Care should be taken where sheet metal is light gauge. High air pressure and/or coarse blasting media can warp the metal.

4. Watch the surface carefully. The blasting might reveal a hole, in which case blast as much of the hole out as possible. Blasting is designed to reveal weak spots like these. Before priming the rusted out area, weld a patch on it.

A

B

C

FIGURE 18-61   Conventional type sand blaster operations: (A) fill the reservoir with adhesive material; (B) aim the gun nozzle; (C) trigger the gun to release the abrasive. *(Courtesy of Truman's Inc.)*

FIGURE 18-62   Typical "dust-free, captive" sand blaster. *(Courtesy of Clements National Co.)*

FIGURE 18-63   Blasting with "captive" sand blaster. *(Courtesy of Clements National Co.)*

5. After the paint has been removed, use an air blow gun to remove the sand from other parts of the vehicle, particularly the glass. If it is not removed, the sand or abrasive will eventually get stuck in windshield wiper blades or window slots and scratch the windows.

6. It is advisable to prime coat the metal as soon as possible after any stripping process, but a sandblast job actually requires that the job be primed almost immediately because the metal is really in a raw state after this treatment and will start rusting if allowed to stand overnight.

Until recently, all sandblasting work was done outdoors. As mentioned in Chapter 4, some of the newer blaster models provide "dust-free, captive" sandblasting (Figure 18-62). They contain a built-in vacuum and filtration system that cleans up and recycles the abrasive, while it blasts away paint, rust, and other debris.

To operate this newer type of blaster, hold the designed nozzle directly against the surface being treated (Figure 18-63). As the abrasive strikes the surface, it is sucked back by the vacuum, along with rust and debris. A rubber nozzle and stiff brush seal in the abrasive and debris to keep them from escaping. The rust and debris fall into an easy-to-empty pail, while the blasting abrasive is recycled and sent back into action.

CHEMICAL STRIPPING

A chemical paint remover is recommended for stripping large areas of paint. It is very effective in those places that a power sander cannot reach and there is no danger of the metal warping.

Before applying paint remover, mask off the area to ensure that the remover does not get on any area that is not to be stripped. Use two or three thicknesses of masking tape to give adequate protection. Cover any crevices to prevent the paint remover from seeping to the undersurface of a panel. Slightly scoring the surface of the paint to be stripped will help the paint remover to penetrate more quickly.

Paint remover should be applied following the manufacturer's instructions. Pay attention to warnings regarding ventilation, smoking, and the use of protective clothing such as PVC or rubber gloves, long sleeve shirts, and safety glasses or goggles. If remover comes in contact with the skin or eyes, it will cause irritation and burning.

To apply, brush on a heavy coat of paint remover in one direction only to the entire area being treated (Figure 18-64). Use a soft bristle brush, but do not brush the material out. Allow the paint remover to stand until the finish is softened. Although paint remover is quickly effective on most vehicle topcoats, some modern car undercoats can prove stubborn. (For example, acrylic lacquer becomes sticky, making it more difficult to remove.) Because the active strength of the paint remover must be held at a safe level to prevent the risk of serious skin and eye injury to the operator, more than one application might be needed.

715

Caution should be taken when removing the loosened paint coatings. Some paint removers are designed to be neutralized by water. Others are more easily removed with a squeegee or scraper (Figure 18–65). Be sure to rinse off any residue that remains using cleaning solvent and steel wool, followed immediately by wiping with a clean rag. This rinsing operation is essential. Many paint removers contain wax, which, if left on the surface, will prevent the refinish paint from adhering, drying, and hardening properly.

CAUTION: Do not use paint remover on fiberglass or other plastic substrates.

FIGURE 18–64 Applying chemical paint remover with a brush. (Courtesy of America Sikkens, Inc.)

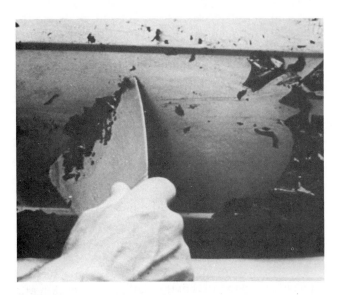

FIGURE 18–65 Removing paint with a scraper. (Courtesy of America Sikkens, Inc.)

Rusting occurs very rapidly on metal that has been chemically stripped. In fact, any bare metal substrate should be treated immediately. But before selecting the type of metal treatment or conditioning system, first consider the types of rust. The least amount of rust might be considered **microscopic rust** (Figure 18–66) that is not really visible to the eye but can be a hazard to the performance of a refinish job. The second type of rust might be called **flash rust** that usually develops when there is moisture or humidity present. The other types of rust are the types that are very visible and might even be large and scabby.

The decision about which metal conditioning system to use depends on the type of rust and the type of substrate.

18.9 BARE METAL SUBSTRATE

Proper bare metal treatment is a critical step in every successful automotive painting operation. Yet it is often ignored or carried out in a haphazard manner. This can only result in poor adhesion, corrosion, and—as a result—customer complaints. Though not noticeable when the original finish has been stripped down to bare metal, it is the single most important factor in original equipment finish life. Recognizing its importance, auto manufacturers devote more attention to this step than they do to priming and topcoating, using a seven-stage zinc phosphate metal treatment process to ensure adhesion of primers to the substrate.

Though the techniques and equipment used on the OEM level are not adaptable to body shops,

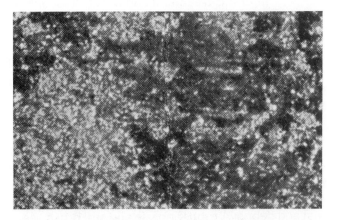

FIGURE 18–66 Rust-pitted sheet steel sanded clean to the naked eye. Under a microscope (enlarged 125 diameters) traces of rust still appear in pits. (Courtesy of PPG Industries, Inc.)

some metal treatment products on the market today can enable the refinisher to simulate original equipment metal treatment.

Why is bare metal treatment so important? Water vapor penetrates all paint films. The fresher the paint and the more humid the weather, the further the vapor penetrates, sometimes reaching the bare metal. Once water droplets form under the paint film, pressure starts to build, causing bubbling, blistering, and loss of adhesion. Rust can also begin to form, further pushing the paint film away from the metal.

The only way to prevent this potentially serious problem is to create such a strong bond between the primer-surfacer and the metal that water vapor cannot penetrate down to the substrate. If the water vapor is not allowed to condense under the paint film, it will return to the surface of the finish and eventually evaporate.

This bond between a negatively charged metal car surface and a positively charged primer can be created electrochemically. All that is needed is the application of an acidic metal treatment system that contains both positive and negative parts. The negative parts are attracted to the metal, while the positive parts are attracted to the primer, forming a superior bond that does not allow water droplets to collect. This type of system is called a conversion coating. The conventional system described in Chapter 15 generally works the best and consists of the following three-step process called metal treating:

- **Cleaning to remove contaminants.** Use a wax and grease remover and apply it to the surface. While the surface is still wet, fold a second clean cloth and wipe dry. Work small areas, 2 to 3 square feet, wetting the surface liberally (Figure 18-67).
- **Cleaning with metal conditioner.** Mix the appropriate cleaner with water in a plastic bucket according to label instruction. Apply with a cloth, sponge, or spray bottle. If rust is present, work the surface with a stiff brush or abrasive plastic pad (Figure 18-68). Then while the surface is still wet, wipe it dry with a clean cloth.
- **Applying conversion coatings.** Pour the appropriate conversion coating into a plastic bucket (Figure 18-69). Using an abrasive pad, brush, or spray bottle, apply the coating to the metal surface. Then leave the conditioner on the surface 2 to 5 mintues. Apply only to an area that can be coated and rinsed before the solution dries. If the surface dries before the rinsing, reapply. Flush the coating

FIGURE 18-67   Applying a wax and grease remover. *(Courtesy of Du Pont Co.)*

FIGURE 18-68   Applying metal conditioner. *(Courtesy of Du Pont Co.)*

from the surface with cold water. Wipe dry with a clean cloth and allow to air dry completely. The desired primer or primer-surfacer can then be applied.

Another type of metal treatment system also can be applied to enhance adhesion and assure corrosion resistance. A washer-primer is a sprayable sur-

FIGURE 18-69 Mixing a conversion coating

face treatment that eliminates the need for a conversion coating. The vinyl resin in the washer primer provides corrosion resistance and the reducer contains phosphoric acid for strong bonding.

A washer-primer with phosphoric acid reducer not only cleans, it also etches the metal and assists the adhesion of the subsequent paint film. It helps prevent the occurrence of rust and also eases sanding marks. The washer-primer is applied by the following procedure:

1. Carefully read the manufacturer's directions and special instructions, which should be closely followed.

2. Pour the washer-primer into a container and add a special washer-primer thinner to achieve a sprayable viscosity. Do not use a metal container because the washer-primer reacts with metal. If applying a two-component washer-primer, the solution must be used within 8 hours after mixing the main and subagents.

3. Pour the mix solution or thinned solution into the spray bottle container and spray the metal immediately. Do not allow any washer-primer to get on any part of the vehicle that is not to be repainted. The gun air pressure and discharge pressure should be kept low and the gun held close to the surface. The area should be masked off to prevent other areas from coming into contact with the washer-primer.

4. Apply a **thin** coat. Too thick an application will result in paint peeling and blistering.

5. The washer-primer should not be allowed to dry on the metal. Should this happen a second application of the material will soften and dissolve the dried residues. After the washer-primer has been applied, wash well with plenty of clean water and dry thoroughly.

6. Wash out the spray gun immediately after spraying washer-primer. Washer-primer left in the spray gun or container will cause a chemical film to form on the metal, making the spray gun useless. Because of this, some manufacturers recommend that washer-primer be used with an acid-resistant brush or sponge.

WARNING: While phosphoric acid metal materials are not considered dangerous chemicals, they do have a drying action on the skin. Although this is comparatively harmless, it might cause chapping and render the skin susceptible to irritants. Rubber or PVC gloves should be worn, and rubber or PVC boots and aprons are recommended to protect the clothing.

Typically, metal conditioning and priming/surfacing are considered separate surface preparation steps. Some new products, however, actually make it possible to combine these steps. "Etching primer-fillers" etch the bare metal to improve paint adhesion and corrosion resistance, while providing the priming and filling properties usually offered by primer-surfacers. Etching primer-fillers work best on lightly sanded surfaces where a slight-to-moderate amount of filling is required. They must be applied as directed by the manufacturer.

SPECIFIC METAL TREATMENTS

The preparation of the various metals used in automotive construction require slightly different techniques. The more common bare metal procedures are for:

Steel-Body Metal (Including Blue Annealed) Preparation

1. Sand metal thoroughly. Remove all visible scale or rust.

2. Clean the surface with wax and grease remover and wipe dry.

3. Use any of the three bare metal treatments—conversion coating, washer-

primer, or etching primer-filler—as previously described.

4. Apply an undercoater (primer or primer-surfacer). If the etching primer-filler is used, this step might not be necessary.

5. Once the undercoat refinish system is dry and sanded, wipe with a tack rag. The surface is ready for the color coat.

Galvanneal, Plymetal, Galvanized, or Other Zinc-coated Metal

1. Follow Steps 1 and 2 of steel-body preparation.

2. Use either a conversion coating or special zinc metal conditioner. Apply the latter according to manufacturer's directions. Never use a washer-primer since it will attack galvanized and other zinc surfaces and must not be allowed to come into contact with them.

3. Apply one wet double coat of epoxy primer. If filling is required, allow the epoxy primer to dry a minimum of 1 hour and then apply a primer-surfacer.

4. Sand the primer-surfacer after a 30-minute dry period. Once the undercoat system is completed (as mentioned later in this chapter), the surface is ready for the topcoat.

New Anodized Aluminum or Untreated Aluminum and Oxidized Aluminum Preparation

1. Follow Steps 1, 2, and 3 of steel-body preparation.

2. Apply one wet double coat of epoxy primer or zinc chromate. If filling is required, allow the material a minimum of 1 hour to dry and then apply a primer-surfacer.

3. Sand the primer-surfacer after a 30-minute dry period. Once the undercoat system is completed, the surface is ready for the color coat.

CHROMIUM PLATING PREPARATION

Chromium presents a very difficult problem and at best the adhesion of a finish to this metal is not lasting. When painting is desired, prepare the surface by cleaning and sanding and proceed with the following system described for stainless steel preparation:

1. Clean the metal thoroughly with a wax and grease remover.

2. Sand metal thoroughly, using #320 wet or dry sandpaper.

3. Reclean with wax and grease remover.

4. Apply any of the metal treatments described earlier in this chapter.

5. Spray two coats of primer-surfacer. Allow 2 to 3 hours drying time before dry sanding.

6. Blow out cracks, then use a tack rag on the entire surface. The final coat can now be applied.

Regardless of the cleaning procedure, once the metal is clean and prepared, it must not be contaminated by fingerprints, so clean cotton industrial gloves should be worn when handling. Sometimes painters rub their hands over an area to determine the effect of the sanding without realizing that they are transferring oil from their hands to the surface. Oil comes from the skin and from shop tools, and even if the hands are freshly washed, a fine oily film will be left on the surface because there are not many people who have oil-free skin. Wiping off the surface with a good wax and grease remover, just before applying the finishing coat, is excellent insurance against peeling and/or blistering.

PREPARING METAL REPLACEMENT PARTS

Many car manufacturers and component suppliers protect panels in a primer. The function of this primer coat is to protect the metal against corrosion. It does not necessarily provide a firm basis for a paint system. Although most primers in use do have this dual function, the supplier should always be consulted. Certain major motor manufacturers supply components in electrocoat primers that are an essential part of their warranty repair systems and should not be removed. They should be suitably prepared for the painting process.

It must be remembered that some replacement parts are provided from the manufacturer with only a coating. This coating is **not** intended to serve as the primer. A primer must be applied to these replacement parts or the color coat will not stick properly. The usual procedure is to clean with wax and grease remover, then examine the part for imperfections such as drips or scratches. If drips or scratches are present, sand these imperfections until smooth but do not try to remove the coating completely. Scuff sand the entire panel, then apply primer before painting. If in doubt about the quality of the coating, check with the manufacturer of the part for the recommended finishing procedures.

Any bare metal replacement panels protected with grease should also be cleaned with a wax and grease solvent. They should be washed with liberal amounts of solvent, changing any rags frequently, then treated with a bare metal conditioner, flushed down with water, and dried off.

18.10 UNDERCOAT REFINISHING SYSTEM

The decision to apply a primer, a primer-sealer, or a primer-surfacer by itself or combined with putty and/or a sealer depends on three factors. These are:

- The condition of the substrate—smooth or rough, bare or painted
- The type of finish on the substrate—if painted
- The type of finish to be used for the topcoat

Full details on the use of undercoats are given in Chapter 16. These products are applied primarily to protect the bare metal against corrosion and to improve adhesion of the topcoats of paint (Figure 18-70). Due to their excellent filling and leveling qualities, they also fill minor sand scratches and level rough edges or depressions that remain after machine sanding. Before applying any undercoater, be sure to treat all bare metal with metal conditioner. Reduce the undercoater chosen according to the manufacturer's instructions. Be careful to select the proper solvent for the weather conditions and mix the material thoroughly.

Apply the first coat of undercoater (Figure 18-71). Allow this coat to flash dry, following the recommendations on the label for flash time. Then apply two or three more medium wet coats for additional film buildup, with flash time between each application. When making a spot repair, extend the undercoater (primer-sealer) several inches around the first coat.

Allow the undercoater to dry thoroughly. Do not apply extra heavy coats to speed up the operation.

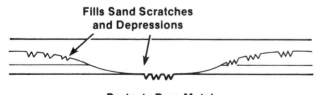

Fills Sand Scratches and Depressions

Protects Bare Metal

FIGURE 18-70   How undercoaters protect bare metal

Film applied in this manner will require more time to dry and can lead to cracking, crazing, pinholes, and poor holdout (Figure 18-72).

After the undercoat is dry, block sand the area until it is smooth (Figure 18-73). For best results, use #320 grit sandpaper. If very fine scratches still appear, another coat of primer-surfacer might be all that is required to fill them.

FIGURE 18-71   Applying the undercoater—in this case a primer-surfacer

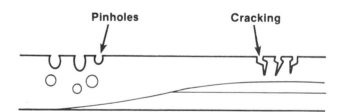

Pinholes   Cracking

FIGURE 18-72   The problems of excessive undercoater

FIGURE 18-73   Block sanding the undercoater

Putty Applications

Some sand scratches might require additional filling with a thin lacquer type glazing putty. This putty is generally used to fill small scratches and pinholes (Figure 18-74), but use it sparingly. To apply the putty, squeeze a small amount from the tube onto the edge of a squeegee (Figure 18-75). Quickly press the putty onto the repair and level it off with a flat scraping motion. Use moderate pressure to assure that the putty fills the depression completely (Figure 18-76). Make additional passes quickly, if necessary.

Allow the putty to air dry until it is hard. Test with a fingernail for hardness before sanding. If it is sanded too soon, the putty will continue to shrink, leaving part of the scratch unfilled (Figure 18-77). Once it hardens, the putty should be dry sanded with #220 grit paper or wet sanded (Figure 18-78). Wet sanding is carried out in the same manner as dry sanding; however, it requires special paper and plenty of water. After sanding the puttied area, clean the surface and then reprime (Figure 18-79). If the putty has been wet sanded, make sure to dry the surface thoroughly before applying primer-surfacer.

FIGURE 18-76   Applying putty to the surface

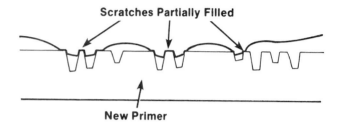

FIGURE 18-77   How putty shrinks

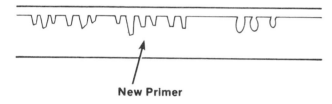

FIGURE 18-74   How lacquer base glazing putty works

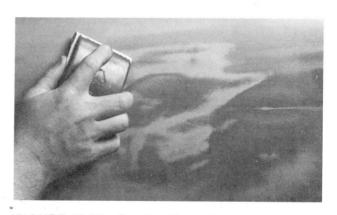

FIGURE 18-78   Sanding the putty

FIGURE 18-75   Applying putty to the squeegee

FIGURE 18-79   Re-priming the puttied area

Lacquer-based glazing putties are being partially replaced by polyester putties, or finishing fillers as they are also called, and by polyester primer/fillers. Both products must be mixed with hardener before starting application and can be applied to filler, metal, or old paint finishes. The use of these high-viscosity, finely textured "fillers" eliminates the traditional primer/putty/primer process. Because they chemically harden, they cure quickly and can be primed and refinished without the worry of sand scratch swelling commonly associated with lacquer-based glazing putties. For complete details on working with all types of putties, see Chapter 8.

COMPOUNDING

Compounding is sometimes done as a final smoothing step to remove light scratches, small dirt particles, and minor grinding or sanding marks before applying a final topcoat. Compounding can be done either by hand or machine. Rubbing compounds are available in various cutting strengths for both hand and machine as a final smoothing operation. A hand-rubbing compound is usually coarser than a machine-rubbing compound. It is used on small spot repairs, but it can be used on an entire car. It is applied with a damp rag to one small area at a time in a straight back-and-forth motion, not in circles. It is then buffed by machine or by hand.

Machine-rubbing compound is made for use with a portable polisher or buffer (see Chapter 4). It is finer than hand-rubbing compound because the machine provides more power. This compound should be thinned with water before it is applied to the surface.

Details on both hand and machine compounds can be found in Chapter 19.

18.11 PLASTIC PARTS PREPARATION

Currently, over 100 types of plastic are being used in the manufacture of vehicles, and approximately 40 need preparation before painting. The painter must be able to identify these plastic parts before refinishing them. Methods of identifying plastic and how to make plastic repairs are given in Chapter 13.

Plastic parts are usually considered either hard (rigid) or flexible (semirigid). Some flexible plastic auto body replacement parts come from the factory

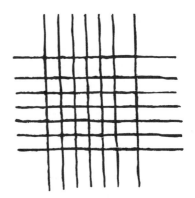

A

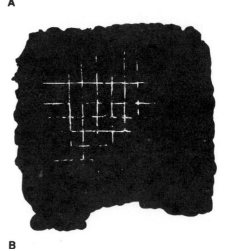

B

FIGURE 18-80 These test panels show the improved adhesion to TPO made possible by the use of a plastic primer. Panel A was primed; Panel B was not. *(Courtesy of Sherwin-Williams Co.)*

already primed, while others are delivered unprimed. If the parts are factory-primed, no additional priming is necessary. If they are not, both rigid and semirigid plastics might benefit from the use of a special plastic primer, primer-sealer, or vinyl washer-primer to improve paint adhesion. TPO, in particular (Figure 18-80), has an extremely slick, waxy surface that makes it difficult for the topcoat to form a strong bond to the substrate unless a primer is used. Adhesion to ABS used in exterior applications also is greatly enhanced by priming.

PREPARATION OF FLEXIBLE PLASTIC

Prepare the surface of semirigid unpainted material as follows:

1. Clean the entire part with a wax, grease, and silicone removing solvent applied with a water dampened cloth. Wipe dry.

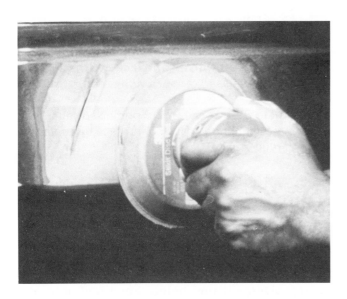

FIGURE 18-81   Featheredging the filler repair

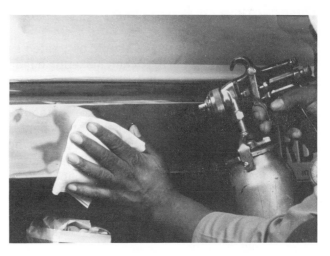

FIGURE 18-82   Applying a flexible primer-surfacer

 **SHOP TALK** _____

Unpainted rigid plastic parts should also be solvent cleaned to remove mold release agents (typically silicones) before a primer or topcoat is applied.

2. Featheredge the scuff or filler repair with #320 sandpaper, blow off dust and tack wipe (Figure 18-81).
3. Mix and apply four medium dry coats of flexible primer-surfacer (Figure 18-82). Follow manufacturer's instructions for specific mix ratios and additives.

 **SHOP TALK** _____

Use a fast evaporating thinner as recommended to reduce the primer-surfacer and do not apply excessively wet coats. Bare flexible plastic surface and/or flexible filler materials have a tendency to swell from thinner absorption, resulting in a visible or "highlighted" repair.

4. Allow to dry at least 1 hour and block sand with #400 sandpaper. Sand the entire part to remove all gloss with #400 sandpaper in preparation for color application.

When undercoaters are modified with a flex additive, the possibility of mixture "pot life" exists; therefore, spray equipment should be emptied and flushed immediately after use. Flex additives are needed for semirigid plastics because they expand, contract, and bend more easily than other substrates. The flex agent will keep the paint film flexible so it can accommodate the movement of the substrate without cracking.

Preparation of Polypropylene Plastic Parts

The system for painting polypropylene parts involves the use of a special primer. Since polypropylene plastic is hard, it can be color coated after priming with conventional interior acrylic lacquer. To prepare the surface, proceed as follows:

 1. Wash the part with a wax and silicone remover solvent. Follow the label directions.
2. Apply a thin, wet coat of polypropylene primer according to label directions. Wetness of primer is determined by observing gloss reflection of spray application in adequate lighting. Be sure primer application includes all edges. Allow primer to flash dry 1 minute minimum and 10 minutes maximum.
3. During the above flash time period (1 to 10 minutes), apply conventional interior acrylic lacquer color as required and allow to dry before installing part. Application of color during above flash time range promotes best adhesion of color coats.

PREPARATION OF RIGID PARTS

Exterior hard (rigid) parts should be treated as fiberglass when in doubt as to their makeup. In fact, fiberglass should be treated much the same—in preparation for a final coat—as body steel. It must be remembered that fiberglass parts do not require chemical conditioners. Replacement or new panels can contain contaminants on the surface due to the mold release agent used in the molds. Several common release agents are composed of silicone oils. These contaminants must be removed.

1. Newly molded parts should be washed with denatured alcohol used liberally on a clean cloth.
2. Thoroughly clean the surface with a wax and grease remover.
3. Sand the exposed fiberglass with #220 or #280 grit paper by hand or #80 to #120 grit with sander.

CAUTION: Do not sand down through the gel coat to the glass fibers that are used to reinforce the plastic. There is generally sufficient gel coating to allow thorough sanding for refinishing.

4. Reclean surface and wipe dry with clean rags.

Alternate Step: If there are joints to be filled or the sanding operation exposes air pockets or glass strands, glaze a coat of body filler over the entire surface (Figure 18-83). Allow to cure, sand, and reclean. Apply a single coat of sealer or a double coat of epoxy chromate primer.

FIGURE 18-83 Applying body filler to a plastic part

5. Apply a primer-surfacer as directed on the label. Allow to dry and sand smooth with fine sandpaper to minimize sand scratches. Blow off with air and tack-rag the surface. If necessary apply another coat of sealer.

Alternate Step: A synthetic primer-surfacer is also recommended if topcoats are to be enamel or acrylic enamel.

6. The surface is now ready for the color coats.

When refinishing previously painted fiberglass parts, care should be taken not to sand through the gel coat, and a sealer should be used. Fiberglass parts are extremely porous. The gel coat keeps topcoat solvents from being absorbed into the substrate.

18.12 MASKING

Masking is a very important step in the painting preparation process. Masking keeps paint mist from contacting areas other than those that are to be repainted (Figure 18-84). This has become even more important since the popular use of acrylic urethane and two-component type paints. Once these types of paints dry, the paint mist cannot be removed with a thinner or other solvent. These paints will have to be removed with a compound or other time-consuming means.

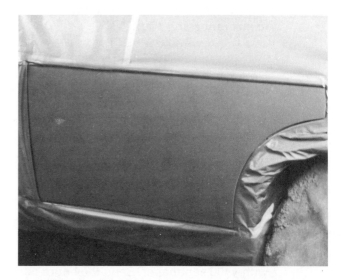

FIGURE 18-84   Car masked for a panel refinishing job. (Courtesy of Du Pont Co.)

MASKING MATERIALS

The basic materials for any masking job are masking paper and tape. Automotive paper comes in various widths—from 3 to 36 inches. Automotive masking paper is heat resistant so that it can be used safely in baking ovens. It also has good wet strength, freedom from loose fibers, and resistance to solvent penetration. **Never** use newspaper for masking a vehicle since it does not meet any of these requirements. Newspaper also has the added disadvantage of containing printing inks that are soluble in some paint solvents. These can be transferred to the underlying finish causing staining.

Automotive masking tape comes in various widths from 1/4 to 2 inches. The most frequently used tapes are shown in Figure 18-85. Larger width tapes are used only occasionally since they are expensive and difficult to handle. Automotive masking tape should not be confused with tapes bought in hardware or paint stores for home use. The latter will

not hold up to the demanding requirements of automotive refinishing. It is interesting to note that the average size vehicle takes 2 to 2-1/2 rolls of tape to be completely masked.

The use of masking paper and tape dispensing equipment (Figure 18-86) makes it easy to pull and tear the exact amount of paper needed. Some masking machines permit tape to adhere to one or both edges of the paper as it is rolled out.

There are several types of masking covers available. One type of cover is the plastic tire cover that eliminates the need for masking off the tire (Figure 18-87). Others include a body cover (Figure 18-88) and a frame cover. Light covers in a variety of sizes and shapes (Figure 18-89) are available to mask light assemblies including headlights and tail lights (Figure 18-90). These various covers can be used as the situation demands.

FIGURE 18-85   Most common sizes of tape used in the paint shop. All widths are in 60-yard rolls.

FIGURE 18-86   Typical masking paper and tape dispensing equipment

FIGURE 18-87   Typical plastic tire covers in use. *(Courtesy of DeVilbiss Co.).*

FIGURE 18-88   Typical plastic car cover. Note the door panel is the area to be painted. *(Courtesy of Fibre Glass Evercoat Co., Inc.)*

FIGURE 18-89 Typical light covers save time masking head and tail lights. (Courtesy of Marson Corp.)

FIGURE 18-90 How the headlight covers are used. (Courtesy of Lenco, Inc.)

How to Mask

Before any masking materials are applied, the vehicle must be completely cleaned and all dust blown from the vehicle. The masking tape will not stick to surfaces that are not clean or dry. It is most important that the tape be pressed down firmly and adhered to the surface. Otherwise, paint solvents will creep under the tape. In the case of a two-color job, where the color break is not hidden by a capping strip or molding, it is **vital** that the masking tape edge is firmly pressed down.

 **SHOP TALK**

It is wise to completely detail the car before the masking job is started and, of course, after the paint job is completed (see Chapter 19). Reason: Improper masking can also cause a dirty paint job if done over a dirty car.

If the paint shop is cold and damp with little air movement, the masking tape probably will not stick to glass or chromium parts because of an almost invisible film of condensation that has formed on these parts. It must be wiped off before the tape will adhere properly.

Masking tape generally will not stick on the black rubber weatherstripping used around the doorjambs and deck lid opening. To mask rubber weatherstripping, apply clear lacquer with a rag, allow it to completely dry, and then apply the tape. When masking doorjambs, be sure to cover both the door lock assembly and the striker bolt.

Although masking tape has an elastic property, it should be stretched only on curved surfaces. This is especially true when masking newly applied finishes that are still soft beneath the surface. It is also wise to avoid stretching the tape because this can increase the degree of tape marking on the finish.

When applying masking tape, most experienced maskers find it is easier to hold and peel the tape in one hand while they use the other hand to guide and secure it (Figure 18-91). This gives tight edges for good adherence and also allows the masker to change directions and go around corners with tape. To cut the masking tape easily, quickly tear upward

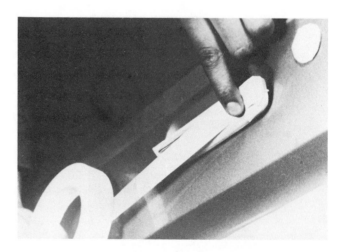

FIGURE 18-91 Proper way to handle masking tape

FIGURE 18-92   Easy method of cutting masking tape

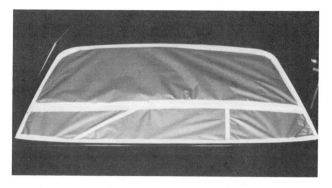

FIGURE 18-94   Masking the rear window

against the thumbnail as shown in Figure 18-92. This procedure will permit a clean cut of the tape without any stretching.

Be careful that the tape does not overlap any of the areas to be painted. Loop or overlap the inner tape edge to make, and follow, curves. The tape will stretch to conform to curves. Difficult areas such as a wheel can be masked using this process, but more often wheel covers are used to save time.

Here are some general recommendations on masking paper and tape size for the various areas of a car to be masked:

- Mask antennas by making a sleeve with pre-taped 3-inch masking paper and secure at the base with masking tape. On windshields, use two widths of either 15- or 18-inch masking paper. The top layer must overlap the bottom to prevent overspray (Figure 18-93).

- Rear windows are masked similarly to windshields with the use of two widths of 15- and 18-inch masking paper (Figure 18-94).
- Apply 12- or 15-inch masking paper to windows for fast, economical protection. On door handles, apply 3/4-inch tape in a lengthwise continuous strip to ensure faster removal. Chrome drip rails and moldings also require 3/4-inch or wider widths of masking tape. Outside mirrors can be masked with 2-inch tape or 6-inch masking paper (Figure 18-95).
- The wide variety of shapes and widths of grilles and bumpers might require various widths of masking paper; 6, 9, 12, and 15 inches are the most popular widths to use (Figure 18-96).
- Mask protective side molding and wheel well molding with two strips of 3/4-inch or greater widths, 1-1/2, 2, or 3 inch as required. For protecting the tire and wheel, wrap two ad-

FIGURE 18-93   Masking an antenna and windshield

FIGURE 18-95   Masking the side window, door handles, and side mirror

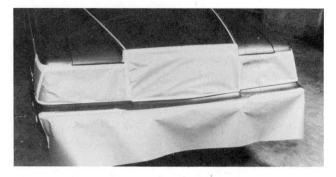

FIGURE 18-96   Masking the grille and the bumper

joining pieces of 18-inch masking paper around the tire.
- Tail lights are masked with 6- or 9-inch masking paper. Mask letter and emblems with 1/8-inch or 1/4-inch tapes (Figure 18-97). A pocket knife is a handy tool to work the tape into place on such small items. If these items are too difficult to mask, they can often be removed during the masking operation and replaced after refinishing.
- Use two or three pieces of 36-inch masking paper to protect the inside of the trunk area. Use clear lacquer to promote tape adhesion when masking weatherstrip (Figure 18-98).

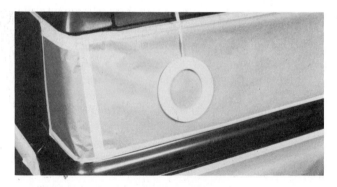

FIGURE 18-97   Masking tail lights

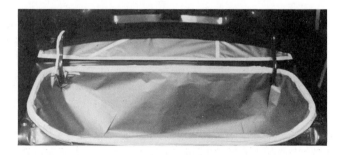

FIGURE 18-98   Masking a trunk

FIGURE 18-99   Masking the doorjambs

- Mask around doorjambs with 6-inch pre-taped masking paper (Figure 18-99).

When masking large areas, such as bumpers, it is easier to manage the paper if it is tacked in the middle of the bumper with tape first. Then each side can be masked without the paper dragging on the floor and getting in the way.

Before masking glass areas, remove such items as wiper blades. The wiper shafts can be protected in the same manner as radio antennas and door handles. Glass areas themselves can be masked by first applying tape along the very top and edges of window moldings. Then, use two pieces of masking paper to cover the glass area. The tape on the edge of the paper should overlap the tape placed on the molding. The top piece of paper should overlap the bottom layer of paper. If necessary, fold and tape any pleats in the paper so that there is no dust seepage. To mask lights that cannot be completely covered by tape or light covers, masking paper can be cut, folded, and worked around before being held down with tape.

One-sixteenth and 3/32-inch fine line tape can be used to protect existing stripes from overspray or damage of adjacent panels (Figure 18-100). Use fine line tape for precise color separation in two tone painting and for painting vivid, clean stripes. Its added flexibility and conformability make painting of curved lines easier, with less reworking (Figure 18-101).

When spraying horizontal surfaces (hood, trunk, and so on), two layers of paper should be used to prevent bleed-through of finish-dulling solvents. Another method to prevent bleed-through is to reverse tape the paper. The paper is taped on the inside and allowed to bellow slightly, which keeps the paper lifted slightly from the surface.

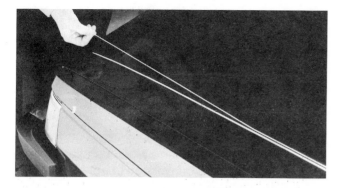

FIGURE 18-100 Fine line tape can also be used to paint stripes; special tapes are available to create custom designs. *(Courtesy of Spartan Plastics Inc.)*

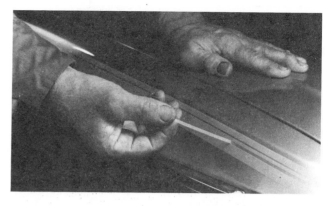

FIGURE 18-101 Using a special masking tape for making stripe painting easier. *(Courtesy of 3M)*

REVERSE MASKING METHOD A

REVERSE MASKING METHOD B

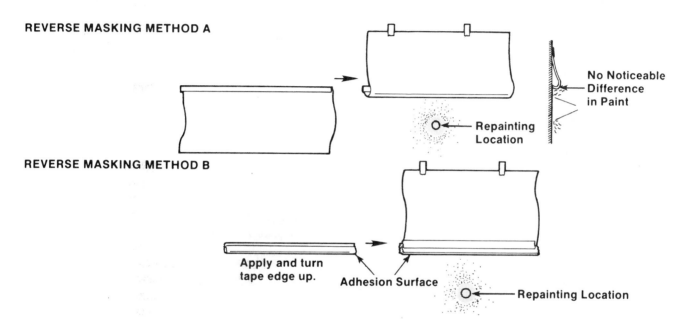

FIGURE 18-102 How to make a reverse mask. *(Courtesy of Toyota Motor Corp.)*

A reverse masking method is often used during spot repainting to restrict the shading area and to make it less noticeable. At times a **line of definition** such as a door edge or a body seam next to a refinished panel will accentuate a slight difference in an otherwise acceptable color match. This is particularly true with metallics. This situation can be avoided by sanding the adjacent panel (crossing the line) when preparing the panel to be refinished. Then reverse mask the adjacent panel and refinish the repaired panel. Now remove the masking paper. If there is a slight difference, just paint across the line and blend in smoothly as with any spot repair. In Figure 18-102, reverse masking method A is used for flat surfaces and method B for curved surfaces.

Inspect the masking very carefully for any overmasked or undermasked areas that will make extra

work after the vehicle is painted. Overmasked areas mean that the painter must touch up the part of the car that should have been painted. On the other hand, undermasked areas must be cleaned with solvent to remove overspray that detracts from the overall appearance of an otherwise good job.

18.13 REVIEW QUESTIONS

1. Technician A uses a dual action sander to remove heavy surface rust, while Technician B uses an air grinder. Who is correct?
   a. Technician A
   b. Technician B
   c. Both A and B
   d. Neither A nor B

2. If the original paint surface is in good condition, Technician A simply washes the car. In the same instance, Technician B washes and scuff sands the vehicle. Who is correct?
   a. Technician A
   b. Technician B
   c. Both A and B
   d. Neither A nor B

3. When filling a dent, Technician A first applies a metal conditioner and then the body filler. Technician B applies the body filler alone. Who is correct?
   a. Technician A
   b. Technician B
   c. Both A and B
   d. Neither A nor B

4. Which of the following methods is used to strip paint from the metal surfaces of a vehicle?
   a. sanding
   b. sandblasting
   c. chemical stripping
   d. all of the above

5. Technician A sandblasts at a 20- to 30-degree angle. Technician B sandblasts holding the hose 8 to 12 inches back from the area being repaired. Who is correct?
   a. Technician A
   b. Technician B
   c. Both A and B
   d. Neither A nor B

6. Technician A brushes paint remover on the surface with a back and forth motion along the body lines. Technician B brushes it on in one direction only. Who is correct?
   a. Technician A
   b. Technician B
   c. Both A and B
   d. Neither A nor B

7. Which method of paint removal is the quickest?
   a. sanding
   b. grinding
   c. sandblasting
   d. chemical stripping

8. Paint removers are _____ .
   a. neutralized and removed with water
   b. removed with a squeegee or scraper
   c. not to be used on fiberglass
   d. all of the above

9. During a wet sanding operation, Technician A lets the surface dry periodically, while Technician B keeps the surface constantly wet. Who is correct?
   a. Technician A
   b. Technician B
   c. Both A and B
   d. Neither A nor B

10. Technician A applies a metal conditioner before applying a conversion coating. Technician B does not. Who is correct?
    a. Technician A
    b. Technician B
    c. Both A and B
    d. Neither A nor B

11. A washer-primer with phosphoric acid
    _____ .
    a. cleans
    b. etches the metal
    c. assists in adhesion
    d. all of the above

12. After the putty hardens, Technician A dry sands it. Technician B wet sands. Who is correct?
    a. Technician A
    b. Technician B
    c. Both A and B
    d. Neither A nor B

13. Lacquer-based glazing putties are being partially replaced by _____ .
    a. polyester putties
    b. finishing fillers
    c. all the above
    d. none of the above

14. Technician A applies compound in a back and forth motion. Technician B uses a circular motion. Who is correct?
    a. Technician A
    b. Technician B
    c. Both A and B
    d. Neither A nor B

15. Newspaper _____ .
    a. has freedom from loose fibers
    b. has resistance to solvent penetration
    c. contains inks that are soluble in some paint solvents
    d. all of the above
    e. none of the above

CHAPTER
19

Application of Color Coats

From the customer's standpoint, the topcoat or color coat is the most important operation in body repair because that is all the customer sees. The expert refinisher takes special pride in producing a beautiful finish on spot, panel, or overall repairs, that matches both the color (or color effect) and the texture of the original finish. Sometimes this color effect can be a basecoat/clear coat finish that more and more customers are viewing as a premium-looking finish. It is the painter's job to satisfy the customer with the paint application. So it is of great importance to fully understand all the working application instructions for applying topcoats. The best place for this, as discussed later in this chapter, is the paint label.

Since the customer sees only the topcoat and judges the quality of the refinisher's work on its appearance and its appearance alone, there is little appreciation for all the work done underneath the topcoat. As already pointed out in previous chapters, the cleaning, filling, and sanding of the substrate must be done very painstakingly. A perfectly smooth surface must be readied before the topcoat is applied. Otherwise, any imperfection—even the smallest—will show in the topcoat.

19.1 TYPE OF PAINT AND REPAINTING PROCESS

The conditions determining the type of topcoat paint to be used are: the extent of the area to be covered, the extent of deterioration of the previous paint film, and whether or not the vehicle had been previously repainted. The type of paint used and the process in which it is applied in accordance with these conditions are very important factors governing work efficiency and speed.

DETERMINING IF THE AUTOMOBILE HAS BEEN REPAINTED

There are two ways to determine if the automobile has been repainted in the past. They are:

- **Sanding method.** Sand an edge on the area to be repainted until the bare metal appears. The make-up of the paint coating will determine whether or not it was repainted previously (Figure 19-1).
- **Paint film thickness measurement method.** A paint film thickness that is greater than the standard for a new vehicle is an indication of

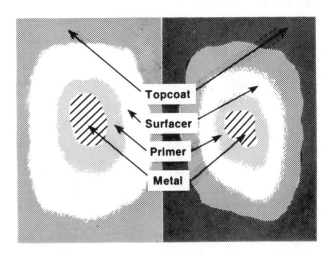

FIGURE 19-1 Sanding method of determining the type of old finish

previous repainting. The standard paint film thicknesses of new vehicles are:

Domestic vehicles	3 to 5 mils
European cars	5 to 8 mils
Japanese vehicles	3 to 5 mils

Normally, an electromagnetic thickness gauge or a mechanical thickness gauge mentioned in Chapter 17 is used to measure the paint film thickness.

19.2 DETERMINING THE TYPE OF PREVIOUS PAINT COATING

If the vehicle has never been repainted (the finish is the original one), determining the paint type is fairly easy. Shop manuals or the so-called "world color" book will identify the topcoat. If it is confirmed that the vehicle had been repainted in the past, it is now necessary to determine what type of paint was used. The methods for doing this include:

1. **Visual inspection method.** If the skin texture near a character line is rough or if what is known as a "polished texture" appears when rubbed (Figure 19-2), it indicates that a polish type paint was used for repainting. If a gloss peculiar to acrylic urethane appears, it can be determined that it was repainted with an acrylic urethane type paint.

2. **Solvent application method.** With this method, the paint film is rubbed with a white shop cloth soaked in lacquer thinner to determine the extent to which it will dis-

FIGURE 19-2   Visual inspection method of determining the type of old finish

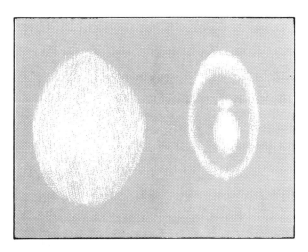

FIGURE 19-4   Heat application method of determining the type of old finish

FIGURE 19-3   Solvent application method of determining the type of old finish

solve the previous film. If the paint film dissolves and leaves a mark on the rag (Figure 19-3), the previous paint is an air-dry type. If it does not dissolve, it is either an oven dried or a two-component reaction type paint. An acrylic urethane lacquer paint film will not dissolve as easily as an air-dried paint, but sometimes the thinner will penetrate sufficiently to blur the paint gloss.

3. **Heat application method.** First, the area is wet sanded with #800 to #1000 grit abrasive paper to dull the paint film. Next, the area is heated with an infrared lamp. If a gloss returns to the dulled appearance, the paint is acrylic lacquer (Figure 19-4).

Table 19-1 classifies standard paints for determining previous painted coating. Table 19-2 lists the types of previously applied paints and those topcoats that can be applied over them.

19.3 COLOR AND TEXTURE MATCHING

Color matching is probably the single most recurring problem in the automotive refinishing industry. Most of the color matching problems are experienced when attempting to match metallic colors. Although some problems are encountered with solid colors, they cause the fewest problems for the average painter.

The first step in the color matching procedure is to learn the original color from the manufacturer's paint code in the vehicle identification number as described in Chapter 16. Keep in mind that this might not be exactly the right color because automotive finishes gradually change color when exposed to light. Each finish also weathers differently depending on its pigment composition. For these reasons, the ability to tint becomes very important.

TINTING COLORS FOR A PERFECT MATCH

There are three basic reasons for tinting colors:

- To adjust color variations in shades for cars of the same color as they come from the manufacturer.
- To adjust color because of aged or weathered finish.

TABLE 19-1: CLASSIFICATION STANDARD FOR PREVIOUS PAINT COATINGS

Previous Paint Coating	Classification Method		
	Visual Inspection	Solvent Method	Heat Application Method
Alkyd enamel	Caulking surface	Does not dissolve	Some softening
Acrylic lacquer	—	Dissolve	Softens
Acrylic enamel	—	—	Some softening
Polyurethane	Polished skin	—	—
Acrylic urethane lacquer	Polished skin	Difficult to dissolve	Some softening
Acrylic urethane enamel	Gloss with some orange peel	—	—

- To make a color for which there is no formula. There are cars painted with bench colors (a color that was never formulated or a color that has no color codes available).

To do color matching, the refinisher must be able to recognize colors as they actually are. It is

TABLE 19-3: HOW COLORS ARE DESCRIBED

Lighter—Darker (called depth)	1. Direct look (panel to panel) 2. Side angle look (panel to panel)
Cast differences	1. Redder 2. Bluer 3. Greener 4. Yellower
Cleanliness	1. Grayer (dirtier or more muddy) 2. Brighter (cleaner appearance)

important not only to see the color that is to be worked on, but also the overtones within that color, including the shades of darkness or lightness and the richness or fullness of the color (Table 19-3).

Tinting should only be used as a last resort. If the color of the refinish paint varies from the original finish, check the following possible reasons for the mismatch before deciding to tint the paint:

- The original may have faded. Check the paint on unexposed areas such as door jambs or under the trunk or hood to determine if the finish has faded. If this is the case, restore the paint's luster by compounding the old finish well beyond the repair area.
- Was the wrong color used? Check the auto manufacturer's code and the paint company's stock number for the color being used to make sure that it is the right one. It may be necessary to know the VIN number as well as

TABLE 19-2: APPLICATION CHART—PREVIOUSLY APPLIED PAINT AND REPAINTING PAINT

Topcoat	Previously Applied Paint					
	Alkyd Enamel	Acrylic Lacquer	Acrylic Enamel	Polyurethane Enamel	Acrylic Urethane Lacquer	Acrylic Urethane Enamel
Alkyd enamel	A	B	A	A	B	A
Acrylic lacquer	A	B	B	A	A	A
Acrylic lacquer enamel	A	B	A	A	A	A
Polyurethane enamel	B	B	B	A	A	A
Acrylic urethane lacquer	B	B	B	A	A	A
Acrylic urethane enamel	A	A	A	A	A	A

A Okay to repaint with
B Okay if primer-surfacer or sealer specified by paint manufacturer is used

the paint code in order to check the manufacturer's code.

- The pigment and/or flakes might not have been mixed thoroughly. Leaving pigment, flake, or pearl in the bottom of the can could cause a mismatch, so agitate thoroughly.
- Has the amount of thinner or reducer been measured carefully? Overthinning will lighten or desaturate a color. Remember that it is easy to add more thinner, but it cannot be taken out.
- Clean and compound the old finish to remove all chalking and oxidation before making a color comparison.
- The type of light in the shop could alter the appearance of the finish. Colors vary depending on the light they are viewed under. When the color match between two paints changes under different lighting conditions, it is referred to as **metamerism.** This is the reason why it is possible for a refinish paint to match the car color under shop lighting conditions, and then show up as a less than perfect match when the car is viewed in natural daylight. The color match seen under shop lighting conditions can vary depending on the type of lights used. For example, incandescent lights tend to give paint a red cast, while fluorescent lights could give paint a yellow or blue cast, depending on the type of fluorescent in the light. Both cool white light and soft white lights can also alter the appearance of paint color; the cast they throw on the finish will vary with the color of the paint.
- When using a test panel, allow the paint enough time to dry. Allow proper flash and dry times for each coat, because paint usually gets darker as it dries. If using a lacquer clear coat, remember that compounding the clear coat will make the paint appear darker. If testing for a base/clear finish, color judgment cannot be made until the clear is applied to the basecoat. Further information on making a test panel is given later in this chapter.
- Vary the spraying technique. The three shades shown in Figure 19-5 were sprayed out of the same gun cup of material. The section on the left was sprayed dry with the gun quite far away. The section in the middle was sprayed with the gun at the normal distance from the panel. The section on the right was sprayed wet with the gun held close. Here is a list of shading adjustments:

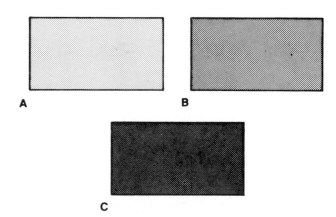

FIGURE 19-5 Matching colors with a spray gun: (A) lighter than normal—dry spray; (B) standard color—normal spray; and (C) darker than standard—wet spray.

Darker
1. Open fluid valve more.
2. Reduce size of fan pattern.
3. Decrease gun distance.
4. Slow down stroke.
5. Allow less flash time.

Lighter
1. Close fluid valve slightly.
2. Increase size of fan pattern.
3. Increase gun distance.
4. Speed up stroke.
5. Increase flash time.

Oddly enough, a mismatch in a panel repair will usually show up more than a mismatch in a spot repair—even though the spot repair is smaller. That is because a panel—such as a car door—has a distinct edge. And the repair, obviously, cuts off at that edge. Any mismatch—as in the case of front and rear doors—will be right next to the adjoining panel and will show a sharp contrast.

A spot repair, on the other hand, is performed by blending the repair into the surrounding area. In spot repairing, the first coat is applied to the immediate area being repaired. Subsequent coats extend beyond this area gradually. Finally, a blend coat extends beyond the color coats. Thus, if there is a slight mismatch, the blend coat and the last color coat will allow enough show through of the old finish to make the color difference a gradual one.

Analyzing Color

Through various application techniques, lightness/darkness, cast, and brightness can be adjusted so that the painter can achieve a good match. To

TABLE 19-4: ADJUSTING LIGHTNESS/DARKNESS		
	To Make Colors	
Variable	**Lighter**	**Darker**
Shop Condition 1. Temperature 2. Humidity 3. Ventilation	1. Increase 2. Decrease 3. Increase	1. Decrease 2. Increase 3. Decrease
Spraying Techniques 1. Gun distance 2. Gun speed 3. Flash time between coats 4. Mist coat	1. Increase distance 2. Increase speed 3. Allow more flash time 4. Will not lighten color	1. Decrease distance 2. Decrease speed 3. Allow less flash time 4. Wetter mist coat
Solvent Usage 1. Type solvent 2. Reduction of color 3. Use of retarder	1. Use faster evaporator solvent 2. Increase amount of solvent 3. Do not use retarder	1. Use slower evaporator solvent 2. Decrease amount of solvent 3. Add retarder to solvent

determine what must be done, the color must first be analyzed to determine whether it is too light or too dark, looking at the finish from an angle and head-on. Then the refinisher must check the cast to see if the color sprayed is redder, bluer, greener, or yellower than the original finish. Before adjusting begins, the color must be checked to see if the finish just sprayed is brighter or grayer than the original. The sprayed portion must always be allowed to dry before any adjustments are made.

Adjustments for lightness or darkness rely primarily on shop conditions, spraying techniques, and solvent usage (Table 19-4). Other variables include the amount of paint applied, the air pressure at the spray gun, and the amount of color added to the mix.

Once the lightness or darkness has been adjusted, tinting might be required to get the right cast. Each color can only vary in cast in two directions.

- Colors that are either greener or redder in cast include:
Blues	Purples
Yellows	Beiges
Golds	Browns
- Colors yellower or bluer in cast are:
Greens	Blacks
Maroons	Grays or Silvers
Whites	
- Colors yellower or redder in cast are:
Bronzes	Reds
Oranges	

- Colors bluer or greener in cast include:
Aqua	Turquoise

Charts and manuals available from manufacturers can help the painter decide on what tint color to use for the appropriate system. Once the color necessary to correctly adjust the cast is determined (Table 19-5), the amount must then be calculated, utilizing the least amount necessary to effectively change the color. The color must be thoroughly mixed; the gun triggered to clear the chamber; and then a small panel can be sprayed, allowed to dry, and checked against the original color.

After the color is correct in lightness/darkness and cast, the color might be made grayer or dirtier. Attempting to make a color brighter at this point will throw off the previous two corrections. To gray the finish, a wet coat must be sprayed followed by a coat sprayed at half trigger at a slightly greater distance and a small amount of white mixed with a very small amount of black.

Use three angles to determine whether or not a color adjustment is necessary:

- **Head-on.** Viewing the repaired area from an angle that is perpendicular to the vehicle.
- **Near spec.** Viewing the repaired area from an angle just past the reflection of the light source.
- **Side tone.** Viewing the repaired area at an angle of less than 45 degrees.

TABLE 19-5: METHOD OF CHANGING CASTS

Color	Add		Cast
Blue	Green	to kill	Red
Blue	Red	to kill	Green
Green	Yellow	to kill	Blue
Green	Blue	to kill	Yellow
Red	Yellow	to kill	Blue
Red	Blue	to kill	Yellow
Gold	Yellow	to kill	Red
Gold	Red	to kill	Yellow
Maroon	Yellow	to kill	Blue
Maroon	Blue	to kill	Yellow
Bronze	Yellow	to kill	Red
Bronze	Red	to kill	Yellow
Orange	Yellow	to kill	Red
Orange	Red	to kill	Yellow
Yellow	Green	to kill	Red
Yellow	Red	to kill	Green
White	White	to kill	Blue
White	White	to kill	Yellow
Beige	Green	to kill	Red
Beige	Red	to kill	Green
Purple	Blue	to kill	Red
Purple	Red	to kill	Blue
Aqua	Blue	to kill	Green
Aqua	Green	to kill	Blue

FIGURE 19-6 One method of determining the overcast of the tinting color

The color of the repaired area should be the same as the rest of the vehicle. If not, correct it until it is the same when viewed from all three angles.

HINTS ON COLOR TINTING

Here are some additional tips that might prove helpful when tinting a color:

- Check the color in daylight as well as artificial light. It might not look the same in both lights. When a refinish color matches in one light but not another, it often indicates that the same pigments were not used in the refinish material as in the original finish. The original equipment supplier is usually very careful to use the same pigments in the refinish material that are used in the original finish. To control the uniformity of colors, every batch is checked for exact color match in three different lights—yellow, blue, and daylight.
- Be sure the panel to be matched is thoroughly cleaned and compounded so the true color can be clearly seen.
- Determine what the color problem is and select the proper tinting colors. Do not use

mixed colors from the bench for this because they probably have overcasts of the wrong shades. Adjust the color to make the hue redder, greener, bluer, or yellower.
- To understand what the overcasts are to a tinting color, put a few drops on a quart lid with a few drops of white, then intermix these two and make a finger smear on the lid. This will allow the refinisher to determine what the overcast of that tinting color is (Figure 19-6).
- Do all tinting systematically.
  —Use a measuring device such as those described in Chapter 17.
  —Keep a list of tinting colors used.
  —Keep a record of the amount used.
- A formula of the color is a help in tinting because it shows the original base colors and indicates which color has faded out and has to be toned down in the refinish material.
- Be sure to mix all tinting colors thoroughly before using; also thoroughly mix the tinting color every time any color is added.
- Add tinting colors in small amounts because it is very easy to overtint. Keep in mind that more color can be added but it cannot be taken out.
- Do not tint the whole can of paint at one time. Make progressive tryouts with small samples until a color match is achieved.
- Be conservative when tinting near the limits of the color range. Correct the most noticeable color differences first.
- Use caution when adding white to metallics or pearls and always use low-strength whites.

FIGURE 19-7   Typical tinting guide and kit that is designed for the refinisher to provide a color matching tool that will help to visualize color changes and develop the experience and skill to accomplish successful color tinting. *(Courtesy of Du Pont Co.)*

- Stay with the same pearls and metallic flakes used in the formula.
- Do not use reduced material when using the drawdown bar.
- An agitator cup should be used when spraying metallics or pearls.
- Allow the color to dry before attempting to adjust it. To shorten dry time, use heat lamps, heat guns, or other drying methods. Be sure the method chosen has been approved for use in the paint/body shop.
- To check the true color, spray out a small panel and allow it to dry. Compare it to the panel to be matched. When it is possible, an old panel from the car to be matched is good to use because it can be masked in the center for an excellent comparison.
- Keep the tint on the light side until the final match is determined. Do not make a final judgment of the color match while the color is wet or still damp because it will change until it is completely dry.
- Once the color is tinted "close enough," complete the repair. Many times that last "just a little bit closer" is the thing that ruins a successful tinting.

Tinting can be divided into two categories: major color tinting and minor color tinting. Major color tinting consists of making up a color for which there is no color mixing formula available. Find a color chip as close as possible to the desired color and look at that formula. Break the formula down into percentages. For example, gold metallic is 45 per-

cent coarse metallic, 20 percent sparkle metallic, 15 percent gold toner, 10 percent yellow gold, 3 percent soft white, 2 percent soft black. Using these percentages, make only half of a can; stir and tint to match the desired color.

Minor color tinting is used to adjust a color in a given repair situation to achieve an acceptable color match. To achieve this, each major paint supplier has a basic color tinting kit, a set of instructions, and a tinting guide that is available to the paint jobber and the paint shop technician (Figure 19-7). Any painter, once familiar with the tinting information and kits that are available, should be able to do minor color tinting to achieve top quality color matches. For more information on the tinting colors and/or for a copy of a company's tinting guide with color chips, contact the shop's local paint jobber or a paint manufacturer's sales and service representative.

MATCHING METALLIC FINISHES

In most cases, solid color finishes—when properly prepared, thinned, and sprayed—will provide a good color match. The matching of metallic (polychrome) finishes, however, is probably the most skillful operation the refinisher has to perform. There are more cars on the road with metallic rather than solid-colored finishes; that means there are more metallic repairs to be made.

The reason much difficulty is experienced in matching metallic color is that metallic colors are made with a pigment and aluminum flake in the binder that allows light to penetrate beyond the surface of the paint film. When viewing a metallic color at right angles or perpendicular to the surface, this is the face of the color (Figure 19-8A). When viewing it at a 45 degree angle or less, it is the pitch or side tone of a color (Figure 19-8B).

As the position of metallic and/or pigment particles changes in a color film, the color shade of the metallic finish changes accordingly. Each metallic particle is like a tiny mirror. That is what changes the appearance of metallic colors when viewed from different angles. Metallic color also appears to be different when viewed under different kinds of light, such as daylight, shade, sun, or artificial light.

In standard color shades, the aluminum and pigment particles are spread uniformly throughout the paint film. Also notice that the metallic particles point in all directions, not just one predominate direction. This random mixing of the tiny mirrors in the paint film causes the light to reflect in all directions. The uniform distribution of pigment particles is what

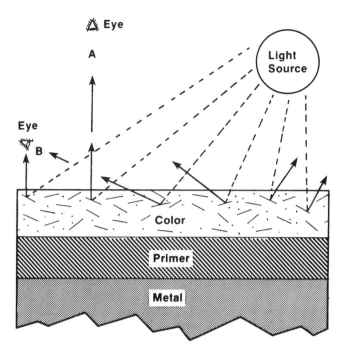

FIGURE 19-8 Metallic color construction showing face and side tone appearance of color. *(Courtesy of General Motors Corp.)*

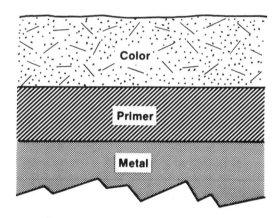

FIGURE 19-9 Standard shade of metallic color. *(Courtesy of General Motors Corp.)*

creates the standard color shade (Figure 19-9). To achieve this standard color proceed as follows:

- Use the label directions for the reduction of the color.
- Use slow evaporating solvents in temperatures of 65 to 85 degrees.
- Use 35 to 40 psi at the gun for lacquer and 50 to 55 psi at the gun for enamels.
- Apply in medium wet color coats with correct flash off time between coats.
- Remember to always be sure the paint material is stirred properly.

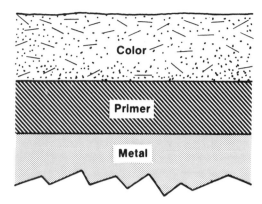

FIGURE 19-10 Light shade of metallic color. *(Courtesy of General Motors Corp.)*

Light Color Shades (Lighter Than Standard)

Light color shades are caused when the aluminum particles lie nearly horizontally at the top of the paint film and hide most of the pigment particles underneath them (Figure 19-10). The flat or horizontal positioning of the tiny metallic mirrors reflects a higher than normal amount of light. This causes lighter than standard color shades of the metallic finish. A match to these shades can be achieved by one or a combination of the following procedures:

 1. Use more solvent than is called for on the label directions.
2. Use medium or fast thinner to reduce acrylic lacquer. Use only fast drying solvents in reducing acrylic enamel.
3. Use a higher than recommended air pressure at the gun.
4. Apply light to medium coats with complete flash off between coats.
5. Hold the spray gun farther from the surface during spraying.
6. Increase speed of spraying applications.

Dark Color Shades (Colors Darker Than Standard)

Dark color shades have a dense flotation of pigment particles near the surface of the paint film. The aluminum flakes are positioned nearly perpendicularly to the surface (Figure 19-11). This effect is achieved on the vertical sides of a car the same as on the horizontal panels and is not simply the settling of the metallic flakes.

Dark shades are produced by very slow solvents and extra wet coats. Darker shades of colors are achieved by one or a combination of the following:

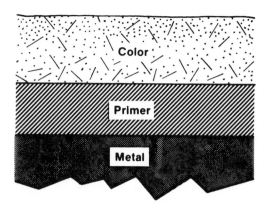

FIGURE 19-11 Dark shade of metallic color. (Courtesy of General Motors Corp.)

- Reduce color with 10 to 25 percent less solvent than the label indicates.
- Use 9 parts slowest solvent to 1 part retarder for color reduction in temperatures of 65 to 85 degrees. Usually a 100 percent reduction works well for dark shades of lacquer metallic colors, 25 percent for acrylic enamels.
- Use lower than normal air pressure for application; 35 to 40 psi is normal for lacquer, 55 to 60 psi for acrylic enamels.

Flip-Flop of Color

Flip-flop is a condition that occurs in metallics involving the positioning of the aluminum particles and the manner in which light is reflected to the observer (Figure 19-12). The cause of this effect results from the percentage of aluminum particles oriented in a specific direction and their depth in the paint film. The direction and intensity of the light being reflected back through the paint film cause the flip-flop phenomenon that is observed.

The first approach to correct the problem is to adjust your spraying technique to compensate for this effect. Spraying the fender a little wetter will slightly darken the appearance when looking directly into the panel. When viewed from an angle, the resulting appearance is lighter. This occurs because the aluminum particles are positioned flatter and deeper in the paint film.

Spraying the panel slightly dryer reverses the effect, giving a light appearance when looking directly at the panel. This is because the aluminum particles are closer to the surface. The result is a darker appearance viewed at the angle, as light becomes trapped. Both of these techniques are a compromise and should be used to correct minor conditions of flip-flop because the match in one direction can be changed too severely to be acceptable.

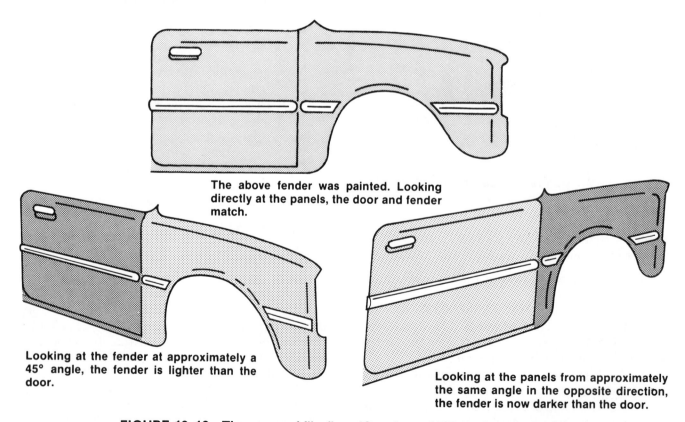

The above fender was painted. Looking directly at the panels, the door and fender match.

Looking at the fender at approximately a 45° angle, the fender is lighter than the door.

Looking at the panels from approximately the same angle in the opposite direction, the fender is now darker than the door.

FIGURE 19-12 The cause of flip-flop. (Courtesy of Martin-Senour Paint)

If spray techniques cannot correct this condition, the addition of a small amount of white will eliminate the sharp contrast from light to dark when the surface is viewed at various angles. The white acts to dull the transparency, giving a more uniform, subdued reflection through the paint film. Care should be taken when adding white since the change occurs quickly. Once too much white is added, recovering the color match becomes virtually impossible.

When confronted with an extremely difficult flip-flop condition, the best method involves adding white, plus blending the color into the adjacent panels. When blending, extend the color in stages. In acrylic lacquer, for example, use a recommended blending clear material, and thin the appropriate color when spraying farther into the adjacent panel. The blending agent protects the metallic edges, eliminating the halo or bright edge where the blend ends.

A good painter must know how to handle metallic colors. They are very sensitive to the solvents with which they are reduced and also sensitive to the air pressure with which they are applied. Metallic colors are also affected by a number of variables. A **variable** is part of the spray painting conditions: such as temperature, humidity, and ventilation, or a part of the spray painting process such as amount of reduction, evaporation, speed of solvents, air pressure, and type of equipment. If a painter is to get good color matches, it is important to understand how certain paint variables affect the shades of metallic colors.

Variables are divided into two categories: positive and negative. Positive variables are those things that a painter does to duplicate the original finish, which in turn results in a good color match. They are:

- Slowness of solvent evaporation. This allows the painter to reproduce the factory finish.
- Wetness of color application.
- Proper spraying technique and the correct air pressure.

Negative variables are those that cause the shades of colors to be off standard. Most common are:

- Improper reduction.
- Improper agitation.
- Improper application; primarily too high or too low air pressure.

In summary, the shades of metallic colors are controlled by:

- Choice of solvents.
- Color reduction.

- Air pressure.
- Wetness of application.
- Spraying techniques.

Test Panels

While a test panel sprayout is merely recommended in many refinish applications, with pearl luster and three-coat finishes it is vital. Test panels for three coats are needed to determine the correct amount of midcoat color. The midcoat color is the most critical portion of the three-coat repair. Gun pressure, reduction, and spray techniques affect the amount of color. The extra time spent spraying one or more test panels will be repaid with a satisfied customer that does not come back with a complaint later.

Make a test panel for a tricoat finish as follows:

 1. Prepare the panel with the same color undercoat being used on the job. If a sealer is going to be used, apply the sealer to the test panel also. Generally, a light color undercoat (or sealer) is preferred for three-coat repairs.

2. Apply the basecoat using the same pressure and spray pattern that will be used on the job. Duplicating the actual spray techniques when preparing the test panel is important. Do not vary the procedures just because the work is a small panel and not a full repair.

3. After the panel has dried, divide it into four equal sections (Figure 19–13). Next, mask off the lower three quarters of the panel, exposing the top quarter.

4. Apply one coat of mica midcoat color over the top quarter of the panel.

5. After the first mica coat has flashed, remove the masking paper and move it down to the middle of the panel, exposing the top half.

6. Apply another coat of mica midcoat color over the exposed top half of the panel.

7. After this second coat has flashed, remove the masking paper and move it down to expose three quarters of the panel.

8. Apply another coat of mica midcoat color over the exposed three quarters of the panel.

9. After flashing, remove the masking paper entirely.

10. Apply a fourth coat of mica midcoat color, again spraying the coat in the same way as would be done on the repair.

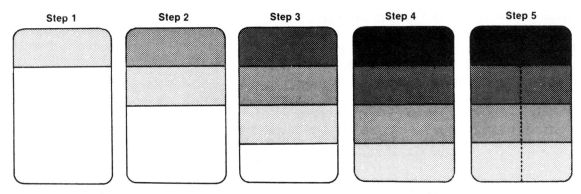

| Step 1 | Step 2 | Step 3 | Step 4 | Step 5 |

FIGURE 19-13   This example shows the step-by-step creation of a three-coat test panel. A test panel is always recommended when spraying paint. However, when spraying three-stage paint, it is necessary in order to achieve a proper color match

11.   After the entire panel has dried, mask off the panel **lengthwise** this time.

12.   Apply the manufacturer's recommended number of coats of clear to the exposed side.

First, clean thoroughly before making a comparison. Lay the test panel on the vehicle to determine the number of mica midcoats needed to match. View the match at different angles and under sunlight, if at all possible.

If the refinisher prefers, instead of using one panel divided into small sections, separate panels can be prepared to provide a larger work area. If separate panels are used, start by spraying all four panels with the midcoat color. Remove one of the panels and then spray the remaining three with a second coat. Spray a third coat on the last two panels and a fourth coat on the last panel only. Then, the panels should be masked vertically and receive the recommended coats of clear.

If, after completing the test panel procedure, a proper color match is still not achieved, recheck the coating with the manufacturer's product number. Be sure to use the correct basecoat color for this match. Slight variations in the basecoat color can produce an unmatchable final finish. So, be sure to follow paint manufacturer's label directions.

Do not mix brands of products. From primer to final clear coat, stay within one manufacturer's system. This system also includes solvents and reducers. Paint company laboratories match colors with a balance of solvents or reducers recommended for their products. Using another manufacturer's thinner might save a few dollars, but will often result in horrendous color matching problems. Keep in mind that individual coating manufacturers might have slightly different techniques and these should be followed carefully.

Once the test panel work is completed, the job is ready for repair. The following are some points to keep in mind when making a spot repair:

 1.   Prepare the surface as you would for any spot repair. Wash the entire panel and surrounding areas with water and a mild detergent soap. Rinse thoroughly and let dry. Then clean the entire panel and surrounding areas with a wax and grease remover. Repair all damaged and bare metal areas. Use a light-colored primer-surfacer or primer-sealer, if possible. Sand the repair area, if necessary. Wet-sand with #400 grit (or finer) sandpaper or dry-sand with #320 grit (or finer) sandpaper. Next, compound the undamaged area of the panel with a fine rubbing compound. Scuff and sand the compounded area with #1200 grit (or finer) sandpaper. Clean the entire panel with a prepaint cleaner to remove the sanding and compound residue. Use an air gun to remove all dirt from the cracks and surfaces of the panel. Complete the preparation job by tacking the entire panel with a clean tack cloth.

2.   Properly reduce the basecoat color by strictly adhering to the paint manufacturer's ratios.

3.   Apply the basecoat over the repair area only, using the blend technique. Apply single coats until proper hiding is achieved using 30 to 40 pounds of air pressure at the gun (or the paint manufacturer's recommended pressure). Normally two to three coats with 5 minutes of flash time between coats will suffice.

4.   Allow 15 minutes of flash time between the basecoat color and mica midcoat color. (It

is not necessary to "melt in" the dry overspray from the basecoat color because the mica midcoat will be applied directly over it.)

5. Tack the entire panel with a clean tack cloth.

6. Properly reduce the mica midcoat color by strictly adhering to the paint manufacturer's ratios. Use the same reduction ratio used when preparing the test panel.

7. Apply the mica midcoat color over the basecoat color and beyond, again using the blend technique. Apply single coats until a color match is achieved based on the test panel. Use 30 to 40 pounds of air pressure at the gun (or the paint manufacturer's recommended pressure) and allow 5 minutes of flash time between coats.

8. Allow 15 minutes of flash time between the mica midcoat color and the clear coat. As with the basecoat, there is no need to "melt in" the mica midcoat dry overspray because the clear coat will be applied directly over it.

9. As with the basecoat and the mica midcoat, carefully follow the manufacturer's recommended mixing procedures. This is especially important with the ratio of clear coat to hardener.

10. Again, tack the entire panel with a clean basecoat/clear coat tack cloth.

11. Apply medium wet coats of clear coat over the entire panel. Unlike application pressures for basecoat and midcoat, the clear coat should be applied using 50 to 55 pounds of air pressure at the gun (or the manufacturer's recommendation). Allow 5 to 10 minutes of flash time between coats. The number of clear coats will vary, depending upon the type of clear coat material being used and the depth of the original finish. If the clear coat must be blended, use the recommended thinner to melt in the dry overspray.

If the repair includes a flexible surface, products and approaches vary. Some coating products require additives in the clear coat, others call for flex agents to be used in the basecoat, midcoat, and clear coat. Still others do not require an additive or flex agent in any of the three coats. It may be necessary to spray a separate test panel with the flexible material if additives are used in any of the three layers of the three-coat procedure because there could be slight color variations caused by the addi-

tives. Pay careful attention to the manufacturer's requirements when three-coating flexible surfaces.

Another method to perform a test panel is the **drawdown bar.** The drawdown bar is a precision tool with a machined blade designed to give an even paint film distribution. To use it, a black and white test panel is taped to a perfectly flat surface, such as an aluminum clipboard. Paint is distributed onto the test panel and the drawdown bar is drawn through the paint, spreading it into a uniform paint thickness. After the first drawdown flashes, the process is repeated until the black and white on the test panel is no longer visible through the paint film. Then the test panel is compared to the car. When working on base/clear, make the drawdown over a strip of clear film (place over a check hiding panel so it will be possible to know when the coating has achieved the desired hiding effect). Turn the clear film over and the result will be a base/clear appearance.

If additional tinting is needed, another drawdown should be made on another test panel. This allows the refinisher to see the direction in which the tint is moving by comparing the panels to each other. When the desired color is achieved, the material can be sprayed and further adjusted through gun techniques and refinishing skills. The drawdown bar eliminates an unnecessary waste of time, material, and labor to adjust color. It is a unique way to tint and is an important tool when applying pearl lusters and three-coat finishes.

19.4 APPLYING TOPCOAT FINISHES

A complete description of various topcoat materials is given in Chapter 16. In this chapter, a general application procedure is given. But, before getting into these application techniques, it would be best to **review** the basic preparation procedures necessary to achieve a satisfactory final finish. They are:

1. Thoroughly wash the car with soap and water.

2. Chemically clean the car with a wax and grease remover to remove wax buildup, tar, and other non-water-soluble grime.

3. Sand the repair area by hand with a block (#400 grit) or machine (#320 grit).

4. Reclean the area with the wax and grease remover.

5. If bare metal is showing, pretreat the area to eliminate any hidden corrosion.

6. Then spot-prime these areas with an epoxy chromate primer.

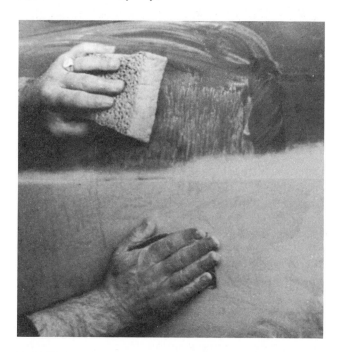

FIGURE 19-14   Wet sanding before applying the topcoat

7.   Apply primer-surfacer as needed to fill low areas and eliminate sand scratches.
8.   Sand primer-surfacer level to the surrounding area and blow off to clear dust. Use #400 grit for hand sanding and #320 grit if machine sanding (Figure 19-14).

After properly masking the vehicle and preparing the surface for repainting as just described, once again blow off any remaining dust with an air gun. Give a final touch-up cleaning with the wax and grease remover and rub the surface with a tack cloth (in this order). From this point on be careful not to touch the surface being refinished.

SPRAYING PROCEDURE

Before the topcoat material can be applied by spraying, it must be:

• Properly stirred or mixed.
• Thinned or reduced with proper solvent to the desired viscosity.
• Checked for surface temperature.

Stirring Paint

The failure to properly stir all the settled pigment into the liquid is a principal cause of paint problems. Stirring or mixing can be done by hand or by machine.

The part of paint that settles is the pigment, which gives the paint its color, opacity, and specific performance properties. These pigments vary greatly as to weight. Some of the commonly used pigments are seven to eight times as heavy as the liquid part of the paint. Because of their weight, the heavy pigments slowly settle and it is impossible to keep them in suspension. Some of the pigments are light and fluffy and have very little tendency to settle. The commonly used pigments that settle quite rapidly are the whites, chrome yellows, chrome oranges, chrome greens, and red and yellow iron oxides.

The consistency or viscosity of the liquid part of the paint has much to do with the rate of settling. The heavier the consistency, the slower the settling. Heavy pigments will settle out of a straight thinner in a few minutes, whereas in a paint vehicle it would take weeks or months. Careful judgment in thinning only sufficient material to do the job and discarding the small amount that is not used is the mark of an experienced painter.

If a color, which contains one or more of the heavy pigments (Table 19-6), is thinned or reduced to spraying consistency and allowed to stand 10 to 15 minutes without being stirred, it will have settled enough in that time to be off color when sprayed.

After a can of paint has been thoroughly agitated, empty out the contents of the can into another container or the gun cap, wash the can clean with a little solvent, and add this to the paint.

If a paint has settled out very hard, the liquid part should be poured off and the residue well broken up. The liquid part should then be slowly poured back with vigorous stirring.

Do not use sharp sticks or screwdrivers for stirring. At least a 1-inch wide flat bottomed, clean stirring paddle or steel spatula should be used.

When using an intermix system, agitate all base mixing colors for a minimum of 15 minutes. Before putting the can on the scale, put in just enough

TABLE 19-6: WEIGHTS OF VARIOUS PIGMENTS	
Name of Pigment	Weight of Solid Gallon Pounds
Toluidine Red	12.0
Indo Maroon	13.1
Carbon Black	14.4
Aluminum Powder	21.0
Titanium Dioxide White	35.0
Red Oxide of Iron	42.7
Chrome Yellow	50.0
Zinc Dust	60.7

universal retarder to cover the bottom. This will prevent small color additions from drying out and not mixing in with the rest of the colors.

There are several important points to remember when mixing basecoat color:

- Always read the label directions first.
- Use only the manufacturer's recommended hardeners and reducers (or basecoat stabilizers, if recommended).
- Use the proper reducer for the shop conditions and size of the job.
- Use only the proper mixing ratios.

The choice of a reducer is an important one. The refinisher must be careful to choose the product to complement the basecoat (and later the clear coat) in relation to the shop's temperature and humidity. Most major paint manufacturers offer a choice of reducers to offset atmospheric conditions that may cause color shifting. Problems such as soak-in (too slow a reducer) or dry overspray (too fast a reducer) can also occur if the incorrect reducer is used.

In the case of some new systems, a basecoat stabilizer or additive replaces the standard reducer. The stabilizer contains a basecoat resin designed to give it a faster recoat time and allow better metallic control. This is especially important if any blending is desired, because it prevents wash-out or a "halo-like" effect at the edge of the repair.

Viscosity

Topcoat paint materials are usually shipped at as high a viscosity as practical to help in slowing down the rate of settling. In order to apply these paint materials, they must be reduced with thinner or reducer to a viscosity that can be properly atomized by the spray gun.

Compared with a two-component reaction, the air-dry type of topcoat has a higher resin viscosity so vaporization is not as rapid. Because the initial drying time is faster, more solvent is required to improve the finish and it is also necessary to increase the spraying air pressure. However, increasing the air pressure will cause the solvent to evaporate faster, resulting in an even faster initial drying time and a defective finish. For preventive measures, it is necessary to consider decreasing the distance between the gun and painting surface, increasing the discharge volume, increasing the number of coats, speeding up the painting operation, and so on.

Two-component reaction type paint can be used with less solvent than air-dry type paint. However, because the acrylic urethane lacquer dries faster than acrylic urethane, more thinner is needed to compensate.

To prevent unevenness, metallic colors with a lower viscosity than solid colors are used. The distance between the gun and the painted surface is greater and there is also more pattern overlap. Application is similar to that for a dry coat.

Clear coat is applied in a method similar to a solid color but care must be taken to avoid a heavy coat. This can cause residual unevenness or other defects.

The method of checking the viscosity of paint is described in Chapter 17. The recommended viscosities for spot repairs, body repairs, and overall paint, as well as spray gun pressure, are given later in this chapter. All spray gun air pressure recommendations in this reading are at the gun.

Temperature

The temperatures of concern when refinishing are the room temperature, the temperature of the surface of the car, and the temperature of the paint. Temperature is especially important in downdraft spray booths. With all the air rushing by, the temperature of the paint applied is raised 6 or 7 degrees almost immediately. If the paint dries too fast, solvents will be trapped in the basecoat. This can cause problems when applying the clear coat. Also be careful when bringing in a car that has been stored outside in the cold. If the surface is too cold, the solvents will not evaporate as quickly as they should. Color matching and paint curing problems can result. A thermometer should be placed on the surface of the car (Figure 19–15). Make sure the surface is at the temperature suggested by the manufacturer before spraying.

19.5 REPAINTING SPRAY METHODS

As mentioned in Chapter 16, repainting spray methods are classified according to the condition of

FIGURE 19–15 A surface thermometer is handy for making sure that the metal temperature will not cause problems when the paint hits the surface.

the previous (original) paint coat, the size of the area to be repainted, and the location. These methods are:

- Spot repair spraying
- Panel repair spraying
- Overall spraying

SPOT AND PANEL SPRAYING

Spot repainting repairs are recommended where a complete panel repair is unjustified, being either uneconomical (size of repair or amount of masking involved) or impractical (difficulty of rendering the repair invisible, particularly in the case of metallic finishes). Shading is necessary so that slight differences in color or texture are not conspicuous.

Panel repainting is done to repair complete panels separated by a definite boundary, such as a door or a fender. Normally, it is not necessary to shade or graduate the paint unless the paint is difficult to match or if it is a metallic color. However, shading is done for such areas as between the quarter panel and roof panel, but this is still referred to as a panel repair.

Spot Repainting With Solid Colors

Definite rules cannot be laid down as to the range or degree of gradation for the shade area. The spot repair method should be used for light damage at the fender edge. In this case, there are two methods of gradation: at the boundary line between the fender and hood (Figure 19-16A) and at the press line. If gradation can be done within the range shown in Figure 19-16B, it will not be necessary to paint the upper portion of the fender where shading shows most conspicuously, thereby avoiding problems with color and texture differences.

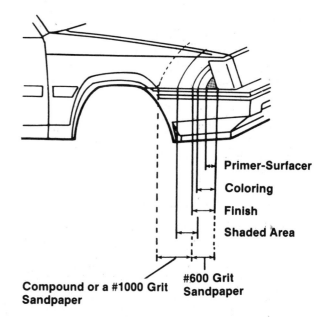

FIGURE 19-17   Preparing for spot repainting

Shown in Figure 19-17, when spot repainting with a solid color lacquer, the shaded area should be treated with compound or sanded using a #1000 grit sandpaper before repainting.

Apply the topcoat with a circular motion, working the spray gun from the center outward (Figure 19-18). This allows each coat to slightly overlap the previous one. An alternative method is to apply the finish in short strokes from the center outward. Again extend each coat so that it slightly overlaps the previous one. But in either method, the spray pattern should be narrowed and the fluid delivery reduced by adjusting the spray controls. To minimize overspray, the air pressure should be reduced, depending on the material to be sprayed. The spray pattern should never be reduced to a completely round jet; otherwise, both the paint control and overlapping of passes become difficult.

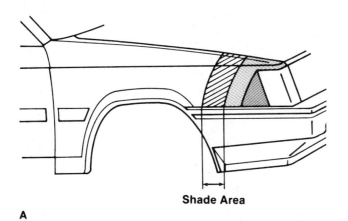

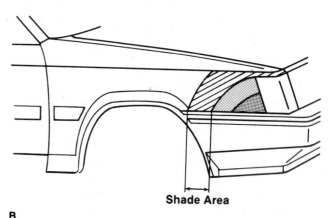

FIGURE 19-16   Range of spot repainting

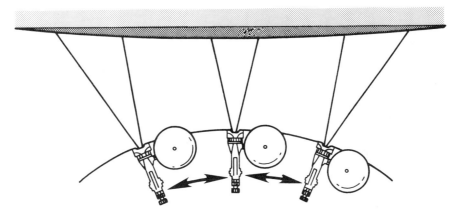

FIGURE 19-18   When spraying a shade area, it might be necessary to break "the arcing pattern" rule, but the arcing should be kept to a minimum.

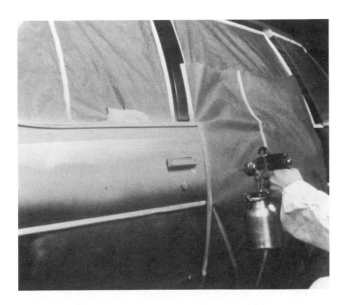

FIGURE 19-19   As the name implies, panel repairs are the usual concern in repainting a panel.

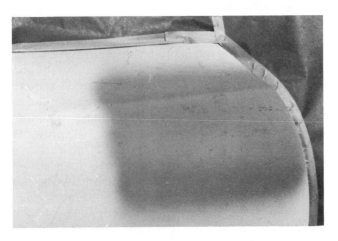

FIGURE 19-20   Once the area has been primed and the surface masked, apply the topcoat(s).

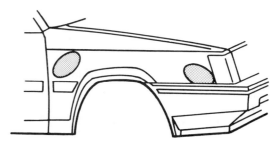

FIGURE 19-21   Panel repainting in two areas

Panel Repairs With Solid Colors

For complete panel or block repair (Figure 19-19), it is wise to properly mask off the area not to be painted (Figure 19-20).

If a panel has damage at two different locations, as shown in Figure 19-21, repairs should be done in a panel style. As shown, shading can be done at the molding area or extended below the molding.

For the quarter panel, it is generally necessary to graduate the shade area into the quarter pillar. If the vehicle has a ventilation louver on the quarter pillar, as shown in Figure 19-22, shading at that area will be less noticeable.

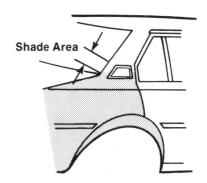

Shade Area

FIGURE 19-22   Repainting of quarter panel

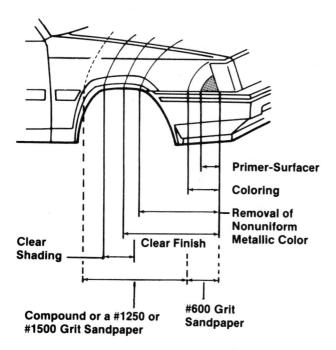

FIGURE 19-23   Spot repainting of metallic colors

Spot Repainting With Metallic Colors

If spot repainting with a metallic color at locations shown in Figure 19–23, skill is required in matching the color tone and bringing out the metallic image through proper distribution of the paint. The shaded area will be less noticeable if it is angled away from the press line (Figure 19–24).

Panel Repairs With Metallic Colors

Unevenness tends to be very noticeable with clear and bright metallic colors. Therefore, if it is

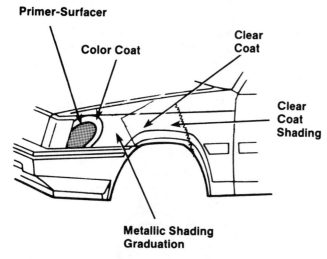

FIGURE 19-24   One method of making a shaded area less noticeable

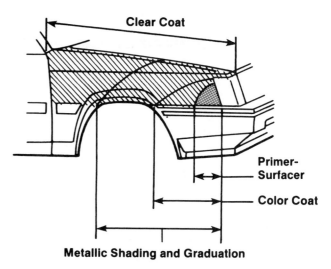

FIGURE 19-25   Panel repainting of metallic colors

impossible to match the paint exactly with the previous coat, extend the shade area over a wide range, as shown in Figure 19–25, to make it less distinguishable.

If one panel has damage at both ends or if the whole panel is to be repainted, shading of metallic paint must extend onto the adjacent panels. As shown in Figure 19–26, the clear coat extends beyond the fender onto one of the adjacent door panels and to the second press line of the hood.

OVERALL SPRAYING

For overall spraying, keep a wet edge while maintaining minimal overspray on the horizontal surfaces. This prevents spray from settling onto areas that have already dried, which would cause a gritty surface. Avoid sags in the overlap line by changing the point of overlapping (Figure 19–27).

Although there is not a single most perfect procedure for repainting a car overall, most refinishers will agree that the diagrams in Figure 19–28 illustrate the best patterns. With a conventional booth, by starting with the top of the car and proceeding to the trunk deck lid, side, and so on, the painter can best keep a wet edge while maintaining minimum overspray on the horizontal surfaces. This prevents spray dust from settling onto areas that have already dried, causing a gritty or contaminated surface. If possible, it is better for two painters to work in a state-of-the-art downdraft booth. The spray pattern is different from that of the conventional booth because of the direction of the airflow (top to bottom). Following the pattern shown in Figure 19–29 allows the three main horizontal surfaces to remain as wet

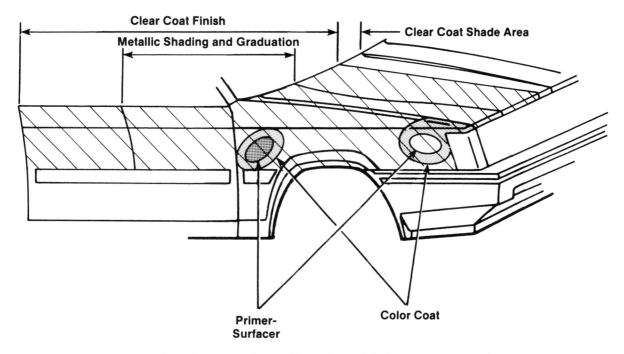

FIGURE 19-26   Panel repairs of metallic colors with damage at more than one area

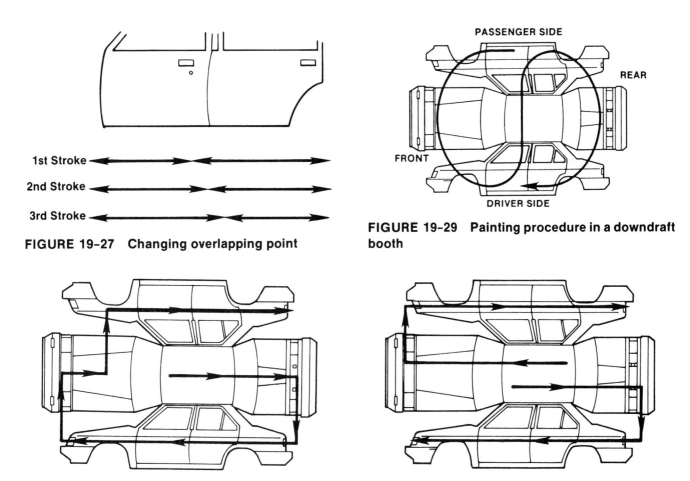

FIGURE 19-27   Changing overlapping point

FIGURE 19-29   Painting procedure in a downdraft booth

PAINTING ORDER FOR 1 PERSON

PAINTING ORDER FOR 2 PERSONS

FIGURE 19-28   Overall painting procedures

as possible while maintaining minimum overspray. These procedures also allow the painter(s) to continue to apply additional coats as needed without a significant loss of time due to flash off between coats.

19.6 TOPCOAT APPLICATIONS

Before applying any topcoat finish, it is necessary to very carefully read the paint manufacturer's directions that appear on the paint container (Figure 19-30). While the basic type of paints—alkyd enamel, acrylic urethane, and so on—have the same general characteristics, each manufacturer has its own formulations for its products. For this reason, the best source of data on how to apply a specific brand of paint is the container label. Another source of good information can be found in the manufacturer's literature.

Some of the more important label and literature data that should be checked include:

- Proper viscosity using either Ford or Zahn cup
- Spray gun pressure
- Use of additives, reducers, thinners, and activators when necessary
- Application techniques
- Number of paint coats required for different refinishing jobs
- Blending and mist coat procedures, if necessary
- Cleanup procedures

FIGURE 19-30 Carefully read the manufacturer's directions that appear on the paint container.

WARNING: Polyurethane and acrylic urethane enamels as well as the two-component or catalyzed type finishes (acrylic and alkyd) use isocyanates as a hardener. Isocyanates, however, are highly reactive and can become health hazards if not handled carefully. Because isocyanates react with many common substances, they must be used, stored, and disposed of with care. All urethane paints and products contain isocyanates and, therefore, share the same potential health hazards regardless of brand.

APPLYING BASECOAT/CLEAR COATS

Basecoat/clear coat systems pose a major challenge to refinishers. To help match and repair basecoat/clear coat systems, paint manufacturers offer special clear coats for use over color basecoats. Since more and more cars have basecoat/clear coat finishes, it is very important to become familiar with them. The application procedures for acrylic enamel and acrylic lacquer basecoats already have been discussed.

When estimating a basecoat/clear coat repair, carefully examine the finish on the area adjacent to the damage. If it is chalked, dulled, or otherwise impaired, matching the old finish might prove impossible. Ideally, such jobs should be performed as overalls. This approach will eliminate many problems in repairing basecoat/clear coat finishes that are severely weathered.

When spraying, two medium coats of basecoat should be applied. The basecoat does not need to be glossy, and only enough should be used so as to achieve hiding. Two or three medium wet coats of clear should be applied next, with at least 15 minutes flash time between coats.

For best results, sanding of the basecoat should be avoided. If sanding must be done because of dirt or imperfections after the first clear coat, it can be done safely after approximately 3 hours at 70 degrees Fahrenheit, 50 percent relative humidity, and in a location where adequate air movement is assured. Wet sanding with #600 to #1200 grit paper will minimize sand scratches. The sanded area must then be given another basecoat to prevent streaking and mottling. Buffing of an acrylic enamel basecoat/clear coat finish is needed only if sanding was done. Several things can be done to help clear coats wear better:

- Do not load clear coats on heavily. Because these finishes are clear, refinishers have a tendency to use too much in an attempt to increase the desired glamour effect. As a result, they "bury" the topcoat.
- Do not use thick clear finishes. Contrary to some opinions, clears do not perform better when they are underreduced. Thin or reduce according to the label instructions.
- Do not use economy thinners or reducers when spraying clear coats. Fast thinners/reducers weaken the performance of clears by trapping solvents and hurting the flow and leveling characteristics. Use a quality thinner/reducer and let each coat flash thoroughly before applying the next one.
- Apply an adhesion promoter over the entire panel to be refinished, or at least past where any color or clear will be applied (Figure 19-31). Apply a clear coat over the entire panel within the adhesion promoter area. If necessary, blend the clear as described earlier. Remember to step out the coats of clear.

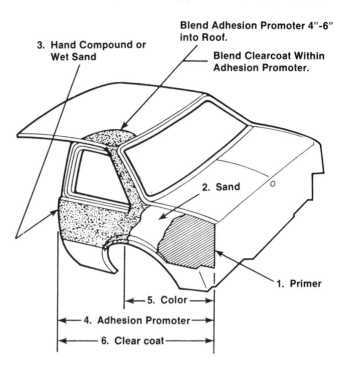

FIGURE 19-31 A typical panel repair using adhesion promoter

 **SHOP TALK**

Recently introduced, fluorine clear coats are designed to provide superior weathering characteristics and paint film durability. This is due to the higher resistance to ultraviolet rays. The result is a finish that requires no waxing. It is reported to keep its gloss and water shedding properties as well as, or better than, conventional clears when waxed regularly. If the vehicle has an OEM fluorine clear topcoat, check the service paint manuals, the finish must be preserved during collision repair. This means that the refinish system must also use a fluorine clear coat. These finishes are now becoming available through domestic paint manufacturers. Some might require slightly different application and blending procedures than the clears now being used. This might include longer care times for basecoats before the clear is applied and before the use of adhesion promoter.

TRI-COAT FINISHES

Although tri-coats require somewhat different refinish procedures and techniques, they are essentially the same as the repairs done on basecoat/clear coat finishes. Following are some key points to keep in mind when performing a tri-coat repair:

- Follow the recommendations for this type of repair furnished by the paint manufacturer.
- Pay close attention when the instructions call for the use of adhesion promoters, antistatic materials, and so on.
- Make a test or let-down panel, as described earlier in this chapter. A mismatch in the basecoat, mica coats, or clear coat can affect the overall finish match.
- Keep the repair area as small as possible.
- Avoid a "halo" effect by applying the first coat of mica to the basecoat only.
- The more intermediate coats that are applied, the darker the finish will appear.
- Allow a larger area in which to blend the mica intermediate coats. They require more room to blend than a standard basecoat.
- Do not try to substitute another type of paint for the recommended basecoat.
- Always check the basecoat color against the OEM basecoat. To do this, find an uncleared mica-free area of the vehicle. Some car companies leave an exposed portion of basecoat beneath the right and left sill plates that is perfect for this.

SHOP TALK _____

Recently introduced, polyoxithane enamels are part of the first isocyanate-free basecoat/clear coat and single stage system. They were developed with health considerations in mind as well as providing the highest quality in OEM color and quality matching. Tests show that these provide excellent hiding, durability against industrial pollution and extreme weather conditions, and protection from fading caused by ultraviolet light. More information about polyoxithane and other nonisocyanate-activated paint systems will be available in the near future, but for now these initial enamels promise to be the answer to one of the refinishing industries' major health problems.

19.7 SPATTER FINISHES

The interior of luggage compartments—the side walls and floor—is often painted with a special latex finish and a lacquer color. The material is water-reducible and can be applied in one heavy or two medium coats. The spatter finish material should be agitated to a minimum. Hand paddle mixing is usually sufficient; do not shake on a paint shaker. When ordering spatter paint from a paint jobber, mention the make of the vehicle and the model year.

The application procedure is as follows:

1. After all metal repair work and priming have been completed, clean the luggage compartment surfaces with a solvent.
2. Mask off the compartment area, as required.

FIGURE 19-32 When removing the masking material, be sure not to touch the paint.

3. Read the label directions carefully and follow them to the letter. As a rule, open the spray fan nozzle to give only 3/4 of the full pattern. The fluid feed should be wide open. Also, use the lowest air pressure that causes the desired spray pattern:
   - For smaller spatters, increase the air pressure.
   - For larger spatters, reduce the air pressure.
4. Apply the coating. If two coats are needed, allow several minutes of flash time. Allow the surface to dry completely before putting the vehicle back into service.

19.8 FINAL DETAILING

Once the topcoat has been applied, begin the final touch-up or **detailing.**

- Removing masking tape and paper
- Polishing the surface
- Repairing small surface defects

REMOVING MASKING MATERIALS

After the topcoat has dried, the masking paper and tape must be removed. If the finish has been force dried, the masking should be removed while the paint finish is still warm. If the finish is allowed to cool, the tape is more difficult to remove and leaves adhesive particles on the paint finish.

The tape should be removed slowly so that it comes off evenly (Figure 19-32). Pull the tape away from the paint edge—never across it. Take care not to touch any painted areas because the paint might not be completely dry. Fingerprints or tape marks could result if the surface is touched. Also, be careful of loosely fitting clothing or belt buckles that could accidentally rub against the paint.

Never allow a lacquer type paint to dry thoroughly before removing the tape as the paint film might peel off along with the tape. It is best to remove the tape immediately after repainting, but when doing so, be careful not to touch the freshly painted surface.

POLISHING

Lacquer paint generally needs a light compounding or polishing to give it the desired gloss and to remove any unevenness (Figure 19-33). If any

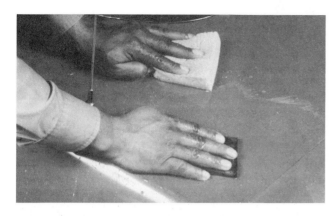

FIGURE 19-33   Use micro fine #1200 grit abrasive paper for leveling newly painted lacquer surface and to produce that "show car" finish. Use micro fine #1500 grit abrasive paper to remove dust nibs in enamel surfaces.

slight defects in new enamel finished surfaces should occur, they should not be compounded until the paint has had a chance to "set up." This could involve a period of several days.

Rubbing Compound and How It Works

Rubbing compounds (Table 19–7) are much like paste and liquid cleaners used before a car is waxed. Whether these rubbing compounds come in paste or liquid form, they contain an abrasive such as pumice that levels the top of the finish, making it smooth and lustrous. Rubbing compounds are available in various cutting strengths for both hand and machine compounding. (Hand compounds are oil based to provide lubrication; machine compounds are water based to disperse the abrasive while using a buffing wheel.)

Generally, compounds with coarse particles are called **rubbing compounds,** while those with fine particles of pumice are called **polishing compounds.**

A rubbing compound works two ways:

- When originally used, the pumice particles cut and smooth the compound.
- This action breaks down the pumice into small particles so it then works as a polish.

Uses of rubbing compounds are:

- To eliminate fine sand scratches around a repair area as described in Chapter 18
- To correct "orange peel" or a gritty surface
- To smooth and bring out the gloss of applied lacquer topcoats (Figure 19–34)

Small areas or blended areas are best done by hand. On large areas, however, machine compound-

TABLE 19-7:   POLISHING AND RUBBING COMPOUNDS

Grade	Liquid	Paste	Use and Application
Very fine	Machine or hand	—	Used to remove swirl marks on topcoat. Spread material evenly with buffing wheel pad before starting compounding.
Fine	Machine or hand	Hand (add water for machine use)	Used to level orange peel. Can also be used to clean, polish, and restore older finishes leaving no wheel marks or swirls.
Medium	Machine or hand	Paste (add water for machine use)	Used for quick-leveling orange peel. Can be used to repair other minor paint defects.
Coarse	Machine	Machine	Used for compounding before final topcoating (see Chapter 18)

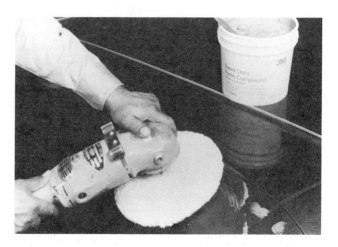

FIGURE 19-34   Rubbing compounds bring out gloss.

ing is recommended. Care must be taken not to cut through styling edges. To avoid cutting through styling edges, apply a strip of masking tape along the edge. After compounding is completed, remove the tape and compound the edge by hand—just enough to produce a smooth finish. Keep in mind that styling edges usually retain less paint than flat surfaces and should get only minimum compounding.

FIGURE 19-35 Always hand polish or compound in a straight direction. *(Courtesy of 3M).*

Hand Compounding

Fold a soft, lint-free, flannel cloth into a thick pad or roll into a ball and apply a small amount of compound to it (Figure 19-35). Rub area to be compounded in straight back and forth strokes using medium-to-hard pressure until desired smoothness is achieved.

When polishing over a blended or shaded area, it is a must to keep the following in mind:

- Rub in the direction shown in Figure 19-36. If rubbed in the opposite direction, there is danger of the shade texture appearing.
- Use either a very fine or extra-fine grain rubbing compound.
- If the shade texture appears, it cannot be corrected.

Hand compounding takes a lot of elbow grease and is time consuming. To keep the final compound-

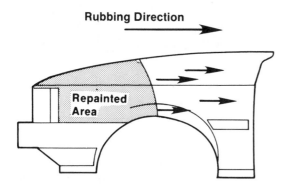

FIGURE 19-36 Polishing direction over shaded area

ing of lacquer topcoats to a minimum, it is important to apply the finish as wet as possible (without sags or runs) by using the right quality lacquer thinner.

Machine Compounding

Compounding/polishing machines are fully described in Chapter 4. Apply machine compound over a small area using a medium-to-coarse bristled paint brush or a squeeze bottle. Then compound using a buffing pad on the machine. Do not try to compound too large an area at one time because the rubbing compound has a tendency to dry out. Do not apply too much pressure and keep the machine moving to prevent cutting through the topcoat to the undercoat. Figure 19-37 shows how to install both buffing and polishing pads.

A

B

FIGURE 19-37 (A) The buffing pad is usually fastened by a washer nut. (B) Most finishers install the polishing pad over the buffing pad for extra softness. The pad is tied in place.

 **SHOP TALK** _____

During polishing, the abrasive material in the rubbing compound gradually crumbles into smaller pieces. The polishing effect is better in the early stages and gradually decreases with the gloss producing effect gradually becoming better. This is why a small amount of compound should be used over small areas without replenishing the compound for each area.

The primary advantages of machine compounding—in addition to saving time—are the achievement of the proper cutting action and the nonclogging of the compounding pad. When the compounding is completed, replace the buffing pad with a polishing pad or lamb's wool bonnet and polish. Remember to keep the machine moving.

 **SHOP TALK** _____

A spray gun should not be used for small repairs of the topcoat. Instead, repairs can be made with a knife (or razor blade) and a whetstone and repainted with a brush.

Repair With a Whetstone and Knife

Protruding defects in the topcoat such as sags or seeds (pieces of dirt) should be first corrected with a whetstone or a knife and then polished with a rubbing compound. Use of either a whetstone or a knife depends on the shape of the defect as shown in Figure 19-38.

If the protrusion is not so apparent, use a #1500 to #2000 FBB whetstone as follows:

1. First, prepare the whetstone by sanding a smooth edge with a #1200 grit abrasive paper to make it flat. Next, round the corners.
2. Place the sanded edge of the whetstone over the protrusion and move it in a left-right direction (Figure 19-39). If necessary, use a little oil to help make the movement smoother.
3. After the protrusion has almost disappeared, blow off the whetstone particles and finish the job with a very fine or extra-fine rubbing compound.

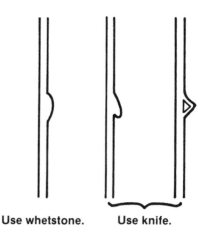

Use whetstone.   Use knife.

FIGURE 19-38   Type of defect and proper repair tool

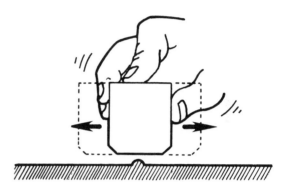

FIGURE 19-39   How to polish defects with a whetstone

FIGURE 19-40   Making surface repair with a knife or razor blade

If the protrusion is rather noticeable, repair with a knife or single-edged razor blade:

1. Being careful not to take off more than necessary, cut off the protrusion with a knife or razor blade (Figure 19-40). The tip of the knife should be pointed slightly upward.
2. Take off the remaining protrusion with a whetstone or #1500 to #2000 grit abrasive paper.
3. Blow off any particles and finish with an extra-fine grain rubbing compound.

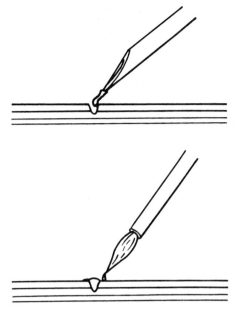

FIGURE 19-41 Making surface repairs with a brush

Repairs With a Brush

A fine brush can be used to repair slight peeling or scratches by filling them in with touch-up paint. Here is the basic procedure:

1. First, degrease the defective area with silicone solvent or comparable material.
2. Lightly dip the tapered tip of a small brush handle into the touch-up paint and quickly allow the paint to drip onto the defective area (Figure 19-41).
3. Dip the brush into lacquer thinner and apply it around the boundary of the touch-up paint. This will cause the touch-up paint to

smooth out and make it less noticeable.
4. Allow to set until completely dry.

 **SHOP TALK** _____

Until a new topcoat has cured at least 60 to 90 days, no automotive finish wax should be applied.

Repair by Filing

Filing will remove surface dirt, runs, and sags. The dirt nib is a tool that has been used in car factories for years. Yet it is new to the collision industry. This tool is useful for removing surface dirt, runs, and sags, and other defects that are on or above the paint surface. They are available commercially, or can be made from a body file (Figure 19-42).

It must be remembered that body files are made from hardened steels. The technician may not be able to break off a piece. Files must be cut with an abrasive saw or plasma arc/cutting torch. Also the ends of the file must be dressed. The sharp edges of the teeth must also be carefully dressed down so that you have smooth, flat teeth resting against the paint. The file can be glued to a wooden block for better grip. It can be sharpened or deburred by gently running the length of the file across a piece of #1200 to #1500 grit sandpaper held flat on a hard, smooth surface.

Use the surface file with short, straight strokes in one direction only. One or two strokes should remove any defect. When used properly, the file will quickly shave off any defect, without causing much damage to the surrounding paint. However, the spot must be sanded to remove any remaining portion of the defect.

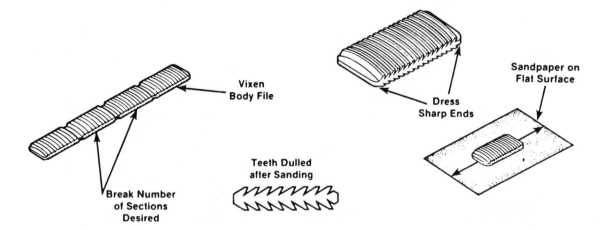

FIGURE 19-42 Making a surface file

19.9 FINESSE FINISHING

Finesse finishing refers to the procedures and products needed to do the finish steps required by basecoat/clear coat high-tech finishes. The objective of finesse finishing is to remove any defects in the refinish paint without damaging the surrounding surface, while keeping the repair as small as possible.

The four basic steps involved in a systemic approach to the finesse finishing process (Table 19–8) can be summarized as follows, beginning with the most aggressive step:

TABLE 19–8:   FINESSE FINISHING PROCEDURES

Paint Type	Paint Condition	Procedure			
		Wet Sanding	Compounding	Machine Glazing	Hand Glazing
Refinish paints: cured enamels/urethanes* (air-dried more than 48 hours or baked)	1. Minor dust nibs or mismatched orange peel (light sanding) 2. Heavy orange peel, dust nibs, paint, runs or sags	1. Fine 1500 2. Fine 1200	1. — 2. Microfinishing compound	1. Finishing material 2. Finishing material	1. Hand glaze 2. Hand glaze
Refinish paints: fresh enamels/urethanes* (air-dried 24 to 48 hours)	1. Minor dust nibs or mismatched orange peel (light sanding) 2. Heavy orange peel, dust nibs, paint runs or sags	1. Fine 1500 2. Fine 1200	1. Microfinishing compound 2. Microfinishing compound	1. Microfinishing glaze 2. Microfinishing glaze	1. Hand glaze 2. Hand galze
Refinish paints: acrylic lacquer	1. Low gloss or overspray 2. Low gloss, minor orange peel, or overspray 3. Low gloss, moderate orange peel, or dust nibs 4. Low gloss, heavy orange peel, paint runs or sags	1. — 2. — 3. Fine 1200 4. Fine 1000	1. — 2. Paste or rubbing compound (heavy cut) 3. Microfinishing compound (medium cut) 4. Paste or rubbing compound (heavy cut)	1. Machine glaze 2. Machine glaze 3. Machine glaze 4. Machine glaze	1. Hand glaze 2. Hand glaze 3. Hand glaze 4. Hand glaze
All factory applied (OEM)	1. New car prep or fine wheel marks 2. Coarse swirl marks, chemical spotting or light oxidation 3. Overspray or medium oxidation 4. Heavy oxidation or minor acid rain pitting 5. Dust nibs, minor scratches, or major acid rain pitting 6. Orange peel, paint runs or sags	1. — 2. — 3. — 4. — 5. Fine 1500 6. Fine 1200 or 1500	1. — 2. — 3. Microfinishing compound (medium cut) 4. Rubbing compound (heavy cut) 5. — 6. Microfinishing compound (medium cut)	1. — 2. Finishing material 3. Finishing material 4. Finishing material 5. Finishing material 6. Finishing material	1. Hand glaze liquid polish 2. Hand glaze 3. Hand glaze 4. Hand glaze 5. Hand glaze 6. Hand glaze

*Enamels/urethanes—as referred to in this chart—are catalyzed paint systems (including acrylic enamel, urethane, acrylic urethanes, acrylic urethane enamels, polyurethane enamels, and polyurethane acrylic enamels) and nonisocyanate-activated paint systems used in color or clear coats.

1. **Wet sanding.** Use very fine (#1000, 1500, 2000) grit sanding papers. Wet sanding is particularly appropriate for dealing initially with heavy or mismatched orange peel, paint runs and sags, dust nibs, minor scratches, and major acid rain pitting on all painted surfaces. Basically, wet sanding removes a defect from the surface. When wet sanding, always keep the area very wet. A small dab of polishing compound can also be used as lubricant. Use light, even strokes, and sand in a circular motion. To check the sanding progress, wipe or squeegee the area frequently.

   Finesse sanding requires a sanding block or backing pad to obtain a smooth, even cutting action (Figure 19-43). There are a number of new types of backing pads available for finesse sanding. There are also small sanding blocks used with half-dollar sized wafers of sandpaper. These wafers have adhesive on the back for mounting to the sanding block.

2. **Compounding.** As the second step in the process, compounding is necessary to remove sanding marks and scratches left on the surface from Step 1. At times, the painter might be able to start the finishing process at Step 2. This would be the case when dealing with a low gloss, minor orange peel, or overspray problem on an acrylic lacquer surface, or with heavy-to-medium oxidation and minor acid rain pitting problems on OEM-painted surfaces.

Again, in the system approach to paint finishing, the paint expert must determine at the beginning of the job both the type of defect involved and the severity of the problem, then base the choice of an appropriate finish step on this information.

When the sand scratches have been removed and there is a uniform glossy finish, move on to the orbital buffing stage (Figure 19-44). Orbital buffing is also new, although detailers have been using it for some time.

3. **Machine glazing.** Step 3 is essential to eliminate the compounding swirl marks produced by the previous step. Machine glazing is critical to the overall success of the finishing process. It is always important to devote enough time to this step to complete it properly. Failure to do so can result in a "die-back" problem, in which the defective work reveals itself weeks or months later, requiring costly rework, as well as damaging a body/paint shop's reputation.

   The choice of both the machine glazing product and the polishing pad is critical. Depending on the type of automotive paint being finished, it is essential to choose the recommended machine glazing product for that particular type of paint.

   It is also essential to use very high-quality polishing pads—pads designed specifically for machine glazing. Use of compounding pads or coarsely fibered polishing pads for machine glazing can result in surface marks that cannot be re-

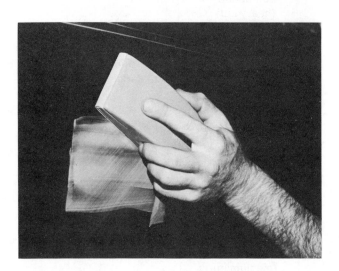

FIGURE 19-43 Finesse sanding requires a sanding block or backing pad.

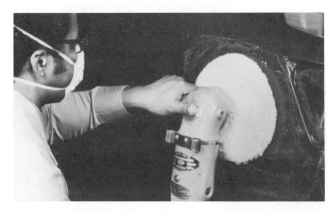

FIGURE 19-44 When doing a buffing job, use an orbital procedure. (Courtesy of 3M)

moved by the final hand glazing. Use glaze material sparingly; it will not take much to do the job. Use the buffing wheel to distribute the material evenly over the area to be buffed before running the wheel. Keep the pad flat against the surface, directly over the spot to be buffed. Use a slow, circular motion and continue on into the surrounding area to blend in the repair.

4. **Hand glazing.** Hand glazing with a sealer/glaze is the final step in achieving a finesse finish. Hand glazing results in an exceptionally high gloss, defect-free finish. When dealing with very minor, superficial finishing problems such as those encountered in new car prep work, hand glazing might be the only required step. However, most refinish situations will require more than one step.

Hand sealer/glazes are applied by hand using a clean terry cloth. Rub thoroughly into the surface, and wipe dry with a clean cloth. Be careful, though, glazes can fill and cover up some fine scratches that should be buffed out. But this is a temporary disappearing act. The scratches will show after a few washes.

Finesse finishing is not a cure-all. It certainly is not a substitute for careful and thorough vehicle preparation. Finesse finishing cannot turn an unacceptable paint job into an acceptable one. However, it may be possible to salvage a job that otherwise may have to be redone.

19.10 PAINTING PROBLEMS

Most refinishing problems can usually be repaired, but the work requires time and money. Therefore it is wise to prevent common paint problems before they occur. Unfortunately, there is a variety of causes for defects occurring in a paint finish, and they usually originate in the preparation of the base metal, painting procedure, environment, paint ingredients, and external influences. If defects are noted, the remedy should be in accordance with the instructions given earlier in this chapter.

If defects are noted while painting, either stop work and take the proper steps immediately or wait until the painting is finished to take the proper remedy. One of the best ways to reduce the likelihood of defects occurring is to closely follow the proper fundamental painting procedures outlined in the paint manufacturer's instructions.

ACID AND ALKALI SPOTTING

Condition

Spotty discoloration that appears on the surface. (Various pigments react differently when in contact with acids or alkalies.)

Causes

Chemical change of pigments resulting from atmospheric contamination, in the presence of moisture (acid rain), due to industrial activity.

Prevention

1. Keep finish away from contaminated atmosphere.
2. Immediately following contamination, the surface should be vigorously flushed with cool water and detergent.

Solution

1. Wash with detergent water and follow with a vinegar bath.
2. Sand and refinish.
3. If contamination has reached the metal or subcoating, the spot must be sanded down to the metal before refinishing.

BLEEDING

Condition

Original finish discoloring—or color seeping through—the new topcoat color.

Causes

Contamination—usually in the form of soluble dyes or pigments on the older finish before it was repainted. (This is especially true with older shades of red.)

Prevention

Thoroughly clean areas to be painted before sanding, especially when applying lighter colors over darker colors. (Avoid using lighter colors over older shades of red without sealing first.)

Solution

Apply two medium coats of bleeder. Seal in accordance with label instructions. Then reapply color coat.

BLISTERING

Condition

Bubbles or pimples appearing in the topcoat film, often months after applications.

Causes

1. Improper surface cleaning or preparation. Tiny specks of dirt left on the surface can act as a sponge and hold moisture. When the finish is exposed to the sun (or abrupt changes in atmospheric pressure), moisture expands and builds up pressure. If the pressure is great enough, blisters form.
2. Wrong thinner or reducer. Use of a fast-dry thinner or reducer, especially when the material is sprayed too dry or at an excessive pressure. Air or moisture can be trapped in the film.
3. Excessive film thickness. Insufficient drying time between coats or too heavy application of the undercoats can trap solvents that escape later and blister the color coat.
4. Contamination of compressed air lines. Oil, water, or dirt in lines.

Prevention

1. Thoroughly clean areas to be painted before sanding. Be sure surface is completely dry before applying either undercoats or topcoats. Do not touch a cleaned area because the oils in the hands will contaminate the surface.
2. Select the thinner or reducer most suitable for existing shop conditions.
3. Allow proper drying time for undercoats and topcoats. Be sure to let each coat flash before applying the next.
4. Drain and clean air pressure regulator daily to remove trapped moisture and dirt. Air compressor tank should also be drained daily.

Solution

If damage is extensive and severe, paint must be removed down to undercoat or metal, depend-

ing on depth of blisters. Then refinish. In less severe cases, blisters can be sanded out, resurfaced, and retopcoated.

BLUSHING

Condition

A milky white haze that appears on lacquer films.

Causes

1. In hot humid weather, moisture droplets become trapped in the wet paint film. Air currents from the spray gun and the evaporation of the thinner tend to make the surface being sprayed lower in temperature than the surrounding atmosphere. This causes moisture in the air to condense on the wet paint film.
2. Excessive air pressure.
3. Too fast a thinner.

Prevention

1. In hot humid weather try to schedule painting early in the morning when temperature and humidity conditions are more suitable.
2. Use proper gun adjustments and techniques.
3. Select the thinner that is suitable for existing shop conditions.

Solution

Add retarder to the thinned color and apply additional coats.

CHALKING

Condition

Formation on the finish caused by pigment powder no longer held by the binder, which makes the finish look dull.

Causes (Other Than Normal Exposure)

1. Wrong thinner or reducer, which can harm topcoat durability.
2. Materials not uniformly mixed.
3. Starved paint film.
4. Excessive mist coats when finishing a metallic color application.

Prevention

1. Select the thinner or reducer that is best suited for existing shop conditions.
2. Stir all pigmented undercoats and top-coats thoroughly.
3. Meet or slightly exceed minimum film thicknesses.
4. Apply metallic color as evenly as possible so that misting is not required. When mist coats are necessary to even out flake, avoid using straight reducer.

Solution

Remove surface in affected area by sanding, then clean and refinish.

CHIPPING

Condition

Small chips of a finish losing adhesion to the substrate, usually caused by impact of stones or hard objects. While refinishers have no control over local road conditions—and thus cannot prevent such occurrences—they can take steps to minimize the effects if they know beforehand that these conditions will exist. (For details on the causes, prevention, and solution for **Chipping,** see **Peeling.**)

CRACKING (LINE CHECKING, MICROCHECKING)

Condition

A series of deep cracks resembling mud cracks in a dry pond. Often in the form of three-legged stars and in no definite pattern, they are usually through the color coat and sometimes the undercoat as well.

Causes

1. Excessive film thickness. Excessively thick topcoats magnify normal stresses and strains that can result in cracking even under normal conditions.
2. Materials not uniformly mixed.
3. Insufficient flash time.
4. Incorrect use of additive.

Prevention

1. Do not pile on topcoats. Allow sufficient flash and dry time between coats. Do not dry by gun fanning.

2. Stir all pigmented undercoats and top-coats thoroughly. Strain and—where necessary—add fish eye eliminator to top-coats.
3. Same as Step 1.
4. Read and carefully follow label instructions. Additives not specifically designed for a color coat can weaken the final paint film and make it more sensitive to cracking.

Solution

The affected areas must be sanded to a smooth finish or, in extreme cases, removed down to the bare metal and refinished.

LINE CHECKING

Condition

Similar to cracking, except that the lines or cracks are more parallel and range from very short up to about 18 inches.

Causes

1. Excessive film thickness.
2. Improper surface preparation. Oftentimes the application of a new finish over an old film that had cracked and was not completely removed.

Prevention

1. Do not pile on topcoats. Allow sufficient flash and dry time. Do not dry by gun fanning.
2. Thoroughly clean areas to be painted before sanding. Be sure the surface is completely dry before applying any undercoats or topcoats.

Solution

Remove color coat down to primer and apply new color coat.

MICROCHECKING

Condition

Appears as severe dulling of the film, but when examined with a magnifying glass, it contains many small cracks that do not touch. Microchecking is the beginning of film breakdown and might be an indication that film failures such as cracking or crazing will develop.

Solution

Sand off the color coat to remove the cracks, then recoat as required.

CRAZING

Condition

Fine splits or small cracks—often called "crows-feet"—that completely checker an area in an irregular manner.

Causes

Shop too cold. Surface tension of original material is under stress and literally shatters under the softening action of the solvents being applied.

Prevention

Select the thinner or reducer that is suitable for existing shop conditions. Schedule painting to avoid temperature and humidity extremes in shop or between temperature of shop and the job. Bring vehicle to room temperature before refinishing.

Solution

1. Continue to apply wet coats of topcoat to melt the crazing and flow pattern together (using the wettest possible thinner shop conditions will allow).
2. Use a fast-flashing thinner, which will allow a bridging of subsequent topcoats over the crazing area. (This is one case where bridging is a cure and not a cause for trouble.)

DIRT IN FINISH

Condition

Foreign particles dried in the paint film.

Causes

1. Improper cleaning, blowing off, and tack ragging of the surface to be painted.
2. Defective air regulator cleaning filter.
3. Dirty working area.

4. Defective or dirty air inlet filters.
5. Dirty spray gun.

Prevention

1. Blow out all cracks and body joints.
2. Solvent clean and tack-rag surface thoroughly.
3. Be sure equipment is clean.
4. Work in clean spray area.
5. Replace inlet air filters if dirty or defective.
6. Strain out foreign matter from paint.
7. Keep all containers closed when not in use to prevent contamination.

Solution

1. Rub out finish with rubbing compounds (not for enamels).
2. If dirt is deep in finish, sand and compound to restore gloss. Metallic finishes might show mottling with this treatment and will then require additional color coats.

DULLED FINISH

Condition

Gloss retards as film dries.

Causes

1. Compounding before thinner evaporates.
2. Using poorly balanced thinner or reducer.
3. Poorly cleaned surface.
4. Topcoats put on wet subcoats.
5. Washing with caustic cleaners.
6. Inferior polishes.

Prevention

1. Clean surface thoroughly.
2. Use recommended materials.
3. Allow all coatings sufficient drying time.

Solution

Allow finish to dry hard and rub with a mild rubbing compound.

FEATHEREDGE SPLITTING

Condition

Appears as stretch marks (or cracking) along the featheredge. Occurs during or shortly after the topcoat is applied over lacquer primer-surfacer.

Causes

1. "Piling on" the undercoat in heavy and wet coats. Solvent is trapped in undercoat layers that have not had sufficient time to set up.
2. Material not uniformly mixed. Because of the high pigment content of primer-surfacers, it is possible for settling to occur after it has been thinned. Delayed use of this material without restirring results in applying a film with loosely held pigment containing voids and crevices throughout, causing the film to act like a sponge.
3. Wrong thinner.
4. Improper surface cleaning or preparation. When not properly cleaned, primer-surfacer coats can crawl or draw away from the edge because of poor wetting and adhesion.
5. Improper drying. Fanning with a spray gun after the primer-surfacer is applied will result in drying the surface before solvent or air from the lower layers is released.
6. Excessive use (and film build) of putty.

Prevention

1. Apply properly reduced primer-surfacer in thin to medium coats with enough time between coats to allow solvents and air to escape.
2. Stir all pigmented undercoats and topcoats thoroughly. Select thinner that is suitable for existing shop conditions.
3. Select only thinners that are recommended for existing shop conditions.
4. Thoroughly clean areas to be painted before sanding.
5. Apply primer-surfacer in thin to medium coats with enough time between coats to allow solvents and air to escape.
6. Lacquer putty should be limited to filling minor imperfections. Putty applied too heavily (or too thick) will eventually shrink causing featheredge splitting.

Solution

Remove finish from the affected areas and refinish.

FISH EYES

Condition

Small, crater-like openings in the finish after it has been applied.

Causes

1. Improper surface cleaning or preparation. Many waxes and polishes contain silicone, the most common cause of fish eyes. Silicones adhere firmly to the paint film and require extra effort for their removal. Even small quantities in sanding dust, rags, or from cars being polished nearby can cause this failure.
2. Effects of the old finish or previous repair. Old finish or previous repair can contain excessive amounts of silicone from additives used during their application. Usually solvent wiping will not remove embedded silicone.
3. Contamination of air lines.

Prevention

1. Precautions should be taken to remove all traces of silicone by thoroughly cleaning with wax and grease solvent. The use of fish eye eliminator is in no way a replacement for good surface preparation.
2. Add fish eye eliminator.
3. Drain and clean air pressure regulator daily to remove trapped moisture and dirt. Air compressor tank should also be drained daily.

Solution

After affected coat has set up, apply another double coat of color containing the recommended amount of fish eye eliminator. In severe cases, affected areas should be sanded down and refinished.

LIFTING

Condition

Surface distortion or shriveling, while the topcoat is being applied or while drying.

Causes

1. Use of incompatible materials. Solvents in new topcoat attack old surface, which results in a distorted or wrinkled effect.
2. Insufficient flash time. Lifting will occur when the paint film is an alkyd enamel and is only partially cured. The solvents from the coat being applied cause localized swelling or partial dissolving that later distorts final surface.
3. Improper dry. When synthetic enamel type undercoats are not thoroughly dry, topcoating with lacquer can result in lifting.
4. Effect of old finish or previous repair. Lacquer applied over a fresh air-dry enamel finish will cause lifting.
5. Improper surface cleaning or preparation. Use of an enamel-type primer or sealer over an original lacquer finish, which is to be topcoated with a lacquer, will result in lifting due to a sandwich effect.
6. Wrong thinner or reducer. The use of lacquer thinners in enamel increases the amount of substrate swelling and distortion, which can lead to lifting, particularly when two-toning or recoating.

Prevention

1. Avoid incompatible materials, such as a thinner with enamel products, or incompatible sealers and primers.
2. Do not pile on topcoats. Allow sufficient flash and dry time. Final topcoat should be applied when the previous coat is still soluble or after it has completely dried and is impervious to topcoat solvents.
3. Same as Steps 1 and 2.
4. Same as Step 1.
5. Same as Step 1.
6. Select the thinner or reducer that is correct for the finish applied and suitable for existing shop conditions.

Solution

Remove finish from affected areas and refinish.

MOTTLING

Condition

Occurs only in metallics when the flakes float together to form spotty or striped appearance.

Causes

1. Wrong thinner or reducer.
2. Materials not uniformly mixed.
3. Spraying too wet.
4. Holding spray gun too close to work.
5. Uneven spray pattern.
6. Low shop temperature.

Prevention

1. Select the thinner or reducer that is suitable for existing shop conditions and mix properly. In cold, damp weather use a faster dry solvent.
2. Stir all pigmented topcoats—especially metallics—thoroughly.
3. Use proper gun adjustments, techniques, and air pressure.
4. Same as Step 3.
5. Keep your spray gun clean (especially the needle fluid tip and air cap) and in good working condition.
6. Same as Step 1.

Solution

Allow color coat to set up and apply a drier double coat or two single coats, depending upon which topcoat is to be applied.

ORANGE PEEL

Condition

Uneven surface formation—much like that of the skin of an orange—that results from poor fusion of atomized paint droplets. Paint droplets dry out before they can flow out and level smoothly together.

Causes

1. Improper gun adjustment and techniques. Too little air pressure, wide fan patterns, or spraying at excessive gun distances cause droplets to become too dry during their travel time to the work surface and they remain as formed by gun nozzle.
2. Extreme shop temperature. When air temperature is too high, droplets lose more solvent and dry out before they can flow and level properly.
3. Improper dry. Gun fanning before paint droplets have a chance to flow together will cause orange peel.

4. Improper flash or recoat time between coats. If first coats of enamel are allowed to become too dry, solvent in the paint droplets of following coats will be absorbed into the first coat before proper flow is achieved.
5. Wrong thinner or reducer. Underdiluted paint or paint thinned with fast evaporating thinners or reducers causes the atomized droplets to become too dry before reaching the surface.
6. Too little thinner or reducer.
7. Materials not uniformly mixed. Many finishes are formulated with components that aid fusion. If these are not properly mixed, orange peel will result.

Prevention

1. Use proper gun adjustments, techniques, and air pressure.
2. Schedule painting to avoid temperature and humidity extremes. Select the thinner or reducer that is suitable for existing conditions. The use of a slower evaporating thinner or reducer will overcome this.
3. Allow sufficient flash and dry time. Do not dry by fanning.
4. Allow proper drying time for undercoats and topcoats (not too long or not too short).
5. Select the thinner or reducer that is most suitable for existing shop conditions to provide good flow and leveling of the topcoat.
6. Reduce to recommended viscosity with proper thinner/reducer.
7. Stir all pigmented undercoats and topcoats thoroughly.

Solution

Compounding might help—a mild polishing compound for enamel, rubbing compound for lacquer. In extreme cases, sand down to smooth surface and refinish, using a slower evaporating thinner or reducer at the correct air pressure.

PEELING

Condition

Loss of adhesion between paint and substrate (topcoat to primer and/or old finish, or primer to metal).

Causes

1. Improper cleaning or preparation. Failure to remove sanding dust and other surface contaminants will keep the finish coat from coming into proper contact with the substrate.
2. Improper metal treatment.
3. Materials not uniformly mixed.
4. Failure to use proper sealer.

Prevention

1. Thoroughly clean areas to be painted. It is always good shop practice to wash the sanding dust off the area to be refinished with clean-up solvent.
2. Use correct metal conditioner and conversion coating.
3. Stir all pigmented undercoats and topcoats thoroughly.
4. In general, sealers are recommended to improve adhesion of topcoats. In certain cases (for example, alkyd enamels over lacquer finishes) sealers are required to prevent peeling.

Solution

Remove finish from an area slightly larger than the affected area and refinish.

PINHOLING

Condition

Tiny holes or groups of holes in the finish, or in putty or body filler, usually are the result of trapped solvents, air, or moisture.

Causes

1. Improper surface cleaning or preparation. Moisture left on primer-surfacers will pass through the wet topcoat to cause pinholing.
2. Contamination of air lines. Moisture or oil in air lines will enter paint while being applied and cause pinholes when released during the drying stage.
3. Wrong gun adjustment or technique. If adjustments or techniques result in application that is too wet, or if the gun is held too close to the surface, pinholes will occur when the air or excessive solvent is released during dry.

4. Wrong thinner or reducer. The use of a solvent that is too fast for shop temperature tends to make the refinisher spray too close to the surface in order to get adequate flow. When the solvent is too slow, it is trapped by subsequent topcoats.

5. Improper dry. Fanning a newly applied finish can drive air into the surface or cause a dry skin—both of which result in pinholing when solvents retained in lower layers come to the surface.

Prevention

1. Thoroughly clean all areas to be painted. Be sure surface is completely dry before applying undercoats or topcoats.

2. Drain and clean air pressure regulator daily to remove trapped moisture and dirt. Air compressor tank should also be drained daily.

3. Use proper gun adjustments, techniques, and air pressure.

4. Select the thinner or reducer that is suitable for existing shop conditions.

5. Allow sufficient flash and dry time. Do not dry by fanning.

Solution

Sand affected area down to smooth finish and refinish.

Plastic Filler Bleed-Through

Condition

Discoloration (normally yellowing) of the topcoat color.

Causes

1. Too much hardener.
2. Applying topcoat before plastic filler is cured.

Prevention

1. Use correct amount of hardener.
2. Allow adequate cure time before refinishing.

Solution

1. Remove patch.
2. Cure topcoat, sand, and refinish.

Plastic Filler Not Drying

Conditions

Plastic filler remains soft after applying.

Causes

1. Insufficient amount of hardener.
2. Hardener exposed to sunlight.

Prevention

1. Add recommended amount of hardener.
2. Be sure hardener is fresh and avoid exposure to sunlight.

Solution

Scrape off plastic filler and reapply.

Runs or Sags

Condition

Heavy application of sprayed material that fails to adhere uniformly to the surface.

Causes

1. Too much thinner or reducer.
2. Wrong thinner or reducer.
3. Excessive film thickness without allowing proper dry time.
4. Low air pressure (causing lack of atomization), holding gun too close, or making too slow a gun pass.
5. Shop or surface too cold.

Prevention

1. Read and carefully follow the instructions on the label.
2. Select proper thinner/reducer.
3. Do not pile on finishes. Allow sufficient flash and dry time in between coats.
4. Use proper gun adjustment, techniques, and air pressure.
5. Allow vehicle surface to warm up to at least room temperature before attempting to refinish. Try to maintain an appropriate shop temperature for paint areas.

Solution

Wash off the affected area and let dry until affected area can be sanded to a smooth surface and refinish.

Rust Under Finish

Condition

The surface will show raised surface spots or peeling or blistering.

Causes

1. Improper metal preparation.
2. Broken paint film allows moisture to creep under surrounding finish.
3. Water in air lines.

Prevention

1. Locate source of moisture and seal off.
2. When replacing ornaments or molding, be careful not to break paint film and allow dissimilar metals to come in contact. This contact can produce electrolysis that might cause a tearing away or loss of good bond with the film.

Solution

1. Seal off entrance of moisture from inner part of panels.
2. Sand down to bare metal, prepare metal, and treat with phosphate before refinishing.

Sand Scratch Swelling

Condition

Enlarged sand scratches caused by swelling action of topcoat solvents.

Causes

1. Improper surface cleaning or preparation. Use of too coarse sandpaper or omitting a sealer in panel repairs greatly exaggerates swelling caused by thinner penetration.
2. Improper thinner or reducer, especially a slow-dry thinner or reducer when sealer has been omitted.
3. Underreduced or wrong thinner (too fast) used in primer-surfacer causes "bridging" of scratches.

Prevention

1. Use appropriate grits of sanding materials for the topcoats being used.
2. Seal to eliminate sand scratch swelling. Select thinner or reducer suitable for existing shop conditions.
3. Use proper thinner and reducer for primer-surfacer.

Solution

Sand affected area down to smooth surface and apply appropriate sealer before refinishing.

Solvent Popping

Condition

Blisters on the paint surface caused by trapped solvents in the topcoats or primer-surfacer—a situation that is further aggravated by force drying or uneven heating.

Causes

1. Improper surface cleaning or preparation.
2. Wrong thinner or reducer. Use of fast-dry thinner or reducer, especially when the material is sprayed too dry or at excessive pressure, can cause solvent popping by trapping air in the film.
3. Excessive film thickness. Insufficient drying time between coats and too heavy application of the undercoats can trap solvents causing popping of the color coat as they later escape.

Prevention

1. Thoroughly clean areas to be painted.
2. Select the thinner or reducer suitable for existing shop conditions.
3. Do not pile on undercoats or topcoats. Allow sufficient flash and dry time. Allow proper drying time for undercoats and topcoats. Allow each coat of primer-surfacer to flash naturally—do not fan.

Solution

If damage is extensive and severe, paint must be removed down to undercoat or metal, depending on depth of blisters; then, refinish. In less severe cases, sand out, resurface, and retopcoat.

STONE BRUISES

Condition

Small chips of paint missing from an otherwise firm finish.

Causes

1. Flying stones from other vehicles.
2. Impact of other car doors in a parking lot.

Solution

1. Thoroughly sand remaining paint film back several inches from damage point.
2. Properly treat metal and refinish.

UNDERCOAT SHOW THROUGH

Condition

Variation in surface color.

Causes

1. Insufficient color coats.
2. Repeated compounding.

Prevention

1. Apply good coverage of color.
2. Avoid excessively compounding or polishing.

Solution

Sand and refinish.

WATER SPOTTING

Condition

General dulling of gloss in spots or masses of spots.

Causes

1. Water evaporating on finish before it is thoroughly dry.
2. Washing finish in bright sunlight.

Prevention

1. Do not apply water to fresh paint job and try to keep newly finished car out of rain. Allow sufficient dry time before delivering car to customer.
2. Wash car in shade and wipe completely dry.

Solution

Compound or polish with rubbing or polishing compound. In severe cases, sand affected areas and refinish.

WET SPOTS

Condition

Discoloration and/or the slow drying of various areas.

Causes

1. Improper cleaning and preparation.
2. Improper drying of excessive undercoat film build.
3. Sanding with contaminated solvent.

Prevention

1. Thoroughly clean all areas to be painted.
2. Allow proper drying time for undercoats.
3. Wet sand with clean water.

Solution

Wash or sand all affected areas thoroughly and then refinish.

WRINKLING

Condition

Surface distortions (or shriveling) that occur while enamel topcoat is being applied (or later during the drying stage).

Causes

1. Improper dry. When a freshly applied topcoat is baked or force dried too soon, softening of the undercoats can occur. This increases topcoat solvent penetration and swelling. In addition, baking or force drying causes surface layers to dry too soon. The combination of these forces causes wrinkling.
2. "Piling on" heavy or wet coats. When enamel coats are too thick, the lower wet coats are not able to release their solvents and set up at the same rate as the surface layer, which results in wrinkling.

3. Improper reducer or incompatible materials. A fast-dry reducer or the use of a lacquer thinner in enamel can cause wrinkling.
4. Improper or rapid change in shop temperature. Drafts of warm air cause enamel surfaces to set up and shrink before sublayers have released their solvents, which results in localized skinning in uneven patterns.

Prevention

1. Allow proper drying time for undercoats and topcoats. When force drying alkyd enamel, baking additive is required to retard surface setup until lower layers harden. Lesser amounts can be used in hot weather. Read and carefully follow label instructions.
2. Do not pile on topcoats. Allow sufficient flash and dry time.
3. Select proper reducer and avoid using incompatible materials such as a reducer with lacquer products or thinner with enamel products.
4. Schedule painting to avoid temperature extremes or rapid changes.

Solution

Remove wrinkled enamel and refinish.

19.11 TOPCOATS FOR PLASTIC AUTOMOTIVE PARTS

After automotive plastic part(s) have been repaired or installed as described in Chapter 13 and the surfaces have been prepared as detailed in Chapter 18, the final color can be applied. Automotive plastics can generally be topcoated using most acrylic lacquers, acrylic enamels (catalyzed or uncatalyzed), and acrylic enamel basecoat/clear coat systems. Follow the manufacturer's recommendations to determine if a particular paint system can be used on a specific type of plastic, or if a special plastic primer or flexibilizing agent is required. Table 19–9 lists the more popular automotive plastics and suggested finishing systems.

Most rigid (hard) plastics generally require no primers. The paint will adhere properly to the plastic. Semirigid (flexible) plastics might require the addition of a "flex agent" to the paint system. The additive is needed because semirigid plastics expand, contract, and bend more easily than other substrates. The flex agent will keep the paint film flexible so it can accommodate the movement of the substrate without cracking.

Some refinish product manufacturers require that different flexible additives be used in the various paint systems. Others offer a universal flexible additive that can be used in a variety of paint systems. These products eliminate the need to stock several flexible additives and help keep costs down. As always, it is best not to mix manufacturers' products. The flexible additive, the topcoat, the undercoat products, and the reducer or thinner used all should be provided by the same manufacturer. Mixing labels or using different manufacturers' products on the same job can result in poor performance.

 **SHOP TALK**

Plastic parts are normally painted before they are installed. However, if painting is done on the car, it is important that the surfaces are properly masked off.

PAINTING RIGID INTERIOR PLASTIC PARTS

Rigid or hard ABS plastic parts generally require no primer or primer-sealer. Interior colors are color keyed to trim combination numbers located on the body number plate (see Chapter 16). Conventional interior acrylic lacquer colors are designed for use only on hard trim parts, such as:

- Steel and fiberglass parts (primer or sealer required on new service parts)
- Hard ABS plastic (no primer necessary)
- Hard polypropylene plastic (special primer required)

Each major paint supplier provides an interior color chart that identifies the stock number, color name, gloss factor, and trim combination number for each conventional interior color. When painting rigid interior surfaces, proceed as follows:

1. Wash the part with a cleaning liquid or solvent.
2. Apply conventional interior acrylic lacquer color according to trim combination (see paint supplier color chart for trim and color code). Apply only enough color for proper hiding to avoid washout of grain effect.
3. Allow to dry, following label directions, and then install part.

TABLE 19-9: FINISHING SYSTEMS FOR POPULAR PLASTICS

KEY I Interior E Exterior P Primer NP No primer SP Special primer/adhesion promoter NA None approved * Flexible primer and/or additive recommended		Standard Lacquer System	Flexible Lacquer/Enamel System	Polypropylene System	Vinyl System	Urethane System
ABS	Acrylonitrile-Butadiene-Styrene	I/NP E/NP				
ABS/PVC	ABS/Vinyl (Soft)		I/NP E/NP		I/NP	
EP I, EP II, or TPO	Ethylene Propylene			E/SP*		
PA	Nylon	E/P				
PC	Lexan	I/NP				
PE	Polyethylene	NA	NA	NA	NA	NA
PP	Polypropylene			I/SP		
PPO	Noryl	I/NP				
PS	Polystyrene	NA	NA	NA	NA	NA
PUR, RIM, or RRIM	Thermoset Polyurethane		E*			E
PVC	Polyvinyl Chloride (Vinyl)		E/NP I/NP		E/NP	E I/NP
SAN	Styrene Acrylonitrile	I/NP				
SMC	Sheet Molded Compound (Polyester)	E/P				
UP	Polyester (Fiberglass)	E/P				
TPUR	Thermoplastic Polyurethane		E*			E
TPR	Thermoplastic Rubber		E*			E

Painting Rigid Exterior Plastic Parts

Painting of rigid exterior plastic parts is basically the same for rigid interior plastic parts. While most rigid exterior plastics do not require a primer, some paint manufacturers recommend giving ABS exterior parts a primer coat before the color coat. When applying a coat to rigid (hard) plastic parts, proceed as follows:

1. Wash the part thoroughly with a cleaning solvent.
2. Color coat the part using the appropriate color of acrylic lacquer, acrylic enamel, urethane, or basecoat/clear coat systems (Figure 19–45).
3. Allow the color coat to dry, and reinstall the part.

In finishing fiberglass after the primer-sealer has been applied, the color or topcoat is applied following the basic procedures as for body steel.

When refinishing a previously painted sheet molded compound (SMC) with either a blend or full panel paint procedure, it is necessary to apply a coat of an adhesion promoter. This must be applied 6 to 8 inches beyond the blend area, when performing a spot repair, or in the event of refinishing a full panel, the entire part must be coated. A flash time of at least

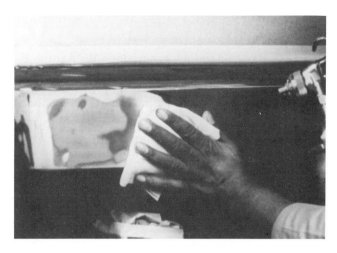

FIGURE 19-45 Apply the desired finish to a rigid exterior plastic part. *(Courtesy of 3M)*

30 minutes is required before applying the base color. This will ensure adequate adhesion of the topcoat.

A spot repair can be accomplished in the following manner. The area that will receive the basecoat color should be sanded with #400 grit wet or dry paper. The blend area that will be clear coated should be sanded with #600 grit or finer wet or dry paper (Figure 19-46). It is important that the adhesion promoter extend beyond the blend area. The application of paint to new parts does not require an adhesion promoter prior to applying the topcoat.

When refinishing rigid plastic parts, a slow-drying lacquer solvent is recommended for reducing the basecoat color. Specific reduction ratios supplied by the paint manufacturer should be followed.

Only enough film thickness to achieve full hiding is necessary, usually two or three medium wet coats are sufficient. The basecoat should be allowed to dry at least 20 minutes before the clear coat is applied. The clear coat can be either lacquer or enamel. The label directions for the product selected should be followed accordingly.

INTERIOR/EXTERIOR FLEXIBLE PLASTIC PARTS

As previously mentioned, most flexible or semi-rigid plastics require an additive to the paint to allow the paint to flex without cracking. There are several flexible or elastomeric topcoat systems available for the painter's selection; in most cases, it is a matter of personal preference. Basecoat/clear coat material can be either enamel or lacquer based. Some manufacturers do not recommend the use of flex additives in their base color material when using a clear topcoat, but do recommend its use for their lacquer and enamel clear coats.

To apply a flexible (elastomeric) finish, proceed as follows:

 1. Thoroughly sand the entire part with #400 grit abrasive paper. Clean the surface with a cleaning solvent.
2. Following the manufacturer's instructions, mix the base color, the flex additive, and the recommended solvent (Figure 19-47). Mix the base color and flex additive thoroughly before adding the amount of solvent best suited for the shop temperature.

FIGURE 19-46 Sanding plastic surface with a #600 grit or finer. *(Courtesy of 3M)*

FIGURE 19-47 Mix basecoat according to manufacturer's instructions.

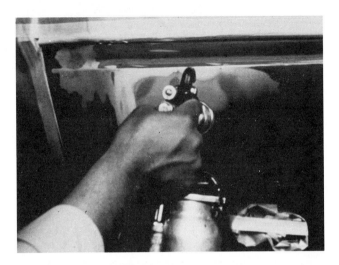

FIGURE 19-48 Apply enough color coats to achieve the proper color match.

Remember to mix only the amount of elastomeric material that is going to be used, since the reduced material cannot be stored.

3. Using the recommended air pressure at the gun, apply a sufficient number of wet double coats to achieve complete hiding and the proper color match (Figure 19-48). Wet double coats are applied as follows: Spray the first pass left to right. Spray the second pass right to left, directly over the first pass. Drop the nozzle so that 50 percent of the pattern overlaps the bottom half of the initial double coat. Continue the pattern until complete. Be sure to allow flash time between coats.

CAUTION: As the paint film builds, it will be necessary to allow more flash time between coats to avoid trapping the thinner. If thinner is trapped, pinholes and bubbles might result.

4. Allow the basecoat 30 to 60 minutes drying time before applying the clear coat. Do not sand the basecoat before applying the clear coat. When not applying a topcoat, air dry for approximately 4 hours before installing or putting the part into service.

5. If sanding of the basecoat is necessary to remove imperfections, such as dirt or sags, sand with #400 grit or finer sandpaper and reclean the area(s). Apply one additional coat of base material and let dry.

Apply the clear coat, if desired, in the following manner:

1. Mix and reduce the material as per the label instructions. Use flex additive if recommended.

2. Strain the mixture and apply 2 to 3 coats at the recommended air pressure at the gun.

3. Allow each coat to flash completely before applying the next one. Allow at least 4 hours air dry time or force dry for 30 minutes with a heat light at 180 degrees Fahrenheit before putting the part back into service.

 **SHOP TALK** _____

Compounding is not necessary when a flexible additive is used in the topcoat; the mixture will dry with acceptable gloss. Compounding dulls the gloss of elastomeric finishes, causing a flat appearance. In this case, the finish cannot be brought back to the same gloss level without applying more paint.

Flexible replacement panels are factory primed with an elastomeric enamel-based primer. The only preparation required prior to topcoating is cleaning with solvent, sanding with #400 grit paper, and a second cleaning after the sanding is completed. In the event the OEM primer is scratched and has left the plastic substrate exposed, or the part has been repaired with a flexible filler material, it is necessary to cover the exposed area with a flexible primer-surfacer prior to topcoating. If the exposed surface is not primed, the area will be highlighted after the topcoats are applied. A fast evaporating solvent should be used to reduce the primer-surfacer and prevent swelling of the base material by absorption.

SHOP TALK _____

Spot repairs on OEM-finished flexible panels and parts are not recommended because of the failure of elastomeric color to flow or "wet out" properly at the blend area.

Keep elastomeric paint material off regular vehicle finishes. If applied to them, there could be a problem color matching the gloss differences. If retopcoated with lacquer, the finish could lift or wrinkle, requiring removal of the affected area. Conversely, keep conventional acrylic lacquers and enamels off all flexible exterior parts. If these finishes are applied to flexible parts, the finish will crack as the parts are flexed and will spoil the appearance of the car.

PAINTING INTERIOR/EXTERIOR POLYPROPYLENE PARTS

The system for painting polypropylene (PP) parts involves the use of a special primer. Since this plastic is hard, it can be color coated after priming with conventional interior acrylic lacquer.

The most common exterior use of polypropylene plastic parts is for bumpers, which come in two types.

- One with a tinted base material (black, gray, or dark gray)
- One that is partially painted, also called a colored bumper (Figure 19-49)

The quality of paint used for PP bumpers is different from that for metal surfaces; adhesive and softening agents are required. Therefore, a special PP primer must be used for the undercoat and a flexing agent added to the topcoat. If not, peeling will result.

If a PP bumper has major structural damage, it must be replaced. Replacement bumpers of this type are usually primed and ready to be painted. If they are not primed, a special PP primer must be applied over the entire bumper. Before starting the painting, be sure to wash the surface with solvent. When applying only a regular color coat, proceed as follows:

1. Apply properly thinned, proportioned, and mixed PP primer and flexible additive as directed by the manufacturer. Allow 1 to 2 hours drying time before applying any color coats.

2. Apply proportioned and mixed acrylic enamel and hardener additive. Flexible additive should not be used in the topcoat.
3. Allow 8 hours (overnight if possible) drying time to assure paint hardness.

If a basecoat/clear coat is being used, read the container labels and proceed as follows:

1. Apply properly thinned and agitated PP primer. Allow 1/2 to 1 hour drying time before the application of acrylic lacquer. Flexible additive should not be used with basecoat/clear coat finishes.
2. Apply properly thinned, proportioned, and mixed acrylic lacquer. Allow 15 to 30 minutes drying time before applying the clear coat.
3. Apply properly thinned, proportioned, and mixed acrylic enamel clear coat and urethane enamel clear hardener. Allow 8 hours to overnight drying time to assure finish coat hardness.

CAUTION: Because polypropylene bumpers are made of thermoplastic resin, force drying at more than 212 degrees Fahrenheit could result in deformation.

Minor surface scratches can usually be repaired by following the same procedures used for finishing replacement PP bumpers, with the following changes:

1. If the scratches do not penetrate the substrate, follow the entire procedure but do not apply primer.
2. If scratches penetrate the substrate, use a lightweight body filler (Figure 19-50) and primer the repair area only.

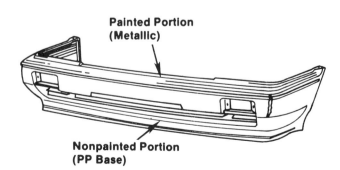

FIGURE 19-49 Typical colored bumper

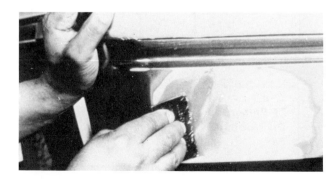

FIGURE 19-50 Applying a thin coat of body filler

A summary of repainting procedures of a PP bumper can be found in Figure 19-51 and Table 19-10.

Repainting of Urethane Bumpers

Urethane bumpers include the colored type that have been painted and the tinted black bumpers. Although both are made of urethane, the black type has been made with an additive that helps prevent deterioration due to sunlight and rain. If painted, a black bumper would change color due to the additive. Light colors such as white would cause a noticeable change. Therefore, black bumpers cannot be painted.

Described here is the procedure for painting a colored urethane bumper:

 1. Mask off the area to be repainted and clean with a silicone solvent. Keep in mind that insufficient cleaning will result in peeling or blistering.

2. Apply a coat of primer-surfacer over the entire surface (Figure 19-52). Repair any scratches with a brush.
3. It is extremely difficult to match the paint for spot repainting, so the entire bumper should be repainted. Prepare the entire surface by wet sanding with a #600 grit abrasive paper.
4. Clean the topcoat surface again.
5. Apply the topcoat over the entire bumper. Use a two-part acrylic urethane paint with a softening agent added (Figure 19-53). For a metallic color, allow a flash time of approximately 5 minutes after application, then apply a clear coat.
6. Follow the dry time recommended by the manufacturer.

A summary of repainting procedures of urethane can be found in Table 19-11.

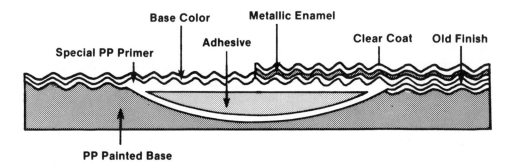

FIGURE 19-51 Repainting damaged PP bumper. *(Courtesy of Toyota Motor Corp.)*

TABLE 19-10   SUMMARY OF THE REPAINTING STAGES OF A PP BUMPER

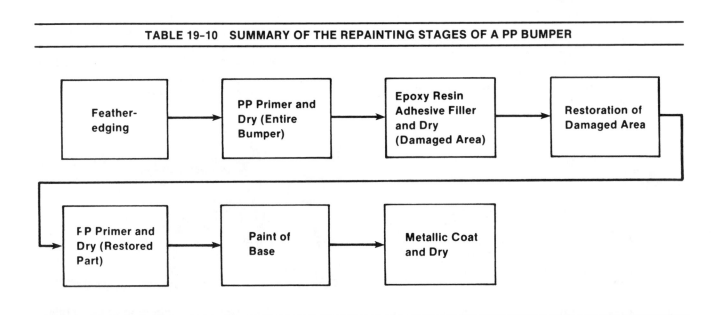

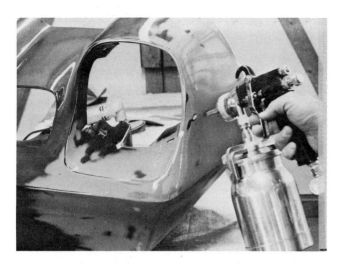

FIGURE 19-52   Applying a coat of special primer to the surface that is to be finished. *(Courtesy of Urethane Supply Co.)*

FIGURE 19-53   The bumper after the topcoat has been applied. *(Courtesy of Urethane Supply Co.)*

PAINTING INTERIOR VINYL AND SOFT ABS PLASTIC PARTS

The outer cover material of flexible instrument panel cover assemblies is made mostly of ABS plastic modified with PVC or vinyl. The same is true of many padded door trim assemblies. The soft cushion padding under ABS covers is urethane foam plastic.

The most widely used flexible vinyls (polyvinyl chloride) are coated fabrics as used in seat trim, some door trim assemblies, headlinings, and sun visors. Examples of hard vinyls are door and front seat back assist handles, coat hooks, and exterior molding inserts.

The paint system for vinyl as well as for interior ABS plastic involves the use of vinyl lacquer. Originally, this heavy-bodied finish was used over painted steel tops to simulate vinyl fabric tops. By changing reductions and air pressures, the vinyl lacquer will dry to a leather-like texture similar in appearance to a fabric textured vinyl top. Also this product is frequently used to restore faded vinyl tops.

More recently vinyl lacquer has been used as a flat black topcoat to produce accent stripes and nonglare hood trim. Vinyl lacquer is also suggested as a basecoat for duplicating the OEM chip-resistant coating on rocker panels. Once dry, most vinyl lacquer can be recoated with acrylic lacquer or acrylic enamel to match the car color. Vinyl system finishes are also usually available in a wide array of colors.

No primer or other undercoat is required. Also no thinning is necessary since vinyl lacquer or color is usually packaged at the proper spray viscosity. The painting procedure is as follows:

1. Always make sure the panels or parts to be colored are free of soil, oils, waxes, food, and all other debris. Synthetic enamel re-

TABLE 19-11   SUMMARY OF THE REPAINTING STAGES OF A URETHANE BUMPER

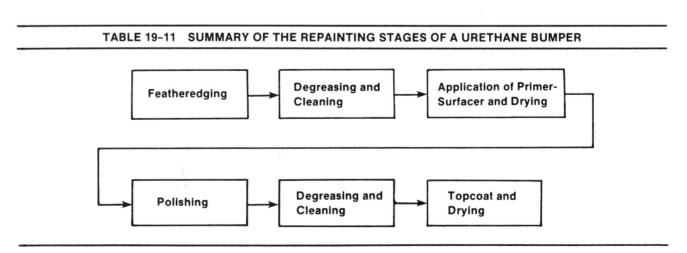

ducer or a vinyl cleaning and preparation solvent should be used to clean vinyl. Isopropyl alcohol will remove ballpoint pen ink. Do not use wax and grease removing solvents; they evaporate too slowly and can cause poor adhesion and cracking of coatings. If an extremely soiled condition exists, detergent and water can be used for a first washing before the solvents are used. Be sure all moisture has completely evaporated before any coatings are applied. Infrared or quartz radiation is the most effective method of evaporation.

2. As soon as the surface dries, apply interior vinyl color in wet coats. Allow flash time between coats according to label directions. Use proper vinyl color shown by interior trim code combination. Apply only enough color for proper hiding to avoid washout of grain effect. Use the air pressure recommended by the finish manufacturer.

3. Before color flashes completely, apply one wet double coat of vinyl clear topcoat. Use topcoat with appropriate gloss level to match adjacent similar components. The clear coat is necessary to control the gloss requirement and to prevent crocking (rubbing off) of the color coat after drying. Remember that instrument panel covers require a nonglare final topcoat.

4. Allow to dry according to label directions before installing part or putting the vehicle back in service.

   Optional procedure. Since acrylic lacquers are available for a perfect, or near perfect, color match to interior surfaces, many painters like to choose the proper acrylic lacquer color then mix it with a proper vinyl system according to the directions on the label. When coloring seats or panels that will be flexed as much as a seat, mix the acrylic lacquer into an equal amount of vinyl system for the proper feel and flexibility. No thinning will be required. If the panels are not as flexible as a seat, such as headliners, trim pads, crash pads, dash panels, kickpanels, and roof coverings, use 3 parts color to 2 parts vinyl system. A little more than a half pint of good acrylic lacquer thinner should be added to this mixture for proper spraying.

Leather interior parts can be refinished in much the same manner as vinyl plastic. It must be remem-

bered that vinyl is not dyed but colored with pigment and coatings. The same is true of leathers used for upholstering vehicles. Leathers are coated in Europe with nitrocellulose lacquers and urethanes. In the United States, leathers are coated with acrylics and urethanes. Vinyl colors are usually used to repaint leather.

 **SHOP TALK** _____

American made cars with leather seats use a vinyl impregnated leather. These can be coated with vinyl color. Do not use on leather generally without testing for scratch off on a test piece after 24 hours curing time.

When painting leather, some interesting applications can be achieved. For example, leather can be given a dual tone accent. This is accomplished by using a basecoat to cover the panel and supply the primary color, then a darker color is applied over the base color in a shadowy manner. Some interior colors have metallic flakes to add sparkle, but some colors have a pearlescent pigment.

Painting Exterior Vinyl Roofs

Exterior vinyl roofs can be painted by using either the vinyl system described for interior vinyl parts or the optional procedure of equal parts of acrylic lacquer and vinyl system material. With either method proceed as follows:

 1. Wash the old top with a bleach-type detergent, a brush, and plenty of water. Rinse the top and entire car thoroughly in clean water.

2. Clean the top thoroughly with paint finish cleaning solvent or with vinyl prep conditioner.

3. Blow out all gap spacing and crevices around the top and tack-wipe the top as required.

4. Be sure masking is carefully done and cover the entire hood and deck lid. The adhesion property of the vinyl system will make overspray difficult to remove.

5. Start the color application with a banding coat at low air pressure and a narrow fan. Spray into drip rails and cracks where windshield and back window molding meet the roof.

6. Then, increase the air pressure as directed by the manufacturer and open the fan to a normal spray pattern. Apply vinyl color, working toward the center.

7. On the opposite side of the car, start at the center and maintain wet application of the near side. Keep the application wet with a full and uniform 50 to 75 percent stroke overlap. Keep the spray gun as perpendicular to the surface as possible. Control the hose by positioning it over the shoulders and back.

8. Apply a second full wet coat for complete hiding and uniformity of wetness. Adjust gun distance and speed for the desired texture. If streaks or dry spots are present, apply a good acrylic lacquer thinner through the spray gun to wet out the dry spots and even out the spray pattern.

9. For the final coat, many manufacturers recommend an application of one wet coat of 200 percent thinned vinyl lacquer (1 part vinyl color to 2 parts lacquer thinner) over the entire vinyl roof area to obtain a uniform appearance.

10. After 1 hour of drying, remove the masking. Allow to dry a minimum of 4 hours before putting the car into service.

Vinyl roof repairs are described in Chapter 14 and should be completed before applying a new finish.

Vinyl Preserver

A clear protective dressing is available for use on vinyl roof tops, upholstery, and other areas covered with vinyl color—floor mats, tires, wires, hoses, and batteries. Its water and dirt repellent film withstands sun, salt, and snow. It is also ideal for spray applications to preclean the engine compartment.

When applying over vinyls, use a thin, even coat of preserver with cellulose sponge or clean soft cloth (Figure 19-54). It dries to the touch in 10 to 20 minutes, is water repellent in 1 hour, and detergent resistant in 1 day. Do not thin the preserver; use it at can consistency.

Retexturing Interior Plastic Parts

Many different textures or grains are found in the average automobile interior. When retexturing a repaired part, it is important to keep in mind that the existing texture does not have to be duplicated. There is no need to spend time and effort trying to

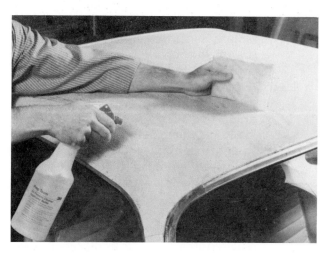

FIGURE 19-54 Applying a vinyl gloss and preserver

get the retextured area to look exactly like the rest of the piece; a variation in the grain is meaningless. Only the coarseness of the grain must be duplicated in order to achieve professional results (Figure 19-55).

Retexturing can be done one of two ways:

- by blending the new texture out into the old
- by retexturing to a natural break line on the panel

Use a refillable aerosol sprayer; the lower pressure will prevent the material from atomizing, which means a faster texture buildup. To achieve a coarse texture, use the material unthinned. For a finer texture, use a small amount of lacquer thinner. A typical retexturing procedure is as follows:

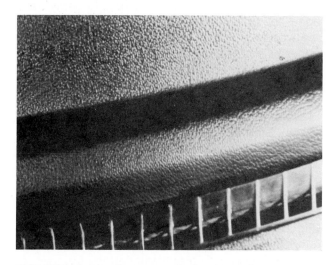

FIGURE 19-55 Retextured plastic surface

1. Mix the texture material as per the manufacturer's instructions. Direct the first coat toward the repaired area only. Hold the sprayer 18 to 24 inches from the surface (Figure 19–56), and always dry spray the material. Spraying it on wet will destroy the grain effect.

2. Allow flash time between coats. As many as eight to ten light coats might be needed to achieve the required buildup. Remember that this is by no means a one-shot application.

3. When buildup has been achieved, begin blending the texture out and away from the repaired area, similar to a color coat. Force-drying between coats speeds up the process.

4. When the texture material has dried, nib sand with #220 grit paper. This will blend the newly textured area into the original texture of the panel (Figure 19–57).

5. If not satisfied with the texture, apply more light coats of material and repeat the sanding.

After retexturing, the part should be blown dust-free in preparation for the refinishing. Do not use any type of cleaner on a newly retextured area. Since the flexible texture material is usually lacquer based, a conventional interior acrylic lacquer is considered the best final color.

19.12 WOODGRAIN TRANSFER REPLACEMENT

Whenever woodgrain overlays are badly damaged, the only solution is replacement. To remove the woodgrain decal, use a heat gun to soften the adhesive on the transfer (Figure 19–58). Start at one edge and slowly peel the decal back. Work the heat over the area until the sheet is completely off.

To remove the woodgrain decal, use a heat gun to soften the adhesive on the transfer (Figure 19–58). Start at one edge and slowly peel the decal back. Keep the heat working over the area until the sheet is completely off.

After the old decal is removed, repair the damaged metal and prime the repair. With either a new panel or a repaired one, sand the surface smooth (Figure 19–59) and then clean with wax and grease remover.

The first step in the reinstallation of the woodgrain decal is to make a template of the area to be

FIGURE 19–56 Using an aerosol sprayer to apply a new finish to a repaired area

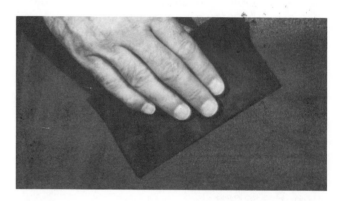

FIGURE 19–57 Checking the blending of original texture with the new

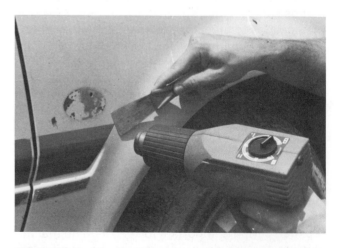

FIGURE 19–58 Removing old transfer (decal) with heat

FIGURE 19-59 Sand the surface smooth before applying the transfer material.

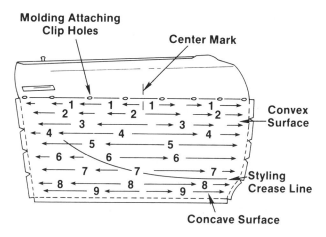

FIGURE 19-60 Transfer installation sequence—right front door shown. (Courtesy of General Motors Corp.)

covered. Using a sheet of masking paper, align it with the centerline of the molding attaching clip holes across the top of the panel. Tack-tape the paper in place.

With the template paper securely taped to the panel, mark the centerline of the panel on both the panel and the template. Smooth the paper flush against the panel and mark the front, rear, and bottom edges of the panel. If the woodgrain transfer on adjacent panels has a plank design, mark the top horizontal plank line on the front and rear edges of the panel.

Remove the template from the panel and lay it out in a flat, clean work surface. Measure 3/4 inches out from the panel outline and mark another perimeter line. Oversizing the template this way will allow room for fitting the transfer to the panel. With a pair of scissors, cut out the template along the perimeter line. Mark the front edge of the template on the backside of the paper.

Now, roll out a sufficient amount of overlay and cut it to length. Lay the transfer face down on the work surface. Turn the template over and place it face down on the transfer. Make sure that the woodgrain is running left to right and that the horizontal planking lines on the template align with plank lines on the transfer (Figure 19-60). Trace the outline of the template on the transfer backing paper and cut the template to shape with a pair of scissors. Align the woodgrain as close as possible.

Hold the transfer cutout against the panel again. Carefully position the top edge of the transfer with the centerline of the trim clip holes and mark the centerline of the transfer with the centerline of the panel.

Lay the transfer face down again on the work surface and peel off the adhesive backing paper. With a sponge and a solution of water and liquid detergent, wet the adhesive side of the woodgrain overlay and the panel.

Align the decal with the clip holes and panel centerline. Lightly press the top of the transfer to the panel, making sure to align any plank lines or grain. With the transfer aligned, squeegee the center 3 or 4 inches of the transfer. Use an upward motion with the squeegee, forcing the liquid solution out along the top. This anchors the transfer in position.

Raise one side of the decal and with short strokes gradually squeegee the top edge of the transfer in place. Make sure the transfer edge stays even with the centerline of the molding clip holes. Then, squeegee the top edge with a long horizontal stroke. Repeat this procedure for the other side top edge. Then raise the transfer and with the squeegee press down another 2 or 3 inches in the center. Use overlapping horizontal strokes to bond another band of decal across the top of the panel. Progressively work down and across the panel in this manner. If the decal gets tacky and sticks to the panel before it is pressed in place, break the grab with a fast firm pull. Periodically, rewet the panel to decrease the tack as well as to make the transfer easier to position.

When reaching the edges of the decal cut 90 degree notches in the corners and V-shaped notches along the edges where necessary to fit the transfer to the panel. Avoid excessive pulling and stretching; the decal can tear.

Apply vinyl trim adhesive to door hem edges. Apply the adhesive sparingly to avoid a lumpy build-up under the transfer. Heat the edges of the door hem flanges and the transfer. Then, wrap the transfer around the flange edge and firmly press it to the backside. Apply heat to any depressions, or hole edges, and firmly press the transfer to ensure a good bond. Cut the excess decal away from panel edges and holes with a razor blade.

Inspect the application from an angle where light reflections will expose any irregularities. Pierce bubbles with a fine needle from an acute angle and press these down firmly. Reinstall all moldings and other hardware (Figure 19-61).

In addition to woodgrain, other decorative effects can be achieved by using decals. For example, many customers like to personalize their car, truck, or van with stripe designs. These stripes and decals are easy to apply as long as supplier directions are followed.

19.13 ADDING THE FINISHING TOUCHES

Before returning the vehicle to the customer, the refinisher must be constantly aware of all those little things that make a big difference to the customer. These include:

- Vacuum the interior of the car carefully. It should be cleaner than when the customer brought it in. To achieve this it might be necessary to use an automobile fabric reconditioner on interior upholstering and carpet surfaces. Most fabric reconditioners are available in several color tints and a clear shampoo. Reduce the reconditioner solution with water according to the ratio on the label.

After all areas to be reconditioned have been cleaned by either a vacuum or air gun, apply the reconditioning solution with a soft wire brush to all soiled spots on seats and door panels. Apply a light coat of premixed reconditioner, using a sponge or bristle brush on both front and rear fabric seats, seat belts, carpets, and door panels. No masking is required because leather, vinyl, and metal surfaces are not affected by most reconditioners. (Check the manufacturer's instructions.) It is important to saturate stains and water marks thoroughly and brush them with a soft wire brush. When an air gun is used, an air pressure of 60 psi is recommended. Hold the air gun 12 to 18 inches from the surface so that the reconditioner contacts the fabric for the best penetration.

After an application of the material, use a highly absorbent turkish towel or cloth and heavy pressure to remove the excess reconditioner from seats, door panels, seat belts, and rugs. Be sure to remove all excess from seat crevices and folds with a dry towel. Heavy toweling removes stains and loosens dirt along with the excess reconditioner. Stubborn stains or water marks remaining after the application can be removed by brushing on an unmixed reconditioner solution. Remove the excess material with an absorbent towel or cloth. Under normal conditions, the entire interior should dry within 12 hours.

- Thoroughly clean all the glass, including windows, mirrors, and lights (Figure 19-62).
- Touch up any overmasked areas and carefully remove any overspray that may have been left on windows or chrome. Touch up overmasking.

FIGURE 19-61 Inspecting a finished application for bubbles

FIGURE 19-62 Clean all glass.

- Clean and polish chrome, moldings, and bumpers. Steel wool should not be used to polish chrome because pieces of the wool can easily become embedded in the new paint. Instead, use a commercial chrome polisher.
- Use a brush with soap and water to clean the tires and wheels. Do not let dirty wheels spoil the appearance of an otherwise quality job.
- Use chassis black to blacken wheel openings, the tail pipe, and any other exposed undercarriage parts since overspray often gets on these areas. The customer generally will not notice this, but it certainly will be noticed if it is not done.
- Replace wipers, moldings, and emblems that were removed before painting. Take the time to clean off old paint that might be on these items and be certain that everything is replaced.
- If the car has a vinyl top, wipe it with a damp cloth or a commercial vinyl top cleaner.
- As a finishing touch, most body shops today clean the engine compartment. The easiest way to do this is to spray the engine and engine compartment with a heavy-duty engine cleaner. Flush out the engine compartment with high-pressure water. (Most modern cleaners do not require steam or flammable solutions.) A clean engine and engine compartment usually makes a big impression on the customer.

Finally, inspect the car with a careful eye. Make the extra effort. If a window is smeared, clean it again. If a piece of masking tape or paper still re-mains, remove it. If an emblem is missing, replace it before the customer asks where it is. If the car gets dirty before the customer arrives, wipe it down with a clean cloth. Always remember that the satisfaction of the customer is the ultimate goal, so make the extra effort (Figure 19–63).

19.14 REVIEW QUESTIONS

1. To achieve a painted surface with a metallic appearance and light color, Technician A sprays on metallic paint dry. To achieve the same effect, Technician B sprays it on wet. Who is correct?
   a. Technician A
   b. Technician B
   c. Both A and B
   d. Neither A nor B

2. Which part of the paint settles in the can?
   a. binder
   b. solvent
   c. resin
   d. pigment

3. Which of the following statements is incorrect?
   a. The objective of blending is to create the illusion that only one color is being seen.
   b. It is not practical to try to get a perfect color match when blending.
   c. When preparing the rest of the car, always prepare the adjacent panels for blending.
   d. None of the above.

4. When working with basecoat/clear coats, _____ .
   a. the need for buffing is all but eliminated
   b. a greater emphasis must be put on cleanliness
   c. streaking is a common problem
   d. both a and b

5. When spot repainting with solid colors, Technician A applies the topcoat with a circular motion from the center outward. Technician B applies the topcoat in short strokes from the center outward. Who is correct?
   a. Technician A
   b. Technician B
   c. Both A and B
   d. Neither A nor B

FIGURE 19–63 Always try to send the customer home satisfied.

6. What can be done during overall spraying to prevent a gritty surface?
   a. keep a dry edge
   b. maintain minimal overspray on the horizontal surfaces
   c. both a and b
   d. neither a nor b

7. Which of the following statements concerning basecoat/clear coat applications is incorrect?
   a. Sanding of the basecoat should be avoided.
   b. Do not thin or reduce clear coats before applying them.
   c. Two medium coats of basecoat are needed.
   d. All of the above

8. After force drying the topcoat, Technician A removes the masking tape while the finish is still warm. Technician B waits to remove it until after the finish has cooled. Who is correct?
   a. Technician A
   b. Technician B
   c. Both A and B
   d. Neither A nor B

9. Which type of compound features coarse particles?
   a. polishing
   b. lacquer
   c. epoxy
   d. rubbing

10. How long should a new topcoat be cured before automotive finish wax is applied?
    a. 24 hours
    b. 1 week
    c. 30 to 45 days
    d. 60 to 90 days

11. When refinishing a rigid plastic part, Technician B uses a lacquer clear coat, while Technician B uses an enamel clear coat. Who is correct?
    a. Technician A
    b. Technician B
    c. Both A and B
    d. Neither A nor B

12. When applying a flexible finish, _____ .
    a. thoroughly sand the entire part with #400 grit adhesive paper
    b. mix the base color and solvent thoroughly before adding the flex additive
    c. store any unused elastomeric material in a covered container
    d. both a and b

13. When painting a polyproplyene part, _____ .
    a. a flexing agent must be added to the topcoat
    b. a special PP primer is required for the undercoat
    c. both a and b
    d. neither a nor b

14. Texture material should be applied with the sprayer _____ .
    a. 18 to 24 inches from the surface and using a wet spray
    b. 6 inches from the surface and using a wet spray
    c. 6 inches from the surface and using a dry spray
    d. 18 to 24 inches from the surface and using a dry spray

15. Technician A paints an exterior vinyl roof by starting with a banding coat and wide spray fan. Technician B starts with a banding coat and narrow spray fan. Who is correct?
    a. Technician A
    b. Technician B
    c. Both A and B
    d. Neither A nor B

16. When spraying a metallic or pearl luster paint, Technician A uses an agitator cup. Technician B does not. Who is correct?
    a. Technician A
    b. Technician B
    c. Both A and B
    d. Neither A nor B

17. When working with a three-coat finish, Technician A never makes a test panel. Technician B always makes a test panel when working with three-coat finishes. Who is correct?
    a. Technician A
    b. Technician B
    c. Both A and B
    d. Neither A nor B

CHAPTER
20

Estimating Auto Body Repair and Refinishing Costs

OBJECTIVES

After reading this chapter, you will be able to:

- explain how damage repair estimates are determined.
- describe the basic procedures of writing up an estimate for the body shop and customer or insurance company.
- outline the sequence for estimating vehicle damage.
- describe the method of determining the repairability of a damaged vehicle based on observation and by consulting appropriate sources.
- begin making damage appraisal judgments about whether or not new parts or repair and straightening procedures are necessary.
- explain the difference between flat-rate labor time and overlap labor time when estimating labor costs.
- convert flat-rate labor time into dollars.
- roughly estimate the time required for painting a given collision repair job.
- estimate material costs based on a refinishing materials list.

Nearly any damaged automobile can be restored if the vehicle owner is willing to pay for the repair. It is this cost that is a major consideration for both the vehicle owner and the auto body shop. Most collision jobs are usually paid for by an insurance company. Insurance companies generally require at least two estimates from two separate auto body shops. In most cases, the shop that submits the lowest estimate will get the work. In some cases the insurance company will send an adjuster to evaluate the damage and determine an agreeable repair price with the vehicle owner and the auto body shop. Therefore, the profit and loss margins for a body shop depend heavily on the accuracy of estimates. Estimates should not be written carelessly, nor be too low (a money loss) or too high (a customer loss). It is very important that any estimate be fair, accurate, and firm.

As stated in Chapter 1, in all but large body shops, one person usually handles the task of making an estimate. In the performance of the duty of a shop estimator, a number of specialized skills must be acquired; each vital in the pursuit of making a fair and accurate estimate. The range of technical knowledge must encompass exterior-interior automobile construction—properties of metals (cast, rolled, forged), painting and refinishing techniques, as well as the design and assembly of drivetrains, including engines, transmissions, rear axles, and the newer transaxles. Operation and design of brakes, steering, and suspension systems must also be included in the estimator's storehouse of technical information. Most of the information in this book is vital to the estimator.

It is not the purpose of this chapter to make a body or refinishing technician into an estimator—although that might be something some professionals of these trades might wish to consider in the future. However, it is very important that shop technicians understand how estimates are determined and, in some cases, how work reports are prepared from them. After all, it is shop technicians who must do the work. Thus, in most successful auto body and refinishing, it is a cooperative effort among the estimator and technicians that leads to a fair and accurate estimate and satisfied customer.

20.1 THE ESTIMATE

Before any decision involving the repair of the damaged vehicle can be made (Figure 20-1), a detailed repair estimate, sometimes called a **damage appraisal** or **damage report,** must be made. Before writing the formal damage report (Figure 20-2), fill in all preliminary information that identifies the owner of the vehicle and who will pay the bill. Also record the make, year, body style or type, license plate number, mileage, and date. The written estimate should also give a detailed description of all the labor operations that must be performed and a complete listing of parts and materials needed to make the necessary repairs. All this information—pricing of labor, parts and materials, and their totals—can help prevent any misunderstanding between the shop and the vehicle owner.

At least two copies of the written estimate should be made. One is kept by the body shop, while the other copy is given to the insurance company or to the customer. An estimate is a firm bid for a given period of time—usually for 30 days. The reason for a given time period is quite obvious: Part prices change and damaged parts can deteriorate.

The written estimate is also considered as the authorization to complete the repair work as listed, but only when it is agreed upon and signed by the owner or by the owner and insurance company adjuster/appraiser. On the estimate form legal conditions are explained under which the repair work is accepted by the body shop and protects the shop against the possibility of undetected damage that might be revealed later as repairs progress.

An important part of any estimate is determining who is going to pay for the repairs to the vehicle. Is the customer or the insurance company or both going to pay for the work done? This must be stated on the estimate form and signed by the responsible party(s). It is good business practice to have the method of payment established.

FIGURE 20-1 Although the damage to this vehicle appears minimal, the repair cost for it was over $1,500 as shown in Figure 20-2.

	B&J Collision Estimating Services 20 WEST BROAD ST. AUBURN, PA 17922 TELEPHONE: (717) 555-7764		ESTIMATE OF REPAIRS № 002128

SHEET NO._____OF_____SHEETS

NAME KAREN Miller	ADDRESS 1143 RailRoad St. Cressona, Pa. 17929	PHONE HOME 395-2719 BUS. 623 7347	DATE 12-17-91

YEAR 1990	MAKE ford	MODEL P.V.	LICENSE NO. MAE 917	MILEAGE 14864	SERIAL/ V.I. NO. 1FTDF15YSGNA69994

INSURANCE COMPANY Amerisure	TYPE OF INSURANCE COL	ADJUSTER	PHONE	CAR LOCATED AT mf6. 4/91

PARTS NECESSARY AND ESTIMATE OF LABOR REQUIRED	PAINT COST ESTIMATE		PARTS COST ESTIMATE		LABOR COST ESTIMATE	
① FRONT FACE BAR Chrome No gds or pads			205	82		.5
① " Stone deflector	1	0	40	50		.5
① Left Headlamp door (with argent Grill)			52	32		2
① " " Shield			3	20		
① " front fender	3	1	133	00	1	6
① " " " APRON			60	47	1	0
② Wheels 15" 55.60 ea.			111	20		6
② Stems and Balance			2	50		5
② HUB CAPS			43	46		—
Repair Radiator Support			—		2	0
Align FRONT End			—		1	5
① Left door trim Panel			73	40		
Stripe Left FRONT fender			15	00		.5
LABOR 23.0 HRS @ 23.00			575	00		
(note may Be FRONT suspension damage)						
PANT MAT.			89	10		
UNdeRCOAT			15	00		
TOTALS			1,529	97		

INSURED PAYS $_____INS. CO. PAYS $_____R. O. NO._____	GRAND TOTAL	1,529.97

INS. CHECK PAYABLE TO_____

The above is an estimate, based on our inspection, and does not cover additional parts or labor which may be required after the work has been opened up. Occasionally, after work has started, worn, broken or damaged parts are discovered which are not evident on first inspection. Quotations on parts and labor are current and subject to change. Not responsible for any delays caused by unavailability of parts or delays in parts shipment by supplier or transporter.

TOWING & STORAGE	

ESTIMATOR _____

AUTHORIZATION FOR REPAIRS. You are hereby authorized to make the above specified repairs to the car described herein.

	TAX	91.80

SIGNED X_____   DATE _____ 19_____

TOTAL OF ESTIMATE	$ 1,621.77

FIGURE 20-2   The damage estimate or damage appraisal for the needed parts and labor to repair the vehicle shown in Figure 20-1

REPAIR ORDER

B & J
Collision Estimating Services
20 WEST BROAD ST.
AUBURN, PA 17922
TELEPHONE: (717) 555-7764

REPAIR ORDER
NO. 004007

SHEET NO. _____ OF _____ SHEETS

CUSTOMER'S NAME	ADDRESS	PHONE	DATE
Karen Miller	1143 Railroad St. Cressona, PA. 17929	HOME 395-2719 BUS. 623-7347	12-17-91

YEAR	MAKE	MODEL	LICENSE NO.	MILEAGE	SERIAL/VIN
1990	Ford	PV	MAE 917	14,864	1FTDF15Y56NA69994

ORDER GENERATED BY	MECHANIC	PAINTER
Bob	JT	Bill

VEHICLE IN BODY SHOP	IN	DATE 6-29	HOUR 0800	VEHICLE IN PAINT SHOP	IN	DATE 7-1	HOUR 0800
	OUT	DATE 6-30	HOUR 1130		OUT	DATE 7-2	HOUR 1430

BODY SHOP

INSTRUCTIONS	NO. OF MECHANICS	PART NO.	PART IN HOUSE	ACTUAL TIME
Repr. Front Bumper	1	E1TZ17757A	6-26	.5
" Stone Deflector	"	E0TZ17779A	"	.6
" L. Headlight Door	"	E2TZ13064B	"	.6
" " " Shield	"	E0TZ13B042B	"	.2
" Frt Fender (Left)	"	E1TZ16006B	"	1.6
" " " Apron	"	E4TZ16055A	"	1.0
" 2 Frt Wheels	"	E7TZ1015C	"	.6
" 2 Hubcaps	"	E2TZ1130A	"	.5
Repair Rad. Support	"			2.5
Align Front End	"			1.5

PAINT SHOP

INSTRUCTIONS	NO. OF PAINTERS	MATERIALS AND PAINT TYPE AND COLOR	PAINT IN HOUSE	ACTUAL TIME
Paint Damabed & Replaced Items	1	W. White – Centari	6.26	2.0
Refinish & Repair	"	Paper, Putty, Tape		3.5
Replace Door Trim Panel	"	E01Z10208971B		.5
Stripe Fender (Left f.)	"	Tape		.5
Undercoat	"	2 Qts		1.0

SHOP FOREMAN _____ DATE _____

FIGURE 20-3 Typical repair order

FIGURE 20-4 Typical crash estimating guides for American-made and import vehicles

Many auto insurance policies contain a deductible clause. This means that the customer (policyholder) is responsible for the first given amount of the estimate (usually $100 to $300) and the remaining cost of the damage repair is paid by the insurance company. In such cases, both the customer and insurance company should authorize the estimate. Remember that the deductible amount is usually paid for by the customer.

Until a few years ago, many body shops gave auto body damage reports or estimates **free.** Because the preparation of an estimate can involve a considerable amount of time and paperwork, this practice is seldom followed. Instead, most body shops charge a flat fee for the estimate or a percentage of the estimated repair costs. However, if the vehicle is repaired by them, this charge is usually deducted from the final bill.

In some parts of the country, so-called courtesy estimates or appraisals are made. These appraisals are generally made because a customer might need two or more estimates for the insurance company. The body shop will submit an appraisal for a small fee knowing quite well that the shop will not get the job. Also, courtesy estimates or appraisals are written for vehicles that might be totally wrecked. The estimator will write up to the total list range. If the vehicle is worth $4,000 and the actual cost of making the repairs would be $3,500, the shop will stop at a $4,000 estimate. When a body shop is a department of a vehicle dealership, courtesy estimates are often made in the hopes of obtaining the sale of a new car.

Another important function of the estimate is that it serves as a basis for preparing the repair work order or operational plan. Usually prepared from the damage appraisal of the estimator (from the written

estimate) and visual inspection by the body shop supervisor and/or a body technician, the repair order (Figure 20-3) outlines the procedures that should be taken to put the vehicle back in top condition. It is also a valuable tool to both the estimator and to the shop foreman since it lists the actual times necessary to do the job.

20.2 ESTIMATING AIDS

Crash estimating guides or collision damage manuals (Figure 20-4) are essential tools of the estimator. They contain such items as vehicle identification information, the price of new parts, amount of time needed to install the parts, identification of almost any part of the car from the front bumper to the rear bumper, and refinishing data such as a paint code reference. These guides are published and updated at different times of the year when manufacturers change prices or make model revisions. Most of the information in these guides is of value to body technicians and refinishers, thus they should be able to read and understand them.

ABBREVIATIONS USED IN ESTIMATING GUIDES

When using crash estimating guides, the body technician and painter, as well as the estimator, must be familiar with the abbreviations that are used. The three most commonly used abbreviations are:

- **R&I: Remove and Reinstall.** The item is removed as an assembly, set aside, and later reinstalled and aligned for a proper fit. This is generally done to gain access to another part. For example, R&I bumper would mean that the bumper assembly would have to be removed to install a new fender or quarter panel.
- **R&R: Remove and Repair.** Remove the old parts, transfer necessary items to new part, replace, and align.
- **O/H: Overhaul.** Remove an assembly from the vehicle, disassemble, clean, inspect, replace parts as needed, then reassemble, install, and adjust (except wheel and suspension alignment). Overhaul time should be used only if the time for the individual parts (less overlap) is more than the overhaul time.

In addition to these abbreviations, Appendix B gives a listing of other terms that are accepted by most estimating guide publishers and estimators in general when filling out written forms.

20.3 COMPUTER ESTIMATING

Computerized estimating and shop management systems are being used by an ever increasing number of body shops. Regardless of size, body shops face concerns that demand increased efficiency and speed. A dramatic increase in the number of individual vehicle makes and models has led to a proliferation of specialty repair shops. Prices are constantly updated and changed. Calculating the needed overlaps and deductions takes precision and accuracy. The time needed to do these jobs is time not spent selling customers or repairing vehicles. Damage report writing, accounting, job costing, time and inventory control, and business analysis can all be performed quicker and easier using a computer.

COMPUTER COMPONENTS AND JARGON

The computer is simply a machine. Just as a driver need not understand the various components of an automobile to drive it, the computer operator need not thoroughly understand the workings of a computer to use it. However, the driver who does have some knowledge of the mechanics of a car might notice early warning signals of a mechanical problem. And the person who understands the computer might detect problems sooner as well.

Like the auto, the computer is made up of various systems and components (Figure 20–5). The input/output devices are items such as cathode ray tubes (CRTs) and printers. The central processing unit (CPU) is where the work—processing of the data—actually takes place.

Most people have probably seen a CRT in the form of a screen. This device serves as both an input device where the data is keyed in and as an output device where the information is displayed on the screen. Information that is keyed in is sent to the CPU to be processed, then the information is returned to the screen for viewing.

An awareness of computer jargon is essential to understanding the computer. The following is a list of definitions to acquaint the damage report writer with computer terminology, increase an understanding of the computer, and serve as a reference guide.

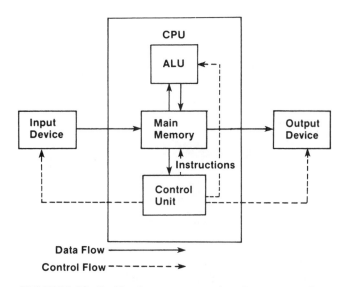

FIGURE 20–5   Basic components of a personal or business computer system

ALU (Arithmetic and Logic Unit) The portion of the CPU (Central Processing Unit) that performs arithmetic and makes logical comparisons. The CPU has two parts: a main memory that holds the computer program and the processing data, and the ALU that actually executes the program's instructions.

Command An instruction to the computer to perform a predefined operation.

Control Unit (of CPU) The portion of the CPU that directs the sequence of operations by electrical signals and governs the actions of the units that make up the computer.

Cursor A movable, blinking marker on the terminal video screen that defines the next point of character entry or change.

Downtime The period of time when a device is not working.

Drive A device that holds a disk or diskette so that the computer can read data from and write data onto it.

Floppy Disk A thin magnetic disk (in protective paper jacket) that stores data or programs. It is erasable and reusable, and comes in several diameters.

Hard Disk A device to store data on magnetic disks that, unlike floppies, is rigid and not readily interchangeable but can store and retrieve data faster than a floppy (Figure 20–6).

Hardware The physical parts of a computer, such as keyboard, screen, disk drives, printer, and so on.

Mainframe Computer A powerful computer capable of storing and processing extremely large

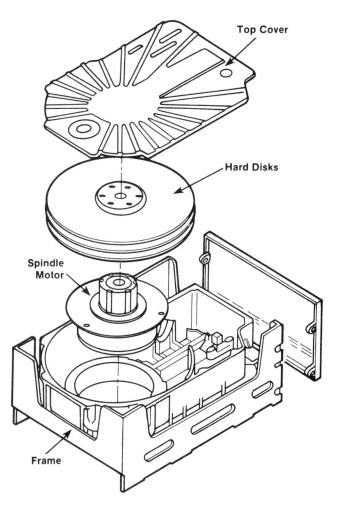

FIGURE 20-6   A hard magnetic disk mounts onto the spindle motor of a system. They are not readily interchangeable but can store and retrieve data faster than a floppy disk.

A

B

FIGURE 20-7   Peripherals are components added to the basic computer such as (A) a printer and (B) a disk drive to load floppy disks.

amounts of data. Also called the "host" computer in some systems.

Main Storage Also known as internal storage, memory, or primary storage unit; the section of the CPU that holds instructions, data, and intermediate and final results during processing.

Menu A displayed list of options from which the user selects an action to be performed.

Peripherals Hardware that can be added to a basic computer, such as a printer, disk drive, or modem, for transferring information by telephone (Figure 20-7).

Secondary Storage Also known as permanent storage; the components of the system, such as magnetic tape or disks, that hold large amounts of "raw" data that can be called up to the CPU for processing.

Software Also known as programs; instructions written in a computer language that tell the computer what the user wants to do. Most programs come on floppy disks for small computers and on magnetic tape for larger ones.

Terminals An input/output device used to enter data into a computer and record the output. Terminals are divided into two categories: hard copy (printers) and soft copy (video terminals).

INFORMATION STORAGE AND RETRIEVAL

An understanding of how information is stored and retrieved within a computer will enable the damage report writer to determine the cause of certain problems encountered within the system. When not in use, information is stored in secondary storage. This is permanent storage as compared to primary

789

storage, which is temporary. Examples of devices used for secondary storage are magnetic tape and magnetic disks.

Information is retrieved from secondary storage and brought into the CPU for processing when requested by the user. For example, the damage report writer can access all pertinent operational and parts price information for a certain vehicle make and model by keying in the request on the CRT terminal. The secondary storage data base can be physically located at the CPU, or accessed from a central remote location using telephone modem hookups.

The CRT terminal is the user's link with the CPU. The CRTs do no processing themselves, but serve as display units for the dialogue between the user and the CPU. The request for information is sent to the CPU, where the control unit takes over. Someone has already written a program that contains a series of instructions directing the computer what to do next.

THE PROCESS

The control unit issues an electronic command that causes the requested data to be found in secondary storage and copied into primary storage. After this transfer is complete, the information is available for use. Note that information is available for use only after it has been transferred into primary storage, never while it is in secondary storage. The program that specifies what must be done to this data is also kept in primary storage.

Rather than rely on magnetic tape or disk data banks compiled from information in the collision estimating guides, some computer software programs allow the user to key in data from the guides into a spreadsheet type program. Although not as fast as fully computerized systems, user keyed data is more flexible. For example, it can be slightly altered to reflect different part prices and labor time projections. Again, once the information is keyed into the computer, it can be used throughout the rest of the job process to print various form letters and work reports.

The two central data bank systems used most by body shops and collision repair facilities are the Audatex and Mitchellmatix systems. These systems interface with the user's computer to provide, among other things, coded estimating worksheets. A special version of the Audatex designed specifically for collision repairers provides access to the same data base used by insurance companies and makes it easier to reach on-the-spot repair settlements. The Mitchellmatix uses its own set of guide books that

utilize computer bar codes for individual parts and labor operations. Users of these systems are guaranteed the most comprehensive, up-to-date data available.

ON-SITE SYSTEMS

Many independent computer software developers have designed programs that allow body shops and adjusters to write estimates on their personal or business computers without using a remote central data bank. The two on-site systems are the manual data entry systems and the on-site data bank systems.

Manual Data Entry

Manual data entry systems require the user to enter parts prices, labor times, labor rates, and other pertinent information into the program using the terminal keyboard. Information must be typed in line by line just as you would enter items on the lines of a handwritten damage report form. Data used with manual entry systems is found in the standard collision estimating guides used to create handwritten reports (Figure 20–8). Once this data is entered into the program format, it can be manipulated and changed to create the damage report. The report can be stored on magnetic disk or tape for future reference or printed out in hard copy form.

Manual data entry systems offer fast, accurate calculations. Line items can be quickly added, deleted, or changed. Since the user manually enters all prices and times, he or she can adjust them to the exact situation. The final printouts are neat and professional looking. And as a group, manual entry systems are the least expensive. Job costing and a full

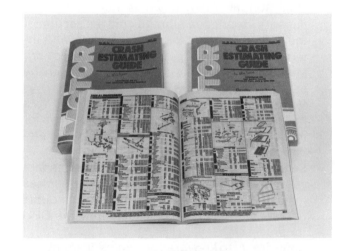

FIGURE 20–8   Standard estimating guide

range of shop management programs are normally available as system components. Finally many manual entry systems can be easily upgraded to on-site data bank systems through the purchase of secondary storage data bases.

The main disadvantage is the time and effort needed to type in the data entries. Because there is no secondary storage in data, information typed in yesterday for Estimate A cannot be called up and used today in creating Estimate B, even if the vehicles are the same and the damage is similar. The operator could modify Estimate A into Estimate B, but then there would be no permanent record of Estimate A stored on magnetic disc or tape. With manual entry systems the accuracy of the data entered is also dependent on the accuracy of the typist or operator. Simple typed errors can generate wildly inaccurate results.

On-Site Data Banks

With on-site data bank systems, the secondary data storage becomes a component of the user's computer system; there is no need for a telephone modem or special hookup. Massive amounts of data can be accessed using several keystrokes. There is no need to type entire line entries. A single keystroke can enter a line of data onto the damage report program sheet.

The three main sources of on-site data bases are Motor (Motorlink™), Mitchell, and Audatex. These companies license their massive data bases to independent computer software suppliers for inclusion in their estimating systems. Users subscribe to the data bank source in exactly the same way they subscribe to the estimating manuals. Updated computer data is provided at regular intervals on magnetic tape or disc and is loaded into the user's secondary storage system. Once the data bank is loaded, it can be used as often as needed to produce damage reports or appraisals.

Advantages of a "resident" data source include:

- No need to worry about transmission errors or breakdowns that can occur with telephone-based linkups. The data is also accessible at the user's convenience, day or night, peak working hours or off periods.
- The ability to factor in many features not user controlled in central data bank systems. The user has the opportunity to view items on the screen before they are selected. There is access to footnotes, procedure pages, refinish times and notes, and lists of included operations.

- The entire estimate can be previewed and any errors or omissions can be corrected **before** printing. With central data bank systems the report is transmitted to and printed at the user location, then reviewed. If there are mistakes due to user or data entry personnel errors, the report must be revised and reprinted while time is wasted.
- The ability to transfer data directly from the data base to the damage report. The system allows the user to add items and alter prices as is necessary. The user controls all phases of what goes on the damage report without sacrificing the speed and convenience of a computerized data base.
- With data banks based on printed estimating guides, the guides can serve as a verifiable source of the computer estimate entries. For example, Motor includes a full subscription to their crash estimating guides with their Motorlink data base. The user can refer to the printed guides to check illustrations, industry nomenclature, parts interchange, and paint code references. The guides also serve as a portable reference away from the computer and a backup in the event of a power loss or system breakdown.

20.4 ESTIMATING SEQUENCE

When estimating any type of damage to a vehicle, whether minor or major, a logical sequence must be followed. The analyzing of damage procedures given in the earlier chapters of this book, especially in Chapter 9, must be followed by both the estimator and the shop's body technicians. A major difference is that an estimator must determine the cost of repairing the vehicle, while body technicians determine how to repair the vehicle in the best and most economical manner. This is why the shop's body technician is a most important part of the estimating sequence.

Before making a written estimate, the estimator should make a visual inspection of the entire vehicle, paying special attention to damaged subassemblies and parts that are mounted to (or part of) a damaged component. The estimator must consider basically the same points as the technician does before making any decision on the repair work. That is, most estimators start from the outside of the car and work inward, listing everything (Figure 20–9) on paper—by car section—that is found bent, broken, crushed, or missing. For example, if the front grille and some

FIGURE 20-9 The estimator must make and item-by-item listing of all parts needed.

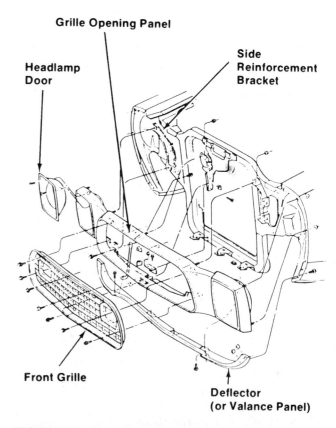

FIGURE 20-10 Typical exploded view of a grille that would be found in shop manuals and other similar industry publications.

of the related parts are damaged, list the repairs or replacements needed as follows:

Front Grille	Replace
Front Grille	Straighten
Opening Panel	and Replace
Deflector (or Valance Panel)	Replace
Headlamp Door	Replace
Grille Opening Panel	Refinish

Notice that the parts to be repaired, straightened, replaced, or refinished are listed in a definite sequence according to factory disassembly operations or exploded views as provided in shop manuals (Figure 20-10) or crash estimating guides.

The estimator must be on constant guard against missing related and hidden damages. As described in Chapter 9, damage that happens to a vehicle during the moment of impact or immediately after impact is referred to as **related damage.** Often, in the case of unibody cars especially, related damage is not near the area of impact but some distance away. For example, during a fender-bender accident, the rear of the vehicle might be hit by an oncoming vehicle unable to stop in time, thereby causing damage to the trunk and rear bumper. Damage to the rear of the vehicle would be called related damage. Another classification would be secondary damage because it is not at or near the fender-bender impact zone but was caused by it.

Hidden or secondary damage, as stressed many times in this book, can occur almost anywhere or to any part or component on a car that has been involved in a collision. Naturally, if the damage is only minor—creased fender, gouge in door, headlamp

assembly smashed, and so forth—the chances of hidden damage occurring are somewhat remote. However, due to the tremendous forces involved in a major, severe collision, the estimator must always suspect some form of hidden damage. For example, crankshafts can snap when the engine stops suddenly by collision forces. Badly damaged fan blades can be the clue to a water pump shaft that is cracked or driven back into the pump housing by the radiator, crushing the internal seals or bearings.

Front motor mounts can be sheared and yet the engine resettles back into position, hiding this type of damage. Castings of the engine, transmission, or bell housing might crack, leaving only a hairline fracture that is difficult to detect even upon close examination.

Spring leafs can crack and be hard to spot, or the parking pawl, located inside the automatic transmission, might have snapped in two if the car was hit with the shift lever in the park position.

Transmission cooler lines running from the engine radiator to the automatic transmission case might have become crushed or pinched. Steering linkage might have become bent and yet because of its unusual configuration, misalignment can be difficult to detect at first glance.

The estimator or technician must look for buckles in frame members. Look for bolts, flat washers, or other types of fasteners that have moved or shifted out of position, leaving unpainted, bare, or shiny metal showing. Look for displaced, cracked, or fractured undercoating underneath the body structure.

As mentioned several times, severe collisions from any direction often cause the frame or unitized body to distort (Figure 20-11). At one time the estimator could check this damage with the naked eye and would be fairly close in giving a repair cost. But in today's auto construction, especially with unibody, the "eyeballing" technique is sometimes not enough to detect misalignment. It is far better to use measuring gauges (Figure 20-12) or devices to check for misalignment. (The use of these tools is a

FIGURE 20-12   Measuring for misalignment with a tram gauge. Uses of gauges in today's automobile construction is essential.

must for frame/body technicians when it comes to misalignment.) However, unless the estimator is thoroughly skilled in such types of estimating, it is wise to consult with the frame/body technician for an appraisal to determine the labor time necessary to get it back into proper alignment.

When estimating a car involved in a severe collision, raise the car off the floor so that a good visual inspection can be made of all underbody and drivetrain components (Figure 20-13). In some unibody vehicles, it might even be necessary to remove the drivetrain and suspension components to make a thorough damage inspection.

FIGURE 20-11   All damage—from minor to severe—must be given very careful inspection by estimator or technician because of the chance of hidden or secondary damage.

FIGURE 20-13   Underbody inspection is best made on a lift or bench. (Courtesy of Car-O-Liner Co.)

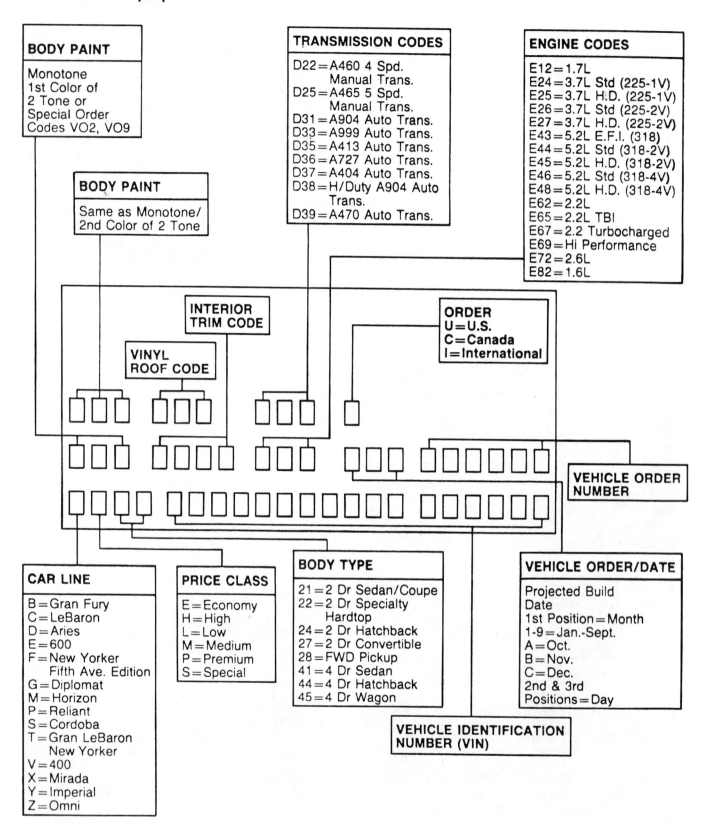

FIGURE 20-14 Typical Chrysler body code plate interpretation. Other vehicle manufacturers follow the same basic system.

> **WARNING:** Never support the car on a hydraulic jack to inspect underbody damage; always use jack stands.

Doors out of alignment and cracked stationary glass are often a solid clue to hidden damage to the frame or underbody structure. The operation of instrument panel gauges and lights, heater, air conditioner, radio, and all other comfort and convenience components must be carefully checked.

In other words, the estimator with the help of the technician must give the entire car—top to bottom and front to rear—a thorough, intensive inspection and take nothing for granted. If something is missed on the original estimate, it often becomes difficult to reopen it later on for further negotiations. Some estimates do include a so-called hidden damage clause that permits added charges to the original estimate when hidden damages are discovered when the work has been opened up for repairs.

As mentioned in Chapter 1, it is important that the body shop technician and the estimator collect all of the necessary information about the vehicle to locate and order the correct parts and paint. The best sources of this information are the VIN number (see Chapter 2), paint tag (see Chapter 16), and the body code plate. Body code plates are located in various places according to the vehicle manufacturer's desires. For example, Chrysler products might have the body code plate located on the left front side shield, the wheelhousing, or on the upper radiator support. The typical Chrysler plate as shown in Figure 20–14 contains five rows of data. The bottom two rows, plus a portion of the center row, are reserved for specific information as depicted in the illustration. Starting at the center row, other sales codes used to build a specific vehicle are listed.

20.5 REPAIRABILITY OF THE VEHICLE

The first critical decision that the estimator must make is the repairability of the vehicle. If the car was involved in a severe collision, there is a strong possibility that the total repair costs might exceed its market value. For example, a car with a market value of $3,150.00 (if undamaged), and an estimate that totals $3,710.00 is one situation where repairs are not practical. More than likely the insurance company adjuster will agree with such a decision and would authorize "totaling" the vehicle.

Naturally, when a car that is totaled is towed into a body shop (for example, frame badly distorted, body crushed, engine transmission severely damaged), there is usually never any doubt that writing a complete estimate is unnecessary. All that is usually necessary is a courtesy estimate.

The auto industry "blue book" (Figure 20–15) or equivalent lists the market value (not the selling price in a used or new car lot) of various model years for all cars. Refer to this publication when such decisions of "repair or scrap" must be made for a badly damaged car. Of course, cars that have been wrapped around trees, smashed almost flat, or sliced in half by extreme collision forces are other

86 **FORD 1986-85**

DOMESTIC CARS

Av'g. Trd-In	BODY TYPE	Model	M.S.R.P.	Wgt.	Av'g. Loan	Av'g. Retail
1986	**LTD CROWN VICTORIA-AT-PS-AC-Continued**					
200	Add Power Windows (Std. 2D & LX)		$282		200	250
200	Add Power Seats				200	250
125	Add Rear Window Defroster		145		125	150
100	Add Luggage Rack (S/W)		110		100	125
150	Add Cruise Control		176		150	200
150	Add Tilt Steering Wheel		115		150	200
150	Add Wire Wheel Covers		205		150	200
275	Add Leather Seats		418		250	350
225	Add Brougham Roof		793		225	300
150	Add Custom or 2-Tone Paint		117		150	200
850	Deduct W/out Air Conditioning				850	850
1986	**THUNDERBIRD-AT-PS-AC**				**Start Oct. 1985**	
THUNDERBIRD-V6	Veh Ident 1FA()P46()()G()100001 Up					
8100	Coupe 2D	46	$11020	3089	7300	9300
9300	Coupe 2D elan	46	12554	3145	8375	10600
THUNDERBIRD-V8	Veh Ident 1FA()P46()()G()100001 Up					
8300	Coupe 2D	46	$11568	3275	7475	9525
9500	Coupe 2D elan	46	13102	3331	8550	10825
THUNDERBIRD-4 Cyl.-AT/5 Spd.	Veh Ident 1FA()P46()()G()100001 Up					
8950	Turbo Coupe 2D	46	$14143	3172	8075	10200
400	Add Power Sunroof		$701		375	475
150	Add AM/FM Stereo/Tape		127		150	200
75	Add Power Door Locks		220		75	100
100	Add Power Windows (Std. elan & Turbo)		207		100	125
100	Add Power Seats				100	125
75	Add Rear Window Defroster		145		75	100
75	Add Cruise Control		176		75	100
75	Add Tilt Steering Wheel		115		75	100
100	Add Wire Wheel Covers		212		100	125
200	Add Leather Seats		415		200	250
100	Add Custom or 2-Tone Paint (Std. Turbo)				100	125
650	Deduct W/out Air Conditioning				650	650
1985	**ESCORT/EXP-AT-PS-FWD**				**Start Sept. 1984, 1985.5 March 1985**	
ESCORT-4 Cyl.	Veh Ident 1FA()P(Model)()()F()100001 Up					
3300	Hatchback 2D	04	$5620 *	1990	2975	4125
3400	Hatchback 4D	13	5827 *	2055	3075	4225
3500	Hatchback 2D L	04	5876 *	1979	3150	4325
3600	Hatchback 4D L	13	6091 *	2044	3250	4450
3750	Station Wagon 4D L	09	6305 *	2071	3375	4600
3775	Hatchback 2D GL	05	6374 *	2047	3400	4650
3875	Hatchback 4D GL	14	6588 *	2114	3500	4750
4025	Station Wagon 4D GL	10	6765 *	2139	3625	4900
4025	Hatchback 4D LX	15	7840 *	2175	3625	4900
4175	Station Wagon 4D LX	11	7931 *	2198	3775	5050
4175	Hatchback 2D GT	07	7585 *	2140	3775	5050
4250	Hatchback 2D Turbo GT	07	8680 *	2172	3825	5150
1985.5 ESCORT-4 Cyl.	Veh Ident 1FA()P(Model)()()F()100001 Up					
3350	Hatchback 2D	31	$5856 *	2142	3025	4175
3550	Hatchback 2D L	31	6127 *		3200	4400
3650	Hatchback 4D L	36	6341 *	2195	3300	4500
3800	Station Wagon 4D L	34	6622 *	2223	3425	4675
3825	Hatchback 2D GL	32	6641 *		3450	4700

DEDUCT FOR RECONDITIONING
1987 APRIL 1987 A

FIGURE 20–15 Page from the auto industry "blue book" that lists the market value of most vehicles. *(Courtesy of National Automobile Dealers Used Car Guide Co.)*

FIGURE 20-16   Example of a totaled vehicle

FIGURE 20-17   A salvage yard is the last resting place for totaled vehicles and is an excellent source of used parts.

examples of cars considered totaled and should be scrapped (Figure 20-16).

Some totaled vehicles have a salvage value. That is, parts of a wrecked car such as the engine, transmission, drive shaft, and body parts might be usable. They can be sold as used parts by salvage yards (Figure 20-17).

20.6 PART PRICES

Once the vehicle is judged repairable, the next decision that the estimator must determine is whether or not the collision damage requires new parts or simply repair and straightening procedures. From an economical (and practical) standpoint, it might be unwise to call for all new parts to replace those that have become bent, twisted, creased, torn, buckled, or broken. Naturally, it would be simple to list only new parts and units in order to restore the damaged vehicle to its precollision condition. But as mentioned, this is sometimes impractical. As a result, the estimator must have the ability to judge the seriousness of damage that a specific part or unit has received and balance the cost of repairs against the cost of new parts or units.

As a rule of thumb, repair costs should never exceed replacement costs. If there is some doubt that repairs and straightening will not produce a quality job, then the estimate should list the required new parts. Remember, too, sheet metal parts usually offer the most opportunities for repair and straightening. As a result, sheet metal repairs, replacement, and refinishing of panels generally account for the largest number of estimate dollars. Of course, sheet metal parts that are considered repairable can be

handled in several different ways. For example, bends can be hammered out; stretched metal can be shrunk through the use of heat plus a hammer and dolly; tears can be welded; and upsets in the metal can be stretched, while low surfaces can be filled with filler compounds.

To reduce parts costs, many insurance appraisers and some customers might want the body shop to use salvage parts. These are parts that were removed from totally wrecked vehicles by salvage yards and they are usually in good condition. But there is always a chance that parts have been previously damaged and repaired. For this reason, it is important that the body shop or parts manager carefully inspect all salvage parts before they are installed to be sure that they are in usable condition. While some customers might object to used parts in their repaired car, it might be necessary, especially on older vehicles, because manufacturers often discontinue a part's availability after a period of time. Many salvage yard dealers offer a free computer parts location service (Figure 20-18).

When writing a damage estimate on late-model cars, it is best to use only the prices for new parts. As a general rule, new parts are easier to install, when compared to salvage parts, but are more expensive.

Each damaged car poses different problems that must be answered in order to arrive at a repair versus replacement final solution. The most difficult questions arise when a vehicle was involved in a major collision. If the frame horns (available separately on some car lines) received extensive damage, for instance, the estimator might want to consider listing their replacement rather than the more costly job of installing a complete new frame assembly. Or, the estimator might wish to list the replacement of a

FIGURE 20–18   Many salvage yard dealers have a free computer parts locator service.

front side rail section or a complete front frame section, both of which are available for a number of the same models. These solutions might be more practical (from a time and cost approach) than making repairs with heat and the use of body and chassis frame straightening equipment.

On the other hand, estimating damage to the body shell is often a much more difficult job. Knowing the corrective forces that would be needed to restore the body shell to its original dimensions and configuration requires on-the-job work experience. If body shell distortion is suspected, such a condition can be checked by careful measurement made prior to listing any necessary repair or straightening procedures. Generally, clues to minor body distortion (twist, sag, sidesway) are apparent if any cracking of stationary glass (windshields/ back window) is noted, yet there is no visible sign of a direct impact with any object. This is commonly termed a "stress crack," which is one that shows no evidence of an impact.

In some situations, such as a severely damaged front end, an estimator might want to consider the purchase and installation of a used front end assembly. In the body repair trade this is referred to as a "front clip" (see Chapter 10). This assembly generally includes the front bumper and supports, grilles and baffles, the radiator and its supporting members, the hood and its hinges (or hood torsion bars), the front fenders and skirts, as well as all front lamps, the wiring, and all parts that are related to each other in this frontal area. Often, this method for collision repairs to the front end will decrease the total time the car is in the shop. Of course, if permitted by the manufacturer, sectioned parts are available and are often used (Figure 20–19).

If vehicle inspection reveals that one or more wheels have severe damage or the lip of the wheel is pushed inward past the first step, then there is no

FIGURE 20–19   Certain sectioned used parts can be used in body repair.

question that a new wheel must be listed on the estimate. Tires should also be given a close inspection both on the outside and inside of the sidewall. If the estimator finds extensive or deep cuts, such damage can affect the basic tire structure (carcass) and thus make it unsafe. A new tire must be listed in the estimate.

Often, wheel damage occurs and yet the tire remains undamaged. However, a check might find a deflated tire (caused by a bent wheel) that does not show any sign of external damage yet it might have received internal damage. In such instances, have someone dismount the tire and make an inspection of the inner surfaces. If a tire must be replaced, the estimator must take into consideration the amount of tread wear it received before the accident. From this information, the owner of the car should then be charged a "betterment" cost for the installation of a new tire. In other words, the owner should be charged for the amount of tread wear on his/her original tire, thus sharing in the purchase price of the new tire.

Collision or estimating guides can be used as a reference for pricing parts. However, never use the guides to determine the **absolute** price. Usually, these guides will list the name of the part, the year of the vehicle it will fit, its part number, the estimated

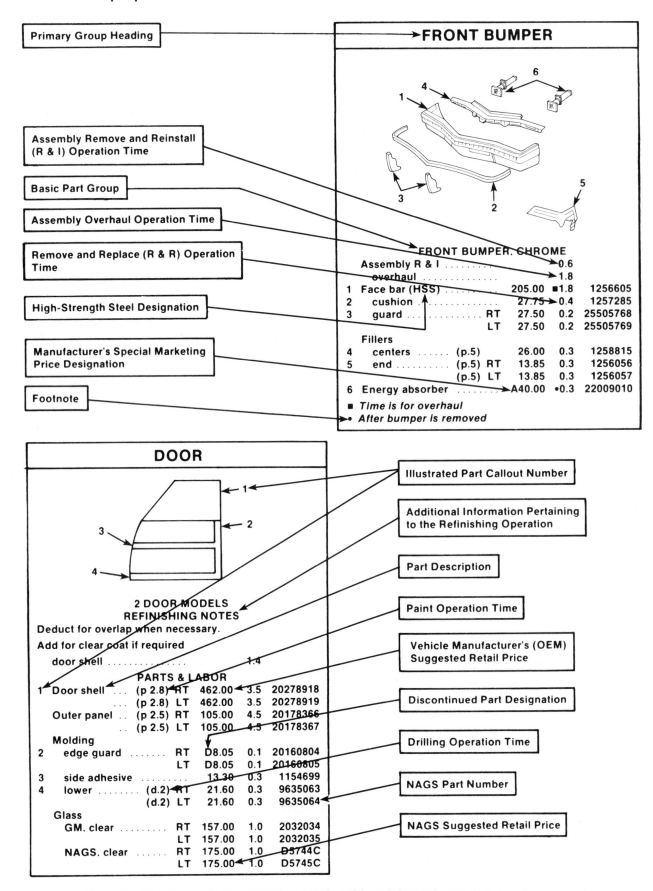

Primary Group Heading

Assembly Remove and Reinstall (R & I) Operation Time

Basic Part Group

Assembly Overhaul Operation Time

Remove and Replace (R & R) Operation Time

High-Strength Steel Designation

Manufacturer's Special Marketing Price Designation

Footnote

FRONT BUMPER

FRONT BUMPER, CHROME

Assembly R & I			0.6	
overhaul			1.8	
1 Face bar (HSS)		205.00	■1.8	1256605
2 cushion		27.75	0.4	1257285
3 guard	RT	27.50	0.2	25505768
	LT	27.50	0.2	25505769
Fillers				
4 centers	(p.5)	26.00	0.3	1258815
5 end	(p.5) RT	13.85	0.3	1256056
	(p.5) LT	13.85	0.3	1256057
6 Energy absorber		A40.00	•0.3	22009010

■ *Time is for overhaul*
• *After bumper is removed*

DOOR

Illustrated Part Callout Number

Additional Information Pertaining to the Refinishing Operation

Part Description

Paint Operation Time

Vehicle Manufacturer's (OEM) Suggested Retail Price

Discontinued Part Designation

Drilling Operation Time

NAGS Part Number

NAGS Suggested Retail Price

2 DOOR MODELS
REFINISHING NOTES

Deduct for overlap when necessary.

Add for clear coat if required

door shell			1.4	
PARTS & LABOR				
1 Door shell	(p 2.8) RT	462.00	3.5	20278918
	(p 2.8) LT	462.00	3.5	20278919
Outer panel	(p 2.5) RT	105.00	4.5	20178366
	(p 2.5) LT	105.00	4.5	20178367
Molding				
2 edge guard	RT	D8.05	0.1	20160804
	LT	D8.05	0.1	20160805
3 side adhesive		13.30	0.3	1154699
4 lower	(d.2) RT	21.60	0.3	9635063
	(d.2) LT	21.60	0.3	9635064
Glass				
GM. clear	RT	157.00	1.0	2032034
	LT	157.00	1.0	2032035
NAGS. clear	RT	175.00	1.0	D5744C
	LT	175.00	1.0	D5745C

FIGURE 20-20 Typical estimating crash guide pricing information and how to use it

time to repair or replace, and the current price (Figure 20-20). These current prices are the factory-suggested list prices. Parts that are no longer available or discontinued by the vehicle manufacturer are usually listed; the price that appears in the guide (proceeded by "D") was the last available one. The prefix "A" in a guide price list indicates that it is included in a special marketing program and does not have a manufacturer's suggested list price. The actual price, which might be higher or lower than the "D" or "A" price listed in the estimating guide, can be determined by contacting a parts dealer in the shop's local area.

Part prices given in estimating guides usually do not include the cost of state and local taxes, shipping from the supplier, bolts, rivets, screws, nuts, washers, clips, fasteners, body repair materials and refinishing, unless otherwise noted.

It is important that estimators take into consideration their place of employment. The facilities of a particular body shop, the type of equipment available, and the ability of body technicians to do the job in a specific time limit, all enter into the final "repair or replace" decision. This will affect the total cost of the estimate.

Once the part prices have been determined, they can be placed on the estimate form.

20.7 LABOR COSTS

The front pages of estimating guides usually provide an explanation of what the flat rate labor time includes and does not include. For example, replacing a panel or fender includes transfer of the part attached to the panel. It does not include the installation of moldings, antennas, refinishing, pin striping, decals, or other accessory parts. Also not considered are rusted bolts, undercoating, and alignment or straightening of damaged adjacent parts or bolts that are inaccessible to the auto body technician.

The flat rate labor time reported in collision damage manuals is to be used as a **guide only.** The times reported are principally based on data reported by vehicle manufacturers who have arrived at them by repeated performance of each operation a sufficient number of times under normal shop conditions. An explanation is listed in the estimating guides (Figure 20-21) of the established requirements for the average mechanic, working under average conditions and following procedures outlined in their service manuals and the "operational times."

The times reported apply only to standard stock models listed in identification sections of the guide.

The labor times do not apply to cars with equipment other than that supplied by the car manufacturer as standard or regular production options. If other equipment is used, the time might be adjusted to compensate for the variables.

All reported flat rate times given in estimating guides include time necessary to ensure proper fit of the individual new part being replaced. The times listed are based on new, undamaged parts installed as an individual operation. Additional time has not been added to compensate for collision damage to the vehicle. Removal and replacement of exchanged or used parts is not considered. If additional aligning or repair must be made, such factors should be considered when making an estimate.

When jobs overlap, reductions in an estimating guide flat rate operation times must be considered. This occurs when replacement of one component duplicates some labor operations required to replace an adjacent component. For example, when replacing a quarter panel and a rear body panel on the same vehicle, that area where these two components join is considered overlap. Where a labor overlap condition exists, less time is required to replace adjoining components collectively than is required when they are replaced individually.

Overlap labor estimating guide information is generally included at the beginning of each group. In those instances where overlap information is not given, appropriate allowances should be negotiated after an on-the-spot evaluation.

Another labor cost reduction is noted as included operations. These are jobs that can be performed individually but are also part of another operation. As an example, when replacing a door, the suggested time for the door replacement would include the replacement of all parts attached to the door, except for the ornamentation. It would be impossible to replace the door without transferring these parts. Consequently, the time involved in transferring these parts would be "included operations" and should be disregarded because the times for the individual items are already included in the door replacement time.

The following individual operations are additional factors to be considered by the estimator when writing an estimate. Such added time is usually negotiated between the shop estimator and the insurance company's appraiser or the customer.

- Time required for the setup of the vehicle on a frame machine and damage diagnosis.
- Time necessary for pushing, pulling, cutting, and so on to remove collision-damaged parts.
- Time required to straighten or align related parts.

1. BUMPER

FRONT OR REAR
NOTE: Disconnect at energy absorber (mounting bracket) or frame mounting.
ASSEMBLY REMOVE AND REINSTALL (R & I)
Included:
- R & I unit as assembly
- Alignment to vehicle

ASSEMBLY OVERHAUL
Included:
- R & I assembly
- Disassemble
- Replace damaged parts
- Reassemble unit
- Align to vehicle

FACE BAR REMOVE AND REPLACE (R & R)
Included:
- R & R face bar
- R & I guards and face bar cushions (unless otherwise noted in text)

ALL BUMPER OPERATIONS
Does Not Include:
- Additional time for frozen or broken fasteners
- Refinishing
- Optional moldings, name plates, emblems, and ornamentation; air bags and lamps
- Stripe tape, decals, overlays
- Removal of hydraulic energy absorbers
- Aim headlamps

2. FRAME

UNITIZED
Included:
- Welding as necessary and electrical wiring
- Floor mats, insulation, and trim (if required)

Does Not Include:
- Setup on frame machine and damage diagnosis
- R & I of all bolted-on parts and body sheet metal
- Wheel alignment
- Refinishing, undercoating, sound deadening material, and anticorrosion protection
- Removal of adjacent panels
- Time for pulling

CONVENTIONAL
Included:
- R & I front sheet metal and body assembly
- Front and rear suspension parts
- Steering parts and powertrain as assembly
- Brake line disconnect and bleed
- R & I fuel tank and bumper assembly
- Control linkage and electrical wiring

Does Not Include:
- Setup on frame machine and damage diagnosis
- Wheel alignment
- Refinishing, undercoating, sound deadening material, and anticorrosion protection
- Time for pulling

FRONT OR REAR SUSPENSION CROSS MEMBERS
Included:
- Welding as necessary

Does Not Include:
- R & I of all bolted on parts
- Wheel alignment

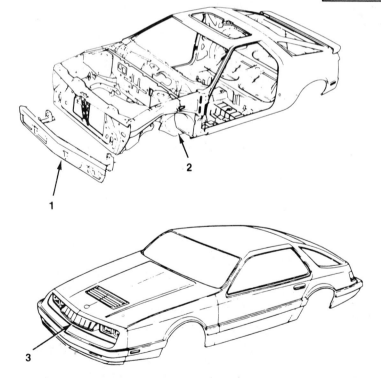

3. GRILLE

Included:
- Grille remove and reinstall
- Lamps (when mounted in grille)
- Standard equipment molding, name plates, and ornamentation

Does Not Include:
- Stripe tape, decals
- Optional molding, name plates, and ornamentation
- Refinishing
- Optional lamps
- Aim headlamps

GRILLE/HEADER PANEL/FASCIA
Included: (unless otherwise noted)
- Grille remove and reinstall
- Lamps
- Alignment to vehicle
- Fillers and extensions

Does Not Include:
- Bumper assembly remove and reinstall
- Refinishing
- Stripe tape, decal, overlays
- Molding, name plates, and ornamentation
- Drill time
- Aim headlamps

FIGURE 20–21   Information found in a typical estimating crash guide "operational times" section

- Time necessary to remove undercoating, tar, grease, and similar materials.
- Time to repair rust or corrosion damage to adjacent parts.
- Time for the free-up of rusted or frozen parts.
- Time for drilling for ornamentation or the fabrication of mounting holes when not provided in new part being installed.
- Time for filling or plugging unneeded holes in new parts.
- Time to repair damaged replacement parts prior to installation.
- Time to check suspension and steering alignment/toe-in.
- Time for removal of shattered glass.
- Time to rebuild, recondition, and install aftermarket components. (Parts replacement time does not include refinishing time.)
- Time for application of sound deadening material, undercoating, caulking, and painting inner areas.

- Time to replace rust resistant anticorrosion material.
- Time to R & I main computer module when excessive temperatures (above 176 degrees Fahrenheit) are necessary in repair operations. Contact manufacturer for recommended removal procedures.
- Time to R & I wheel or hub cap locks.
- Time to replace such accessories as trailer hitches, sun roofs, fender flares, and so forth.
- Time to spend on previous repairs or damage.

It is easy for even an experienced estimator to overlook the removal of exterior trim and body sheet metal hardware. These parts must often be removed prior to bumping or painting operations and then replaced after their completion. This is a labor cost that should not be overlooked (Figure 20-22). One more often overlooked job: Any repairs or replacement of front end parts should include a headlight

---

1. DECALS, STRIPE TAPE, AND OVERLAYS

Included:
- Installation of material only

Does Not Include:
- Removal of old material (estimate accordingly)
- R & R or R & I of moldings, name plates, and ornamentation
- Straightening or repairing damaged panels
- R & I outside door hardware
- Refinishing prior to application

---

2. ADHESIVE TYPE MOLDING

Panel replacement time does not include time for installation of molding, name plates, or ornamentation.

If new parts are used on a new panel, add one half the replacement time. If old parts are used on a new panel, add entire replacement time.

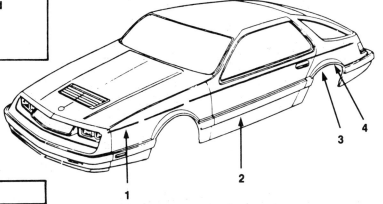

---

3. BOLT OR CLIP-ON MOLDING

Panel replacement time does not include time for installation of molding, name plates, ornamentation, or for the drilling of mounting holes.

If new parts are used on a new panel, add drilling time and one half the replacement time. If old parts are used on a new panel, add drilling time and entire replacement time.

---

4. DRILLING OPERATIONS

Time to drill mounting holes is listed in parentheses next to part description; (d.2) indicates .2 for drilling. Times shown are for round holes only. If holes must be other than round, estimate time accordingly.

If new parts are used on a new panel, add drilling time and one half the replacement time. If old parts are used on a new panel, add drilling time and entire replacement time.

FIGURE 20-22 Typical "operational times" for molding, decal, and overlay installation

TABLE 20-1: TIME/DOLLAR CONVERSION TABLE*

Dollar Per Hour Rates

Time	$.50	$1.00	$10.00	$15.00	$20.00	$25.00	$30.00	$35.00	$40.00	$45.00	$50.00
0.6	.30	.60	6.00	9.00	12.00	15.00	18.00	21.00	24.00	27.00	30.00
0.7	.35	.70	7.00	10.50	14.00	17.50	21.00	24.50	28.00	31.50	35.00
0.8	.40	.80	8.00	12.00	16.00	20.00	24.00	28.00	32.00	36.00	40.00
0.9	.45	.90	9.00	13.50	18.00	22.50	27.00	31.50	36.00	40.50	45.00
1.0	.50	1.00	10.00	15.00	20.00	25.00	30.00	35.00	40.00	45.00	50.00
1.1	.55	1.10	11.00	16.50	22.00	27.50	33.00	38.50	44.00	49.50	55.00
1.2	.60	1.20	12.00	18.00	24.00	30.00	36.00	42.00	48.00	54.00	60.00
1.3	.65	1.30	13.00	19.50	26.00	32.50	39.00	45.50	52.00	58.50	65.00
1.4	.70	1.40	14.00	21.00	28.00	35.00	42.00	49.00	56.00	63.00	70.00
1.5	.75	1.50	15.00	22.50	30.00	37.50	45.00	52.50	60.00	67.50	75.00
1.6	.80	1.60	16.00	24.00	32.00	40.00	48.00	56.00	64.00	72.00	80.00
1.7	.85	1.70	17.00	25.50	34.00	42.50	51.00	59.50	68.00	76.50	85.00
1.8	.90	1.80	18.00	27.00	36.00	45.00	54.00	63.00	72.00	81.00	90.00
1.9	.95	1.90	19.00	28.50	38.00	47.50	57.00	66.50	76.00	85.50	95.00
2.0	1.00	2.00	20.00	30.00	40.00	50.00	60.00	70.00	80.00	90.00	100.00
2.1	1.05	2.10	21.00	31.50	42.00	52.50	63.00	73.50	84.00	94.50	105.00
2.2	1.10	2.20	22.00	33.00	44.00	55.00	66.00	77.00	88.00	99.00	110.00
2.3	1.15	2.30	23.00	34.50	46.00	57.50	69.00	80.50	92.00	103.50	115.00
2.4	1.20	2.40	24.00	36.00	48.00	60.00	72.00	84.00	96.00	108.00	120.00
2.5	1.25	2.50	25.00	37.50	50.00	62.50	75.00	87.50	100.00	112.50	125.00
2.6	1.30	2.60	26.00	39.00	52.00	65.00	78.00	91.00	104.00	117.00	130.00
2.7	1.35	2.70	27.00	40.50	54.00	67.50	81.00	94.50	108.00	121.50	135.00
2.8	1.40	2.80	28.00	42.00	56.00	70.00	84.00	98.00	112.00	126.00	140.00
2.9	1.45	2.90	29.00	43.50	58.00	72.50	87.00	101.50	116.00	130.50	145.00
3.0	1.50	3.00	30.00	45.00	60.00	75.00	90.00	105.00	120.00	135.00	150.00
3.1	1.55	3.10	31.00	46.50	62.00	77.50	93.00	108.50	124.00	139.50	155.00
3.2	1.60	3.20	32.00	48.00	64.00	80.00	96.00	112.00	128.00	144.00	160.00
3.3	1.65	3.30	33.00	49.50	66.00	82.50	99.00	115.50	132.00	148.50	165.00
3.4	1.70	3.40	34.00	51.00	68.00	85.00	102.00	119.00	136.00	153.00	170.00
3.5	1.75	3.50	35.00	52.50	70.00	87.50	105.00	122.50	140.00	157.50	175.00
3.6	1.80	3.60	36.00	54.00	72.00	90.00	108.00	126.00	144.00	162.00	180.00
3.7	1.85	3.70	37.00	55.50	74.00	92.50	111.00	129.50	148.00	166.50	185.00
3.8	1.90	3.80	38.00	57.00	76.00	95.00	114.00	133.00	152.00	171.00	190.00
3.9	1.95	3.90	39.00	58.50	78.00	97.50	117.00	136.50	156.00	175.50	195.00
4.0	2.00	4.00	40.00	60.00	80.00	100.00	120.00	140.00	160.00	180.00	200.00
4.1	2.05	4.10	41.00	61.50	82.00	102.50	123.00	143.50	164.00	184.50	205.00
4.2	2.10	4.20	42.00	63.00	84.00	105.00	126.00	147.00	168.00	189.00	210.00
4.3	2.15	4.30	43.00	64.50	86.00	107.50	129.00	150.50	172.00	193.50	215.00
4.4	2.20	4.40	44.00	66.00	88.00	110.00	132.00	154.00	176.00	198.00	220.00
4.5	2.25	4.50	45.00	67.50	90.00	112.50	135.00	157.50	180.00	202.50	225.00
4.6	2.30	4.60	46.00	69.00	92.00	115.00	138.00	161.00	184.00	207.00	230.00
4.7	2.35	4.70	47.00	70.50	94.00	117.50	141.00	164.50	188.00	211.50	235.00
4.8	2.40	4.80	48.00	72.00	96.00	120.00	144.00	168.00	192.00	216.00	240.00
4.9	2.45	4.90	49.00	73.50	98.00	122.50	147.00	171.50	196.00	220.50	245.00
5.0	2.50	5.00	50.00	75.00	100.00	125.00	150.00	175.00	200.00	225.00	250.00
5.1	2.55	5.10	51.00	76.50	102.00	127.50	153.00	178.50	204.00	229.50	255.00
5.2	2.60	5.20	52.00	78.00	104.00	130.00	156.00	182.00	208.00	234.00	260.00
5.3	2.65	5.30	53.00	79.50	106.00	132.50	159.00	185.50	212.00	238.50	265.00
5.4	2.70	5.40	54.00	81.00	108.00	135.00	162.00	189.00	216.00	243.00	270.00
5.5	2.75	5.50	55.00	82.50	110.00	137.50	165.00	192.50	220.00	247.50	275.00
5.6	2.80	5.60	56.00	84.00	112.00	140.00	168.00	196.00	224.00	252.00	280.00
5.7	2.85	5.70	57.00	85.50	114.00	142.50	171.00	199.50	228.00	256.50	285.00
5.8	2.90	5.80	58.00	87.00	116.00	145.00	174.00	203.00	232.00	261.00	290.00
5.9	2.95	5.90	59.00	88.50	118.00	147.50	177.00	206.50	236.00	265.50	295.00
6.0	3.00	6.00	60.00	90.00	120.00	150.00	180.00	210.00	240.00	270.00	300.00

*Complete time/dollar conversion can be found in most crash guides.

alignment. Remember that the estimator must charge out every job function needed to restore the vehicle to its precollision operation, safety, and value.

In recent years, estimators must also consider the special materials—plastic and steel—used in cars that require special handling by the body technician. For example, the use of lightweight, high-strength steel in various locations throughout vehicles, as noted in earlier chapters of this book, requires specific repair procedures.

It is not always possible or practical to accurately identify the correct locations on a vehicle where HSLA/HSS steel is used. However, when this information is available, estimating guides generally will identify this type of steel with an HSS designation next to the description. When in doubt, it is recommended to contact the automobile manufacturer for the specific location(s) of high-strength steel and the required repair procedures.

TOTAL ESTIMATED LABOR COSTS

Once all the repairs and labor times have been entered on the estimate form, then it is necessary to refer to Table 20-1. This conversion table can be used to convert flat rate labor time into dollars to fit local labor or operating rates per hour.

When establishing flat labor rates, the shop overhead (including such items as rent, management and supervision, supplies, and depreciation on equipment) must be determined. Then the actual labor cost of all employees (including office help) and the profit required to keep the business operating must be added to the shop overhead to obtain a dollar flat rate for repairs. This flat rate cost is usually figured on an hourly basis.

 **SHOP TALK** _____

When using a conversion table such as Table 20-1, read across from the labor time column to the appropriate flat labor rate column. For time or dollar rates not listed, use a combination of columns given in the table. For dollar rates ending with 50 cents, add 50 from the cent column to the appropriate rate column.

Labor times shown in all collision estimating guides are listed in hours and tenths of an hour. If a

vehicle requires a new right front fender, a new wheel opening molding, and a new nameplate ornament, the total labor replacement time, according to a leading estimating guide (Figure 20–23), is:

FENDER

FENDER
REFINISHING NOTES
Deduct for overlap when necessary. See GUIDE to ESTIMATING pages.
Add for clear coat

fender			1.1	

PARTS & LABOR

1 Fender	(p2.2)	RT	242.43 #	3.0	E4ZZ16005A
	(p2.2)	LT	242.43 #	3.0	E4ZZ16006A
Transfer					
silver			8.17 †	0.3	E4ZZ16720B
black			8.17 †	0.3	E4ZZ16720A
Mouldings					
side, rear	84	RT	8.45	0.2	E4ZZ16A038B
	84	LT	8.45	0.2	E4ZZ16A039B
	85-86	RT	8.45	0.2	E5ZZ16A038CP
	85-86	LT	8.45	0.2	E5ZZ16A039CP
2 Brace			3.86		D9ZZ16A023A
Rear mount bracket			2.51		D8BZ16C078A
3 Splash shield		RT	51.70	0.5	E6ZZ16102A
		LT	51.70	0.5	E6ZZ16103A
4 Wheelhouse w/siderail					
	(p1.0) 84-85	RT	217.15 §	6.5	E7ZZ16054A
	(p1.0) 84-85	LT	217.15 §	6.5	E6ZZ16055A
	(p1.0) 86	RT	217.15 §	6.5	E7ZZ16054A
	(p1.0) 86	LT	217.15 §	6.5	E6ZZ16055A
5 front extension	84-85	RT	29.68 ‡	2.0	E4LY16054B
	84-85	LT	29.68 ‡	2.0	E7ZZ16055B
	86	RT	29.68 ‡	2.0	E7ZZ16054B
	86	LT	29.68 ‡	2.0	E7ZZ16055B
reinforcement					
upper		RT	12.23		E6ZZ16154A
		LT	11.71		D8BZ16155A
lower		RT	11.59		D9ZZ16060A
		LT	11.43		E6ZZ16060A
6 Sound absorber		RT	7.92		D9ZZ16071A
		LT	7.92		D9ZZ16072A

ANTENNA

Antenna assembly		15.00	0.5	E3AZ18813A

\# *With antenna add .5.*
§ *After fender, radiator support, & front suspension crossmember are detached.*
† *Time does not include removal of old transfer.*
‡ *After fender and necessary parts are removed.*

FIGURE 20-23   A simple method of figuring refinishing and labor cost

Front right fender	3.0 hours
Wheel opening molding	0.2 hours
Installation of nameplate	0.2 hours
Total labor	3.4 hours

But remember, there is a drilling time of 0.1 hours (d.2) involved when installing the new molding on the new fender; thus, the total labor time is 3.5 hours. Referring to Table 20–1 and knowing that the shop's dollar per hour operating rate is (for this example) $25.00, the total estimated labor cost would be $87.50. When the dollar labor costs are determined, they are written on the estimate form.

With the introduction of unibody construction, the task of the estimator to make an accurate estimate has become more difficult. As mentioned earlier in the chapter, the five zone concept developed by the Inter-Industry Conference on Auto Collision Repair is a logical continuation of damage identification and a good unibody estimate guideline. The five damage zones of a unibody vehicle and the types of damage can be broken down in two parts:

- Operations that can be flat rated
- Operations that must be truly estimated

On the whole, flat-rated operations comprise all work in which components must be removed and replaced (Figure 20–24). Estimated work is work done to straighten and/or repair body members. However, it is not always that simple. Sometimes there are combinations. A good example of this is when body members must be straightened first before cutting them off (Figure 20–25) to make sure the new member will line up before welding. The

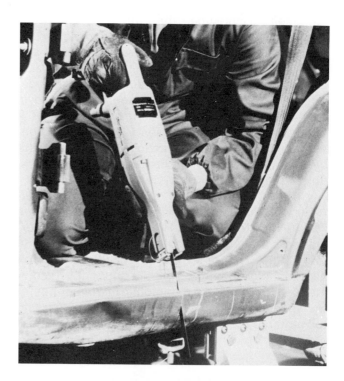

FIGURE 20–25 Cutting a sectioned part

procedure for this operation, even though it is a flat rated R & R, must have some extra time (that must be estimated) added on to the total time for the procedure.

20.8 REFINISHING TIME

Making a correct estimate of the amount of labor time required to refinish panels, doors, hoods, and so forth is a vital part of an estimator's job function. Although the wide range of materials and conditions sometimes makes it difficult to arrive at a precise refinishing cost, there are a number of generally approved concepts that will help an estimator arrive at a fair judgment of the amount of materials that will be needed for the job.

Flat rate manuals published by the major United States car manufacturers list a labor time plus a materials allowance (in dollars) for a multitude of individual paint operations. However, independently published estimating guides and crash books list paint labor times but not the dollar value of the materials required.

In most estimating guides, the time required for painting is shown in the parentheses adjacent to the

FIGURE 20–24 Typical manufacturer's sectional replacement panel

part name. For the fender shown in Figure 20–23, the p 2.2, for example, indicates that 2.2 hours are needed to paint it. The basic color coat application generally **includes:**

- Clean panel/light sanding
- Mask adjacent panels
- Prime/scuff sand
- Final sand/clean
- Mix paint/load sprayer
- Apply color coat
- Remove masking
- Buff or compound (if required)
- Clean equipment

The basic color coat application generally **does not include:**

- Cost of paints or materials
- Matching and/or tinting color
- Grinding, filling, and smoothing welded seams
- Blending into adjacent panels
- Removal of protective coatings
- Spatter paint
- Custom painting
- Undercoating
- Anticorrosion materials
- Sound deadening
- Edging panel
- Underside of hood or trunk lids
- Covering **entire** vehicle prior to refinishing if necessary
- Protective coatings
- Additional time to produce custom, non-OEM finishes

Painting times given in most estimates are for one color on new replacement parts **outer surfaces only.** Additions to paint times are usually made for the following operations:

Underside of hood	Add 0.6
Underside of trunk lid	Add 0.6
Edging new part	
First panel	Add 0.5
Each additional	Add 0.3
Anticorrosion coating	Add 0.3
Two-tone operations	
(unless otherwise specified in text)	
First panel	Add 0.6
Each adjacent	Add 0.4
Stone chip (protective material)	
First panel	Add 0.5
Each additional	Add 0.3

- Clear coat (basecoat/clear coat) **after deduction for overlap**

First major panel	Add 50%
Each additional	Add 25%

 **SHOP TALK** _____

Clear Coat Test. *Lightly sand a painted surface. If the sandpaper shows a whitish dust, it is clear. If sandpaper shows color, it is standard. Refer to paint code reference guide given in Chapter 19.*

Reductions to paint times can be considered when

- Overlap—Adjacent parts

First major panel	Full time
Each additional (except extensions)	Deduct 0.4
Extensions	Deduct 0.2

- Overlap—

Additional parts	(nonadjacent)
First major panel	Full time
Each additional	Deduct 0.2

As previously noted, the labor allowance given in a collision manual does not include any material costs. These must be estimated using a refinishing materials list (locally compiled) or one that is accepted on a national or regional basis. The use of a guide (Table 20–2) permits shop owners and estimators to place a fair evaluation on the refinish materials actually used.

To see how a guide such as this is used, assume that the car must have the entire trunk lid, the left rear quarter panel, and the rocker panel refinished after repairs have been completed. Looking up the labor times in one of the published guides reveals that the trunk lid requires 2.5 hours, the left rear quarter panel states 3.0 hours, while the rocker panel lists only 1.0 hour. Adding them up the total is 6.5 hours. Looking at Table 20–2, note that the total falls within the figures 6.1 through 6.5, which indicates that 2-3/4 quarts of refinish materials are needed to complete the job.

If the total amount of labor figures out to 14.0 hours on a two door sedan or 16.0 hours on a four door sedan, then a complete refinishing job should be considered. One final item that must not be over-

| **B&J** | | | ESTIMATE OF REPAIRS |
| Collision Estimating Services | | | No. 031865 |

20 WEST BROAD ST.
AUBURN, PA 17922
TELEPHONE: (717) 555-7764

SHEET NO. _____1_____ OF __1__ SHEETS

NAME	ADDRESS	PHONE (717)	DATE
CARDINAL SYSTEMS INC.	R.D.1. Rt.61/Sch. Haven/Pa./17972	HOME BUS. 385-4733	1/8/91

YEAR	MAKE	MODEL	LICENSE NO.	MILEAGE	SERIAL/ V.I. NO.
90	Ford	TAURUS 4DR.	MDS-109	08825	1FABP30U1GG197857

INSURANCE COMPANY	TYPE OF INSURANCE	ADJUSTER	PHONE	CAR LOCATED AT
AMERISURE		Ruth Kercher		

PARTS NECESSARY AND ESTIMATE OF LABOR REQUIRED	PAINT COST ESTIMATE		PARTS COST ESTIMATE		LABOR COST ESTIMATE	
1 WHEEL + VALVE + BAL RR			128	15	0	5
1 " TRIM RING			23	37		
1 TIRE P205/70R14 w/w MTS GOODYEAR			85	17		
INVICTA 89⁶⁵ less BRT						
CHECK + ALIGN REAR SUSP.			—		1	5
" BUMPER COVER REAR			—		—	
1 " MLdg			11	33	0	3
1 QUARTER PANEL RR + LOCKPILLAR (SECTION)			193	17	10	0
CHECK QUARTER wh/housg			—		2	0
" " STRIPE	17	50	—		—	
1 DOOR ASSY RR			378	95	4	8
" MLdg SIDE			37	53	0	3
" " BELT			26	47	—	
" HANDLE			7	88		
" Hinges ALIGN			—		0	4
" STRIPE	17	50	—		—	
CHECK ROCKER PANEL RT			—		2	5
1 ROCKER MLdg FR			78	98	0	4
CHECK " " REAR			12	98	0	2
REFINISH DAMAGED PARTS + CLEAR COAT			—		12	1
ALL MATERIALS	121	00				
UNDERCOAT RRQ	5	00			0	5
RUST PROOF	25	00				
TOTALS	186	00	983	98	35	5

INSURED PAYS $_____ INS. CO. PAYS $_____ R.O. NO._____	GRAND TOTAL	1,986.48
INS. CHECK PAYABLE TO_____		
The above is an estimate, based on our inspection, and does not cover additional parts or labor which may be required after the work has been opened up. Occasionally, after work has started, worn, broken or damaged parts are discovered which are not evident on first inspection. Quotations on parts and labor are current and subject to change. Not responsible for any delays caused by unavailability of parts or delays in parts shipment by supplier or transporter.	TOWING & STORAGE	—
ESTIMATOR_____		
AUTHORIZATION FOR REPAIRS. You are hereby authorized to make the above specified repairs to the car described herein.	TAX	119.19
SIGNED X_____ DATE_____ 19___	TOTAL OF ESTIMATE	$ 2,105.67

FIGURE 20-26   A total estimate

TABLE 20-2: REFINISH MATERIALS COST GUIDE (TYPICAL)

Hours	Amount of Material In Quarts	Cost of Material†
0.5 to 1.0	1	$10.00
1.1 to 1.5	1-1/4	12.50
1.6 to 2.0	1-1/2	15.50
2.1 to 2.5	1-3/4	17.00
2.6 to 3.0	2	19.70
3.1 to 3.5	2-1/4	21.90
3.6 to 4.0	2-1/2	22.80
4.1 to 4.5	2-3/4	24.00
4.6 to 5.0	3	29.30
5.1 to 5.5	3-1/4	30.00
5.6 to 6.0	3-1/2	33.00
6.1 to 6.5	3-3/4	34.00
6.6 to 7.0	4	38.00
7.1 to 7.5	4-1/4	43.20
7.6 to 8.0	4-1/2	45.00
8.1 to 8.5	4-3/4	46.10
8.6 to 9.0	5	50.00
9.1 to 9.5	5-1/4	52.00
9.6 to 10.0	5-1/2	55.00
10.1 to 10.5	5-3/4	58.00
10.6 to 11.0	6	59.00
11.1 to 11.5	6-1/4	60.00
11.6 to 12.0	6-1/2	62.00
12.1 to 12.5	6-3/4	63.00
12.6 to 13.0	7	66.00
13.1 to 13.5	7-1/4	68.00
13.6 to 14.0	7-1/2	70.00
14.1 to 14.5	7-3/4	72.00
14.6 to 15.0	8	74.00
15.1 to 15.5	8-1/2	75.00
15.6 to 16.0		76.00

†Cost of materials varies across United States. Some colors, including metallics, are often priced higher.

looked in the refinish estimate has to do with preparation materials, such as plastic body filler, solvents, sanding discs, file sandpaper, forming blades, sealers, undercoat, tape, masking paper, welding supplies, as well as rivets, nuts, bolts, and so forth. Many body shop estimators recommend a charge of $3.00 to $5.00 per refinisher's hours in order to cover such material costs. The paint/material estimate might be listed on the damage report as individual operations or as a sum total of the entire refinishing job.

20.9 ESTIMATE TOTAL

Once all the columns of the estimating form—parts, labor, and refinishing costs—are filled out,

they can be added together for a subtotal. To this figure, add any extra charges such as wrecker and towing charges, as well as storage fee, and state and local taxes. These figures, plus the subtotal figure, will give the grand total estimate of the repair (Figure 20–26).

While more and more larger body shops are doing repair jobs such as wheel alignment, rust-proofing, and tire replacement, smaller operations still "farm" or "sublet" these jobs to specialty organizations. When this is done, the specialty shop bills the body shop for the work. Generally, this is done at a rate less than the normal retail labor cost for work. In this way, the body shop can charge the normal retail cost and still make a small profit. Shops that farm out work usually have a column—Sublet—where the retail labor cost is marked. This sublet figure is added to others to obtain the grand total of the estimate.

If the owner wants to have "extra" work performed (damage that occurred prior to the collision), this should be noted as "customer requested" (C/R) repairs. As a general rule, the insurance company will not pay for customer requested repairs. Often a separate estimate must be made for the customer in such cases.

20.10 REVIEW QUESTIONS

1. Technician A uses the flat rate labor times reported in collision damage manuals only as a guide for estimating. Technician B uses these exact times in the estimates. Who is correct?
   a. Technician A
   b. Technician B
   c. Both A and B
   d. Neither A nor B

2. How long does an estimate usually remain a firm bid?
   a. 1 year
   b. 6 months
   c. 90 days
   d. 30 days

3. Which of the following abbreviations found in crash estimating guides means that the item in question should be removed as an assembly, set aside, and later reinstalled?
   a. R & R
   b. R & I
   c. O & H
   d. O/H

4. Which computer estimating system is preferred by most body shops?
   a. microfilm
   b. resident
   c. dial-up

5. Technician A supports a vehicle on jack stands to inspect for underbody damage. Technician B uses a hydraulic jack. Who is correct?
   a. Technician A
   b. Technician B
   c. Both A and B
   d. Neither A nor B

6. Which of the following conditions is a good sign of minor body distortion?
   a. stress cracking
   b. front clip
   c. side clip
   d. all of the above

7. In a crash estimating guide price list, which prefix means that the part in question does not have a manufacturer's suggested list price?
   a. A
   b. B
   c. C
   d. D

8. What is the name given to jobs that can be performed individually but are also part of another operation?
   a. R & R
   b. overlapping procedures
   c. included operations
   d. flat rate

9. What is the smallest increment in which labor times are listed in crash estimating guides?
   a. hours
   b. half hours
   c. quarter hours
   d. tenths of an hour

10. Which of the following is considered in crash estimating guides to be part of the basic color coat application?
    a. matching and/or tinting
    b. masking adjacent panels
    c. cleaning/light sanding
    d. both b and c

11. Technician A says a totaled vehicle has no salvage value. Technician B says that a totaled vehicle often does have salvage value. Who is correct?
    a. Technician A
    b. Technician B
    c. Both A and B
    d. Neither A nor B

12. Which of the following is not included in the refinishing times for painting a new panel?
    a. removing moldings
    b. featheredging body putty
    c. masking handles
    d. all of the above

13. Which of the following operations is included in the refinishing times listed in the crash manuals?
    a. scuff sanding the repair area
    b. masking the complete vehicle to prevent overspray damage
    c. tinting the color coat
    d. all of the above

14. Printed estimating guides produced from the same data base as the computer program _____ .
    a. serve as a verification check for data used to generate the computer estimate
    b. serve as a backup system in the event of breakdown or power loss
    c. serve as a portable reference guide and a source of additional useful information
    d. all of the above

15. A computer program or instructions written in a computer language that tell the computer what to do is also known as _____ .
    a. hardware
    b. jargon
    c. software
    d. menu

16. Central data bank estimating/management computer systems _____ .
    a. dispense data to users from a single location using modems or special hookups
    b. supply periodic data packages for loading into end user computer systems
    c. both a and b
    d. none of the above

Appendix A
Auto Body Shop Terms

Abrasive A substance used to wear away a surface by friction.

Accessible area An area that can be reached without parts being removed from the vehicle.

Adhesion The ability of one substance to stick to another.

Air drying Allowing paint to dry at ambient (surrounding) temperatures without the aid of an external heat source.

Airless spraying A method of spray application in which atomization is affected by forcing the paint under high pressure through a very small orifice in the spray gun cap. On emerging, the paint instantly expands breaking up into very fine particles.

Align To adjust to a line or predetermined relative position.

Alignment gap The space between panels.

Anchor To hold in place.

Assembly A number of auto body parts that are either bolted or welded together forming a single unit.

Atomize The extent to which the air at the spray gun nozzle breaks up the paint and solvent into fine particles.

Axle A theoretical or actual crossbar supporting vehicle and on which one or more wheels turn.

Ball joint A flexible joint consisting of a ball within a socket; used in front suspension systems and valve train rocker arms.

Basecoat The coat of paint upon which the final coats will be applied.

Basecoat and clear coat A paint system in which the color effect is given by a highly pigmented basecoat. Gloss and durability are given by a subsequent clear coat. The basecoat can be either straight color or metallic.

Belt line The horizontal molding or crown along the side of the vehicle.

Binder The ingredient in a paint that holds the pigment particles together.

Bleeding An older color showing through after a new topcoat has been applied.

Body The apparent viscosity of a paint as assessed when stirring it.

Body filler A heavy-bodied plastic material that cures very hard and is used to fill small dents in metal.

Body panels Sheets of steel that are fastened together to form the car body.

Bounce-back Atomized particles of paint that rebound from the surface being sprayed and contribute to overspray.

Bracket An attachment used to secure parts to the body or frame.

Brittle Lack of flexibility; usually combined with a lack of toughness.

Buffing compound A soft paste containing fine abrasive in a neutral medium, used to eliminate fine scratches and polish lacquer.

Bulge A high crown or area of stretched metal.

Burnishing To polish or buff a finish by hand or machine using a compound or liquid manufactured for this purpose.

Butt weld Weld is made along a line where two pieces are put edge to edge.

Camber The inward or outward tilt of the wheel at the top. It is the tire wearing angle measured in degrees and is the amount the centerline of the wheel is tilted from true vertical.

Cardan universal joint A ball-and-socket type of universal joint. A constant velocity (CV) joint.

Caster The backward or forward tilt of the king pin or spindle support arm at the top. It is the directional control angle measured in degrees and is the amount the centerline of the spindle support arm is tilted from the true vertical.

Catalyst A substance that causes or speeds up a chemical reaction when mixed with another substance but does not change by itself.

Caulking compound A sealing substance used on cracks and air and water leaks.

Centering gauge Used in sets of four, this frame gauge is for locating horizontal datum planes and centerlines on a vehicle.

Chassis The assembly of mechanisms that makes up the major operating systems of the vehicle; usually assumed to include everything except the car body.

Clearance The amount of space between adjacent panels.

Clear coat A top coating on a painted surface that is transparent so that the color coat beneath it is visible.

Closed structural members Boxed-in sections, typically accessible only from the outside, such as rails, pillars, and so forth.

Coatings Covering material used to protect an area.

Color The visual appearance of a material: red, blue, green, and so on. Colors are seen differently by different people.

Compounding The action of using an abrasive material—either by hand or machine—to smooth and bring out the gloss of the applied lacquer topcoat.

Cone concept A way of looking and thinking about the progress of damage in a collision.

Contaminants Foreign substances on the surface to be painted (or in the paint) that would adversely affect the finish.

Control points Points on a vehicle, including holes, flats, or other identifying areas, used to position panels and rails during the manufacturing and redimensioning of vehicles.

Conventional frame An auto body construction type in which the engine and body are bolted to a separate frame.

Conventional points Points on the unibody used as a reference to make a repair.

Corrosion The chemical reaction of air, moisture, or corrosive materials on a metal surface. Usually referred to as rusting or oxidation.

Coverage The area a given amount of paint will cover.

Cowl panels Panels forward of the passenger compartment to which the fenders, hood, and dashboard are bolted.

Cure The process of drying or hardening of a paint film.

Datum line An imaginary line that appears on frame blueprints or charts to help determine correct frame height.

Decarburization Using too much heat resulting in a softening of the metal.

Dedicated fixture measuring systems A bench with fixtures that are set in specific points for body measurement.

Degreasing Cleaning a substrate (usually metallic) by removing greases, oils, and other surface contaminants.

Depression An inward (concave) dent.

Diamond A vehicle body damage condition where one side of the vehicle has been moved to the rear or front causing the frame/body to be out of square.

Direct damage The damage that occurs to the area that is in direct contact with the damaging force or impact.

Dog tracking Off-center tracking of rear wheels as related to the front wheels.

Double coat Spray first pass left to right, spray second pass right to left directly over first pattern.

Drier A catalyst added to a paint to speed up the cure or dry.

Drivetrain Engine, transmission, and shafts.

Drying The process of change of a coat of paint from the liquid to the solid state due to evaporation of solvent, chemical reaction of the binding medium, or a combination of these causes.

Dry spray An imperfect coat, usually caused by spraying too far from the surface being painted or on too hot a surface.

Enamel A type of paint that dries in two stages: first by evaporation of the solvent and then by oxidation of the paint film.

Epoxy A class of resins characterized by good chemical resistance.

Evaporation Solvents in the paint escaping to the air.

Factory specifications Data as supplied by the individual car manufacturer covering all measurements and areas of the vehicle.

Fan The spray pattern of a spray gun.

Fatigue failure A type of metal failure resulting from repeated stress that finally alters the character of the metal so that it cracks.

Featheredge Tapering the edges of the damaged area with sandpaper or special solvents.

Fiberglass A spun-glass material used on some cars instead of sheet metal.

Filler Any material used to fill (level) a damaged area.

Film A very thin continuous sheet of material. Paint forms a film on the surface to which it is applied.

Finish A protective coating of paint; to apply a paint or paint system.

Fixtures A set of accessories for a dedicated measuring system designed to attach to a bench to fit the control points for a specific family of body styles.

Flash The first stage of drying where some of the solvents evaporate, which dulls the surface from an exceedingly high gloss to a normal gloss.

Flat Lacking in gloss.

Frame The heavy metal structure that supports the auto body and other external components.

Frame alignment The procedure by which the frame of a car, truck, or bus that has been damaged in an accident or from wear is restored to the manufacturer's specifications.

Frame gauges Gauges that can be hung from the car frame to check its alignment.

Frame straightener A pneumatic-powered machine used to align and straighten a distorted frame or body.

Front end drive A vehicle having its drive wheels located on the front axle.

Full body section Simultaneous section repairs to both rocker panels, windshield pillars, and floorpan; required to join the undamaged front half of one vehicle to the replacement undamaged half of another vehicle.

Galvanized Metal coated with zinc.

Gap The distance between two points.

Gauge A measure of the thickness of sheet metal.

Gloss The ability of a paint to reflect images when polished.

Grille Parallel bars or similar metal constructions used to protect the radiator of the car.

Grit A measure of the size of particles on sandpaper or discs.

Hardener A curing agent used in plastics.

Header bar The framework or inner construction that joins the upper sections of the windshield, pillars, forms the upper portion of the windshield opening, and reinforces the turret top panel.

Headlining The cloth or plastic material covering the ceiling area in the passenger compartment.

High-strength steel A low-allow steel that is much stronger than hot-rolled or cold-rolled sheet steels that normally are used in the manufacture of car body frames.

Hinge pillar The framework or inner construction to which the door hinges fasten.

Hood panel The large metal panel that generally fills in the space between the two fenders and closes off the engine compartment so that rain cannot fall on the engine.

Hot spot An unprotected area subject to corrosion.

HSLA High Strength Low Alloy steel, used in unibody construction.

HSS High Strength Steel, used in unibody construction.

Hue The characteristic by which one color differs from another, such as red, blue, green, and so on.

Independent front suspension The conventional front suspension system in which each front wheel moves independently of the other.

Independent rear suspension Rear suspension that has no cross axle shaft. Each wheel and related suspension is allowed to act individually.

Information sheet Used to record step-by-step measurements during repair.

Interior trim All the upholstery and molding on the inside of the vehicle.

Jig A mechanical device for holding work in its exact position while it is being welded.

Joint The point where or line along which two pieces are connected.

Jounce Rebound force or push down and release.

Lacquer A type of paint that dries by solvent evaporation. Can be rubbed to improve appearance.

Lap weld A weld is made along the edge of an overlapping piece.

Laser system A type of universal measuring system that uses laser optics in part or total vehicle redimensioning.

Lead A metal commonly used in the manufacture of driers and pigments. All lead compounds are extremely toxic. Lead driers promote thorough drying.

Mash A vehicle body damage condition where the length of any section or frame member is shorter than factory specifications.

Masking Using tape and paper to protect an area that will not be painted.

Mechanical components Powertrain, accessories, and suspension system.

Member Any essential part of a machine or assembly.

Metal conditioner A chemical cleaner that removes rust and corrosion from bare metal and helps prevent further rusting.

Metallic paint Finish-paint colors that contain metallic flakes in addition to pigment.

Misaligned Having uneven spacing, as between body panels.

Model year The production period for new motor vehicles or new engines, designated by the calendar year in which the period ends.

Monocoque A type of vehicle construction in which the sheet metal of the body supports most of the structural strength of the vehicle.

Multiple-pull systems Pulling in two or more directions to correct damage to a unibody.

OEM Original Equipment Manufacturer

Open structural members Flat panels, typically accessible from both sides, such as floorpans and trunk floors.

Outer panels Sheet metal sections that, when attached to the inner panels, form the auto's exterior.

Oven A piece of equipment used to bake finishes.

Overall repainting A type of refinish repair in which the car is completely repainted.

Overlap The amount of the spray pattern that covers the previous spray stroke.

Overpulling Stretching the metal too much resulting in the need to replace the part.

Overspray Paint that falls on the area next to the one being painted.

Paint film The actual thickness of the paint on a surface.

Panel repair A type of refinish repair job in which a complete section (door, hood, rear deck, and so on) is repainted.

Parallelogram linkage A steering system in which a short idler arm is mounted on the right side so that it is parallel to the pitman arm.

Parent metals Original metals in the unibody.

Partial section One or more section repairs performed on the same vehicle.

Perimeter frame Frame designed to surround the passenger compartment.

Plastic filler A compound of resin and fiberglass used to fill dents on car bodies.

Plug weld Adding metal into a hole and fusing all the metal.

Primary damage Local damage that occurs at the point of impact on the vehicle.

Prime coat The first coat in a paint system—its main purpose being to impart adhesion.

Primer An undercoat applied to bare metal to promote adhesion of the topcoat.

Primer-sealer An undercoat that improves adhesion of the topcoat and seals old painted surfaces that have been sanded.

Primer-surfacer A high-solids primer that fills small imperfections in the substrate and usually must be sanded.

Pulling Applying force to a part to make a change.

Putty A material made for filling small holes or sand scratches.

Quarter panel The side panel, which in four door sedans, is generally a quarter of the total length of the automobile and extends from the rear door to the end of the car.

Rack-and-pinion steering gear   A steering gear in which a pinion on the end of the steering shaft meshes with a rack on the steering linkage.

Rear camber   Inclination of a rear wheel in or out at the top as seen from the side of the rear wheel.

Rear toe condition   The rotation of the rear wheel in or out at the front of the wheel as seen from the side of the rear wheel.

Reducer   The solvent combination used to thin enamel is usually referred to as a reducer.

Refinish   To remove or seal the old finish and apply a new topcoat; to repaint.

Resistance welding   Welds made by passing an electric current through metal between the electrodes of the welding gun.

Respirator   A device worn over the mouth to filter particles and fumes out of the air being breathed.

Retarder   A slow evaporating thinner used to retard drying.

Rim   The metal part of the wheel upon which a tire is fitted.

Rocker panel   The narrow, outer panel attached below the car door.

Roof rails   The framework or inner construction that reinforces and supports the sides of the roof panel or turret top.

Rust   A form of corrosion in which oxygen combines with metal, causing it to turn brown in color and deteriorate.

Sag   A type of frame damage in which one or both side rails bend and sag at the cowl, causing buckles to be formed on the top of the side rails.

Scuff   To rough up a surface by rubbing lightly with sandpaper to provide a suitable surface for painting.

Sealer   An intercoat between the topcoat and the primer or old finish, giving better adhesion.

Secondary damage   Damage that occurs due to misplaced energy that causes stresses in suspension and/or body dimensions at areas other than the primary impact zone.

Section repair   A repair made by cutting a component somewhere along its length, removing the damaged portion; and replacing it with an undam-

aged component according to specific methods for cutting, joining, and welding.

Service manual   A book published annually by each vehicle manufacturer, listing the specifications and service procedures for each make and model of vehicle. Also called a **shop manual.**

Shim   A small metal spacer used behind panels to bring them into alignment.

Shock absorber   A device placed at each vehicle wheel to regulate spring rebound and compression.

Show through   Sand scratches in the undercoat that are visible through the topcoat.

Shroud   A sheet metal or plastic part used on cars to direct the suction of the cooling fan.

Sidesway   Damage that results when either the front, center, or rear of the vehicle has been pushed sideways out of alignment, causing the structural linear alignment of the vehicle to be altered.

Single coat   Spray first pass left to right. Drop nozzle to 50 percent of spray pattern overlapping bottom half of original pass, returning right to left.

Single pull systems   Pulling one way at a time.

Solvents   That which puts a paint into solution for application; a single such ingredient. Thinners and reducers are composed of one or several solvents.

Specifications   Information provided by the manufacturer that describes each automotive system and its components, operation, and measurement.

Spot putty   A special fast drying substance for filling dings and small imperfections.

Spot repair   A type of refinish repair job in which a section of a car smaller than a panel is refinished (often called **ding** and **dent** work).

Spray   Paint is atomized in a spray gun and the stream of atomized paint is directed at the part to be painted.

Spray gun   A painting tool powered by air pressure that atomizes liquids.

Squeegee   A rubber block used to wipe off wet sanded areas and to apply putty.

Steering system   The mechanism that enables the driver to turn the wheels for changing the direction of vehicle movement.

Straight-in damage   Damage resulting from a direct hit, a collision for example, rather than from a glancing hit.

Stress relieving Taking tension off a part.

Structural member Any primary load-bearing portion of the body structure that affects its over-the-road performance or crash-worthiness.

Structural panels Panels used in the unibody that become part of the whole unit and are vital to the strength of the unibody.

Strut suspension MacPherson strut attached to tower and camber reference angle.

Stub frame A unitized body frame with only front and rear stub sections of side rail and no center side rail portions.

Subassembly Several parts put together before the "whole" is attached.

Substrate The surface that is to be finished (painted). It can be anything from an old finish or primer to an unpainted surface.

Suspension system The springs and other parts that support the upper part of a vehicle on its axles and wheels.

Symmetrical design A design in which both sides of a unibody are identical in structure.

Tack cloth A cheesecloth that has been treated with nondrying varnish to make it tacky. Used to pick up dust and lint from the surface to be painted.

Thinner The solvent combination used to thin lacquers and acrylics to spraying viscosity is usually called thinner.

Tint A very light color, usually a pastel. To add color to another color or to white.

Toe condition The rotation of the wheel in or out as seen at the front of the wheel looking from the side.

Toe-in The distance the front of the front wheels is closer together than rear of the front wheels.

Toe-out The distance the front of the front wheels is farther apart than the rear of the front wheels.

Tolerances The acceptable alteration limit of the vehicle dimensions as provided by the manufacturer (for example, ±3 mm is typical).

Topcoat The last or final color coat.

Tram gauges Gauges used to accurately measure and diagnose body and frame collision damages for all conventional and unitized vehicles.

Trim Decorative metal pieces on a car body.

Turning radius A tire wearing angle measured in degrees. It is the amount one front wheel turns sharper than the other on turns.

Twist A type of frame damage in which both side rails are bent out of alignment, so that they do not run horizontally parallel to one another.

Two-part A paint or lacquer supplied in two parts that must be mixed together in the correct proportions before use. The mixture will then remain usable for a limited period only.

Undercoat A first coat: primer, sealer, or surfacer.

Unibody Vehicle in which the parts for the body structure serve as the support for the overall vehicle components.

Universal measuring system A measuring system that has devices mounted on a frame that can be adjusted for various vehicle bodies. This system can utilize laser systems, universal benches, or mechanical gauges.

Vehicle identification number (VIN) The number assigned to each vehicle by its manufacturer, primarily for registration and identification purposes.

Weld To join two metal or plastic pieces together by bringing them to their melting points, often involving use of a welding rod to add metal to the joint.

Wheel alignment Positioning the suspension and steering components to assure a vehicle's proper handling and optimum tire wear.

Wheel balancing The proper distribution of weight around a tire and wheel assembly to counteract centrifugal forces acting upon the heavy areas in order to maintain a true running wheel perpendicular to its rotating axis.

Wheelbase The distance between the centerlines of the front and rear axles. For trucks with tandem rear axles, the rear centerline is considered to be midway between the two rear axles.

Wheelhouses The deep curved panels that form the compartments in which the wheels rotate. They are generally bolted to the front fenders and spot welded to the rear quarter panels.

Zoning A method of systematically observing a damaged vehicle. It includes checking primary damage, secondary damage, then the suspension, steering and mechanics, the interior components, and, lastly, the exterior paint and trim of the vehicle.

Appendix B

Abbreviations Used by Body Technicians and Estimators

It is important that the estimator and body shop technician be able to communicate verbally as well as in writing. Both in estimates and work procedure reports most estimators use abbreviations. Generally, these abbreviations are the same as those used in the estimating crash guides. Some abbreviations are even used verbally. For example, three of the most commonly used abbreviations in a body shop are:

- **R&I: Remove and Reinstall.** The item is removed as an assembly, set aside, and later reinstalled and aligned for a proper fit. This is generally done to gain access to another part. For example, R&I bumper would mean that the bumper assembly would have to be removed to install a new fender or quarter panel.
- **R&R: Remove and Repair.** Remove the old parts, transfer necessary items to new part, replace, and align.
- **O/H: Overhaul.** Remove an assembly from the vehicle, disassemble, clean, inspect, replace parts as needed, then reassemble, install and adjust (except wheel and suspension alignment).

In addition to these abbreviations, the following terms are those accepted by most estimating guides, shop manuals, and estimators. They are the ones used in most written forms.

A	Manufacturer has no list price for the part.	c/mbr	cross member	div	division
		cntr	center	Dlxe	DeLuxe
AC	Air Conditioner	col	column	dr	door
ACRS	Air Cushion Restraint System	comp	compressor		
		compt	compartment	ea	each
adj	adjuster or adjustable	cond	conditioning or conditioner	elec	electric
AIR	Air Injector Reactor			emiss	emission
alt	alternator	cont	control	eng	engine
alum	aluminum	conv	converter or convertible	EP	Exhaust Purging
amp	ampere	cor	corner	equip	equipment
assy	assembly	cov	cover	evap	evaporator
AT	Automatic Trans	Cpe	Coupe	exc	except
auto	automatic	C/R	Customer Request	exh	exhaust
aux	auxiliary	crossmbr	cross member	extn	extension
		c/shaft	crankshaft		
bbl	barrel	ctl	control	flr	floor
bk	back	Ctry	Country	Fndr	Fender
blwr	blower	Cust	Custom	Fr & Rr	Front & Rear
bmpr	bumper	cyl	cylinder	frm	from
brg	bearing			fr or rr	front or rear
brkt	bracket	D	Discontinued part	ft	foot
Bro	Brougham	d	drilling operational time		
btry	battery	dbl	double	gal	gallon
btwn	between	def	deflector	gen	generator
B-U	Back-Up	dehyd	dehydrator	grds	guards
bush	bushing	desc	description	grv	groove
		dia	diameter		
Calif	California	diag	diagonal	H'back	Hatchback
chnl	channel	dist	distributor	HD	Heavy Duty

HDC	Heavy Duty Cooling	OD	Outside diameter	stab	stabilizer
hdr	header	OEM	Original Equipment	stat	stationary
HEI	High Energy Ignition		Manufacturer	Std	Standard
Hi Per	High Performance	OH	Overhaul	stl	steel
horiz	horizontal	opng	opening	strg	steering
H.P.	High Performance	orna	ornament	Sub	Suburban
hsg	housing	otr	outer	sup	super
HSLA	High Strength			supt	support
	Alloy Steel	p	paint operational time	surr	surround
HSS	High Strength Steel	pass	passenger	susp	suspension
HT	Hard Top	pkg	package	SW	Station Wagon
H'Top	Hard Top	plr	pillar		
hyd	hydraulic	pnl	panel	tach	tachometer
Hydra	Hydramatic	pos	positive	t & t	tilt & telescope or tilt
		PS	Power Steering		& travel
ign	ignition	Pwr	Power	TE	Thermactor Emission
in	inch			tel	telescope
incl	includes	qtr	quarter	trans	transmission
inr	inner				
inst	instrument	R	Right	upr	upper
inter	intermediate	rad	radiator		
		R & R	Remove & Reinstall	vent	ventilator
L	Left	R-L	Right or Left	vert	vertical
lic	license	rec	receiver	vib	vibration
lp	lamp	refl	reflector	VIR	Valve-In-Receiver
lwr	lower	reg	regulator		
		reinf	reinforcement	w/	with
max	maximum	reson	resonator	WB	Wheelbase
mdl	model	Rr	Rear	WD	Wheel Drive
mldg	molding			Wgn	Wagon
MT	Manual Transmission	Sed	Sedan	w'house	wheelhouse
mtd	mounted	ser	serial or series	whl	wheel
mtg	mounting	shld	shield	whlse	wheelhouse
muff	muffler	sidembr	side member	wndo	window
		sig	single	wo/	without
NAGS	National Auto Glass	spd	speed	wshd	windshield
	Specification	spec	special	w'strip	weatherstrip
neg	negative	Sta	Station		

Appendix C
Decimal and Metric Equivalents

DECIMAL AND METRIC EQUIVALENTS

Fractions	Decimal (in.)	Metric (mm)	Fractions	Decimal (in.)	Metric (mm)
1/64	.015625	.397	33/64	.515625	13.097
1/32	.03125	.794	17/32	.53125	13.494
3/64	.046875	1.191	35/64	.546875	13.891
1/16	.0625	1.588	9/16	.5625	14.288
5/64	.078125	1.984	36/64	.578125	14.684
3/32	.09375	2.381	19/32	.59375	15.081
7/64	.109375	2.778	39/64	.609375	15.478
1/8	.125	3.175	5/8	.625	15.875
9/64	.140625	3.572	41/64	.640625	16.272
5/32	.15625	3.969	21/32	.65625	16.669
11/64	.171875	4.366	43/64	.671875	17.066
3/16	.1875	4.763	11/16	.6875	17.463
13/64	.203125	5.159	45/64	.703125	17.859
7/32	.21875	5.556	23/32	.71875	18.256
15/64	.234275	5.953	47/64	.734375	18.653
1/4	.250	6.35	3/4	.750	19.05
17/64	.265625	6.747	49/64	.765625	19.447
9/32	.28125	7.144	25/32	.78125	19.844
19/64	.296875	7.54	51/64	.796875	20.241
5/16	.3125	7.938	13/16	.8125	20.638
21/64	.328125	8.334	53/64	.828125	21.034
11/32	.34375	8.731	27/32	.84375	21.431
23/64	.359375	9.128	55/64	.859375	21.828
3/8	.375	9.525	7/8	.875	22.225
25/64	.390625	9.922	57/64	.890625	22.622
13/32	.40625	10.319	29/32	.90625	23.019
27/64	.421875	10.716	59/64	.921875	23.416
7/16	.4375	11.113	15/16	.9375	23.813
29/64	.453125	11.509	61/64	.953125	24.209
15/32	.46875	11.906	31/32	.96875	24.606
31/64	.484375	12.303	63/64	.984375	25.003
1/2	.500	12.7	1	1.00	25.4

Index